THE HARBRACE
ANTHOLOGY OF
DRAMA

THE HARBRACE ANTHOLOGY OF DRAMA

SENIOR EDITORS

JON C. STOTT

RAYMOND E. JONES

RICK BOWERS

CONTRIBUTING EDITORS

GLENN BURGER

WILLIAM CONNOR

KATHERINE KOLLER

JAMES NELSON

DAPHNE READ

GLENNIS STEPHENSON

BRUCE STOVEL

University of Alberta

Harcourt Brace & Company, Canada

HARCOURT
BRACE
CANADA

Toronto Montreal Orlando Fort Worth San Diego
Philadelphia London Sydney Tokyo

Copyright 1994
Harcourt Brace & Company Canada, Ltd.
All rights reserved

No part of this publication may be reproduced or transmitted in any form or by any means, electronic or mechanical, including photocopy, recording, or any information storage and retrieval system, without permission in writing from the publisher.

Requests for permission to make copies of any part of the work should be mailed to: Permissions, College Division, Harcourt Brace & Company Canada, 55 Horner Avenue, Toronto, Ontario M8Z 4X6.

Every reasonable effort has been made to acquire permission for copyright material used in this text, and to acknowledge all such indebtedness accurately. Any errors and omissions called to the publisher's attention will be corrected in future printings.

Canadian Cataloguing in Publication Data

Main entry under title:

The Harbrace anthology of drama

Includes bibliographical references and index.

ISBN 0-7747-3352-7

1. English drama. I. Stott, Jon C., 1939-
II. Jones, Raymond E. III. Bowers, Rick.

PN6112.H3 1994   822.008   C94-930105-1

Editorial Director: *Heather McWhinney*
Acquisitions Editor: *Heather McWhinney*
Developmental Editors: *Deborah Adamczyk, Dianne Horton*
Editorial Assistant: *Debra Jarrett-Chase*
Director of Publishing Services: *Steve Lau*
Editorial Manager: *Liz Radojkovic*
Editorial Co-ordinator: *Marcel Chiera*
Production Manager: *Sue-Ann Becker*
Production Co-ordinator: *Denise Wake*
Copy Editor: *Cy Strom*
Cover and Interior Design: *Landgraff Design Associates*
Typesetting and Assembly: *True to Type Inc.*
Printing and Binding: *Best Gagné Book Manufacturers*

Cover Art: *French Doors I* by Joseph Plaskett. Courtesy of Bau-Xi Gallery, Toronto and Vancouver, Canada.

∞   This book was printed in Canada on acid-free paper.

1 2 3 4 5   98 97 96 95 94

PREFACE

"We imagine ourselves, we create ourselves, we touch ourselves into being with words, words that are important to us," writes native North American author Gerald Vizenor. One means by which we imagine or create ourselves is through the reading of literature.

The Harbrace Anthology of Literature uses three approaches to encourage its readers in this activity. First, it presents significant and representative works from the increasingly widening canon of literature in English. Second, it provides strategies to assist readers in their appreciation of works of literature. Third, by introducing readers to the language of literature, both simple and complex, and by suggesting methods for articulating responses, it provides opportunities to explore literature and to respond to language in its rich and varied forms.

Although no anthology can include all of its readers' favourite works, the editors have attempted to make their selections as varied and diverse as possible. Thus, *The Harbrace Anthology of Literature* offers many contemporary poems, plays, and short stories, by men and women alike, from a variety of cultures and backgrounds, in addition to many of those works that have always formed an integral part of the accepted canon of literature in English. It also includes a large sampling of English Canadian literature in the belief that Canadian students should have the opportunity to experience the major works of their literary tradition both on their own terms and within the larger context of literature written in English.

Individual works in *The Harbrace Anthology of Literature* mirror the diversity of backgrounds and interests of Canadian students as well as reflecting an expanded canon. The poems, plays, and short stories reveal many of the characteristic themes and artistic techniques of their authors; they also reflect the cultural and social contexts in which they were written. In particular they embody, as the eighteenth-century poet Alexander Pope observed, "what oft was thought but ne'er so well expressed." Most readers of this anthology will find its works speaking directly to them and addressing their most deeply felt concerns.

The Harbrace Anthology of Literature is organized by genre, beginning with poetry. Its poetry selections span eleven hundred years, the longest period of the three genres presented in the anthology. It continues with drama and concludes with short stories, the most recent of the three genres to develop. Selections within each genre are chronological, according to the birth dates of their authors. Following a selection, its date of publication is printed in parentheses on the right; when it differs significantly and is known, the date of composition appears in parentheses on the left. Such an organizational pattern, based on chronology rather than on pedagogical or theoretical concerns, invites a broad range of responses to a work, unencumbered by artificial or purely technical groupings based on content or theme. It does, of course, implicitly suggest an historical continuity in literature: that works from a specific period often have technical and thematic similarities; and that earlier works and authors can influence later ones.

The General Introduction considers the reading of literature both as a personal, necessary lifelong activity and as a discipline. It explores how reading poems, plays, and short stories allows individuals to understand their own lives and responses to literature in relation to those of other people. It also demonstrates how readers can engage more deeply with a text, experiencing it more fully and relating it more completely to their own lives.

The introduction to each genre focuses directly on the characteristics and conventions of the genre, using examples from the literature presented in *The Harbrace Anthology of Literature*. Discussions of individual characteristics are intended not to offer explanations or explications, but to indicate ways in which authors have used the various elements of the genre. For the reader, an awareness of these characteristics may assist in engagement with the text and lead to a broader range of responses.

Each work or, in the case of poetry, each group of poems by the same author is prefaced by a brief headnote establishing a biographical and literary context. The headnote may also touch on technique or theme. Explanatory footnotes identify historical, fictional, and mythological personages, literary and artistic works, real and fictional places, and terms not usually found in standard dictionaries. This material provides resources to assist readers in the personal creation of meaning — not to impose a critical viewpoint or to force interpretation in a specific, narrow direction.

Reading literature invites writing about it. The chapter entitled "Writing Essays about Literature" explores some of the challenges that writing about literature poses, without prescribing a recipe or rigid format for writing. It offers constructive suggestions to assist readers and writers in articulating responses — intellectual, aesthetic, or emotional — to works of literature.

The Glossary offers definitions of key terms, providing for readers both an awareness of essential concepts and a standard vocabulary for use in discussing literature.

The compilation of this anthology was a co-operative venture of the ten colleagues whose names appear on the title page; however, no book, even one developed by ten people, is ever created in a vacuum. During the planning, compiling, writing, and editing stages of *The Harbrace Anthology of Literature*, many people offered suggestions and made valuable comments. We wish to acknowledge the contributions and suggestions of our colleagues from the University of Alberta and reviewers from other universities: Claude G. Arnold, Richard Arnold, Diana Austin, William Benzie, William Blackburn, Sylvia Bowerbank, Mervin Butovsky, George J. Casey, Lorelei Cederstrom, Diane T. Edwards, Ian W. Fairclough, James Hart, Ron

Johnson, W.B. Lambert, Edward Lobb, T.J. Matheson, Lee McLeod, Craig W. McLuckie, Edward Mullaly, Victor A. Neufeldt, Andrew Parkin, Victor Ramraj, Constance Rooke, Eric J. Savoy, John F. Secker, Tony Steele, S. Warren Stevenson, J.E. Svilpis, Peter A. Taylor, B.F. Tyson, Paul S. Upton, Aritha van Herk, Lorraine York, and Edward R. Zietlow. As well, we thank Heather McWhinney, Nancy Ennis, Dianne Horton, Deborah Adamczyk, Marcel Chiera, Debra Jarrett-Chase, Graeme Whitley, and Michael Young at Harcourt Brace. These people have made this a better anthology; the responsibility for its limitations is our own.

PUBLISHER'S NOTE TO STUDENTS AND INSTRUCTORS

This textbook is a key component of your course. If you are the instructor of this course, you undoubtedly considered a number of texts carefully before choosing this as the one that would work best for your students and you. The authors and publishers spent considerable time and money to ensure its high quality, and we appreciate your recognition of this effort and accomplishment. Please note the copyright statement.

If you are a student, we are confident that this text will help you to meet the objectives of your course. It will also become a valuable addition to your personal library.

Since we want to hear what you think about this book, please be sure to send us the stamped reply card at the end of the text. Your input will help us to continue to publish high-quality books for your courses.

A NOTE ON THE HARBRACE ANTHOLOGIES OF POETRY, DRAMA, AND SHORT FICTION

The success of *The Harbrace Anthology of Literature* provides the publisher with an ideal opportunity to print individual anthologies of each of the three genres presented in *The Harbrace Anthology of Literature*. These are *The Harbrace Anthology of Poetry*, *The Harbrace Anthology of Drama*, and *The Harbrace Anthology of Short Fiction*. The new one-genre anthologies will offer greater choice to instructors teaching courses in these individual genres. Each of the one-genre anthologies incorporates the following elements from *The Harbrace Anthology of Literature*:
- the general introduction to literature
- the introduction to the specific genre
- the glossary of literary terms
- the chapter on writing essays about literature
- the index.

Each of the anthologies also contains the entire table of contents for *The Harbrace Anthology of Literature*. This will give instructors who choose to use one or more of the one-genre anthologies the opportunity to refer to all works in the other anthologies.

ACKNOWLEDGEMENTS

ALLEN, WOODY: *God*. From *Without Feathers* by Woody Allen. Copyright © 1972, 1973, 1974, 1975 by Woody Allen. Reprinted by permission of Random House, Inc..

AMMONS, A.R.: "Dunes" is reprinted from *The Selected Poems, 1951-1977*, by A.R. Ammons, by permission of W.W. Norton & Company, Inc. Copyright © 1977, 1975, 1974, 1972, 1971, 1970, 1966, 1965, 1964, 1955 by A.R. Ammons.

ANONYMOUS MEDIEVAL LYRICS: "Western Wind" from *Early English Lyrics*, 1967, published by October House. Copyright © 1966 and reprinted by permission of Sidgwick and Jackson Limited.

ANONYMOUS MEDIEVAL LYRICS: "I Sing of a Maiden," "Sunset on Calvary," "Alison," and "The Cuckoo Song" from *One Hundred Middle English Lyrics*, edited by R.D. Stevick (Indianapolis: The Bobbs-Merrill Company/Macmillan Publishing Company, 1964).

ANONYMOUS MEDIEVAL POPULAR BALLADS: "Sir Patrick Spens," "Get Up and Bar the Door," "Lord Randall," "The Twa Corbies," and "The Birth of Robin Hood." Reprinted from Arthur Quiller-Couch, editor. *The Oxford Book of Ballads* (London: Oxford University Press, 1910).

ARNOLD, MATTHEW: "Isolation: To Marguerite" and "Dover Beach" by Matthew Arnold. Reprinted from C.B. Tinker and H.F. Lowry, editors. *Arnold: Poetical Works* (Oxford: Oxford University Press, 1950).

ATWOOD, MARGARET: "Progressive Insanities of a Pioneer," "The Animals in That Country," "Further Arrivals," and "you fit into me." From Margaret Atwood's *Selected Poems 1966-1984*, copyright© Margaret Atwood, 1990, reprinted by permission of Oxford University Press Canada. "Variations on the Word *Love*," "A Women's Issue," and "Interlunar." From Margaret Atwood's *Selected Poems 1966–1984*, copyright © Margaret Atwood 1990, reprinted by permission of Oxford University Press Canada. "The Resplendent Quetzal." From *Dancing Girls* by Margaret Atwood. Used by permission of the Canadian Publishers, McClelland & Stewart, Toronto.

AUDEN, W.H.: "Musée des Beaux Arts," "The Unknown Citizen," "In Memory of William Butler Yeats," and "The Shield of Achilles." From W. H. Auden, *Collected Shorter Poems 1927–1957* (London: Faber and Faber, 1966). Reprinted with the permission of Faber and Faber Limited. "After Reading a Child's Guide to Modern Physics" and "Lullaby." From Edward Mendelson, editor. *Collected Poems of W.H. Auden* (London: Faber and Faber, 1976). Reprinted with the permission of Faber and Faber Limited.

BARTHELME, DONALD: "Jaws." Reprinted by permission of the Putnam Publishing Group from *Forty Stories* by Donald Barthelme. Copyright © 1988 by Donald Barthelme.

BEHN, APHRA: "Song (*Amyntas* led me to a Grove)" and *The Rover*. Reprinted from Montague Summers, editor. *The Works of Aphra Behn* (6 vols.) (London: Heinemann, 1915).

BENNETT, LOUISE: " Colonization in Reverse." Reprinted from Louise Bennett, *Jamaica Labrish* (Sangster's, 1966), with the permission of the author.

BETJEMAN, JOHN: "In Westminster Abbey" and "Upper Lambourne." From *John Betjeman's Collected Poems*, enlarged edition (London: John Murray, 1970), compiled by the Earl of Birkenhead. Reprinted by permission of John Murray Publishers.

BIRNEY, EARLE: "Vancouver Lights," "Anglosaxon Street," "Mappemounde," and "Bushed." From *The Collected Poems of Earle Birney*, 2 vols., by Earle Birney. Used by permission of the Canadian Publishers, McClelland & Stewart, Toronto.

BLAKE, WILLIAM: Songs of Innocence: "The Lamb," "The Little Black Boy," "The Chimney Sweeper," "Holy Thursday," and "Nurse's Song," and Songs of Experience: "The Tyger," "The Chimney Sweeper," "Holy Thursday," "Nurse's Song," "The Sick Rose," "London," and "Auguries of Innocence" reprinted from David V. Erdman, editor. *The Complete Poetry and Prose of William Blake*, revised edition (New York: Doubleday, 1962).

BRADSTREET, ANNE: "The Author to her Book," "To my Dear and loving Husband," and "Upon the burning of our house, July 10, 1966." Reprinted from Robert Hutchinson, editor. *Poems of Anne Bradstreet* (New York: Dover Publications, 1969).

BRAND, DIONNE: "Eurocentric." From Dionne Brand, *Chronicles of the Hostile Sun* (Stratford, Ontario: Williams-Wallace, 1984). Copyright © 1984 Dionne Brand. Reprinted by permission of Williams-Wallace Publishers.

BURNS, ROBERT: "To A Mouse: On Turning Her Up in Her Nest, with the Plough, November, 1785" and "Holy Willie's Prayer." Reprinted from James Kinsley, editor. *The Poems and Songs of Robert Burns* (Oxford: Clarendon Press, 1968).

BYRON, GEORGE GORDON, LORD: "She Walks in Beauty," "Who kill'd John Keats?", and "On This Day I Complete My Thirty-Sixth Year." Reprinted from Robert F. Gleckner, editor. *The Poetical Works of Byron* (Boston: Houghton Mifflin, 1975).

CARVER, RAYMOND: "Cathedral." From *Cathedral* by Raymond Carver. Copyright © 1983 by Raymond Carver. Reprinted by permission of Alfred A. Knopf, Inc.

CATHER, WILLA: "Paul's Case." Reprinted from *Willa Cather's Collected Short Fiction, 1892-1912*, edited by Virginia Faulkner, introduction by Mildred R. Bennett, by permission of University of Nebraska Press. Copyright © 1965, 1970 by the University of Nebraska Press.

CHAUCER, GEOFFREY: "General Prologue" and "The Miller's Prologue and Tale." Reprinted from Robinson, F.N. (Editor). *The Works of Geoffrey Chaucer*. Copyright © 1957 by Houghton Mifflin Company. Used with permission.

CHEEVER, JOHN: "Goodbye, My Brother." Copyright 1951 by John Cheever. Reprinted from *The Stories of John Cheever*, by permission of Alfred A. Knopf, Inc.

CHOPIN, KATE: "The Story of an Hour" by Kate Chopin reprinted from *The Complete Works of Kate Chopin*, vol. 1 (Baton Rouge: Louisiana State University Press, 1969).

CLARKE, AUSTIN C.: "The Motor Car." From *When He Was Free and Young and He Used to Wear Silks* by Austin C. Clarke. Reprinted by permission of Harold Ober Associates Incorporated. Copyright © 1971, 1972, 1973 by Austin C. Clarke.

COHEN, LEONARD: "I Have Not Lingered in European Monasteries." "For E.J.P.," and "Suzanne Takes You Down." From *Selected Poems 1950–1975* by Leonard Cohen. Used by permission of the Canadian Publishers, McClelland & Stewart, Toronto.

COLERIDGE, SAMUEL TAYLOR: "Kubla Khan," "Frost at Midnight," and "The Rime of the Ancient Mariner." Reprinted from Ernest Hartley Coleridge, editor. *Coleridge: The Complete Poetical Works* (Oxford: Oxford University Press, 1912).

CONRAD, JOSEPH: "An Outpost of Progress" by Joseph Conrad reprinted from *The Medallion Edition of the Works of Joseph Conrad*, vol. 1 (London: Gresham Publishing, 1925).

CRANE, STEPHEN: "The Open Boat" by Stephen Crane reprinted from *The Open Boat and Other Stories* (London: Heinemann, 1898).

CREELEY, ROBERT: "Ballad of the Despairing Husband" and "The Rhythm." From Robert Creeley, *Collected Poems of Robert Creeley, 1945–1975* (Berkeley: University of California Press, 1983). Copyright © 1983 The Regents of the University of California. Reprinted by permission of the University of California Press.

CUMMINGS, E.E.: "anyone lived in a pretty how town," "it may not always be so; and i say," "in Just-spring," and "next to of course god america i." Reprinted from *Complete Poems, 1913–1962*, by E.E. Cummings, by permission of Liveright Publishing Corporation. Copyright © 1923, 1925, 1931, 1935, 1938, 1939, 1940, 1944, 1945, 1946, 1947, 1948, 1949, 1950, 1951, 1952, 1953, 1954, 1955, 1956, 1957, 1958, 1959, 1960, 1961, 1962 by the Trustees for the E.E. Cummings Trust. Copyright © 1961, 1963, 1968 by Marion Morehouse Cummings.

DE LA MARE, WALTER: "The Listeners" from *The Complete Poems of Walter de la Mare* (London: Faber and Faber, 1969). Reprinted with the permission of The Literary Trustees of Walter de la Mare and The Society of Authors as their representative.

DICKINSON, EMILY: "There's a certain Slant of light," "I'm Nobody! Who are you?", "The Soul selects her own Society," "A Bird came down the Walk — ," "I heard a Fly buzz — when I died — ," "I started early — took my Dog — ," and "As imperceptibly as Grief." Reprinted by permission of the publishers and the Trustees of Amherst College from *The Poems of Emilly Dickinson*, Thomas H. Johnson, editor, Cambridge, MA: The Belknap Press of Harvard University Press, Copyright 1951, © 1955, 1979, 1983 by the President and Fellows of Harvard College.

DONNE, JOHN: "The Ecstasy." Reprinted from A.J. Smith, editor. *John Donne: The Complete English Poems* (Harmondsworth: Penguin, 1971).

DUNCAN, ROBERT: "Bending the Bow" and "My Mother Would Be a Falconress." From Robert Duncan: *Bending the Bow.* Copyright © 1968 by Robert Duncan. Reprinted by permission of New Directions Publishing Corporation.

ELIOT, T.S.: "The Hollow Men," "Journey of the Magi," "The Love Song of J. Alfred Prufrock," and "Preludes." From T.S. Eliot, *The Complete Poems and Plays 1909–1950* (London: Faber and Faber, 1971). Reprinted with the permission of Faber and Faber Limited.

FAULKNER, WILLIAM: "A Rose for Emily." Copyright 1930 and renewed 1958 by William Faulkner. Reprinted from *Collected Stories of William Faulkner*, by permission of Random House, Inc.

FERLINGHETTI, LAWRENCE: "Constantly Risking Absurdity." From Lawrence Ferlinghetti: *A Coney Island of the Mind*. Copyright © 1958 by Lawrence Ferlinghetti. Reprinted by permission of New Directions Publishing Corporation.

FRENCH, DAVID: *Leaving Home* by David French (Toronto: New Press, 1972). Copyright © 1972 by David French. Reproduced with the permission of Stoddart Publishing Co. Limited, 34 Lesmill Rd., Don Mills, Ontario, Canada.

FROST, ROBERT: "Stopping by Woods on a Snowy Evening," "After Apple-Picking," "Design," "An Old Man's Winter Night," "Acquainted with the Night," and "For Once, Then, Something." From *The Poetry of Robert Frost* edited by Edward Connery Lathem. Copyright 1923, 1928 © 1964 by Lesley Frost Ballantine. Reprinted by permission of Henry Holt and Company.

FUGARD, ATHOL: *"MASTER HAROLD"* . . . *and the boys*. From *"MASTER HAROLD"* . . . *and the boys* by Athol Fugard. Copyright © 1982 by Athol Fugard. Reprinted by permission of Alfred A. Knopf, Inc.

GALLANT, MAVIS: "My Heart Is Broken." Reprinted by permission of Georges Borchardt Inc. for the author. Copyright © 1957 by Mavis Gallant.

GILMAN, CHARLOTTE PERKINS: "The Yellow Wallpaper" by Charlotte Perkins Gilman reprinted from *The Charlotte Perkins Gilman Reader*, vol.1 (New York: Pantheon, 1980).

GINSBERG, ALLEN: "A Supermarket in California" by Allen Ginsberg from *Collected Poems 1947–1980* by Allen Ginsberg. Copyright © 1984 by Allen Ginsberg. Reprinted by permission of HarperCollins Publishers Inc.

GRAVES, ROBERT: "The Cool Web" and "The Naked and the Nude." From Robert Graves, *New Collected Poems* (London: A.P. Watt, 1977). Reprinted with the permission of A.P. Watt Ltd. on behalf of The Trustees of the Robert Graves Copyright Trust.

GRAY, THOMAS: "Elegy Written in a Country Church-Yard." Reprinted from H.W. Starr and J.R. Hendrickson, editors. *The Complete Poems of Thomas Gray* (Oxford: Clarendon Press, 1966).

GUNN, THOM: "On the Move," "To Yvor Winters, 1955," and "Moly" by Thom Gunn. From *Selected Poems 1950–1975* (London: Faber and Faber, 1979). Reprinted by permission of Faber and Faber Limited.

HARDY, THOMAS: "Hap," "The Darkling Thrush," "New Year's Eve," "The Convergence of the Twain," "The Ruined Maid," and "Afterwards." Reprinted from James Gibson, editor. *The Complete Poems of Thomas Hardy* (London: Macmillan, 1976).

HAWTHORNE, NATHANIEL: "My Kinsman, Major Molineux" by Nathaniel Hawthorne reprinted from *Centenary Edition of the Works of Nathaniel Hawthorne*, vol. XI (Columbus, OH: Ohio State University Press).

HEANEY, SEAMUS: "Personal Helicon" and "Death of a Naturalist" from Seamus Heaney, *Selected Poems 1965–1975* (London: Faber and Faber, 1981). Reprinted by permission of Faber and Faber Limited. "The Singer's House," "The Harvest Bow," "The Otter," and "Casualty" from Seamus Heaney, *Field Work* (London: Faber and Faber, 1980). Reprinted by permission of Faber and Faber Limited.

HECHT, ANTHONY: "The Dover Bitch." From *Collected Earlier Poems* by Anthony Hecht. Copyright © 1990 by Anthony E. Hecht. Reprinted by permission of Alfred A. Knopf, Inc.

HEMINGWAY, ERNEST: "A Clean, Well-Lighted Place." Reprinted with persmission of Charles Scribner's Sons, an imprint of Macmillan Publishing Company from *The Short Stories of Ernest Hemingway* by Ernest Hemingway. Copyright 1933 by Charles Scribner's Sons; renewal copyright © 1961 by Mary Hemingway.

HODGINS, JACK: "The Concert Stages of Europe." From *The Barclay Family Theatre* by Jack Hodgins. Copyright © 1981 by Jack Hodgins. Reprinted by permission of Macmillan of Canada, A Division of Canada Publishing Corporation.

HOGAN, LINDA: "The Sand Roses." From *Seeing Through the Sun* by Linda Hogan (Amherst: University of Massachusetts Press, 1985), copyright © 1985 by Linda Hogan. Reprinted by permission of the University of Massachusetts Press.

HOPKINS, GERARD MANLEY: "Pied Beauty," Sonnet 65, "The Windhover," and "God's Grandeur." Reprinted from W.H. Gardiner and N.H. Mackenzie, editors. *The Poems of Gerald Manley Hopkins* (Oxford: Oxford University Press, 1967).

HOUSMAN, A.E.: "Loveliest of trees, the cherry now," "When I was one-and-twenty," and "To an Athlete Dying Young." From *Collected Poems*. Reprinted by permission of The Society of Authors as the literary representative of the Estate of A.E. Housman and Jonathan Cape Ltd., publishers of A.E. Housman's *Collected Poems*.

HUGHES, TED: "Wind," "Pike," and "Hawk Roosting" by Ted Hughes from *Selected Poems 1957–1967.* Copyright © 1972 by Ted Hughes. Reprinted by permission of HarperCollins Publishers Inc.

JAMES, HENRY: "The Real Thing" by Henry James. Reprinted from Leon Edel, editor. *The Complete Tales of Henry James*, vol. 8 (New York: Lippincott, 1963).

JOHNSON, PAULINE: "The Derelict" by Pauline Johnson reprinted from *The Moccasin Maker* (Toronto: Ryerson, 1913).

JONSON, BEN: "Song: To Celia," "Queen and huntress," "Come, my Celia," and "On My First Son." Reprinted from Harry Levin, editor. *Ben Jonson: Selected Works* (New York: Random House, 1938).

JOYCE, JAMES: "The Dead" from *The Dubliners* by James Joyce. Copyright 1916 by B.W. Huebsch. Definitive text copyright © 1967 by the Estate of James Joyce. Used by permission of Viking Penguin, a division of Penguin Books USA, Inc.

KEATS, JOHN: "Ode to a Nightingale," "Ode on a Grecian Urn," "To Autumn," "La Belle Dame sans Merci," "When I have fears," "On First Looking into Chapman's Homer," and Sonnet: "Bright star!" reprinted from H.W. Garrod, editor. *The Poetical Works of John Keats* (Oxford: Clarendon Press, 1958).

KLEIN, A.M.: "Heirloom" and "Portrait of the Poet as Landscape" by A.M. Klein. From *A. M. Klein: Complete Poems, parts 1 and 2*, edited by Zailig Pollock. Copyright © 1990 by University of Toronto Press. Reprinted by permission of University of Toronto Press.

LARKIN, PHILIP: "Church Going," "Lines of a Young Lady's Photograph Album," "Toads," "An Arundel Tomb," and "Next, Please" by Philip Larkin are reprinted from *The Less Deceived* by permission of the Marvel Press, England.

LAURENCE, MARGARET: "The Loons." From *A Bird in the House* by Margaret Laurence. Reprinted by permission of the Canadian Publishers, McClelland & Stewart, Toronto.

LAWRENCE, D.H.: "Piano" and "Snake." From *The Complete Poems of D. H. Lawrence* (London: Heinemann, 1964, 1972). Reprinted with the permission of Laurence Pollinger Limited, Authors' Agents, and the Estate of Frieda Lawrence Ravagli. "The Horse Dealer's Daughter." From *The Complete Short Stories of D. H. Lawrence* (London: Heinemann, 1955). Reprinted with the permission of Laurence Pollinger Limited, Authors' Agents, and the Estate of Frieda Lawrence Ravagli.

LAYTON, IRVING: "The Birth of Tragedy" and "Keine Lazarovich, 1870–1959." From *Collected Poems* by Irving Layton. Used by permission of the Canadian Publishers, McClelland & Stewart, Toronto.

LePAN, DOUGLAS: "A Country Without a *Mythology*" by Douglas LePan. From *Weathering It* by Douglas LePan. Used by permission of the Canadian Publishers, McClelland & Stewart, Toronto.

LESSING, DORIS: "A Woman on a Roof." Copyright © 1963 Doris Lessing. Reprinted by permission of Jonathan Clowes Ltd, London, on behalf of Doris Lessing.

LEVERTOV, DENISE: "The Ache of Marriage" and "What Were They Like?" From Denise Levertov: *Poems 1960–1967*. Copyright © 1964, 1966 by Denise Levertov Goodman. Reprinted by permission of New Directions Publishing Corporation.

LIVESAY, DOROTHY: "Bartok and the Geranium" and "The Three Emilys" by Dorothy Livesay. Reprinted from *Collected Poems: The Two Seasons* (Toronto: McGraw-Hill Ryerson, 1972). Copyright © and reprinted with the permission of Dorothy Livesay.

LOWELL, ROBERT: "Skunk Hour" from *Life Studies* by Robert Lowell. Copyright © 1956, 1959 by Robert Lowell. Renewal copyright © 1981, 1986, 1987 by Harriet W. Lowell, Caroline Lowell and Sheridan Lowell. Reprinted by permission of Farrar, Straus and Giroux, Inc. "After the Surprising Conversion" in *Lord Weary's Castle* copyright 1946 and renewed 1974 by Robert Lowell, reprinted by permission of Harcourt Brace Jovanovich, Inc.

MacEWEN, GWENDOLYN: "Dark Pines Under Water." From Gwendolyn MacEwen, *The Shadow-Maker* (Toronto: Macmillan, 1969). Reprinted with the permission of the author's family. "The Real Enemies" reprinted by permission of Mosaic Press, 1252 Speers Rd., Units 1 & 2, Oakville, Ontario, L6L 5N9, from *The T. E. Lawrence Poems*. "But." From *Afterworlds* by Gwendolyn MacEwen. Used by permission of the Canadian Publishers, McClelland & Stewart, Toronto.

MANSFIELD, KATHERINE: "Bliss" by Katherine Mansfield reprinted from *Bliss and Other Stories* (New York: Knopf, 1931).

MARLOWE, CHRISTOPHER: *Doctor Faustus*. Reprinted from *The Plays of Christopher Marlowe* (Cleveland and New York: World Publishing, 1962).

McGRATH, ELIZABETH: "Fogbound in Avalon." Reprinted by permission; © 1980 The New Yorker Magazine, Inc.

MILTON, JOHN: "How soon hath Time" from John Milton: *Complete Poems and Major Prose*, edited by Merritt Y. Hughes (New York: Macmillan Publishing Company, 1985).

MILTON, JOHN: "When I consider how my light is spent," "On the Late Massacre in Piedmont," "Methought I saw my late espousèd saint," "Lycidas." Reprinted from D. Masson, editor. *The Poetical Works of John Milton* (London: Macmillan, 1891).

MOURÉ, ERIN: "Miss Chatelaine" and "The Producers." From Erin Mouré, *Furious* (Toronto: House of Anansi, 1987). These selections were reproduced with the permission of Stoddart Publishing Co. Limited, 34 Lesmill Rd., Don Mills, Ontario, Canada. "Bends" and "Safety." From Erin Mouré, *Domestic Fuel* (Toronto: House of Anansi, 1985). These selections were reproduced with the permission of Stoddart Publishing Co. Limited, 34 Lesmill Rd., Don Mills, Ontario, Canada.

MUKHERJEE, BHARATI: "The Tenant." From *The Middleman and Other Stories*. Copyright © 1988 by Bharati Mukherjee. Reprinted by permission of Penguin Books Canada Limited.

MUNRO, ALICE: "Mrs. Cross and Mrs. Kidd." From *The Moons of Jupiter* by Alice Munro. Copyright © 1983 by Alice Munro. Reprinted by permission of Macmillan of Canada, A Division of Canada Publishing Corporation.

NOWLAN, ALDEN: "The Bull Moose." From *An Exchange of Gifts* (Toronto: Irwin, 1985). Copyright © by Alden Nowlan. This selection was reproduced with the permission of Stoddart Publishing Co. Limited, 34 Lesmill Rd., Don Mills, Ontario, Canada.

O'CONNOR, FLANNERY: "Everything that Rises Must Converge" from *Everything that Rises Must Converge* by Flannery O'Connor. Copyright © 1965 by the Estate of Mary Flannery O'Connor. Reprinted by permission of Farrar, Straus and Giroux, Inc.

OLSON, CHARLES: "Maximus, to himself" by Charles Olson. From George Butterick, editor. *The Maximus Poems* (Berkeley: University of California Press, 1983). Copyright © 1983 The Regents of the University of California. Reprinted by permission of the University of California Press.

ONDAATJE, MICHAEL: "Elizabeth," "White Dwarfs," "Letters and Other Worlds," and "Bearhug." From *There's a Trick with a Knife I'm Learning to Do: Poems 1963–1978* by Michael Ondaatje. Used by permission of the Canadian Publishers, McClelland & Stewart, Toronto. "The Cinnamon Peeler," "To a Sad Daughter," and "When you drive the Queensborough roads at midnight." From *Secular Love* (Toronto: Coach House, 1984). Copyright © 1984 and reprinted by permission of the author.

OODGEROO OF THE TRIBE NOONUCCAL, CUSTODIAN OF THE LAND MINJERRIBAH: "Nona" and "We Are Going" by Oodgeroo of the tribe Noonuccal. Reprinted from *My People* (Milton, Queensland: The Jacaranda Press, 1964) with the permission of The Jacaranda Press.

OWEN, WILFRED: "Strange Meeting," "Anthem for Doomed Youth," and *"Dulce et Decorum Est."* From Jon Stallworthy, editor. *The Complete Poems and Fragments*, vol. 1 (London: The Hogarth Press, 1983). Reprinted with the permission of the Estate of Wilfred Owen and The Hogarth Press.

PAGE, P.K.: "The Stenographers," "Stories of Snow," and "Photos of a Salt Mine" copyright © P.K. Page. Reprinted with the permission of the author from *The Glass Air: Selected Poems* (Toronto: Oxford University Press, 1985).

PINTER, HAROLD: *The Homecoming.* Copyright © 1965 Harold Pinter. Reprinted by permission of Faber and Faber Limited.

PLATH, SYLVIA: "Daddy," "Lady Lazarus," and "Spider." From *Ariel* by Sylvia Plath (London: Faber and Faber, 1966). Reprinted by permission of Faber and Faber Limited.

POLLOCK, SHARON: *Blood Relations* from *Blood Relations and Other Plays*. Reprinted by permission of NeWest Publishers Limited, Edmonton.

POPE, ALEXANDER: "The Rape of the Lock." Reprinted from Geoffrey Tillotson, editor. *The Rape of the Lock and Other Poems*, vol. 2 of *The Poems of Alexander Pope*, 3rd edition (London: Methuen, 1962). Excerpt from "Essay on Man," Epistle II. Reprinted from Maynard Mack, editor. *An Essay on Man*, vol. 3 of *The Poems of Alexander Pope*, 3rd edition (London: Methuen, 1962). Reprinted with the permission of Routledge Publishers.

PORTER, KATHERINE ANN: "Rope" from *Flowering Judas and Other Stories*, copyright 1930 and renewed 1958 by Katherine Ann Porter, reprinted by permission of Harcourt Brace Jovanovich, Inc.

POUND, EZRA: "An Immorality." From Ezra Pound: *Collected Earlier Poems*. Copyright © 1976 by the Trustees of the Ezra Pound Literary Property Trust. Reprinted by permission of New Directions Publishing Corporation. "The Seafarer," "Ancient Music," "In a Station of the Metro," "The River Merchant's Wife: A Letter," and "There died a myriad." From Ezra Pound: *Personae*. Copyright 1926 by Ezra Pound. Reprinted by permission of New Directions Publishing Corporation.

PRATT, E.J.: "From Stone to Steel" and "The Truant" by E.J. Pratt from *E. J. Pratt: Complete Poems*, edited by Sandra Djwa and R.G. Moyles, copyright © 1989 University of Toronto Press. Reprinted by permission of University of Toronto Press.

PURDY, AL: "The Country North of Belleville" and "Lament for the Dorsets." From *Being Alive: Poems 1958–78* by Al Purdy. Used by permission of the Canadian Publishers, McClelland & Stewart, Toronto.

RICH, ADRIENNE: "Aunt Jennifer's Tigers," "Living in Sin," "Snapshots of a Daughter-in-Law," "Diving into the Wreck," and "Transit." Reprinted from *The Fact of a Doorframe, Poems Selected and New, 1950–1984*, by Adrienne Rich, by permission of W.W. Norton & Company, Inc. Copyright © 1984 by Adrienne Rich. Copyright © 1975, 1978 by W.W. Norton & Company, Inc. Copyright © 1981 by Adrienne Rich.

ROBERTS, SIR CHARLES G.D. "Tantramar Revisited," "The Potato Harvest," "The Winter Fields," and "The Herring Weir" by Sir Charles G.D. Roberts. Reprinted from *The Collected Poems of Sir Charles G. D. Roberts* (Wolfville, N.S.: The Wombat Press, 1985). Copyright © by Mary Pacey and Lady Joan Roberts. Reprinted by permission of The Wombat Press.

ROBINSON, EDWIN ARLINGTON: "Richard Cory" from *The Children of the Night* by Edwin Arlington Robinson (New York: Charles Scribner's Sons, 1897). "Mr. Flood's Party" from *Collected Poems* by Edwin Arlington Robinson. Copyright 1921 by Edwin Arlington Robinson, renewed 1949 by Ruth Nivison. "Eros Turannos" from *Collected Poems* by Edwin Arlington Robinson. Copyright 1916 by Edwin Arlington Robinson, renewed 1944 by Ruth Nivison.

ROCHESTER, JOHN WILMOT, EARL OF: "A Satire against Mankind." Reprinted from David M. Vieth, editor. *The Complete Poems of John Wilmot, Earl of Rochester*. Copyright © 1968 and reprinted with the permission of Yale University Press.

ROETHKE, THEODORE: "Root Cellar" copyright 1943 by Modern Poetry Association. "The Waking" copyright 1948 by Theodore Roethke. "My Papa's Waltz" copyright 1942 by Hearst Magazines, Inc. "The Minimal" copyright 1942 by Theodore Roethke. From *The Collected Poems of Theodore Roethke* by Theodore Roethke. Used by permission of Doubleday, a division of Bantam Doubleday Dell Publishing Group, Inc.

ROSENBERG, ISAAC: "Break of Day in the Trenches." Reprinted from *The Collected Poems of Isaac Rosenberg* (London: Chatto and Windus, 1949).

ROSS, SINCLAIR: "The Lamp at Noon." From *The Lamp at Noon and Other Stories* by Sinclair Ross. Used by permission of the Canadian Publishers, McClelland & Stewart, Toronto.

ROSSETTI, CHRISTINA: "The World," "Song" ("When I am dead, my dearest"), and "In an Artist's Studio." Reprinted from William Michael Rossetti, editor. *The Poetical Works of Christina Georgina Rossetti* (London: Macmillan, 1908).

ROTH, PHILIP: "The Conversion of the Jews." From *Goodbye, Columbus* by Philip Roth. Copyright © 1959 by Philip Roth. Reprinted by permission of Houghton Mifflin Company. All rights reserved.

SASSOON, SIEGFRIED: "Dreamers." Reprinted from Siegfried Sassoon, *Poems Newly Selected 1916–1935* (London: Faber and Faber, 1940). By permission of George Sassoon.

SCOTT, DUNCAN CAMPBELL: "The Onondaga Madonna," "The Forsaken," and "Night Hymns on Lake Nipigon." Reprinted from *The Poems of Duncan Campbell Scott* (Toronto: McClelland and Stewart, 1926). The Work of Duncan Campbell Scott is printed with the permission of John G. Aylen, Ottawa, Canada.

SCOTT, F.R.: "The Canadian Authors Meet," "Saturday Sundae," and "Trans Canada." From *Collected Poems* by F.R. Scott. Used by permission of the Canadian Publishers, McClelland & Stewart, Toronto.

SHAKESPEARE, WILLIAM: *Antony and Cleopatra.* Reprinted from George Lyman Kittredge and Irving Ribner, editors. *The Tragedy of Antony and Cleopatra* (Waltham, MA: Blaisdell, 1966). *The Tempest.* Reprinted from George Lyman Kittredge and Irving Ribner, editors. *The Tempest* (Waltham, MA: Blaisdell, 1966).

SHAW, BERNARD: *Caesar and Cleopatra.* Copyright 1913 by George Bernard Shaw. Reprinted by permission of The Society of Authors on behalf of the Estate of Bernard Shaw.

SILKO, LESLIE: "Storyteller." Copyright © 1981 by Leslie Marmon Silko. Reprinted from *Storyteller* by Leslie Marmon Silko, published by Seaver Books, New York, New York.

SMITH, STEVIE: "Our Bog is Dood" and "Not Waving But Drowning." From Stevie Smith: *Collected Poems of Stevie Smith.* Copyright © 1972 by Stevie Smith. Reprinted by permission of New Directions Publishing Corporation.

SPENDER, STEPHEN: "The Truly Great" and "An Elementary School Classroom in a Slum" from Stephen Spender, *Collected Poems 1928–1953* (London: Faber and Faber, 1955). Reprinted by permission of Faber and Faber Limited.

STEVENS, WALLACE: "The Idea of Order at Key West," "Sunday Morning," "Thirteen Ways of Looking at a Blackbird," and "Study of Two Pears." From *The Collected Poems of Wallace Stevens* by Wallace Stevens. Copyright 1923 and renewed 1951 by Wallace Stevens. Reprinted by permission of Alfred A. Knopf, Inc.

SWIFT, JONATHAN: "A Description of the Morning" and "A Satirical Elegy on the Death of a Late Famous General." Reprinted from Harold Williams, editor. *The Poems of Jonathan Swift*, 3rd edition (Oxford: Clarendon Press, 1958).

TAN, AMY: "Two Kinds." Reprinted by permission of The Putnam Publishing Group from *The Joy Luck Club* by Amy Tan. Copyright © 1989 by Amy Tan.

TAYLOR, EDWARD: "Upon a Spider Catching a Fly" and "Huswifery" reprinted with permission from *The Poems of Edward Taylor*. Copyright © 1960, 1988 by Donald E. Stanford.

THOMAS, DYLAN: "And Death Shall Have No Dominion," "The Force That through the Green Fuse Drives the Flower," "The Hunchback in the Park," "Fern Hill," "In My Craft or Sullen Art," and "Do Not Go Gentle into That Good Night" by Dylan Thomas. From *Dylan Thomas: The Poems* (London: J.M. Dent, 1971). Reprinted by permission of David Higham Associates.

UPDIKE, JOHN: "A & P." From *Pigeon Feathers and Other Stories* by John Updike. Copyright © 1962 by John Updike. Reprinted by permission of Alfred A. Knopf, Inc. Originally appeared in *The New Yorker*.

VANDERHAEGHE, GUY: "Cages." From *Man Descending* by Guy Vanderhaeghe. Copyright © 1982 by Guy Vanderhaeghe. Reprinted by permission of Macmillan of Canada, A Division of Canada Publishing Corporation.

WADDINGTON, MIRIAM: "Conserving" from Miriam Waddington's *Collected Poems*, copyright © Miriam Waddington 1986. Reprinted by permission of Oxford University Press Canada.

WALKER, ALICE: "Everyday Use" from *In Love & Trouble: Stories of Black Women*, copyright © 1973 by Alice Walker, reprinted by permission of Harcourt Brace Jovanovich, Inc.

WEBB, PHYLLIS: "Marvell's Garden" and "The Glass Castle" by Phyllis Webb. From Sharon Thesen, editor. *The Vision Tree: Selected Poems* (Vancouver: Talonbooks, 1982, 1985). Copyright © 1982 and reprinted with the permission of Phyllis Webb. "Treblinka Gas Chamber" from *Wilson's Bowl* by Phyllis Webb (Toronto: Coach House Press, 1980). Copyright © 1980 and reprinted with the permission of the author.

WELTY, EUDORA: "Why I Live at the P.O." from *A Curtain of Green and Other Stories*, copyright © 1941 and renewed 1969 by Eudora Welty, reprinted by permission of Harcourt Brace Jovanovich, Inc.

WHITMAN, WALT: "One's-Self I Sing," "Out of the Cradle Endlessly Rocking," "There Was a Child Went Forth," and "When Lilacs Last in the Dooryard Bloom'd" from *Leaves of Grass: Comprehensive Reader's Edition*, edited by Harold W. Blodgett and Sculley Bradley, reprinted by permission of New York University Press. Copyright © 1965 by New York University.

WIEBE, RUDY: "Chinook Christmas." From *The Angel of the Tar Sands and Other Stories* by Rudy Wiebe. Used by permission of the Canadian Publishers, McClelland & Stewart, Toronto.

WILDE, OSCAR: *The Importance of Being Earnest.* Reprinted from R. Ross, editor. *The First Collected Edition of the Works of Oscar Wilde,* vol. 3 (London: Dawson of Pall Mall, 1969).

WILLIAMS, TENNESSEE: *Cat on a Hot Tin Roof.* Copyright 1954, 1955, 1971, 1975 by Tennessee Williams. Reprinted by permission of New Directions Publishing Corporation. Canadian rights.

WILLIAMS, WILLIAM CARLOS: "Portrait of a Lady," "Tract," "The Red Wheelbarrow," and "Spring and All." From William Carlos Williams: *The Collected Poems of William Carlos Williams, 1909–1939,* vol. 1. Copyright 1938 by New Directions Publishing Corporation. Reprinted by permission of New Directions Publishing Corporation.

WINCHELSEA, ANNE FINCH, COUNTESS OF: "The Introduction." Reprinted from Denys Thompson, editor. *Anne Finch, Countess of Winchelsea: Selected Poems.* Copyright © 1987 and reprinted with the permission of Carcanet Press Ltd.

WINTERS, YVOR: "By the Road to the Air-Base" and "The Slow Pacific Swell." From Yvor Winters: *The Collected Poems of Yvor Winters.* Copyright 1943 by New Directions Publishing Corporation. Reprinted by permission of New Directions Publishing Corporation.

WORDSWORTH, WILLIAM: "Michael: A Pastoral Poem," "Lines Composed a Few Miles above Tintern Abbey," "Composed upon Westminster Bridge, September 3, 1802," Sonnet: "It is a beauteous evening, calm and free," "London, 1802," Sonnet: "The world is too much with us," and "I wandered lonely as a cloud." Reprinted from Ernest de Selincourt, editor. *The Poetical Works of Wordsworth,* new edition, revised (Oxford: Oxford University Press, 1953).

YEATS, WILLIAM BUTLER: "The Second Coming," "Easter 1916," "Sailing to Byzantium," "Among School Children," "Crazy Jane Talks with the Bishop," "Lapis Lazuli." "The Circus Animals' Desertion," and "The Old Men Admiring Themselves in the Water." Reprinted from *The Poems of William Butler Yeats* (London: Macmillan, 1933).

Contents

DRAMA

INTRODUCTION

"*P*art of the beauty of all literature," commented novelist and short story writer F. Scott Fitzgerald, is that "you discover that your longings are universal longings, that you're not lonely and isolated from anyone. You belong." Sharing experience through the creation and reception of stories, poems, and plays is a very old, basic, and necessary human activity, as necessary to human existence as food, shelter, and clothing. The literary critic Northrop Frye further emphasized the importance of literature, observing that "whenever a society is reduced to the barest primary requirements of food and sex and shelter, the arts, including poetry, stand out sharply in relief as ranking with those primary requirements." The need to bring order, through language and stories, to human experience seems to be fundamental to all societies and cultures.

While some literature may simply entertain or allow escape from everyday lives, the works that ultimately stay with their readers are those that challenge, engage, or make demands. Well-crafted literature invites its readers to laugh, to cry, to wonder, to analyze, to explore, to understand.

Throughout our lives, we seek to understand ourselves, our emotions, our experiences, and our relationships with others. We also attempt to define our connections to larger social and cultural institutions. One way that we can do so is through literature, for works of literature are the records of individual response to the world in which we live.

Because of our own experiences, we are able to understand the self-doubts and uncertainties expressed in T.S. Eliot's "The Love Song of J. Alfred Prufrock," the mixed emotions of love and hate of the title characters in William Shakespeare's *Antony and Cleopatra*, the social obligations and friendships in Alice Munro's "Mrs. Cross and Mrs. Kidd," and the anguish of Phyllis Webb's "Treblinka Gas Chamber." The specific experiences may be different from our own, but we recognize similarities in the thoughts and emotions of the characters; examination and reflection may lead to clearer insights into our own lives.

Because works of literature are often demanding, they offer great rewards. Readers come to fuller awareness of themselves and others. They discover both the uniqueness and the universality of human experience; they explore both their own world and worlds they may never otherwise see. Through critical response to literature, readers question a work, examine their relationship to the author, consider the author's role, and develop an appreciation of the work, both on its own terms and as an expression of the author's vision of life. Readers may also explore a work in the context of its times, whether social, historical, or ideological.

Until fairly recently, much of the literature studied in English courses was chosen from a list of works deemed important by a majority of critics and scholars, a list referred to as the canon of English literature. Like most of these critics and scholars, most of the writers were white, male, and British or of British descent. The list usually began with the anonymous creator of the Anglo-Saxon epic "Beowulf" and ended with such earlier twentieth-century writers as T.S. Eliot, W.H. Auden, and Dylan Thomas. Because it included very few works by women, members of ethnic minorities, or writers from the British colonies, however, it could not be said to reflect the diversity of writing in English.

The past 25 years have seen a remarkable change in our society as a whole: the recognition of the equal place of all people in it, regardless of gender or ethnic origin. As a consequence, many literary scholars and critics have vigorously sought to expand the canon so that it speaks to everyone. They have demanded the inclusion of the many voices whose stories, poems, and dramas are worthy of study, both on their own merits and because of the insights they offer into a very large segment of the population of the English-speaking world. Such critics have argued that literature should certainly present universal human concerns but should also help readers understand how gender, cultural background, and social position influence responses to life. The works in this anthology reflect this expanded canon.

Reading and reflecting on works of literature reveal human similarities as well as differences. Aphra Behn's drama *The Rover* makes us aware of the position of women in the male-dominated upper-class English society of the late seventeenth century. Athol Fugard's *"MASTER HAROLD"* . . . *and the boys* delineates the political and racial tensions of mid-twentieth-century South Africa. The poetry of Oodgeroo of the tribe Noonuccal (Kath Walker) reveals a modern Australian aboriginal woman examining her people's past and its troubled relationships with both government and newcomers.

Readers who come actively to such works with an open, questioning mind will be able to join with their authors in making explicit the implicit. They will appreciate that an author has used language connotatively, choosing words that, in addition to their dictionary meanings, suggest a range of emotions, ideas, or associations. They will recognize the symbolic nature of actions, characters, and objects. As the German literary critic Wolfgang Iser has commented, literary texts are incomplete; they contain gaps that readers fill in or bridge to create meaning. Readers anticipate, make inferences, draw conclusions; in short, they actively work with the language of a piece of literature to arrive at meaning.

Reading for meaning is a very personal act. It is not simply a matter of paraphrasing or summarizing a story or play, of transforming poetry into prose, or of examining literary technique or metaphorical language. Each reader is unique and will, therefore, respond differently — perhaps slightly, perhaps dramatically — to a work. A Dubliner will no doubt react differently to James Joyce's "The Dead" than will a Winnipegger; a man about to retire will react differently to Shakespeare's *The Tempest* than will a young woman who has just left home for first-year college or university; a woman will react differently to Margaret Atwood's "The Resplendent Quetzal" than will a man. People who have read widely in each of these three authors or who have a well-developed knowledge of literature would likely have a different and broader interpretation of these three works than someone who seldom reads. Readers draw on personal experience, knowledge, and awareness of both specific literature and literary techniques to appreciate and interpret a literary work.

There is no one simple process for interpreting literature; different readers develop different approaches, some of which will be more useful for some works than for others. That said, interpretation of a literary work begins with the words of the text themselves. Readers question the choice and arrangement of details and ponder their significance. Such active inquiry may commence on reading the title or during a first reading. Individual interpretation will change with each rereading as readers observe more details, acquire more information about them, and perceive new relationships among them.

Readers bring their own experiences to their interpretation of literature. Basing interpretation on the words of the text, they can compare and contrast their own responses to life with those of authors and characters. Readers who have had intense family conflicts will be able to make inferences about the domestic arguments in Eudora Welty's "Why I Live at the P.O." Reciprocally, interpretation of literature can enrich experiences of life. Younger readers will not have had the experiences of the elderly women in Alice Munro's "Mrs. Cross and Mrs. Kidd," but a reading of that story may bring empathy towards the elderly people in their lives. Recalling personal experience while reading a work for the first time can assist in its interpretation.

Readers also bring considerable literary experience to their reading of literature: an understanding of the ways in which authors use language and the general patterns of the major literary genres (poetry, drama, and fiction), awareness of important themes, and, frequently, familiarity with other works by the same writer. For example, knowledge of Shakespeare's use of blank verse, his creation of patterns of imagery, and the nature of his tragic heroes will make study of *Antony and Cleopatra* more rewarding. Reflection on the myths surrounding men and women will aid in the interpretation of Adrienne Rich's "Diving into the Wreck." Readers draw on what they already know and on critical literature to expand their interpretation of a literary work.

While readers bring considerable knowledge and experience to a literary work, they must also be conscious of the creative intelligence behind the selection and arrangement of its elements. General techniques and genre characteristics, as well as cultural or other forces at play during the writing, may influence some of the selection and arrangement, but most choices arise from the author's purpose in writing the work. Although readers may not find this purpose apparent on first reading, speculation on purpose, based on attention to details and their sequence, may reveal potentially deeper meanings in a work.

Understanding is enhanced as readers acquire more relevant background information and apply it to the text. Knowledge of the actual people and literary or mythological characters mentioned in the text, of allusions to historical events and episodes in other works, and of geographical or architectural settings will clarify their function in a work. In "Fogbound in Avalon," for example, Annie, the narrator, reads a magazine article about the painter Edvard Munch. Examining that artist's works may reveal a clearer picture of Annie's state of mind.

Literary works often reflect events and conflicts in the lives of their authors; awareness of such personal details can enhance a reader's understanding of how and why authors have written as they have. For example, James Joyce, in "The Dead," William Wordsworth, in "Tintern Abbey," and Amy Tan, in "Two Kinds," drew on facts from their own lives. What is perhaps most interesting is the way in which an author has taken such raw materials of life and shaped them to meet the needs of the work.

Literary works are also products of the times in which they were written, for nearly all writers have been sensitive to and influenced by the literary, intellectual, political, and social forces around them. Ernest Hemingway's attitude towards the rejection by many of traditional moral and religious values during and after World War I helps to explain the actions of the two waiters and the elderly man in "A Clean, Well-Lighted Place." Familiarity with Margaret Atwood's musings on being a woman writer will enrich interpretations of her poetry and such short stories as "The Resplendent Quetzal."

Finally, readers should remember that just as it is impossible to understand completely another person or even oneself, so there is no such thing as a final, complete, or totally correct interpretation of a work of literature. To successive readings of a work readers bring different frames of mind, other personal experiences, new literary or other factual knowledge, and greater familiarity with the work. Thus, with each reading, fuller, more rewarding, and potentially new interpretations are possible.

To assist readers in the creation of meaning, the introductions to the three genres in this anthology — poetry, drama, and short stories — discuss technical aspects of literary works. Headnotes and footnotes provide information about authors and their works and about names, places, and obscure terms mentioned in the texts. The Glossary defines terms frequently used in discussing literature.

Critical response to literature often involves writing about poems, stories, and dramas. Through writing, readers explore the parts and the whole of a work, examine their previous interpretations and test their validity, evaluate the significance of relationships among parts of a work, and create new meanings. Of course, new interpretations may not be final ones; indeed, they may be modified several times during the writing process. Exploration of apparently contradictory information may provide fresh insights into a work. If, in creating an interpretation, the writer has based the statements on the text, has provided evidence and not ignored contradictory evidence, and has argued logically and clearly, then the interpretation is valid. For those seeking assistance in the writing of interpretive essays, the chapter entitled "Writing Essays about Literature" offers a number of suggestions and guidelines.

What are the rewards of becoming active readers and interpreters? An answer can be found by returning to this introduction's opening discussion of essential human needs. Poems, plays, and short stories are artistic and articulate responses to life that offer emotional, intellectual, and imaginative nourishment to their readers. Anthologies such as this provide exposure to literature that enhances the readers' knowledge of themselves and the world outside of themselves. Such experiences can lead to self-discovery and a life-long love of reading.

DRAMA

INTRODUCTION TO DRAMA

DRAMA, ACTION, AND LIFE

*T*he very word *drama* comes from a Greek root meaning "to do," "to perform." Thus the word means essentially what it is: action. Drama is action. But more: drama is communication between human beings that conveys meaning through language, gesture, position, costume, expression. In fact, the Greek root for *theatre* has to do with *seeing*, and so a dramatic text comprises a set of directions for theatrical completion. The action can be visualized in the reader's imagination or realized on the actor's stage. In both cases the drama is seen and interpreted, and a spectator or reader is necessary for the communication of meaning. A reader of drama thus constitutes an audience that collaborates with the script in actively interpreting action and meaning; the reader becomes an actor/director of the mind.

Drama communicates at a human level that is at once primitive and profound. It is pre-philosophical, pre-literate, even pre-structural. Before the first stories were told, before the first songs were sung, human beings had enacted drama. Their physical gestures and movements were themselves a kind of dramatic language that represented where the hunt was held, re-created acts of bravery and heroism, celebrated the blessings of a benign spirit, expressed pleasure, disappointment, outrage, and loss. These enactments, codified and performed as ritual, explain a society in terms of its social action. And the actions that are performed are the actions and orientations of human life: birth, death, maturity, sexual interaction, seasonal change, societal history, criticism, and accomplishment. These actions and social perspectives, celebrated through ritual, communicate unifying truths about a people. At their essence, they state: "Our tribe 'acts' in this manner; this is the way we 'do' things."

At another, conscious, level, we humans discover that we can imagine ourselves as other than what we really *are*. This dramatic realization sets humans apart as a species. We celebrate and indulge our imaginations, mythologies, and aesthetic impulses because they are fundamental to our human nature and provide the metaphorical nourishment that only human beings can appreciate. We thus enact rituals to order our lives and reinforce our mythologies. Rituals, however, while they do not feed us or physically protect us, do something equally important: they represent us as we believe or wish ourselves to be, as people with social structures and spiritual insights that have meaning beyond animal instinct and physical sensation. In primitive societies, costumed performers assume the form of benign and malevolent gods: the performers represent the gods in relation to themselves and to their society; they actively develop the mythology of the people. In such religious representation, performers and audience are mutually involved social participants. When performers and audience perceive that there is a distinct difference between them, ritual has become drama. And yet the shared experience of human creativity, meaning, and assertion remains. Drama represents the insights of human beliefs and social interaction.

In the English experience, drama grew out of the rituals of the early Christian church. The *Regularis Concordia* (c. A.D. 970) of St. Ethelwold, Bishop of Winchester, includes directions for an interaction between priests at the end of matins on Easter Sunday. Known as the *Quem Quaeritis* ("Whom do you seek?") play, the dialogue dramatizes the information of the angel and the joy of the three Marys at news of the resurrection of Christ reported in the gospels of the New Testament. Medieval mystery plays (so called because they were performed by various civic "mysteries" or trade groups such as carpenters, bakers, or drapers) emphasized social involvement and expression on a larger scale. Popular from about 1380 to the second half of the sixteenth century, these plays involved entire cities in the annual performance of biblical stories. These enactments celebrated and communicated the sacred history of an early European society, from the creation of the world by an all-powerful deity to the human action of that deity in the person of Christ, to the resurrection of all human souls at the end of time.

Actively ignored if not suppressed, Catholic church drama under Henry VIII eventuated in allegorical moral dramas that enacted themes of sin, wickedness, repentance, faith, and human conduct in general. The way was already prepared for them before Henry's break with Rome: such titles as *Youth* (c. 1513), *Magnificence* (c. 1516), and *The World and the Child* (c. 1520) suggest stereotyped conflict between figures with indicative names such as Pride, Riot, Humility, Sad Circumspection, Conscience, and Perseverance. The performers of such plays were no longer participants in the civic ritual, but actors practising a craft whose venues included the feast halls of the nobility and the public market square.

A production such as Christopher Marlowe's *Doctor Faustus* in 1592 could reach back to earlier morality representations for such action as the dance of the Seven Deadly Sins, the high jinks of asinine irreverence, or the torment of spiritual suffering in general. But Marlowe's drama also looked forward to more fully psychologized human conflicts of hope, doubt, delusion, achievement, betrayal, and grief. The standard medieval prop representing hell as a monstrous mouth emitting fire and smoke can be suggested through a stage trap (see *Doctor Faustus*, 5.2.111), but Marlowe also makes it clear that hell is a state of mind. The Good and Bad Angels represent moral stereotypes in Faustus's conscience, but the title character also seeks power, significance, meaning. The play represents human possibility and striving in the character of Faustus, but it also expresses the misery of failure and damnation as understood in the context of Christian Renaissance Europe.

Drama, in fact, always expresses active human orientation. And we need not speculate exclusively in the performance possibilities of Renaissance plays or in the mists of spiritual impulse. Everywhere today, drama is a medium of expression that orders reality for the human mind. A ritual warm-up and introduction precedes hockey games and orchestral performances alike; royal coronations, ribbon-cutting ceremonies; graduation exercises, and funerals proceed according to script; advertising and news reportage on television owe much to dramatic techniques; the wedding party in the centre aisle, dancers on the dance floor, and fashion models on the runway all conform to a loose spatial pattern in the service of dramatization. A classroom or public meeting often reflects a spectator-performer orientation. Business, political, and military strategists all proceed according to "scenarios." Children learn "roles" through which their social and emotional development is patterned by dramatic improvisation, and which they call "play." It is also a dramatically suggestive coincidence that some modern social and philosophical thinkers such as Sartre, Beckett, Shaw, and Brecht are also playwrights; that Shakespeare is a word for literary and cultural significance as much as it is the name of a Renaissance actor and playwright; that one of Plato's contributions to philosophy is titled *Dialogues*; that Freudian psychology sees the plot of the ancient Greek play *Oedipus the King* as pattern and paradigm for modern subconscious reality. Drama explains and drama entertains; it concretizes, represents, and translates the complexities of human nature and existence.

CONFLICT, CHARACTER, AND EXPOSITION

Because drama "means" action, it needs, at all points, dramatic **conflict**. Life itself can be seen as a competitive struggle for physical, emotional, and spiritual survival, and drama represents such struggle through conflict and its resolution. Adversarial forces within a character or between characters provide the stress and tension that keep the action interesting. **Dialogue**, as a struggle for meaning between diverse, often antagonistic, points of view, is also a kind of conflict. Such struggle goes beyond the simple Antagonist versus Protagonist opposition of the Villain and the Hero. All the characters of *The Homecoming* relate to one another in terms of overt or insidious conflict. Implicit in the very title *"MASTER HAROLD"* . . . *and the boys* is a conflict of hopes, expectations, and relative worth. In *Antony and Cleopatra* the title characters, though clearly in love, are also in conflict. In fact the three-cornered political conflict of Antony, Octavius Caesar, and Cleopatra suggests the widespread military conflict of Shakespeare's play. One might say that Brick in *Cat on a Hot Tin Roof* is in conflict with himself as much as he is with Maggie, Big Daddy, and the hypocrisy of the situation in general on Big Daddy's birthday. Dramatic conflict suggests a variety of differences in attitude, allegiance, situation, opinion, and expression. Characters in drama argue, deny, insult, reject, and insinuate. They also try to resolve conflict when they embrace one another, take sides, share knowledge, or face the future.

The oppositions in character and action that ensure conflict are also basic elements of dramatic exposition. **Exposition** is the background information about characters, situations, and relationships that acts as a starting point for understanding the drama that ensues. The Prologue to *Doctor Faustus* contains a biographical summary of the humble childhood and early scholastic promise of Faustus. Then, in the first scene, Faustus himself informs us of his past success and present dissatisfaction with conventional learning. This expository information establishes aspects of the character of Faustus at the same time as it explains the situation in which the reader discovers him at the beginning of the play. But exposition is not always so overt. Ben and Mary's secret interaction early in *Leaving Home* makes it clear that, because he has not been invited to his own son's graduation, Jacob has been left out of the family once again. Prospero, by lecturing in turn to Miranda and Ariel in the second scene of *The Tempest*, actually sets forth the exposition of family and island history. Exposition can occur later in a play, too, and can be just as revealing. The retrospective description by Enobarbus in *Antony and Cleopatra* (act 2, scene 2), beginning "The barge she sat in, like a burnish'd throne, / Burn'd on the water," effectively reports Cleopatra's political upstaging of Antony, her supposed conqueror. The description of Cleopatra charms and excites Enobarbus's associates back at headquarters; it also presents, for the audience, the exposition of Antony and Cleopatra's significant first meeting. Expository information "fills in the blanks"; it provides past details of character and situation that are relevant if the audience is to understand the present action.

"Who are these people? What are they doing?" These are basic questions concerning character; good exposition provides clues to their answers. But a character is more than just a name in the *dramatis personae*. **Characters** in drama are agents of action. They signify the attitudes, psychological impulses, and moral conditions of separate human minds as well as the actions for which their minds are agent. They can be complex and unpredictable, though credible, as Hally is in *"MASTER HAROLD" . . . and the boys*, or relatively simple, flat and unsurprising, as is Mae in *Cat on a Hot Tin Roof*. Mae, however, is a character important for her antagonistic relationship to the complex characters of Maggie and Big Daddy. Hally and Sam in *"MASTER HAROLD" . . . and the boys* are a pair of complex characters with highly developed racial, business and personal relationships.

Characters in drama reveal their characteristics through interaction with others, but are further exposed through their own words and actions. Every line, every word, even every pause in the text says something about the character involved. Caesar's benign, logical, somewhat paternalistic pacifism in *Caesar and Cleopatra* is reinforced by virtually his every utterance, just as Cleopatra's self-willed, scheming immaturity is by hers. Jacob's strong Newfoundland accent in *Leaving Home*, emphasized near the outset by his little performance of "I's the b'y that builds the boat," establishes the traditional values of his character as much as his later reminiscences of Bay Roberts and his violent arguments with his educated son. Character is exposed and intensified not only by *what* is said, but throughout by *how* things are said. This represents the linguistic and motivational essence of acting. The script provokes questions at every point about why and how things are said and performed. Consequently, an active reader of drama must pose, consider, and respond to such questions at every point in the play.

PLOT AND SETTING

The **plot** of the play is the sequence of events through which the action proceeds. It represents the playwright's selection of actions to be staged and the order in which they are staged. Thus the plot of a play, as a moment-by-moment occurrence in time, conforms to an overall pattern. The **action** moves forward in time, complicated by various interactions of character and situation, as well as by happenings of subplot and the ideas that stem from these interactions and secondary plots. Then, after a **climax** of recognition, revelation, or discovery, the play draws itself rhetorically to a satisfying conclusion. This standard pattern is usually outlined in terms of the **Freytag Pyramid**, a structural diagram devised by the nineteenth-century German playwright and critic Gustav Freytag. His terms correspond to the five-act structure:

3. Climax

2. Rising Action   4. Falling Action

1. Exposition   5. Resolution

This pattern, however, is rarely a simple one. The plot of a play is usually more lateral and complicated than the rising-and-falling movement suggested by Freytag's diagram. In *Leaving Home*, both brothers are in the process of leaving, and for very different reasons. The relatively simple plot of Florinda's desire for Belvile in *The Rover* is countered and thwarted throughout by various subplots, misalliances, and misrepresentations. One might say that the "climax" of *Blood Relations* occurs in the very last line spoken, or that "resolution," as the final explanation or consolidation of the plot, is an absolute impossibility in *The Homecoming*.

The plot of a play always acts as commentary on the play itself, whether tightly drawn to an unassailable conclusion, as in *The Importance of Being Earnest*, or rendered through the tacit gambits of random conversation, suggestion, and meaningful pauses as in *The Homecoming*. Often, aspects of exposure and discovery are foreshadowed through plot for dramatic effect. In *Blood Relations*, Harry makes early reference to cutting kindling; he re-enters with the hatchet and hands it to Mr. Borden, who slams the weapon into the table at the end of the first act while resolving to decapitate all of Lizzie's pet birds: these are significant plotted actions in a play about the social and ethical complications surrounding a famous axe murder.

Drama occurs in an eternally present tense of representation that makes plot a kind of unifying tendency for the action. Thus, the reader takes active part in reconstructing the plot of a drama. In *Blood Relations*, the "plot" of Lizzie Borden's alleged parricide is perceived, patterned, and developed through an actress playing an actress who is playing Lizzie's part. The activity of playing Lizzie is the actual plot of the play. The reader must visualize an actress *now* playing the part of an actress in 1902, who is performing what had actually happened some ten years earlier. Similarly, in terms of space, the plot of *Antony and Cleopatra* moves through Antony's actions in Alexandria, Rome, and beyond. The many short scenes of acts 3 and 4 are effective in plotting the confusion, variousness, frustration, and uncertainty of love in combination with world struggle.

A plot contains a variety of actions and situations that need an environment in which to occur. This environment, at once physical and psychological, is known as the **setting**. It is a background, context, or location that contributes much to the plot. And the setting of a drama can be technically prescriptive, as in *The Homecoming*:

> *In the room a window, R. Odd tables, chairs. Two large armchairs. A large sofa, L. Against R. wall a large sideboard, the upper half of which contains a mirror. U.L., a radiogram.*

A reader or audience begins immediately to work with the play in asking what such a technical prescription signifies. The setting can also be expressed within the play as time and place, as in *Blood Relations*: "*The time proper is late Sunday afternoon and evening, late fall, in Fall River, 1902.*" The audience thus has a concrete setting to consider in terms of prevailing social mores and expectations. But setting can also be attentive to the nuances and subtleties of atmosphere, as indicated in Tennessee Williams's "Notes for the Designer," prefixed to *Cat on a Hot Tin Roof*: "The room must evoke some ghosts; it is gently and poetically haunted by a relationship that must have involved a tenderness which was uncommon." He continues:

> *I once saw a reproduction of a faded photograph of the verandah of Robert Louis Stevenson's home on that Samoan Island where he spent his last years, and there was a quality of tender light on weathered wood, such as porch furniture made of bamboo and wicker, exposed to tropical suns and tropical rains, which came to mind when I thought about the set for this play, bringing also to mind the grace and comfort of light, the reassurance it gives, on a late and fair afternoon in summer, the way that no matter what, even dread of death, is gently touched and soothed by it.*

This certainly suggests a mood and atmosphere in which the characters of the drama can move within the reader's imagination. But it also raises technical and aesthetic questions: How would such a setting be realized onstage? Why? What is it supposed to evoke for reader and audience? for actor? director? character?

Translating such effects onstage is most often the job of character. Onstage, setting can be effectively intuited from the words and actions of various characters: Cleopatra's "Give me some music! music, moody food / Of us that trade in love" (*Antony and Cleopatra*, 2.5.1–2) would seem to indicate that she is at home in her boudoir, restless in Antony's absence. Representing her present frame of mind is thus a challenge to any actor, director, costumer, reader. Likewise, the "feminine" repartee of Florinda and Hellena at the outset of *The Rover* establishes the setting as comfortable but also restrictive for its female participants. How might such a combination of comfort and restriction be realized? Setting is as much physical, environmental realization as it is emotional, atmospheric suggestion. One might say that the setting of *Doctor Faustus* is a professor's office; but the setting is also circumscribed by the complex wish fulfilment of an aspiring mind.

IRONY AND CHARACTER

In a sense, drama is an extended **irony** of representation. Character, plot, setting — none of it "exists" except on the stage as a patterned imitative enactment, or in the imagination of a sensitive reader. Dramatic irony occurs when the reader or audience knows more about a situation than the characters in that situation do. Such irony occurs in the first exploratory meeting between Caesar and Cleopatra. Shaw crafts the scene so that Caesar and the reader/audience are aware of the situation while Cleopatra is not. Safely within the shrine of a Sphinx, the queen of Egypt exposes her character unreservedly to a person whom she considers to be a kindly old gentleman, sharing her fears about the "monster," Julius Caesar. Only at the end of the scene, when the Roman soldiers troop into Cleopatra's throne room with shouts of "Hail, Caesar" directed towards their leader, is Cleopatra fully informed. The audience relishes the comic irony of her belated understanding. But the irony of withheld information can also work in an opposite way. It is most pronounced near the conclusion of Shakespeare's *Antony and Cleopatra* when Cleopatra sends word to Antony of her death. We, as reader/audience, know that the information is false but are powerless to intercede; Antony believes the report, and his desperate actions follow as a consequence. Irony of this sort heightens suspense and emphasizes, for this play, tragic misunderstanding.

But irony of representation occurs for characters within a play, too. Their self-deception and mistaken identity are features of irony pleasing to an audience. Thus, an extended comic irony of withheld information virtually comprises the plot of *The Importance of Being Earnest*. It also informs the role-play of Jack — representing himself as Ernest — and Algernon, who also represents himself as Ernest. The character "Ernest," of course, does not really exist, but the other characters of the play do not know this. The climactic visual irony of the play follows in act 2, as Jack enters in mourning for the supposedly dead Ernest, while Algernon — very much alive — is impersonating Ernest in another part of the garden. Such ironic disguise and role-play is a comic staple of television sitcoms and popular film. It also heightens the irony of characters and their representation in Woody Allen's *God*. Here, the conventions of ancient Greek tragedy — the Fates, the Chorus, the *deus ex machina* — are literalized in ironic and anachronistic absurdity. Characters arrive from other plays, from other periods of history, even from the audience, to help the play represent itself effectively. In *Blood Relations*, however, role-play is a grimly ironic basis of character as the Actress portrays Lizzie, and Lizzie herself portrays Bridget. Antony and Cleopatra, in Shakespeare's play, constantly play off each other in a variety of lovers' private roles as well as leaders' public personas.

Irony occurs in plot too, as circumstances twist themselves and turn out to be quite different from what a character — or sometimes the audience — expects. Irony operates in the gap between expectation and actuality, between what is said and what is meant, between what is intended and what occurs. In *Antony and Cleopatra*, Antony returns to Rome for his wife's funeral and ends up marrying another Roman woman while Cleopatra waits for him impatiently back in Egypt. In *Leaving Home*, the central irony of the play involves the fact that Bill and Kathy *must* get married because of her pregnancy. But Kathy has had a miscarriage, and that changes matters for everyone. In *Doctor Faustus*, the title character unequivocally states: "I think hell's a fable." And yet a representative of that very place is standing before him. Likewise, Faustus sells his soul for extra-worldly power and yet ends up involved in very worldly things: a roughhouse at the Vatican, a peep-show for the German emperor, a series of illusionistic self-mutilations. In *The Tempest*, Miranda's marvellous insight, "O brave new world / That has such people in't!" is undercut by the irony of Prospero's response: "'Tis new to thee" (5.1.183–84). The audience intellectually savours the added significance, incongruity, or paradox that irony constantly presents in drama.

THEME, SYMBOL, AND EFFECT

It might be said that drama lacks narration because it proceeds primarily through dialogue. As noted in the section on exposition, however, characters do sometimes narrate. Most often, though, narrative, as the story of the plot in time, is assembled in the imagination of the reader or audience. And inasmuch as drama is a participatory theatrical script, it is also a literary text with features of figurative language to be considered. Just as the plot is a perceived chain of events in the play, so the **theme** is an interpretation suggested by the plot. Basically, the plot of *Caesar and Cleopatra* concerns Julius

Caesar's consolidation of power in Egypt and his fatherly instruction of Cleopatra in affairs of state. But issues of imperialism, political logic, and benign despotism inevitably suggest themselves, as do overall themes of education and growth of awareness. In *The Homecoming*, plot is signalled by the title, but themes of mental, emotional, and sexual violence pervade the drama. Likewise, *Leaving Home*: the title might seem self-explanatory, but it raises many questions about what and how, and even who is actually "leaving home." In *The Importance of Being Earnest*, too, the plot involves a rather trivial farce of deception but suggests thematic complexity in terms of how people actually represent themselves to others and to themselves. The enduring freshness of drama as a form is due in large part to its active assembly, destruction, or consideration of situation through thematic and metaphorical suggestiveness.

Theme is conveyed powerfully through **symbol** and **metaphor** in the drama. Consider the symbolic visual significance of the hatchet in *Blood Relations*, along with the image of Lizzie's decapitated birds. Irrational violence? Sudden terror? Freedom destroyed? All three, and more, suggest themselves. In *The Rover*, the masks and disguises which the characters continually put on signify physical deception as a controlling theme of the play. Brick, in *Cat on a Hot Tin Roof*, moves around on a crutch, suggesting other "crutches" on which he desperately depends. In terms of language, notice the clipped, unmetaphorical efficiency of the very lines that Caesar speaks in *Antony and Cleopatra*:

> Go forth, Agrippa, and begin the fight.
> Our will is Antony be took alive.
> Make it known.
>
> (4.6.1–3)

Compare it with Antony's richer emotional and poetic complexity as he addresses his soldiers:

> Tend me to-night.
> May be it is the period of your duty.
> Haply you shall not see me more; or if,
> A mangled shadow. Perchance to-morrow
> You'll serve another master. I look on you
> As one that takes his leave.
>
> (4.2.24–29)

Caesar symbolizes cold calculation; Antony appeals to the heart. In *Doctor Faustus*, the appearance of Helen of Troy symbolizes the ultimate in sensual desirability. But the sexy vision is — like everything else Faustus achieves — an illusion. This may very well be "the face that launch'd a thousand ships" (5.1.92); it also metaphorically *sinks* Faustus's soul. Magic in the play represents tantalizing, transcendent wisdom at the same time as it suggests debilitating loss of agency in the title character. The book, at once a key stage property and a literalized visual symbol, suggests issues of learning along with its limits and misapplication. Damnation itself, in terms of Faustus's tragedy, is an overwhelmingly symbolic state.

In addition to words, symbols, and metaphors, drama also presents special physical and aural effects that enhance and complicate meaning. One can easily envisage a nude extra in a spotlight playing Helen in *Doctor Faustus*. As well, Helen could be represented simply by the spotlight. An effect true to the script would still be created in terms of attractive illusion. In addition to lighting, costume (or lack of costume) creates effect of character and atmosphere. Faustus could wear the period costume of Elizabethan England, the scholar's gown of a Victorian pedant, or the campus casual outfit of a young professor today. In *The Homecoming*, scripted pauses, blackouts, and re-starts of interaction and dialogue purposely create an effect of discontinuity. In *Antony and Cleopatra*, Shakespeare's direction *"music of the hautboys is under the stage"* (4.3.11) creates an eerie effect of ominous confusion as the spirit of Hercules abandons Antony.

SCRIPT AND MEANING

In drama, the time is always *now*, the mood is always imperative. The script is a set of textual instructions to be followed, interpreted, and performed. A reader mediates in the manner of an actor or director to construct meaning from the text. Drama involves plot, but there is no first-person or third-person narrative guide with a ready-made **point of view** for the reader's consideration. Instead, the reader of drama must discern general themes from a multiplicity of points of view provided by the words and actions of various characters. Thus, a reader of drama provides narration mentally in terms of plot, and performs the play imaginatively in terms of action. As a result, the reading of drama can never be passive. There is too much to do and consider: Imagine yourself performing a specific character or two. Read an especially emotional speech or dialogue aloud, and listen to what is created by the words. Consider yourself a director, and imagine how you would stage a specific scene in terms of movement, timing, costume. How do these various effects relate to each other? to character, action, and theme? The reading of drama, as opposed to the theatrical performance of it, allows a reader time to analyze, time to re-read, reconsider, and reinterpret dramatic possibilities. In fact — as every actor and director knows — no drama can be performed without a complex variety of interpretive prior "readings."

Variety, possibility, and surprise combine to make drama an eternally vital medium of communication. The script exists as a recipe and a suggestion because nothing is finalized; everything must be interpreted and created. This form of mental construction is a fundamental activity of the human mind and explains the enduring importance of drama to human beings. It represents the way we are. It expresses our social interactions as well as our deepest personal fears and hopes. We live our lives in a variety of roles and contexts as daughters, sons, students, parents, spectators, activists. In every one of our daily roles we must create a context in which to speak and act, and then we must perform. We must also interpret the performances of others. This is not to say that everything is illusion — not at all. Everything is action. Drama is human action. To read drama effectively is to re-create and interpret human social activity in order to broaden our understanding, refine our sympathy, and inform our prejudices about what it means to be human.

CHRISTOPHER MARLOWE

(1564–1593)

*B*orn in the same year as Shakespeare, Christopher Marlowe took a very different route to the professional London stage. He received the M.A. degree from Cambridge, and became playwright for the theatrical company known as the Admiral's Men sometime around 1587 with the début of his titanic play Tamburlaine The Great. *This was followed by* Doctor Faustus *and further stage triumphs in a short-lived theatrical career. He seems to have been involved in some sort of espionage as early as his university days, and was also one of Sir Walter Ralegh's irreverent circle of skeptics and free-thinkers. Brilliant, violent, homosexual, Marlowe clearly had a penchant for strong opinion and unconventional behaviour — a combination which got him into trouble with civic and ecclesiastical authorities, and led to a Privy Council warrant for his arrest issued on May 18, 1593. Before he could be brought to trial, however, he was killed under suspicious and controversial circumstances in a tavern east of London.*

Marlowe was a gifted dramatist who, through the energy of his verse, transformed the plodding, didactic stage into an inspired and exciting place for action and ideas. In fact, as noted in the Poetry section of this text, Marlowe's unprecedented "mighty line" became the standard metre for Shakespeare and later Renaissance drama.

INTRODUCTION TO *DOCTOR FAUSTUS*

*T*he earliest references to Marlowe's play occur in the records of theatrical entrepreneur Philip Henslowe, dating from 1594 to 1598. During this period the play triumphed at the Rose Theatre where it was performed by the Lord Admiral's Men with Edward Alleyn in the title role. Marlowe himself did not share in the play's success; he had been killed in 1593. Historical information about the play is further obscured and complicated by the fact that the earliest printed text of *Doctor Faustus* is dated 1604. A second and greatly expanded version is dated 1616. Modern bibliographical research has proven that the 1616 B-text, although textually corrupt in some places, is the authoritative version, with the 1604 A-text representing an abridged and uncertain version of the longer script. The version of *Doctor Faustus* printed here follows the 1616 B-text established by editor Leo Kirschbaum in 1962. The A-text expletives of the fifth act have been restored, as have one or two incidentals.

The primary medium of the play is epic blank verse: unrhymed iambic pentameter. Marlowe was not the first to use this measure in English, but he was certainly the first to demonstrate its breadth and power. Full of exciting imagery, rhythmic vitality, and rhetorical freshness, Marlowe's verse became the standard idiom for the Elizabethan stage. He even announced his departure from previous poetic practice of "jigging" fourteeners and incessant rhyming in a manifesto that served as prologue to *Tamburlaine The Great* (1587), his first dramatic success:

> From jigging veins of rhyming mother wits,
> And such conceits as clownage keeps in pay,
> We'll lead you to the stately tent of war,
> Where you shall hear the Scythian Tamburlaine
> Threat'ning the world with high astounding terms
> And scourging kingdoms with his conquering sword.
> View but his picture in this tragic glass,
> And then applaud his fortunes as you please.

Shakespeare was indebted to this style of poetry, and Milton would use it as the medium for his epic.

Stylistically and thematically, Marlowe's drama represents the sort of powerful Renaissance change that mediates between a medieval world of divinely ordained authority and a modern world of legitimate dissident questioning. The play documents the tragic career of Doctor John Faustus, brilliant academic at the university at Wittenberg where Martin Luther had taught. Thus the symbolism of iconoclastic inquiry and revolutionary theological theories is established at the very outset of the play. Faustus stands alone in conflict with his own aspirations, hopes, fantasies; but, as a social and spiritual renegade, his status is thrown in doubt. A gifted scholar with all the enlightenment of early Renaissance humanism, Faustus has improved himself; but, by seeking power beyond his human means, he goes too far. He mortgages his soul to the Devil in return for 24 years of magical power. Here — in terms of a scorned but comfortable past, a hopeful but uncertain future, and a desperate present pact — the very nature of his existence is placed in question.

In addition to this tragic pattern of choice and uncertainty, temptation and fall, Marlowe injects much in the way of irony, paradox, and conflict: Faustus is constantly warned of his ruin, but he just as constantly disregards these warnings; he considers himself at all points as the Devil's intellectual, even spiritual, superior; his early dreams of power and prestige get lost in petty displays of magic for the entertainment of the German emperor, the Duke of Vanholt, and, vicariously, for us as audience. His actions are as desperate as they are inconsequential. And the comic effects of the middle scenes are bracketed by lengthy monologues wherein Faustus effectively condemns himself to his own miserable conclusion. The power of the language in these passages reinforces images of cosmic significance, tragic choice, and utter personal grief.

The play, however, is more than just the effect of its admittedly powerful language. Marlowe's dramaturgy in *Doctor Faustus* looks back to the medieval morality plays and forward to modern psychologized drama. The pageant of the Seven Deadly Sins (2.2.105–57) is strictly representational and dramatically unsophisticated, as is the conflict of the Good and Bad Angels. But, although they represent personified abstractions in the manner of the early morality plays, the Good and Bad Angels also double as Faustus's conscience (2.2.12–20). Likewise, the Old Man who chastises Faustus near the conclusion (5.1.32–62) has his allegorical features but is not a moral type in the manner of "Mercy" or "Truth" or "Virtuous Life," as he might have been called in the earlier drama. He is simply an aged human whose soul is out of danger because of the strength of his faith. The Devil cannot harm him, as Mephostophilis says:

> His faith is great. I cannot touch his soul.
> But what I may afflict his body with
> I will attempt, which is but little worth.
>
> (5.1.80–82)

Physical facts have no bearing on spiritual health. Yet Marlowe provides the literalized stage property of the moralities — "Hell is discovered" (5.2.114 s.d.) — as well as the standard descriptions of demonic punishment and torment involving much heat and darkness and gnashing of teeth. At the same time, the play insists that hell is a state of mind. Mephostophilis (who should know) claims:

> Hell hath no limits nor is circumscrib'd
> In one self place, but where we are is Hell,
> And where Hell is there must we ever be.
>
> (2.1.114–16)

Faustus's prosaic response, "I think Hell's a fable" (2.1.124), is both a sophisticate's rejection and an unconscious statement of spiritual limitation that links up with the contrasts of the play overall: pride and shame, humanity and spirituality, seriousness and irresponsibility, heaven and hell. Such suggestive and basic dramatic conflicts are promised at the very outset of Doctor Faustus, described in the prologue as "The form of Faustus' fortunes, good or bad" (8). And Marlowe's sense of energetic theatre ensures that Faustus's fortunes will not be merely narrated or figuratively represented; they will be physically and psychologically performed.

The Tragical History of the Life and Death of Doctor Faustus

SPEAKING CHARACTERS

CHORUS

DOCTOR FAUSTUS

WAGNER, *his servant*

GOOD ANGEL

BAD ANGEL

VALDES ⎫
CORNELIUS ⎭ *magicians*

THREE SCHOLARS

LUCIFER

MEPHOSTOPHILIS

ROBIN, *called the Clown*

BELZEBUB

PRIDE

COVETOUSNESS

ENVY

WRATH ⎬ *the Seven Deadly Sins*

GLUTTONY

SLOTH

LECHERY

DICK, *a clown, hostler at an inn*

POPE ADRIAN

RAYMOND, *King of Hungary*

BRUNO, *rival Pope appointed by the* EMPEROR

TWO CARDINALS

ARCHIBISHOP OF RHEIMS

FRIARS

VINTNER'S BOY

MARTINO ⎫
FREDERICK ⎬ *gentlemen at the* EMPEROR's *court*
BENVOLIO ⎭

THE GERMAN EMPEROR, CHARLES THE FIFTH

DUKE OF SAXONY

TWO SOLDIERS

HORSE-COURSER, *a clown*

CARTER, *a clown*

HOSTESS OF TAVERN

DUKE OF VANHOLT

DUCHESS OF VANHOLT

SERVANT

OLD MAN

MUTE CHARACTERS

DARIUS, ALEXANDER THE GREAT, HIS PARAMOUR, HELEN OF TROY, DEVILS, PIPER, CARDINALS, MONKS, FRIARS, ATTENDANTS, SOLDIERS, SERVANTS, TWO CUPIDS

(Enter CHORUS.*)*

Not marching in the fields of Trasimene
Where Mars did mate[1] the warlike Carthagens,
Nor sporting in the dalliance of love
In courts of kings where state is overturn'd,
Nor in the pomp of proud audacious deeds
Intends our muse to vaunt his heavenly verse.
Only this, gentles: We must now perform
The form of Faustus' fortunes, good or bad,
And now to patient judgments we appeal
And speak for Faustus in his infancy.   *10*
Now is he born of parents base of stock
In Germany within a town call'd Rhode;
At riper years to Wittenberg he went
Whereas his kinsmen chiefly brought him up.
So much he profits in divinity
That shortly he was grac'd with doctor's name,
Excelling all, and sweetly can dispute
In th' heavenly matters of theology —
Till swoll'n with cunning, of a self-conceit,
His waxen wings did mount above his reach   *20*
And melting, Heavens conspir'd his overthrow!
For falling to a devilish exercise
And glutted now with learning's golden gifts
He surfeits upon cursed necromancy:
Nothing so sweet as magic is to him
Which he prefers before his chiefest bliss[2] . . .
And this the man that in his study sits.

1 *encounter.*
2 *salvation.*

ACT ONE

SCENE 1.

([CHORUS points to curtains in back of stage. They are drawn to discover] FAUSTUS in his study. [CHORUS exit.])

FAUSTUS: Settle thy studies Faustus, and begin
To sound the depth of that thou wilt profess.
Having commenc'd,[1] be a Divine in show —
Yet level[2] at the end of every art
And live and die in Aristotle's works.
Sweet Analytics,[3] 'tis thou hast ravish'd me. . . .

[Opens a book and turns over pages.]

Bene disserere est finis logices.[4]
Is to dispute well logic's chiefest end?
Affords this art no greater miracle?
Then read no more, thou hast attain'd that end.   10
A greater subject fitteth Faustus' wit:
Bid *on kai me on*[5] farewell, and Galen[6] come:

[Opens another book.]

Be a physician, Faustus, heap up gold,
And be eterniz'd for some wondrous cure.
Summum bonum medicinae sanitas,[7]
The end of physic is our body's health.
Why Faustus, hast thou not attain'd that end?
Are not thy bills[8] hung up as monuments
Whereby whole cities have escap'd the plague
And thousand desperate maladies been cur'd?   20
Yet art thou still but Faustus and a man.
Could'st thou make men to live eternally
Or being dead raise them to life again,
Then this profession were to be esteem'd.
Physic farewell! Where is Justinian?[9]

---

1 *graduated.* 2 *aim.* 3 *title of Aristotle's two treatises on logic.* 4 *To argue well is the end of logic.* 5 *being and not being.* 6 *Greek medical authority of the second century* A.D. 7 *The greatest good of medicine is health.* 8 *prescriptions.* 9 *Roman legal code of the sixth century* A.D., *named for the emperor Justinian.*

[*Opens another book.*]

Si una eademque res legatur duobus, alter rem, alter valorem rei, et cetera.[10]
A petty case of paltry legacies. . . .
Exhereditare filium non potest pater, nisi — [11]
Such is the subject of the Institute   30
And universal body of the law!
This study fits a mercenary drudge
Who aims at nothing but external trash,
Too servile and illiberal for me.
When all is done, divinity is best.
Jerome's Bible,[12] Faustus, view it well.

[*Opens another book.*]

Stipendium peccati mors est. Ha! *Stipendium et cetera* . . .
The reward of sin is death?[13] That's hard: *Si peccasse negamus,*
fallimur, et nulla est in nobis veritas. If we say that we have no
sin, we deceive ourselves, and there is no truth in us, Why,   40
then belike, we must sin, and so consequently die.
Ay, we must die an everlasting death.
What doctrine call you this? *Che serà, serà:*[14]
What will be, shall be! Divinity, adieu!
These metaphysics of magicians

[*Opens another book raptly.*]

And necromantic books are heavenly;
Lines, circles, letters, characters —
Ay, these are those that Faustus most desires!
O, what a world of profit and delight,
Of power, of honor, and omnipotence   50
Is promis'd to the studious artisan!
All things that move between the quiet poles
Shall be at my command. Emperors and kings
Are but obey'd in their several provinces
But his dominion that exceeds in this[15]
Stretcheth as far as doth the mind of man —
A sound magician is a demi-god!
Here tire my brains to get a deity!

[*Reads awhile with delight.*]

---

10 *If one thing is bequeathed to two persons, one of them gets the thing itself, the other the value of the thing.*
11 *A father cannot disinherit his son, unless —*
12 *the vulgate, a Latin translation done by Jerome in the fourth century. Still the authorized Latin text of the Roman Catholic Church.*
13 *here and following, Faustus provides translation for part of Romans 6:23 and I John 1:8.*
14 *Italian proverb; translated next sentence.*
15 *i.e., in magic.*

(Enter WAGNER.)

Wagner, commend me to my dearest friends,
The German Valdes and Cornelius.   60
Request them earnestly to visit me.
WAGNER: I will, sir.

(Exit.)

FAUSTUS: Their conference will be a greater help to me.
Than all my labors, plod I ne'er so fast.

[*He reads.*]

(Enter the [GOOD] ANGEL *and* SPIRIT [*i.e.,* BAD ANGEL].*)*

GOOD ANGEL: O Faustus, lay that damned book aside
And gaze not on it lest it tempt thy soul
And heap God's heavy wrath upon thy head!
Read, read the Scriptures — that[16] is blasphemy!
BAD ANGEL: Go forward Faustus, in that famous art
Wherein all nature's treasure is contain'd.   70
Be thou on earth as Jove is in the sky,
Lord and commander of these elements!

(Exeunt.)

FAUSTUS: How am I glutted with conceit of this![17]

[*Raises head from book.*]

Shall I make spirits fetch me what I please?
Resolve me of all ambiguities?
Perform what desperate enterprise I will?
I'll have them fly to India for gold,
Ransack the ocean for orient pearl,
And search all corners of the new-found world
For pleasant fruits and princely delicates;   80
I'll have them read me strange philosophy
And tell the secrets of all foreign kings;
I'll have them wall all Germany with brass
And make swift Rhine circle fair Wittenberg;
I'll have them fill the public schools with silk
Wherewith the students shall be bravely clad.

16 *i.e., Faustus's book of magic.*
17 *i.e., the notion of magical power.*

I'll levy soldiers with the coin they bring
And chase the Prince of Parma[18] from our land
And reign sole king of all our provinces!
Yea, stranger engines for the brunt of war   90
Than was the fiery keel at Antwerp's bridge
I'll make my servile spirits to invent.

(Enter VALDES *and* CORNELIUS *[with books].)*

Come German Valdes and Cornelius
And make me blest with your sage conference.
Valdes, sweet Valdes, and Cornelius,
Know that your words have won me at the last
To practice magic and concealed arts.
Philosophy is odious and obscure,
Both law and physic are for petty wits,
Divinity is basest of the three —   100
Unpleasant, harsh, contemptible, and vile.
'Tis magic, magic, that hath ravish'd me!
Then, gentle friends, aid me in this attempt
And I, that have with subtle syllogisms
Gravell'd[19] the pastors of the German church
And made the flow'ring pride of Wittenberg
Swarm to my problems as th' infernal spirits
On sweet Musaeus[20] when he came to Hell,
Will be as cunning as Agrippa[21] was,
Whose shadows made all Europe honor him.   110
VALDES: Faustus, these books, thy wit, and our experience
Shall make all nations to canonize us.
As Indian Moors[22] obey their Spanish lords,
So shall the spirits of every element
Be always serviceable to us three:
Like lions shall they guard us when we please,
Like Almain rutters[23] with their horsemen's staves
Or Lapland giants trotting by our sides;
Sometimes like women or unwedded maids
Shadowing more beauty in their airy brows   120
Than has the white breasts of the queen of love;
From Venice shall they drag huge argosies
And from America the golden fleece
That yearly stuffs old Philip's[24] treasury —
If learned Faustus will be resolute.
FAUSTUS: Valdes, as resolute am I in this
As thou to live; therefore object it not.

---

18 *Spanish governor general of the Low Countries, including northern Germany (1579–92).* **19** *confounded.* **20** *poet in Greek mythology.* **21** *Cornelius Agrippa (1486–1535), author of a book on magic and a reputed magician himself.* **22** *i.e., North American native people.* **23** *German cavalry officers.* **24** *king of Spain (1527–98).*

CORNELIUS: The miracles that magic will perform
    Will make thee vow to study nothing else.
    He that is grounded in astrology,   *130*
    Enrich'd with tongues, well seen in minerals,
    Hath all the principles magic doth require.
    Then doubt not Faustus but to be renown'd
    And more frequented for this mystery
    Than heretofore the Delphian oracle.[25]
    The spirits tell me they can dry the sea
    And fetch the treasure of all foreign wracks,
    Yea, all the wealth that our forefathers hid
    Within the massy entrails of the earth.
    Then tell me Faustus, what shall we three want?   *140*
FAUSTUS: Nothing, Cornelius! O, this cheers my soul!
    Come, show me some demonstrations magical
    That I may conjure in some bushy grove
    And have these joys in full possession.
VALDES: Then haste thee to some solitary grove,
    And bear wise Bacon's and Albanus'[26] works,
    The Hebrew Psalter, and New Testament;
    And whatsoever else is requisite
    We will inform thee ere our conference cease.
CORNELIUS: Valdes, first let him know the words of art,   *150*
    And then, all other ceremonies learn'd,
    Faustus may try his cunning by himself.
VALDES: First I'll instruct thee in the rudiments,
    And then wilt thou be perfecter than I.
FAUSTUS: Then come and dine with me, and after meat
    We'll canvass every quiddity[27] thereof —
    For ere I sleep I'll try what I can do.
    This night I'll conjure though I die therefor!

(Exeunt omnes.)[28]

    SCENE 2. *(Enter two* SCHOLARS.*)*

1 SCHOLAR: I wonder what's become of Faustus that was wont to make
    our schools ring with *sic probo*.[1]

(Enter WAGNER *[with a bottle].)*

2 SCHOLAR: That shall we presently know. Here comes his boy.
1 SCHOLAR: How now sirrah,[2] where's thy master?

25 *legendary oracle of Apollo at Delphi.*
26 *Roger Bacon and Pietro D'Albano, medieval scientists and reputed magicians.*
27 *essential detail.*
28 *all go out.*

1 *thus I prove it.*
2 *form of address directed toward an inferior.*

WAGNER: God in Heaven knows.

2 SCHOLAR: Why, dost not thou know then?

WAGNER: Yes, I know, but that follows not.

1 SCHOLAR: Go to sirrah, leave your jesting and tell us where he is.

WAGNER: That follows not by force of argument, which you, being licentiates,[3] should stand upon; therefore acknowledge your error and be   10
attentive.

2 SCHOLAR: Then you will not tell us?

WAGNER: You are deceiv'd, for I will tell you. Yet if you were not dunces, you would never ask me such a question. For is he not *corpus naturale*?[4] And is not that *mobile*?[5] Then wherefore should you ask me such a question? But that I am by nature phlegmatic, slow to wrath, and prone to lechery — to love, I would say — it were not for you to come within forty foot of the place of execution[6] — although I do not doubt but to see you both hang'd the next sessions. Thus, having triumphed over you, I will set my countenance like a precisian[7]   20
and begin to speak thus: Truly, my dear brethren, my master is within at dinner, with Valdes and Cornelius, as this wine, if it could speak, would inform your worships; and so, the Lord bless you, preserve you, and keep you, my dear brethren.

(Exit.)

1 SCHOLAR: O Faustus, then I fear that which I have long suspected,
That thou art fall'n into that damned art
For which they two are infamous through the world.

2 SCHOLAR: Were he a stranger, not allied to me,
The danger of his soul would make me mourn.
But come, let us go and inform the Rector.[8]   30
It may be his grave counsel may reclaim him.

1 SCHOLAR: I fear me nothing will reclaim him now.

2 SCHOLAR: Yet let us see what we can do.

(Exeunt.)

> SCENE 3. *(Thunder. Enter* LUCIFER *and four* DEVILS *[above]:* FAUSTUS *[in magician's robe] to them with this speech:)*

FAUSTUS: Now that the gloomy shadow of the night,
Longing to view Orion's[1] drizzling look,
Leaps from th' antarctic world unto the sky
And dims the welkin[2] with her pitchy breath,

---

3 *i.e., graduate students.*
4 *a natural body.*
5 *movable.*
6 *i.e., the place where Faustus is dining.*
7 *puritan.*
8 *head of the university.*

1 *winter constellation that portends rain in northern Europe.*
2 *sky.*

Faustus, begin thine incantations
And try if devils will obey thy hest,
Seeing thou hast pray'd and sacrific'd to them.
Within this circle is Jehovah's name
Forward and backward anagrammatiz'd,
Th' abbreviated names of holy saints,   10
Figures of every adjunct to the heavens,
And characters of signs and erring stars,
By which the spirits are enforc'd to rise:
Then fear not, Faustus, to be resolute
And try the uttermost magic can perform.

(Thunder)

*Sint mihi dei Acherontis propitii! Valeat numen triplex Iehovae! Ignei, aerii, aqua-
tici, spiritus, salvete! Orientis princeps, Belzebub inferni ardentis monarcha, et
Demogorgon, propitiamus vos ut appareat et surgat Mephostophilis! Quid tu mora-
ris? Per Iehovam, Gehennam, et consecratam aquam quam nunc spargo, signumque
crucis quod nunc facio, et per vota nostra, ipse nunc surgat nobis dicatus*   20
Mephostophilis![3]

(Enter a DEVIL [i.e., a dragon-head rises from the open trap. FAUSTUS recoils].)

I charge thee to return and change thy shape,
Thou art too ugly to attend on me.
Go, and return an old Franciscan friar:
That holy shape becomes a devil best.

(Exit DEVIL [i.e., dragon-head sinks].)

I see there's virtue in my heavenly words.
Who would not be proficient in this art?
How pliant is this Mephostophilis,
Full of obedience and humility,
Such is the force of magic and my spells!   30

(Enter MEPHOSTOPHILIS [from the back as an elderly friar].)

MEPHOSTOPHILIS: Now Faustus, what wouldst thou have me do?
FAUSTUS: I charge thee wait upon me whilst I live
    To do whatever Faustus shall command,
    Be it to make the moon drop from her sphere
    Or the ocean to overwhelm the world.
MEPHOSTOPHILIS: I am a servant to great Lucifer
    And may not follow thee without his leave.
    No more than he commands must we perform.

---

3 *May the gods of Acheron (one of the rivers in Hades) be propitious to me! Away with the trinity of Jehovah!
Hail, spirits of fire, air, water! Prince of the East, Belzebub monarch of burning hell, and Demogorgon, we ask
your favour that Mephostophilis may appear and rise! Why do you delay? By Jehovah, Gehenna, and the holy
water which I now sprinkle, and the sign of the cross which I now make, and by our vows, may Mephostophilis
himself rise at our command!*

FAUSTUS: Did not he charge thee to appear to me?
MEPHOSTOPHILIS: No, I came now hither of mine own accord.   40
FAUSTUS: Did not my conjuring raise thee? Speak.
MEPHOSTOPHILIS: That was the cause, but yet *per accidens*:[4]
    For when we hear one rack the name of God,
    Abjure the Scriptures and his savior Christ,
    We fly in hope to get his glorious soul.
    Nor will we come unless he use such means
    Whereby he is in danger to be damn'd.
    Therefore the shortest cut for conjuring
    Is stoutly to abjure the Trinity
    And pray devoutly to the Prince of Hell.   50
FAUSTUS: So Faustus hath already done, and holds this principle,
    There is no chief but only Belzebub:
    To whom Faustus doth dedicate himself.
    This word *damnation* terrifies not me
    For I confound Hell in Elysium:[5]
    My ghost[6] be with the old[7] philosophers!
    But leaving these vain trifles of men's souls,
    Tell me, what is that Lucifer thy lord?
MEPHOSTOPHILIS: Arch-Regent and Commander of All Spirits.
FAUSTUS: Was not that Lucifer an angel once?   60
MEPHOSTOPHILIS: Yes Faustus, and most dearly lov'd of God.
FAUSTUS: How comes it then that he is Prince of Devils?
MEPHOSTOPHILIS: O, by aspiring pride and insolence,
    For which God threw him from the face of Heaven.
FAUSTUS: And what are you that live with Lucifer?
MEPHOSTOPHILIS: Unhappy spirits that fell with Lucifer,
    Conspir'd against our God with Lucifer,
    And are for ever damn'd with Lucifer.
FAUSTUS: Where are you damn'd?
MEPHOSTOPHILIS: In Hell.   70
FAUSTUS: How comes it then that thou art out of Hell?
MEPHOSTOPHILIS: Why this is Hell, nor am I out of it. . . .
    Think'st thou that I who saw the face of God
    And tasted the eternal joys of Heaven
    Am not tormented with ten thousand Hells
    In being depriv'd of everlasting bliss?
    O Faustus, leave these frivolous demands
    Which strike a terror to my fainting soul!
FAUSTUS: What, is great Mephostophilis so passionate
    For being deprived of the joys of Heaven?   80
    Learn thou of Faustus manly fortitude
    And scorn those joys thou never shalt possess.
    Go bear these tidings to great Lucifer:

---

4 *by chance.*
5 *i.e., do not distinguish between Christian hell and pagan Elysium, the place of ideal comfort in Greek and Roman mythology.*
6 *soul, spirit.*
7 *i.e., pre-Christian.*

Seeing Faustus hath incurr'd eternal death
By desperate thoughts against Jove's deity,
Say he surrenders up to him his soul
So he will spare him four and twenty years,
Letting him live in all voluptuousness,
Having thee ever to attend on me,
To give me whatsoever I shall ask,   90
To tell me whatsoever I demand,
To slay mine enemies and to aid my friends
And always be obedient to my will.
Go and return to mighty Lucifer
And meet me in my study at midnight,
And then resolve me of thy master's mind.
MEPHOSTOPHILIS: I will, Faustus.

(Exit.)

FAUSTUS: Had I as many souls as there be stars
I'd give them all for Mephostophilis!
By him I'll be great emperor of the world   100
And make a bridge thorough[8] the moving air
To pass the ocean with a band of men;
I'll join the hills that bind the Afric shore
And make that country continent to Spain,
And both contributary to my crown;
The Emperor shall not live but by my leave,
Nor any potentate of Germany.
Now that I have obtain'd what I desir'd
I'll live in speculation of this art
Till Mephostophilis return again.   110

(Exit.)

SCENE 4. *(Enter* WAGNER *and* [ROBIN] *the* CLOWN.*)*

WAGNER: Come hither, sirrah boy.
ROBIN: Boy! O, disgrace to my person! Zounds, boy in your face! You
   have seen many boys with such pickadevants,[1] I am sure.
WAGNER: Sirrah, hast thou no comings in?[2]
ROBIN: Yes, and goings out too, you may see sir.
WAGNER: Alas, poor slave! See how poverty jests in his nakedness. I
   know the villain's out of service, and so hungry that I know he
   would give his soul to the Devil for a shoulder of mutton, though it
   were blood-raw.
ROBIN: Not so, neither! I had need to have it well roasted, and good   10
   sauce to it, if I pay so dear, I can tell you.

---

8 *i.e., through.*

1 *pointed beards.*

2 *i.e., income.*

WAGNER: Sirrah, wilt thou be my man and wait on me? And I will make
thee go like *Qui mihi discipulus*.[3]
ROBIN: What, in verse?
WAGNER: No, slave, in beaten[4] silk and stavesacre.[5]
ROBIN: Stavesacre? That's good to kill vermin! Then, belike, if I serve
you I shall be lousy.
WAGNER: Why, so thou shalt be, whether thou dost it or no; for sirrah, if
thou dost not presently bind thyself to me for seven years, I'll turn
all the lice about thee into familiars[6] and make them tear thee in   20
pieces.
ROBIN: Nay sir, you may save yourself a labor, for they are as familiar
with me as if they paid for their meat and drink, I can tell you.
WAGNER: Well sirrah, leave your jesting and take these guilders.[7]
ROBIN: Yes marry sir, and I thank you too.
WAGNER: So, now thou art to be at an hour's warning whensoever and
wheresoever the Devil shall fetch thee.
ROBIN: Here, take your guilders, I'll none of 'em.
WAGNER: Not I, thou art press'd. Prepare thyself, for I will presently raise
up two devils to carry thee away. Banio! Belcher! [*Makes magical*   30
gestures.]
ROBIN: Belcher! And Belcher come here I'll belch him. I am not afraid of
a devil!

(*Enter two* DEVILS [*and the* CLOWN *runs about*].)

WAGNER: How now sir, will you serve me now?
ROBIN: Ay, good Wagner, take away the Devil then.
WAGNER: Spirits, away! [*Exeunt.*] Now, sirrah, follow me.
ROBIN: I will sir! But hark you master, will you teach me this conjuring
occupation?
WAGNER: Ay sirrah, I'll teach thee to turn thyself to a dog or a cat or a
mouse or a rat or anything.
ROBIN: A dog or a cat or a mouse or a rat? O brave Wagner!   40
WAGNER: Villain, call me Master Wagner. And see that you walk atten-
tively, and let your right eye be always diametrally[8] fixed upon my
left heel, that thou mayst *quasi vestigiis nostris insistere*.[9]
ROBIN: Well sir, I warrant you.

(*Exeunt.*)

---

3 *You who are my pupil.* **4** *embroidered.* **5** *lice powder.* **6** *attendant demons.* **7** *Dutch currency.* **8** *directly.* **9** *as*
it were, walk in our footsteps.

ACT TWO

SCENE 1. *(Enter* FAUSTUS *in his study.)*

FAUSTUS: Now, Faustus, must thou needs be damn'd, canst thou not be
  sav'd!
  What boots it then to think on God or Heaven?
  Away with such vain fancies, and despair —
  Despair in God and trust in Belzebub!
  Now go not backward. Faustus, be resolute!
  Why waver'st thou? O something soundeth in mine ear,
  "Abjure this magic, turn to God again. . . ."
  Why, He loves thee not —
  The god thou serv'st is thine own appetite
  Wherein is fix'd the love of Belzebub!   10
  To him I'll build an altar and a church
  And offer lukewarm blood of newborn babes!

(Enter the two ANGELS.*)*

BAD ANGEL: Go forward, Faustus, in that famous art.
GOOD ANGEL: Sweet Faustus, leave that execrable art.
FAUSTUS: Contrition, prayer, repentance, what of these?
GOOD ANGEL: O, they are means to bring thee unto Heaven.
BAD ANGEL: Rather illusions, fruits of lunacy,
  That make men foolish that do use them most.
GOOD ANGEL: Sweet Faustus, think of Heaven and heavenly things.
BAD ANGEL: No Faustus, think of honor and of wealth.   20
FAUSTUS: Wealth!
  Why, the signory of Emden[1] shall be mine!
  When Mephostophilis shall stand by me
  What power can hurt me? Faustus, thou art safe.
  Cast no more doubts! Mephostophilis, come,
  And bring glad tidings from great Lucifer.
  Is't not midnight? Come Mephostophilis,
  Veni,[2] *veni, Mephostophilis!*

(Enter MEPHOSTOPHILIS.*)*

  Now tell me, what saith Lucifer thy lord?
MEPHOSTOPHILIS: That I shall wait on Faustus whilst he lives,   30
  So he will buy my service with his soul.
FAUSTUS: Already Faustus hath hazarded that for thee.
MEPHOSTOPHILIS: But now thou must bequeath it solemnly
  And write a deed of gift with thine own blood,
  For that security craves Lucifer.
  If thou deny it I must back to Hell.

1 *wealthy port in northwest Germany.*
2 *come.*

FAUSTUS: Stay Mephostophilis and tell me
    What good my soul will do thy lord?
MEPHOSTOPHILIS: Enlarge his kingdom.
FAUSTUS: Is that the reason why he tempts us thus?   40
MEPHOSTOPHILIS: *Solamen miseris socios habuisse doloris.*[3]
FAUSTUS: Why, have you any pain that torture other?
MEPHOSTOPHILIS: As great as have the human souls of men.
    But tell me, Faustus, shall I have thy soul —
    And I will be thy slave and wait on thee
    And give thee more than thou hast wit to ask?
FAUSTUS: Ay Mephostophilis, I'll give it him.[4]
MEPHOSTOPHILIS: Then, Faustus, stab thy arm courageously
    And bind thy soul that at some certain day
    Great Lucifer may claim it as his own.   50
    And then be thou as great as Lucifer!
FAUSTUS: Lo, Mephostophilis, for love of thee

[FAUSTUS *cuts his arm, dips a pen in his blood, and writes.*]

Faustus hath cut his arm and with his proper[5] blood
Assures his soul to be great Lucifer's,
Chief lord and regent of perpetual night.
View here this blood that trickles from mine arm
And let it be propitious for my wish.
MEPHOSTOPHILIS: But Faustus,
    Write it in manner of a deed of gift.
FAUSTUS: Ay so I do — But Mephostophilis,   60
    My blood congeals and I can write no more!
MEPHOSTOPHILIS: I'll fetch thee fire to dissolve it straight.

(Exit.)

FAUSTUS: What might the staying of my blood portend?
    Is it unwilling I should write this bill?[6]
    Why streams it not that I may write afresh:
    "Faustus gives to thee his soul"? O there it stay'd. . . .
    Why shouldst thou not? Is not thy soul thine own?
    Then write again: "Faustus gives to thee his soul."

(Enter MEPHOSTOPHILIS *with the chafer*[7] *of fire.)*

MEPHOSTOPHILIS: See Faustus, here is fire. Set it on.

[FAUSTUS *puts his arm over the fire.*]

---

3 *It is a solace to the wretched to have had companions in grief (i.e., "Misery loves company").*
4 *i.e., to Lucifer.*
5 *own.*
6 *contract.*
7 *portable grate.*

FAUSTUS: So, now the blood begins to clear again.   70
    Now will I make an end immediately.
MEPHOSTOPHILIS: [aside.] (What will not I do to obtain his soul!)
FAUSTUS: Consummatum est![8] This bill is ended:
    And Faustus hath bequeath'd his soul to Lucifer.
    — But what is this inscription on mine arm?
    Homo fuge![9] Whither should I fly?
    If unto God, He'll throw me down to Hell.
    — My senses are deceiv'd, here's nothing writ.
    — O yes, I see it plain! Even here is writ
    Homo fuge! Yet shall not Faustus fly!   80
MEPHOSTOPHILIS: [aside.] (I'll fetch him somewhat to delight his mind.)

(Exit.)

(Enter DEVILS giving crowns and rich apparel to FAUSTUS. They dance and then depart.)

(Enter MEPHOSTOPHILIS.)

FAUSTUS: What means this show? Speak, Mephostophilis.
MEPHOSTOPHILIS: Nothing Faustus, but to delight thy mind
    And let thee see what magic can perform.
FAUSTUS: But may I raise such spirits when I please?
MEPHOSTOPHILIS: Ay Faustus, and do greater things than these.
FAUSTUS: Then, Mephostophilis, receive this scroll,
    A deed of gift of body and of soul —
    But yet conditionally that thou perform
    All covenants and articles between us both.   90
MEPHOSTOPHILIS: Faustus, I swear by Hell and Lucifer
    To effect all promises between us both.
FAUSTUS: Then hear me read it, Mephostophilis:
    On these conditions following — First, that Faustus may be a spirit in form and substance. Secondly, that Mepohostophilis shall be his servant and be by him commanded. Thirdly, that Mephostophilis shall do for him and bring him whatsoever. Fourthly, that he shall be in his chamber or house invisible. Lastly, that he shall appear to the said John Faustus at all times in what form or shape soever he please:
    I, John Faustus of Wittenberg, Doctor, by these presents, do give both body and soul to Lucifer, Prince of the East, and his minister Mephostophilis, and furthermore grant unto them that, four and twenty years being expired, and these articles above written being inviolate, full power to fetch or carry the said John Faustus, body and soul, flesh, blood, into their habitation wheresoever.   100
                                  By me, John Faustus.
MEPHOSTOPHILIS: Speak Faustus, do you deliver this as your deed?
FAUSTUS: Ay, take it, and the Devil give thee good of it!
MEPHOSTOPHILIS: So now Faustus, ask me what thou wilt.

8 It is finished. (A daring repetition of Christ's last words on the cross; see John 19:30.)
9 Flee, man!

FAUSTUS: First will I question with thee about Hell.
  Tell me, where is the place that men call Hell?
MEPHOSTOPHILIS: Under the heavens.
FAUSTUS: Ay, so are all things else, but whereabouts? *110*
MEPHOSTOPHILIS: Within the bowels of these elements
  Where we are tortur'd and remain forever.
  Hell hath no limits nor is circumscrib'd
  In one self place, but where we are is Hell,
  And where Hell is there must we ever be.
  And to be short, when all the world dissolves
  And every creature shall be purifi'd
  All places shall be Hell that is not Heaven!
FAUSTUS: I think Hell's a fable.
MEPHOSTOPHILIS: Ay, think so still — till experience change thy mind! *120*
FAUSTUS: Why, dost thou think that Faustus shall be damn'd?
MEPHOSTOPHILIS: Ay, of necessity, for here's the scroll
  In which thou hast given thy soul to Lucifer.
FAUSTUS: Ay, and body too — but what of that?
Think'st thou that Faustus is so fond¹⁰ to imagine
  That after this life there is any pain?
  No, these are trifles and mere old wives' tales.
MEPHOSTOPHILIS: But I am an instance to prove the contrary,
  For I tell thee I am damn'd and now in Hell!
FAUSTUS: Nay, and this be Hell, I'll willingly be damn'd — *130*
  What, sleeping, eating, walking, and disputing? But leaving this, let
  me have a wife, the fairest maid in Germany, for I am wanton and
  lascivious and cannot live without a wife.
MEPHOSTOPHILIS: Well Faustus, thou shalt have a wife.

(He fetches in a WOMAN DEVIL.)

FAUSTUS: What sight is this?
MEPHOSTOPHILIS: Now Faustus, wilt thou have a wife?
FAUSTUS: Here's a hot whore indeed! No, I'll no wife.
MEPHOSTOPHILIS: Marriage is but a ceremonial toy,

[SHE-DEVIL *exit.*]

  And if thou lovest me, think no more of it.
  I'll cull thee out the fairest courtesans *140*
  And bring them every morning to thy bed.
  She whom thine eye shall like thy heart shall have,
  Were she as chaste as was Penelope,¹¹
  As wise as Saba,¹² or as beautiful
  As was bright Lucifer before his fall.
  Here, take this book, peruse it well.
  The iterating of these lines brings gold;

10 *foolish.*
11 *faithful wife of Ulysses.*
12 *queen of Sheba.*

[*Points to certain pages.*]

The framing of this circle on the ground
Brings thunder, whirlwinds, storm, and lightning;
Pronounce this thrice devoutly to thyself,   150
And men in harness shall appear to thee,
Ready to execute what thou command'st.

[*He gives* FAUSTUS *the book.*]

FAUSTUS: Thanks Mephostophilis for this sweet book.
     This will I keep as chary as my life.

(*Exeunt.*)

[*Apparently at this point there occurred a comic scene, which is now lost.*]

SCENE 2. (*Enter* FAUSTUS *in his study and* MEPHOSTOPHILIS.)

FAUSTUS: When I behold the heavens, then I repent —
     And curse thee, wicked Mephostophilis,
     Because thou hast depriv'd me of those joys.
MEPHOSTOPHILIS: 'Twas thine own seeking Faustus, thank thyself.
     But think'st thou Heaven is such a glorious thing?
     I tell thee, Faustus, it is not half so fair
     As thou or any man that breathe on earth.
FAUSTUS: How prov'st thou that?
MEPHOSTOPHILIS: 'Twas made for man: then he's more excellent.
FAUSTUS: If Heaven was made for man, 'twas made for me!   10
     I will renounce this magic and repent.

(*Enter the two* ANGELS.)

GOOD ANGEL: Faustus, repent: yet God will pity thee!
BAD ANGEL: Thou art a spirit: God cannot pity thee!
FAUSTUS: Who buzzeth in mine ears I am a spirit?
     Be I a devil, yet God may pity me —
     Yea, God will pity me if I repent.
BAD ANGEL: Ay, but Faustus never shall repent.

(*Exeunt* ANGELS.)

FAUSTUS: My heart is harden'd, I cannot repent.
     Scarce can I name salvation, faith, or Heaven,
     Swords, poison, halters, and envenom'd steel   20
     Are laid before me to dispatch myself.
     And long ere this I should have done the deed
     Had not sweet pleasure conquer'd deep despair.
     Have not I made blind Homer sing to me

Of Alexander's love and Oenon's death?[1]
And hath not he[2] that built the walls of Thebes
With ravishing sound of his melodious harp
Made music with my Mephostophilis?
Why should I die then or basely despair? —
I am resolv'd Faustus shall not repent! —   30
Come Mephostophilis, let us dispute again
And reason of divine astrology.
Speak, are there many spheres above the moon?
Are all celestial bodies but one globe
As is the substance of this centric earth?
MEPHOSTOPHILIS: As are the elements, such are the heavens,
Even from the moon unto the empyreal orb
Mutually folded in each others' spheres —
And jointly move upon one axle-tree,
Whose termine[3] is termed the world's wide pole.   40
Nor are the names of Saturn, Mars, or Jupiter
Feign'd but are erring stars.
FAUSTUS: But have they all one motion, both *situ et tempore?*[4]
MEPHOSTOPHILIS: All move from east to west in four and twenty hours
    upon the poles of the world but differ in their motions upon the
    poles of the zodiac.
FAUSTUS: These slender questions Wagner can decide. Hath Mephosto-
    philis no greater skill? Who knows not the double motion of the
    planets? — That the first is finish'd in a natural day. The second
    thus: Saturn in thirty years; Jupiter in twelve; Mars in four; the sun,   50
    Venus, and Mercury in a year; the moon in twenty-eight days.
    These are freshmen's suppositions. But tell me, hath every sphere a
    dominion or *intelligentia?*[5]
MEPHOSTOPHILIS: Ay.
FAUSTUS: How many heavens or spheres are there?
MEPHOSTOPHILIS: Nine: the seven planets, the firmament, and the empy-
    real heaven.
FAUSTUS: But is there not *coelum igneum* and *crystallinum?*[6]
MEPHOSTOPHILIS: No Faustus, they be but fables.
FAUSTUS: Resolve me then in this one question. Why are not conjunc-   60
    tions, oppositions, aspects, eclipses all at one time, but in some years
    we have more, in some less?
MEPHOSTOPHILIS: *Per inaequalem motum respectu totius.*[7]
FAUSTUS: Well, I am answer'd. Now tell me, who made the world?
MEPHOSTOPHILIS: I will not.
FAUSTUS: Sweet Mephostophilis, tell me.

---

1 *also known as Paris, Alexander loved but deserted Oenon for Helen of Troy, thus precipitating the Trojan War, of which Homer "sings" in the* Iliad. **2** *Amphion, mythological musician.* **3** *limit.* **4** *in space and time.* **5** *governing intelligence.* **6** *a heaven of fire and crystal?* **7** *because of their unequal motion with respect to the whole.*

MEPHOSTOPHILIS: Move[8] me not, Faustus!
FAUSTUS: Villain, have not I bound thee to tell me anything?
MEPHOSTOPHILIS: Ay, that is not against our kingdom. This is. Thou art
    damn'd. Think thou of Hell!   70
FAUSTUS: Think, Faustus, upon God, that made the world.
MEPHOSTOPHILIS: Remember this!

    (Exit.)

FAUSTUS: Ay, go accursed spirit to ugly Hell!
    'Tis thou hast damn'd distressed Faustus' soul. —
    Is't not too late?

    (Enter the two ANGELS.)

BAD ANGEL: Too late.
GOOD ANGEL: Never too late, if Faustus will repent.
BAD ANGEL: If thou repent, devils will tear thee in pieces.
GOOD ANGEL: Repent, and they shall never raze[9] thy skin.

    (Exeunt ANGELS.)

FAUSTUS: O Christ, my savior, my savior! Help to save distressed Faus-   80
    tus' soul.

    (Enter LUCIFER, BELZEBUB, and MEPHOSTOPHILIS [from trap. LUCIFER menaces
    FAUSTUS].)

LUCIFER: Christ cannot save thy soul, for He is just.
    There's none but I have interest in the same.
FAUSTUS: [retreating.] O, what art thou that look'st so terribly?
LUCIFER: I am Lucifer
    And this is my companion prince in Hell.
FAUSTUS: [wildly.] O Faustus, they are come to fetch thy soul!
BELZEBUB: We are come to tell thee thou dost injure us.
LUCIFER: Thou call'st on Christ contrary to thy promise.
BELZEBUB: Thou should'st not think on God.   90
LUCIFER: Think on the Devil.
BELZEBUB: And his dam[10] too.
FAUSTUS: Nor will Faustus henceforth. Pardon him for this,
    And Faustus vows never to look to Heaven!
LUCIFER: So shalt thou show thyself an obedient servant, and we will
    highly gratify thee for it.
BELZEBUB: Faustus, we are come from Hell in person to show thee some
    pastime. Sit down and thou shalt behold the Seven Deadly Sins
    appear to thee in their own proper shapes and likeness.

8 urge.
9 scratch.
10 dame, mother.

FAUSTUS: That sight will be as pleasant to me as Paradise was to Adam   *100*
    the first day of his creation.
LUCIFER: Talk not of Paradise or creation but mark the show. Go
    Mephostophilis, fetch them in.

[MEPHOSTOPHILIS *goes to one of the entrances and beckons.*]

(Enter the SEVEN DEADLY SINS *[led by a* PIPER].*)*

BELZEBUB: Now Faustus, question them of their names and dispositions.
FAUSTUS: That shall I soon. What art thou, the first?
PRIDE: I am Pride. I disdain to have any parents. I am like to Ovid's flea,[11]
    I can creep into every corner of a wench: sometimes, like a periwig I
    sit upon her brow; next, like a necklace I hang about her neck; then,
    like a fan of feathers I kiss her; and then, turning myself to a
    wrought[12] smock, do what I list. . . . But fie, what a smell is here! I'll   *110*
    not speak a word more for a king's ransom unless the ground be
    perfum'd and cover'd with cloth of arras.[13]
FAUSTUS: Thou art a proud knave indeed. What art thou, the second?
COVETOUSNESS: I am Covetousness, begotten of an old churl in a leather
    bag. — And might I now obtain my wish, this house, you and all,
    should turn to gold that I might lock you safe into my chest. O my
    sweet gold!
FAUSTUS: And what art thou, the third?
ENVY: I am Envy, begotten of a chimney-sweeper and an oyster-wife. I
    cannot read and therefore wish all books burn'd. I am lean with see-   *120*
    ing others eat. O, that there would come a famine over all the world
    that all might die and I live alone! Then thou shouldst see how fat
    I'd be. But must thou sit and I stand? Come down, with a
    vengeance!
FAUSTUS: Out, envious wretch! But what art thou, the fourth?
WRATH: I am Wrath. I had neither father nor mother. I leapt out of a
    lion's mouth when I was scarce an hour old and ever since have run
    up and down the world with these case[14] of rapiers, wounding
    myself when I could get none to fight withal. I was born in Hell!
    And [*to audience*] look to it, for some of you shall be my father.   *130*
FAUSTUS: And what art thou, the fifth?
GLUTTONY: I am Gluttony. My parents are all dead, and the devil a
    penny they have left me, but a small pension: and that buys me
    thirty meals a day and ten bevers,[15] a small trifle to suffice nature. I
    come of a royal pedigree. My father was a gammon of bacon, and
    my mother was a hogshead of claret wine. My godfathers were
    these: Peter Pickl'd-Herring and Martin Martlemas-Beef.[16] But my
    godmother, O, she was an ancient gentlewoman: her name was
    Mistress Margery March-Beer. Now Faustus, thou hast heard all my
    progeny, wilt thou bid me to supper?   *140*

---

*11 featured in an erotic Latin poem once thought to have been written by Ovid. **12** embroidered. **13** tapestry.*
*14 pair. **15** light snacks. **16** beef cattle slaughtered at Martinmas (November 11) and salted down for the winter.*

FAUSTUS: Not I.

GLUTTONY: Then the Devil choke thee!

FAUSTUS: Choke thyself, glutton! What art thou, the sixth?

SLOTH: Heigh-ho! I am Sloth. I was begotten on a sunny bank. Heigh-ho, I'll not speak a word more for a king's ransom.

FAUSTUS: And what are you, Mistress Minx, the seventh and last?

LECHERY: Who, I, I sir? I am one that loves an inch of raw mutton[17] better than an ell[18] of fried stockfish. . . . And the first letter of my name begins with Lechery.

LUCIFER: Away to Hell, away! On, piper!   150

(Exeunt the SEVEN SINS.)

FAUSTUS: O, how this sight doth delight my soul.

LUCIFER: But Faustus, in Hell is all manner of delight.

FAUSTUS: O, might I see Hell and return again safe, how happy were I then!

LUCIFER: Faustus, thou shalt. At midnight I will send for thee. Meanwhile peruse this book and view it thoroughly, and thou shalt turn thyself into what shape thou wilt.

FAUSTUS: Thanks mighty Lucifer. This will I keep as chary as my life.

LUCIFER: Now Faustus, farewell.

FAUSTUS: Farewell great Lucifer. Come Mephostophilis.   160

(Exeunt omnes several ways.)

SCENE 3. *(Enter the CLOWN [ROBIN, with a book].)*

ROBIN: [*to off-stage*] What, Dick, look to the horses there till I come again! [*to audience*] I have gotten one of Doctor Faustus' conjuring books, and now we'll have such knavery as't passes.

(Enter DICK.)

DICK: What, Robin, you must come away and walk the horses.

ROBIN: I walk the horses? I scorn't, 'faith. I have other matters in hand. Let the horses walk themselves an they will.

[*Chants, making a circle.*]

A per se — a; t, h, e — the; o per se — o; deny orgon — gorgon.[1] Keep further from me, O thou illiterate and unlearned hostler!

DICK: 'Snails,[2] what hast thou got there? A book! Why, thou canst not tell ne'er a word on't.   10

---

17 *i.e., erect penis.*

18 *45 inches (114 centimetres).*

1 *Robin, an illiterate, is trying hard to read from Faustus's conjuring book: "A" by itself spells 'a'; t, h, e, spells 'the'; o by itself spells 'o'." Then he struggles with the pronunciation of "Demogorgon."*

2 *i.e., By God's nails.*

ROBIN: That thou shalt see presently. Keep out of the circle, I say, lest I
    send you into the hostry[3] with a vengeance.

DICK: That's like, 'faith! You had best leave your foolery, for an my mas-
    ter come, he'll conjure you, 'faith.

ROBIN: My master conjure me? I'll tell thee what. An my master come
    here, I'll clap as fair a pair of horns on's head as e'er thou sawest in
    thy life.

DICK: Thou need'st not do that, for my mistress hath done it.

ROBIN: Ay, there be of us here have waded as deep into matters as other
    men — if they were disposed to talk.   20

DICK: A plague take you! I thought you did not sneak up and down after
    her for nothing. But I prithee tell me in good sadness[4] Robin, is that
    a conjuring book?

ROBIN: Do but speak what thou't have me to do, and I'll do't. If thou't
    dance naked, put off thy clothes, and I'll conjure thee about pres-
    ently. Or if thou't go but to the tavern with me, I'll give thee white
    wine, red wine, claret wine, sack, muscadine, malmesey, and whip-
    pincrust[5] — hold-belly-hold. And we'll not pay one penny for it!

[*Pats his stomach at "hold-belly-hold."*]

DICK: O brave! Prithee let's to it presently, for I am as dry as a dog.

ROBIN: Come then, let's away. *(Exeunt.)*   30

(Enter the CHORUS.*)*

Learned Faustus,
To find the secrets of astronomy
Graven in the book of Jove's high firmament,
Did mount him up to scale Olympus' top:
Where, sitting in a chariot burning bright
Drawn by the strength of yoked dragons' necks,
He views the clouds, the planets, and the stars,
The tropics, zones, and quarters of the sky,
From the bright circle of the horned moon
Even to the height of *primum mobile:*[6]   40
And whirling round with this circumference
Within the concave compass of the pole,
From east to west his dragons swiftly glide
And in eight days did bring him home again.
Not long he stay'd within his quiet house
To rest his bones after his weary toil
But new exploits do hale him out again.
And mounted then upon a dragon's back,
That with his wings did part the subtle air,

---

3 *hostelry, inn.*
4 *seriousness.*
5 *folksy pronunciation of "hippocras," a spiced wine.*
6 *first moving thing.*

He now is gone to prove cosmography,   50
That measures coasts and kingdoms of the earth,
And as I guess will first arrive in Rome
To see the Pope and manner of his court
And take some part of holy Peter's feast,
The which this day is highly solemniz'd.

(Exit.)

ACT THREE

SCENE 1. *(Enter* FAUSTUS *and* MEPHOSTOPHILIS.*)*

FAUSTUS: Having now, my good Mephostophilis,
    Pass'd with delight the stately town of Trier,
    Environ'd round with airy mountain tops,
    With walls of flint, and deep-entrenched lakes,
    Not to be won by any conquering prince:
    From Paris next, coasting the realm of France,
    We saw the river Main fall into Rhine,
    Whose banks are set with groves of fruitful vines:
    Then up to Naples, rich Campania,
    Whose buildings fair and gorgeous to the eye,   10
    The streets straight forth and pav'd with finest brick,
    Quarters the town in four equivalents.
    There saw we learned Maro's[1] golden tomb,
    The way he cut an English mile in length
    Thorough a rock of stone in one night's space.
    From thence to Venice, Padua, and the rest,
    In one of which a sumptuous temple stands
    That threats the stars with her aspiring top,
    Whose frame is pav'd with sundry color'd stones
    And roof'd aloft with curious work in gold.   20
    Thus hitherto hath Faustus spent his time.
    But tell me now, what resting-place is this?
    Hast thou, as erst I did command,
    Conducted me within the walls of Rome?
MEPHOSTOPHILIS: I have, my Faustus, and for proof thereof
    This is the goodly palace of the Pope,
    And 'cause we are no common guests
    I choose his privy chamber for our use.
FAUSTUS: I hope His Holiness will bid us welcome.
MEPHOSTOPHILIS: All's one, for we'll be bold with his venison.   30
    But now my Faustus, that thou may'st perceive
    What Rome contains for to delight thine eyes,
    Know that this city stands upon seven hills
    That underprop the groundwork of the same:
    Just through the midst runs flowing Tiber's stream

---

1 *Virgil. The classical poet's full name was Publius Vergilius Maro.*

With winding banks that cut it in two parts,
Over the which four stately bridges lean
That make safe passage to each part of Rome.
Upon the bridge call'd Ponte Angelo
Erected is a castle passing strong   40
Where thou shalt see such store of ordinance
As that the double cannons forg'd of brass
Do match the number of the days contain'd
Within the compass of one complete year,
Beside the gates and high pyramides
That Julius Caesar brought from Africa.
FAUSTUS: Now, by the kingdoms of infernal rule,
Of Styx, of Acheron, and the fiery lake
Of ever-burning Phlegethon,[2] I swear
That I do long to see the monuments   50
And situation of bright-splendent Rome.
Come therefore, let's away!
MEPHOSTOPHILIS: Nay stay my Faustus. I know you'd see the Pope
And take some part of holy Peter's feast,
The which this day with high solemnity,
This day, is held through Rome and Italy
In honor of the Pope's triumphant victory.
FAUSTUS: Sweet Mephostophilis, thou pleasest me.
Whilst I am here on earth let me be cloy'd
With all things that delight the heart of man.
My four and twenty years of liberty   60
I'll spend in pleasure and in dalliance,
That Faustus' name, whilst this bright frame doth stand,
May be admired through the furthest land.
MEPHOSTOPHILIS: 'Tis well said, Faustus, come then, stand by me
And thou shalt see them come immediately.
FAUSTUS: Nay stay, my gentle Mephostophilis,
And grant me my request, and then I go.
Thou know'st, within the compass of eight days
We view'd the face of Heaven, of Earth, and Hell —   70
So high our dragons soar'd into the air
That looking down the earth appear'd to me
No bigger than my hand in quantity —
There did we view the kingdoms of the world,
And what might please mine eye I there beheld.
Then in this show let me an actor be
That this proud Pope may Faustus' cunning see!
MEPHOSTOPHILIS: Let it be so, my Faustus, but first stay
And view their triumphs[3] as they pass this way.
And then devise what best contents thy mind   80
By cunning in thine art to cross the Pope
Or dash the pride of this solemnity —

2 *Styx, Acheron, and Phlegethon are rivers in Hades.*
3 *spectacular ceremonies.*

To make his monks and abbots stand like apes[4]
And point like antics[5] at his triple crown,
To beat the beads about the friars' pates,
Or clap huge horns upon the cardinals' heads,
Or any villainy thou canst devise —
And I'll perform it, Faustus. Hark, they come!
This day shall make thee be admir'd in Rome!

[*They stand aside.*]

(*Enter the* CARDINALS *and* BISHOPS, *some bearing crosiers, some the pillars;*[6] MONKS
and FRIARS *singing their procession; then the* POPE *and* RAYMOND *King of Hungary,
with* BRUNO[7] *led in chains.*)

POPE: Cast down our footstool.   90
RAYMOND: Saxon Bruno, stoop,
    Whilst on thy back His Holiness ascends
    Saint Peter's chair and state pontifical.
BRUNO: Proud Lucifer, that state belongs to me —
    But thus I fall to Peter, not to thee!

[*He lies flat.*]

POPE: To me and Peter shalt thou grov'lling lie
    And crouch before the papal dignity!
    Sound trumpets then, for thus Saint Peter's heir
    From Bruno's back ascends Saint Peter's chair!

(*A flourish*[8] *while he ascends* [*stepping on* BRUNO].)

Thus as the gods creep on with feet of wool   100
Long ere with iron hands they punish men,
So shall our sleeping vengeance now arise
And smite with death thy hated enterprise.

[BRUNO *rises.*]

Lord Cardinals of France and Padua,
Go forthwith to our holy consistory
And read amongst the Statutes Decretal
What by the holy council held at Trent[9]
The sacred synod hath decreed for him
That doth assume the papal government

---

4 *subhuman dolts.*
5 *grotesque clowns, buffoons.*
6 *ornamental symbols of support and power.*
7 *the emperor's failed nominee for the papacy (see line 122 of this scene).*
8 *fanfare.*
9 *ecclesiastical council which sat intermittently between 1545 and 1563.*

Without election and a true consent.   *110*
Away, and bring us word with speed!
1 CARDINAL: We go my lord.

(Exeunt [two] CARDINALS.*)*

POPE: Lord Raymond. . . . [*Talks to him in pantomime.*]
FAUSTUS: [*coming forward.*] Go haste thee, gentle Mephostophilis
    Follow the cardinals to the consistory
    And as they turn their superstitious books
    Strike them with sloth and drowsy idleness
    And make them sleep so sound that in their shapes
    Thyself and I may parley with this Pope,
    This proud confronter of the Emperor!   *120*
    — And in despite of all his holiness
    Restore this Bruno to his liberty
    And bear him to the states of Germany!
MEPHOSTOPHILIS: Faustus, I go.
FAUSTUS: Dispatch it soon.
    The Pope shall curse that Faustus came to Rome.

(Exeunt FAUSTUS *and* MEPHOSTOPHILIS.*)*

BRUNO: Pope Adrian, let me have some right of law:
    I was elected by the Emperor.
POPE: We will depose the Emperor for that deed
    And curse the people that submit to him.   *130*
    Both he and thou shalt stand excommunicate
    And interdict from church's privilege
    And all society of holy men.
    He grows too proud in his authority,
    Lifting his lofty head above the clouds,
    And like a steeple overpeers the church.
    But we'll pull down his haughty insolence.
    And as Pope Alexander, our progenitor,[10]
    Trod on the neck of German Frederick,
    Adding this golden sentence to our praise: *140*
    That Peter's heirs should tread on emperors
    And walk upon the dreadful adder's back,
    Treading the lion and the dragon down,
    And fearless spurn the killing basilisk[11] —
    So will we quell that haughty schismatic
    And by authority apostolical
    Depose him from his regal government.
BRUNO: Pope Julius swore to princely Sigismond,
    For him and the succeeding Popes of Rome,
    To hold the Emperors their lawful lords.   *150*

---

10 *predecessor.*
11 *deadly mythological reptile able to kill with a glance.*

POPE: Pope Julius did abuse the church's rites
   And therefore none of his decrees can stand.
   Is not all power on earth bestowed on us?
   And therefore though we would, we cannot err.
   Behold this silver belt whereto is fix'd
   Seven golden keys fast seal'd with seven seals
   In token of our sevenfold power from Heaven
   To bind or loose, lock fast, condemn, or judge,
   Resign[12] or seal, or whatso pleaseth us.
   Then he and thou and all the world shall stoop —   *160*
   Or be assured of our dreadful curse
   To light as heavy as the pains of Hell.

   (Enter FAUSTUS *and* MEPHOSTOPHILIS *like the* [*two*] CARDINALS.*)*

MEPHOSTOPHILIS: [*aside.*] (Now tell me Faustus, are we not fitted well?)
FAUSTUS: [*aside.*] (Yes Mephostophilis, and two such cardinals
   Ne'er serv'd a holy Pope as we shall do.
   But whilst they sleep within the consistory
   Let us salute his reverend Fatherhood.)
RAYMOND: Behold my lord, the cardinals are return'd.
POPE: Welcome grave fathers, answer presently,
   What have our holy council there decreed   *170*
   Concerning Bruno and the Emperor
   In quittance of their late conspiracy
   Against our state and papal dignity?
FAUSTUS: Most sacred patron of the church of Rome,
   By full consent of all the synod
   Of priests and prelates it is thus decreed:
   That Bruno and the German Emperor
   Be held as lollards[13] and bold schismatics
   And proud disturbers of the church's peace.
   And if that Bruno by his own assent,   *180*
   Without enforcement of the German peers,
   Did seek to wear the triple diadem
   And by your death to climb Saint Peter's chair,
   The Statutes Decretal have thus decreed:
   He shall be straight condemn'd of heresy
   And on a pile of fagots burnt to death.
POPE: It is enough. Here, take him to your charge
   And bear him straight to Ponte Angelo
   And in the strongest tower enclose him fast.
   Tomorrow, sitting in our consistory   *190*
   With all our college of grave cardinals
   We will determine of his life or death.
   Here, take his triple crown along with you

   [*Removes tiara from* BRUNO *and gives it to* FAUSTUS.]

---

12 *cancel.*
13 *i.e., heretics.*

And leave it in the church's treasury.
Make haste again, my good lord cardinals,
And take our blessing apostolical.
MEPHOSTOPHILIS: [*aside.*] (So, so! Was never devil thus bless'd before.)
FAUSTUS: [*aside.*] (Away sweet Mephostophilis, be gone!
The cardinals will be plagu'd for this anon.)

(*Exeunt* FAUSTUS *and* MEPHOSTOPHILIS [*with* BRUNO].)

POPE: Go presently and bring a banquet forth,   200
That we may solemnize Saint Peter's feast
And with Lord Raymond, King of Hungary,
Drink to our late and happy victory.

(*Exeunt.*)

> SCENE 2. (*A sennet*[1] *while the banquet is brought in, and then enter* FAUSTUS
> *and* MEPHOSTOPHILIS *in their own shapes.*)

MEPHOSTOPHILIS: Now Faustus, come prepare thyself for mirth.
The sleepy cardinals are hard at hand
To censure Bruno, that is posted hence,
And on a proud-pac'd steed as swift as thought
Flies o'er the Alps to fruitful Germany,
There to salute the woeful Emperor.
FAUSTUS: The Pope will curse them for their sloth today
That slept both Bruno and his crown away!
But now, that Faustus may delight his mind
And by their folly make some merriment,   10
Sweet Mephostophilis, so charm me here
That I may walk invisible to all
And do whate'er I please unseen of any.
MEPHOSTOPHILIS: [*takes a wand and a girdle from beneath his robe.*]
Faustus, thou shalt. Then kneel down presently,
>   *Whilst on thy head I lay my hand*
>   *And charm thee with this magic wand.*
>   *First wear this girdle, then appear*
>   *Invisible to all are here:*
>   *The planets seven, the gloomy air,*
>   *Hell, and the furies*[2] *forked hair,*   20
>   *Pluto's blue fire, and Hecat's*[3] *tree*
>   *With magic spells so compass thee*
>   *That no eye may thy body see.*
So Faustus, now for all their holiness,
Do what thou wilt, thou shalt not be discern'd.
FAUSTUS: Thanks Mephostophilis. Now friars, take heed [*Puts on girdle.*]
Lest Faustus make your shaven crowns to bleed.

---

1 *trumpet fanfare.*
2 *mythological avengers whose "hair" consisted of snakes.*
3 *triple goddess of earth, moon, and underworld.*

MEPHOSTOPHILIS: Faustus, no more. See where the cardinals come.

(*Enter* POPE [*and* FRIARS] *and all the* LORDS [*with* KING RAYMOND *and the*
ARCHBISHOP OF RHEIMS]. *Enter the* [*two*] CARDINALS *with a book.*)

POPE: Welcome lord cardinals. Come, sit down.
    Lord Raymond, take your seat. Friars, attend,   *30*
    And see that all things be in readiness
    As best beseems this solemn festival.
1 CARDINAL: First may it please Your Sacred Holiness
    To view the sentence of the reverend synod
    Concerning Bruno and the Emperor.
POPE: What needs this question? Did I not tell you
    Tomorrow we would sit i' th' consistory
    And there determine of his punishment?
    You brought us word, even now, it was decreed
    That Bruno and the cursed Emperor   *40*
    Were by the holy council both condemn'd
    For loathed lollards and base schismatics.
    Then wherefore would you have me view that book?
1 CARDINAL: Your Grace mistakes. You gave us no such charge.
RAYMOND: Deny it not. We all are witnesses
    That Bruno here was late deliver'd you
    With his rich triple crown to be reserv'd
    And put into the church's treasury.
BOTH CARDINALS: By holy Paul we saw them not!
POPE: By Peter you shall die   *50*
    Unless you bring them forth immediately!
    Hale them to prison, lade their limbs with gyves.[4]
    False prelates, for this hateful treachery
    Curs'd be your souls to hellish misery.

[*Two* CARDINALS *are removed.*]

FAUSTUS: [*aside.*] (So, they are safe. Now Faustus, to the feast.
    The Pope had never such a frolic guest.)
POPE: Lord Archbishop of Rheims, sit down with us.
ARCHBISHOP: I thank Your Holiness.
FAUSTUS: Fall to,[5] the Devil choke you an you spare!
POPE: Who's that spoke? Friars, look about. Lord Raymond, pray fall to. I   *60*
    am beholding to the Bishop of Milan for this so rare a present.
FAUSTUS: [*aside.*] (I thank you, sir!)

[*Snatches the dish.*]

POPE: How now! Who snatch'd the meat from me? Villains, why speak
    you not? — My good Lord Archbishop, here's a most dainty dish
    was sent me from a cardinal in France.

4 *chains and manacles.*
5 *i.e., dig in.*

FAUSTUS: [*aside.*] (I'll have that too!)

[*Snatches the dish.*]

POPE: What lollards do attend our Holiness that we receive such great
　　indignity! Fetch me some wine.
FAUSTUS: [*aside.*] (Ay, pray do, for Faustus is adry.)

[*Wine is served.*]

POPE: Lord Raymond, I drink unto Your Grace.   70
FAUSTUS: [*aside.*] (I pledge Your Grace!) [*Snatches the goblet.*]
POPE: My wine gone too? Ye lubbers, look about and find the man that
　　doth this villainy, or by our sanctitude you all shall die. — I pray, my
　　lords, have patience at this troublesome banquet.
ARCHBISHOP: Please it Your Holiness, I think it be some ghost crept out
　　of purgatory, and now is come unto Your Holiness for his pardon.
POPE: It may be so. Go then, command our priests to sing a dirge to lay
　　the fury of this same troublesome ghost.

[*One of the* SERVITORS *exit.*]

[*The* POPE *crosses himself before beginning to eat. He takes a bite and then crosses
himself again.*]

FAUSTUS: How now! Must every bit be spiced with a cross? Nay then
　　take that!   80

[FAUSTUS *strikes the* POPE.]

POPE: O, I am slain! Help me my lords! O come and help to bear my
　　body hence. Damn'd be this soul for ever for this deed!

(*Exeunt the* POPE [*supported*] *and his* TRAIN.)

MEPHOSTOPHILIS: Now Faustus, what will you do now? For I can tell
　　you, you'll be curs'd with bell, book, and candle.[6]
FAUSTUS: Bell, book, and candle. Candle, book, and bell.
　　Forward and backward, to curse Faustus to Hell!

(*Enter the* FRIARS, *with bell, book, and candle for the dirge.*)

1 FRIAR: Come brethren, let's about our business with good devotion.
　　Cursed be he that stole away His Holiness' meat from the table.
　　　Maledicat Dominus![7]

---

6 *implements used in the ceremony of formal excommunication.*
7 *May the Lord curse him.*

Cursed be he that struck His Holiness a blow on the face.   90
    Maledicat Dominus!

[FAUSTUS *strikes a* FRIAR *and moves among them, disturbing them.*]

Cursed be he that took Friar Sandelo a blow on the pate.
    Maledicat Dominus!
Cursed be he that disturbeth our holy dirge.
    Maledicat Dominus!
Cursed be he that took away His Holiness' wine.
    Maledicat Dominus!

([FAUSTUS *and* MEPHOSTOPHILIS] *beat the* FRIARS, *fling fireworks among them and exeunt.*)

    SCENE 3. *(Enter* CLOWN [ROBIN] *and* DICK *with a cup.)*

DICK: Sirrah Robin, we were best look that your Devil can answer the stealing of this same cup, for the vintner's boy follows us at the hard heels.[1]
ROBIN: 'Tis no matter, let him come! An he follow us I'll so conjure him as he was never conjur'd in his life, I warrant him. Let me see the cup.

(Enter VINTNER['S BOY].*)*

DICK: Here 'tis. Yonder he comes. Now Robin, now or never show thy cunning.
BOY: O, are you here? I am glad I have found you. You are a couple of fine companions! Pray, where's the cup you stole from the tavern?   10
ROBIN: How, how! We steal a cup? Take heed what you say. We look not like cup-stealers, I can tell you.
BOY: Never deny't, for I know you have it, and I'll search you.
ROBIN: Search me? Ay, and spare not! [*Aside*] (Hold the cup, Dick!) [*To* BOY] Come, come. Search me, search me.

[ROBIN *behind his back gives cup to* DICK. BOY *searches* ROBIN.]

BOY: Come on sirrah, let me search you now.
DICK: Ay ay, do do. [*Aside*] (Hold the cup, Robin!) [*To* BOY] I fear not your searching. We scorn to steal your cups, I can tell you. [DICK *behind his back gives cup to* ROBIN. BOY *searches* DICK.]
BOY: Never outface me for the matter, for sure the cup is between you two.   20
ROBIN: Nay, there you lie! 'Tis beyond us both.

[*Behind his back* ROBIN *flings cup away.*]

---

1 *i.e., hard at our heels.*

BOY: A plague take you. I thought 'twas your knavery to take it away.
Come, give it me again.
ROBIN: Ay, much! When, can you tell? [*Aside*] (Dick, make me a circle
and stand close at my back and stir not for thy life.)

[DICK *makes a circle enclosing him and* ROBIN. ROBIN *addresses* BOY.]

Vintner, you shall have your cup anon. [*Aside*] (Say nothing, Dick!)
O per se, o; Demogorgon, Belcher, and Mephostophilis!

(*Enter* MEPHOSTOPHILIS [*from trap.* BOY *rushes off frightened*].)

MEPHOSTOPHILIS: You princely legions of infernal rule,
How am I vexed by these villains' charms!
From Constantinople have they brought me now   30
Only for pleasure of these damned slaves.
ROBIN: By lady sir, you have had a shrewd² journey of it. Will it please
you to take a shoulder of mutton to supper and a tester³ in your
purse and go back again?
DICK: Ay, I pray you heartily, sir. For we called you but in jest, I promise
you.
MEPHOSTOPHILIS: To purge the rashness of this cursed deed,

[*Turns to* DICK.]

First be thou turned to this ugly shape,
For apish deeds transformed to an ape.

[DICK *grimaces, acts like a monkey.*]

ROBIN: O brave! An ape! I pray sir, let me have the carrying of him about   40
to show some tricks.
MEPHOSTOPHILIS: And so thou shalt. Be thou transform'd to a dog.

[*Turns to* ROBIN, *who gets down on all fours, acts like a dog.*]

and carry him upon thy back. Away, be gone!
ROBIN: A dog! That's excellent. Let the maids look well to their
porridge-pots, for I'll into the kitchen presently. Come Dick, come.
(*Exeunt the two* CLOWNS [, DICK *on* ROBIN'S *back*].)
MEPHOSTOPHILIS: Now with the flames of ever-burning fire
I'll wing myself and forthwith fly amain
Unto my Faustus, to the Great Turk's court.

(*Exit.*)

2 *rough.*
3 *sixpence.*

(Enter CHORUS.*)*

When Faustus had with pleasure ta'en the view
Of rarest things and royal courts of kings,   50
He stay'd his course and so returned home,
Where such as bare his absence but with grief,
I mean his friends and nearest companions,
Did gratulate his safety with kind words.
And in their conference of what befell
Touching his journey through the world and air
They put forth questions of astrology
Which Faustus answer'd with such learned skill
As they admir'd and wond'red at his wit.
Now is his fame spread forth in every land.   60
Amongst the rest the Emperor is one,
Carolus the Fifth, at whose palace now
Faustus is feasted 'mongst his noblemen.
What there he did in trial of his art
I leave untold, your eyes shall see perform'd. *(Exit.)*

ACT FOUR

SCENE 1. *(Enter* MARTINO *and* FREDERICK *at several doors.)*

MARTINO: What ho, officers, gentlemen!
Hie to the presence[1] to attend the Emperor.
Good Frederick, see the rooms be voided straight,[2]
His Majesty is coming to the hall.
Go back and see the state in readiness.

[FREDERICK *opens curtains at back, revealing throne.*]

FREDERICK: But where is Bruno, our elected Pope,
That on a fury's back came post from Rome?
Will not His Grace consort[3] the Emperor?
MARTINO: O yes, and with him comes the German conjurer,
The learned Faustus, fame of Wittenberg,   10
The wonder of the world for magic art:
And he intends to show great Carolus
The race of all his stout progenitors
And bring in presence of His Majesty
The royal shapes and warlike semblances
Of Alexander and his beauteous paramour.[4]
FREDERICK: Where is Benvolio?

1 *stateroom or presence chamber.*
2 *cleared immediately.*
3 *accompany.*
4 *i.e., Alexander the Great and his paramour, Thaïs.*

MARTINO: Fast asleep, I warrant you.
    He took his rouse[5] with stoups[6] of Rhenish wine
    So kindly yesternight to Bruno's health   20
    That all this day the sluggard keeps his bed.
FREDERICK: See, see, his window's ope. We'll call to him.
MARTINO: What ho, Benvolio!

(Enter BENVOLIO *above at a window, in his night-cap, buttoning.)*

BENVOLIO: What a devil ail you two?
MARTINO: Speak softly sir, lest the Devil hear you,
    For Faustus at the court is late arriv'd
    And at his heels a thousand furies wait
    To accomplish whatsoever the doctor please.
BENVOLIO: What of this?
MARTINO: Come, leave thy chamber first, and thou shalt see   30
    This conjurer perform such rare exploits
    Before the Pope[7] and royal Emperor
    As never yet was seen in Germany.
BENVOLIO: Has not the Pope enough of conjuring yet?
    He was upon the Devil's back late enough!
    And if he be so far in love with him
    I would he would post with him to Rome again.
FREDERICK: Speak, wilt thou come and see this sport?
BENVOLIO: Not I.
MARTINO: Wilt thou stand in thy window and see it then?   40
BENVOLIO: Ay, and I fall not asleep i' th' meantime.
MARTINO: The Emperor is at hand, who comes to see
    What wonders by black spells may compass'd be.
BENVOLIO: Well, go you attend the Emperor. I am content for this once
    to thrust my head out at a window, for they say if a man be drunk
    overnight the Devil cannot hurt him in the morning. If that be true,
    I have a charm in my head shall control him as well as the conjurer,
    I warrant you.

(Exit [MARTINO *and* FREDERICK. BENVOLIO *remains above at window].)*

(A sennet. CHARLES THE GERMAN EMPEROR, BRUNO [*wearing tiara*], [*the* DUKE
OF] SAXONY, FAUSTUS, MEPHOSTOPHILIS [*invisible*], FREDERICK, MARTINO, *and
attendants.* [EMPEROR *seats himself.*])

EMPEROR: Wonder of men, renown'd magician,
    Thrice-learned Faustus, welcome to our court.   50
    This deed of thine in setting Bruno free
    From his and our professed enemy,
    Shall add more excellence unto thine art
    Than if by powerful necromantic spells

---

5 *drinking bout.*
6 *full goblets.*
7 *i.e., the emperor's "pope," Bruno.*

Thou could'st command the world's obedience.
For ever be belov'd of Carolus!
And if this Bruno thou hast late redeem'd
In peace possess the triple diadem
And sit in Peter's chair despite of chance,
Thou shalt be famous through all Italy   60
And honor'd of the German Emperor.
FAUSTUS: These gracious words, most royal Carolus,
    Shall make poor Faustus to his utmost power
    Both love and serve the German Emperor
    And lay his life at holy Bruno's feet.
    For proof whereof, if so Your Grace be pleas'd,
    The doctor stands prepar'd by power of art
    To cast his magic charms that shall pierce through
    The ebon gates of ever-burning Hell,
    And hale the stubborn furies from their caves   70
    To compass whatsoe'er Your Grace commands.
BENVOLIO: Blood! He speaks terribly! But for all that I do not greatly
    believe him. He looks as like a conjurer as the Pope to a
    costermonger.[8]
EMPEROR: Then Faustus, as thou late didst promise us,
    We would behold that famous conqueror
    Great Alexander and his paramour
    In their true shapes and state majestical,
    That we may wonder at their excellence.
FAUSTUS: Your Majesty shall see them presently.   80
    [Aside] (Mephostophilis away,
    And with a solemn noise of trumpets' sound
    Present before this royal Emperor
    Great Alexander and his beauteous paramour.)
MEPHOSTOPHILIS: [aside.] (Faustus, I will.) [Exit.]
BENVOLIO: Well master doctor, an your devils come not away quickly,
    you shall have me asleep presently. Zounds,[9] I could eat myself for
    anger to think I have been such an ass all this while to stand gaping
    after the devils' governor and can see nothing.
FAUSTUS: [aside, looking up.] (I'll make you feel something anon if my art   90
    fail me not!)
    My lord, I must forewarn Your Majesty
    That when my spirits present the royal shapes
    Of Alexander and his paramour,
    Your Grace demand no questions of the King
    But in dumb silence let them come and go.
EMPEROR: Be it as Faustus please. We are content.
BENVOLIO: Ay ay, and I am content too. An thou bring Alexander and
    his paramour before the Emperor, I'll be Actaeon[10] and turn myself
    to a stag.   100

8 *fruit merchant.*
9 *i.e., by God's wounds.*
10 *mythological hunter who, having seen Diana and her nymphs bathing, was transformed into a stag and pursued
    by his own hounds.*

FAUSTUS: [*aside.*] (And I'll play Diana and send you the horns presently.)

[*During ensuing dumb-show,* BENVOLIO *puts his head on his arms and falls asleep.* MEPHOSTOPHILIS *fastens horns on* BENVOLIO'S *head.*]

(*Sennet. Enter at one* [*door*] *the* EMPEROR ALEXANDER, *at the other* DARIUS.[11] *They meet.* DARIUS *is thrown down.* ALEXANDER *kills him, takes off his crown, and offering to go out, his* PARAMOUR *meets him. He embraceth her and sets* DARIUS' *crown upon her head, and coming back both salute the* EMPEROR; *who leaving his state* [*i.e., throne*] *offers to embrace them, which* FAUSTUS *seeing suddenly stays him. Then trumpets cease and music sounds.*)

My gracious lord, you do forget yourself.
These are but shadows, not substantial.
EMPEROR: O pardon me, my thoughts are so ravish'd
With sight of this renowned Emperor,
That in mine arms I would have compass'd[12] him.
But Faustus, since I may not speak to them,
To satisfy my longing thoughts at full,
Let me this tell thee: I have heard it said
That this fair lady whilst she liv'd on earth,   *110*
Had on her neck a little wart or mole.
How may I prove that saying to be true?
FAUSTUS: Your Majesty may boldly go and see.
EMPEROR: Faustus, I see it plain!
And in this sight thou better pleasest me
Than if I gain'd another monarchy.
FAUSTUS: Away, be gone!

(*Exit show.*)

See, see, my gracious lord, what strange beast is yon that thrusts his
head out at the window!
EMPEROR: O wondrous sight! See, Duke of Saxony, two spreading horns   *120*
most strangely fasten'd upon the head of young Benvolio.
SAXONY: What, is he asleep or dead?
FAUSTUS: He sleeps my lord, but dreams not of his horns.
EMPEROR: This sport is excellent. We'll call and wake him.
What ho, Benvolio!
BENVOLIO: A plague upon you! Let me sleep awhile.
EMPEROR: I blame thee not to sleep much, having such a head of thine
own.
SAXONY: Look up, Benvolio! 'Tis the Emperor calls.
BENVOLIO: The Emperor! Where? O zounds, my head!   *130*

---

11 *king of Persia.*
12 *encompassed, embraced.*

[*He tries to pull his head in but width of horns prevents him. Puts hand to head in pain.*]

EMPEROR: Nay, an thy horns hold, 'tis no matter for thy head, for that's
    arm'd sufficiently.
FAUSTUS: Why, how now Sir Knight? What, hang'd by the horns? This
    is most horrible! Fie fie, pull in your head for shame! Let not all the
    world wonder at you.
BENVOLIO: Zounds doctor, is this your villainy?
FAUSTUS: Oh, say not so sir: The doctor has no skill,
    No art, no cunning to present these lords
    Or bring before this Royal Emperor
    The mighty monarch, warlike Alexander.   *140*
    If Faustus do it, you are straight resolv'd
    In bold Actaeon's shape to turn a stag.
    And therefore my lord, so please Your Majesty,
    I'll raise a kennel of hounds shall hunt him so
    As all his footmanship shall scarce prevail
    To keep his carcass from their bloody fangs.
    Ho, Belimote, Argiron, Asterote!
BENVOLIO: Hold, hold! Zounds, he'll raise up a kennel of devils I think,
    anon. Good my lord, entreat for me. 'Sblood,[13] I am never able to
    endure these torments. [*Tries to pull off horns.*]   *150*
EMPEROR: Then good master doctor,
    Let me entreat you to remove his horns.
    He has done penance now sufficiently!
FAUSTUS: My gracious lord, not so much for injury done to me, as to
    delight Your Majesty with some mirth, hath Faustus justly requited
    this injurious knight — which being all I desire, I am content to
    remove his horns. [*Aside to* MEPHOSTOPHILIS, *who appears behind*
    BENVOLIO.] (Mephostophilis, transform him.) [MEPHOSTOPHILIS
    removes horns and exit.] And hereafter sir, look you speak well of
    scholars.   *160*
BENVOLIO: [*aside.*] (Speak well of ye! 'Sblood, an scholars be such
    cuckold-makers to clap horns of honest men's heads o' this order, I'll
    ne'er trust smooth faces[14] and small ruffs[15] more. But an I be not
    reveng'd for this, would I might be turned to a gaping oyster and
    drink nothing but salt water.) [*Exit from window.*]
EMPEROR: Come Faustus, while the Emperor lives,
    In recompense of this thy high desert,
    Thou shalt command the state of Germany
    And live belov'd of mighty Carolus.

(*Exeunt omnes.*)

---

13 *i.e., by God's blood.*
14 *i.e., beardless scholars.*
15 *unpretentious frilled collars worn by students.*

SCENE 2. *(Enter* BENVOLIO, MARTINO, FREDERICK, *and* SOLDIERS. *[Trees at the back.])*

MARTINO: Nay, sweet Benvolio, let us sway thy thoughts
    From this attempt against the conjurer.
BENVOLIO: Away! You love me not to urge me thus.
    Shall I let slip so great an injury
    When every servile groom jests at my wrongs
    And in their rustic gambols proudly say,
    "Benvolio's head was grac'd with horns today"?
    O, may these eyelids never close again
    Till with my sword I have that conjurer slain!
    If you will aid me in this enterprise,   10
    Then draw your weapons and be resolute;
    If not, depart. Here will Benvolio die
    But[1] Faustus' death shall quit[2] my infamy.
FREDERICK: Nay, we will stay with thee, betide what may,
    And kill that doctor if he come this way.
BENVOLIO: Then, gentle Frederick, hie thee to the grove
    And place our servants and our followers
    Close in an ambush there behind the trees.
    By this, I know, the conjurer is near.
    I saw him kneel and kiss the Emperor's hand   20
    And take his leave laden with rich rewards.
    Then soldiers, boldly fight. If Faustus die,
    Take you the wealth, leave us the victory.
FREDERICK: Come soldiers, follow me unto the grove.
Who kills him shall have gold and endless love.

(Exit FREDERICK *with the* SOLDIERS.*)*

BENVOLIO: My head is lighter than it was by th' horns —
    But yet my heart more ponderous than my head,
    And pants until I see that conjurer dead.
MARTINO: Where shall we place ourselves, Benvolio?
BENVOLIO: Here will we stay to bide the first assault.   30
    O, were that damned hell-hound but in place
    Thou soon should'st see me quit my foul disgrace.

(Enter FREDERICK.*)*

FREDERICK: Close, close! The conjurer is at hand
    And all alone comes walking in his gown.
    Be ready then and strike the peasant down!
BENVOLIO: Mine be that honor then! Now sword, strike home!

[Draws his sword.]

For horns he gave I'll have his head anon.

1 *unless.*
2 *requite, avenge.*

(Enter FAUSTUS *with the false head.)*

MARTINO: See see, he comes.
BENVOLIO: No words. This blow ends all!

[Strikes FAUSTUS *with sword.* FAUSTUS *falls to his knees.]*

    Hell take his soul, his body thus must fall.   40
FAUSTUS: O!
FREDERICK: Groan you, master doctor?
BENVOLIO: Break may his heart with groans! Dear Frederick, see,
    Thus will I end his griefs immediately.

[Cuts FAUSTUS' *false head off.* FAUSTUS *falls flat.]*

MARTINO: Strike with a willing hand! His head is off.
BENVOLIO: The devil's dead, the furies now may laugh.
FREDERICK: Was this that stern aspect, that awful frown,
    Made the grim monarch of infernal spirits
    Tremble and quake at his commanding charms?
MARTINO: Was this that damned head whose heart conspir'd   50
    Benvolio's shame before the Emperor?
BENVOLIO: Ay, that's the head, and here the body lies
    Justly rewarded for his villainies.
FREDERICK: Come let's devise how we may add more shame
    To the black scandal of his hated name.
BENVOLIO: First, on his head in quittance of my wrongs

*[*BENVOLIO *lifts false head by hair.]*

    I'll nail huge forked horns and let them hang
    Within the window where he yok'd me first
    That all the world may see my just revenge.
MARTINO: What use shall we put his beard to?   60
BENVOLIO: We'll sell it to a chimney-sweeper. It will wear out ten bir-
    chen brooms, I warrant you.
FREDERICK: What shall eyes do?
BENVOLIO: We'll put out his eyes, and they shall serve for buttons to his
    lips to keep his tongue from catching cold.
MARTINO: An excellent policy! And now sirs, having divided him, what
    shall the body do?

*[*FAUSTUS *rises without a head.]*

BENVOLIO: Zounds, the devil's alive again!
FREDERICK: Give him his head for God's sake!
FAUSTUS: Nay keep it. Faustus will have heads and hands,   70
    Ay, all your hearts, to recompense this deed.
    Knew you not, traitors, I was limited

[FAUSTUS *shows his own head.*]

For four and twenty years to breathe on earth?
And had you cut my body with your swords
Or hew'd this flesh and bones as small as sand,
Yet in a minute had my spirit return'd
And I had breath'd a man made free from harm.
But wherefore do I dally my revenge?
Asteroth, Belimoth, Mephostophilis!

(Enter MEPHOSTOPHILIS *and other* DEVILS *[from trap].)*

Go horse these traitors on your fiery backs   80
And mount aloft with them as high as Heaven,
Thence pitch them headlong to the lowest Hell.
Yet stay, the world shall see their misery,
And Hell shall after plague their treachery.
Go Belimoth, and take this caitiff³ hence
And hurl him in some lake of mud and dirt:

[BELIMOTH *grasps* FREDERICK.]

Take thou this other, drag him through the woods
Amongst the pricking thorns and sharpest briars:

[ASTEROTH *grasps* MARTINO.]

Whilst with my gentle Mephostophilis
This traitor flies unto some steepy rock   90
That rolling down may break the villain's bones
As he intended to dismember me.

[MEPHOSTOPHILIS *grasps* BENVOLIO.]

Fly hence, dispatch my charge immediately!
FREDERICK: Pity us, gentle Faustus, save our lives!
FAUSTUS: Away!
FREDERICK: He must needs go that the Devil drives.

(Exeunt SPIRITS *with the* KNIGHTS.*)*

(Enter the ambushed SOLDIERS.*)*

1 SOLDIER: Come sirs, prepare yourselves in readiness.
Make haste to help these noble gentlemen.
I heard them parley with the conjurer.
2 SOLDIER: See where he comes. Dispatch, and kill the slave!   100

3 *wretch.*

FAUSTUS: What's here, an ambush to betray my life?
　　Then Faustus, try thy skill. Base peasants, stand!
　　For lo, these trees remove at my command [*Motions with hands.*]
　　And stand as bulwarks 'twixt yourselves and me
　　To shield me from your hated treachery!

[*Trees move between* FAUSTUS *and* SOLDIERS.]

　　Yet to encounter this your weak attempt
　　Behold an army comes incontinent.[4]

(FAUSTUS *strikes the door, and enter a* DEVIL *playing on a drum, after him another bearing an ensign, and divers[5] with weapons:* MEPHOSTOPHILIS *with fireworks: they set upon the* SOLDIERS *and drive them out.* [*Exeunt all.*])

Enter at several doors BENVOLIO, FREDERICK, *and* MARTINO, *their heads and faces bloody and besmeared with mud and dirt, all having horns on their heads.*)

MARTINO: What ho, Benvolio!
BENVOLIO: Here! What, Frederick, ho!
FREDERICK: O, help me gentle friend. Where is Martino?　　　　　110
MARTINO: Dear Frederick, here,
　　Half smother'd in a lake of mud and dirt,
　　Through which the furies dragg'd me by the heels.
FREDERICK: Martino, see, Benvolio's horns again.
MARTINO: O misery! How now Benvolio?
BENVOLIO: Defend me, Heaven! Shall I be haunted still?
MARTINO: Nay fear not man, we have no power to kill.
BENVOLIO: My friends transformed thus! O hellish spite,
　　Your heads are all set with horns.
FREDERICK: You hit it right:　　　　　120
　　It is your own you mean. Feel on your head.
BENVOLIO: Zounds, horns again!

　　[BENVOLIO *feels horns.*]

MARTINO: Nay chafe[6] not man, we all are sped.[7]
BENVOLIO: What devil attends this damn'd magician,
　　That spite of spite our wrongs are doubled?
FREDERICK: What may we do that we may hide our shames?
BENVOLIO: If we should follow him to work revenge
　　He'd join long asses' ears to these huge horns
　　And make us laughing-stocks to all the world.
MARTINO: What shall we then do, dear Benvolio?　　　　　130
BENVOLIO: I have a castle joining near these woods,
　　And thither we'll repair and live obscure

4　*without delay.*
5　*i.e., various others.*
6　*complain.*
7　*humiliated, requited.*

Till time shall alter this our brutish shapes.
Sith[8] black disgrace hath thus eclips'd our fame,
We'll rather die with grief than live with shame.

(Exeunt omnes.)

SCENE 3. *(Enter* FAUSTUS *and the* HORSE-COURSER[1] *[with money in his hand].)*

HORSE-COURSER: I beseech your worship, accept of these forty dollars.
FAUSTUS: Friend, thou canst not buy so good a horse for so small a price. I have no great need to sell him, but if thou likest him for ten dollars more, take him, because I see thou hast a good mind to him.
HORSE-COURSER: I beseech you sir, accept of this. I am a very poor man and have lost very much of late by horse-flesh, and this bargain will set me up again.
FAUSTUS: Well, I will not stand[2] with thee. Give me the money.

[Takes money.]

Now sirrah, I must tell you that you may ride him o'er hedge and ditch and spare him not. But, do you hear, in any case ride him not   *10* into the water.
HORSE-COURSER: How sir, not into the water! Why, will he not drink of all waters?[3]
FAUSTUS: Yes, he will drink of all waters, but ride him not into the water: o'er hedge and ditch or where thou wilt, but not into the water. Go bid the hostler deliver him unto you, and remember what I say.
HORSE-COURSER: I warrant you sir. O joyful day! Now am I a made man forever. *(Exit.)*
FAUSTUS: What art thou, Faustus, but a man condemn'd to die?   *20*
Thy fatal time draws to a final end . . .
Despair doth drive distrust into my thoughts.
Confound these passions with a quiet sleep.
Tush, Christ did call the thief upon the cross!
Then rest thee Faustus, quiet in conceit.[4]

(He sits to sleep.)

(Enter the HORSE-COURSER *wet.)*

HORSE-COURSER: O what a cozening[5] doctor was this! I riding my horse into the water, thinking some hidden mystery had been in the horse — I had nothing under me but a little straw and had much ado to escape drowning! Well, I'll go rouse him and make him give me my forty dollars again. Ho, sirrah doctor, you cozening scab! Master   *30*

---

8 *since.*

1 *horse dealer.*
2 *haggle.*
3 *i.e., go anywhere.*
4 *i.e., in a quiet state of mind.*
5 *cheating, deceiving.*

doctor, awake and rise, and give me my money again, for your horse is turned to a bottle⁶ of hay. Master doctor — . *(He pulls off his leg.)*

Alas, I am undone! What shall I do? I have pull'd off his leg.

FAUSTUS: O help, help! The villain hath murder'd me!

HORSE-COURSER: Murder or not murder, now he has but one leg I'll outrun him, and cast this leg into some ditch or other. [*Exit with the leg.*]

FAUSTUS: Stop him, stop him, stop him! — Ha, ha, ha! Faustus hath his leg again, and the horse-courser a bundle of hay for his forty dollars.

(Enter WAGNER.*)*

How now, Wagner? What news with thee?   40

WAGNER: If it please you, the Duke of Vanholt doth earnestly entreat your company, and hath sent some of his men to attend you with provision fit for your journey.

FAUSTUS: The Duke of Vanholt's an honorable gentleman, and one to whom I must be no niggard of my cunning. Come, away!

(Exeunt.)

SCENE 4. *(Enter* CLOWN [ROBIN], DICK, HORSE-COURSER, *and a* CARTER.*)*

CARTER: Come my masters, I'll bring you to the best beer in Europe. What ho, hostess! Where be these whores?

(Enter HOSTESS.*)*

HOSTESS: How now? What lack you? What, my old guests, welcome.

ROBIN: [*aside.*] (Sirrah Dick, dost thou know why I stand so mute?)

DICK: [*aside.*] (No Robin, why is't?)

ROBIN: [*aside.*] I am eighteen pence on the score.¹ But say nothing. See if she have forgotten me.)

HOSTESS: Who's this that stands so solemnly by himself? What, my old guest!

ROBIN: O, hostess, how do you? I hope my score stands still.   10

HOSTESS: Ay, there's no doubt of that, for methinks you make no haste to wipe it out.

DICK: Why hostess, I say, fetch us some beer!

HOSTESS: You shall, presently. — Look up into th' hall, there, ho! [*To someone off-stage*] *(Exit.)*

DICK: Come sirs, what shall we do now till mine hostess comes?

6 bundle.

1 on the tab (i.e., in debt).

CARTER: Marry sir, I'll tell you the bravest tale how a conjurer served me. You know Doctor Fauster?

HORSE-COURSER: Ay, a plague take him! Here's some on's have cause to know him. Did he conjure thee too?

CARTER: I'll tell you how he serv'd me. As I was going to Wittenberg   20
t'other day with a load of hay, he met me and asked me what he should give me for as much hay as he could eat. Now sir, I thinking that a little would serve his turn, bad him take as much as he would for three farthings. So he presently gave me my money and fell to eating; and as I am a cursen[2] man, he never left eating till he had eat up all my load of hay.

ALL: O monstrous, eat a whole load of hay!

ROBIN: Yes yes, that may be, for I have heard of one that has eat a load of logs.

[HOSTESS *enters and serves drinks, then exit.*]

HORSE-COURSER: Now sirs, you shall hear how villainously he served   30
me. I went to him yesterday to buy a horse of him, and he would by no means sell him under forty dollars. So sir, because I knew him to be such a horse as would run over hedge and ditch and never tire, I gave him his money. So, when I had my horse, Doctor Fauster bad me ride him night and day and spare him no time. "But," quoth he, "in any case ride him not into the water." Now sir, I thinking the horse had had some quality that he would not have me know of, what did I but rid him into a great river — and when I came just in the midst, my horse vanish'd away and I sate straddling upon a bot-tle of hay!   40

ALL: O brave doctor!

HORSE-COURSER: But you shall hear how bravely I serv'd him for it. I went me home to his house, and there I found him asleep. I kept ahallowing and whooping in his ears, but all could not wake him. I seeing that, took him by the leg and never rested pulling till I had pull'd me his leg quite off, and now 'tis at home in mine hostry.

DICK: And has the doctor but one leg then? That's excellent, for one of his devils turned me into the likeness of an ape's face.

CARTER: Some more drink, hostess!

ROBIN: Hark you, we'll into another room and drink awhile, and then   50
we'll go seek out the doctor.

(Exeunt omnes.)

SCENE 5. *(Enter the* DUKE OF VANHOLT, *his [pregnant]* DUCHESS, FAUSTUS, *and* MEPHOSTOPHILIS *[invisible, and* SERVANTS].*)*

DUKE: Thanks master doctor, for these pleasant sights. Nor know I how sufficiently to recompense your great deserts in erecting that enchanted castle in the air, the sight whereof so delighted me, as nothing in the world could please me more.

2 *i.e., Christian (folksy dialect).*

FAUSTUS: I do think myself, my good lord, highly recompens'd in that it
    pleaseth Your Grace to think but well of that which Faustus hath
    perform'd. — But gracious lady, it may be that you have taken no
    pleasure in those sights. Therefore I pray you tell me what is the
    thing you most desire to have: be it in the world it shall be yours. I
    have heard that great-bellied women do long for things are rare and   *10*
    dainty.
DUCHESS: True master doctor, and since I find you so kind, I will make
    known unto you what my heart desires to have: and were it now
    summer, as it is January, a dead time of the winter, I would request
    no better meat[1] than a dish of ripe grapes.
FAUSTUS: This is but a small matter. — [*Aside*] (Go Mephostophilis,
    away!)

(*Exit* MEPHOSTOPHILIS.)

Madam, I will do more than this for your content.

(*Enter* MEPHOSTOPHILIS [*invisible*] *again with the grapes* [, *hands them to* FAUSTUS,
who gives them to DUCHESS].)

Here, now taste ye these. They should be good, for they come from
    a far country, I can tell you.   *20*
DUKE: This makes me wonder more than all the rest, that at this time of
    the year when every tree is barren of his fruit, from whence you
    had these ripe grapes.
FAUSTUS: Please it Your Grace, the year is divided into two circles over
    the whole world, so that when it is winter with us, in the contrary
    circle it is likewise summer with them, as in India, Saba, and such
    countries that lie far east, where they have fruit twice a year. From
    whence, by means of a swift spirit that I have, I had these grapes
    brought as you see.
DUCHESS: And trust me, they are the sweetest grapes that e'er I tasted.   *30*

(*The* CLOWN [S — ROBIN, DICK, CARTER, *and* HORSE-COURSER *who are all drunk*
—] *bounce* [*i.e., thump*] *at the gate within.*)

DUKE: What rude disturbers have we at the gate?
    Go pacify their fury, set it ope,
    And then demand of them what they would have.

(*They knock again and call out* [*off-stage*] *to talk with* FAUSTUS. [*They ad-lib in
calling out.*])

A SERVANT: [*at back of stage.*] Why, how now masters, what a coil[2] is there!

1 *food.*
2 *noise.*

What is the reason you disturb the Duke?

DICK: [*off-stage.*] We have no reason for it, therefore a fig[3] for him!

SERVANT: Why saucy varlets, dare you be so bold!

HORSE-COURSER: [*off-stage.*] I hope sir, we have wit enough to be more bold than welcome.

SERVANT: [*at back of stage.*] It appears so. Pray be bold elsewhere and trouble not the Duke.

DUKE: What would they have?

SERVANT: They all cry out to speak with Doctor Faustus.

CARTER: [*off-stage.*] Ay, and we will speak with him.

DUKE: Will you sir? Commit the rascals.

DICK: [*off-stage.*] Commit[4] with us! He were as good commit with his father as commit with us!

FAUSTUS: I do beseech Your Grace, let them come in.
They are good subject for a merriment.

DUKE: Do as thou wilt, Faustus. I give thee leave.

FAUSTUS: I thank Your Grace.

(*Enter the* CLOWN [ROBIN], DICK, CARTER, *and* HORSE-COURSER.)

Why, how now my good friends? 'Faith, you are too outrageous.
But come near, I have procur'd your pardons. Welcome all!

ROBIN: Nay sir, we will be welcome for our money, and we will pay for what we take. What ho, give's half a dozen of beer here, and be hang'd!

FAUSTUS: Nay, hark you, can you tell me where you are?

CARTER: Ay, marry can I, we are under Heaven.

SERVANT: Ay, but Sir Sauce-Box, know you in what place?

HORSE-COURSER: Ay ay, the house is good enough to drink in. Zounds, fill us some beer, or we'll break all the barrels in the house and dash out all your brains with your bottles.

FAUSTUS: Be not so furious. Come, you shall have beer. — My lord, beseech you give me leave awhile; I'll gage[5] my credit 'twill content Your Grace.

DUKE: With all my heart, kind doctor, please thyself. Our servants and our court's at thy command.

FAUSTUS: I humbly thank Your Grace. — Then fetch some beer. [*To* SERVANTS, *some of whom exeunt.* MEPHOSTOPHILIS *also exit.*]

HORSE-COURSER: Ay marry, there spake a doctor indeed! And 'faith, I'll drink a health to thy wooden leg for that word.

FAUSTUS: My wooden leg? What dost thou mean by that?

CARTER: Ha, ha, ha, dost thou hear him Dick? He has forgot his leg.

HORSE-COURSES: Ay, ay, he does not stand much upon that.

FAUSTUS: No, 'faith, not much upon a wooden leg.

---

3 *Dick puns on the preceding line (reason pronounced "raison"), and it leads him to the expression "fig" with the appropriate obscene gesture in which the thumb is thrust out between the first two fingers of a clenched fist.*

4 *in the previous line "commit" means imprison. Dick puns on the slang meaning of commit: to have sexual intercourse.*

5 *engage, pledge.*

CARTER: Good lord, that flesh and blood should be so frail with your worship! Do not you remember a horse-courser you sold a horse to?

FAUSTUS: Yes, I remember I sold one a horse.

CARTER: And do you remember you bid he should not ride into the water?   80

FAUSTUS: Yes, I do very well remember that.

CARTER: And do you remember nothing of your leg?

FAUSTUS: No, in good sooth.

CARTER: Then I pray remember your curtsy.[6]

FAUSTUS: I thank you sir [*bows*].

CARTER: 'Tis not so much worth. I pray you tell me one thing.

FAUSTUS: What's that?

CARTER: Be both your legs bedfellows every night together?

FAUSTUS: Would'st thou make a colossus[7] of me that thou askest me such questions?   90

CARTER: No, truly sir, I would make nothing of you, but I would fain know that.

(*Enter* [MEPHOSTOPHILIS *invisible leading astonished*] HOSTESS *with drink.*)

FAUSTUS: Then I assure thee certainly they are.

CARTER: I thank you, I am fully satisfied.

FAUSTUS: But wherefore dost thou ask?

CARTER: For nothing, sir, but methinks you should have a wooden bed-fellow of one of 'em.

HORSE-COURSER: Why, do you hear sir, did not I pull off one of your legs when you were asleep?   100

FAUSTUS: But I have it again now I am awake. [*Opens robe*] Look you here sir.

ALL: O horrible! Had the doctor three legs?

CARTER: Do you remember sir, how you cozened me and eat up my load of —

(FAUSTUS *charms him dumb.*)

DICK: Do you remember how you made me wear an ape's — [*Same.*]

HORSE-COURSER: You whoreson conjuring scab! Do you remember how you cozened me of a ho — [*Same.*]

ROBIN: Ha' you forgotten me? You think to carry it away with your *hey-pass* and *re-pass*?[8] Do you remember the dog's fa — [*Same.*]   110

(*Exeunt* CLOWNS [*rigidly, like automata*].)

HOSTESS: Who pays for the ale? Hear you master doctor, now you have sent away my guests, I pray who shall pay me for my a —

---

6 *play on meaning from two lines previous: to "curtsy" is to "make a leg."*

7 *i.e., the Colossus of Rhodes: one of the wonders of the ancient world, a gigantic statue between whose legs ships were said to pass into the port of Rhodes.*

8 *magical expressions.*

[FAUSTUS *charms her.*] *(Exit* HOSTESS.*)*

DUCHESS: My lord,
We are much beholding to this learned man.
DUKE: So are we madam, which we will recompense
With all the love and kindness that we may:
His artful sport drives all sad thoughts away.

(Exeunt.)

ACT FIVE

SCENE 1. *(Thunder and lightning. Enter* DEVILS *with covered dishes:*
MEPHOSTOPHILIS *leads them into* FAUSTUS' *study. Then enter* WAGNER.*)*

WAGNER: I think my master means to die shortly. He has made his will
and given me his wealth: his house, his goods, and store of golden
plate — besides two thousand ducats ready coin'd. I wonder what he
means. If death were nigh, he would not frolic thus. He's now at
supper with the scholars, where there's such belly-cheer as Wagner
in his life ne'er saw the like! And see where they come. Belike[1] the
feast is done. *(Exit.)*

(Enter FAUSTUS, MEPHOSTOPHILIS *[invisible], and two or three* SCHOLARS.*)*

1 SCHOLAR: Master Doctor Faustus, since our conference about fair
ladies, which was the beautifulest in all the world, we have determin'd with ourselves that Helen of Greece was the admirablest lady   10
that ever liv'd. Therefore master doctor, if you will do us so much
favor as to let us see that peerless dame of Greece, whom all the
world admires for majesty, we should think ourselves much behold-
ing unto you.
FAUSTUS: Gentlemen,
For that I know your friendship is unfeign'd,
It is not Faustus' custom to deny
The just request of those that wish him well:
You shall behold that peerless dame of Greece
No otherwise for pomp and majesty   20
Than when Sir Paris cross'd the seas with her
And brought the spoils to rich Dardania.[2]
Be silent then, for danger is in words.

[He *motions to* MEPHOSTOPHILIS.]

(Music sounds. MEPHOSTOPHILIS *brings in* HELEN: *she passeth over the stage.)*

1 *most likely.*
2 *Troy.*

2 SCHOLAR: Was this fair Helen, whose admir'd worth
    Made Greece with ten years' wars afflict poor Troy?
3 SCHOLAR: Too simple is my wit to tell her worth,
    Whom all the world admires for majesty.
1 SCHOLAR: Now we have seen the pride of nature's work,
    We'll take our leaves, and for this blessed sight
    Happy and blest be Faustus evermore!   30
FAUSTUS: Gentlemen, farewell! The same I wish to you.

    (Exeunt SCHOLARS.*)*

    (Enter an OLD MAN.*)*

OLD MAN: O gentle Faustus, leave this damned art,
    This magic that will charm thy soul to Hell
    And quite bereave thee of salvation.
    Though thou hast now offended like a man,
    Do not persever in it like a devil.
    Yet, yet, thou hast an amiable[3] soul
    If sin by custom grow not into nature.
    Then, Faustus, will repentance come too late!
    Then, thou art banish'd from the sight of Heaven!   40
    No mortal can express the pains of Hell!
    It may be this my exhortation
    Seems harsh and all unpleasant. Let it not.
    For gentle son, I speak it not in wrath
    Or envy of thee but in tender love
    And pity of thy future misery:
    And so have hope that this my kind rebuke,
    Checking[4] thy body, may amend thy soul.
FAUSTUS: Where art thou, Faustus? Wretch, what hast thou done?

    *(*MEPHOSTOPHILIS *gives him a dagger* [*which* FAUSTUS *seems about to use*]*.)*

    Hell claims his right and with a roaring voice   50
    Says "Faustus, come, thine hour is almost come!"
    And Faustus now will come to do thee right!
OLD MAN: O stay, good Faustus, stay thy desperate steps!

    [*Holds out hand to stop him.*]

    I see an angel hover o'er thy head,
    And with a vial full of precious grace
    Offers to pour the same into thy soul:
    Then call for mercy and avoid despair.

3 *lovable.*
4 *criticizing.*

FAUSTUS: O friend, I feel
    Thy words to comfort my distressed soul:
    Leave me awhile to ponder on my sins. 60
OLD MAN: Faustus, I leave thee, but with grief of heart,
    Fearing the enemy of thy hapless soul. *(Exit.)*
FAUSTUS: Accursed Faustus! Wretch, what hast thou done!
    I do repent, and yet I do despair:
    Hell strives with grace for conquest in my breast!
    What shall I do to shun the snares of death? [*Stares at dagger in his hand.*]
MEPHOSTOPHILIS: Thou traitor Faustus, I arrest thy soul [*Advances.*]
    For disobedience to my sovereign lord.
    Revolt,[5] or I'll in piecemeal tear thy flesh.
FAUSTUS: I do repent I e'er offended him. [*Retreats, frightened.*] 70
    Sweet Mephostophilis, entreat thy lord
    To pardon my unjust presumption,
    And with my blood again I will confirm
    The former vow I made to Lucifer.
MEPHOSTOPHILIS: Do it then, Faustus, with unfeigned heart
    Lest greater dangers do attend thy drift.
FAUSTUS: Torment, sweet friend, that base and aged man
    That durst dissuade me from thy Lucifer,
    With greatest torment that our Hell affords.
MEPHOSTOPHILIS: His faith is great. I cannot touch his soul. 80
    But what I may afflict his body with
    I will attempt, which is but little worth.
FAUSTUS: One thing, good servant, let me crave of thee
    To glut the longing of my heart's desire:
    That I may have unto my paramour
    That heavenly Helen which I saw of late,
    Whose sweet embraces may extinguish clear
    Those thoughts that do dissuade me from my vow,
    And keep mine oath I made to Lucifer.
MEPHOSTOPHILIS: This or what else my Faustus shall desire 90
    Shall be perform'd in twinkling of an eye.

(Enter HELEN *again, passing over between two* CUPIDS.*)*

FAUSTUS: Was this the face that launch'd a thousand ships
    And burnt the topless[6] towers of Ilium?[7]
    Sweet Helen, make me immortal with a kiss. [*Kisses her.*]
    Her lips suck forth my soul. See where it flies!
    Come Helen, come, give me my soul again. [*Kisses again.*]
    Here will I dwell, for Heaven is in these lips [*Embraces her.*]
    And all is dross that is not Helena.
    I will be Paris, and for love of thee

5 *i.e., back again to Lucifer.*
6 *i.e., incredibly high.*
7 *Troy.*

Instead of Troy shall Wittenberg be sack'd;   100
And I will combat with weak Menelaus[8]
And wear thy colors on my plumed crest. —
Yea, I will wound Achilles[9] in the heel
And then return to Helen for a kiss!
O, thou art fairer than the evening's air
Clad in the beauty of a thousand stars,
Brighter art thou than flaming Jupiter
When he appear'd to hapless Semele,[10]
More lovely than the monarch of the sky
In wanton Arethusa's[11] azure arms,   110
And none but thou shalt be my paramour.

(Exeunt.)

> SCENE 2. *(Thunder. Enter* LUCIFER, BELZEBUB, *and* MEPHOSTOPHILIS *[from trap and then go above, where they watch all this scene].)*

LUCIFER: Thus from infernal Dis do we ascend
To view the subjects of our monarchy,
Those souls which sin seals the black sons of Hell.
'Mong which as chief, Faustus, we come to thee,
Bringing with us lasting damnation
To wait upon thy soul. The time is come
Which makes it forfeit.
MEPHOSTOPHILIS: And this gloomy night
Here in this room will wretched Faustus be.
BELZEBUB: And here we'll stay   10
To mark him how he doth demean himself.
MEPHOSTOPHILIS: How should he but in desperate lunacy?
Fond[1] worldling, now his heart blood dries with grief,
His conscience kills it, and his laboring brain
Begets a world of idle fantasies
To overreach the Devil — but all in vain:
His store of pleasures must be sauc'd with pain!
He and his servant Wagner are at hand.
Both come from drawing Faustus' latest will.
See where they come!   20

(Enter FAUSTUS *and* WAGNER.*)*

FAUSTUS: Say Wagner, thou hast perus'd my will;
How dost thou like it?
WAGNER: Sir, so wondrous well
As in all humble duty I do yield
My life and lasting service for your love.

---

8 *Greek king and husband of Helen. She deserted him for Paris, the Trojan.*
9 *most famous of Greek warriors in the Trojan War.*
10 *Semele begged her lover Jupiter to show his full, divine splendour. His bolts of lightning disintegrated her.*
11 *wood nymph turned into a spring by Artemis. Marlowe imagines Jupiter, "the monarch of the sky," as reflected in her waters.*

1 *foolish.*

(Enter the SCHOLARS.*)*

FAUSTUS: Gramercies,[2] Wagner. — Welcome gentlemen.

[*Exit* WAGNER.]

1 SCHOLAR: Now worthy Faustus, methinks your looks are chang'd.
FAUSTUS: O gentlemen!
2 SCHOLAR: What ails Faustus?
FAUSTUS: Ah my sweet chamber-fellow, had I liv'd with thee, then had I   *30*
    liv'd still! — But now must die eternally. Look sirs, comes he not,
    comes he not? [*Points at trap.*]
1 SCHOLAR: O my dear Faustus, what imports this fear?
2 SCHOLAR: Is all our pleasure turned to melancholy?
3 SCHOLAR: He is not well with being over-solitary.
2 SCHOLAR: If it be so, we'll have physicians and Faustus shall be cur'd.
3 SCHOLAR: 'Tis but a surfeit[3] sir, fear nothing.
FAUSTUS: A surfeit of deadly sin that hath damn'd both body and soul!
2 SCHOLAR: Yet Faustus, look up to Heaven and remember mercy is
    infinite.   *40*
FAUSTUS: But Faustus' offense can ne'er be pardoned. The serpent that
    tempted Eve may be saved, but not Faustus! O gentlemen, hear with
    patience and tremble not at my speeches. Though my heart pant
    and quiver to remember that I have been a student here these thirty
    years, O, would I had never seen Wittenberg, never read book. —
    And what wonders I have done all Germany can witness, yea all the
    world! — For which Faustus hath lost both Germany and the world,
    yea Heaven itself — Heaven, the seat of God, the throne of the
    blessed, the kingdom of joy — and must remain in Hell forever!
    Hell, O Hell forever! Sweet friends, what shall become of Faustus   *50*
    being in Hell forever?
2 SCHOLAR: Yet Faustus, call on God.
FAUSTUS: On God, whom Faustus hath abjur'd? On God, whom Faustus
    hath blasphem'd? O my God, I would weep, but the Devil draws in
    my tears! Gush forth blood instead of tears, yea life and soul! O, he
    stays my tongue! I would lift up my hands, but see, they hold 'em,
    they hold 'em!
ALL: Who, Faustus?
FAUSTUS: Why, Lucifer and Mephostophilis. O gentlemen, I gave them
    my soul for my cunning.   *60*
ALL: O, God forbid!
FAUSTUS: God forbade it indeed, but Faustus hath done it. For the vain
    pleasure of four and twenty years hath Faustus lost eternal joy and
    felicity. I writ them a bill with mine own blood. The date is expired.
    This is the time. And he will fetch me.
1 SCHOLAR: Why did not Faustus tell us of this before, that Divines
    might have pray'd for thee?

2 *great thanks.*
3 *i.e., indigestion.*

FAUSTUS: Oft have I thought to have done so, but the Devil threaten'd to
    tear me in pieces if I nam'd God — to fetch me body and soul if I
    once gave ear to divinity. And now 'tis too late! Gentlemen, away,   *70*
    lest you perish with me.
2 SCHOLAR: O, what may we do to save Faustus?
FAUSTUS: Talk not of me but save yourselves and depart.
3 SCHOLAR: God will strengthen me! I will stay with Faustus.
1 SCHOLAR: Tempt not God, sweet friend, but let us into the next room
    and pray for him.
FAUSTUS: Ay, pray for me, pray for me. And what noise soever you hear,
    come not unto me, for nothing can rescue me.
2 SCHOLAR: Pray thou, and we will pray, that God may have mercy upon
    thee.   *80*
FAUSTUS: Gentlemen, farewell! If I live till morning, I'll visit you. If not,
    Faustus is gone to Hell.
ALL: Faustus, farewell.

(Exeunt SCHOLARS. [MEPHOSTOPHILIS *descends to stage.*])

MEPHOSTOPHILIS: Ay, Faustus, now thou hast no hope of Heaven.
    Therefore, despair! Think only upon Hell,
    For that must be thy mansion, there to dwell.
FAUSTUS: O thou bewitching fiend, 'twas thy temptation
    Hath robb'd me of eternal happiness.
MEPHOSTOPHILIS: I do confess it Faustus, and rejoice.
    'Twas I, that when thou wert i' the way to Heaven   *90*
    Damm'd up thy passage. When thou took'st the book
    To view the Scriptures, then I turn'd the leaves
    And led thine eye.
    What, weep'st thou! 'Tis too late, despair, farewell!
    Fools that laugh on earth, most weep in Hell.

(Exit.)

(Enter the GOOD ANGEL *and the* BAD ANGEL *at several doors.)*

GOOD ANGEL: O Faustus, if thou hadst given ear to me
    Innumerable joys had followed thee.
    But thou did'st love the world.
BAD ANGEL: — Gave ear to me,
    And now must taste Hell's pains perpetually.   *100*
GOOD ANGEL: O, what will all thy riches, pleasures, pomps
    Avail thee now?
BAD ANGEL: — Nothing but vex thee more,
    To want in Hell, that had on earth such store.

(Music while the throne[4] *descends.)*

---

4 *symbolic of what Faustus might have occupied in heaven.*

GOOD ANGEL: O, thou hast lost celestial happiness,
    Pleasures unspeakable, bliss without end.
    Had'st thou affected[5] sweet Divinity,
    Hell or the Devil had had no power on thee.
    Had'st thou kept on that way, Faustus behold
    In what resplendent glory thou had'st sat   *110*
    In yonder throne, like those bright shining saints,
    And triumphed over Hell! That hast thou lost. [*Throne ascends.*]
    And now, poor soul, must thy good angel leave thee,
    The jaws of Hell are open to receive thee.

    (Exit.)

    (Hell is discovered. [*Trap opens: fire and smoke come out as* BAD ANGEL *points down in it.*]*)*

BAD ANGEL: Now Faustus, let thine eyes with horror stare
    Into that vast perpetual torture-house.

    [FAUSTUS *stares into trap.*]

    There are the furies, tossing damned souls
    On burning forks. Their bodies boil in lead.
    There are live quarters broiling on the coals,
    That ne'er can die. This ever-burning chair   *120*
    Is for o'er-tortur'd souls to rest them in.
    These that are fed with sops of flaming fire
    Were gluttons and lov'd only delicates
    And laughed to see the poor starve at their gates.
    But yet all these are nothing. Thou shalt see
    Ten thousand tortures that more horrid be.
FAUSTUS: O, I have seen enough to torture me.
BAD ANGEL: Nay, thou must feel them, taste the smart of all —
    He that loves pleasure must for pleasure fall.
    And so I leave thee Faustus, till anon: *130*
    Then wilt thou tumble in confusion.

    (Exit.)

    (The clock strikes eleven.)

FAUSTUS: O Faustus!
    Now hast thou but one bare hour to live
    And then thou must be damn'd perpetually!
    Stand still, you ever-moving spheres of Heaven
    That time may cease and midnight never come:
    Fair nature's eye, rise, rise again and make
    Perpetual day, or let this hour be but a year,
    A month, a week, a natural day —
    That Faustus may repent and save his soul!   *140*
    O lente lente currite noctis equi![6]
    The stars move still, time runs, the clock will strike:
    The Devil will come, and Faustus must be damn'd!

5 *preferred.*
6 *Run slowly, slowly, O horses of the night. (Quoted from Ovid,* Amores, *I.13.40.)*

O, I'll leap up to my God! Who pulls me down?
See, see where Christ's blood streams in the firmament!
One drop of blood will save me. O, my Christ!
— Rend not my heart for naming of my Christ!
Yet will I call on Him! O spare me, Lucifer!
Where is it now? 'Tis gone!
And see a threat'ning arm, an angry brow!   150
Mountains and hills, come, come and fall on me
And hide me from the heavy wrath of God!
No?
Then will I headlong run into the earth.
Gape earth! O no, it will not harbor me.
You stars that reign'd at my nativity,
Whose influence hath allotted death and Hell,
Now draw up Faustus like a foggy mist
Into the entrails of yon laboring cloud
That when you vomit forth into the air,   160
My limbs may issue from your smoky mouths —
But let my soul mount and ascend to Heaven!

(The watch strikes.)

O half the hour is pass'd! 'Twill all be pass'd anon!
O God. If thou wilt not have mercy on my soul,
Yet for Christ's sake, whose blood hath ransom'd me,
Impose some end to my incessant pain!
Let Faustus live in Hell a thousand years,
A hundred thousand, and at last be sav'd!
No end is limited to damned souls!
Why wert thou not a creature wanting soul?   170
Or why is this immortal that thou hast?
O, Pythagoras' metempsychosis,⁷ were that true
This soul should fly from me and I be chang'd
Unto some brutish beast. — All beasts are happy
For when they die
Their souls are soon dissolv'd in elements.
But mine must live still to be plagu'd in Hell!
Curs'd be the parents that engender'd me!
No Faustus, curse thyself, curse Lucifer
That hath depriv'd thee of the joys of Heaven. . . .   180

(The clock strikes twelve.)

It strikes, it strikes! Now body, turn to air,
Or Lucifer will bear thee quick⁸ to Hell!
O soul, be changed into small water-drops
And fall into the ocean, ne'er be found.

---

7 *transmigration of souls: doctrine held by Pythagoras, Greek philosopher of the sixth century* B.C.
8 *alive.*

(Thunder, and enter the DEVILS.*)*

My God, my God! Look not so fierce on me!
Adders and serpents! Let me breathe awhile!
Ugly Hell, gape not! Come not Lucifer!
I'll burn my books! — O Mephostophilis. . . .

(Exeunt [DEVILS *with* FAUSTUS *into the trap. He is heard shrieking. Then his limbs
are thrown up.* DEVILS *above exeunt*]*.)*

SCENE 3. *(Enter the* SCHOLARS.*)*

1 SCHOLAR: Come gentlemen, let us go visit Faustus
For such a dreadful night was never seen
Since first the world's creation did begin!
Such fearful shrieks and cries were never heard!
Pray Heaven, the doctor have escaped the danger.
2 SCHOLAR: O, help us Heaven, see, here are Faustus' limbs
All torn asunder by the hand of death!
3 SCHOLAR: The devils whom Faustus serv'd have torn him thus:
For 'twixt the hours of twelve and one, methought
I heard him shriek and call aloud for help,   10
At which self[1] time the house seem'd all on fire
With dreadful horror of these damned fiends.
2 SCHOLAR: Well gentlemen, though Faustus' end be such
As every Christian heart laments to think on,
Yet for he was a scholar once admir'd
For wondrous knowledge in our German schools,
We'll give his mangled limbs due burial;
And all the students, cloth'd in mourning black,
Shall wait[2] upon his heavy funeral.

(Exeunt [*with limbs*]*.)*

(Enter CHORUS.*)*

Cut is the branch that might have grown full straight   20
And burned is Apollo's laurel bough
That sometime grew within this learned man.
Faustus is gone. Regard his hellish fall!
— Whose fiendful fortune may exhort the wise
Only to wonder at unlawful things
Whose deepness doth entice such forward wits
To practice more than heavenly power permits.

[*Exit.*]

---

1 *same.*
2 *i.e., attend.*

WILLIAM SHAKESPEARE

(1564–1616)

*A*lthough little is known for certain about Shakespeare's early life and education, his entire professional life as actor and playwright was spent with the Lord Chamberlain's Men, who were renamed the King's Men in 1604 upon the accession of James I. He was thus, along with his colleagues, under direct patronage of the royal household. The King's Men were the pre-eminent performing company of the day. They acted plays by Ben Jonson, John Fletcher, and others, but Shakespeare was their most sustained playwright.

Shakespeare retired in comfort after 1611, having made a substantial living as actor, playwright, and investor in the Globe Theatre. His plays were first collected after his death by fellow actors John Heminges and Henry Condell into Mr. William Shakespeare's Comedies, Histories, and Tragedies, *better known as the First Folio of 1623. Half of the texts (including the two reprinted here) had never been previously published.*

INTRODUCTION TO *ANTONY AND CLEOPATRA*

*B*y the time Shakespeare came to write *Antony and Cleopatra* (in 1606 or 1607), he had already penned the four great tragedies *Hamlet, Othello, Macbeth,* and *King Lear.* His comic ventures such as *Twelfth Night* and *A Midsummer Night's Dream* were behind him, as were the problematic dramas *Troilus and Cressida* and *Measure for Measure,* as well as another tale of doomed love, *Romeo and Juliet.* He was clearly at the height of his power as a playwright. Having been connected with the professional London theatre for some twenty years, Shakespeare knew both the power and the limitations of the stage. He would put both to work in achieving the massively political yet intimately emotional quality of *Antony and Cleopatra.*

Based largely on Sir Thomas North's translation of Plutarch's *Lives of the Noble Grecians and Romans* (1579), the play centres on the exalted, deified, yet ultimately doomed love of the title characters. Antony is representative of Mars, Roman god of war; Cleopatra is (in Antony's belief system) Venus, the goddess of love. He is descended of Hercules, rich in associations of virility, strength, and endurance. She embodies Isis, Egyptian goddess of fertility and the moon. Together, Antony and Cleopatra are transcendent in their love — as all lovers purport to be — but earthly reality and responsibility impinge upon them. Because they are heads of state and charismatic leaders with important social responsibilities, their love can never be insulated from the world around them. Antony is a ruling Roman triumvir with political pressures and conjugal attachments back in Rome. Cleopatra is the deific Egyptian queen who has allied herself wisely in the past to such figures as Julius Caesar and Pompey the Great. "The nobleness of life / Is to do thus," declares Antony in the first scene as he and Cleopatra embrace (36–37). He commands the world to acknowledge them "peerless" (40), but the world is a complex and relativistic entity, and their love is an emotionally complex entity, too.

Antony and Cleopatra represent two very different political and cultural systems: the Roman and the Egyptian. Egypt is the land of the fluctuating Nile where predictability gives way to flood and fertility, colour and emotion, variety and passion. This is a land of beauty and excitement and feminine verve that is embodied in its ruler and chief goddess Cleopatra. Rome, on the other hand, is rational, imperialist, militaristic, and absolute. This is a masculine world that is strictly task- and goal-oriented and that is embodied in the rigid policy of Octavius Caesar. Antony, with his love for both Egypt and Rome, straddles the two systems, and it is within his conflicting loyalties that much of the dramatic conflict takes place. He had crushed the revolutionaries who assassinated Julius Caesar, endorsed the eminence of Octavius, and gone eastward as military leader to maintain Roman influence and empire. He was supposed to make Egypt a part of Rome and degrade Cleopatra to the status of Roman puppet. He now knows this is politically impossible. For him, it is emotionally undesirable. In fact, Antony's discovery of a world of elegance, of leisured sophistication, ultimately of love, becomes the basis for questions about his real political and emotional loyalties.

To the Roman mind, reality is dictated by the iron logic that Octavius Caesar applies to every circumstance. He draws the necessary conclusions from reliable information. As the messenger who greets him first in the play says,

> Thy biddings have been done, and every hour,
> Most noble Caesar, shalt thou have report
> How 'tis abroad.
>
> (1.4.34–36)

Cleopatra's correspondence with Antony — "He shall have every day a several greeting, / Or I'll unpeople Egypt" (1.5.77–78) — is not nearly so efficient or thorough. But it is truly felt. She is given to supposition and emotional outburst, as in her mistreatment of the messenger who brings news of Antony's marriage to Octavia. Her overstated reactions provide comic incident throughout in swift mood changes and in her repeated action with the same cowed messenger in act 3 scene 3. Octavius, by contrast, treats all messengers with unprejudiced distance because of the amoral power of their information. He succeeds through the logistical narrowing of possibility. Emotion plays no part beyond public necessity. By the time Antony is reduced to whipping Caesar's messenger in act 3 scene 13, it is clear that the once-great Roman general is on the downside of his fortunes. Caesar reads Antony's desperation accurately, and sends the most dishonorable message of all:

> My messenger
> He hath whipp'd with rods; dares me to personal combat,
> Caesar to Antony. Let the old ruffian know
> I have many other ways to die, meantime
> Laugh at his challenge.

(4.1.2–6)

It is little surprise that Antony's patron and mythological forebear Hercules should leave him in the touchingly beautiful scene that follows his receipt of Caesar's message.

But just as much as the play is personal on the level of character conflict and interaction, so too is it political and world-scale in terms of military struggle. If "all the world's a stage," so too the stage can be a world, and Shakespeare's conception of this play is in many ways epic. The whole "world" of the Mediterranean Roman empire is its setting, with specific action in Egypt, North Africa, Greece, Italy, Rome. The many and massive scene shifts of the third act take us to Syria, to Rome, to Actium, to Alexandria. The record fifteen scenes of act 4 take us back and forth between the warring camps and on to Cleopatra's "monument." These many scenes were interpreted as dramatic weakness in the past, but are self-consciously playable and accessible on the stage once the assumptions of cinematic realism are suspended. In fact nearly all the "action," from Cleopatra's exotic first meeting with Antony on the River Cydnus to the variety of military conflict on land and sea, is reported rather than performed. As audience, we are distanced and we watch players performing parts in the world theatre of politics: Octavius Caesar, the young master, his cold rationality and instinct for power ever aiming at the main chance; Antony, the old lion, capable of eliciting passionate allegiance but just as capable of massive misjudgement because of his depth of feeling; Cleopatra, Egyptian queen, a woman of complex, sometimes comical, and always self-consciously intuitive political manipulation. The fifth act is all hers. With Antony very much on her mind, she proceeds, through her suicide, to outmanoeuvre Octavius, fully realizing the political caricature to which both she and her lover will be put in Roman triumph:

> The quick comedians
> Extemporally will stage us and present
> Our Alexandrian revels. Antony
> Shall be brought drunken forth, and I shall see
> Some squeaking Cleopatra boy my greatness
> I' th' posture of a whore.

(5.2.216–21)

This dramatically dangerous self-reference makes certain that the boy actor who performed Cleopatra on Shakespeare's stage did not "squeak." It also effectively suspends realism at this crucial point to remind the audience that it has not witnessed a caricatured "posture of a whore." Cleopatra then follows Antony in noble death rather than Caesar in paltry alliance. It is her death that reinforces their lost passionate grandeur.

Antony and Cleopatra

DRAMATIS PERSONAE

MARK ANTONY
OCTAVIUS CAESAR   } *Triumvirs*
M. AEMILIUS LEPIDUS
SEXTUS POMPEIUS
DOMITIUS ENOBARBUS
VENTIDIUS
EROS
SCARUS   } *friends to* ANTONY
DECRETAS
DEMETRIUS
PHILO
CANIDIUS, *Lieutenant-General to* ANTONY
MAECENAS
AGRIPPA
DOLABELLA
PROCULEIUS   } *friends to* CAESAR
THIDIAS
GALLUS
TAURUS, *Lieutenant-General to* CAESAR
MENAS
MENECRATES   } *friends to* POMPEY
VARRIUS
SILIUS, *an Officer in the army of* VENTIDIUS
EUPHRONIUS, *an Ambassador from* ANTONY *to* CAESAR
ALEXAS
MARDIAN
SELEUCUS   } *attendants on* CLEOPATRA
DIOMEDES
A SOOTHSAYER
A CLOWN

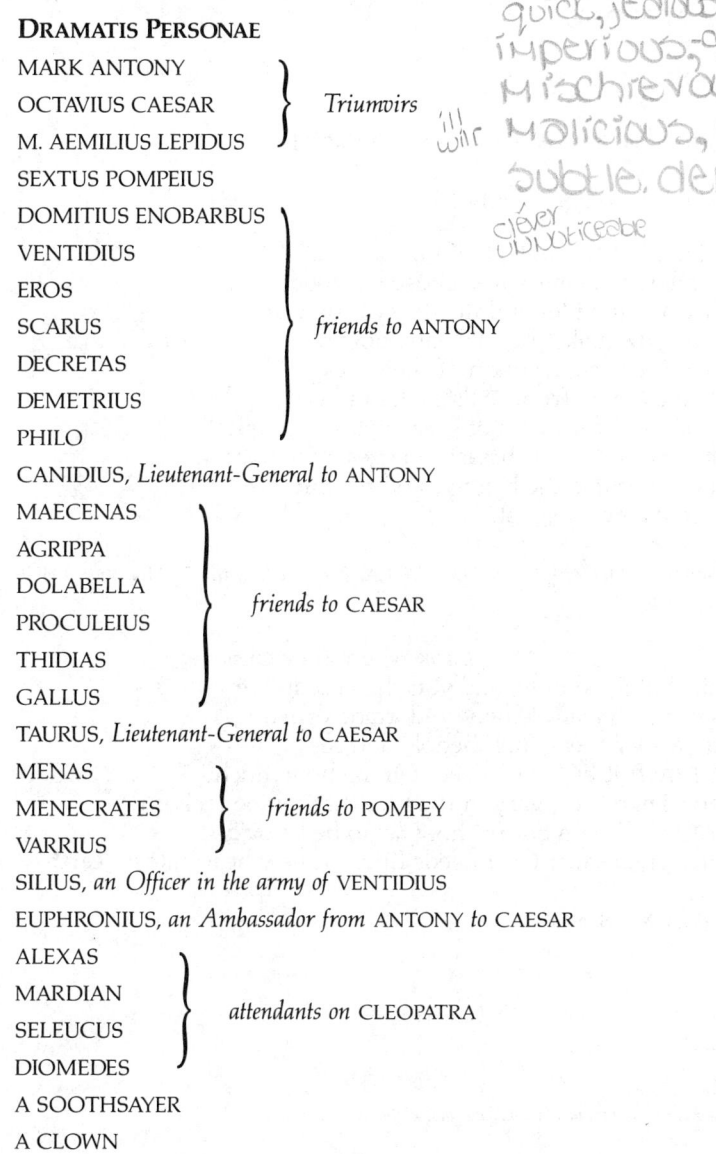

(handwritten annotation:) quick, jealous, imperious, commanding, arrogant, Mischrevous, conspicuous, ill badly will Malicious, flagrant, subtle, delicate, clever, noticeable

CLEOPATRA, *Queen of Egypt*

OCTAVIA, *sister to* CAESAR *and wife to* ANTONY

CHARMIAN   }

IRAS   }   *ladies attending on* CLEOPATRA

OFFICERS, SOLDIERS, MESSENGERS, ATTENDANTS

SCENE. — *In several parts of the Roman empire.*

ACT ONE

SCENE 1.

[Alexandria. A room in CLEOPATRA's *Palace.]*

(Enter DEMETRIUS *and* PHILO.*)*

PHILO: Nay, but this dotage of our general's
    O'erflows the measure. Those his goodly eyes
    That o'er the files and musters of the war
    Have glow'd like plated[1] Mars, now bend, now turn
    The office and devotion of their view
    Upon a tawny front.[2] His captain's heart,
    Which in the scuffles of great fights hath burst
    The buckles on his breast, reneges all temper[3]
    And is become the bellows and the fan
    To cool a gypsy's lust.

(Flourish. Enter ANTONY, CLEOPATRA, *her* LADIES, *the* TRAIN, *with* EUNUCHS *fanning her.)*

                    Look where they come!   10
    Take but good note, and you shall see in him
    The triple pillar of the world[4] transform'd
    Into a strumpet's fool. Behold and see.
CLEOPATRA: If it be love indeed, tell me how much.
ANTONY: There's beggary in the love that can be reckon'd.
CLEOPATRA: I'll set a bourn[5] how far to be belov'd.
ANTONY: Then must thou needs find out new heaven, new earth.

(Enter a MESSENGER.*)*

---

1 *armoured.*
2 *face.*
3 *discipline, self-control.*
4 *i.e., the ruling triumvirate (with Lepidus and Octavius Caesar).*
5 *limit.*

MESSENGER: News, my good lord, from Rome.
ANTONY: Grates me! The sum.
CLEOPATRA: Nay, hear them, Antony.
Fulvia[6] perchance is angry; or who knows   20
If the scarce-bearded Caesar have not sent
His pow'rful mandate to you: "Do this, or this;
Take in that kingdom, and enfranchise that.
Perform't, or else we damn thee."
ANTONY: How, my love?
CLEOPATRA: Perchance? Nay, and most like:
You must not stay here longer; your dismission
Is come from Caesar; therefore hear it, Antony.
Where's Fulvia's process? Caesar's I would say — both?
Call in the messengers. As I am Egypt's Queen,
Thou blushest, Antony, and that blood of thine   30
Is Caesar's homager! Else so thy cheek pays shame
When shrill-tongu'd Fulvia scolds. The messengers!
ANTONY: Let Rome in Tiber melt and the wide arch
Of the rang'd[7] empire fall! Here is my space.
Kingdoms are clay; our dungy earth alike
Feeds beast as man. The nobleness of life
Is to do thus [embracing]; when such a mutual pair
And such a twain can do't, in which I bind,
On pain of punishment, the world to weet[8]
We stand up peerless.
CLEOPATRA: Excellent falsehood!   40
Why did he marry Fulvia, and not love her?
I'll seem the fool I am not. Antony
Will be himself.
ANTONY: But stirr'd by Cleopatra.
Now for the love of Love and her soft hours,
Let's not confound the time with conference harsh.
There's not a minute of our lives should stretch
Without some pleasure now. What sport to-night?
CLEOPATRA: Hear the ambassadors.
ANTONY: Fie, wrangling queen!
Whom everything becomes — to chide, to laugh,
To weep; whose every passion fully strives   50
To make itself, in thee, fair and admir'd!
No messenger but thine, and all alone
To-night we'll wander through the streets and note
The qualities of people. Come, my queen;
Last night you did desire it. — Speak not to us.

(Exeunt [ANTONY and CLEOPATRA] with the TRAIN.)

---

6 Antony's wife.
7 extended, well-arranged.
8 acknowledge.

DEMETRIUS: Is Caesar with Antonius priz'd so slight?
PHILO: Sir, sometimes when he is not Antony
    He comes too short of that great property
    Which still should go with Antony.
DEMETRIUS: I am full sorry
    That he approves the common liar,[9] who   60
    Thus speaks of him at Rome; but I will hope
    Of better deeds to-morrow. Rest you happy! *(Exeunt.)*

SCENE 2.

[Alexandria. Another room in CLEOPATRA's *Palace.]*

(Enter a SOOTHSAYER, CHARMIAN, IRAS, *and* ALEXAS.*)*

CHARMIAN: Lord Alexas, sweet Alexas, most anything Alexas, almost
    most absolute Alexas, where's the soothsayer that you prais'd so to
    th' Queen? O that I knew this husband which, you say, must
    charge[1] his horns[2] with garlands!
ALEXAS: Soothsayer!
SOOTHSAYER: Your will?
CHARMIAN: Is this the man? Is't you, sir, that know things?
SOOTHSAYER: In nature's infinite book of secrecy
    A little I can read.
ALEXAS: Show him your hand.

[Enter ENOBARBUS.]

ENOBARBUS: Bring in the banquet quickly; wine enough   10
    Cleopatra's health to drink.
CHARMIAN: Good sir, give me good fortune.
SOOTHSAYER: I make not, but foresee.
CHARMIAN: Pray then, foresee me one.
SOOTHSAYER: You shall be yet far fairer than you are.
CHARMIAN: He means in flesh.
IRAS: No, you shall paint when you are old.
CHARMIAN: Wrinkles forbid!
ALEXAS: Vex not his prescience; be attentive.
CHARMIAN: Hush!   20
SOOTHSAYER: You shall be more beloving than beloved.
CHARMIAN: I had rather heat my liver[3] with drinking.
ALEXAS: Nay, hear him.
CHARMIAN: Good now, some excellent fortune! Let me be married to
    three kings in a forenoon and widow them all. Let me have a child
    at fifty, to whom Herod of Jewry may do homage. Find me to marry
    me with Octavius Caesar, and companion me with my mistress.

9 *i.e., gossips, rumour-mongers.*

1 *decorate.*
2 *i.e., cuckold's horns.*
3 *supposed internal organ of passion.*

SOOTHSAYER: You shall outlive the lady whom you serve.

CHARMIAN: O excellent! I love long life better than figs.

SOOTHSAYER: You have seen and prov'd a fairer former fortune   30
    Than that which is to approach.

CHARMIAN: Then belike my children shall have no names. Prithee, how
    many boys and wenches must I have?

SOOTHSAYER: If every of your wishes had a womb,
    And fertile every wish, a million.

CHARMIAN: Out, fool! I forgive thee for a witch.

ALEXAS: You think none but your sheets are privy to your wishes.

CHARMIAN: Nay, come, tell Iras hers.

ALEXAS: We'll know all our fortunes.

ENOBARBUS: Mine, and most of our fortunes, to-night, shall be — drunk   40
    to bed.

IRAS: There's a palm presages chastity, if nothing else.

CHARMIAN: E'en as the o'erflowing Nilus⁴ presageth famine.

IRAS: Go, you wild bedfellow, you cannot soothsay.

CHARMIAN: Nay, if an oily palm be not a fruitful prognostication, I can-
    not scratch mine ear. Prithee tell her but a workyday⁵ fortune.

SOOTHSAYER: Your fortunes are alike.

IRAS: But how, but how? Give me particulars.

SOOTHSAYER: I have said.

IRAS: Am I not an inch of fortune better than she?   50

CHARMIAN: Well, if you were but an inch of fortune better than I, where
    would you choose it?

IRAS: Not in my husband's nose.

CHARMIAN: Our worser thoughts heavens mend! Alexas — come, his
    fortune, his fortune! O, let him marry a woman that cannot go,
    sweet Isis,⁶ I beseech thee! and let her die too, and give him a worse!
    and let worse follow worse till the worst of all follow him laughing
    to his grave, fiftyfold a cuckold! Good Isis, hear me this prayer,
    though thou deny me a matter of more weight; good Isis, I beseech
    thee!   60

IRAS: Amen. Dear goddess, hear that prayer of the people! For, as it is a
    heartbreaking to see a handsome man loose-wiv'd, so it is a deadly
    sorrow to behold a foul knave uncuckolded. Therefore, dear Isis,
    keep decorum, and fortune him accordingly!

CHARMIAN: Amen.

ALEXAS: Lo now, if it lay in their hands to make me a cuckold, they
    would make themselves whores but they'ld do't!

ENOBARBUS: Hush! Here comes Antony.

(Enter CLEOPATRA.*)*

CHARMIAN: Not he! the Queen.

CLEOPATRA: Saw you my lord?

---

4 *Nile.*

5 *common, uncomplicated.*

6 *Egyptian goddess of fertility.*

ENOBARBUS: No, lady.
CLEOPATRA: Was he not here?
CHARMIAN: No, madam.   70
CLEOPATRA: He was dispos'd to mirth; but on the sudden
   A Roman thought hath struck him. Enobarbus!
ENOBARBUS: Madam?
CLEOPATRA: Seek him, and bring him hither. Where's Alexas?
ALEXAS: Here at your service. My lord approaches.

   (Enter ANTONY *with a* MESSENGER *[and* ATTENDANTS].*)*

CLEOPATRA: We will not look upon him. Go with us.

   (Exeunt [CLEOPATRA, ENOBARBUS *and the rest].)*

MESSENGER: Fulvia thy wife first came into the field.
ANTONY: Against my brother Lucius?
MESSENGER: Ay.
   But soon that war had end, and the time's state   80
   Made friends of them, jointing their force 'gainst Caesar,
   Whose better issue[7] in the war from Italy
   Upon the first encounter drave them.
ANTONY: Well, what worst?
MESSENGER: The nature of bad news infects the teller.
ANTONY: When it concerns the fool or coward. On!
   Things that are past are done with me. 'Tis thus:
   Who tells me true, though in his tale lie death,
   I hear him as he flatter'd.
MESSENGER: Labienus[8]
   (This is stiff news) hath with his Parthian force
   Extended Asia from Euphrates,   90
   His conquering banner shook from Syria
   To Lydia and to Ionia,
   Whilst —
ANTONY: Antony, thou wouldst say,
MESSENGER: O, my lord!
ANTONY: Speak to me home. Mince not the general tongue.
   Name Cleopatra as she is call'd in Rome.
   Rail thou in Fulvia's phrase, and taunt my faults
   With such full license as both truth and malice
   Have power to utter. O, then we bring forth weeds
   When our quick minds lie still, and our ills told us
   Is as our earing.[9] Fare thee well awhile.   100
MESSENGER: At your noble pleasure. *(Exit.)*
ANTONY: From Sicyon, ho, the news! Speak there!
1. ATTENDANT: The man from Sicyon — is there such an one?

7 *i.e., military superiority.*
8 *an ally of Brutus and Cassius in their failed struggle after the assassination of Julius Caesar. Having obtained a*
  force from the king of Parthia, he began military action against Roman territories in Asia Minor.
9 *ploughing; i.e., hearing our own faults plainly is like ploughing under and exterminating weeds.*

To such whose place is under us, requires   *180*
Our quick remove from hence.
ENOBARBUS: I shall do't. [*Exeunt.*]

SCENE 3.

[*Alexandria. Another room in* CLEOPATRA's *Palace.*]

(*Enter* CLEOPATRA, CHARMIAN, ALEXAS, *and* IRAS.)

CLEOPATRA: Where is he?
CHARMIAN: I did not see him since.[1]
CLEOPATRA: See where he is, who's with him, what he does.
   I did not send you. If you find him sad,
   Say I am dancing; if in mirth, report
   That I am sudden sick. Quick, and return!

   [*Exit* ALEXAS.]

CHARMIAN: Madam, methinks, if you did love him dearly,
   You do not hold the method to enforce
   The like from him.
CLEOPATRA: What should I do, I do not?
CHARMIAN: In each thing give him way, cross him in nothing.
CLEOPATRA: Thou teachest like a fool: the way to lose him!   *10*
CHARMIAN: Tempt him not so too far; I wish, forbear.
   In time we hate that which we often fear.

   (*Enter* ANTONY.)

   But here comes Antony.
CLEOPATRA: I am sick and sullen.
ANTONY: I am sorry to give breathing[2] to my purpose —
CLEOPATRA: Help me away, dear Charmian! I shall fall.
   It cannot be thus long; the sides of nature[3]
   Will not sustain it.
ANTONY: Now, my dearest queen —
CLEOPATRA: Pray you stand farther from me.
ANTONY: What's the matter?
CLEOPATRA: I know by that same eye there's some good news.
   What, says the married woman you may go?   *20*
   Would she had never given you leave to come!
   Let her not say 'tis I that keep you here.
   I have no power upon you; hers you are.
ANTONY: The gods best know —

1 *recently.*
2 *voice.*
3 *i.e., natural human strength.*

CLEOPATRA: O, never was there queen
  So mightily betray'd! Yet at the first
  I saw the treasons planted.
ANTONY: Cleopatra —
CLEOPATRA: Why should I think you can be mine, and true,
  Though you in swearing shake the throned gods,
  Who have been false to Fulvia? Riotous madness,
  To be entangled with those mouth-made vows   30
  Which break themselves in swearing!
ANTONY: Most sweet queen —
CLEOPATRA: Nay, pray you seek no colour[4] for your going,
  But bid farewell, and go. When you su'd[5] staying,
  Then was the time for words. No going then!
  Eternity was in our lips and eyes,
  Bliss in our brows' bent, none our parts so poor
  But was a race of heaven. They are so still,
  Or thou, the greatest soldier of the world,
  Art turn'd the greatest liar.
ANTONY: How now, lady?
CLEOPATRA: I would I had thy inches! Thou shouldst know   40
  There were a heart in Egypt.[6]
ANTONY: Hear me, Queen.
  The strong necessity of time commands
  Our services awhile; but my full heart
  Remains in use with you. Our Italy
  Shines o'er with civil swords.[7] Sextus Pompeius
  Makes his approaches to the port of Rome.
  Equality of two domestic powers
  Breed scrupulous faction. The hated, grown to strength,
  Are newly grown to love. The condemn'd Pompey,
  Rich in his father's honour, creeps apace   50
  Into the hearts of such as have not thriv'd
  Upon the present state, whose numbers threaten;
  And quietness, grown sick of rest, would purge
  By any desperate change. My more particular,[8]
  And that which most with you should safe my going,
  Is Fulvia's death.
CLEOPATRA: Though age from folly could not give me freedom,
  It does from childishness. Can Fulvia die?
ANTONY: She's dead, my queen.
  Look here, and at thy sovereign leisure read   60
  The garboils[9] she awak'd. At the last, best,
  See when and where she died.

4 pretext.
5 begged.
6 i.e., the queen of Egypt, as well as the country itself.
7 i.e., swords drawn for civil war.
8 i.e., particular reason.
9 disturbances.

CLEOPATRA: O most false love!
  Where be the sacred vials thou shouldst fill
  With sorrowful water? Now I see, I see,
  In Fulvia's death, how mine receiv'd shall be.
ANTONY: Quarrel no more, but be prepar'd to know
  The purposes I bear; which are, or cease,
  As you shall give the advice. By the fire[10]
  That quickens Nilus' slime, I go from hence
  Thy soldier, servant, making peace or war   70
  As thou affects.[11]
CLEOPATRA: Cut my lace,[12] Charmian, come!
  But let it be. I am quickly ill, and well —
  So Antony loves.
ANTONY: My precious queen, forbear,
  And give true evidence to his love, which stands
  An honourable trial.
CLEOPATRA: So Fulvia told me.
  I prithee turn aside and weep for her;
  Then bid adieu to me, and say the tears
  Belong to Egypt. Good now, play one scene
  Of excellent dissembling, and let it look
  Like perfect honour.
ANTONY: You'll heat my blood. No more!   80
CLEOPATRA: You can do better yet; but this is meetly.[13]
ANTONY: Now by my sword —
CLEOPATRA: And target.[14] Still he mends;
  But this is not the best. Look, prithee, Charmian,
  How this Herculean Roman does become
  The carriage of his chafe.[15]
ANTONY: I'll leave you, lady.
CLEOPATRA: Courteous lord, one word.
  Sir, you and I must part — but that's not it.
  Sir, you and I have lov'd — but there's not it.
  That you know well. Something it is I would —
  O, my oblivion is a very Antony,   90
  And I am all forgotten!
ANTONY: But that your royalty
  Holds idleness[16] your subject, I should take you
  For idleness itself.
CLEOPATRA: 'Tis sweating labour
  To bear such idleness so near the heart
  As Cleopatra this. But, sir, forgive me;
  Since my becomings[17] kill me when they do not
  Eye well to you. Your honour calls you hence;
  Therefore be deaf to my unpitied folly,
  And all the gods go with you! Upon your sword

---

10 *the sun.* **11** *i.e., as you order.* **12** *i.e., the laces of her bodice.* **13** *appropriate.* **14** *shield.* **15** *i.e., acts out his anger. (Antony claimed direct descent from Hercules.)* **16** *frivolity, coquettishness.* **17** *charms.*

Sit laurel victory, and smooth success   *100*
Be strew'd before your feet!
ANTONY: Let us go. Come.
   Our separation so abides and flies
   That thou, residing here, goes yet with me,
   And I, hence fleeting, here remain with thee.
   Away! *(Exeunt.)*

   SCENE 4 [*Rome.* CAESAR's *house.*]

(Enter OCTAVIUS [CAESAR], *reading a letter,* LEPIDUS, *and their* TRAIN.*)*

CAESAR: You may see, Lepidus, and henceforth know
   It is not Caesar's natural vice to hate
   Our great competitor.¹ From Alexandria
   This is the news: he fishes, drinks, and wastes
   The lamps of night in revel; is not more manlike
   Than Cleopatra, nor the queen of Ptolemy²
   More womanly than he; hardly gave audience, or
   Vouchsaf'd to think he had partners. You shall find there
   A man who is the abstract³ of all faults
   That all men follow.
LEPIDUS: I must not think there are   *10*
   Evils enow⁴ to darken all his goodness.
   His faults, in him, seem as the spots of heaven,
   More fiery by night's blackness; hereditary
   Rather than purchas'd;⁵ what he cannot change
   Than what he chooses.
CAESAR: You are too indulgent. Let us grant it is not
   Amiss to tumble on the bed of Ptolemy,
   To give a kingdom for a mirth, to sit
   And keep the turn of tippling with a slave,
   To reel the streets at noon, and stand the buffet   *20*
   With knaves that smell of sweat. Say this becomes him
   (As his composure must be rare indeed
   Whom these things cannot blemish), yet must Antony
   No way excuse his foils⁶ when we do bear
   So great weight in his lightness. If he fill'd
   His vacancy⁷ with his voluptuousness,
   Full surfeits and the dryness of his bones
   Call on⁸ him for't! But to confound such time
   That drums⁹ him from his sport and speaks as loud

---

1 *partner; i.e., Antony.* 2 *Cleopatra had been nominally married to her brother, the late Ptolemy*
XII. 3 *embodiment, summary.* 4 *enough.* 5 *acquired.* 6 *shortcomings.* 7 *spare time.* 8 *reprimand.* 9 *compels,*
recalls.

As his own state and ours — 'tis to be chid   30
As we rate[10] boys who, being mature in knowledge,
Pawn their experience to their present pleasure
And so rebel to judgment.

(Enter a MESSENGER.)

LEPIDUS: Here's more news.
MESSENGER: Thy biddings have been done, and every hour,
    Most noble Caesar, shalt thou have report
    How 'tis abroad. Pompey is strong at sea,
    And it appears he is belov'd of those
    That only have fear'd Caesar. To the ports
    The discontents[11] repair, and men's reports
    Give[12] him much wrong'd.
CAESAR: I should have known no less.   40
    It hath been taught us from the primal state[13]
    That he which is[14] was wish'd until he were;[15]
    And the ebb'd man, ne'er lov'd till ne'er worth love,
    Comes dear'd by being lack'd. This common body,[16]
    Like to a vagabond flag[17] upon the stream,
    Goes to and back, lackeying the varying tide,
    To rot itself with motion.
MESSENGER: Caesar, I bring thee word
    Menecrates and Menas, famous pirates,
    Make the sea serve them, which they ear[18] and wound
    With keels of every kind. Many hot inroads   50
    They make in Italy; the borders maritime
    Lack blood to think on't, and flush youth revolt.
    No vessel can peep forth but 'tis as soon
    Taken as seen; for Pompey's name strikes more
    Than could his war resisted.
CAESAR: Antony,
    Leave thy lascivious wassails. When thou once
    Was beaten from Modena, where thou slew'st
    Hirtius and Pansa, consuls, at thy heel
    Did famine follow; whom thou fought'st against
    (Though daintily brought up) with patience more   60
    Than savages could suffer. Thou didst drink
    The stale[19] of horses and the gilded[20]puddle
    Which beasts would cough at. Thy palate then did deign
    The roughest berry on the rudest hedge.
    Yea, like the stag when snow the pasture sheets,

---

10 scold, berate. 11 malcontents. 12 represent. 13 i.e., the very first government. 14 i.e., in power. 15 i.e., came to power. 16 populace. 17 iris. 18 plough. 19 urine. 20 yellowed.

The barks of trees thou browsed. On the Alps
It is reported thou didst eat strange flesh,
Which some did die to look on. And all this
(It wounds thine honour that I speak it now)
Was borne so like a soldier that thy cheek   70
So much as lank'd[21] not.
LEPIDUS: It is pity of him.
CAESAR: Let his shames quickly
      Drive him to Rome. 'Tis time we twain
      Did show ourselves i' th' field; and to that end
      Assemble we immediate council. Pompey
      Thrives in our idleness.
LEPIDUS: To-morrow, Caesar,
      I shall be furnish'd to inform you rightly
      Both what by sea and land I can be able
      To front[22] this present time.
CAESAR: Till which encounter,
      It is my business too. Farewell.   80
LEPIDUS: Farewell, my lord. What you shall know meantime
      Of stirs abroad, I shall beseech you, sir,
      To let me be partaker.
CAESAR: Doubt not, sir;
      I knew it for my bond.[23]

(Exeunt.)

      SCENE 5

[Alexandria. A room in CLEOPATRA's Palace.]

(Enter CLEOPATRA, CHARMIAN, IRAS, and MARDIAN.)

CLEOPATRA: Charmian!
CHARMIAN: Madam?
CLEOPATRA: Ha, ha!
      Give me to drink mandragora.[1]
CHARMIAN: Why, madam?
CLEOPATRA: That I might sleep out this great gap of time
      My Antony is away.
CHARMIAN: You think of him too much.
CLEOPATRA: O, 'tis treason!
CHARMIAN: Madam, I trust, not so.
CLEOPATRA: Thou, eunuch Mardian!
MARDIAN: What's your Highness' pleasure?
CLEOPATRA: Not now to hear thee sing. I take no pleasure
      In aught an eunuch has. 'Tis well for thee   10

21 thinned.
22 provide for.
23 duty.

1 a narcotic.

That, being unseminar'd,[2] thy freer thoughts
May not fly forth of Egypt. Hast thou affections?
MARDIAN: Yes, gracious madam.
CLEOPATRA: Indeed?
MARDIAN: Not in deed, madam; for I can do nothing
But what indeed is honest to be done.
Yet have I fierce affections, and think
What Venus did with Mars.[3]
CLEOPATRA: O Charmian!
Where think'st thou he is now? Stands he, or sits he?
Or does he walk? or is he on his horse?   20
O happy horse, to bear the weight of Antony!
Do bravely, horse! for wot'st thou whom thou mov'st?
The demi-Atlas[4] of this earth, the arm
And burgonet[5] of men. He's speaking now,
Or murmuring "Where's my serpent of old Nile?"
For so he calls me. Now I feed myself
With most delicious poison. Think on me,
That am with Phoebus'[6] amorous pinches black
And wrinkled deep in time? Broad-fronted Caesar,[7]
When thou wast here above the ground, I was   30
A morsel for a monarch; and great Pompey
Would stand and make his eyes grow in my brow;
There would he anchor his aspect,[8] and die
With looking on his life.

(Enter ALEXAS.*)*

ALEXAS: Sovereign of Egypt, hail!
CLEOPATRA: How much unlike art thou Mark Antony!
Yet, coming from him, that great med'cine hath
With his tinct[9] gilded[10] thee.
How goes it with my brave Mark Antony?
ALEXAS: Last thing he did, dear Queen,
He kiss'd — the last of many doubled kisses —   40
This orient pearl. His speech sticks in my heart.
CLEOPATRA: Mine ear must pluck it thence.
ALEXAS: "Good friend," quoth he,
"Say the firm Roman to great Egypt sends
This treasure of an oyster; at whose foot,
To mend the petty present, I will piece[11]
Her opulent throne with kingdoms. All the East,
Say thou, shall call her mistress." So he nodded,

---

2 *castrated.* 3 *in Roman mythology, the goddess of love and the god of war were lovers.* 4 *in mythology, Atlas supported the world on his shoulders.* 5 *military helmet.* 6 *the sun's.* 7 *Julius Caesar.* 8 *gaze.* 9 *medicinal properties.* 10 *i.e., turned to gold. The "great medicine" or philosopher's stone were key ingredients sought by alchemists in their attempts to turn base metal into gold.* 11 *add to.*

And soberly did mount an arm-gaunt[12] steed,
Who neigh'd so high that what I would have spoke
Was beastly dumb'd[13] by him.

CLEOPATRA: What, was he sad or merry?   50

ALEXAS: Like to the time o' th' year between the extremes
    Of hot and cold. He was nor sad nor merry.

CLEOPATRA: O well-divided disposition! Note him,
    Note him, good Charmian; 'tis the man; but note him!
    He was not sad, for he would shine on those
    That make their looks by his; he was not merry,
    Which seem'd to tell them his remembrance lay
    In Egypt with his joy; but between both.
    O heavenly mingle! Be'st thou sad or merry,
    The violence of either thee becomes,   60
    So does it no man else. — Met'st thou my posts?[14]

ALEXAS: Ay, madam, twenty several[15] messengers.
    Why do you send so thick?

CLEOPATRA: Who's born that day
    When I forget to send to Antony
    Shall die a beggar. Ink and paper, Charmian.
    Welcome, my good Alexas, Did I, Charmian,
    Ever love Caesar so?

CHARMIAN: O that brave Caesar!

CLEOPATRA: Be chok'd with such another emphasis!
    Say "the brave Antony."

CHARMIAN: The valiant Caesar!

CLEOPATRA: By Isis, I will give thee bloody teeth   70
    If thou with Caesar paragon[16] again
    My man of men!

CHARMIAN: By your most gracious pardon,
    I sing but after you.

CLEOPATRA: My salad days,
    When I was green in judgment, cold in blood,
    To say as I said then. But come, away!
    Get me ink and paper.
    He shall have every day a several greeting,
    Or I'll unpeople Egypt. *(Exeunt.)*

ACT TWO

SCENE 1 [*Messina.* POMPEY's *house.*]

(Enter POMPEY, MENECRATES, *and* MENAS, *in warlike manner.)*

---

12 *battle-trained; lean and mean.*
13 *silenced.*
14 *messengers.*
15 *separate.*
16 *compare.*

POMPEY: If the great gods be just, they shall assist
    The deeds of justest men.
MENECRATES: Know, worthy Pompey,
    That what they do delay, they not deny.
POMPEY: Whiles we are suitors to their throne, decays
    The thing we sue for.
MENECRATES: We, ignorant of ourselves,
    Beg often our own harms, which the wise pow'rs
    Deny us for our good. So find we profit
    By losing of our prayers.
POMPEY: I shall do well.
    The people love me, and the sea is mine;
    My powers are crescent,[1] and my auguring hope   *10*
    Says it will come to th' full. Mark Antony
    In Egypt sits at dinner, and will make
    No wars without doors. Caesar gets money where
    He loses hearts. Lepidus flatters both,
    Of both is flatter'd; but he neither loves,
    Nor either cares for him.
MENAS: Caesar and Lepidus
    Are in the field; a mighty strength they carry.
POMPEY: Where have you this? 'Tis false.
MENAS: From Silvius, sir.
POMPEY: He dreams. I know they are in Rome together,
    Looking for Antony. But all the charms of love,   *20*
    Salt[2] Cleopatra, soften thy wan'd[3] lip!
    Let witchcraft join with beauty, lust with both!
    Tie up the libertine in a field of feasts,
    Keep his brain fuming. Epicurean cooks
    Sharpen with cloyless sauce his appetite,
    That sleep and feeding may prorogue[4] his honour
    Even till a Lethe'd[5] dullness!

    (Enter VARRIUS.*)*

                How now, Varrius?
VARRIUS: This is most certain that I shall deliver:
    Mark Antony is every hour in Rome
    Expected. Since he went from Egypt 'tis   *30*
    A space for farther travel.
POMPEY: I could have given less matter
    A better ear. Menas, I did not think
    This amorous surfeiter would have donn'd his helm
    For such a petty war. His soldiership
    Is twice the other twain. But let us rear

1 *increasing.*
2 *lusty.*
3 *faded.*
4 *suspend.*
5 *oblivious. Lethe is a river in Hades. According to Roman mythology, the dead drink from it to obliterate the*
  memory of life.

The higher our opinion,⁶ that our stirring
Can from the lap of Egypt's widow pluck
The ne'er-lust-wearied Antony.
MENAS: I cannot hope
Caesar and Antony shall well greet together.
His wife that's dead did trespasses to Caesar;   40
His brother warr'd upon him; although, I think,
Not mov'd by Antony.
POMPEY: I know not, Menas,
How lesser enmities may give way to greater.
Were't not that we stand up against them all,
'Twere pregnant⁷ they should square between themselves,
For they have entertained cause enough
To draw their swords; but how the fear of us
May cement their divisions and bind up
The petty difference we yet not know.
Be't as our gods will have't! It only stands   50
Our lives upon to use our strongest hands.
Come, Menas. (Exeunt.)

SCENE 2 [*Rome. The house of* LEPIDUS.]

(*Enter* ENOBARBUS *and* LEPIDUS.)

LEPIDUS: Good Enobarbus, 'tis a worthy deed,
And shall become you well, to entreat your captain
To soft and gentle speech.
ENOBARBUS: I shall entreat him
To answer like himself. If Caesar move¹ him,
Let Antony look over Caesar's head
And speak as loud as Mars. By Jupiter,
Were I the wearer of Antonius' beard,
I would not shave't to-day!
LEPIDUS: 'Tis not a time
For private stomaching.²
ENOBARBUS: Every time
Serves for the matter that is then born in't.   10
LEPIDUS: But small to greater matters must give way.
ENOBARBUS: Not if the small come first.
LEPIDUS: Your speech is passion;
But pray you stir no embers up. Here comes
The noble Antony.

(*Enter* ANTONY *and* VENTIDIUS.)

ENOBARBUS: And yonder, Caesar.

---

6 *i.e., self-esteem.*
7 *probable.*

1 *anger, irritate.*
2 *i.e., personal resentment.*

(Enter CAESAR, MAECENAS, *and* AGRIPPA.*)*

ANTONY: If we compose³ well here, to Parthia.
    Hark, Ventidius.
CAESAR: I do not know,
    Maecenas. Ask Agrippa.
LEPIDUS: Noble friends,
    That which combin'd us was most great, and let not
    A leaner action rend us. What's amiss,
    May it be gently heard. When we debate   20
    Our trivial difference loud, we do commit
    Murder in healing wounds. Then, noble partners,
    The rather for I earnestly beseech,
    Touch you the sourest points with sweetest terms,
    Nor curstness grow to th' matter.
ANTONY: 'Tis spoken well.
    Were we before our armies, and to fight,
    I should do thus.

(Flourish.)

CAESAR: Welcome to Rome.
ANTONY: Thank you.
CAESAR: Sit.
ANTONY: Sit, sir.
CAESAR: Nay then.

    [*They sit.*]

ANTONY: I learn you take things ill which are not so,
    Or being, concern you not.
CAESAR: I must be laugh'd at   30
    If, or for nothing or a little, I
    Should say myself offended, and with you
    Chiefly i' th' world: more laugh'd at that I should
    Once name you derogately⁴ when to sound your name
    It not concern'd me.
ANTONY: My being in Egypt, Caesar,
    What was't to you?
CAESAR: No more than my residing here at Rome
    Might be to you in Egypt. Yet if you there
    Did practise on my state,⁵ your being in Egypt
    Might be my question.
ANTONY: How intend you? practis'd?   40
CAESAR: You may be pleas'd to catch at mine intent
    By what did here befall me. Your wife and brother
    Made wars upon me, and their contestation
    Was theme for you; you were the word of war.
ANTONY: You do mistake your business. My brother never
    Did urge me in his act. I did inquire it

---

3 *agree.*
4 *disparagingly.*
5 *i.e., plot against my administration.*

And have my learning from some true reports[6]
That drew their swords with you. Did he not rather
Discredit my authority with yours,
And make the wars alike against my stomach,[7]   50
Having alike your cause? Of this my letters
Before did satisfy you. If you'll patch a quarrel,
As matter whole you have not to make it with,
It must not be with this.
CAESAR: You praise yourself
    By laying defects of judgment to me; but
    You patch'd up your excuses.
ANTONY: Not so, not so!
    I know you could not lack, I am certain on't,
    Very necessity of this thought, that I,
    Your partner in the cause 'gainst which he fought,
    Could not with graceful eyes attend those wars   60
    Which fronted[8] mine own peace. As for my wife,
    I would you had her spirit in such another!
    The third o' th' world is yours, which with a snaffle[9]
    You may pace easy, but not such a wife.
ENOBARBUS: Would we had all such wives, that the men might go to
    wars with the women!
ANTONY: So much uncurbable, her garboils, Caesar,
    Made out of her impatience, — which not wanted
    Shrewdness of policy too, — I grieving grant
    Did you too much disquiet. For that you must   70
    But say I could not help it.
CAESAR: I wrote to you
    When rioting in Alexandria. You
    Did pocket up my letters, and with taunts
    Did gibe my missive[10] out of audience.
ANTONY: Sir,
    He fell upon me ere admitted. Then
    Three kings I had newly feasted, and did want
    Of what I was i' th' morning; but next day
    I told him of myself,[11] which was as much
    As to have ask'd him pardon. Let this fellow
    Be nothing of our strife. If we contend,   80
    Out of our question wipe him.
CAESAR: You have broken
    The article of your oath, which you shall never
    Have tongue to charge me with.
LEPIDUS: Soft, Caesar!

---

6 reporters.
7 liking.
8 confronted.
9 bridle.
10 messenger.
11 i.e., my condition.

ANTONY: No,
   Lepidus; let him speak.
   The honour is sacred which he talks on now,
   Supposing that I lack'd it. But on, Caesar.
   The article of my oath —
CAESAR: To lend me arms and aid when I requir'd them,
   The which you both denied.
ANTONY: Neglected rather;
   And then when poisoned hours had bound me up   90
   From mine own knowledge. As nearly as I may,
   I'll play the penitent to you; but mine honesty
   Shall not make poor my greatness, nor my power
   Work without it. Truth is, that Fulvia,
   To have me out of Egypt, made wars here,
   For which myself, the ignorant motive, do
   So far ask pardon as befits mine honour
   To stoop in such a case.
LEPIDUS: 'Tis noble spoken.
MAECENAS: If it might please you to enforce no further
   The griefs between ye — to forget them quite   100
   Were to remember that the present need
   Speaks to atone[12] you.
LEPIDUS: Worthily spoken, Maecenas.
ENOBARBUS: Or, if you borrow one another's love for the instant, you
   may, when you hear no more words of Pompey, return it again. You
   shall have time to wrangle in when you have nothing else to do.
ANTONY: Thou are a soldier only. Speak no more.
ENOBARBUS: That truth should be silent I had almost forgot.
ANTONY: You wrong this presence; therefore speak no more.
ENOBARBUS: Go to, then! your considerate stone.
CAESAR: I do not much dislike the matter, but   110
   The manner of his speech; for 't cannot be
   We shall remain in friendship, our conditions
   So diff'ring in their acts. Yet if I knew
   What hoop should hold us staunch, from edge to edge
   O' th' world I would pursue it.
AGRIPPA: Give me leave, Caesar.
CAESAR: Speak, Agrippa.
AGRIPPA: Thou hast a sister by the mother's side.
   Admir'd Octavia. Great Mark Antony
   Is now a widower.
CAESAR: Say not so, Agrippa.
   If Cleopatra heard you, your reproof   120
   Were well deserv'd of rashness.[13]
ANTONY: I am not married, Caesar. Let me hear
   Agrippa further speak.
AGRIPPA: To hold you in perpetual amity,
   To make you brothers, and to knit your hearts

12 *reconcile.*
13 *i.e., rash response.*

With an unslipping knot, take Antony
Octavia to his wife; whose beauty claims
No worse a husband than the best of men;
Whose virtue and whose general graces speak
That which none else can utter. By this marriage   *130*
All little jealousies, which now seem great,
And all great fears, which now import their dangers,
Would then be nothing. Truths would be tales,
Where now half-tales be truths. Her love to both
Would each to other, and all loves to both,
Draw after her. Pardon what I have spoke;
For 'tis a studied, not a present thought,
By duty ruminated.
ANTONY: Will Caesar speak?
CAESAR: Not till he hears how Antony is touch'd
    With what is spoke already.
ANTONY: What power is in Agrippa,   *140*
    If I would say "Agrippa, be it so,"
    To make this good?
CAESAR: The power of Caesar, and
    His power unto Octavia.
ANTONY: May I never
    To this good purpose, that so fairly shows,
    Dream of impediment! Let me have thy hand.
    Further this act of grace; and from this hour
    The heart of brothers govern in our loves
    And sway our great designs!
CAESAR: There is my hand.
    A sister I bequeath you, whom no brother
    Did ever love so dearly. Let her live   *150*
    To join our kingdoms and our hearts; and never
    Fly off our loves again!
LEPIDUS: Happily, amen!
ANTONY: I did not think to draw my sword 'gainst Pompey;
    For he hath laid strange courtesies and great
    Of late upon me. I must thank him only,
    Lest my remembrance suffer ill report;
    At heel of that, defy him.
LEPIDUS: Time calls upon's.
    Of us must Pompey presently be sought,
    Or else he seeks out us.
ANTONY: Where lies he?
CAESAR: About the Mount Misenum.[14]   *160*
ANTONY: What is his strength by land?
CAESAR: Great and increasing; but by sea
    He is an absolute master.

---

14 *hilly cape on the Bay of Naples.*

ANTONY: So is the fame.[15]
　　Would we had spoke together! Haste we for it.
　　Yet, ere we put ourselves in arms, dispatch we
　　The business we have talk'd of.
CAESAR: With most gladness;
　　And do invite you to my sister's view,
　　Whither straight I'll lead you.
ANTONY: Let us, Lepidus,
　　Not lack your company.
LEPIDUS: Noble Antony,
　　Not sickness should detain me.   170

(Flourish. Exeunt. Manent[16] ENOBARBUS, AGRIPPA, MAECENAS.)

MAECENAS: Welcome from Egypt, sir.
ENOBARBUS: Half the heart of Caesar, worthy Maecenas! My honoura-
　　ble friend, Agrippa!
AGRIPPA: Good Enobarbus!
MAECENAS: We have cause to be glad that matters are so well digested.
　　You stay'd well by't in Egypt.
ENOBARBUS: Ay, sir; we did sleep day out of countenance and made the
　　night light with drinking.
MAECENAS: Eight wild boars roasted whole at a breakfast, and but
　　twelve persons there. Is this true?   180
ENOBARBUS: This was but as a fly by an eagle. We had much more mon-
　　strous matter of feast, which worthily deserved noting.
MAECENAS: She's a most triumphant lady, if report be square[17] to her.
ENOBARBUS: When she first met Mark Antony, she purs'd up[18] his heart,
　　upon the river of Cydnus.
AGRIPPA: There she appear'd indeed; or my reporter devis'd[19] well for
　　her.
ENOBARBUS: I will tell you.
　　The barge she sat in, like a burnish'd throne,
　　Burn'd on the water. The poop was beaten gold;   190
　　Purple the sails, and so perfumed that
　　The winds were lovesick with them; the oars were silver,
　　Which to the tune of flutes kept stroke, and made
　　The water which they beat to follow faster,
　　As amorous of their strokes. For her own person,
　　It beggar'd all description. She did lie
　　In her pavilion, cloth-of-gold of tissue,
　　O'erpicturing that Venus where we see
　　The fancy[20] outwork nature. On each side her

15　rumour, report.
16　i.e., they remain (Latin).
17　true.
18　took up, took possession of.
19　invented.
20　imagination.

Stood pretty dimpled boys, like smiling Cupids,   *200*
With divers-colour'd fans, whose wind did seem
To glow the delicate cheeks which they did cool,
And what they undid did.
AGRIPPA: O, rare for Antony!
ENOBARBUS: Her gentlewomen, like the Nereides,[21]
   So many mermaids, tended her i' th' eyes,
   And made their bends adornings. At the helm
   A seeming mermaid steers. The silken tackle
   Swell with the touches of those flower-soft hands
   That yarely[22] frame the office. From the barge
   A strange invisible perfume hits the sense   *210*
   Of the adjacent wharfs. The city cast
   Her people out upon her; and Antony,
   Enthron'd i' th' market place, did sit alone,
   Whistling to th' air; which, but for vacancy,
   Had gone to gaze on Cleopatra too,
   And made a gap in nature.
AGRIPPA: Rare Egyptian!
ENOBARBUS: Upon her landing, Antony sent to her,
   Invited her to supper. She replied,
   It should be better he became her guest;
   Which she entreated. Our courteous Antony,   *220*
   Whom ne'er the word of "no" woman heard speak,
   Being barber'd ten times o'er, goes to the feast,
   And for his ordinary[23] pays his heart
   For what his eyes eat only.
AGRIPPA: Royal wench!
   She made great Caesar lay his sword to bed.
   He plough'd her, and she cropp'd.
ENOBARBUS: I saw her once
   Hop forty paces through the public street;
   And having lost her breath, she spoke, and panted,
   That she did make defect perfection
   And, breathless, pow'r breathe forth.   *230*
MAECENAS: Now Antony must leave her utterly.
ENOBARBUS: Never! He will not.
   Age cannot wither her nor custom stale
   Her infinite variety. Other women cloy
   The appetites they feed, but she makes hungry
   Where most she satisfies; for vilest things
   Become themselves in her, that the holy priests
   Bless her when she is riggish.[24]
MAECENAS: If beauty, wisdom, modesty, can settle
   The heart of Antony, Octavia is   *240*

---

21 *sea nymphs, daughters of the water god Nereus.*
22 *skilfully.*
23 *meal; usually refers to an informal meal at the public table of a tavern.*
24 *lusty, lewd.*

A blessed lottery²⁵ to him.
AGRIPPA: Let us go.
Good Enobarbus, make yourself my guest
Whilst you abide here.
ENOBARBUS: Humbly, sir, I thank you.

(Exeunt.)

SCENE 3. [*Rome.* CAESAR's *house.*]

(Enter ANTONY, CAESAR, OCTAVIA *between them.)*

ANTONY: The world and my great office will sometimes
Divide me from your bosom.
OCTAVIA: All which time
Before the gods my knees shall bow my prayers
To them for you.
ANTONY: Good night, sir. My Octavia,
Read not my blemishes in the world's report.
I have not kept my square; but that to come
Shall all be done by th' rule. Good night, dear lady.
OCTAVIA: Good night, sir.
CAESAR: Good night. *(Exit [with* OCTAVIA].)*

(Enter SOOTHSAYER.)*

ANTONY: Now, sirrah,¹ you do wish yourself in Egypt?   10
SOOTHSAYER: Would I had never come from thence, nor you thither!
ANTONY: If you can, your reason!
SOOTHSAYER: I see it in my motion,² have it not in my tongue.
But yet hie you to Egypt again.
ANTONY: Say to me,
Whose fortunes shall rise higher, Caesar's or mine?
SOOTHSAYER: Caesar's.
Therefore, O Antony, stay not by his side!
Thy demon,³ that thy spirit which keeps thee, is
Noble, courageous, high, unmatchable,
Where Caesar's is not; but near him thy angel   20
Becomes a fear, as being o'erpow'r'd. Therefore
Make space enough between you.
ANTONY: Speak this no more.
SOOTHSAYER: To none but thee; no more but when to thee.
If thou dost play with him at any game,
Thou art sure to lose; and of that natural luck
He beats thee 'gainst the odds. Thy lustre thickens⁴

---

25 *prize.*

1 *sir (addressed to an inferior).*
2 *mind.*
3 *i.e., guardian angel.*
4 *dims.*

When he shines by. I say again, thy spirit
Is all afraid to govern thee near him;
But he away, 'tis noble.
ANTONY: Get thee gone.
Say to Ventidius I would speak with him.   30

(Exit [SOOTHSAYER].)

He shall to Parthia. — Be it art or hap,[5]
He hath spoken true. The very dice obey him,
And in our sports my better cunning faints
Under his chance.[6] If we draw lots, he speeds;[7]
His cocks do win the battle still of mine
When it is all to naught, and his quails ever
Beat mine, inhoop'd,[8] at odds. I will to Egypt;
And though I make this marriage for my peace,
I' th' East my pleasure lies.

political deceit

(Enter VENTIDIUS.)

                          O, come, Ventidius,
You must to Parthia. Your commission's ready;   40
Follow me, and receive't. (Exeunt.)

SCENE 4. [Rome. A Street.]

(Enter LEPIDUS, MAECENAS, and AGRIPPA.)

LEPIDUS: Trouble yourselves no further. Pray you, hasten
     Your generals after.
AGRIPPA: Sir, Mark Antony
     Will e'en but kiss Octavia, and we'll follow.
LEPIDUS: Till I shall see you in your soldier's dress,
     Which will become you both, farewell.
MAECENAS: We shall,
     As I conceive the journey, be at th' Mount[1]
     Before you, Lepidus.
LEPIDUS: Your way is shorter;
     My purposes do draw me much about.
     You'll win two days upon me.
BOTH: Sir, good success!
LEPIDUS: Farewell. (Exeunt.)   10

5 skill or luck.
6 luck.
7 wins.
8 enclosed in a ring.

1 Misenum (see 2.2.160).

SCENE 5. [*Alexandria.* CLEOPATRA's *Palace.*]

(*Enter* CLEOPATRA, CHARMIAN, IRAS, *and* ALEXAS.)

CLEOPATRA: Give me some music! music, moody food
    Of us that trade in love.
OMNES: [1]   The music, ho!

(*Enter* MARDIAN *the* EUNUCH.)

[handwritten margin note: strikes and i interrogates the messenger who brings news of Antony's to Marriage to Octavia.]

CLEOPATRA: Let it alone! Let's to billiards. Come, Charmian.
CHARMIAN: My arm is sore; best play with Mardian.
CLEOPATRA: As well a woman with an eunuch play'd
    As with a woman. Come, you'll play with me, sir?
MARDIAN: As well as I can, madam.
CLEOPATRA: And when good will is show'd, though 't come too short,
    The actor may plead pardon. I'll none now.
    Give me mine angle![2] we'll to th' river. There,   10
    My music playing far off, I will betray
    Tawny-finn'd fishes. My bended hook shall pierce
    Their slimy jaws; and as I draw them up,
    I'll think them every one an Antony,
    And say, "Ah, ha! y'are caught!"
CHARMIAN: 'Twas merry when
    You wager'd on your angling, when your diver
    Did hang a salt fish on his hook, which he
    With fervency drew up.
CLEOPATRA: That time? O times!
    I laugh'd him out of patience; and that night
    I laugh'd him into patience; and next morn   20
    Ere the ninth hour I drunk him to his bed,
    Then put my tires[3] and mantles on him, whilst
    I wore his sword Philippan.[4]

(*Enter a* MESSENGER.)

               O, from Italy!
    Ram thou thy fruitful tidings in mine ears,
    That long time have been barren.
MESSENGER: Madam, madam —
CLEOPATRA: Antony's dead! If thou say so, villain,
    Thou kill'st thy mistress; but well and free,
    If thou so yield him, there is gold, and here
    My bluest veins to kiss — a hand that kings

---

1 *all (Latin).*
2 *fishing tackle.*
3 *headdresses.*
4 *the sword with which Antony defeated Brutus and Cassius at the Battle of Philippi.*

Have lipp'd, and trembled kissing.   30
MESSENGER: First, madam, he is well.
CLEOPATRA: Why, there's more gold.
    But, sirrah, mark, we use
    To say the dead are well. Bring it to that,
    The gold I give thee will I melt and pour
    Down thy ill-uttering throat.
MESSENGER: Good madam, hear me.
CLEOPATRA: Well, go to, I will.
    But there's no goodness in thy face. If Antony
    Be free and healthful, why so tart a favour⁵
    To trumpet such good tidings? If not well,
    Thou shouldst come like a Fury⁶ crown'd with snakes,   40
    Not like a formal man.
MESSENGER: Will't please you hear me?
CLEOPATRA: I have a mind to strike thee ere thou speak'st.
    Yet, if thou say Antony lives, is well,
    Or friends with Caesar or not captive to him,
    I'll set thee in a shower of gold and hail
    Rich pearls upon thee.
MESSENGER: Madam, he's well.
CLEOPATRA: Well said.
MESSENGER: And friends with Caesar.
CLEOPATRA: Th'art an honest man.
MESSENGER: Caesar and he are greater friends than ever.
CLEOPATRA: Make thee a fortune from me!
MESSENGER: But yet, madam —   50
CLEOPATRA: I do not like "but yet." It does allay⁷
    The good precedence. Fie upon "but yet"!
    "But yet" is as a jailer to bring forth
    Some monstrous malefactor. Prithee, friend,
    Pour out the pack of matter to mine ear,
    The good and bad together. He's friends with Caesar;
    In state of health thou say'st; and thou say'st free.
MESSENGER: Free, madam? No; I made no such report.
    He's bound unto Octavia.
CLEOPATRA: For what good turn?
MESSENGER: For the best turn i' th' bed.
CLEOPATRA: I am pale, Charmian.
MESSENGER: Madam, he's married to Octavia.   60
CLEOPATRA: The most infectious pestilence upon thee!

    (Strikes him down.)

MESSENGER: Good madam, patience.

5 *face, expression.*
6 *in mythology, an avenging deity.*
7 *qualify.*

CLEOPATRA: What say you? *(Strikes him.)*
                                                Hence,
   Horrible villain! or I'll spurn[8] thine eyes
   Like balls before me. I'll unhair thy head!

(She hales[9] him up and down.)

   Thou shalt be whipp'd with wire and stew'd in brine,
   Smarting in ling'ring pickle.[10]
MESSENGER: Gracious madam,
   I that do bring the news made not the match.
CLEOPATRA: Say 'tis not so, a province I will give thee
   And make thy fortunes proud. The blow thou hadst
   Shall make thy peace for moving me to rage;   70
   And I will boot[11] thee with what gift beside
   Thy modesty can beg.
MESSENGER: He's married, madam.
CLEOPATRA: Rogue, thou hast liv'd too long. *(Draws a knife.)*
MESSENGER: Nay, then I'll run.
   What mean you, madam? I have made no fault. *(Exit.)*
CHARMIAN: Good madam, keep yourself within yourself.
   The man is innocent.
CLEOPATRA: Some innocents scape not the thunderbolt.
   Melt Egypt into Nile! and kindly creatures
   Turn all to serpents! Call the slave again.
   Though I am mad, I will not bite him. Call!   80
CHARMIAN: He is afeard to come.
CLEOPATRA: I will not hurt him.
   These hands do lack nobility, that they strike
   A meaner than myself; since I myself
   Have given myself the cause.

(Enter the MESSENGER *again.)*

                                                Come hither, sir.
   Though it be honest, it is never good
   To bring bad news. Give to a gracious message
   An host of tongues, but let ill tidings tell
   Themselves when they be felt.
MESSENGER: I have done my duty.
CLEOPATRA: Is he married?
   I cannot hate thee worser than I do   90
   If thou again say yes.
MESSENGER: He's married, madam.

8 kick.
9 drags.
10 i.e., pickling solution.
11 provide.

CLEOPATRA: The gods confound thee! Dost thou hold there still?
MESSENGER: Should I lie, madam?
CLEOPATRA: O, I would thou didst,
   So[12] half my Egypt were submerg'd and made
   A cistern for scal'd snakes! Go get thee hence!
   Hadst thou Narcissus[13] in thy face, to me
   Thou wouldst appear most ugly. He is married?
MESSENGER: I crave your Highness' pardon.
CLEOPATRA: He is married?
MESSENGER: Take no offence that I would not offend you.
   To punish me for what you make me do   100
   Seems much unequal.[14] He's married to Octavia.
CLEOPATRA: O, that his fault should make a knave of thee,
   That art not what th' art sure of! Get thee hence.
   The merchandise which thou hast brought from Rome
   Are all too dear for me. Lie they upon thy hand,
   And be undone by 'em! [Exit MESSENGER.]
CHARMIAN: Good your Highness, patience.
CLEOPATRA: In praising Antony I have disprais'd Caesar.
CHARMIAN: Many times, madam.
CLEOPATRA: I am paid for't now.
   Lead me from hence,
   I faint. O Iras, Charmian! 'Tis no matter.   110
   Go to the fellow, good Alexas. Bid him
   Report the feature[15] of Octavia, her years,
   Her inclinations; let him not leave out
   The colour of her hair. Bring me word quickly.

   [Exit ALEXAS.]

   Let him for ever go! — let him not! — Charmian,
   Though he be painted one way like a Gorgon,[16]
   The other way's a Mars — [To MARDIAN] Bid you Alexas
   Bring me word how tall she is. — Pity me, Charmian,
   But do not speak to me. Lead me to my chamber.

   (Exeunt.)

---

12 even if.
13 in mythology, a young man so beautiful that he fell in love with his own reflection.
14 unjust.
15 features.
16 in Greek mythology, three hideous tusked women with snakes for hair and glaring eyes, who turned to stone anyone who dared to meet their gaze.

SCENE 6. [*Near Misenum.*]

(*Flourish. Enter* POMPEY [*and*] MENAS *at one door, with Drum and Trumpet: at another,* CAESAR, LEPIDUS, ANTONY, ENOBARBUS, MAECENAS, AGRIPPA, *with* SOLDIERS *marching.*)

POMPEY: Your hostages I have, so have you mine;
  And we shall talk before we fight.
CAESAR: Most meet[1]
  That first we come to words; and therefore have we
  Our written purposes before us sent;
  Which if thou hast considered, let us know
  If 'twill tie up thy discontented sword
  And carry back to Sicily much tall[2] youth
  That else must perish here.
POMPEY: To you all three,
  The senators alone of this great world,
  Chief factors[3] for the gods: I do not know   10
  Wherefore my father should revengers want,
  Having a son and friends, since Julius Caesar,
  Who at Philippi the good Brutus ghosted,
  There saw you labouring for him. What was't
  That mov'd pale Cassius to conspire? and what
  Made the all-honour'd honest Roman, Brutus,
  With the arm'd rest, courtiers of beauteous freedom,
  To drench the Capitol, but that they would
  Have one man but a man? And that is it
  Hath made me rig my navy, at whose burden   20
  The anger'd ocean foams; with which I meant
  To scourge th' ingratitude that despiteful Rome
  Cast on my noble father.
CAESAR: Take your time.
ANTONY: Thou canst not fear[4] us, Pompey, with thy sails.
  We'll speak with thee at sea. At land thou know'st
  How much we do o'ercount[5] thee.
POMPEY: At land indeed
  Thou dost o'ercount[6] me of my father's house!
  But since the cuckoo builds not for himself,
  Remain in't as thou mayst.
LEPIDUS: Be pleas'd to tell us
  (For this is from the present)[7] how you take   30
  The offers we have sent you.
CAESAR: There's the point.

---

1 *appropriate.* 2 *brave, able.* 3 *agents.* 4 *frighten.* 5 *outnumber.* 6 *cheat. (Pompey puns on Antony's use in the preceding line.)* 7 *i.e., beside the point.*

ANTONY: Which do not be entreated to, but weigh
    What it is worth embrac'd.
CAESAR: And what may follow,
    To try a larger fortune.
POMPEY: You have made me offer
    Of Sicily, Sardinia; and I must
    Rid all the sea of pirates; then, to send
    Measures of wheat to Rome; this 'greed upon,
    To part with unhack'd edges[8] and bear back
    Our targes[9] undinted.
OMNES: That's our offer.
POMPEY: Know then
    I came before you here a man prepar'd   40
    To take this offer; but Mark Antony
    Put me to some impatience. Though I lose
    The praise of it by telling, you must know,
    When Caesar and your brother were at blows,
    Your mother came to Sicily and did find
    Her welcome friendly.
ANTONY: I have heard it, Pompey,
    And am well studied[10] for a liberal thanks,
    Which I do owe you.
POMPEY: Let me have your hand.
    I did not think, sir, to have met you here.
ANTONY: The beds i' th' East are soft; and thanks to you,   50
    That call'd me timelier than my purpose hither;
    For I have gain'd by 't.
CAESAR: Since I saw you last
    There is a change upon you.
POMPEY: Well, I know not
    What counts[11] harsh fortune casts upon my face;
    But in my bosom shall she never come
    To make my heart her vassal.
LEPIDUS: Well met here.
POMPEY: I hope so, Lepidus. Thus we are agreed.
    I crave our composition[12] may be written,
    And seal'd between us.
CAESAR: That's the next to do.
POMPEY: We'll feast each other ere we part, and let's   60
    Draw lots who shall begin.
ANTONY: That will I, Pompey.
POMPEY: No, Antony, take the lot;
    But, first or last, your fine Egyptian cookery
    Shall have the fame. I have heard that Julius Caesar
    Grew fat with feasting there.

---

8 *swords.*
9 *shields.*
10 *prepared.*
11 *accounts (wrinkles).*
12 *conciliation.*

ANTONY: You have heard much.
POMPEY: I have fair meanings, sir.
ANTONY: And fair words to them.
POMPEY: Then so much have I heard;
    And I have heard Apollodorus[13] carried —
ENOBARBUS: No more of that! He did so.
POMPEY: What, I pray you?
ENOBARBUS: A certain queen to Caesar in a mattress.   70
POMPEY: I know thee now. How far'st thou, soldier?
ENOBARBUS: Well;
    And well am like to do, for I perceive
    Four feasts are toward.[14]
POMPEY: Let me shake thy hand.
    I never hated thee. I have seen thee fight
    When I have envied thy behaviour.
ENOBARBUS: Sir,
    I never lov'd you much; but I ha' prais'd ye
    When you have well deserv'd ten times as much
    As I have said you did.
POMPEY: Enjoy thy plainness;
    It nothing ill becomes thee.
    Aboard my galley I invite you all.   80
    Will you lead, lords?
ALL: Show us the way, sir.
POMPEY: Come.

(Exeunt. Manent ENOBARBUS *and* MENAS.*)*

MENAS: [*aside*] Thy father, Pompey, would ne'er have made this treaty. —
    You and I have known,[15] sir.
ENOBARBUS: At sea, I think.
MENAS: We have, sir.
ENOBARBUS: You have done well by water.
MENAS: And you by land.
ENOBARBUS: I will praise any man that will praise me; though it cannot
    be denied what I have done by land.
MENAS: Nor what I have done by water.   90
ENOBARBUS: Yes, something you can deny for your own safety. You have
    been a great thief by sea.
MENAS: And you by land.
ENOBARBUS: There I deny my land service. But give me your hand,
    Menas. If our eyes had authority,[16] here they might take two thieves
    kissing.

13 *the biographer Plutarch reports that Cleopatra was wrapped in a bedcover and carried in secret to Julius Caesar on the back of her servant Apollodorus.*
14 *ready.*
15 *met.*
16 *authority to make an arrest.*

MENAS: All men's faces are true,[17] whatsome'er their hands are.

ENOBARBUS: But there is never a fair woman has a true face.

MENAS: No slander. They steal hearts.

ENOBARBUS: We came hither to fight with you.   100

MENAS: For my part, I am sorry it is turn'd to a drinking. Pompey doth
    this day laugh away his fortune.

ENOBARBUS: If he do, sure he cannot weep't back again.

MENAS: Y'have said, sir. We look'd not for Mark Antony here. Pray you,
    is he married to Cleopatra?

ENOBARBUS: Caesar's sister is call'd Octavia.

MENAS: True, sir. She was the wife of Caius Marcellus.

ENOBARBUS: But she is now the wife of Marcus Antonius.

MENAS: Pray ye, sir?

ENOBARBUS: 'Tis true.   110

MENAS: Then is Caesar and he for ever knit together.

ENOBARBUS: If I were bound to divine of this unity, I would not proph-
    esy so.

MENAS: I think the policy of that purpose made more in the marriage
    than the love of the parties.

ENOBARBUS: I think so too. But you shall find the band that seems to tie
    their friendship together will be the very strangler of their amity.
    Octavia is of a holy, cold, and still conversation.

MENAS: Who would not have his wife so?

ENOBARBUS: Not he that himself is not so; which is Mark Antony. He   120
    will to his Egyptian dish again. Then shall the sighs of Octavia blow
    the fire up in Caesar, and, as I said before, that which is the
    strength of their amity shall prove the immediate author of their
    variance. Antony will use his affection where it is. He married but
    his occasion[18] here.

MENAS: And thus it may be. Come, sir, will you aboard? I have a health
    for you.

ENOBARBUS: I shall take it, sir. We have us'd our throats in Egypt.

MENAS: Come, let's away. (Exeunt.)

SCENE 7.

[On board POMPEY's galley, off Misenum.]

(Music plays. Enter two or three SERVANTS, with a banquet.)

1. SERVANT: Here they'll be, man. Some o' their plants are ill-rooted
    already; the least wind i' th' world will blow them down.

2. SERVANT: Lepidus is high-colour'd.

1. SERVANT: They have made him drink alms-drink.[1]

2. SERVANT: As they pinch one another by the disposition, he cries out
    "No more!" reconciles them to his entreaty and himself to th' drink.

17 honest.
18 i.e., political necessity.

1 i.e., more than his share.

1. SERVANT: But it raises the greater war between him and his discretion.

2. SERVANT: Why, this it is to have a name in great men's fellowship. I had as lief have a reed that will do me no service, as a partisan[2] I could not heave.

1. SERVANT: To be call'd into a huge sphere and not to be seen to move in't, are the holes where eyes should be, which pitifully disaster the cheeks.

(A sennet[3] sounded. Enter CAESAR, ANTONY, POMPEY, LEPIDUS, AGRIPPA, MAECENAS, ENOBARBUS, MENAS, *with other* CAPTAINS.)

ANTONY: [*to* CAESAR] Thus do they, sir: they take the flow o' th' Nile
By certain scales i' th' pyramid. They know
By th' height, the lowness, or the mean, if dearth
Or foison[4] follow. The higher Nilus swells,
The more it promises. As it ebbs, the seedsman
Upon the slime and ooze scatters his grain,
And shortly comes to harvest.

LEPIDUS: Y'have strange serpents there.

ANTONY: Ay, Lepidus.

LEPIDUS: Your serpent of Egypt is bred now of your mud by the operation of your sun; so is your crocodile.

ANTONY: They are so.

POMPEY: Sit — and some wine! A health to Lepidus!

LEPIDUS: I am not so well as I should be, but I'll ne'er out.[5]

ENOBARBUS: Not till you have slept. I fear me you'll be in till then.

LEPIDUS: Nay, certainly, I have heard the Ptolemies' pyramises are very goodly things. Without contradiction I have heard that.

MENAS: [*aside to* POMPEY] Pompey, a word.

POMPEY: [*aside to* MENAS] Say in mine ear. What is't?

MENAS: [*aside to* POMPEY] Forsake thy seat, I do beseech thee, Captain,
And hear me speak a word.

POMPEY: [*aside to* MENAS] Forbear me till anon.[6]

(Whispers in's ear.)

This wine for Lepidus!

LEPIDUS: What manner o' thing is your crocodile?

ANTONY: It is shap'd, sir, like itself, and it is as broad as it hath breadth. It is just so high as it is, and moves with its own organs. It lives by that which nourisheth it, and the elements once out of it, it transmigrates.

LEPIDUS: What colour is it of?

---

2 *long-handled spear.*
3 *trumpet fanfare.*
4 *abundance.*
5 *i.e., drop out of the drinking turns.*
6 *soon.*

ANTONY: Of its own colour too.

LEPIDUS: 'Tis a strange serpent.

ANTONY: 'Tis so. And the tears of it are wet.

CAESAR: Will this description satisfy him?

ANTONY: With the health that Pompey gives him; else he is a very
  epicure.

POMPEY: [*aside to* MENAS] Go hang, sir, hang! Tell me of that?
      Away!
    Do as I bid you. — Where's this cup I call'd for?

MENAS: [*aside to* POMPEY] If for the sake of merit thou wilt hear
      me,
    Rise from thy stool.

POMPEY: [*aside to* MENAS]   I think th'art mad.

[*Rises and walks aside.*]

                                    The matter?   50

MENAS: I have ever held my cap off to thy fortunes.

POMPEY: Thou hast serv'd me with much faith. What's else to say? —
    Be jolly, lords.

ANTONY: These quicksands, Lepidus,
    Keep off them, for you sink.

MENAS: Wilt thou be lord of all the world?

POMPEY: What say'st thou?

MENAS: Wilt thou be lord of the whole world? That's twice.

POMPEY: How should that be?

MENAS: But entertain[7] it,
    And though thou think me poor, I am the man
    Will give thee all the world.

POMPEY: Hast thou drunk well?

MENAS: No, Pompey, I have kept me from the cup.   60
    Thou art, if thou dar'st be, the earthly Jove.
    Whate'er the ocean pales,[8] or sky inclips,[9]
    Is thine, if thou wilt ha't.

POMPEY: Show me which way.

MENAS: These three world-sharers, these competitors,
    Are in thy vessel. Let me cut the cable;
    And when we are put off, fall to their throats.
    All there is thine.

POMPEY: Ah, this thou shouldst have done,
    And not have spoke on't! In me 'tis villainy;
    In thee 't had been good service. Thou must know,
    'Tis not my profit that does lead mine honour;   70
    Mine honour, it. Repent that e'er thy tongue
    Hath so betray'd thine act. Being done unknown,

7 *accept.*
8 *encloses.*
9 *embraces.*

I should have found it afterwards well done,
But must condemn it now. Desist, and drink.
MENAS: [*aside*] For this,
     I'll never follow thy pall'd[10] fortunes more.
     Who seeks, and will not take when once 'tis offer'd,
     Shall never find it more.
POMPEY: This health to Lepidus!
ANTONY: Bear him ashore. I'll pledge it for him, Pompey.
ENOBARBUS: Here's to thee, Menas!
MENAS: Enobarbus, welcome!   80
POMPEY: Fill till the cup be hid.
ENOBARBUS: There's a strong fellow, Menas.

[*Points to the* SERVANT *who carries off* LEPIDUS.]

MENAS: Why?
ENOBARBUS: 'A[11] bears the third part of the world, man; see'st not?
MENAS: The third part, then, is drunk. Would it were all,
     That it might go on wheels![12]
ENOBARBUS: Drink thou. Increase the reels.
MENAS: Come.
POMPEY: This is not yet an Alexandrian feast.
ANTONY: It ripens towards it. Strike the vessels,[13] ho!   90
     Here's to Caesar!
CAESAR: I could well forbear't.
     It's monstrous labour when I wash my brain
     And it grows fouler.
ANTONY: Be a child o' th' time.
CAESAR: Possess it;[14] I'll make answer.
     But I had rather fast from, all four days,
     Than drink so much in one.
ENOBARBUS: [*to* ANTONY]   Ha, my brave emperor!
     Shall we dance now the Egyptian Bacchanals[15]
     And celebrate our drink?
POMPEY: Let's ha't, good soldier.
ANTONY: Come, let's all take hands
     Till that the conquering wine hath steep'd our sense   100
     In soft and delicate Lethe.[16]
ENOBARBUS: All take hands.
     Make battery to our ears with the loud music.
     The while I'll place you; then the boy shall sing.
     The holding[17] every man shall bear as loud
     As his strong sides can volley.

---

10 *weakened.* 11 *he.* 12 *i.e., run smoothly.* 13 *i.e., open the wine casks.* 14 *i.e., drink it.* 15 *wild dance in honour of Bacchus, god of wine.* 16 *obliviousness (see 2.1.27).* 17 *chorus.*

(*Music plays.* ENOBARBUS *places them hand in hand.*)

(*The Song.*)

> Come, thou monarch of the vine,
> Plumpy Bacchus with pink eyne!
> In thy fats our cares be drown'd,
> With thy grapes our hairs be crown'd.
> Cup us till the world go round,   110
> Cup us till the world go round!

CAESAR: What would you more? Pompey, good night. Good brother,
Let me request you off.[18] Our graver business
Frowns at this levity. Gentle lords, let's part;
You see we have burnt our cheeks. Strong Enobarb
Is weaker than the wine, and mine own tongue
Splits what it speaks. The wild disguise[19] hath almost
Antick'd[20] us all. What needs more words? Good night.
Good Antony, your hand.
POMPEY: I'll try you[21] on the shore.
ANTONY: And shall, sir. — Give's your hand.
POMPEY: O Antony,   120
You have my father's house — but what? We are friends!
Come, down into the boat.
ENOBARBUS: Take heed you fall not.

[*Exeunt all but* ENOBARBUS *and* MENAS.]

Menas, I'll not on shore.
MENAS: No, to my cabin.
These drums! these trumpets, flutes! what!
Let Neptune hear we bid a loud farewell
To these great fellows. Sound and be hang'd, sound out!

(*Sound a flourish, with drums.*)

ENOBARBUS: Hoo! says 'a. There's my cap.
MENAS: Hoo! Noble Captain, come. (*Exeunt.*)

18 *i.e., off ship.*
19 *revelry.*
20 *crazed.*
21 *i.e., test your drinking power.*

ACT THREE

SCENE 1. [*A plain in Syria.*]

(Enter VENTIDIUS *as it were in triumph,* [*with* SILIUS *and other* ROMANS, OFFICERS, *and* SOLDIERS;] *the dead body of* PACORUS *borne before him.)*

VENTIDIUS: Now, darting[1] Parthia, art thou struck, and now
    Pleas'd fortune does of Marcus Crassus'[2] death
    Make me revenger. Bear the King's son's body
    Before our army. Thy Pacorus,[3] Orodes,
    Pays this for Marcus Crassus.
SILIUS: Noble Ventidius,
    Whilst yet with Parthian blood thy sword is warm,
    The fugitive Parthians follow. Spur through Media,
    Mesopotamia, and the shelters whither
    The routed fly. So thy grand captain, Antony,
    Shall set thee on triumphant chariots and   10
    Put garlands on thy head.
VENTIDIUS: O Silius, Silius,
    I have done enough. A lower place, note well,
    May make too great an act. For learn this, Silius:
    Better to leave undone than by our deed
    Acquire too high a fame when him we serve's away.
    Caesar and Antony have ever won
    More in their officer than person. Sossius,
    One of my place[4] in Syria, his[5] lieutenant,
    For quick accumulation of renown,
    Which he achiev'd by th' minute, lost his favour.   20
    Who does i' th' wars more than his captain can
    Becomes his captain's captain; and ambition,
    The soldier's virtue, rather makes choice of loss
    Than gain which darkens him.
    I could do more to do Antonius good,
    But 'twould offend him; and in his offence
    Should my performance perish.
SILIUS: Thou hast, Ventidius, that
    Without the which a soldier and his sword
    Grants scarce distinction. Thou wilt write to Antony?
VENTIDIUS: I'll humbly signify what in his name,   30
    That magical word of war, we have effected;
    How with his banners and his well-paid ranks

---

1 shooting (the Parthians were renowned archers).
2 Roman general and member of the first trimvirate along with the elder Pompey and Julius Caesar. He was
  treacherously killed by Orodes, king of Parthia.
3 son of Orodes, king of Parthia.
4 rank.
5 Antony's.

The ne'er-yet-beaten horse of Parthia
We have jaded out o' th' field.

SILIUS: Where is he now?

VENTIDIUS: He purposeth to Athens; whither, with what haste
The weight we must convey with 's will permit,
We shall appear before him. — On, there! Pass along!

(*Exeunt.*)

SCENE 2. [*Rome.* CAESAR's *house.*]

(*Enter* AGRIPPA *at one door,* ENOBARBUS *at another.*)

AGRIPPA: What, are the brothers parted?

ENOBARBUS: They have dispatch'd with Pompey; he is gone;
The other three are sealing.[1] Octavia weeps
To part from Rome; Caesar is sad; and Lepidus
Since Pompey's feast, as Menas says, is troubled
With the green-sickness.[2]

AGRIPPA: 'Tis a noble Lepidus.

ENOBARBUS: A very fine one. O, how he loves Caesar!

AGRIPPA: Nay, but how dearly he adores Mark Antony!

ENOBARBUS: Caesar? Why, he's the Jupiter of men.

AGRIPPA: What's Antony? The god of Jupiter.   10

ENOBARBUS: Spake you of Caesar? Hoo! the nonpareil!

AGRIPPA: O Antony! O thou Arabian bird![3]

ENOBARBUS: Would you praise Caesar, say "Caesar" — go no further.

AGRIPPA: Indeed he plied them both with excellent praises.

ENOBARBUS: But he loves Caesar best. Yet he loves Antony!
Hoo! hearts, tongues, figures, scribes, bards, poets, cannot
Think, speak, cast, write, sing, number — hoo! —
His love to Antony. But as for Caesar,
Kneel down, kneel down, and wonder!

AGRIPPA: Both he loves.

ENOBARBUS: They are his shards,[4] and he their beetle. [*Trumpet within.*]
So —   20
This is to horse. Adieu, noble Agrippa.

AGRIPPA: Good fortune, worthy soldier, and farewell!

(*Enter* CAESAR, ANTONY, LEPIDUS, *and* OCTAVIA.)

ANTONY: No further, sir.

---

1 *i.e., sealing the agreement.*
2 *anemia of lovesick young women. Here, Lepidus's hangover.*
3 *i.e., the Phoenix, a mythical bird that cremates itself and is reborn out of its own ashes; hence, unique and immortal.*
4 *insect wings, or dungy sustenance.*

CAESAR: You take from me a great part of myself;
    Use me well in't. Sister, prove such a wife
    As my thoughts make thee, and as my farthest band
    Shall pass on thy approof. Most noble Antony,
    Let not the piece of virtue which is set
    Betwixt us as the cement of our love
    To keep it builded, be the ram to batter   30
    The fortress of it; for better might we
    Have lov'd without this mean,⁵ if on both parts
    This be not cherish'd.
ANTONY: Make me not offended
    In your distrust.
CAESAR: I have said.
ANTONY: You shall not find,
    Though you be therein curious, the least cause
    For what you seem to fear. So the gods keep you
    And make the hearts of Romans serve your ends!
    We will here part.
CAESAR: Farewell, my dearest sister, fare thee well.
    The elements be kind to thee and make   40
    Thy spirits all of comfort! Fare thee well.
OCTAVIA: My noble brother!
ANTONY: The April's in her eyes. It is love's spring,
    And these the showers to bring it on. Be cheerful.
OCTAVIA: Sir, look well to my husband's house; and —
CAESAR: What,
    Octavia?
OCTAVIA: I'll tell you in your ear.
ANTONY: Her tongue will not obey her heart, nor can
    Her heart inform her tongue — the swan's down-feather
    That stands upon the swell at full of tide,
    And neither way inclines.   50
ENOBARBUS: [aside to AGRIPPA] Will Caesar weep?
AGRIPPA: [aside to ENOBARBUS]   He has a cloud in's face.
ENOBARBUS: [aside to AGRIPPA] He were the worse for that, were he a
        horse;
    So is he, being a man.
AGRIPPA: [aside to ENOBARBUS] Why, Enobarbus,
    When Antony found Julius Caesar dead,
    He cried almost to roaring; and he wept
    When at Philippi he found Brutus slain.
ENOBARBUS: [aside to AGRIPPA] That year indeed he was troubled with a
        rheum.⁶
    What willingly he did confound he wail'd,
    Believe 't, till I wept too.

---

5 means.
6 head cold.

CAESAR: No, sweet Octavia,
 You shall hear from me still. The time shall not   60
 Outgo my thinking on you.
ANTONY: Come, sir, come.
 I'll wrestle with you in my strength of love.
 Look, here I have you; thus I let you go,
 And give you to the gods.
CAESAR: Adieu, be happy!
LEPIDUS: Let all the number of the stars give light
 To thy fair way!
CAESAR: Farewell, farewell!

        (Kisses OCTAVIA.*)*

ANTONY: Farewell!

(Trumpets sound. Exeunt.)

SCENE 3. [*Alexandria.* CLEOPATRA's *Palace.*]

(Enter CLEOPATRA, CHARMIAN, IRAS, *and* ALEXAS.*)*

CLEOPATRA: Where is the fellow?
ALEXAS: Half afeard to come.
CLEOPATRA: Go to, go to!

(Enter the MESSENGER, *as before.)*

   Come hither, sir.
ALEXAS: Good Majesty,
 Herod of Jewry dare not look upon you
 But when you are well pleas'd.
CLEOPATRA: That Herod's head
 I'll have! But how, when Antony is gone
 Through whom I might command it? Come thou near.
MESSENGER: Most gracious Majesty!
CLEOPATRA: Didst thou behold Octavia?
MESSENGER: Ay, dread Queen.
CLEOPATRA: Where?   10
MESSENGER: Madam, in Rome.
 I look'd her in the face, and saw her led
 Between her brother and Mark Antony.
CLEOPATRA: Is she as tall as me?
MESSENGER: She is not, madam.
CLEOPATRA: Didst hear her speak? Is she shrill-tongu'd or low?

[handwritten margin note: interrogates the messenger about Octavia.*]*

MESSENGER: Madam, I heard her speak. She is low-voic'd.
CLEOPATRA: That's not so good! He cannot like her long.
CHARMIAN: Like her? O Isis! 'tis impossible.
CLEOPATRA: I think so, Charmian. Dull of tongue, and dwarfish!
    What majesty is in her gait? Remember, 20
    If e'er thou look'st on majesty.
MESSENGER: She creeps!
    Her motion and her station are as one.
    She shows a body rather than a life,
    A statue than a breather.
CLEOPATRA: Is this certain?
MESSENGER: Or I have no observance.
CHARMIAN: Three in Egypt
    Cannot make better note.
CLEOPATRA: He's very knowing;
    I do perceive't. There's nothing in her yet.
    The fellow has good judgment.
CHARMIAN: Excellent.
CLEOPATRA: Guess at her years, I prithee.
MESSENGER: Madam,
    She was a widow —
CLEOPATRA: Widow? Charmian, hark! 30
MESSENGER: And I do think she's thirty.
CLEOPATRA: Bear'st thou her face in mind? Is't long or round?
MESSENGER: Round even to faultiness.
CLEOPATRA: For the most part, too, they are foolish that are so.
    Her hair, what colour?
MESSENGER: Brown, madam; and her forehead
    As low as she would wish it.
CLEOPATRA: There's gold for thee.
    Thou must not take my former sharpness ill.
    I will employ thee back again; I find thee
    Most fit for business. Go, make thee ready; 40
    Our letters are prepar'd. [*Exit* MESSENGER.]
CHARMIAN: A proper man.
CLEOPATRA: Indeed he is so. I repent me much
    That so I harried him. Why, methinks, by him,
    This creature's no such thing.[1]
CHARMIAN: Nothing, madam.
CLEOPATRA: The man hath seen some majesty, and should know.
CHARMIAN: Hath he seen majesty? Isis else defend,
    And serving you so long!
CLEOPATRA: I have one thing more to ask him yet, good Charmian.
    But 'tis no matter. Thou shalt bring him to me
    Where I will write. All may be well enough. 50
CHARMIAN: I warrant you, madam. *(Exeunt.)*

---

1 *i.e., nothing much.*

SCENE 4. [*Athens.* ANTONY's *house.*]

(*Enter* ANTONY *and* OCTAVIA.)

ANTONY: Nay, nay, Octavia; not only that —
    That were excusable, that and thousands more
    Of semblable[1] import — but he hath wag'd
    New wars 'gainst Pompey; made his will, and read it
    To public ear;
    Spoke scantly of me: when perforce he could not
    But pay me terms of honour, cold and sickly
    He vented them, most narrow measure lent me;
    When the best hint was given him, he not took't,
    Or did it from his teeth.[2]
OCTAVIA: O, my good lord,   *10*
    Believe not all; or if you must believe,
    Stomach[3] not all. A more unhappy lady,
    If this division chance, ne'er stood between,
    Praying for both parts.
    The good gods will mock me presently
    When I shall pray "O, bless my lord and husband!"
    Undo that prayer by crying out as loud
    "O, bless my brother!" Husband win, win brother,
    Prays, and destroys the prayer; no midway
    'Twixt these extremes at all.
ANTONY: Gentle Octavia,   *20*
    Let your best love draw to that point which seeks
    Best to preserve it. If I lose mine honour,
    I lose myself. Better I were not yours
    Than yours so branchless. But, as you requested,
    Yourself shall go between 's. The mean time, lady,
    I'll raise the preparation of a war
    Shall stain your brother. Make your soonest haste;
    So your desires are yours.
OCTAVIA: Thanks to my lord.
    The Jove of power make me most weak, most weak,
    Your reconciler! Wars 'twixt you twain would be   *30*
    As if the world should cleave, and that slain men
    Should solder up the rift.
ANTONY: When it appears to you where this begins,
    Turn your displeasure that way, for our faults
    Can never be so equal that your love
    Can equally move with them. Provide your going;
    Choose your own company, and command what cost
    Your heart has mind to. (*Exeunt.*)

1 *similar.*
2 *i.e., grudgingly.*
3 *resent.*

SCENE 5. [*Athens. Another room in* ANTONY's *house.*]

(*Enter* ENOBARBUS *and* EROS, [*meeting*]).

ENOBARBUS: How now, friend Eros?
EROS: There's strange news come, sir.
ENOBARBUS: What, man?
EROS: Caesar and Lepidus have made wars upon Pompey.
ENOBARBUS: This is old. What is the success?[1]
EROS: Caesar, having made use of him in the wars 'gainst Pompey, pres-
    ently denied him rivality,[2] would not let him partake in the glory of
    the action; and not resting here, accuses him of letters he had for-
    merly wrote to Pompey; upon his own appeal, seizes him. So the
    poor third is up[3] 'till death enlarge his confine.   10
ENOBARBUS: Then, world, thou hast a pair of chaps,[4] no more;
    And throw between them all the food thou hast,
    They'll grind the one the other. Where's Antony?
EROS: He's walking in the garden thus, and spurns
    The rush that lies before him; cries "Fool Lepidus!"
    And threats the throat of that his officer
    That murd'red Pompey.[5]
ENOBARBUS: Our great navy 's rigg'd.
EROS: For Italy and Caesar. More, Domitius:
    My lord desires you presently. My news
    I might have told hereafter.
ENOBARBUS: 'Twill be naught;   20
    But let it be. Bring me to Antony.
EROS: Come, sir. (*Exeunt.*)

SCENE 6. [*Rome.* CAESAR's *house.*]

(*Enter* AGRIPPA, MAECENAS, *and* CAESAR.)

CAESAR: Contemning Rome, he has done all this and more
    In Alexandria. Here's the manner of't:
    I' th' market place on a tribunal silver'd
    Cleopatra and himself in chairs of gold
    Were publicly enthron'd. At the feet sat
    Caesarion,[1] whom they call my father's son,
    And all the unlawful issue that their lust
    Since then hath made between them. Unto her
    He gave the stablishment of Egypt; made her

---

1 *outcome.* **2** *partnership.* **3** *i.e., locked up.* **4** *jaws.* **5** *according to Plutarch, Pompey was murdered by Titus, one of Antony's lieutenants.*

---

1 *illegitimate son of Julius Caesar and Cleopatra. Octavius had been officially adopted by Julius Caesar.*

Of lower Syria, Cyprus, Lydia,   *10*
    Absolute queen.
MAECENAS: This in the public eye?
CAESAR: I' th' common show-place, where they exercise.
    His sons he there proclaim'd the kings of kings:
    Great Media, Parthia, and Armenia
    He gave to Alexander; to Ptolemy he assign'd
    Syria, Cilicia, and Phoenicia. She
    In th' habiliments of the goddess Isis
    That day appear'd; and oft before gave audience,
    As 'tis reported, so.
MAECENAS: Let Rome be thus
    Inform'd.
AGRIPPA: Who, queasy with his insolence   *20*
    Already, will their good thoughts call from him.
CAESAR: The people knows it, and have now receiv'd
    His accusations.
AGRIPPA: Who does he accuse?
CAESAR: Caesar; and that, having in Sicily
    Sextus Pompeius spoil'd, we had not rated[2] him
    His part o' th' isle. Then does he say he lent me
    Some shipping unrestor'd. Lastly, he frets
    That Lepidus of the triumvirate
    Should be depos'd; and, being, that we detain
    All his revenue.
AGRIPPA: Sir, this should be answer'd.   *30*
CAESAR: 'Tis done already, and the messenger gone.
    I have told him Lepidus was grown too cruel,
    That he his high authority abus'd
    And did deserve his change. For what I have conquer'd,
    I grant him part; but then in his Armenia,
    And other of his conquer'd kingdoms, I
    Demand the like.
MAECENAS: He'll never yield to that.
CAESAR: Nor must not then be yielded to in this.

(Enter OCTAVIA *with her* TRAIN.*)*

OCTAVIA: Hail, Caesar, and my lord! hail, most dear Caesar!
CAESAR: That ever I should call thee castaway!   *40*
OCTAVIA: You have not call'd me so, nor have you cause.
CAESAR: Why have you stol'n upon us thus? You come not
    Like Caesar's sister. The wife of Antony
    Should have an army for an usher, and
    The neighs of horse to tell of her approach
    Long ere she did appear. The trees by th' way
    Should have borne men, and expectation fainted,

---

2 *allotted.*

Longing for what it had not. Nay, the dust
Should have ascended to the roof of heaven,
Rais'd by your populous troops. But you are come 50
A market-maid to Rome, and have prevented
The ostentation of our love, which, left unshown,
Is often left unlov'd. We should have met you
By sea and land, supplying every stage
With an augmented greeting.
OCTAVIA: Good my lord,
To come thus was I not constrain'd, but did it
On my free will. My lord, Mark Antony,
Hearing that you prepar'd for war, acquainted
My grieved ear withal; whereon I begg'd
His pardon for return. 60
CAESAR: Which soon he granted,
Being an abstract[3] 'tween his lust and him.
OCTAVIA: Do not say so, my lord.
CAESAR: I have eyes upon him,
And his affairs come to me on the wind.
Where is he now?
OCTAVIA: My lord, in Athens.
CAESAR: No, my most wronged sister. Cleopatra
Hath nodded him to her. He hath given his empire
Up to a whore, who now are levying
The kings o' th' earth for war. He hath assembled
Bocchus, the king of Libya; Archelaus,
Of Cappadocia; Philadelphos, king 70
Of Paphlagonia; the Thracian king, Adallas;
King Malchus of Arabia; King of Pont;
Herod of Jewry; Mithridates, king
Of Comagene; Polemon and Amyntas,
The kings of Mede and Lycaonia, with a
More larger list of sceptres.
OCTAVIA: Ay me most wretched,
That have my heart parted betwixt two friends
That does afflict each other!
CAESAR: Welcome hither.
Your letters did withhold our breaking forth,
Till we perceiv'd both how you were wrong led 80
And we in negligent danger. Cheer your heart!
Be you not troubled with the time, which drives
O'er your content these strong necessities;
But let determin'd things to destiny
Hold unbewail'd their way. Welcome to Rome,
Nothing more dear to me! You are abus'd
Beyond the mark of thought; and the high gods,

---

3 *obstruction.*

To do you justice, makes his ministers
Of us and those that love you. Best of comfort,
And ever welcome to us!
AGRIPPA: Welcome, lady.   *90*
MAECENAS: Welcome, dear madam.
    Each heart in Rome does love and pity you.
    Only th' adulterous Antony, most large
    In his abominations, turns you off
    And gives his potent regiment to a trull
    That noises it against us.
OCTAVIA: Is it so, sir?
CAESAR: Most certain. Sister, welcome. Pray you
    Be ever known to patience. My dear'st sister! *(Exeunt.)*

SCENE 7 [ANTONY's *camp, near Actium.*]

(Enter CLEOPATRA *and* ENOBARBUS.*)*

CLEOPATRA: I will be even with thee, doubt it not.
ENOBARBUS: But why, why, why?
CLEOPATRA: Thou hast forspoke my being in these wars,
    And say'st it is not fit.
ENOBARBUS: Well, is it, is it?
CLEOPATRA: Is't not denounc'd[1] against us? Why should not we
    Be there in person?
ENOBARBUS: [*aside*]   Well, I could reply:
    If we should serve with horse and mares together,
    The horse were merely[2] lost; the mares would bear
    A soldier and his horse.
CLEOPATRA: What is't you say?
ENOBARBUS: Your presence needs must puzzle Antony;   *10*
    Take from his heart, take from his brain, from 's time,
    What should not then be spar'd. He is already
    Traduc'd for levity; and 'tis said in Rome
    That Photinus an eunuch and your maids
    Manage this war.
CLEOPATRA: Sink Rome, and their tongues rot
    That speak against us! A charge we bear i' th' war
    And, as the president of my kingdom, will
    Appear there for a man. Speak not against it.
    I will not stay behind!

(Enter ANTONY *and* CANIDIUS.*)*

ENOBARBUS: Nay, I have done.
    Here comes the Emperor.

1 *declared.*
2 *simply, utterly.*

ANTONY: Is it not strange, Canidius,   *20*
    That from Tarentum and Brundusium
    He could so quickly cut the Ionian sea
    And take in Toryne? — You have heard on't, sweet?
CLEOPATRA: Celerity is never more admir'd
    Than by the negligent.
ANTONY: A good rebuke,
    Which might have well becom'd the best of men
    To taunt at slackness. Canidius, we
    Will fight with him by sea.
CLEOPATRA: By sea? What else?
CANIDIUS: Why will my lord do so?
ANTONY: For that he dares us to 't.
ENOBARBUS: So hath my lord dar'd him to single fight.   *30*
CANIDIUS: Ay, and to wage this battle at Pharsalia,
    Where Caesar fought with Pompey. But these offers,
    Which serve not for his vantage, he shakes off;
    And so should you.
ENOBARBUS: Your ships are not well mann'd;
    Your mariners are muleters,[3] reapers, people
    Ingross'd by swift impress.[4] In Caesar's fleet
    Are those that often have 'gainst Pompey fought;
    Their ships are yare;[5] yours, heavy. No disgrace
    Shall fall you for refusing him at sea,
    Being prepar'd for land.
ANTONY: By sea, by sea!   *40*
ENOBARBUS: Most worthy sir, you therein throw away
    The absolute soldiership you have by land;
    Distract[6] your army, which doth most consist
    Of war-mark'd footmen; leave unexecuted
    Your own renowned knowledge; quite forgo
    The way which promises assurance, and
    Give up yourself merely to chance and hazard
    From firm security.
ANTONY: I'll fight at sea.
CLEOPATRA: I have sixty sails, Caesar none better.
ANTONY: Our overplus of shipping will we burn,   *50*
    And with the rest full-mann'd, from th' head of Actium[7]
    Beat the approaching Caesar. But if we fail,
    We then can do 't at land.

    (Enter a MESSENGER.*)*

---

3 *mule drivers.*
4 *conscription.*
5 *swift, seaworthy.*
6 *divide.*
7 *on the west coast of Greece. The Battle of Actium was fought in 31* B.C.

Thy business?
MESSENGER: The news is true, my lord. He is descried;
    Caesar has taken Toryne.
ANTONY: Can he be there in person? 'Tis impossible;
    Strange that his power should be! Canidius,
    Our nineteen legions thou shalt hold by land
    And our twelve thousand horse. We'll to our ship
    Away, my Thetis!⁸

(Enter a SOLDIER.)

               How now, worthy soldier?   60
SOLDIER: O noble Emperor, do not fight by sea!
    Trust not to rotten planks. Do you misdoubt
    This sword and these my wounds? Let the Egyptians
    And the Phoenicians go a-ducking. We
    Have us'd to conquer standing on the earth
    And fighting foot to foot.
ANTONY: Well, well. Away!

(Exeunt ANTONY, CLEOPATRA, and ENOBARBUS.)

SOLDIER: By Hercules, I think I am i' th' right.
CANIDIUS: Soldier, thou art; but his whole action grows
    Not in the power on't. So our leader's led,
    And we are women's men.
SOLDIER: You keep by land   70
    The legions and the horse whole, do you not?
CANIDIUS: Marcus Octavius, Marcus Justeius,
    Publicola, and Caelius are for sea;
    But we keep whole by land. This speed of Caesar's
    Carries beyond belief.
SOLDIER: While he was yet in Rome,
    His power went out in such distractions⁹ as
    Beguil'd all spies.
CANIDIUS: Who's his lieutenant, hear you?
SOLDIER: They say, one Taurus.
CANIDIUS: Well I know the man.

(Enter a MESSENGER.)

MESSENGER: The Emperor calls Canidius.
CANIDIUS: With news the time's with labour and throws forth   80
    Each minute some.¹⁰ *(Exeunt.)*

---

8 *a sea goddess.*
9 *separate units.*
10 *i.e., more news.*

SCENE 8. [*A plain near Actium.*]

(*Enter* CAESAR, *with his* ARMY, *marching.*)

CAESAR: Taurus!
TAURUS: My lord?
CAESAR: Strike not by land; keep whole: provoke not battle
    Till we have done at sea. Do not exceed
    The prescript of this scroll. Our fortune lies
    Upon this jump.[1] (*Exeunt.*)

SCENE 9. [*Another part of the plain.*]

(*Enter* ANTONY *and* ENOBARBUS.)

ANTONY: Set we our squadrons on yond side o' th' hill
    In eye of Caesar's battle;[1] from which place
    We may the number of the ships behold,
    And so proceed accordingly. (*Exeunt.*)

SCENE 10. [*Another part of the plain.*]

(CANIDIUS *marcheth with his land army one way over the stage, and* TAURUS, *the Lieutenant of* CAESAR, *the other way. After their going in, is heard the noise of a sea-fight. Alarum. Enter* ENOBARBUS.)

ENOBARBUS: Naught, naught, all naught! I can behold no longer.
    Th' Antoniad, the Egyptian admiral,[1]
    With all their sixty, fly and turn the rudder.
    To see't mine eyes are blasted.

(*Enter* SCARUS.)

SCARUS: Gods and goddesses,
    All the whole synod[2] of them!
ENOBARBUS: What's thy passion?
SCARUS: The greater cantle[3] of the world is lost
    With very ignorance. We have kiss'd away
    Kingdoms and provinces.
ENOBARBUS: How appears the fight?

1 *risk, strategy.*
1 *battle line.*
1 *flagship.*
2 *assembly.*
3 *portion.*

SCARUS: On our side like the token'd[4] pestilence
  Where death is sure. Yon ribaudred[5] nag of Egypt   *10*
  (Whom leprosy o'ertake!) i' th' midst o' th' fight,
  When vantage like a pair of twins appear'd,
  Both as the same, or rather ours the elder. —
  The breese[6] upon her, like a cow in June, —
  Hoist sails, and flies.
ENOBARBUS: That I beheld.
  Mine eyes did sicken at the sight and could not
  Endure a further view.
SCARUS: She once being loof'd,[7]
  The noble ruin of her magic, Antony,
  Claps on his sea-wing, and (like a doting mallard)   *20*
  Leaving the fight in height, flies after her.
  I never saw an action of such shame.
  Experience, manhood, honour, ne'er before
  Did violate so itself.
ENOBARBUS: Alack, alack!

(Enter CANIDIUS.*)*

CANIDIUS: Our fortune on the sea is out of breath
  And sinks most lamentably. Had our general
  Been what he knew himself,[8] it had gone well.
  O, he has given example for our flight
  Most grossly by his own!
ENOBARBUS: Ay, are you thereabouts?
  Why then, good night indeed.   *30*
CANIDIUS: Toward Peloponnesus are they fled.
SCARUS: 'Tis easy to't; and there I will attend
  What further comes.
CANIDIUS: To Caesar will I render
  My legions and my horse. Six kings already
  Show me the way of yielding.
ENOBARBUS: I'll yet follow
  The wounded chance[9] of Antony, though my reason
  Sits in the wind against me. *(Exeunt.)*

SCENE 11. [*Alexandria.* CLEOPATRA's *palace.*]

(Enter ANTONY *with* ATTENDANTS.*)*

4 *signalled, symptomatic.*
5 *ribald, lewd.*
6 *stinging gadfly.*
7 *away.*
8 *i.e., true to himself.*
9 *fortunes*

ANTONY: Hark! the land bids me tread no more upon't!
　　It is asham'd to bear me! Friends, come hither.
　　I am so lated¹ in the world that I
　　Have lost my way for ever. I have a ship
　　Laden with gold. Take that; divide it. Fly,
　　And make your peace with Caesar.
OMNES:　　　　　　　　　　　　　　　　Fly? Not we!
ANTONY: I have fled myself, and have instructed cowards
　　To run and show their shoulders. Friends, be gone.
　　I have myself resolv'd upon a course
　　Which has no need of you. Be gone.　　　　　　　　　　10
　　My treasure 's in the harbour. Take it! O,
　　I follow'd that² I blush to look upon.
　　My very hairs do mutiny; for the white
　　Reprove the brown for rashness, and they them
　　For fear and doting. Friends, be gone. You shall
　　Have letters from me to some friends that will
　　Sweep your way for you. Pray you look not sad
　　Nor make replies of loathness. Take the hint³
　　Which my despair proclaims. Let that be left
　　Which leaves itself. To the seaside straightway!　　　　20
　　I will possess you of that ship and treasure.
　　Leave me, I pray, a little; pray you now!
　　Nay, do so; for indeed I have lost command;
　　Therefore I pray you. I'll see you by and by. *(Sits down.)*

(Enter CLEOPATRA *led by* CHARMIAN *and* IRAS, [EROS *following*].*)*

EROS: Nay, gentle madam, to him! comfort him!
IRAS: Do, most dear Queen.
CHARMIAN: Do? Why, what else?
CLEOPATRA: Let me sit down. O Juno!
ANTONY: No, no, no, no, no!
EROS: See you here, sir?　　　　　　　　　　　　　　　　30
ANTONY: O fie, fie, fie!
CHARMIAN: Madam!
IRAS: Madam, O good Empress!
EROS: Sir, sir!
ANTONY: Yes, my lord, yes! He⁴ at Philippi kept
　　His sword e'en like a dancer, while I struck
　　The lean and wrinkled Cassius; and 'twas I
　　That the mad Brutus ended. He alone
　　Dealt on lieutenantry and no practice had

1 *i.e., left out late.*
2 *i.e., that which.*
3 *opportunity.*
4 *i.e., Octavius.*

In the brave squares of war. Yet now — No matter.   40
CLEOPATRA: Ah, stand by!
EROS: The Queen, my lord, the Queen!
IRAS: Go to him, madam, speak to him.
    He is unqualitied with very shame.
CLEOPATRA: Well then, sustain me. O!
EROS: Most noble sir, arise. The Queen approaches.
    Her head 's declin'd, and death will seize her, but[5]
    Your comfort makes the rescue.
ANTONY: I have offended reputation[6] —
    A most unnoble swerving.
EROS: Sir, the Queen.   50
ANTONY: O, whither hast thou led me, Egypt? See
    How I convey my shame out of thine eyes
    By looking back what I have left behind
    Stroy'd[7] in dishonour.
CLEOPATRA: O my lord, my lord,
    Forgive my fearful sails! I little thought
    You would have followed.
ANTONY: Egypt, thou knew'st too well
    My heart was to thy rudder tied by th' strings,
    And thou shouldst tow me after. O'er my spirit
    Thy full supremacy thou knew'st, and that
    Thy beck might from the bidding of the gods   60
    Command me.
CLEOPATRA: O, my pardon!
ANTONY: Now I must
    To the young man send humble treaties, dodge
    And palter in the shifts of lowness, who
    With half the bulk o' th' world play'd as I pleas'd,
    Making and marring fortunes. You did know
    How much you were my conqueror, and that
    My sword, made weak by my affection, would
    Obey it on all cause.
CLEOPATRA: Pardon, pardon!
ANTONY: Fall[8] not a tear, I say. One of them rates[9]
    All that is won and lost. Give me a kiss.   70
    Even this repays me. We sent our schoolmaster.[10]
    Is 'a come back? Love, I am full of lead.
    Some wine, within there, and our viands! Fortune knows
    We scorn her most when most she offers blows.

    (Exeunt.)

---

5 *unless.*
6 *honour.*
7 *destroyed.*
8 *Let fall.*
9 *equals.*
10 *Plutarch records that Euphronius, the tutor of Antony and Cleopatra's children, was sent to Caesar as emissary.*

SCENE 12. [CAESAR's *camp in Egypt.*]

(Enter CAESAR, AGRIPPA, DOLABELLA, [THIDIAS,] *with others.)*

CAESAR: Let him appear that's come from Antony.
  Know you him?
DOLABELLA: Caesar, 'tis his schoolmaster.
  An argument that he is pluck'd, when hither
  He sends so poor a pinion of his wing,
  Which had superfluous kings for messengers
  Not many moons gone by.

(Enter [EUPHRONIUS,] AMBASSADOR *from* ANTONY.*)*

CAESAR: Approach and speak.
AMBASSADOR: Such as I am, I come from Antony.
  I was of late as petty to his ends
  As is the morn-dew on the myrtle leaf
  To his grand sea.
CAESAR: Be't so. Declare thine office.   *10*
AMBASSADOR: Lord of his fortunes he salutes thee, and
  Requires¹ to live in Egypt; which not granted,
  He lessens his requests and to thee sues
  To let him breathe between the heavens and earth,
  A private man in Athens. This for him.
  Next, Cleopatra does confess thy greatness,
  Submits her to thy might, and of thee craves
  The circle² of the Ptolemies for her heirs,
  Now hazarded to thy grace.
CAESAR: For Antony,
  I have no ears to his request. The Queen   *20*
  Of audience nor desire shall fail, so she
  From Egypt drive her all-disgraced friend
  Or take his life there. This if she perform,
  She shall not sue unheard. So to them both.
AMBASSADOR: Fortune pursue thee!
CAESAR: Bring him through the bands.

[*Exit* AMBASSADOR.]

[*To* THIDIAS] To try thy eloquence now 'tis time. Dispatch.
  From Antony win Cleopatra. Promise,
  And in our name, what she requires; add more,
  From thine invention, offers. Women are not
  In their best fortunes strong, but want will perjure³   *30*

---

1 *requests.*
2 *crown.*
3 *corrupt.*

The ne'er-touch'd Vestal. Try thy cunning, Thidias.
Make thine own edict for thy pains, which we
Will answer as a law.
THIDIAS: Caesar, I go.
CAESAR: Observe how Antony becomes his flaw,
    And what thou think'st his very action speaks
    In every power that moves.
THIDIAS: Caesar, I shall. *(Exeunt.)*

SCENE 13. [*Alexandria.* CLEOPATRA'S *Palace.*]

(Enter CLEOPATRA, ENOBARBUS, CHARMIAN, *and* IRAS.*)*

CLEOPATRA: What shall we do, Enobarbus?
ENOBARBUS: Think, and die.
CLEOPATRA: Is Antony or we in fault for this?
ENOBARBUS: Antony only, that would make his will
    Lord of his reason. What though you fled
    From that great face of war whose several ranges
    Frighted each other? Why should he follow?
    The itch of his affection should not then
    Have nick'd his captainship, at such a point,
    When half to half the world oppos'd, he being
    The meered question.[1] 'Twas a shame no less   10
    Than was his loss, to course[2] your flying flags
    And leave his navy gazing.
CLEOPATRA: Prithee peace!

(Enter the AMBASSADOR [EUPHRONIUS] *with* ANTONY.*)*

ANTONY: Is that his answer?
AMBASSADOR: Ay, my lord.
ANTONY: The Queen shall then have courtesy, so she
    Will yield us up.
AMBASSADOR: He says so.
ANTONY: Let her know't.
    To the boy Caesar send this grizzled head,
    And he will fill thy wishes to the brim
    With principalities.
CLEOPATRA: That head, my lord?
ANTONY: To him again! Tell him he wears the rose   20
    Of youth upon him; from which the world should note
    Something particular. His coin, ships, legions
    May be a coward's, whose ministers would prevail
    Under the service of a child as soon

1 *i.e., the main question or issue.*
2 *pursue.*

As i' th' command of Caesar. I dare him therefore
To lay his gay³ comparisons apart
And answer me declin'd,⁴ sword against sword,
Ourselves alone. I'll write it. Follow me.

[*Exeunt* ANTONY *and* AMBASSADOR.]

ENOBARBUS: [*aside*] Yes, like enough high-battled⁵ Caesar will
    Unstate his happiness and be stag'd to th' show   30
    Against a sworder! I see men's judgments are
    A parcel of their fortunes, and things outward
    Do draw the inward quality after them
    To suffer all alike. That he should dream,
    Knowing all measures, the full Caesar will
    Answer his emptiness! Caesar, thou hast subdu'd
    His judgment too.

(*Enter a* SERVANT.)

SERVANT: A messenger from Caesar.
CLEOPATRA: What, no more ceremony? See, my women!
    Against the blown rose may they stop their nose
    That kneel'd unto the buds. Admit him, sir.   40

[*Exit* SERVANT.]

ENOBARBUS: [*aside*] Mine honesty and I begin to square.¹
    The loyalty well held to fools does make
    Our faith mere folly. Yet he that can endure
    To follow with allegiance a fall'n lord
    Does conquer him that did his master conquer
    And earns a place i' th' story.

(*Enter* THIDIAS.)

CLEOPATRA: Caesar's will?
THIDIAS: Hear it apart.
CLEOPATRA: None but friends. Say boldly.
THIDIAS: So haply⁷ are they friends to Antony.
ENOBARBUS: He needs as many, sir, as Caesar has,
    Or needs not us. If Caesar please, our master   50
    Will leap to be his friend. For us, you know

---

3 *splendid.*
4 *diminished.*
5 *militarily superior.*
6 *quarrel, square off.*
7 *perhaps.*

Whose he is we are, and that is Caesar's.
THIDIAS: So.
Thus them, thou most renown'd: Caesar entreats
Not to consider in what case thou stand'st
Further than he is Caesar.[8]
CLEOPATRA: Go on. Right royal!
THIDIAS: He knows that you embrace not Antony
    As you did love, but as you fear'd him.
CLEOPATRA: O!
THIDIAS: The scars upon your honour, therefore, he
    Does pity, as constrained blemishes,
    Not as deserv'd.
CLEOPATRA: He is a god, and knows   60
    What is most right. Mine honour was not yielded,
    But conquer'd merely.
ENOBARBUS: [aside] To be sure of that,
    I will ask Antony. Sir, sir, thou art so leaky
    That we must leave thee to thy sinking, for
    Thy dearest quit thee. (Exit)
THIDIAS: Shall I say to Caesar
    What you require of him? For he partly begs
    To be desir'd to give. It much would please him
    That of his fortunes you should make a staff
    To lean upon. But it would warm his spirits
    To hear from me you had left Antony   70
    And put yourself under his shroud,[9]
    The universal landlord.
CLEOPATRA: What's your name?
THIDIAS: My name is Thidias.
CLEOPATRA: Most kind messenger,
    Say to great Caesar this: in deputation
    I kiss his conqu'ring hand. Tell him I am prompt
    To lay my crown at's feet, and there to kneel.
    Tell him, from his all-obeying breath I hear
    The doom[10] of Egypt.
THIDIAS: 'Tis your noblest course.
    Wisdom and fortune combating together,
    If that the former dare but what it can,   80
    No chance may shake it. Give me grace to lay
    My duty on your hand.
CLEOPATRA: Your Caesar's father oft,
    When he hath mus'd of taking kingdoms in,
    Bestow'd his lips on that unworthy place
    As[11] it rain'd kisses.

8 i.e., unbeatable but generous.
9 protection.
10 judgement.
11 as if.

(Enter ANTONY *and* ENOBARBUS.*)*

ANTONY: Favours, by Jove that thunders!
   What art thou, fellow?
THIDIAS: One that but performs
   The bidding of the fullest man, and worthiest
   To have command obey'd.
ENOBARBUS: [*aside*] You will be whipp'd.
ANTONY: Approach there! — Ah, you kite!¹² — Now, gods and devils!
   Authority melts from me. Of late, when I cried "Ho!"   *90*
   Like boys unto a muss,¹³ kings would start forth
   And cry "Your will?" Have you no ears? I am
   Antony yet.

(Enter SERVANTS.*)*

          Take hence this Jack¹⁴ and whip him.
ENOBARBUS: [*aside*] 'Tis better playing with a lion's whelp
   Than with an old one dying.
ANTONY: Moon and stars!
   Whip him. Were't twenty of the greatest tributaries
   That do acknowledge Caesar, should I find them
   So saucy with the hand of she here — what's her name
   Since she was Cleopatra? Whip him, fellows,
   Till like a boy you see him cringe his face   *100*
   And whine aloud for mercy. Take him hence.
THIDIAS: Mark Antony —
ANTONY: Tug him away. Being whipp'd,
   Bring him again. This Jack of Caesar's shall
   Bear us an errand to him.

(Exeunt [SERVANTS] *with* THIDIAS.*)*

   You were half blasted ere I knew you. Ha!
   Have I my pillow left unpress'd in Rome,
   Forborne the getting of a lawful race,
   And by a gem of women, to be abus'd
   By one that looks on feeders?¹⁵
CLEOPATRA: Good my lord —
ANTONY: You have been a boggler¹⁶ ever.   *110*
   But when we in our viciousness grow hard
   (O misery on't!) the wise gods seel¹⁷ our eyes,

12 *scavenging hawk, whore.*
13 *scramble, roughhouse.*
14 *knave, rascal.*
15 *servants, menials.*
16 *fickle dissembler.*
17 *sew up.*

In our own filth drop our clear judgments, make us
Adore our errors, laugh at's while we strut
To our confusion.

CLEOPATRA: O, is't come to this?

ANTONY: I found you as a morsel cold upon
Dead Caesar's trencher.[18] Nay, you were a fragment[19]
Of Gneius Pompey's, besides what hotter hours,
Unregist'red in vulgar fame, you have
Luxuriously[20] pick'd out: for I am sure,   120
Though you can guess what temperance should be,
You know not what it is.

CLEOPATRA: Wherefore is this?

ANTONY: To let a fellow that will take rewards,
And say "God quit[21] you!" be familiar with
My playfellow, your hand, this kingly seal
And plighter of high hearts! O that I were
Upon the hill of Basan to outroar
The horned herd![22] for I have savage cause,
And to proclaim it civilly were like
A halter'd neck which does the hangman thank   130
For being yare[23] about him.

(Enter a SERVANT *with* THIDIAS.*)*

                      Is he whipp'd?

SERVANT: Soundly, my lord.

ANTONY: Cried he? and begg'd 'a pardon?

SERVANT: He did ask favour.

ANTONY: If that thy father live, let him repent
Thou wast not made his daughter; and be thou sorry
To follow Caesar in his triumph, since
Thou hast been whipp'd for following him. Henceforth
The white hand of a lady fever thee!
Shake thou to look on't! Get thee back to Caesar;
Tell him thy entertainment. Look thou say   140
He makes me angry with him; for he seems
Proud and disdainful, harping on what I am,
Not what he knew I was. He makes me angry;
And at this time most easy 'tis to do't,
When my good stars that were my former guides
Have empty left their orbs[24] and shot their fires
Into th' abysm of hell. If he mislike
My speech and what is done, tell him he has
Hipparchus, my enfranched[25] bondman, whom

---

18 *wooden dish.* **19** *leftover.* **20** *lecherously.* **21** *reward.* **22** *Antony considers himself cuckolded, a horned beast like the biblical bulls of Bashan (Psalms 22:12).* **23** *quick, effective.* **24** *spheres.* **25** *enfranchised, freed.*

He may at pleasure whip or hang or torture,   *150*
As he shall like, to quit me. Urge it thou.
Hence with thy stripes, be gone! *(Exit* THIDIAS.*)*
CLEOPATRA: Have you done yet?
ANTONY: Alack, our terrene[26] moon
   Is now eclips'd, and it portends alone
   The fall of Antony!
CLEOPATRA: I must stay his time.
ANTONY: To flatter Caesar, would you mingle eyes
   With one that ties his points[27]
CLEOPATRA: Not know me yet?
ANTONY: Cold-hearted toward me?
CLEOPATRA: Ah, dear, if I be so,
   From my cold heart let heaven engender hail,
   And poison it in the source, and the first stone   *160*
   Drop in my neck; as it determines, so
   Dissolve my life! The next Caesarion smite!
   Till by degrees the memory[28] of my womb,
   Together with my brave Egyptians all,
   By the discandying[29] of this pelleted storm,
   Lie graveless, till the flies and gnats of Nile
   Have buried them for prey!
ANTONY: I am satisfied.
   Caesar sits down in Alexandria, where
   I will oppose his fate. Our force by land
   Hath nobly held; our sever'd navy too   *170*
   Have knit again, and fleet,[30] threat'ning most sea-like.
   Where hast thou been, my heart? Dost thou hear, lady?
   If from the field I shall return once more
   To kiss these lips, I will appear in blood.
   I and my sword will earn our chronicle.
   There's hope in't yet.
CLEOPATRA: That's my brave lord!
ANTONY: I will be treble-sinewed, hearted, breath'd,
   And fight maliciously. For when mine hours
   Were nice and lucky, men did ransom lives   *180*
   Of me for jests; but now I'll set my teeth
   And send to darkness all that stop me. Come,
   Let's have one other gaudy[31] night. Call to me
   All my sad captains; fill our bowls once more.
   Let's mock the midnight bell.

26 *earthly.*
27 *i.e., a valet; one who laces Caesar's garments.*
28 *i.e., children.*
29 *melting.*
30 *float.*
31 *festive.*

CLEOPATRA: It is my birthday.
   I had thought t' have held it poor; but since my lord
   Is Antony again, I will be Cleopatra.
ANTONY: We will yet do well.
CLEOPATRA: Call all his noble captains to my lord.
ANTONY: Do so, we'll speak to them; and to-night I'll force   190
   The wine peep through their scars. Come on, my queen,
   There's sap in't yet! The next time I do fight,
   I'll make Death love me; for I will contend
   Even with his pestilent scythe.

   (Exeunt [all but ENOBARBUS].*)*

ENOBARBUS: Now he'll outstare the lightning. To be furious
   Is to be frighted out of fear, and in that mood
   The dove will peck the estridge.³² I see still
   A diminution in our captain's brain
   Restores his heart. When valour preys on reason,
   It eats the sword it fights with. I will seek   200
   Some way to leave him. *(Exit.)*

ACT FOUR

SCENE 1. [CAESAR's *camp before Alexandria.*]

(Enter CAESAR, AGRIPPA, *and* MAECENAS, *with his* ARMY; CAESAR *reading a letter.)*

CAESAR: He calls me boy, and chides as he had power
   To beat me out of Egypt. My messenger
   He hath whipp'd with rods; dares me to personal combat,
   Caesar to Antony. Let the old ruffian know
   I have many other ways to die, meantime
   Laugh at his challenge.
MAECENAS: Caesar must think,
   When one so great begins to rage, he's hunted
   Even to falling. Give him no breath, but now
   Make boot¹ of his distraction. Never anger
   Made good guard for itself.
CAESAR: Let our best heads   10
   Know that to-morrow the last of many battles
   We mean to fight. Within our files² there are,
   Of those that serv'd Mark Antony but late,

---

32 *goshawk.*

1 *take advantage.*
2 *ranks.*

Enough to fetch him in. See it done;
And feast the army. We have store to do't,
And they have earn'd the waste. Poor Antony! *(Exeunt.)*

SCENE 2. [*Alexandria.* CLEOPATRA's *Palace.*]

(Enter ANTONY, CLEOPATRA, ENOBARBUS, CHARMIAN, IRAS, ALEXAS, *with others.)*

ANTONY: He will not fight with me, Domitius?
ENOBARBUS: No.
ANTONY: Why should he not?
ENOBARBUS: He thinks, being twenty times of better fortune,
    He is twenty men to one.
ANTONY: To-morrow, soldier,
    By sea and land I'll fight. Or I will live,
    Or bathe my dying honour in the blood
    Shall make it live again. Woo't[1] thou fight well?
ENOBARBUS: I'll strike, and cry "Take all!"
ANTONY: Well said. Come on.
    Call forth my household servants. Let's to-night
    Be bounteous at our meal.

(Enter three or four SERVITORS.*)*

                                Give me thy hand,   10
    Thou hast been rightly honest. So hast thou;
    And thou, and thou, and thou. You have serv'd me well,
    And kings have been your fellows.
CLEOPATRA: [*aside to* ENOBARBUS]   What means this?
ENOBARBUS: [*aside to* CLEOPATRA] 'Tis one of those odd tricks which sor-
        row shoots
    Out of the mind.
ANTONY: And thou art honest too.
    I wish I could be made so many men,
    And all of you clapp'd up together in
    An Antony, that I might do you service
    So good as you have done.
OMNES: The gods forbid!
ANTONY: Well, my good fellows, wait on me to-night.   20
    Scant not my cups, and make as much of me

---

1 *would.*

As when mine empire was your fellow too
And suffer'd my command.
CLEOPATRA: [*aside to* ENOBARBUS]   What does he mean?
ENOBARBUS: [*aside to* CLEOPATRA] To make his followers weep.
ANTONY: Tend me to-night.
    May be it is the period[2] of your duty.
    Haply[3] you shall not see me more; or if,
    A mangled shadow. Perchance to-morrow
    You'll serve another master. I look on you
    As one that takes his leave. Mine honest friends,
    I turn you not away; but, like a master   30
    Married to your good service, stay till death.
    Tend me to-night two hours, I ask no more,
    And the gods yield you for't!
ENOBARBUS: What mean you, sir,
    To give them this discomfort? Look, they weep,
    And I, an ass, am onion-ey'd. For shame!
    Transform us not to women.
ANTONY: Ho, ho, ho!
    Now the witch take me if I meant it thus!
    Grace grow where those drops fall! My hearty friends,
    You take me in too dolorous a sense;
    For I spake to you for your comfort, did desire you   40
    To burn this night with torches. Know, my hearts,
    I hope well of to-morrow, and will lead you
    Where rather I'll expect victorious life
    Than death and honour. Let's to supper come,
    And drown consideration. *(Exeunt.)*

SCENE 3. [*Alexandria. Before* CLEOPATRA'S *Palace.*]

(Enter a COMPANY *of* SOLDIERS.*)*

1. SOLDIER: Brother, good night. To-morrow is the day.
2. SOLDIER: It will determine one way. Fare you well.
    Heard you of nothing strange about the streets?
1. SOLDIER: Nothing. What news?
2. SOLDIER: Belike[1] 'tis but a rumour. Good night to you.
1. SOLDIER: Well, sir, good night.

(They meet other SOLDIERS.*)*

2. SOLDIER: Soldiers, have careful watch.
3. SOLDIER: And you. Good night, good night.

2 *end.*
3 *perhaps.*

1 *probably.*

(They place themselves in every corner of the stage.)

4. SOLDIER: Here we. And if to-morrow
    Our navy thrive, I have an absolute hope
    Our landmen will stand up.
3. SOLDIER: 'Tis a brave army,   10
    And full of purpose.

(Music of the hautboys[2] is under the stage.)

2. SOLDIER: Peace! What noise?
1. SOLDIER: List, list!
2. SOLDIER: Hark!
1. SOLDIER: Music i' th' air.
3. SOLDIER: Under the earth.
4. SOLDIER: It signs well, does it not?
3. SOLDIER: No.
1. SOLDIER: Peace, I say!
    What should this mean?
2. SOLDIER: 'Tis the god Hercules, whom Antony lov'd,
    Now leaves him.
1. SOLDIER: Walk. Let's see if other watchmen
    Do hear what we do.
2. SOLDIER: How now, masters?
OMNES: *(speak together)*   How now?
    How now? Do you hear this?
1. SOLDIER: Ay. Is't not strange?
3. SOLDIER: Do you hear, masters? Do you hear?
1. SOLDIER: Follow the noise so far as we have quarter.   20
    Let's see how it will give off.[3]
OMNES: Content. 'Tis strange. *(Exeunt.)*

SCENE 4. *[Alexandria. CLEOPATRA's Palace.]*

(Enter ANTONY and CLEOPATRA, [CHARMIAN, IRAS,] with others.)

ANTONY: Eros! mine armour, Eros!
CLEOPATRA: Sleep a little.
ANTONY: No, my chuck.[1] Eros! Come, mine armour, Eros!

(Enter EROS [with armour].)

Come, good fellow, put thine iron on.
If fortune be not ours to-day, it is
Because we brave[2] her. Come.

2 *oboes.*
3 *finish.*

1 *chick.*
2 *defy.*

CLEOPATRA: Nay, I'll help too.
What's this for?
ANTONY: Ah, let be, let be! Thou art
The armourer of my heart. False,[3] false! This, this!
CLEOPATRA: Sooth, la, I'll help. Thus it must be.
ANTONY: Well, well.
We shall thrive now. Seest thou, my good fellow?
Go put on thy defences.
EROS: Briefly,[4] sir.   10
CLEOPATRA: Is not this buckled well?
ANTONY: Rarely, rarely!
He that unbuckles this, till we do please
To daff't[5] for our repose, shall hear a storm.
Thou fumblest, Eros, and my queen's a squire
More tight at this than thou. Dispatch. O love,
That thou couldst see my wars to-day, and knew'st
The royal occupation![6] Thou shouldst see
A workman[7] in't.

(Enter an armed SOLDIER.*)*

                         Good morrow to thee! Welcome.
Thou look'st like him that knows a warlike charge.
To business that we love we rise betime   20
And go to't with delight.
SOLDIER: A thousand, sir,
Early though 't be, have on their riveted trim
And at the port[8] expect you.

(Shout. Trumpets. Flourish. Enter CAPTAINS *and* SOLDIERS.*)*

CAPTAIN: The morn is fair. Good morrow, General.
ALL: Good morrow, General.
ANTONY: 'Tis well blown, lads.
This morning, like the spirit of a youth
That means to be of note, begins betimes.
So, so. Come, give me that! This way. Well said.
Fare thee well, dame, whate'er becomes of me.
This is a soldier's kiss. Rebukable   30
And worthy shameful check it were to stand
On more mechanic[9] compliment. I'll leave thee
Now like a man of steel. You that will fight,
Follow me close; I'll bring you to't. Adieu.

---

3 *i.e., in the wrong place.* **4** *soon.* **5** *remove it.* **6** *i.e., warfare.* **7** *professional.* **8** *portal, gate.* **9** *common, belaboured.*

(Exeunt [ANTONY, EROS, CAPTAINS, and SOLDIERS].)

CHARMIAN: Please you retire to your chamber?
CLEOPATRA: Lead me.
  He goes forth gallantly. That he and Caesar might
  Determine this great war in single fight!
  Then Antony — but now — Well, on! *(Exeunt.)*

SCENE 5. *[Alexandria. ANTONY's camp.]*

(Trumpets sound. Enter ANTONY and EROS. [a SOLDIER meeting them].)

SOLDIER: The gods make this a happy day to Antony!
ANTONY: Would thou and those thy scars had once prevail'd
  To make me fight at land!
SOLDIER: Hadst thou done so,
  The kings that have revolted and the soldier
  That has this morning left thee would have still
  Followed thy heels.
ANTONY: Who's gone this morning?
SOLDIER: Who?
  One ever near thee. Call for Enobarbus,
  He shall not hear thee, or from Caesar's camp
  Say "I am none of thine."
ANTONY: What sayest thou?
SOLDIER: Sir,
  He is with Caesar.
EROS: Sir, his chests and treasure   10
  He has not with him.
ANTONY: Is he gone?
SOLDIER: Most certain.
ANTONY: Go, Eros, send his treasure after. Do it;
  Detain no jot, I charge thee. Write to him
  (I will subscribe)¹ gentle adieus and greetings.
  Say that I wish he never find more cause
  To change a master. O, my fortunes have
  Corrupted honest men! Dispatch. Enobarbus! *(Exeunt.)*

SCENE 6. *[Alexandria. CAESAR's camp.]*

(Flourish. Enter AGRIPPA, CAESAR, with ENOBARBUS, and DOLABELLA.)

CAESAR: Go forth, Agrippa, and begin the fight.
  Our will is Antony be took alive.
  Make it so known.
AGRIPPA: Caesar, I shall. *[Exit.]*

---

1 *sign.*

CAESAR: The time of universal peace is near.
    Prove this a prosp'rous day, the three-nook'd[1] world
    Shall bear the olive freely.

(Enter a MESSENGER.*)*

MESSENGER: Antony
    Is come into the field.
CAESAR: Go charge Agrippa
    Plant those that have revolted in the vant,[2]
    That Antony may seem to spend his fury   10
    Upon himself.

(Exeunt [all but ENOBARBUS].*)*

ENOBARBUS: Alexas did revolt and went to Jewry on
    Affairs of Antony; there did dissuade[3]
    Great Herod to incline himself to Caesar
    And leave his master Antony. For this pains
    Caesar hath hang'd him. Canidius and the rest
    That fell away have entertainment, but
    No honourable trust. I have done ill,
    Of which I do accuse myself so sorely,
    That I will joy no more.

(Enter a SOLDIER *of* CAESAR's.*)*

SOLDIER: Enobarbus, Antony   20
    Hath after thee sent all thy treasure, with
    His bounty overplus. The messenger
    Came on my guard and at thy tent is now
    Unloading of his mules.
ENOBARBUS: I give it you!
SOLDIER: Mock not, Enobarbus.
    I tell you true. Best you saf'd[4] the bringer
    Out of the host. I must attend mine office
    Or would have done't myself. Your emperor
    Continues still a Jove. *(Exit.)*
ENOBARBUS: I am alone the villain of the earth,   30
    And feel I am so most. O Antony,
    Thou mine of bounty, how wouldst thou have paid
    My better service, when my turpitude
    Thou dost so crown with gold! This blows[5] my heart.

---

1 *three-cornered: Europe, Asia, Africa.*
2 *vanguard, front line.*
3 *persuade.*
4 *ensured safety for.*
5 *swells.*

If swift thought[6] break it not, a swifter mean
Shall outstrike thought; but thought will do't, I feel.
I fight against thee? No! I will go seek
Some ditch wherein to die; the foul'st best fits
My latter part of life. *(Exit.)*

SCENE 7. *[Field of battle between the camps.]*

(Alarum. Drums and trumpets. Enter AGRIPPA *[and others].)*

AGRIPPA: Retire. We have engag'd ourselves too far.
    Caesar himself has work,[1] and our oppression[2]
    Exceeds what we expected. *(Exeunt.)*

(Alarums. Enter ANTONY, *and* SCARUS *wounded.)*

SCARUS: O my brave Emperor, this is fought indeed!
    Had we done so at first, we had droven them home
    With clouts[3] about their heads.
ANTONY: Thou bleed'st apace.
SCARUS: I had a wound here that was like a T,
    But now 'tis made an H.

([Sound retreat] far off.)

ANTONY: They do retire.
SCARUS: We'll beat 'em into bench-holes.[4] I have yet
    Room for six scotches[5] more.

(Enter EROS.)

EROS: They are beaten, sir, and our advantage serves
    For a fair victory.
SCARUS: Let us score their backs
    And snatch 'em up, as we take hares, behind!
    'Tis sport to maul a runner.
ANTONY: I will reward thee
    Once for thy sprightly comfort, and tenfold
    For thy good valour. Come thee on!
SCARUS: I'll halt[6] after.

(Exeunt.)

10

---

6 *grief.*

1 *difficulty.* 2 *opposition.* 3 *cloth bandages.* 4 *holes in an outdoor privy.* 5 *slashes.* 6 *limp.*

SCENE 8. [*Under the walls of Alexandria.*]

(*Alarum. Enter* ANTONY *again in a march;* SCARUS, *with others.*)

ANTONY: We have beat him to his camp. Run one before
    And let the Queen know of our gests.[1] To-morrow
    Before the sun shall see 's, we'll spill the blood
    That has to-day escap'd. I thank you all;
    For doughty-handed are you, and have fought
    Not as you serv'd the cause, but as 't had been
    Each man's like mine. You have shown all Hectors.[2]
    Enter the city, clip[3] your wives, your friends,
    Tell them your feats, whilst they with joyful tears
    Wash the congealment from your wounds and kiss   10
    The honour'd gashes whole.

(*Enter* CLEOPATRA [*attended*].)

                                   [*to* SCARUS] Give me thy hand. —
    To this great fairy[4] I'll commend thy acts,
    Make her thanks bless thee. [*To* CLEOPATRA] O thou day o' th' world,
    Chain mine arm'd neck! Leap thou, attire and all,
    Through proof of harness[5] to my heart, and there
    Ride on the pants triumphing!
CLEOPATRA: Lord of lords!
    O infinite virtue, com'st thou smiling from
    The world's great snare uncaught?
ANTONY: My nightingale,
    We have beat them to their beds. What, girl! though grey
    Do something mingle with our younger brown, yet ha' we   20
    A brain that nourishes our nerves, and can
    Get goal for goal of youth. Behold this man.
    Commend unto his lips thy favouring hand. —
    Kiss it, my warrior! — He hath fought to-day
    As if a god in hate of mankind had
    Destroyed in such a shape.
CLEOPATRA: I'll give thee, friend,
    An armour all of gold. It was a king's.
ANTONY: He has deserv'd it, were it carbuncled
    Like holy Phoebus' car.[6] Give me thy hand.

---

1 *deeds.*
2 *i.e., fought like Hector, famous Trojan warrior and son of Priam, king of Troy.*
3 *embrace.*
4 *enchantress.*
5 *impenetrable armour.*
6 *chariot of the sun god.*

Through Alexandria make a jolly march;   30
Bear our hack'd targets[7] like the men that owe[8] them.
Had our great palace the capacity
To camp this host, we all would sup together
And drink carouses to the next day's fate,
Which promises royal peril. Trumpeters,
With brazen din blast you the city's ear;
Make mingle with our rattling tabourines,
That heaven and earth may strike their sounds together,
Applauding our approach. *(Exeunt.)*

SCENE 9. [CAESAR's *camp.*]

(Enter a SENTRY *and his* COMPANY. ENOBARBUS *follows.)*

SENTRY: If we be not reliev'd within this hour,
   We must return to th' court of guard. The night
   Is shiny, and they say we shall embattle
   By th' second hour i' th' morn.
1. WATCHMAN: This last day was
   A shrewd one to's.
ENOBARBUS: O, bear me witness, night —
2. WATCHMAN: What man is this?
1. WATCHMAN: Stand close, and list him.
ENOBARBUS: Be witness to me, O thou blessed moon,
   When men revolted shall upon record
   Bear hateful memory, poor Enobarbus did
   Before thy face repent!
SENTRY: Enobarbus?
2. WATCHMAN: Peace!   10
   Hark further.
ENOBARBUS: O sovereign mistress[1] of true melancholy,
   The poisonous damp of night disponge upon me,
   That life, a very rebel to my will,
   May hang no longer on me! Throw my heart
   Against the flint and hardness of my fault,
   Which, being dried with grief, will break to powder,
   And finish all foul thoughts. O Antony,
   Nobler than my revolt is infamous,
   Forgive me in thine own particular,[2]   20
   But let the world rank me in register
   A master-leaver and a fugitive!
   O Antony! O Antony! [*Dies.*]
1. WATCHMAN: Let's speak
   To him.

7 *shields.*
8 *own.*

1 *i.e., the moon.*
2 *personally.*

SENTRY: Let's hear him, for the things he speaks
    May concern Caesar.
2. WATCHMAN: Let's do so. But he sleeps.
SENTRY: Swoons rather; for so bad a prayer as his
    Was never yet for sleep.
1. WATCHMAN: Go we to him.
2. WATCHMAN: Awake, sir, awake! Speak to us!
1. WATCHMAN: Hear you, sir?
SENTRY: The hand of death hath raught³ him. *(Drums afar off.)* Hark! The   30
    drums
    Demurely wake the sleepers. Let us bear him
    To th' court of guard. He is of note. Our hour
    I fully out.
2. WATCHMAN: Come on then.
    He may recover yet. *(Exeunt [with the body].)*

SCENE 10. *[Between the two camps.]*

(Enter ANTONY *and* SCARUS, *with their* ARMY.)

ANTONY: Their preparation is to-day by sea;
    We please them not by land.
SCARUS: For both, my lord.
ANTONY: I would they'd fight i' th' fire or i' th' air;
    We'd fight there too. But this it is, our foot
    Upon the hills adjoining to the city
    Shall stay with us — order for sea is given;
    They have put forth the haven —
    Where their appointment we may best discover
    And look on their endeavour. *(Exeunt.)*

SCENE 11. *[Between the camps.]*

(Enter CAESAR *and his* ARMY.)

CAESAR: But¹ being charg'd, we will be still by land,
    Which, as I take't, we shall; for his best force
    Is forth to man his galleys. To the vales,
    And hold our best advantage. *(Exeunt.)*

SCENE 12. *[Hill adjoining Alexandria.]*

(Enter ANTONY *and* SCARUS.)

ANTONY: Yet they are not join'd.¹ Where yond pine does stand

---

3 *reached.*

1 *unless.*

1 *i.e., in battle.*

I shall discover all. I'll bring thee word
Straight how 'tis like to go. *(Exit.)*
SCARUS: Swallows have built
In Cleopatra's sails their nests. The augurers
Say they know not, they cannot tell; look grimly
And dare not speak their knowledge. Antony
Is valiant, and dejected; and by starts
His fretted fortunes give him hope and fear
Of what he has and has not.

(Alarum afar off, as at a sea-fight.)

(Enter ANTONY.*)*

ANTONY: All is lost!   10
This foul Egyptian hath betrayed me!
My fleet hath yielded to the foe, and yonder
They cast their caps up and carouse together
Like friends long lost. Triple-turn'd whore!² 'tis thou
Hast sold me to this novice, and my heart
Makes only wars on thee. Bid them all fly!
For when I am reveng'd upon my charm,³
I have done all. Bid them all fly; begone!

[Exit SCARUS.*]*

O sun, thy uprise shall I see no more.
Fortune and Antony part here; even here
Do we shake hands. All come to this? The hearts   20
That spaniel'd me at heels, to whom I gave
Their wishes, do discandy, melt their sweets
On blossoming Caesar; and this pine is bark'd,
That overtopp'd them all. Betray'd I am.
O this false soul of Egypt! this grave charm⁴ —
Whose eye beck'd forth my wars and call'd them home,
Whose bosom was my crownet, my chief end —
Like a right gypsy hath at fast and loose
Beguil'd me to the very heart of loss!
What, Eros, Eros!

(Enter CLEOPATRA.*)*

                    Ah, thou spell! Avaunt!   30
CLEOPATRA: Why is my lord enrag'd against his love?

2 *i.e., from Pompey the Elder, to Julius Caesar, to Antony.*
3 *charmer (Cleopatra).*
4 *deadly witch.*

ANTONY: Vanish, or I shall give thee thy deserving
       And blemish Caesar's triumph. Let him take thee
       And hoist thee up to the shouting plebeians.
       Follow his chariot, like the greatest spot[5]
       Of all thy sex. Most monster-like be shown
       For poor'st diminutives, for dolts, and let
       Patient Octavia plough thy visage up
       With her prepared nails.

       (Exit CLEOPATRA.)

                              'Tis well th'art gone,
       If it be well to live; but better 'twere   40
       Thou fell'st into my fury, for one death
       Might have prevented many. Eros, ho!
       The shirt of Nessus[6] is upon me. Teach me,
       Alcides,[7] thou mine ancestor, thy rage.
       Let me lodge Lichas[8] on the horns o' th' moon
       And with those hands that grasp'd the heaviest club
       Subdue my worthiest self. The witch shall die.
       To the young Roman boy she hath sold me, and I fall
       Under this plot. She dies for't. Eros, ho! *(Exit.)*

       SCENE 13. [*Alexandria.* CLEOPATRA's *Palace.*]

       (Enter CLEOPATRA, CHARMIAN, IRAS, MARDIAN.*)*

CLEOPATRA: Help me, my women! O, he is more mad
       Than Telamon[1] for his shield. The boar of Thessaly[2]
       Was never so emboss'd.[3]
CHARMIAN: To th' monument!
       There lock yourself, and send him word you are dead.
       The soul and body rive[4] not more in parting
       Than greatness going off.
CLEOPATRA: To th' monument!
       Mardian, go tell him I have slain myself.
       Say that the last I spoke was "Antony"
       And word it, prithee, piteously. Hence, Mardian,

---

5 blot, blemish. 6 a shirt, charmed by the centaur Nessus, which drove Hercules mad and eventually killed him after he had put it on. 7 Hercules. 8 servant of Hercules who innocently presented him with the shirt of Nessus. In his agony, Hercules threw Lichas into the sea.

1 Ajax, who went mad with resentment after the shield of Achilles was awarded to Ulysses instead of to himself. 2 a monstrous boar sent by Diana to ravage neglectful worshippers. 3 frenzied. 4 rend, divide.

And bring me how he takes my death. To th' monument!   *10*

(Exeunt.)

SCENE 14. [CLEOPATRA's *Palace. Another room.*]

(Enter ANTONY *and* EROS.*)*

ANTONY: Eros, thou yet behold'st me?
EROS: Ay, noble lord.
ANTONY: Sometime we see a cloud that's dragonish;
    A vapour sometime like a bear or lion,
    A tower'd citadel, a pendent rock,
    A forked mountain, or blue promontory
    With trees upon't that nod unto the world
    And mock our eyes with air. Thou hast seen these signs;
    They are black Vesper's pageants.
EROS: Ay, my lord.
ANTONY: That which is now a horse, even with a thought
    The rack dislimns, and makes it indistinct   *10*
    As water is in water.
EROS: It does, my lord.
ANTONY: My good knave Eros, now thy captain is
    Even such a body. Here I am Antony;
    Yet cannot hold this visible shape, my knave.
    I made these wars for Egypt; and the Queen —
    Whose heart I thought I had, for she had mine,
    Which, whilst it was mine, had annex'd unto't
    A million moe,[1] now lost — she, Eros, has
    Pack'd cards with Caesar and false-play'd my glory
    Unto an enemy's triumph.   *20*
    Nay, weep not, gentle Eros. There is left us
    Ourselves to end ourselves.

(Enter MARDIAN.*)*

                                       O, thy vile lady!
    She has robb'd me of my sword.
MARDIAN: No, Antony.
    My mistress lov'd thee and her fortunes mingled
    With thine entirely.
ANTONY: Hence, saucy eunuch! Peace!
    She hath betray'd me and shall die the death.
MARDIAN: Death of one person can be paid but once,
    And that she has discharg'd. What thou wouldst do

---

1 *more.*

Is done unto thy hand.[2] The last she spake
Was, "Antony! most noble Antony!"   30
Then in the midst a tearing groan did break
The name of Antony; it was divided
Between her heart and lips. She rend'red[3] life,
Thy name so buried in her.
ANTONY: Dead, then?
MARDIAN: Dead.
ANTONY: Unarm, Eros. The long day's task is done,
    And we must sleep. [*To* MARDIAN] That thou depart'st hence safe
    Does pay thy labour richly. Go. (*Exit* MARDIAN.)
                            Off, pluck off!
    The sevenfold shield of Ajax cannot keep
    The battery[4] from my heart. O, cleave, my sides!
    Heart, once be stronger than thy continent,[5]   40
    Crack thy frail case! Apace, Eros, apace. —
    No more a soldier. Bruised pieces, go;
    You have been nobly borne. — From me awhile.

(*Exit* EROS.)

I will o'ertake thee, Cleopatra, and
Weep for my pardon. So it must be, for now
All length is torture. Since the torch is out,
Lie down, and stray no farther. Now all labour
Mars what it does; yea, very force entangles
Itself with strength. Seal then, and all is done.
Eros! — I come, my queen. — Eros! — Stay for me.   50
Where souls do couch on flowers, we'll hand in hand
And with our sprightly port[6] make the ghosts gaze.
Dido and her Aeneas[7] shall want troops,[8]
And all the haunt be ours. — Come, Eros, Eros!

(*Enter* EROS.)

EROS: What would my lord?
ANTONY: Since Cleopatra died
    I have liv'd in such dishonour that the gods
    Detest my baseness. I, that with my sword
    Quarter'd the world and o'er green Neptune's back
    With ships made cities, condemn myself to lack
    The courage of a woman — less noble mind   60
    Than she which by her death our Caesar tells

2 *i.e., done for you already.* 3 *surrendered.* 4 *battering.* 5 *container.* 6 *deportment.* 7 *lovers from Virgil's*
Aeneid. 8 *i.e., lack admirers.*

"I am conqueror of myself." Thou art sworn, Eros,
That, when the exigent⁹ should come (which now
Is come indeed) when I should see behind me
Th' inevitable prosecution of
Disgrace and horror, that, on my command,
Thou then wouldst kill me. Do't; the time is come.
Thou strik'st not me; 'tis Caesar thou defeat'st.
Put colour in thy cheek.

EROS: The gods withhold me! 70
  Shall I do that which all the Parthian darts,
  Though enemy, lost aim and could not?

ANTONY: Eros,
  Wouldst thou be window'd in great Rome and see
  Thy master thus with pleach'd¹⁰ arms, bending down
  His corrigible¹¹ neck, his face subdu'd
  To penetrative shame, whilst the wheel'd seat
  Of fortunate Caesar, drawn before him, branded
  His baseness that ensu'd?

EROS: I would not see't.

ANTONY: Come then; for with a wound I must be cur'd.
  Draw that thy honest sword, which thou hast worn
  Most useful for thy country.

EROS: O sir, pardon me! 80

ANTONY: When I did make thee free, swor'st thou not then
  To do this when I bade thee? Do it at once,
  Or thy precedent services are all
  But accidents unpurpos'd. Draw, and come.

EROS: Turn from me then that noble countenance
  Wherein the worship of the whole world lies.

ANTONY: Lo thee!   [*Turns from him.*]

EROS: My sword is drawn.

ANTONY: Then let it do at once
  The thing why thou hast drawn it.

EROS: My dear master,
  My captain, and my emperor, let me say, 90
  Before I strike this bloody stroke, farewell.

ANTONY: 'Tis said, man; and farewell.

EROS: Farewell, great chief. Shall I strike now?

ANTONY: Now, Eros.

EROS: Why, there then! Thus I do escape the sorrow
  Of Antony's death. (*Kills himself.*)

ANTONY: Thrice nobler than myself!
  Thou teachest me, O valiant Eros, what
  I should, and thou couldst not. My queen and Eros

---

9 *necessity.*
10 *folded.*
11 *submissive.*

Have by their brave instruction got upon me
A nobleness in record. But I will be
A bridegroom in my death and run into't   100
As to a lover's bed. Come then; and, Eros,
Thy master dies thy scholar. To do thus

[*Falls on his sword.*]

I learn'd of thee. How? not dead? not dead? —
The guard, ho! O, dispatch me!

(*Enter* [DECRETAS *and*] *a* GUARD.)

1. GUARDSMAN: What's the noise?
ANTONY: I have done my work ill, friends. O, make an end
    Of what I have begun.
2. GUARDSMAN: The star is fall'n.
1. GUARDSMAN: And time is at his period.[12]
ALL: Alas, and woe!
ANTONY: Let him that loves me strike me dead.
1. GUARDSMAN: Not I.
2. GUARDSMAN: Nor I.
3. GUARDSMAN: Nor any one.   110

(*Exeunt* [GUARD].)

DECRETAS: Thy death and fortunes bid thy followers fly.
    This sword but shown to Caesar, with this tidings,
    Shall enter[13] me with him.

(*Enter* DIOMEDES.)

DIOMEDES: Where's Antony?
DECRETAS: There, Diomed, there.
DIOMEDES: Lives he?
    Wilt thou not answer, man?

[*Exit* DECRETAS.]

ANTONY: Art thou there, Diomed? Draw thy sword and give me
    Sufficing strokes for death.
DIOMEDES: Most absolute lord,
    My mistress Cleopatra sent me to thee.
ANTONY: When did she send thee?
DIOMEDES: Now, my lord.

12 *end.*
13 *recommend, endear.*

ANTONY: Where is she?
DIOMEDES: Lock'd in her monument. She had a prophesying fear   120
    Of what hath come to pass; for when she saw
    (Which never shall be found) you did suspect
    She had dispos'd[14] with Caesar, and that your rage
    Would not be purg'd, she sent you word she was dead;
    But, fearing since how it might work, hath sent
    Me to proclaim the truth; and I am come,
    I dread, too late.
ANTONY: Too late, good Diomed. Call my guard, I prithee.
DIOMEDES: What ho! the Emperor's guard! the guard, what ho!
    Come, your lord calls!   130

(Enter four or five of the GUARD *of* ANTONY.*)*

ANTONY: Bear me, good friends, where Cleopatra bides.
    'Tis the last service that I shall command you.
1. GUARDSMAN: Woe, woe are we, sir, you may not live to wear
    All your true followers out.
ALL: Most heavy day!
ANTONY: Nay, good my fellows, do not please sharp fate
    To grace it with your sorrows. Bid that welcome
    Which comes to punish us, and we punish it,
    Seeming to bear it lightly. Take me up.
    I have led you oft; carry me now, good friends.
    And have my thanks for all.   140

(Exeunt, bearing ANTONY.*)*

SCENE 15. [*Alexandria. A monument.*]

(Enter CLEOPATRA *and her* MAIDS *aloft, with* CHARMIAN *and* IRAS.*)*

CLEOPATRA: O Charmian, I will never go from hence.
CHARMIAN: Be comforted, dear madam.
CLEOPATRA: No, I will not.
    All strange and terrible events are welcome,
    But comforts we despise. Our size of sorrow,
    Proportion'd to our cause, must be as great
    As that which makes it.

(Enter DIOMED [*below*].*)*

                          How now? Is he dead?

14 *made terms.*

DIOMEDES: His death's upon him, but not dead.
    Look out o' th' other side your monument.
    His guard have brought him thither.

(Enter, [below,] ANTONY and the GUARD [bearing him].)

CLEOPATRA: O sun,   10
    Burn the great sphere thou mov'st in! Darkling stand
    The varying shore o' th' world! O Antony,
    Antony, Antony! Help, Charmian; help, Iras; help!
    Help, friends below! Let's draw him hither.
ANTONY: Peace!
    Not Caesar's valour hath o'erthrown Antony,
    But Antony's hath triumph'd on itself.
CLEOPATRA: So it should be, that none but Antony
    Should conquer Antony; but woe 'tis so!
ANTONY: I am dying, Egypt, dying; only
    I here importune death awhile, until
    Of many thousand kisses the poor last   20
    I lay upon thy lips.
CLEOPATRA: I dare not, dear.
    Dear my lord, pardon! I dare not,
    Lest I be taken. Not th' imperious show
    Of the full-fortun'd Caesar ever shall
    Be brooch'd¹ with me! If knife, drugs, serpents have
    Edge, sting, or operation, I am safe.
    Your wife Octavia, with her modest eyes
    And still conclusion, shall acquire no honour
    Demuring² upon me. But come, come, Antony!
    Help me, my women. We must draw thee up.   30
    Assist, good friends.
ANTONY: O, quick, or I am gone.
CLEOPATRA: Here's sport indeed! How heavy weighs my lord!
    Our strength is all gone into heaviness;³
    That makes the weight. Had I great Juno's power,
    The strong-wing'd Mercury should fetch thee up
    And set thee by Jove's side. Yet come a little!
    Wishers were ever fools. O, come, come, come!

(They heave ANTONY aloft to CLEOPATRA.)

    And welcome, welcome! Die when thou hast liv'd!
    Quicken⁴ with kissing. Had my lips that power,

1 *ornamented.*
2 *i.e., looking down.*
3 *sorrow.*
4 *revive.*

Thus would I wear them out.
ALL: A heavy sight!   40
ANTONY: I am dying, Egypt, dying.
  Give me some wine, and let me speak a little.
CLEOPATRA: No, let me speak; and let me rail so high
  That the false huswife⁵ Fortune break her wheel,
  Provok'd by my offence.
ANTONY: One word, sweet queen.
  Of Caesar seek your honour, with your safety. O!
CLEOPATRA: They do not go together.
ANTONY: Gentle, hear me.
  None about Caesar trust but Proculeius.
CLEOPATRA: My resolution and my hands I'll trust;
  None about Caesar.   50
ANTONY: The miserable change now at my end
  Lament nor sorrow at; but please your thoughts
  In feeding them with those my former fortunes,
  Wherein I liv'd the greatest prince o' th' world,
  The noblest; and do now not basely die,
  Not cowardly put off my helmet to
  My countryman — a Roman by a Roman
  Valiantly vanquish'd. Now my spirit is going.
  I can no more.
CLEOPATRA: Noblest of men, woo't die?
  Hast thou no care of me? Shall I abide   60
  In this dull world, which in thy absence is
  No better than a sty? O, see, my women, [ANTONY *dies*.]
  The crown o' th' earth doth melt. My lord!
  O, wither'd is the garland of the war,
  The soldier's pole is fall'n! Young boys and girls
  Are level now with men. The odds⁶ is gone,
  And there is nothing left remarkable
  Beneath the visiting moon. [*Swoons.*]
CHARMIAN: O, quietness, lady!
IRAS: She's dead too, our sovereign.
CHARMIAN: Lady!
IRAS: Madam!
CHARMIAN: O madam, madam, madam!
IRAS: Royal Egypt!   70
  Empress!
CHARMIAN: Peace, peace, Iras!
CLEOPATRA: No more but e'en a woman, and commanded
  By such poor passion as the maid that milks
  And does the meanest chares.⁷ It were for me

---

5 *hussy, whore.*
6 *differences, advantages.*
7 *chores.*

To throw my sceptre at the injurious gods,
To tell them that this world did equal theirs
Till they had stol'n our jewel. All 's but naught.
Patience is sottish,[8] and impatience does
Become a dog that's mad. Then is it sin   80
To rush into the secret house of death
Ere death dare come to us? How do you, women?
What, what! good cheer! Why, how now, Charmian?
My noble girls! Ah, women, women, look!
Our lamp is spent, it's out! Good sirs,[9] take heart.
We'll bury him; and then, what's brave, what's noble,
Let's do it after the high Roman fashion
And make death proud to take us. Come, away!
This case of that huge spirit now is cold.
Ah, women, women! Come; we have no friend   90
But resolution and the briefest end.

(Exeunt, bearing off ANTONY's body.)

ACT FIVE

SCENE 1. [*Alexandria.* CAESAR's *camp.*]

(*Enter* CAESAR, AGRIPPA, DOLABELLA, MAECENAS, [GALLUS, PROCULEIUS, *and others*], *his* COUNCIL *of* WAR.)

CAESAR: Go to him, Dolabella; bid him yield.
   Being so frustrate, tell him he mocks
   The pauses that he makes.
DOLABELLA: Caesar, I shall. [*Exit.*]

(*Enter* DECRETAS, *with the sword of* ANTONY.)

CAESAR: Wherefore is that? And what art thou that dar'st
   Appear thus to us?
DECRETAS: I am call'd Decretas.
   Mark Antony I serv'd, who best was worthy
   Best to be serv'd. Whilst he stood up and spoke,
   He was my master, and I wore my life
   To spend upon his haters. If thou please
   To take me to thee, as I was to him   10
   I'll be to Caesar; if thou pleasest not,
   I yield thee up my life.
CAESAR: What is't thou say'st?

8 *foolish.*
9 *i.e., ladies.*

DECRETAS: I say, O Caesar, Antony is dead.
CAESAR: The breaking of so great a thing should make
    A greater crack. The round world
    Should have shook lions into civil streets
    And citizens to their dens. The death of Antony
    Is not a single doom; in the name lay
    A moiety[1] of the world.
DECRETAS: He is dead, Caesar,
    Not by a public minister of justice   20
    Nor by a hired knife; but that self[2] hand
    Which writ his honour in the acts it did
    Hath, with the courage which the heart did lend it,
    Splitted the heart. This is his sword.
    I robb'd his wound of it. Behold it stain'd
    With his most noble blood.
CAESAR: Look you sad, friends?
    The gods rebuke me but it is tidings
    To wash the eyes of kings!
AGRIPPA: And strange it is
    That nature must compel us to lament
    Our most persisted deeds.
MAECENAS: His taints and honours   30
    Wag'd equal with him.
AGRIPPA: A rarer spirit never
    Did steer humanity; but you gods will give us
    Some faults to make us men. Caesar is touch'd.
MAECENAS: When such a spacious mirror 's set before him,
    He needs must see himself.
CAESAR: O Antony,
    I have followed thee to this! But we do lanch[3]
    Diseases in our bodies. I must perforce
    Have shown to thee such a declining day
    Or look on thine: we could not stall[4] together
    In the whole world. But yet let me lament   40
    With tears as sovereign as the blood of hearts
    That thou, my brother, my competitor
    In top of all design, my mate in empire,
    Friend and companion in the front of war,
    The arm of mine own body, and the heart
    Where mine his thoughts did kindle — that our stars,
    Unreconciliable, should divide
    Our equalness to this. Hear me, good friends —

(Enter an EGYPTIAN.)

1 *half.*
2 *selfsame.*
3 *lance.*
4 *dwell.*

But I will tell you at some meeter season.
The business of this man looks out of him;   50
We'll hear him what he says. Whence are you?
EGYPTIAN: A poor Egyptian yet.[5] The Queen my mistress,
　　Confin'd in all she has, her monument,
　　Of thy intents desires instruction,
　　That she preparedly may frame herself
　　To th' way she's forced to.
CAESAR:　　　　　　　　　　　Bid her have good heart.
　　She soon shall know of us, by some of ours,
　　How honourable and how kindly we
　　Determine for her; for Caesar cannot live
　　To be ungentle.
EGYPTIAN:　　　　　　　So the gods preserve thee! *(Exit.)*   60
CAESAR: Come hither, Proculeius. Go and say
　　We purpose her no shame. Give her what comforts
　　The quality of her passion[6] shall require,
　　Lest, in her greatness, by some mortal stroke
　　She do defeat us; for her life in Rome
　　Would be eternal in our triumph. Go,
　　And with your speediest bring us what she says
　　And how you find of her.
PROCULEIUS:　　　　　　　　Caesar, I shall. *(Exit.)*
CAESAR: Gallus, go you along. Where's Dolabella. [*Exit* GALLUS.]
　　To second Proculeius?
ALL:　　　　　　　　　　Dolabella!   70
CAESAR: Let him alone, for I remember now
　　How he's employ'd. He shall in time be ready.
　　Go with me to my tent; where you shall see
　　How hardly[7] I was drawn into this war,
　　How calm and gentle I proceeded still
　　In all my writings. Go with me and see
　　What I can show in this. *(Exeunt.)*

　　　SCENE 2. [*Alexandria. The monument.*]

　　(Enter CLEOPATRA, CHARMIAN, IRAS, *and* MARDIAN.*)*

CLEOPATRA: My desolation does begin to make
　　A better life. 'Tis paltry to be Caesar.
　　Not being Fortune, he's but Fortune's knave,
　　A minister of her will. And it is great
　　To do that thing that ends all other deeds,
　　Which shackles accidents and bolts up change,
　　Which sleeps, and never palates[1] more then dung,
　　The beggar's nurse and Caesar's.

5 *still.*
6 *grief.*
7 *reluctantly.*

1 *tastes.*

(Enter PROCULEIUS.*)*

PROCULEIUS: Caesar sends greeting to the Queen of Egypt,
    And bids thee study on what fair demands   10
    Thou mean'st to have him grant thee.
CLEOPATRA: What's thy name?
PROCULEIUS: My name is Proculeius.
CLEOPATRA: Antony
    Did tell me of you, bade me trust you; but
    I do not greatly care to be deceiv'd,
    That have no use for trusting. If your master
    Would have a queen his beggar, you must tell him
    That majesty, to keep decorum, must
    No less beg than a kingdom. If he please
    To give me conquer'd Egypt for my son,
    He gives me so much of mine own as I   20
    Will kneel to him with thanks.
PROCULEIUS: Be of good cheer;
    Y'are fall'n into a princely hand; fear nothing.
    Make your full reference freely to my lord,
    Who is so full of grace that it flows over
    On all that need. Let me report to him
    Your sweet dependency, and you shall find
    A conqueror that will pray in aid² for kindness.
    Where he for grace is kneel'd to.
CLEOPATRA: Pray you tell him
    I am his fortune's vassal and I send him
    The greatness he has got. I hourly learn   30
    A doctrine of obedience, and would gladly
    Look him i' th' face.
PROCULEIUS: This I'll report, dear lady.
    Have comfort, for I know your plight is pitied
    Of him that caus'd it.

[*Enter* SOLDIERS, *who seize* CLEOPATRA.]

    You see how easily she may be surpris'd.
    Guard her till Caesar come.
IRAS: Royal Queen!
CHARMIAN: O Cleopatra! thou art taken, Queen!
CLEOPATRA: Quick, quick, good hands!

[*Draws a dagger.*]

PROCULEIUS: Hold, worthy lady, hold!

[*Disarms her.*]

---

2 addition.

Do not yourself such wrong, who are in this   40
Reliev'd, but not betray'd.
CLEOPATRA: What, of death too,
That rids our dogs of languish?[3]
PROCULEIUS: Cleopatra,
Do not abuse my master's bounty by
Th' undoing of yourself. Let the world see
His nobleness well acted, which your death
Will never let come forth.
CLEOPATRA: Where art thou, death?
Come hither, come! Come, come, and take a queen
Worth many babes and beggars!
PROCULEIUS: O, temperance, lady!
CLEOPATRA: Sir, I will eat no meat; I'll not drink, sir;
If idle talk will once be necessary,   50
I'll not sleep neither. This mortal house I'll ruin,
Do Caesar what he can. Know, sir, that I
Will not wait pinion'd[4] at your master's court
Nor once be chastis'd with the sober eye
Of dull Octavia. Shall they hoist me up
And show me to the shouting varlotry[5]
Of censuring Rome? Rather a ditch in Egypt
Be gentle grave unto me! Rather on Nilus' mud
Lay me stark-nak'd and let the waterflies
Blow me into abhorring! Rather make   60
My country's high pyramides my gibbet
And hang me up in chains!
PROCULEIUS: You do extend
These thoughts of horror further than you shall
Find cause in Caesar.

(Enter DOLABELLA.*)*

DOLABELLA: Proculeius,
What thou hast done thy master Caesar knows,
And he hath sent for thee. For the Queen,
I'll take her to my guard.
PROCULEIUS: So, Dolabella,
It shall content me best. Be gentle to her.
[*To* CLEOPATRA] To Caesar I will speak what you shall please,
If you'll employ me to him.
CLEOPATRA: Say, I would die.   70

(Exeunt PROCULEIUS [*and* SOLDIERS].*)*

---

3 *lingering misery.*
4 *i.e., with clipped wings.*
5 *rabble.*

DOLABELLA: Most noble Empress, you have heard of me?
CLEOPATRA: I cannot tell.
DOLABELLA: Assuredly you know me.
CLEOPATRA: No matter, sir, what I have heard or known.
    You laugh when boys or women tell their dreams;
    Is't not your trick?[6]
DOLABELLA: I understand not, madam.
CLEOPATRA: I dreamt there was an Emperor Antony —
    O, such another sleep, that I might see
    But such another man!
DOLABELLA: If it might please ye —
CLEOPATRA: His face was as the heav'ns, and therein stuck
    A sun and moon, which kept their course and lighted   80
    The little O, the earth.
DOLABELLA: Most sovereign creature —
CLEOPATRA: His legs bestrid the ocean; his rear'd arm
    Crested the world. His voice was propertied
    As all the tuned[7] spheres, and that to friends;
    But when he meant to quail and shake the orb,
    He was as rattling thunder. For his bounty,
    There was no winter in't; an autumn 'twas
    That grew the more by reaping. His delights
    Were dolphin-like: they show'd his back above
    The element they liv'd in. In his livery[8]   90
    Walk'd crowns and crownets.[9] Realms and islands were
    As plates[10] dropp'd from his pocket.
DOLABELLA: Cleopatra —
CLEOPATRA: Think you there was or might be such a man
    As this I dreamt of?
DOLABELLA: Gentle madam, no.
CLEOPATRA: You lie, up to the hearing of the gods!
    But, if there be or ever were one such,
    It's past the size of dreaming. Nature wants stuff
    To vie strange forms with fancy; yet t' imagine
    An Antony were nature's piece[11] 'gainst fancy,
    Condemning shadows quite.   100
DOLABELLA: Hear me, good madam.
    Your loss is as yourself, great; and you bear it
    As answering to the weight. Would I might never
    O'ertake pursu'd success, but I do feel,
    By the rebound of yours, a grief that smites
    My very heart at root.

---

6 i.e., special menial talent.
7 musical. Pre-Copernican astronomy held that concentric spheres about the earth moved in a harmony that was too
   beautiful for humans to hear.
8 service (literally: distinctive uniform of followers or servants).
9 i.e., kings and princes.
10 silver coins.
11 masterpiece.

CLEOPATRA: I thank you, sir.
    Know you what Caesar means to do with me?
DOLABELLA: I am loath to tell you what I would you knew.
CLEOPATRA: Nay, pray you, sir.
DOLABELLA: Though he be honourable —
CLEOPATRA: He'll lead me, then, in triumph?
DOLABELLA: Madam, he will. I know't. *(Flourish.)*   *110*
    [*Shout within.*] "Make way there! Caesar!"

(*Enter* CAESAR; PROCULEIUS, GALLUS, MAECENAS, [SELEUCUS,] *and others of his*
TRAIN.)

CAESAR: Which is the Queen of Egypt?
DOLABELLA: It is the Emperor, madam.

(CLEOPATRA *kneels.*)

CAESAR: Arise! You shall not kneel.
    I pray you rise. Rise, Egypt.
CLEOPATRA: Sir, the gods
    Will have it thus. My master and my lord
    I must obey.
CAESAR: Take to you no hard thoughts.
    The record of what injuries you did us,
    Though written in our flesh, we shall remember
    As things but done by chance.
CLEOPATRA: Sole sir o' th' world,   *120*
    I cannot project¹² mine own cause so well
    To make it clear; but do confess I have
    Been laden with like frailties which before
    Have often sham'd our sex.
CAESAR: Cleopatra, know
    We will extenuate rather than enforce.
    If you apply¹³ yourself to our intents,
    Which towards you are most gentle, you shall find
    A benefit in this change; but if you seek
    To lay on me a cruelty by taking
    Antony's course, you shall bereave yourself   *130*
    Of my good purposes, and put your children
    To that destruction which I'll guard them from
    If thereon you rely. I'll take my leave.
CLEOPATRA: And may, through all the world! 'Tis yours, and we,
    Your scutcheons¹⁴ and your signs of conquest, shall
    Hang in what place you please. Here, my good lord.
CAESAR: You shall advise me in all for Cleopatra.

12 *explain.*
13 *submit, conform.*
14 *i.e., shields bearing his coat of arms.*

CLEOPATRA: This is the brief[15] of money, plate, and jewels
    I am possess'd of. 'Tis exactly valued,
    Not petty things admitted. Where's Seleucus?   140
SELEUCUS: Here, madam.
CLEOPATRA: This is my treasurer. Let him speak, my lord,
    Upon his peril, that I have reserv'd
    To myself nothing. Speak the truth, Seleucus.
SELEUCUS: Madam,
    I had rather seal my lips than to my peril
    Speak that which is not.
CLEOPATRA: What have I kept back?
SELEUCUS: Enough to purchase what you have made known.
CAESAR: Nay, blush not, Cleopatra. I approve
    Your wisdom in the deed.
CLEOPATRA: See, Caesar! O, behold,   150
    How pomp is followed! Mine will now be yours;
    And should we shift estates, yours would be mine.
    The ingratitude of this Seleucus does
    Even make me wild. O slave, of no more trust
    Than love that's hir'd! What, goest thou back? Thou shalt
    Go back, I warrant thee; but I'll catch thine eyes,
    Though they had wings. Slave, soulless villain, dog!
    O rarely base!
CAESAR: Good Queen, let us entreat you.
CLEOPATRA: O Caesar, what a wounding shame is this,
    That thou vouchsafing here to visit me,   160
    Doing the honour of thy lordliness
    To one so meek, that mine own servant should
    Parcel[16] the sum of my disgraces by
    Addition of his envy! Say, good Caesar,
    That I some lady trifles have reserv'd,
    Immoment[17] toys, things of such dignity
    As we greet modern friends withal; and say
    Some nobler token I have kept apart
    For Livia[18] and Octavia, to induce
    Their mediation — must I be unfolded[19]   170
    With[20] one that I have bred? The gods! It smites me
    Beneath the fall I have. [To SELEUCUS] Prithee go hence!
    Or I shall show the cinders of my spirits
    Through th' ashes of my chance.[21] Wert thou a man,
    Thou wouldst have mercy on me.
CAESAR: Forbear, Seleucus.

[*Exit* SELEUCUS.]

---

15 list. **16** wrap up. **17** inconsequential. **18** Caesar's wife. **19** exposed. **20** by. **21** fortune.

CLEOPATRA: Be it known that we, the greatest, are misthought
    For things that others do; and when we fall,
    We answer others' merits in our name,
    Are therefore to be pitied.
CAESAR: Cleopatra,
    Not what you have reserv'd, nor what acknowledg'd,   *180*
    Put we i' th' roll of conquest. Still be't yours,
    Bestow it at your pleasure; and believe
    Caesar's no merchant, to make prize with you
    Of things that merchants sold. Therefore be cheer'd;
    Make not your thoughts your prisons. No, dear Queen;
    For we intend so to dispose you as
    Yourself shall give us counsel. Feed and sleep.
    Our care and pity is so much upon you
    That we remain your friend; and so adieu.
CLEOPATRA: My master and my lord!
CAESAR: Not so. Adieu.   *190*

(Flourish. Exeunt CAESAR *and his* TRAIN.*)*

CLEOPATRA: He words me, girls, he words me, that I should not
    Be noble to myself! But hark thee, Charmian.

[*Whispers to* CHARMIAN.]

IRAS: Finish, good lady. The bright day is done,
    And we are for the dark.
CLEOPATRA: Hie thee again.
    I have spoke already, and it is provided.
    Go put it to the haste.
CHARMIAN: Madam, I will.

(Enter DOLABELLA.*)*

DOLABELLA: Where is the Queen?
CHARMIAN: Behold, sir.

                      [*Exit.*]

CLEOPATRA: Dolabella!
DOLABELLA: Madam, as thereto sworn, by your command
    (Which my love makes religion to obey)
    I tell you this: Caesar through Syria
    Intends his journey, and within three days   *200*
    You with your children will he send before.
    Make your best use of this. I have perform'd
    Your pleasure and my promise.
CLEOPATRA: Dolabella,
    I shall remain your debtor.

DOLABELLA: I your servant.
Adieu, good Queen; I must attend on Caesar.
CLEOPATRA: Farewell, and thanks.

(Exit [DOLABELLA].)

Now Iras, what think'st thou?
Thou, an Egyptian puppet, shall be shown
In Rome as well as I. Mechanic slaves,
With greasy aprons, rules, and hammers, shall   210
Uplift us to the view. In their thick breaths,
Rank of gross diet, shall we be enclouded,
And forc'd to drink their vapour.
IRAS: The gods forbid!
CLEOPATRA: Nay, 'tis most certain, Iras. Saucy lictors[22]
Will catch at us like strumpets, and scald[23] rhymers
Ballad us out o' tune. The quick comedians
Extemporally will stage us and present
Our Alexandrian revels. Antony
Shall be brought drunken forth, and I shall see
⌐Some squeaking Cleopatra boy[24] my greatness⌐   220
⌊I' th' posture of a whore.
IRAS: O the good gods!
CLEOPATRA: Nay, that's certain.
IRAS: I'll never see't; for I am sure my nails
Are stronger than mine eyes.
CLEOPATRA: Why, that's the way
To fool their preparation and to conquer
Their most absurd intents.

(Enter CHARMIAN.)

Now, Charmian!
Show me, my women, like a queen. Go fetch
My best attires. I am again for Cydnus,
To meet Mark Antony. Sirrah Iras, go.
Now, noble Charmian, we'll dispatch indeed;   230
And when thou hast done this chare,[25] I'll give thee leave
To play till doomsday. — Bring our crown and all.

(A noise within.)

[*Exit* IRAS.]

---

22 *officers.*
23 *vulgar.*
24 *i.e., performed by a boy (as women's parts were on the English Renaissance stage).*
25 *chore.*

Wherefore's this noise?

(Enter a GUARDSMAN.*)*

GUARDSMAN: Here is a rural fellow
  That will not be denied your Highness' presence.
  He brings you figs.
CLEOPATRA: Let him come in.

(Exit GUARDSMAN.*)*

                              What poor an instrument
  May do a noble deed! He brings me liberty.
  My resolution's plac'd, and I have nothing
  Of woman in me. Now from head to foot
  I am marble-constant. Now the fleeting moon   240
  No planet is of mine.

(Enter GUARDSMAN *and* CLOWN[26] *[with basket].)*

GUARDSMAN: This is the man.
CLEOPATRA: Avoid,[27] and leave him.

(Exit GUARDSMAN.*)*

  Hast thou the pretty worm[28] of Nilus there
  That kills and pains not?
CLOWN: Truly I have him. But I would not be the party that should
  desire you to touch him, for his biting is immortal. Those that do
  die of it do seldom or never recover.
CLEOPATRA: Remember'st thou any that have died on't?
CLOWN: Very many, men and women too. I heard of one of them no
  longer than yesterday; a very honest woman, but something given   250
  to lie, as a woman should not do but in the way of honesty — how
  she died of the biting of it, what pain she felt. Truly, she makes a
  very good report o' th' worm; but he that will believe all that they
  say shall never be saved by half that they do. But this is most fallia-
  ble, the worm's an odd worm.
CLEOPATRA: Get thee hence; farewell.
CLOWN: I wish you all joy of the worm.

  [Sets down his basket.]

CLEOPATRA: Farewell.
CLOWN: You must think this, look you, that the worm will do his kind.
CLEOPATRA: Ay, ay; farewell.   260

26 *country rustic.*
27 *depart.*
28 *serpent, asp.*

CLOWN: Look you, the worm is not to be trusted but in the keeping of wise people; for indeed there is no goodness in the worm.

CLEOPATRA: Take thou no care; it shall be heeded.

CLOWN: Very good. Give it nothing, I pray you, for it is not worth the feeding.

CLEOPATRA: Will it eat me?

CLOWN: You must not think I am so simple but I know the devil himself will not eat a woman. I know that a woman is a dish for the gods, if the devil dress her not. But truly, these same whoreson devils do the gods great harm in their women; for in every ten that they   *270* make, the devils mar five.

CLEOPATRA: Well, get thee gone; farewell.

CLOWN: Yes, forsooth, I wish you joy o' th' worm. *(Exit.)*

[*Enter* IRAS *with a robe, crown, etc.*]

CLEOPATRA: Give me my robe, put on my crown. I have
Immortal longings in me. Now no more
The juice of Egypt's grape shall moist this lip.
Yare, yare, good Iras; quick. Methinks I hear
Antony call. I see him rouse himself
To praise my noble act. I hear him mock
The luck of Caesar, which the gods give men   *280*
To excuse their after wrath. Husband, I come!
Now to that name my courage prove my title!
I am fire and air; my other elements
I give to baser life. So, have you done?
Come then and take the last warmth of my lips.
Farewell, kind Charmian. Iras, long farewell.

[*Kisses them.* IRAS *falls and dies.*]

Have I the aspic[29] in my lips? Dost fall?
If thou and nature can so gently part,
The stroke of death is as a lover's pinch,
Which hurts, and is desir'd. Dost thou lie still?   *290*
If thus thou vanishest, thou tell'st the world
It is not worth leave-taking.

CHARMIAN: Dissolve, thick cloud, and rain, that I may say
The gods themselves do weep!

CLEOPATRA: This proves me base.
If she first meet the curled Antony,
He'll make demand of her, and spend that kiss
Which is my heaven to have. Come, thou mortal wretch,

[*To an asp, which she applies to her breast.*]

---

29 *i.e., asp's poison.*

With thy sharp teeth this knot intrinsicate[30]
Of life at once untie. Poor venomous fool,
Be angry, and dispatch. O, couldst thou speak,   *300*
That I might hear thee call great Caesar ass
Unpolicied!
CHARMIAN: O Eastern star!
CLEOPATRA: Peace, peace!
Dost thou not see my baby at my breast,
That sucks the nurse asleep?
CHARMIAN: O, break! O, break!
CLEOPATRA: As sweet as balm, as soft as air, as gentle —
O Antony! Nay, I will take thee too:

[*Applies another asp to her arm.*]

What should I stay — *(Dies.)*
CHARMIAN: In this wild world? So fare thee well.
Now boast thee, death, in thy possession lies
A lass unparallel'd. Downy windows, close;   *310*
And golden Phoebus[31] never be beheld
Of eyes again so royal! Your crown's awry.
I'll mend it, and then play —

(Enter the GUARD, *rustling in.)*

1. GUARDSMAN: Where is the Queen?
CHARMIAN: Speak softly, wake her not.
1. GUARDSMAN: Caesar hath sent —
CHARMIAN: Too slow a messenger.

[*Applies an asp.*]

O, come apace, dispatch. I partly feel thee.
1. GUARDSMAN: Approach, ho! All's not well. Caesar's beguil'd.
2. GUARDSMAN: There's Dolabella sent from Caesar. Call him.
1. GUARDSMAN: What work is here! Charmian, is this well done?
CHARMIAN: It is well done, and fitting for a princess   *320*
Descended of so many royal kings.
Ah, soldier! (CHARMIAN *dies.*)

(Enter DOLABELLA.*)*

DOLABELLA: How goes it here?
2. GUARDSMAN: All dead.
DOLABELLA: Caesar, thy thoughts
Touch their effects[32] in this. Thyself art coming

---

30 *intricate.*
31 *sun god.*
32 *i.e., meet their realization.*

To see perform'd the dreaded act which thou
So sought'st to hinder.
[*Shout within.*]   A way there, a way for Caesar!

(*Enter* CAESAR *and all his* TRAIN.)

DOLABELLA: O sir, you are too sure an augurer:
That you did fear is done.
CAESAR: Bravest at the last!
She levell'd at our purposes, and being royal,
Took her own way. The manner of their deaths?   330
I do not see them bleed.
DOLABELLA: Who was last with them?
1. GUARDSMAN: A simple countryman, that brought her figs.
This was his basket.
CAESAR: Poison'd, then.
1. GUARDSMAN: O Caesar,
This Charmian liv'd but now; she stood and spake.
I found her trimming up the diadem
On her dead mistress. Tremblingly she stood,
And on the sudden dropp'd.
CAESAR: O noble weakness!
If they had swallow'd poison, 'twould appear
By external swelling; but she looks like sleep,
As she would catch another Antony   340
In her strong toil[33] of grace.
DOLABELLA: Here on her breast
There is a vent of blood, and something blown;[34]
The like is on her arm.
1. GUARDSMAN: This is an aspic's trail; and these fig leaves
Have slime upon them, such as th' aspic leaves
Upon the caves of Nile.
CAESAR: Most probable
That so she died; for her physician tells me
She hath pursu'd conclusions infinite
Of easy ways to die. Take up her bed,
And bear her women from the monument.   350
She shall be buried by her Antony.
No grave upon the earth shall clip in it
A pair so famous. High events as these
Strike those that make them; and their story is
No less in pity than his glory which
Brought them to be lamented. Our army shall
In solemn show attend this funeral,
And then to Rome. Come, Dolabella, see
High order in this great solemnity.

(*Exeunt omnes.*)

33 *net.*
34 *swollen.*

INTRODUCTION TO *THE TEMPEST*

*L*ike *Antony and Cleopatra*, the earliest printed text of *The Tempest* appears in the first collection of Shakespeare's plays, the First Folio of 1623. Shakespeare did not see either play printed in his lifetime. A record shows that *The Tempest* was produced at court on November 1, 1611, and was likely quite new at that point. Two topical pamphlets of the year before have a clear bearing on the play: *A Discovery of the Bermudas* by Sylvester Jourdain, and *The True Declaration of the estate of the Colony of Virginia* issued by the Virginia Company, which was then headed by the earls of Pembroke and Southampton, Shakespeare's patrons. These reports, along with a testamentary letter dated July 15, 1610, tell of the wreck and survival of an English crew off the Bermudas in 1609. The survivors fashioned crude sailing vessels and arrived in Jamestown, Virginia, a year after being lost. Their experience was an unprecedented one of survival and endurance, but what was even more noteworthy was their report of Bermuda as an island paradise. Shakespeare seems to have drawn a measure of inspiration from these pamphlets in crafting the utopian island of *The Tempest* — a fantastic place in which to explore comic themes such as discovery, good government, love, freedom, and reconciliation.

No clear source exists for the plot of *The Tempest*, but the pattern is a virtual archetype for comedy: the challenged paradise adapted to social needs, the triumphant but sad return home after self-discovery, the hopes that reside in a new generation of people. The plot thus shares many characteristics with mythologies, folktales, and sophisticated children's stories: testing the fidelity of character, revealing unsuspected evil, asserting self-discovery, moving from trepidation to safety through shades of good and evil and their subsequent realignment after testing. Here, all is not quite as it seems: Prospero is not the inflexible, overbearing father that Ferdinand takes him to be; Miranda is not merely an island beauty; the shipwrecked European nobles are far from noble; Caliban himself is "savage and deformed" only when judged by the standards of European civilization. And yet all is resolved at the conclusion, in a comic understanding that goes beyond the trite "happily-ever-after" notion to express a sense of human value and endurance.

In plotting his drama, Shakespeare had no way of knowing the 300 years of colonialism and emigration that were to follow the new world's discovery, but he did know of aboriginal people in Africa and the Americas. Caliban is suggestive of just such a native whose land has been taken away, and David Suchet triumphed in interpreting the character thus in the 1978 season of the Royal Shakespeare Company. Fiercely hateful of his oppressors, Caliban can also be lyrically sensitive and touched by beauty, as when he describes his island to the drunks whom he has mistaken for supernaturals. The isle is indeed "full of noises," along with countless other possibilities in effecting comic resolution in terms of survival, reintegration, and restored stability.

Good government — personal and political — is itself a key issue of the play. Prospero is the deposed Duke of Milan, and the survivors of the wreck are mostly his political enemies: his usurping brother Antonio, Alonso King of Naples, and Sebastian, Alonso's ambitious brother. But the trusty councillor Gonzalo is also a member of the survivors, and his good-natured fantasies about the ideal state in act 2 scene 1 are roundly lampooned through the literalism and dim hopes of the others. This, as the same time as Antonio counsels Sebastian on the merits of assassinating his brother and usurping his throne. In another part of the island, Caliban, Stephano, and Trinculo drunkenly plan to assassinate Prospero and take over the island. Prospero, of course, sees all — through closed-circuit TV, in the 1950s production of the Yale Dramatic Association — and achieves political reconciliation through reuniting all the victims of the shipwreck and effecting the marriage of Miranda and Ferdinand. Their love, and the survival of the others, is both a discovery and an effect of Prospero's government. Prospero himself has come a long way politically and personally from the arm's-length ineffectuality that saw him deposed back in Milan.

In a sense, satisfied isolation on the island has allowed Prospero the freedom to effect desirable political change. For him, however, this change is belated. Not so for the others in the play who achieve their personal and political freedom. Ariel, in his first exchange with Prospero, demands his liberty and has it granted to him at the play's conclusion. For Ferdinand and Miranda, freedom is found in their love-at-first-sight togetherness. Caliban is aware of his lack of freedom, as he declares to Prospero: "I am all the subjects that you have, / Which first was mine own king" (1.2.341–42), and in his euphoric drunken slogan: "Freedom, high-day! high-day, freedom!" (2.2.162). Like Prospero in a way, who recovers his dukedom, Caliban gets his island back and he is free to chart its future. Prospero himself, in the tender epilogue that concludes the play, asks the audience for freedom.

The dominating effect of Prospero's character has led to allegorical interpretations of the play which see him as a figure for Shakespeare himself at the end of his dramatic career. Some of his lines on the nature of art and drama are richly suggestive, but to locate Prospero as a direct mouthpiece for the playwright simplifies his power within the play. This strategy also simplifies the play in terms of strict causality in order to explain the rich aesthetic effect that the play communicates. And yet the play itself, through amorphous themes of love, embitterment, magical possibility, and human forgiveness, resists such reductive interpretation.

In The Tempest everything is forgiven; anything is possible; comic rein-tegration ties all the loose ends of the play together. And yet confusion, at once blissful and disturbing, is suggested and sustained throughout by the sheer theatricality of the play. The variety of music, dance, and special effects constantly interrupts the plot and varies the pace. There is much room for costume, pageantry, and farce. The "happy" ending of the play, however, is not a transparent theatrical victory: Prospero's desire for revenge is tempered by the extra-human plea of Ariel: Ferdinand must labour like a peasant and prove his kingly love through abstinence; Caliban learns the folly of uncritical trust once more. All three face their futures with varying measures of hope and resolve at the conclusion, a conclusion that signifies hope and possibility for every character involved.

The Tempest

NAMES OF THE ACTORS

ALONSO, *King of Naples*

SEBASTIAN, *his brother*

PROSPERO, *the right Duke of Milan*

ANTONIO, *his brother, the usurping Duke of Milan*

FERDINAND, *son to the King of Naples*

GONZALO, *an honest old councillor*

ADRIAN *and* FRANCISCO, *lords*

CALIBAN, *a salvage*[1] *and deformed slave*

TRINCULO, *a jester*

STEPHANO, *a drunken butler*

MASTER OF A SHIP, BOATSWAIN, MARINERS

MIRANDA, *daughter to* PROSPERO

ARIEL, *an airy spirit*

IRIS

CERES

JUNO   } [*presented by spirits*]

NYMPHS

REAPERS

[*Other* SPIRITS *attending on* PROSPERO]

---

1 *savage, uncivilized.*

THE SCENE. — [*On board a ship at sea; afterwards*] *an uninhabited island.*

ACT ONE

SCENE 1. [*On board a ship at sea.*]

(*A tempestuous noise of thunder and lightning heard.*
Enter a SHIPMASTER *and a* BOATSWAIN.)

MASTER: Boatswain!

BOATSWAIN: Here, master. What cheer?

MASTER: Good, speak to th' mariners! Fall to't — yarely,[1] or we run ourselves aground! Bestir, bestir! (*Exit.*)

(*Enter* MARINERS)

BOATSWAIN: Heigh, my hearts! Cheerly, cheerly, my hearts! Yare, yare!
Take in the topsail! Tend to th' master's whistle! Blow till thou burst
thy wind, if room enough!

(*Enter* ALONSO, SEBASTIAN, ANTONIO, FERDINAND, GONZALO, *and others.*)

ALONSO: Good boatswain, have care. Where's the master? Play the men.

BOATSWAIN: I pray now, keep below.

ANTONIO: Where is the master, bos'n? 10

BOATSWAIN: Do you not hear him? You mar our labour. Keep your cab-
ins! You do assist the storm.

GONZALO: Nay, good, be patient.

BOATSWAIN: When the sea is. Hence! What cares these roarers for the
name of king? To cabin! Silence! Trouble us not!

GONZALO: Good, yet remember whom thou hast aboard.

BOATSWAIN: None that I more love than myself. You are a Councillor. If
you can command these elements to silence and work the peace of
the present, we will not hand a rope more; use your authority. If
you cannot, give thanks you have liv'd so long, and make yourself 20
ready in your cabin for the mischance of the hour, if it so hap. —
Cheerly, good hearts! — Out of our way, I say. (*Exit.*)

GONZALO: I have great comfort from this fellow. Methinks he hath no
drowning mark upon him; his complexion[2] is perfect gallows.[3] Stand
fast, good Fate, to his hanging! Make the rope of his destiny our
cable, for our own doth little advantage. If he be not born to be
hang'd, our case is miserable. (*Exeunt.*)

---

1 *smartly, briskly.*
2 *attitude.*
3 *proverbial: he that is born to be hanged need have no fear of drowning.*

(Enter BOATSWAIN.*)*

BOATSWAIN: Down with the topmast! Yare! Lower, lower! Bring her to
try with maincourse![4] *(A cry within.)* A plague upon this howling!
They are louder than the weather or our office.   30

(Enter SEBASTIAN, ANTONIO, *and* GONZALO.*)*

Yet again? What do you here? Shall we give o'er and drown? Have
you a mind to sink?
SEBASTIAN: A pox o' your throat, you bawling, blasphemous, incharita-
ble dog!
BOATSWAIN: Work you then.
ANTONIO: Hang, cur, hang, you whoreson, insolent noisemaker! We are
less afraid to be drown'd than thou art.
GONZALO: I'll warrant[5] him for drowning, though the ship were no
stronger than a nutshell and as leaky as an unstanched wench.
BOATSWAIN: Lay her ahold, ahold! Set her two courses! Off to sea again!   40
Lay her off!

(Enter MARINERS *wet.)*

MARINERS: All lost! To prayers, to prayers! All lost! [*Exeunt.*]
BOATSWAIN: What, must our mouths be cold?
GONZALO: The King and Prince at prayers! Let's assist them,
    For our case is as theirs.
SEBASTIAN: I am out of patience.
ANTONIO: We are merely cheated of our lives by drunkards.
    This wide-chopp'd[6] rascal — would thou mightst lie drowning
    The washing of ten tides!
GONZALO: He'll be hang'd yet,
    Though every drop of water swear against it
    And gape at wid'st to glut him.   50
        (A confused noise within:) "Mercy on us! —
        We split, we split! — Farewell, my wife and children! —
        Farewell, brother! — We split, we split, we split!"

[*Exit* BOATSWAIN]

ANTONIO: Let's all sink with th' King.
SEBASTIAN: Let's take leave of him.

(Exeunt [ANTONIO *and* SEBASTIAN].*)*

4 *mainsail.*
5 *guarantee against.*
6 *bigmouthed.*

GONZALO: Now would I give a thousand furlongs of sea for an acre of
  barren ground — long heath, brown furze, anything. The wills
  above be done! but I would fain die a dry death. (*Exit.*)

  SCENE 2. [*The island. Before* PROSPERO's *cell.*]

(*Enter* PROSPERO *and* MIRANDA.)

MIRANDA: If by your art, my dearest father, you have
  Put the wild waters in this roar, allay them.
  The sky, it seems, would pour down stinking pitch
  But that the sea, mounting to th' welkin's[1] cheek,
  Dashes the fire out. O, I have suffered
  With those that I saw suffer! a brave vessel
  (Who had no doubt some noble creature in her)
  Dash'd all to pieces! O, the cry did knock
  Against my very heart! Poor souls, they perish'd!
  Had I been any god of power, I would   10
  Have sunk the sea within the earth or ere
  It should the good ship so have swallow'd and
  The fraughting[2] souls within her.
PROSPERO: Be collected.
  No more amazement. Tell your piteous heart
  There's no harm done.
MIRANDA: O, woe the day!
PROSPERO: No harm.
  I have done nothing but in care of thee,
  Of thee my dear one, thee my daughter, who
  Art ignorant of what thou art, naught knowing
  Of whence I am; nor that I am more better
  Than Prospero, master of a full poor cell,   20
  And thy no greater father.
MIRANDA: More to know
  Did never meddle with my thoughts.
PROSPERO: 'Tis time
  I should inform thee farther. Lend thy hand
  And pluck my magic garment from me. So,

[*Lays down his robe.*]

  Lie there, my art. Wipe thou thine eyes; have comfort.
  The direful spectacle of the wrack,[3] which touch'd
  The very virtue of compassion in thee,
  I have with such provision in mine art.
  So safely ordered that there is no soul —

1 *sky's.*
2 *freighted.*
3 *wreck.*

No, not so much perdition[4] as an hair   30
Betid[5] to any creature in the vessel
Which thou heard'st cry, which thou saw'st sink. Sit down;
For thou must now know farther.
MIRANDA: You have often
Begun to tell me what I am; but stopp'd
And left me to a bootless[6] inquisition,
Concluding, "Stay! Not yet."
PROSPERO: The hour's now come;
The very minute bids thee ope thine ear.
Obey, and be attentive. Canst thou remember
A time before we came unto this cell?
I do not think thou canst, for then thou wast not   40
Out three years old.
MIRANDA: Certainly, sir, I can.
PROSPERO: By what? By any other house or person?
Of any thing the image tell me that
Hath kept with thy remembrance.
MIRANDA: 'Tis far off,
And rather like a dream than an assurance
That my remembrance warrants. Had I not
Four or five women once that tended me?
PROSPERO: Thou hadst, and more, Miranda. But how is it
That this lives in thy mind? What seest thou else
In the dark backward and abysm of time?   50
If thou rememb'rest aught ere thou cam'st here,
How thou cam'st here thou mayst.
MIRANDA: But that I do not.
PROSPERO: Twelve year since, Miranda, twelve year since,
Thy father was the Duke of Milan and
A prince of power.
MIRANDA: Sir, are not you my father?
PROSPERO: Thy mother was a piece of virtue, and
She said thou wast my daughter; and thy father
Was Duke of Milan; and his only heir
A princess — no worse issued.
MIRANDA: O the heavens!
What foul play had we that we came from thence?   60
Or blessed was't we did?
PROSPERO: Both, both, my girl!
By foul play, as thou say'st, were we heav'd thence,
But blessedly holp[7] hither.
MIRANDA: O, my heart bleeds
To think o' th' teen[8] that I have turn'd you to,

4 *loss, damage.*
5 *happened.*
6 *pointless.*
7 *helped.*
8 *trouble.*

Which is from my remembrance! Please you, farther.
PROSPERO: My brother, and thy uncle, call'd Antonio —
    I pray thee mark me — that a brother should
    Be so perfidious! — he whom next thyself
    Of all the world I lov'd, and to him put
    The manage of my state, as at that time   70
    Through all the signories[9] it was the first,
    And Prospero the prime duke, being so reputed
    In dignity, and for the liberal arts
    Without a parallel; those being all my study,
    The government I cast upon my brother
    And to my state grew stranger, being transported
    And rapt in secret studies — thy false uncle —
    Dost thou attend me?
MIRANDA: Sir, most heedfully.
PROSPERO: Being once perfected how to grant suits,
    How to deny them, who t' advance, and who   80
    To trash for over-topping, new created
    The creatures that were mine, I say, or chang'd 'em,
    Or else new-form'd 'em; having both the key
    Of officer and office, set all hearts i' th' state
    To what tune pleas'd his ear, that now he was
    The ivy which had hid my princely trunk
    And suck'd my verdure[10] out on't. Thou attend'st not!
MIRANDA: O, good sir, I do.
PROSPERO: I pray thee mark me.
    I thus neglecting worldly ends, all dedicated
    To closeness, and the bettering of my mind
    With that which, but by being so retir'd,   90
    O'er-priz'd all popular rate,[11] in my false brother
    Awak'd an evil nature, and my trust,
    Like a good parent, did beget of him
    A falsehood in its contrary as great
    As my trust was, which had indeed no limit,
    A confidence sans[12] bound. He being thus lorded,
    Not only with what my revenue yielded
    But what my power might else exact, like one
    Who having unto truth, by telling of it,   100
    Made such a sinner of his memory
    To credit his own lie, he did believe
    He was indeed the Duke, out o' th' substitution
    And executing th' outward face of royalty
    With all prerogative. Hence his ambition growing —
    Dost thou hear?
MIRANDA: Your tale, sir, would cure deafness.

---

9 *dukedoms, city states.*
10 *vitality, strength.*
11 *i.e., overran all usual interests in state and politics.*
12 *without.*

PROSPERO: To have no screen between this part he play'd
    And him he play'd it for, he needs will be
    Absolute Milan.[13] Me (poor man) my library
    Was dukedom large enough! Of temporal royalties   *110*
    He thinks me now incapable; confederates[14]
    (So dry he was for sway)[15] with th' King of Naples
    To give him annual tribute, do him homage,
    Subject his coronet to his crown, and bend
    The dukedom yet unbow'd (alas, poor Milan!)
    To most ignoble stooping.
MIRANDA: O, the heavens!
PROSPERO: Mark his condition,[16] and th' event; then tell me
    If this might be a brother.
MIRANDA: I should sin
    To think but nobly of my grandmother.
    Good wombs have borne bad sons.
PROSPERO: Now the condition.   *120*
    This King of Naples, being an enemy
    To me inveterate, hearkens my brother's suit;
    Which was, that he, in lieu o' th' premises,
    Of homage and I know not how much tribute,
    Should presently extirpate me and mine
    Out of the dukedom and confer fair Milan,
    With all the honours, on my brother. Whereon,
    A treacherous army levied, one midnight
    Fated to th' purpose, did Antonio open
    The gates of Milan; and, i' th' dead of darkness,   *130*
    The ministers[17] for th' purpose hurried thence
    Me and thy crying self.
MIRANDA: Alack, for pity!
    I, not rememb'ring how I cried out then,
    Will cry it o'er again. It is a hint[18]
    That wrings mine eyes to't.
PROSPERO: Hear a little further,
    And then I'll bring thee to the present business
    Which now 's upon 's; without the which this story
    Were most impertinent.[19]
MIRANDA: Wherefore did they not
    That hour destroy us?
PROSPERO: Well demanded, wench.
    My tale provokes that question. Dear, they durst not,   *140*
    So dear the love my people bore me; nor set
    A mark so bloody on the business; but

---

13 *i.e., the actual Duke of Milan.* 14 *makes alliance.* 15 *power, influence.* 16 *terms of agreement.* 17 *agents.* 18 *occasion.* 19 *inappropriate, irrelevant.*

With colours fairer painted their foul ends.
In few, they hurried us aboard a bark,
Bore us some leagues to sea; where they prepar'd
A rotten carcass of a butt,²⁰ not rigg'd,
Nor tackle, sail, nor mast; the very rats
Instinctively have quit it. There they hoist us,
To cry to th' sea, that roar'd to us; to sigh
To th' winds, whose pity, sighing back again,   150
Did us but loving wrong.
MIRANDA: Alack, what trouble
Was I then to you!
PROSPERO: O, a cherubin
Thou wast that did preserve me! Thou didst smile,
Infused with a fortitude from heaven,
When I have deck'd the sea with drops²¹ full salt,
Under my burden groan'd; which rais'd in me
An undergoing stomach, to bear up
Against what should ensue.
MIRANDA: How came we ashore?
PROSPERO: By providence divine.
Some food we had, and some fresh water, that   160
A noble Neapolitan, Gonzalo,
Out of his charity, who being then appointed
Master of this design, did give us, with
Rich garments, linens, stuffs, and necessaries
Which since have steaded²² much. So, of his gentleness,
Knowing I lov'd my books, he furnish'd me
From mine own library with volumes that
I prize above my dukedom.
MIRANDA: Would I might
But ever see that man!
PROSPERO: Now I arise.
Sit still, and hear the last of our sea-sorrow.   170
Here in this island we arriv'd; and here
Have I, thy schoolmaster, made thee more profit
Than other princess can, that have more time
For vainer hours, and tutors not so careful.
MIRANDA: Heavens thank you for't! And now I pray you, sir, —
For still 'tis beating in my mind, — your reason
For raising this sea-storm?
PROSPERO: Know thus far forth.
By accident most strange, bountiful Fortune
(Now my dear lady) hath mine enemies
Brought to this shore; and by my prescience   180
I find my zenith²³ doth depend upon

20 *tub; small, barely seaworthy boat.*
21 *tears.*
22 *helped; benefited.*
23 *i.e., highest point of good fortune.*

A most auspicious star, whose influence
If now I court not, but omit,[24] my fortunes
Will ever after droop. Here cease more questions.
Thou art inclin'd to sleep. 'Tis a good dullness,
And give it way. I know thou canst not choose.

[MIRANDA *sleeps*.]

Come away, servant, come! I am ready now.
Approach, my Ariel. Come!

(*Enter* ARIEL.)

ARIEL: All hail, great master! Grave sir, hail! I come
    To answer thy best pleasure; be't to fly,   *190*
    To swim, to dive into the fire, to ride
    On the curl'd clouds. To thy strong bidding task
    Ariel and all his quality.
PROSPERO: Hast thou, spirit,
    Perform'd to point the tempest that I bade thee?
ARIEL: To every article.
    I boarded the King's ship. Now on the beak,
    Now in the waist, the deck, in every cabin,
    I flam'd amazement. Sometime I'd divide
    And burn in many places; on the topmast,
    The yards, and boresprit would I flame distinctly,   *200*
    Then meet and join. Jove's lightnings, the precursors
    O' th' dreadful thunderclaps, more momentary
    And sight-outrunning were not. The fire and cracks
    Of sulphurous roaring the most mighty Neptune
    Seem to besiege and make his bold waves tremble;
    Yea, his dread trident shake.
PROSPERO: My brave spirit!
    Who was so firm, so constant, that this coil[25]
    Would not infect his reason?
ARIEL: Not a soul
    But felt a fever of the mad and play'd
    Some tricks of desperation. All but mariners   *210*
    Plung'd in the foaming brine and quit the vessel,
    Then all afire with me. The King's son Ferdinand,
    With hair up-staring[26] (then like reeds, not hair),
    Was the first man that leapt; cried "Hell is empty,
    And all the devils are here!"
PROSPERO: Why, that's my spirit!
    But was not this nigh shore?

24 *ignore.*
25 *uproar, excitement.*
26 *i.e., standing on end.*

ARIEL: Close by, my master.
PROSPERO: But are they, Ariel, safe?
ARIEL: Not a hair perish'd.
  On their sustaining²⁷ garments not a blemish,
  But fresher than before; and as thou bad'st me,
  In troops I have dispers'd them 'bout the isle.   220
  The King's son have I landed by himself,
  Whom I left cooling of the air with sighs
  In an odd angle of the isle, and sitting,
  His arms in this sad knot.
PROSPERO: Of the King's ship
  The mariners say how thou hast dispos'd,
  And all the rest o' th' fleet.
ARIEL: Safely in harbour
  Is the King's ship; in the deep nook where once
  Thou call'dst me up at midnight to fetch dew
  From the still-vex'd Bermoothes,²⁸ there she's hid;
  The mariners all under hatches stow'd,   230
  Who, with a charm join'd to their suff'red labour,
  I have left asleep; and for the rest o' th' fleet,
  Which I dispers'd, they all have met again,
  And are upon the Mediterranean flote²⁹
  Bound sadly home for Naples,
  Supposing that they saw the King's ship wrack'd
  And his great person perish.
PROSPERO: Ariel, thy charge
  Exactly is perform'd; but there's more work.
  What is the time o' th' day?
ARIEL: Past the mid season.
PROSPERO: At least two glasses.³⁰ The time 'twixt six and now   240
  Must by us both be spent most preciously.
ARIEL: Is there more toil? Since thou dost give me pains,
  Let me remember³¹ thee what thou hast promis'd,
  Which is not yet perform'd me.
PROSPERO: How now? moody?
  What is't thou canst demand?
ARIEL: My liberty.
PROSPERO: Before the time be out? No more!
ARIEL: I prithee,
  Remember I have done thee worthy service,
  Told thee no lies, made no mistakings, serv'd
  Without or grudge or grumblings. Thou didst promise
  To bate³² me a full year.

27 *buoying.*
28 *Bermudas.*
29 *sea.*
30 *i.e., 2:00 P.M.*
31 *remind.*
32 *rebate.*

PROSPERO: Dost thou forget   *250*
  From what a torment I did free thee?
ARIEL: No.
PROSPERO: Thou dost; and think'st it much to tread the ooze
  Of the salt deep,
  To run upon the sharp wind of the North,
  To do me business in the veins o' th' earth
  When it is bak'd with frost.
ARIEL: I do not, sir.
PROSPERO: Thou liest, malignant thing! Hast thou forgot
  The foul witch Sycorax, who with age and envy
  Was grown into a hoop? Hast thou forgot her?
ARIEL: No, sir.
PROSPERO: Thou hast. Where was she born? Speak! Tell me!   *260*
ARIEL: Sir, in Argier.[33]
PROSPERO: O, was she so? I must
  Once in a month recount what thou hast been,
  Which thou forget'st. This damn'd witch Sycorax,
  For mischiefs manifold, and sorceries terrible
  To enter human hearing, from Argier
  Thou know'st was banish'd. For one thing she did
  They would not take her life. Is not this true?
ARIEL: Ay, sir.
PROSPERO: This blue-ey'd hag was hither brought with child
  And here was left by th' sailors. Thou, my slave,   *270*
  As thou report'st thyself, wast then her servant;
  And, for thou wast a spirit too delicate
  To act her earthy and abhorr'd commands,
  Refusing her grand hests,[34] she did confine thee,
  By help of her more potent ministers,
  And in her most unmitigable rage,
  Into a cloven pine; within which rift
  Imprison'd thou didst painfully remain
  A dozen years; within which space she died
  And left thee there; where thou didst vent thy groans   *280*
  As fast as millwheels strike. Then was this island
  (Save for the son that she did litter here,
  A freckled whelp, hag-born) not honour'd with
  A human shape.
ARIEL: Yes, Caliban her son.
PROSPERO: Dull thing, I say so! He, that Caliban
  Whom now I keep in service. Thou best know'st
  What torment I did find thee in. Thy groans
  Did make wolves howl and penetrate the breasts
  Of ever-angry bears. It was a torment
  To lay upon the damn'd, which Sycorax   *290*
  Could not again undo. It was mine art,

33 *Algiers.*
34 *behests.*

When I arriv'd and heard thee, that made gape
The pine, and let thee out.
ARIEL: I thank thee, master.
PROSPERO: If thou more murmur'st, I will rend an oak
     And peg thee in his knotty entrails till
     Thou hast howl'd away twelve winters.
ARIEL: Pardon, master.
     I will be correspondent[35] to command
     And do my spriting gently.
PROSPERO: Do so; and after two days
     I will discharge thee.
ARIEL: That's my noble master!
     What shall I do? Say what! What shall I do?   *300*
PROSPERO: Go make thyself like a nymph o' th' sea. Be subject
     To no sight but thine and mine; invisible
     To every eyeball else. Go take this shape
     And hither come in't. Go! Hence with diligence!

(*Exit* [ARIEL].)

     Awake, dear heart, awake! Thou hast slept well.
     Awake!
MIRANDA: The strangeness of your story put
     Heaviness in me.
PROSPERO: Shake it off. Come on.
     We'll visit Caliban, my slave, who never
     Yields us kind answer.
MIRANDA: 'Tis a villain, sir,
     I do not love to look on.
PROSPERO: But as 'tis,   *310*
     We cannot miss him. He does make our fire,
     Fetch in our wood, and serves in offices
     That profit us. What, ho! slave! Caliban!
     Thou earth, thou! Speak!
CALIBAN: (*within*)   There's wood enough within.
PROSPERO: Come forth, I say! There's other business for thee.
     Come, thou tortoise! When?[36]

(*Enter* ARIEL *like a water nymph.*)

     Fine apparition! My quaint Ariel,
     Hark in thine ear. [*whispers*]
ARIEL: My lord, it shall be done. (*Exit.*)
PROSPERO: Thou poisonous slave, got by the devil himself
     Upon thy wicked dam, come forth!   *320*

---

35 *obedient.*
36 *Hurry up; Come on (an expression of impatience).*

(Enter CALIBAN.*)*

CALIBAN: As wicked dew as e'er my mother brush'd
    With raven's feather from unwholesome fen
    Drop on you both! A south-west blow on ye
    And blister you all o'er!
PROSPERO: For this, be sure, to-night thou shalt have cramps,
    Side-stitches that shall pen thy breath up; urchins
    Shall, for that vast of night that they may work,
    All exercise on thee; thou shalt be pinch'd
    As thick as honeycomb, each pinch more stinging
    Than bees that made 'em.
CALIBAN: I must eat my dinner.   *330*
    This island's mine by Sycorax my mother,
    Which thou tak'st from me. When thou camest first,
    Thou strok'dst me and mad'st much of me; wouldst give me
    Water with berries in't; and teach me how
    To name the bigger light, and how the less,
    That burn by day, and night; and then I lov'd thee
    And show'd thee all the qualities o' th' isle,
    The fresh springs, brine-pits, barren place and fertile.
    Cursed be I that did so! All the charms
    Of Sycorax — toads, beetles, bats light on you!   *340*
    For I am all the subjects that you have,
    Which first was mine own king; and here you sty me
    In this hard rock, whiles you do keep from me
    The rest o' th' island.
PROSPERO: Thou most lying slave,
    Whom stripes[37] may move, not kindness! I have us'd thee,
    (Filth as thou art) with humane care, and lodg'd thee
    In mine own cell till thou didst seek to violate
    The honour of my child.
CALIBAN: O ho, O ho! Would 't had been done!
    Thou didst prevent me; I had peopled else   *350*
    This isle with Calibans.
MIRANDA: Abhorred slave,
    Which any print of goodness wilt not take,
    Being capable of all ill! I pitied thee,
    Took pains to make thee speak, taught thee each hour
    One thing or other. When thou didst not, savage,
    Know thine own meaning, but wouldst gabble like
    A thing most brutish, I endow'd thy purposes
    With words that made them known. But thy vile race,
    Though thou didst learn, had that in't which good natures
    Could not abide to be with. Therefore wast thou   *360*
    Deservedly confin'd into this rock, who hadst
    Deserv'd more than a prison.

37 *lashes.*

CALIBAN: You taught me language, and my profit on't
    Is, I know how to curse. The red plague rid you
    For learning me your language!
PROSPERO: Hag-seed, hence!
    Fetch us in fuel; and be quick, thou'rt best,[38]
    To answer other business. Shrug'st thou, malice?
    If thou neglect'st or dost unwillingly
    What I command, I'll rack thee with old cramps,
    Fill all thy bones with achës, make thee roar   *370*
    That beasts shall tremble at thy din.
CALIBAN: No, pray thee.
    [*Aside*] I must obey. His art is of such pow'r
    It would control my dam's god, Setebos,
    And make a vassal of him.
PROSPERO: So, slave; hence!

(Exit CALIBAN.*)*

(Enter FERDINAND; *and* ARIEL *(invisible), playing and singing.)*

    Ariel's song.

    Come unto these yellow sands,
       And then take hands.
    Curtsied when you have and kiss'd,
       The wild waves whist,
    Foot it featly here and there;
    And, sweet sprites, the burden[39] bear.   *380*
       Hark, hark!
         (Burden, dispersedly.)[40] Bowgh, wawgh!
    The watchdogs bark.
         (Burden, dispersedly.) Bowgh, wawgh.
    Hark, hark! I hear
    The strain of strutting chanticleer
       Cry, cock-a-diddle-dowe.

FERDINAND: Where should this music be? I' th' air, or th' earth?
    It sounds no more; and sure it waits upon
    Some god o' th' island. Sitting on a bank,
    Weeping again the King my father's wrack,   *390*
    This music crept by me upon the waters,
    Allaying both their fury and my passion[41]
    With its sweet air. Thence I have follow'd it,
    Or it hath drawn me rather; but 'tis gone.
    No, it begins again.

---

38 *i.e., you'd better (a warning).*
39 *refrain.*
40 *coming from various directions.*
41 *sorrow, grief.*

Ariel's song.

Full fathom five thy father lies;
   Of his bones are coral made;
Those are pearls that were his eyes;
   Nothing of him that doth fade
But doth suffer a sea-change   400
Into something rich and strange.
Sea nymphs hourly ring his knell;
   (*Burden.*) Ding-dong.
Hark! now I hear them — Ding-dong bell.

FERDINAND: The ditty does remember my drown'd father.
   This is no mortal business, nor no sound
   That the earth owes.[42] I hear it now above me.
PROSPERO: The fringed curtains of thine eye advance[43]
   And say what thou seest yond.
MIRANDA: What is't? a spirit?
   Lord, how it looks about! Believe me, sir,   410
   It carries a brave form. But 'tis a spirit.
PROSPERO: No, wench. It eats, and sleeps, and hath such senses
   As we have, such. This gallant which thou seest
   Was in the wrack; and, but he's something stain'd
   With grief (that's beauty's canker), thou mightst call him
   A goodly person. He hath lost his fellows
   And strays about to find 'em.
MIRANDA: I might call him
   A thing divine; for nothing natural
   I ever saw so noble.
PROSPERO: [*aside*]   It goes on, I see,
   As my soul prompts it. Spirit, fine spirit! I'll free thee   420
   Within two days for this.
FERDINAND: Most sure, the goddess
   On whom these airs attend! Vouchsafe my pray'r
   May know if you remain upon this island,
   And that you will some good instruction give
   How I may bear me here. My prime request,
   Which I do last pronounce, is (O you wonder!)
   If you be maid or no?
MIRANDA: No wonder, sir,
   But certainly a maid.
FERDINAND: My language? Heavens!
   I am the best of them that speak this speech,
   Were I but where 'tis spoken.
PROSPERO: How? the best?   430
   What wert thou if the King of Naples heard thee?
FERDINAND: A single thing, as I am now, that wonders
   To hear thee speak of Naples. He does hear me;

42 *owns.*
43 *raise.*

And that he does I weep. Myself am Naples,
Who with mine eyes, never since at ebb, beheld
The King my father wrack'd.
MIRANDA: Alack, for mercy!
FERDINAND: Yes, faith, and all his lords, the Duke of Milan
    And his brave son being twain.
PROSPERO: [aside]   The Duke of Milan
    And his more braver daughter could control thee,
    If now 'twere fit to do't. At the first sight   440
    They have chang'd eyes.[44] Delicate Ariel,
    I'll set thee free for this! — A word, good sir.
    I fear you have done yourself some wrong.[45] A word!
MIRANDA: Why speaks my father so ungently? This
    Is the third man that e'er I saw; the first
    That e'er I sigh'd for. Pity move my father
    To be inclin'd my way!
FERDINAND: O, if a virgin,
    And your affection not gone forth, I'll make you
    The Queen of Naples.
PROSPERO: Soft, sir! one word more.
    [Aside] They are both in either's pow'rs. But this swift business   450
    I must uneasy make, lest too light winning
    Make the prize light. — One word more! I charge thee
    That thou attend me. Thou dost here usurp
    The name thou ow'st[46] not, and hast put thyself
    Upon this island as a spy, to win it
    From me, the lord on't.
FERDINAND: No, as I am a man!
MIRANDA: There's nothing ill can dwell in such a temple.
    If the ill spirit have so fair a house,
    Good things will strive to dwell with't.
PROSPERO: Follow me. —
    Speak not you for him; he's a traitor. — Come!   460
    I'll manacle thy neck and feet together;
    Sea water shalt thou drink; thy food shall be
    The fresh-brook mussels, wither'd roots, and husks
    Wherein the acorn cradled. Follow.
FERDINAND: No.
    I will resist such entertainment till
    Mine enemy has more power.

    (He draws, and is charmed from moving.)

MIRANDA: O dear father,
    Make not too rash a trial of him, for
    He's gentle, and not fearful.

44 *i.e., exchanged loving glances.*
45 *i.e., done (or said) something mistaken.*
46 *ownest.*

PROSPERO: What, I say,
  My foot[47] my tutor? — Put thy sword up, traitor!
  Who mak'st a show but dar'st not strike, thy conscience   470
  Is so possess'd with guilt. Come, from thy ward![48]
  For I can here disarm thee with this stick
  And make thy weapon drop.
MIRANDA: Beseech you, father!
PROSPERO: Hence! Hang not on my garments.
MIRANDA: Sir, have pity.
  I'll be his surety.
PROSPERO: Silence! One word more
  Shall make me chide thee, if not hate thee. What,
  An advocate for an impostor? Hush!
  Thou think'st there is no more such shapes as he,
  Having seen but him and Caliban. Foolish wench!
  To th' most of men this is a Caliban,   480
  And they to him are angels.
MIRANDA: My affections
  Are then most humble. I have no ambition
  To see a goodlier man.
PROSPERO: [To FERDINAND]   Come on, obey!
  Thy nerves[49] are in their infancy again
  And have no vigour in them.
FERDINAND: So they are.
  My spirits, as in a dream, are all bound up.
  My father's loss, the weakness which I feel,
  The wrack of all my friends, nor this man's threats
  To whom I am subdu'd, are but light to me,
  Might I but through my prison once a day   490
  Behold this maid. All corners else o' th' earth
  Let liberty make use of. Space enough
  Have I in such a prison.
PROSPERO: [aside]   It works. [To FERDINAND] Come
        on. —
  Thou hast done well, fine Ariel! [To FERDINAND] Follow me. —
  [To ARIEL] Hark what thou else shalt do me.
MIRANDA: Be of comfort.
  My father 's of a better nature, sir,
  Than he appears by speech. This is unwonted
  Which now came from him.
PROSPERO: Thou shalt be as free
  As mountain winds; but then exactly do
  All points of my command.
ARIEL: To th' syllable.   500
PROSPERO: Come, follow. — Speak not for him.

  (Exeunt.)

47 inferior.
48 defensive posture; this is the challenge, "On guard!"
49 sinews.

ACT TWO

SCENE 1. [*Another part of the island.*]

(*Enter* ALONSO, SEBASTIAN, ANTONIO, GONZALO, ADRIAN, FRANCISCO, *and others.*)

GONZALO: Beseech you, sir, be merry. You have cause
    (So have we all) of joy; for our escape
    Is much beyond our loss. Our hint of woe
    Is common. Every day some sailor's wife,
    The masters of some merchant,[1] and the merchant,
    Have just our theme of woe; but for the miracle,
    I mean our preservation, few in millions
    Can speak like us. Then wisely, good sir, weigh
    Our sorrow with our comfort.
ALONSO: Prithee peace.
SEBASTIAN: He receives comfort like cold porridge.   *10*
ANTONIO: The visitor[2] will not give him o'er so.
SEBASTIAN: Look, he's winding up the watch of his wit; by-and-by it will
    strike.
GONZALO: Sir —
SEBASTIAN: One. Tell.[3]
GONZALO: When every grief is entertain'd,
    That's offer'd comes to th' entertainer —
SEBASTIAN: A dollar.
GONZALO: Dolour comes to him, indeed. You have spoken truer than
    you purpos'd.   *20*
SEBASTIAN: You have taken it wiselier than I meant you should.
GONZALO: Therefore, my lord —
ANTONIO: Fie, what a spendthrift is he of his tongue!
ALONSO: I prithee spare.
GONZALO: Well, I have done. But yet —
SEBASTIAN: He will be talking.
ANTONIO: Which, of he or Adrian, for a good wager, first begins to
    crow?
SEBASTIAN: The old cock.[4]
ANTONIO: The cock'rel.[5]   *30*
SEBASTIAN: Done! The wager?
ANTONIO: A laughter.
SEBASTIAN: A match!
ADRIAN: Though this island seem to be desert —
ANTONIO: Ha, ha, ha!

1 *i.e., merchant ship.*
2 *spiritual advisor (sarcastic reference to Gonzalo).*
3 *count.*
4 *i.e., Gonzalo.*
5 *i.e., Adrian.*

SEBASTIAN: So, you're paid.
ADRIAN: Uninhabitable and almost inaccessible —
SEBASTIAN: Yet —
ADRIAN: Yet —
ANTONIO: He could not miss't.   40
ADRIAN: It must needs be of subtle, tender, and delicate temperance.
ANTONIO: Temperance was a delicate wench.
SEBASTIAN: Ay, and a subtle, as he most learnedly deliver'd.
ADRIAN: The air breathes upon us here most sweetly.
SEBASTIAN: As if it had lungs, and rotten ones.
ANTONIO: Or as 'twere perfum'd by a fen.
GONZALO: Here is everything advantageous to life.
ANTONIO: True; save means to live.
SEBASTIAN: Of that there's none, or little.
GONZALO: How lush and lusty the grass looks! how green!   50
ANTONIO: The ground indeed is tawny.
SEBASTIAN: With an eye[6] of green in't.
ANTONIO: He misses not much.
SEBASTIAN: No; he doth but mistake the truth totally.
GONZALO: But the rarity of it is — which is indeed almost beyond
    credit —
SEBASTIAN: As many vouch'd rarities are.
GONZALO: That our garments, being, as they were, drench'd in the sea,
    hold, notwithstanding, their freshness and glosses, being rather
    new-dy'd than stain'd with salt water.   60
ANTONIO: If but one of his pockets could speak, would it not say he lies?
SEBASTIAN: Ay, or very falsely pocket up his report.
GONZALO: Methinks our garments are now as fresh as when we put
    them on first in Afric, at the marriage of the King's fair daughter
    Claribel to the King of Tunis.
SEBASTIAN: 'Twas a sweet marriage, and we prosper well in our return.
ADRIAN: Tunis was never grac'd before with such a paragon to their
    queen.
GONZALO: Not since widow Dido's time.
ANTONIO: Widow? A pox o' that! How came that "widow" in?   70
    Widow Dido![7]
SEBASTIAN: What if he had said "widower Aeneas" too? Good Lord, how
    you take it!
ADRIAN: "Widow Dido," said you? You make me study of that. She was
    of Carthage, not of Tunis.
GONZALO: This Tunis, sir, was Carthage.
ADRIAN: Carthage?
GONZALO: I assure you, Carthage.
ANTONIO: His word is more than the miraculous harp.[8]

6 spot.
7 Dido, queen of Carthage and lover of Aeneas, is not usually thought of as widow of Sichaeus.
8 in mythology, the music of the harp of Amphion rebuilt the walls of Thebes. (Antonio and Sebastian make fun of
    Gonzalo's error in associating modern Tunis with ancient Carthage.)

SEBASTIAN: He hath rais'd the wall, and houses too.   80
ANTONIO: What impossible matter will he make easy next?
SEBASTIAN: I think he will carry this island home in his pocket and give
    it his son for an apple.
ANTONIO: And, sowing the kernels of it in the sea, bring forth more
    islands.
GONZALO: Ay!
ANTONIO: Why, in good time!
GONZALO: Sir, we were talking that our garments seem now as fresh as
    when we were at Tunis at the marriage of your daughter, who is
    now Queen.   90
ANTONIO: And the rarest that e'er came there.
SEBASTIAN: Bate,[9] I beseech you, widow Dido.
ANTONIO: O, widow Dido? Ay, widow Dido!
GONZALO: Is not, sir, my doublet as fresh as the first day I wore it?
    I mean, in a sort.
ANTONIO: That "sort" was well fish'd for.
GONZALO: When I wore it at your daughter's marriage.
ALONSO: You cram these words into mine ears against
    The stomach[10] of my sense. Would I had never
    Married my daughter there! for, coming thence,   100
    My son is lost; and, in my rate,[11] she too,
    Who is so far from Italy remov'd
    I ne'er again shall see her. O thou mine heir
    Of Naples and of Milan, what strange fish
    Hath made his meal on thee?
FRANCISCO: Sir, he may live.
    I saw him beat the surges under him
    And ride upon their backs. He trod the water,
    Whose enmity he flung aside, and breasted
    The surge most swol'n that met him. His bold head
    'Bove the contentious waves he kept, and oar'd   110
    Himself with his good arms in lusty stroke
    To th' shore, that o'er his wave-worn basis bow'd,
    As stooping to relieve him. I not doubt
    He came alive to land.
ALONSO: No, no, he's gone.
SEBASTIAN: Sir, you may thank yourself for this great loss,
    That would not bless our Europe with your daughter,
    But rather loose her to an African,
    Where she, at least, is banish'd from your eye
    Who hath cause to wet the grief on't.
ALONSO: Prithee peace.

9 *except.*
10 *desire.*
11 *opinion.*

SEBASTIAN: You were kneel'd to and importun'd otherwise   *120*
    By all of us; and the fair soul herself
    Weigh'd, between loathness and obedience, at
    Which end o' th' beam should bow. We have lost your son,
    I fear, for ever. Milan and Naples have
    Moe[12] widows in them of this business' making
    Than we bring men to comfort them.
    The fault's your own.
ALONSO: So is the dear'st o' th' loss.
GONZALO: My Lord Sebastian,
    The truth you speak doth lack some gentleness,
    And time to speak it in. You rub the sore   *130*
    When you should bring the plaster.
SEBASTIAN: Very well.
ANTONIO: And most chirurgeonly.[13]
GONZALO: It is foul weather in us all, good sir,
    When you are cloudy.
SEBASTIAN: Foul weather?
ANTONIO: Very foul.
GONZALO: Had I plantation of this isle, my lord —
ANTONIO: He'd sow't with nettle seed.
SEBASTIAN: Or docks, or mallows.
GONZALO: And were the king on't, what would I do?
SEBASTIAN: Scape being drunk, for want of wine.
GONZALO: I' th' commonwealth I would by contraries[14]
    Execute all things; for no kind of traffic[15]   *140*
    Would I admit; no name of magistrate;
    Letters should not be known; riches, poverty,
    And use of service,[16] none; contract, succession,
    Bourn, bound of land, tilth,[17] vineyard, none;
    No use of metal, corn, or wine, or oil;
    No occupation; all men idle, all;
    And women too, but innocent and pure;
    No sovereignty.
SEBASTIAN: Yet he would be king on't.
ANTONIO: The latter end of his commonwealth forgets the beginning.
GONZALO: All things in common nature should produce   *150*
    Without sweat or endeavour. Treason, felony,
    Sword, pike, knife, gun, or need of any engine
    Would I not have; but nature should bring forth,
    Of it own kind, all foison,[18] all abundance,
    To feed my innocent people.
SEBASTIAN: No marrying mong his subjects?
ANTONIO: None, man! All idle — whores and knaves.

---

12 *more.* 13 *like a surgeon.* 14 *i.e., by the opposite of customary practices.* 15 *business,*
trade. 16 *servants.* 17 *tillage, agriculture.* 18 *plenty.*

GONZALO: I would with such perfection govern, sir,
    T' excel the golden age.
SEBASTIAN: Save his Majesty!
ANTONIO: Long live Gonzalo!
GONZALO: And — do you mark me, sir?   160
ALONSO: Prithee no more. Thou dost talk nothing to me.
GONZALO: I do well believe your Highness; and did it to minister[19] occa-
    sion to these gentlemen, who are of such sensible and nimble lungs
    that they always use to laugh at nothing.
ANTONIO: 'Twas you we laugh'd at.
GONZALO: Who in this kind of merry fooling am nothing to you. So you
    may continue, and laugh at nothing still.
ANTONIO: What a blow was there given!
SEBASTIAN: An[20] it had not fall'n flatlong.[21]
GONZALO: You are gentlemen of brave metal. You would lift the moon   170
    out of her sphere if she would continue in it five weeks without
    changing.

(Enter ARIEL, *[invisible,] playing solemn music.)*

SEBASTIAN: We would so, and then go a-batfowling.[22]
ANTONIO: Nay, good my lord, be not angry.
GONZALO: No, I warrant you. I will not adventure my discretion so
    weakly. Will you laugh me asleep, for I am very heavy?
ANTONIO: Go sleep, and hear us.

[*All sleep except* ALONSO, SEBASTIAN, *and* ANTONIO.]

ALONSO: What, all so soon asleep? I wish mine eyes
    Would, with themselves, shut up my thoughts. I find
    They are inclin'd to do so.
SEBASTIAN: Please you, sir,   180
    Do not omit[23] the heavy offer of it.
    It seldom visits sorrow; when it doth,
    It is a comforter.
ANTONIO: We two, my lord,
    Will guard your person while you take your rest,
    And watch your safety.
ALONSO: Thank you. Wondrous heavy.

[ALONSO *sleeps. Exit* ARIEL.]

SEBASTIAN: What a strange drowsiness possesses them!

---

19 *provide.*
20 *if.*
21 *along the flat of the blade (as opposed to the slicing edge).*
22 *knocking birds out of the air after attracting them with a light.*
23 *neglect.*

ANTONIO: It is the quality o' th' climate.

SEBASTIAN: Why
    Doth it not then our eyelids sink? I find not
    Myself dispos'd to sleep.

ANTONIO: Nor I. My spirits are nimble.
    They fell together all, as by consent.   *190*
    They dropp'd as by a thunder-stroke. What might,
    Worthy Sebastian — O, what might? — No more!
    And yet methinks I see it in thy face,
    What thou shouldst be. Th' occasion speaks thee, and
    My strong imagination sees a crown
    Dropping upon thy head.

SEBASTIAN: What? Art thou waking?

ANTONIO: Do you not hear me speak?

SEBASTIAN: I do; and surely
    It is a sleepy language, and thou speak'st
    Out of thy sleep. What is it thou didst say?
    This is a strange repose, to be asleep   *200*
    With eyes wide open; standing, speaking, moving —
    And yet so fast asleep.

ANTONIO: Noble Sebastian,
    Thou let'st thy fortune sleep — die, rather; wink'st
    Whiles thou art waking.

SEBASTIAN: Thou dost snore distinctly;
    There's meaning in thy snores.

ANTONIO: I am more serious than my custom. You
    Must be so too, if heed me; which to do
    Trebles[24] thee o'er.

SEBASTIAN: Well, I am standing water.

ANTONIO: I'll teach you how to flow.

SEBASTIAN: Do so. To ebb
    Hereditary sloth instructs me.

ANTONIO: O,   *210*
    If you but knew how you the purpose[25] cherish
    Whiles thus you mock it; how, in stripping it,
    You more invest it! Ebbing men indeed
    (Most often) do so near the bottom run
    By their own fear or sloth.

SEBASTIAN: Prithee say on.
    The setting of thine eye and cheek proclaim
    A matter from thee; and a birth, indeed,
    Which throes[26] thee much to yield.

ANTONIO: Thus, sir:
    Although this lord[27] of weak remembrance, this

---

24 triples (in influence, prestige over Antonio, Ferdinand, Alonso).
25 i.e., the gaining of political power.
26 pains, discomforts.
27 i.e., Gonzalo.

Who shall be of as little memory   *220*
When he is earth'd,[28] hath here almost persuaded
(For he's a spirit of persuasion, only
Professes to persuade) the King his son's alive,
'Tis as impossible that he's undrown'd
As he that sleeps here swims.
SEBASTIAN: I have no hope
   That he's undrown'd.
ANTONIO: O, out of that no hope
   What great hope have you! No hope that way is
   Another way so high a hope that even
   Ambition cannot pierce a wink beyond,
   But doubt discovery there. Will you grant with me   *230*
   That Ferdinand is drown'd?
SEBASTIAN: He's gone.
ANTONIO: Then tell me,
   Who's the next heir of Naples?
SEBASTIAN: Claribel.
ANTONIO: She that is Queen of Tunis; she that dwells
   Ten leagues beyond man's life; she that from Naples
   Can have no note, unless the sun were post[29] —
   The man i' th' moon 's too slow — till new-born chins
   Be rough and razorable; she that from whom
   We all were sea-swallow'd, though some cast[30] again,
   And, by that destiny, to perform an act
   Whereof what's past is prologue, what to come,   *240*
   In yours and my discharge.[31]
SEBASTIAN: What stuff is this? How say you?
   'Tis true my brother's daughter's Queen of Tunis;
   So is she heir of Naples; 'twixt which regions
   There is some space.
ANTONIO: A space whose ev'ry cubit
   Seems to cry out "How shall that Claribel
   Measure us back to Naples? Keep in Tunis,
   And let Sebastian wake!" Say this were death
   That now hath seiz'd them, why, they were no worse
   Than now they are. There be that can rule Naples
   As well as he that sleeps; lords that can prate   *250*
   As amply and unnecessarily
   As this Gonzalo. I myself could make
   A chough[32] of as deep chat. O, that you bore
   The mind that I do! What a sleep were this
   For your advancement! Do you understand me?
SEBASTIAN: Methinks I do.

---

28 *buried.*
29 *messenger.*
30 *cast upon shore, cast for performance.*
31 *action, performance.*
32 *member of the crow family; birds that can be taught to mimic a few words.*

ANTONIO: And how does your content[33]
   Tender your own good fortune?
SEBASTIAN: I remember
   You did supplant your brother Prospero.
ANTONIO: True.
   And look how well my garments sit upon me,
   Much feater[34] than before! My brother's servants   260
   Were then my fellows; now they are my men.
SEBASTIAN: But, for your conscience —
ANTONIO: Ay, sir! Where lies that? If 'twere a kibe,[35]
   'Twould put me to my slipper; but I feel not
   This deity in my bosom. Twenty consciences
   That stand 'twixt me and Milan, candied be they
   And melt, ere they molest! Here lies your brother,
   No better than the earth he lies upon
   If he were that which now he's like — that's dead;
   Whom I with this obedient steel (three inches of it)   270
   Can lay to bed for ever; whiles you, doing thus,
   To the perpetual wink[36] for aye might put
   This ancient morsel, this Sir Prudence, who
   Should not upbraid our course. For all the rest,
   They'll take suggestion as a cat laps milk;
   They'll tell the clock to any business that
   We say befits the hour.
SEBASTIAN: Thy case, dear friend,
   Shall be my precedent. As thou got'st Milan,
   I'll come by Naples. Draw thy sword. One stroke
   Shall free thee from the tribute which thou payest,   280
   And I the King shall love thee.
ANTONIO: Draw together;
   And when I rear my hand, do you the like,
   To fall it on Gonzalo. [They draw.]
SEBASTIAN: O, but one word!

[They converse apart.]

(Enter ARIEL, [invisible,] with music and song.)

ARIEL: My master through his art foresees the danger
   That you, his friend, are in, and sends me forth
   (For else his project dies) to keep them living.

(Sings in GONZALO's ear.)

33 inclination.
34 better, more appropriately.
35 chilblain.
36 sleep.

> While you here do snoring lie,
> Open-ey'd conspiracy
>   His time doth take.
> If of life you keep a care,   290
> Shake off slumber and beware.
>   Awake, Awake!

ANTONIO: Then let us both be sudden.
GONZALO: [*wakes*]   Now good angels
    Preserve the King!
ALONSO: Why, how now? Ho, awake! — Why are you drawn?
    Wherefore this ghastly looking?
GONZALO: What's the matter?
SEBASTIAN: Whiles we stood here securing your repose,
    Even now, we heard a hollow burst of bellowing
    Like bulls, or rather lions. Did't not wake you?
    It struck mine ear most terribly.
ALONSO: I heard nothing.   300
ANTONIO: O, 'twas a din to fright a monster's ear,
    To make an earthquake! Sure it was the roar
    Of a whole herd of lions.
ALONSO: Heard you this, Gonzalo?
GONZALO: Upon mine honour, sir, I heard a humming,
    And that a strange one too, which did awake me.
    I shak'd you, sir, and cried. As mine eyes open'd,
    I saw their weapons drawn. There was a noise;
    That's verily.³⁷ 'Tis best we stand upon our guard,
    Or that we quit this place. Let's draw our weapons.
ALONSO: Lead off this ground, and let's make further search   310
    For my poor son.
GONZALO: Heavens keep him from these beasts!
    For he is sure i' th' island.
ALONSO: Lead away.
ARIEL: Prospero my lord shall know what I have done.
    So, King, go safely on to seek thy son. (*Exeunt.*)

SCENE 2. [*Another part of the island.*]

(*Enter* CALIBAN *with a burden of wood. A noise of thunder heard.*)

CALIBAN: All the infections that the sun sucks up
    From bogs, fens, flats, on Prosper fall and make him
    By inchmeal¹ a disease! His spirits hear me,
    And yet I needs must curse. But they'll nor pinch,
    Fright me with urchin-shows,² pitch me i' th' mire,

---

37 *true.*

1 *i.e., inch by inch.*
2 *goblin-like hallucinations.*

Nor lead me, like a firebrand,[3] in the dark
Out of my way, unless he bid 'em; but
For every trifle are they set upon me;
Sometime like apes that mow[4] and chatter at me,
And after bite me; then like hedgehogs which   10
Lie tumbling in my barefoot way and mount
Their pricks at my footfall; sometime am I
All wound with adders, who with cloven tongues
Do hiss me into madness.

(Enter TRINCULO*)*

Lo, now, lo!
Here comes a spirit of his, and to torment me
For bringing wood in slowly. I'll fall flat.
Perchance he will not mind me. [*Lies down.*]

TRINCULO: Here's neither bush nor shrub to bear[5] off any weather at all,
and another storm brewing. I hear it sing i' th' wind. Yond same
black cloud, yond huge one, looks like a foul bombard[6] that would   20
shed his liquor. If it should thunder as it did before, I know not
where to hide my head. Yond same cloud cannot choose but fall by
pailfuls. What have we here? a man or a fish? dead or alive? A fish:
he smells like a fish; a very ancient and fishlike smell; a kind of, not
of the newest, poor-John.[7] A strange fish! Were I in England now, as
once I was, and had but this fish painted, not a holiday fool there
but would give a piece of silver. There would this monster make a
man. Any strange beast there makes a man. When they will not give
a doit[8] to relieve a lame beggar, they will lay out ten to see a dead
Indian. Legg'd like a man! and his fins like arms! Warm, o' my troth!   30
I do now let loose my opinion, hold it no longer: this is no fish, but
an islander, that hath lately suffered by a thunderbolt. [*Thunder.*]
Alas, the storm is come again! My best way is to creep under his
gaberdine. There is no other shelter hereabout. Misery acquaints a
man with strange bedfellows. I will here shroud till the dregs of the
storm be past. [*Creeps under* CALIBAN's *garment.*]

(Enter STEPHANO, *singing;* [*a bottle in his hand*]*.)*

STEPHANO: I shall no more to sea, to sea;
        Here shall I die ashore.

3 *will-o-the-wisp,* ignis fatuus — *bizarre light effects of swamp gas.*
4 *scowl, grimace.*
5 *ward.*
6 *leather jug.*
7 *dried cod or hake.*
8 *coin.*

This is a very scurvy tune to sing at a man's funeral.
Well, here's my comfort. *(Drinks.)*   40

> The master, the swabber, the boatswain, and I,
>   The gunner, and his mate,
> Lov'd Mall, Meg, and Marian, and Margery,
>   But none of us car'd for Kate.
>   For she had a tongue with a tang,
>   Would cry to a sailor "Go hang!"
> She lov'd not the savour of tar nor of pitch;
> Yet a tailor might scratch her where'er she did itch.
>   Then to sea, boys, and let her go hang!

This is a scurvy tune too; but here's my comfort. *(Drinks.)*   50
CALIBAN: Do not torment me! O!
STEPHANO: What's the matter? Have we devils here? Do you put tricks
　　upon 's with salvages and men of Inde, ha? I have not scap'd drown-
　　ing to be afeared now of your four legs; for it hath been said, "As
　　proper a man as ever went on four legs cannot make him give
　　ground"; and it shall be said so again, while Stephano breathes at'
　　nostrils.
CALIBAN: The spirit torments me. O!
STEPHANO: This is some monster of the isle, with four legs, who hath
　　got, as I take it, an ague.[9] Where the devil should he learn our lan-   60
　　guage? I will give him some relief, if it be but for that. If I can
　　recover him, and keep him tame, and get to Naples with him, he's a
　　present for any emperor that ever trod on neat's leather.[10]
CALIBAN: Do not torment me prithee! I'll bring my wood home faster.
STEPHANO: He's in his fit now and does not talk after the wisest. He
　　shall taste of my bottle. If he have never drunk wine afore, it will go
　　near to remove his fit. If I can recover him and keep him tame, I will
　　not take too much for him; he shall pay for him that hath him, and
　　that soundly.
CALIBAN: Thou dost me yet but little hurt.   70
　　Thou wilt anon;[11] I know it by thy trembling.
　　Now Prosper works upon thee.
STEPHANO: Come on your ways. Open your mouth. Here is that which
　　will give language to you, cat. Open your mouth. This will shake
　　your shaking, I can tell you, and that soundly. [*Gives* CALIBAN *drink.*]
　　You cannot tell who's your friend. Open your chaps[12] again.
TRINCULO: I should know that voice. It should be — but he is drown'd;
　　and these are devils. O, defend me!
STEPHANO: Four legs and two voices — a most delicate monster! His
　　forward voice now is to speak well of his friend; his backward voice   80
　　is to utter foul speeches and to detract. If all the wine in my bottle

9 *fever.*
10 *cowhide.*
11 *soon.*
12 *chops, jaws.*

will recover him, I will help his ague. Come! [*Gives drink.*] Amen! I
will pour some in thy other mouth.

TRINCULO: Stephano!

STEPHANO: Doth thy other mouth call me? Mercy, mercy! This is a
devil, and no monster. I will leave him; I have no long spoon.[13]

TRINCULO: Stephano! If thou beest Stephano, touch me and speak to
me; for I am Trinculo — be not afeard — thy good friend Trinculo.

STEPHANO: If thou beest Trinculo, come forth. I'll pull thee by the lesser
legs. If any be Trinculo's legs, these are they. [*Draws him out from   90
under* CALIBAN's *garment.*] Thou art very Trinculo indeed! How cam'st
thou to be the siege[14] of this mooncalf? Can he vent Trinculos?

TRINCULO: I took him to be kill'd with a thunderstroke. But art thou not
drown'd, Stephano? I hope now thou art not drown'd. Is the storm
overblown? I hid me under the dead mooncalf's gaberdine for fear
of the storm. And art thou living, Stephano? O Stephano, two Nea-
politans scap'd?

STEPHANO: Prithee do not turn me about. My stomach is not constant.

CALIBAN: [*aside*] These be fine things, an if they be not sprites.
That's a brave god and bears celestial liquor.   100
I will kneel to him.

STEPHANO: How didst thou scape? How cam'st thou hither? Swear by
this bottle how thou cam'st hither. I escap'd upon a butt of sack
which the sailor's heaved o'erboard, by this bottle! which I made of
the bark of a tree with mine own hands since I was cast ashore.

CALIBAN: I'll swear upon that bottle to be thy true subject, for the liquor
is not earthly.

STEPHANO: Here! Swear then how thou escap'dst.

TRINCULO: Swum ashore, man, like a duck. I can swim like a duck, I'll be
sworn.   110

STEPHANO: Here, kiss the book. [*Gives him drink.*] Though thou canst
swim like a duck, thou art made like a goose.

TRINCULO: O Stephano, hast any more of this?

STEPHANO: The whole butt, man. My cellar is in a rock by th' seaside,
where my wine is hid. How now, mooncalf? How does thine ague?

CALIBAN: Hast thou not dropp'd from heaven?

STEPHANO: Out o' th' moon, I do assure thee. I was the Man i' th' Moon
when time was.[15]

CALIBAN: I have seen thee in her, and I do adore thee.
My mistress show'd me thee, and thy dog, and thy bush.[16]   120

STEPHANO: Come, swear to that; kiss the book. I will furnish it anon
with new contents. Swear. [CALIBAN *drinks.*]

TRINCULO: By this good light, this is a very shallow monster! I afeard of
him? A very weak monster! The Man i' th' Moon? A most poor
credulous monster! Well drawn,[17] monster, in good sooth.

---

13 *proverbial: He who eats with the Devil must have a long spoon.*
14 *excrement.*
15 *i.e., once upon a time.*
16 *legendary: The Man in the Moon, along with his dog and some brushwood, was banished from earth for
gathering firewood on Sunday.*
17 *drunk.*

CALIBAN: I'll show thee every fertile inch o' th' island;
    And I will kiss thy foot. I prithee be my god.
TRINCULO: By this light, a most perfidious and drunken monster!
    When's god's asleep he'll rob his bottle.
CALIBAN: I'll kiss thy foot. I'll swear myself thy subject.   130
STEPHANO: Come on then. Down, and swear!
TRINCULO: I shall laugh myself to death at this puppy-headed monster. A
    most scurvy monster! I could find in my heart to beat him —
STEPHANO: Come, kiss.
TRINCULO: But that the poor monster 's in drink. An abominable
    monster!
CALIBAN: I'll show thee the best springs; I'll pluck thee berries;
    I'll fish for thee, and get thee wood enough.
    A plague upon the tyrant that I serve!
    I'll bear him no more sticks, but follow thee,   140
    Thou wondrous man.
TRINCULO: A most ridiculous monster, to make a wonder of a poor
    drunkard!
CALIBAN: I prithee let me bring thee where crabs[18] grow;
    And I with my long nails will dig thee pignuts,[19]
    Show thee a jay's nest, and instruct thee how
    To snare the nimble marmoset; I'll bring thee
    To clust'ring filberts, and sometimes I'll get thee
    Young scamels[20] from the rock. Wilt thou go with me?
STEPHANO: I prithee now lead the way without any more talking.   150
    Trinculo, the King and all our company else being drown'd, we will
    inherit here. Here, bear my bottle. Fellow Trinculo, we'll fill him by-
    and-by again.

    (CALIBAN *sings drunkenly.*)

CALIBAN: Farewell, master; farewell, farewell!
TRINCULO: A howling monster! a drunken monster!
CALIBAN: No more dams I'll make for fish,
        Nor fetch in firing
        At requiring,
    Nor scrape trenchering,[21] nor wash dish.
        'Ban, 'Ban, Ca — Caliban   160
        Has a new master. Get a new man.

    Freedom, high-day! high-day, freedom! freedom, high-day, freedom!
STEPHANO: O brave monster! lead the way. *(Exeunt.)*

---

18 *crab apples.*
19 *peanuts.*
20 *sea birds (perhaps shellfish).*
21 *wooden plates and bowls.*

ACT THREE

SCENE 1. [*Before* PROSPERO's *cell*.]

(*Enter* FERDINAND, *bearing a log*.)

FERDINAND: There be some sports are painful, and their labour
    Delight in them sets off; some kinds of baseness
    Are nobly undergone, and most poor matters
    Point to rich ends. This my mean task
    Would be as heavy to me as odious, but
    The mistress which I serve quickens[1] what's dead
    And makes my labours pleasures. O, she is
    Ten times more gentle than her father's crabbed;
    And he's compos'd of harshness! I must remove
    Some thousands of these logs and pile them up,   10
    Upon a sore injuction.[2] My sweet mistress
    Weeps when she sees me work, and says such baseness
    Had never like executor. I forget;
    But these sweet thoughts do even refresh my labours
    Most busy, least when I do it.

(*Enter* MIRANDA; *and* PROSPERO [*behind, unseen*].)

MIRANDA: Alas, now pray you
    Work not so hard! I would the lightning had
    Burnt up those logs that you are enjoin'd to pile!
    Pray set it down and rest you. When this burns,
    'Twill weep[3] for having wearied you. My father
    Is hard at study. Pray now rest yourself.   20
    He's safe for these three hours.
FERDINAND: O most dear mistress,
    The sun will set before I shall discharge
    What I must strive to do.
MIRANDA: If you'll sit down,
    I'll bear your logs the while. Pray give me that.
    I'll carry it to the pile.
FERDINAND: No, precious creature.
    I had rather crack my sinews, break my back,
    Than you should such dishonour undergo
    While I sit lazy by.
MIRANDA: It would become me
    As well as it does you; and I should do it

---

1 *enlivens.*
2 *harsh command.*
3 *i.e., run sap.*

> With much more ease; for my good will is to it,   30
> And yours it is against.

PROSPERO: [aside]   Poor worm, thou art infected!
> This visitation shows it.

MIRANDA: You look wearily.

FERDINAND: No, noble mistress. 'Tis fresh morning with me
> When you are by at night. I do beseech you,
> Chiefly that I might set it in my prayers,
> What is your name?

MIRANDA: Miranda. O my father,
> I have broke your hest⁴ to say so!

FERDINAND: Admir'd Miranda!
> Indeed the top of admiration, worth
> What's dearest to the world! Full many a lady
> I have ey'd with best regard, and many a time   40
> Th' harmony of their tongues hath into bondage
> Brought my too diligent ear; for several virtues
> Have I lik'd several women; never any
> With so full soul but some defect in her
> Did quarrel with the noblest grace she ow'd,⁵
> And put it to the foil; but you, O you,
> So perfect and so peerless, are created
> Of every creature's best!

MIRANDA: I do not know
> One of my sex; no woman's face remember,
> Save, from my glass, mine own; nor have I seen   50
> More that I may call men than you, good friend,
> And my dear father. How features are abroad
> I am skilless⁶ of; but, by my modesty
> (The jewel in my dower), I would not wish
> Any companion in the world but you;
> Nor can imagination form a shape,
> Besides yourself, to like of.⁷ But I prattle
> Something too wildly, and my father's precepts
> I therein do forget.

FERDINAND: I am, in my condition,
> A prince, Miranda; I do think, a king   60
> (I would not so!), and would no more endure
> This wooden slavery than to suffer
> The fleshfly blow my mouth. Hear my soul speak!
> The very instant that I saw you, did
> My heart fly to your service; there resides,
> To make me slave to it; and for your sake
> Am I this patient log-man.

4 *behest, command.*
5 *owned.*
6 *ignorant.*
7 *i.e., to like, admire.*

MIRANDA: Do you love me?
FERDINAND: O heaven, O earth, bear witness to this sound,
     And crown what I profess with kind event[8]
     If I speak true! if hollowly, invert   70
     What best is boded[9] me to mischief! I,
     Beyond all limit of what else i' th' world,
     Do love, prize, honour you.
MIRANDA: I am a fool
     To weep at what I am glad of.
PROSPERO: [aside]   Fair encounter
     Of two most rare affections! Heavens rain grace
     On that which breeds between 'em!
FERDINAND: Wherefore weep you?
MIRANDA: At mine unworthiness, that dare not offer
     What I desire to give, and much less take
     What I shall die to want. But this is trifling;
     And all the more it seeks to hide itself,   80
     The bigger bulk it shows. Hence, bashful cunning!
     And prompt me plain and holy innocence!
     I am your wife, if you will marry me;
     If not, I'll die your maid. To be your fellow[10]
     You may deny me; but I'll be your servant,
     Whether you will or no.
FERDINAND: My mistress, dearest!
     And I thus humble ever.
MIRANDA: My husband then?
FERDINAND: Ay, with a heart as willing
     As bondage e'er of freedom. Here's my hand.
MIRANDA: And mine, with my heart in't; and now farewell   90
     Till half an hour hence.
FERDINAND: A thousand thousand!

(*Exeunt* [FERDINAND *and* MIRANDA *severally*[11]].)

PROSPERO: So glad of this as they I cannot be,
     Who are surpris'd withal; but my rejoicing
     At nothing can be more. I'll to my book;
     For yet ere supper time must I perform
     Much business appertaining.

(*Exit.*)

---

8 *outcome.*
9 *destined, promised by fate.*
10 *friend.*
11 *i.e., in different directions.*

SCENE 2. [*Another part of the island.*]

(*Enter* CALIBAN, STEPHANO, *and* TRINCULO.)

STEPHANO: Tell not me! When the butt is out, we will drink water; not a drop before. Therefore bear up and board 'em![1] Servant monster, drink to me.

TRINCULO: Servant monster? The folly of this island! They say there's but five upon this isle. We are three of them. If th' other two be brain'd like us, the state totters.

STEPHANO: Drink, servant monster, when I bid thee. Thy eyes are almost set in thy head.

TRINCULO: Where should they be set else? He were a brave monster indeed if they were set in his tail. 10

STEPHANO: My man-monster hath drown'd his tongue in sack. For my part, the sea cannot drown me. I swam, ere I could recover the shore, five-and-thirty leagues off and on, by this light. Thou shalt be my lieutenant, monster, or my standard.[2]

TRINCULO: Your lieutenant, if you list; he's no standard.

STEPHANO: We'll not run, Monsieur Monster.

TRINCULO: Nor go neither; but you'll lie like dogs,and yet say nothing neither.

STEPHANO: Mooncalf, speak once in thy life, if thou beest a good mooncalf. 20

CALIBAN: How does thy honour? Let me lick thy shoe. I'll not serve him; he is not valiant.

TRINCULO: Thou liest, most ignorant monster! I am in case[3] to justle a constable. Why, thou debosh'd fish thou, was there ever man a coward that hath drunk so much sack as I to-day? Wilt thou tell a monstrous lie, being but half a fish and half a monster?

CALIBAN: Lo, how he mocks me! Wilt thou let him, my lord?

TRINCULO: "Lord" quoth he? That a monster should be such a natural![4]

CALIBAN: Lo, lo, again! Bite him to death I prithee.

STEPHANO: Trinculo, keep a good tongue in your head. If you prove a 30 mutineer — the next tree! The poor monster's my subject, and he shall not suffer indignity.

CALIBAN: I thank my noble lord. Wilt thou be pleas'd
To hearken once again to the suit I made to thee?

STEPHANO: Marry,[5] will I. Kneel and repeat it; I will stand, and so shall Trinculo.

(*Enter* ARIEL, *invisible.*)

1 i.e., Drink up!
2 standard-bearer.
3 shape, fit condition.
4 congenital idiot.
5 i.e., By the Virgin Mary (a common expletive).

CALIBAN: As I told thee before, I am subject to a tyrant,
    A sorcerer, that by his cunning hath
    Cheated me of the island.
ARIEL: Thou liest.
CALIBAN: Thou liest, thou jesting monkey thou!   40
    I would my valiant master would destroy thee.
    I do not lie.
STEPHANO: Trinculo, if you trouble him any more in's tale, by this hand,
    I will supplant some of your teeth.
TRINCULO: Why, I said nothing.
STEPHANO: Mum then, and no more. — Proceed.
CALIBAN: I say by sorcery he got this isle;
    From me he got it. If thy greatness will
    Revenge it on him — for I know thou dar'st,
    But this thing[6] dare not —   50
STEPHANO: That's most certain.
CALIBAN: Thou shalt be lord of it, and I'll serve thee.
STEPHANO: How now shall this be compass'd?
    Canst thou bring me to the party?
CALIBAN: Yea, yea, my lord! I'll yield him thee asleep,
    Where thou mayst knock a nail into his head.
ARIEL: Thou liest; thou canst not.
CALIBAN: What a pied[7] ninny's this! Thou scurvy patch![8]
    I do beseech thy greatness give him blows
    And take his bottle from him. When that's gone,   60
    He shall drink naught but brine, for I'll not show him
    Where the quick freshes[9] are.
STEPHANO: Trinculo, run into no further danger. Interrupt the monster
    one word further and, by this hand, I'll turn my mercy out o' doors
    and make a stockfish[10] of thee.
TRINCULO: Why, what did I? I did nothing. I'll go farther off.
STEPHANO: Didst thou not say he lied?
ARIEL: Thou liest.
STEPHANO: Do I so? Take thou that! [Strikes TRINCULO.] As you like this,
    give me the lie another time.   70
TRINCULO: I did not give the lie. Out o' your wits, and hearing too? A
    pox o' your bottle! This can sack and drinking do. A murrain[11] on
    your monster, and the devil take your fingers!
CALIBAN: Ha, ha, ha!
STEPHANO: Now forward with your tale. — Prithee stand further off.
CALIBAN: Beat him enough. After a little time
    I'll beat him too.
STEPHANO: Stand farther. — Come, proceed.

---

6 i.e., Trinculo.
7 particoloured.
8 jester.
9 freshwater springs.
10 dried, pulverized fish.
11 disease (especially of cattle).

CALIBAN: Why, as I told thee, 'tis a custom with him
    I' th' afternoon to sleep. There thou mayst brain him,
    Having first seiz'd his books, or with a log   *80*
    Batter his skull, or paunch him with a stake,
    Or cut his wesand[12] with thy knife. Remember
    First to possess his books; for without them
    He's but a sot, as I am, nor hath not
    One spirit to command. They all do hate him
    As rootedly as I. Burn but his books.
    He has brave utensils (for so he calls them)
    Which, when he has a house, he'll deck withal.
    And that most deeply to consider is
    The beauty of his daughter. He himself   *90*
    Calls her a nonpareil. I never saw a woman
    But only Sycorax my dam and she;
    But she as far surpasseth Sycorax
    As great'st does least.
STEPHANO: Is it so brave a lass?
CALIBAN: Ay, lord. She will become thy bed, I warrant,
    And bring thee forth brave brood.
STEPHANO: Monster, I will kill this man. His daughter and I will be king
    and Queen, save our Graces! and Trinculo and thyself shall be vice-
    roys. Dost thou like the plot, Trinculo?
TRINCULO: Excellent.   *100*
STEPHANO: Give me thy hand. I am sorry I beat thee; but while thou
    liv'st, keep a good tongue in thy head.
CALIBAN: Within this half hour will he be asleep.
    Wilt thou destroy him then?
STEPHANO: Ay, on mine honour.
ARIEL: This will I tell my master.
CALIBAN: Thou mak'st me merry; I am full of pleasure.
    Let us be jocund. Will you troll[13] the catch[14]
    You taught me but whilere?[15]
STEPHANO: At thy request, monster, I will do reason, any reason. Come
    on, Trinculo, let us sing. *(Sings.)*   *110*

        Flout 'em and scout[16] 'em
        And scout 'em and flout 'em!
        Thought is free.

CALIBAN: That's not the tune.

---

12 *windpipe.*
13 *sing.*
14 *three-part song.*
15 *a while ago.*
16 *jeer, scoff.*

(ARIEL *plays the tune on a tabor*[17] *and pipe.*)

STEPHANO: What is this same?

TRINCULO: This is the tune of our catch, play'd by the picture of Nobody.

STEPHANO: If thou beest a man, show thyself in thy likeness. If thou
beest a devil, take't as thou list.

TRINCULO: O, forgive me my sins!   120

STEPHANO: He that dies pays all debts. I defy thee. Mercy upon us!

CALIBAN: Art thou afeard?

STEPHANO: No, monster, not I.

CALIBAN: Be not afeard. The isle is full of noises,
    Sounds and sweet airs that give delight and hurt not.
    Sometimes a thousand twangling instruments
    Will hum about mine ears; and sometime voices
    That, if I then had wak'd after long sleep,
    Will make me sleep again; and then, in dreaming,
    The clouds methought would open and show riches   130
    Ready to drop upon me, that, when I wak'd,
    I cried to dream again.

STEPHANO: This will prove a brave kingdom to me, where I shall have
    my music for nothing.

CALIBAN: When Prospero is destroy'd.

STEPHANO: That shall be by-and-by. I remember the story.

TRINCULO: The sound is going away. Let's follow it, and after do our
    work.

STEPHANO: Lead, monster; we'll follow. I would I could see this taborer!
    He lays it on.   140

TRINCULO: Wilt come? I'll follow, Stephano. (*Exeunt.*)

SCENE 3. [*Another part of the island.*]

(*Enter* ALONSO, SEBASTIAN, ANTONIO, GONZALO, ADRIAN, FRANCISCO, *etc.*)

GONZALO: By'r Lakin,[1] I can go no further, sir!
    My old bones ache. Here's a maze trod indeed
    Through forthrights[2] and meanders. By your patience,
    I needs must rest me.

ALONSO: Old lord, I cannot blame thee,
    Who am myself attach'd with weariness
    To th' dulling of my spirits. Sit down and rest.
    Even here I will put off my hope, and keep it
    No longer for my flatterer. He is drown'd
    Whom thus we stray to find; and the sea mocks
    Our frustrate search on land. Well, let him go.   10

17 *small drum.*

1 *By our Lady.*
2 *straight paths.*

ANTONIO: [*aside to* SEBASTIAN] I am right glad that he's so out of hope.
    Do not for one repulse forgo the purpose
    That you resolv'd t' effect.
SEBASTIAN: [*aside to* ANTONIO]   The next advantage
    We will take throughly.[3]
ANTONIO: [*aside to* SEBASTIAN]   Let it be to-night;
    For, now they are oppress'd with travel, they
    Will not nor cannot use such vigilance
    As when they are fresh.
SEBASTIAN: [*aside to* ANTONIO]   I say to-night. No more.

    (*Solemn and strange music; and* PROSPERO *on the top*[4] *(invisible).*)

ALONSO: What harmony is this? My good friends, hark!
GONZALO: Marvellous sweet music!

    (*Enter several strange* SHAPES, *bringing in a banquet; and dance about it with gentle
    actions of salutations; and, inviting the* KING *etc. to eat, they depart.*)

ALONSO: Give us kind keepers,[5] heavens! What were these?   20
SEBASTIAN: A living drollery.[6] Now I will believe
    That there are unicorns; that in Arabia
    There is one tree, the phoenix' throne; one phoenix
    At this hour reigning there.
ANTONIO: I'll believe both;
    And what does else want credit,[7] come to me,
    And I'll be sworn 'tis true. Travellers ne'er did lie,
    Though fools at home condemn 'em.
GONZALO: If in Naples
    I should report this now, would they believe me?
    If I should say, I saw such islanders
    (For certes[8] these are people of the island),   30
    Who, though they are of monstrous shape, yet, note,
    Their manners are more gentle, kind, than of
    Our human generation you shall find
    Many — nay, almost any.
PROSPERO: [*aside*]   Honest lord,
    Thou hast said well; for some of you there present
    Are worse than devils.
ALONSO: I cannot too much muse[9]
    Such shapes, such gesture, and such sound, expressing
    (Although they want the use of tongue) a kind
    Of excellent dumb discourse.

3 *thoroughly.* 4 *upper stage.* 5 *guardian angels.* 6 *puppet show.* 7 *belief.* 8 *certainly.* 9 *wonder at.*

PROSPERO: [*aside*]   Praise in departing.
FRANCISCO: They vanish'd strangely.
SEBASTIAN: No matter, since   40
    They have left their viands behind; for we have stomachs.
    Will't please you taste of what is here?
ALONSO: Not I.
GONZALO: Faith, sir, you need not fear. When we were boys,
    Who would believe that there were mountaineers
    Dewlapp'd like bulls, whose throats had hanging at 'em
    Wallets of flesh?[10] or that there were such men
    Whose heads stood in their breasts? which now we find
    Each putter-out of five for one[11] will bring us
    Good warrant of.
ALONSO: I will stand to, and feed;
    Although my last, no matter, since I feel   50
    The best is past. Brother, my lord the Duke,
    Stand to, and do as we.

(*Thunder and lightning. Enter* ARIEL, *like a harpy; claps his wings upon the table; and with a quaint device the banquet vanishes.*)

ARIEL: You are three men of sin, whom destiny —
    That hath to instrument[12] this lower world
    And what is in't — the never surfeited sea
    Hath caus'd to belch up you, and on this island,
    Where man doth not inhabit — you 'mongst men
    Being most unfit to live. I have made you mad;
    And even with such-like valour men hang and drown
    Their proper selves.

[ALONSO, SEBASTIAN, *etc. draw their swords.*]

                You fools! I and my fellows   60
Are ministers of Fate. The elements,
Of whom your swords are temper'd, may as well
Wound the loud winds, or with bemock'd-at stabs
Kill the still-closing waters, as diminish
One dowle[13] that's in my plume. My fellow ministers
Are like invulnerable. If you could hurt,
Your swords are now too massy for your strengths
And will not be uplifted. But remember
(For that's my business to you) that you three
From Milan did supplant good Prospero;   70
Expos'd unto the sea, which hath requit it,[14]

---

10 *i.e., goiter (from which Swiss mountaineers especially were said to suffer).*
11 *a traveller, whose insured deposit was repaid fivefold if alive upon return to collect it.*
12 *i.e., as its instrument.*
13 *downy feather.*
14 *i.e., repaid the crime of supplanting Prospero.*

Him and his innocent child; for which foul deed
The powers, delaying (not forgetting), have
Incens'd the seas and shores, yea, all the creatures,
Against your peace. Thee of thy son, Alonso,
They have bereft; and do pronounce by me
Ling'ring perdition (worse than any death
Can be at once) shall step by step attend
You and your ways; whose[15] wraths to guard you from,
Which here, in this most desolate isle, else falls   80
Upon your heads, is nothing but heart's sorrow[16]
And a clear life ensuing.

(He vanishes in thunder; then, to soft music, enter the SHAPES *again, and dance, with mocks and mows,[17] and carrying out the table.)*

PROSPERO: [*aside*] Bravely the figure of this harpy hast thou
Perform'd, my Ariel; a grace it had, devouring.[18]
Of my instruction hast thou nothing bated[19]
In what thou hadst to say. So, with good life
And observation strange,[20] my meaner ministers[21]
Their several kinds[22] have done. My high charms work,
And these, mine enemies, are all knit up
In their distractions. They now are in my pow'r;   90
And in these fits I leave them, while I visit
Young Ferdinand, whom they suppose is drown'd,
And his and mine lov'd darling. [*Exit above.*]
GONZALO: I' th' name of something holy, sir, why stand you
In this strange stare?
ALONSO: O, it is monstrous, monstrous!
Methought the billows spoke and told me of it;
The winds did sing it to me; and the thunder,
That deep and dreadful organ pipe, pronounc'd
The name of Prosper. It did bass my trespass.
Therefore my son i' th' ooze is bedded; and   100
I'll seek him deeper than e'er plummet sounded
And with him there lie mudded. *(Exit.)*
SEBASTIAN: But one fiend at a time,
I'll fight their legions o'er![23]
ANTONIO: I'll be thy second.

*(Exeunt [*SEBASTIAN *and* ANTONIO].*)*

GONZALO: All three of them are desperate. Their great guilt,
Like poison given to work a great time after,

---

15 i.e., the "powers" of line 73. **16** repentance. **17** mocking gestures and grimaces. **18** i.e., making the banquet disappear. **19** abated. **20** i.e., close observance. **21** spirits (inferior to Ariel). **22** duties. **23** i.e., to the last.

Now 'gins to bite the spirits. I do beseech you,
That are of suppler joints, follow them swiftly
And hinder them from what this ecstasy[24]
May now provoke them to.
ADRIAN: Follow, I pray you.

(Exeunt omnes.)

ACT FOUR

SCENE 1. [*Before* PROSPERO's *cell.*]

(Enter PROSPERO, FERDINAND, *and* MIRANDA.*)*

PROSPERO: If I have too austerely punish'd you,
    Your compensation makes amends; for I
    Have given you here a third of mine own life,
    Or that for which I live; who once again
    I tender to thy hand. All thy vexations
    Were but my trials of thy love, and thou
    Hast strangely[1] stood the test. Here, afore heaven,
    I ratify this my rich gift. O Ferdinand,
    Do not smile at me that I boast her off,
    For thou shalt find she will outstrip all praise   10
    And make it halt behind her.
FERDINAND: I do believe it
    Against an oracle.[2]
PROSPERO: Then, as my gift, and thine own acquisition
    Worthily purchas'd, take my daughter. But
    If thou dost break her virgin-knot before
    All sanctimonious ceremonies may
    With full and holy rite be minist'red,
    No sweet aspersion[3] shall the heavens let fall
    To make this contract grow; but barren hate,
    Sour-ey'd disdain, and discord shall bestrew   20
    The union of your bed with weeds so loathly
    That you shall hate it both. Therefore take heed,
    As Hymen's[4] lamps shall light you!
FERDINAND: As I hope
    For quiet days, fair issue, and long life,

24 *madness.*

1 *wonderfully, remarkably.*
2 *i.e., even though an oracle declared otherwise.*
3 *blessing.*
4 *god of marriage.*

With such love as 'tis now, the murkiest den,
The most opportune place, the strong'st suggestion[5]
Our worser genius can,[6] shall never melt
Mine honour into lust, to take away
The edge of that day's celebration
When I shall think or Phoebus'[7] steeds are founder'd[8]
Or Night kept chain'd below.

PROSPERO: Fairly spoke.
Sit then and talk with her; she is thine own.
What, Ariel! my industrious servant, Ariel!

(Enter ARIEL.*)*

ARIEL: What would my potent master? Here I am.
PROSPERO: Thou and thy meaner fellows your last service
Did worthily perform; and I must use you
In such another trick. Go bring the rabble,[9]
O'er whom I give thee pow'r, here to this place.
Incite them to quick motion; for I must
Bestow upon the eyes of this young couple
Some vanity of mine art. It is my promise,
And they expect it from me.

ARIEL: Presently?
PROSPERO: Ay, with a twink.
ARIEL: Before you can say "Come" and "Go,"
And breathe twice and cry, "So, so,"
Each one, tripping on his toe,
Will be here with mop and mow.[10]
Do you love me, master? No?
PROSPERO: Dearly, my delicate Ariel. Do not approach
Till thou dost hear me call.

ARIEL: Well! I conceive. *(Exit.)*
PROSPERO: Look thou be true. Do not give dalliance
Too much the rein. The strongest oaths are straw
To th' fire i' th' blood. Be more abstemious,
Or else good night your vow!

FERDINAND: I warrant you, sir.
The white cold virgin snow upon my heart
Abates the ardour of my liver.[11]

PROSPERO: Well.
Now come, my Ariel! Bring a corollary[12]
Rather than want a spirit. Appear, and pertly!
No tongue! All eyes! Be silent. *(Soft music.)*

30

40

50

---

5 *temptation.* 6 *i.e., can offer.* 7 *sun god.* 8 *lamed.* 9 *lesser spirits ("thy meaner fellows," line 35).* 10 *mocking gestures and grimaces.* 11 *supposed internal organ of passion.* 12 *extra.*

(Enter IRIS.[13]*)*

IRIS: Ceres,[14] most bounteous lady, thy rich leas[15]   60
    Of wheat, rye, barley, fetches,[16] oats, and pease;
    Thy turfy mountains, where live nibbling sheep,
    And flat meads thatch'd with stover,[17] them to keep;
    Thy banks with pioned[18] and twilled[19] brims,
    Which spongy April at thy hest betrims
    To make cold nymphs chaste crowns; and thy broom groves,
    Whose shadow the dismissed bachelor loves,
    Being lasslorn; thy pole-clipt[20] vineyard;
    And thy sea-marge, sterile and rocky-hard,
    Where thou thyself dost air — the queen o' th' sky,[21]   70
    Whose wat'ry arch and messenger am I,
    Bids thee leave these, and with her sovereign grace,
    Here on this grass-plot, in this very place,
    To come and sport. Her peacocks fly amain.[22]
    Approach, rich Ceres, her to entertain.

(Enter CERES.*)*

CERES: Hail, many-coloured messenger, that ne'er
    Dost disobey the wife of Jupiter,
    Who, with thy saffron wings, upon my flow'rs
    Diffusest honey drops, refreshing show'rs,
    And with each end of thy blue bow dost crown   80
    My bosky[23] acres and my unshrubb'd down,
    Rich scarf to my proud earth — why hath thy queen
    Summon'd me hither to this short-grass'd green?
IRIS: A contract of true love to celebrate
    And some donation freely to estate[24]
    On the bless'd lovers.
CERES: Tell me, heavenly bow,
    If Venus or her son,[25] as thou dost know,
    Do now attend the Queen. Since they did plot
    The means that dusky Dis[26] my daughter got,
    Her and her blind boy's scandal'd company   90
    I have forsworn.
IRIS: Of her society
    Be not afraid. I met her Deity
    Cutting the clouds towards Paphos,[27] and her son
    Dove-drawn with her. Here thought they to have done
    Some wanton charm upon this man and maid,

---

13 *goddess of the rainbow and messenger of Juno.* **14** *goddess of agriculture.* **15** *meadows.* **16** *vetches,*
fodder. **17** *hay.* **18** *trenched.* **19** *ridged.* **20** *pruned or pole-clinging.* **21** *i.e.,*
Juno. **22** *swiftly.* **23** *wooded.* **24** *grant, bestow.* **25** *Cupid.* **26** *Pluto, who abducted Ceres's daughter Proserpine*
with the complicity of Venus and Cupid. **27** *a town in Cyprus; a centre of Venus-worship.*

Whose vows are, that no bed-right shall be paid
Till Hymen's torch be lighted; but in vain.
Mars's hot minion[28] is return'd again;
Her waspish-headed son has broke his arrows,
Swears he will shoot no more, but play with sparrows   100
And be a boy right out.[29]

[*Enter* JUNO.]

CERES: Highest queen of state,
    Great Juno, comes; I know her by her gait.
JUNO: How does my bounteous sister? Go with me
    To bless this twain, that they may prosperous be
    And honour'd in their issue.

(*They sing.*)

JUNO: Honour, riches, marriage blessing,
                Long continuance, and increasing,
                Hourly joys be still upon you!
                Juno sings her blessings on you.
CERES: Earth's increase, foison[30] plenty,   110
                Barns and garners never empty,
                Vines with clust'ring bunches growing,
                Plants with goodly burden bowing;
                Spring come to you at the farthest
                In the very end of harvest!
                Scarcity and want shall shun you,
                Ceres' blessing so is on you.

FERDINAND: This is a most majestic vision, and
    Harmonious charmingly. May I be bold
    To think these spirits?
PROSPERO: Spirits, which by mine art   120
    I have from their confines call'd to enact
    My present fancies.
FERDINAND: Let me live here ever!
    So rare a wond'red[31] father and a wise
    Makes this place Paradise.

(JUNO *and* CERES *whisper, and send* IRIS *on employment.*)

---

28 *mistress (i.e., Venus).*
29 *outright (i.e., an ordinary boy).*
30 *abundance.*
31 *wondrous, wonderful.*

PROSPERO: Sweet now, silence!
   Juno and Ceres whisper seriously.
   There's something else to do. Hush and be mute,
   Or else our spell is marr'd.
IRIS: You nymphs, call'd Naiades, of the wand'ring brooks,
   With your sedg'd crowns and ever-harmless looks,
   Leave your crisp³² channels, and on this green land   130
   Answer your summons. Juno does command.
   Come, temperate nymphs, and help to celebrate
   A contract of true love. Be not too late.

(Enter certain NYMPHS.*)*

   You sunburn'd sicklemen, of August weary,
   Come hither from the furrow and be merry.
   Make holiday. Your rye-straw hats put on,
   And these fresh nymphs encounter every one
   In country footing.³³

(Enter certain REAPERS, *properly habited. They join with the* NYMPHS *in a graceful
dance; towards the end whereof* PROSPERO *starts suddenly and speaks; after which, to a
strange, hollow, and confused noise, they heavily³⁴ vanish.)*

PROSPERO: [*aside*] I had forgot that foul conspiracy
   Of the beast Caliban and his confederates   140
   Against my life. The minute of their plot
   Is almost come. — [*To the* SPIRITS] Well done! Avoid!³⁵ No more!
FERDINAND: This is strange. Your father's in some passion
   That works him strongly.
MIRANDA: Never till this day
   Saw I him touch'd with anger so distemper'd.
PROSPERO: You do look, my son, in a mov'd sort,
   As if you were dismay'd. Be cheerful, sir.
   Our revels now are ended. These our actors,
   As I foretold you, were all spirits and
   Are melted into air, into thin air;   150
   And, like the baseless fabric of this vision,
   The cloud-capp'd towers, the gorgeous palaces,
   The solemn temples, the great globe itself,
   Yea, all which it inherit,³⁶ shall dissolve,
   And, like this insubstantial pageant faded,
   Leave not a rack³⁷ behind. We are such stuff

---

32 *rippling.*
33 *dancing.*
34 *reluctantly, mopingly.*
35 *Begone!*
36 *occupies, possesses.*
37 *shred, wisp of cloud.*

As dreams are made on, and our little life
Is rounded with a sleep. Sir, I am vex'd.
Bear with my weakness. My old brain is troubled.
Be not disturb'd with my infirmity.   160
If you be pleas'd, retire into my cell
And there repose. A turn or two I'll walk
To still my beating mind.
FERDINAND, MIRANDA: We wish you peace. *(Exeunt.)*

(Enter ARIEL.*)*

PROSPERO: Come with a thought! I thank thee, Ariel. Come.
ARIEL: Thy thoughts I cleave to. What's thy pleasure?
PROSPERO: Spirit,
We must prepare to meet with Caliban.
ARIEL: Ay, my commander. When I presented Ceres,
I thought to have told thee of it, but I fear'd
Lest I might anger thee.
PROSPERO: Say again, where didst thou leave these varlets?   170
ARIEL: I told you, sir, they were red-hot with drinking;
So full of valour that they smote the air
For breathing in their faces, beat the ground
For kissing of their feet; yet always bending
Towards their project.[38] Then I beat my tabor;
At which like unback'd[39] colts they prick'd their ears,
Advanc'd their eyelids, lifted up their noses
As they smelt music. So I charm'd their ears
That calf-like they my lowing follow'd through
Tooth'd briers, sharp furzes, pricking goss,[40] and thorns,   180
Which ent'red their frail shins. At last I left them
I' th' filthy mantled[41] pool beyond your cell,
There dancing up to th' chins, that the foul lake
O'erstunk their feet.
PROSPERO: This was well done, my bird.
Thy shape invisible retain thou still.
The trumpery[42] in my house, go bring it hither
For stale[43] to catch these thieves.
ARIEL: I go, I go. *(Exit.)*
PROSPERO: A devil, a born devil, on whose nature
Nurture can never stick! on whom my pains,
Humanely taken, all, all lost, quite lost!   190
And as with age his body uglier grows,
So his mind cankers. I will plague them all,
Even to roaring.

38 *i.e., the murder of Prospero.*
39 *unbroken, unridden.*
40 *gorse.*
41 *scummed.*
42 *finery (the* glistering apparel *of the next stage direction).*
43 *bait.*

(Enter ARIEL, *loaden with glistering apparel, etc.)*

Come, hang them on this line.

[PROSPERO *and* ARIEL *remain, invisible*]

(Enter CALIBAN, STEPHANO, *and* TRINCULO, *all wet.)*

CALIBAN: Pray you tread softly, that the blind mole may not
    Hear a foot fall. We now are near his cell.
STEPHANO: Monster, your fairy, which you say is a harmless fairy, has
    done little better than play'd the Jack[44] with us.
TRINCULO: Monster, I do smell all horse-piss, at which my nose is in
    great indignation.
STEPHANO: So is mine. Do you hear, monster? If I should take a dis-   *200*
    pleasure against you, look you —
TRINCULO: Thou wert but a lost monster.
CALIBAN: Good my lord, give me thy favour still.
    Be patient, for the prize I'll bring thee to
    Shall hoodwink[45] this mischance. Therefore speak softly.
    All's hush'd as midnight yet.
TRINCULO: Ay, but to lose our bottles in the pool —
STEPHANO: There is not only disgrace and dishonour in that, monster,
    but an infinite loss.
TRINCULO: That's more to me than my wetting. Yet this is your harm-   *210*
    less fairy, monster.
STEPHANO: I will fetch off my bottle, though I be o'er ears for my
    labour.
CALIBAN: Prithee, my king, be quiet. Seest thou here?
    This is the mouth o' th' cell. No noise, and enter.
    Do that good mischief which may make this island
    Thine own for ever, and I, thy Caliban,
    For aye thy foot-licker.
STEPHANO: Give me thy hand. I do begin to have bloody thoughts.
TRINCULO: O King Stephano! O peer! O worthy Stephano, look what a   *220*
    wardrobe here is for thee!
CALIBAN: Let it alone, thou fool! It is but trash.
TRINCULO: O, ho, monster! we know what belongs to a frippery.[46] O
    King Stephano!
STEPHANO: Put off that gown, Trinculo. By this hand, I'll have that
    gown!
TRINCULO: Thy Grace shall have it.
CALIBAN: The dropsy drown this fool! What do you mean
    To dote thus on such luggage?[47] Let't alone,
    And do the murder first. If he awake,

44 *knave.*
45 *put out of sight (and mind).*
46 *second-hand clothing store.*
47 *bulky encumbrance.*

From toe to crown he'll fill our skins with pinches,   230
Make us strange stuff.
STEPHANO: Be you quiet, monster. Mistress line, is not this my jerkin?[48]
[*Takes it down.*] Now is the jerkin under the line.[49] Now, jerkin, you
are like to lose your hair and prove a bald jerkin.
TRINCULO: Do, do! We steal by line and level,[50] an't like your Grace.
STEPHANO: I thank thee for that jest. Here's a garment for't. Wit shall
not go unrewarded while I am king of this country. 'Steal by line
and level' is an excellent pass of pate.[51] There's another garment
for't.
TRINCULO: Monster, come put some lime[52] upon your fingers, and away   240
with the rest!
CALIBAN: I will have none on't. We shall lose our time
And all be turn'd to barnacles, or to apes
With foreheads villainous low.
STEPHANO: Monster, lay-to your fingers. Help to bear this away where
my hogshead of wine is, or I'll turn you out of my kingdom. Go to,
carry this.
TRINCULO: And this.
STEPHANO: Ay, and this.

(*A noise of hunters heard. Enter divers*[53] SPIRITS *in shape of dogs and hounds, hunting
them about,* PROSPERO *and* ARIEL *setting them on.*)

PROSPERO: Hey, Mountain, hey!   250
ARIEL: Silver! there it goes, Silver!
PROSPERO: Fury, Fury! There, Tyrant, there! Hark, Hark!

[CALIBAN, STEPHANO, *and* TRINCULO *are driven out.*]

Go, charge my goblins that they grind their joints
With dry convulsions, shorten up their sinews
With aged cramps, and more pinch-spotted make them
Than pard[54] or cat o' mountain.
ARIEL: Hark, they roar.
PROSPERO: Let them be hunted soundly. At this hour
Lie at my mercy all mine enemies.
Shortly shall all my labours end, and thou
Shalt have the air at freedom. For a little   260
Follow, and do me service. (*Exeunt.*)

---

48 *jacket.* **49** *clothes line, tree, equator. The joke that follows involves the popular understanding that tropical
diseases contracted south of the equator involved loss of hair.* **50** *plumb line and carpenter's level; i.e., with
professional skill.* **51** *wit.* **52** *sticky substance.* **53** *diverse.* **54** *leopard.*

ACT FIVE

SCENE 1. [*Before the cell of* PROSPERO.]

(Enter PROSPERO *in his magic robes, and* ARIEL.*)*

PROSPERO: Now does my project gather to a head.
    My charms crack not, my spirits obey, and time
    Goes upright with his carriage. How's the day?
ARIEL: On the sixth hour, at which time, my lord,
    You said our work should cease.
PROSPERO: I did say so
    When first I rais'd the tempest. Say, my spirit,
    How fares the King and's followers?
ARIEL: Confin'd together
    In the same fashion as you gave in charge,
    Just as you left them — all prisoners, sir,
    In the line grove which weather-fends[1] your cell.   10
    They cannot budge till your release.[2] The King,
    His brother, and yours abide all three distracted,
    And the remainder mourning over them,
    Brimful of sorrow and dismay; but chiefly
    Him that you term'd, sir, the good old Lord Gonzalo.
    His tears runs down his beard like winter's drops
    From eaves of reeds.[3] Your charm so strongly works 'em,
    That if you now beheld them, your affections
    Would become tender.
PROSPERO: Dost thou think so, spirit?
ARIEL: Mine would, sir, were I human.
PROSPERO: And mine shall.   20
    Hast thou, which art but air, a touch, a feeling
    Of their afflictions, and shall not myself,
    One of their kind, that relish all as sharply
    Passion as they, be kindlier mov'd than thou art?
    Though with their high wrongs I am struck to th' quick,
    Yet with my nobler reason 'gainst my fury
    Do I take part. The rarer action is
    In virtue than in vengeance. They being penitent,
    The sole drift of my purpose doth extend
    Not a frown further. Go, release them, Ariel.   30
    My charms I'll break, their senses I'll restore,
    And they shall be themselves.
ARIEL: I'll fetch them, sir. *(Exit.)*
PROSPERO: [*makes a magic circle with his staff*] Ye elves of hills,
        brooks, standing lakes, and groves,

1 *acts as windbreak.*
2 *i.e., released by you.*
3 *i.e., thatched roofs.*

And ye that on the sands with printless foot
Do chase the ebbing Neptune, and do fly him
When he comes back; you demi-puppets that
By moonshine do the green sour ringlets[4] make,
Whereof the ewe not bites; and you whose pastime
Is to make midnight mushrumps,[5] that rejoice
To hear the solemn curfew; by whose aid   40
(Weak masters though ye be) I have bedimm'd
The noontide sun, call'd forth the mutinous winds,
And 'twixt the green sea and the azur'd vault
Set roaring war; to the dread rattling thunder
Have I given fire and rifted Jove's stout oak
With his own bolt; the strong-bas'd promontory
Have I made shake and by the spurs[6] pluck'd up
The pine and cedar; graves at my command
Have wak'd their sleepers, op'd, and let 'em forth
By my so potent art. But this rough magic   50
I here abjure; and when I have requir'd
Some heavenly music (which even now I do)
To work mine end upon their senses that
This airy charm is for, I'll break my staff,
Bury it certain fathoms in the earth,
And deeper than did ever plummet sound
I'll drown my book. *(Solemn music.)*

(Here enters ARIEL *before; then* ALONSO, *with a frantic gesture, attended by*
GONZALO; SEBASTIAN *and* ANTONIO *in like manner, attended by* ADRIAN *and*
FRANCISCO. *They all enter the circle which* PROSPERO *had made, and there stand*
charm'd; which PROSPERO *observing, speaks.)*

A solemn air, and the best comforter
To an unsettled fancy, cure thy brains,
Now useless, boil'd within thy skull! There stand,   60
For you are spell-stopp'd.
Holy Gonzalo, honourable man,
Mine eyes, ev'n sociable to the show of thine,
Fall fellowly drops.[7] The charm dissolves apace;
And as the morning steals upon the night,
Melting the darkness, so their rising senses
Begin to chase the ignorant fumes that mantle
Their clearer reason. O good Gonzalo,
My true preserver, and a loyal sir
To him thou follow'st! I will pay thy graces   70
Home[8] both in word and deed. Most cruelly

---

4 *fairy rings.*
5 *mushrooms.*
6 *roots.*
7 *sympathetic tears.*
8 *i.e., thoroughly, completely.*

Didst thou, Alonso, use me and my daughter.
Thy brother was a furtherer in the act.
Thou art pinch'd for't now, Sebastian. Flesh and blood,
You, brother mine, that entertain'd ambition,
Expell'd remorse and nature; who, with Sebastian
(Whose inward pinches therefore are most strong),
Would here have kill'd your king, I do forgive thee,
Unnatural though thou art. Their understanding
Begins to swell, and the approaching tide   80
Will shortly fill the reasonable shore,
That now lies foul and muddy. Not one of them
That yet looks on me or would know me. Ariel,
Fetch me the hat and rapier in my cell.
I will discase[9] me, and myself present
As I was sometime Milan.[10] Quickly, spirit!
Thou shalt ere long be free.

[*Exit* ARIEL *and returns immediately.*]

(ARIEL *sings and helps to attire him.*)

ARIEL: Where the bee sucks, there suck I;
                          In a cowslip's bell I lie;
                          There I couch when owls do cry.   90
                          On the bat's back I do fly
                          After summer merrily.
                     Merrily, merrily shall I live now
                     Under the blossom that hangs on the bough.

PROSPERO: Why, that's my dainty Ariel! I shall miss thee,
     But yet thou shalt have freedom. So, so, so.
     To the King's ship, invisible as thou art!
     There shalt thou find the mariners asleep
     Under the hatches. The master and the boatswain
     Being awake, enforce them to this place,   100
     And presently,[11] I prithee.
ARIEL: I drink the air before me, and return
     Or ere your pulse twice beat. *(Exit.)*
GONZALO: All torment, trouble, wonder, and amazement
     Inhabits here. Some heavenly power guide us
     Out of this fearful country!
PROSPERO: Behold, sir King,
     The wronged Duke of Milan, Prospero.

9 *disrobe.*
10 *i.e., the former Duke of Milan.*
11 *immediately.*

For more assurance that a living prince
Does now speak to thee, I embrace thy body,
And to thee and thy company I bid   *110*
A hearty welcome.
ALONSO: Whe'r[12] thou be'st he or no,
Or some enchanted trifle[13] to abuse me,
As late I have been, I not know. Thy pulse
Beats, as of flesh and blood; and, since I saw thee,
Th' affliction of my mind amends, with which,
I fear, a madness held me. This must crave[14]
(An if this be at all) a most strange story.
Thy dukedom I resign and do entreat
Thou pardon me my wrongs. But how should Prospero
Be living and be here?
PROSPERO: First, noble friend,   *120*
Let me embrace thine age, whose honour cannot
Be measur'd or confin'd.
GONZALO: Whether this be
Or be not, I'll not swear.
PROSPERO: You do yet taste
Some subtleties o' th' isle, that will not let you
Believe things certain. Welcome, my friends all.
[*Aside to* SEBASTIAN *and* ANTONIO] But you, my brace of lords, were I
        so minded,
I here could pluck his Highness' frown upon you,
And justify[15] you traitors. At this time
I will tell no tales.
SEBASTIAN: [*aside*]   The devil speaks in him.
PROSPERO: No.
For you, most wicked sir, whom to call brother   *130*
Would even infect my mouth, I do forgive
Thy rankest fault — all of them; and require
My dukedom of thee, which perforce I know
Thou must restore.
ALONSO: If thou beest Prospero,
Give us particulars of thy preservation;
How thou hast met us here, who three hours since
Were wrack'd upon this shore; where I have lost
(How sharp the point of this remembrance is!)
My dear son Ferdinand.
PROSPERO: I am woe[16] for't, sir.
ALONSO: Irreparable is the loss, and patience   *140*
Says it is past her cure.

---

12 *whether.*
13 *trick, apparition.*
14 *require.*
15 *prove.*
16 *sorry.*

PROSPERO: I rather think
    You have not sought her help, of whose soft grace
    For the like loss I have her sovereign aid
    And rest myself content.
ALONSO: You the like loss?
PROSPERO: As great to me as late;[17] and, supportable
    To make the dear[18] loss, have I means much weaker
    Than you may call to comfort you; for I
    Have lost my daughter.
ALONSO: A daughter?
    O heavens, that they were living both in Naples,
    The King and Queen there! That they were, I wish   150
    Myself were mudded in that oozy bed
    Where my son lies. When did you lose your daughter?
PROSPERO: In this last tempest. I perceive these lords
    At this encounter do so much admire[19]
    That they devour their reason, and scarce think
    Their eyes do offices of truth, their words
    Are natural breath. But, howsoev'r you have
    Been justled from your senses, know for certain
    That I am Prospero, and that very duke
    Which was thrust forth of Milan, who most strangely   160
    Upon this shore, where you were wrack'd, was landed
    To be the lord on't. No more yet of this;
    For 'tis a chronicle of day by day,
    Not a relation for a breakfast, nor
    Befitting this first meeting. Welcome, sir.
    This cell's my court. Here have I few attendants,
    And subjects none abroad.[20] Pray you look in.
    My dukedom since you have given me again,
    I will requite you with as good a thing,
    At least bring forth a wonder to content ye   170
    As much as me my dukedom.

(*Here* PROSPERO *discovers*[21] FERDINAND *and* MIRANDA *playing at chess.*)

MIRANDA: Sweet lord, you play me false.
FERDINAND: No, my dearest love,
    I would not for the world.
MIRANDA: Yes, for a score of kingdoms you should wrangle,
    And I would call it fair play.

17 *recent.*
18 *deeply felt, intensified.*
19 *wonder, marvel.*
20 *i.e., on the rest of the island.*
21 *reveals.*

ALONSO: If this prove
    A vision of the island, one dear son
    Shall I twice lose.
SEBASTIAN: A most high miracle!
FERDINAND: Though the seas threaten, they are merciful.
    I have curs'd them without cause. [*Kneels.*]
ALONSO: Now all the blessings
    Of a glad father compass thee about!   180
    Arise, and say how thou cam'st here.
MIRANDA: O, wonder!
    How many goodly creatures are there here!
    How beauteous mankind is! O brave new world
    That has such people in't!
PROSPERO: 'Tis new to thee.
ALONSO: What is this maid with whom thou wast at play?
    Your eld'st[22] acquaintance cannot be three hours.
    Is she the goddess that hath sever'd us
    And brought us thus together?
FERDINAND: Sir, she is mortal;
    But by immortal providence she's mine.
    I chose her when I could not ask my father   190
    For his advice, nor thought I had one. She
    Is daughter to this famous Duke of Milan,
    Of whom so often I have heard renown
    But never saw before; of whom I have
    Receiv'd a second life; and second father
    This lady makes him to me.
ALONSO: I am hers.
    But, O, how oddly will it sound that I
    Must ask my child forgiveness!
PROSPERO: There, sir, stop.
    Let us not burden our remembrance with
    A heaviness that's gone.
GONZALO: I have inly wept,   200
    Or should have spoke ere this. Look down, you gods,
    And on this couple drop a blessed crown!
    For it is you that have chalk'd forth the way
    Which brought us hither.
ALONSO: I say amen, Gonzalo.
GONZALO: Was Milan thrust from Milan that his issue
    Should become kings of Naples? O, rejoice
    Beyond a common joy, and set it down
    With gold on lasting pillars: In one voyage
    Did Claribel her husband find at Tunis,
    And Ferdinand her brother found a wife   210
    Where he himself was lost; Prospero his dukedom
    In a poor isle; and all of us ourselves
    When no man was his own.

22 *longest.*

ALONSO: [to FERDINAND and MIRANDA] Give me your hands.
    Let grief and sorrow still[23] embrace his heart
    That doth not wish you joy.
GONZALO: Be it so! Amen!

(Enter ARIEL, with the MASTER and BOATSWAIN amazedly following.)

    O, look, sir; look, sir! Here is more of us!
    I prophesied, if a gallows were on land,
    This fellow could not drown. Now, blasphemy,[24]
    That swear'st grace o'erboard, not an oath on shore?
    Hast thou no mouth by land? What is the news?   220
BOATSWAIN: The best news is that we have safely found
    Our king and company; the next, our ship,
    Which, but three glasses[25] since, we gave out split,
    Is tight and yare[26] and bravely rigg'd as when
    We first put out to sea.
ARIEL: [aside to PROSPERO]   Sir, all this service
    Have I done since I went.
PROSPERO: [aside to ARIEL]   My tricksy spirit!
ALONSO: These are not natural events; they strengthen
    From strange to stranger. Say, how came you hither?
BOATSWAIN: If I did think, sir, I were well awake,
    I'd strive to tell you. We were dead of sleep   230
    And (how we know not) all clapp'd under hatches;
    Where, but even now, with strange and several noises
    Of roaring, shrieking, howling, jingling chains,
    And moe[27] diversity of sounds, all horrible,
    We were awak'd; straightway at liberty;
    Where we, in all her trim, freshly beheld
    Our royal, good, and gallant ship; our master
    Cap'ring[28] to eye her. On a trice, so please you,
    Even in a dream, were we divided from them
    And were brought moping[29] hither.
ARIEL: [aside to PROSPERO]   Was't well done?   240
PROSPERO: [aside to ARIEL] Bravely, my diligence. Thou shalt be free.
ALONSO: This is as strange a maze as e'er men trod,
    And there is in this business more than nature
    Was ever conduct[30] of. Some oracle
    Must rectify our knowledge.
PROSPERO: Sir, my liege,
    Do not infest your mind with beating on
    The strangeness of this business. At pick'd leisure,
    Which shall be shortly, single I'll resolve you
    (Which to you shall seem probable) of every

---

23 always, forever. **24** i.e., blasphemous fellow. **25** hours. **26** shipshape. **27** more. **28** i.e., dancing with joy. **29** dazed. **30** conductor.

These happen'd accidents; till when, be cheerful   *250*
And think of each thing well. [*Aside to* ARIEL] Come hither, spirit.
Set Caliban and his companions free.
Untie the spell. [*Exit* ARIEL.] How fares my gracious sir?
There are yet missing of your company
Some few odd lads that you remember not.

(*Enter* ARIEL, *driving in* CALIBAN, STEPHANO, *and* TRINCULO, *in their stol'n apparel.*)

STEPHANO: Every man shift for all the rest, and let no man take care for
    himself; for all is but fortune. Coragio,³¹ bully-monster, coragio!
TRINCULO: If these be true spies which I wear in my head, here's a
    goodly sight.
CALIBAN: O Setebos, these be brave spirits indeed!   *260*
    How fine my master is! I am afraid
    He will chastise me.
SEBASTIAN: Ha, ha!
    What things are these, my Lord Antonio?
    Will money buy 'em?
ANTONIO: Very like. One of them
    Is a plain fish and no doubt marketable.
PROSPERO: Mark but the badges³² of these men, my lords,
    Then say if they be true.³³ This misshapen knave,
    His mother was a witch, and one so strong
    That could control the moon, make flows and ebbs,
    And deal in her³⁴ command without³⁵ her power.   *270*
    These three have robb'd me, and this demi-devil
    (For he's a bastard one) had plotted with them
    To take my life. Two of these fellows you
    Must know and own; this thing of darkness I
    Acknowledge mine.
CALIBAN: I shall be pinch'd to death.
ALONSO: Is not this Stephano, my drunken butler?
SEBASTIAN: He is drunk now. Where had he wine?
ALONSO: And Trinculo is reeling ripe. Where should they
    Find this grand liquor that hath gilded 'em?
    How cam'st thou in this pickle?   *280*
TRINCULO: I have been in such a pickle, since I saw you last, that I fear
    me will never out of my bones. I shall not fear fly-blowing.³⁶

---

31 *courage.*
32 *insignia indicating the allegiance of a servant (in this case, stolen clothes indicate untrustworthiness and*
    rascality).
33 *honest.*
34 *i.e., the moon's.*
35 *beyond.*
36 *rotting (he is well pickled).*

SEBASTIAN: Why, how now, Stephano?
STEPHANO: O, touch me not! I am not Stephano, but a cramp.
PROSPERO: You'd be king o' the isle, sirrah?[37]
STEPHANO: I should have been a sore one then.
ALONSO: This is as strange a thing as e'er I look'd on.
PROSPERO: He is as disproportion'd in his manners
    As in his shape. Go, sirrah, to my cell;
    Take with you your companions. As you look   *290*
    To have my pardon, trim it handsomely.
CALIBAN: Ay, that I will; and I'll be wise hereafter,
    And seek for grace. What a thrice-double ass
    Was I to take this drunkard for a god
    And worship this dull fool!
PROSPERO: Go to! Away!
ALONSO: Hence, and bestow your luggage where you found it.
SEBASTIAN: Or stole it rather.

    [*Exeunt* CALIBAN, STEPHANO, *and* TRINCULO.]

PROSPERO: Sir, I invite your Highness and your train
    To my poor cell, where you shall take your rest
    For this one night; which, part of it, I'll waste[38]   *300*
    With such discourse as, I not doubt, shall make it
    Go quick away — the story of my life,
    And the particular accidents[39] gone by
    Since I came to this isle; and in the morn
    I'll bring you to your ship, and so to Naples,
    Where I have hope to see the nuptial
    Of these our dear-belov'd solemnized;
    And thence retire me to my Milan, where
    Every third thought shall be my grave.
ALONSO: I long
    To hear the story of your life, which must   *310*
    Take the ear strangely.
PROSPERO: I'll deliver[40] all;
    And promise you calm seas, auspicious gales,
    And sail[41] so expeditious that shall catch
    Your royal fleet far off. [*Aside to* ARIEL] My Ariel, chick,
    That is thy charge. Then to the elements
    Be free, and fare thou well — Please you draw near.

    (*Exeunt omnes.*)

37 *sir (addressed to an inferior).*
38 *spend.*
39 *incidents, occurrences.*
40 *tell, report.*
41 *course, voyage.*

EPILOGUE

(Spoken by PROSPERO.*)*

Now my charms are all o'erthrown,
And what strength I have's mine own,
Which is most faint. Now 'tis true
I must be here confin'd by you,
Or sent to Naples. Let me not,
Since I have my dukedom got
And pardon'd the deceiver, dwell
In this bare island by your spell;
But release me from my bands[42]
With the help of your good hands.[43]   10
Gentle breath[44] of yours my sails
Must fill, or else my project fails,
Which was to please. Now I want[45]
Spirits to enforce, art to enchant;
And my ending is despair
Unless I be reliev'd by prayer,[46]
Which pierces so that it assaults
Mercy itself and frees all faults.
As you from crimes would pardon'd be,
Let your indulgence set me free.   20

(Exit.)

---

42 *bonds.*
43 *i.e., applause.*
44 *commentary, acclaim.*
45 *lack.*
46 *i.e., this epilogue, petition.*

APHRA BEHN

(1640–1689)

See the biographical note for Aphra Behn in the Poetry section.

INTRODUCTION TO *THE ROVER*

*T*he *Rover* (1677) was Behn's most successful play and one of the very few plays written by a woman to be acted frequently on the English stage. First performed in the presence of King Charles II (who was highly amused by it), it was very popular: Behn produced a sequel, *The Second Part of the Rover*, in 1681. *The Rover* was frequently performed until 1760. By then, tastes had grown more fastidious, and the play was dropped from the repertoire of the English acting companies; in 1790, the actor and manager John Philip Kemble produced an adaptation, entitled *Love in Many Masks*, which, he claimed, "purified" the play of its earthy action and racy language. After falling out of favour in the nineteenth century and the first half of the twentieth, it is once again enjoying popularity.

Though the play was first performed in 1677, it is set in the years before 1660, the date when the English people rejected the Puritan austerity of the Commonwealth, which had come to power under Oliver Cromwell in 1649, and restored the monarchy, in the person of Charles II. The leading men in the play are, as the play's subtitle and opening scenes make clear, "banished cavaliers" — royalist supporters of Charles II whose estates have been seized and who are thus social and economic freebooters. The Puritans, who had suppressed most forms of amusement, including public theatres, had become hated by the time they were driven out; Behn's play celebrates the aristocratic, pleasure-loving, anti-Puritan rule of Charles II, "the Merry Monarch." By setting her play in Naples (like most of Italy, part of the Spanish Empire in the seventeenth century) and during carnival-time, Behn accentuates her play's uninhibited, anti-Puritanical world.

More than simply the monarchy was restored in 1660. The Church of England, rule by Parliament, and the public theatres also returned to British life. But the new British stage was very different from what it had been: female roles were now played by actresses instead of by young boys, and the proscenium stage replaced the Elizabethan and Jacobean thrust stage. Even more importantly, the Restoration stage was primarily a court amusement. Whereas there had been about seventeen theatres in Shakespeare's London, the much larger city of Behn's time had only two theatres; whereas Shakespeare's Globe Theatre held about 3000 people and was attended by people from all walks of life, Behn's Dorset Garden Theatre held 500 to 600 and was dominated by the aristocracy. Significantly, the Prologue to Behn's play was written by "a Person of Quality" (that is, one of rank), and there is an opposition throughout between aristocratic and commercial values — between "quality" and money. Moreover, *The Rover* exemplifies the kind of play dominant in the cavalier and hedonistic Restoration theatre: the sex-comedy. Characterized by complex and interwoven intrigues, tough-minded inquiry into conventional sexual ethics, and an attempt to harmonize the claims of impulse and morality (as Willmore and Hellena eventually do), these plays present a world in which prose is the norm and poetry a departure from that norm.

As a woman, Behn handles this standard form distinctively. Her leading man, Willmore, like other heroes of Restoration comedy, is gallant, generous, scheming, unscrupulous, sexually predatory: his name says it all. Behn's heroine Hellena, however, is a striking departure. She is like other comic heroines in that she is witty and intelligent, high-spirited and independent-minded; what makes her different is Behn's emphasis upon her struggle to find a way of life that expresses her active energies, one that is socially acceptable and yet avoids the two obvious (and equally passive) alternatives — chaste retirement from the world as a nun, or an arranged marriage that amounts to prostitution. Even more indicative of Behn's female per-spective are the acts of violence, real and threatened, directed against women in the play and the sympathetic portrayal of Angelica Bianca, the prostitute. In fact, Angelica's sign, a hugh image of herself as a commodity, dominates the stage when the play is performed, and the problems that she raises have hardly been resolved by the play's conclusion. To a very large degree, it is Behn's special perspective as a woman writer that makes *The Rover* so significant for readers and playgoers of our age.

The Rover
or The Banished Cavaliers

DRAMATIS PERSONAE

MEN

DON ANTONIO, *the Vice-Roy's Son*

DON PEDRO, *a Noble Spaniard, his Friend*

BELVILE, *an English Colonel in love with* FLORINDA

WILLMORE, *the Rover*

FREDERICK, *an English Gentleman, and Friend to* BELVILE *and* BLUNT

BLUNT, *an English Country Gentleman*

STEPHANO, *Servant to* DON PEDRO

PHILIPPO, LUCETTA's *Gallant*

SANCHO, *Pimp to* LUCETTA

BISKY *and* SEBASTIAN, *two Bravoes*[1] *to* ANGELICA

DIEGO, *Page to* DON ANTONIO

PAGE to HELLENA

BOY, *Page to* BELVILE

BLUNT'S MAN

OFFICERS *and* SOLDIERS

WOMEN

FLORINDA, *Sister to* DON PEDRO

HELLENA, *a gay young Woman design'd for a Nun, and Sister to* FLORINDA

VALERIA, *a Kinswoman to* FLORINDA

ANGELICA BIANCA, *a famous Curtezan*[2]

MORETTA, *her Woman*

CALLIS, *Governess to* FLORINDA *and* HELLENA

LUCETTA, *a jilting Wench*

THE SCENE — *Naples, in Carnival-time.*

PROLOGUE

Written by a Person of Quality

WITS, *like Physicians, never can agree,*
When of a different Society;
And Rabel's Drops[1] *were never more cry'd down*
By all the Learned Doctors of the Town,
Than a new Play, whose Author is unknown:
Nor can those Doctors with more Malice sue
(And powerful Purses) the dissenting Few,
Than those with an insulting Pride do rail
At all who are not of their own Cabal.[2]
  If a Young Poet hit your Humour right,   10
You judge him then out of Revenge and Spite;
So amongst Men there are ridiculous Elves,[3]
Who Monkeys hate for being too like themselves:
So that the Reason of the Grand Debate,
Why Wit so oft is damn'd, when good Plays take,
Is, that you censure as you love or hate.
Thus, like a learned Conclave, Poets sit

1 *hired ruffians, desperadoes.*
2 *courtesan.*

1 *a popular patent medicine.*
2 *secret group.*
3 *devils, malicious persons.*

Catholick Judges both of Sense and Wit,
And damn or save, as they themselves think fit.
Yet those who to others Faults are so severe,   20
Are not so perfect, but themselves may err.
Some write correct indeed, but then the whole
(Bating[4] *their own dull Stuff i' th' Play) is stole:*
As Bees do suck from Flowers their Honey-dew,
So they rob others, striving to please you.
    Some write their Characters genteel and fine,
But then they do so toil for every Line,
That what to you does easy seem, and plain,
Is the hard issue of their labouring Brain.
And some th' Effects of all their Pains we see,   30
Is but to mimick good Extempore.
Others by long Converse about the Town,
Have Wit enough to write a leud Lampoon,
But their chief Skill lies in a Baudy Song.
In short, the only Wit that's now in Fashion
Is but the Gleanings of good Conversation.
As for the Author of this coming Play,
I ask'd him what he thought fit I should say,
In thanks for your good Company to day:
He call'd me Fool, and said it was well known,   40
You came not here for our sakes, but your own.
New Plays are stuff'd with Wits, and with Debauches,
That crowd and sweat like Cits[5] *in May-day Coaches.*[6]

ACT ONE

SCENE 1. *(A chamber.)*

(Enter FLORINDA *and* HELLENA.*)*

FLORINDA: What an impertinent thing is a young Girl bred in a
    Nunnery! How full of Questions! Prithee no more, *Hellena;* I have
    told thee more than thou understand'st already.
HELLENA: The more's my Grief; I wou'd fain know as much as you,
    which makes me so inquisitive; nor is't enough to know you're a
    Lover, unless you tell me too, who 'tis you sigh for.
FLORINDA: When you are a Lover, I'll think you fit for a Secret of that
    nature.
HELLENA: 'Tis true, I was never a Lover yet — but I begin to have a
    shreud Guess, what 'tis to be so, and fancy it very pretty to sigh,   10
    and sing, and blush and wish, and dream and wish, and long and

---

4 *excepting.*
5 *middle-class citizens.*
6 *on May Day (May 1), Londoners paraded around Hyde Park.*

wish to see the Man; and when I do, look pale and tremble; just as you did when my Brother brought home the fine *English* Colonel to see you — what do you call him? Don *Belvile*.

FLORINDA: Fie, *Hellena*.

HELLENA: That Blush betrays you — I am sure 'tis so — or is it Don *Antonio* the Vice-Roy's Son? — or perhaps the rich old Don *Vincentio*, whom my father designs for your Husband? — Why do you blush again?

FLORINDA: With Indignation; and how near soever my Father thinks I am to marrying that hated Object, I shall let him see I understand better what's due to my Beauty, Birth and Fortune, and more to my Soul, than to obey those unjust Commands.

HELLENA: Now hang me, if I don't love thee for that dear Disobedience. I love Mischief strangely, as most of our Sex do, who are come to love nothing else — But tell me, dear *Florinda*, don't you love that fine *Anglese?*[1] — for I vow next to loving him my self, 'twill please me most that you do so, for he is so gay and so handsome.

FLORINDA: *Hellena*, a Maid design'd for a Nun ought not to be so curious in a Discourse of Love.

HELLENA: And dost thou think that ever I'll be a Nun? Or at least till I'm so old, I'm fit for nothing else. Faith no, Sister; and that which makes me long to know whether you love *Belvile*, is because I hope he has some mad Companion or other, that will spoil my Devotion; nay I'm resolv'd to provide my self this Carnival, if there be e'er a handsome Fellow of my Humour above Ground, tho I ask first.[2]

FLORINDA: Prithee be not so wild.

HELLENA: Now you have provided your self with a Man, you take no Care for poor me — Prithee tell me, what dost thou see about me that is unfit for Love — have not I a world of Youth? a Humour gay? a Beauty passable? a Vigour desirable? well shap'd? clean limb'd? sweet breath'd? and Sense enough to know how all these ought to be employ'd to the best Advantage: yes, I do and will. Therefore lay aside your Hopes of my Fortune, by my being a Devotee, and tell me how you came acquainted with this *Belvile*; for I perceive you knew him before he came to *Naples*.

FLORINDA: Yes, I knew him at the Siege of *Pampelona*, he was then a Colonel of *French* Horse, who when the Town was ransack'd, nobly treated my Brother and my self, preserving us from all Insolencies; and I must own, (besides great Obligations) I have I know not what, that pleads kindly for him about my Heart, and will suffer no other to enter — But see my Brother.

(*Enter* DON PEDRO, STEPHANO, *with a Masquing Habit,*[3] *and* CALLIS.)

---

1 *Englishman.*
2 *even if I have to do the asking.*
3 *masquerade costume.*

PEDRO: Good morrow, Sister. Pray, when saw you your Lover Don
    Vincentio?

FLORINDA: I know not, Sir — *Callis*, when was he here? for I consider it
    so little, I know not when it was.

PEDRO: I have a Command from my Father here to tell you, you ought
    not to despise him, a Man of so vast a Fortune, and such a Passion
        for you — *Stephano*, my things — *(Puts on his Masquing Habit.)*

FLORINDA: A Passion for me! 'tis more than e'er I saw, or had a desire   60
    should be known — I hate *Vincentio*, and I would not have a Man so
    dear to me as my Brother follow the ill Customs of our Country,
    and make a Slave of his Sister — And Sir, my Father's Will, I'm
    sure, you may divert.

PEDRO: I know not how dear I am to you, but I wish only to be rank'd in
    your Esteem, equal with the *English* Colonel *Belvile* — Why do you
    frown and blush? Is there any Guilt belongs to the Name of that
    Cavalier?

FLORINDA: I'll not deny I value *Belvile*: when I was expos'd to such
    Dangers as the licens'd Lust of common Soldiers threatned, when   70
    Rage and Conquest flew thro the City — then *Belvile*, this Criminal
    for my sake, threw himself into all Dangers to save my Honour, and
    will you not allow him my Esteem?

PEDRO: Yes, pay him what you will in Honour — but you must consider
    Don *Vincentio's* Fortune, and the Jointure[4] he'll make you.

FLORINDA: Let him consider my Youth, Beauty and Fortune; which
    ought not to be thrown away on his Age and Jointure.

PEDRO: 'Tis true, he's not so young and fine a Gentleman as that *Belvile*
    — but what Jewels will that Cavalier present you with? those of his
    Eyes and Heart?   80

HELLENA: And are not those better than any Don *Vincentio* has brought
    from the *Indies?*

PEDRO: Why how now! Has your Nunnery-breeding taught you to
    understand the Value of Hearts and Eyes?

HELLENA: Better than to believe *Vincentio* deserves Value from any
    woman — He may perhaps encrease her Bags, but not her Family.

PEDRO: This is fine — Go up to your Devotion, you are not design'd for
    the Conversation of Lovers.

HELLENA: *(Aside.)* Nor Saints yet a while I hope — Is't not enough you
    make a Nun of me, but you must cast my Sister away too, exposing   90
    her to a worse Confinement than a religious Life?

PEDRO: The Girl's mad — Is it a Confinement to be carry'd into the
    Country, to an antient Villa belonging to the Family of the *Vincentio's*
    these five hundred Years, and have no other Prospect than that
    pleasing one of seeing all her own that meets her Eyes — a fine Air,
    large Fields and Gardens, where she may walk and gather Flowers?

HELLENA: When? By Moon-Light? For I'm sure she dares not encounter
    with the heat of the Sun; that were a Task only for Don *Vincentio*
    and his *Indian* Breeding, who loves it in the Dog-days[5] — And if

---

4 *estate settled on a wife that she possesses after her husband's death.*
5 *the hottest days of summer, so called because Sirius, the Dog Star, is overhead.*

these be her daily Divertisements, what are those of the Night? to   *100*
lie in a wide Moth-eaten Bed-Chamber with Furniture in Fashion in
the Reign of King *Sancho* the First;[6] the Bed that which his Forefa-
thers liv'd and dy'd in.

PEDRO: Very well.

HELLENA: This Apartment (new furbisht and fitted out for the young
   Wife) he (out of Freedom) makes his Dressing-room; and being a
   frugal and a jealous Coxcomb, instead of a Valet to uncase his feeble
   Carcase, he desires you to do that Office — Signs of Favour, I'll
   assure you, and such as you must not hope for, unless your Woman
   be out of the way.   *110*

PEDRO: Have you done yet?

HELLENA: That Honour being past, the Giant stretches it self, yawns and
   sighs a Belch or two as loud as a Musket, throws himself into Bed,
   and expects you in his foul Sheets, and e'er you can get your self
   undrest, calls you with a Snore or two — And are not these fine
   Blessings to a young Lady?

PEDRO: Have you done yet?

HELLENA: And this man you must kiss, nay, you must kiss none but him
   too — and nuzle thro his Beard to find his Lips — and this you
   must submit to for threescore Years, and all for a Jointure.   *120*

PEDRO: For all your Character of Don *Vincentio*, she is as like to marry
   him as she was before.

HELLENA: Marry Don *Vincentio*! hang me, such a Wedlock would be
   worse than Adultery with another Man: I had rather see her in the
   Hostel de Dieu,[7] to waste her Youth there in Vows, and be a Handmaid
   to Lazers[8] and Cripples, than to lose it in such a Marriage.

PEDRO: You have consider'd, Sister, that *Belvile* has no Fortune to bring
   you to, is banisht his Country, despis'd at home, and pity'd abroad.

HELLENA: What then? the Vice-Roy's Son is better than that Old Sir
   Fifty. Don *Vincentio*! Don *Indian*! he thinks he's trading to *Gambo*[9] still,   *130*
   and wou'd barter himself (that Bell and Bawble) for your Youth and
   Fortune.

PEDRO: *Callis*, take her hence, and lock her up all this Carnival, and at
   Lent she shall begin her everlasting Penance in a Monastery.

HELLENA: I care not, I had rather be a Nun, than be oblig'd to marry as
   you wou'd have me, if I were design'd for't.

PEDRO: Do not fear the Blessing of that Choice — you shall be a Nun.

HELLENA: *(Aside.)* Shall I so? you may chance to be mistaken in my way
   of Devotion — A Nun! yes I am like to make a fine Nun! I have an
   excellent Humour for a Grate: No, I'll have a Saint of my own to   *140*
   pray to shortly, if I like any that dares venture on me.

---

6 *king of Spain in the tenth century.*
7 *hospital for the poor operated by a religious order.*
8 *beggars afflicted with an infectious disease such as leprosy.*
9 *a British colony in western Africa.*

PEDRO: *Callis*, make it your Business to watch this wild Cat. As for you,
    Florinda, I've only try'd you all this while, and urg'd my Father's Will;
    but mine is, that you would love *Antonio*, he is brave and young, and
    all that can compleat the Happiness of a gallant Maid — This
    Absence of my Father will give us opportunity to free you from
    Vincentio, by marrying here, which you must do to morrow.
FLORINDA: To morrow!
PEDRO: To morrow, or 'twill be too late — 'tis not my Friendship to
    Antonio, which makes me urge this, but Love to thee, and Hatred to   *150*
    Vincentio — therefore resolve upon't to morrow.
FLORINDA: Sir, I shall strive to do, as shall become your Sister.
PEDRO: I'll both believe and trust you — Adieu.

(Exit PEDRO *and* STEPHANO.*)*

HELLENA: As becomes his Sister! — That is, to be as resolved your way,
    as he is his — *(*HELLENA *goes to* CALLIS.*)*
FLORINDA: I ne'er till now perceiv'd my Ruin near,
    I've no Defence against *Antonio's* Love,
    For he has all the Advantages of Nature,
    The moving Arguments of Youth and Fortune.
HELLENA: But hark you, *Callis*, you will not be so cruel to lock me up   *160*
    indeed: will you?
CALLIS: I must obey the Commands I hate — besides, do you consider
    what a Life you are going to lead?
HELLENA: Yes, *Callis*, that of a Nun: and till then I'll be indebted a World
    of Prayers to you, if you let me now see, what I never did, the Div-
    ertisements of a Carnival.
CALLIS: What, go in Masquerade? 'twill be a fine farewell to the World I
    take it — pray what wou'd you do there?
HELLENA: That which all the World does, as I am told, be as mad as the
    rest, and take all innocent Freedom — Sister, you'll go too, will you   *170*
    not? come prithee be not sad — We'll out-wit twenty Brothers, if
    you'll be ruled by me — Come put off this dull Humour with your
    Clothes, and assume one as gay, and as fantastick as the Dress my
    Cousin *Valeria* and I have provided, and let's ramble.
FLORINDA: *Callis*, will you give us leave to go?
CALLIS: *(Aside.)* I have a youthful Itch of going myself — Madam, if I
    thought your Brother might not know it, and I might wait on you,
    for by my troth I'll not trust young Girls alone.
FLORINDA: Thou see'st my Brother's gone already, and thou shalt attend
    and watch us.   *180*

(Enter STEPHANO.*)*

STEPHANO: Madam, the Habits are come, and your Cousin Valeria is
    drest, and stays for you.

FLORINDA: 'Tis well — I'll write a Note, and if I chance to see *Belvile*, and want an opportunity to speak to him, that shall let him know what I've resolv'd in favour of him.

HELLENA: Come, let's in and dress us. *(Exeunt.)*

SCENE 2. *(A Long Street.)*

(Enter BELVILE, *melancholy,* BLUNT *and* FREDERICK.*)*

FREDERICK: Why, what the Devil ails the Colonel, in a time when all the World is gay, to look like mere Lent thus? Hadst thou been long enough in *Naples* to have been in love, I should have sworn some such Judgment had befall'n thee.

BELVILE: No, I have made no new Amours since I came to Naples.

FREDERICK: You have left none behind you in Paris.

BELVILE: Neither.

FREDERICK: I can't divine the Cause then; unless the old Cause, the want of Money.

BLUNT: And another old Cause, the want of a Wench — Wou'd not that revive you?   10

BELVILE: You're mistaken, *Ned*.

BLUNT: Nay, 'Sheartlikins,[1] then thou art past Cure.

FREDERICK: I have found it out; thou hast renew'd thy Acquaintance with the Lady that cost thee so many Sighs at the Siege of *Pampelona* — pox on't, what d'ye call her — her Brother's a noble *Spaniard* — Nephew to the dead General — *Florinda* — ay, *Florinda* — And will nothing serve thy turn but that damn'd virtuous Woman, whom on my Conscience thou lov'st in spite too, because thou seest little or no possibility of gaining her?   20

BELVILE: Thou art mistaken, I have Interest enough in that lovely Virgin's Heart, to make me proud and vain, were it not abated by the Severity of a Brother, who perceiving my Happiness —

FREDERICK: Has civilly forbid thee the House?

BELVILE: 'Tis so, to make way for a powerful Rival, the Vice-Roy's Son, who has the advantage of me, in being a Man of Fortune, a *Spaniard*, and her Brother's Friend; which gives him liberty to make his Court, whilst I have recourse only to Letters, and distant Looks from her Window, which are as soft and kind as those which Heav'n sends down on Penitents.   30

BLUNT: Hey day! 'Sheartlikins, Simile! by this Light the Man is quite spoil'd — *Frederick*, what the Devil are we made of, that we cannot be thus concern'd for a Wench? — 'Sheartlikins, our *Cupids* are like the Cooks of the Camp, they can roast or boil a Woman, but they have none of the fine Tricks to set 'em off, no Hogoes to make the Sauce pleasant, and the Stomach sharp.

---

1 *by God's heart (a mild oath).*

FREDERICK: I dare swear I have had a hundred as young, kind and hand-some as this *Florinda*; and Dogs eat me, if they were not as trouble-some to me i'th' Morning as they were welcome o'er night.

BLUNT: And yet, I warrant, he wou'd not touch another Woman, if he might have her for nothing.

BELVILE: That's thy Joy, a cheap Whore.

BLUNT: Why, 'dsheartlikins, I love a frank Soul — When did you ever hear of an honest Woman that took a Man's Money? I warrant 'em good ones — But, Gentlemen, you may be free, you have been kept so poor with Parliaments and Protectors, that the little Stock you have is not worth preserving — but I thank my Stars, I have more Grace than to forfeit my Estate by Cavaliering.[2]

BELVILE: Methinks only following the Court should be sufficient to enti-tle 'em to that.

BLUNT: 'Sheartlikins, they know I follow it to do it no good, unless they pick a hole in my Coat for lending you Money now and then; which is a greater Crime to my Conscience, Gentlemen, than to the Common-wealth.

(Enter WILLMORE.*)*

WILLMORE: Ha! dear *Belvile!* noble Colonel!

BELVILE: *Willmore!* welcome ashore, my dear Rover! — what happy Wind blew us this good Fortune?

WILLMORE: Let me salute you my dear *Fred*, and then command me — How is't honest Lad?

FREDERICK: Faith, Sir, the old Complement, infinitely the better to see my dear mad *Willmore* again — Prithee why camest thou ashore? and where's the Prince?[3]

WILLMORE: He's well, and reigns still Lord of the watery Element — I must aboard again within a Day or two, and my Business ashore was only to enjoy my self a little this Carnival.

BELVILE: Pray know our new Friend, Sir, he's but bashful, a raw Travel-ler, but honest, stout, and one of us. *(Embraces* BLUNT.*)*

WILLMORE: That you esteem him, gives him an Interest here.

BLUNT: Your Servant, Sir.

WILLMORE: But well — Faith I'm glad to meet you again in a warm Cli-mate, where the kind Sun has its god-like Power still over the Wine and Woman. — Love and Mirth are my Business in *Naples*; and if I mistake not the Place, here's an excellent Market for Chapmen[4] of my Humour.

BELVILE: See here be those kind Merchants of Love you look for.

---

2 *during the English Civil War, many Royalist ("Cavalier") estates were confiscated by order of the Puritan government of Oliver Cromwell, Lord Protector of England.*

3 *Prince Charles, leader of the Royalist forces, who became Charles II in 1660.*

4 *pedlars, merchants.*

(Enter several Men in masquing Habits, some playing on Musick, others dancing after; Women drest like Curtezans, with Papers pinn'd to their Breasts, and Baskets of Flowers in their Hands.)

BLUNT: 'Sheartlikins, what have we here!

FREDERICK: Now the Game begins.

WILLMORE: Fine pretty Creatures! may a stranger have leave to look and love? — What's here — *Roses for every Month! (Reads the Paper.)*

BLUNT: Roses for every Month! what means that?   80

BELVILE: They are, or wou'd have you think they're Curtezans, who here in *Naples* are to be hir'd by the Month.

WILLMORE: Kind and obliging to inform us — Pray where do these Roses grow? I would fain plant some of 'em in a Bed of mine.

WOMAN: Beware such Roses, Sir.

WILLMORE: A Pox of fear: I'll be bak'd with thee between a pair of Sheets, and that's thy proper Still, so I might but strow such Roses over me and under me — Fair one, wou'd you wou'd give me leave to gather at your Bush this idle Month, I wou'd go near to make some Body smell of it all the Year after.   90

BELVILE: And thou hast need of such a Remedy, for thou stinkest of Tar and Rope-ends, like a Dock or Pesthouse.

(The Woman puts her self into the Hands of a Man, and they Exit.)

WILLMORE: Nay, nay, you shall not leave me so.

BELVILE: By all means use no Violence here.

WILLMORE: Death! just as I was going to be damnably in love, to have her led off! I could pluck that Rose out of his Hand, and even kiss the Bed, the Bush it grew in.

FREDERICK: No Friend to Love like a long Voyage at Sea.

BLUNT: Except a Nunnery, *Fred.*

WILLMORE: Death! but will they not be kind, quickly be kind? Thou   100
know'st I'm no tame Sigher, but a rampant Lion of the Forest.

(Two Men drest all over with Horns[5] of several sorts, making Grimaces at one another, with Papers pinn'd on their Backs, advance from the farther end of the Scene.)

BELVILE: Oh the fantastical Rogues, how they are dress'd! 'tis a Satire against the whole Sex.

WILLMORE: Is this a Fruit that grows in this warm Country?

BELVILE: Yes: 'Tis pretty to see these *Italians* start, swell, and stab at the Word *Cuckold*, and yet stumble at Horns on every Threshold.

WILLMORE: See what's on their Back *(Reads.) Flowers for every Night.* — Ah Rogue! And more sweet than Roses of ev'ry Month! This is a Gar-diner of *Adam's* own breeding. *(They dance.)*

BELVILE: What think you of those grave People? — is a Wake in *Essex* half   110
so mad or extravagant?

---

5 *horns were the traditional emblem of a cuckold.*

WILLMORE: I like their sober grave way, 'tis a kind of legal authoriz'd Fornication, where the Men are not chid for't, nor the Women despis'd,
as amongst our dull *English*; even the Monsieurs[6] want that part of
good Manners.

BELVILE: But here in *Italy* a Monsieur is the humblest best-bred Gentleman — Duels are so baffled by Bravoes that an age shews not one,
but between a *Frenchman* and a Hang-man, who is as much too hard
for him on the Piazza, as they are for a *Dutchman* on the new Bridge
— But see another Crew. 120

(Enter FLORINDA, HELLENA, *and* VALERIA, *drest like Gipsies;* CALLIS *and*
STEPHANO, LUCETTA, PHILIPPO *and* SANCHO *in Masquerade.)*

HELLENA: Sister, there's your *Englishman*, and with him a handsome
proper Fellow — I'll to him, and instead of telling him his Fortune,
try my own.

WILLMORE: Gipsies, on my Life — Sure these will prattle if a Man cross
their Hands.[7] *(Goes to* HELLENA*)* — Dear pretty (and I hope) young
Devil, will you tell an amorous Stranger what Luck he's like to
have?

HELLENA: Have a care how you venture with me, Sir, lest I pick your
Pocket, which will more vex your *English* Humour, than an *Italian*
Fortune will please you. 130

WILLMORE: How the Devil cam'st thou to know my Country and
Humour?

HELLENA: The first I guess by a certain forward Impudence, which does
not displease me at this time; and the Loss of your Money will vex
you, because I hope you have but very little to lose.

WILLMORE: Egad Child, thou'rt i'th' right; it is so little, I dare not offer it
thee for a Kindness — But cannot you divine what other things of
more value I have about me, that I would more willingly part with?

HELLENA: Indeed no, that's the Business of a Witch, and I am but a
Gipsy yet — Yet, without looking in your Hand, I have a parlous 140
Guess, 'tis some foolish Heart you mean, an inconstant *English*
Heart, as little worth stealing as your Purse.

WILLMORE: Nay, then thou dost deal with the Devil, that's certain —
Thou hast guess'd as right as if thou hadst been one of that
Number it has languisht for — I find you'll be better acquainted
with it; nor can you take it in a better time, for I am come from Sea,
Child; and *Venus* not being propitious to me in her own Element,[8] I
have a world of Love in store — Wou'd you would be good-natur'd,
and take some on't off my Hands.

HELLENA: Why — I could be inclin'd that way — but for a foolish Vow I 150
am going to make — to die a Maid.

---

6 *the French.*
7 *gives them money.*
8 *Venus, the Roman goddess of love, was born from the sea.*

WILLMORE: Then thou art damn'd without Redemption; and as I am a good Christian, I ought in charity to divert so wicked a Design — therefore prithee, dear Creature, let me know quickly when and where I shall begin to set a helping hand to so good a Work.

HELLENA: If you should prevail with my tender Heart (as I begin to fear you will, for you have horrible loving Eyes) there will be difficulty in't that you'll hardly undergo for my sake.

WILLMORE: Faith, Child, I have been bred in Dangers, and wear a Sword that has been employ'd in a worse Cause, than for a handsome kind Woman — Name the Danger — let it be any thing but a long Siege, and I'll undertake it. 160

HELLENA: Can you storm?

WILLMORE: Oh, most furiously.

HELLENA: What think you of a Nunnery-wall? for he that wins me, must gain that first.

WILLMORE: A Nun! Oh how I love thee for't! there's no Sinner like a young Saint — Nay, now there's no denying me: the old Law had no Curse (to a Woman) like dying a Maid; witness *Jephtha's* Daughter.[9] 170

HELLENA: A very good Text this, if well handled; and I perceive, Father Captain, you would impose no severe Penance on her who was inclin'd to console her self before she took Orders.

WILLMORE: If she be young and handsome.

HELLENA: Ay, there's it — but if she be not —

WILLMORE: By this Hand, Child, I have an implicit Faith, and dare venture on thee with all Faults — besides, 'tis more meritorious to leave the World when thou hast tasted and prov'd the Pleasure on't; then 'twill be a Virtue in thee, which now will be pure Ignorance.

HELLENA: I perceive, good Father Captain, you design only to make me fit for Heaven — but if on the contrary you should quite divert me from it, and bring me back to the World again, I should have a new Man to seek I find; and what a grief that will be — for when I begin, I fancy I shall love like any thing: I never try'd yet. 180

WILLMORE: Egad, and that's kind — Prithee, dear Creature, give me Credit for a Heart, for faith, I'm a very honest Fellow — Oh, I long to come first to the Banquet of Love; and such a swinging[10] Appetite I bring — Oh, I'm impatient. Thy Lodging, Sweetheart, thy Lodging, or I'm a dead man.

HELLENA: Why must we be either guilty of Fornication or Murder, if we converse with you Men? — And is there no difference between leave to love me, and leave to lie with me? 190

WILLMORE: Faith, Child, they were made to go together.

LUCETTA: Are you sure this is the Man? (*Pointing to* BLUNT.)

SANCHO: When did I mistake your Game?

---

9 *Jephtha, a judge of Israel, sacrificed his daughter and only child to fulfil a vow made before going into battle (see Judges 11:1–12:7).*

10 *huge, powerful.*

LUCETTA: This is a stranger, I know by his gazing; if he be brisk he'll venture to follow me; and then, if I understand my Trade, he's mine: he's *English* too, and they say that's a sort of good natur'd loving People, and have generally so kind an opinion of themselves, that a Woman with any Wit may flatter 'em into any sort of Fool she pleases.

BLUNT: 'Tis so — she is taken — I have Beauties which my false Glass at home did not discover.

(She often passes by BLUNT *and gazes on him; he struts, and cocks,*[11] *and walks, and gazes on her.)*

FLORINDA: This woman watches me so, I shall get no Opportunity to discover my self to him, and so miss the intent of my coming — But as I was saying, Sir — by this Line you should be a Lover. *(Looking in his Hand.)*

BELVILE: I thought how right you guess'd, all Men are in love, or pretend to be so — Come, let me go, I'm weary of this fooling. *(Walks away.)*

FLORINDA: I will not, till you have confess'd whether the Passion that you have vow'd *Florinda* be true or false. *(She holds him, he strives to get from her.)*

BELVILE: *Florinda*! *(Turns quick towards her.)*

FLORINDA: Softly.

BELVILE: Thou hast nam'd one will fix me here for ever.

FLORINDA: She'll be disappointed then, who expects you this Night at the Garden-gate, and if you'll fail not — as let me see the other Hand — you will go near to do — she vows to die or make you happy. *(Looks on* CALLIS, *who observes 'em.)*

BELVILE: What canst thou mean?

FLORINDA: That which I say — Farewel. *(Offers to go.)*

BELVILE: Oh charming Sybil,[12] stay, complete that Joy, which, as it is, will turn into Distraction! — Where must I be? at the Garden-gate? I know it — at night you say — I'll sooner forfeit Heaven than disobey.

(Enter DON PEDRO *and other Masquers, and pass over the Stage.)*

CALLIS: Madam, your Brother's here.

FLORINDA: Take this to instruct you farther. *(Gives him a Letter, and goes off.)*

FREDERICK: Have a care, Sir, what you promise; this may be a Trap laid by her Brother to ruin you.

BELVILE: Do not disturb my Happiness with Doubts.
(Opens the Letter.)

WILLMORE: My dear pretty Creature, a Thousand Blessings on thee; still in this Habit, you say, and after Dinner at this Place.

---

11 *stands up jauntily, like a rooster.*
12 *prophetess.*

HELLENA: Yes, if you will swear to keep your Heart, and not bestow it between this time and that.

WILLMORE: By all the little Gods of Love I swear, I'll leave it with you; and if you run away with it, those Deities of Justice will revenge me.

(Exeunt all the Women except LUCETTA.)

FREDERICK: Do you know the Hand?

BELVILE: 'Tis *Florinda's*. All Blessings fall upon the virtuous Maid.   240

FREDERICK: Nay, no Idolatry, a sober Sacrifice I'll allow you.

BELVILE: Oh Friends! the welcom'st News, the softest Letter! — nay, you shall see it; and could you now be serious, I might be made the happiest Man the Sun shines on.

WILLMORE: The Reason of this mighty Joy.

BELVILE: See how kindly she invites me to deliver her from the threaten'd Violence of her Brother — will you not assist me?

WILLMORE: I know not what thou mean'st, but I'll make one at any Mischief where a Woman's concern'd — but she'll be grateful to us for the Favour, will she not?   250

BELVILE: How mean you?

WILLMORE: How should I mean? Thou know'st there's but one way for a Woman to oblige me.

BELVILE: Don't prophane — the Maid is nicely[13] virtuous.

WILLMORE: Who, pox, then she's fit for nothing but a Husband; let her e'en go, Colonel.

FREDERICK: Peace, she's the Colonel's Mistress, Sir.

WILLMORE: Let her be the Devil; if she be thy Mistress, I'll serve her — name the way.

BELVILE: Read here this Postscript. *(Gives him a letter.)*   260

WILLMORE: *(Reads.)* At Ten at night — at the Garden-Gate — of which, if I cannot get the Key, I will contrive a way over the Wall — come attended with a Friend or two. — Kind heart, if we three cannot weave a String to let her down a Garden-Wall, 'twere pity but the Hangman wove one for us all.

FREDERICK: Let her alone for that: your Woman's Wit, your fair kind Woman, will out-trick a Brother or a Jew, and contrive like a Jesuit in Chains — but see, *Ned Blunt* is stoln out after the Lure of a Damsel. *(Exeunt BLUNT and LUCETTA.)*

BELVILE: So he'll scarce find his way home again, unless we get him cry'd   270
by the Bell-man[14] in the Market-place, and 'twou'd sound prettily — a lost *English* Boy of Thirty.

FREDERICK: I hope 'tis some common crafty Sinner, one that will fit him; it may be she'll sell him for *Peru*, the Rogue's sturdy and would work well in a Mine; at least I hope she'll dress him for our Mirth; cheat him of all, then have him well-favour'dly bang'd,[15] and turn'd out naked at Midnight.

---

13 *scrupulously.*
14 *town crier.*
15 *soundly beaten.*

WILLMORE: Prithee what Humour is he of, that you wish him so well?

BELVILE: Why, of an *English* Elder Brother's Humour, educated in a
Nursery, with a Maid to tend him till Fifteen, and lies with his   280
Grand-mother till he's of Age; one that knows no Pleasure beyond
riding to the next Fair, or going up to *London* with his right Worship-
ful Father in Parliament-time; wearing gay Clothes, or making honourable Love to his Lady Mother's Laundry-Maid; gets drunk at a
Hunting-Match, and ten to one then gives some Proofs of his Prow-
ess — A pox upon him, he's our Banker, and has all our Cash about
him, and if he fail we are all broke.

FREDERICK: Oh let him alone for that matter, he's of a damn'd stingy
Quality, that will secure our Stock. I know not in what Danger it
were indeed, if the Jilt should pretend she's in love with him, for 'tis   290
a kind believing Coxcomb; otherwise if he part with more than a
Piece of Eight[16] — geld him: for which offer he may chance to be
beaten, if she be a Whore of the first Rank.

BELVILE: Nay the Rogue will not be easily beaten, he's stout enough; perhaps if they talk beyond his Capacity, he may chance to exercise his
Courage upon some of them; else I'm sure they'll find it as difficult
to beat as to please him.

WILLMORE: 'Tis a lucky Devil to light upon so kind a Wench!

FREDERICK: Thou hadst a great deal of talk with thy little Gipsy, coud'st
thou do no good upon her? for mine was hard-hearted.   300

WILLMORE: Hang her, she was some damn'd honest Person of Quality,
I'm sure, she was so very free and witty. If her Face be but answera-
ble to her Wit and Humour, I would be bound to Constancy this
Month to gain her. In the mean time, have you made no kind
Acquaintance since you came to Town? — You do not use to be
honest[17] so long, Gentlemen.

FREDERICK: Faith, Love has kept us honest: we have been all fir'd with a
Beauty newly come to Town, the famous *Paduana*[18] *Angelica Bianca*.

WILLMORE: What, the Mistress of the dead *Spanish* General?

BELVILE: Yes, she's now the only ador'd Beauty of all the Youth in *Naples*,   310
who put on all their Charms to appear lovely in her sight, their
Coaches, Liveries, and themselves, all gay, as on a Monarch's Birth-
Day, to attract the Eyes of this fair Charmer, while she has the
Pleasure to behold all languish for her that see her.

FREDERICK: 'Tis pretty to see with how much Love the Men regard her,
and how much Envy the Women.

WILLMORE: What Gallant has she?

BELVILE: None, she's exposed to Sale, and four Days in the Week she's
yours — for so much a Month.

WILLMORE: The very Thought of it quenches all manner of Fire in me   320
— yet prithee let's see her.

---

16 *a Spanish coin, a dollar.*
17 *chaste.*
18 *woman from Padua.*

BELVILE: Let's first to Dinner, and after that we'll pass the Day as you please — but at Night ye must all be at my Devotion.

WILLMORE: I will not fail you. *(Exeunt.)*

ACT TWO

SCENE 1. *(The Long Street.)*

(Enter BELVILE *and* FREDERICK *in Masquing-Habits, and* WILLMORE *in his own Clothes, with a Vizard[1] in his Hand.)*

WILLMORE: But why thus disguis'd and muzzl'd?

BELVILE: Because whatever Extravagances we commit in these Faces, our own may not be oblig'd to answer 'em.

WILLMORE: I should have chang'd my Eternal Buff[2] too: but no matter, my little Gipsy wou'd not have found me out then: for if she should change hers, it is impossible I should know her, unless I should hear her prattle — A Pox on't, I cannot get her out of my Head: Pray Heaven, if ever I do see her again, she prove damnable ugly, that I may fortify my self against her Tongue.

BELVILE: Have a care of Love, for o' my conscience she was not of a   10
Quality to give thee any hopes.

WILLMORE: Pox on 'em, why do they draw a Man in then? She has play'd with my Heart so, that 'twill never lie still till I have met with some kind Wench, that will play the Game out with me — Oh for my Arms full of soft, white, kind — Woman! such as I fancy *Angelica*.

BELVILE: This is her House, if you were but in stock[3] to get admittance; they have not din'd yet; I perceive the Picture is not out.

(Enter BLUNT.*)*

WILLMORE: I long to see the Shadow of the fair Substance, a Man may gaze on that for nothing.   20

BLUNT: Colonel, thy Hand — and thine, *Fred.* I have been an Ass, a deluded Fool, a very Coxcomb from my Birth till this Hour, and heartily repent my little Faith.

BELVILE: What the Devil's the matter with thee *Ned*?

BLUNT: Oh, such a Mistress, *Fred.* Such a Girl!

WILLMORE: Ha! where?

FREDERICK: Ay where!

BLUNT: So fond, so amorous, so toying and fine! and all for sheer Love, ye Rogue! Oh how she lookt and kiss'd! and sooth'd my Heart from my Bosom. I cannot think I was awake, and yet methinks I see and   30
feel her Charms still — *Fred.* — Try if she have not left the taste of her balmy Kisses upon my Lips — *(Kisses him.)*

BELVILE: Ha, ha, ha!

1 *face-mask attached to a stick.*
2 *military coat made of tough leather.*
3 *costume.*

WILLMORE: Death Man, where is she?

BLUNT: What a Dog was I to stay in dull *England* so long — How have I laught at the Colonel when he sigh'd for Love! but now the little Archer has reveng'd him, and by his own Dart, I can guess at all his Joys, which then I took for Fancies, mere Dreams and Fables — Well, I'm resolved to sell all in *Essex*, and plant here for ever.

BELVILE: What a Blessing 'tis, thou hast a Mistress thou dar'st boast of; for I know thy Humour is rather to have a proclaim'd Clap, than a secret Amour.

WILLMORE: Dost know her Name?

BLUNT: Her Name? No, 'sheartlikins: what care I for Names? — She's fair, young, brisk and kind, even to ravishment: and what a Pox care I for knowing her by another Title?

WILLMORE: Didst give her anything?

BLUNT: Give her! — Ha, ha, ha! why, she's a Person of Quality — That's a good one, give her! 'sheartlikins dost think such Creatures are to be bought? Or are we provided for such a Purchase? Give her, quoth ye? Why she presented me with this Bracelet, for the Toy of a Diamond I us'd to wear: No, Gentlemen, *Ned Blunt* is not every Body — She expects me again to night.

WILLMORE: Egad that's well; we'll all go.

BLUNT: Not a Soul: No, Gentlemen, you are Wits; I am a dull Country Rogue, I.

FREDERICK: Well, Sir, for all your Person of Quality, I shall be very glad to understand your Purse be secure; 'tis our whole Estate at present, which we are loth to hazard in one Bottom:[4] come, Sir, unload.

BLUNT: Take the necessary Trifle, useless now to me, that am belov'd by such a Gentlewoman — 'sheartlikins Money! Here take mine too.

FREDERICK: No, keep that to be cozen'd,[5] that we may laugh.

WILLMORE: Cozen'd! — Death! wou'd I cou'd meet with one, that wou'd cozen me of all the Love I cou'd spare to night.

FREDERICK: Pox 'tis some common Whore upon my Life.

BLUNT: A Whore! yes with such Clothes! such Jewels! such a House! such Furniture, and so attended! a Whore!

BELVILE: Why yes, Sir, they are Whores, tho they'll neither entertain you with Drinking, Swearing, or Baudy; are Whores in all those gay Clothes, and right[6] Jewels; are Whores with great Houses richly furnisht with Velvet Beds, Store of Plate,[7] handsome Attendance, and fine Coaches, are Whores and errant[8] ones.

WILLMORE: Pox on't, where do these fine Whores live?

BELVILE: Where no Rogue in Office yclep'd[9] Constables dare give 'em laws, nor the Wine-inspired Bullies of the Town break their Windows; yet they are Whores, tho this *Essex* Calf believe them Persons of Quality.

BLUNT: 'Sheartlikins, y'are all Fools, there are things about this *Essex* Calf, that shall take with the Ladies, beyond all your Wits and Parts

4 *ship (punningly).*
5 *tricked, cheated.*
6 *genuine.*
7 *silver utensils.*
8 *errant (thorough; through and through).*
9 *called.*

— This Shape and Size, Gentlemen, are not to be despis'd; my   80
Waste[10] tolerably long, with other inviting Signs, that shall be
nameless.

WILLMORE: Egad I believe he may have met with some Person of Quality
that may be kind to him.

BELVILE: Dost thou perceive any such tempting things about him, should
make a fine Woman, and of Quality, pick him out from all Mankind,
to throw away her Youth and Beauty upon, nay, and her dear Heart
too? — no, no, *Angelica* has rais'd the Price too high.

WILLMORE: May she languish for Mankind till she die, and be damn'd
for that one Sin alone.   90

(Enter two Bravoes, and hang up a great Picture of ANGELICA'S, *against the Balcony,
and two little ones at each side of the Door.)*

BELVILE: See there the fair Sign to the Inn, where a Man may lodge
that's Fool enough to give her Price. *(WILLMORE gazes on the Picture.)*

BLUNT: 'Sheartlikins, Gentlemen, what's this?

BELVILE: A famous Curtezan that's to be sold.

BLUNT: How! to be sold! nay then I have nothing to say to her — sold!
what Impudence is practis'd in this Country? — With Order and
Decency Whoring's established here by virtue of the Inquisition —
Come let's be gone, I'm sure we're no Chapmen for this
Commodity.

FREDERICK: Thou art none, I'm sure, unless thou could'st have her in thy   100
Bed at the Price of a Coach in the Street.

WILLMORE: How wondrous fair she is — a Thousand Crowns a Month
— by Heaven as many Kingdoms were too little. A plague of this
Poverty — of which I ne'er complain, but when it hinders my
Approach to Beauty, which Virtue ne'er could purchase. *(Turns from
the Picture.)*

BLUNT: What's this? — *(Reads) A Thousand Crowns a Month!*
— 'Sheartlikins, here's a Sum! sure 'tis a mistake.
— Hark you, Friend, does she take or give so much by the Month!

FREDERICK: A Thousand Crowns! Why, 'tis a Portion for the *Infanta*.[11]   110

BLUNT: Hark ye, Friends, won't she trust?

BRAVO: This is a Trade, Sir, that cannot live by Credit.

(Enter DON PEDRO *in Masquerade, follow'd by* STEPHANO.*)*

BELVILE: See, here's more Company, let's walk off a while.

(Exeunt ENGLISH.*) (*PEDRO *Reads.)*

PEDRO: Fetch me a Thousand Crowns, I never wish to buy this Beauty
at an easier Rate. *(Passes off.)*

---

10 *waist.*
11 *a dowry for the Princess of Spain.*

(Enter ANGELICA *and* MORETTA *in the Balcony, and draw a Silk Curtain.)*

ANGELICA: Prithee what said those Fellows to thee?

BRAVO: Madam the first were Admirers of Beauty only, but no purchasers; they were merry with your Price and Picture, laught at the Sum, and so past off.

ANGELICA: No matter, I'm not displeas'd with their rallying; their Wonder feeds my Vanity, and he that wishes to buy, gives me more Pride, than he that gives my Price can make me Pleasure.   120

BRAVO: Madam, the last I knew thro all his disguises to be Don *Pedro*, Nephew to the General, and who was with him in *Pampelona*.

ANGELICA: Don *Pedro*! my old Gallant's Nephew! When his Uncle dy'd, he left him a vast Sum of Money; it is he who was so in love with me at *Padua*, and who us'd to make the General so jealous.

MORETTA: Is this he that us'd to prance before our Window and take such care to shew himself an amorous Ass? if I am not mistaken, he is the likeliest Man to give your Price.   130

ANGELICA: The Man is brave and generous, but of an Humour so uneasy and inconstant, that the victory over his Heart is as soon lost as won; a Slave that can add little to the Triumph of the Conqueror: but inconstancy's the Sin of all Mankind, therefore I'm resolved that nothing but Gold shall charm my Heart.

MORETTA: I'm glad on't; 'tis only interest that Women of our Profession ought to consider: tho I wonder what has kept you from that general Disease of our Sex so long, I mean that of being in Love.

ANGELICA: A kind, but sullen Star, under which I had the Happiness to be born; yet I have had no time for Love; the bravest and noblest of   140
Mankind have purchas'd my Favours at so dear a Rate, as if no Coin but Gold were current with our Trade — But here's Don *Pedro* again, fetch me my Lute — for 'tis for him or Don *Antonio* the Vice-Roy's Son, that I have spread my Nets.

(Enter at one Door DON PEDRO, *and* STEPHANO; DON ANTONIO *and* DIEGO [*his page*], *at the other Door, with People following him in Masquerade, antickly*[12] *attir'd, some with Musick: they both go up to the Picture.)*

ANTONIO: A thousand Crowns! had not the Painter flatter'd her, I should not think it dear.

PEDRO: Flatter'd her! by Heaven he cannot. I have seen the Original, nor is there one Charm here more than adorns her Face and Eyes; all this soft and sweet, with a certain languishing Air, that no Artist can represent.   150

ANTONIO: What I heard of her Beauty before had fir'd my Soul, but this confirmation of it has blown it into a flame.

PEDRO: Ha!

12 *grotesquely.*

PAGE: Sir, I have known you throw away a Thousand Crowns on a
    worse Face, and tho y' are near your Marriage, you may venture a
    little Love here; *Florinda* — will not miss it.
PEDRO: *(Aside.)* Ha! *Florinda*! Sure 'tis *Antonio*.
ANTONIO: *Florinda*! name not those distant Joys, there's not one thought
    of her will check my Passion here.
PEDRO: *(Aside.) Florinda* scorn'd! and all my Hopes defeated of the Posses-   160
    sion of *Angelica*! *(A noise of a Lute above.* ANTONIO *gazes up.)* Her Injuries
    by Heaven he shall not boast of.

(Song to a Lute above.)

SONG

When Damon *first began to love,*
He languisht in a soft Desire,
And knew not how the Gods to move,
To lessen or increase his Fire,
For Caelia *in her charming Eyes*
Wore all Love's Sweet, and all his Cruelties.

II

But as beneath a Shade he lay,
Weaving of Flow'rs for Caelia's *Hair,*   170
She chanc'd to lead her Flock that way,
And saw the am'rous Shepherd there.
She gaz'd around upon the Place,
And saw the Grove (resembling Night)
To all the Joys of Love invite,
Whilst guilty Smile and Blushes drest her Face.
At this the bashful youth all Transport grew,
And with kind Force he taught the Virgin how
To yield what all his Sighs cou'd never do.

ANTONIO: By Heav'n she's charming fair!   180

*(*ANGELICA *throws open the Curtains, and bows to* ANTONIO, *who pulls off his
Vizard, and bows and blows up Kisses.* PEDRO *unseen looks in his Face.)*

PEDRO: 'Tis he, the false *Antonio*!
ANTONIO: *(To the* BRAVO.*)* Friend, where must I pay my offering of Love?
    My Thousand Crowns I mean.
PEDRO: That Offering I have design'd to make
    And yours will come too late.
ANTONIO: Prithee be gone, I shall grow angry else,
    And then thou art not safe.
PEDRO: My Anger may be fatal, Sir, as yours;
    And he that enters here may prove this Truth.

ANTONIO: I know not who thou art, but I am sure thou'rt worth my kil-   *190*
    ling, and aiming at *Angelica. (They draw and fight.)*

(Enter WILLMORE *and* BLUNT, *who draw and part 'em.)*

BLUNT: 'Sheartlikins, here's fine doings.
WILLMORE: Tilting for the Wench I'm sure — nay gad, if that wou'd win
    her, I have as good a Sword as the best of ye — Put up — put up,
    and take another time and place, for this is design'd for Lovers only.
    (They all put up.)
PEDRO: We are prevented; dare you meet me to morrow on the *Molo?*[13]
    For I've a Title to a better quarrel,
    That of *Florinda*, in whose credulous Heart
    Thou'st made an Int'rest, and destroy'd my Hopes.   *200*
ANTONIO: Dare?
    I'll meet thee there as early as the Day.
PEDRO: We will come thus disguis'd, that whosoever chance to get the
    better, he may escape unknown.
ANTONIO: It shall be so. *(Exeunt* PEDRO *and* STEPHANO.*)*
    Who shou'd this Rival be? unless the *English* Colonel, of whom I've
    often heard Don *Pedro* speak; it must be he, and time he were
    removed, who lays a Claim to all my Happiness.

*(*WILLMORE *having gaz'd all this while on the Picture, pulls down a little one.)*

WILLMORE: This posture's loose and negligent,
    The sight on't wou'd beget a warm desire   *210*
    In Souls, whom Impotence and Age had chill'd.
    — This must along with me.
BRAVO: What means this rudeness, Sir? — restore the Picture.
ANTONIO: Ha! Rudeness committed to the fair *Angelica!* — Restore the
    Picture, Sir.
WILLMORE: Indeed I will not, Sir.
ANTONIO: By Heav'n but you shall.
WILLMORE: Nay, do not shew your Sword; if you do, by this dear Beauty
    — I will shew mine too.
ANTONIO: What right can you pretend to't?   *220*
WILLMORE: That of Possession which I will maintain — you perhaps
    have 1000 Crowns to give for the Original.
ANTONIO: No matter, Sir, you shall restore the Picture.
ANGELICA: Oh, *Moretta!* what's the matter? *(*ANGELICA *and* MORETTA *above.)*
ANTONIO: Or leave your Life behind.
WILLMORE: Death! you lye — I will do neither.
ANGELICA: Hold, I command you, if for me you fight.

(They fight, the SPANIARDS *join with* ANTONIO, BLUNT *laying on like mad.)*
(They leave off and bow.)

---

13 *mall, promenade.*

WILLMORE: How heavenly fair she is! — ah Plague of her Price.

ANGELICA: You Sir in Buff, you that appear a Soldier, that first began this Insolence. 230

WILLMORE: 'Tis true, I did so, if you call it Insolence for a Man to preserve himself; I saw your charming Picture, and was wounded: quite thro my Soul each pointed Beauty ran; and wanting a Thousand Crowns to procure my remedy, I laid this little Picture to my Bosom — which if you cannot allow me, I'll resign.

ANGELICA: No, you may keep the Trifle.

ANTONIO: You shall first ask my leave, and this. (Fight again as before.)

(Enter BELVILE and FREDERICK, who join with the English.)

ANGELICA: Hold; will you ruin me? — Bisky, Sebastian, part them. (The SPANIARDS are beaten off.)

MORETTA: Oh Madam, we're undone, a pox upon that rude Fellow, he's 240 set on to ruin us: we shall never see good days, till all these fighting poor Rogues are sent to the Gallies.[14]

(Enter BELVILE, BLUNT, FREDERICK and WILLMORE, with his shirt bloody.)

BLUNT: 'Sheartlikins, beat me at this Sport, and I'll ne'er wear Sword more.

BELVILE: The Devil's in thee for a mad Fellow, thou art always one at an unlucky Adventure. — Come, let's be gone whilst we're safe, and remember these are Spaniards, a sort of People that know how to revenge an Affront.

FREDERICK: You bleed; I hope you are not wounded. (To WILLMORE.)

WILLMORE: Not much: — a plague upon your Dons, if they fight no bet- 250 ter they'll ne'er recover Flanders.[15] — What the Devil was't to them that I took down the Picture?

BLUNT: Took it! 'Sheartlikins, we'll have the great one too; 'tis ours by Conquest. — Prithee, help me up, and I'll pull it down. —

ANGELICA: Stay, Sir, and e'er you affront me further, let me know how you durst commit this Outrage — To you I speak, Sir, for you appear like a Gentleman.

WILLMORE: To me, Madam? — Gentlemen, your Servant. (BELVILE stays him.)

BELVILE: Is the Devil in thee? Do'st know the danger of entring the 260 house of an incens'd Curtezan?

WILLMORE: I thank you for your care — but there are other matters in hand, there are, tho we have no great Temptation. — Death! let me go.

FREDERICK: Yes, to your Lodging, if you will, but not in here. — Damn these gay Harlots — by this Hand I'll have as sound and handsome a Whore for a Patacoone.[16] — Death, Man, she'll murder thee.

---

14 galleys: large rowing ships powered by slaves and criminals.
15 France had recently annexed part of Flanders in the Spanish Netherlands.
16 a Spanish coin of little value.

By Heaven, bright Creature — I would not for the World
Thy Fame were half so fair as is thy Face.

(Turns her away from him.)

ANGELICA: *(Aside.)* His words go thro me to the very Soul.
   — If you have nothing else to say to me.
WILLMORE: Yes, you shall hear how infamous you are —
   For which I do not hate thee:
   But that secures my Heart, and all the Flames it feels
   Are but so many Lusts,
   I know it by their sudden bold intrusion.
   The Fire's impatient and betrays, 'tis false —
   For had it been the purer Flame of Love,
   I should have pin'd and languish'd at your Feet,
   Ere found the Impudence to have discover'd it.
   I now dare stand your Scorn, and your Denial.
MORETTA: Sure she's bewitcht, that she can stand thus tamely, and hear
   his saucy railing. — Sirrah, will you be gone?
ANGELICA: *(To Moretta.)* How dare you take this liberty? — Withdraw.
   — Pray, tell me, Sir, are not you guilty of the same mercenary
   Crime? When a Lady is proposed to you for a Wife, you never ask
   how fair, discreet, or virtuous she is; but what's her Fortune —
   which if but small, you cry — She will not do my business — and
   basely leave her, tho she languish for you. — Say, is not this as
   poor?
WILLMORE: It is a barbarous Custom, which I will scorn to defend in our
   Sex, and do despise in yours.
ANGELICA: Thou art a brave Fellow! put up thy Gold, and know,
   That were thy Fortune large, as is thy Soul,
   Thou shouldst not buy my Love,
   Couldst thou forget those mean Effects of Vanity,
   Which set me out to sale; and as a Lover, prize
   My yielding Joys.
   Canst thou believe they'l be entirely thine,
   Without considering they were mercenary?
WILLMORE: I cannot tell, I must bethink me first *(Aside.)* — ha,
   Death, I'm going to believe her.
ANGELICA: Prithee, confirm that Faith — or if thou canst not — flatter
   me a little, 'twill please me from thy Mouth.
WILLMORE: *(Aside.)*Curse on thy charming Tongue! dost thou return
   My feign'd Contempt with so much subtilty?
   Thou'st found the easiest way into my Heart,
   Tho I yet know that all thou say'st is false.

(Turning from her in a Rage.)

ANGELICA: By all that's good 'tis real,
 I never lov'd before, tho oft a Mistress.   *110*
 — Shall my first Vows be slighted?
WILLMORE: *(Aside.)* What can she mean?
ANGELICA: *(In an angry tone.)* I find you cannot credit me.
WILLMORE: I know you take me for an errant Ass,
 An Ass that may be sooth'd into Belief,
 And then be us'd at pleasure.
 — But, Madam I have been so often cheated
 By perjur'd, soft, deluding Hypocrites,
 That I've no Faith left for the cozening Sex,
 Especially for Women of your Trade.   *120*
ANGELICA: The low esteem you have of me, perhaps,
 May bring my Heart again:
 For I have Pride that yet surmounts my Love.

(She turns with Pride, he holds her.)

WILLMORE: Throw off this Pride, this Enemy to Bliss,
 And shew the Power of Love: 'tis with those Arms
 I can be only vanquisht, made a Slave.
ANGELICA: Is all my mighty Expectation vanisht?
 — No, I will not hear thee talk, — thou hast a Charm
 In every word, that draws my Heart away.
 And all the thousand Trophies I design'd,   *130*
 Thou hast undone — Why art thou soft?
 Thy Looks are bravely rough, and meant for War.
 Could thou not storm on still?
 I then perhaps had been as free as thou.
WILLMORE: *(Aside.)* Death! how she throws her Fire about my Soul!
 — Take heed, fair Creature, how you raise my Hopes,
 Which once assum'd pretend to all Dominion.
 There's not a Joy thou hast in store
 I shall not then command:
 For which I'll pay thee back my Soul, my Life.   *140*
 Come, let's begin th' account this happy minute.
ANGELICA: And will you pay me then the Price I ask?
WILLMORE: Oh, why dost thou draw me from an awful[4] Worship,
 By shewing thou art no Divinity?
 Conceal the Fiend, and shew me all the Angel;
 Keep me but ignorant, and I'll be devout,
 And pay my Vows for ever at this Shrine.

(Kneels, and kisses her Hand.)

---

4 *awe-inspiring.*

ANGELICA: The Pay I mean is but thy Love for mine.
— Can you give that?
WILLMORE: Intirely — come, let's withdraw: where I'll renew my Vows,   *150*
— and breathe 'em with such Ardour, thou shalt not doubt my
Zeal.
ANGELICA: Thou hast a Power too strong to be resisted.

(Exeunt WILLMORE *and* ANGELICA.*)*

MORETTA: Now my Curse go with you — Is all our Project fallen to
this? to love the only Enemy to our Trade? Nay, to love such a
Shameroon,⁵ a very Beggar; nay, a Pirate-Beggar, whose Business is
to rifle and be gone, a No-Purchase, No-Pay Tatterdemalion, an
English Piccaroon;⁶ a Rogue that fights for daily Drink, and takes a
Pride in being loyally lousy — Oh, I could curse now, if I durst —
This is the Fate of most Whores.   *160*
   Trophies, which from believing Fops we win,
   Are Spoils to those who cozen us again. (Exit.)

ACT THREE

SCENE 1. *(A Street.)*

(Enter FLORINDA, VALERIA, HELLENA, *in antick¹ different Dresses from what they
were in before,* CALLIS *attending.)*

FLORINDA: I wonder what should make my Brother in so ill a Humour: I
hope he has not found out our Ramble this Morning.
HELLENA: No, if he had, we should have heard on't at both Ears, and
have been mew'd up² this Afternoon; which I would not for the
World should have happen'd — Hey ho! I'm sad as a Lover's Lute.
VALERIA: Well, methinks we have learnt this Trade of Gipsies as readily
as if we had been bred upon the Road to *Loretto*:³ and yet I did so
fumble, when I told the Stranger his Fortune, that I was afraid I
should have told my own and yours by mistake — But methinks
Hellena has been very serious ever since.   *10*
FLORINDA: I would give my Garters she were in love, to be reveng'd
upon her, for abusing me — How is't, *Hellena*?
HELLENA: Ah! — would I had never seen my mad Monsieur — and yet
for all your laughing I am not in love — and yet this small
Acquaintance, o'my Conscience, will never out of my Head.

---

5 *cheat, imposter.*
6 *confidence trickster.*

1 *bizarre.*
2 *caged, confined.*
3 *an Italian town, site of a famous shrine and so a centre for gypsies.*

VALERIA: Ha, ha, ha — I laugh to think how thou art fitted with a Lover, a Fellow that, I warrant, loves every new Face he sees.

HELLENA: Hum — he has not kept his Word with me here — and may be taken up — that thought is not very pleasant to me — what the Duce should this be now that I feel?   20

VALERIA: What is't like?

HELLENA: Nay, the Lord knows — but if I should be hanged, I cannot chuse but be angry and afraid, when I think that mad Fellow should be in love with any Body but me — What to think of my self I know not — Would I could meet with some true damn'd Gipsy, that I might know my Fortune.

VALERIA: Know it! why there's nothing so easy; thou wilt love this wandring Inconstant till thou find'st thy self hanged about his Neck, and then be as mad to get free again.

FLORINDA: Yes, *Valeria*; we shall see her bestride his Baggage-horse, and   30 follow him to the Campaign.

HELLENA: So, so; now you are provided for, there's no care taken of poor me — But since you have set my Heart a wishing, I am resolv'd to know for what. I will not die of the Pip,[4] so I will not.

FLORINDA: Art thou mad to talk so? Who will like thee well enough to have thee, that hears what a mad Wench thou art?

HELLENA: Like me! I don't intend every he that likes me shall have me, but he that I like: I shou'd have staid in the Nunnery still, if I had lik'd my Lady Abbess as well as she lik'd me. No, I came thence, not (as my wise Brother imagines) to take an eternal Farewel of the   40 World, but to love and to be belov'd; and I will be belov'd, or I'll get one of your Men, so I will.

VALERIA: Am I put into the Number of Lovers?

HELLENA: You! why Coz, I know thou art too good natur'd to leave us in any Design: Thou wou't venture a Cast, tho thou comest off a Loser, especially with such a Gamester — I observ'd your Man, and your willing Ears incline that way; and if you are not a Lover, 'tis an Art soon learnt — that I find. *(Sighs.)*

FLORINDA: I wonder how you learnt to love so easily, I had a thousand Charms to meet my Eyes and Ears, ere I cou'd yield; and 'twas the   50 knowledge of *Belvile's* Merit, not the surprising Person, took my Soul — Thou art too rash to give a Heart at first sight.

HELLENA: Hang your considering Lover; I ne'er thought beyond the Fancy, that 'twas a very pretty, idle, silly kind of Pleasure to pass one's time with, to write little, soft, nonsensical Billets, and with great difficulty and danger receive Answers; in which I shall have my Beauty prais'd, my Wit admir'd (tho little or none) and have the

---

4 *a vague minor ailment or a fit of bad temper.*

Vanity and Power to know I am desirable; then I have the more
Inclination that way, because I am to be a Nun, and so shall not be
suspected to have any such earthly Thoughts about me — But
when I walk thus — and sigh thus — they'll think my Mind's upon
my Monastery, and cry, how happy 'tis she's so resolv'd! — But not
a Word of Man.

FLORINDA: What a mad Creature's this!

HELLENA: I'll warrant, if my Brother hears either of you sigh, he cries
(gravely) — "I fear you have the Indiscretion to be in love, but take
heed of the Honour of our House, and your own unspotted Fame;"
and so he conjures on till he has laid the soft-wing'd God in your
Hearts, or broke the Bird's-nest — But see here comes your Lover:
but where's my inconstant? let's step aside, and we may learn something. *(Go aside.)*

(Enter BELVILE, FREDERICK *and* BLUNT.*)*

BELVILE: What means this? the Picture's taken in.

BLUNT: It may be the Wench is good-natur'd, and will be kind *gratis*. Your
Friend's a proper handsom Fellow.

BELVILE: I rather think she has cut his Throat and is fled: I am mad he
should throw himself into Dangers — Pox on't, I shall want him to
night — let's knock and ask for him.

HELLENA: My heart goes a-pit a-pat, for fear 'tis my Man they talk of.
(Knock, MORETTA *above.)*

MORETTA: What would you have?

BELVILE: Tell the Stranger that enter'd here about two Hours ago, that
his Friends stay here for him.

MORETTA: A curse upon him for *Moretta*,[5] would he were at the Devil —
but he's coming to you. *(Enter* WILLMORE.*)*

HELLENA: I, I, 'tis he. Oh how this vexes me.

BELVILE: And how, and how, dear Lad, has Fortune smil'd? Are we to
break her Windows, or raise up Altars to her! hah!

WILLMORE: Does not my Fortune sit triumphant on my Brow? dost not
see the little wanton God there all gay and smiling? have I not an
Air about my Face and Eyes, that distinguish me from the Croud of
common Lovers? By Heav'n, *Cupid's* Quiver has not half so many
Darts as her Eyes — Oh such a *Bona Roba*,[6] to sleep in her Arms is
lying in Fresco,[7] all perfum'd Air about me.

HELLENA: *(Aside.)* Here's fine encouragement for me to fool on.

WILLMORE: Hark ye, where didst thou purchase that rich Canary[8] we
drank to-day? Tell me, that I may adore the Spigot, and sacrifice to
the Butt: the Juice was divine, into which I must dip my Rosary, and
then bless all things that I would have bold or fortunate.

5 *from Moretta.*
6 *willing wench.*
7 *in the fresh air.*
8 *sweet wine from the Canary Islands.*

BELVILE: Well, Sir, let's go take a Bottle, and hear the Story of your
    Success.   100
FREDERICK: Would not *French* Wine do better?
WILLMORE: Damn the hungry Balderdash;[9] cheerful Sack[10] has a gener-
    ous Virtue in't, inspiring a successful Confidence, gives Eloquence
    to the Tongue, and Vigour to the Soul; and has in a few Hours
    compleated all my Hopes and Wishes. There's nothing left to raise a
    new Desire in me — Come let's be gay and wanton — and, Gentle-
    men, study, study what you want, for here are Friends *(Jingles coins.)*
    — that will supply, Gentlemen, — hark! what a charming sound
    they make — 'tis he and she Gold whilst here, shall beget new
    Pleasures every moment.   110
BLUNT: But hark ye, Sir, you are not married, are you?
WILLMORE: All the Honey of Matrimony, but none of the Sting, Friend.
BLUNT: 'Sheartlikins, thou'rt a fortunate Rogue.
WILLMORE: I am so, Sir, let these inform you. — Ha, how sweetly they
    chime! Pox of Poverty, it makes a Man a Slave, makes Wit and Hon-
    our sneak. My Soul grew lean and rusty for want of Credit.
BLUNT: 'Sheartlikins, this I like well, it looks like my lucky Bargain! Oh
    how I long for the Approach of my Squire, that is to conduct me to
    her House again. Why! here's two provided for.
FREDERICK: By this light y're happy Men.   120
BLUNT: Fortune is pleased to smile on us, Gentlemen, — to smile on us.

(Enter SANCHO, *and pulls* BLUNT *by the Sleeve. They go aside.)*

SANCHO: Sir, my Lady expects you — she has remov'd all that might
    oppose your Will and Pleasure — and is impatient till you come.
BLUNT: Sir, I'll attend you — Oh the happiest Rogue! I'll take no leave,
    lest they either dog me, or stay me. *(Exit with* SANCHO.*)*
BELVILE: But then the little Gipsy is forgot?
WILLMORE: A Mischief on thee for putting her into my thoughts; I had
    quite forgot her else, and this Night's Debauch had drunk her quite
    down.
HELLENA: Had it so, good Captain? *(Claps him on the Back.)*   130
WILLMORE: *(Aside.)* Ha! I hope she did not hear.
HELLENA: What, afraid of such a Champion?
WILLMORE: Oh! you're a fine Lady of your word, are you not? to make a
    Man languish a whole day —
HELLENA: In tedious search of me.
WILLMORE: Egad, Child, thou'rt in the right, hadst thou seen what a
    melancholy Dog I have been ever since I was a Lover, how I have
    walkt the Streets like a *Capuchin*,[11] with my Hands in my Sleeves —
    Faith, Sweetheart, thou wouldst pity me.

9 *worthless mixture of wines.*
10 *sherry.*
11 *Franciscan friar.*

HELLENA: Now, if I should be hang'd, I can't be angry with him, he dis-   *140*
 sembles so heartily — Alas, good Captain, what pains you have
 taken — Now were I ungrateful not to reward so true a Servant.

WILLMORE: Poor Soul! that's kindly said, I see thou bearest a Conscience
 — come then for a beginning shew me thy dear Face.

HELLENA: I'm afraid, my small Acquaintance, you have been staying[12]
 that swinging stomach you boasted of this morning; I remember
 then my little Collation[13] would have gone down with you, without
 the Sauce of a handsome Face — Is your Stomach so queasy now?

WILLMORE: Faith long fasting, Child, spoils a Man's Appetite — yet if
 you durst treat, I could so lay about me still.   *150*

HELLENA: And would you fall to, before a Priest says Grace?

WILLMORE: Oh fie, fie, what an old out-of-fashion'd thing hast thou
 nam'd? Thou could'st not dash me more out of Countenance,
 shouldst thou shew me an ugly Face.

(*Whilst he is seemingly courting* HELLENA, *enter* ANGELICA, MORETTA, BISKY, *and*
SEBASTIAN, *all in Masquerade:* ANGELICA *sees* WILLMORE *and starts.*)

ANGELICA: Heavens, is't he? and passionately fond to see another
 Woman?

MORETTA: What cou'd you less expect from such a Swaggerer?

ANGELICA: Expect! as much as I paid him, a Heart intire,
 Which I had pride enough to think when e'er I gave
 It would have rais'd the Man above the Vulgar,   *160*
 Made him all Soul, and that all soft and constant.

HELLENA: You see, Captain, how willing I am to be Friends with you, till
 Time and Ill-luck make us Lovers; and ask you the Question first,
 rather than put your Modesty to the blush, by asking me: for alas, I
 know you Captains are such strict Men, severe Observers of your
 Vows to Chastity, that 'twill be hard to prevail with your tender
 Conscience to marry a young willing Maid.

WILLMORE: Do not abuse me, for fear I should take thee at thy word,
 and marry thee indeed, which I'm sure will be Revenge sufficient.

HELLENA: O' my Conscience, that will be our Destiny, because we are   *170*
 both of one humour; I am as inconstant as you, for I have considered, Captain, that a handsome Woman has a great deal to do whilst
 her Face is good, for then is our Harvest-time to gather Friends; and
 should I in these days of my Youth, catch a fit of foolish Constancy,
 I were undone; 'tis loitering by day-light in our great Journey: therefore declare, I'll allow but one year for Love, one year for Indifference, and one year for Hate — and then — go hang your self — for
 I profess myself the gay, the kind, and the inconstant — the Devil's
 in't if this won't please you.

WILLMORE: Oh most damnably! — I have a Heart with a hole quite thro   *180*
 it too, no Prison mine to keep a Mistress in.

12 *appeasing.*
13 *light meal*

ANGELICA: *(Aside.)* Perjur'd Man! how I believe thee now!

HELLENA: Well, I see our Business as well as Humours are alike, yours to cozen as many Maids as will trust you, and I as many Men as have Faith — See if I have not as desperate a lying look, as you can have for the heart of you. *(Pulls off her Vizard; he starts.)*
— How do you like it, Captain?

WILLMORE: Like it! by Heav'n, I never saw so much Beauty. Oh the Charms of those sprightly black Eyes, that strangely fair Face, full of Smiles and Dimples! those soft round melting cherry Lips! and small even white Teeth! not to be exprest, but silently adored! — Oh one Look more, and strike me dumb, or I shall repeat nothing else till I am mad.

(He seems to court her to pull off her Vizard: she refuses.)

ANGELICA: I can endure no more — nor is it fit to interrupt him; for if I do, my Jealousy has so destroy'd my Reason, — I shall undo him — Therefore I'll retire. And you *Sebastian (To one of her Bravoes)* follow that Woman, and learn who 'tis; while you *(To the other Bravo.)* tell the Fugitive, I would speak to him instantly. *(Exit.)*

(This while FLORINDA *is talking to* BELVILE, *who stands sullenly.* FREDERICK *courting* VALERIA.*)*

VALERIA: *(To* BELVILE.*)* Prithee, dear Stranger, be not so sullen; for tho you have lost your Love, you see my Friend frankly offers you hers, to play with in the mean time.

BELVILE: Faith, Madam, I am sorry I can't play at her Game.

FREDERICK: *(To* VALERIA.*)* Pray leave your Intercession, and mind your own Affair, they'll better agree apart; he's a model Sigher in Company, but alone no Woman escapes him.

FLORINDA: *(Aside.)* Sure he does but rally[14] — yet if it should be true — I'll tempt him farther — Believe me, noble Stranger, I'm no common Mistress — and for a little proof on't — wear this Jewel[15] — nay, take it, Sir, 'tis right, and Bills of Exchange[16] may sometimes miscarry.

BELVILE: Madam, why am I chose out of all Mankind to be the Object of your Bounty?

VALERIA: There's another civil Question askt.

FREDERICK: *(Aside.)* Pox of's Modesty, it spoils his own Markets, and hinders mine.

FLORINDA: Sir, from my Window I have often seen you; and Women of Quality have so few opportunities for Love, that we ought to lose none.

---

14 *tease, banter.*
15 *valuable ornament; here, a locket.*
16 *money orders.*

FREDERICK: *(To* VALERIA.*)* Ay, this is something! here's a Woman! — When
    shall I be blest with so much kindness from your fair Mouth? *(Aside*
    to BELVILE.*)* Take the Jewel, Fool.   220
BELVILE: You tempt me strangely, Madam, every way.
FLORINDA: *(Aside.)* So, if I find him false, my whole Repose is gone.
BELVILE: And but for a Vow I've made to a very fine Lady, this Goodness
    had subdu'd me.
FREDERICK: Pox on't be kind, in pity to me be kind, for I am to thrive
    here but as you treat her Friend.
HELLENA: Tell me what did you in yonder House, and I'll unmasque.
WILLMORE: Yonder House — oh — I went to — a — to — why, there's a
    Friend of mine lives there.
HELLENA: What a she, or a he Friend?   230
WILLMORE: A Man upon my Honour! a Man — A She Friend! no, no,
    Madam, you have done my Business, I thank you.
HELLENA: And was't your Man Friend, that had more Darts in's Eyes
    than *Cupid* carries in a whole Budget[17] of Arrows?
WILLMORE: So —
HELLENA: "Ah such a *Bona Roba*: to be in her Arms is lying in *Fresco*, all
    perfumed Air about me" — Was this your Man Friend too?
WILLMORE: So —
HELLENA: That gave you the He, and the She — Gold, that begets young
    Pleasures.   240
WILLMORE: Well, well, Madam, then you see there are Ladies in the
    World, that will not be cruel — there are, Madam, there are —
HELLENA: And there be Men too as fine, wild, inconstant Fellows as
    your self, there be, Captain, there be, if you go to that now —
    therefore I'm resolv'd —
WILLMORE: Oh!
HELLENA: To see your Face no more —
WILLMORE: Oh!
HELLENA: Till to morrow.
WILLMORE: Egad you frighted me.   250
HELLENA: Nor then neither, unless you'l swear never to see that Lady
    more.
WILLMORE: See her! — why! never to think of Womankind again.
HELLENA: Kneel, and swear. *(Kneels, she gives him her hand.)*
WILLMORE: I do, never to think — to see — to love — nor lie with any
    but thy self.
HELLENA: Kiss the Book.
WILLMORE: Oh, most religiously. *(Kisses her Hand.)*
HELLENA: Now what a wicked Creature am I, to damn a proper Fellow.
CALLIS: *(To* FLORINDA.*)* Madam, I'll stay no longer, 'tis e'en dark.   260
FLORINDA: However, Sir, I'll leave this with you — that when I'm gone,
    you may repent the opportunity you have lost by your modesty.
    (Gives him the Jewel, which is her Picture, and Exit. He gazes after her.)

---

17 *quiver.*

WILLMORE: *(To* HELLENA.*)* Twill be an Age till to morrow, — and till then I will most impatiently expect you — Adieu, my dear pretty Angel. *(Exeunt all the* WOMEN.*)*

BELVILE: Ha! *Florinda's* Picture! 'twas she her self — what a dull Dog was I? I would have given the World for one minute's discourse with her. —

FREDERICK: This comes of your Modesty, — ah pox on your Vow, 'twas   270
ten to one but we had lost the Jewel by't.

BELVILE: *Willmore!* the blessed'st Opportunity lost! — *Florinda,* Friends, *Florinda!*

WILLMORE: Ah Rogue! such black Eyes, such a Face, such a Mouth, such Teeth, — and so much Wit!

BELVILE: All, all, and a thousand Charms besides.

WILLMORE: Why, dost thou know her?

BELVILE: Know her! ay, ay, and a Pox take me with all my Heart for being Modest.

WILLMORE: But hark ye, Friend of mine, are you my Rival? and have I   280
been only beating the Bush all this while?

BELVILE: I understand thee not — I'm mad — see here — *(Shews the Picture.)*

WILLMORE: Ha! whose Picture is this? — 'tis a fine Wench.

FREDERICK: The Colonel's Mistress, Sir.

WILLMORE: Oh, oh, here *(Gives the Picture back.)* — I thought it had been another Prize — come, come, a Bottle will set thee right again.

BELVILE: I am content to try, and by that time 'twill be late enough for our Design.

WILLMORE: Agreed.   290
Love does all day the Soul's great Empire keep,
But Wine at night lulls the soft God asleep. (Exeunt.)

SCENE 2. *(*LUCETTA's *House.)*

(Enter BLUNT *and* LUCETTA *with a Light.)*

LUCETTA: Now we are safe and free, no fears of the coming home of my old jealous Husband, which made me a little thoughtful when you came in first — but now Love is all the business of my Soul.

BLUNT: I am transported — *(Aside.)* Pox on't, that I had but some fine things to say to her, such as Lovers use — I was a Fool not to learn of *Frederick* a little by Heart before I came — something I must say. —

'Sheartlikins, sweet Soul, I am not us'd to complement, but I'm an honest Gentleman, and thy humble Servant.

LUCETTA: I have nothing to pay for so great a Favour, but such a Love as cannot but be great, since at first sight of that sweet Face and Shape   10
it made me your absolute Captive.

BLUNT: *(Aside.)* Kind heart, how prettily she talks! Egad I'll show her Husband a *Spanish* Trick; send him out of the World, and marry her:

she's damnably in love with me, and will ne'er mind Settlements,[1] and so there's that sav'd.

LUCETTA: Well, Sir, I'll go and undress me, and be with you instantly.

BLUNT: Make haste then, for 'dsheartlikins, dear Soul, thou canst not guess at the pain of a longing Lover, when his Joys are drawn within the compass of a few minutes.

LUCETTA: You speak my Sense, and I'll make haste to provide it. *(Exit.)*   20

BLUNT: 'Tis a rare Girl, and this one night's enjoyment with her will be worth all the days I ever past in Essex. — Would she'd go with me into *England*, tho to say truth, there's plenty of Whores there already. — But a pox on 'em they are such mercenary prodigal Whores, that they want such a one as this, that's free and generous, to give 'em good Examples: — Why, what a House she has! how rich and fine!

(Enter SANCHO.)

SANCHO: Sir, my Lady has sent me to conduct you to her Chamber.

BLUNT: Sir, I shall be proud to follow — *(Aside.)* Here's one of her Servants too: 'dsheartlikins, by his Garb and Gravity he might be a Justice of Peace in *Essex*, and is but a Pimp here. *(Exeunt.)*   30

(The Scene changes to a Chamber with an Alcove-Bed in it, a Table, &c. LUCETTA in Bed. Enter SANCHO and BLUNT, who takes the Candle of SANCHO at the Door.)

SANCHO: Sir, my Commission reaches no farther.

BLUNT: Sir, I'll excuse your Complement — what, in Bed, my sweet Mistress?

LUCETTA: You see, I still out-do you in kindness.

BLUNT: And thou shalt see what haste I'll make to quit scores — oh the luckiest Rogue! *(Undresses himself.)*

LUCETTA: Shou'd you be false or cruel now!

BLUNT: False, 'Sheartlikins, what dost thou take me for a *Jew*? an insensible Heathen, — A Pox of thy old jealous Husband: and he were dead, egad, sweet Soul, it shou'd be none of my fault, if I did not   40 marry thee.

LUCETTA: It never shou'd be mine.

BLUNT: Good Soul, I'm the fortunatest Dog!

LUCETTA: Are you not undrest yet?

BLUNT: As much as my Impatience will permit.

(Goes towards the Bed in his Shirt and Drawers.)

LUCETTA: Hold, Sir, put out the Light, it may betray us else.

BLUNT: Any thing, I need no other Light but that of thine Eyes! — *(Aside.)* 'sheartlikins, there I think I had it.

(Puts out the Candle, the Bed descends, he gropes about to find it.)

---

1 *marriage contracts guaranteeing the wife a separate income.*

— Why — why — where am I got? what, not yet? — where are you
sweetest? — ah, the Rogue's silent now — a pretty Love-trick this   50
— how she'll laugh at me anon! — you need not, my dear Rogue!
you need not! I'm all on a fire already — come, come, now call me
in for pity — Sure I'm enchanted! I have been round the Chamber,
and can find neither Woman, nor Bed — I lockt the Door, I'm sure
she cannot go that way; or if she cou'd, the Bed cou'd not —
Enough, enough, my pretty Wanton, do not carry the Jest too far —
Ha, betray'd! Dogs! Rogues! Pimps! help! help! *(Lights on a Trap, and is
let down.)*

(Enter LUCETTA, PHILIPPO, *and* SANCHO *with a Light.)*

PHILIPPO: Ha, ha, ha, he's dispatcht finely.

LUCETTA: Now, Sir, had I been coy, we had mist of this Booty.   60

PHILIPPO: Nay when I saw 'twas a substantial Fool, I was mollified; but
　　when you doat upon a Serenading Coxcomb, upon a Face, fine
　　Clothes, and a Lute, it makes me rage.

LUCETTA: You know I never was guilty of that Folly, my dear *Philippo*, but
　　with your self — But come let's see what we have got by this.

PHILIPPO: A rich Coat! — Sword and Hat! — these Breeches too — are
　　well lin'd! — see here a Gold Watch! — a Purse — ha! Gold! — at
　　least two hundred Pistoles! a bunch of Diamond Rings; and one
　　with the Family Arms! — A Gold Box! — with a Medal of his King!
　　and his Lady Mother's Picture! — these were sacred Reliques,   70
　　believe me! — see, the Wasteband of his Breeches have a Mine of
　　Gold! — Old Queen *Bess's*. We have a Quarrel to her ever since
　　Eighty Eight,[2] and may therefore justify the Theft; the Inquisition
　　might have committed it.

LUCETTA: See, a Bracelet of bow'd[3] Gold, these his Sister ty'd about his
　　Arm at parting — but well — for all this, I fear his being a Stranger
　　may make a noise, and hinder our Trade with them hereafter.

PHILIPPO: That's our security; he is not only a Stranger to us, but to the
　　Country too — the Common-Shore[4] into which he is descended,
　　thou know'st, conducts him into another Street, which this Light   80
　　will hinder him from ever finding again — he knows neither your
　　Name, nor the Street where your House is, nay, nor the way to his
　　own Lodgings.

LUCETTA: And art not thou an unmerciful Rogue, not to afford him one
　　Night for all this? — I should not have been such a *Jew*.

PHILIPPO: Blame not me, *Lucetta*, to keep as much of thee as I can to my
　　self — come, that thought makes me wanton, — let's to Bed, —
　　Sancho, lock up these.

---

2 *1588, the year in which the Spanish Armada was defeated by England.*
3 *bent.*
4 *sewer.*

This is the Fleece which Fools do bear,
Design'd for witty Men to shear. (Exeunt.)

(The Scene changes, and discovers BLUNT, *creeping out of a Common Shore, his Face*
&c., all dirty.)

BLUNT: Oh Lord! *(Climbing up.)*
I am got out at last, and (which is a Miracle) without a Clue — and
now to Damning and Cursing, — but if that would ease me, where
shall I begin? with my Fortune, my self, or the Quean[5] that cozen'd
me — What a dog was I to believe in Women! Oh Coxcomb —
ignorant conceited Coxcomb! to fancy she cou'd be enamour'd with
my Person, at the first sight enamour'd — Oh, I'm a cursed Puppy,
'tis plain, Fool was writ upon my Forehead, she perceiv'd it, — saw
the *Essex* Calf there — for what Allurements could there be in this
Countenance? which I can indure, because I'm acquainted with it — 100
Oh, dull silly Dog! to be thus sooth'd into a Cozening! Had I been
drunk, I might fondly have credited the young Quean! but as I was
in my right Wits, to be thus cheated, confirms I am a dull believing
English Country Fop. — But my Comrades! Death and the Devil,
there's the worst of all — then a Ballad will be sung to Morrow on
the *Prado,*[6] to a lousy Tune of the enchanted Squire, and the annihi-
lated Damsel — But *Frederick* that Rogue, and the Colonel, will abuse
me beyond all Christian patience — had she left me my Clothes, I
have a Bill of Exchange at home wou'd have sav'd my Credit — but
now all hope is taken from me — Well, I'll home (if I can find the 110
way) with this Consolation, that I am not the first kind believing
Coxcomb; but there are, Gallants, many such good Natures
amongst ye.
And tho you've better Arts to hide your Follies,
Adsheartlikins, y'are all as errant Cullies.[7]

SCENE 3. *(The Garden, in the Night.)*

(Enter FLORINDA *undress'd,*[1] *with a Key, and a little Box.)*

FLORINDA: Well, thus far I'm in my way to Happiness; I have got my self
free from *Callis;* my Brother too, I find by yonder light, is gone into
his Cabinet,[2] and thinks not of me: I have by good Fortune got the
Key of the Garden Back-door, — I'll open it, to prevent *Belvile's*
knocking, — a little noise will now alarm my Brother. Now am I as
fearful as a young Thief. *(Unlocks the Door.)* — Hark, — what noise is
that? — Oh, 'twas the Wind that plaid amongst the Boughs. —

5 *slut.*
6 *promenade.*
7 *dupes.*

1 *in undress, dressed informally.*
2 *study.*

Belvile stays long, methinks — it's time — stay — for fear of a surprize, I'll hide these Jewels in yonder Jessamin.³ *(She goes to lay down the Box.)*   10

(Enter WILLMORE *drunk.)*

WILLMORE: What the Devil is become of these Fellows, *Belvile* and *Frederick*? They promis'd to stay at the next corner for me, but who the Devil knows the corner of a full Moon? — Now — whereabouts am I? — hah — what have we here? a Garden! — a very convenient place to sleep in — hah — what has God sent us here? — a Female — by this light, a Woman; I'm a Dog if it be not a very Wench. —

FLORINDA: He's come! — hah — who's there?

WILLMORE: Sweet Soul, let me salute thy Shoe-string.

FLORINDA: 'Tis not my *Belvile* — good Heavens, I know him not. — Who   20
are you, and from whence come you?

WILLMORE: Prithee — prithee, Child — not so many hard Questions —
let it suffice I am here, Child — Come, come kiss me.

FLORINDA: Good Gods! what luck is mine?

WILLMORE: Only good luck, Child, parlous⁴ good luck. — Come hither,
— 'tis a delicate shining Wench, — by this Hand she's perfum'd, and smells like any Nosegay. — Prithee, dear Soul, let's not play the Fool, and lose time, — precious time — for as Gad shall save me, I'm as honest a Fellow as breathes, tho I am a little disguis'd at present. — Come, I say, — why, thou may'st be free with me, I'll be   30
very secret. I'll not boast who 'twas oblig'd me, not I — for hang me if I know thy Name.

FLORINDA: Heavens! what a filthy beast is this!

WILLMORE: I am so, and thou oughtst the sooner to lie with me for that reason, — for look you, Child, there will be no Sin in't, because 'twas neither design'd nor premeditated; 'tis pure Accident on both sides — that's a certain thing now — Indeed should I make love to you, and you vow Fidelity — and swear and lye till you believ'd and yielded — Thou art therefore (as thou art a good Christian) oblig'd in Conscience to deny me nothing. Now — come, be kind, without   40
any more idle prating.

FLORINDA: Oh, I am ruin'd — wicked Man, unhand me.

WILLMORE: Wicked! Egad, Child, a Judge, were he young and vigorous, and saw those Eyes of thine, would know 'twas they gave the first blow — the first provocation. — Come, prithee let's lose no time, I say — this is a fine convenient place.

FLORINDA: Sir, let me go, I conjure you, or I'll call out.

WILLMORE: Ay, ay, you were best to call Witness to see how finely you treat me — do. —

---

3 *a box perfumed with jasmine.*
4 *extremely.*

FLORINDA: I'll cry Murder, Rape, or any thing, if you do not instantly let   50
me go.
WILLMORE: A Rape! Come, come, you lye, you Baggage, you lye: What,
I'll warrant you would fain have the World believe now that you are
not so forward as I. No, not you, — why at this time of Night was
your Cobweb-door set open, dear Spider — but to catch Flies? —
Hah! Come — or I shall be damnably angry. — Why what a Coil⁵ is
here. —
FLORINDA: Sir, can you think —
WILLMORE: That you'd do it for nothing? oh, oh, I find what you'd be at
— look here, here's a Pistole for you — here's a work indeed —   60
here — take it, I say. —
FLORINDA: For Heaven's sake, Sir, as you're a Gentleman —
WILLMORE: So — now — she would be wheedling me for more — what,
you will not take it then — you're resolv'd you will not. — Come,
come, take it, or I'll put it up again; for, look ye, I never give more.
— Why, how now, Mistress, are you so high i'th' Mouth, a Pistole
won't down with you? — hah — why, what a work's here — in
good time — come, no struggling, be gone — But an y'are good at a
dumb Wrestle, I'm for ye, — look ye, — I'm for ye. — *(She struggles
with him.)*   70

(Enter BELVILE *and* FREDERICK.*)*

BELVILE: The Door is open, a Pox of this mad Fellow, I'm angry that
we've lost him, I durst have sworn he had follow'd us.
FREDERICK: But you were so hasty, Colonel, to be gone.
FLORINDA: Help, help, — Murder! — help — oh, I'm ruin'd.
BELVILE: Ha, sure that's *Florinda's* Voice. *(Comes up to them.)*
— A Man! Villain, let go that Lady.

(A noise; WILLMORE *turns and draws;* FREDERICK *interposes.)*

FLORINDA: *Belvile!* Heavens! my Brother too is coming, and 'twill be
impossible to escape. — *Belvile,* I conjure you to walk under my
Chamber-window, from whence I'll give you some instructions   80
what to do — This rude Man has undone us. *(Exit.)*
WILLMORE: *Belvile!*

(Enter PEDRO, STEPHANO, *and other Servants with Lights.)*

PEDRO: I'm betray'd; run, *Stephano,* and see if *Florinda* be safe. *(Exit*
STEPHANO.*)*
So whoe'er they be, all is not well, I'll to *Florinda's* Chamber. *(They
fight, and* PEDRO'S *Party beats 'em out; going out, meets* STEPHANO.*)*

5 *commotion.*

STEPHANO: You need not, Sir, the poor Lady's fast asleep, and thinks no harm: I wou'd not wake her, Sir, for fear of frightning her with your danger.

PEDRO: I'm glad she's there — Rascals, how came the Garden-Door open? 90

STEPHANO: That Question comes too late, Sir: some of my Fellow-Servants Masquerading I'll warrant.

PEDRO: Masquerading! a lewd Custom to debauch our Youth — there's something more in this than I imagine. *(Exeunt.)*

SCENE 4. *(Changes to the Street.)*

(Enter BELVILE *in a Rage,* FREDERICK *holding him, and* WILLMORE *melancholy.)*

WILLMORE: Why, how the Devil shou'd I know *Florinda*?

BELVILE: Ah plague of your ignorance! if it had not been *Florinda*, must you be a Beast? — a Brute, a senseless Swine?

WILLMORE: Well, Sir, you see I am endu'd with Patience — I can bear — tho egad y're very free with me methinks, — I was in good hopes the Quarrel wou'd have been on my side, for so uncivilly interrupting me.

BELVILE: Peace, Brute, whilst thou'rt safe — oh, I'm distracted.

WILLMORE: Nay, nay, I'm an unlucky Dog, that's certain.

BELVILE: Ah curse upon the Star that rul'd my Birth! or whatsoever 10 other Influence that makes me still so wretched.

WILLMORE: Thou break'st my Heart with these Complaints; there is no Star in fault, no Influence but Sack, the cursed Sack I drank.

FREDERICK: Why, how the Devil came you so drunk?

WILLMORE: Why, how the Devil came you so sober?

BELVILE: A curse upon his thin Skull, he was always before-hand that way.

FREDERICK: Prithee, dear Colonel, forgive him, he's sorry for his fault.

BELVILE: He's always so after he has done a mischief — a plague on all such Brutes. 20

WILLMORE: By this Light I took her for an errant Harlot.

BELVILE: Damn your debaucht Opinion: tell me, Sot, hadst thou so much sense and light about thee to distinguish her to be a Woman, and could'st not see something about her Face and Person, to strike an awful Reverence into thy Soul?

WILLMORE: Faith no, I consider'd her as mere a Woman as I could wish.

BELVILE: 'Sdeath I have no patience — draw, or I'll kill you.

WILLMORE: Let that alone till to morrow, and if I set not all right again, use your Pleasure.

BELVILE: To morrow, damn it. 30
    The spiteful Light will lead me to no happiness.
    To morrow is *Antonio's*, and perhaps
    Guides him to my undoing; — oh that I could meet
    This Rival, this powerful Fortunate.

WILLMORE: What then?

BELVILE: Let thy own Reason, or my Rage instruct thee.

WILLMORE: I shall be finely inform'd then, no doubt; hear me, Colonel — hear me — shew me the Man and I'll do his Business.[1]

BELVILE: I know him no more than thou, or if I did, I should not need thy aid.

WILLMORE: This you say is *Angelica's* House, I promis'd the kind Baggage to lie with her to Night. (*Offers to go in.*)

(*Enter* ANTONIO *and his* PAGE. ANTONIO *knocks on the Hilt of his Sword.*)

ANTONIO: You paid the thousand Crowns I directed?

PAGE: To the Lady's old Woman, Sir, I did.

WILLMORE: Who the Devil have we here?

BELVILE: I'll now plant my self under *Florinda's* Window, and if I find no comfort there, I'll die. (*Exeunt* BELVILE *and* FREDERICK.)

(*Enter* MORETTA.)

MORETTA: Page!

PAGE: Here's my Lord.

WILLMORE: How is this, a Piccaroon going to board my Frigate! here's one Chase-Gun[2] for you.

(*Drawing his Sword, justles* ANTONIO, *who turns and draws. They fight,* ANTONIO *falls.*)

MORETTA: Oh, bless us, we are all undone! (*Runs in, and shuts the Door.*)

PAGE: Help, Murder!

(BELVILE *returns at the noise of fighting.*)

BELVILE: Ha, the mad Rogue's engag'd in some unlucky Adventure again.

(*Enter two or three Masqueraders.*)

MASQUERADER: Ha, a Man kill'd!

WILLMORE: How! a Man kill'd! then I'll go home to sleep. (*Puts up, and reels out. Exeunt Masqueraders another way.*)

BELVILE: Who shou'd it be! pray Heaven the Rogue is safe, for all my Quarrel to him. (*As* BELVILE *is groping about, enter an Officer and six Soldiers.*)

SOLDIER: Who's there?

---

1 *take care of him (i.e., kill him).*
2 *ship's cannon.*

OFFICER: So, here's one dispatcht — secure the Murderer.

BELVILE: Do not mistake my Charity for Murder:
  I came to his Assistance. *(Soldiers seize on* BELVILE.*)*

OFFICER: That shall be tried, Sir. — St. *Jago,*[3] Swords drawn in the Carnival time! *(Goes to* ANTONIO.*)*

ANTONIO: Thy Hand prithee.

OFFICER: Ha, Don *Antonio!* look well to the Villain there. — How is't,
  Sir?   70

ANTONIO: I'm hurt.

BELVILE: Has my Humanity made me a Criminal?

OFFICER: Away with him.

BELVILE: What a curst Chance is this! *(Exeunt Soldiers with* BELVILE.*)*

ANTONIO: This is the Man that has set upon me twice — *(To the Officer.)*
  carry him to my Apartment till you have further Orders from me.

(Exit ANTONIO, *led.)*

ACT FOUR

SCENE 1. *(A fine Room.)*

(Discovers BELVILE, *as by Dark alone.)*

BELVILE: When shall I be weary of railing on Fortune, who is resolv'd
  never to turn with Smiles upon me? — Two such Defeats in one
  Night — none but the Devil and that mad Rogue could have con-
  triv'd to have plagued me with — I am here a Prisoner — but
  where? — Heaven knows — and if there be Murder done, I can
  soon decide the Fate of a Stranger in a Nation without Mercy — Yet
  this is nothing to the Torture my Soul bows with, when I think of
  losing my fair, my dear *Florinda.* — Hark — my Door opens — a
  Light — a Man — and seems of Quality — arm'd too. — Now shall
  I die like a Dog without defence.   10

(Enter ANTONIO *in a Night-Gown, with a Light; his Arm in a Scarf, and a Sword
under his Arm: He sets the Candle on the Table.)*

ANTONIO: Sir, I am come to know what Injuries I have done you, that
  could provoke you to so mean an Action, as to attack me basely,
  without allowing time for my Defence.

BELVILE: Sir, for a Man in my Circumstances to plead Innocence, would
  look like Fear — but view me well, and you will find no marks of a
  Coward on me, nor any thing that betrays the Brutality you accuse
  me of.

ANTONIO: In vain, Sir, you impose upon my Sense,
  You are not only he who drew on me last Night,

---

3 *by St. James (especially venerated in Spain).*

But yesterday before the same House, that of *Angelica*.   20
Yet there is something in your Face and Mien —
BELVILE: I own I fought to day in the defence of a Friend of mine, with
whom you (if you're the same) and your Party were first engag'd.
Perhaps you think this Crime enough to kill me,
But if you do, I cannot fear you'll do it basely.
ANTONIO: No, Sir, I'll make you fit for a Defence with this. *(Gives him the
Sword.)*
BELVILE: This Gallantry surprizes me — nor know I how to use this
Present, Sir, against a Man so brave.
ANTONIO: You shall not need;   30
For know, I come to snatch you from a Danger
That is decreed against you;
Perhaps your Life, or long Imprisonment.
And 'twas with so much Courage you offended,
I cannot see you punisht.
BELVILE: How shall I pay this Generosity?
ANTONIO: It had been safer to have kill'd another,
Than have attempted me.
To shew your Danger, Sir, I'll let you know my Quality;[1]
And 'tis the Vice-Roy's Son whom you have wounded.   40
BELVILE: The Vice-Roy's Son! *(Aside.)*
Death and Confusion! was this Plague reserved
To compleat all the rest? — oblig'd by him!
The Man of all the World I would destroy.
ANTONIO: You seem disorder'd, Sir.
BELVILE: Yes, trust me, Sir, I am, and 'tis with pain
That Man receives such Bounties,
Who wants the pow'r to pay 'em back again.
ANTONIO: To gallant Spirits 'tis indeed uneasy;
— But you may quickly over-pay me, Sir.   50
BELVILE: Then I am well — *(Aside.)* kind Heaven! but set us even,
That I may fight with him, and keep my Honour safe.
— Oh, I'm impatient, Sir, to be discounting[2]
The mighty Debt I owe you; command me quickly —
ANTONIO: I have a Quarrel with a Rival, Sir,
About the Maid we love.
BELVILE: *(Aside.)* Death, 'tis *Florinda* he means —
That Thought destroys my Reason, and I shall kill him —
ANTONIO: My Rival, Sir.
Is one has all the Virtues Man can boast of.   60
BELVILE: *(Aside.)* Death! who shou'd this be?
ANTONIO: He challeng'd me to meet him on the *Molo*,
As soon as Day appear'd; but last Night's quarrel
Has made my Arm unfit to guide a Sword.

1 *rank.*
2 *paying back.*

BELVILE: I apprehend you, Sir, you'd have me kill the Man
    That lays a claim to the Maid you speak of.
    — I'll do't — I'll fly to do it.
ANTONIO: Sir, do you know her?
BELVILE: — No, Sir, but 'tis enough she is admired by you.
ANTONIO: Sir, I shall rob you of the Glory on't,   70
    For you must fight under my Name and Dress.
BELVILE: That Opinion must be strangely obliging that makes
    You think I can personate the brave *Antonio*,
    Whom I can but strive to imitate.
ANTONIO: You say too much to my Advantage.
    Come, Sir, the Day appears that calls you forth.
    Within, Sir, is the Habit. *(Exit* ANTONIO.*)*
BELVILE: Fantastick Fortune, thou deceitful Light,
    That cheats the wearied Traveller by Night,
    Tho on a Precipice each step you tread,   80
    I am resolv'd to follow where you lead. *(Exit.)*

SCENE 2. *(The Molo.)*

(Enter FLORINDA *and* CALLIS *in Masques, with* STEPHANO.*)*

FLORINDA: *(Aside.)* I'm dying with my fears; *Belvile's* not coming,
    As I expected, underneath my Window,
    Makes me believe that all those Fears are true.
    — Canst thou not tell with whom my Brother fights?
STEPHANO: No, Madam, they were both in Masquerade, I was by when
    they challeng'd one another, and they had decided the Quarrel then,
    but were prevented by some Cavaliers; which made 'em put it off till
    now — but I am sure 'tis about you they fight.
FLORINDA: *(Aside.)* Nay, then 'tis with *Belvile*, for what other Lover have I
    that dares fight for me, except *Antonio*? and he is too much in favour   10
    with my Brother — If it be he, for whom shall I direct my Prayers to
    Heaven?
STEPHANO: Madam, I must leave you; for if my Master see me, I shall be
    hang'd for being your Conductor. — I escap'd narrowly for the
    Excuse I made for you last night i'th' Garden.
FLORINDA: And I'll reward thee for't — prithee no more. *(Exit* STEPHANO.*)*

(Enter DON PEDRO *in his Masquing Habit.)*

PEDRO: *Antonio's* late to day, the place will fill, and we may be prevented.
    (Walks about.)
FLORINDA: *(Aside.) (Antonio!* sure I heard amiss.
PEDRO: But who will not excuse a happy Lover   20
    When soft fair Arms confine the yielding Neck;
    And the kind Whisper languishingly breathes,

"Must you be gone so soon?"
Sure I had dwelt for ever on her Bosom.
— But stay, he's here.

(Enter BELVILE *drest in* ANTONIO's *Clothes.)*

FLORINDA: *(Aside.)* 'Tis not *Belvile*, half my Fears are vanisht.
PEDRO: *Antonio!* —
BELVILE: *(Aside.)* This must be he.
    You're early, Sir; I do not use to be out-done this way.
PEDRO: The wretched, Sir, are watchful, and 'tis enough   *30*
    You have the advantage of me in *Angelica.*
BELVILE: *(Aside.) Angelica!*
    Or[1] I've mistook my Man! Or else *Antonio,*
    Can he forget his Interest in *Florinda,*
    And fight for common Prize?
PEDRO: Come, Sir, you know our terms —
BELVILE: *(Aside.)* By Heaven, not I.
    — No talking, I am ready, Sir.
    (Offers to fight. FLORINDA *runs in.)*
FLORINDA: *(To* BELVILE.*)* Oh, hold! whoe'er you be, I do conjure you hold.   *40*
    If you strike here — I die —
PEDRO: *Florinda!*
BELVILE: *Florinda* imploring for my Rival!
PEDRO: Away, this Kindness is unseasonable.

(Puts her by, they fight; she runs in just as BELVILE *disarms* PEDRO.*)*

FLORINDA: Who are you, Sir, that dare deny my Prayers?
BELVILE: Thy Prayers destroy him; if thou wouldst preserve him.
    Do that thou'rt unacquainted with, and curse him. *(She holds him.)*
FLORINDA: By all you hold most dear, by her you love,
    I do conjure you, touch him not.
BELVILE: By her I love?   *50*
    See — I obey — and at your Feet resign
    The useless Trophy of my Victory. *(Lays his sword at her Feet.)*
PEDRO: *Antonio,* you've done enough to prove you love *Florinda.*
BELVILE: Love *Florinda!*
    Does Heaven love Adoration, Pray'r, or Penitence?
    Love her! here Sir, — your Sword again. *(Snatches up the Sword, and*
        gives it him.)
    Upon this Truth I'll fight my Life away.
PEDRO: No, you've redeem'd my Sister, and my Friendship.

(He gives him FLORINDA, *and pulls off his Vizard to shew his Face, and puts it on
again.)*

BELVILE: Don *Pedro!*   *60*

---

1 *either.*

PEDRO: Can you resign your Claims to other Women,
 And give your Heart intirely to *Florinda*?
BELVILE: Intire, as dying Saints' Confessions are.
 I can delay my happiness no longer.
 This minute let me make *Florinda* mine:
PEDRO: This minute let it be — no time so proper,
 This Night my Father will arrive from *Rome*,
 And possibly may hinder what we purpose.
FLORINDA: Oh Heavens! this Minute?

(Enter Masqueraders, and pass over.)

BELVILE: Oh, do not ruin me!   70
PEDRO: The place begins to fill; and that we may not be observ'd, do you
 walk off to St. *Peter's* Church, where I will meet you, and conclude
 your Happiness.
BELVILE: I'll meet you there — *(Aside.)* if there be no more Saints
 Churches in *Naples*
FLORINDA: Oh stay, Sir, and recall your hasty Doom:
 Alas I have not yet prepar'd my Heart
 To entertain so strange a Guest.
PEDRO: Away, this silly Modesty is assum'd too late.
BELVILE: Heaven, Madam! what do you do?   80
FLORINDA: Do? despise the Man that lays a Tyrant's Claim
 To what he ought to conquer by Submission.
BELVILE: You do not know me — move a little this way. *(Draws her aside.)*
FLORINDA: Yes, you may even force me to the Altar,
 But not the holy Man that offers there
 Shall force me to be thine. *(*PEDRO *talks to* CALLIS *this while.)*
BELVILE: Oh do not lose so blest an opportunity!
 See — 'tis your *Belvile* — not *Antonio*,
 Whom your mistaken Scorn and Anger ruins. *(Pulls off his Vizard.)*
FLORINDA: *Belvile!*   90
 Where was my Soul it cou'd not meet thy Voice,
 And take this knowledge in?

(As they are talking, enter WILLMORE *finely drest, and* FREDERICK.*)*

WILLMORE: No Intelligence! no News of *Belvile* yet — well I am the most
 unlucky Rascal in Nature — ha! — am I deceiv'd — or is it he —
 look, *Frederick.* — 'tis he — my dear *Belvile.*

(Runs and embraces him. BELVILE'S *Vizard falls out on's Hand.)*

BELVILE: Hell and Confusion seize thee!
PEDRO: Ha! *Belvile!* I beg your Pardon, Sir. *(Takes* FLORINDA *from him.)*

BELVILE: Nay, touch her not, she's mine by Conquest, Sir.
　　I won her by my Sword.

WILLMORE: Did'st thou so? — and egad, Child, we'll keep her by the　　100
　　Sword. *(Draws on* PEDRO, BELVILE *goes between.)*

BELVILE: Stand off!
　　Thou'rt so profanely lewd, so curst by Heaven,
　　All Quarrels thou espousest must be fatal.

WILLMORE: Nay, an² you be so hot, my Valour's coy,
　　And shall be courted when you want it next. *(Puts up his Sword.)*

BELVILE: *(To* PEDRO.*)* You know I ought to claim a Victor's Right,
　　But you're the Brother to divine *Florinda*,
　　To whom I'm such a Slave — to purchase her,
　　I durst not hurt the Man she holds so dear.　　110

PEDRO: 'Twas by *Antonio's*, not by *Belvile's* Sword,
　　This Question should have been decided, Sir:
　　I must confess much to your Bravery's due,
　　Both now, and when I met you last in Arms.
　　But I am nicely³ punctual in my word,
　　As Men of Honour ought, and beg your Pardon.
　　— For this Mistake another Time shall clear.
　　— *(Aside to* FLORINDA, *as they are going out.)* This was
　　some Plot between you and *Belvile*:
　　But I'll prevent you.　　120

*(*BELVILE *looks after her, and begins to walk up and down in a Rage.)*

WILLMORE: Do not be modest now, and lose the Woman:
　　but if we shall fetch her back, so —

BELVILE: Do not speak to me.

WILLMORE: Not speak to you! — Egad, I'll speak to you, and will be
　　answered too.

BELVILE: Will you, Sir?

WILLMORE: I know I've done some mischief, but I'm so dull a Puppy, that
　　I am the Son of a Whore, if I know how, or where — prithee
　　inform my Understanding. —

BELVILE: Leave me I say, and leave me instantly!　　130

WILLMORE: I will not leave you in this humour, nor till I know my
　　Crime.

BELVILE: Death, I'll tell you, Sir —

(Draws and runs at WILLMORE; *he runs out*, BELVILE *after him;* FREDERICK
interposes.)

(Enter ANGELICA, MORETTA, *and* SEBASTIAN.*)*

ANGELICA: Ha — *Sebastian* — Is not that *Willmore*? haste, haste, and bring
　　him back.

2 *if.*
3 *scrupulously.*

FREDERICK: *(Aside.)* The Colonel's mad — I never saw him thus before;
　　　I'll after 'em, lest he do some mischief, for I am sure *Willmore* will
　　　not draw on him. *(Exit.)*
ANGELICA: I am all Rage! my first desires defeated
　　　For one, for ought he knows, that has no　　　　　　　　　　140
　　　Other Merit than her Quality, —
　　　Her being Don *Pedro's* Sister — He loves her:
　　　I know 'tis so — dull, dull, insensible —
　　　He will not see me now tho oft invited;
　　　And broke his Word last night — false perjur'd Man!
　　　— He that but yesterday fought for my Favours,
　　　And would have made his Life a Sacrifice
　　　To've gain'd one Night with me,
　　　Must now be hired and courted to my Arms.
MORETTA: I told you what wou'd come on't, but *Moretta's* an old doating　150
　　　Fool — Why did you give him five hundred Crowns, but to set him-
　　　self out for other Lovers? You shou'd have kept him poor, if you
　　　had meant to have had any good from him.
ANGELICA: Oh, name not such mean Trifles. — Had I given him all
　　　My Youth has earn'd from Sin,
　　　I had not lost a Thought nor Sigh upon't.
　　　But I have given him my eternal Rest,
　　　My whole Repose, my future Joys, my Heart;
　　　My Virgin Heart. *Moretta!* oh 'tis gone!
MORETTA: Curse on him, here he comes;　　　　　　　　　　　　160
　　　How fine she has made him too!

(Enter WILLMORE *and* SEBASTIAN. ANGELICA *turns and walks away.)*

WILLMORE: How now, turn'd Shadow?
　　　Fly when I pursue, and follow when I fly!

[*Sings.*]

　　　　Stay gentle Shadow of my Dove,
　　　　　And tell me ere I go,
　　　　Whether the Substance may not prove
　　　　　A fleeting Thing like you.

There's a soft kind Look remaining yet.

(As she turns she looks on him.)

ANGELICA: Well, Sir, you may be gay; all Happiness, all Joys pursue you
　　　still. Fortune's your Slave, and gives you every hour choice of new　170
　　　Hearts and Beauties, till you are cloy'd with the repeated Bliss,
　　　which others vainly languish for — But know, false Man, that I shall
　　　be reveng'd. *(Turns away in a Rage.)*

WILLMORE: So, 'gad, there are of those faint-hearted Lovers, whom such a sharp Lesson next their Hearts would make as impotent as Four-score — pox o' this whining — my Bus'ness is to laugh and love — a pox on't; I hate your sullen Lover, a Man shall lose as much time to put you in Humour now, as would serve to gain a new Woman.

ANGELICA: I scorn to cool that Fire I cannot raise,
Or do the Drudgery of your virtuous Mistress.   *180*

WILLMORE: A virtuous Mistress! Death, what a thing thou hast found out for me! why what the Devil should I do with a virtuous Woman? — a sort of ill-natur'd Creatures, that take a Pride to torment a Lover. Virtue is but an Infirmity in Women, a Disease that renders even the handsome ungrateful; whilst the ill-favour'd, for want of Sollicitations and Address, only fancy themselves so. — I have lain with a Woman of Quality, who has all the while been railing at Whores.

ANGELICA: I will not answer for your Mistress's Virtue,
Tho she be young enough to know no Guilt: *190*
And I could wish you would persuade my Heart,
'Twas the two hundred thousand Crowns you courted.

WILLMORE: Two hundred thousand Crowns! what Story's this? — what Trick? — what Woman? — ha.

ANGELICA: How strange you make it! have you forgot the Creature you entertain'd on the Piazza last night?

WILLMORE: *(Aside.)* Ha, my Gipsy worth two hundred thousand Crowns! — oh how I long to be with her — pox, I knew she was of Quality.

ANGELICA: False Man, I see my Ruin in thy Face.
How many vows you breath'd upon my Bosom,   *200*
Never to be unjust — have you forgot so soon?

WILLMORE: Faith no, I was just coming to repeat 'em — but here's a Humour indeed — would make a Man a Saint — *(Aside.)* Wou'd she'd be angry enough to leave me, and command me not to wait on her.

(Enter HELLENA, drest in Man's Clothes.)

HELLENA: *(Aside.)* This must be *Angelica*, I know it by her mumping[4] Matron here — Ay, ay, 'tis she: my mad Captain's with her too, for all his swearing — how this unconstant Humour makes me love him: — pray, good grave Gentlewoman, is not this *Angelica*?

MORETTA: My too young Sir, it is — I hope 'tis one from Don *Antonio*.   *210*
(Goes to ANGELICA.)

HELLENA: *(Aside.)* Well, something I'll do to vex him for this.

ANGELICA: I will not speak with him; am I in humour to receive a Lover?

WILLMORE: Not speak with him? why I'll be gone — and wait your idler minutes — Can I shew less Obedience to the thing I love so fondly?
(Offers to go.)

---

4 *grimacing, sullen.*

ANGELICA: A fine Excuse this — stay —

WILLMORE: And hinder your Advantage: should I repay your Bounties
  so ungratefully?

ANGELICA: *(To* HELLENA.*)* Come hither, Boy, — *(To* WILLMORE.*)* that I may   220
  let you see
  How much above the Advantages you name
  I prize one Minute's Joy with you.

WILLMORE: Oh, you destroy me with this Endearment. *(Impatient to be
  gone.)*
  — Death, how shall I get away? — Madam, 'twill not be fit I should
  be seen with you — besides, it will not be convenient — and I've a
  Friend — that's dangerously sick.

ANGELICA: I see you're impatient — yet you shall stay.

WILLMORE: *(Aside.)* And miss my Assignation with my Gipsy. *(Walks about*   230
  impatiently.)

HELLENA: Madam, *(*MORETTA *brings* HELLENA, *who addresses herself to*
       ANGELICA.*)*
  You'l hardly pardon my Intrusion,
  When you shall know my Business;
  And I'm too young to tell my Tale with Art:
  But there must be a wondrous store of Goodness
  Where so much Beauty dwells.

ANGELICA: A pretty Advocate, whoever sent thee,
  — Prithee proceed — Nay, Sir, you shall not go. *(To* WILLMORE *who is*   240
  stealing off.)

WILLMORE: *(Aside.)* Then I shall lose my dear Gipsy for ever.
  — Pox on't, she stays me out of spite.

HELLENA: I am related to a Lady, Madam,
  Young, rich, and nobly born, but has the fate
  To be in love with a young *English* Gentleman.
  Strangely she loves him, at first sight she lov'd him,
  But did adore him when she heard him speak;
  For he, she said, had Charms in every word,
  That fail'd not to surprize, to wound, and conquer —   250

WILLMORE: *(Aside.)* Ha, Egad I hope this concerns me.

ANGELICA: 'Tis my false Man, he means — wou'd he were gone. *(Aside.)*
  This Praise will raise his Pride and ruin me — *(To* WILLMORE.*)* Well,
  Since you are so impatient to be gone,
  I will release you, Sir.

WILLMORE: *(Aside.)* Nay, then I'm sure 'twas me he spoke of, this cannot
  be the Effects of Kindness in her.
  — No, Madam, I've consider'd better on't,
  And will not give you cause of Jealousy.

ANGELICA: But, Sir, I've — business, that —   260

WILLMORE: This shall not do, I know 'tis but to try me.

ANGELICA: Well, to your Story, Boy, — *(Aside.)* tho 'twill undo me.

HELLENA: With this Addition to his other Beauties,
  He won her unresisting tender Heart,

He vow'd and sigh'd, and swore he lov'd her dearly;
And she believ'd the cunning Flatterer,
And thought her self the happiest Maid alive:
To day was the appointed time by both,
To consummate their Bliss;
The Virgin, Altar, and the Priest were drest,   270
And whilst she languisht for the expected Bridegroom,
She heard, he paid his broken Vows to you.

WILLMORE: *(Aside.)* So, this is some dear Rogue that's in love with me,
and this way lets me know it; or if it be not me, he means some one
whose place I may supply.

ANGELICA: Now I perceive
The cause of thy Impatience to be gone,
And all the business of this glorious Dress.

WILLMORE: Damn the young Prater, I know not what he means.

HELLENA: Madam,   280
In your fair Eyes I read too much concern
To tell my farther Business.

ANGELICA: Prithee, sweet Youth, talk on thou may'st perhaps
Raise here a Storm that may undo my Passion,
And then I'll grant thee any thing.

HELLENA: Madam, 'tis to intreat you, (oh unreasonable!)
You wou'd not see this Stranger;
For if you do, she vows you are undone,
Tho Nature never made a Man so excellent;
And sure he'ad been a God, but for Inconstancy.   290

WILLMORE: *(Aside.)* Ah, Rogue, how finely he's instructed!
— 'Tis plain some Woman that has seen me *en passant*.

ANGELICA: Oh, I shall burst with Jealousy! do you know the Man you
speak of? —

HELLENA: Yes, Madam, he us'd to be in Buff and Scarlet.

ANGELICA: *(To* WILLMORE.*)* Thou, false as Hell, what canst thou say to
this?

WILLMORE: By Heaven —

ANGELICA: Hold, do not damn thy self —

HELLENA: Nor hope to be believ'd. *(He walks about, they follow.)*   300

ANGELICA: Oh, perjur'd Man!
Is't thus you pay my generous Passion back?

HELLENA: Why wou'd you, Sir, abuse my Lady's Faith?

ANGELICA: And use me so inhumanly?

HELLENA: A Maid so young, so innocent —

WILLMORE: Ah, young Devil!

ANGELICA: Dost thou not know thy Life is in my Power?

HELLENA: Or think my Lady cannot be reveng'd?

WILLMORE: *(Aside.)* So, so, the Storm comes finely on.

ANGELICA: Now thou art silent, Guilt has struck thee dumb.   310
Oh, hadst thou still been so, I'd liv'd in safety. *(She turns away and
weeps.)*

WILLMORE: *(Aside to* HELLENA.*)* Sweetheart, the Lady's Name and House
  — quickly: I'm impatient to be with her. — *(Looks toward* ANGELICA *to watch her turning; and as she comes towards them, he meets her.)*
HELLENA: *(Aside.)* So now is he for another woman.
WILLMORE: The impudent'st young thing in Nature!
  I cannot persuade him out of his Error, Madam.
ANGELICA: I know he's in the right, — yet thou'st a Tongue   320
  That wou'd persuade him to deny his Faith. *(In Rage walks away.)*
WILLMORE: Her Name, her Name, dear Boy — *(Said softly to* HELLENA.*)*
HELLENA: Have you forgot it, Sir?
WILLMORE: *(Aside.)* Oh, I perceive he's not to know I am a Stranger to
  his Lady.
  — Yes, yes, I do know — but — I have forgot the — (ANGELICA
  turns.)
  — By Heaven, such early confidence I never saw.
ANGELICA: Did I not charge you with this Mistress, Sir?
  Which you denied, tho I beheld your Perjury.   330
  This little Generosity of thine has render'd back my Heart. *(Walks away.)*
WILLMORE: So, you have made sweet work here, my little mischief;
  Look your Lady be kind and good-natur'd now, or
  I shall have but a cursed Bargain on't. *(*ANGELICA *turns towards them.)*
  — The Rogue's bred up to Mischief,
  Art thou so great a Fool to credit him?
ANGELICA: Yes, I do; and you in vain impose upon me.
  — Come hither, Boy — Is not this he you speak of?
HELLENA: I think — it is; I cannot swear, but I vow he has just such   340
  another lying Lover's look. *(*HELLENA *looks in his Face, he gazes on her.)*
WILLMORE: *(Aside.)* Hah! do not I know that Face? —
  By Heaven, my little Gipsy! what a dull Dog was I?
  Had I but lookt that way, I'd known her.
  Are all my hopes of a new Woman banisht?
  — Egad, if I don't fit thee for this, hang me.
  — Madam, I have found out the Plot.
HELLENA: *(Aside.)* Oh Lord, what does he say, am I discover'd now?
WILLMORE: Do you see this young Spark here?
HELLENA: *(Aside.)* He'll tell her who I am.   350
WILLMORE: Who do you think this is?
HELLENA: *(Aside.)* Ay, ay, he does know me. — Nay, dear Captain,
  I'm undone if you discover me.
WILLMORE: Nay, nay, no cogging;[5] she shall know what a precious Mis-
  tress I have.
HELLENA: Will you be such a Devil!

---

5 *wheedling.*

WILLMORE: Nay, nay, I'll teach you to spoil sport you will not make. — This small Ambassador comes not from a Person of Quality, as you imagine, and he says; but from a very errant Gipsy, the talkingst, pratingst, cantingst little Animal thou ever saw'st.   *360*

ANGELICA: What news you tell me! that's the thing I mean.

HELLENA: *(Aside.)* Wou'd I were well off the place. — If ever I go a Captain-hunting again. —

WILLMORE: Mean that thing? that Gipsy thing? thou may'st as well be jealous of thy Monkey, or Parrot as her: a *German* Motion[6] were worth a dozen of her, and a Dream were a better Enjoyment, a Creature of Constitution fitter for Heaven than Man.

HELLENA: *(Aside.)* Tho I'm sure he lyes, yet this vexes me.

ANGELICA: You are mistaken, she's a *Spanish* Woman
Made up of no such dull Materials.   *370*

WILLMORE: Materials! Egad, and she be made of any that will either dispense, or admit of Love, I'll be bound to continence.

HELLENA: *(Aside to him.)* Unreasonable Man, do you think so?

WILLMORE: You may Return, my little Brazen Head, and tell your Lady, that till she be handsome enough to be belov'd, or I dull enough to be religious, there will be small hopes of me.

ANGELICA: Did you not promise then to marry her?

WILLMORE: Not I, by Heaven.

ANGELICA: You cannot undeceive my fears and torments, till you have vow'd you will not marry her.   *380*

HELLENA: *(Aside.)* If he swears that, he'll be reveng'd on me indeed for all my Rogueries.

ANGELICA: I know what Arguments you'll bring against me: Fortune and Honour.

WILLMORE: Honour! I tell you, I hate it in your Sex; and those that fancy themselves possest of that Foppery, are the most impertinently troublesome of all Woman-kind, and will transgress nine Commandments to keep one: and to satisfy your Jealousy I swear —

HELLENA: *(Aside to him.)* Oh, no swearing, dear Captain —

WILLMORE: If it were possible I should ever be inclin'd to marry, it   *390*
should be some kind young Sinner, one that has Generosity enough to give a favour handsomely to one that can ask it discreetly, one that has Wit enough to manage an Intrigue of Love — oh, how civil such a Wench is, to a Man that does her the Honour to marry her.

ANGELICA: By Heaven, there's no Faith in any thing he says.

(Enter SEBASTIAN.*)*

SEBASTIAN: Madam, *Don Antonio* —

ANGELICA: Come hither.

HELLENA: *(Aside.)* Ha, *Antonio!* he may be coming hither, and he'll certainly discover me. I'll therefore retire without a Ceremony. *(Exit* HELLENA.*)*

---

6 *puppet show.*

ANGELICA: I'll see him, get my Coach ready.   400
SEBASTIAN: It waits you, Madam.
WILLMORE: This is lucky: what, Madam, now I may be gone and leave
    you to the enjoyment of my Rival?
ANGELICA: Dull Man, that canst not see how ill, how poor
    That false dissimulation looks — Be gone,
    And never let me see thy cozening Face again,
    Lest I relapse and kill thee.
WILLMORE: Yes, you can spare me now, — farewell till you are in a better
    Humour — I'm glad of this release — *(Aside.)*
    Now for my Gipsy: 410
    For tho to worse we change, yet still we find
    New Joys, New Charms, in a new Miss that's kind. *(Exit* WILLMORE.*)*
ANGELICA: He's gone, and in this Ague of My Soul
    The shivering Fit returns;
    Oh with what willing haste he took his leave,
    As if the long'd for Minute were arriv'd,
    Of some blest Assignation.
    In vain I have consulted all my Charms,
    In vain this Beauty priz'd, in vain believ'd
    My eyes cou'd kindle any lasting Fires.   420
    I had forgot my Name, my Infamy,
    And the Reproach that Honour lays on those
    That dare pretend a sober passion here.
    Nice Reputation, tho it leave behind
    More Virtues than inhabit where that dwells,
    Yet that once gone, those virtues shine no more.
    — Then since I am not fit to be belov'd,
    I am resolv'd to think on a Revenge
    On him that sooth'd me thus to my undoing. *(Exeunt.)*

SCENE 3. *(A Street.)*

(Enter FLORINDA *and* VALERIA *in Habits different from what they have been seen in.)*

FLORINDA: We're happily escap'd, yet I tremble still.
VALERIA: A Lover and fear! why, I am but half a one, and yet I have
    Courage for any Attempt. Would *Hellena* were here. I wou'd fain
    have had her as deep in this Mischief as we; she'll fare but ill else, I
    doubt.
FLORINDA: She pretended a Visit to the *Augustine* Nuns,[1] but I believe
    some other design carried her out; pray Heavens we light on her.
    — Prithee what didst do with *Callis*?
VALERIA: When I saw no Reason wou'd do good on her, I follow'd her
    into the Wardrobe, and as she was looking for something in a great

---

1 *an order of nuns following the Rule of St. Augustine, which enjoined poverty, prayer, obedience, and chastity.*

Chest, I tumbled her in by the Heels, snatched the Key of the Apartment where you were confin'd, lockt her in, and left her bawling for help.

FLORINDA: 'Tis well you resolve to follow my Fortunes, for thou darest never appear at home again after such an Action.

VALERIA: That's according as the young Stranger and I shall agree — But to our business — I deliver'd your Note to *Belvile* when I got out under pretence of going to Mass. I found him at his Lodging, and believe me it came seasonably; for never was Man in so desperate a Condition. I told him of your Resolution of making your escape to   20
day, if your Brother would be absent long enough to permit you; if not, die rather than be *Antonio's*.

FLORINDA: Thou shou'dst have told him I was confin'd to my Chamber upon my Brother's suspicion, that the Business on the *Molo* was a Plot laid between him and I.

VALERIA: I said all this, and told him your Brother was now gone to his Devotion, and he resolves to visit every Church till he find him; and not only undeceive him in that, but caress him so as shall delay his return home.

FLORINDA: Oh Heavens! he's here, and *Belvile* with him too. *(They put on   30
their Vizards.)*

(Enter DON PEDRO, BELVILE, WILLMORE; BELVILE *and* DON PEDRO *seeming in serious Discourse.)*

VALERIA: Walk boldly by them; I'll come at a distance, lest he suspect us. *(She walks by them, and looks back on them.)*

WILLMORE: Ha! A Woman! and of an excellent Mien!

PEDRO: She throws a kind look back on you.

WILLMORE: Death, tis a likely Wench, and that kind look shall not be cast away — I'll follow her.

BELVILE: Prithee do not.

WILLMORE: Do not! By Heavens to the Antipodes, with such an Invitation. *(She goes out, and* WILLMORE *follows her.)*   40

BELVILE: 'Tis a mad Fellow for a Wench.

(Enter FREDERICK.*)*

FREDERICK: Oh Colonel, such News.

BELVILE: Prithee what?

FREDERICK: News that will make you laugh in spite of Fortune.

BELVILE: What, *Blunt* has had some damn'd Trick put upon him? Cheated, bang'd, or clapt?

FREDERICK: Cheated, Sir, rarely cheated of all but his Shirt and Drawers; the unconscionable Whore too turn'd him out before Consummation, so that traversing the Streets at Midnight, the Watch found him in this *Fresco*, and conducted him home: By Heaven 'tis such a   50
slight, and yet I durst as well have been hang'd as laugh at him, or

pity him; he beats all that do but ask him a Question, and is in such
an Humour —

PEDRO: Who is't has met with this ill usage, Sir?

BELVILE: A Friend of ours, whom you must see for Mirth's sake. *(Aside.)*
I'll imploy him to give *Florinda* time for an escape.

PEDRO: Who is he?

BELVILE: A young Countryman of ours, one that has been educated at so
plentiful a rate he yet ne'er knew the want of Money, and 'twill be a
great Jest to see how simply he'll look without it. For my part I'll   60
lend him none, and the Rogue knows not how to put on a borrow-
ing Face, and ask first. I'll let him see how good 'tis to play our parts
whilst I play his — Prithee, *Fred*, do go home and keep him in that
posture till we come. *(Exeunt.)*

(Enter FLORINDA from the farther end of the Scene, looking behind her.)

FLORINDA: I am follow'd still — hah — my Brother too advancing this
way good Heavens defend me from being seen by him. *(She goes off.)*

(Enter WILLMORE, and after him VALERIA, at a little distance.)

WILLMORE: Ah! There she sails, she looks back as she were willing to be
boarded; I'll warrant her Prize. *(He goes out, VALERIA following.)*

(Enter HELLENA, just as he goes out, with a Page.)

HELLENA: Hah, is not that my Captain that has a Woman in chase? —
'tis not *Angelica*. Boy, follow those People at a distance, and bring me   70
an Account where they go in. — *(Exit Page.)* I'll find his Haunts, and
plague him every where. — ha — my Brother!

(BELVILE, WILLMORE, PEDRO cross the Stage: HELLENA runs off.)

(Scene changes to another Street. Enter FLORINDA.)

FLORINDA: What shall I do? My Brother now pursues me.
Will no kind Power protect me from his Tyranny?
— Hah, here's a Door open, I'll venture in, since nothing can be
worse than to fall into his Hands, my Life and Honour are at stake,
and my Necessity has no choice. *(She goes in.)*

(Enter VALERIA, and HELLENA's PAGE peeping after FLORINDA.)

PAGE: Here she went in, I shall remember this House. *(Exit Boy.)*

VALERIA: This is *Belvile's* Lodgings; she's gone in as readily as if she knew
it — hah — here's that mad Fellow again; I dare not venture in —   80
I'll watch my Opportunity. *(Goes aside.)*

(Enter WILLMORE, *gazing about him.)*

WILLMORE: I have lost her hereabouts — Pox on't she must not scape me so. *(Goes out.)*

(Scene changes to BLUNT's *Chamber, discovers him sitting on a Couch in his Shirt and Drawers, reading.)*

BLUNT: So, now my Mind's a little at Peace, since I have resolv'd Revenge — A Pox on this Taylor tho, for not bringing home the Clothes I bespoke; and a Pox of all poor Cavaliers, a Man can never keep a spare Suit for 'em; and I shall have these Rogues come in and find me naked; and then I'm undone; but I'm resolv'd to arm my self — the Rascals shall not insult over me too much.

(Puts on an old rusty Sword and Buff-Belt.)

— Now, how like a Morrice-Dancer[2] I am equipt — a fine Lady-like   *90* Whore to cheat me thus, without affording me a Kindness for my Money, a Pox light on her, I shall never be reconciled to the Sex more, she has made me as faithless as a Physician, as uncharitable as a Churchman, and as ill-natur'd as a Poet. O how I'll use all Women-kind hereafter! what wou'd I give to have one of 'em within my reach now! any Mortal thing in Petticoats, kind Fortune, send me; and I'll forgive thy last Night's Malice — Here's a cursed Book too — a Warning to all young Travellers — that can instruct me how to prevent such Mischiefs now 'tis too late. Well 'tis a rare con-venient thing to read a little now and then, as well as hawk and   *100* hunt. *(Sits down again and reads.)*

(Enter to him FLORINDA.)

FLORINDA: This House is haunted sure, 'tis well furnisht and no living thing inhabits it — hah — a Man! Heavens how he's attir'd! sure 'tis some Rope-dancer, or Fencing-Master; I tremble now for fear, and yet I must venture now to speak to him — Sir, if I may not inter-rupt your Meditations — *(He starts up and gazes.)*
BLUNT: Hah — what's here? Are my wishes granted? and is not that a she Creature? 'Adsheartlikins 'tis! what wretched thing art thou — hah!
FLORINDA: Charitable Sir, you've told your self already what I am; a very   *110* wretched Maid, forc'd by a strange unlucky Accident, to seek a safety here, and must be ruin'd, if you do not grant it.
BLUNT: Ruin'd! Is there any Ruin so inevitable as that which now threat-ens thee? Dost thou know, miserable Woman, into what Den of Mischiefs thou art fall'n? what a Bliss of Confusion? — hah — dost

---

2 *morris dances are British folk dances performed by dancers wearing antique and fantastical costumes to represent legendary characters.*

not see something in my looks that frights thy guilty Soul, and
makes thee wish to change that Shape of Woman for any humble
Animal, or Devil? for those were safer for thee, and less
mischievous.

FLORINDA: Alas, what mean you, Sir? I must confess your Looks have   120
something in 'em makes me fear; but I beseech you, as you seem a
Gentleman, pity a harmless Virgin, that takes your House for
Sanctuary.

BLUNT: Talk on, talk on, and weep too, till my faith return. Do, flatter
me out of my Senses again — a harmless Virgin with a Pox, as
much one as t'other, 'adsheartlikins. Why, what the Devil can I not
be safe in my House for you? not in my Chamber? nay, even being
naked too cannot secure me? This is an Impudence greater than has
invaded me yet. — Come, no Resistance. *(Pulls her rudely.)*

FLORINDA: Dare you be so cruel?   130

BLUNT: Cruel, 'adsheartlikins as a Galley-slave, or a *Spanish* Whore:
Cruel, yes, I will kiss and beat thee all over; kiss, and see thee all
over; thou shalt lie with me too, not that I care for the Injoyment,
but to let you see I have ta'en deliberated Malice to thee, and will be
revenged on one Whore for the Sins of another; I will smile and
deceive thee, flatter thee, and beat thee, kiss and swear, and lye to
thee, imbrace thee and rob thee, as she did me, fawn on thee, and
strip thee stark naked, then hang thee out at my Window by the
Heels, with a Paper of scurvey Verses fasten'd to thy Breast, in
praise of damnable Women — Come, come along.   140

FLORINDA: Alas, Sir, must I be sacrific'd for the Crimes of the most infamous of my Sex? I never understood the Sins you name.

BLUNT: Do, persuade the Fool you love him, or that one of you can be
just or honest; tell me I was not an easy Coxcomb, or any strange
impossible Tale: it will be believ'd sooner than thy false Showers or
Protestations. A Generation of damn'd Hypocrites, to flatter my
very Clothes from my back! dissembling Witches! are these the
Returns you make an honest Gentleman that trusts, believes, and
loves you? — But if I be not even with you — Come along, or I
shall — *(Pulls her again.)*   150

(Enter FREDERICK.)

FREDERICK: Hah, what's here to do?

BLUNT: 'Adsheartlikins, *Fred* I am glad thou art come, to be a Witness of
my dire Revenge.

FREDERICK: What's this, a Person of Quality too, who is upon the Ramble to supply the Defects of some grave impotent Husband?

BLUNT: No, this has another Pretence, some very unfortunate Accident
brought her hither, to save a Life pursued by I know not who, or
why, and forc'd to take Sanctuary here at Fool's Haven. 'Adsheartlikins to me of all Mankind for Protection? Is the Ass to be cajol'd
again, think ye? No, young one, no Prayers or Tears shall mitigate   160

my Rage; therefore prepare for both my Pleasure of Enjoyment and Revenge, for I am resolved to make up my Loss here on thy Body: I'll take it out in kindness and in beating.

FREDERICK: Now, Mistress of mine, what do you think of this?

FLORINDA: I think he will not — dares not be so barbarous.

FREDERICK: Have a care, *Blunt*, she fetch'd a deep Sigh; she is inamour'd with thy Shirt and Drawers, she'll strip thee even of that. There are of her Calling such unconscionable Baggages, and such dexterous Thieves, they'll flea³ a Man, and he shall ne'er miss his Skin, till he feels the Cold. There was a Country-man of ours robb'd of a Row of Teeth whilst he was sleeping, which the Jilt made him buy again when he wak'd — You see, Lady, how little Reason we have to trust you.

BLUNT: 'Dsheartlikins, why, this is most abominable!

FLORINDA: Some such Devils there may be, but by all that's holy I am none such, I entered here to save a Life in danger.

BLUNT: For no goodness, I'll warrant her.

FREDERICK: Faith, Damsel, you had e'en confess the plain Truth, for we are Fellows not to be caught twice in the same Trap: Look on that Wreck, a tight Vessel when he set out of Haven, well trim'd and laden, and see how a Female Piccaroon of this Island of Rogues has shatter'd him, and canst thou hope for any Mercy?

BLUNT: No, no, Gentlewoman, come along, 'adsheartlikins we must be better acquainted — we'll both lie with her, and then let me alone to bang her.

FREDERICK: I am ready to serve you in matters of Revenge; that has a double Pleasure in't.

BLUNT: Well said. You hear, little one, how you are condemn'd by publick Vote to the Bed within; there's no resisting your Destiny, Sweetheart. *(Pulls her.)*

FLORINDA: Stay, Sir, I have seen you with *Belvile*, an *English* Cavalier. For his sake use me kindly; you know him, Sir.

BLUNT: *Belvile!* why, yes, Sweeting, we do know *Belvile*, and wish he were with us now. He's a Cormorant at Whore and Bacon,⁴ he'd have a Limb or two of thee, my Virgin Pullet: but 'tis no matter, we'll leave him the Bones to pick.

FLORINDA: Sir, if you have any Esteem for that *Belvile*, I conjure you to treat me with more Gentleness; he'll thank you for the Justice.

FREDERICK: Hark ye, *Blunt*, I doubt we are mistaken in this matter.

FLORINDA: Sir, If you find me not worth *Belvile's* Care, use me as you please; and that you may think I merit better treatment than you threaten — pray take this Present —

(Gives him a Ring: He looks on it.)

BLUNT: Hum — A Diamond! why, 'tis a wonderful Virtue now that lies in this Ring, a mollifying Virtue; 'adsheartlikins there's more persuasive Rhetorick in't, than all her Sex can utter.

3 *flay.*
4 *i.e., he has a ravenous sexual appetite.*

FREDERICK: I begin to suspect something; and 'twou'd anger us vilely to
be truss'd up for a Rape upon a Maid of Quality, when we only
believe we ruffle a Harlot.

BLUNT: Thou art a credulous Fellow, but 'adsheartlikins I have no Faith
yet; why, my Saint prattled as parlously as this does, she gave me a   210
Bracelet too, a Devil on her: but I sent my Man to sell it to day for
Necessaries, and it prov'd as counterfeit as her Vows of Love.

FREDERICK: However, let it reprieve her till we see *Belvile.*

BLUNT: That's hard, yet I will grant it.

(Enter a Servant.)

SERVANT: Oh, Sir, the Colonel is just come in with his new Friend and a
Spaniard of Quality, and talks of having you to Dinner with 'em.

BLUNT: 'Dsheartlikins, I'm undone — I would not see 'em for the World:
Harkye, *Fred,* lock up the Wench in your Chamber.

FREDERICK: Fear nothing, Madam, whate'er he threatens, you're safe
whilst in my Hands. *(Exeunt FREDERICK and FLORINDA.)*   220

BLUNT: And, Sirrah — upon your Life, say — I am not at home — or
that I am asleep — or — or anything — away — I'll prevent them
coming this way. *(Locks the Door and Exeunt.)*

ACT FIVE

SCENE 1. *(BLUNT's Chamber.)*

*(After a great knocking as at his Chamber-door, enter BLUNT softly, crossing the Stage
in his Shirt and Drawers, as before.)*

VOICES: *(Calls within.)* Ned! Ned Blunt! Ned Blunt!

BLUNT: The Rogues are up in Arms; 'dsheartlikins, this villainous
Frederick has betray'd me: they have heard of my blessed Fortune.

VOICES: *Ned Blunt, Ned, Ned — (and knocking within.)*

BELVILE: Why, he's dead, Sir, without dispute dead, he has not been seen
to day; let's break open the Door — here — Boy —

BLUNT: Ha, break open the Door! 'dsheartlikins that mad Fellow will be
as good as his word.

BELVILE: Boy, bring something to force the Door.

(A great noise within at the Door again.)

BLUNT: So, now must I speak in my own Defence; I'll try what Rhetor-   10
ick will do — hold — hold, what do you mean, Gentlemen, what do
you mean?

BELVILE: Oh Rogue, art alive? prithee open the Door, and convince us.

BLUNT: Yes, I am alive, Gentlemen — but at present a little busy.

BELVILE: *(Within.)* How! *Blunt* grown a man of Business! come, come, open, and let's see this Miracle.

BLUNT: No, no, no, no, Gentlemen, 'tis no great Business — but — I am — at — my Devotion, — 'dsheartlikins, will you not allow a man time to pray?

BELVILE: *(Within.)* Turn'd religious! a greater Wonder than the first, therefore open quickly, or we shall unhinge, we shall.

BLUNT: *(Aside.)* This won't do — Why, hark ye, Colonel; to tell you the plain Truth, I am about a necessary Affair of Life. — I have a Wench with me — you apprehend me? the Devil's in't if they be so uncivil as to disturb me now.

WILLMORE: *(Within.)* How, a Wench! Nay, then we must enter and partake; no Resistance, — unless it be your Lady of Quality, and then we'll keep our distance.

BLUNT: So, the Business is out.

WILLMORE: *(Within.)* Come, come, lend more hands to the Door, — now heave altogether — so, well done, my Boys — *(Breaks open the Door.)*

(Enter BELVILE, WILLMORE, FREDERICK, PEDRO, *and* BELVILE's *Page:* BLUNT *looks simply;[1] they all laugh at him, he lays his hand on his Sword, and comes up to* WILLMORE.*)*

BLUNT: Hark ye, Sir, laugh out your laugh quickly, d'ye hear, and be gone, I shall spoil your sport else; 'dsheartlikins, Sir, I shall — the Jest has been carried on too long, — *(Aside.)* a Plague upon my Taylor —

WILLMORE: 'Sdeath, how the Whore has drest him! Faith, Sir, I'm sorry.

BLUNT: Are you so, Sir? keep't to your self then, Sir, I advise you, d'ye hear? for I can as little endure your Pity as his Mirth. *(Lays his Hand on's Sword.)*

BELVILE: Indeed, *Willmore,* thou wert a little too rough with *Ned Blunt's* Mistress; call a Person of Quality Whore, and one so young, so handsome, and so eloquent! — ha, ha, ha.

BLUNT: Hark ye, Sir, you know me, and know I can be angry; have a care — for 'dsheartlikins I can fight too — I can, Sir, — do you mark me — no more.

BELVILE: Why so peevish, good *Ned?* some Disappointments, I'll warrant — What! did the jealous Count her Husband return just in the nick?

BLUNT: Or the Devil, Sir, — *(They laugh.)* d'ye laugh? Look ye, settle me a good sober Countenance, and that quickly too, or you shall know *Ned Blunt* is not —

BELVILE: Not every Body, we know that.

BLUNT: Not an Ass, to be laught at, Sir.

---

1 *foolishly.*

WILLMORE: Unconscionable Sinner, to bring a Lover so near his Happiness, a vigorous passionate Lover, and then not only cheat him of his Moveables, but his Desires too.

BELVILE: Ah, Sir, a Mistress is a Trifle with *Blunt*, he'll have a dozen the next time he looks aboad; his Eyes have Charms not to be resisted: There needs no more than to expose that taking Person to the view of the Fair, and he leads 'em all in Triumph. 60

PEDRO: Sir, tho I'm a stranger to you, I'm ashamed at the rudeness of my Nation; and could you learn who did it, would assist you to make an Example of 'em.

BLUNT: Why, ay, there's one speaks sense now, and handsomely; and let me tell you Gentlemen, I should not have shew'd my self like a Jack-Pudding,[2] thus to have made you Mirth, but that I have revenge within my power; for know, I have got into my possession a Female, who had better have fallen under any Curse, than the Ruin I design her: 'dsheartlikins, she assaulted me here in my own Lodgings, and hast doubtless committed a Rape upon me, had not this Sword 70 defended me.

FREDERICK: I knew not that, but o' my Conscience thou hadst ravisht her, had she not redeem'd her self with a Ring — let's see't, *Blunt*. (BLUNT *shews the Ring.*)

BELVILE: *(Aside.)* Hah! — the Ring I gave *Florinda* when we exchang'd our Vows! — hark ye, *Blunt* — *(Goes to whisper to him.)*

WILLMORE: No whispering, good Colonel, there's a Woman in the case, no whispering.

BELVILE: Hark ye, Fool, be advis'd, and conceal both the Ring and the Story, for your Reputation's sake; don't let people know what des- 80 pis'd Cullies we *English* are: to be cheated and abus'd by one Whore, and another rather bribe thee than be kind to thee, is an Infamy to our Nation.

WILLMORE: Come, come, where's the Wench? we'll see her, let her be what she will, we'll see her.

PEDRO: Ay, ay, let us see her, I can soon discover whether she be of Quality, or for your Diversion.

BLUNT: She's in *Fred's* Custody.

WILLMORE: Come, come, the Key. *(To* FREDERICK, *who gives him the Key; they are going.)* 90

BELVILE: *(Aside.)* Death! what shall I do? — stay, Gentlemen — *(Aside.)* yet if I hinder 'em, I shall discover all — hold, let's go one at once[3] — give me the Key.

WILLMORE: Nay, hold there, Colonel, I'll go first.

FREDERICK: Nay, no Dispute, *Ned* and I have the property of her.

WILLMORE: Damn Property — then we'll draw Cuts. (BELVILE *goes to whisper* WILLMORE.)
Nay, no Corruption, good Colonel: come, the longest Sword carries her. — *(They all draw, forgetting* DON PEDRO, *being a* Spaniard, *had the longest.)* 100

2 *clown.*
3 *one at a time.*

BLUNT: I yield up my Interest to you Gentlemen, and that will be
Revenge sufficient.
WILLMORE: *(To* PEDRO.*)* The Wench is yours — *(Aside.)* Pox of his *Toledo*,[4] I
had forgot that.
FREDERICK: Come, Sir, I'll conduct you to the Lady.

(Exeunt FREDERICK *and* PEDRO.*)*

BELVILE: *(Aside.)* To hinder him will certainly discover her —
Dost know, dull Beast, what Mischief thou hast done?
*(*WILLMORE, *walking up and down out of Humour.)*
WILLMORE: Ay, ay, to trust our Fortune to Lots, a Devil on't, 'twas mad-
ness, that's the Truth on't.   110
BELVILE: Oh intolerable Sot!

(Enter FLORINDA, *running masqu'd,* PEDRO *after her,* WILLMORE *gazing round her.)*

FLORINDA: *(Aside.)* Good Heaven, defend me from discovery.
PEDRO: 'Tis but in vain to fly me, you are fallen to my Lot.
BELVILE: *(Aside.)* Sure she is undiscover'd yet, but now I fear there is no
way to bring her off.
WILLMORE: *(Aside.)* Why, what a Pox is not this my Woman, the same I
follow'd but now?

*(*PEDRO *talking to* FLORINDA, *who walks up and down.)*

PEDRO: As if I did not know ye, and your Business here.
FLORINDA: *(Aside.)* Good Heaven! I fear he does indeed —
PEDRO: Come, pray be kind, I know you meant to be so when you   120
enter'd here, for these are proper Gentlemen.
WILLMORE: But, Sir — perhaps the Lady will not be impos'd upon, she'll
chuse her Man.
PEDRO: I am better bred, than not to leave her Choice free.

(Enter VALERIA, *and is surpriz'd at the Sight of* DON PEDRO.*)*

VALERIA: *(Aside.)* Don *Pedro* here! there's no avoiding him.
FLORINDA: *(Aside.)* Valeria! then I'm undone —
VALERIA: Oh! have I found you, Sir — *(To* PEDRO, *running to him.)*
— The strangest Accident — if I had breath — to tell it.
PEDRO: Speak — is *Florinda* safe? *Hellena* well?
VALERIA: Ay, ay, Sir — *Florinda* — is safe — *(Aside.)* from any fears of you.   130
PEDRO: Why, where's *Florinda*? — speak.
VALERIA: Ay, where indeed, Sir? I wish I could inform you, — But to
hold you no longer in doubt —
FLORINDA: *(Aside.)* Oh, what will she say!
VALERIA: She's fled away in the Habit of one of her Pages, Sir — but
Callis thinks you may retrieve her yet, if you make haste away; she'll
tell you, Sir, the rest — *(Aside.)* if you can find her out.

---

4 *sword (Toledo in Spain was known for its fine swords).*

PEDRO: Dishonourable Girl, she has undone my Aim — Sir — you see
my necessity of leaving you, and I hope you'll pardon it: my Sister, I
know, will make her flight to you; and if she do, I shall expect she   *140*
should be render'd back.

BELVILE: I shall consult my Love and Honour, Sir. *(Exit* PEDRO.*)*

FLORINDA: *(To* VALERIA.*)* My dear Preserver, let me imbrace thee.

WILLMORE: What the Devil's all this?

BLUNT: Mystery by this Light.

VALERIA: Come, come, make haste and get your selves married quickly,
for your Brother will return again.

BELVILE: I am so surpriz'd with Fears and Joys, so amaz'd to find you
here in safety, I can scarce persuade my Heart into a Faith of what I
see —   *150*

WILLMORE: Harkye, Colonel, is this that Mistress who has cost you so
many Sighs, and me so many Quarrels with you?

BELVILE: *(To* FLORINDA.*)* It is — Pray give him the Honour of your Hand.

WILLMORE: Thus it must be receiv'd then. *(Kneels and kisses her Hand.)*
And with it give your Pardon too.

FLORINDA: The Friend to *Belvile* may command me anything.

WILLMORE: *(Aside.)* Death, wou'd I might, 'tis a surprizing Beauty.

BELVILE: Boy, run and fetch a Father instantly. *(Exit* BOY.*)*

FREDERICK: So, now do I stand like a Dog, and have not a Syllable to
plead my own Cause with: by this Hand, Madam, I was never thor-   *170*
owly confounded before, nor shall I ever more dare look up with
Confidence, till you are pleased to pardon me.

FLORINDA: Sir, I'll be reconcil'd to you on one Condition, that you'll follow the Example of your Friend, in marrying a Maid that does not
hate you, and whose Fortune (I believe) will not be unwelcome to
you.

FREDERICK: Madam, had I no Inclinations that way, I shou'd obey your
kind Commands.

BELVILE: Who, *Fred* marry? he has so few Inclinations for Womankind,
that had he been possest of Paradise, he might have continu'd there   *170*
to this Day, if no Crime but Love cou'd have disinherited him.

FREDERICK: Oh, I do not use to boast of my Intrigues.

BELVILE: Boast! why thou do'st nothing but boast; and I dare swear, wer't
thou as innocent from the Sin of the Grape, as thou art from the
Apple, thou might'st yet claim that right in *Eden* which our first Parents lost by too much loving.

FREDERICK: I wish this Lady would think me so modest a Man.

VALERIA: She shou'd be sorry then, and not like you half so well, and I
shou'd be loth to break my Word with you; which was, That if your
Friend and mine are agreed, it shou'd be a Match between you and   *180*
I. *(She gives him her Hand.)*

FREDERICK: Bear witness, Colonel, 'tis a Bargain. *(Kisses her Hand.)*

BLUNT: *(To* FLORINDA.*)* I have a Pardon to beg too; but 'adsheartlikins I
am so out of Countenance, that I am a Dog if I can say any thing to
purpose.

FLORINDA: Sir, I heartily forgive you all.

BLUNT: That's nobly said, sweet Lady — *Belvile*, prithee present her her
Ring again, for I find I have not Courage to approach her my self.
(Gives him the Ring, he gives it to FLORINDA.*)*

(Enter BOY.*)*

BOY: Sir, I have brought the Father that you sent for. *(Exit* BOY.*)*

BELVILE: 'Tis well, and now my dear *Florinda*, let's fly to compleat that   190
mighty Joy we have so long wish'd and sigh'd for. — Come, *Fred*
you'll follow?

FREDERICK: Your Example, Sir, 'twas ever my Ambition in War, and
must be so in Love.

WILLMORE: And must not I see this juggling⁵ Knot ty'd?

BELVILE: No, thou shalt do us better Service, and be our Guard, lest Don
Pedro's sudden Return interrupt the Ceremony.

WILLMORE: Content; I'll secure this Pass.

(Exeunt BELVILE, FLORINDA, FREDERICK, *and* VALERIA.*)*

(Enter BOY.*)*

BOY: *(To* WILLMORE.*)* Sir, there's a Lady without wou'd speak to you.

WILLMORE: Conduct her in, I dare not quit my Post.   200

BOY: *(To* BLUNT.*)*And, Sir, your Taylor waits you in your Chamber.

BLUNT: Some comfort yet, I shall not dance naked at the Wedding.

(Exeunt BLUNT *and* BOY.*)*

(Enter again the BOY, *conducting in* ANGELICA *in her masquing Habit and a Vizard.*
WILLMORE *runs to her.)*

WILLMORE: This can be none but my pretty Gipsy — Oh, I see you can
follow as well as fly — Come, confess thy self the most malicious
Devil in Nature; you think you have done my Bus'ness with
Angelica —

ANGELICA: Stand off, base Villain — *(She draws a Pistol and holds it to his*
Breast.)

WILLMORE: Hah, 'tis not she: who art thou? and what's thy Business?

ANGELICA: One thou hast injur'd, and who comes to kill thee for't.

WILLMORE: What the Devil canst thou mean?   210

ANGELICA: By all my Hopes to kill thee —
Holds still the Pistol to his Breast, he going back, she following still.)

WILLMORE: Prithee on what Acquaintance? for I know thee not.

ANGELICA: Behold this Face! — so lost to thy Remembrance!
And then call all thy Sins about thy Soul,
And let them die with thee. *(Pulls off her Vizard.)*

---

5 *cheating (of Florinda's family).*

WILLMORE: *Angelica!*

ANGELICA: Yes, Traitor.
Does not thy guilty Blood run shivering thro thy Veins?
Hast thou no Horrour at this Sight, that tells thee,   220
Thou hast not long to boast thy shameful Conquest?

WILLMORE: Faith, no Child, my Blood keeps its old Ebbs and Flows still,
and that usual Heat too, that cou'd oblige thee with a Kindness, had
I but opportunity.

ANGELICA: Devil! dost wanton with my Pain — have at thy Heart!

WILLMORE: Hold, dear Virago! hold thy Hand a little,
I am not now at leisure to be kill'd — hold and hear me — *(Aside.)*
Death, I think she's in earnest.

ANGELICA: *(Aside, turning from him.)* Oh if I take not heed,
My coward Heart will leave me to his Mercy.   230
— What have you, Sir, to say? — but should I hear thee,
Thoud'st talk away all that is brave about me: *(Follows him with the Pistol to his Breast.)*
And I have vow'd thy Death, by all that's sacred.

WILLMORE: Why, then there's an end of a proper handsome Fellow, that
might have liv'd to have done good Service yet: — That's all I can
say to't.

ANGELICA: *(Pausingly.)* Yet — I wou'd give thee — time for Penitence.

WILLMORE: Faith, Child, I thank God, I have ever took care to lead a
good, sober, hopeful Life, and am of a Religion that teaches me to   240
believe, I shall depart in Peace.

ANGELICA: So will the Devil: tell me
How many poor believing Fools thou hast undone;
How many Hearts thou hast betray'd to ruin!
— Yet these are little Mischiefs to the Ills
Thou'st taught mine to commit: thou'st taught it Love.

WILLMORE: Egad, 'twas shrewdly⁶ hurt the while.

ANGELICA: — Love, that has robb'd it of its Unconcern,
Of all that Pride that taught me how to value it,
And in its room a mean submissive Passion was convey'd,   250
That made me humbly bow, which I ne'er did
To any thing but Heaven.
— Thou, perjur'd Man, didst this, and with thy Oaths,
Which on thy Knees thou didst devoutly make,
Soften'd my yielding Heart — And then, I was a Slave —
Yet still had been content to've worn my Chains,
Worn 'em with Vanity and Joy for ever,
Hadst thou not broke those Vows that put them on.
— 'Twas then I was undone. *(All this while follows him with a Pistol to his Breast.)*   260

WILLMORE: Broke my Vows! why, where hast thou lived?
Amongst the Gods? For I never heard of mortal Man,
That has not broke a thousand Vows.

---

6 *painfully.*

ANGELICA: Oh, Impudence!

WILLMORE: *Angelica*! that Beauty has been too long tempting,
    Not to have made a thousand Lovers languish,
    Who in the amorous Favour, no doubt have sworn
    Like me; did they all die in that Faith? still adoring?
    I do not think they did.

ANGELICA: No, faithless Man: had I repaid their Vows, as I did thine, I   *270*
    wou'd have kill'd the ungrateful that had abandon'd me.

WILLMORE: This old General has quite spoil'd thee; nothing makes a
    Woman so vain, as being flatter'd; your old Lover ever supplies the
    Defects of Age, with intolerable Dotage, vast Charge, and that
    which you call Constancy; and attributing all this to your own Mer-
    its, you domineer, and throw your Favours in's Teeth, upbraiding
    him still with the Defects of Age, and cuckold him as often as he
    deceives your Expectations. But the gay, young, brisk Lover, that
    brings his equal Fires, and can give you Dart for Dart, he'll be as
    nice[7] as you sometimes.   *280*

ANGELICA: All this thou'st made me know, for which I hate thee.
    Had I remain'd in innocent Security,
    I shou'd have thought all Men were born my Slaves;
    And worn my Pow'r like Lightning in my Eyes,
    To have destroy'd at Pleasure when offended.
    — But when Love held the Mirror, the undeceiving Glass
    Reflected all the Weakness of my Soul, and made me know,
    My richest Treasure being lost, my Honour,
    All the remaining Spoil cou'd not be worth
    The Conqueror's Care or Value.   *290*
    — Oh how I fell like a long worship'd Idol,
    Discovering all the Cheat!
    Wou'd not the Incense and rich Sacrifice,
    Which blind Devotion offer'd at my Altars,
    Have fall'n to thee?
    Why woud'st thou then destroy my fancy'd Power?

WILLMORE: By Heaven thou art brave, and I admire thee strangely.
    I wish I were that dull, that constant thing,
    Which thou woud'st have, and Nature never meant me:
    I must, like chearful Birds, sing in all Groves,   *300*
    And perch on every Bough,
    Billing the next kind She that flies to meet me;
    Yet after all cou'd build my Nest with thee,
    Thither repairing when I'd lov'd my round,
    And still reserve a tributary Flame.
    — To gain your Credit, I'll pay you back your Charity,
    And be oblig'd for nothing but for Love. *(Offers her a Purse of Gold.)*

ANGELICA: Oh that thou wert in earnest!
    So mean a Thought of me,
    Wou'd turn my Rage to Scorn, and I shou'd pity thee,   *310*

---

7 *fastidious.*

And give thee leave to live;
Which for the publick Safety of our Sex,
And my own private Injuries, I dare not do.
Prepare — *(Follows still, as before.)*
— I will no more be tempted with Replies.
WILLMORE: Sure —
ANGELICA: Another Word will damn thee! I've heard thee talk too long.
(She follows him with a Pistol ready to shoot: he retires still amaz'd.)

(Enter DON ANTONIO, *his Arm in a Scarf, and lays hold on the Pistol.)*

ANTONIO: Hah! *Angelica!*
ANGELICA: *Antonio!* What Devil brought thee hither?   320
ANTONIO: Love and Curiosity, seeing your Coach at Door. Let me dis-
    arm you of this unbecoming Instrument of Death. — *(Takes away the
    Pistol.)*
    Amongst the Number of your Slaves, was there not one worthy the
    Honour to have fought your Quarrel?
    — Who are you, Sir, that are so very wretched
    To merit Death from her?
WILLMORE: One, Sir, that cou'd have made a better End of an amorous
    Quarrel without you, than with you.
ANTONIO: Sure 'tis some Rival — hah — the very Man took down her   330
    Picture yesterday — the very same that set on me last night — Blest
    opportunity — *(Offers to shoot him.)*
ANGELICA: Hold, you're mistaken, Sir.
ANTONIO: By Heaven the very same!
    — Sir, what pretensions have you to this Lady?
WILLMORE: Sir, I don't use to be examin'd, and am ill at all Disputes but
    this — *(Draws,* ANTONIO *offers to shoot.)*
ANGELICA: *(To* WILLMORE.*)* Oh, hold! you see he's arm'd with certain
    Death:
    — And you, *Antonio,* I command you hold,   340
    By all the Passion you've so lately vow'd me.

(Enter DON PEDRO, *sees* ANTONIO, *and stays.)*

PEDRO: *(Aside.)* Hah, *Antonio!* and *Angelica!*
ANTONIO: When I refuse Obedience to your Will,
    May you destroy me with your mortal Hate.
    By all that's Holy I adore you so,
    That even my Rival, who has Charms enough
    To make him fall a Victim to my Jealousy,
    Shall live, nay, and have leave to love on still.
PEDRO: *(Aside.)* What's this I hear?
ANGELICA: *(Pointing to* WILLMORE.*)* Ah thus, 'twas thus he talk'd, and I   350
    believ'd.
    — *Antonio,* yesterday,

I'd not have sold my Interest in his Heart,
For all the Sword has won and lost in Battle.
— But now to show my utmost of Contempt,
I give thee Life — which if thou would'st preserve,
Live where my Eyes may never see thee more,
Live to undo some one, whose Soul may prove
So bravely constant to revenge my Love.

(Goes out. ANTONIO *follows, but* PEDRO *pulls him back.)*

PEDRO: *Antonio* — stay.   370
ANTONIO: Don *Pedro* —
PEDRO: What Coward Fear was that prevented thee
    From meeting me this Morning on the *Molo*?
ANTONIO: Meet thee?
PEDRO: Yes me; I was the Man that dar'd thee to't.
ANTONIO: Hast thou so often seen me fight in War,
    To find no better Cause to excuse my Absence?
    — I sent my Sword and one to do thee Right,
    Finding my self uncapable to use a Sword.
PEDRO: But 'twas *Florinda's* Quarrel that we fought,   380
    And you to shew how little you esteem'd her,
    Sent me your Rival, giving him your Interest.
    — But I have found the Cause of this Affront,
    And when I meet you fit for the Dispute,
    — I'll tell you my Resentment.
ANTONIO: I shall be ready, Sir, e'er long to do you Reason. *(Exit*
    ANTONIO.*)*
PEDRO: If I cou'd find *Florinda*, now, whilst my Anger's high, I think I
    shou'd be kind, and give her to *Belvile* in Revenge.
WILLMORE: Faith, Sir, I know not what you wou'd do, but I believe the   390
    Priest within has been so kind.
PEDRO: How! my Sister married?
WILLMORE: I hope by this time she is, and bedded too, or he has not my
    longings about him.
PEDRO: Dares he do thus? Does he not fear my Pow'r?
WILLMORE: Faith not at all. If you will go in, and thank him for the
    Favour he has done your Sister, so; if not, Sir, my Power's greater in
    this House than yours; I have a damn'd surly Crew here, that will
    keep you till the next Tide, and then clap you on board my Prize;
    my Ship lies but a League off the *Molo*, and we shall show your   400
    Donship a damn'd *Tramontana* Rover's[8] Trick.

(Enter BELVILE.*)*

8 *foreign (here, English) pirate's.*

BELVILE: This Rogue's in some new Mischief — hah, *Pedro* return'd!
PEDRO: Colonel *Belvile*, I hear you have married my Sister.
BELVILE: You have heard truth then, Sir.
PEDRO: Have I so? then, Sir, I wish you Joy.
BELVILE: How!
PEDRO: By this Embrace I do, and I glad on't.
BELVILE: Are you in earnest?
PEDRO: By our long Friendship and my Obligations to thee, I am. The
sudden Change I'll give you Reasons for anon. Come lead me in to   410
my Sister, that she may know I now approve her Choice. *(Exit* BEL-
VILE *with* PEDRO.*)*

*(*WILLMORE *goes to follow them. Enter* HELLENA *as before in Boy's Clothes, and pulls him back.)*

WILLMORE: Ha! my Gipsy — Now a thousand Blessings on thee for this
Kindness. Egad, Child, I was e'en in despair of ever seeing thee
again; my Friends are all provided for within, each Man his kind
Woman.
HELLENA: Hah! I thought they had serv'd me some such Trick.
WILLMORE: And I was e'en resolv'd to go aboard, condemn my self to my
lone Cabin, and the Thoughts of thee.
HELLENA: And cou'd you have left me behind? wou'd you have been so   420
ill-natur'd?
WILLMORE: Why, 'twou'd have broke my Heart, Child — but since we
are met again, I defy foul Weather to part us.
HELLENA: And wou'd you be a faithful Friend now, if a Maid shou'd
trust you?
WILLMORE: For a Friend I cannot promise: thou art of a Form so excellent, a Face and Humour too good for cold dull Friendship. I am parlously afraid of being in love, Child; and you have not forgot how
severely you have us'd me?
HELLENA: That's all one; such Usage you must still look for, to find out   430
all your Haunts, to rail at you to all that love you, till I have made
you love only me in your Defence, because no body else will love you.
WILLMORE: But hast thou no better Quality to recommend thy self by?
HELLENA: Faith none, Captain — Why, 'twill be the greater Charity to
take me for thy Mistress. I am a lone Child, a kind of Orphan
Lover; and why I shou'd die a Maid, and in a Captain's Hands too, I
do not understand.
WILLMORE: Egad, I was never claw'd away with Broad-Sides from any
Female before. Thou hast one Virtue I adore, good-Nature; I hate a
coy demure Mistress, she's as troublesome as a Colt; I'll break none;   440
no, give me a mad Mistress when mew'd, and in flying one I dare
trust upon the Wing, that whilst she's kind will come to the Lure.[9]
HELLENA: Nay, as kind as you will, good Captain, whilst it lasts; but let's
lose no time.

9 *a falconer's device for recalling a hawk.*

WILLMORE: My time's as precious to me, as thine can be; therefore, dear
Creature, since we are so well agreed, let's retire to my Chamber,
and if ever thou wert treated with such savory Love — Come —
My Bed's prepar'd for such a Guest, all clean and sweet as thy fair
self; I love to steal a Dish and a Bottle with a Friend, and hate long
Graces — Come, let's retire and fall to.   450

HELLENA: 'Tis but getting my Consent, and the Business is soon done;
let but old Gaffer[10] *Hymen* and his Priest say Amen to't, and I dare
lay my Mother's Daughter by as proper a Fellow as your Father's
Son, without fear or blushing.

WILLMORE: Hold, hold, no Bugg[11] Words, Child. Priest and *Hymen*: prithee add Hangman to 'em to make up the Consort — No, no, we'll
have no Vows but Love, Child, nor Witness but the Lover; the kind
Deity injoins naught but love and enjoy. *Hymen* and Priest wait still
upon Portion, and Joynture; Love and Beauty have their own Ceremonies. Marriage is as certain a Bane to Love, as lending Money is   460
to Friendship: I'll neither ask nor give a Vow, tho I could be content
to turn Gipsy, and become a Left-hand[12] Bridegroom, to have the
Pleasure of working that great Miracle of making a Maid a Mother,
if you durst venture; 'tis upse[13] Gipsy that, and if I miss, I'll lose my
Labour.

HELLENA: And if you do not lose, what shall I get? A Cradle full of
Noise and Mischief, with a Pack of Repentance at my Back? Can
you teach me to weave Incle[14] to pass my time with? 'Tis upse Gipsy
that too.

WILLMORE: I can teach thee to weave a true Love's Knot better.   470

HELLENA: So can my Dog.

WILLMORE: Well, I see we are both upon our Guard, and I see there's no
way to conquer good Nature, but by yielding — here — give me thy
Hand — one Kiss and I am thine —

HELLENA: One Kiss! How like my Page he speaks; I am resolv'd you shall
have none, for asking such a sneaking Sum — He that will be satisfied with one Kiss, will never die of that Longing; good Friend
single-Kiss, is all your talking come to this? A Kiss, a Caudle![15]
farewel, Captain single-Kiss. *(Going out he stays her.)*

WILLMORE: Nay, if we part so, let me die like a Bird upon a Bough, at the   480
Sheriff's Charge. By Heaven, both the *Indies* shall not buy thee from
me. I adore thy Humour and will marry thee, and we are so of one
Humour, it must be a Bargain — give me thy Hand — *(Kisses her
hand.)* And now let the blind ones (Love and Fortune) do their
worst.

HELLENA: Why, God-a-mercy, Captain!

WILLMORE: But harkye — The Bargain is now made; but is it not fit we
should know each other's Names? That when we have Reason to

10 *grandfather.*
11 *scary (as in "bogy" and "bugbear").*
12 *common-law.*
13 *in the manner of.*
14 *linen tape.*
15 *warm gruel for invalids.*

curse one another hereafter, and People ask me who 'tis I give to the
Devil, I may at least be able to tell what Family you came of.

HELLENA: Good reason, Captain; and where I have cause, (as I doubt not   490
but I shall have plentiful) that I may know at whom to throw my —
Blessings — I beseech ye your Name.

WILLMORE: I am call'd *Robert the Constant.*

HELLENA: A very fine Name! pray was it your Faulkner[16] or Butler that
christen'd you? Do they not use to whistle when they call you?

WILLMORE: I hope you have a better, that a Man may name without
crossing himself, you are so merry with mine.

HELLENA: I am call'd *Hellena the Inconstant*

(*Enter* PEDRO, BELVILE, FLORINDA, FREDERICK, VALERIA.*)*

PEDRO: Hah! *Hellena!*

FLORINDA: *Hellena!*   500

HELLENA: The very same — hah my Brother! now, Captain, shew your
Love and Courage; stand to your Arms, and defend me bravely, or I
am lost for ever.

PEDRO: What's this I hear? false Girl, how came you hither, and what's
your Business? Speak! (*Goes roughly to her.*)

WILLMORE: Hold off, Sir; you have leave to parley only. (*Puts himself
between.*)

HELLENA: I had e'en as good tell it, as you guess it. Faith, Brother, my
Business is the same with all living Creatures of my Age, to love,
and be loved, and here's the Man.   510

PEDRO: Perfidious Maid, hast thou deceiv'd me too, deceiv'd thy self and
Heaven?

HELLENA: 'Tis time enough to make my Peace with that: Be you but
kind, let me alone with Heaven.

PEDRO: *Belvile,* I did not expect this false Play from you; was't not enough
you'd gain *Florinda* (which I pardon'd), but your lewd Friends too
must be inrich'd with the Spoils of a noble Family?

BELVILE: Faith, Sir, I am as much surpriz'd at this as you can be: Yet, Sir,
my Friends are Gentlemen, and ought to be esteem'd for their Mis-
fortunes, since they have the Glory to suffer with the best of Men   520
and Kings; 'tis true, he's a Rover of Fortune, yet a Prince aboard his
little wooden World.

PEDRO: What's this to the maintenance of a Woman of her Birth and
Quality?

WILLMORE: Faith, Sir, I can boast of nothing but a Sword which does me
Right where-e'er I come, and has defended a worse Cause than a
Woman's: and since I lov'd her before I either knew her Birth or
Name, I must pursue my Resolution, and marry her.

PEDRO: And is all your holy Intent of becoming a Nun debauch'd into a
Desire of Man?   530

HELLENA: Why — I have consider'd the matter, Brother, and find the
Three hundred thousand Crowns my Uncle left me (and you can-

16 *falconer, hawk-keeper.*

not keep from me) will be better laid out in Love than in Religion, and turn to as good an Account — let most Voices carry it, for Heaven or the Captain?

(ALL *cry.*) A Captain! a Captain!

HELLENA: Look ye, Sir, 'tis a clear Case.

PEDRO: Oh I am mad — *(Aside.)* if I refuse, my Life's in Danger — — Come — There's one motive induces me — take her — I shall now be free from the fears of her Honour; guard it you now, if you can; I have been a Slave to't long enough. *(Gives her to him.)*   540

WILLMORE: Faith, Sir, I am of a Nation, that are of opinion a Woman's Honour is not worth guarding when she has a mind to part with it.

HELLENA: Well said, Captain.

PEDRO: *(To* VALERIA.*)* This was your Plot, Mistress, but I hope you have married one that will revenge my Quarrel to you —

VALERIA: There's no altering Destiny, Sir.

PEDRO: Sooner than a Woman's Will; therefore I forgive you all — and wish you may get my Father's Pardon as easily; which I fear.

(Enter BLUNT *drest in a* Spanish *Habit, looking very ridiculously; his Man adjusting his Band.)*

MAN: 'Tis very well, Sir.   550

BLUNT: Well, Sir, 'dsheartlikins I tell you 'tis damnable ill, Sir — a Spanish Habit, good Lord! cou'd the Devil and my Taylor devise no other Punishment for me, but the Mode of a Nation I abominate?

BELVILE: What's the matter, *Ned?*

BLUNT: Pray view me round, and judge — *(Turns round.)*

BELVILE: I must confess thou art a kind of odd Figure.

BLUNT: In a Spanish Habit with a Vengeance! I had rather be in the Inquisition for Judaism, than in this Doublet[17] and Breeches; a Pillory were an easy Collar to this, three Handfuls high; and these Shoes too are worse than the Stocks, with the Sole an Inch shorter   560 than my Foot: In fine, Gentlemen, methinks I look altogether like a Bag of Bays[18] stuff'd full of Fool's Flesh.

BELVILE: Methinks 'tis well, and makes thee look *en Cavalier:* Come, Sir, settle your Face, and salute our Friends, Lady —

BLUNT: Hah! Say'st thou so, my little Rover? *(To* HELLENA.*)* Lady — (if you be one) give me leave to kiss your Hand, and tell you, adsheartlikins, for all I look so, I am your humble Servant — A Pox of my *Spanish* Habit!

WILLMORE: Hark — what's this? *(Musick is heard to Play.)*

(Enter BOY.*)*

BOY: Sir, as the Custom is, the gay People in Masquerade, who make   570 every Man's House their own, are coming up.

17 *undercoat.*
18 *a spice-bag.*

(Enter several Men and Women in masquing Habits, with Musick; they put themselves
in order and dance.)

BLUNT: Adsheartlikins, wou'd 'twere lawful to pull off their false Faces,
that I might see if my Doxy[19] were not amongst 'em.
BELVILE: *(To the Masquers.)* Ladies and Gentlemen, since you are come so *a*
propos, you must take a small Collation with us.
WILLMORE: *(To* HELLENA.*)* Whilst we'll to the Good Man within, who
stays to give us a Cast of his Office.[20] — Have you no trembling at
the near approach?
HELLENA: No more than you have in an Engagement or a Tempest.
WILLMORE: Egad, thou'rt a brave Girl, and I admire thy Love and   580
Courage.
Lead on, no other Dangers they can dread,
Who venture in the Storms o' th' Marriage-Bed. (Exeunt.)

EPILOGUE.

THE banisht Cavaliers! a Roving Blade![1]
A popish Carnival! a Masquerade!
The Devil's in't if this will please the Nation,
In these our blessed Times of Reformation,
When Conventicling[2] is so much in Fashion.
And yet —
That mutinous Tribe less Factions do beget,
Than your continual differing in Wit;
Your Judgment's (as your Passions) a Disease:
Nor Muse or Miss your Appetite can please;   10
You're grown as nice as queasy Consciences,
Whose each Convulsion, when the Spirit moves,
Damns every thing that Maggot[3] disapproves.
    With canting Rule you wou'd the Stage refine,
And to dull Method all our Sense confine.
With th' Insolence of Common-wealths you rule,
Where each gay Fop, and politick brave Fool
On Monarch Wit impose without controul.
As for the last,[4] who seldom sees a Play,
Unless it be the old Black-Fryers[5] way,   20
Shaking his empty Noddle[6] o'er Bamboo,[7]
He crys — "Good Faith, these Plays will never do.
    — Ah, Sir, in my young days, what lofty Wit,

---

19 *wench.*
20 *a sample of his work.*

1 *rake.*
2 *a conventicle was a chapel attended by Dissenting or nonconforming (i.e., strict and puritanical) Protestants.*
3 *whim or caprice; here, the inner light that Dissenters claimed as their guide.*
4 *i.e., the "politick brave Fool."*
5 *Blackfriars, a London theatre popular in the early 1600s and destroyed under the Puritans.*
6 *head.*
7 *a cane.*

What high-strain'd Scenes of Fighting there were writ:
These are slight airy Toys. But tell me, pray
What has the House of Commons *done to day?"*
Then shews his Politicks, to let you see
Of State Affairs he'll judge as notably,
As he can do of Wit and Poetry.
    The younger Sparks, who hither do resort,   30
Cry —
"Pox o' your gentle things, give us more Sport;
— Damn me, I'm sure 'twill never please the Court."
    Such Fops are never pleas'd, unless the Play
Be stuff'd with Fools, as brisk and dull as they.
Such might the Half-Crown spare, and in a Glass
At home behold a more accomplisht Ass.
Where they may set their Cravats, Wigs and Faces,
And practice all their Buffoonry Grimaces;
See how this — Huff becomes — this Dammy[8] — stare —   40
Which they at home may act, because they dare,
But — must with prudent Caution do elsewhere.
Oh that our Nokes, *or* Tony Lee[9] *could show*
A Fop but half so much to th' Life as you.

---

8 *Damn me.*
9 *James Nokes and Tony Lee were popular comic actors on the Restoration stage.*

OSCAR WILDE

(1854–1900)

*W*ilde was born in Ireland and spent his early years there. His interest in art and literature began while he studied Classics at Trinity College, Dublin, and developed during his subsequent years at Oxford. Graduating with first-class honours in 1878, Wilde went to London to pursue the artistic career he had begun at Oxford. His body of work includes plays, the collections of poems entitled Poems *(1881)* and The Sphinx *(1894)*, his famous novel The Picture of Dorian Gray *(1891)*, and a volume of essays, Intentions *(1891)*. In 1882, Wilde toured America as a lecturer.

From his university days, he was identified with aestheticism,[1] and his early writings dealt with this late nineteenth-century movement in France and England. The general public judged the movement for the most part on its external features, such as the dress and postures, or "attitudes," of its devotees, whose affectations are satirized in Gilbert and Sullivan's Patience.

Wilde wrote his best plays in the 1890s: Lady Windermere's Fan *(1892)*, A Woman of No Importance *(1893)*, An Ideal Husband *(1895)*, and The Importance of Being Earnest *(1895)*. The first three resemble many drawing-room comedies of the time, but surpass most of them in several respects. In structure, they show the influence of the well-made play formula[2] created by nineteenth-century French playwright Eugène Scribe. The plays' frequent epigrams and crisp dialogue also demonstrate Wilde's wit, whose target is often the hypocrisies of the society of his time. In the history of English theatre, the plays belong, in many respects, to the tradition of the comedy of manners;[3] yet while he handles this form deftly, Wilde also exposes some of its weaknesses.

INTRODUCTION TO *THE IMPORTANCE OF BEING EARNEST*

*T*he Importance of Being Earnest opened at the St. James's Theatre in London on February 14, 1895. It was an instant success with both the public and most critics, including George Bernard Shaw, who admired and supported Wilde's work.

1 The belief in beauty as the main standard of value in human life. The aesthetic movement originated on the Continent and was introduced into England by Walter Pater. Artifice and pleasurable sensations were stressed by the aesthetes and the phrase "the love of art for art's sake" was a rallying cry. The movement's followers frequently dressed in an unconventional manner that reflected their love of beauty.

2 The plot of this kind of play depends on a secret which is known to only some of the characters. The revelation of the secret comes at the play's climax and usually leads to the exposure of the villain and the triumph of the hero. The action of the play builds with a series of reversals which only end at the climax. Letters containing vital information are used and many misunderstandings exist. The plot is carefully structured, often manipulated but always believable; therefore, the climax has been prepared for in a sure and careful way.

3 This term emerged in the late seventeenth century to describe a type of comedy that was based on the love intrigues of a sophisticated and witty aristocratic society. Much humour was also created by characters who, as would-be wits, attempted to imitate the wit and manners of the aristocratic true-wits.

For many reasons, this is the play for which Wilde is best remembered. In *Lady Windermere's Fan*, he used some of the devices of the well-made play with his tongue in his cheek; but in *Earnest* he holds such devices up to ridicule in an inspired way. The discovery scene, centred on the notion of a baby in a handbag in the waiting-room of a railway station, is a brilliant invention. If the well-made play formula was intended to ensure dovetailing developments and smooth transitions, this play simultaneously surpasses other plays built on the formula, and exposes their conventionality for what it is.

One of the main functions of a play in the tradition of the comedy of manners is to reflect the society of its time; *Earnest*, more than any other play of the 1890s, resembles those plays that were first given this label at the end of the seventeenth century. Wilde's heroes are direct descendants of the Restoration beaux and fops, but they are also very much of their own time in their reflection of the aesthetes and dandies of the 1890s.

The title, as a good title should, captures an important thread of plot and establishes the tone. The reader not only enjoys the word-play, but is also alerted to the whimsical idea that prompts the heroes to seek christening — or re-christening.

The main focus of the play is on Jack and Algernon and how they behave and must behave: their strictly codified roles and how they play them. The whole business of Bunburying, in fact, provides them with time to rest, away from the demanding theatricals of the social scene. Wilde knew his audiences would be thinking of the aesthetes, their affectations, and their excesses; once again, his wit triumphs as he encapsulates all these things in the dialogue and stage business that surrounds the cucumber sandwiches and muffins.

To many, the young women seem comparatively insipid, but they, like the men, modulate the roles assigned to them by society. They cannot sparkle like the dandies or scheme as freely; society would not allow it, nor, indeed, would the dandies. Although they, too, must follow a code and play artificial roles, things are not so difficult and demanding for them. Indeed, they frequently serve the function of setting the males off; while the heroines flutter, the poise of the heroes is emphasized.

In constructing this play, Wilde achieves a remarkable symmetry. In the cast, we have the two young couples, and with brilliant economy Wilde creates a third couple: Canon Chasuble and Miss Prism. Lady Bracknell stands alone as commentator, arbiter of decorum, and comic obstacle to romantic happiness. A direct descendant of the imposing females in the great comedies of manners, such as Lady Wishfort in William Congreve's *The Way of the World* (1700), she, perhaps, is the most memorable of all.

Earnest enjoyed a successful run and, nearly a century later, it is still performed as a classic of English comedy — indeed, in the opinion of many, the greatest English comedy.

The Importance of Being Earnest

THE PERSONS OF THE PLAY
JOHN WORTHING, J.P.

ALGERNON MONCRIEFF

REV. CANON CHASUBLE, D.D.

MERRIMAN, *Butler*

LANE, *Manservant*

LADY BRACKNELL

HON. GWENDOLEN FAIRFAX

CECILY CARDEW

MISS PRISM, *Governess*

THE SCENES OF THE PLAY

ACT I
Algernon Moncrieff's flat in Half-Moon Street, W.

ACT II
The garden at the Manor House, Woolton

ACT III
Drawing-Room at the Manor House, Woolton
TIME
The Present

FIRST ACT

SCENE

Morning-room in Algernon's flat in Half-Moon Street.[1] The room is luxuriously and artistically furnished. The sound of a piano is heard in the adjoining room.

(LANE *is arranging afternoon tea on the table and, after the music has ceased,* ALGERNON *enters.*)

ALGERNON: Did you hear what I was playing, Lane?
LANE: I didn't think it polite to listen, sir.

---

1 *a street in London's fashionable West End.*

ALGERNON: I'm sorry for that, for your sake. I don't play accurately —
anyone can play accurately — but I play with wonderful expression.
As far as the piano is concerned, sentiment is my forte. I keep
science for Life.

LANE: Yes, sir.

ALGERNON: And, speaking of the science of Life, have you got the
cucumber sandwiches cut for Lady Bracknell?

LANE: Yes, sir. *(Hands them on a salver.)*

ALGERNON *(Inspects them, takes two, and sits down on the sofa)*: Oh! . . . by the
way, Lane, I see from your book that on Thursday night, when Lord
Shoreman and Mr Worthing were dining with me, eight bottles of
champagne are entered as having been consumed.

LANE: Yes, sir; eight bottles and a pint.

ALGERNON: Why is it that at a bachelor's establishment the servants
invariably drink the champagne? I ask merely for information.

LANE: I attribute it to the superior quality of the wine, sir. I have often
observed that in married households the champagne is rarely of a
first-rate brand.

ALGERNON: Good heavens! Is marriage so demoralising as that?

LANE: I believe it *is* a very pleasant state, sir. I have had very little experience of it myself up to the present. I have only been married once.
That was in consequence of a misunderstanding between myself
and a young person.

ALGERNON *(languidly)*: I don't know that I am much interested in your
family life, Lane.

LANE: No, sir; it is not a very interesting subject. I never think of it
myself.

ALGERNON: Very natural, I am sure. That will do, Lane, thank you.

LANE: Thank you, sir.

(LANE goes out.)

ALGERNON: Lane's views on marriage seem somewhat lax. Really, if the
lower orders don't set us a good example, what on earth is the use
of them? They seem, as a class, to have absolutely no sense of
moral responsibility.

(Enter LANE.)

LANE: Mr Ernest Worthing.

(Enter JACK. LANE goes out.)

ALGERNON: How are you, my dear Ernest? What brings you up to
town?

JACK: Oh, pleasure, pleasure! What else should bring one anywhere?
Eating as usual, I see, Algy!

ALGERNON (stiffly): I believe it is customary in good society to take some slight refreshment at five o'clock. Where have you been since last Thursday?

JACK (sitting down on the sofa): In the country.

ALGERNON: What on earth do you do there?

JACK (pulling off his gloves): When one is in town one amuses oneself. When one is in the country one amuses other people. It is excessively boring.

ALGERNON: And who are the people you amuse?

JACK (airily): Oh, neighbours, neighbours.

ALGERNON: Got nice neighbours in your part of Shropshire?[2]

JACK: Perfectly horrid! Never speak to one of them.

ALGERNON: How immensely you must amuse them! (Goes over and takes sandwich.) By the way, Shropshire is your county, is it not?

JACK: Eh? Shropshire? Yes, of course. Hallo! Why all these cups? Why cucumber sandwiches? Why such reckless extravagance in one so young? Who is coming to tea?

ALGERNON: Oh! merely Aunt Augusta and Gwendolen.

JACK: How perfectly delightful!

ALGERNON: Yes, that is all very well; but I am afraid Aunt Augusta won't quite approve of your being here.

JACK: May I ask why?

ALGERNON: My dear fellow, the way you flirt with Gwendolen is perfectly disgraceful. It is almost as bad as the way Gwendolen flirts with you.

JACK: I am in love with Gwendolen. I have come up to town expressly to propose to her.

ALGERNON: I thought you had come up for pleasure? . . . I call that business.

JACK: How utterly unromantic you are!

ALGERNON: I really don't see anything romantic in proposing. It is very romantic to be in love. But there is nothing romantic about a definite proposal. Why, one may be accepted. One usually is, I believe. Then the excitement is all over. The very essence of romance is uncertainty. If ever I get married, I'll certainly try to forget the fact.

JACK: I have no doubt about that, dear Algy. The Divorce Court was specially invented for people whose memories are so curiously constituted.

ALGERNON: Oh! there is no use speculating on that subject. Divorces are made in Heaven — (JACK puts out his hand to take a sandwich. ALGERNON at once interferes.) Please don't touch the cucumber sandwiches. They are ordered specially for Aunt Augusta. (Takes one and eats it.)

JACK: Well, you have been eating them all the time.

ALGERNON: That is quite a different matter. She is my aunt. (Takes plate from below.) Have some bread and butter. The bread and butter is for Gwendolen. Gwendolen is devoted to bread and butter.

---

2 Jack lives in Hertfordshire but has chosen to say Shropshire because of its distance from London, on the Welsh border.

JACK (*advancing to table and helping himself*): And very good bread and butter it is too.

ALGERNON: Well, my dear fellow, you need not eat as if you were going to eat it all. You behave as if you were married to her already. You are not married to her already, and I don't think you ever will be.

JACK: Why on earth do you say that?

ALGERNON: Well, in the first place, girls never marry the men they flirt with. Girls don't think it right.

JACK: Oh, that is nonsense!

ALGERNON: It isn't. It is a great truth. It accounts for the extraordinary number of bachelors that one sees all over the place. In the second place, I don't give my consent.

JACK: Your consent!

ALGERNON: My dear fellow, Gwendolen is my first cousin. And before I allow you to marry her, you will have to clear up the whole question of Cecily. (*Rings bell.*)

JACK: Cecily! What on earth do you mean? What do you mean, Algy, by Cecily! I don't know any one of the name of Cecily.

(*Enter* LANE.)

ALGERNON: Bring me that cigarette case Mr Worthing left in the smoking-room the last time he dined here.

LANE: Yes, sir.

(*LANE goes out.*)

JACK: Do you mean to say you have had my cigarette case all this time? I wish to goodness you had let me know. I have been writing frantic letters to Scotland Yard about it. I was very nearly offering a large reward.

ALGERNON: Well, I wish you would offer one. I happen to be more than usually hard up.

JACK: There is no good offering a large reward now that the thing is found.

(*Enter* LANE *with the cigarette case on a salver.* ALGERNON *takes it at once.* LANE *goes out.*)

ALGERNON: I think that is rather mean of you, Ernest, I must say. (*Opens case and examines it.*) However, it makes no matter, for, now that I look at the inscription inside, I find that the thing isn't yours after all.

JACK: Of course it's mine. (*Moving to him.*) You have seen me with it a hundred times, and you have no right whatsoever to read what is written inside. It is a very ungentlemanly thing to read a private cigarette case.

ALGERNON: Oh! it is absurd to have a hard and fast rule about what one should read and what one shouldn't. More than half of modern culture depends on what one shouldn't read.

JACK: I am quite aware of the fact, and I don't propose to discuss modern culture. It isn't the sort of thing one should talk of in private. I simply want my cigarette case back.

ALGERNON: Yes; but this isn't your cigarette case. This cigarette case is a present from someone of the name of Cecily, and you said you didn't know anyone of that name.

JACK: Well, if you want to know, Cecily happens to be my aunt.

ALGERNON: Your aunt!

JACK: Yes. Charming old lady she is, too. Lives at Tunbridge Wells. Just give it back to me, Algy.

ALGERNON (retreating to back of sofa): But why does she call herself little Cecily if she is your aunt and lives at Tunbridge Wells? (Reading.) 'From little Cecily with her fondest love.'

JACK (moving to sofa and kneeling upon it): My dear fellow, what on earth is there in that? Some aunts are tall, some aunts are not tall. That is a matter that surely an aunt may be allowed to decide for herself. You seem to think that every aunt should be exactly like your aunt! That is absurd! For Heaven's sake give me back my cigarette case. (Follows ALGERNON round the room.)

ALGERNON: Yes. But why does your aunt call you her uncle? 'From little Cecily, with her fondest love to her dear Uncle Jack.' There is no objection, I admit, to an aunt being a small aunt, but why an aunt, no matter what her size may be, should call her own nephew her uncle, I can't quite make out. Besides, your name isn't Jack at all; it is Ernest.

JACK: It isn't Ernest; it's Jack.

ALGERNON: You have always told me it was Ernest. I have introduced you to everyone as Ernest. You answer to the name of Ernest. You look as if your name was Ernest. You are the most earnest-looking person I ever saw in my life. It is perfectly absurd your saying that your name isn't Ernest. It's on your cards. Here is one of them. (Taking it from case.) 'Mr Ernest Worthing, B.4, The Albany.' I'll keep this as a proof that your name is Ernest if ever you attempt to deny it to me, or to Gwendolen, or to anyone else. (Puts the card in his pocket.)

JACK: Well, my name is Ernest in town and Jack in the country, and the cigarette case was given to me in the country.

ALGERNON: Yes, but that does not account for the fact that your small Aunt Cecily, who lives at Tunbridge Wells, calls you her dear uncle. Come, old boy, you had much better have the thing out at once.

JACK: My dear Algy, you talk exactly as if you were a dentist. It is very vulgar to talk like a dentist when one isn't a dentist. It produces a false impression.

ALGERNON: Well, that is exactly what dentists always do. Now, go on! Tell me the whole thing. I may mention that I have always suspected

you of being a confirmed and secret Bunburyist; and I am quite
sure of it now.

JACK: Bunburyist? What on earth do you mean by a Bunburyist?

ALGERNON: I'll reveal to you the meaning of that incomparable expression as soon as you are kind enough to inform me why you are
Ernest in town and Jack in the country.

JACK: Well, produce my cigarette case first.

ALGERNON: Here it is. *(Hands cigarette case.)* Now produce your explanation, and pray make it improbable. *(Sits on sofa.)*

JACK: My dear fellow, there is nothing improbable about my explanation
at all. In fact it's perfectly ordinary. Old Mr Thomas Cardew, who
adopted me when I was a little boy, made me in his will guardian to
his grand-daughter, Miss Cecily Cardew. Cecily, who addresses me
as her uncle from motives of respect that you could not possibly
appreciate, lives at my place in the country under the charge of her
admirable governess, Miss Prism.

ALGERNON: Where is that place in the country, by the way?

JACK: That is nothing to you, dear boy. You are not going to be
invited. . . . I may tell you candidly that the place is not in
Shropshire.

ALGERNON: I suspected that, my dear fellow! I have Bunburyed all over
Shropshire on two separate occasions. Now, go on. Why are you
Ernest in town and Jack in the country?

JACK: My dear Algy, I don't know whether you will be able to understand my real motives. You are hardly serious enough. When one is
placed in the position of guardian, one has to adopt a very high
moral tone on all subjects. It's one's duty to do so. And as a high
moral tone can hardly be said to conduce very much to either one's
health or one's happiness, in order to get up to town I have always
pretended to have a younger brother of the name of Ernest, who
lives in the Albany, and gets into the most dreadful scrapes. That,
my dear Algy, is the whole truth pure and simple.

ALGERNON: The truth is rarely pure and never simple. Modern life
would be very tedious if it were either, and modern literature a
complete impossibility!

JACK: That wouldn't be at all a bad thing.

ALGERNON: Literary criticism is not your forte, my dear fellow. Don't try
it. You should leave that to people who haven't been at a University.
They do it so well in the daily papers. What you really are is a Bunburyist. I was quite right in saying you were a Bunburyist. You are
one of the most advanced Bunburyists I know.

JACK: What on earth do you mean?

ALGERNON: You have invented a very useful younger brother called Ernest, in order that you may be able to come up to town as often as
you like. I have invented an invaluable permanent invalid called Bunbury, in order that I may be able to go down into the country whenever I choose. Bunbury is perfectly invaluable. If it wasn't for Bunbury's extraordinary bad health, for instance, I wouldn't be able to

dine with you at Willis's[3] tonight, for I have been really engaged to Aunt Augusta for more than a week.

JACK: I haven't asked you to dine with me anywhere tonight.

ALGERNON: I know. You are absurdly careless about sending out invitations. It is very foolish of you. Nothing annoys people so much as not receiving invitations.

JACK: You had much better dine with your Aunt Augusta.

ALGERNON: I haven't the smallest intention of doing anything of the kind. To begin with, I dined there on Monday, and once a week is quite enough to dine with one's own relations. In the second place, whenever I do dine there I am always treated as a member of the family, and sent down with either no woman at all, or two. In the third place, I know perfectly well whom she will place me next to, tonight. She will place me next Mary Farquhar, who always flirts with her own husband across the dinner-table. That is not very pleasant. Indeed, it is not even decent . . . and that sort of thing is enormously on the increase. The amount of women in London who flirt with their own husbands is perfectly scandalous. It looks so bad. It is simply washing one's clean linen in public. Besides, now that I know you to be a confirmed Bunburyist I naturally want to talk to you about Bunburying. I want to tell you the rules.

JACK: I'm not a Bunburyist at all. If Gwendolen accepts me, I am going to kill my brother, indeed I think I'll kill him in any case. Cecily is a little too much interested in him. It is rather a bore. So I am going to get rid of Ernest. And I strongly advise you to do the same with Mr . . . with your invalid friend who has the absurd name.

ALGERNON: Nothing will induce me to part with Bunbury, and if you ever get married, which seems to me extremely problematic, you will be very glad to know Bunbury. A man who marries without knowing Bunbury has a very tedious time of it.

JACK: That is nonsense. If I marry a charming girl like Gwendolen, and she is the only girl I ever saw in my life that I would marry, I certainly won't want to know Bunbury.

ALGERNON: Then your wife will. You don't seem to realize, that in married life three is company and two is none.

JACK (sententiously): That, my dear young friend, is the theory[4] that the corrupt French Drama has been propounding for the last fifty years.

ALGERNON: Yes; and that the happy English home has proved in half the time.

JACK: For heaven's sake, don't try to be cynical. It's perfectly easy to be cynical.

ALGERNON: My dear fellow, it isn't easy to be anything nowadays. There's such a lot of beastly competition about. (The sound of an electric bell is heard.) Ah! that must be Aunt Augusta. Only relatives, or creditors, ever ring in that Wagnerian manner.[5] Now, if I get her out

---

3 a fashionable restaurant.
4 this refers to the recurrent theme of marital infidelity.
5 the loud music of the operas of Richard Wagner.

of the way for ten minutes, so that you can have an opportunity for proposing to Gwendolen, may I dine with you tonight at Willis's?

JACK: I suppose so, if you want to.

ALGERNON: Yes, but you must be serious about it. I hate people who are not serious about meals. It is so shallow of them.

(Enter LANE.)

LANE: Lady Bracknell and Miss Fairfax.

(ALGERNON goes forward to meet them. Enter LADY BRACKNELL and GWENDOLEN.)

LADY BRACKNELL: Good afternoon, dear Algernon, I hope you are behaving very well.

ALGERNON: I'm feeling very well, Aunt Augusta.

LADY BRACKNELL: That's not quite the same thing. In fact the two things rarely go together. *(Sees JACK and bows to him with icy coldness.)*

ALGERNON *(to GWENDOLEN)*: Dear me, you are smart![6]

GWENDOLEN: I am always smart! Am I not, Mr Worthing?

JACK: You're quite perfect, Miss Fairfax.

GWENDOLEN: Oh! I hope I am not that. It would leave no room for developments, and I intend to develop in many directions.

(GWENDOLEN and JACK sit down together in the corner.)

LADY BRACKNELL: I'm sorry if we are a little late, Algernon, but I was obliged to call on dear Lady Harbury. I hadn't been there since her poor husband's death. I never saw a woman so altered; she looks quite twenty years younger. And now I'll have a cup of tea, and one of those nice cucumber sandwiches you promised me.

ALGERNON: Certainly, Aunt Augusta. *(Goes over to tea-table.)*

LADY BRACKNELL: Won't you come and sit here, Gwendolen?

GWENDOLEN: Thanks, mamma, I'm quite comfortable where I am.

ALGERNON *(picking up empty plate in horror)*: Good heavens! Lane! Why are there no cucumber sandwiches? I ordered them specially.

LANE *(gravely)*: There were no cucumbers in the market this morning, sir. I went down twice.

ALGERNON: No cucumbers!

LANE: No, sir. Not even for ready money.

ALGERNON: That will do, Lane, thank you.

LANE: Thank you, sir. *(Goes out.)*

ALGERNON: I am greatly distressed, Aunt Augusta, about there being no cucumbers, not even for ready money.

LADY BRACKNELL: It really makes no matter, Algernon. I had some

6 *well-dressed.*

crumpets[7] with Lady Harbury, who seems to me to be living entirely for pleasure now.

ALGERNON: I hear her hair has turned quite gold from grief.

LADY BRACKNELL: It certainly has changed its colour. From what cause I, of course, cannot say. (ALGERNON *crosses and hands tea.*) Thank you, I've quite a treat for you tonight, Algernon. I am going to send you down with Mary Farquhar. She is such a nice woman, and so attentive to her husband. It's delightful to watch them.

ALGERNON: I am afraid, Aunt Augusta, I shall have to give up the pleasure of dining with you tonight after all.

LADY BRACKNELL (*frowning*): I hope not, Algernon. It would put my table completely out. Your uncle would have to dine upstairs. Fortunately he is accustomed to that.

ALGERNON: It is a great bore, and, I need hardly say, a terrible disappointment to me, but the fact is I have just had a telegram to say that my poor friend Bunbury is very ill again. (*Exchanges glances with* JACK.) They seem to think I should be with him.

LADY BRACKNELL: It is very strange. This Mr Bunbury seems to suffer from curiously bad health.

ALGERNON: Yes; poor Bunbury is a dreadful invalid.

LADY BRACKNELL: Well, I must say, Algernon, that I think it is high time that Mr Bunbury made up his mind whether he was going to live or to die. This shilly-shallying with the question is absurd. Nor do I in any way approve of the modern sympathy with invalids. I consider it morbid. Illness of any kind is hardly a thing to be encouraged in others. Health is the primary duty of life. I am always telling that to your poor uncle, but he never seems to take much notice . . . as far as any improvement in his ailments goes. I should be much obliged if you would ask Mr Bunbury, from me, to be kind enough not to have a relapse on Saturday, for I rely on you to arrange my music for me. It is my last reception, and one wants something that will encourage conversation, particularly at the end of the season when everyone has practically said whatever they had to say, which, in most cases, was probably not much.

ALGERNON: I'll speak to Bunbury, Aunt Augusta, if he is still conscious, and I think I can promise you he'll be all right by Saturday. Of course the music is a great difficulty. You see, if one plays good music, people don't listen, and if one plays bad music people don't talk. But I'll run over the programme I've drawn out, if you will kindly come into the next room for a moment.

LADY BRACKNELL: Thank you, Algernon. It is very thoughtful of you. (*Rising, and following* ALGERNON.) I'm sure the programme will be delightful, after a few expurgations. French songs I cannot possibly allow. People always seem to think that they are improper, and either look shocked, which is vulgar, or laugh, which is worse. But German sounds a thoroughly respectable language, and indeed, I believe is so. Gwendolen, you will accompany me.

GWENDOLEN: Certainly mamma.

---

7 *a soft cake like a waffle, usually toasted.*

(LADY BRACKNELL *and* ALGERNON *go into the music-room,* GWENDOLEN *remains behind.*)

JACK: Charming day it has been, Miss Fairfax.

GWENDOLEN: Pray don't talk to me about the weather, Mr Worthing. Whenever people talk to me about the weather, I always feel quite certain that they mean something else. And that makes me so nervous.

JACK: I do mean something else.

GWENDOLEN: I thought so. In fact, I am never wrong.

JACK: And I would like to be allowed to take advantage of Lady Bracknell's temporary absence . . .

GWENDOLEN: I would certainly advise you to do so. Mamma has a way of coming back suddenly into a room that I have often had to speak to her about.

JACK (*nervously*): Miss Fairfax, ever since I met you I have admired you more than any girl . . . I have ever met since . . . I met you.

GWENDOLEN: Yes, I am quite well aware of the fact. And I often wish that in public, at any rate, you had been more demonstrative. For me you have always had an irresistible fascination. Even before I met you I was far from indifferent to you. (JACK *looks at her in amazement.*) We live, as I hope you know, Mr Worthing, in an age of ideals. The fact is constantly mentioned in the more expensive monthly magazines, and has reached the provincial pulpits, I am told; and my ideal has always been to love someone of the name of Ernest. There is something in that name that inspires absolute confidence. The moment Algernon first mentioned to me that he had a friend called Ernest, I knew I was destined to love you.

JACK: You really love me, Gwendolen?

GWENDOLEN: Passionately!

JACK: Darling! You don't know how happy you've made me.

GWENDOLEN: My own Ernest!

JACK: But you don't really mean to say that you couldn't love me if my name wasn't Ernest?

GWENDOLEN: But your name is Ernest.

JACK: Yes, I know it is. But supposing it was something else? Do you mean to say you couldn't love me then?

GWENDOLEN (*glibly*): Ah! that is clearly a metaphysical speculation, and like most metaphysical speculations has very little reference at all to the actual facts of real life, as we know them.

JACK: Personally, darling, to speak quite candidly, I don't much care about the name of Ernest. . . . I don't think the name suits me at all.

GWENDOLEN: It suits you perfectly. It is a divine name. It has music of its own. It produces vibrations.

JACK: Well, really, Gwendolen, I must say that I think there are lots of other much nicer names. I think Jack, for instance, a charming name.

GWENDOLEN: Jack? . . . No, there is very little music in the name Jack, if any at all, indeed. It does not thrill. It produces absolutely no vibrations. . . . I have known several Jacks, and they all, without exception, were more than usually plain. Besides, Jack is a notorious domesticity for John! And I pity any woman who is married to a man called John. She would probably never be allowed to know the entrancing pleasure of a single moment's solitude. The only really safe name is Ernest.

JACK: Gwendolen, I must get christened at once — I mean we must get married at once. There is no time to be lost.

GWENDOLEN: Married, Mr Worthing?

JACK (astounded): Well . . . surely. You know that I love you, and you led me to believe, Miss Fairfax, that you were not absolutely indifferent to me.

GWENDOLEN: I adore you. But you haven't proposed to me yet. Nothing has been said at all about marriage. The subject has not even been touched on.

JACK: Well . . . may I propose to you now?

GWENDOLEN: I think it would be an admirable opportunity. And to spare you any possible disappointment, Mr Worthing, I think it only fair to tell you quite frankly beforehand that I am fully determined to accept you.

JACK: Gwendolen!

GWENDOLEN: Yes, Mr Worthing, what have you got to say to me?

JACK: You know what I have got to say to you.

GWENDOLEN: Yes, but you don't say it.

JACK: Gwendolen, will you marry me? (Goes on his knees.)

GWENDOLEN: Of course I will, darling. How long you have been about it! I am afraid you have had very little experience in how to propose.

JACK: My own one, I have never loved anyone in the world but you.

GWENDOLEN: Yes, but men often propose for practice. I know my brother Gerald does. All my girl-friends tell me so. What wonderfully blue eyes you have, Ernest! They are quite, quite, blue. I hope you will always look at me just like that, especially when there are other people present.

(Enter LADY BRACKNELL.)

LADY BRACKNELL: Mr Worthing! Rise, sir, from this semi-recumbent posture. It is most indecorous.

GWENDOLEN: Mamma! (He tries to rise; she restrains him.) I must beg you to retire. This is no place for you. Besides, Mr Worthing has not quite finished yet.

LADY BRACKNELL: Finished what, may I ask?

GWENDOLEN: I am engaged to Mr Worthing, mamma. (They rise together.)

LADY BRACKNELL: Pardon me, you are not engaged to anyone. When you do become engaged to some one, I, or your father, should his health permit him, will inform you of the fact. An engagement should come on a young girl as a surprise, pleasant or unpleasant, as the case may be. It is hardly a matter that she could be allowed to arrange for herself. . . . And now I have a few questions to put to you, Mr Worthing. While I am making these inquiries, you, Gwendolen, will wait for me below in the carriage.

GWENDOLEN *(reproachfully)*: Mamma!

LADY BRACKNELL: In the carriage, Gwendolen! *(GWENDOLEN goes to the door. She and JACK blow kisses to each other behind LADY BRACKNELL's back. LADY BRACKNELL looks vaguely about as if she could not understand what the noise was. Finally turns round.)* Gwendolen, the carriage!

GWENDOLEN: Yes, mamma. *(Goes out, looking back at JACK.)*

LADY BRACKNELL *(sitting down)*: You can take a seat, Mr Worthing.

(Looks in her pocket for note-book and pencil.)

JACK: Thank you, Lady Bracknell, I prefer standing.

LADY BRACKNELL *(pencil and note-book in hand)*: I feel bound to tell you that you are not down on my list of eligible young men, although I have the same list as the dear Duchess of Bolton has. We work together, in fact. However, I am quite ready to enter your name, should your answers be what a really affectionate mother requires. Do you smoke?

JACK: Well, yes, I must admit I smoke.

LADY BRACKNELL: I am glad to hear it. A man should always have an occupation of some kind. There are far too many idle men in London as it is. How old are you?

JACK: Twenty-nine.

LADY BRACKNELL: A very good age to be married at. I have always been of opinion that a man who desires to get married should know either everything or nothing. Which do you know?

JACK *(after some hesitation)*: I know nothing, Lady Bracknell.

LADY BRACKNELL: I am pleased to hear it. I do not approve of anything that tampers with natural ignorance. Ignorance is like a delicate exotic fruit; touch it and the bloom is gone. The whole theory of modern education is radically unsound. Fortunately in England, at any rate, education produces no effect whatsoever. If it did, it would prove a serious danger to the upper classes, and probably lead to acts of violence in Grosvenor Square.[8] What is your income?

JACK: Between seven and eight thousand a year.

LADY BRACKNELL *(makes a note in her book)*: In land, or in investments?

JACK: In investments, chiefly.

LADY BRACKNELL: That is satisfactory. What between the duties expected of one during one's lifetime, and the duties[9] exacted from one after one's death, land has ceased to be either a profit or a pleasure. It gives one position, and prevents one from keeping it up. That's all that can be said about land.

---

8 *a fashionable area of London.*
9 *taxes.*

JACK: I have a country house with some land, of course, attached to it, about fifteen hundred acres, I believe; but I don't depend on that for my real income. In fact, as far as I can make out, the poachers are the only people who make anything out of it.

LADY BRACKNELL: A country house! How many bedrooms? Well, that point can be cleared up afterwards. You have a town house, I hope? A girl with a simple, unspoiled nature, like Gwendolen, could hardly be expected to reside in the country.

JACK: Well, I own a house in Belgrave Square, but it is let by the year to Lady Bloxham. Of course, I can get it back whenever I like, at six months' notice.

LADY BRACKNELL: Lady Bloxham? I don't know her.

JACK: Oh, she goes about very little. She is a lady considerably advanced in years.

LADY BRACKNELL: Ah, nowadays that is no guarantee of respectability of character. What number in Belgrave Square?

JACK: 149.

LADY BRACKNELL (shaking her head): The unfashionable side. I thought there was something. However, that could easily be altered.

JACK: Do you mean the fashion, or the side?

LADY BRACKNELL (sternly): Both, if necessary, I presume. What are your politics?

JACK: Well, I am afraid I really have none. I am a Liberal Unionist.

LADY BRACKNELL: Oh, they count as Tories. They dine with us. Or come in the evening, at any rate. Now to minor matters. Are your parents living?

JACK: I have lost both my parents.

LADY BRACKNELL: To lose one parent, Mr Worthing, may be regarded as a misfortune; to lose both looks like carelessness. Who was your father? He was evidently a man of some wealth. Was he born in what the Radical papers call the purple of commerce,[10] or did he rise from the ranks of the aristocracy?

JACK: I am afraid I really don't know. The fact is, Lady Bracknell, I said I had lost my parents. It would be nearer the truth to say that my parents seem to have lost me. . . . I don't actually know who I am by birth. I was . . . well, I was found.

LADY BRACKNELL: Found!

JACK: The late Mr Thomas Cardew, an old gentleman of a very charitable and kindly disposition, found me, and gave me the name of Worthing, because he happened to have a first-class ticket for Worthing in his pocket at the time. Worthing is a place in Sussex. It is a seaside resort.

LADY BRACKNELL: Where did the charitable gentleman who had a first-class ticket for this seaside resort find you?

JACK (gravely): In a hand-bag.

LADY BRACKNELL: A hand-bag?

---

10 "born in the purple": of royal birth.

JACK (*very seriously*): Yes, Lady Bracknell. I was in a hand-bag — a somewhat large, black leather hand-bag, with handles to it — an ordinary hand-bag in fact.

LADY BRACKNELL: In what locality did this Mr James, or Thomas, Cardew come across this ordinary hand-bag?

JACK: In the cloak-room at Victoria Station. It was given to him in mistake for his own.

LADY BRACKNELL: The cloak-room at Victoria Station?

JACK: Yes. The Brighton line.

LADY BRACKNELL: The line is immaterial. Mr Worthing, I confess I feel somewhat bewildered by what you have just told me. To be born, or at any rate bred, in a hand-bag, whether it had handles or not, seems to me to display a contempt for the ordinary decencies of family life that reminds one of the worst excesses of the French Revolution. And I presume you know what that unfortunate movement led to? As for the particular locality in which the hand-bag was found, a cloak-room at a railway station might serve to conceal a social indiscretion — has probably, indeed, been used for that purpose before now — but it could hardly be regarded as an assured basis for a recognised position in good society.

JACK: May I ask you then what you would advise me to do? I need hardly say I would do anything in the world to ensure Gwendolen's happiness.

LADY BRACKNELL: I would strongly advise you, Mr Worthing, to try and acquire some relations as soon as possible, and to make a definite effort to produce at any rate one parent, of either sex, before the season is quite over.

JACK: Well, I don't see how I could possibly manage to do that. I can produce the hand-bag at any moment. It is in my dressing-room at home. I really think that should satisfy you, Lady Bracknell.

LADY BRACKNELL: Me, sir! What has it to do with me? You can hardly imagine that I and Lord Bracknell would dream of allowing our only daughter — a girl brought up with the utmost care — to marry into a cloak-room, and form an alliance with a parcel? Good morning, Mr Worthing!

(LADY BRACKNELL *sweeps out in majestic indignation.*)

JACK: Good morning! (ALGERNON, *from the other room, strikes up the Wedding March.* JACK *looks perfectly furious, and goes to the door.*) For goodness' sake don't play that ghastly tune, Algy! How idiotic you are!

(*The music stops and* ALGERNON *enters cheerily.*)

ALGERNON: Didn't it go off all right, old boy? You don't mean to say Gwendolen refused you? I know it is a way she has. She is always refusing people. I think it is most ill-natured of her.

JACK: Oh, Gwendolen is as right as a trivet.[11] As far as she is concerned, we are engaged. Her mother is perfectly unbearable. Never met such a Gorgon. . . . I don't really know what a Gorgon is like, but I am quite sure that Lady Bracknell is one. In any case, she is a monster, without being a myth, which is rather unfair. . . . I beg your pardon, Algy, I suppose I shouldn't talk about your own aunt in that way before you.

ALGERNON: My dear boy, I love hearing my relations abused. It is the only thing that makes me put up with them at all. Relations are simply a tedious pack of people, who haven't got the remotest knowledge of how to live, nor the smallest instinct about when to die.

JACK: Oh, that is nonsense!

ALGERNON: It isn't!

JACK: Well, I won't argue about the matter. You always want to argue about things.

ALGERNON: That is exactly what things were originally made for.

JACK: Upon my word, if I thought that, I'd shoot myself. . . . (A pause.) You don't think there is any chance of Gwendolen becoming like her mother in about a hundred and fifty years, do you, Algy?

ALGERNON: All women become like their mothers. That is their tragedy. No man does. That's his.

JACK: Is that clever?

ALGERNON: It is perfectly phrased! and quite as true as any observation in civilised life should be.

JACK: I am sick to death of cleverness. Everybody is clever nowadays. You can't go anywhere without meeting clever people. The thing has become an absolute public nuisance. I wish to goodness we had a few fools left.

ALGERNON: We have.

JACK: I should extremely like to meet them. What do they talk about?

ALGERNON: The fools? Oh! about the clever people, of course.

JACK: What fools!

ALGERNON: By the way, did you tell Gwendolen the truth about your being Ernest in town, and Jack in the country?

JACK (in a very patronizing manner): My dear fellow, the truth isn't quite the sort of thing one tells to a nice, sweet, refined girl. What extraordinary ideas you have about the way to behave to a woman!

ALGERNON: The only way to behave to a woman is to make love to her, if she is pretty, and to someone else, if she is plain.

JACK: Oh, that is nonsense.

ALGERNON: What about your brother? What about the profligate Ernest?

JACK: Oh, before the end of the week I shall have got rid of him. I'll say he died in Paris of apoplexy. Lots of people die of apoplexy, quite suddenly, don't they?

---

11 a trivet is a three- or four-legged stand for a hot pot or a teapot. The allusion is that it must be level and standing firmly on its legs ("right").

ALGERNON: Yes, but it's hereditary, my dear fellow. It's a sort of thing that runs in families. You had much better say a severe chill.

JACK: You are sure a severe chill isn't hereditary, or anything of that kind?

ALGERNON: Of course it isn't!

JACK: Very well, then. My poor brother Ernest is carried off suddenly, in Paris, by a severe chill. That gets rid of him.

ALGERNON: But I thought you said that . . . Miss Cardew was a little too much interested in your poor brother Ernest? Won't she feel his loss a good deal?

JACK: Oh, that is all right. Cecily is not a silly romantic girl, I am glad to say. She has got a capital appetite, goes on long walks, and pays no attention at all to her lessons.

ALGERNON: I would rather like to see Cecily.

JACK: I will take very good care you never do. She is excessively pretty, and she is only just eighteen.

ALGERNON: Have you told Gwendolen yet that you have an excessively pretty ward who is only just eighteen?

JACK: Oh! one doesn't blurt these things out to people. Cecily and Gwendolen are perfectly certain to be extremely great friends. I'll bet you anything you like that half an hour after they have met, they will be calling each other sister.

ALGERNON: Women only do that when they have called each other a lot of other things first. Now, my dear boy, if we want to get a good table at Willis's, we really must go and dress. Do you know it is nearly seven?

JACK (*irritably*): Oh! it always is nearly seven.

ALGERNON: Well, I'm hungry.

JACK: I never knew you when you weren't. . . .

ALGERNON: What shall we do after dinner? Go to a theatre?

JACK: Oh no! I loathe listening.

ALGERNON: Well, let us go to the Club?

JACK: Oh, no! I hate talking.

ALGERNON: Well, we might trot round to the Empire[12] at ten?

JACK: Oh, no! I can't bear looking at things. It is so silly.

ALGERNON: Well, what shall we do?

JACK: Nothing!

ALGERNON: It is awfully hard work doing nothing. However, I don't mind hard work where there is no definite object of any kind.

(*Enter* LANE.)

LANE: Miss Fairfax.

(*Enter* GWENDOLEN. LANE *goes out.*)

ALGERNON: Gwendolen, upon my word!

---

12 *a London music hall.*

GWENDOLEN: Algy, kindly turn your back. I have something very particular to say to Mr Worthing.
ALGERNON: Really, Gwendolen, I don't think I can allow this at all.
GWENDOLEN: Algy, you always adopt a strictly immoral attitude towards
life. You are not quite old enough to do that. (ALGERNON *retires to the
fireplace.*)
JACK: My own darling!
GWENDOLEN: Ernest, we may never be married. From the expression on
mamma's face I fear we never shall. Few parents nowadays pay any
regard to what their children say to them. The old-fashioned respect
for the young is fast dying out. Whatever influence I ever had over
mamma, I lost at the age of three. But although she may prevent us
from becoming man and wife, and I may marry someone else, and
marry often, nothing that she can possibly do can alter my eternal
devotion to you.
JACK: Dear Gwendolen!
GWENDOLEN: The story of your romantic origin, as related to me by
mamma, with unpleasing comments, has naturally stirred the
deeper fibres of my nature. Your Christian name has an irresistible
fascination. The simplicity of your character makes you exquisitely
incomprehensible to me. Your town address at the Albany I have.
What is your address in the country?
JACK: The Manor House, Woolton, Hertfordshire.

(ALGERNON, *who has been carefully listening, smiles to himself, and writes the address
on his shirt-cuff. Then picks up the Railway Guide.*)

GWENDOLEN: There is a good postal service, I suppose? It may be neces-
sary to do something desperate. That of course will require serious
consideration. I will communicate with you daily.
JACK: My own one!
GWENDOLEN: How long do you remain in town?
JACK: Till Monday.
GWENDOLEN: Good! Algy, you may turn round now.
ALGERNON: Thanks, I've turned round already.
GWENDOLEN: You may also ring the bell.
JACK: You will let me see you to your carriage, my own darling?
GWENDOLEN: Certainly.
JACK(*to* LANE, *who now enters*): I will see Miss Fairfax out.
LANE: Yes, sir. (JACK *and* GWENDOLEN *go off.*)

(LANE *presents several letters on a salver, to* ALGERNON. *It is to be surmised that they
are bills, as* ALGERNON, *after looking at the envelopes, tears them up.*)

ALGERNON: A glass of sherry, Lane.
LANE: Yes, sir.
ALGERNON: Tomorrow, Lane, I'm going Bunburying.

LANE: Yes, sir.

ALGERNON: I shall probably not be back till Monday. You can put up my dress clothes, my smoking jacket, and all the Bunbury suits . . .

LANE: Yes, sir. *(Handing sherry.)*

ALGERNON: I hope tomorrow will be a fine day, Lane.

LANE: It never is, sir.

ALGERNON: Lane, you're a perfect pessimist.

LANE: I do my best to give satisfaction, sir.

(Enter JACK. LANE *goes off.)*

JACK: There's a sensible, intellectual girl! the only girl I ever cared for in my life. *(*ALGERNON *is laughing immoderately.)* What on earth are you so amused at?

ALGERNON: Oh, I'm a little anxious about poor Bunbury, that is all.

JACK: If you don't take care, your friend Bunbury will get you into a serious scrape some day.

ALGERNON: I love scrapes. They are the only things that are never serious.

JACK: Oh, that's nonsense, Algy. You never talk anything but nonsense.

ALGERNON: Nobody ever does.

*(*JACK *looks indignantly at him, and leaves the room.* ALGERNON *lights a cigarette, reads his shirt-cuff, and smiles.)*

ACT DROP

SECOND ACT

SCENE

Garden at the Manor House. A flight of grey stone steps leads up to the house. The garden, an old-fashioned one, full of roses. Time of year, July. Basket chairs, and a table covered with books, are set under a large yew-tree.

*(*MISS PRISM *discovered seated at the table.* CECILY *is at the back watering flowers.)*

MISS PRISM *(calling)*: Cecily, Cecily! Surely such a utilitarian occupation as the watering of flowers is rather Moulton's duty than yours? Especially at a moment when intellectual pleasures await you. Your German grammar is on the table. Pray open it at page fifteen. We will repeat yesterday's lesson.

CECILY *(coming over very slowly)*: But I don't like German. It isn't at all a becoming language. I know perfectly well that I look quite plain after my German lesson.

MISS PRISM: Child, you know how anxious your guardian is that you should improve yourself in every way. He laid particular stress on your German, as he was leaving for town yesterday. Indeed, he always lays stress on your German when he is leaving for town.

CECILY: Dear Uncle Jack is so very serious! Sometimes he is so serious that I think he cannot be quite well.

MISS PRISM *(drawing herself up)*: Your guardian enjoys the best of health, and his gravity of demeanour is especially to be commended in one so comparatively young as he is. I know no one who has a higher sense of duty and responsibility.

CECILY: I suppose that is why he often looks a little bored when we three are together.

MISS PRISM: Cecily! I am surprised at you. Mr Worthing has many troubles in his life. Idle merriment and triviality would be out of place in his conversation. You must remember his constant anxiety about that unfortunate young man his brother.

CECILY: I wish Uncle Jack would allow that unfortunate young man, his brother, to come down here sometimes. We might have a good influence over him, Miss Prism. I am sure you certainly would. You know German, and geology, and things of that kind influence a man very much. *(CECILY begins to write in her diary.)*

MISS PRISM *(shaking her head)*: I do not think that even I could produce any effect on a character that according to his own brother's admission is irretrievably weak and vacillating. Indeed I am not sure that I would desire to reclaim him. I am not in favour of this modern mania for turning bad people into good people at a moment's notice. As a man sows so let him reap. You must put away your diary, Cecily. I really don't see why you should keep a diary at all.

CECILY: I keep a diary in order to enter the wonderful secrets of my life. If I didn't write them down, I should probably forget all about them.

MISS PRISM: Memory, my dear Cecily, is the diary that we all carry about with us.

CECILY: Yes, but it usually chronicles the things that have never happened, and couldn't possibly have happened. I believe that Memory is responsible for nearly all the three-volume novels that Mudie[1] sends us.

MISS PRISM: Do not speak slightingly of the three-volume novel, Cecily. I wrote one myself in earlier days.

CECILY: Did you really, Miss Prism? How wonderfully clever you are! I hope it did not end happily? I don't like novels that end happily. They depress me so much.

MISS PRISM: The good ended happily, and the bad unhappily. That is what Fiction means.

---

1 *a well-known circulating library and bookstore.*

CECILY: I suppose so. But it seems very unfair. And was your novel ever published?

MISS PRISM: Alas! no. The manuscript unfortunately was abandoned. *(CECILY starts.)* I use the word in the sense of lost or mislaid. To your work, child, these speculations are profitless.

CECILY *(smiling)*: But I see dear Dr Chasuble coming up through the garden.

MISS PRISM *(rising and advancing)*: Dr Chasuble! This is indeed a pleasure.

(Enter CANON CHASUBLE.)

CHASUBLE: And how are we this morning? Miss Prism, you are, I trust, well?

CECILY: Miss Prism has just been complaining of a slight headache. I think it would do her so much good to have a short stroll with you in the Park, Dr Chasuble.

MISS PRISM: Cecily, I have not mentioned anything about a headache.

CECILY: No, dear Miss Prism, I know that, but I felt instinctively that you had a headache. Indeed I was thinking about that, and not about my German lesson, when the Rector came in.

CHASUBLE: I hope, Cecily, you are not inattentive.

CECILY: Oh, I am afraid I am.

CHASUBLE: That is strange. Were I fortunate enough to be Miss Prism's pupil, I would hang upon her lips. *(MISS PRISM glares.)* I spoke metaphorically. — My metaphor was drawn from bees. Ahem! Mr Worthing, I suppose, has not returned from town yet?

MISS PRISM: We do not expect him till Monday afternoon.

CHASUBLE: Ah yes, he usually likes to spend his Sunday in London. He is not one of those whose sole aim is enjoyment, as, by all accounts, that unfortunate young man his brother seems to be. But I must not disturb Egeria[2] and her pupil any longer.

MISS PRISM: Egeria? My name is Laetitia, Doctor.

CHASUBLE *(bowing)*: A classical allusion merely, drawn from the Pagan authors. I shall see you both no doubt at Evensong?

MISS PRISM: I think, dear Doctor, I will have a stroll with you. I find I have a headache after all, and a walk might do it good.

CHASUBLE: With pleasure, Miss Prism, with pleasure. We might go as far as the schools and back.

MISS PRISM: That would be delightful. Cecily, you will read your Political Economy in my absence. The chapter on the Fall of the Rupee[3] you may omit. It is somewhat too sensational. Even these metallic problems have their melodramatic side.

(Goes down the garden with DR CHASUBLE.)

CECILY *(picks up books and throws them back on table)*: Horrid Political Economy! Horrid Geography! Horrid, horrid German!

2 *in Roman mythology, a nymph who was the wife and instructor of a Roman king and who was transformed into a fountain at his death.*
3 *the basic unit of money in India and Pakistan, part of the British Empire in Wilde's time.*

(Enter MERRIMAN *with a card on a salver.)*

MERRIMAN: Mr Ernest Worthing has just driven over from the station.
He has brought his luggage with him.

CECILY *(takes the card and reads it)*: 'Mr Ernest Worthing, B.4, The Albany,
W.' Uncle Jack's brother! Did you tell him Mr Worthing was in
town?

MERRIMAN: Yes, Miss. He seemed very much disappointed. I mentioned
that you and Miss Prism were in the garden. He said he was anxious to speak to you privately for a moment.

CECILY: Ask Mr Ernest Worthing to come here. I suppose you had better
talk to the housekeeper about a room for him.

MERRIMAN: Yes, Miss. (MERRIMAN *goes off.)*

CECILY: I have never met any really wicked person before. I feel rather
frightened. I am so afraid he will look just like every one else.

(Enter ALGERNON, *very gay and debonair.)*

He does!

ALGERNON *(raising his hat)*: You are my little cousin Cecily, I'm sure.

CECILY: You are under some strange mistake. I am not little. In fact, I
believe I am more than usually tall for my age. (ALGERNON *is rather
taken aback.)* But I am your cousin Cecily. You, I see from your card,
are Uncle Jack's brother, my cousin Ernest, my wicked cousin
Ernest.

ALGERNON: Oh! I am not really wicked at all, cousin Cecily. You mustn't
think that I am wicked.

CECILY: If you are not, then you have certainly been deceiving us all in a
very inexcusable manner. I hope you have not been leading a double
life, pretending to be wicked and being really good all the time. That
would be hypocrisy.

ALGERNON *(looks at her in amazement)*: Oh! Of course I have been rather
reckless.

CECILY: I am glad to hear it.

ALGERNON: In fact, now you mention the subject, I have been very bad
in my own small way.

CECILY: I don't think you should be so proud of that, though I am sure it
must have been very pleasant.

ALGERNON: It is much pleasanter being here with you.

CECILY: I can't understand how you are here at all. Uncle Jack won't be
back till Monday afternoon.

ALGERNON: That is a great disappointment. I am obliged to go up by the
first train on Monday morning. I have a business appointment that I
am anxious . . . to miss!

CECILY: Couldn't you miss it anywhere but in London?

ALGERNON: No: the appointment is in London.

CECILY: Well, I know, of course, how important it is not to keep a business engagement, if one wants to retain any sense of the beauty of
life, but still I think you had better wait till Uncle Jack arrives. I
know he wants to speak to you about your emigrating.

ALGERNON: About my what?

CECILY: Your emigrating. He has gone up to buy your outfit.

ALGERNON: I certainly wouldn't let Jack buy my outfit. He has no taste in neckties at all.

CECILY: I don't think you will require neckties. Uncle Jack is sending you to Australia.

ALGERNON: Australia! I'd sooner die.

CECILY: Well, he said at dinner on Wednesday night, that you would have to choose between this world, the next world, and Australia.

ALGERNON: Oh, well! The accounts I have received of Australia and the next world are not particularly encouraging. This world is good enough for me, cousin Cecily.

CECILY: Yes, but are you good enough for it?

ALGERNON: I'm afraid I'm not that. That is why I want you to reform me. You might make that your mission, if you don't mind, cousin Cecily.

CECILY: I'm afraid I've no time, this afternoon.

ALGERNON: Well, would you mind my reforming myself this afternoon?

CECILY: It is rather Quixotic of you. But I think you should try.

ALGERNON: I will. I feel better already.

CECILY: You are looking a little worse.

ALGERNON: That is because I am hungry.

CECILY: How thoughtless of me. I should have remembered that when one is going to lead an entirely new life, one requires regular and wholesome meals. Won't you come in?

ALGERNON: Thank you. Might I have a buttonhole[4] first? I never have any appetite unless I have a buttonhole first.

CECILY: A Maréchal Niel?[5] *(Picks up scissors.)*

ALGERNON: No, I'd sooner have a pink rose.

CECILY: Why? *(Cuts a flower.)*

ALGERNON: Because you are like a pink rose, Cousin Cecily.

CECILY: I don't think it can be right for you to talk to me like that. Miss Prism never says such things to me.

ALGERNON: Then Miss Prism is a short-sighted old lady. *(CECILY puts the rose in his buttonhole.)* You are the prettiest girl I ever saw.

CECILY: Miss Prism says that all good looks are a snare.

ALGERNON: They are a snare that every sensible man would like to be caught in.

CECILY: Oh, I don't think I would care to catch a sensible man. I shouldn't know what to talk to him about.

(They pass into the house. MISS PRISM and DR CHASUBLE return.)

MISS PRISM: You are too much alone, dear Dr Chasuble. You should get married. A misanthrope I can understand — a woman-thrope, never!

4 *a flower worn on a jacket lapel.*
5 *an exotic breed of rose.*

CHASUBLE (*with a scholar's shudder*): Believe me, I do not deserve so neologistic a phrase. The precept as well as the practice of the Primitive Church was distinctly against matrimony.

MISS PRISM (*sententiously*: That is obviously the reason why the Primitive Church has not lasted up to the present day. And you do not seem to realize, dear Doctor, that by persistently remaining single, a man converts himself into a permanent public temptation. Men should be more careful; this very celibacy leads weaker vessels astray.

CHASUBLE: But is a man not equally attractive when married?

MISS PRISM: No married man is ever attractive except to his wife.

CHASUBLE: And often, I've been told, not even to her.

MISS PRISM: That depends on the intellectual sympathies of the woman. Maturity can always be depended on. Ripeness can be trusted. Young women are green. (DR CHASUBLE *starts.*) I spoke horticulturally. My metaphor was drawn from fruits. But where is Cecily?

CHASUBLE: Perhaps she followed us to the schools.

(Enter JACK *slowly from the back of the garden. He is dressed in the deepest mourning, with crape hatband and black gloves.*)

MISS PRISM: Mr Worthing!

DR CHASUBLE: Mr Worthing?

MISS PRISM: This is indeed a surprise. We did not look for you till Monday afternoon.

JACK (*shakes* MISS PRISM's *hand in a tragic manner*): I have returned sooner than I expected. Dr Chasuble, I hope you are well?

CHASUBLE: Dear Mr Worthing, I trust this garb of woe does not betoken some terrible calamity?

JACK: My brother.

MISS PRISM: More shameful debts and extravagance?

CHASUBLE: Still leading his life of pleasure?

JACK (*shaking his head*: Dead!

CHASUBLE: Your brother Ernest dead?

JACK: Quite dead.

MISS PRISM: What a lesson for him! I trust he will profit by it.

CHASUBLE: Mr Worthing, I offer you my sincere condolence. You have at least the consolation of knowing that you were always the most generous and forgiving of brothers.

JACK: Poor Ernest! He had many faults, but it is a sad, sad blow.

CHASUBLE: Very sad indeed. Were you with him at the end?

JACK: No. He died abroad; in Paris, in fact. I had a telegram last night from the manager of the Grand Hotel.

CHASUBLE: Was the cause of death mentioned?

JACK: A severe chill, it seems.

MISS PRISM: As a man sows, so shall he reap.

CHASUBLE (*raising his hand*): Charity, dear Miss Prism, charity! None of us are perfect. I myself am peculiarly susceptible to draughts. Will the interment take place here?

JACK: No. He seems to have expressed a desire to be buried in Paris.

CHASUBLE: In Paris! *(Shakes his head.)* I fear that hardly points to any very serious state of mind at the last. You would no doubt wish me to make some slight allusion to this tragic domestic affliction next Sunday. *(JACK presses his hand convulsively.)* My sermon on the meaning of the manna in the wilderness can be adapted to almost any occasion, joyful, or, as in the present case, distressing. *(All sigh.)* I have preached it at harvest celebrations, christenings, confirmations, on days of humiliation and festal days. The last time I delivered it was in the Cathedral, as a charity sermon on behalf of the Society for the Prevention of Discontent among the Upper Orders. The Bishop, who was present, was much struck by some of the analogies I drew.

JACK: Ah! that reminds me, you mentioned christenings I think, Dr Chasuble? I suppose you know how to christen all right? *(DR CHASUBLE looks astounded.)* I mean, of course, you are continually christening, aren't you?

MISS PRISM: It is, I regret to say, one of the Rector's most constant duties in this parish. I have often spoken to the poorer classes on the subject. But they don't seem to know what thrift is.

CHASUBLE: But is there any particular infant in whom you are interested, Mr Worthing? Your brother was, I believe, unmarried, was he not?

JACK: Oh, yes.

MISS PRISM *(bitterly)*: People who live entirely for pleasure usually are.

JACK: But it is not for any child, dear Doctor. I am very fond of children. No! the fact is, I would like to be christened myself, this afternoon, if you have nothing better to do.

CHASUBLE: But surely, Mr Worthing, you have been christened already?

JACK: I don't remember anything about it.

CHASUBLE: But have you any grave doubts on the subject?

JACK: I certainly intend to have. Of course I don't know if the thing would bother you in any way, or if you think I am a little too old now.

CHASUBLE: Not at all. The sprinkling, and, indeed, the immersion of adults is a perfectly canonical practice.

JACK: Immersion!

CHASUBLE: You need have no apprehensions. Sprinkling is all that is necessary, or indeed I think advisable. Our weather is so changeable. At what hour would you wish the ceremony performed?

JACK: Oh, I might trot round about five if that would suit you.

CHASUBLE: Perfectly, perfectly! In fact I have two similar ceremonies to perform at that time. A case of twins that occurred recently in one of the outlying cottages on your own estate. Poor Jenkins the carter, a most hard-working man.

JACK: Oh! I don't see much fun in being christened along with other babies. It would be childish. Would half-past five do?

CHASUBLE: Admirably! Admirably! *(Takes out watch.)* And now, dear Mr Worthing, I will not intrude any longer into a house of sorrow. I would merely beg you not to be too much bowed down by grief. What seem to us bitter trials are often blessings in disguise.

MISS PRISM: This seems to me a blessing of an extremely obvious kind.

(Enter CECILY from the house.)

CECILY: Uncle Jack! Oh, I am pleased to see you back. But what horrid clothes you have got on! Do go and change them.

MISS PRISM: Cecily!

CHASUBLE: My child! my child! *(CECILY goes towards JACK; he kisses her brow in a melancholy manner.)*

CECILY: What is the matter, Uncle Jack? Do look happy! You look as if you had toothache, and I have got such a surprise for you. Who do you think is in the dining-room? Your brother!

JACK: Who?

CECILY: Your brother Ernest. He arrived about half an hour ago.

JACK: What nonsense! I haven't got a brother.

CECILY: Oh, don't say that. However badly he may have behaved to you in the past he is still your brother. You couldn't be so heartless as to disown him. I'll tell him to come out. And you will shake hands with him, won't you, Uncle Jack? *(Runs back into the house.)*

CHASUBLE: These are very joyful tidings.

MISS PRISM: After we had all been resigned to his loss, his sudden return seems to me peculiarly distressing.

JACK: My brother is in the dining-room? I don't know what it all means. I think it is perfectly absurd.

(Enter ALGERNON and CECILY hand in hand. They come slowly up to JACK.)

JACK: Good heavens! *(Motions ALGERNON away.)*

ALGERNON: Brother John, I have come down from town to tell you that I am very sorry for all the trouble I have given you, and that I intend to lead a better life in the future. *(JACK glares at him and does not take his hand.)*

CECILY: Uncle Jack, you are not going to refuse your own brother's hand?

JACK: Nothing will induce me to take his hand. I think his coming down here disgraceful. He knows perfectly well why.

CECILY: Uncle Jack, do be nice. There is some good in everyone. Ernest has just been telling me about his poor invalid friend Mr Bunbury whom he goes to visit so often. And surely there must be much good in one who is kind to an invalid, and leaves the pleasures of London to sit by a bed of pain.

JACK: Oh! he has been talking about Bunbury, has he?

CECILY: Yes, he has told me all about poor Mr Bunbury, and his terrible state of health.

JACK: Bunbury! Well, I won't have him talk to you about Bunbury or about anything else. It is enough to drive one perfectly frantic.

ALGERNON: Of course I admit that the faults were all on my side. But I must say that I think that Brother John's coldness to me is peculiarly

painful. I expected a more enthusiastic welcome, especially considering it is the first time I have come here.

CECILY: Uncle Jack, if you don't shake hands with Ernest I will never forgive you.

JACK: Never forgive me?

CECILY: Never, never, never!

JACK: Well, this is the last time I shall ever do it. *(Shakes hands with
ALGERNON and glares.)*

CHASUBLE: It's pleasant, is it not, to see so perfect a reconciliation? I
think we might leave the two brothers together.

MISS PRISM: Cecily, you will come with us.

CECILY: Certainly, Miss Prism. My little task of reconciliation is over.

CHASUBLE: You have done a beautiful action today, dear child.

MISS PRISM: We must not be premature in our judgments.

CECILY: I feel very happy. *(They all go off except JACK and ALGERNON.)*

JACK: You young scoundrel, Algy, you must get out of this place as soon
as possible. I don't allow any Bunburying here.

(Enter MERRIMAN.)

MERRIMAN: I have put Mr Ernest's things in the room next to yours, sir.
I suppose that is all right?

JACK: What?

MERRIMAN: Mr Ernest's luggage, sir. I have unpacked it and put it in the
room next to your own.

JACK: His luggage?

MERRIMAN: Yes, sir. Three portmanteaus, a dressing-case, two hat-
boxes, and a large luncheon-basket.

ALGERNON: I am afraid I can't stay more than a week this time.

JACK: Merriman, order the dog-cart[6] at once. Mr Ernest has been suddenly called back to town.

MERRIMAN: Yes, sir. *(Goes back into the house.)*

ALGERNON: What a fearful liar you are, Jack. I have not been called back
to town at all.

JACK: Yes, you have.

ALGERNON: I haven't heard anyone call me.

JACK: Your duty as a gentleman calls you back.

ALGERNON: My duty as a gentleman has never interfered with my pleasures in the smallest degree.

JACK: I can quite understand that.

ALGERNON: Well, Cecily is a darling.

JACK: You are not to talk of Miss Cardew like that. I don't like it.

ALGERNON: Well, I don't like your clothes. You look perfectly ridiculous
in them. Why on earth don't you go up and change? It is perfectly
childish to be in deep mourning for a man who is actually staying
for a whole week with you in your house as a guest. I call it
grotesque.

---

6 *a small two-wheeled cart with two seats.*

JACK: You are certainly not staying with me for a whole week as a guest or anything else. You have got to leave . . . by the four-five train.

ALGERNON: I certainly won't leave you so long as you are in mourning. It would be most unfriendly. If I were in mourning you would stay with me, I suppose. I should think it very unkind if you didn't.

JACK: Well, will you go if I change my clothes?

ALGERNON: Yes, if you are not too long. I never saw anybody take so long to dress, and with such little result.

JACK: Well, at any rate, that is better than being always over-dressed as you are.

ALGERNON: If I am occasionally a little over-dressed, I make up for it by being always immensely over-educated.

JACK: Your vanity is ridiculous, your conduct an outrage, and your presence in my garden utterly absurd. However, you have got to catch the four-five, and I hope you will have a pleasant journey back to town. This Bunburying, as you call it, has not been a great success for you.

(Goes into the house.)

ALGERNON: I think it has been a great success. I'm in love with Cecily, and that is everything.

(Enter CECILY *at the back of the garden. She picks up the can and begins to water the flowers.)*

But I must see her before I go, and make arrangements for another Bunbury. Ah, there she is.

CECILY: Oh, I merely came back to water the roses. I thought you were with Uncle Jack.

ALGERNON: He's gone to order the dog-cart for me.

CECILY: Oh, is he going to take you for a nice drive?

ALGERNON: He's going to send me away.

CECILY: Then have we got to part?

ALGERNON: I am afraid so. It's a very painful parting.

CECILY: It is always painful to part from people whom one has known for a very brief space of time. The absence of old friends one can endure with equanimity. But even a momentary separation from any one to whom one has just been introduced is almost unbearable.

ALGERNON: Thank you.

(Enter MERRIMAN.*)*

MERRIMAN: The dog-cart is at the door, sir.

*(*ALGERNON *looks appealingly at* CECILY.*)*

CECILY: It can wait, Merriman . . . for . . . five minutes.
MERRIMAN: Yes, miss.

(Exit MERRIMAN.*)*

ALGERNON: I hope, Cecily, I shall not offend you if I state quite frankly
and openly that you seem to me to be in every way the visible personification of absolute perfection.
CECILY: I think your frankness does you great credit, Ernest. If you will
allow me, I will copy your remarks into my diary. *(Goes over to table
and begins writing in diary.)*
ALGERNON: Do you really keep a diary? I'd give anything to look at it.
May I?
CECILY: Oh no. *(Puts her hand over it.)* You see, it is simply a very young
girl's record of her own thoughts and impressions, and consequently meant for publication. When it appears in volume form I
hope you will order a copy. But pray, Ernest, don't stop. I delight in
taking down from dictation. I have reached 'absolute perfection.'
You can go on. I am quite ready for more.
ALGERNON*(somewhat taken aback)*: Ahem! Ahem!
CECILY: Oh, don't cough, Ernest. When one is dictating one should speak
fluently and not cough. Besides, I don't know how to spell a cough.
(Writes as ALGERNON *speaks.)*
ALGERNON *(speaking very rapidly)*: Cecily, ever since I first looked upon your
wonderful and incomparable beauty, I have dared to love you wildly,
passionately, devotedly, hopelessly.
CECILY: I don't think that you should tell me that you love me wildly,
passionately, devotedly, hopelessly. Hopelessly doesn't seem to make
much sense, does it?
ALGERNON: Cecily!

(Enter MERRIMAN.*)*

MERRIMAN: The dog-cart is waiting, sir.
ALGERNON: Tell it to come round next week, at the same hour.
MERRIMAN *(looks at* CECILY, *who makes no sign)*: Yes, sir.

*(*MERRIMAN *retires.)*

CECILY: Uncle Jack would be very much annoyed if he knew you were
staying on till next week, at the same hour.
ALGERNON: Oh, I don't care about Jack. I don't care for anybody in the
whole world but you. I love you, Cecily. You will marry me, won't
you?
CECILY: You silly boy! Of course. Why, we have been engaged for the
last three months.

ALGERNON: For the last three months?

CECILY: Yes, it will be exactly three months on Thursday.

ALGERNON: But how did we become engaged?

CECILY: Well, ever since dear Uncle Jack first confessed to us that he had a younger brother who was very wicked and bad, you of course have formed the chief topic of conversation between myself and Miss Prism. And of course a man who is much talked about is always very attractive. One feels there must be something in him, after all. I daresay it was foolish of me, but I fell in love with you, Ernest.

ALGERNON: Darling! And when was the engagement actually settled?

CECILY: On the 14th of February last. Worn out by your entire ignorance of my existence, I determined to end the matter one way or the other, and after a long struggle with myself I accepted you under this dear old tree here. The next day I bought this little ring in your name, and this is the little bangle with the true lover's knot I promised you always to wear.

ALGERNON: Did I give you this? It's very pretty, isn't it?

CECILY: Yes, you've wonderfully good taste, Ernest. It's the excuse I've always given for your leading such a bad life. And this is the box in which I keep all your dear letters. *(Kneels at table, opens box, and produces letters tied up with blue ribbon.)*

ALGERNON: My letters! But, my own sweet Cecily, I have never written you any letters.

CECILY: You need hardly remind me of that, Ernest. I remember only too well that I was forced to write your letters for you. I wrote always three times a week, and sometimes oftener.

ALGERNON: Oh, do let me read them, Cecily?

CECILY: Oh, I couldn't possibly. They would make you far too conceited. *(Replaces box.)* The three you wrote me after I had broken off the engagement are so beautiful, and so badly spelled, that even now I can hardly read them without crying a little.

ALGERNON: But was our engagement ever broken off?

CECILY: Of course it was. On the 22nd of last March. You can see the entry if you like. *(Shows diary.)* 'Today I broke off my engagement with Ernest. I feel it is better to do so. The weather still continues charming.'

ALGERNON: But why on earth did you break it off? What had I done? I had done nothing at all. Cecily, I am very much hurt indeed to hear you broke it off. Particularly when the weather was so charming.

CECILY: It would hardly have been a really serious engagement if it hadn't been broken off at least once. But I forgave you before the week was out.

ALGERNON *(crossing to her, and kneeling)*: What a perfect angel you are, Cecily.

CECILY: You dear romantic boy. *(He kisses her, she puts her fingers through his hair.)* I hope your hair curls naturally, does it?

ALGERNON: Yes, darling, with a little help from others.

CECILY: I am so glad.

ALGERNON: You'll never break off our engagement again, Cecily?

CECILY: I don't think I could break it off now that I have actually met you. Besides, of course, there is the question of your name.

ALGERNON: Yes, of course. *(Nervously.)*

CECILY: You must not laugh at me, darling, but it had always been a girlish dream of mine to love some one whose name was Ernest. *(ALGERNON rises, CECILY also.)* There is something in that name that seems to inspire absolute confidence. I pity any poor married woman whose husband is not called Ernest.

ALGERNON: But, my dear child, do you mean to say you could not love me if I had some other name?

CECILY: But what name?

ALGERNON: Oh, any name you like — Algernon — for instance . . .

CECILY: But I don't like the name of Algernon.

ALGERNON: Well, my own dear, sweet, loving little darling, I really can't see why you should object to the name of Algernon. It is not at all a bad name. In fact, it is rather an aristocratic name. Half of the chaps who get into the Bankruptcy Court are called Algernon. But seriously, Cecily . . . *(moving to her)* . . . if my name was Algy, couldn't you love me?

CECILY *(rising)*: I might respect you, Ernest, I might admire your character, but I fear that I should not be able to give you my undivided attention.

ALGERNON: Ahem! Cecily! *(Picking up hat.)* Your Rector here is, I suppose, thoroughly experienced in the practice of all the rites and ceremonials of the Church?

CECILY: Oh, yes, Dr Chasuble is a most learned man. He has never written a single book, so you can imagine how much he knows.

ALGERNON: I must see him at once on a most important christening — I mean on most important business.

CECILY: Oh!

ALGERNON: I shan't be away more than half an hour.

CECILY: Considering that we have been engaged since February the 14th, and that I only met you today for the first time, I think it is rather hard that you should leave me for so long a period as half an hour. Couldn't you make it twenty minutes?

ALGERNON: I'll be back in no time. *(Kisses her and rushes down the garden.)*

CECILY: What an impetuous boy he is! I like his hair so much. I must enter his proposal in my diary.

(Enter MERRIMAN.)

MERRIMAN: A Miss Fairfax has just called to see Mr Worthing. On very important business, Miss Fairfax states.

CECILY: Isn't Mr Worthing in his library?

MERRIMAN: Mr Worthing went over in the direction of the Rectory some time ago.

CECILY: Pray ask the lady to come out here; Mr Worthing is sure to be back soon. And you can bring tea.

MERRIMAN: Yes, Miss.

(Goes out.)

CECILY: Miss Fairfax! I suppose one of the many good elderly women who are associated with Uncle Jack in some of his philanthropic work in London. I don't quite like women who are interested in philanthropic work. I think it is so forward of them.

(Enter MERRIMAN.*)*

MERRIMAN: Miss Fairfax.

(Enter GWENDOLEN. *Exit* MERRIMAN.*)*

CECILY *(advancing to meet her)*: Pray let me introduce myself to you. My name is Cecily Cardew.

GWENDOLEN: Cecily Cardew? *(Moving to her and shaking hands.)* What a very sweet name! Something tells me that we are going to be great friends. I like you already more than I can say. My first impressions of people are never wrong.

CECILY: How nice of you to like me so much after we have known each other such a comparatively short time. Pray sit down.

GWENDOLEN *(still standing up)*: I may call you Cecily, may I not?

CECILY: With pleasure!

GWENDOLEN: And you will always call me Gwendolen, won't you?

CECILY: If you wish.

GWENDOLEN: Then that is all quite settled, is it not?

CECILY: I hope so. *(A pause. They both sit down together.)*

GWENDOLEN: Perhaps this might be a favourable opportunity for my mentioning who I am. My father is Lord Bracknell. You have never heard of papa, I suppose?

CECILY: I don't think so.

GWENDOLEN: Outside the family circle, papa, I am glad to say, is entirely unknown. I think that is quite as it should be. The home seems to me to be the proper sphere for the man. And certainly once a man begins to neglect his domestic duties he becomes painfully effeminate, does he not? And I don't like that. It makes men so very attractive. Cecily, mamma, whose views on education are remarkably strict, has brought me up to be extremely short-sighted; it is part of her system; so do you mind my looking at you through my glasses?

CECILY: Oh! not at all, Gwendolen. I am very fond of being looked at.

GWENDOLEN *(after examining* CECILY *carefully through a lorgnette)*: You are here on a short visit, I suppose.

CECILY: Oh no! I live here.

GWENDOLEN *(severely)*: Really? Your mother, no doubt, or some female relative of advanced years, resides here also?

CECILY: Oh no! I have no mother, nor, in fact, any relations.

GWENDOLEN: Indeed?

CECILY: My dear guardian, with the assistance of Miss Prism, has the arduous task of looking after me.

GWENDOLEN: Your guardian?

CECILY: Yes, I am Mr Worthing's ward.

GWENDOLEN: Oh! It is strange he never mentioned to me that he had a ward. How secretive of him! He grows more interesting hourly. I am not sure, however, that the news inspires me with feelings of unmixed delight. *(Rising and going to her.)* I am very fond of you, Cecily; I have liked you ever since I met you! But I am bound to state that now that I know that you are Mr Worthing's ward, I cannot help expressing a wish you were — well, just a little older than you seem to be — and not quite so very alluring in appearance. In fact, if I may speak candidly —

CECILY: Pray do! I think that whenever one has anything unpleasant to say, one should always be quite candid.

GWENDOLEN: Well, to speak with perfect candour, Cecily, I wish that you were fully forty-two, and more than usually plain for your age. Ernest has a strong upright nature. He is the very soul of truth and honour. Disloyalty would be as impossible to him as deception. But even men of the noblest possible moral character are extremely susceptible to the influence of the physical charms of others. Modern, no less than Ancient History, supplies us with many most painful examples of what I refer to. If it were not so, indeed, History would be quite unreadable.

CECILY: I beg your pardon, Gwendolen, did you say Ernest?

GWENDOLEN: Yes.

CECILY: Oh, but it is not Mr Ernest Worthing who is my guardian. It is his brother — his elder brother.

GWENDOLEN *(sitting down again)*: Ernest never mentioned to me that he had a brother.

CECILY: I am sorry to say they have not been on good terms for a long time.

GWENDOLEN: Ah! that accounts for it. And now that I think of it I have never heard any man mention his brother. The subject seems distasteful to most men. Cecily, you have lifted a load from my mind. I was growing almost anxious. It would have been terrible if any cloud had come across a friendship like ours, would it not? Of course you are quite, quite sure that it is not Mr Ernest Worthing who is your guardian?

CECILY: Quite sure. *(A pause.)* In fact, I am going to be his.

GWENDOLEN *(inquiringly)*: I beg your pardon?

CECILY *(rather shy and confidingly)*: Dearest Gwendolen, there is no reason why I should make a secret of it to you. Our little county newspaper is sure to chronicle the fact next week. Mr Ernest Worthing and I are engaged to be married.

GWENDOLEN (*quite politely, rising*): My darling Cecily, I think there must be some slight error. Mr Ernest Worthing is engaged to me. The announcement will appear in the *Morning Post* on Saturday at the latest.

CECILY (*very politely, rising*): I am afraid you must be under some misconception. Ernest proposed to me exactly ten minutes ago. (*Shows diary.*)

GWENDOLEN (*examines diary through her lorgnette carefully*): It is very curious, for he asked me to be his wife yesterday afternoon at 5:30. If you would care to verify the incident, pray do so. (*Produces diary of her own.*) I never travel without my diary. One should always have something sensational to read in the train. I am so sorry, dear Cecily, if it is any disappointment to you, but I am afraid I have the prior claim.

CECILY: It would distress me more than I can tell you, dear Gwendolen, if it caused you any mental or physical anguish, but I feel bound to point out that since Ernest proposed to you he clearly has changed his mind.

GWENDOLEN (*meditatively*): If the poor fellow has been entrapped into any foolish promise I shall consider it my duty to rescue him at once, and with a firm hand.

CECILY (*thoughtfully and sadly*): Whatever unfortunate entanglement my dear boy may have got into, I will never reproach him with it after we are married.

GWENDOLEN: Do you allude to me, Miss Cardew, as an entanglement? You are presumptuous. On an occasion of this kind it becomes more than a moral duty to speak one's mind. It becomes a pleasure.

CECILY: Do you suggest, Miss Fairfax, that I entrapped Ernest into an engagement? How dare you? This is no time for wearing the shallow mask of manners. When I see a spade I call it a spade.

GWENDOLEN (*satirically*): I am glad to say that I have never seen a spade. It is obvious that our social spheres have been widely different.

(*Enter* MERRIMAN, *followed by the footman. He carries a salver, table cloth, and plate stand.* CECILY *is about to retort. The presence of the servants exercises a restraining influence, under which both girls chafe.*)

MERRIMAN: Shall I lay tea here as usual, Miss?

CECILY (*sternly, in a calm voice*): Yes, as usual. (MERRIMAN *begins to clear table and lay cloth. A long pause.* CECILY *and* GWENDOLEN *glare at each other.*)

GWENDOLEN: Are there many interesting walks in the vicinity, Miss Cardew?

CECILY: Oh! yes! a great many. From the top of one of the hills quite close one can see five counties.

GWENDOLEN: Five counties! I don't think I should like that; I hate crowds.

CECILY (*sweetly*): I suppose that is why you live in town? (GWENDOLEN *bites her lip, and beats her foot nervously with her parasol.*)

GWENDOLEN (*looking around*): Quite a well-kept garden this is, Miss Cardew.

CECILY: So glad you like it, Miss Fairfax.

GWENDOLEN: I had no idea there were any flowers in the country.

CECILY: Oh, flowers are as common here, Miss Fairfax, as people are in London.

GWENDOLEN: Personally I cannot understand how anybody manages to exist in the country, if anybody who is anybody does. The country always bores me to death.

CECILY: Ah! This is what the newspapers call agricultural depression, is it not? I believe the aristocracy are suffering very much from it just at present. It is almost an epidemic amongst them, I have been told. May I offer you some tea, Miss Fairfax?

GWENDOLEN (with elaborate politeness): Thank you. (Aside.) Detestable girl! But I require tea!

CECILY (sweetly): Sugar?

GWENDOLEN (superciliously): No, thank you. Sugar is not fashionable any more. (CECILY looks angrily at her, takes up the tongs and puts four lumps of sugar into the cup.)

CECILY (severely): Cake or bread and butter?

GWENDOLEN (in a bored manner): Bread and butter, please. Cake is rarely seen at the best houses nowadays.

CECILY (cuts a very large slice of cake and puts it on the tray): Hand that to Miss Fairfax.

(MERRIMAN does so, and goes out with footman. GWENDOLEN drinks the tea and makes a grimace. Puts down cup at once, reaches out her hand to the bread and butter, looks at it, and finds it is cake. Rises in indignation.)

GWENDOLEN: You have filled my tea with lumps of sugar, and though I asked most distinctly for bread and butter, you have given me cake. I am known for the gentleness of my disposition, and the extraordinary sweetness of my nature, but I warn you, Miss Cardew, you may go too far.

CECILY (rising): To save my poor, innocent, trusting boy from the machinations of any other girl there are no lengths to which I would not go.

GWENDOLEN: From the moment I saw you I distrusted you. I felt that you were false and deceitful. I am never deceived in such matters. My first impressions of people are invariably right.

CECILY: It seems to me, Miss Fairfax, that I am trespassing on your valuable time. No doubt you have many other calls of a similar character to make in the neighbourhood.

(Enter JACK.)

GWENDOLEN (catching sight of him): Ernest! My own Ernest!

JACK: Gwendolen! Darling! (Offers to kiss her.)

GWENDOLEN (drawing back): A moment! May I ask if you are engaged to be married to this young lady? (Points to CECILY.)

JACK (laughing): To dear little Cecily! Of course not! What could have put such an idea into your pretty little head?

GWENDOLEN: Thank you. You may! *(Offers her cheek.)*

CECILY *(very sweetly)*: I knew there must be some misunderstanding, Miss Fairfax. The gentleman whose arm is at present round your waist is my guardian, Mr John Worthing.

GWENDOLEN: I beg your pardon?

CECILY: This is Uncle Jack.

GWENDOLEN *(receding)*: Jack! Oh!

(Enter ALGERNON.)

CECILY: Here is Ernest.

ALGERNON *(goes straight over to CECILY without noticing anyone else)*: My own love! *(Offers to kiss her.)*

CECILY *(drawing back)*: A moment, Ernest! May I ask you — are you engaged to be married to this young lady?

ALGERNON *(looking round)*: To what young lady? Good heavens! Gwendolen!

CECILY: Yes! to good heavens, Gwendolen, I mean to Gwendolen.

ALGERNON *(laughing)*: Of course not! What could have put such an idea into your pretty little head?

CECILY: Thank you. *(Presenting her cheek to be kissed.)* You may. *(ALGERNON kisses her.)*

GWENDOLEN: I felt there was some slight error, Miss Cardew. The gentleman who is now embracing you is my cousin, Mr Algernon Moncrieff.

CECILY *(breaking away from Algernon)*: Algernon Moncrieff! Oh! *(The two girls move towards each other and put their arms round each other's waists as if for protection.)*

CECILY: Are you called Algernon?

ALGERNON: I cannot deny it.

CECILY: Oh!

GWENDOLEN: Is your name really John?

JACK *(standing rather proudly)*: I could deny it if I liked. I could deny anything if I liked. But my name certainly is John. It has been John for years.

CECILY *(to GWENDOLEN)*: A gross deception has been practised on both of us.

GWENDOLEN: My poor wounded Cecily!

CECILY: My sweet wronged Gwendolen!

GWENDOLEN *(slowly and seriously)*: You will call me sister, will you not? *(They embrace. JACK and ALGERNON groan and walk up and down.)*

CECILY *(rather brightly)*: There is just one question I would like to be allowed to ask my guardian.

GWENDOLEN: An admirable idea! Mr Worthing, there is just one question I would like to be permitted to put to you. Where is your brother Ernest? We are both engaged to be married to your brother Ernest, so it is a matter of some importance to us to know where your brother Ernest is at present.

JACK *(slowly and hesitatingly)*: Gwendolen — Cecily — it is very painful for me to be forced to speak the truth. It is the first time in my life that I have ever been reduced to such a painful position, and I am really quite inexperienced in doing anything of the kind. However, I will tell you quite frankly that I have no brother Ernest. I have no brother at all. I never had a brother in my life, and I certainly have not the smallest intention of ever having one in the future.

CECILY (surprised): No brother at all?

JACK (cheerily): None!

GWENDOLEN (severely): Had you never a brother of any kind?

JACK (pleasantly): Never. Not even of any kind.

GWENDOLEN: I am afraid it is quite clear, Cecily, that neither of us is engaged to be married to anyone.

CECILY: It is not a very pleasant position for a young girl suddenly to find herself in. Is it?

GWENDOLEN: Let us go into the house. They will hardly venture to come after us there.

CECILY: No, men are so cowardly, aren't they?

(They retire into the house with scornful looks.)

JACK: This ghastly state of things is what you call Bunburying, I suppose?

ALGERNON: Yes, and a perfectly wonderful Bunbury it is. The most wonderful Bunbury I have ever had in my life.

JACK: Well, you've no right whatsoever to Bunbury here.

ALGERNON: That is absurd. One has a right to Bunbury anywhere one chooses. Every serious Bunburyist knows that.

JACK: Serious Bunburyist? Good heavens!

ALGERNON: Well, one must be serious about something, if one wants to have any amusement in life. I happen to be serious about Bunburying. What on earth you are serious about I haven't got the remotest idea. About everything, I should fancy. You have such an absolutely trivial nature.

JACK: Well, the only small satisfaction I have in the whole of this wretched business is that your friend Bunbury is quite exploded. You won't be able to run down to the country quite so often as you used to do, dear Algy. And a very good thing too.

ALGERNON: Your brother is a little off colour, isn't he, dear Jack? You won't be able to disappear to London quite so frequently as your wicked custom was. And not a bad thing either.

JACK: As for your conduct towards Miss Cardew, I must say that your taking in a sweet, simple, innocent girl like that is quite inexcusable. To say nothing of the fact that she is my ward.

ALGERNON: I can see no possible defence at all for your deceiving a brilliant, clever, thoroughly experienced young lady like Miss Fairfax. To say nothing of the fact that she is my cousin.

JACK: I wanted to be engaged to Gwendolen, that is all. I love her.

ALGERNON: Well, I simply wanted to be engaged to Cecily. I adore her.

JACK: There is certainly no chance of your marrying Miss Cardew.

ALGERNON: I don't think there is much likelihood, Jack, of you and Miss Fairfax being united.

JACK: Well, that is no business of yours.

ALGERNON: If it was my business, I wouldn't talk about it. *(Begins to eat muffins.)* It is very vulgar to talk about one's business. Only people like stockbrokers do that, and then merely at dinner parties.

JACK: How can you sit there, calmly eating muffins when we are in this horrible trouble, I can't make out. You seem to me to be perfectly heartless.

ALGERNON: Well, I can't eat muffins in an agitated manner. The butter would probably get on my cuffs. One should always eat muffins quite calmly. It is the only way to eat them.

JACK: I say it's perfectly heartless your eating muffins at all, under the circumstances.

ALGERNON: When I am in trouble, eating is the only thing that consoles me. Indeed, when I am in really great trouble, as any one who knows me intimately will tell you, I refuse everything except food and drink. At the present moment I am eating muffins because I am unhappy. Besides, I am particularly fond of muffins. *(Rising.)*

JACK *(rising)*: Well, that is no reason why you should eat them all in that greedy way. *(Takes muffins from* ALGERNON.*)*

ALGERNON *(offering tea-cake)*: I wish you would have tea-cake instead. I don't like tea-cake.

JACK: Good heavens! I suppose a man may eat his own muffins in his own garden.

ALGERNON: But you have just said it was perfectly heartless to eat muffins.

JACK: I said it was perfectly heartless of you, under the circumstances. That is a very different thing.

ALGERNON: That may be. But the muffins are the same. *(He seizes the muffin-dish from* JACK.*)*

JACK: Algy, I wish to goodness you would go.

ALGERNON: You can't possibly ask me to go without having some dinner. It's absurd. I never go without my dinner. No one ever does, except vegetarians and people like that. Besides I have just made arrangements with Dr Chasuble to be christened at a quarter to six under the name of Ernest.

JACK: My dear fellow, the sooner you give up that nonsense the better. I made arrangements this morning with Dr Chasuble to be christened myself at 5.30, and I naturally will take the name of Ernest. Gwendolen would wish it. We cannot both be christened Ernest. It's absurd. Besides, I have a perfect right to be christened if I like. There is no evidence at all that I ever have been christened by anybody. I should think it extremely probable I never was, and so does Dr Chasuble. It is entirely different in your case. You have been christened already.

ALGERNON: Yes, but I have not been christened for years.

JACK: Yes, but you have been christened. That is the important thing.

ALGERNON: Quite so. So I know my constitution can stand it. If you are not quite sure about your ever having been christened, I must say I think it rather dangerous your venturing on it now. It might make you very unwell. You can hardly have forgotten that someone very closely connected with you was very nearly carried off this week in Paris by a severe chill.

JACK: Yes, but you said yourself that a severe chill was not hereditary.

ALGERNON: It usen't to be, I know — but I daresay it is now. Science is always making wonderful improvements in things.

JACK *(picking up the muffin-dish)*: Oh, that is nonsense; you are always talking nonsense.

ALGERNON: Jack, you are at the muffins again! I wish you wouldn't. There are only two left. *(Takes them.)* I told you I was particularly fond of muffins.

JACK: But I hate tea-cake.

ALGERNON: Why on earth then do you allow tea-cake to be served up for your guests? What ideas you have of hospitality!

JACK: Algernon! I have already told you to go. I don't want you here. Why don't you go!

ALGERNON: I haven't quite finished my tea yet! and there is still one muffin left. *(JACK groans, and sinks into a chair. ALGERNON continues eating.)*

ACT DROP

THIRD ACT

SCENE

Drawing-room at the Manor House

(GWENDOLEN and CECILY are at the window, looking out into the garden.)

GWENDOLEN: The fact that they did not follow us at once into the house, as anyone else would have done, seems to me to show that they have some sense of shame left.

CECILY: They have been eating muffins. That looks like repentance.

GWENDOLEN *(after a pause)*: They don't seem to notice us at all. Couldn't you cough?

CECILY: But I haven't got a cough.

GWENDOLEN: They're looking at us. What effrontery!

CECILY: They're approaching. That's very forward of them.

GWENDOLEN: Let us preserve a dignified silence.

CECILY: Certainly. It's the only thing to do now.

(Enter JACK followed by ALGERNON. They whistle some dreadful popular air from a British Opera.)

GWENDOLEN: This dignified silence seems to produce an unpleasant effect.

CECILY: A most distasteful one.

GWENDOLEN: But we will not be the first to speak.

CECILY: Certainly not.

GWENDOLEN: Mr Worthing, I have something very particular to ask you. Much depends on your reply.

CECILY: Gwendolen, your common sense is invaluable. Mr Moncrieff, kindly answer me the following question. Why did you pretend to be my guardian's brother?

ALGERNON: In order that I might have an opportunity of meeting you.

CECILY (to GWENDOLEN): That certainly seems a satisfactory explanation, does it not?

GWENDOLEN: Yes, dear, if you can believe him.

CECILY: I don't. But that does not affect the wonderful beauty of his answer.

GWENDOLEN: True. In matters of grave importance, style, not sincerity, is the vital thing. Mr Worthing, what explanation can you offer to me for pretending to have a brother? Was it in order that you might have an opportunity of coming up to town to see me as often as possible?

JACK: Can you doubt it, Miss Fairfax?

GWENDOLEN: I have the gravest doubts upon the subject. But I intend to crush them. This is not the moment for German scepticism.[1] (Moving to CECILY.) Their explanations appear to be quite satisfactory, especially Mr Worthing's. That seems to me to have the stamp of truth upon it.

CECILY: I am more than content with what Mr Moncrieff said. His voice alone inspires one with absolute credulity.

GWENDOLEN: Then you think we should forgive them?

CECILY: Yes. I mean no.

GWENDOLEN: True! I had forgotten. There are principles at stake that one cannot surrender. Which of us should tell them? The task is not a pleasant one.

CECILY: Could we not both speak at the same time?

GWENDOLEN: An excellent idea! I nearly always speak at the same time as other people. Will you take the time from me?

CECILY: Certainly. (GWENDOLEN beats time with uplifted finger.)

GWENDOLEN and CECILY (speaking together): Your Christian names are still an insuperable barrier. That is all!

JACK and ALGERNON (speaking together): Our Christian names! Is that all? But we are going to be christened this afternoon.

GWENDOLEN (to JACK): For my sake you are prepared to do this terrible thing?

JACK: I am.

---

1 skepticism holds that no knowledge is absolute and that doubt is necessary to achieve an approximation of certainty. German theological writings at this time were considered especially skeptical in the English popular mind.

CECILY *(to* ALGERNON*)*: To please me you are ready to face this fearful ordeal?

ALGERNON: I am!

GWENDOLEN: How absurd to talk about the equality of the sexes! Where questions of self-sacrifice are concerned, men are infinitely beyond us.

JACK: We are. *(Clasps hands with* ALGERNON*.)*

CECILY: They have moments of physical courage of which we women know absolutely nothing.

GWENDOLEN *(to* JACK*)*: Darling!

ALGERNON *(to* CECILY*)*: Darling! *(They fall into each other's arms.)*

(Enter MERRIMAN*. When he enters he coughs loudly, seeing the situation.)*

MERRIMAN: Ahem! Ahem! Lady Bracknell!

JACK: Good heavens!

(Enter LADY BRACKNELL*. The couples separate in alarm. Exit* MERRIMAN*.)*

LADY BRACKNELL: Gwendolen! What does this mean?

GWENDOLEN: Merely that I am engaged to be married to Mr Worthing, mamma.

LADY BRACKNELL: Come here. Sit down. Sit down immediately. Hesitation of any kind is a sign of mental decay in the young, of physical weakness in the old. *(Turns to* JACK*.)* Apprised, sir, of my daughter's sudden flight by her trusty maid, whose confidence I purchased by means of a small coin, I followed her at once by a luggage train. Her unhappy father is, I am glad to say, under the impression that she is attending a more than usually lengthy lecture by the University Extension Scheme on the Influence of a permanent income on Thought. I do not propose to undeceive him. Indeed I have never undeceived him on any question. I would consider it wrong. But of course, you will clearly understand that all communication between yourself and my daughter must cease immediately from this moment. On this point, as indeed on all points, I am firm.

JACK: I am engaged to be married to Gwendolen, Lady Bracknell!

LADY BRACKNELL: You are nothing of the kind, sir. And now as regards Algernon! . . . Algernon!

ALGERNON: Yes, Aunt Augusta.

LADY BRACKNELL: May I ask if it is in this house that your invalid friend Mr Bunbury resides?

ALGERNON *(stammering)*: Oh! No! Bunbury doesn't live here. Bunbury is somewhere else at present. In fact, Bunbury is dead.

LADY BRACKNELL: Dead! When did Mr Bunbury die? His death must have been extremely sudden.

ALGERNON *(airily)*: Oh! I killed Bunbury this afternoon. I mean poor Bunbury died this afternoon.

LADY BRACKNELL: What did he die of?

ALGERNON: Bunbury? Oh, he was quite exploded.

LADY BRACKNELL: Exploded! Was he the victim of a revolutionary outrage? I was not aware that Mr Bunbury was interested in social leg-
islation. If so, he is well punished for his morbidity.

ALGERNON: My dear Aunt Augusta, I mean he was found out! The doctors found out that Bunbury could not live, that is what I mean —
so Bunbury died.

LADY BRACKNELL: He seems to have had great confidence in the opinion
of his physicians. I am glad, however, that he made up his mind at
the last to some definite course of action, and acted under proper
medical advice. And now that we have finally got rid of this Mr
Bunbury, may I ask, Mr Worthing, who is that young person whose
hand my nephew Algernon is now holding in what seems to me a
peculiarly unnecessary manner?

JACK: That lady is Miss Cecily Cardew, my ward. (LADY BRACKNELL *bows
coldly to* CECILY.)

ALGERNON: I am engaged to be married to Cecily, Aunt Augusta.

LADY BRACKNELL: I beg your pardon?

CECILY: Mr Moncrieff and I are engaged to be married, Lady Bracknell.

LADY BRACKNELL (*with a shiver, crossing to the sofa and sitting down*): I do not
know whether there is anything peculiarly exciting in the air of this
particular part of Hertfordshire, but the number of engagements
that go on seems to me considerably above the proper average that
statistics have laid down for our guidance. I think some preliminary
inquiry on my part would not be out of place. Mr Worthing, is Miss
Cardew at all connected with any of the larger railway stations in
London? I merely desire information. Until yesterday I had no idea
that there were any families or persons whose origin was a Termi-
nus. (JACK *looks perfectly furious, but restrains himself.*)

JACK (*in a cold, clear voice*): Miss Cardew is the grand-daughter of the late
Mr Thomas Cardew of 149 Belgrave Square, S.W.; Gervase Park,
Dorking, Surrey; and the Sporran, Fifeshire, N.B.

LADY BRACKNELL: That sounds not unsatisfactory. Three addresses
always inspire confidence, even in tradesmen. But what proof have I
of their authenticity?

JACK: I have carefully preserved the Court Guides[2] of the period. They
are open to your inspection, Lady Bracknell.

LADY BRACKNELL (*grimly*): I have known strange errors in that publication.

JACK: Miss Cardew's family solicitors are Messrs Markby, Markby, and
Markby.

LADY BRACKNELL: Marky, Markby, and Markby? A firm of the very
highest position in their profession. Indeed I am told that one of the
Mr Markby's is occasionally to be seen at dinner parties. So far I am
satisfied.

JACK (*very irritably*): How extremely kind of you, Lady Bracknell! I have
also in my possession, you will be pleased to hear, certificates of
Miss Cardew's birth, baptism, whooping cough, registration, vaccination,

---

2 *publication that lists social position.*

confirmation, and the measles; both the German and the English variety.

LADY BRACKNELL: Ah! A life crowded with incident, I see; though perhaps somewhat too exciting for a young girl. I am not myself in favour of premature experiences. *(Rises, looks at her watch.)* Gwendolen! the time approaches for our departure. We have not a moment to lose. As a matter of form, Mr Worthing, I had better ask you if Miss Cardew has any little fortune?

JACK: Oh! about a hundred and thirty thousand pounds in the Funds.[3] That is all. Good-bye, Lady Bracknell. So pleased to have seen you.

LADY BRACKNELL *(sitting down again)*: A moment, Mr Worthing. A hundred and thirty thousand pounds! And in the Funds! Miss Cardew seems to me a most attractive young lady, now that I look at her. Few girls of the present day have any really solid qualities, any of the qualities that last, and improve with time. We live, I regret to say, in an age of surfaces. *(To CECILY.)* Come over here, dear. *(CECILY goes across.)* Pretty child! your dress is sadly simple, and your hair seems almost as Nature might have left it. But we can soon alter all that. A thoroughly experienced French maid produces a really marvellous result in a very brief space of time. I remember recommending one to young Lady Lancing, and after three months her own husband did not know her.

JACK: And after six months nobody knew her.

LADY BRACKNELL *(glares at JACK for a few moments. Then bends, with a practised smile, to CECILY)*: Kindly turn round, sweet child. *(CECILY turns completely round.)* No, the side view is what I want. *(CECILY presents her profile.)* Yes, quite as I expected. There are distinct social possibilities in your profile. The two weak points in our age are its want of principle and its want of profile. The chin a little higher, dear. Style largely depends on the way the chin is worn. They are worn very high, just at present. Algernon!

ALGERNON: Yes, Aunt Augusta!

LADY BRACKNELL: There are distinct social possibilities in Miss Cardew's profile.

ALGERNON: Cecily is the sweetest, dearest, prettiest girl in the whole world. And I don't care twopence about social possibilities.

LADY BRACKNELL: Never speak disrespectfully of Society, Algernon. Only people who can't get into it do that. *(To CECILY.)* Dear child, of course you know that Algernon has nothing but his debts to depend upon. But I do not approve of mercenary marriages. When I married Lord Bracknell I had no fortune of any kind. But I never dreamed for a moment of allowing that to stand in my way. Well, I suppose I must give my consent.

ALGERNON: Thank you, Aunt Augusta.

LADY BRACKNELL: Cecily, you may kiss me!

CECILY *(kisses her)*: Thank you, Lady Bracknell.

LADY BRACKNELL: You may also address me as Aunt Augusta for the future.

3 *government bonds.*

CECILY: Thank you, Aunt Augusta.

LADY BRACKNELL: The marriage, I think, had better take place quite soon.

ALGERNON: Thank you, Aunt Augusta.

CECILY: Thank you, Aunt Augusta.

LADY BRACKNELL: To speak frankly, I am not in favour of long engagements. They give people the opportunity of finding out each other's character before marriage, which I think is never advisable.

JACK: I beg your pardon for interrupting you, Lady Bracknell, but this engagement is quite out of the question. I am Miss Cardew's guardian, and she cannot marry without my consent until she comes of age. That consent I absolutely decline to give.

LADY BRACKNELL: Upon what grounds, may I ask? Algernon is an extremely, I may almost say ostentatiously, eligible young man. He has nothing, but he looks everything. What more can one desire?

JACK: It pains me very much to have to speak frankly to you, Lady Bracknell, about your nephew, but the fact is that I do not approve at all of his moral character. I suspect him of being untruthful. *(ALGERNON and CECILY look at him in indignant amazement.)*

LADY BRACKNELL: Untruthful! My nephew Algernon? Impossible! He is an Oxonian.[4]

JACK: I fear there can be no possible doubt about the matter. This afternoon during my temporary absence in London on an important question of romance, he obtained admission to my house by means of the false pretence of being my brother. Under an assumed name he drank, I've just been informed by my butler, an entire pint bottle of my Perrier-Jouet, Brut, '89; wine I was specially reserving for myself. Continuing his disgraceful deception, he succeeded in the course of the afternoon in alienating the affections of my only ward. He subsequently stayed to tea, and devoured every single muffin. And what makes his conduct all the more heartless is, that he was perfectly well aware from the first that I have no brother, that I never had a brother, and that I don't intend to have a brother, not even of any kind. I distinctly told him so myself yesterday afternoon.

LADY BRACKNELL: Ahem! Mr Worthing, after careful consideration I have decided entirely to overlook my nephew's conduct to you.

JACK: That is very generous of you, Lady Bracknell. My own decision, however, is unalterable. I decline to give my consent.

LADY BRACKNELL *(to CECILY)*: Come here, sweet child. *(CECILY goes over.)* How old are you, dear?

CECILY: Well, I am really only eighteen, but I always admit to twenty when I go to evening parties.

LADY BRACKNELL: You are perfectly right in making some slight alteration. Indeed, no woman should ever be quite accurate about her age. It looks so calculating. . . . *(In a meditative manner.)* Eighteen, but admitting to twenty at evening parties. Well, it will not be very long before you are of age and free from the restraints of tutelage. So I

---

4 *a graduate of Oxford University.*

don't think your guardian's consent is, after all, a matter of any importance.

JACK: Pray excuse me, Lady Bracknell, for interrupting you again, but it is only fair to tell you that according to the terms of her grandfather's will Miss Cardew does not come legally of age till she is thirty-five.

LADY BRACKNELL: That does not seem to me to be a grave objection. Thirty-five is a very attractive age. London society is full of women of the very highest birth who have, of their own free choice, remained thirty-five for years. Lady Dumbleton is an instance in point. To my own knowledge she has been thirty-five ever since she arrived at the age of forty, which was many years ago now. I see no reason why our dear Cecily should not be even still more attractive at the age you mention than she is at present. There will be a large accumulation of property.

CECILY: Algy, could you wait for me till I was thirty-five?

ALGERNON: Of course I could, Cecily. You know I could.

CECILY: Yes, I felt it instinctively, but I couldn't wait all that time. I hate waiting even five minutes for anybody. It always makes me rather cross. I am not punctual myself, I know, but I do like punctuality in others, and waiting, even to be married, is quite out of the question.

ALGERNON: Then what is to be done, Cecily?

CECILY: I don't know, Mr Moncrieff.

LADY BRACKNELL: My dear Mr Worthing, as Miss Cardew states positively that she cannot wait till she is thirty-five — a remark which I am bound to say seems to me to show a somewhat impatient nature — I would beg of you to reconsider your decision.

JACK: But my dear Lady Bracknell, the matter is entirely in your own hands. The moment you consent to my marriage with Gwendolen, I will most gladly allow your nephew to form an alliance with my ward.

LADY BRACKNELL (*rising and drawing herself up*): You must be quite aware that what you propose is out of the question.

JACK: Then a passionate celibacy is all that any of us can look forward to.

LADY BRACKNELL: That is not the destiny I propose for Gwendolen. Algernon, of course, can choose for himself. (*Pulls out her watch.*) Come, dear (GWENDOLEN *rises*), we have already missed five, if not six, trains. To miss any more might expose us to comment on the platform.

(*Enter* DR CHASUBLE.)

CHASUBLE: Everything is quite ready for the christenings.

LADY BRACKNELL: The christenings, sir! Is not that somewhat premature?

CHASUBLE(*looking rather puzzled, and pointing to* JACK *and* ALGERNON*)*: Both these gentlemen have expressed a desire for immediate baptism.

LADY BRACKNELL: At their age? The idea is grotesque and irreligious! Algernon, I forbid you to be baptized. I will not hear of such excesses. Lord Bracknell would be highly displeased if he learned that that was the way in which you wasted your time and money.

CHASUBLE: Am I to understand then that there are to be no christenings at all this afternoon?

JACK: I don't think that, as things are now, it would be of much practical value to either of us, Dr Chasuble.

CHASUBLE: I am grieved to hear such sentiments from you, Mr Worthing. They savour of the heretical views of the Anabaptists,[5] views that I have completely refuted in four of my unpublished sermons. However, as your present mood seems to be one peculiarly secular, I will return to the church at once. Indeed, I have just been informed by the pew-opener[6] that for the last hour and a half Miss Prism has been waiting for me in the vestry.

LADY BRACKNELL (*starting*): Miss Prism! Did I hear you mention a Miss Prism?

CHASUBLE: Yes, Lady Bracknell. I am on my way to join her.

LADY BRACKNELL: Pray allow me to detain you for a moment. This matter may prove to be one of vital importance to Lord Bracknell and myself. Is this Miss Prism a female of repellent aspect, remotely connected with education?

CHASUBLE (*somewhat indignantly*): She is the most cultivated of ladies, and the very picture of respectability.

LADY BRACKNELL: It is obviously the same person. May I ask what position she holds in your household?

CHASUBLE (*severely*): I am a celibate, madam.

JACK (*interposing*): Miss Prism, Lady Bracknell, has been for the last three years Miss Cardew's esteemed governess and valued companion.

LADY BRACKNELL: In spite of what I hear of her, I must see her at once. Let her be sent for.

CHASUBLE (*looking off*): She approaches; she is nigh.

(*Enter* MISS PRISM *hurriedly.*)

MISS PRISM: I was told you expected me in the vestry, dear Canon. I have been waiting for you there for an hour and three-quarters. (*Catches sight of* LADY BRACKNELL, *who has fixed her with a stony glare.* MISS PRISM *grows pale and quails. She looks anxiously round as if desirous to escape.*)

LADY BRACKNELL (*in a severe, judicial voice*): Prism! (MISS PRISM *bows her head in shame.*) Come here, Prism! (MISS PRISM *approaches in a humble manner.*) Prism! Where is that baby? (*General consternation. The* CANON *starts back in horror.* ALGERNON *and* JACK *pretend to be anxious to shield* CECILY *and* GWENDOLEN *from hearing the details of a terrible public scandal.*) Twenty-eight years ago, Prism, you left Lord Bracknell's house, Number

---

5 a Protestant sect that opposed infant baptism and required a second or adult baptism.
6 at one time, the pews in churches were enclosed boxes of seats that were reserved for particular families.

104, Upper Grosvenor Street, in charge of a perambulator that contained a baby of the male sex. You never returned. A few weeks later, through the elaborate investigations of the Metropolitan police, the perambulator was discovered at midnight standing by itself in a remote corner of Bayswater. It contained the manuscript of a three-volume novel of more than usually revolting sentimentality. *(MISS PRISM starts in involuntary indignation.)* But the baby was not there! *(Everyone looks at MISS PRISM.)* Prism! Where is that baby? *(A pause.)*

MISS PRISM: Lady Bracknell, I admit with shame that I do not know. I only wish I did. The plain facts of the case are these. On the morning of the day you mention, a day that is for ever branded on my memory, I prepared as usual to take the baby out in its perambulator. I had also with me a somewhat old, but capacious hand-bag in which I intended to place the manuscript of a work of fiction that I had written during my few unoccupied hours. In a moment of mental abstraction, for which I never can forgive myself, I deposited the manuscript in the bassinette, and placed the baby in the hand-bag.

JACK *(who has been listening attentively)*: But where did you deposit the hand-bag?

MISS PRISM: Do not ask me, Mr Worthing.

JACK: Miss Prism, this is a matter of no small importance to me. I insist on knowing where you deposited the hand-bag that contained that infant.

MISS PRISM: I left it in the cloak-room of one of the larger railway stations in London.

JACK: What railway station?

MISS PRISM *(quite crushed)*: Victoria. The Brighton line. *(Sinks into a chair.)*

JACK: I must retire to my room for a moment. Gwendolen, wait here for me.

GWENDOLEN: If you are not too long, I will wait here for you all my life.

(Exit JACK in great excitement.)

CHASUBLE: What do you think this means, Lady Bracknell?

LADY BRACKNELL: I dare not even suspect, Dr Chasuble. I need hardly tell you that in families of high position strange coincidences are not supposed to occur. They are hardly considered the thing.

(Noises heard overhead as if someone was throwing trunks about. Everyone looks up.)

CECILY: Uncle Jack seems strangely agitated.

CHASUBLE: Your guardian has a very emotional nature.

LADY BRACKNELL: This noise is extremely unpleasant. It sounds as if he was having an argument. I dislike arguments of any kind. They are always vulgar, and often convincing.

CHASUBLE *(looking up)*: It has stopped now. *(The noise is redoubled.)*

LADY BRACKNELL: I wish he would arrive at some conclusion.

GWENDOLEN: This suspense is terrible. I hope it will last.

(Enter JACK with a hand-bag of black leather in his hand.)

JACK (*rushing over to* MISS PRISM): Is this the hand-bag, Miss Prism? Examine it carefully before you speak. The happiness of more than one life depends on your answer.

MISS PRISM (*calmly*): It seems to be mine. Yes, here is the injury it received through the upsetting of a Gower Street omnibus in younger and happier days. Here is the stain on the lining caused by the explosion of a temperance beverage, an incident that occurred at Leamington. And here, on the lock, are my initials. I had forgotten that in an extravagant mood I had had them placed there. The bag is undoubtedly mine. I am delighted to have it so unexpectedly restored to me. It has been a great inconvenience being without it all these years.

JACK (*in a pathetic voice*): Miss Prism, more is restored to you than this hand-bag. I was the baby you placed in it.

MISS PRISM (*amazed*): You?

JACK (*embracing her*): Yes . . . mother!

MISS PRISM (*recoiling in indignant astonishment*): Mr Worthing! I am unmarried!

JACK: Unmarried! I do not deny that is a serious blow. But after all, who has the right to cast a stone against one who has suffered? Cannot repentance wipe out an act of folly? Why should there be one law for men, and another for women? Mother, I forgive you. (*Tries to embrace her again.*)

MISS PRISM (*still more indignant*): Mr Worthing, there is some error. (*Pointing to* LADY BRACKNELL.) There is the lady who can tell you who you really are.

JACK (*after a pause*): Lady Bracknell, I hate to seem inquisitive, but would you kindly inform me who I am?

LADY BRACKNELL: I am afraid that the news I have to give you will not altogether please you. You are the son of my poor sister, Mrs Moncrieff, and consequently Algernon's elder brother.

JACK: Algy's elder brother! Then I have a brother after all. I knew I had a brother! I always said I had a brother! Cecily — how could you have ever doubted that I had a brother? (*Seizes hold of* ALGERNON.) Dr Chasuble, my unfortunate brother. Miss Prism, my unfortunate brother. Gwendolen, my unfortunate brother. Algy, you young scoundrel, you will have to treat me with more respect in the future. You have never behaved to me like a brother in all your life.

ALGERNON: Well, not till today, old boy, I admit. I did my best, however, though I was out of practice.

(*Shakes hands.*)

GWENDOLEN (*to* JACK): My own! But what own are you? What is your Christian name, now that you have become someone else?

JACK: Good heavens! . . . I had quite forgotten that point. Your decision on the subject of my name is irrevocable, I suppose?

GWENDOLEN: I never change, except in my affections.

CECILY: What a noble nature you have, Gwendolen!

JACK: Then the question had better be cleared up at once. Aunt Augusta, a moment. At the time when Miss Prism left me in the hand-bag, had I been christened already?

LADY BRACKNELL: Every luxury that money could buy, including christening, had been lavished on you by your fond and doting parents.

JACK: Then I was christened! That is settled. Now, what name was I given? Let me know the worst.

LADY BRACKNELL: Being the eldest son you were naturally christened after your father.

JACK *(irritably)*: Yes, but what was my father's Christian name?

LADY BRACKNELL *(meditatively)*: I cannot at the present moment recall what the General's Christian name was. But I have no doubt he had one. He was eccentric, I admit. But only in later years. And that was the result of the Indian climate, and marriage, and indigestion, and other things of that kind.

JACK: Algy! Can't you recollect what our father's Christian name was?

ALGERNON: My dear boy, we were never even on speaking terms. He died before I was a year old.

JACK: His name would appear in the Army Lists of the period, I suppose, Aunt Augusta?

LADY BRACKNELL: The General was essentially a man of peace, except in his domestic life. But I have no doubt his name would appear in any military directory.

JACK: The Army Lists of the last forty years are here. These delightful records should have been my constant study. *(Rushes to bookcase and tears the books out.)* M. Generals . . . Mallam, Maxbohm, Magley — what ghastly names they have — Markby, Migsby, Mobbs, Moncrieff! Lieutenant 1840, Captain, Lieutenant-Colonel, Colonel, General 1869, Christian names, Ernest John. *(Puts book very quietly down and speaks quite calmly.)* I always told you, Gwendolen, my name was Ernest, didn't I? Well, it is Ernest after all. I mean it naturally is Ernest.

LADY BRACKNELL: Yes, I remember now that the General was called Ernest. I knew I had some particular reason for disliking the name.

GWENDOLEN: Ernest! My own Ernest! I felt from the first that you could have no other name!

JACK: Gwendolen, it is a terrible thing for a man to find out suddenly that all his life he has been speaking nothing but the truth. Can you forgive me?

GWENDOLEN: I can. For I feel that you are sure to change.

JACK: My own one!

CHASUBLE *(to MISS PRISM)*Laetitia! *(Embraces her.)*

MISS PRISM *(enthusiastically)*: Frederick! At last!

ALGERNON: Cecily! *(Embraces her.)* At last!

JACK: Gwendolen! *(Embraces her.)*: At last!

LADY BRACKNELL: My nephew, you seem to be displaying signs of triviality.

JACK: On the contrary, Aunt Augusta, I've now realised for the first time in my life the vital Importance of Being Earnest.

TABLEAU

CURTAIN

GEORGE BERNARD SHAW

(1856–1950)

haw was born and raised in Dublin, Ireland, and left for London in 1876. He started his career as a novelist, but when he did not achieve success in this genre he turned to journalism and was soon reviewing books and writing art and music criticism; eventually, he turned to dramatic criticism. He also became an active socialist and was drawn to the Fabian movement.[1]

Through his dramatic criticism he became familiar with the London stage, where he found much to criticize. He urged many reforms in staging and a movement away from nineteenth-century forms and conventions.

He welcomed the plays of the Norwegian playwright Henrik Ibsen enthusiastically because he saw in them a drama of ideas and discussion, two things he wanted to see on the English stage. In Ibsen he also saw an iconoclast presenting problems and solutions in a new and stimulating way. Shaw was in the forefront, along with critic William Archer, a translator of Ibsen's plays, and J.T. Grein, founder of the Independent Theatre, in fostering productions of Ibsen's plays in private performances.[2]

Shaw's early plays Widowers' Houses *(1892) and* Mrs Warren's Profession *(1893) reveal a coming together of his socialism and the drama of ideas and discussion. He deliberately set out, often pugnaciously, to deal with controversial subjects, and his approach to the playwright's craft was unconventional, even playful. For these reasons, many of his plays were not given public performances; he published them with long prefaces in which he discussed the ideas they contain in the context of the time.*

Shaw's plays span the years from 1892 to 1947, and his impressive output makes him one of the greatest English dramatists since Shakespeare. He received the Nobel Prize in 1925.

INTRODUCTION TO CAESAR AND CLEOPATRA

aesar and Cleopatra was written in 1899 and published in 1901 in a volume with two other plays, *The Devil's Disciple* and *Captain Brassbound's Conversion*.[3] In the preface to this volume, which he entitled *Plays for Puritans*, he deplores the predominance of romantic plays and declares that the play of ideas is the proper sort of play, since it provides edification. He surveys the audience of his time and finds too great a variety of people wanting to be pleased.

---

1 *The Fabian Society was founded in England in 1884. Its aim was to bring about socialism by gradual reform rather than by revolution.*
2 *Ibsen's plays were refused licences by the censor, the Examiner of Plays in the office of the Lord Chamberlain.*
3 Three Plays for Puritans *(London: Constable and Co. Ltd., 1929).*

He claims that in the romantic plays produced to gratify this audience, paradoxically, love is kept off the stage and "an intolerable perversion of human conduct" (xvi) is the result. He then lists the romantic clichés in these plays and calls upon the Puritans who once before rescued the theatre to rescue it again from "sensuous ecstasy" and to re-establish "intellectual activity and honesty." (xix).

When he turns to Shakespearean productions of the time, he sees mutilated texts and a great deal of "stage ritualism" (x) and sensualism. He irreverently entitles this section of his preface "Better Than Shakespear?" and fires a Shavian opening broadside:

> *The very name of Cleopatra suggests at once a tragedy of Circe, with the horrible difference that whereas the ancient myth rightly represents Circe as turning heroes into hogs, the modern romantic convention would represent her as turning hogs into heroes.* Shakespear's Antony and Cleopatra *must needs be as intolerable in the true Puritan as it is vaguely distressing to the ordinary healthy citizen, because, after giving a faithful picture of the soldier broken down by debauchery, and the typical wanton in whose arms such men perish, Shakespear finally strains all his huge command of rhetoric and stage pathos to give a theatrical sublimity to the wretched end of the business, and to persuade foolish spectators the world was well lost by the twain. (xxvii–xxviii)*

He continues: "I have a technical objection to making sexual infatuation a tragic theme. Experience proves that it is only effective in the comic spirit" (xxix) and adds: "Shakespear, who knew human weakness so well, never knew human strength of the Caesarian type" (xxix). So Shaw claims that he is offering his own Caesar to the public as an improvement on Shakespeare's portrayal of him. Anticipating the shock for those who see in Shakespeare "Perfection and Infallibility" (xxx), he dismisses such a stance as "Bardolatry" (xxxi). Maintaining his right to criticize, he claims that he does not write better-crafted plays, but rather that he is trying to change the outlook on life in Shakespeare's plays.

In *Caesar and Cleopatra*, Shaw takes a realistic approach rather than the romantic one he deplored. His theme is a serious one as he stresses through Caesar that power has responsibility and that vengeance is not only dangerous but also irrational. Caesar's clemency both puzzles and exasperates his fellow Romans. He emerges as a plain-speaking leader whose actions are always decisive; eventually his moral sense triumphs, and he achieves self-fulfilment.

Cleopatra appears as an enticing young woman, but Caesar is impervious to her charms. Instead of succumbing, he sets out to show her how to be a good and wise queen, and he consistently instructs her in the ways of common sense and candour. Thus Caesar is in control at all times, and Cleopatra cannot manipulate him as the historical sources suggest she did. On the other hand, Shaw's references to Antony suggest that he, unlike Caesar, is controlled by passion and will be ruled by Cleopatra.

Shaw's purpose went beyond being anti-romantic. His focus on Caesar indicates his interest in figures of power whom he called "life shapers." Some of these characters in other plays are Napoleon in *Man of Destiny* (1897), Andrew Undershaft, the munitions manufacturer in *Major Barbara* (1905), and Joan of Arc, in what many consider to be his greatest play, *Saint Joan* (1923).

In his preface to *Plays for Puritans*, Shaw says:

> *Human faculty being what it is, is it likely that in our time any advance, except in external conditions, will take place in the arts of expression sufficient to enable an author, without making himself ridiculous, to undertake to say what he has to say better than Homer or Shakespear? But the humblest author, and much more a rather arrogant one like myself, may profess to have something to say by this time that neither Homer nor Shakespear said. And the playgoer may reasonably ask to have historical events and persons presented to him in the light of his own time, even though Homer and Shakespear have already shown them in the light of their time. (xxxiv)*

So Shaw expands once more on the reasons for following his own path in tracing the story of Cleopatra. He also explains why Cleopatra is referred to as a "new woman,"[4] while his own time is also anachronistically represented by his characters Britannus and Apollodorus.

Shaw delights in presenting Britannus, who is full of praise for his northern land and delivers this praise frequently and always uncritically. In this way, many aspects of English life in Shaw's time and many British complacent attitudes are ridiculed.

Apollodorus also reflects Shaw's world. With Oscar Wilde and the aesthetic movement[5] in mind, Shaw describes Apollodorus as "dressed with deliberate aestheticism in the most delicate purple and dove grey."

The aristocratic carpet merchant reflects the same movement as he calls his shop "a temple of the arts" and states his motto as "Art for Art's sake."

---

4 *When Shaw was writing, the term "new woman" referred to an emancipated woman.*

5 *The aesthetic movement originated on the Continent. Walter Pater is usually credited with introducing it into England. The movement stressed artifice and a fostering of pleasurable sensations. Beauty was given a high value and the phrase "the love of art for art's sake" became a cry of the movement. English followers of the movement frequently dressed in an unconventional manner that reflected their love of beauty.*

To conclude with this brief discussion of the playful side of Shaw is fitting, since in almost all his plays he finds moments to send up the excesses and the general pomposity of the English.

Caesar and Cleopatra

PROLOGUE

In the doorway of the temple of Ra[1] in Memphis.[2] Deep gloom. An august personage with a hawk's head is mysteriously visible by his own light in the darkness within the temple. He surveys the modern audience with great contempt; and finally speaks the following words to them.

Peace! Be silent and hearken unto me, ye quaint little islanders. Give ear, ye men with white paper on your breasts and nothing written thereon (to signify the innocency of your minds). Hear me, ye women who adorn yourselves alluringly and conceal your thoughts from your men, leading them to believe that ye deem them wondrous strong and masterful whilst in truth ye hold them in your hearts as children without judgment. Look upon my hawk's head; and know that I am Ra, who was once in Egypt a mighty god. Ye cannot kneel nor prostrate yourselves; for ye are packed in rows without freedom to move, obstructing one another's vision; neither do any of ye regard it as seemly to do aught until ye see all the rest do so too; wherefore it commonly happens that in great emergencies ye do nothing, though each telleth his fellow that something must be done. I ask you not for worship, but for silence. Let not your men speak nor your women cough; for I am come to draw you back two thousand years over the graves of sixty generations. Ye poor posterity, think not that ye are the first. Other fools before ye have seen the sun rise and set, and the moon change her shape and her hour. As they were so ye are; and yet not so great; for the pyramids my people built stand to this day; whilst the dustheaps on which ye slave, and which ye call empires, scatter in the wind even as ye pile your dead sons' bodies on them to make yet more dust.

Hearken to me then, oh ye compulsorily educated ones. Know that even as there is an old England and a new, and ye stand perplexed between the twain; so in the days when I was worshipped was there an old Rome and a new, and men standing perplexed between them.

---

1 *Egyptian sun god.*
2 *capital of ancient Egypt, fifteen kilometres south of present-day Cairo.*

And the old Rome was poor and little, and greedy and fierce, and evil in many ways; but because its mind was little and its work was simple, it knew its own mind and did its own work; and the gods pitied it and helped it and strengthened it and shielded it; for the gods are patient with littleness. Then the old Rome, like the beggar on horseback, presumed on the favor of the gods, and said, "Lo! there is neither riches nor greatness in our littleness: the road to riches and greatness is through robbery of the poor and slaughter of the weak." So they robbed their own poor until they became great masters of that art, and knew by what laws it could be made to appear seemly and honest. And when they had squeezed their own poor dry, they robbed the poor of other lands, and added those lands to Rome until there came a new Rome, rich and huge. And I, Ra, laughed; for the minds of the Romans remained the same size whilst their dominion spread over the earth.

Now mark me, that ye may understand what ye are presently to see. Whilst the Romans still stood between the old Rome and the new, there arose among them a mighty soldier: Pompey the Great. And the way of the soldier is the way of death; but the way of the gods is the way of life; and so it comes that a god at the end of his way is wise and a soldier at the end of his way is a fool. So Pompey held by the old Rome, in which only soldiers could become great; but the gods turned to the new Rome, in which any man with wit enough could become what he would. And Pompey's friend Julius Caesar was on the side of the gods; for he saw that Rome had passed beyond the control of the little old Romans. This Caesar was a great talker and a politician: he bought men with words and with gold, even as ye are bought. And when they would not be satisfied with words and gold, and demanded also the glories of war, Caesar in his middle age turned his hand to that trade; and they that were against him when he sought their welfare, bowed down before him when he became a slayer and a conqueror; for such is the nature of you mortals. And as for Pompey, the gods grew tired of his triumphs and his airs of being himself a god; for he talked of law and duty and other matters that concerned not a mere human worm. And the gods smiled on Caesar; for he lived the life they had given him boldly, and was not forever rebuking us for our indecent ways of creation, and hiding our handiwork as a shameful thing. Ye know well what I mean; for this is one of your own sins.

And thus it fell out between the old Rome and the new, that Caesar said, "Unless I break the law of old Rome, I cannot take my share in ruling her; and the gift of ruling that the gods gave me will perish without fruit." But Pompey said, "The law is above all; and if thou break it thou shalt die." Then said Caesar, "I will break it: kill me who can." And he broke it. And Pompey went for him, as ye say, with a great army to slay him and uphold the old Rome. So Caesar fled across the Adriatic sea; for the high gods had a lesson to teach him, which lesson they shall also teach you in due time if ye continue to forget them and to worship that cad among gods, Mammon. Therefore before they raised Caesar to be master of the world, they were minded to throw him down into the dust, even beneath the feet of Pompey, and blacken his face before the nations. And Pompey they raised higher than ever, he and his laws and his high mind that aped the gods, so that his fall might be the more terrible. And Pompey followed Caesar, and overcame him with all the majesty of old Rome, and stood over him and over the whole world even as ye stand over it with your fleet that covers thirty miles of the sea. And when Caesar was brought down to utter nothingness, he made a last stand to die honorably, and did not despair; for he said, "Against me there is Pompey, and the old Rome, and the law and the legions: all all against me; but high above these are the gods; and Pompey is a fool." And the gods laughed and approved; and on the field of Pharsalia the impossible came to pass; the blood and iron ye pin your faith on fell before the spirit of man; for the spirit of man is the will of the gods; and Pompey's power crumbled in his hand, even as the power of imperial Spain crumbled when it was set against your fathers in the days when England was little, and knew her own mind, and had a mind to know instead of a circulation of newspapers. Wherefore look to it, lest some little people whom ye would enslave rise up and become in the hand of God the scourge of your boastings and your injustices and your lusts and stupidities.

And now, would ye know the end of Pompey, or will ye sleep while a god speaks? Heed my words well; for Pompey went where ye have gone, even to Egypt, where there was a Roman occupation even as there was but now a British one. And Caesar pursued Pompey to Egypt: a Roman fleeing, and a Roman pursuing: dog eating dog. And the Egyptians said, "Lo: these Romans which have lent money to our kings and levied a distraint upon us with their arms, call for ever upon us to be loyal to them by betraying our own country to them. But now behold two Romes! Pompey's Rome and Caesar's Rome! To which of the twain shall we pretend to be loyal?" So they turned in their perplexity to a soldier that had once served Pompey, and that knew the ways of Rome and was full of her lusts. And they said to him, "Lo: in thy country dog eats dog; and both dogs are coming to eat us: what counsel hast thou to give us?" And this soldier, whose name was Lucius Septimius, and whom ye shall presently see before ye, replied, "Ye shall diligently consider which is the bigger dog of the two; and ye shall kill the other dog for his sake and thereby earn his favor." And the Egyptians said, "Thy counsel is expedient; but if we kill a man outside the law we set ourselves in the place of the gods; and this we dare not do. But thou, being a Roman, art accustomed to this kind of killing; for thou hast imperial instincts. Wilt thou therefore kill the lesser dog for us?" And he said, "I will; for I have made my home in Egypt; and I desire consideration and influence among you." And they said, "We knew well thou wouldst not do it for nothing: thou shalt have thy reward." Now when Pompey came, he came alone in a little galley, putting his trust in the law and the constitution. And it was plain to the people of Egypt that Pompey was now but a very small dog. So when he set his foot on the shore he was greeted by his old comrade Lucius Septimius, who welcomed him with one hand and with the other smote off his head, and kept it as it were a pickled cabbage to make a present to Caesar.

And mankind shuddered; but the gods laughed; for Septimius was but a knife that Pompey had sharpened; and when it turned against his own throat they said that Pompey had better have made Septimius a ploughman than so brave and readyhanded a slayer. Therefore again I bid you beware, ye who would all be Pompeys if ye dared; for war is a wolf that may come to your own door.

Are ye impatient with me? Do ye crave for a story of an unchaste woman? Hath the name of Cleopatra tempted ye hither? Ye foolish ones; Cleopatra is as yet but a child that is whipped by her nurse. And what I am about to shew you for the good of your souls is how Caesar, seeking Pompey in Egypt, found Cleopatra; and how he received that present of a pickled cabbage that was once the head of Pompey; and what things happened between the old Caesar and the child queen before he left Egypt and battled his way back to Rome to be slain there as Pompey was slain, by men in whom the spirit of Pompey still lived. All this ye shall see; and ye shall marvel, after your ignorant manner, that men twenty centuries ago were already just such as you, and spoke and lived as ye speak and live, no worse and no better, no wiser and no sillier. And the two thousand years that have past are to me, the god Ra, but a moment; nor is this day any other than the day in which Caesar set foot in the land of my people. And now I leave you; for ye are a dull folk, and instruction is wasted on you; and I had not spoken so much but that it is in the nature of a god to struggle for ever with the dust and the darkness, and to drag from them, by the force of his longing for the divine, more life and more light. Settle ye therefore in your seats and keep silent; for ye are about to hear a man speak, and a great man he was, as ye count greatness. And fear not that I shall speak to you again: the rest of the story must ye learn from them that lived it. Farewell; and do not presume to applaud me. *(The temple vanishes in utter darkness.)*

(1912)

AN ALTERNATIVE TO THE PROLOGUE

An October night on the Syrian border of Egypt towards the end of the XXXIII Dynasty, in the year 706 by Roman computation, afterwards reckoned by Christian computation as 48 B.C. A great radiance of silver fire, the dawn of a moonlit night, is rising in the east. The stars and the cloudless sky are our own contemporaries, nineteen and a half centuries younger than we know them; but you would not guess that from their appearance. Below them are two notable drawbacks of civilization: a palace, and soldiers. The palace, an old, low, Syrian building of whitened mud, is not so ugly as Buckingham Palace; and the officers in the courtyard are more highly civilized than modern English officers: for example, they do not dig up the corpses of their dead enemies and mutilate them, as we dug up Cromwell and the Mahdi.[3] They are in two groups:

3 *a spiritual and temporal leader whose coming is expected by some Muslims. The followers of a leader claiming to be the Mahdi were defeated by the British in the Sudan in 1898.*

one intent on the gambling of their captain BELZANOR, *a warrior of fifty, who, with his spear on the ground beside his knee, is stooping to throw dice with a sly-looking young* PERSIAN RECRUIT; *the other gathered about a guardsman who has just finished telling a naughty story (still current in English barracks) at which they are laughing uproariously. They are about a dozen in number, all highly aristocratic young Egyptian guardsmen, handsomely equipped with weapons and armor, very unEnglish in point of not being ashamed of and uncomfortable in their professional dress; on the contrary, rather ostentatiously and arrogantly warlike, as valuing themselves on their military caste.*

BELZANOR *is a typical veteran, tough and wilful; prompt, capable and crafty where brute force will serve; helpless and boyish when it will not: an active sergeant, an incompetent general, a deplorable dictator. Would, if influentially connected, be employed in the two last capacities by a modern European State on the strength of his success in the first. Is rather to be pitied just now in view of the fact that Julius Caesar is invading his country. Not knowing this, is intent on his game with the* PERSIAN, *whom, as a foreigner, he considers quite capable of cheating him.*

His subalterns are mostly handsome young fellows whose interest in the game and the story symbolize with tolerable completeness the main interests in life of which they are conscious. Their spears are leaning against the walls, or lying on the ground ready to their hands. The corner of the courtyard forms a triangle of which one side is the front of the palace, with a doorway, the other a wall with a gateway. The storytellers are on the palace side: the gamblers, on the gateway side. Close to the gateway, against the wall, is a stone block high enough to enable a NUBIAN SENTINEL, *standing on it, to look over the wall. The yard is lighted by a torch stuck in the wall. As the laughter from the group round the storyteller dies away, the kneeling* PERSIAN, *winning the throw, snatches up the stake from the ground.*

BELZANOR: By Apis, Persian, thy gods are good to thee.
THE PERSIAN: Try yet again, O captain. Double or quits!
BELZANOR: No more. I am not in the vein.
THE SENTINEL: *(poising his javelin as he peers over the wall)* Stand. Who goes there?

(They all start, listening. A strange voice replies from without.)

VOICE: The bearer of evil tidings.
BELZANOR: *(calling to the* SENTRY*)* Pass him.
THE SENTINEL: *(grounding his javelin)* Draw near, O bearer of evil tidings.
BELZANOR: *(pocketing the dice and picking up his spear)* Let us receive this man with honor. He bears evil tidings.

(The GUARDSMEN *seize their spears and gather about the gate, leaving a way through for the new comer.)*

PERSIAN: *(rising from his knee)* Are evil tidings, then, so honorable?

BELZANOR: O barbarous Persian, hear my instruction. In Egypt the bearer of good tidings is sacrificed to the gods as a thank offering; but no god will accept the blood of the messenger of evil. When we have good tidings, we are careful to send them in the mouth of the cheapest slave we can find. Evil tidings are borne by young noblemen who desire to bring themselves into notice. *(They join the rest at that gate.)*

THE SENTINEL: Pass. O young captain; and bow the head in the House of the Queen.

VOICE: Go anoint thy javelin with fat of swine, O Blackamoor: for before morning the Romans will make thee eat it to the very butt.

(The owner of the voice, a fairhaired dandy, dressed in a different fashion from that affected by the GUARDSMEN, but no less extravagantly, comes through the gateway laughing. He is somewhat battlestained; and his left forearm, bandaged, comes through a torn sleeve. In his right hand he carries a Roman sword in its sheath. He swaggers down the courtyard, the PERSIAN on his right, BELZANOR on his left, and the GUARDSMEN crowding down behind him.)

BELZANOR: Who are thou that laughest in the House of Cleopatra the Queen, and in the teeth of Belzanor, the captain of her guard?

THE NEW COMER: I am Bel Affris, descended from the gods.

BELZANOR: *(ceremoniously)* Hail, cousin!

ALL: *(except the PERSIAN)* Hail, cousin!

PERSIAN: All the Queen's guards are descended from the gods, O stranger, save myself. I am Persian, and descended from many kings.

BEL AFFRIS: *(to the GUARDSMEN)* Hail, cousins! *(To the PERSIAN, condescendingly)* Hail, mortal!

BELZANOR: You have been in battle, Bel Affris; and you are a soldier among soldiers. You will not let the Queen's women have the first of your tidings.

BEL AFFRIS: I have no tidings, except that we shall have our throats cut presently, women, soldiers, and all.

PERSIAN: *(To BELZANOR)* I told you so.

THE SENTINEL: *(who had been listening)* Woe, alas!

BEL AFFRIS: *(calling to him)* Peace, peace, poor Ethiop: destiny is with the gods who painted thee black. *(To BELZANOR)* What has this mortal *(indicating the PERSIAN)* told you?

BELZANOR: He says that the Roman Julius Caesar, who has landed on our shores with a handful of followers, will make himself master of Egypt. He is afraid of the Roman soldiers. *(The GUARDSMEN laugh with boisterous scorn.)* Peasants, brought up to scare crows and follow the plough! Sons of smiths and millers and tanners! And we nobles, consecrated to arms, descended from the gods!

PERSIAN: Belzanor: the gods are not always good to their poor relations.

BELZANOR: *(hotly, to the PERSIAN)* Man to man, are we worse than the slaves of Caesar?

BEL AFFRIS: *(stepping between them)* Listen, cousin. Man to man, we Egyptians are as gods above the Romans.

THE GUARDSMEN: *(exultantly)* Aha!

BEL AFFRIS: But this Caesar does not pit man against man: he throws a legion at you where you are weakest as he throws a stone from a catapult; and that legion is as a man with one head, a thousand arms, and no religion. I have fought against them; and I know.

BELZANOR: *(derisively)* Were you frightened, cousin?

(The GUARDSMEN roar with laughter, their eyes sparkling at the wit of their captain.)

BEL AFFRIS: No, cousin; but I was beaten. They were frightened (perhaps); but they scattered us like chaff.

(The GUARDSMEN, much damped, utter a growl of contemptuous disgust.)

BELZANOR: Could you not die?

BEL AFFRIS: No: that was too easy to be worthy of a descendant of the gods. Besides, there was no time: all was over in a moment. The attack came just where we least expected it.

BELZANOR: That shews that the Romans are cowards.

BEL AFFRIS: They care nothing about cowardice, these Romans: they fight to win. The pride and honor of war are nothing to them.

PERSIAN: Tell us the tale of the battle. What befell?

THE GUARDSMEN: *(gathering eagerly round BEL AFFRIS)* Ay: the tale of the battle.

BEL AFFRIS: Know then, that I am a novice in the guard of the temple of Ra in Memphis, serving neither Cleopatra nor her brother Ptolemy, but only the high gods. We went a journey to inquire of Ptolemy why he had driven Cleopatra into Syria, and how we of Egypt should deal with the Roman Pompey, newly come to our shores after his defeat by Caesar at Pharsalia. What, think ye, did we learn? Even that Caesar is coming also in hot pursuit of his foe, and that Ptolemy has slain Pompey, whose severed head he holds in readiness to present to the conqueror. *(Sensation among the GUARDSMEN.)* Nay, more: we found that Caesar is already come; for we had not made half a day's journey on our way back when we came upon a city rabble flying from his legions, whose landing they had gone out to withstand.

BELZANOR: And ye, the temple guard! did ye not withstand these legions?

BEL AFFRIS: What man could, that we did. But there came the sound of a trumpet whose voice was as the cursing of a black mountain. Then saw we a moving wall of shields coming towards us. You know how the heart burns when you charge a fortified wall; but how if the fortified wall were to charge you?

THE PERSIAN: *(exalting in having told them so)* Did I not say it?

BEL AFFRIS: When the wall came nigh, it changed into a line of men — common fellows enough, with helmets, leather tunics, and breastplates. Every man of them flung his javelin: the one that came my way drove through my shield as through a papyrus — lo there! *(he points to the bandage on his left arm)* and would have gone through my neck had I not stooped. They were charging at the double then, and were upon us with short swords almost as soon as their javelins. When a man is close to you with such a sword, you can do nothing with our weapons; they are all too long.

THE PERSIAN: What did you do?

BEL AFFRIS: Doubled my fist and smote my Roman on the sharpness of his jaw. He was but mortal after all: he lay down in a stupor; and I took his sword and laid it on. *(Drawing the sword)* Lo! a Roman sword with Roman blood on it!

THE GUARDSMEN: *(approvingly)* Good! *(They take the sword and hand it round, examining it curiously.)*

THE PERSIAN: And your men?

BEL AFFRIS: Fled. Scattered like sheep.

BELZANOR: *(furiously)* The cowardly slaves! Leaving the descendants of the gods to be butchered!

BEL AFFRIS: *(with acid coolness)* The descendants of the gods did not stay to be butchered, cousin. The battle was not to the strong; but the race was to the swift. The Romans, who have no chariots, sent a cloud of horsemen in pursuit, and slew multitudes. Then our high priest's captain rallied a dozen descendants of the gods and exhorted us to die fighting. I said to myself: surely it is safer to stand than to lose my breath and be stabbed in the back; so I joined our captain and stood. Then the Romans treated us with respect; for no man attacks a lion when the field is full of sheep, except for the pride and honor of war, of which these Romans know nothing. So we escaped with our lives; and I am come to warn you that you must open your gates to Caesar; for his advance guard is scarce an hour behind me; and not an Egyptian warrior is left standing between you and his legions.

THE SENTINEL: Woe, alas! *(He throws down his javelin and flies into the palace.)*

BELZANOR: Nail him to the door, quick. *(The GUARDSMEN rush for him with their spears; but he is too quick for them.)* Now this news will run through the palace like fire through stubble.

BEL AFFRIS: What shall we do to save the women from the Romans?

BELZANOR: Why not kill them?

PERSIAN: Because we should have to pay blood money for some of them. Better let the Romans kill them: it is cheaper.

BELZANOR: *(awestruck at his brain power)* O subtle one! O serpent!

BEL AFFRIS: But your Queen?

BELZANOR: True: we must carry off Cleopatra.

BEL AFFRIS: Will ye not await her command?

BELZANOR: Command! a girl of sixteen! Not we. At Memphis ye deem her a Queen: here we know better. I will take her on the crupper of my horse. When we soldiers have carried her out of Caesar's reach, then the priests and the nurses and the rest of them can pretend she is a queen again, and put their commands into her mouth.

PERSIAN: Listen to me, Belzanor.

BELZANOR: Speak, O subtle beyond thy years.

THE PERSIAN: Cleopatra's brother Ptolemy is at war with her. Let us sell her to him.

THE GUARDSMEN: O subtle one! O serpent!

BELZANOR: We dare not. We are descended from the gods; but Cleopatra is descended from the river Nile; and the lands of our fathers will grow no grain if the Nile rises not to water them. Without our father's gifts we should live the lives of dogs.

PERSIAN: It is true: the Queen's guard cannot live on its pay. But hear me further, O ye kinsmen of Osiris.[4]

THE GUARDSMEN: Speak, O subtle one. Hear the serpent begotten!

PERSIAN: Have I heretofore spoken truly to you of Caesar, when you thought I mocked you?

GUARDSMEN: Truly, truly.

BELZANOR: *(reluctantly admitting it)* So Bel Affris says.

PERSIAN: Hear more of him, then. This Caesar is a great lover of women: he makes them his friends and counsellors.

BELZANOR: Faugh! This rule of women will be the ruin of Egypt.

PERSIAN: Let it rather be the ruin of Rome! Caesar grows old now: he is past fifty and full of labours and battles. He is too old for the young women; and the old women are too wise to worship him.

BEL AFFRIS: Take heed, Persian. Caesar is by this time almost within earshot.

PERSIAN: Cleopatra is not yet a woman: neither is she wise. But she already troubles men's wisdom.

BELZANOR: Ay: that is because she is descended from the river Nile and a black kitten of the sacred White Cat. What then?

PERSIAN: Why, sell her secretly to Ptolemy, and then offer ourselves to Caesar as volunteers to fight for the overthrow of her brother and the rescue of our Queen, the Great Grand-daughter of the Nile.

THE GUARDSMEN: O serpent!

PERSIAN: He will listen to us if we come with her picture in our mouths. He will conquer and kill her brother, and reign in Egypt with Cleopatra for his Queen. And we shall be her guard.

GUARDSMEN: O subtlest of all the serpents! O admiration! O wisdom!

BEL AFFRIS: He will also have arrived before you have done talking, O word spinner.

BELZANOR: That is true. *(An affrighted uproar in the palace interrupts him.)* Quick: the flight has begun: guard the door. *(They rush to the door and form a cordon before it with their spears. A mob of women-servants and nurses surges out. Those in front recoil from the spears, screaming to those behind to keep back.* BELZANOR's *voice dominates the disturbance as he shouts)* Back there. In again, unprofitable cattle.

THE GUARDSMEN: Back, unprofitable cattle.

BELZANOR: Send us out Ftatateeta, the Queen's chief nurse.

THE WOMEN: *(calling into the palace)* Ftatateeta, Ftatateeta. Come, come. Speak to Belzanor.

A WOMAN: Oh, keep back. You are thrusting me on the spearheads.

(A huge grim woman, her face covered with a network of tiny wrinkles, and her eyes old, large, and wise; sinewy handed, very tall, very strong; with the mouth of a bloodhound and the jaws of a bulldog, appears on the threshold. She is dressed like a person of consequence in the palace, and confronts the guardsmen insolently.)

---

4 *god and judge of the dead; chief deity of ancient Egypt.*

FTATATEETA: Make way for the Queen's chief nurse.

BELZANOR: *(with solemn arrogance)* Ftatateeta: I am Belzanor, the captain of the Queen's guard, descended from the gods.

FTATATEETA: *(retorting his arrogance with interest)* Belzanor: I am Ftatateeta, the Queen's chief nurse; and your divine ancestors were proud to be painted on the wall in the pyramids of the kings whom my fathers served. *(The women laugh triumphantly.)*

BELZANOR: *(with grim humor)* Ftatateeta: daughter of a long-tongued, swivel-eyed chameleon, the Romans are at hand. *(A cry of terror from the women: they would fly but for the spears.)* Not even the descendants of the gods can resist them; for they have each man seven arms, each carrying seven spears. The blood in their veins is boiling quick-silver; and their wives become mothers in three hours, and are slain and eaten the next day.

(A shudder of horror from the women. FTATATEETA, despising them and scorning the soldiers, pushes her way through the crowd and confronts the spear points undismayed.)

FTATATEETA: Then fly and save yourselves, O cowardly sons of the cheap clay gods that are sold to fish porters; and leave us to shift for ourselves.

BELZANOR: Not until you have first done our bidding, O terror of manhood. Bring out Cleopatra the Queen to us; and then go wither you will.

FTATATEETA: *(with a derisive laugh)* Now I know why the gods have taken her out of our hands. *(The GUARDSMEN start and look at one another.)* Know, thou foolish soldier, that the Queen has been missing since an hour past sundown.

BELZANOR: *(furiously)* Hag: you have hidden her to sell to Caesar or her brother. *(He grasps her by the left wrist, and drags her, helped by a few of the guard, to the middle of the courtyard, where, as they fling her on her knees, he draws a murderous looking knife.)* Where is she? Where is she? or — *(he threatens to cut her throat).*

FTATATEETA: *(savagely)* Touch me, dog; and the Nile will not rise on your fields for seven times seven years of famine.

BELZANOR: *(frightened, but desperate)* I will sacrifice: I will pay. Or stay. *(To the PERSIAN)* You, O subtle one: your father's lands lie far from the Nile. Slay her.

PERSIAN: *(threatening her with his knife)* Persia has but one god; yet he loves the blood of old women. Where is Cleopatra?

FTATATEETA: Persian: as Osiris lives, I do not know. I chid her for bringing evil days upon us by talking to the sacred cats of the priests, and carrying them in her arms. I told her she would be left alone here when the Romans came as a punishment for her disobedience. And now she is gone — run away — hidden. I speak the truth. I call Osiris to witness —

THE WOMEN: *(protesting officiously)* She speaks the truth, Belzanor.

BELZANOR: You have frightened the child: she is hiding. Search — quick — into the palace — search every corner.

(The GUARDS, led by BELZANOR, shoulder their way into the palace through the flying crowd of women, who escape through the courtyard gate.)

FTATATEETA: *(screaming)* Sacrilege! Men in the Queen's chambers! Sa — *(her voice dies away as the PERSIAN puts his knife to her throat.)*

BEL AFFRIS: *(laying a hand on* FTATATEETA's *left shoulder)* Forbear her yet a moment, Persian. *(To* FTATATEETA, *very significantly)* Mother: your gods are asleep or away hunting; and the sword is at your throat. Bring us to where the Queen is hid, and you shall live.

FTATATEETA: *(comtemptuously)* Who shall stay the sword in the hand of a fool, if the high gods put it there? Listen to me, ye young men without understanding. Cleopatra fears me; but she fears the Romans more. There is but one power greater in her eyes than the wrath of the Queen's nurse and the cruelty of Caesar; and that is the power of the Sphinx that sits in the desert watching the way to the sea. What she would have it know, she tells into the ears of the sacred cats; and on her birthday she sacrifices to it and decks it with poppies. Go ye therefore into the desert and seek Cleopatra in the shadow of the Sphinx; and on your heads see to it that no harm comes to her.

BEL AFFRIS: *(to the* PERSIAN*)* May we believe this, O subtle one?

PERSIAN: Which way come the Romans?

BEL AFFRIS: Over the desert, from the sea, by this very Sphinx.

PERSIAN: *(to* FTATATEETA*)* O mother of guile! O aspic's tongue! You have made up this tale so that we two may go into the desert and perish on the spears of the Romans. *(Lifting his knife)* Taste death.

FTATATEETA: Not from thee, baby. *(She snatches his ankle from under him and flies stooping along the palace wall, vanishing in the darkness within its precinct.* BEL AFFRIS *roars with laughter as the* PERSIAN *tumbles. The* GUARDSMEN *rush out of the palace with* BELZANOR *and a mob of fugitives, mostly carrying bundles.)*

PERSIAN: Have you found Cleopatra?

BELZANOR: She is gone. We have searched every corner.

THE NUBIAN[5] SENTINEL: *(appearing at the door of the palace)* Woe! Alas! Fly, fly!

BELZANOR: What is the matter now?

THE NUBIAN SENTINEL: The sacred white cat has been stolen.

ALL: Woe! woe! *(General panic. They all fly with cries of consternation. The torch is thrown down and extinguished in the rush. The noise of the fugitives dies away. Darkness and dead silence.)*

ACT ONE

The same darkness into which the temple of Ra and the Syrian palace vanished. The same silence. Suspense. Then the blackness and stillness break softly into silver mist and strange airs as the windswept harp of Memnon[1] plays at the dawning of the moon. It rises full over the desert; and a vast horizon comes into relief, broken by a huge shape which soon reveals itself in the spreading radiance as a Sphinx pedestalled on the sands. The light still clears, until the upraised eyes of the image are distinguished looking straight forward and upward in infinite fearless vigil, and a mass of color between its great paws defines itself as a heap of red poppies on which a girl lies motionless, her silken vest heaving gently and regularly with the breathing of a dreamless sleeper, and her braided hair glittering in a shaft of moonlight like a bird's wing.

5 *the Nubians were an ethnic group in southern Egypt.*

1 *an ancient Ethiopian king.*

Suddenly there comes from afar a vaguely fearful sound (it might be the bellow of a Minotaur[2] softened by great distance) and Memnon's music stops. Silence: then a few faint high-ringing trumpet notes. Then silence again. Then a man comes from the south with stealing steps, ravished by the mystery of the night, all wonder, and halts, lost in contemplation, opposite the left flank of the Sphinx, whose bosom, with its burden, is hidden from him by its massive shoulder.

THE MAN: Hail, Sphinx: salutation from Julius Caesar! I have wandered in many lands, seeking the lost regions from which my birth into this world exiled me, and the company of creatures such as I myself. I have found flocks and pastures, men and cities, but no other Caesar, no air native to me, no man kindred to me, none who can do my day's deed, and think my night's thought. In the little world yonder, Sphinx, my place is as high as yours in this great desert; only I wander, and you sit still; I conquer, and you endure; I work and wonder, you watch and wait; I look up and am dazzled, look down and am darkened, look round and am puzzled, whilst your eyes never turn from looking out — out of the world — to the lost region — the home from which we have strayed. Sphinx, you and I, strangers to the race of men, are no strangers to one another: have I not been conscious of you and of this place since I was born? Rome is a madman's dream: this is my Reality. These starry lamps of yours I have seen from afar in Gaul, in Britain, in Spain, in Thessaly, signalling great secrets to some eternal sentinel below, whose post I never could find. And here at last is their sentinel — an image of the constant and immortal part of my life, silent, full of thoughts, alone in the silver desert. Sphinx, Sphinx: I have climbed mountains at night to hear in the distance the stealthy footfall of the winds that chase your sands in forbidden play — our invisible children, O Sphinx, laughing in whispers. My way hither was the way of destiny; for I am he of whose genius you are the symbol: part brute, part woman, and part god — nothing of man in me at all. Have I read your riddle, Sphinx?

THE GIRL: *(who has wakened, and peeped cautiously from her nest to see who is speaking)* Old Gentleman.

CAESAR: *(starting violently, and clutching his sword)* Immortal gods!

THE GIRL: Old gentleman: dont run away.

CAESAR: *(stupefied)* "Old gentleman: dont run away"!!! This! to Julius Caesar!

THE GIRL: *(urgently)* Old gentleman.

CAESAR: Sphinx: you presume on your centuries. I am younger than you, though your voice is but a girl's voice as yet.

THE GIRL: Climb up here, quickly; or the Romans will come and eat you.

CAESAR: *(running forward past the Sphinx's shoulder, and seeing her)* A child at its breast! a divine child!

THE GIRL: Come up quickly. You must get up at its side and creep round.

CAESAR: *(amazed)* Who are you?

THE GIRL: Cleopatra, Queen of Egypt.

---

2 *a half-human, half-bull creature in Greek mythology.*

CAESAR: Queen of the Gypsies, you mean.

CLEOPATRA: You must not be disrespectful to me, or the Sphinx will let the Romans eat you. Come up. It is quite cosy here.

CAESAR: *(to himself)* What a dream! What a magnificent dream! Only let me not wake, and I will conquer ten continents to pay for dreaming it out to the end. *(He climbs to the Sphinx's flank, and presently reappears to her on the pedestal, stepping round its right shoulder.)*

CLEOPATRA: Take care. That's right. Now sit down: you may have its other paw. *(She seats herself comfortably on its left paw.)* It is very powerful and will protect us; but *(shivering, and with plaintive loneliness)* it would not take any notice of me or keep me company. I am glad you have come: I was very lonely. Did you happen to see a white cat anywhere?

CAESAR: *(sitting slowly down on the right paw in extreme wonderment)* Have you lost one?

CLEOPATRA: Yes: the sacred white cat: is it not dreadful? I brought him here to sacrifice him to the Sphinx; but when we got a little way from the city a black cat called him, and he jumped out of my arms and ran away to it. Do you think that the black cat can have been my great-great-great-grandmother?

CAESAR: *(staring at her)* Your great-great-great-grandmother! Well, why not? Nothing would surprise me on this night of nights.

CLEOPATRA: I think it must have been. My great-grandmother's great-grandmother was a black kitten of the sacred white cat; and the river Nile made her his seventh wife. That is why my hair is so wavy. And I always want to be let do as I like, no matter whether it is the will of the gods or not: that is because my blood is made with Nile water.

CAESAR: What are you doing here at this time of night? Do you live here?

CLEOPATRA: Of course not: I am the Queen; and I shall live in the palace at Alexandria when I have killed my brother, who drove me out of it. When I am old enough I shall do just what I like. I shall be able to poison the slaves and see them wriggle, and pretend to Ftatateeta that she is going to be put into the fiery furnace.

CAESAR: Hm! Meanwhile why are you not at home and in bed?

CLEOPATRA: Because the Romans are coming to eat us all. You are not at home and in bed either.

CAESAR: *(with conviction)* Yes I am. I live in a tent; and I am now in that tent, fast asleep and dreaming. Do you suppose that I believe you are real, you impossible little dream witch?

CLEOPATRA: *(giggling and leaning trustfully towards him)* You are a funny old gentleman. I like you.

CAESAR: Ah, that spoils the dream. Why dont you dream that I am young?

CLEOPATRA: I wish you were; only I think I should be more afraid of you. I like men, especially young men with round strong arms; but I am afraid of them. You are old and rather thin and stringy; but you have a nice voice; and I like to have somebody to talk to, though I think you are a little mad. It is the moon that makes you talk to yourself in that silly way.

CAESAR: What! you heard that, did you? I was saying my prayers to the great Sphinx.

CLEOPATRA: But this isnt the great Sphinx.

CAESAR: *(much disappointed, looking up at the statue)* What!

CLEOPATRA: This is only a dear little kitten of a Sphinx. Why, the great Sphinx is so big that it has a temple between its paws. This is my pet Sphinx. Tell me: do you think the Romans have any sorcerers who could take us away from the Sphinx by magic?

CAESAR: Why? Are you afraid of the Romans?

CLEOPATRA: *(very seriously)* Oh, they would eat us if they caught us. They are barbarians. Their chief is called Julius Caesar. His father was a tiger and his mother a burning mountain; and his nose is like an elephant's trunk. *(CAESAR involuntarily rubs his nose.)* They all have long noses, and ivory tusks, and little tails, and seven arms with a hundred arrows in each; and they live on human flesh.

CAESAR: Would you like me to shew you a real Roman?

CLEOPATRA: *(terrified)* No. You are frightening me.

CAESAR: No matter: this is only a dream —

CLEOPATRA: *(excitedly)* It is not a dream: it is not a dream. See, see. *(She plucks a pin from her hair and jabs it repeatedly into his arm.)*

CAESAR: Ffff — Stop. *(Wrathfully)* How dare you?

CLEOPATRA: *(abashed)* You said you were dreaming. *(Whimpering)* I only wanted to shew you —

CAESAR: *(gently)* Come, come: dont cry. A queen mustnt cry. *(He rubs his arm, wondering at the reality of the smart.)* Am I awake? *(He strikes his hand against the Sphinx to test its solidity. It feels so real that he begins to be alarmed, and says perplexedly)* Yes, I — *(quite panicstricken)* no: impossible: madness, madness! *(Desperately)* Back to camp — to camp. *(He rises to spring down from the pedestal.)*

CLEOPATRA: *(flinging her arms in terror round him)* No: you shant leave me. No, no, no: dont go. I'm afraid — afraid of the Romans.

CAESAR: *(as the conviction that he is really awake forces itself on him)* Cleopatra: can you see my face well?

CLEOPATRA: Yes. It is so white in the moonlight.

CAESAR: Are you sure it is the moonlight that makes me look whiter than an Egyptian? *(Grimly)* Do you notice that I have a rather long nose?

CLEOPATRA: *(recoiling, paralysed by a terrible suspicion)* Oh!

CAESAR: It is a Roman nose, Cleopatra.

CLEOPATRA: Ah! *(With a piercing scream she springs up; darts round the left shoulder of the Sphinx; scrambles down to the sand; and falls on her knees in frantic supplication, shrieking)* Bite him in two, Sphinx: bite him in two. I meant to sacrifice the white cat — I did indeed — I *(CAESAR, who has slipped down from the pedestal, touches her on the shoulder)* — Ah! *(She buries her head in her arms.)*

CAESAR: Cleopatra: shall I teach you a way to prevent Caesar from eating you?

CLEOPATRA: *(clinging to him piteously)* Oh do, do, do. I will steal Ftatateeta's jewels and give them to you. I will make the river Nile water your lands twice a year.

CAESAR: Peace, peace, my child. Your gods are afraid of the Romans: you see the Sphinx dare not bite me, nor prevent me carrying you off to Julius Caesar.

CLEOPATRA: *(in pleading murmurings)* You wont, you wont. You said you wouldnt.

CAESAR: Caesar never eats women.

CLEOPATRA: *(springing up full of hope)* What!

CAESAR: *(impressively)* But he eats girls *(she relapses)* and cats. Now you are a silly little girl; and you are descended from the black kitten. You are both a girl and a cat.

CLEOPATRA: *(trembling)* And will he eat me?

CAESAR: Yes; unless you make him believe that you are a woman.

CLEOPATRA: Oh, you must get a sorcerer to make a woman of me. Are you a sorcerer?

CAESAR: Perhaps. But it will take a long time; and this very night you must stand face to face with Caesar in the palace of your fathers.

CLEOPATRA: No, no. I darent.

CAESAR: Whatever dread may be in your soul — however terrible Caesar may be to you — you must confront him as a brave woman and a great queen; and you must feel no fear. If your hand shakes: if your voice quavers; then — night and death! *(She moans.)* But if he thinks you worthy to rule, he will set you on the throne by his side and make you the real ruler of Egypt.

CLEOPATRA: *(despairingly)* No: he will find me out: he will find me out.

CAESAR: *(rather mournfully)* He is easily deceived by women. Their eyes dazzle him; and he sees them not as they are, but as he wishes them to appear to him.

CLEOPATRA: *(hopefully)* Then we will cheat him. I will put on Ftatateeta's head-dress; and he will think me quite an old woman.

CAESAR: If you do that he will eat you at one mouthful.

CLEOPATRA: But I will give him a cake with my magic opal and seven hairs of the white cat baked in it; and —

CAESAR: *(abruptly)* Pah! you are a little fool. He will eat your cake and you too. *(He turns contemptuously from her.)*

CLEOPATRA: *(running after him and clinging to him)* Oh please, please! I will do whatever you tell me. I will be good. I will be your slave. *(Again the terrible bellowing note sounds across the desert, now closer at hand. It is the bucina, the Roman war trumpet.)*

CAESAR: Hark!

CLEOPATRA: *(trembling)* What was that?

CAESAR: Caesar's voice.

CLEOPATRA: *(pulling at his hand)* Let us run away. Come. Oh, come.

CAESAR: You are safe with me until you stand on your throne to receive Caesar. Now lead me thither.

CLEOPATRA: *(only too glad to get away)* I will, I will. *(Again the bucina.)* Oh come, come, come: the gods are angry. Do you feel the earth shaking?

CAESAR: It is the tread of Caesar's legions.

CLEOPATRA: *(drawing him away)* This way, quickly. And let us look for the white cat as we go. It is he that has turned you into a Roman.

CAESAR: Incorrigible, oh, incorrigible! Away! *(He follows her, the bucina sounding louder as they steal across the desert. The moonlight wanes: the horizon again shews black against the sky, broken only by the fantastic silhouette of the Sphinx. The sky itself vanishes in darkness, from which there is no relief until the gleam of a distant torch falls on great Egyptian pillars supporting the roof of a majestic corridor. At the further end of this corridor a* NUBIAN SLAVE *appears carrying the torch.* CAESAR, *still led by* CLEOPATRA, *follows him. They come down the corridor,* CAESAR *peering keenly about at the strange architecture, and at the pillar shadows between which, as the passing torch makes them hurry noiselessly backwards, figures of men with wings and hawks' heads, and vast black marble cats, seem to flit in and out of ambush. Further along, the wall turns a corner and makes a spacious transept in which* CAESAR *sees, on his right, a throne, and behind the throne a door. On each side of the throne is a slender pillar with a lamp on it.)*

CAESAR: What place is this?

CLEOPATRA: This is where I sit on the throne when I am allowed to wear my crown and robes. *(The* SLAVE *holds his torch to shew the throne.)*

CAESAR: Order the slave to light the lamps.

CLEOPATRA: *(shyly)* Do you think I may?

CAESAR: Of course. You are the Queen. *(She hesitates.)* Go on.

CLEOPATRA: *(timidly, to the slave)* Light all the lamps.

FTATATEETA: *(suddenly coming from behind the throne)* Stop. *(The* SLAVE *stops. She turns sternly to* CLEOPATRA, *who quails like a naughty child.)* Who is this you have with you; and how dare you order the lamps to be lighted without my permission? *(*CLEOPATRA *is dumb with apprehension.)*

CAESAR: Who is she?

CLEOPATRA: Ftatateeta.

FTATATEETA: *(arrogantly)* Chief nurse to —

CAESAR: *(cutting her short)* I speak to the Queen. Be silent. *(To* CLEOPATRA*)* Is this how your servants know their places? Send her away; and do you *(to the slave)* do as the Queen has bidden. *(The* SLAVE *lights the lamps. Meanwhile* CLEOPATRA *stands hesitating, afraid of* FTATATEETA.*)* You are the Queen: send her away.

CLEOPATRA: *(cajoling)* Ftatateeta, dear: you must go away — just for a little.

CAESAR: You are not commanding her to go away: you are begging her. You are no Queen. You will be eaten. Farewell. *(He turns to go.)*

CLEOPATRA: *(clutching him)* No, no, no. Dont leave me.

CAESAR: A Roman does not stay with queens who are afraid of their slaves.

CLEOPATRA: I am not afraid. Indeed I am not afraid.

FTATATEETA: We shall see who is afraid here. *(Menacingly)* Cleopatra —

CAESAR: On your knees, woman: am I also a child that you dare trifle with me? *(He points to the floor at* CLEOPATRA's *feet.* FTATATEETA, *half cowed, half savage, hesitates.* CAESAR *calls to the* NUBIAN.*)* Slave. *(The* NUBIAN *comes to him)* Can you cut off a head? *(The* NUBIAN *nods and grins ecstatically, showing all his teeth.* CAESAR *takes his sword by the scabbard, ready to offer the hilt to the* NUBIAN, *and turns again to* FTATATEETA, *repeating his gesture.)* Have you remembered yourself, mistress?

*(*FTATATEETA, *crushed, kneels before* CLEOPATRA, *who can hardly believe her eyes.)*

FTATATEETA: *(hoarsely)* O Queen, forget not thy servant in the days of thy greatness.

CLEOPATRA: *(blazing with excitement)* Go. Begone. Go away. *(*FTATATEETA *rises with stooped head, and moves backwards towards the door.* CLEOPATRA *watches her submission eagerly, almost clapping her hands, which are trembling. Suddenly she cries)* Give me something to beat her with. *(She snatches a snake-skin from the throne and dashes after* FTATATEETA, *whirling it like a scourge in the air.* CAESAR *makes a bound and manages to catch her and hold her while* FTATATEETA *escapes.)*

CAESAR: You scratch, kitten, do you?

CLEOPATRA: *(breaking from him)* I will beat somebody. I will beat him. *(She attacks the slave.)* There, there, there! *(The* SLAVE *flies for his life up the corridor and vanishes. She throws the snake-skin away and jumps on the step of the throne with her arms waving, crying)* I am a real Queen at last — a real, real Queen! Cleopatra the Queen! *(*CAESAR *shakes his head dubiously, the advantage of the change seeming open to question from the point of view of the general welfare of Egypt. She turns and looks at him exultantly. Then she jumps down from the steps, runs to him, and flings her arms round him rapturously, crying)* Oh, I love you for making me a Queen.

CAESAR: But queens love only kings.

CLEOPATRA: I will make all the men I love kings. I will make you a king. I will have many young kings, with round, strong arms; and when I am tired of them I will whip them to death; but you shall always be my king: my nice, kind, wise, good old king.

CAESAR: Oh, my wrinkles, my wrinkles! And my child's heart! You will be the most dangerous of all Caesar's conquests.

CLEOPATRA: *(appalled)* Caesar! I forgot Caesar. *(Anxiously)* You will tell him that I am a Queen, will you not? — a real Queen. Listen! *(stealthily coaxing him)*: let us run away and hide until Caesar is gone.

CAESAR: If you fear Caesar, you are no true queen; and though you were to hide beneath a pyramid, he would go straight to it and lift it with one hand. And then — ! *(he chops his teeth together.)*

CLEOPATRA: *(trembling)* Oh!

CAESAR: Be afraid if you dare. *(The note of the bucina resounds again in the distance. She moans with fear.* CAESAR *exults in it, exclaiming)* Aha! Caesar approaches the throne of Cleopatra. Come: take your place. *(He takes her hand and leads her to the throne. She is too downcast to speak.)* Ho, there, Teetatota. How do you call your slaves?

CLEOPATRA: *(spiritlessly, as she sinks on the throne and cowers there, shaking)* Clap your hands.

(He claps his hands. FTATATEETA *returns.)*

CAESAR: Bring the Queen's robes, and her crown, and her women; and prepare her.

CLEOPATRA: *(eagerly — recovering herself a little)* Yes, the crown, Ftatateeta: I shall wear the crown.

FTATATEETA: For whom must the Queen put on her state?

CAESAR: For a citizen of Rome. A king of kings, Totateeta.

CLEOPATRA: *(stamping at her)* How dare you ask questions? Go and do as you are told. *(*FTATATEETA *goes out with a grim smile.* CLEOPATRA *goes on eagerly, to*

CAESAR) Caesar will know that I am a Queen when he sees my crown and robes, will he not?

CAESAR: No. How shall he know that you are not a slave dressed up in the Queen's ornaments?

CLEOPATRA: You must tell him.

CAESAR: He will not ask me. He will know Cleopatra by her pride, her courage, her majesty, and her beauty. (She looks very doubtful) Are you trembling?

CLEOPATRA: (shivering with dread) No, I — I — (in a very sickly voice) No.

(FTATATEETA and three women come in with the regalia.)

FTATATEETA: Of all the Queen's women, these three alone are left. The rest are fled. (They begin to deck CLEOPATRA, who submits, pale and motionless.)

CAESAR: Good, good. Three are enough. Poor Caesar generally has to dress himself.

FTATATEETA: (contemptuously) The queen of Egypt is not a Roman barbarian. (To CLEOPATRA) Be brave, my nursling. Hold up your head before this stranger.

CAESAR: (admiring CLEOPATRA, and placing the crown on her head) Is it sweet or bitter to be a Queen, Cleopatra?

CLEOPATRA: Bitter.

CAESAR: Cast out fear; and you will conquer Caesar. Tota: are the Romans at hand?

FTATATEETA: They are at hand; and the guard has fled.

THE WOMEN: (wailing subduedly) Woe to us!

(The NUBIAN comes running down the hall.)

NUBIAN: The Romans are in the courtyard. (He bolts through the door. With a shriek, the WOMEN, fly after him. FTATATEETA's jaw expresses savage resolution: she does not budge. CLEOPATRA can hardly restrain herself from following them. CAESAR grips her wrist, and looks steadfastly at her. She stands like a martyr).

CAESAR: The Queen must face Caesar alone. Answer "So be it."

CLEOPATRA: (white) So be it.

CAESAR: (releasing her) Good.

(A tramp and tumult of armed men is heard. CLEOPATRA's terror increases. The bucina sounds close at hand, followed by a formidable clangor of trumpets. This is too much for CLEOPATRA: she utters a cry and darts towards the door. FTATATEETA stops her ruthlessly.)

FTATATEETA: You are my nursling. You have said "So be it"; and if you die for it, you must make the Queen's word good. (She hands CLEOPATRA to CAESAR, who takes her back, almost beside herself with apprehension, to the throne.)

CAESAR: Now, if you quail — ! (He seats himself on the throne.)

(She stands on the step, all but unconscious, waiting for death. The Roman soldiers troop in tumultuously through the corridor, headed by their ensign with his eagle, and their bucinator, a burly fellow with his instrument coiled round his body, its brazen bell shaped like the head of a howling wolf. When they reach the transept, they stare in amazement at the throne; dress into ordered rank opposite it; draw their swords and lift them in the air with a shout of Hail, Caesar. CLEOPATRA *turns and stares wildly at* CAESAR; *grasps the situation; and, with a great sob of relief, falls into his arms.)*

ACT TWO

Alexandria. A hall on the first floor of the Palace, ending in a loggia approached by two steps. Through the arches of the loggia the Mediterranean can be seen, bright in the morning sun. The clean lofty walls, painted with a procession of the Egyptian theocracy, presented in profile as flat ornament, and the absence of mirrors, sham perspectives, stuffy upholstery and textiles, make the place handsome, wholesome, simple and cool, or, as a rich English manufacturer would express it, poor, bare, ridiculous and unhomely. For Tottenham Court Road civilization is to this Egyptian civilization as glass bead and tattoo civilization is to Tottenham Court Road.[1]

The young king PTOLEMY DIONYSUS *(aged ten) is at the top of the steps, on his way in through the loggia, led by his guardian* POTHINUS, *who has him by the hand. The court is assembled to receive him. It is made up of men and women (some of the women being officials) of various complexions and races, mostly Egyptian; some of them, comparatively fair, from lower Egypt, some, much darker, from upper Egypt; with a few Greeks and Jews. Prominent in a group on* PTOLEMY's *right hand is* THEODOTUS, PTOLEMY's *tutor. Another group, on* PTOLEMY's *left, is headed by* ACHILLAS, *the general of* PTOLEMY's *troops.* THEODOTUS *is a little old man, whose features are as cramped and wizened as his limbs, except his tall straight forehead, which occupies more space than all the rest of his face. He maintains an air of magpie keenness and profundity, listening to what the others say with the sarcastic vigilance of a philosopher listening to the exercises of his disciples.* ACHILLAS *is a tall handsome man of thirty-five, with a fine black beard curled like the coat of a poodle. Apparently not a clever man, but distinguished and dignified.* POTHINUS *is a vigorous man of fifty, a eunuch, passionate, energetic and quick witted, but of common mind and character; impatient and unable to control his temper. He has fine tawny hair, like fur.* PTOLEMY, *the King, looks much older than an English boy of ten; but he has the childish air, the habit of being in leading strings, the mixture of impotence and petulance, the appearance of being excessively washed, combed and dressed by other hands, which is exhibited by court-bred princes of all ages.*

All receive the KING *with reverences. He comes down the steps to a chair of state which stands a little to his right, the only seat in the hall. Taking his place before it, he*

---

1 From the early nineteenth century this street has been the centre for the furniture manufacturing industry in Britain and is still known for its fashionable furniture.

looks nervously for instructions to POTHINUS, *who places himself at his left hand.*

POTHINUS: The king of Egypt has a word to speak.

THEODOTUS: *(in a squeak which he makes impressive by sheer self-opinionativeness)* Peace for the King's word!

PTOLEMY: *(without any vocal inflexions: he is evidently repeating a lesson)* Take notice of this all of you. I am the first-born son of Auletes the Flute Blower who was your King. My sister Berenice drove him from his throne and reigned in his stead but — but — *(he hesitates)* —

POTHINUS: *(stealthily prompting)* — but the gods would not suffer —

PTOLEMY: Yes — the gods would not suffer — not suffer — *(He stops; then, crestfallen)* I forget what the gods would not suffer.

THEODOTUS: Let Pothinus, the King's guardian, speak for the King.

POTHINUS: *(suppressing his impatience with difficulty)* The King wished to say that the gods would not suffer the impiety of his sister to go unpunished.

PTOLEMY: *(hastily)* Yes: I remember the rest of it. *(He resumes his monotone.)* Therefore the gods sent a stranger one Mark Antony a Roman captain of horsemen across the sands of the desert and he set my father again upon the throne. And my father took Berenice my sister and struck her head off. And now that my father is dead yet another of his daughters my sister Cleopatra would snatch the kingdom from me and reign in my place. But the gods would not suffer — *(POTHINUS coughs admonitorily)* — the gods — the gods would not suffer —

POTHINUS: *(prompting)* — will not maintain —

PTOLEMY: Oh yes — will not maintain such iniquity they will give her head to the axe even as her sister's. But with the help of the witch Ftatateeta she hath cast a spell on the Roman Julius Caesar to make him uphold her false pretence to rule in Egypt. Take notice then that I will not suffer — that I will not suffer — *(pettishly, to POTHINUS)* What is it that I will not suffer?

POTHINUS: *(suddenly exploding with all the force and emphasis of political passion)* The King will not suffer a foreigner to take from him the throne of our Egypt. *(A shout of applause.)* Tell the King, Achillas, how many soldiers and horsemen follow the Roman?

THEODOTUS: Let the King's general speak!

ACHILLAS: But two Roman legions, O King. Three thousand soldiers and scarce a thousand horsemen.

(The court breaks into derisive laughter; and a great chattering begins, amid which RUFIO, *a Roman officer, appears in the loggia. He is a burly, black-bearded man of middle age, very blunt, prompt and rough, with small clear eyes, and plump nose and cheeks, which, however, like the rest of his flesh, are in ironhard condition.)*

RUFIO: *(from the steps)* Peace, ho! *(The laughter and chatter cease abruptly.)* Caesar approaches.

THEODOTUS: *(with much presence of mind)* The King permits the Roman commander to enter!

(CAESAR, *plainly dressed, but wearing an oak wreath to conceal his baldness, enters from the loggia, attended by* BRITANNUS, *his secretary, a Briton, about forty, tall, solemn, and already slightly bald, with a heavy, drooping, hazel-colored moustache trained so as to lose its ends in a pair of trim whiskers. He is carefully dressed in blue, with portfolio, inkhorn, and reed pen at his girdle. His serious air and sense of the importance of the business in hand is in marked contrast to the kindly interest of* CAESAR, *who looks at the scene, which is new to him, with the frank curiosity of a child, and then turns to the king's chair:* BRITANNUS *and* RUFIO *posting themselves near the steps at the other side.*)

CAESAR: *(looking at* POTHINUS *and* PTOLEMY*)* Which is the King? the man or the boy?

POTHINUS: I am Pothinus, the guardian of my lord the King.

CAESAR: *(patting* PTOLEMY *kindly on the shoulder)* So you are the King. Dull work at your age, eh? *(To* POTHINUS*)* Your servant, Pothinus. *(He turns away unconcernedly and comes slowly along the middle of the hall, looking from side to side at the courtiers until he reaches* ACHILLAS.*)* And this gentleman?

THEODOTUS: Achillas, the King's general.

CAESAR: *(to* ACHILLAS, *very friendly)* A general, eh? I am a general myself. But I began too old, too old. Health and many victories, Achillas!

ACHILLAS: As the gods will, Caesar.

CAESAR: *(turning to* THEODOTUS*)* And you, sir, are — ?

THEODOTUS: Theodotus, the King's tutor.

CAESAR: You teach men how to be kings, Theodotus. That is very clever of you. *(Looking at the gods on the walls as he turns away from* THEODOTUS, *and goes up again to* POTHINUS*)* And this place?

POTHINUS: The council chamber of the chancellors of the King's treasury, Caesar.

CAESAR: Ah! that reminds me. I want some money.

POTHINUS: The King's treasury is poor, Caesar.

CAESAR: Yes: I notice that there is but one chair in it.

RUFIO: *(shouting gruffly)* Bring a chair there, some of you, for Caesar.

PTOLEMY: *(rising shyly to offer his chair)* Caesar —

CAESAR: *(kindly)* No, no, my boy: that is your chair of state. Sit down.

(*He makes* PTOLEMY *sit down again. Meanwhile* RUFIO, *looking about him, sees in the nearest corner an image of the god Ra, represented as a seated man with the head of a hawk. Before the image is a bronze tripod, about as large as a three-legged stool, with a stick of incense burning on it.* RUFIO, *with Roman resourcefulness and indifference to foreign superstitions, promptly seizes the tripod; shakes off the incense; blows away the ash; and dumps it down behind* CAESAR, *nearly in the middle of the hall.*)

RUFIO: Sit on that, Caesar.

(*A shiver runs through the court, followed by a hissing whisper of* Sacrilege!)

CAESAR: *(seating himself)* Now, Pothinus, to business. I am badly in want of money.

BRITANNUS: *(disapproving of these informal expressions)* My master would say that there is a lawful debt due to Rome by Egypt, contracted by the King's deceased father to the Triumvirate;[2] and that it is Caesar's duty to his country to require immediate payment.

CAESAR: *(blandly)* Ah, I forgot. I have not made my companions known here. Pothinus: this is Britannus, my secretary. He is an islander from the western end of the world, a day's voyage from Gaul. *(BRITANNUS bows stiffly.)* This gentleman is Rufio, my comrade in arms. *(RUFIO nods.)* Pothinus: I want 1,600 talents.

(The courtiers, appalled, murmur loudly, and THEODOTUS *and* ACHILLAS *appeal mutely to one another against so monstrous a demand.)*

POTHINUS: *(aghast)* Forty million sesterces! Impossible. There is not so much money in the King's treasury.

CAESAR: *(encouragingly)* Only sixteen hundred talents, Pothinus. Why count it in sesterces? A sestertius is only worth a loaf of bread.

POTHINUS: And a talent is worth a racehorse. I say it is impossible. We have been at strife here, because the King's sister Cleopatra falsely claims his throne. The King's taxes have not been collected for a whole year.

CAESAR: Yes they have, Pothinus. My officers have been collecting them all morning. *(Renewed whisper and sensation, not without some stifled laughter, among the courtiers.)*

RUFIO: *(bluntly)* You must pay, Pothinus. Why waste words? You are getting off cheaply enough.

POTHINUS: *(bitterly)* Is it possible that Caesar, the conqueror of the world, has time to occupy himself with such a trifle as our taxes?

CAESAR: My friend: taxes are the chief business of a conqueror of the world.

POTHINUS: Then take warning, Caesar. This day, the treasures of the temple and the gold of the King's treasury shall be sent to the mint to be melted down for our ransom in the sight of the people. They shall see us sitting under bare walls and drinking from wooden cups. And their wrath be on your head, Caesar, if you force us to this sacrilege!

CAESAR: Do not fear, Pothinus: the people know how well wine tastes in wooden cups. In return for your bounty, I will settle this dispute about the throne for you, if you will. What say you?

POTHINUS: If I say no, will that hinder you?

RUFIO: *(defiantly)* No.

CAESAR: You say the matter has been at issue for a year, Pothinus. May I have ten minutes at it?

POTHINUS: You will do your pleasure, doubtless.

CAESAR: Good! But first, let us have Cleopatra here.

THEODOTUS: She is not in Alexandria: she is fled into Syria.

CAESAR: I think not. *(To* RUFIO*)* Call Totateeta.

RUFIO: *(calling)* Ho there, Teetatota.

2 *unofficial Roman political coalition of Julius Caesar, Pompey, and Crassus.*

(FTATATEETA *enters the loggia, and stands arrogantly at the top of the steps.*)

FTATATEETA: Who pronounces the name of Ftatateeta, the Queen's chief nurse?
CAESAR: Nobody can pronounce it, Tota, except yourself. Where is your mistress?

(CLEOPATRA, *who is hiding behind* FTATATEETA, *peeps out at them, laughing.* CAESAR *rises.*)

CAESAR: Will the Queen favor us with her presence for a moment?
CLEOPATRA: *(pushing* FTATATEETA *aside and standing haughtily on the brink of the steps)* Am I to behave like a Queen?
CAESAR: Yes.

(CLEOPATRA *immediately comes down to the chair of state; seizes* PTOLEMY; *drags him out of his seat; then takes his place in the chair.* FTATATEETA *seats herself on the step of the loggia, and sits there, watching the scene with sibylline intensity.*)

PTOLEMY: *(mortified, and struggling with his tears)* Caesar: this is how she treats me always. If I am king why is she allowed to take everything from me?
CLEOPATRA: You are not to be King, you little cry-baby. You are to be eaten by the Romans.
CAESAR: *(touched by* PTOLEMY's *distress)* Come here, my boy, and stand by me.

(PTOLEMY *goes over to* CAESAR, *who, resuming his seat on the tripod, takes the boy's hand to encourage him.* CLEOPATRA, *furiously jealous, rises and glares at them.*)

CLEOPATRA: *(with flaming cheeks)* Take your throne: I dont want it. *(She flings away from the chair, and approaches* PTOLEMY, *who shrinks from her.)* Go this instant and sit down in your place.
CAESAR: Go, Ptolemy. Always take a throne when it is offered to you.
RUFIO: I hope you will have the good sense to follow your own advice when we return to Rome, Caesar.

(PTOLEMY *slowly goes back to the throne, giving* CLEOPATRA *a wide berth, in evident fear of her hands. She takes his place beside* CAESAR.)

CAESAR: Pothinus —
CLEOPATRA: *(interrupting him)* Are you not going to speak to me?
CAESAR: Be quiet. Open your mouth again before I give you leave, and you shall be eaten.
CLEOPATRA: I am not afraid. A queen must not be afraid. Eat my husband there, if you like: he is afraid.
CAESAR: *(starting)* Your husband! What do you mean?
CLEOPATRA: *(pointing to* PTOLEMY) That little thing.

(The two Romans and the Briton stare at one another in amazement.)

THEODOTUS: Caesar: you are a stranger here, and not conversant with our laws. The kings and queens of Egypt may not marry except with their own royal blood. Ptolemy and Cleopatra are born king and consort just as they are born brother and sister.

BRITANNUS: *(shocked)* Caesar: this is not proper.

THEODOTUS: *(outraged)* How!

CAESAR: *(recovering his self-possession)* Pardon him, Theodotus: he is a barbarian, and thinks that the customs of his tribe and island are the laws of nature.

BRITANNUS: On the contrary, Caesar, it is these Egyptians who are barbarians; and you do wrong to encourage them. I say it is a scandal.

CAESAR: Scandal or not, my friend, it opens the gate of peace. *(He addresses POTHINUS seriously.)* Pothinus: hear what I propose.

RUFIO: Hear Caesar there.

CAESAR: Ptolemy and Cleopatra shall reign jointly in Egypt.

ACHILLAS: What of the King's younger brother and Cleopatra's younger sister?

RUFIO: *(explaining)* There is another little Ptolemy, Caesar: so they tell me.

CAESAR: Well, the little Ptolemy can marry the other sister; and we will make them both a present of Cyprus.

POTHINUS: *(impatiently)* Cyprus is of no use to anybody.

CAESAR: No matter: you shall have it for the sake of peace.

BRITANNUS: *(unconsciously anticipating a later statesman)* Peace with honor, Pothinus.

POTHINUS: *(mutinously)* Caesar: be honest. The money you demand is the price of our freedom. Take it; and leave us to settle our own affairs.

THE BOLDER COURTIERS: *(encouraged by POTHINUS's tone and CAESAR's quietness)* Yes, yes. Egypt for the Egyptians!

(The conference now becomes an altercation, the Egyptians becoming more and more heated. CAESAR remains unruffled; but RUFIO grows fiercer and doggeder, and BRITANNUS haughtily indignant.)

RUFIO: *(contemptuously)* Egypt for the Egyptians! Do you forget that there is a Roman army of occupation here, left by Aulus Gabinius when he set up your toy king for you?

ACHILLAS: *(suddenly asserting himself)* And now under my command. I am the Roman general here, Caesar.

CAESAR: *(tickled by the humor of the situation)* And also the Egyptian general, eh?

POTHINUS: *(triumphantly)* That is so, Caesar.

CAESAR: *(to ACHILLAS)* So you can make war on the Egyptians in the name of Rome, and on the Romans — on me, if necessary — in the name of Egypt?

ACHILLAS: That is so, Caesar.

CAESAR: And which side are you on at present, if I may presume to ask, general?

ACHILLAS: On the side of the right and of the gods.

CAESAR: Hm! How many men have you?

ACHILLAS: That will appear when I take the field.

RUFIO: (truculently) Are your men Romans? If not, it matters not how many there are, provided you are no stronger than 500 to ten.

POTHINUS: It is useless to try to bluff us, Rufio. Caesar has been defeated before and may be defeated again. A few weeks ago Caesar was flying for his life before Pompey: a few months hence he may be flying for his life before Cato and Juba of Numidia, the African King.

ACHILLAS: (following up POTHINUS's speech menacingly) What can you do with 4,000 men?

THEODOTUS: (following up ACHILLAS's speech with a raucous squeak) And without money? Away with you.

ALL THE COURTIERS: (shouting fiercely and crowding towards CAESAR) Away with you. Egypt for the Egyptians! Begone.

(RUFIO bites his beard, too angry to speak. CAESAR sits as comfortably as if he were at breakfast, and the cat were clamoring for a piece of Finnan-haddie.[3])

CLEOPATRA: Why do you let them talk to you like that, Caesar? Are you afraid?

CAESAR: Why, my dear, what they say is quite true.

CLEOPATRA: But if you go away, I shall not be Queen.

CAESAR: I shall not go away until you are Queen.

POTHINUS: Achillas: if you are not a fool, you will take that girl whilst she is under your hand.

RUFIO: (daring them) Why not take Caesar as well, Achillas?

POTHINUS: (retorting the defiance with interest) Well said, Rufio. Why not?

RUFIO: Try, Achillas. (Calling) Guard there.

(The loggia immediately fills with CAESAR's soldiers, who stand, sword in hand, at the top of the steps, waiting the word to charge from their centurion, who carries a cudgel. For a moment the Egyptians face them proudly: then they retire sullenly to their former places.)

BRITANNUS: You are Caesar's prisoners, all of you.

CAESAR: (benevolently) Oh no, no, no. By no means. Caesar's guests, gentlemen.

CLEOPATRA: Wont you cut their heads off?

CAESAR: What! Cut off your brother's head?

CLEOPATRA: Why not? He would cut off mine, if he got the chance. Wouldnt you, Ptolemy?

PTOLEMY: (pale and obstinate) I would. I will, too, when I grow up.

(CLEOPATRA is rent by a struggle between her newly-acquired dignity as a queen, and a strong impulse to put out her tongue at him. She takes no part in the scene which

3 smoked haddock.

follows, but watches it with curiosity and wonder, fidgeting with the restlessness of a child, and sitting down on CAESAR's *tripod when he rises.)*

POTHINUS: Caesar: if you attempt to detain us —

RUFIO: He will succeed, Egyptian: make up your mind to that. We hold the palace, the beach, and the eastern harbor. The road to Rome is open; and you shall travel it if Caesar chooses.

CAESAR: *(courteously)* I could do no less, Pothinus, to secure the retreat of my own soldiers. I am accountable for every life among them. But you are free to go. So are all here, and in the palace.

RUFIO: *(aghast at this clemency)* What! Renegades and all?

CAESAR: *(softening the expression)* Roman army of occupation and all, Rufio.

POTHINUS: *(bewildered)* But — but — but —

CAESAR: Well, my friend?

POTHINUS: You are turning us out of our own palace into the streets; and you tell us with a grand air that we are free to go! It is for you to go.

CAESAR: Your friends are in the street, Pothinus. You will be safer there.

POTHINUS: This is a trick. I am the king's guardian: I refuse to stir. I stand on my right here. Where is your right?

CAESAR: It is in Rufio's scabbard, Pothinus. I may not be able to keep it there if you wait too long.

(Sensation.)

POTHINUS: *(bitterly)* And this is Roman justice!

THEODOTUS: But not Roman gratitude, I hope.

CAESAR: Gratitude! Am I in your debt for any service, gentlemen?

THEODOTUS: Is Caesar's life of so little account to him that he forgets that we have saved it?

CAESAR: My life! Is that all?

THEODOTUS: Your life. Your laurels. Your future.

POTHINUS: It is true. I can call a witness to prove that but for us, the Roman army of occupation, led by the greatest soldier in the world, would now have Caesar at its mercy. *(Calling through the loggia)* Ho, there, Lucius Septimius (CAESAR *starts, deeply moved)*: if my voice can reach you, come forth and testify before Caesar.

CAESAR: *(shrinking)* No, no.

THEODOTUS: Yes, I say. Let the military tribune bear witness.

(LUCIUS SEPTIMIUS, a clean shaven, trim athlete of about 40, with symmetrical features, resolute mouth, and handsome, thin Roman nose, in the dress of a Roman officer, comes in through the loggia and confronts CAESAR, who hides his face with his robe for a moment; then, mastering himself, drops it, and confronts the tribune with dignity.)

POTHINUS: Bear witness, Lucius Septimius. Caesar came hither in pursuit of his foe. Did we shelter his foe?

LUCIUS: As Pompey's foot touched the Egyptian shore, his head fell by the stroke of my sword.

THEODOTUS: *(with viperish relish)* Under the eyes of his wife and child! Remember that, Caesar! They saw it from the ship he had just left. We have given you a full and sweet measure of vengeance.

CAESAR: *(with horror)* Vengeance!

POTHINUS: Our first gift to you, as your galley came into the roadstead, was the head of your rival for the empire of the world. Bear witness, Lucius Septimius: is it not so?

LUCIUS: It is so. With this hand, that slew Pompey, I placed his head at the feet of Caesar.

CAESAR: Murderer! So would you have slain Caesar, had Pompey been victorious at Pharsalia.

LUCIUS: Woe to the vanquished, Caesar! When I served Pompey, I slew as good men as he, only because he conquered them. His turn came at last.

THEODOTUS: *(flatteringly)* The deed was not yours, Caesar, but ours — nay, mine; for it was done by my counsel. Thanks to us, you keep your reputation for clemency, and have your vengeance too.

CAESAR: Vengeance! Vengeance!! Oh, if I could stoop to vengeance, what would I not exact from you as the price of this murdered man's blood? *(They shrink back, appalled and disconcerted.)* Was he not my son-in-law, my ancient friend, for 20 years the master of great Rome, for 30 years the compeller of victory? Did not I, as a Roman, share his glory? Was the Fate that forced us to fight for the mastery of the world, of our making? Am I Julius Caesar, or am I a wolf, that you fling to me the grey head of the old soldier, the laurelled conqueror, the mighty Roman, treacherously struck down by this callous ruffian, and then claim my gratitude for it! *(To* LUCIUS SEPTIMIUS*)* Begone: you fill me with horror.

LUCIUS: *(cold and undaunted)* Pshaw! You have seen severed heads before, Caesar, and severed right hands too, I think; some thousands of them, in Gaul, after you vanquished Vercingetorix. Did you spare him, with all your clemency? Was that vengeance?

CAESAR: No, by the gods! would that it had been! Vengeance at least is human. No, I say: those severed right hands, and the brave Vercingetorix basely strangled in a vault beneath the Capitol were *(with shuddering satire)* a wise severity, a necessary protection to the commonwealth, a duty of statesmanship — follies and fictions ten times bloodier than honest vengeance! What a fool was I then! To think that men's lives should be at the mercy of such fools! *(Humbly)* Lucius Septimius, pardon me: why should the slayer of Vercingetorix rebuke the slayer of Pompey? You are free to go with the rest. Or stay if you will: I will find a place for you in my service.

LUCIUS: The odds are against you, Caesar. I go. *(He turns to go out through the loggia.)*

RUFIO: *(full of wrath at seeing his prey escaping)* That means that he is a Republican.

LUCIUS: *(turning defiantly on the loggia steps)* And what are you?

RUFIO: A Caesarian, like all Caesar's soldiers.

CAESAR: *(courteously)* Lucius: believe me, Caesar is no Caesarian. Were Rome a true republic, then were Caesar the first of Republicans. But you have made your choice. Farewell.

LUCIUS: Farewell. Come, Achillas, whilst there is yet time.

(CAESAR, *seeing that* RUFIO's *temper threatens to get the worse of him, puts his hand on his shoulder and brings him down the hall out of harm's way,* BRITANNUS *accompanying them and posting himself on* CAESAR's *right hand. This movement brings the three in a little group to the place occupied by* ACHILLAS, *who moves haughtily away and joins* THEODOTUS *on the other side.* LUCIUS SEPTIMIUS *goes out through the soldiers in the loggia.* POTHINUS, THEODOTUS *and* ACHILLAS *follow him with the courtiers, very mistrustful of the soldiers, who close up in their rear and go out after them, keeping them moving without much ceremony. The* KING *is left in his chair, piteous, obstinate, with twitching face and fingers. During these movements* RUFIO *maintains an energetic grumbling, as follows:* —)

RUFIO: *(as* LUCIUS *departs)* Do you suppose he would let us go if he had our heads in his hands?

CAESAR: I have no right to suppose that his ways are any baser than mine.

RUFIO: Psha!

CAESAR: Rufio: if I take Lucius Septimius for my model, and become exactly like him, ceasing to be Caesar, will you serve me still?

BRITANNUS: Caesar: this is not good sense. Your duty to Rome demands that her enemies should be prevented from doing further mischief. (CAESAR, *whose delight in the moral eye-to-business of his British secretary is inexhaustible, smiles indulgently.)*

RUFIO: It is no use talking to him, Britannus: you may save your breath to cool your porridge. But mark this, Caesar. Clemency is very well for you; but what is it for your soldiers, who have to fight tomorrow the men you spared yesterday? You may give what orders you please; but I tell you that your next victory will be a massacre, thanks to your clemency. I, for one, will take no prisoners. I will kill my enemies in the field; and then you can preach as much clemency as you please: I shall never have to fight them again. And now, with your leave, I will see these gentry off the premises. *(He turns to go.)*

CAESAR: *(turning also and seeing* PTOLEMY*)* What! have they left the boy alone! Oh shame, shame!

RUFIO: *(taking* PTOLEMY's *hand and making him rise)* Come, your majesty!

PTOLEMY: *(To* CAESAR, *drawing away his hand from* RUFIO*)* Is he turning me out of my palace?

RUFIO: *(grimly)* You are welcome to stay if you wish.

CAESAR: *(kindly)* Go, my boy. I will not harm you; but you will be safer away, among your friends. Here you are in the lion's mouth.

PTOLEMY: *(turning to go)* It is not the lion I fear, but *(looking at* RUFIO*)* the jackal. *(He goes out through the loggia.)*

CAESAR: *(laughing approvingly)* Brave boy!

CLEOPATRA: *(jealous of* CAESAR's *approbation, calling after* PTOLEMY) Little silly. You think that very clever.

CAESAR: Britannus: attend the King. Give him in charge to that Pothinus fellow. *(*BRITANNUS *goes out after* PTOLEMY.)

RUFIO: *(pointing to* CLEOPATRA) And this piece of goods? What is to be done with her? However, I suppose I may leave that to you. *(He goes out through the loggia.)*

CLEOPATRA: *(flushing suddenly and turning on* CAESAR) Did you mean me to go with the rest?

CAESAR: *(a little preoccupied, goes with a sigh to* PTOLEMY's *chair, whilst she waits for his answer with red cheeks and clenched fists)* You are free to do just as you please, Cleopatra.

CLEOPATRA: Then you do not care whether I stay or not?

CAESAR: *(smiling)* Of course I had rather you stayed.

CLEOPATRA: Much, much rather?

CAESAR: *(nodding)* Much, much rather.

CLEOPATRA: Then I consent to stay, because I am asked. But I do not want to, mind.

CAESAR: That is quite understood. *(Calling)* Totateeta.

*(*FTATATEETA, *still seated, turns her eyes on him with a sinister expression, but does not move.)*

CLEOPATRA: *(with a splutter of laughter)* Her name is not Totateeta: it is Ftatateeta. *(Calling)* Ftatateeta. *(*FTATATEETA *instantly rises and comes to* CLEOPATRA.)

CAESAR: *(stumbling over the name)* Tfatafeeta will forgive the erring tongue of a Roman. Tota: the Queen will hold her state here in Alexandria. Engage women to attend upon her; and do all that is needful.

FTATATEETA: Am I then the mistress of the Queen's household?

CLEOPATRA: *(sharply)* No: I am the mistress of the Queen's household. Go and do as you are told, or I will have you thrown into the Nile this very afternoon, to poison the poor crocodiles.

CAESAR: *(shocked)* Oh no, no.

CLEOPATRA: Oh yes, yes. You are very sentimental, Caesar; but you are clever; and if you do as I tell you, you will soon learn to govern.

*(*CAESAR, *quite dumbfounded by this impertinence, turns in his chair and stares at her.* FTATATEETA, *smiling grimly, and shewing a splendid set of teeth, goes, leaving them alone together.)*

CAESAR: Cleopatra: I really think I must eat you, after all.

CLEOPATRA: *(kneeling beside him and looking at him with eager interest, half real, half affected to shew how intelligent she is)* You must not talk to me now as if I were a child.

CAESAR: You have been growing up since the sphinx introduced us the other night; and you think you know more than I do already.

CLEOPATRA: *(taken down, and anxious to justify herself)* No: that would be very silly of me: of course I know that. But — *(suddenly)* are you angry with me?

CAESAR: No.

CLEOPATRA: *(only half believing him)* Then why are you so thoughtful?

CAESAR: *(rising)* I have work to do, Cleopatra.

CLEOPATRA: *(drawing back)* Work! *(Offended)* You are tired of talking to me; and that is your excuse to get away from me.

CAESAR: *(sitting down again to appease her)* Well, well: another minute. But then — work!

CLEOPATRA: Work! what nonsense! You must remember that you are a king now: I have made you one. Kings dont work.

CAESAR: Oh! Who told you that, little kitten? Eh?

CLEOPATRA: My father was King of Egypt; and he never worked. But he was a great king, and cut off my sister's head because she rebelled against him and took the throne from him.

CAESAR: Well; and how did he get his throne back again?

CLEOPATRA: *(eagerly, her eyes lighting up)* I will tell you. A beautiful young man, with strong round arms, came over the desert with many horsemen, and slew my sister's husband and gave my father back his throne. *(Wistfully)* I was only twelve then. Oh, I wish he would come again, now that I am a queen. I would make him my husband.

CAESAR: It might be managed, perhaps; for it was I who sent that beautiful young man to help your father.

CLEOPATRA: *(enraptured)* You know him!

CAESAR: *(nodding)* I do.

CLEOPATRA: Has he come with you? *(CAESAR shakes his head: she is cruelly disappointed.)* Oh, I wish he had, I wish he had. If only I were a little older; so that he might not think me a mere kitten, as you do! But perhaps that is because you are old. He is many many years younger than you, is he not?

CAESAR: *(as if swallowing a pill)* He is somewhat younger.

CLEOPATRA: Would he be my husband, do you think, if I asked him?

CAESAR: Very likely.

CLEOPATRA: But I should not like to ask him. Could you not persuade him to ask me — without knowing that I wanted him to?

CAESAR: *(touched by her innocence of the beautiful young man's character)* My poor child!

CLEOPATRA: Why do you say that as if you were sorry for me? Does he love anyone else?

CAESAR: I am afraid so.

CLEOPATRA: *(tearfully)* Then I shall not be his first love.

CAESAR: Not quite the first. He is greatly admired by women.

CLEOPATRA: I wish I could be the first. But if he loves me, I will make him kill all the rest. Tell me: is he still beautiful? Do his strong round arms shine in the sun like marble?

CAESAR: He is in excellent condition — considering how much he eats and drinks.

CLEOPATRA: Oh, you must not say common, earthly things about him; for I love him. He is a god.

CAESAR: He is a great captain of horsemen, and swifter of foot than any other Roman.

CLEOPATRA: What is his real name?

CAESAR: *(puzzled)* His real name?

CLEOPATRA: Yes. I always call him Horus, because Horus is the most beautiful of our gods. But I want to know his real name.

CAESAR: His name is Mark Antony.

CLEOPATRA: *(musically)* Mark Antony, Mark Antony, Mark Antony! What a beautiful name! *(She throws her arms round CAESAR's neck.)* Oh, how I love you for sending him to help my father! Did you love my father very much?

CAESAR: No, my child; but your father, as you say, never worked. I always work. So when he lost his crown he had to promise me 16,000 talents to get it back for him.

CLEOPATRA: Did he ever pay you?

CAESAR: Not in full.

CLEOPATRA: He was quite right: it was too dear. The whole world is not worth 16,000 talents.

CAESAR: That is perhaps true, Cleopatra. Those Egyptians who work paid as much of it as he could drag from them. The rest is still due. But as I most likely shall not get it, I must go back to my work. So you must run away for a little and send my secretary to me.

CLEOPATRA: *(coaxing)* No: I want to stay and hear you talk about Mark Antony.

CAESAR: But if I do not get to work, Pothinus and the rest of them will cut us off from the harbor; and then the way from Rome will be blocked.

CLEOPATRA: No matter: I dont want you to go back to Rome.

CAESAR: But you want Mark Antony to come from it.

CLEOPATRA: *(springing up)* Oh yes, yes, yes: I forgot. Go quickly and work, Caesar; and keep the way over the sea open for my Mark Antony. *(She runs out through the loggia, kissing her hand to Mark Antony across the sea.)*

CAESAR: *(going briskly up the middle of the hall to the loggia steps)* Ho, Britannus. *(He is startled by the entry of a wounded ROMAN SOLDIER, who confronts him from the upper step).* What now?

SOLDIER: *(pointing to his bandaged head)* This, Caesar; and two of my comrades killed in the market place.

CAESAR: *(quiet, but attending)* Ay. Why?

SOLDIER: There is an army come to Alexandria, calling itself the Roman army.

CAESAR: The Roman army of occupation. Ay?

SOLDIER: Commanded by one Achillas.

CAESAR: Well?

SOLDIER: The citizens rose against us when the army entered the gates. I was with two others in the market place when the news came. They set upon us. I cut my way out; and here I am.

CAESAR: Good. I am glad to see you alive. *(RUFIO enters the loggia hastily, passing behind the soldier to look out through one of the arches at the quay beneath.)* Rufio: we are besieged.

RUFIO: What! Already?

CAESAR: Now or tomorrow: what does it matter? We shall be besieged.

(BRITANNUS *runs in.*)

BRITANNUS: Caesar —
CAESAR: *(anticipating him)* Yes: I know. (RUFIO *and* BRITANNUS *come down the hall from the loggia at opposite sides, past* CAESAR, *who waits for a moment near the step to say to the soldier)* Comrade: give the word to turn out on the beach and stand by the boats. Get your wound attended to. Go. *(The* SOLDIER *hurries out.* CAESAR *comes down the hall between* RUFIO *and* BRITANNUS*)* Rufio: we have some ships in the west harbor. Burn them.
RUFIO: *(staring)* Burn them!!
CAESAR: Take every boat we have in the east harbor, and seize the Pharos — that island with the lighthouse. Leave half our men behind to hold the beach and the quay outside this palace: that is the way home.
RUFIO: *(disapproving strongly)* Are we to give up the city?
CAESAR: We have not got it, Rufio. This palace we have; and — what is that building next door?
RUFIO: The theatre.
CAESAR: We will have that too: it commands the strand. For the rest, Egypt for the Egyptians!
RUFIO: Well, you know best, I suppose. Is that all?
CAESAR: That is all. Are those ships burnt yet?
RUFIO: Be easy: I shall waste no more time. *(He runs out.)*
BRITANNUS: Caesar: Pothinus demands speech of you. In my opinion he needs a lesson. His manner is most insolent.
CAESAR: Where is he?
BRITANNUS: He waits without.
CAESAR: Ho there! admit Pothinus.

(POTHINUS *appears in the loggia, and comes down the hall very haughtily to* CAESAR'S *left hand.*)

CAESAR: Well, Pothinus?
POTHINUS: I have brought you our ultimatum, Caesar.
CAESAR: Ultimatum! The door was open: you should have gone out through it before you declared war. You are my prisoner now. *(He goes to the chair and loosens his toga.)*
POTHINUS: *(scornfully)* I your prisoner! Do you know that you are in Alexandria, and that King Ptolemy, with an army outnumbering your little troop a hundred to one, is in possession of Alexandria?
CAESAR: *(unconcernedly taking off his toga and throwing it on the chair)* Well, my friend, get out if you can. And tell your friends not to kill any more Romans in the market place. Otherwise my soldiers, who do not share my celebrated clemency, will probably kill you. Britannus: pass the word to the guard; and fetch my armor. (BRITANNUS *runs out.* RUFIO *returns.*) Well?

RUFIO: *(pointing from the loggia to a cloud of smoke drifting over the harbor)* See there! *(POTHINUS runs eagerly up the steps to look out.)*

CAESAR: What, ablaze already! Impossible!

RUFIO: Yes, five good ships, and a barge laden with oil grappled to each. But it is not my doing: the Egyptians have saved me the trouble. They have captured the west harbor.

CAESAR: *(anxiously)* And the east harbor? The lighthouse, Rufio?

RUFIO: *(with a sudden splutter of raging ill usage, coming down to CAESAR and scolding him)* Can I embark a legion in five minutes? The first cohort is already on the beach. We can do no more. If you want faster work, come and do it yourself.

CAESAR: *(soothing him)* Good, good. Patience, Rufio, patience.

RUFIO: Patience! Who is impatient here, you or I? Would I be here, if I could not oversee them from that balcony?

CAESAR: Forgive me, Rufio; and *(anxiously)* hurry them as much as —

(He is interrupted by an outcry as of an old man in the extremity of misfortune. It draws near rapidly; and THEODOTUS rushes in, tearing his hair, and squeaking the most lamentable exclamations. RUFIO steps back to stare at him, amazed at his frantic condition. POTHINUS turns to listen.)

THEODOTUS: *(on the steps, with uplifted arms)* Horror unspeakable! Woe, alas! Help!

RUFIO: What now?

CAESAR: *(frowning)* Who is slain?

THEODOTUS: Slain! Oh, worse than the death of ten thousand men! Loss irreparable to mankind!

RUFIO: What has happened, man?

THEODOTUS: *(rushing down the hall between them)* The fire has spread from your ships. The first of the seven wonders of the world perishes. The library of Alexandria is in flames.

RUFIO: Psha! *(Quite relieved, he goes up to the loggia and watches the preparations of the troops on the beach.)*

CAESAR: Is that all?

THEODOTUS: *(unable to believe his senses)* All! Caesar: will you go down to posterity as a barbarous soldier too ignorant to know the value of books?

CAESAR: Theodotus: I am an author myself; and I tell you it is better that the Egyptians should live their lives than dream them away with the help of books.

THEODOTUS: *(kneeling, with genuine literary emotion: the passion of the pedant)* Caesar: once in ten generations of men, the world gains an immortal book.

CAESAR: *(inflexible)* If it did not flatter mankind, the common executioner would burn it.

THEODOTUS: Without history, death will lay you beside your meanest soldier.

CAESAR: Death will do that in any case. I ask no better grave.

THEODOTUS: What is burning there is the memory of mankind.

CAESAR: A shameful memory. Let it burn.

THEODOTUS: *(wildly)* Will you destroy the past?

CAESAR: Ay, and build the future with its ruins. *(THEODOTUS, in despair, strikes himself on the temples with his fists.)* But harken, Theodotus, teacher of kings: you who valued Pompey's head no more than a shepherd values an onion, and who now kneel to me, with tears in your old eyes, to plead for a few sheepskins scrawled with errors. I cannot spare you a man or a bucket of water just now; but you shall pass freely out of the palace. Now, away with you to Achillas; and borrow his legions to put out the fire. *(He hurries him to the steps.)*

POTHINUS: *(significantly)* You understand, Theodotus: I remain a prisoner.

THEODOTUS: A prisoner!

CAESAR: Will you stay to talk whilst the memory of mankind is burning? *(Calling through the loggia)* Ho there! Pass Theodotus out. *(To THEODOTUS)* Away with you.

THEODOTUS: *(to POTHINUS)* I must go to save the library. *(He hurries out.)*

CAESAR: Follow him to the gate, Pothinus. Bid him urge your people to kill no more of my soldiers, for your sake.

POTHINUS: My life will cost you dear if you take it, Caesar. *(He goes out after THEODOTUS.)*

(RUFIO, absorbed in watching the embarkation, does not notice the departure of the two Egyptians.)

RUFIO: *(shouting from the loggia to the beach)* All ready, there?

A CENTURION: *(from below)* All ready. We wait for Caesar.

CAESAR: Tell them Caesar is coming — the rogues! *(Calling)* Britannicus. *(This magniloquent version of his secretary's name is one of CAESAR's jokes. In later years it would have meant, quite seriously and officially, Conqueror of Britain.)*

RUFIO: *(calling down)* Push off, all except the longboat. Stand by it to embark, Caesar's guard there. *(He leaves the balcony and comes down into the hall.)* Where are those Egyptians? Is this more clemency? Have you let them go?

CAESAR: *(chuckling)* I have let Theodotus go to save the library. We must respect literature, Rufio.

RUFIO: *(raging)* Folly on folly's head! I believe if you could bring back all the dead of Spain, Gaul, and Thessaly to life, you would do it that we might have the trouble of fighting them over again.

CAESAR: Might not the gods destroy the world if their only thought were to be at peace next year? *(RUFIO, out of all patience, turns away in anger. CAESAR suddenly grips his sleeve, and adds slyly in his ear)* Besides, my friend: every Egyptian we imprison means imprisoning two Roman soldiers to guard him. Eh?

RUFIO: Agh! I might have known there was some fox's trick behind your fine talking. *(He gets away from CAESAR with an ill-humored shrug, and goes to the balcony for another look at the preparations; finally goes out.)*

CAESAR: Is Britannus asleep? I sent him for my armor an hour ago. *(Calling)* Britannicus, thou British islander. Britannicus!

(CLEOPATRA *runs in through the loggia with* CAESAR's *helmet and sword, snatched from* BRITANNUS, *who follows her with a cuirass and greaves. They come down to* CAESAR, *she to his left hand,* BRITANNUS *to his right.*)

CLEOPATRA: I am going to dress you, Caesar. Sit down. (*He obeys.*) These Roman helmets are so becoming! (*She takes off his wreath.*) Oh! (*She bursts out laughing at him.*)

CAESAR: What are you laughing at?

CLEOPATRA: Youre bald (*beginning with a big B, and ending with a splutter*).

CAESAR: (*almost annoyed*) Cleopatra! (*He rises, for the convenience of* BRITANNUS, *who puts the cuirass on him.*)

CLEOPATRA: So that is why you wear the wreath — to hide it.

BRITANNUS: Peace, Egyptian: they are the bays of the conqueror. (*He buckles the cuirass.*)

CLEOPATRA: Peace, thou: islander! (*To* CAESAR) You should rub your head with strong spirits of sugar, Caesar. That will make it grow.

CAESAR: (*with a wry face*) Cleopatra: do you like to be reminded that you are very young?

CLEOPATRA: (*pouting*) No.

CAESAR: (*sitting down again, and setting out his leg for* BRITANNUS, *who kneels to put on his greaves.*) Neither do I like to be reminded that I am — middle aged. Let me give you ten of my superfluous years. That will make you 26, and leave me only — no matter. Is it a bargain?

CLEOPATRA: Agreed. 26, mind. (*She puts the helmet on him.*) Oh! How nice! You look only about 50 in it!

BRITANNUS: (*looking up severely at* CLEOPATRA) You must not speak in this manner to Caesar.

CLEOPATRA: Is it true that when Caesar caught you on that island, you were painted all over blue?

BRITANNUS: Blue is the color worn by all Britons of good standing. In war we stain our bodies blue; so that though our enemies may strip us of our clothes and our lives, they cannot strip us of our respectability. (*He rises.*)

CLEOPATRA: (*with* CAESAR's *sword*) Let me hang this on. Now you look splendid. Have they made any statues of you in Rome?

CAESAR: Yes, many statues.

CLEOPATRA: You must send for one and give it to me.

RUFIO: (*coming back into the loggia, more impatient than ever*) Now Caesar: have you done talking? The moment your foot is aboard there will be no holding our men back: the boats will race one another for the lighthouse.

CAESAR: (*drawing his sword and trying the edge*) Is this well set today, Britannicus? At Pharsalia it was as blunt as a barrel-hoop.

BRITANNUS: It will split one of the Egyptian's hairs today, Caesar. I have set it myself.

CLEOPATRA: (*suddenly throwing her arms in terror round* CAESAR) Oh, you are not really going into battle to be killed?

CAESAR: No, Cleopatra. No man goes to battle to be killed.

CLEOPATRA: But they do get killed. My sister's husband was killed in battle. You must not go. Let him go *(pointing to* RUFIO. *They all laugh at her.)* Oh please, please dont go. What will happen to me if you never come back?

CAESAR: *(gravely)* Are you afraid?

CLEOPATRA: *(shrinking)* No.

CAESAR: *(with quiet authority)* Go to the balcony; and you shall see us take the Pharos. You must learn to look on battles. Go. *(She goes, downcast, and looks out from the balcony.)* That is well. Now, Rufio. March.

CLEOPATRA: *(suddenly clapping her hands)* Oh, you will not be able to go!

CAESAR: Why? What now?

CLEOPATRA: They are drying up the harbor with buckets — a multitude of soldiers — over there *(pointing out across the sea to her left)* — they are dipping up the water.

RUFIO: *(hastening to look)* It is true. The Egyptian army! Crawling over the edge of the west harbor like locusts. *(With sudden anger he strides down to* CAESAR.*)* This is your accursed clemency, Caesar. Theodotus has brought them.

CAESAR: *(delighted at his own cleverness)* I meant him to, Rufio. They have come to put out the fire. The library will keep them busy whilst we seize the lighthouse. Eh? *(He rushes out buoyantly through the loggia, followed by* BRITANNUS.*)*

RUFIO: *(disgustedly)* More foxing! Agh! *(He rushes off. A shout from the soldiers announces the appearance of* CAESAR *below).*

CENTURION: *(below)* All aboard. Give way there. *(Another shout).*

CLEOPATRA: *(waving her scarf through the loggia arch)* Goodbye, goodbye, dear Caesar. Come back safe. Goodbye!

ACT THREE

The edge of the quay in front of the palace, looking out west over the east harbor of Alexandria to Pharos island, just off the end of which, and connected with it by a narrow mole, is the famous lighthouse, a gigantic square tower of white marble diminishing in size storey by storey to the top, on which stands a cresset beacon. The island is joined to the main land by the Heptastadium, a great mole or causeway five miles long bounding the harbor on the south.

In the middle of the quay a ROMAN SENTINEL *stands on guard, pilum in hand, looking out to the lighthouse with strained attention, his left hand shading his eyes. The pilum is a stout wooden shaft 4½ feet long, with an iron spit about three feet long fixed in it. The* SENTINEL *is so absorbed that he does not notice the approach from the north end of the quay of four Egyptian* MARKET PORTERS *carrying rolls of carpet, preceded by* FTATATEETA *and* APOLLODORUS *the Sicilian.* APOLLODORUS *is a dashing young man of about 24, handsome and debonair, dressed with deliberate aestheticism in the most delicate purples and dove greys, with ornaments of bronze, oxydized silver, and stones of jade and agate. His sword, designed as carefully as a medieval cross, has a blued blade shewing through an openwork scabbard of purple leather and filigree. The* PORTERS, *conducted by* FTATATEETA, *pass along the quay behind the sentinel to the steps of the palace, where they put down their bales and squat on the ground.*

APOLLODORUS *does not pass along with them: he halts, amused by the preoccupation of the* SENTINEL.

APOLLODORUS: *(calling to the* SENTINEL*)* Who goes there, eh?

SENTINEL: *(starting violently and turning with his pilum at the charge, revealing himself as a small, wiry, sandy-haired, conscientious young man with an elderly face)* Whats this? Stand. Who are you?

APOLLODORUS: I am Apollodorus the Sicilian. Why, man, what are you dreaming of? Since I came through the lines beyond the theatre there, I have brought my caravan past three sentinels, all so busy staring at the lighthouse that not one of them challenged me. Is this Roman discipline?

SENTINEL: We are not here to watch the land but the sea. Caesar has just landed on the Pharos. *(Looking at* FTATATEETA*)* What have you here? Who is this piece of Egyptian crockery?

FTATATEETA: Apollodorus: rebuke this Roman dog; and bid him bridle his tongue in the presence of Ftatateeta, the mistress of the Queen's household.

APOLLODORUS: My friend: this is a great lady, who stands high with Caesar.

SENTINEL: *(not at all impressed, pointing to the carpets)* And what is all this truck?

APOLLODORUS: Carpets for the furnishing of the Queen's apartments in the palace. I have picked them from the best carpets in the world; and the Queen shall choose the best of my choosing.

SENTINEL: So you are the carpet merchant?

APOLLODORUS: *(hurt)* My friend: I am a patrician.

SENTINEL: A patrician! A patrician keeping a shop instead of following arms!

APOLLODORUS: I do not keep a shop. Mine is a temple of the arts. I am a worshipper of beauty. My calling is to choose beautiful things for beautiful queens. My motto is Art for Art's sake.

SENTINEL: That is not the password.

APOLLODORUS: It is a universal password.

SENTINEL: I know nothing about universal passwords. Either give me the password for the day or get back to your shop.

(FTATATEETA, *roused by his hostile tone, steals towards the edge of the quay with the step of a panther, and gets behind him.)*

APOLLODORUS: How if I do neither?

SENTINEL: Then I will drive this pilum through you.

APOLLODORUS: At your service, my friend. *(He draws his sword, and springs to his guard with unruffled grace.)*

FTATATEETA: *(suddenly seizing the* SENTINEL'S *arms from behind)* Thrust your knife into the dog's throat, Apollodorus. *(The chivalrous* APOLLODORUS *laughingly shakes his head; breaks ground away from the* SENTINEL *towards the palace; and lowers his point.)*

SENTINEL: *(struggling vainly)* Curse on you! Let me go. Help ho!

FTATATEETA: *(lifting him from the ground)* Stab the little Roman reptile. Spit him on your sword.

(A couple of Roman SOLDIERS, *with a* CENTURION, *come running along the edge of the quay from the north end. They rescue their comrade, and throw off* FTATATEETA, *who is sent reeling away on the left hand of the* SENTINEL.*)*

CENTURION: *(an unattractive man of fifty, short in his speech and manners, with a vine-wood cudgel in his hand)* How now? What is all this?

FTATATEETA: *(to* APOLLODORUS*)* Why did you not stab him? There was time!

APOLLODORUS: Centurion: I am here by order of the Queen to —

CENTURION: *(interrupting him)* The Queen! Yes, yes: *(to the sentinel)* pass him in. Pass all these bazaar people in to the Queen, with their goods. But mind you pass no one out that you have not passed in — not even the Queen herself.

SENTINEL: This old woman is dangerous: she is as strong as three men. She wanted the merchant to stab me.

APOLLODORUS: Centurion: I am not a merchant. I am a patrician and a votary of art.

CENTURION: Is the woman your wife?

APOLLODORUS: *(horrified)* No, no! *(Correcting himself politely)* Not that the lady is not a striking figure in her own way. But *(emphatically)* she is not my wife.

FTATATEETA: *(to the* CENTURION*)* Roman: I am Ftatateeta, the mistress of the Queen's household.

CENTURION: Keep your hands off our men, mistress; or I will have you pitched into the harbor, though you were as strong as ten men. *(To his men)* To your posts: march! *(He returns with his men the way they came.)*

FTATATEETA: *(looking malignantly after him)* We shall see whom Isis[1] loves best: her servant Ftatateeta or a dog of a Roman.

SENTINEL: *(to* APOLLODORUS, *with a wave of his pilum towards the palace)* Pass in there; and keep your distance. *(Turning to* FTATATEETA*)* Come within a yard of me, you old crocodile; and I will give you this *(the pilum)* in your jaws.

CLEOPATRA: *(calling from the palace)* Ftatateeta, Ftatateeta.

FTATATEETA: *(looking up, scandalized)* Go from the window, go from the window. There are men here.

CLEOPATRA: I am coming down.

FTATATEETA: *(distracted)* No, no. What are you dreaming of? O ye gods, ye gods! Apollodorus: bid your men pick up your bales; and in with me quickly.

APOLLODORUS: Obey the mistress of the Queen's household.

FTATATEETA: *(impatiently, as the* PORTERS *stoop to lift the bales)* Quick, quick: she will be out upon us. *(*CLEOPATRA *comes from the palace and runs across the quay to* FTATATEETA.*)* Oh that ever I was born!

CLEOPATRA: *(eagerly)* Ftatateeta: I have thought of something. I want a boat — at once.

FTATATEETA: A boat! No, no: you cannot. Apollodorus: speak to the Queen.

APOLLODORUS: *(gallantly)* Beautiful queen: I am Apollodorus the Sicilian, your servant, from the bazaar. I have brought you the three most beautiful Persian carpets in the world to choose from.

---

1 *wife and queen of Osiris, she was a deity with knowledge of everything that happened on earth and in heaven.*

CLEOPATRA: I have no time for carpets today. Get me a boat.

FTATATEETA: What whim is this? You cannot go on the water except in the royal barge.

APOLLODORUS: Royalty, Ftatateeta, lies not in the barge but in the Queen. *(To* CLEOPATRA*)* The touch of your majesty's foot on the gunwhale of the meanest boat in the harbor will make it royal. *(He turns to the harbor and calls seaward)* Ho there, boatman! Pull in to the steps.

CLEOPATRA: Apollodorus: you are my perfect knight; and I will always buy my carpets through you. *(*APOLLODORUS *bows joyously. An oar appears above the quay; and the* BOATMAN, *a bullet-headed, vivacious, grinning fellow, burnt almost black by the sun, comes up a flight of steps from the water on the* SENTINEL's *right, oar in hand, and waits at the top.)* Can you row, Apollodorus?

APOLLODORUS: My oars shall be your majesty's wings. Whither shall I row my Queen?

CLEOPATRA: To the lighthouse. Come. *(She makes for the steps.)*

SENTINEL: *(opposing her with his pilum at the charge)* Stand. You cannot pass.

CLEOPATRA: *(flushing angrily)* How dare you? Do you know that I am the Queen?

SENTINEL: I have my orders. You cannot pass.

CLEOPATRA: I will make Caesar have you killed if you do not obey me.

SENTINEL: He will do worse to me if I disobey my officer. Stand back.

CLEOPATRA: Ftatateeta: strangle him.

SENTINEL: *(alarmed — looking apprehensively at* FTATATEETA, *and brandishing his pilum)* Keep off, there.

CLEOPATRA: *(running to* APOLLODORUS*)* Apollodorus: make your slaves help us.

APOLLODORUS: I shall not need their help, lady. *(He draws his sword.)* Now, soldier: choose which weapon you will defend yourself with. Shall it be sword against pilum, or sword against sword?

SENTINEL: Roman against Sicilian, curse you. Take that. *(He hurls his pilum at* APOLLODORUS, *who drops expertly on one knee. The pilum passes whizzing over his head and falls harmless.* APOLLODORUS, *with a cry of triumph, springs up and attacks the* SENTINEL, *who draws his sword and defends himself, crying)* Ho there, guard. Help!

*(*CLEOPATRA, *half frightened, half delighted, takes refuge near the palace, where the* PORTERS *are squatting among the bales. The* BOATMAN, *alarmed, hurries down the steps out of harm's way, but stops, with his head just visible above the edge of the quay, to watch the fight. The* SENTINEL *is handicapped by his fear of an attack in the rear from* FTATATEETA. *His swordsmanship, which is of a rough and ready sort, is heavily taxed, as he has occasionally to strike at her to keep her off between a blow and a guard with* APOLLODORUS. *The* CENTURION *returns with several* SOLDIERS. APOLLODORUS *springs back towards* CLEOPATRA *as this reinforcement confronts him.)*

CENTURION: *(coming to the* SENTINEL's *right hand)* What is this? What now?

SENTINEL: *(panting)* I could do well enough by myself if it werent for the old woman. Keep her off me: that is all the help I need.

CENTURION: Make your report, soldier. What has happened?

FTATATEETA: Centurion: he would have slain the Queen.

SENTINEL: *(bluntly)* I would, sooner than let her pass. She wanted to take boat, and go — so she said — to the lighthouse. I stopped her, as I was ordered to; and she set this fellow on me. *(He goes to pick up his pilum and returns to his place with it.)*

CENTURION: *(turning to* CLEOPATRA*)* Cleopatra: I am loth to offend you; but without Caesar's express order we dare not let you pass beyond the Roman lines.

APOLLODORUS: Well, Centurion; and has not the lighthouse been within the Roman lines since Caesar landed there?

CLEOPATRA: Yes, yes. Answer that, if you can.

CENTURION: *(to* APOLLODORUS*)* As for you, Apollodorus, you may thank the gods that you are not nailed to the palace door with a pilum for your meddling.

APOLLODORUS: *(urbanely)* My military friend, I was not born to be slain by so ugly a weapon. When I fall, it will be *(holding up his sword)* by this white queen of arms, the only weapon fit for an artist. And now that you are convinced that we do not want to go beyond the lines, let me finish killing your sentinel and depart with the Queen.

CENTURION: *(as the* SENTINEL *makes an angry demonstration)* Peace there, Cleopatra: I must abide by my orders, and not by the subtleties of this Sicilian. You must withdraw into the palace and examine your carpets there.

CLEOPATRA: *(pouting)* I will not: I am the Queen. Caesar does not speak to me as you do. Have Caesar's centurions changed manners with his scullions?

CENTURION: *(sulkily)* I do my duty. That is enough for me.

APOLLODORUS: Majesty: when a stupid man is doing something he is ashamed of, he always declares that it is his duty.

CENTURION: *(angry)* Apollodorus —

APOLLODORUS: *(interrupting him with defiant elegance)* I will make amends for that insult with my sword at fitting time and place. Who says artist, says duellist. *(To* CLEOPATRA*)* Hear my counsel, star of the east. Until word comes to these soldiers from Caesar himself, you are a prisoner. Let me go to him with a message from you, and a present; and before the sun has stooped half way to the arms of the sea, I will bring you back Caesar's order of release.

CENTURION: *(sneering at him)* And you will sell the Queen the present, no doubt.

APOLLODORUS: Centurion: the Queen shall have from me, without payment, as the unforced tribute of Sicilian taste to Egyptian beauty, the richest of these carpets for her present to Caesar.

CLEOPATRA: *(exultantly, to the* CENTURION*)* Now you see what an ignorant common creature you are!

CENTURION: *(curtly)* Well, a fool and his wares are soon parted. *(He turns to his men)* Two more men to this post here; and see that no one leaves the palace but this man and his merchandize. If he draws his sword again inside the lines, kill him. To your posts. March.

(He goes out, leaving two AUXILIARY SENTINELS *with the other.)*

APOLLODORUS: *(with polite goodfellowship)* My friends: will you not enter the palace and bury our quarrel in a bowl of wine? *(He takes out his purse, jingling the coins in it).* The Queen has presents for you all.

SENTINEL: *(very sulky)* You heard our orders. Get about your business.

FIRST AUXILIARY: Yes: you ought to know better. Off with you.

SECOND AUXILIARY: *(looking longingly at the purse — this sentinel is a hooknosed man, unlike his comrade, who is squab faced)* Do not tantalize a poor man.

APOLLODORUS: *(to* CLEOPATRA*)* Pearl of Queens: the centurion is at hand; and the Roman soldier is incorruptible when his officer is looking. I must carry your word to Caesar.

CLEOPATRA: *(who has been meditating among the carpets)* Are these carpets very heavy?

APOLLODORUS: It matters not how heavy. There are plenty of porters.

CLEOPATRA: How do they put the carpets into boats? Do they throw them down?

APOLLODORUS: Not into small boats, majesty. It would sink them.

CLEOPATRA: Not into that man's boat, for instance? *(pointing to the* BOATMAN*).*

APOLLODORUS: No. Too small.

CLEOPATRA: But you can take a carpet to Caesar in it if I send one?

APOLLODORUS: Assuredly.

CLEOPATRA: And will you have it carried gently down the steps and take great care of it?

APOLLODORUS: Depend on me.

CLEOPATRA: Great, great care?

APOLLODORUS: More than of my own body.

CLEOPATRA: You will promise me not to let the porters drop it or throw it about?

APOLLODORUS: Place the most delicate glass goblet in the palace in the heart of the roll, Queen; and if it be broken, my head shall pay for it.

CLEOPATRA: Good. Come, Ftatateeta. *(*FTATATEETA *comes to her.* APOLLODORUS *offers to squire them into the palace).* No, Apollodorus, you must not come. I will choose a carpet for myself. You must wait here. *(She runs into the palace.)*

APOLLODORUS: *(to the* PORTERS*)* Follow this lady *(indicating* FTATATEETA*)* and obey her.

(The PORTERS *rise and take up their bales.)*

FTATATEETA: *(addressing the* PORTERS *as if they were vermin)* This way. And take your shoes off before you put your feet on those stairs.

(She goes in, followed by the PORTERS *with the carpets. Meanwhile* APOLLODORUS *goes to the edge of the quay and looks out over the harbor. The* SENTINELS *keep their eyes on him malignantly.)*

APOLLODORUS: *(addressing the* SENTINEL*)* My friend —

SENTINEL: *(rudely)* Silence there.

FIRST AUXILIARY: Shut your muzzle, you.

SECOND AUXILIARY: *(in a half whisper, glancing apprehensively towards the north end of the quay)* Cant you wait a bit?

APOLLODORUS: Patience, worthy three-headed donkey. *(They mutter ferociously; but he is not at all intimidated.)* Listen: were you set here to watch me, or to watch the Egyptians?

SENTINEL: We know our duty.

APOLLODORUS: Then why dont you do it? There is something going on over there *(pointing southwestward to the mole).*

SENTINEL: *(sulkily)* I do not need to be told what to do by the like of you.

APOLLODORUS: Blockhead. *(He begins shouting)* Ho there, Centurion. Hoiho!

SENTINEL: Curse your meddling. *(Shouting)* Hoiho! Alarm! Alarm!

FIRST AND SECOND AUXILIARIES: Alarm! alarm! Hoiho!

(The CENTURION comes running in with his guard.)

CENTURION: What now? Has the old woman attacked you again? *(Seeing APOLLODORUS)* Are you here still?

APOLLODORUS: *(pointing as before)* See there. The Egyptians are moving. They are going to recapture the Pharos. They will attack by sea and land: by land along the great mole; by sea from the west harbor. Stir yourselves, my military friends: the hunt is up. *(A clangor of trumpets from several points along the quay.)* Aha! I told you so.

CENTURION: *(quickly)* The two extra men pass the alarm to the south posts. One man keep guard here. The rest with me — quick.

(The two AUXILIARY SENTINELS run off to the south. The CENTURION and his guard run off northward; and immediately afterwards the bucina sounds. The four PORTERS come from the palace carrying a carpet, followed by FTATATEETA.)

SENTINEL: *(handling his pilum apprehensively)* You again! *(The PORTERS stop.)*

FTATATEETA: Peace, Roman fellow: you are now single-handed. Apollodorus: this carpet is Cleopatra's present to Caesar. It has rolled up in it ten precious goblets of the thinnest Iberian crystal, and a hundred eggs of the sacred blue pigeon. On your honor, let none of them be broken.

APOLLODORUS: On my head be it! *(To the PORTERS)* Into the boat with them carefully.

(The PORTERS carry the carpet to the steps.)

FIRST PORTER: *(looking down at the boat)* Beware what you do, sir. Those eggs of which the lady speaks must weigh more than a pound apiece. This boat is too small for such a load.

BOATMAN: *(excitedly rushing up the steps)* Oh thou injurious porter! Oh thou unnatural son of a she-camel! *(To APOLLODORUS)* My boat, sir, hath often carried five men. Shall it not carry your lordship and a bale of pigeon's eggs? *(To the* PORTER*)* Thou mangey dromedary, the gods shall punish thee for this envious wickedness.

FIRST PORTER: *(stolidly)* I cannot quit this bale now to beat thee; but another day I will lie in wait for thee.

APOLLODORUS: *(going between them)* Peace there. If the boat were but a single plank, I would get to Caesar on it.

FTATATEETA: *(anxiously)* In the name of the gods, Apollodorus, run no risks with that bale.

APOLLODORUS: Fear not, thou venerable grotesque: I guess its great worth. *(To the* PORTERS*)* Down with it, I say; and gently; or ye shall eat nothing but stick for ten days.

(The BOATMAN *goes down the steps, followed by the* PORTERS *with the bale:* FTATATEETA *and* APOLLODORUS *watching from the edge.)*

APOLLODORUS: Gently, my sons, my children — *(with sudden alarm)* gently, ye dogs. Lay it level in the stern — so — tis well.

FTATATEETA: *(screaming down at one of the* PORTERS*)* Do not step on it, do not step on it. Oh thou brute beast!

FIRST PORTER: *(ascending)* Be not excited, mistress: all is well.

FTATATEETA: *(panting)* All well! Oh, thou hast given my heart a turn! *(She clutches her side, gasping.)*

(The four PORTERS *have now come up and are waiting at the stairhead to be paid.)*

APOLLODORUS: Here, ye hungry ones.

(He gives money to the first PORTER, *who holds it in his hand to shew to the others. They crowd greedily to see how much it is, quite prepared, after the Eastern fashion, to protest to heaven against their patron's stinginess. But his liberality overpowers them.)*

FIRST PORTER: O bounteous prince!

SECOND PORTER: O lord of the bazaar!

THIRD PORTER: O favored of the gods!

FOURTH PORTER: O father to all the porters of the market!

SENTINEL: *(enviously, threatening them fiercely with his pilum)* Hence, dogs: off. Out of this. *(They fly before him northward along the quay.)*

APOLLODORUS: Farewell, Ftatateeta. I shall be at the lighthouse before the Egyptians. *(He descends the steps.)*

FTATATEETA: The gods speed thee and protect my nursling!

(The SENTRY *returns from chasing the* PORTERS *and looks down at the boat, standing near the stairhead lest* FTATATEETA *should attempt to escape.)*

APOLLODORUS: *(from beneath, as the boat moves off)* Farewell, valiant pilum pitcher.

SENTINEL: Farewell, shopkeeper.

APOLLODORUS: Ha, ha! Pull, thou brave boatman, pull. Soho-o-o-o-o! *(He begins to sing in barcarolle² measure to the rhythm of the oars)*

> My heart, my heart, spread out thy wings:
> Shake off thy heavy load of love —

Give me the oars, O son of a snail.

SENTINEL: *(threatening* FTATATEETA*)* Now mistress: back to your henhouse. In with you.

FTATATEETA: *(falling on her knees and stretching her hands over the waters)* Gods of the seas, bear her safely to the shore!

SENTINEL: Bear who safely? What do you mean?

FTATATEETA: *(looking darkly at him)* Gods of Egypt and of Vengeance, let this Roman fool be beaten like a dog by his captain for suffering her to be taken over the waters.

SENTINEL: Accursed one: is she then in the boat? *(He calls over the sea)* Hoiho, there, boatman! Hoiho!

APOLLODORUS: *(singing in the distance)*

> My heart, my heart, be whole and free:
> Love is thine only enemy.

(Meanwhile RUFIO, *the morning's fighting done, sits munching dates on a faggot of brushwood outside the door of the lighthouse, which towers gigantic to the clouds on his left. His helmet, full of dates, is between his knees; and a leathern bottle of wine is by his side. Behind him the great stone pedestal of the lighthouse is shut in from the open sea by a low stone parapet, with a couple of steps in the middle to the broad coping. A huge chain with a hook hangs down from the lighthouse crane above his head. Faggots like the one he sits on lie beneath it ready to be drawn up to feed the beacon.*

CAESAR is standing on the step at the parapet looking out anxiously, evidently ill at ease. BRITANNUS *comes out of the lighthouse door.)*

RUFIO: Well, my British islander. Have you been up to the top?

BRITANNUS: I have. I reckon it at 200 feet high.

RUFIO: Anybody up there?

BRITANNUS: One elderly Tyrian³ to work the crane; and his son, a well conducted youth of 14.

RUFIO: *(looking at the chain)* What! An old man and a boy work that! Twenty men, you mean.

BRITANNUS: Two only, I assure you. They have counterweights, and a machine with boiling water in it which I do not understand: it is not of British design. They use it to haul up barrels of oil and faggots to burn in the brazier on the roof.

---

2 *musical rhythm based on songs of Venetian gondoliers.*
3 *citizen of Tyre, a seaport in Phoenicia (now Lebanon).*

RUFIO: But —

BRITANNUS: Excuse me: I came down because there are messengers coming along the mole to us from the island. I must see what their business is. *(He hurries out past the lighthouse.)*

CAESAR: *(coming away from the parapet, shivering and out of sorts)* Rufio: this has been a mad expedition. We shall be beaten. I wish I knew how our men are getting on with that barricade across the great mole.

RUFIO: *(angrily)* Must I leave my food and go starving to bring you a report?

CAESAR: *(soothing him nervously)* No, Rufio, no. Eat, my son, eat. *(He takes another turn,* RUFIO *chewing dates meanwhile.)* The Egyptians cannot be such fools as not to storm the barricade and swoop down on us here before it is finished. It is the first time I have ever run an avoidable risk. I should not have come to Egypt.

RUFIO: An hour ago you were all for victory.

CAESAR: *(apologetically)* Yes: I was a fool — rash, Rufio — boyish.

RUFIO: Boyish! Not a bit of it. Here *(offering him a handful of dates)*.

CAESAR: What are these for?

RUFIO: To eat. Thats whats the matter with you. When a man comes to your age, he runs down before his midday meal. Eat and drink; and then have another look at our chances.

CAESAR: *(taking the dates)* My age! *(He shakes his head and bites a date.)* Yes, Rufio: I am an old man — worn out now — true, quite true. *(He gives way to melancholy contemplation, and eats another date.)* Achillas is still in his prime: Ptolemy is a boy. *(He eats another date, and plucks up a little.)* Well, every dog has his day; and I have had mine: I cannot complain. *(With sudden cheerfulness)* These dates are not bad, Rufio. *(*BRITANNUS *returns, greatly excited, with a leathern bag.* CAESAR *is himself again in a moment.)* What now?

BRITANNUS: *(triumphantly)* Our brave Rhodian[4] mariners have captured a treasure. There! *(He throws the bag down at* CAESAR's *feet.)* Our enemies are delivered into our hands.

CAESAR: In that bag?

BRITANNUS: Wait till you hear, Caesar. This bag contains all the letters which have passed between Pompey's party and the army of occupation here.

CAESAR: Well?

BRITANNUS: *(impatient of* CAESAR's *slowness to grasp the situation)* Well, we shall now know who your foes are. The name of every man who has plotted against you since you crossed the Rubicon[5] may be in these papers, for all we know.

CAESAR: Put them in the fire.

BRITANNUS: Put them — *(he gasps)!!!!*

CAESAR: In the fire. Would you have me waste the next three years of my life in proscribing and condemning men who will be my friends when I have proved that my friendship is worth more than Pompey's was — than Cato's is. O incorrigible British islander: am I a bull dog, to seek quarrels merely to shew how stubborn my jaws are?

BRITANNUS: But your honor — the honor of Rome —

---

4 *from Rhodes, an island in the Aegian sea near Turkey.*

5 *a stream in northern Italy. By crossing it, Caesar committed himself to war against Pompey and the Roman Senate.*

CAESAR: I do not make human sacrifices to my honor, as your Druids do. Since you will not burn these, at least I can drown them. *(He picks up the bag and throws it over the parapet into the sea.)*

BRITANNUS: Caesar: this is mere eccentricity. Are traitors to be allowed to go free for the sake of a paradox?

RUFIO: *(rising)* Caesar: when the islander has finished preaching, call me again. I am going to have a look at the boiling water machine. *(He goes into the lighthouse.)*

BRITANNUS: *(with genuine feeling)* O Caesar, my great master, if I could but persuade you to regard life seriously, as men do in my country!

CAESAR: Do they truly do so, Britannus?

BRITANNUS: Have you not been there? Have you not seen them? What Briton speaks as you do in your moments of levity? What Briton neglects to attend the services at the sacred grove? What Briton wears clothes of many colors as you do, instead of plain blue, as all solid, well esteemed men should? These are moral questions with us.

CAESAR: Well, well, my friend: some day I shall settle down and have a blue toga, perhaps. Meanwhile, I must get on as best I can in my flippant Roman way. *(APOLLODORUS comes past the lighthouse.)* What now?

BRITANNUS: *(turning quickly, and challenging the stranger with official haughtiness)* What is this? Who are you? How did you come here?

APOLLODORUS: Calm yourself, my friend: I am not going to eat you. I have come by boat, from Alexandria, with precious gifts for Caesar.

CAESAR: From Alexandria!

BRITANNUS: *(severely)* That is Caesar, sir.

RUFIO: *(appearing at the lighthouse door)* Whats the matter now?

APOLLODORUS: Hail, great Caesar! I am Apollodorus the Sicilian, an artist.

BRITANNUS: An artist! Why have they admitted this vagabond?

CAESAR: Peace, man. Apollodorus is a famous patrician amateur.

BRITANNUS: *(disconcerted)* I crave the gentleman's pardon. *(To* CAESAR*)* I understood him to say that he was a professional. *(Somewhat out of countenance, he allows* APOLLODORUS *to approach* CAESAR, *changing places with him.* RUFIO, *after looking* APOLLODORUS *up and down with marked disparagement, goes to the other side of the platform.)*

CAESAR: You are welcome, Apollodorus. What is your business?

APOLLODORUS: First, to deliver to you a present from the Queen of Queens.

CAESAR: Who is that?

APOLLODORUS: Cleopatra of Egypt.

CAESAR: *(taking him into his confidence in his most winning manner)* Apollodorus: this is no time for playing with presents. Pray you, go back to the Queen, and tell her that if all goes well I shall return to the palace this evening.

APOLLODORUS: Caesar: I cannot return. As I approached the lighthouse, some fool threw a great leathern bag into the sea. It broke the nose of my boat; and I had hardly time to get myself and my charge to the shore before the poor little cockleshell sank.

CAESAR: I am sorry, Apollodorus. The fool shall be rebuked. Well, well: what have you brought me? The Queen will be hurt if I do not look at it.

RUFIO: Have we time to waste on this trumpery? The Queen is only a child.

CAESAR: Just so: that is why we must not disappoint her. What is the present, Apollodorus?

APOLLODORUS: Caesar: it is a Persian carpet — a beauty! And in it are — so I am told — pigeons' eggs and crystal goblets and fragile precious things. I dare not for my head have it carried up that narrow ladder from the causeway.

RUFIO: Swing it up by the crane, then. We will send the eggs to the cook, drink our wine from the goblets; and the carpet will make a bed for Caesar.

APOLLODORUS: The crane! Caesar: I have sworn to tender this bale of carpet as I tender my own life.

CAESAR: (cheerfully) Then let them swing you up at the same time; and if the chain breaks, you and the pigeons' eggs will perish together. (He goes to the chain and looks up along it, examining it curiously.)

APOLLODORUS: (to BRITANNUS) Is Caesar serious?

BRITANNUS: His manner is frivolous because he is an Italian; but he means what he says.

APOLLODORUS: Serious or not, he spake well. Give me a squad of soldiers to work the crane.

BRITANNUS: Leave the crane to me. Go and await the descent of the chain.

APOLLODORUS: Good. You will presently see me there (turning to them all and pointing with an eloquent gesture to the sky above the parapet) rising like the sun with my treasure.

(He goes back the way he came. BRITANNUS goes into the lighthouse.)

RUFIO: (ill-humoredly) Are you really going to wait here for this foolery, Caesar?

CAESAR: (backing away from the crane as it gives signs of working) Why not?

RUFIO: The Egyptians will let you know why not if they have the sense to make a rush from the shore end of the mole before our barricade is finished. And here we are waiting like children to see a carpet full of pigeons' eggs.

(The chain rattles, and is drawn up high enough to clear the parapet. It then swings round out of sight behind the lighthouse.)

CAESAR: Fear not, my son Rufio. When the first Egyptian takes his first step along the mole, the alarm will sound; and we two will reach the barricade from our end before the Egyptians reach it from their end — we two, Rufio: I, the old man, and you, his biggest boy. And the old man will be there first. So peace; and give me some more dates.

APOLLODORUS: (from the causeway below) Soho, haul away. So-ho-o-o-o! (The chain is drawn up and comes round again from behind the lighthouse. APOLLODORUS is swinging in the air with his bale of carpet at the end of it. He breaks into song as he soars above the parapet)

Aloft, aloft, behold the blue
That never shone in woman's eyes —

Easy there: stop her. *(He ceases to rise.)* Further round! *(The chain comes forward above the platform.)*
RUFIO: *(calling up)* Lower away there. *(The chain and its load begin to descend.)*
APOLLODORUS: *(calling up)* Gently — slowly — mind the eggs.
RUFIO: *(calling up)* Easy there — slowly — slowly.

(APOLLODORUS and the bale are deposited safely on the flags in the middle of the platform. RUFIO and CAESAR help APOLLODORUS to cast off the chain from the bale.)

RUFIO: Haul up.

(The chain rises clear of their heads with a rattle. BRITANNUS comes from the lighthouse and helps them to uncord the carpet.)

APOLLODORUS: *(when the cords are loose)* Stand off, my friends: let Caesar see. *(He throws the carpet open.)*
RUFIO: Nothing but a heap of shawls. Where are the pigeons' eggs?
APOLLODORUS: Approach, Caesar; and search for them among the shawls.
RUFIO: *(drawing his sword)* Ha, treachery! Keep back, Caesar: I saw the shawl move: there is something alive there.
BRITANNUS: *(drawing his sword)* It is a serpent.
APOLLODORUS: Dares Caesar thrust his hand into the sack where the serpent moves?
RUFIO: *(turning on him)* Treacherous dog —
CAESAR: Peace. Put up your swords. Apollodorus: your serpent seems to breathe very regularly. *(He thrusts his hand under the shawls and draws out a bare arm.)* This is a pretty little snake.
RUFIO: *(drawing out the other arm)* Let us have the rest of you.

(They pull CLEOPATRA up by the wrists into a sitting position. BRITANNUS, scandalized, sheathes his sword with a drive of protest.)

CLEOPATRA: *(gasping)* Oh, I'm smothered. Oh, Caesar, a man stood on me in the boat; and a great sack of something fell upon me out of the sky; and then the boat sank; and then I was swung up into the air and bumped down.
CAESAR: *(petting her as she rises and takes refuge on his breast)* Well, never mind: here you are safe and sound at last.
RUFIO: Ay; and now that she is here, what are we to do with her?
BRITANNUS: She cannot stay here, Caesar, without the companionship of some matron.
CLEOPATRA: *(jealously, to CAESAR, who is obviously perplexed)* Arnt you glad to see me?
CAESAR: Yes, yes; I am very glad. But Rufio is very angry; and Britannus is shocked.

CLEOPATRA: *(contemptuously)* You can have their heads cut off, can you not?

CAESAR: They would not be so useful with their heads cut off as they are now, my sea bird.

RUFIO: *(to CLEOPATRA)* We shall have to go away presently and cut some of your Egyptians' heads off. How will you like being left here with the chance of being captured by that little brother of yours if we are beaten?

CLEOPATRA: But you mustnt leave me alone. Caesar: you will not leave me alone, will you?

RUFIO: What! not when the trumpet sounds and all our lives depend on Caesar's being at the barricade before the Egyptians reach it? Eh?

CLEOPATRA: Let them lose their lives: they are only soldiers.

CAESAR: *(gravely)* Cleopatra: when that trumpet sounds, we must take every man his life in his hand, and throw it in the face of Death. And of my soldiers who have trusted me there is not one whose hand I shall not hold more sacred than your head. *(CLEOPATRA is overwhelmed. Her eyes fill with tears.)* Apollodorus: you must take her back to the palace.

APOLLODORUS: Am I a dolphin, Caesar, to cross the seas with young ladies on my back? My boat is sunk: all yours are either at the barricade or have returned to the city. I will hail one if I can: that is all I can do. *(He goes back to the causeway.)*

CLEOPATRA: *(struggling with her tears)* It does not matter. I will not go back. Nobody cares for me.

CAESAR: Cleopatra —

CLEOPATRA: You want me to be killed.

CAESAR: *(still more gravely)* My poor child: your life matters little here to anyone but yourself. *(She gives way altogether at this, casting herself down on the faggots weeping. Suddenly a great tumult is heard in the distance, bucinas and trumpets sounding through a storm of shouting. BRITANNUS rushes to the parapet and looks along the mole. CAESAR and RUFIO turn to one another with quick intelligence.)*

CAESAR: Come, Rufio.

CLEOPATRA: *(scrambling to her knees and clinging to him)* No no. Do not leave me, Caesar. *(He snatches his skirt from her clutch.)* Oh!

BRITANNUS: *(from the parapet)* Caesar: we are cut off. The Egyptians have landed from the west harbor between us and the barricade!!!

RUFIO: *(running to see)* Curses! It is true. We are caught like rats in a trap.

CAESAR: *(ruthfully)* Rufio, Rufio: my men at the barricade are between the sea party and the shore party. I have murdered them.

RUFIO: *(coming back from the parapet to CAESAR's right hand)* Ay: that comes of fooling with this girl here.

APOLLODORUS: *(coming up quickly from the causeway)* Look over the parapet, Caesar.

CAESAR: We have looked, my friend. We must defend ourselves here.

APOLLODORUS: I have thrown the ladder into the sea. They cannot get in without it.

RUFIO: Ay; and we cannot get out. Have you thought of that?

APOLLODORUS: Not get out! Why not? You have ships in the east harbor.

BRITANNUS: *(hopefully, at the parapet)* The Rhodian galleys are standing in towards us already. (CAESAR *quickly joins* BRITANNUS *at the parapet.)*

RUFIO: *(to* APOLLODORUS, *impatiently)* And by what road are we to walk to the galleys, pray?

APOLLODORUS: *(with gay, defiant rhetoric)* By the road that leads everywhere — the diamond path of the sun and moon. Have you never seen the child's shadow play of The Broken Bridge? "Ducks and geese with ease get over" — eh? *(He throws away his cloak and cap, and binds his sword on his back.)*

RUFIO: What are you talking about?

APOLLODORUS: I will shew you. *(Calling to* BRITANNUS*)* How far off is the nearest galley?

BRITANNUS: Fifty fathom.

CAESAR: No, no: they are further off than they seem in this clear air to your British eyes. Nearly quarter of a mile, Apollodorus.

APOLLODORUS: Good. Defend yourselves here until I send you a boat from that galley.

RUFIO: Have you wings, perhaps?

APOLLODORUS: Water wings, soldier. Behold!

(He runs up the steps between CAESAR *and* BRITANNUS *to the coping of the parapet; springs into the air; and plunges head foremost into the sea.)*

CAESAR: *(like a schoolboy — wildly excited)* Bravo, bravo! *(Throwing off his cloak)* By Jupiter, I will do that too.

RUFIO: *(seizing him)* You are mad. You shall not.

CAESAR: Why not? Can I not swim as well as he?

RUFIO: *(frantic)* Can an old fool dive and swim like a young one? He is twenty-five and you are fifty.

CAESAR: *(breaking loose from* RUFIO*)* Old!!!

BRITANNUS: *(shocked)* Rufio: you forget yourself.

CAESAR: I will race you to the galley for a week's pay, father Rufio.

CLEOPATRA: But me! me!! me!!! what is to become of me?

CAESAR: I will carry you on my back to the galley like a dolphin. Rufio: when you see me rise to the surface, throw her in: I will answer for her. And then in with you after her, both of you.

CLEOPATRA: No, no, NO. I shall be drowned.

BRITANNUS: Caesar: I am a man and a Briton, not a fish. I must have a boat. I cannot swim.

CLEOPATRA: Neither can I.

CAESAR: *(to* BRITANNUS*)* Stay here, then, alone, until I recapture the light-house: I will not forget you. Now, Rufio.

RUFIO: You have made up your mind to this folly?

CAESAR: The Egyptians have made it up for me. What else is there to do? And mind where you jump: I do not want to get your fourteen stone in the small of my back as I come up. *(He runs up the steps and stands on the coping.)*

BRITANNUS: *(anxiously)* One last word, Caesar. Do not let yourself be seen in the fashionable part of Alexandria until you have changed your clothes.

CAESAR: *(calling over the sea)* Ho, Apollodorus: *(he points skyward and quotes the barcarolle)*

The white upon the blue above —

APOLLODORUS: *(swimming in the distance)*

Is purple on the green below —

CAESAR: *(exultantly)* Aha! *(He plunges into the sea.)*

CLEOPATRA: *(running excitedly to the steps)* Oh, let me see. He will be drowned *(RUFIO seizes her)* — Ah — ah — ah — ah! *(He pitches her screaming into the sea. RUFIO and BRITANNUS roar with laughter.)*

RUFIO: *(looking down after her)* He has got her. *(To BRITANNUS)* Hold the fort, Briton. Caesar will not forget you. *(He springs off.)*

BRITANNUS: *(running to the steps to watch them as they swim)* All safe, Rufio?

RUFIO: *(swimming)* All safe.

CAESAR: *(swimming further off)* Take refuge up there by the beacon; and pile the fuel on the trap door, Britannus.

BRITANNUS: *(calling in reply)* I will first do so, and then commend myself to my country's gods. *(A sound of cheering from the sea. BRITANNUS gives full vent to his excitement.)* The boat has reached him: Hip, hip, hip, hurrah!

ACT FOUR

CLEOPATRA's *sousing in the east harbor of Alexandria was in October 48 B.C. In March 47 she is passing the afternoon in her boudoir in the palace, among a bevy of her ladies, listening to a slave girl who is playing the harp in the middle of the room. The harpist's master, an old* MUSICIAN, *with a lined face, prominent brows, white beard, moustache and eyebrows twisted and horned at the ends, and a consciously keen and pretentious expression, is squatting on the floor close to her on her right, watching her performance.* FTATATEETA *is in attendance near the door, in front of a group of female slaves. Except the harp player all are seated:* CLEOPATRA *in a chair opposite the door on the other side of the room; the rest on the ground.* CLEOPATRA's *ladies are all young, the most conspicuous being* CHARMIAN *and* IRAS, *her favorites.* CHARMIAN *is a hatchet faced, terra cotta colored little goblin, swift in her movements, and neatly finished at the hands and feet.* IRAS *is a plump, goodnatured creature, rather fatuous, with a profusion of red hair, and a tendency to giggle on the slightest provocation.*

CLEOPATRA: Can I —

FTATATEETA: *(insolently, to the player)* Peace, thou! The Queen speaks. *(The player stops.)*

CLEOPATRA: *(to the old musician)* I want to learn to play the harp with my own hands. Caesar loves music. Can you teach me?

MUSICIAN: Assuredly I and no one else can teach the queen. Have I not discovered the lost method of the ancient Egyptians, who could make a pyramid tremble by touching a bass string? All the other teachers are quacks: I have exposed them repeatedly.

CLEOPATRA: Good: you shall teach me. How long will it take?

MUSICIAN: Not very long: only four years. Your Majesty must first become proficient in the philosophy of Pythagoras.

CLEOPATRA: Has she *(indicating the slave)* become proficient in the philosophy of Pythagoras?

MUSICIAN: Oh, she is but a slave. She learns as a dog learns.

CLEOPATRA: Well, then, I will learn as a dog learns; for she plays better than you. You shall give me a lesson every day for a fortnight. *(The MUSICIAN hastily scrambles to his feet and bows profoundly.)* After that, whenever I strike a false note you shall be flogged; and if I strike so many that there is not time to flog you, you shall be thrown into the Nile to feed the crocodiles. Give the girl a piece of gold; and send them away.

MUSICIAN: *(much taken aback)* But true art will not be thus forced.

FTATATEETA: *(pushing him out)* What is this? Answering the Queen, forsooth. Out with you.

(He is pushed out by FTATATEETA, the girl following with her harp, amid the laughter of the ladies and slaves.)

CLEOPATRA: Now, can any of you amuse me? Have you any stories or any news?

IRAS: Ftatateeta —

CLEOPATRA: Oh, Ftatateeta, Ftatateeta, always Ftatateeta. Some new tale to set me against her.

IRAS: No: this time Ftatateeta has been virtuous. *(All the ladies laugh — not the slaves.)* Pothinus has been trying to bribe her to let him speak with you.

CLEOPATRA: *(wrathfully)* Ha! you all sell audiences with me, as if I saw whom you please, and not whom I please. I should like to know how much of her gold piece that harp girl will have to give up before she leaves the palace.

IRAS: We can easily find out that for you.

(The ladies laugh.)

CLEOPATRA: *(frowning)* You laugh; but take care, take care. I will find out some day how to make myself served as Caesar is served.

CHARMIAN: Old hooknose! *(They laugh again.)*

CLEOPATRA: *(revolted)* Silence. Charmian: do not you be a silly little Egyptian fool. Do you know why I allow you all to chatter impertinently just as you please, instead of treating you as Ftatateeta would treat you if she were Queen?

CHARMIAN: Because you try to imitate Caesar in everything; and he lets everybody say what they please to him.

CLEOPATRA: No; but because I asked him one day why he did so; and he said "Let your women talk; and you will learn something from them." What have I to learn from them? I said. "What they are," said he; and oh! you should have seen his eye as he said it. You would have curled up, you shallow things. *(They laugh. She turns fiercely on* IRAS.*)* At whom are you laughing — at me or at Caesar?

IRAS: At Caesar.

CLEOPATRA: If you were not a fool, you would laugh at me; and if you were not a coward you would not be afraid to tell me so. *(*FTATATEETA *returns.)* Ftatateeta: they tell me that Pothinus has offered you a bribe to admit him to my presence.

FTATATEETA: *(protesting)* Now by my father's gods —

CLEOPATRA: *(cutting her short despotically)* Have I not told you not to deny things? You would spend the day calling your father's gods to witness to your virtues if I let you. Go take the bribe; and bring in Pothinus. *(*FTATATEETA *is about to reply.)* Dont answer me. Go.

*(*FTATATEETA *goes out; and* CLEOPATRA *rises and begins to prowl to and fro between her chair and the door, meditating. All rise and stand.)*

IRAS: *(as she reluctantly rises)* Heigho! I wish Caesar were back in Rome.

CLEOPATRA: *(threateningly)* It will be a bad day for you all when he goes. Oh, if I were not ashamed to let him see that I am as cruel at heart as my father, I would make you repent that speech! Why do you wish him away?

CHARMIAN: He makes you so terribly prosy and serious and learned and philosophical. It is worse than being religious at our ages. *(The ladies laugh.)*

CLEOPATRA: Cease that endless cackling, will you. Hold your tongues.

CHARMIAN: *(with mock resignation)* Well, well: we must try to live up to Caesar.

(They laugh again. CLEOPATRA *rages silently as she continues to prowl to and fro.* FTATATEETA *comes back with* POTHINUS, *who halts on the threshold.)*

FTATATEETA: *(at the door)* Pothinus craves the ear of the —

CLEOPATRA: There, there: that will do: let him come in. *(She resumes her seat. All sit down except* POTHINUS, *who advances to the middle of the room.* FTATATEETA *takes her former place.)* Well, Pothinus: what is the latest news from your rebel friends?

POTHINUS: *(haughtily)* I am no friend of rebellion. And a prisoner does not receive news.

CLEOPATRA: You are no more a prisoner than I am — than Caesar is. These six months we have been besieged in this palace by my subjects. You are allowed to walk on the beach among the soldiers. Can I go further myself, or can Caesar?

POTHINUS: You are but a child, Cleopatra, and do not understand these matters.

(The ladies laugh. CLEOPATRA *looks inscrutably at him.)*

CHARMIAN: I see you do not know the latest news, Pothinus.

POTHINUS: What is that?

CHARMIAN: That Cleopatra is no longer a child. Shall I tell you how to grow much older, and much, much wiser in one day?

POTHINUS: I should prefer to grow wiser without growing older.

CHARMIAN: Well, go up to the top of the lighthouse; and get somebody to take you by the hair and throw you into the sea. *(The ladies laugh.)*

CLEOPATRA: She is right, Pothinus: you will come to the shore with much conceit washed out of you. *(The ladies laugh.* CLEOPATRA *rises impatiently.)* Begone, all of you. I will speak with Pothinus alone. Drive them out, Ftatateeta. *(They run out laughing.* FTATATEETA *shuts the door on them.)* What are you waiting for?

FTATATEETA: It is not meet that the Queen remain alone with —

CLEOPATRA: *(interrupting her)* Ftatateeta: must I sacrifice you to your father's gods to teach you that I am Queen of Egypt, and not you?

FTATATEETA: *(indignantly)* You are like the rest of them. You want to be what these Romans call a New Woman. *(She goes out, banging the door.)*

CLEOPATRA: *(sitting down again)* Now, Pothinus: why did you bribe Ftatateeta to bring you hither?

POTHINUS: *(studying her gravely)* Cleopatra: what they tell me is true. You are changed.

CLEOPATRA: Do you speak with Caesar every day for six months: and you will be changed.

POTHINUS: It is the common talk that you are infatuated with this old man?

CLEOPATRA: Infatuated? What does that mean? Made foolish, is it not? Oh no: I wish I were.

POTHINUS: You wish you were made foolish! How so?

CLEOPATRA: When I was foolish, I did what I liked, except when Ftatateeta beat me; and even then I cheated her and did it by stealth. Now that Caesar has made me wise, it is no use my liking or disliking: I do what must be done, and have no time to attend to myself. That is not happiness; but it is greatness. If Caesar were gone, I think I could govern the Egyptians; for what Caesar is to me, I am to the fools around me.

POTHINUS: *(looking hard at her)* Cleopatra: this may be the vanity of youth.

CLEOPATRA: No, no: it is not that I am so clever, but that the others are so stupid.

POTHINUS: *(musingly)* Truly, that is the great secret.

CLEOPATRA: Well, now tell me what you came to say?

POTHINUS: *(embarrassed)* I! Nothing.

CLEOPATRA: Nothing!

POTHINUS: At least — to beg for my liberty: that is all.

CLEOPATRA: For that you would have knelt to Caesar. No, Pothinus: you came with some plan that depended on Cleopatra being a little nursery kitten. Now that Cleopatra is a Queen, the plan is upset.

POTHINUS: *(bowing his head submissively)* It is so.

CLEOPATRA: *(exultant)* Aha!

POTHINUS: *(raising his eyes keenly to hers)* Is Cleopatra then indeed a Queen, and no longer Caesar's prisoner and slave?

CLEOPATRA: Pothinus: we are all Caesar's slaves — all we in this land of Egypt — whether we will or no. And she who is wise enough to know this will reign when Caesar departs.

POTHINUS: You harp on Caesar's departure.

CLEOPATRA: What if I do?

POTHINUS: Does he not love you?

CLEOPATRA: Love me! Pothinus: Caesar loves no one. Who are those we love? Only those whom we do not hate: all people are strangers and enemies to us except those we love. But it is not so with Caesar. He has no hatred in him: he makes friends with everyone as he does with dogs and children. His kindness to me is a wonder: neither mother, father, nor nurse have ever taken so much care for me, or thrown open their thoughts to me so freely.

POTHINUS: Well: is not this love?

CLEOPATRA: What! when he will do as much for the first girl he meets on his way back to Rome? Ask his slave, Britannus: he has been just as good to him. Nay, ask his very horse! His kindness is not for anything in me: it is in his own nature.

POTHINUS: But how can you be sure that he does not love you as men love women?

CLEOPATRA: Because I cannot make him jealous. I have tried.

POTHINUS: Hm! Perhaps I should have asked, then, do you love him?

CLEOPATRA: Can one love a god? Besides, I love another Roman: one whom I saw long before Caesar — no god, but a man — one who can love and hate — one whom I can hurt and who would hurt me.

POTHINUS: Does Caesar know this?

CLEOPATRA: Yes.

POTHINUS: And he is not angry?

CLEOPATRA: He promises to send him to Egypt to please me!

POTHINUS: I do not understand this man.

CLEOPATRA: *(with superb contempt)* You understand Caesar! How could you? *(Proudly)* I do — by instinct.

POTHINUS: *(deferentially, after a moment's thought)* Your Majesty caused me to be admitted today. What message has the Queen for me?

CLEOPATRA: This. You think that by making my brother king, you will rule in Egypt, because you are his guardian and he is a little silly.

POTHINUS: The Queen is pleased to say so.

CLEOPATRA: The Queen is pleased to say this also. That Caesar will eat up you, and Achillas, and my brother, as a cat eats up mice; and that he will put on this land of Egypt as a shepherd puts on his garment. And when he has done that, he will return to Rome, and leave Cleopatra here as his viceroy.

POTHINUS: *(breaking out wrathfully)* That he shall never do. We have a thousand men to his ten; and we will drive him and his beggarly legions into the sea.

CLEOPATRA: *(with scorn, getting up to go)* You rant like any common fellow. Go, then, and marshal your thousands; and make haste; for Mithridates of Pergamos is at hand with reinforcements for Caesar. Caesar has held you at bay with two legions: we shall see what he will do with twenty.

POTHINUS: Cleopatra —

CLEOPATRA: Enough, enough: Caesar has spoiled me for talking to weak things like you. *(She goes out.* POTHINUS, *with a gesture of rage, is following, when* FTATATEETA *enters and stops him.)*

POTHINUS: Let me go forth from this hateful place.

FTATATEETA: What angers you?

POTHINUS: The curse of all the gods of Egypt be upon her! She has sold her country to the Roman, that she may buy it back from him with her kisses.

FTATATEETA: Fool: did she not tell you that she would have Caesar gone?

POTHINUS: You listened?

FTATATEETA: I took care that some honest woman should be at hand whilst you were with her.

POTHINUS: Now by the gods —

FTATATEETA: Enough of your gods! Caesar's gods are all powerful here. It is no use you coming to Cleopatra: you are only an Egyptian. She will not listen to any of her own race: she treats us all like children.

POTHINUS: May she perish for it!

FTATATEETA: *(balefully)* May your tongue wither for that wish! Go! send for Lucius Septimius, the slayer of Pompey. He is a Roman: may be she will listen to him. Begone!

POTHINUS: *(darkly)* I know to whom I must go now.

FTATATEETA: *(suspiciously)* To whom, then?

POTHINUS: To a greater Roman than Lucius. And mark this, mistress. You thought, before Caesar came, that Egypt should presently be ruled by you and your crew in the name of Cleopatra. I set myself against it —

FTATATEETA: *(interrupting him — wrangling)* Ay; that it might be ruled by you and your crew in the name of Ptolemy.

POTHINUS: Better me, or even you, than a woman with a Roman heart; and that is what Cleopatra is now become. Whilst I live, she shall never rule. So guide yourself accordingly. *(He goes out.)*

(It is by this time drawing on to dinner time. The table is laid on the roof of the palace; and thither RUFIO *is now climbing, ushered by a majestic* PALACE OFFICIAL, *wand of office in hand, and followed by a slave carrying an inlaid stool. After many stairs they emerge at last into a massive colonnade on the roof. Light curtains are drawn between the columns on the north and east to soften the westering sun. The* OFFICIAL *leads* RUFIO *to one of these shaded sections. A cord for pulling the curtains apart hangs down between the pillars.)*

THE OFFICIAL: *(bowing)* The Roman commander will await Caesar here.

(The slave sets down the stool near the southernmost column, and slips out through the curtains.)

RUFIO: *(sitting down, a little blown)* Pouf! That was a climb. How high have we come?

THE OFFICIAL: We are on the palace roof, O Beloved of Victory!

RUFIO: Good! the Beloved of Victory has no more stairs to get up.

(A SECOND OFFICIAL *enters from the opposite end, walking backwards.)*

THE SECOND OFFICIAL: Caesar approaches.

*(*CAESAR, *fresh from the bath, clad in a new tunic of purple silk, come in, beaming and festive, followed by two slaves carrying a light couch, which is hardly more than an elaborately designed bench. They place it near the northmost of the two curtained columns. When this is done they slip out through the curtains; and the two* OFFICIALS, *formally bowing, follow them.* RUFIO *rises to receive* CAESAR.*)*

CAESAR: *(coming over to him)* Why, Rufio! *(Surveying his dress with an air of admiring astonishment)* A new baldrick! A new golden pommel to your sword! And you have had your hair cut! But not your beard — ? impossible! *(He sniffs at* RUFIO'S *beard.)* Yes, perfumed, by Jupiter Olympus!

RUFIO: *(growling)* Well: is it to please myself?

CAESAR: *(affectionately)* No, my son Rufio, but to please me — to celebrate my birthday.

RUFIO: *(contemptuously)* Your birthday! You always have a birthday when there is a pretty girl to be flattered or an ambassador to be conciliated. We had seven of them in ten months last year.

CAESAR: *(contritely)* It is true, Rufio! I shall never break myself of these petty deceits.

RUFIO: Who is to dine with us — besides Cleopatra?

CAESAR: Apollodorus the Sicilian.

RUFIO: That popinjay!

CAESAR: Come! the popinjay is an amusing dog — tells a story; sings a song; and saves us the trouble of flattering the Queen. What does she care for old politicians and camp-fed bears like us? No: Apollodorus is good company, Rufio, good company.

RUFIO: Well, he can swim a bit and fence a bit: he might be worse, if he only knew how to hold his tongue.

CAESAR: The gods forbid he should ever learn! Oh, this military life! this tedious, brutal life of action! That is the worst of us Romans: we are mere doers and drudgers: a swarm of bees turned into men. Give me a good talker — one with wit and imagination enough to live without continually doing something!

RUFIO: Ay! a nice time he would have of it with you when dinner was over! Have you noticed that I am before my time?

CAESAR: Aha! I thought that meant something. What is it?

RUFIO: Can we be overheard here?

CAESAR: Our privacy invites eavesdropping. I can remedy that. *(He claps his hands twice. The curtains are drawn, revealing the roof garden with a banqueting table set across in the middle for four persons, one at each end, and two side by side. The side next* CAESAR *and* RUFIO *is blocked with golden wine vessels and basins. A gorgeous*

MAJOR-DOMO *is superintending the laying of the table by a staff of slaves. The colonnade goes round the garden at both sides to the further end, where a gap in it, like a
great gateway, leaves the view open to the sky beyond the western edge of the roof, except
in the middle, where a life size image of Ra, seated on a huge plinth, towers up, with
hawk head and crown of asp and disk. His altar, which stands at his feet, is a single
white stone.)* Now everybody can see us, nobody will think of listening to
us. *(He sits down on the bench left by the two slaves.)*

RUFIO: *(sitting down on his stool)* Pothinus wants to speak to you. I advise you to
see him: there is some plotting going on here among the women.

CAESAR: Who is Pothinus?

RUFIO: The fellow with hair like squirrel's fur — the little King's bear leader,
whom you kept prisoner.

CAESAR: *(annoyed)* And has he not escaped?

RUFIO: No.

CAESAR: *(rising imperiously)* Why not? You have been guarding this man
instead of watching the enemy. Have I not told you always to let prisoners escape unless there are special orders to the contrary? Are there not
enough mouths to be fed without him?

RUFIO: Yes; and if you would have a little sense and let me cut his throat,
you would save his rations. Anyhow, he wont escape. Three sentries
have told him they would put a pilum through him if they saw him
again. What more can they do? He prefers to stay and spy on us. So
would I if I had to do with generals subject to fits of clemency.

CAESAR: *(resuming his seat, argued down)* Hm! And so he wants to see me.

RUFIO: Ay. I have brought him with me. He is waiting there *(jerking his thumb
over his shoulder)* under guard.

CAESAR: And you want me to see him?

RUFIO: *(obstinately)* I dont want anything. I daresay you will do what you like.
Dont put it on to me.

CAESAR: *(with an air of doing it expressly to indulge* RUFIO*)* Well, well: let us have
him.

RUFIO: *(calling)* Ho there, guard! Release your man and send him up.
(beckoning) Come along!

*(*POTHINUS *enters and stops mistrustfully between the two, looking from one to the
other.)*

CAESAR: *(graciously)* Ah, Pothinus! You are welcome. And what is the news
this afternoon?

POTHINUS: Caesar: I come to warn you of a danger, and to make you an
offer.

CAESAR: Never mind the danger. Make the offer.

RUFIO: Never mind the offer. Whats the danger?

POTHINUS: Caesar: you think that Cleopatra is devoted to you.

CAESAR: *(gravely)* My friend: I already know what I think. Come to your
offer.

POTHINUS: I will deal plainly. I know not by what strange gods you have
been enabled to defend a palace and a few yards of beach against a city
and an army. Since we cut you off from Lake Mareotis, and you dug

wells in the salt sea sand and brought up buckets of fresh water from them, we have known that your gods are irresistible, and that you are a worker of miracles. I no longer threaten you —

RUFIO: *(sarcastically)* Very handsome of you, indeed.

POTHINUS: So be it: you are the master. Our gods sent the north west winds to keep you in our hands; but you have been too strong for them.

CAESAR: *(gently urging him to come to the point)* Yes, yes, my friend. But what then?

RUFIO: Spit it out, man. What have you to say?

POTHINUS: I have to say that you have a traitress in your camp. Cleopatra —

THE MAJOR-DOMO: *(at the table, announcing)* The Queen! *(CAESAR and RUFIO rise.)*

RUFIO: *(aside to POTHINUS)* You should have spat it out sooner, you fool. Now it is too late.

(CLEOPATRA, in gorgeous raiment, enters in state through the gap in the colonnade, and comes down past the image of Ra and past the table to CAESAR. Her retinue, headed by FTATATEETA, joins the staff at the table. CAESAR gives CLEOPATRA his seat, which she takes.)

CLEOPATRA: *(quickly, seeing POTHINUS)* What is he doing here?

CAESAR: *(seating himself beside her, in the most amiable of tempers)* Just going to tell me something about you. You shall hear it. Proceed, Pothinus.

POTHINUS: *(disconcerted)* Caesar — *(he stammers)*

CAESAR: Well, out with it.

POTHINUS: What I have to say is for your ear, not for the Queen's.

CLEOPATRA: *(with subdued ferocity)* There are means of making you speak. Take care.

POTHINUS: *(defiantly)* Caesar does not employ those means.

CAESAR: My friend: when a man has anything to tell in this world, the difficulty is not to make him tell it, but to prevent him from telling it too often. Let me celebrate my birthday by setting you free. Farewell: we shall not meet again.

CLEOPATRA: *(angrily)* Caesar: this mercy is foolish.

POTHINUS: *(to CAESAR)* Will you not give me a private audience? Your life may depend on it. *(CAESAR rises loftily.)*

RUFIO: *(aside to POTHINUS)* Ass! Now we shall have some heroics.

CAESAR: *(oratorically)* Pothinus —

RUFIO: *(interrupting him)* Caesar: the dinner will spoil if you begin preaching your favorite sermon about life and death.

CLEOPATRA: *(priggishly)* Peace, Rufio. I desire to hear Caesar.

RUFIO: *(bluntly)* Your Majesty has heard it before. You repeated it to Apollodorus last week; and he thought it was all your own. *(CAESAR's dignity collapses. Much tickled, he sits down again and looks roguishly at CLEOPATRA, who is furious. RUFIO calls as before)* Ho there, guard! Pass the prisoner out. He is released. *(To POTHINUS)* Now off with you. You have lost your chance.

POTHINUS: *(his temper overcoming his prudence)* I will speak.

CAESAR: *(to* CLEOPATRA*)* You see. Torture would not have wrung a word from him.

POTHINUS: Caesar: you have taught Cleopatra the arts by which the Romans govern the world.

CAESAR: Alas! they cannot even govern themselves. What then?

POTHINUS: What then? Are you so besotted with her beauty that you do not see that she is impatient to reign in Egypt alone, and that her heart is set on your departure?

CLEOPATRA: *(rising)* Liar!

CAESAR: *(shocked)* What! Protestations! Contradictions!

CLEOPATRA: *(ashamed, but trembling with suppressed rage)* No. I do not deign to contradict. Let him talk. *(She sits down again.)*

POTHINUS: From her own lips I have heard it. You are to be her catspaw: you are to tear the crown from her brother's head and set it on her own, delivering us all into her hand — delivering yourself also. And then Caesar can return to Rome, or depart through the gate of death, which is nearer and surer.

CAESAR: *(calmly)* Well, my friend; and is not this very natural?

POTHINUS: *(astonished)* Natural! Then you do not resent treachery?

CAESAR: Resent! O thou foolish Egyptian, what have I to do with resentment? Do I resent the wind when it chills me, or the night when it makes me stumble in the darkness? Shall I resent youth when it turns from age, and ambition when it turns from servitude? To tell me such a story as this is but to tell me that the sun will rise tomorrow.

CLEOPATRA: *(unable to contain herself)* But it is false — false. I swear it.

CAESAR: It is true, though you swore it a thousand times, and believed all you swore. *(She is convulsed with emotion. To screen her, he rises and takes* POTHINUS *to* RUFIO, *saying)* Come, Rufio: let us see Pothinus past the guard. I have a word to say to him. *(Aside to them)* We must give the Queen a moment to recover herself. *(Aloud)* Come. *(He takes* POTHINUS *and* RUFIO *out with him, conversing with them meanwhile.)* Tell your friends, Pothinus, that they must not think I am opposed to a reasonable settlement of the country's affairs — *(They pass out of hearing.)*

CLEOPATRA: *(in a stifled whisper)* Ftatateeta, Ftatateeta.

FTATATEETA: *(hurrying to her from the table and petting her)* Peace, child: be comforted —

CLEOPATRA: *(interrupting her)* Can they hear us?

FTATATEETA: No, dear heart, no.

CLEOPATRA: Listen to me. If he leaves the Palace alive, never see my face again.

FTATATEETA: He? Poth —

CLEOPATRA: *(striking her on the mouth)* Strike his life out as I strike his name from your lips. Dash him down from the wall. Break him on the stones. Kill, kill, kill him.

FTATATEETA: *(shewing all her teeth)* The dog shall perish.

CLEOPATRA: Fail in this, and you go out from before me for ever.

FTATATEETA: *(resolutely)* So be it. You shall not see my face until his eyes are darkened.

(CAESAR comes back, with APOLLODORUS, *exquisitely dressed, and* RUFIO.*)*

CLEOPATRA: *(to* FTATATEETA*)* Come soon — soon. *(*FTATATEETA *turns her meaning eyes for a moment on her mistress; then goes grimly away past Ra and out.* CLEOPATRA *runs like a gazelle to* CAESAR*)* So you have come back to me, Caesar. *(Caressingly)* I thought you were angry. Welcome, Apollodorus. *(She gives him her hand to kiss, with her other arm about* CAESAR.*)*

APOLLODORUS: Cleopatra grows more womanly beautiful from week to week.

CLEOPATRA: Truth, Apollodorus?

APOLLODORUS: Far, far short of the truth! Friend Rufio threw a pearl into the sea: Caesar fished up a diamond.

CAESAR: Caesar fished up a touch of rheumatism, my friend. Come: to dinner! to dinner! *(They move towards the table.)*

CLEOPATRA: *(skipping like a young fawn)* Yes, to dinner. I have ordered such a dinner for you, Caesar!

CAESAR: Ay? What are we to have?

CLEOPATRA: Peacocks' brains.

CAESAR: *(as if his mouth watered)* Peacocks' brains, Apollodorus!

APOLLODORUS: Not for me. I prefer nightingales' tongues. *(He goes to one of the two covers set side by side.)*

CLEOPATRA: Roast boar, Rufio!

RUFIO: *(gluttonously)* Good! *(He goes to the seat next* APOLLODORUS, *on his left).*

CAESAR: *(looking at his seat, which is at the end of the table, to Ra's left hand)* What has become of my leathern cushion?

CLEOPATRA: *(at the opposite end)* I have got new ones for you.

THE MAJOR-DOMO: These cushions, Caesar, are of Maltese gauze, stuffed with rose leaves.

CAESAR: Rose leaves! Am I a caterpillar? *(He throws the cushions away and seats himself on the leather mattress underneath.)*

CLEOPATRA: What a shame! My new cushions!

THE MAJOR-DOMO: *(at* CAESAR's *elbow)* What shall we serve to whet Caesar's appetite?

CAESAR: What have you got?

THE MAJOR-DOMO: Sea hedgehogs, black and white sea acorns, sea nettles, beccaficoes, purple shellfish —

CAESAR: Any oysters?

THE MAJOR-DOMO: Assuredly.

CAESAR: British oysters?

THE MAJOR-DOMO: *(assenting)* British oysters, Caesar.

CAESAR: Oysters, then. *(The* MAJOR-DOMO *signs to a slave at each order; and the slave goes out to execute it.)* I have been in Britain — that western land of romance — the last piece of earth on the edge of the ocean that surrounds the world. I went there in search of its famous pearls. The British pearl was a fable; but in searching for it I found the British oyster.

APOLLODORUS: All posterity will bless you for it. *(To the* MAJOR-DOMO*)* Sea hedgehogs for me.

RUFIO: Is there nothing solid to begin with?

THE MAJOR-DOMO: Fieldfares with asparagus —

CLEOPATRA: *(interrupting)* Fattened fowls! have some fattened fowls, Rufio.

RUFIO: Ay, that will do.

CLEOPATRA: *(greedily)* Fieldfares for me.

THE MAJOR-DOMO: Caesar will deign to choose his wine? Sicilian, Lesbian, Chian —

RUFIO: *(contemptuously)* All Greek.

APOLLODORUS: Who would drink Roman wine when he could get Greek. Try the Lesbian, Caesar.

CAESAR: Bring me my barley water.

RUFIO: *(with intense disgust)* Ugh! Bring me my Falernian. *(The Falernian is presently brought to him)*.

CLEOPATRA: *(pouting)* It is waste of time giving you dinners, Caesar. My scullions would not condescend to your diet.

CAESAR: *(relenting)* Well, well: let us try the Lesbian. *(The MAJOR-DOMO fills CAESAR's goblet; then CLEOPATRA's and APOLLODORUS's.)* But when I return to Rome, I will make laws against these extravagances. I will even get the laws carried out.

CLEOPATRA: *(coaxingly)* Never mind. Today you are to be like other people: idle, luxurious, and kind. *(She stretches her hand to him along the table.)*

CAESAR: Well, for once I will sacrifice my comfort — *(kissing her hand)* there! *(He takes a draught of wine.)* Now are you satisfied?

CLEOPATRA: And you no longer believe that I long for your departure for Rome?

CAESAR: I no longer believe anything. My brains are asleep. Besides, who knows whether I shall return to Rome?

RUFIO: *(alarmed)* How? Eh? What?

CAESAR: What has Rome to shew me that I have not seen already? One year of Rome is like another, except that I grow older, whilst the crowd in the Appian Way[1] is always the same age.

APOLLODORUS: It is no better here in Egypt. The old men, when they are tired of life, say "We have seen everything except the source of the Nile."

CAESAR: *(his imagination catching fire)* And why not see that? Cleopatra; will you come with me and track the flood to its cradle in the heart of the regions of mystery? Shall we leave Rome behind us — Rome, that has achieved greatness only to learn how greatness destroys nations of men who are not great! Shall I make you a new kingdom, and build you a holy city there in the great unknown?

CLEOPATRA: *(rapturously)* Yes, yes. You shall.

RUFIO: Ay: now he will conquer Africa with two legions before we come to the roast boar.

APOLLODORUS: Come: no scoffing. This is a noble scheme: in it Caesar is no longer merely the conquering soldier, but the creative poet-artist. Let us name the holy city, and consecrate it with Lesbian wine.

CAESAR: Cleopatra shall name it herself.

CLEOPATRA: It shall be called Caesar's Gift to his Beloved.

---

1 *the main road leading south from Rome.*

APOLLODORUS: No, no. Something vaster than that — something universal, like the starry firmament.

CAESAR: *(prosaically)* Why not simply The Cradle of the Nile?

CLEOPATRA: No: the Nile is my ancestor; and he is a god. Oh! I have thought of something. The Nile shall name it himself. Let us call upon him. *(To the* MAJOR-DOMO*)* Send for him. *(The three men stare at one another; but the* MAJOR-DOMO *goes out as if he had received the most matter-of-fact order.)* And *(to the retinue)* away with you all.

(The retinue withdraws, making obeisance.

A priest enters, carrying a miniature sphinx with a tiny tripod before it. A morsel of incense is smoking in the tripod. The priest comes to the table and places the image in the middle of it. The light begins to change to the magenta purple of the Egyptian sunset, as if the god had brought a strange colored shadow with him. The three men are determined not to be impressed; but they feel curious in spite of themselves.)

CAESAR: What hocus-pocus is this?

CLEOPATRA: You shall see. And it is not hocus-pocus. To do it properly, we should kill something to please him; but perhaps he will answer Caesar without that if we spill some wine to him.

APOLLODORUS: *(turning his head to look up over his shoulder at Ra)* Why not appeal to our hawkheaded friend here?

CLEOPATRA: *(nervously)* Sh! He will hear you and be angry.

RUFIO: *(phlegmatically)* The source of the Nile is out of his district, I expect.

CLEOPATRA: No: I will have my city named by nobody but my dear little sphinx, because it was in its arms that Caesar found me asleep. *(She languishes at* CAESAR *then turns curtly to the priest.)* Go. I am a priestess, and have power to take your charge from you. *(The priest makes a reverence and goes out.)* Now let us call on the Nile all together. Perhaps he will rap on the table.

CAESAR: What! table rapping! Are such superstitions still believed in this year 707 of the Republic?

CLEOPATRA: It is no superstition: our priests learn lots of things from the tables. Is it not so, Apollodorus?

APOLLODORUS: Yes: I profess myself a converted man. When Cleopatra is priestess, Apollodorus is devotee. Propose the conjuration.

CLEOPATRA: You must say with me "Send us thy voice, Father Nile."

ALL FOUR: *(holding their glasses together before the idol)* Send us thy voice, Father Nile.

(The death cry of a man in mortal terror and agony answers them. Appalled, the men set down their glasses, and listen. Silence. The purple deepens in the sky. CAESAR, *glancing at* CLEOPATRA, *catches her pouring out her wine before the god, with gleaming eyes, and mute assurances of gratitude and worship.* APOLLODORUS *springs up and runs to the edge of the roof to peer down and listen.)*

CAESAR: *(looking piercingly at* CLEOPATRA*)* What was that?

CLEOPATRA: *(petulantly)* Nothing. They are beating some slave.

CAESAR: Nothing.

RUFIO: A man with a knife in him, I'll swear.

CAESAR: *(rising)* A murder!

APOLLODORUS: *(at the back, waving his hand for silence)* S-sh! Silence. Did you hear that?

CAESAR: Another cry?

APOLLODORUS: *(returning to the table)* No, a thud. Something fell on the beach, I think.

RUFIO: *(grimly, as he rises)* Something with bones in it, eh?

CAESAR: *(shuddering)* Hush, hush, Rufio. *(He leaves the table and returns to the colonnade: RUFIO following at his left elbow, and APOLLODORUS at the other side.)*

CLEOPATRA: *(still in her place at the table)* Will you leave me, Caesar? Apollodorus: are you going?

APOLLODORUS: Faith, dearest Queen, my appetite is gone.

CAESAR: Go down to the courtyard, Apollodorus; and find out what has happened.

(APOLLODORUS nods and goes out, making for the staircase by which RUFIO ascended.)

CLEOPATRA: Your soldiers have killed somebody, perhaps. What does it matter?

(The murmur of a crowd rises from the beach below. CAESAR and RUFIO look at one another.)

CAESAR: This must be seen to. *(He is about to follow APOLLODORUS when RUFIO stops him with a hand on his arm as FTATATEETA comes back by the far end of the roof, with dragging steps, a drowsy satiety in her eyes and in the corners of the bloodhound lips. For a moment CAESAR suspects that she is drunk with wine. Not so RUFIO: he knows well the red vintage that has inebriated her).*

RUFIO: *(in a low tone)* There is some mischief between these two.

FTATATEETA: The Queen looks again on the face of her servant.

(CLEOPATRA looks at her for a moment with an exultant reflection of her murderous expression. Then she flings her arms round her; kisses her repeatedly and savagely; and tears off her jewels and heaps them on her. The two men turn from the spectacle to look at one another. FTATATEETA drags herself sleepily to the altar; kneels before Ra; and remains there in prayer. CAESAR goes to CLEOPATRA, leaving RUFIO in the colonnade.)

CAESAR: *(with searching earnestness)* Cleopatra: what has happened?

CLEOPATRA: *(in mortal dread of him, but with her utmost cajolery)* Nothing, dearest Caesar. *(With sickly sweetness, her voice almost failing)* Nothing. I am innocent. *(She approaches him affectionately)* Dear Caesar: are you angry with me? Why do you look at me so? I have been here with you all the time. How can I know what has happened?

CAESAR: *(reflectively)* That is true.

CLEOPATRA: *(greatly relieved, trying to caress him)* Of course it is true. *(He does not respond to the caress)* You know it is true, Rufio.

(The murmur without suddenly swells to a roar and subsides.)

RUFIO: I shall know presently. *(He makes for the altar in the burly trot that serves him for a stride, and touches* FTATATEETA *on the shoulder.)* Now, mistress: I shall want you. *(He orders her, with a gesture, to go before him.)*

FTATATEETA: *(rising and glowering at him)* My place is with the Queen.

CLEOPATRA: She has done no harm, Rufio.

CAESAR: *(to* RUFIO*)* Let her stay.

RUFIO: *(sitting down on the altar)* Very well. Then my place is here too; and you can see what is the matter for yourself. The city is in a pretty uproar, it seems.

CAESAR: *(with grave displeasure)* Rufio: there is a time for obedience.

RUFIO: And there is a time for obstinacy. *(He folds him arms doggedly.)*

CAESAR: *(to* CLEOPATRA*)* Send her away.

CLEOPATRA: *(whining in her eagerness to propitiate him)* Yes, I will. I will do whatever you ask me, Caesar, always, because I love you. Ftatateeta: go away.

FTATATEETA: The Queen's word is my will. I shall be at hand for the Queen's call. *(She goes out past Ra, as she came.)*

RUFIO: *(following her)* Remember, Caesar, your bodyguard is also within call. *(He follows her out.)*

(CLEOPATRA, presuming upon CAESAR's submission to RUFIO, leaves the table and sits down on the bench in the colonnade.)

CLEOPATRA: Why do you allow Rufio to treat you so? You should teach him his place?

CAESAR: Teach him to be my enemy, and to hide his thoughts from me as you are now hiding yours.

CLEOPATRA: *(her fears returning)* Why do you say that, Caesar? Indeed, indeed, I am not hiding anything. You are wrong to treat me like this. *(She stifles a sob.)* I am only a child; and you turn into stone because you think some one has been killed. I cannot bear it. *(She purposely breaks down and weeps. He looks at her with profound sadness and complete coldness. She looks up to see what effect she is producing. Seeing that he is unmoved, she sits up, pretending to struggle with her emotion and to put it bravely away.)* But there: I know you hate tears: you shall not be troubled with them. I know you are not angry, but only sad; only I am so silly, I cannot help being hurt when you speak coldly. Of course you are quite right: it is dreadful to think of anyone being killed or even hurt; and I hope nothing really serious has — *(her voice dies away under his contemptuous penetration.)*

CAESAR: What has frightened you into this? What have you done? *(A trumpet sounds on the beach below.)* Aha! that sounds like the answer.

CLEOPATRA: *(sinking back trembling on the bench and covering her face with her hands)* I have not betrayed you, Caesar: I swear it.

CAESAR: I know that. I have not trusted you. *(He turns from her, and is about to go out when* APOLLODORUS *and* BRITANNUS *drag in* LUCIUS SEPTIMIUS *to him.* RUFIO *follows.* CAESAR *shudders.)* Again, Pompey's murderer!

RUFIO: The town has gone mad, I think. They are for tearing the palace down and driving us into the sea straight away. We laid hold of this renegade in clearing them out of the courtyard.

CAESAR: Release him. *(They let go his arms.)* What has offended the citizens, Lucius Septimius?

LUCIUS: What did you expect, Caesar? Pothinus was a favorite of theirs.

CAESAR: What has happened to Pothinus? I set him free, here, not half an hour ago. Did they not pass him out?

LUCIUS: Ay, through the gallery arch sixty feet above ground, with three inches of steel in his ribs. He is as dead as Pompey. We are quits now, as to killing — you and I.

CAESAR: *(shocked)* Assassinated! — our prisoner, our guest! *(He turns reproachfully on* RUFIO*)* Rufio —

RUFIO: *(emphatically — anticipating the question)* Whoever did it was a wise man and a friend of yours (CLEOPATRA *is greatly emboldened)*; but none of us had a hand in it. So it is no use to frown at me. *(*CAESAR *turns and looks at* CLEOPATRA.*)*

CLEOPATRA: *(violently — rising)* He was slain by order of the Queen of Egypt. I am not Julius Caesar the dreamer, who allows every slave to insult him. Rufio has said I did well: now the others shall judge me too. *(She turns to the others.)* This Pothinus sought to make me conspire with him to betray Caesar to Achillas and Ptolemy. I refused; and he cursed me and came privily to Caesar to accuse me of his own treachery. I caught him in the act; and he insulted me — me, the Queen! to my face. Caesar would not avenge me: he spoke him fair and set him free. Was I right to avenge myself? Speak, Lucius.

LUCIUS: I do not gainsay it. But you will get little thanks from Caesar for it.

CLEOPATRA: Speak, Apollodorus. Was I wrong?

APOLLODORUS: I have only one word of blame, most beautiful. You should have called upon me, your knight; and in fair duel I should have slain the slanderer.

CLEOPATRA: *(passionately)* I will be judged by your very slave, Caesar. Britannus: speak. Was I wrong?

BRITANNUS: Were treachery, falsehood, and disloyalty left unpunished, society must become like an arena full of wild beasts, tearing one another to pieces. Caesar is in the wrong.

CAESAR: *(with quiet bitterness)* And so the verdict is against me, it seems.

CLEOPATRA: *(vehemently)* Listen to me, Caesar. If one man in all Alexandria can be found to say that I did wrong, I swear to have myself crucified on the door of the palace by my own slaves.

CAESAR: If one man in all the world can be found, now or forever, to know that you did wrong, that man will have either to conquer the world as I have, or be crucified by it. *(The uproar in the streets again reaches them.)* Do you hear? These knockers at your gate are also believers in vengeance and in stabbing. You have slain their leader: it is right that they shall slay you. If you doubt it, ask your four counsellors here. And then in the name of that right *(he emphasizes the word with great scorn)* shall I not slay them for murdering their Queen, and be slain in my turn by their countrymen as the invader of their fatherland? Can Rome do less then than slay these slayers, too, to shew the world how Rome avenges her sons and her honor. And so, to the end of history, murder shall breed murder, always in the name of right and honor and peace, until the gods are tired of blood and create a race that can understand. *(Fierce uproar.* CLEOPATRA *becomes white with terror.)* Hearken, you who must not be insulted. Go near enough to catch their words: you will find them bitterer than the tongue of Pothinus. *(Loftily, wrapping himself up in an impenetrable dignity)* Let the Queen of Egypt now give her orders for vengeance, and take her measures for defence; for she has renounced Caesar. *(He turns to go.)*

CLEOPATRA: *(terrified, running to him and falling on her knees)* You will not desert me, Caesar. You will defend the palace.

CAESAR: You have taken the powers of life and death upon you. I am only a dreamer.

CLEOPATRA: But they will kill me.

CAESAR: And why not?

CLEOPATRA: In pity —

CAESAR: Pity! What! has it come to this so suddenly, that nothing can save you now but pity? Did it save Pothinus?

(She rises, wringing her hands, and goes back to the bench in despair. APOLLODORUS *shews his sympathy with her by quietly posting himself behind the bench. The sky has by this time become the most vivid purple, and soon begins to change to a glowing pale orange, against which the colonnade and the great image shew darklier and darklier.)*

RUFIO: Caesar: enough of preaching. The enemy is at the gate.

CAESAR: *(turning on him and giving way to his wrath)* Ay; and what has held him baffled at the gate all these months? Was it my folly, as you deem it, or your wisdom? In this Egyptian Red Sea of blood, whose hand has held all your heads above the waves? *(Turning to* CLEOPATRA*)* And yet, when Caesar says to such an one, "Friend, go free," you, clinging for your little life to my sword, dare steal out and stab him in the back? And you, soldiers and gentlemen, and honest servants as you forget that you are, applaud this assassination, and say "Caesar is in the wrong." By the gods, I am tempted to open my hand and let you all sink into the flood.

CLEOPATRA: *(with a ray of cunning hope)* But, Caesar, if you do, you will perish yourself.

(CAESAR's eyes blaze.)

RUFIO: *(greatly alarmed)* Now, by great Jove, you filthy little Egyptian rat, that is the very word to make him walk out alone into the city and leave us here to be cut to pieces. *(Desperately, to* CAESAR*)* Will you desert us because

we are a parcel of fools? I mean no harm by killing: I do it as a dog kills
a cat, by instinct. We are all dogs at your heels; but we have served you
faithfully.

CAESAR: *(relenting)* Alas, Rufio, my son, my son: as dogs we are like to perish
now in the streets.

APOLLODORUS: *(at his post behind* CLEOPATRA's *seat)* Caesar: what you say has an
Olympian ring in it: it must be right; for it is fine art. But I am still on
the side of Cleopatra. If we must die, she shall not want the devotion of
a man's heart nor the strength of a man's arm.

CLEOPATRA: *(sobbing)* But I dont want to die.

CAESAR: *(sadly)* Oh, ignoble, ignoble!

LUCIUS: *(coming forward between* CAESAR *and* CLEOPATRA*)* Hearken to me, Caesar.
It may be ignoble; but I also mean to live as long as I can.

CAESAR: Well, my friend, you are likely to outlive Caesar. Is it any magic of
mine, think you, that has kept your army and this whole city at bay for
so long? Yesterday, what quarrel had they with me that they should risk
their lives against me? But today we have flung them down their hero,
murdered; and now every man of them is set upon clearing out this
nest of assassins — for such we are and no more. Take courage then;
and sharpen your sword. Pompey's head has fallen; and Caesar's head is
ripe.

APOLLODORUS: Does Caesar despair?

CAESAR: *(with infinite pride)* He who has never hoped can never despair. Caesar, in good or bad fortune, looks his fate in the face.

LUCIUS: Look it in the face, then; and it will smile as it always has on Caesar.

CAESAR: *(with involuntary haughtiness)* Do you presume to encourage me?

LUCIUS: I offer you my services. I will change sides if you will have me.

CAESAR: *(suddenly coming down to earth again, and looking sharply at him, divining that
there is something behind the offer)* What! At this point?

LUCIUS: *(firmly)* At this point.

RUFIO: Do you suppose Caesar is mad, to trust you?

LUCIUS: I do not ask him to trust me until he is victorious. I ask for my life,
and for a command in Caesar's army. And since Caesar is a fair dealer, I
will pay in advance.

CAESAR: Pay! How?

LUCIUS: With a piece of good news for you.

*(*CAESAR *divines the news in a flash.)*

RUFIO: What news?

CAESAR: *(with an elate and buoyant energy which makes* CLEOPATRA *sit up and stare)*
What news! What news, did you say, my son Rufio? The relief has
arrived: what other news remains for us? Is it not so, Lucius Septimius?
Mithridates of Pergamos is on the march.

LUCIUS: He has taken Pelusium.[2]

CAESAR: *(delighted)* Lucius Septimius: you are henceforth my officer. Rufio:
the Egyptians must have sent every soldier from the city to prevent

2 *in northern Sinai, near the Nile Delta.*

Mithridates crossing the Nile. There is nothing in the streets now but mob — mob!

LUCIUS: It is so, Mithridates is marching by the great road to Memphis to cross above the Delta. Achillas will fight him there.

CAESAR: *(all audacity)* Achillas shall fight Caesar there. See, Rufio. *(He runs to the table; snatches a napkin; and draws a plan on it with his finger dipped in wine, whilst RUFIO and LUCIUS SEPTIMIUS crowd about him to watch, all looking closely, for the light is now almost gone).* Here is the palace *(pointing to his plan)*: here is the theatre. You *(to RUFIO)* take twenty men and pretend to go by that street *(pointing it out)*; and whilst they are stoning you, out go the cohorts by this and this. My streets are right, are they, Lucius?

LUCIUS: Ay, that is the fig market —

CAESAR: *(too much excited to listen to him)* I saw them the day we arrived. Good! *(He throws the napkin on the table, and comes down again into the colonnade).* Away, Britannus: tell Petronius that within an hour half our forces must take ship for the western lake. See to my horse and armor. *(BRITANNUS runs out.)* With the rest, I shall march round the lake and up the Nile to meet Mithridates. Away, Lucius; and give the word. *(LUCIUS hurries out after BRITANNUS)* Apollodorus: lend me your sword and your right arm for this campaign.

APOLLODORUS: Ay, and my heart and life to boot.

CAESAR: *(grasping his hand)* I accept both. *(Mighty handshake.)* Are you ready for work?

APOLLODORUS: Ready for Art — the Art of War *(he rushes out after LUCIUS, totally forgetting CLEOPATRA).*

RUFIO: Come! this is something like business.

CAESAR: *(buoyantly)* Is it not, my only son? *(He claps his hands. The slaves hurry in to the table.)* No more of this mawkish revelling: away with all this stuff: shut it out of my sight and be off with you. *(The slaves begin to remove the table; and the curtains are drawn, shutting in the colonnade).* You understand about the streets, Rufio?

RUFIO: Ay, I think I do. I will get through them, at all events.

(The bucina sounds busily in the courtyard beneath.)

CAESAR: Come, then: we must talk to the troops and hearten them. You down to the beach: I to the courtyard. *(He makes for the staircase.)*

CLEOPATRA: *(rising from her seat, where she has been quite neglected all this time, and stretching out her hands timidly to him)* Caesar.

CAESAR: *(turning)* Eh?

CLEOPATRA: Have you forgotten me?

CAESAR: *(indulgently)* I am busy now, my child, busy. When I return your affairs shall be settled. Farewell; and be good and patient.

(He goes, preoccupied and quite indifferent. She stands with clenched fists, in speechless rage and humiliation.)

RUFIO: That game is played and lost, Cleopatra. The woman always gets the worst of it.

CLEOPATRA: *(haughtily)* Go. Follow your master.

RUFIO: *(in her ear, with rough familiarity)* A word first. Tell your executioner that if Pothinus had been properly killed — in the throat — he would not have called out. Your man bungled his work.

CLEOPATRA: *(enigmatically)* How do you know it was a man?

RUFIO: *(startled, and puzzled)* It was not you: you were with us when it happened. *(She turns her back scornfully on him. He shakes his head, and draws the curtains to go out. It is now a magnificent moonlit night. The table has been removed.* FTA-TATEETA *is seen in the light of the moon and stars, again in prayer before the white altar-stone of Ra.* RUFIO *starts; closes the curtains again softly; and says in a low voice to* CLEOPATRA*)* Was it she? with her own hand?

CLEOPATRA: *(threateningly)* Whoever it was, let my enemies beware of her. Look to it, Rufio, you who dare make the Queen of Egypt a fool before Caesar.

RUFIO: *(looking grimly at her)* I will look to it, Cleopatra. *(He nods in confirmation of the promise, and slips out through the curtains, loosening his sword in its sheath as he goes.)*

ROMAN SOLDIERS: *(in the courtyard below)* Hail, Caesar! Hail, hail!

*(*CLEOPATRA *listens. The bucina sounds again, followed by several trumpets.)*

CLEOPATRA: *(wringing her hands and calling)* Ftatateeta. Ftatateeta. It is dark; and I am alone. Come to me. *(Silence)* Ftatateeta. *(Louder)* Ftatateeta. *(Silence. In a panic she snatches the cord and pulls the curtains apart).*

*(*FTATATEETA *is lying dead on the altar of Ra, with her throat cut. Her blood deluges the white stone.)*

ACT FIVE

High noon. Festival and military pageant on the esplanade before the palace. In the east harbor Caesar's galley, so gorgeously decorated that it seems to be rigged with flowers, is alongside the quay, close to the steps Apollodorus descended when he embarked with the carpet. A Roman guard is posted there in charge of a gangway, whence a red floorcloth is laid down the middle of the esplanade, turning off to the north opposite the central gate in the palace front, which shuts in the esplanade on the south side. The broad steps of the gate, crowded with Cleopatra's ladies, all in their gayest attire, are like a flower garden. The façade is lined by her guard, officered by the same gallants to whom Bel Affris announced the coming of Caesar six months before in the old palace on the Syrian border. The north side is lined by Roman soldiers, with the townsfolk on tiptoe behind them, peering over their heads at the cleared esplanade, in which the officers stroll about, chatting. Among these are BELZANOR *and the* PERSIAN; *also the* CENTURION, *vinewood cudgel in hand, battle worn, thick-booted, and much outshone, both socially and decoratively, by the Egyptian officers.*

APOLLODORUS *makes his way through the townsfolk and calls to the officers from behind the Roman line.*

APOLLODORUS: Hullo! May I pass?

CENTURION: Pass Apollodorus the Sicilian there! *(The soldiers let him through.)*

BELZANOR: Is Caesar at hand?

APOLLODORUS: Not yet. He is still in the market place. I could not stand any more of the roaring of the soldiers! After half an hour of the enthusiasm of an army, one feels the need of a little sea air.

PERSIAN: Tell us the news. Hath he slain the priests?

APOLLODORUS: Not he. They met him in the market place with ashes on their heads and their gods in their hands. They placed the gods at his feet. The only one that was worth looking at was Apis: a miracle of gold and ivory work. By my advice he offered the chief priest two talents for it.

BELZANOR: *(appalled)* Apis the all-knowing for two talents! What said the chief Priest?

APOLLODORUS: He invoked the mercy of Apis, and asked for five.

BELZANOR: There will be famine and tempest in the land for this.

PERSIAN: Pooh! Why did not Apis cause Caesar to be vanquished by Achillas? Any fresh news from the war, Apollodorus?

APOLLODORUS: The little King Ptolemy was drowned.

BELZANOR: Drowned! How?

APOLLODORUS: With the rest of them. Caesar attacked them from three sides at once and swept them into the Nile. Ptolemy's barge sank.

BELZANOR: A marvellous man, this Caesar! Will he come soon, think you?

APOLLODORUS: He was settling the Jewish question when I left.

(A flourish of trumpets from the north, and commotion among the townsfolk, announces the approach of CAESAR.*)*

PERSIAN: He has made short work of them. Here he comes. *(He hurries to his post in front of the Egyptian lines.)*

BELZANOR: *(following him)* Ho there! Caesar comes.

(The soldiers stand at attention, and dress their lines. APOLLODORUS *goes to the Egyptian line.)*

CENTURION: *(hurrying to the gangway guard)* Attention there! Caesar comes.

*(*CAESAR *arrives in state with* RUFIO: BRITANNUS *following. The soldiers receive him with enthusiastic shouting.)*

CAESAR: I see my ship awaits me. The hour of Caesar's farewell to Egypt has arrived. And now, Rufio, what remains to be done before I go?

RUFIO: *(at his left hand)* You have not yet appointed a Roman governor for this province.

CAESAR: *(looking whimsically at him, but speaking with perfect gravity)* What say you to Mithridates of Pergamos, my reliever and rescuer, the great son of Eupator?

RUFIO: Why, that you will want him elsewhere. Do you forget that you have some three or four armies to conquer on your way home?

CAESAR: Indeed! Well, what say you to yourself?

RUFIO: *(incredulously)* I! I a governor! What are you dreaming of? Do you not know that I am only the son of a freedman?

CAESAR: *(affectionately)* Has not Caesar called you his son? *(Calling to the whole assembly)* Peace awhile there; and hear me.

THE ROMAN SOLDIERS: Hear Caesar.

CAESAR: Hear the service, quality, rank and name of the Roman governor. By service, Caesar's shield; by quality, Caesar's friend; by rank, a Roman soldier. *(The Roman soldiers give a triumphant shout.)* By name, Rufio. *(They shout again.)*

RUFIO: *(kissing CAESAR's hand)* Ay: I am Caesar's shield; but of what use shall I be when I am no longer on Caesar's arm? Well, no matter — *(He becomes husky, and turns away to recover himself.)*

CAESAR: Where is that British Islander of mine?

BRITANNUS: *(coming forward on CAESAR's right hand)* Here, Caesar.

CAESAR: Who bade you, pray, thrust yourself into the battle of the Delta, uttering the barbarous cries of your native land, and affirming yourself a match for any four of the Egyptians, to whom you applied unseemly epithets?

BRITANNUS: Caesar: I ask you to excuse the language that escaped me in the heat of the moment.

CAESAR: And how did you, who cannot swim, cross the canal with us when we stormed the camp?

BRITANNUS: Caesar: I clung to the tail of your horse.

CAESAR: These are not the deeds of a slave, Britannicus, but of a free man.

BRITANNUS: Caesar: I was born free.

CAESAR: But they call you Caesar's slave.

BRITANNUS: Only as Caesar's slave have I found real freedom.

CAESAR: *(moved)* Well said. Ungrateful that I am, I was about to set you free; but now I will not part from you for a million talents. *(He claps him friendly on the shoulder. BRITANNUS, gratified, but a trifle shamefaced, takes his hand and kisses it sheepishly.)*

BELZANOR: *(to the PERSIAN)* This Roman knows how to make men serve him.

PERSIAN: Ay: men too humble to become dangerous rivals to him.

BELZANOR: O subtle one! O cynic!

CAESAR: *(seeing APOLLODORUS in the Egyptian corner, and calling to him)* Apollodorus: I leave the art of Egypt in your charge. Remember: Rome loves art and will encourage it ungrudgingly.

APOLLODORUS: I understand, Caesar. Rome will produce no art itself; but it will buy up and take away whatever the other nations produce.

CAESAR: What! Rome product no art! Is peace not an art? is war not an art? is government not an art? is civilization not an art? All these we give you in exchange for a few ornaments. You will have the best of the bargain. *(Turning to* RUFIO*)* And now, what else have I to do before I embark? *(Trying to recollect)* There is something I cannot remember: what can it be? Well, well: it must remain undone: we must not waste this favorable wind. Farewell, Rufio.

RUFIO: Caesar: I am loth to let you go to Rome without your shield. There are too many daggers there.

CAESAR: It matters not: I shall finish my life's work on my way back; and then I shall have lived long enough. Besides: I have always disliked the idea of dying: I had rather be killed. Farewell.

RUFIO: *(with a sigh, raising his hands and giving* CAESAR *up as incorrigible)* Farewell. *(They shake hands.)*

CAESAR: *(waving his hand to* APOLLODORUS*)* Farewell, Apollodorus, and my friends, all of you. Aboard!

(The gangway is run out from the quay to the ship. As CAESAR *moves towards it,* CLEOPATRA, *cold and tragic, cunningly dressed in black, without ornaments or decoration of any kind, and thus making a striking figure among the brilliantly dressed bevy of ladies as she passes through it, comes from the palace and stands on the steps.* CAESAR *does not see her until she speaks.)*

CLEOPATRA: Has Cleopatra no part in this leavetaking?

CAESAR: *(enlightened)* Ah, I knew there was something. *(To* RUFIO*)* How could you let me forget her, Rufio? *(Hastening to her)* Had I gone without seeing you, I should never have forgiven myself. *(He takes her hands, and brings her into the middle of the esplanade. She submits stonily.)* Is this mourning for me?

CLEOPATRA: No.

CAESAR: *(remorsefully)* Ah, that was thoughtless of me! It is for your brother.

CLEOPATRA: No.

CAESAR: For whom, then?

CLEOPATRA: Ask the Roman governor whom you have left us.

CAESAR: Rufio?

CLEOPATRA: Yes: Rufio. *(She points at him with deadly scorn.)* He who is to rule here in Caesar's name, in Caesar's way, according to Caesar's boasted laws of life.

CAESAR: *(dubiously)* He is to rule as he can, Cleopatra. He has taken the work upon him, and will do it in his own way.

CLEOPATRA: Not in your way, then?

CAESAR: *(puzzled)* What do you mean by my way?

CLEOPATRA: Without punishment. Without revenge. Without judgment.

CAESAR: *(approvingly)* Ay: that is the right way, the great way, the only possible way in the end. *(To* RUFIO*)* Believe it, Rufio, if you can.

RUFIO: Why, I believe it, Caesar. You have convinced me of it long ago. But look you. You are sailing for Numidia[3] today. Now tell me: if you meet a hungry lion there, you will not punish it for wanting to eat you?

CAESAR: *(wondering what he is driving at)* No.

RUFIO: Nor revenge upon it the blood of those it has already eaten.

3 *in north Africa, now part of Algeria.*

CAESAR: No.

RUFIO: Nor judge it for its guiltiness.

CAESAR: No.

RUFIO: What, then, will you do to save your life from it?

CAESAR: (promptly) Kill it, man, without malice, just as it would kill me. What does this parable of the lion mean?

RUFIO: Why, Cleopatra had a tigress that killed men at her bidding. I thought she might bid it kill you some day. Well, had I not been Caesar's pupil, what pious things might I not have done to that tigress! I might have punished it. I might have revenged Pothinus on it.

CAESAR: (interjects) Pothinus!

RUFIO: (continuing) I might have judged it. But I put all these follies behind me; and, without malice, only cut its throat. And that is why Cleopatra comes to you in mourning.

CLEOPATRA: (vehemently) He has shed the blood of my servant Ftatateeta. On your head be it as upon his, Caesar, if you hold him free of it.

CAESAR: (energetically) On my head be it, then; for it was well done. Rufio: had you set yourself in the seat of the judge, and with hateful ceremonies and appeals to the gods handed that woman over to some hired executioner to be slain before the people in the name of justice, never again would I have touched your hand without a shudder. But this was natural slaying: I feel no horror at it.

(RUFIO, satisfied, nods at CLEOPATRA, mutely inviting her to mark that.)

CLEOPATRA: (pettish and childish in her impotence) No: not when a Roman slays an Egyptian. All the world will now see how unjust and corrupt Caesar is.

CAESAR: (taking her hands coaxingly) Come: do not be angry with me. I am sorry for that poor Totateeta. (She laughs in spite of herself.) Aha! you are laughing. Does that mean reconciliation?

CLEOPATRA: (angry with herself for laughing) No, no, NO!! But it is so ridiculous to hear you call her Totateeta.

CAESAR: What! As much a child as ever, Cleopatra! Have I not made a woman of you after all?

CLEOPATRA: Oh, it is you who are a great baby: you make me seem silly because you will not behave seriously. But you have treated me badly; and I do not forgive you.

CAESAR: Bid me farewell.

CLEOPATRA: I will not.

CAESAR: (coaxing) I will send you a beautiful present from Rome.

CLEOPATRA: (proudly) Beauty from Rome to Egypt indeed! What can Rome give me that Egypt cannot give me?

APOLLODORUS: That is true, Caesar. If the present is to be really beautiful, I shall have to buy it for you in Alexandria.

CAESAR: You are forgetting the treasures for which Rome is most famous, my friend. You cannot buy them in Alexandria.

APOLLODORUS: What are they, Caesar?

CAESAR: Her sons. Come, Cleopatra: forgive me and bid me farewell; and I will send you a man, Roman from head to heel and Roman of the noblest; not old and ripe for the knife; not lean in the arms and cold in the heart; not hiding a bald head under his conqueror's laurels; not stooped with the weight of the world on his shoulders; but brisk and fresh, strong and young, hoping in the morning, fighting in the day, and revelling in the evening. Will you take such an one in exchange for Caesar?

CLEOPATRA: *(palpitating)* His name, his name?

CAESAR: Shall it be Mark Antony? *(She throws herself into his arms.)*

RUFIO: You are a bad hand at a bargain, mistress, if you will swop Caesar for Antony.

CAESAR: So now you are satisfied.

CLEOPATRA: You will not forget.

CAESAR: I will not forget. Farewell: I do not think we shall meet again. Farewell. *(He kisses her on the forehead. She is much affected and begins to sniff. He embarks.)*

THE ROMAN SOLDIERS: *(as he sets his foot on the gangway)* Hail, Caesar; and farewell!

(He reaches the ship and returns RUFIO's wave of the hand.)

APOLLODORUS: *(to CLEOPATRA)* No tears, dearest Queen: they stab your servant to the heart. He will return some day.

CLEOPATRA: I hope not. But I cant help crying, all the same. *(She waves her handkerchief to CAESAR; and the ship begins to move.)*

THE ROMAN SOLDIERS: *(drawing their swords and raising them in the air)* Hail, Caesar!

TENNESSEE WILLIAMS

(1911–1983)

*B*orn Thomas Lanier Williams in Columbus, Mississippi, Tennessee Williams remained a Southerner even though his education eventually took him to the University of Iowa where he began writing plays. The influence of his family on the themes and characters of his plays is always apparent. His mother, an example of perfect Southern gentility, is reflected in Amanda Wingfield, the mother in The Glass Menagerie (1945). Her daughter, the fragile and sensitive Laura, is, in part, a portrait of his sister Rose. Other female characters in later plays display similar gentility or sensitivity. His father, who was an aggressive, domineering, and powerful man whom Williams feared, influenced some of his dominant male characters such as Stanley Kowalski in A Streetcar Named Desire and Big Daddy in Cat on a Hot Tin Roof.

When his play The Glass Menagerie opened in New York, it received critical acclaim. Of the thirteen plays he wrote between 1945 and 1968, the major successes — critically and financially — were The Glass Menagerie, A Streetcar Named Desire, and Cat on a Hot Tin Roof (1955). All three plays received the Drama Critics' Circle Award; A Streetcar Named Desire and Cat on a Hot Tin Roof won Pulitzer prizes. Although he is best known for his plays, he also wrote short stories, poetry, film scripts, including Baby Doll (1956), and a novel, Moise and the World of Reason, which was published in 1975, the same year as his Memoirs.

Almost all his work deals with human sexuality and the pleasure and suffering it brings; the emphasis is placed most often upon the suffering. His protagonists who suffer are portrayed frequently as victims and many of them are responsible, at least partially, for their own fates. Intensely aware of their sufferings, they often try to escape through a world of illusions.

The words lyrical and poetic are characteristically used to describe his work, and are applied fittingly to such things as authentic rhythms of speech and his metaphors and symbols. As well, Williams's sense of theatre pervades Cat on a Hot Tin Roof with its powerful moments created by a combination of lighting, language, musical leitmotifs, and significant entrances and exits.

The settings in all Williams's plays exhibit many similarities. The South always looms large: hot weather and hothouse emotions brood over all Williams's theatrical worlds, producing an almost overwhelming languor and an aura of physical and moral decay. Settings and atmosphere serve the plays well; yet the remarkable fusion of these elements evident in his major plays is not always achieved in the later works.

INTRODUCTION TO *CAT ON A HOT TIN ROOF*

ennessee Williams's early dramatic success continued with *Cat on a Hot Tin Roof* (1955), which won for him his second Pulitzer Prize. This immediate "hit" in the theatre translated well onto the big screen. Metro-Goldwyn-Mayer paid half a million dollars for the film rights, producing a full-length motion picture in 1958 with Elizabeth Taylor, Paul Newman, and Burl Ives in the cast.

Cat on a Hot Tin Roof surpasses the expressionist symbolism and poetic reach of Williams's earlier plays to represent his broadest dramatic sympathy and most fully explored, realist dramatic situation. He enunciates his primary concern in a lengthy interpretive note in act 2 of the play:

> *The bird that I hope to catch in the net of this play is not the solution of one man's psychological problem. I'm trying to catch the true quality of experience in a group of people, that cloudy, flickering evanescent — fiercely charged! — interplay of live human beings in the thundercloud of a common crisis. (2.1168 s.d.)*

The "common crisis" of the play involves the true nature of Big Daddy's medical condition on his sixty-fifth birthday, Brick's drunken detachment from the family and especially from his wife Maggie, and the fraudulent attentions of Mae and Gooper as inheritors of Big Daddy's estate. In one emotionally charged night, convenient "truths" long ago elevated to unchallengeable status are torn down, bashed about, and interrogated by the Pollitt family.

Mendacity, according to Big Daddy "one of them five dollar words that cheap politicians throw back and forth at each other," (2.1165), represents the central theme of the play. Everyone at the Pollitt family estate consciously suppresses truth. Their false emotionality, polite pretension, and self-deceit leads to generalized self-delusion, a comfortable, collective, sincere self-delusion that easily replaces painful fact. Thus, through Big Daddy's birthday party, the family tries desperately to celebrate and reinforce his health, despite the fact that everyone, except Big Mama and Big Daddy himself, knows he is dying of cancer. They all cling to the acceptable "truth" that he suffers merely from a spastic colon — a significant metaphorical condition, considering the play's many falsehoods and Big Daddy's own favourite declarative: "Crap!" Mae and Gooper encourage his show of virility through exaggerated affection, all the while planning to benefit from the inheritance which they know to be imminent. Big Mama, too, uninformed but hoping blindly for the best, encourages Big Daddy's forced show of vigour, which manifests itself in vulgar unceremoniousness and private sexual daydreams. Brick, alone, refuses to take part in the family charade, but he is himself living in the falsity of his former glory as football star and life-buddy of Skipper, his dead teammate. The fact that Brick has broken his ankle on the Glorious Hill High School athletic field might seem to indicate his refusal to admit the "hill" which he is now well over as an adult and an alcoholic. Significantly, the immature action responsible for his injury the night before has provided him with a literal crutch, which he does not hesitate to use as a weapon on his wife, whom he blames for his grieving condition towards Skipper.

The situation of act 1 sets up conflicts to be dramatically explored. In act 2, Brick and Big Daddy confront each other on topics of truth, lies, communication — family mendacity in general. The two characters probe and evade a shared disgust, a generalized disgust that suppresses truth for psychological purposes as opposed to the calculating mendacity of the active liars in the household. Big Daddy wants to get at the root of Brick's drinking, which Brick wants to further evade his responsibilities as son, heir, and husband. Brick claims to drink out of "DISGUST," but Big Daddy itemizes the disgust with which he has lived his 65 years. In fact, only as Big Daddy probes the issue of Maggie's involvement with Skipper and the homosexual nature of Skipper's devotion and suicide does the truth of Brick's generalized "disgust" become any clearer. Threatened, Brick trades truth for truth, hinting at the extent of Big Daddy's terminal condition, and their discussion falls apart in raging expletives.

And yet their discussion is itself a form of mendacity in the play because real communication is so difficult to accomplish. "Why is it so damn hard for people to talk?" (2.1155) asks Big Daddy, and Brick responds noncommittally "Yeah. . . . " Later, Brick declares "Communication is — awful hard between people an' — somehow between you and me, it just don't — happen" (2.1157) Their dialogue itself is often dissonant, noncommunicative, tentative, unsure, touching on main themes of mortality, mendacity, sexuality, and the social pretension and responsibility from which both seek to escape. Brick and Big Daddy, however, develop prominence and some sympathy within the play, at the same time as they come to a gradual realization of their shared evasions concerning ambition, marriage, and family allegiance — evasions that impede effective communication.

Most communicative and probably most sympathetic, the character of Maggie is developed as central to the conflicts of Cat on a Hot Tin Roof. Indeed, the image of nervous instability suggested by the play's title relates most closely to Maggie's character. She wants to reclaim Brick as her husband and gain for both of them their rightful inheritance of the Pollitt estate. Although a childless outsider (and she is often reminded of this), Maggie demonstrates commitment to her husband and to the family in general that clearly exceeds Mae and Gooper's cozy family posturing. She detests the grasping self-interest of her in-laws at the same time as she comforts Big Mama in her confusion and loathing. But Maggie herself is not beyond half-truth in her own startling announcement near the play's conclusion. Clearly Big Daddy's favourite "daughter," Maggie refuses to jump off the "hot tin roof" of her situation until her will has been effected, she and

Brick are reconciled, and "Big Daddy's Dream Come True" of a grandchild from their union is assured. Her final assertion of love and life in the face of hypocrisy and death is something not even Brick contradicts, suggesting ambivalent interpretive possibilities.

Tennessee Williams best summarizes the realistic ambivalence throughout *Cat on a Hot Tin Roof* in the conclusion to his interpretive note previously quoted:

> *Some mystery should be left in the revelation of character in a play, just as a great deal of mystery is always left in the revelation of character in life, even in one's own character to himself. This does not absolve the playwright of his duty to observe and probe as clearly and deeply as he* legitimately *can: but it should steer him away from "pat" conclusions, facile definitions which make a play just a play, not a snare for the truth of human experience. (2.1168)*

Cat on a Hot Tin Roof

CHARACTERS OF THE PLAY

MARGARET

BRICK

MAE, *sometimes called Sister Woman*

BIG MAMA

DIXIE, *a little girl*

BIG DADDY

REVEREND TOOKER

GOOPER, *sometimes called Brother Man*

DOCTOR BAUGH, *pronounced "Baw"*

LACEY, *a Negro servant*

SOOKEY, *another*

CHILDREN

Notes for the Designer

The set is the bed-sitting-room of a plantation home in the Mississippi Delta. It is along an upstairs gallery which probably runs around the entire house; it has two pairs of very wide doors opening onto the gallery, showing white balustrades against a fair summer sky that fades into dusk and night during the course of the play, which occupies precisely the time of its performance, excepting, of course, the fifteen minutes of intermission.

Perhaps the style of the room is not what you would expect in the home of the Delta's biggest cotton-planter. It is Victorian with a touch of the Far East. It hasn't changed much since it was occupied by the original owners of the place, Jack Straw and Peter Ochello, a pair of old bachelors who shared this room all their lives together. In other words, the room must evoke some ghosts; it is gently and poetically haunted by a relationship that must have involved a tenderness which was uncommon. This may be irrelevant or unnecessary, but I once saw a reproduction of a faded photograph of the verandah of Robert Louis Stevenson's home on that Samoan Island where he spent his last years, and there was a quality of tender light on weathered wood, such as porch furniture made of bamboo and wicker, exposed to tropical suns and tropical rains, which came to mind when I thought about the set for this play, bringing also to mind the grace and comfort of light, the reassurance it gives, on a late and fair afternoon in summer, the way that no matter what, even dread of death, is gently touched and soothed by it. For the set is the background for a play that deals with human extremities of emotion, and it needs that softness behind it.

The bathroom door, showing only pale-blue tile and silver towel racks, is in one side wall; the hall door in the opposite wall. Two articles of furniture need mention: a big double bed which staging should make a functional part of the set as often as suitable, the surface of which should be slightly raked to make figures on it seen more easily; and against the wall space between the two huge double doors upstage: a monumental monstrosity peculiar to our times, a *huge* console combination of radio-phonograph (hi-fi with three speakers) TV set *and* liquor cabinet, bearing and containing many glasses and bottles, all in one piece, which is a composition of muted silver tones, and the opalescent tones of reflecting glass, a chromatic link, this thing, between the sepia (tawny gold) tones of the interior and the cool (white and blue) tones of the gallery and sky. This piece of furniture (?!), this monument, is a very complete and compact little shrine to virtually all the comforts and illusions behind which we hide from such things as the characters in the play are faced with. . . .

The set should be far less realistic than I have so far implied in this description of it. I think the walls below the ceiling should dissolve mysteriously into air; the set should be roofed by the sky; stars and moon suggested by traces of milky pallor, as if they were observed through a telescope lens out of focus.

Anything else I can think of? Oh, yes, fanlights (transoms shaped like an open glass fan) above all the doors in the set, with panes of blue and amber, and above all, the designer should take as many pains to give the actors room to move about freely (to show their restlessness, their passion for breaking out) as if it were a set for a ballet.

An evening in summer. The action is continuous, with two intermissions.

ACT ONE

At the rise of the curtain someone is taking a shower in the bathroom, the door of which is half open. A pretty young woman, with anxious lines in her face, enters the bedroom and crosses to the bathroom door.

MARGARET *(shouting above roar of water)*: One of those no-neck monsters hit me with a hot buttered biscuit so I have t' change!

(MARGARET's voice is both rapid and drawling. In her long speeches she has the vocal tricks of a priest delivering a liturgical chant, the lines are almost sung, always continuing a little beyond her breath so she has to gasp for another. Sometimes she intersperses the lines with a little wordless singing, such as "Da-da-daaaa!")

(Water turns off and BRICK calls out to her, but is still unseen. A tone of politely feigned interest, masking indifference, or worse, is characteristic of his speech with MARGARET.)

BRICK: Wha'd you say, Maggie? Water was on s' loud I couldn't hearya. . . .
MARGARET: Well, I! — just remarked that! — one of th' no-neck monsters messed up m' lovely lace dress so I got t' — cha-a-ange. . . .

(She opens and kicks shut drawers of the dresser.)

BRICK: Why d'ya call Gooper's kiddies no-neck monsters?
MARGARET: Because they've got no necks! Isn't that a good enough reason?
BRICK: Don't they have any necks?
MARGARET: None visible. Their fat little heads are set on their fat little bodies without a bit of connection.
BRICK: That's too bad.
MARGARET: Yes, it's too bad because you can't wring their necks if they've got no necks to wring! Isn't that right, honey?

(She steps out of her dress, stands in a slip of ivory satin and lace.)

Yep, they're no-neck monsters, all no-neck people are monsters. . . .

(Children shriek downstairs.)

Hear them? Hear them screaming? I don't know where their voice boxes are located since they don't have necks. I tell you I got so nervous at that table tonight I thought I would throw back my head and utter a scream you could hear across the Arkansas border an' parts of Louisiana an' Tennessee. I said to your charming sister-in-law, Mae, honey, couldn't you feed those precious little things at a separate table with an oilcloth cover? They make such a mess an' the lace cloth looks *so* pretty! She made enormous eyes at me and said, "Ohhh, noooooo! On Big Daddy's birthday? Why, he would never forgive me!" Well, I want you to know, Big Daddy hadn't been at the table two minutes with those five no-neck monsters slobbering and drooling over their food before he threw down his fork an' shouted, "Fo' God's sake, Gooper, why don't you put them pigs at a trough in th' kitchen?" — Well, I swear, I simply could have di-ieed!

Think of it, Brick, they've got five of them and number six is coming. They've brought the whole bunch down here like animals to display at a county fair. Why, they have those children doin' tricks all the time! "Junior, show Big Daddy how you do this, show Big Daddy how you do that, say your little piece fo' Big Daddy, Sister. Show your dimples, Sugar. Brother, show Big Daddy how you stand on your head!" — It goes on all the time, along with constant little remarks and innuendos about the fact that you and I have not produced any children, are totally childless and therefore totally useless! — Of course it's comical but it's also disgusting since it's so obvious what they're up to!

BRICK (*without interest*): What are they up to, Maggie?

MARGARET: Why, you know what they're up to!

BRICK (*appearing*): No, I don't know what they're up to.

(*He stands there in the bathroom doorway drying his hair with a towel and hanging onto the towel rack because one ankle is broken, plastered and bound. He is still slim and firm as a boy. His liquor hasn't started tearing him down outside. He has the additional charm of that cool air of detachment that people have who have given up the struggle. But now and then, when disturbed, something flashes behind it, like lightning in a fair sky, which shows that at some deeper level he is far from peaceful. Perhaps in a stronger light he would show some signs of deliquescence, but the fading, still warm, light from the gallery treats him gently.*)

MARGARET: I'll tell you what they're up to, boy of mine! — They're up to cutting you out of your father's estate, and —

(*She freezes momentarily before her next remark. Her voice drops as if it were somehow a personally embarrassing admission.*)

— Now we know that Big Daddy's dyin' of — *cancer.* . . .

(*There are voices on the lawn below: long-drawn calls across distance.* MARGARET *raises her lovely bare arms and powders her armpits with a light sigh.*)

(She adjusts the angle of a magnifying mirror to straighten an eyelash, then rises fretfully saying:)

There's so much light in the room it —
BRICK *(softly but sharply)*: Do we?
MARGARET: Do we what?
BRICK: Know Big Daddy's dyin' of cancer?
MARGARET: Got the report today.
BRICK: Oh . . .
MARGARET *(letting down bamboo blinds which cast long, gold-fretted shadows over the room)*: Yep, got th' report just now . . . it didn't surprise me, Baby. . . .

(Her voice has range, and music; sometimes it drops low as a boy's and you have a sudden image of her playing boy's games as a child.)

I recognized the symptoms soon's we got here last spring and I'm wil-lin' to bet you that Brother Man and his wife were pretty sure of it, too. That more than likely explains why their usual summer migration to the coolness of the Great Smokies was passed up this summer in favor of — hustlin' down here ev'ry whipstitch with their whole screamin' tribe! And why so many allusions have been made to Rainbow Hill lately. You know what Rainbow Hill is? Place that's famous for treatin' alcoholics an' dope fiends in the movies!
BRICK: I'm not in the movies.
MARGARET: No, and you don't take dope. Otherwise you're a perfect candi-date for Rainbow Hill, Baby, and that's where they aim to ship you — over my dead body! Yep, over my dead body they'll ship you there, but nothing would please them better. Then Brother Man could get a-hold of the purse strings and dole out remittances to us, maybe get power of attorney and sign checks for us and cut off our credit wherever, when-ever he wanted! Son-of-a-bitch! — How'd you like that, Baby? — Well, you've been doin' just about ev'rything in your power to bring it about, you've just been doin' ev'rything you can think of to aid and abet them in this scheme of theirs! Quittin' work, devoting yourself to the occupa-tion of drinkin'! — Breakin' your ankle last night on the high school athletic field: doin' what? Jumpin' hurdles? At two or three in the morn-ing? Just fantastic! Got in the paper. *Clarksdale Register* carried a nice little item about it, human interest story about a well-known former athlete stagin' a one-man track meet on the Glorious Hill High School athletic field last night, but was slightly out of condition and didn't clear the first hurdle! Brother Man Gooper claims he exercised his influence t' keep it from goin' out over AP or UP or every goddam "P."
But Brick? You still have one big advantage!

(During the above swift flood of words, BRICK has reclined with contrapuntal leisure on the snowy surface of the bed and has rolled over carefully on his side or belly.)

BRICK *(wryly)*: Did you *say* something, Maggie?

MARGARET: Big Daddy dotes on you, honey. And he can't stand Brother
  Man and Brother Man's wife, that monster of fertility, Mae. Know how
  I know? By little expressions that flicker over his face when that woman
  is holding fo'th on one of her choice topics such as — how she refused
  twilight sleep! — when the twins were delivered! Because she feels
  motherhood's an experience that a woman ought to experience fully! —
  in order to fully appreciate the wonder and beauty of it! HAH! — and
  how she made Brother Man come in an' stand beside her in the delivery
  room so he would not miss out on the "wonder and beauty" of it either!
  — producin' those no-neck monsters. . . .

(A speech of this kind would be antipathetic from almost anybody but MARGARET; *she
makes it oddly funny, because her eyes constantly twinkle and her voice shakes with
laughter which is basically indulgent.)*

— Big Daddy shares my attitude toward those two! As for me, well — I
  give him a laugh now and then and he tolerates me. In fact! — I some-
  times suspect that Big Daddy harbors a little unconscious "lech" fo'
  me. . . .
BRICK: What makes you think that Big Daddy has a lech for you, Maggie?
MARGARET: Way he always drops his eyes down my body when I'm talkin' to
  him, drops his eyes to my boobs an' licks his old chops! Ha ha!
BRICK: That kind of talk is disgusting.
MARGARET: Did anyone ever tell you that you're an ass-aching Puritan,
  Brick?
  I think it's mighty fine that that ole fellow, on the doorstep of death,
  still takes in my shape with what I think is deserved appreciation!
  And you wanta know something else? Big Daddy didn't know how
  many little Maes and Goopers had been produced! "How many kids
  have you got?" he asked at the table, just like Brother Man and his wife
  were new acquaintances to him! Big Mama said he was jokin', but that
  ole boy wasn't jokin', Lord no!
  And when they infawmed him that they had five already and were
  turning out number six! — the news seemed to come as a sort of
  unpleasant surprise . . .

(Children yell below.)

Scream, monsters!

(Turns to BRICK *with a sudden, gay, charming smile which fades as she notices that he
is not looking at her but into fading gold space with a troubled expression.)*

(It is constant rejection that makes her humor "bitchy.")

Yes, you should of been at that supper-table, Baby.

(Whenever she calls him "baby" the word is a soft caress.)

Y'know, Big Daddy, bless his ole sweet soul, he's the dearest ole thing in the world, but he does hunch over his food as if he preferred not to notice anything else. Well, Mae an' Gooper were side by side at the table, direckly across from Big Daddy, watchin' his face like hawks while they jawed an' jabbered about the cuteness an' brillance of th' no-neck monsters!

(She giggles with a hand fluttering at her throat and her breast and her long throat arched.)

(She comes downstage and recreates the scene with voice and gesture.)

And the no-neck monsters were ranged around the table, some in high chairs and some on th' *Books of Knowledge*, all in fancy little paper caps in honor of Big Daddy's birthday, and all through dinner, well, I want you to know that Brother Man an' his partner never once, for one moment, stopped exchanging pokes an' pinches an' kicks an' signs an' signals! — Why, they were like a couple of cardsharps fleecing a sucker. — Even Big Mama, bless her ole sweet soul, she isn't th' quickest an' brightest thing in the world, she finally noticed, at last, an' said to Gooper, "Gooper, what are you an' Mae makin' all these signs at each other about?" — I swear t' goodness, I nearly choked on my chicken!

(MARGARET, back at the dressing table, still doesn't see BRICK. He is watching her with a look that is not quite definable — Amused? shocked? contemptuous? — part of those and part of something else.)

Y'know — your brother Gooper still cherishes the illusion he took a giant step up on the social ladder when he married Miss Mae Flynn of the Memphis Flynns.

But I have a piece of Spanish news for Gooper. The Flynns never had a thing in this world but money and they lost that, they were nothing at all but fairly successful climbers. Of course, Mae Flynn came out in Memphis eight years before I made my debut in Nashville, but I had friends at Ward-Belmont who came from Memphis and they used to come to see me and I used to go to see them for Christmas and spring vacations, and so I know who rates an' who doesn't rate in Memphis society. Why, y'know ole Papa Flynn, he barely escaped doing time in the Federal pen for shady manipulations on th' stock market when his chain stores crashed, and as for Mae having been a cotton carnival queen, as they remind us so often, lest we forget, well, that's one honor that I don't envy her for! — Sit on a brass throne on a tacky float an' ride down Main Street, smilin', bowin', and blowin' kisses to all the trash on the street —

(She picks out a pair of jeweled sandals and rushes to the dressing table.)

Why, year before last, when Susan McPheeters was singled out fo' that honor, y' know what happened to her? Y'know what happened to poor little Susie McPheeters?

BRICK *(absently)*: No. What happened to little Susie McPheeters?

MARGARET: Somebody spit tobacco juice in her face.

BRICK *(dreamily)*: Somebody spit tobacco juice in her face?

MARGARET: That's right, some old drunk leaned out of a window in the Hotel Gayoso and yelled, "Hey, Queen, hey, hey, there, Queenie!" Poor Susie looked up and flashed him a radiant smile and he shot out a squirt of tobacco juice right in poor Susie's face.

BRICK: Well, what d'you know about that.

MARGARET *(gaily)*: What do I know about it? I was there, I saw it!

BRICK *(absently)*: Must have been kind of funny.

MARGARET: Susie didn't think so. Had hysterics. Screamed like a banshee. They had to stop th' parade an' remove her from her throne an' go on with —

(She catches sight of him in the mirror, gasps slightly, wheels about to face him. Count ten.)

— Why are you looking at me like that?

BRICK *(whistling softly, now)*: Like what, Maggie?

MARGARET *(intensely, fearfully)*: The way y' were lookin' at me just now, befo' I caught your eye in the mirror and you started t' whistle! I don't know how t' describe it but it froze my blood! — I've caught you lookin' at me like that so often lately. What are you thinkin' of when you look at me like that?

BRICK: I wasn't conscious of lookin' at you, Maggie.

MARGARET: Well, I was conscious of it! What were you thinkin'?

BRICK: I don't remember thinking of anything, Maggie.

MARGARET: Don't you think I know that — ? Don't you — ? — Think I know that — ?

BRICK *(coolly)*: Know *what*, Maggie?

MARGARET *(struggling for expression)*: That I've gone through this — *hideous!* — *transformation*, become — *hard! Frantic!*

(Then she adds, almost tenderly:)

— *cruel!!*

That's what you've been observing in me lately. How could y' help but observe it? That's all right. I'm not — thin-skinned any more, can't afford t' be thin-skinned any more.

(She is now recovering her power.)

— But Brick? Brick?

BRICK: Did you say something?

MARGARET: I was *goin'* t' say something: that I get — lonely. Very!

BRICK: Ev'rybody gets that . . .

MARGARET: Living with someone you love can be lonelier — than living entirely *alone*! — if the one that y' love doesn't love you. . . .

(There is a pause. BRICK *hobbles downstage and asks, without looking at her:)*

BRICK: Would you like to live alone, Maggie?

(Another pause: then — after she has caught a quick, hurt breath:)

MARGARET: *No! — God! — I wouldn't!*

(Another gasping breath. She forcibly controls what must have been an impulse to cry out. We see her deliberately, very forcibly, going all the way back to the world in which you can talk about ordinary matters.)

Did you have a nice shower?

BRICK: Uh-huh.

MARGARET: Was the water cool?

BRICK: No.

MARGARET: But it made y' feel fresh, huh?

BRICK: Fresher. . . .

MARGARET: I know something would make y' feel *much* fresher!

BRICK: What?

MARGARET: An alcohol rub. Or cologne, a rub with cologne!

BRICK: That's good after a workout but I haven't been workin' out, Maggie.

MARGARET: You've kept in good shape, though.

BRICK *(indifferently)*: You think so, Maggie?

MARGARET: I always thought drinkin' men lost their looks, but I was plainly mistaken.

BRICK *(wryly)*: Why, thanks, Maggie.

MARGARET: You're the only drinkin' man I know that it never seems t' put fat on.

BRICK: I'm gettin' softer, Maggie.

MARGARET: Well, sooner or later it's bound to soften you up. It was just beginning to soften up Skipper when —

(She stops short.)

I'm sorry. I never could keep my fingers off a sore — I wish you *would* lose your looks. If you did it would make the martyrdom of Saint Maggie a little more bearable. But no such goddam luck. I actually believe you've gotten better looking since you've gone on the bottle. Yeah, a person who didn't know you would think you'd never had a tense nerve in your body or a strained muscle.

(There are sounds of croquet on the lawn below: the click of mallets, light voices, near and distant.)

Of course, you always had that detached quality as if you were playing a game without much concern over whether you won or lost, and now that you've lost the game, not lost but just quit playing, you have that rare sort of charm that usually only happens in very old or hopelessly sick people, the charm of the defeated. — You look so cool, so cool, so enviably cool.

REVEREND TOOKER *(off stage right)*: Now looka here, boy, lemme show you how to get outa that!

MARGARET: They're playing croquet. The moon has appeared and it's white, just beginning to turn a little bit yellow . . . .

You were a wonderful lover. . . .

Such a wonderful person to go to bed with, and I think mostly because you were really indifferent to it. Isn't that right? Never had any anxiety about it, did it naturally, easily, slowly, with absolute confidence and perfect calm, more like opening a door for a lady or seating her at a table than giving expression to any longing for her. Your indifference made you wonderful at lovemaking — *strange?* — but true. . . .

REVEREND TOOKER: Oh! That's a beauty.

DOCTOR BAUGH: Yeah. I got you boxed.

MARGARET: You know, if I thought you would never, never, *never* make love to me again — I would go downstairs to the kitchen and pick out the longest and sharpest knife I could find and stick it straight into my heart, I swear that I would!

REVEREND TOOKER: Watch out, you're gonna miss it.

DOCTOR BAUGH: You just don't know me, boy!

MARGARET: But one thing I don't have is the charm of the defeated, my hat is still in the ring, and I am determined to win!

(There is the sound of croquet mallets hitting croquet balls.)

REVEREND TOOKER: Mmm — You're too slippery for me.

MARGARET: — What is the victory of a cat on a hot tin roof? — I wish I knew. . . .

Just staying on it, I guess, as long as she can. . . .

DOCTOR BAUGH: Jus' like an eel, boy, jus' like an eel!

(More croquet sounds.)

MARGARET: Later tonight I'm going to tell you I love you an' maybe by that time you'll be drunk enough to believe me. Yes, they're playing croquet . . .

Big Daddy is dying of cancer. . . .

What were you thinking of when I caught you looking at me like that? Were you thinking of Skipper?

(BRICK takes up his crutch, rises.)

Oh, excuse me, forgive me, but laws of silence don't work! No, laws of silence don't work. . . .

(BRICK crosses to the bar, takes a quick drink, and rubs his head with a towel.)

Laws of silence don't work. . . .
    When something is festering in your memory or your imagination, laws of silence don't work, it's just like shutting a door and locking it on a house on fire in hope of forgetting that the house is burning. But not facing a fire doesn't put it out. Silence about a thing just magnifies it. It grows and festers in silence, becomes malignant. . . .

(He drops his crutch.)

BRICK: Give me my crutch.

(He has stopped rubbing his hair dry but still stands hanging onto the towel rack in a white towel-cloth robe.)

MARGARET: Lean on me.
BRICK: No, just give me my crutch.
MARGARET: Lean on my shoulder.
BRICK: *I don't want to lean on your shoulder, I want my crutch!*

(This is spoken like sudden lightning.)

Are you going to give me my crutch or do I have to get down on my knees on the floor and —
MARGARET: *Here, here, take it, take it!*

(She has thrust the crutch at him.)

BRICK *(hobbling out)*: Thanks . . .
MARGARET: We mustn't scream at each other, the walls in this house have ears. . . .

(He hobbles directly to liquor cabinet to get a new drink.)

— but that's the first time I've heard you raise your voice in a long time, Brick. A crack in the wall? — Of composure?
    — I think that's a good sign. . . .
    A sign of nerves in a player on the defensive!

(BRICK turns and smiles at her coolly over his fresh drink.)

BRICK: It just hasn't happened yet, Maggie.

MARGARET: What?

BRICK: The click I get in my head when I've had enough of this stuff to make me peaceful. . . .

   Will you do me a favor?

MARGARET: Maybe I will. What favor?

BRICK: Just, just keep your voice down!

MARGARET *(in a hoarse whisper)*: I'll do you that favor, I'll speak in a whisper, if not shut up completely, if *you* will do *me* a favor and make that drink your last one till after the party.

BRICK: What party?

MARGARET: Big Daddy's birthday party.

BRICK: Is this Big Daddy's birthday?

MARGARET: You know this is Big Daddy's birthday!

BRICK: No, I don't, I forgot it.

MARGARET: Well, I remembered it for you. . . .

(They are both speaking as breathlessly as a pair of kids after a fight, drawing deep exhausted breaths and looking at each other with faraway eyes, shaking and panting together as if they had broken apart from a violent struggle.)

BRICK: Good for you, Maggie.

MARGARET: You just have to scribble a few lines on this card.

BRICK: You scribble something, Maggie.

MARGARET: It's got to be your handwriting; it's your present, I've given him my present; it's got to be your handwriting!

(The tension between them is building again, the voices becoming shrill once more.)

BRICK: I didn't get him a present.

MARGARET: I got one for you.

BRICK: All right. You write the card, then.

MARGARET: And have him know you didn't remember his birthday?

BRICK: I didn't remember his birthday.

MARGARET: You don't have to prove you didn't!

BRICK: I don't want to fool him about it.

MARGARET: Just write "Love, Brick!" for God's —

BRICK: No.

MARGARET: You've *got* to!

BRICK: I don't have to do anything I don't want to do. You keep forgetting the conditions on which I agreed to stay on living with you.

MARGARET *(out before she knows it)*: I'm not living with you. We occupy the same cage.

BRICK: You've got to remember the conditions agreed on.

SONNY *(off stage)*: Mommy, give it to me. I had it first.

MAE: Hush.

MARGARET: They're impossible conditions!

BRICK: Then why don't you — ?

SONNY: I want it, I want it!

MAE: Get away!

MARGARET: HUSH! Who is out there? Is somebody at the door?

(There are footsteps in hall.)

MAE *(outside)*: May I enter a moment?

MARGARET: Oh, *you!* Sure. Come in, Mae.

(MAE enters bearing aloft the bow of a young lady's archery set.)

MAE: Brick, is this thing yours?

MARGARET: Why, Sister Woman — that's my Diana Trophy. Won it at the intercollegiate archery contest on the Ole Miss[1] campus.

MAE: It's a mighty dangerous thing to leave exposed round a house full of nawmal rid-blooded children attracted t'weapons.

MARGARET: "Nawmal rid-blooded children attracted t'weapons" ought t'be taught to keep their hands off things that don't belong to them.

MAE: Maggie, honey, if you had children of your own you'd know how funny that is. Will you please lock this up and put the key out of reach?

MARGARET: Sister Woman, nobody is plotting the destruction of your kiddies. — Brick and I still have our special archers' license. We're goin' deer-huntin' on Moon Lake as soon as the season starts. I love to run with dogs through chilly woods, run, run leap over obstructions —

(She goes into the closet carrying the bow.)

MAE: How's the injured ankle, Brick?

BRICK: Doesn't hurt. Just itches.

MAE: Oh, my! Brick — Brick, you should've been downstairs after supper! Kiddies put on a show. Polly played the piano, Buster an' Sonny drums, an' then they turned out the lights an' Dixie an' Trixie puhfawmed a toe dance in fairy costume with *spahkluhs!* Big Daddy just beamed! He just beamed!

MARGARET *(from the closet with a sharp laugh)*: Oh, I bet. It breaks my heart that we missed it!

(She reenters.)

But Mae? Why did y'give dawgs' names to all your kiddies?

MAE: *Dogs'* names?

MARGARET *(sweetly)*: Dixie, Trixie, Buster, Sonny, Polly! — Sounds like four dogs and a parrot . . .

MAE: Maggie?

(MARGARET turns with a smile.)

---

1 *University of Mississippi.*

Why are you so catty?

MARGARET: Cause I'm a cat! But why can't *you* take a joke, Sister Woman?

MAE: Nothin' pleases me more than a joke that's funny. You know the real names of our kiddies. Buster's real name is Robert. Sonny's real name is Saunders. Trixie's real name is Marlene and Dixie's —

(GOOPER *downstairs calls for her.* "Hey, Mae! Sister Woman, intermission is over!" *— She rushes to door, saying:*)

Intermission is over! See ya later!

MARGARET: I wonder what Dixie's real name is?

BRICK: Maggie, being catty doesn't help things any . . .

MARGARET: I know! *WHY*! — Am I so catty? — Cause I'm consumed with envy an' eaten up with longing? — Brick, I'm going to lay out your beautiful Shantung silk suit from Rome and one of your mono-grammed silk shirts. I'll put your cuff links in it, those lovely star sap-phires I get you to wear so rarely. . . .

BRICK: I can't get trousers on over this plaster cast.

MARGARET: Yes, you can, I'll help you.

BRICK: I'm not going to get dressed, Maggie.

MARGARET: Will you just put on a pair of white silk pajamas?

BRICK: Yes, I'll do that, Maggie.

MARGARET: *Thank* you, thank you so *much!*

BRICK: Don't mention it.

MARGARET: *Oh, Brick!* How long does it have t' go on? This punishment? Haven't I done time enough, haven't I served my term, can't I apply for a — pardon?

BRICK: Maggie, you're spoiling my liquor. Lately your voice always sounds like you'd been running upstairs to warn somebody that the house was on fire!

MARGARET: Well, no wonder, no wonder. Y'know what I feel like, Brick? *I feel all the time like a cat on a hot tin roof!*

BRICK: Then jump off the roof, jump off it, cats can jump off roofs and land on their four feet uninjured!

MARGARET: Oh, yes!

BRICK: Do it! — fo' God's sake, do it . . .

MARGARET: Do what?

BRICK: Take a lover!

MARGARET: I can't see a man but you! Even with my eyes closed, I just see you! Why don't you get ugly, Brick, why don't you please get fat or ugly or something so I could stand it?

(She rushes to hall door, opens it, listens.)

The concert is still going on! Bravo, no-necks, bravo!

(She slams and locks door fiercely.)

BRICK: What did you lock the door for?

MARGARET: To give us a little privacy for a while.

BRICK: You know better, Maggie.

MARGARET: No, I don't know better . . . .

(She rushes to gallery doors, draws the rose-silk drapes across them.)

BRICK: Don't make a fool of yourself.

MARGARET: I don't mind makin' a fool of myself over you!

BRICK: I mind, Maggie. I feel embarrassed for you.

MARGARET: Feel embarrassed! But don't continue my torture. I can't live on and on under these circumstances.

BRICK: You agreed to —

MARGARET: I know but —

BRICK: — Accept that condition!

MARGARET: *I CAN'T! CAN'T! CAN'T!*

(She seizes his shoulder.)

BRICK: Let go!

(He breaks away from her and seizes the small boudoir chair and raises it like a lion-tamer facing a big circus cat.)

(Count five. She stares at him with her fist pressed to her mouth, then bursts into shrill, almost hysterical laughter. He remains grave for a moment, then grins and puts the chair down.)

(BIG MAMA calls through closed door.)

BIG MAMA: Son? Son? Son?

BRICK: What is it, Big Mama?

BIG MAMA *(outside)*: Oh, son! We got the most wonderful news about Big Daddy. I just had t' run up an' tell you right this —

(She rattles the knob.)

— What's this door doin', locked, faw? You all think there's robbers in the house?

MARGARET: Big Mama, Brick is dressin', he's not dressed yet.

BIG MAMA: That's all right, it won't be the first time I've seen Brick not dressed. Come on, open this door!

(MARGARET, with a grimace, goes to unlock and open the hall door, as BRICK hobbles rapidly to the bathroom and kicks the door shut. BIG MAMA has disappeared from the hall.)

MARGARET: Big Mama?

(BIG MAMA *appears through the opposite gallery doors behind* MARGARET, *huffing and puffing like an old bulldog. She is a short, stout woman; her sixty years and 170 pounds have left her somewhat breathless most of the time; she's always tensed like a boxer, or rather, a Japanese wrestler. Her "family" was maybe a little superior to* BIG DADDY's, *but not much. She wears a black or silver lace dress and at least half a million in flashy gems. She is very sincere.*)

BIG MAMA (*loudly, startling* MARGARET): Here — I come through Gooper's and Mae's gall'ry door. Where's Brick? *Brick* — Hurry on out of there, son, I just have a second and want to give you the news about Big Daddy. — I hate locked doors in a house. . . .

MARGARET (*with affected lightness*): I've noticed you do, Big Mama, but people have got to have *some* moments of privacy, don't they?

BIG MAMA: No, ma'am, not in *my* house. (*without pause*) Whacha took off you' dress faw? I thought that little lace dress was so sweet on yuh, honey.

MARGARET: I thought it looked sweet on me, too, but one of m' cute little table-partners used it for a napkin so — !

BIG MAMA (*picking up stockings on floor*): What?

MARGARET: You know, Big Mama, Mae and Gooper's so touchy about those children — thanks, Big Mama . . .

(BIG MAMA *has thrust the picked-up stockings in* MARGARET's *hand with a grunt.*)

— that you just don't dare to suggest there's any room for improvement in their —

BIG MAMA: Brick, hurry out! — Shoot, Maggie, you just don't like children.

MARGARET: I do SO like children! Adore them! — well brought up!

BIG MAMA (*gentle — loving*): Well, why don't you have some and bring them up well, then, instead of all the time pickin' on Gooper's an' Mae's?

GOOPER (*shouting up the stairs*): Hey, hey, Big Mama, Betsy an' Hugh got to go, waitin' t' tell yuh g'by!

BIG MAMA: Tell 'em to hold their hawses, I'll be right down in a jiffy!

GOOPER: Yes ma'am!

(*She turns to the bathroom door and calls out.*)

BIG MAMA: Son? Can you hear me in there?

(*There is a muffled answer.*)

We just got the full report from the laboratory at the Ochsner Clinic, completely negative, son, ev'rything negative, right on down the line! Nothin' a-tall's wrong with him but some little functional thing called a spastic colon. Can you hear me, son?

MARGARET: He can hear you, Big Mama.

BIG MAMA: Then why don't he say something? God Almighty, a piece of news like that should make him shout. It made *me* shout, I can tell you. I shouted and sobbed and fell right down on my knees! — Look!

(She pulls up her skirt.)

See the bruises where I hit my kneecaps? Took both doctors to haul me back on my feet!

(She laughs — she always laughs like hell at herself.)

Big Daddy was furious with me! But ain't that wonderful news?

(Facing bathroom again, she continues:)

After all the anxiety we been through to git a report like that on Big Daddy's birthday? Big Daddy tried to hide how much of a load that news took off his mind, but didn't fool *me*. He was mighty close to crying about it *himself!*

(Goodbyes are shouted downstairs, and she rushes to door.)

GOOPER: Big Mama!
BIG MAMA: *Hold those people down there, don't let them go!* — Now, git dressed, we're all comin' up to this room fo' Big Daddy's birthday party because of your ankle. — How's his ankle, Maggie?
MARGARET: Well, he broke it, Big Mama.
BIG MAMA: I know he broke it.

(A phone is ringing in hall. A Negro voice answers: "Mistuh Polly's res'dence.")

I mean does it hurt him much still.
MARGARET: I'm afraid I can't give you that information, Big Mama. You'll have to ask Brick if it hurts much still or not.
SOOKEY *(in the hall)*: It's Memphis, Mizz Polly, it's Miss Sally in Memphis.
BIG MAMA: Awright, Sookey.

(BIG MAMA rushes into the hall and is heard shouting on the phone:)

Hello, Miss Sally. How are you, Miss Sally? — Yes, well, I was just gonna call you about it. *Shoot!* —
MARGARET: Brick, don't!

(BIG MAMA raises her voice to a bellow.)

BIG MAMA: *Miss Sally? Don't ever call me from the Gayoso Lobby, too much talk goes on in that hotel lobby, no wonder you can't hear me!* Now listen, Miss Sally. They's nothin' serious wrong with Big Daddy. We got the report just now, they's nothin' wrong but a thing called a — spastic! *SPASTIC!* — colon . . .

(She appears at the hall door and calls to MARGARET.)

— Maggie, come out here and talk to that fool on the phone. I'm shouted breathless!

MARGARET *(goes out and is heard sweetly at phone)*: Miss Sally? This is Brick's wife, Maggie. So nice to hear your voice. Can you hear *mine?* Well, *good!* — Big Mama just wanted you to know that they've got the report from the Ochsner Clinic and what Big Daddy has is a spastic colon. Yes. Spastic colon, Miss Sally. That's right, spastic colon. *G'bye, Miss Sally, hope I'll see you real soon!*

(Hangs up a little before Miss Sally was probably ready to terminate the talk. She returns through the hall door.)

She heard me perfectly. I've discovered with deaf people the thing to do is not shout at them but just enunciate clearly. My rich old Aunt Cornelia was deaf as the dead but I could make her hear me just by sayin' each word slowly, distinctly, close to her ear. I read her the *Commercial Appeal* ev'ry night, read her the classified ads in it, even, she never missed a word of it. But was she a mean ole thing! Know what I got when she died? Her unexpired subscriptions to five magazines and the Book-of-the-Month Club and a LIBRARY full of ev'ry dull book ever written! All else went to her hellcat of a sister . . . meaner than she was, even!

(BIG MAMA has been straightening things up in the room during this speech.)

BIG MAMA *(closing closet door on discarded clothes)*: Miss Sally sure is a case! Big Daddy says she's always got her hand out fo' something. He's not mistaken. That poor ole thing always has her hand out fo' somethin'. I don't think Big Daddy gives her as much as he should.

GOOPER: Big Mama! Come on now! Betsy and Hugh can't wait no longer!

BIG MAMA *(shouting)*: I'm comin'!

(She starts out. At the hall door, turns and jerks a forefinger, first toward the bathroom door, then toward the liquor cabinet, meaning: "Has Brick been drinking?" MARGARET *pretends not to understand, cocks her head and raises her brows as if the pantomimic performance was completely mystifying to her.)*

(BIG MAMA rushes back to MARGARET:)

Shoot! Stop playin' so dumb! — I mean has he been drinkin' that stuff much yet?

MARGARET *(with a little laugh)*: Oh! I think he had a highball after supper.

BIG MAMA: Don't laugh about it! — Some single men stop drinkin' when they git married and others start! Brick never touched liquor before he — !

MARGARET (crying out): *THAT'S NOT FAIR!*

BIG MAMA: Fair or not fair I want to ask you a question, one question: D'you make Brick happy in bed?

MARGARET: Why don't you ask if he makes *me* happy in bed?

BIG MAMA: Because I know that —

MARGARET: *It works both ways!*

BIG MAMA: Something's not right! You're childless and my son drinks!

GOOPER: Come on, Big Mama!

(GOOPER *has called her downstairs and she has rushed to the door on the line above. She turns at the door and points at the bed.*)

— When a marriage goes on the rocks, the rocks are *there*, right *there!*

MARGARET: *That's —*

(BIG MAMA *has swept out of the room and slammed the door.*)

— not — *fair* . . .

(MARGARET *is alone, completely alone, and she feels it. She draws in, hunches her shoulders, raises her arms with fists clenched, shuts her eyes tight as a child about to be stabbed with a vaccination needle. When she opens her eyes again, what she sees is the long oval mirror and she rushes straight to it, stares into it with a grimace and says: "Who are you?" — Then she crouches a little and answers herself in a different voice which is high, thin, mocking: "I am Maggie the Cat!" — Straightens quickly as bathroom door opens a little and* BRICK *calls out to her.*)

BRICK: Has Big Mama gone?

MARGARET: She's gone.

(He opens the bathroom door and hobbles out, with his liquor glass now empty, straight to the liquor cabinet. He is whistling softly. MARGARET's head pivots on her long, slender throat to watch him.)

(She raises a hand uncertainly to the base of her throat, as if it was difficult for her to swallow, before she speaks:)

You know, our sex life didn't just peter out in the usual way, it was cut off short, long before the natural time for it to, and it's going to revive again, just as sudden as that. I'm confident of it. That's what I'm keeping myself attractive for. For the time when you'll see me again like other men see me. Yes, like other men see me. They still see me, Brick, and they like what they see. Uh-huh. Some of them would give their —

Look, Brick!

(She stands before the long oval mirror, touches her breast and then her hips with her two hands.)

How high my body stays on me! — Nothing has fallen on me — not a fraction. . . .

(Her voice is soft and trembling: a pleading child's. At this moment as he turns to glance at her — a look which is like a player passing a ball to another player, third down and goal to go — she has to capture the audience in a grip so tight that she can hold it till the first intermission without any lapse of attention.)

Other men still want me. My face looks strained, sometimes, but I've kept my figure as well as you've kept yours, and men admire it. I still turn heads on the street. Why, last week in Memphis everywhere that I went men's eyes burned holes in my clothes, at the country club and in restaurants and department stores, there wasn't a man I met or walked by that didn't just eat me up with his eyes and turn around when I passed him and look back at me. Why, at Alice's party for her New York cousins, the best-lookin' man in the crowd — followed me upstairs and tried to force his way in the powder room with me, followed me to the door and tried to force his way in!

BRICK: Why didn't you let him, Maggie?

MARGARET: Because I'm not that common, for one thing. Not that I wasn't almost tempted to. You like to know who it was? It was Sonny Boy Maxwell, that's who!

BRICK: Oh, yeah, Sonny Boy Maxwell, he was a good end-runner but had a little injury to his back and had to quit.

MARGARET: He has no injury now and has no wife and still has a lech for me!

BRICK: I see no reason to lock him out of a powder room in that case.

MARGARET: And have someone catch me at it? I'm not that stupid. Oh, I might sometime cheat on you with someone, since you're so insultingly eager to have me do it! — But if I do, you can be damned sure it will be in a place and a time where no one but me and the man could possibly know. Because I'm not going to give you any excuse to divorce me for being unfaithful or anything else. . . .

BRICK: Maggie, I wouldn't divorce you for being unfaithful or anything else. Don't you know that? Hell. I'd be relieved to know that you'd found yourself a lover.

MARGARET: Well, I'm taking no chances. No, I'd rather stay on this hot tin roof.

BRICK: A hot tin roof's 'n uncomfo'table place t' stay on. . . .

(He starts to whistle softly.)

MARGARET *(through his whistle)*: Yeah, but I can stay on it just as long as I have to.

BRICK: You could leave me, Maggie.

(He resumes whistle. She wheels about to glare at him.)

MARGARET: *Don't want to and will not!* Besides if I did, you don't have a cent to pay for it but what you get from Big Daddy and he's dying of cancer!

(For the first time a realization of BIG DADDY'S *doom seems to penetrate to* BRICK'S *consciousness, visibly, and he looks at* MARGARET.*)*

BRICK: Big Mama just said he *wasn't*, that the report was okay.
MARGARET: That's what she thinks because she got the same story that they gave Big Daddy. And was just as taken in by it as he was, poor ole things. . . .
　　But tonight they're going to tell her the truth about it. When Big Daddy goes to bed, they're going to tell her that he is dying of cancer.

(She slams the dresser drawer.)

— It's malignant and it's terminal.
BRICK: Does Big Daddy know it?
MARGARET: Hell, do they *ever* know it? Nobody says, "You're dying." You have to fool them. They have to fool *themselves*.
BRICK: Why?
MARGARET: *Why?* Because human beings dream of life everlasting, that's the reason! But most of them want it on earth and not in heaven.

(He gives a short, hard laugh at her touch of humor.)

Well. . . . *(She touches up her mascara.)* That's how it is, anyhow. . . . *(She looks about.)* Where did I put down my cigarette? Don't want to burn up the home-place, at least not with Mae and Gooper and their five monsters in it!

(She has found it and sucks at it greedily. Blows out smoke and continues:)

So this is Big Daddy's last birthday. And Mae and Gooper, they know it, oh, *they* know it, all right. They got the first information from the Ochsner Clinic. That's why they rushed down here with their no-neck monsters. Because. Do you know something? Big Daddy's made no will? Big Daddy's never made out any will in his life, and so this campaign's afoot to impress him, forcibly as possible, with the fact that you drink and I've borne no children!

(He continues to stare at her a moment, then mutters something sharp but not audible and hobbles rather rapidly out onto the long gallery in the fading, much faded, gold light.)

MARGARET *(continuing her liturgical chant)*: Y'know, I'm *fond* of Big Daddy, I am
genuinely fond of that old man, I really *am*, you know. . . .

BRICK *(faintly, vaguely)*: Yes, I know you are. . . .

MARGARET: I've always sort of admired him in spite of his coarseness, his
four-letter words and so forth. Because Big Daddy *is* what he *is*, and he
makes no bones about it. He hasn't turned gentleman farmer, he's still a
Mississippi redneck, as much of a redneck as he must have been when
he was just overseer here on the old Jack Straw and Peter Ochello place.
But he got hold of it an' built it into th' biggest an' finest plantation in
the Delta. — I've always *liked* Big Daddy. . . .

(She crosses to the proscenium.)

Well, this is Big Daddy's last birthday. I'm sorry about it. But I'm facing
the facts. It takes money to take care of a drinker and that's the office
that I've been elected to lately.

BRICK: You don't have to take care of me.

MARGARET: Yes, I do. Two people in the same boat have got to take care of
each other. At least you want money to buy more Echo Spring when
this supply is exhausted, or will you be satisfied with a ten-cent beer?

Mae an' Gooper are plannin' to freeze us out of Big Daddy's estate
because you drink and I'm childless. But we can defeat that plan. We're
going to defeat that plan!

Brick, y'know, I've been so God damn disgustingly poor all my life! — That's the
truth, Brick!

BRICK: I'm not sayin' it isn't.

MARGARET: Always had to suck up to people I couldn't stand because they
had money and I was poor as Job's turkey. You don't know what that's
like. Well, I'll tell you, it's like you would feel a thousand miles away
from Echo Spring! — And had to get back to it on that broken
ankle . . . without a crutch!

That's how it feels to be as poor as Job's turkey and have to suck up
to relatives that you hated because they had money and all you had was
a bunch of hand-me-down clothes and a few old moldly three-per-cent
government bonds. My daddy loved his liquor, he fell in love with his
liquor the way you've fallen in love with Echo Spring! — And my poor
Mama, having to maintain some semblance of social position, to keep
appearances up, on an income of one hundred and fifty dollars a month
on those old government bonds!

When I came out, the year that I made my debut, I had just two evening dresses! One Mother made me from a pattern in *Vogue*, the other a
hand-me-down from a snotty rich cousin I hated!

— The dress that I married you in was my grandmother's weddin'
gown. . . .

So that's why I'm like a cat on a hot tin roof!

(BRICK is still on the gallery. Someone below calls up to him in a warm Negro voice, "Hiya, Mistuh Brick, how yuh feelin'?" BRICK raises his liquor glass as if that answered the question.)

MARGARET: You can be young without money, but you can't be old without it. You've got to be old *with* money because to be old without it is just too awful, you've got to be one or the other, either *young* or *with money*, you can't be old and *without* it. — That's the *truth*, Brick. . . .

(BRICK whistles softly, vaguely.)

Well, now I'm dressed, I'm all dressed, there's nothing else for me to do.

(Forlornly, almost fearfully.)

I'm dressed, all dressed, nothing else for me to do. . . .

(She moves about restlessly, aimlessly, and speaks, as if to herself.)

What am I — ? Oh! — my bracelets. . . .

(She starts working a collection of bracelets over her hands onto her wrists, about six on each, as she talks.)

I've thought a whole lot about it and now I know when I made my mistake. Yes, I made my mistake when I told you the truth about that thing with Skipper. Never should have confessed it, a fatal error, tellin' you about that thing with Skipper.

BRICK: Maggie, shut up about Skipper. I mean it, Maggie; you got to shut up about Skipper.

MARGARET: You ought to understand that Skipper and I —

BRICK: You don't think I'm serious, Maggie? You're fooled by the fact that I am saying this quiet? Look, Maggie. What you're doing is a dangerous thing to do. You're — you're — you're — foolin' with something that — nobody ought to fool with.

MARGARET: This time I'm going to finish what I have to say to you. Skipper and I made love, if love you could call it, because it made both of us feel a little bit closer to you. You see, you son of a bitch, you asked too much of people, of me, of him, of all the unlucky poor damned sons of bitches that happen to love you, and there was a whole pack of them, yes, there was a pack of them besides me and Skipper, you asked too goddam much of people that loved you, you — superior creature! — you godlike being! — And so we made love to each other to dream it was you, both of us! Yes, yes, yes! Truth, truth! What's so awful about it? I like it, I think the truth is — yeah! I shouldn't have told you . . . .

BRICK *(holding his head unnaturally still and uptilted a bit)*: It was Skipper that told me about it. Not you, Maggie.

MARGARET: I told you!

BRICK: After he told me!

MARGARET: What does it matter who — ?

DIXIE: I got your mallet, I got your mallet.

TRIXIE: Give it to me, give it to me. IT's mine.

(BRICK *turns suddenly out upon the gallery and calls:*)

BRICK: Little girl! Hey, little girl!

LITTLE GIRL (*at a distance*): What, Uncle Brick?

BRICK: Tell the folks to come up! — Bring everybody upstairs!

TRIXIE: It's mine, it's mine.

MARGARET: I can't stop myself! I'd go on telling you this in front of them all, if I had to!

BRICK: Little girl! Go on, go on, will you? Do what I told you, call them!

DIXIE: Okay.

MARGARET: Because it's got to be told and you, you! — you never let me!

(*She sobs, then controls herself, and continues almost calmly.*)

It was one of those beautiful, ideal things they tell about in the Greek legends, it couldn't be anything else, you being you, and that's what made it so sad, that's what made it so awful, because it was love that never could be carried through to anything satisfying or even talked about plainly.

BRICK: Maggie, you gotta stop this.

MARGARET: Brick, I tell you, you got to believe me, Brick, I *do* understand all about it! I — I think it was — *noble!* Can't you tell I'm sincere when I say I respect it? My only point, the only point that I'm making, is life has got to be allowed to continue even after the *dream* of life is — all — over. . . .

(BRICK *is without his crutch. Leaning on furniture, he crosses to pick it up as she continues as if possessed by a will outside herself:*)

Why I remember when we double-dated at college, Gladys Fitzgerald and I and you and Skipper, it was more like a date between you and Skipper. Gladys and I were just sort of tagging along as if it was necessary to chaperone you! — to make a good public impression —

BRICK (*turns to face her, half lifting his crutch*): Maggie, you want me to hit you with this crutch? Don't you know I could kill you with this crutch?

MARGARET: Good Lord, man, d' you think I'd care if you did?

BRICK: One man has one great good true thing in his life. One great good thing which is true! — I had friendship with Skipper. — You are naming it dirty!

MARGARET: I'm not naming it dirty! I am naming it clean.

BRICK: Not love with you, Maggie, but friendship with Skipper was that one great true thing, and you are naming it dirty!

MARGARET: Then you haven't been listenin', not understood what I'm saying! I'm naming it so damn clean that it killed poor Skipper! — You two
had something that had to be kept on ice, yes, incorruptible, yes! — and
death was the only icebox where you could keep it. . . .

BRICK: I married you, Maggie. Why would I marry you, Maggie, if I
was — ?

MARGARET: Brick, let me finish! — I know, believe me I know, that it was
only Skipper that harbored even any *unconscious* desire for anything not
perfectly pure between you two! — Now let me skip a little. You married me early that summer we graduated out of Ole Miss, and we were
happy, weren't we, we were blissful, yes, hit heaven together ev'ry time
that we loved! But that fall you an' Skipper turned down wonderful
offers of jobs in order to keep on bein' football heroes — pro-football
heroes. You organized the Dixie Stars that fall, so you could keep on
bein' teammates forever! But somethin' was not right with it! — *Me
included!* — between you. Skipper began hittin' the bottle . . . you got a
spinal injury — couldn't play the Thanksgivin' game in Chicago,
watched it on TV from a traction bed in Toledo. I joined Skipper. The
Dixie Stars lost because poor Skipper was drunk. We drank together
that night all night in the bar of the Blackstone and when cold day was
comin' up over the Lake an' we were comin' out drunk to take a dizzy
look at it, I said, "SKIPPER! STOP LOVIN' MY HUSBAND OR TELL
HIM HE'S GOT TO LET YOU ADMIT IT TO HIM!" — one way or
another!

HE SLAPPED ME HARD ON THE MOUTH! — then turned and
ran without stopping once, I am sure, all the way back into his room at
the Blackstone. . . .

— When I came to his room that night, with a little scratch like a shy
little mouse at his door, he made that pitiful, ineffectual little attempt to
prove that what I had said wasn't true. . . .

(BRICK *strikes at her with crutch, a blow that shatters the gemlike lamp on the table.*)

— In this way, I destroyed him, by telling him truth that he and his
world which he was born and raised in, yours and his world, had told
him could not be told?

— From then on Skipper was nothing at all but a receptacle for liquor and drugs. . . .

— *Who shot cock robin? I with my* —

(*She throws back her head with tight shut eyes.*)

— *merciful arrow!*

(BRICK *strikes at her; misses.*)

Missed me! — Sorry, — I'm not tryin' to whitewash my behavior,
Christ, no! Brick, I'm not good. I don't know why people have to pre-

tend to be good, nobody's good. The rich or the well-to-do can afford to respect moral patterns, conventional moral patterns, but I could never afford to, yeah, but — I'm honest! Give me credit for just that, will you *please?* — Born poor, raised poor, expect to die poor unless I manage to get us something out of what Big Daddy leaves when he dies of cancer! But Brick?! — *Skipper is dead! I'm alive!* Maggie the cat is —

(BRICK *hops awkwardly forward and strikes at her again with his crutch.*)

— *alive! I am alive, alive! I am* . . .

(*He hurls the crutch at her, across the bed she took refuge behind, and pitches forward on the floor as she completes her speech.*)

— *alive!*

(*A little girl,* DIXIE, *bursts into the room, wearing an Indian war bonnet and firing a cap pistol at* MARGARET *and shouting: "Bang, bang, bang!"*)

(*Laughter downstairs floats through the open hall door.* MARGARET *had crouched gasping to bed at child's entrance. She now rises and says with cool fury:*)

Little girl, your mother or someone should teach you — (*gasping*) — to knock at a door before you come into a room. Otherwise people might think that you — lack — good breeding. . . .

DIXIE: Yanh, yanh, yanh, what is Uncle Brick doin' on th' floor?

BRICK: I tried to kill your Aunt Maggie, but I failed — and I fell. Little girl, give me my crutch so I can get up off th' floor.

MARGARET: Yes, give your uncle his crutch, he's a cripple, honey, he broke his ankle last night jumping hurdles on the high school athletic field!

DIXIE: What were you jumping hurdles for, Uncle Brick?

BRICK: Because I used to jump them, and people like to do what they used to do, even after they've stopped being able to do it. . . .

MARGARET: That's right, that's your answer, now go away, little girl.

(DIXIE *fires cap pistol at* MARGARET *three times.*)

Stop, you stop that, monster! You little no-neck monster!

(*She seizes the cap pistol and hurls it through gallery doors.*)

DIXIE (*with a precocious instinct for the cruelest thing*): You're jealous! — You're just jealous because you can't have babies!

(*She sticks out her tongue at* MARGARET *as she sashays past her with her stomach stuck out, to the gallery.* MARGARET *slams the gallery doors and leans panting against them.*

There is a pause. BRICK *has replaced his spilt drink and sits, faraway, on the great four-poster bed.)*

MARGARET: You see? — they gloat over us being childless, even in front of their five little no-neck monsters!

(Pause, Voices approach on the stairs.)

Brick? — I've been to a doctor in Memphis, a — a gynecologist. . . .
　　I've been completely examined, and there is no reason why we can't have a child whenever we want one. And this is my time by the calendar to conceive. Are you listening to me? Are you? Are you LISTENING TO ME!
BRICK: Yes. I hear you, Maggie.

(His attention returns to her inflamed face.)

— But how in hell on earth do you imagine — that you're going to have a child by a man that can't stand you?
MARGARET: That's a problem that I will have to work out.

(She wheels about to face the hall door.)

MAE *(off stage left)*: Come on, Big Daddy. We're all goin' up to Brick's room.

(From off stage left, voices: REVEREND TOOKER, DOCTOR BAUGH, MAE.*)*

MARGARET: *Here they come!*

(The lights dim.)

CURTAIN

ACT TWO

There is no lapse of time. MARGARET *and* BRICK *are in the same positions they held at the end of Act 1.*

MARGARET *(at door)*: Here they come!

*(*BIG DADDY *appears first, a tall man with a fierce, anxious look, moving carefully not to betray his weakness even, or especially, to himself.)*

GOOPER: I read in the *Register* that you're getting a new memorial window.

(Some of the people are approaching through the hall, others along the gallery: voices from both directions. GOOPER *and* REVEREND TOOKER *become visible outside gallery doors, and their voices come in clearly.)*

(They pause outside as GOOPER *lights a cigar.)*

REVEREND TOOKER *(vivaciously)*: Oh, but St. Paul's in Grenada has three memorial windows, and the latest one is a Tiffany stained-glass window that cost twenty-five hundred dollars, a picture of Christ the Good Shepherd with a Lamb in His arms.

MARGARET: Big Daddy.

BIG DADDY: Well, Brick.

BRICK: Hello Big Daddy. — Congratulations!

BIG DADDY: — Crap. . . .

GOOPER: Who give that window, Preach?

REVEREND TOOKER: Clyde Fletcher's widow. Also presented St. Paul's with a baptismal font.

GOOPER: Y'know what somebody ought t' give your church is a *coolin'* system, Preach.

MAE *(almost religiously)*: — Let's see now, they've had their *tyyy*-phoid shots, and their tetanus shots, their diphtheria shots and their hepatitis shots and their polio shots, they got *those* shots every month from May through September, and — Gooper? Hey! Gooper! — What all have the kiddies been shot faw?

REVEREND TOOKER: Yes, siree, Bob! And y'know what Gus Hamma's family gave in his memory to the church at Two Rivers? A complete new stone parish-house with a basketball court in the basement and a —

BIG DADDY *(uttering a loud barking laugh which is far from truly mirthful)*: Hey, Preach! What's all this talk about memorials, Preach? Y' think somebody's about t' kick off around here? 'S that it?

(Startled by this interjection, REVEREND TOOKER *decides to laugh at the question almost as loud as he can.)*

(How he would answer the question we'll never know, as he's spared that embarrassment by the voice of GOOPER's *wife,* MAE, *rising high and clear as she appears with "DOC" BAUGH, the family doctor, through the hall door.)*

MARGARET *(overlapping a bit)*: Turn on the hi-fi, Brick! Let's have some music t' start off th' party with!

BRICK: You turn it on, Maggie.

(The talk becomes so general that the room sounds like a great aviary of chattering birds. Only BRICK *remains unengaged, leaning upon the liquor cabinet with his faraway smile, an ice cube in a paper napkin with which he now and then rubs his forehead. He doesn't respond to* MARGARET's *command. She bounds forward and stoops over the instrument panel of the console.)*

GOOPER: We gave 'em that thing for a third anniversary present, got three speakers in it.

(*The room is suddenly blasted by the climax of a Wagnerian opera or a Beethoven symphony.*)

BIG DADDY: *Turn that dam thing off!*

(*Almost instant silence, almost instantly broken by the shouting charge of* BIG MAMA, *entering through hall door like a charging rhino.*)

BIG MAMA: *Wha's my Brick, wha's mah precious baby!!*
BIG DADDY: *Sorry! Turn it back on!*

(*Everyone laughs very loud.* BIG DADDY *is famous for his jokes at* BIG MAMA's *expense, and nobody laughs louder at these jokes than* BIG MAMA *herself, though sometimes they're pretty cruel and* BIG MAMA *has to pick up or fuss with something to cover the hurt that the loud laugh doesn't quite cover.*)

(*On this occasion, a happy occasion because the dread in her heart has also been lifted by the false report on* BIG DADDY's *condition, she giggles, grotesquely, coyly, in* BIG DADDY's *direction and bears down upon* BRICK, *all very quick and alive.*)

BIG MAMA: Here he is, here's my precious baby! What's that you've got in your hand? You put that liquor down, son, your hand was made fo' holdin' somethin' better than that!
GOOPER: Look at Brick put it down!

(BRICK *has obeyed* BIG MAMA *by draining the glass and handing it to her. Again everyone laughs, some high, some low.*)

BIG MAMA: Oh, you bad boy, you, you're my bad little boy. Give Big Mama a kiss, you bad boy, you! — Look at him shy away, will you? Brick never liked bein' kissed or made a fuss over, I guess because he's always had too much of it!
　　Son, you turn that thing off!

(BRICK *has switched on the TV set.*)

I can't stand TV, radio was bad enough but TV has gone it one better, I mean — (*plops wheezing in chair*) — one worse, ha ha! Now what'm I sittin' down here faw? I want t' sit next to my sweetheart on the sofa, hold hands with him and love him up a little!

(BIG MAMA *has on a black and white figured chiffon. The large irregular patterns, like the markings of some massive animal, the luster of her great diamonds and many pearls,*

the brilliants set in the silver frames of her glasses, her riotous voice, booming laugh,
have dominated the room since she entered. BIG DADDY *has been regarding her with a*
steady grimace of chronic annoyance.)

BIG MAMA (*still louder)*: Preacher, Preacher, hey, Preach! Give me you' hand an'
   help me up from this chair!
REVEREND TOOKER: None of your tricks, Big Mama!
BIG MAMA: What tricks? You give me you' hand so I can get up an' —

(REVEREND TOOKER *extends her his hand. She grabs it and pulls him into her lap*
with a shrill laugh that spans an octave in two notes.)

Ever seen a preacher in a fat lady's lap? Hey, hey, folks! Ever seen a
preacher in a fat lady's lap?

(BIG MAMA *is notorious throughout the Delta for this sort of inelegant horseplay.*
MARGARET *looks on with indulgent humor, sipping Dubonnet "on the rocks" and*
watching BRICK, *but* MAE *and* GOOPER *exchange signs of humorless anxiety over these*
antics, the sort of behavior which MAE *thinks may account for their failure to quite get*
in with the smartest young married set in Memphis, despite all. One of the Negroes,
LACY *or* SOOKEY, *peeks in, cackling. They are waiting for a sign to bring in the cake*
and champagne. But BIG DADDY's *not amused. He doesn't understand why, in spite of*
the infinite mental relief he's received from the doctor's report, he still has these same old
fox teeth in his guts. "This spastic condition is something else," he says to himself, but
aloud he roars at BIG MAMA:)

BIG DADDY: BIG MAMA, WILL YOU QUIT HORSIN'? — You're too old
   an' too fat fo' that sort of crazy kid stuff an' besides a woman with your
   blood pressure — she had two hundred last spring! — is riskin' a stroke
   when you mess around like that. . . .

(MAE *blows on a pitch pipe.)*

BIG MAMA: *Here comes Big Daddy's birthday!*

(NEGROES *in white jackets enter with an enormous birthday cake ablaze with candles*
and carrying buckets of champagne with satin ribbons about the bottle necks.)

(MAE *and* GOOPER *strike up song, and everybody, including the* NEGROES *and*
CHILDREN, *joins in. Only* BRICK *remains aloof.)*

EVERYONE: Happy birthday to you.
   Happy birthday to you.
   Happy birthday, Big Daddy —

(Some sing: "Dear, Big Daddy!")

Happy birthday to you.

(Some sing: "How old are you?")

(MAE has come down center and is organizing her children like a chorus. She gives them a barely audible: "One, two, three!" and they are off in the new tune.)

CHILDREN: Skinamarinka — dinka — dink
Skinamarinka — do
We love you.
Skinamarinka — dinka — dink
Skinamarinka–do.

(All together, they turn to BIG DADDY.)

Big Daddy, you!

(They turn back front, like a musical comedy chorus.)

We love you in the morning;
We love you in the night.
We love you when we're with you,
And we love you out of sight.
Skinamarinka–dinka–dink
Skinamarinka — do.

(MAE turns to BIG MAMA.)

Big Mama, too!

(BIG MAMA bursts into tears. The NEGROES leave.)

BIG DADDY: Now Ida, what the hell is the matter with you?
MAE: She's just so happy.
BIG MAMA: I'm just so happy, Big Daddy, I have to cry or something.

(Sudden and loud in the hush:)

Brick, do you know the wonderful news that Doc Baugh got from the clinic about Big Daddy? Big Daddy's one hundred per cent!
MARGARET: Isn't that wonderful?
BIG MAMA: He's just one hundred per cent. Passed the examination with flying colors. Now that we know there's nothing wrong with Big Daddy but a spastic colon, I can tell you something. I was worried sick, half out of my mind, for fear that Big Daddy might have a thing like —

(MARGARET *cuts through this speech, jumping up and exclaiming shrilly:*)

MARGARET: Brick, honey, aren't you going to give Big Daddy his birthday present?

(*Passing by him, she snatches his liquor glass from him.*)

(*She picks up a fancily wrapped package.*)

Here it is, Big Daddy, this is from Brick!

BIG MAMA: This is the biggest birthday Big Daddy's ever had, a hundred presents and bushels of telegrams from —

MAE (*at same time*): What is it, Brick?

GOOPER: I bet 500 to 50 that Brick don't *know* what it is.

BIG MAMA: The fun of presents is not knowing what they are till you open the package. Open your present, Big Daddy.

BIG DADDY: Open it you'self. I want to ask Brick somethin! Come here, Brick.

MARGARET: Big Daddy's callin' you, Brick.

(*She is opening the package.*)

BRICK: Tell Big Daddy I'm crippled.

BIG DADDY: I see you're crippled. I want to know how you got crippled.

MARGARET (*making diversionary tactics*): Oh, look, oh, look, why, it's a cashmere robe!

(*She holds the robe up for all to see.*)

MAE: You sound surprised, Maggie.

MARGARET: I never saw one before.

MAE: That's funny. — Hah!

MARGARET (*turning on her fiercely, with a brilliant smile*): Why is it funny? All my family ever had was family — and luxuries such as cashmere robes still surprise me!

BIG DADDY (*ominously*): Quiet!

MAE (*heedless in her fury*): I don't see how you could be so surprised when you bought it yourself at Loewenstein's in Memphis last Saturday. You know how I know?

BIG DADDY: I said, Quiet!

MAE: — I know because the salesgirl that sold it to you waited on me and said, Oh, Mrs. Pollitt, your sister-in-law just bought a cashmere robe for your husband's father!

MARGARET: Sister Woman! Your talents are wasted as a housewife and mother, you really ought to be with the FBI or —

BIG DADDY: QUIET!

(REVEREND TOOKER's *reflexes are slower than the others'. He finishes a sentence after the bellow.*)

REVEREND TOOKER (*to* DOC BAUGH): — the Stork and the Reaper are running neck and neck!

(*He starts to laugh gaily when he notices the silence and* BIG DADDY's *glare. His laugh dies falsely.*)

BIG DADDY: Preacher, I hope I'm not butting in on more talk about memorial stained-glass windows, am I, Preacher?

(REVEREND TOOKER *laughs feebly, then coughs dryly in the embarrassed silence.*)

Preacher?

BIG MAMA: Now, Big Daddy, don't you pick on Preacher!

BIG DADDY (*raising his voice*): You ever hear that expression all hawk and no spit? You bring that expression to mind with that little dry cough of yours, all hawk an' no spit. . . .

(*The pause is broken only by a short startled laugh from* MARGARET, *the only one there who is conscious of and amused by the grotesque.*)

MAE (*raising her arms and jangling her bracelets*): I wonder if the mosquitoes are active tonight?

BIG DADDY: What's that, Little Mama? Did you make some remark?

MAE: Yes, I said I wondered if the mosquitoes would eat us alive if we went out on the gallery for a while.

BIG DADDY: Well, if they do, I'll have your bones pulverized for fertilizer!

BIG MAMA (*quickly*): Last week we had an airplane spraying the place and I think it done some good, at least I haven't had a —

BIG DADDY (*cutting her speech*): Brick, they tell me, if what they tell me is true, that you done some jumping last night on the high school athletic field?

BIG MAMA: Brick, Big Daddy is talking to you, son.

BRICK (*smiling vaguely over his drink*): What was that, Big Daddy?

BIG DADDY: They said you done some jumping on the high school track field last night.

BRICK: That's what they told me, too.

BIG DADDY: Was it jumping or humping that you were doing out there? What were doing out there at three A.M., layin' a woman on that cinder track?

BIG MAMA: Big Daddy, you are off the sick-list, now, and I'm not going to excuse you for talkin' so —

BIG DADDY: Quiet!

BIG MAMA: — nasty in front of Preacher and–

BIG DADDY: QUIET! — I ast you, Brick, if you was cuttin' you'self a piece o' poon-tang last night on that cinder track? I thought maybe you were chasin' poon-tang on that track an' tripped over something in the heat of the chase — 'sthat it?

(GOOPER *laughs, loud and false, others nervously following suit.* BIG MAMA *stamps her foot, and purses her lips, crossing to* MAE *and whispering something to her as* BRICK *meets his father's hard, intent, grinning stare with a slow, vague smile that he offers all situations from behind the screen of his liquor.*)

BRICK: No, sir, I don't think so. . . .
MAE (*at the same time, sweetly*): Reverend Tooker, let's you and I take a stroll on the widow's walk.

(*She and the preacher go out on the gallery as* BIG DADDY *says:*)

BIG DADDY: Then what the hell were you doing out there at three o'clock in the morning?
BRICK: Jumping the hurdles, Big Daddy, runnin' and jumpin' the hurdles, but those high hurdles have gotten too high for me, now.
BIG DADDY: Cause you was drunk?
BRICK (*his vague smile fading a little*): Sober I wouldn't have tried to jump the *low* ones. . . .
BIG MAMA (*quickly*): Big Daddy, blow out the candles on your birthday cake!
MARGARET (*at the same time*): I want to propose a toast to Big Daddy Pollitt on his sixty-fifth birthday, the biggest cotton planter in —
BIG DADDY (*bellowing with fury and disgust*): I told you to stop it, now stop it, quit this — !
BIG MAMA (*coming in front of* BIG DADDY *with the cake*): Big Daddy, I will not allow you to talk that way, not even on your birthday, I —
BIG DADDY: I'll talk like I want to on my birthday, Ida, or any other goddam day of the year and anybody here that don't like it knows what they can do!
BIG MAMA: You don't mean that!
BIG DADDY: What makes you think I don't mean it?

(*Meanwhile various discreet signals have been exchanged and* GOOPER *has also gone out on the gallery.*)

BIG MAMA: I just know you don't mean it.
BIG DADDY: You don't know a goddam thing and you never did!
BIG MAMA: Big Daddy, you don't mean that.
BIG DADDY: Oh, yes, I do, oh, yes, I do, I mean it! I put up with a whole lot of crap around here because I thought I was dying. And you thought I was dying and you started taking over, well, you can stop taking over now, Ida, because I'm not gonna die, you can just stop now this business of taking over because you're not taking over because I'm not dying, I went through the laboratory and the goddam exploratory operation and there's nothing wrong with me but a spastic colon. And I'm not dying of cancer which you thought I was dying of. Ain't that so? Didn't you think that I was dying of cancer, Ida?

(Almost everybody is out on the gallery but the two old people glaring at each other across the blazing cake.)

(BIG MAMA's chest heaves and she presses a fat fist to her mouth.)

(BIG DADDY continues, hoarsely:)

Ain't that so, Ida? Didn't you have an idea I was dying of cancer and now you could take control of this place and everything on it? I got that impression, I seemed to get that impression. Your loud voice everywhere, your fat old body butting in here and there!
BIG MAMA: Hush! The Preacher!
BIG DADDY: Fuck the goddam preacher!

(BIG MAMA gasps loudly and sits down on the sofa which is almost too small for her.)

Did you hear what I said? I said fuck the goddam preacher!

(Somebody closes the gallery doors from outside just as there is a burst of fireworks and excited cries from the children.)

BIG MAMA: I never seen you act like this before and I can't think what's got in you!
BIG DADDY: I went through all that laboratory and operation and all just so I would know if you or me was boss here! Well, now it turns out that I am and you ain't — and that's my birthday present — and my cake and champagne! — because for three years now you been gradually taking over. Bossing. Talking. Sashaying your fat old body around the place I made! I made this place! I was overseer on it! I was the overseer on the old Straw and Ochello plantation. I quit school at ten! I quit school at ten years old and went to work like a nigger in the fields. And I rose to be overseer of the Straw and Ochello plantation. And old Straw died and I was Ochello's partner and the place got bigger and bigger and bigger and bigger and bigger! I did all that myself with no goddam help from you, and now you think you're just about to take over. Well, I am just about to tell you that you are not just about to take over, you are not just about to take over a God damn thing. Is that clear to you, Ida? Is that very plain to you, now? Is that understood completely? I been through the laboratory from A to Z. I've had the goddam exploratory operation, and nothing is wrong with me but a spastic colon — made spastic, I guess, by *disgust!* By all the goddam lies and liars that I have had to put up with, and all the goddam hypocrisy that I lived with all these forty years that we been livin' together!
 Hey! Ida!! Blow out the candles on the birthday cake! Purse up your lips and draw a deep breath and blow out the goddam candles on the cake!
BIG MAMA: Oh, Big Daddy, oh, oh, oh, Big Daddy!

BIG DADDY: What's the matter with you?

BIG MAMA: *In all these years you never believed that I loved you??*

BIG DADDY: Huh?

BIG MAMA: *And I did, I did so much, I did love you!* — I even loved your hate and your hardness, Big Daddy!

(She sobs and rushes awkwardly out onto the gallery.)

BIG DADDY *(to himself)*: *Wouldn't it be funny if that was true. . . .*

(A pause is followed by a burst of light in the sky from the fireworks.)

BRICK! HEY, BRICK!

(He stands over his blazing birthday cake.)

(After some moments, BRICK *hobbles in on his crutch, holding his glass.)*

*(*MARGARET *follows him with a bright, anxious smile.)*

I didn't call you, Maggie. I called Brick.

MARGARET: I'm just delivering him to you.

(She kisses BRICK *on the mouth which he immediately wipes with the back of his hand. She flies girlishly back out.* BRICK *and his father are alone.)*

BIG DADDY: Why did you do that?

BRICK: Do what, Big Daddy?

BIG DADDY: Wipe her kiss off your mouth like she'd spit on you.

BRICK: I don't know. I wasn't conscious of it.

BIG DADDY: That woman of yours has a better shape on her than Gooper's but somehow or other they got the same look about them.

BRICK: What sort of look is that, Big Daddy?

BIG DADDY: I don't know how to describe it but it's the same look.

BRICK: They don't look peaceful, do they?

BIG DADDY: No, they sure in hell don't.

BRICK: They look nervous as cats?

BIG DADDY: That's right, they look nervous as cats.

BRICK: Nervous as a couple of cats on a hot tin roof?

BIG DADDY: That's right, boy, they look like a couple of cats on a hot tin roof. It's funny that you and Gooper being so different would pick out the same type of woman.

BRICK: Both of us married into society, Big Daddy.

BIG DADDY: Crap . . . I wonder what gives them both that look?

BRICK: Well. They're sittin' in the middle of a big piece of land, Big Daddy, twenty-eight thousand acres is a pretty big piece of land and so they're squaring off on it, each determined to knock off a bigger piece of it than the other whenever you let it go.

BIG DADDY: I got a surprise for those women. I'm not gonna let it go for a long time yet if that's what they're waiting for.

BRICK: That's right, Big Daddy. You just sit tight and let them scratch each other's eyes out. . . .

BIG DADDY: You bet your life I'm going to sit tight on it and let those sons of bitches scratch their eyes out, ha ha ha. . . .

But Gooper's wife's a good breeder, you got to admit she's fertile. Hell, at supper tonight she had them all at the table and they had to put a couple of extra leafs in the table to make room for them, she's got five head of them, now, and another one's comin'.

BRICK: Yep, number six is comin'. . . .

BIG DADDY: Six hell, she'll probably drop a litter next time. Brick, you know, I swear to God, I don't know the way it happens?

BRICK: The way what happens, Big Daddy?

BIG DADDY: You git you a piece of land, by hook or crook, an' things start growin' on it, things accumulate on it, and the first thing you know it's completely out of hand, completely out of hand!

BRICK: Well, they say nature hates a vacuum, Big Daddy.

BIG DADDY: That's what they say, but sometimes I think that a vacuum is a hell of a lot better than some of the stuff that nature replaces it with.

Is someone out there by that door?

GOOPER: Hey Mae.

BRICK: Yep.

BIG DADDY: Who?

(He has lowered his voice.)

BRICK: Someone int'rested in what we say to each other.

BIG DADDY: Gooper? — *GOOPER!*

(After a discreet pause, MAE *appears in the gallery door.)*

MAE: Did you call Gooper, Big Daddy?

BIG DADDY: Aw, it was you.

MAE: Do you want Gooper, Big Daddy?

BIG DADDY: No, and I don't want you. I want some privacy here, while I'm having a confidential talk with my son Brick. Now it's too hot in here to close them doors, but if I have to close those fuckin' doors in order to have a private talk with my son Brick, just let me know and I'll close 'em. Because I hate eavesdroppers, I don't like any kind of sneakin' an' spyin'.

MAE: Why, Big Daddy —

BIG DADDY: You stood on the wrong side of the moon, it threw your shadow!

MAE: I was just —

BIG DADDY: You was just nothing but *spyin'* an' you *know* it!

MAE *(begins to sniff and sob)*: Oh, Big Daddy, you're so unkind for some reason to those that really love you!

BIG DADDY: Shut up, shut up, shut up! I'm going to move you and Gooper out of that room next to this! It's none of your goddam business what goes on in here at night between Brick an' Maggie. You listen at night like a couple of rutten peekhole spies and go and give a report on what you hear to Big Mama an' she comes to me and says they say such and such and so and so about what they heard goin' on between Brick an' Maggie, and Jesus, it makes me sick. I'm goin' to move you an' Gooper out of that room, I can't stand sneakin' an' spyin', it makes me puke. . . .

(MAE throws back her head and rolls her eyes heavenward and extends her arms as if invoking God's pity for this unjust martyrdom; then she presses a handkerchief to her nose and flies from the room with a loud swish of skirts.)

BRICK *(now at the liquor cabinet)*: They listen, do they?
BIG DADDY: Yeah. They listen and give reports to Big Mama on what goes on in here between you and Maggie. They say that —

(He stops as if embarrassed.)

— You won't sleep with her, that you sleep on the sofa. Is that true or not true? If you don't like Maggie, get rid of Maggie! — What are you doin' there now?
BRICK: Fresh'nin' up my drink.
BIG DADDY: Son, you know you got a real liquor problem?
BRICK: Yes, sir, yes, I know.
BIG DADDY: Is that why you quit sports-announcing, because of this liquor problem?
BRICK: Yes, sir, yes, sir, I guess so.

(He smiles vaguely and amiably at his father across his replenished drink.)

BIG DADDY: Son, don't guess about it, it's too important.
BRICK *(vaguely)*: Yes, sir.
BIG DADDY: And listen to me, don't look at the damn chandelier. . . .

(Pause. BIG DADDY's voice is husky.)

— Somethin' else we picked up at th' big fire sale in Europe.

(Another pause.)

Life is important. There's nothing else to hold onto. A man that drinks is throwing his life away. Don't do it, hold onto your life. There's nothing else to hold onto. . . .
  Sit down over here so we don't have to raise our voices, the walls have ears in this place.

BRICK (*hobbling over to sit on the sofa beside him*): All right, Big Daddy.

BIG DADDY: Quit! — how'd that come about? Some disappointment?

BRICK: I don't know. Do you?

BIG DADDY: I'm askin' you, God damn it! How in hell would I know if you don't?

BRICK: I just got out there and found that I had a mouth full of cotton. I was always two or three beats behind what was goin' on on the field and so I —

BIG DADDY: Quit!

BRICK (*amiably*): Yes, quit.

BIG DADDY: Son?

BRICK: Huh?

BIG DADDY (*inhales loudly and deeply from his cigar; then bends suddenly a little forward, exhaling loudly and raising a hand to his forehead*): — Whew! — ha ha! — I took in too much smoke, it made me a little lightheaded. . . .

(The mantel clock chimes.)

Why is it so damn hard for people to talk?

BRICK: Yeah. . . .

(The clock goes on sweetly chiming till it has completed the stroke of ten.)

— Nice peaceful-soundin' clock, I like to hear it all night. . . .

(He slides low and comfortable on the sofa; BIG DADDY sits up straight and rigid with some unspoken anxiety. All his gestures are tense and jerky as he talks. He wheezes and pants and sniffs through his nervous speech, glancing quickly, shyly, from time to time, at his son.)

BIG DADDY: We got that clock the summer we wint to Europe, me an' Big Mama on that damn Cook's Tour, never had such an awful time in my life, I'm tellin' you, son, those gooks over there, they gouge your eyeballs out in their grand hotels. And Big Mama bought more stuff than you could haul in a couple of boxcars, that's no crap. Everywhere she wint on this whirlwind tour, she bought, bought, bought. Why, half that stuff she bought is still crated up in the cellar, under water last spring!

(He laughs.)

That Europe is nothin' on earth but a great big auction, that's all it is, that bunch of old worn-out places, it's just a big fire-sale, the whole fuckin' thing, an' Big Mama wint wild in it, why, you couldn't hold that woman with a mule's harness! Bought, bought, bought! — lucky I'm a rich man, yes siree, Bob, an' half that stuff is mildewin' in th' basement. It's lucky I'm a rich man, it sure is lucky, well, I'm a rich man, Brick, yep, I'm a mighty rich man.

(His eyes light up for a moment.)

Y'know how much I'm worth? Guess, Brick! Guess how much I'm worth!

(BRICK smiles vaguely over his drink.)

Close on ten million in cash an' blue-chip stocks, outside, mind you, of twenty-eight thousand acres of the richest land this side of the valley Nile!

But a man can't buy his life with it, he can't buy back his life with it when his life has been spent, that's one thing not offered in the Europe fire-sale or in the American markets or any markets on earth, a man can't buy his life with it, he can't buy back his life when his life is finished . . . .

That's a sobering thought, a very sobering thought, and that's a thought that I was turning over in my head, over and over and over — until today. . . .

I'm wiser and sadder, Brick, for this experience which I just gone through. They's one thing else that I remember in Europe.

BRICK: What is that, Big Daddy?

BIG DADDY: The hills around Barcelona in the country of Spain and the children running over those bare hills in their bare skins beggin' like starvin' dogs with howls and screeches, and how fat the priests are on the streets of Barcelona, so many of them and so fat and so pleasant, ha ha! — Y'know I could feed that country? I got money enough to feed that goddam country, but the human animal is a selfish beast and I don't reckon the money I passed out there to those howling children in the hills around Barcelona would more than upholster the chairs in this room, I mean pay to put a new cover on this chair!

Hell, I threw them money like you'd scatter feed corn for chickens, I threw money at them just to get rid of them long enough to climb back into th' car and — drive away. . . .

And then in Morocco, them Arabs, why, I remember one day in Marrakech, that old walled Arab city, I set on a broken-down wall to have a cigar, it was fearful hot there and this Arab woman stood in the road and looked at me till I was embarrassed, she stood stock still in the dusty hot road and looked at me till I was embarrassed. But listen to this. She had a naked child with her, a little naked girl with her, barely able to toddle, and after a while she set this child on the ground and give her a push and whispered something to her.

This child come toward me, barely able t' walk, come toddling up to me and —

Jesus, it makes you sick t' remember a thing like this! It stuck out its hand and tried to unbutton my trousers!

That child was not yet five! Can you believe me? Or do you think that I am making this up? I wint back to the hotel and said to Big Mama, Git packed! We're clearing out of this country. . . .

BRICK: Big Daddy, you're on a talkin' jag tonight.

BIG DADDY *(ignoring this remark)*: Yes, sir, that's how it is, the human animal is a beast that dies but the fact that he's dying don't give him pity for others, no, sir, it —

— Did you say something?

BRICK: Yes.

BIG DADDY: What?

BRICK: Hand me over that crutch so I can get up.

BIG DADDY: Where you goin'?

BRICK: I'm takin' a little short trip to Echo Spring.

BIG DADDY: To where?

BRICK: Liquor cabinet. . . .

BIG DADDY: Yes, sir, boy —

(He hands BRICK the crutch.)

— the human animal is a beast that dies and if he's got money he buys and buys and buys and I think the reason he buys everything he can buy is that in the back of his mind he has the crazy hope that one of his purchases will be life everlasting! — Which it never can be. . . . The human animal is a beast that —

BRICK *(at the liquor cabinet)*: Big Daddy, you sure are shootin' th' breeze here tonight.

(There is a pause and voices are heard outside.)

BIG DADDY: I been quiet here lately, spoke not a word, just sat and stared into space. I had something heavy weighing on my mind but tonight that load was took off me. That's why I'm talking. — The sky looks dif-f'rent to me. . . .

BRICK: You know what I like to hear most?

BIG DADDY: What?

BRICK: Solid quiet. Perfect unbroken quiet.

BIG DADDY: Why?

BRICK: Because it's more peaceful.

BIG DADDY: Man, you'll hear a lot of that in the grave.

(He chuckles agreeably.)

BRICK: Are you through talkin' to me?

BIG DADDY: Why are you so anxious to shut me up?

BRICK: Well, sir, ever so often you say to me, Brick, I want to have a talk with you, but when we talk, it never materializes. Nothing is said. You sit in a chair and gas about this and that and I look like I listen. I try to look like I listen, but I don't listen, not much. Communication is — awful hard between people an' — somehow between you and me, it just don't — happen.

BIG DADDY: Have you ever been scared? I mean have you ever felt down-
right terror of something?

(He gets up.)

Just one moment.

(He looks off as if he were going to tell an important secret.)

BIG DADDY: Brick?
BRICK: What?
BIG DADDY: Son, I thought I had it!
BRICK: Had what? Had what, Big Daddy?
BIG DADDY: Cancer!
BRICK: Oh . . .
BIG DADDY: I thought the old man made out of bones had laid his cold and
heavy hand on my shoulder!
BRICK: Well, Big Daddy, you kept a tight mouth about it.
BIG DADDY: A pig squeals. A man keeps a tight mouth about it, in spite of a
man not having a pig's advantage.
BRICK: What advantage is that?
BIG DADDY: Ignorance — of mortality — is a comfort. A man don't have that
comfort, he's the only living thing that conceives of death, that knows
what it is. The others go without knowing which is the way that anything living should go, go without knowing, without any knowledge of
it, and yet a pig squeals, but a man sometimes, he can keep a tight
mouth about it. Sometimes he —

(There is a deep, smoldering, ferocity in the old man.)

— can keep a tight mouth about it. I wonder if —
BRICK: What, Big Daddy?
BIG DADDY: A whiskey highball would injure this spastic condition?
BRICK: No, sir, it might do it good.
BIG DADDY *(grins suddenly, wolfishly)*: Jesus, I can't tell you! The sky is open! Christ, it's
open again! It's open, boy, it's open!

*(*BRICK *looks down at his drink.)*

BRICK: You feel better, Big Daddy?
BIG DADDY: Better? Hell! I can breathe! — All of my life I been like a
doubled up fist. . . .

(He pours a drink.)

— Poundin', smashin', drivin'! — now I'm going to loosen these
doubled-up hands and touch things *easy* with them. . . .

(He spreads his hands as if caressing the air.)

You know what I'm contemplating?
BRICK *(vaguely)*: No, sir. What are you contemplating?
BIG DADDY: Ha ha! — *Pleasure!* — pleasure with *women!*

(BRICK's smile fades a little but lingers.)

— Yes, boy. I'll tell you something that you might not guess. I still have
desire for women and this is my sixty-fifth birthday.
BRICK: I think that's mighty remarkable, Big Daddy.
BIG DADDY: Remarkable?
BRICK: *Admirable*, Big Daddy.
BIG DADDY: You're damn right it is, remarkable and admirable both. I realize
now that I never had me enough. I let many chances slip by because of
scruples about it, scruples, convention — crap. . . . All that stuff is bull,
bull, bull! — It took the shadow of death to make me see it. Now that
shadow's lifted, I'm going to cut loose and have, what is it they call it,
have me a — ball!
BRICK: A ball, huh?
BIG DADDY: That's right, a ball, a ball! Hell! — I slept with Big Mama till,
let's see, five years ago, till I was sixty and she was fifty-eight, and never
even liked her, never did!

(The phone has been ringing down the hall. BIG MAMA *enters, exclaiming:)*

BIG MAMA: Don't you men hear that phone ring? I heard it way out on the
gall'ry.
BIG DADDY: There's five rooms off this front gall'ry that you could go
through. Why do you go through this one?

(BIG MAMA makes a playful face as she bustles out the hall door.)

Hunh! — Why, when Big Mama goes out of a room, I can't remember
what that woman looks like —
BIG MAMA: Hello.
BIG DADDY: — But when Big Mama comes back into the room, boy, then I
see what she looks like, and I wish I didn't!

*(Bends over laughing at this joke till it hurts his guts and he straightens with a
grimace. The laugh subsides to a chuckle as he puts the liquor glass a little distrustfully
down the table.)*

BIG MAMA: Hello, Miss Sally.

(BRICK has risen and hobbled to the gallery doors.)

BIG DADDY: Hey! Where you goin'?

BRICK: Out for a breather.

BIG DADDY: Not yet you ain't. Stay here till this talk is finished, young
fellow.

BRICK: I thought it was finished, Big Daddy.

BIG DADDY: It ain't even begun.

BRICK: My mistake. Excuse me. I just wanted to feel that river breeze.

BIG DADDY: Set back down in that chair.

(BIG MAMA's voice rises, carrying down the hall.)

BIG MAMA: Miss Sally, you're a case! You're a caution, Miss Sally.

BIG DADDY: Jesus, she's talking to my old maid sister again.

BIG MAMA: Why didn't you give me a chance to explain it to you?

BIG DADDY: Brick, this stuff burns me.

BIG MAMA: Well, goodbye, now, Miss Sally. You come down real soon. Big
Daddy's dying to see you.

BIG DADDY: Crap!

BIG MAMA: Yaiss, goodbye, Miss Sally. . . .

*(She hangs up and bellows with mirth. BIG DADDY groans and covers his ears as she
approaches.)*

(Bursting in:)

Big Daddy, that was Miss Sally callin' from Memphis again! You know
what she done, Big Daddy? She called her doctor in Memphis to git
him to tell her what that spastic thing is! Ha-*HAAAA!* — And called
back to tell me how relieved she was that — Hey! Let me in!

(BIG DADDY has been holding the door half closed against her.)

BIG DADDY: Naw I ain't. I told you not to come and go through this room.
You just back out and go through those five other rooms.

BIG MAMA: Big Daddy? Big Daddy? Oh, big Daddy! — You didn't mean
those things you said to me, did you?

(He shuts door firmly against her but she still calls.)

Sweetheart? Sweetheart? Big Daddy? You didn't mean those awful
things you said to me? — I know you didn't. I know you didn't mean
those things in your heart. . . .

*(The childlike voice fades with a sob and her heavy footsteps retreat down the hall.
BRICK has risen once more on his crutches and starts for the gallery again.)*

BIG DADDY: All I ask of that woman is that she leave me alone. But she can't admit to herself that she makes me sick. That comes of having slept with her too many years. Should of quit much sooner but that old woman she never got enough of it — and I was good in bed . . . I never should of wasted so much of it on her . . . . They say you got just so many and each one is numbered. Well, I got a few left in me, a few, and I'm going to pick me a good one to spend 'em on! I'm going to pick me a choice one, I don't care how much she costs, I'll smother her in — minks! Ha ha! I'll strip her naked and smother her in minks and choke her with diamonds! Ha ha! I'll strip her naked and choke her with diamonds and smother her with minks and hump her from hell to breakfast. *Ha aha ha ha ha!*

MAE *(gaily at door)*: Who's that laughin' in there?

GOOPER: Is Big Daddy laughin' in there?

BIG DADDY: Crap! — them two — *drips. . . .*

(He goes over and touches BRICK's shoulder.)

Yes, son. Brick, boy. — I'm — *happy!* I'm happy, son, I'm happy!

(He chokes a little and bites his under lip, pressing his head quickly, shyly against his son's head and then, coughing with embarrassment, goes uncertainly back to the table where he set down the glass. He drinks and makes a grimace as it burns his guts. BRICK sighs and rises with effort.)

What makes you so restless? Have you got ants in your britches?

BRICK: Yes, sir . . .

BIG DADDY: Why?

BRICK: — Something — hasn't — happened. . . .

BIG DADDY: Yeah? What is that!

BRICK *(sadly)*: — the click. . . .

BIG DADDY: Did you say click?

BRICK: Yes, click.

BIG DADDY: What click?

BRICK: A click that I get in my head that makes me peaceful.

BIG DADDY: I sure in hell don't know what you're talking about, but it disturbs me.

BRICK: It's just a mechanical thing.

BIG DADDY: What is a mechanical thing?

BRICK: This click that I get in my head that makes me peaceful. I got to drink till I get it. It's just a mechanical thing, something like a — like a — like a —

BIG DADDY: Like a —

BRICK: Switch clicking off in my head, turning the hot light off and the cool night on and —

(He looks up, smiling sadly.)

— all of a sudden there's — peace!

BIG DADDY (*whistles long and soft with astonishment; he goes back to* BRICK *and clasps his son's two shoulders*): Jesus! I didn't know it had gotten that bad with you. Why, boy, you're — *alcoholic!*

BRICK: That's the truth, Big Daddy. I'm alcoholic.

BIG DADDY: This shows how I — let things go!

BRICK: I have to hear that little click in my head that makes me peaceful. Usually I hear it sooner than this, sometimes as early as — noon, but — — Today it's — dilatory. . . . — I just haven't got the right level of alcohol in my bloodstream yet!

(*This last statement is made with energy as he freshens his drink.*)

BIG DADDY: Uh — huh. Expecting death made me blind. I didn't have no idea that a son of mine was turning into a drunkard under my nose.

BRICK (*gently*): Well, now you do, Big Daddy, the news has penetrated.

BIG DADDY: UH-huh, yes, now I do, the news has — penetrated. . . .

BRICK: And so if you'll excuse me —

BIG DADDY: No, I won't excuse you.

BRICK: — I'd better sit by myself till I hear that click in my head, it's just a mechanical thing but it don't happen except when I'm alone or talking to no one. . . .

BIG DADDY: You got a long, long time to sit still, boy, and talk to no one, but now you're talkin' to me. At least I'm talking to you. And you set there and listen until I tell you the conversation is over!

BRICK: But this talk is like all the others we've ever had together in our lives! It's nowhere, nowhere! — it's — it's *painful*, Big Daddy. . . .

BIG DADDY: All right, then let it be painful, but don't you move from that chair! — I'm going to remove that crutch. . . .

(*He seizes the crutch and tosses it across the room.*)

BRICK: I can hop on one foot, and if I fall, I can crawl!

BIG DADDY: If you ain't careful you're gonna crawl off this plantation and then, by Jesus, you'll have to hustle your drinks along Skid Row!

BRICK: That'll come, Big Daddy.

BIG DADDY: Naw, it won't. You're my son and I'm going to straighten you out; now that *I'm* straightened out, I'm going to straighten out you!

BRICK: Yeah?

BIG DADDY: Today the report come in from Ochsner Clinic. Y'know what they told me?

(*His face glows with triumph.*)

The only thing that they could detect with all the instruments of science in that great hospital is a little spastic condition of the colon! And nerves torn to pieces by all that worry about it.

(A little girl bursts into room with a sparkler clutched in each fist, hops and shrieks like a monkey gone mad and rushes back out again as BIG DADDY *strikes at her.)*

(Silence. The two men stare at each other. A woman laughs gaily outside.)

I want you to know I breathed a sigh of relief almost as powerful as the Vicksburg tornado!

(There is laughter outside, running footsteps, the soft, plushy sound and light of exploding rockets.)

*(*BRICK *stares at him soberly for a long moment; then makes a sort of startled sound in his nostrils and springs up on one foot and hops across the room to grab his crutch, swinging on the furniture for support. He gets the crutch and flees as if in horror for the gallery. His father seizes him by the sleeve of his white silk pajamas.)*

Stay here, you son of a bitch! — till I say go!
BRICK: I can't.
BIG DADDY: You sure in hell will, God damn it.
BRICK: No, I can't. We talk, you talk, in — circles! We get no where, no where! It's always the same, you say you want to talk to me and don't have a fuckin' thing to say to me!
BIG DADDY: Nothin' to say when I'm tellin' you I'm going to live when I thought I was dying?!
BRICK: Oh — *that!* — Is that what you have to say to me?
BIG DADDY: Why, you son of a bitch! Ain't that, ain't that — *important?!*
BRICK: Well, you said that, that's said, and now I —
BIG DADDY: Now you set back down.
BRICK: You're all balled up, you —
BIG DADDY: I ain't balled up!
BRICK: You are, you're all balled up!
BIG DADDY: Don't tell me what I am, you drunken whelp! I'm going to tear this coat sleeve off if you don't set down!
BRICK: Big Daddy —
BIG DADDY: Do what I tell you! I'm the boss here, now! I want you to know I'm back in the driver's seat now!

*(*BIG MAMA *rushes in, clutching her great heaving bosom.)*

BIG MAMA: Big Daddy!
BIG DADDY: What in hell do you want in here, Big Mama?
BIG MAMA: Oh, Big Daddy! Why are you shouting like that? I just cain't stainnnnnnnd — it. . . .
BIG DADDY *(raising the back of his hand above his head)*: GIT! — outa here.

(She rushes back out, sobbing.)

BRICK *(softly, sadly)*: Christ . . . .
BIG DADDY *(fiercely)*: Yeah! Christ! — is right . . . .

(BRICK breaks loose and hobbles toward the gallery.)

(BIG DADDY jerks his crutch from under BRICK so he steps with the injured ankle. He utters a hissing cry of anguish, clutches a chair and pulls it over on top of him on the floor.)

Son of a — tub of — hog fat. . . .
BRICK: Big Daddy! Give me my crutch.

(BIG DADDY throws the crutch out of reach.)

Give me that crutch, Big Daddy.
BIG DADDY: Why do you drink?
BRICK: Don't know, give me my crutch!
BIG DADDY: You better think why you drink or give up drinking!
BRICK: Will you please give me my crutch so I can get up off this floor?
BIG DADDY: First you answer my question. Why do you drink? Why are you throwing your life away, boy, like somethin' disgusting you picked up on the street?
BRICK *(getting onto his knees)*: Big Daddy, I'm in pain, I stepped on that foot.
BIG DADDY: Good! I'm glad you're not too numb with the liquor in you to feel some pain!
BRICK: You — spilled my — drink. . . .
BIG DADDY: I'll make a bargain with you. You tell me why you drink and I'll hand you one. I'll pour you the liquor myself and hand it to you.
BRICK: Why do I drink?
BIG DADDY: Yea! Why?
BRICK: Give me a drink and I'll tell you.
BIG DADDY: Tell me first!
BRICK: I'll tell you in one word.
BIG DADDY: What word?
BRICK: DISGUST!

(The clock chimes softly, sweetly. BIG DADDY gives it a short, outraged glance.)

Now how about that drink?
BIG DADDY: What are you disgusted with? You got to tell me that, first. Otherwise being disgusted don't make no sense!
BRICK: Give me my crutch.
BIG DADDY: You heard me, you got to tell me what I asked you first.
BRICK: I told you, I said to kill my disgust!
BIG DADDY: DISGUST WITH WHAT!
BRICK: You strike a hard bargain.
BIG DADDY: What are you disgusted with? — an' I'll pass you the liquor.
BRICK: I can hop on one foot, and if I fall, I can crawl.

BIG DADDY: You want liquor that bad?

BRICK (*dragging himself up, clinging to bedstead*): Yeah, I want it that bad.

BIG DADDY: If I give you a drink, will you tell me what it is you're disgusted with, Brick?

BRICK: Yes, sir, I will try to.

(*The old man pours him a drink and solemnly passes it to him.*)

(*There is silence as* BRICK *drinks.*)

Have you ever heard the word "mendacity"?

BIG DADDY: Sure. Mendacity is one of them five dollar words that cheap politicians throw back and forth at each other.

BRICK: You know what it means?

BIG DADDY: Don't it mean lying and liars?

BRICK: Yes, sir, lying and liars.

BIG DADDY: Has someone been lying to you?

CHILDREN (*chanting in chorus offstage*):
    We want Big Dad-dee!
    We want Big Dad-dee!

(GOOPER *appears in the gallery door.*)

GOOPER: Big Daddy, the kiddies are shouting for you out there.

BIG DADDY (*fiercely*): Keep out, Gooper!

GOOPER: 'Scuse *me!*

(BIG DADDY *slams the doors after* GOOPER.)

BIG DADDY: Who's been lying to you, has Margaret been lying to you, has your wife been lying to you about something, Brick?

BRICK: Not her. That wouldn't matter.

BIG DADDY: Then who's been lying to you, and what about?

BRICK: No one single person and no one lie. . . .

BIG DADDY: Then what, what then, for Christ's sake?

BRICK: — The whole, the whole — thing. . . .

BIG DADDY: Why are you rubbing your head? You got a headache?

BRICK: No, I'm tryin' to —

BIG DADDY: — Concentrate, but you can't because your brain's all soaked with liquor, it that the trouble? Wet brain!

(*He snatches the glass from* BRICK'S *hand.*)

What do you know about this mendacity thing? Hell! I could write a book on it! Don't you know that? I could write a book on it and still not cover the subject? Well, I could, I could write a goddam book on it and still not cover the subject anywhere near enough!! — Think of all the lies I got to put up with! — Pretenses! Ain't that mendacity? Having to pretend stuff you don't think or feel or have any idea of? Having for instance to act like I care for Big Mama! — I haven't been able to stand the sight, sound, or smell of that woman for forty years now! — even when I *laid* her! — regular as a piston. . . .

Pretend to love that son of a bitch of a Gooper and his wife Mae and those five same screechers out there like parrots in a jungle? Jesus! Can't stand to look at 'em!

Church! — it bores the bejesus out of me but I go! — I go an' sit there and listen to the fool preacher!

Clubs! — Elks! Masons! Rotary! — *crap!*

(A spasm of pain makes him clutch his belly. He sinks into a chair and his voice is softer and hoarser.)

You I *do* like for some reason, did always have some kind of real feeling for — affection — respect — yes, always. . . .

You and being a success as a planter is all I ever had any devotion to in my whole life! — and that's the truth. . . .

I don't know why, but it is!

I've lived with mendacity! — Why can't *you* live with it? Hell, you *got* to live with it, there's nothing *else* to *live* with except mendacity, is there?

BRICK: Yes, sir. Yes, sir there is something else that you can live with!

BIG DADDY: What?

BRICK *(lifting his glass)*: This! — Liquor. . . .

BIG DADDY: That's not living, that's dodging away from life.

BRICK: I want to dodge away from it.

BIG DADDY: Then why don't you kill yourself, man?

BRICK: I like to drink. . . .

BIG DADDY: Oh, God, I can't talk to you. . . .

BRICK: I'm sorry, Big Daddy.

BIG DADDY: Not as sorry as I am. I'll tell you something. A little while back when I thought my number was up —

(This speech should have torrential pace and fury.)

— before I found out it was just this — spastic — colon. I thought about you. Should I or should I not, if the jig was up, give you this place when I go — since I hate Gooper an' Mae an' know that they hate me, and since all five same monkeys are little Maes an' Goopers. — And I thought, No! — Then I thought, Yes! — I couldn't make up my mind. I hate Gooper and his five same monkeys and that bitch Mae! Why should I turn over twenty-eight thousand acres of the richest land this side of the valley Nile to not my kind? — But why in hell, on the other hand, Brick — should I subsidize a goddam fool on the bottle? — Liked or not liked, well, maybe even — *loved!* — Why should I do that? — Subsidize worthless behavior? Rot? Corruption?

BRICK *(smiling)*: I understand.

BIG DADDY: Well, if you do, you're smarter than I am, God damn it, because I don't understand. And this I will tell you frankly. I didn't make up my mind at all on that question and still to this day I ain't made out no will! — Well, now I don't *have* to. The pressure is gone. I can just wait and see if you pull yourself together or if you don't.

BRICK: That's right, Big Daddy.

BIG DADDY: You sound like you thought I was kidding.

BRICK *(rising)*: No, sir, I know you're not kidding.

BIG DADDY: But you don't care — ?

BRICK *(hobbling toward the gallery door)*: No, sir, I don't care. . . .

(He stands in the gallery doorway as the night sky turns pink and green and gold with successive flashes of light.)

BIG DADDY: *WAIT!* — Brick. . . .

(His voice drops. Suddenly there is something shy, almost tender, in his restraining gesture.)

Don't let's — leave it like this, like them other talks we've had, we've always — talked around things, we've — just talked around things for some fuckin' reason, I don't know what, it's always like something was left not spoken, something avoided because neither of us was honest enough with the — other. . . .

BRICK: I never lied to you, Big Daddy.

BIG DADDY: Did I ever to *you?*

BRICK: No, sir. . . .

BIG DADDY: Then there is at least two people that never lied to each other.

BRICK: But we've never *talked* to each other.

BIG DADDY: We can *now.*

BRICK: Big Daddy, there don't seem to be anything much to say.

BIG DADDY: You say that you drink to kill your disgust with lying.

BRICK: You said to give you a reason.

BIG DADDY: Is liquor the only thing that'll kill this disgust?

BRICK: Now. Yes.

BIG DADDY: But not once, huh?

BRICK: Not when I was still young an' believing. A drinking man's someone who wants to forget he isn't still young an' believing.

BIG DADDY: Believing what?

BRICK: Believing. . . .

BIG DADDY: Believing *what?*

BRICK *(stubbornly evasive)*: Believing. . . .

BIG DADDY: I don't know what the hell you mean by believing and I don't think you know what you mean by believing, but if you still got sports in your blood, go back to sports announcing and —

BRICK: Sit in a glass box watching games I can't play? Describing what I can't do while players do it? Sweating out their disgust and confusion in contests I'm not fit for? Drinkin' a coke, half bourbon, so I can stand it?

That's no goddam good any more, no help — time just outran me, Big
  Daddy — got there first. . . .
BIG DADDY: I think you're passing the buck.
BRICK: You know many drinkin' men?
BIG DADDY (*with a slight, charming smile*): I have known a fair number of that
  species.
BRICK: Could any of them tell you why he drank?
BIG DADDY: Yep, you're passin' the buck to things like time and disgust with
  "mendacity" and — crap! — if you got to use that kind of language
  about a thing, it's ninety-proof bull, and I'm not buying any.
BRICK: I had to give you a reason to get a drink!
BIG DADDY: You started drinkin' when your friend Skipper died.

(*Silence for five beats. Then* BRICK *makes a startled movement, reaching for his crutch.*)

BRICK: What are you suggesting?
BIG DADDY: I'm suggesting nothing.

(*The shuffle and clop of* BRICK'S *rapid hobble away from his father's steady, grave
attention.*)

— But Gooper an' Mae suggested that there was something not right
  exactly in your —
BRICK (*stopping short downstage as if backed to a wall*): "Not right"?
BIG DADDY: Not, well, exactly *normal* in your friendship with —
BRICK: They suggested that, too? I thought that was Maggie's suggestion.

(BRICK'S *detachment is at last broken through. His heart is accelerated; his forehead
sweat-beaded; his breath becomes more rapid and his voice hoarse. The thing they're
discussing, timidly and painfully on the side of* BIG DADDY, *fiercely, violently on* BRICK'S
side, is the inadmissible thing that SKIPPER *died to disavow between them. The fact that
if it existed it had to be disavowed to "keep face" in the world they lived in, may be at
the heart of the "mendacity" that* BRICK *drinks to kill his disgust with. It may be the
root of his collapse. Or maybe it is only a single manifestation of it, not even the most
important. The bird that I hope to catch in the net of this play is not the solution of one
man's psychological problem. I'm trying to catch the true quality of experience in a
group of people, that cloudy, flickering, evanescent — fiercely charged! — interplay of
live human beings in the thundercloud of a common crisis. Some mystery should be left
in the revelation of character in a play, just as a great deal of mystery is always left in
the revelation of character in life, even in one's own character to himself. This does not
absolve the playwright of his duty to observe and probe as clearly and deeply as he
legitimately* can: *but it should steer him away from "pat" conclusions, facile
definitions which make a play just a play, not a snare for the truth of human experience.*)

(*The following scene should be played with great concentration, with most of the power
leashed but palpable in what is left unspoken.*)

Who else's suggestion is it, is it *yours?* How many others thought that
Skipper and I were —
BIG DADDY *(gently)*: Now, hold on, hold on a minute, son. — I knocked
around in my time.
BRICK: What's that got to do with —
BIG DADDY: I said "Hold on!" — I bummed, I bummed this country till I
was —
BRICK: Whose suggestion, who else's suggestion is it?
BIG DADDY: Slept in hobo jungles and railroad Y's and flophouses in all cities
before I —
BRICK: Oh, *you* think so, too, you call me your son and a queer. Oh! Maybe
that's why you put Maggie and me in this room that was Jack Straw's
and Peter Ochello's, in which that pair of old sisters slept in a double
bed where both of 'em died!
BIG DADDY: *Now just don't go throwing rocks at* —

(*Suddenly* REVEREND TOOKER *appears in the gallery doors, his head slightly, playfully,
fatuously cocked, with a practised clergyman's smile, sincere as a bird call blown on a
hunter's whistle, the living embodiment of the pious, conventional lie.*)

(BIG DADDY *gasps a little at this perfectly timed, but incongruous, apparition.*)

— What're you lookin' for, Preacher?
REVEREND TOOKER: The gentleman's lavatory, ha ha! — heh, heh . . .
BIG DADDY *(with strained courtesy)*: — Go back out and walk down to the other
end of the gallery, Reverend Tooker, and use the bathroom connected
with my bedroom, and if you can't find it, ask them where it is!
REVEREND TOOKER: Ah, thanks.

(*He goes out with a deprecatory chuckle.*)

BIG DADDY: It's hard to talk in this place. . . .
BRICK: Son of a — !
BIG DADDY *(leaving a lot unspoken)*: — I seen all things and understood a lot of
them, till 1910. Christ, the year that — I had worn my shoes through,
hocked my — I hopped off a yellow dog freight car half a mile down
the road, slept in a wagon of cotton outside the gin — Jack Straw an'
Peter Ochello took me in. Hired me to manage this place which grew
into this one. — When Jack Straw died — why, old Peter Ochello quit
eatin' like a dog does when its master's dead, and died, too!
BRICK: Christ!
BIG DADDY: I'm just saying I understand such —
BRICK *(violently)*: Skipper is dead. I have not quit eating!
BIG DADDY: No, but you started drinking.

(BRICK *wheels on his crutch and hurls his glass across the room shouting.*)

BRICK: YOU THINK SO, TOO?

(Footsteps run on the gallery. There are women's calls.)

(BIG DADDY goes toward the door.)

(BRICK is transformed, as if a quiet mountain blew suddenly up in volcanic flame.)

BRICK: You think so, too? You think so, too? You think me an' Skipper did, did, did! — *sodomy!* — together?
BIG DADDY: Hold — !
BRICK: That what you —
BIG DADDY: — *ON* — a minute!
BRICK: You think we did dirty things between us, Skipper an' —
BIG DADDY: Why are you shouting like that? Why are you —
BRICK: — Me, is that what you think of Skipper, is that —
BIG DADDY: — so excited? I don't think nothing. I don't know nothing. I'm simply telling you what —
BRICK: You think that Skipper and me were a pair of dirty old men?
BIG DADDY: Now that's —
BRICK: Straw? Ochello? A couple of —
BIG DADDY: Now just —
BRICK: — fucking sissies? Queers? Is that what you —
BIG DADDY: Shhh.
BRICK: — think?

(He loses his balance and pitches to his knees without noticing the pain. He grabs the bed and drags himself up.)

BIG DADDY: Jesus! — Whew. . . . Grab my hand!
BRICK: Naw, I don't want your hand. . . .
BIG DADDY: Well, I want yours. Git up!

(He draws him up, keeps an arm about him with concern and affection.)

You broken out in a sweat! You're panting like you'd run a race with —
BRICK *(freeing himself from his father's hold)*: Big Daddy, you shock me, Big Daddy, you, you — *shock* me! Talkin' so —

(He turns away from his father.)

— casually! — about a — thing like that. . . .
    — Don't you know how people *feel* about things like that? How, how *disgusted* they are by things like that? Why, at Ole Miss when it was discovered a pledge to our fraternity, Skipper's and mine, did a, *attempted* to do a, unnatural thing with —
    We not only dropped him like a hot rock! — We told him to git off the campus, and he did, he got! — All the way to —

(He halts, breathless.)

BIG DADDY: — Where?

BRICK: — North Africa, last I heard!

BIG DADDY: Well, I have come back from further away than that, I have just now returned from the other side of the moon, death's country, son, and I'm not easy to shock by anything here.

(He comes downstage and faces out.)

Always, anyhow, lived with too much space around me to be infected by ideas of other people. One thing you can grown on a big place more important than cotton! — is *tolerance!* — I grown it.

(He returns toward BRICK.)

BRICK: Why can't exceptional friendship, *real, real, deep, deep friendship!* between two men be respected as something clean and decent without being thought of as —

BIG DADDY: It can, it is, for God's sake.

BRICK: — *Fairies.* . . .

(In his utterance of this word, we gauge the wide and profound reach of the conventional mores he got from the world that crowned him with early laurel.)

BIG DADDY: I told Mae an' Gooper —

BRICK: Frig Mae and Gooper, frig all dirty lies and liars! — Skipper and me had a clean, true thing between us! — had a clean friendship, practically all our lives, till Maggie got the idea you're talking about. Normal? No! — It was too rare to be normal, any true thing between two people is too rare to be normal. Oh, once in a while he put his hand on my shoulder or I'd put mine on his, oh, maybe even, when we were touring the country in pro-football an' shared hotel-rooms we'd reach across the space between the two beds and shake hands to say goodnight, yeah, one or two times we —

BIG DADDY: Brick, nobody thinks that that's not normal!

BRICK: Well, they're mistaken, it was! It was a pure an' true thing an' that's not normal.

MAE *(off stage)*: Big Daddy, they're startin' the fireworks.

(They both stare straight at each other for a long moment. The tension breaks and both turn away as if tired.)

BIG DADDY: Yeah, it's — hard t' — talk. . . .

BRICK: All right, then, let's — let it go. . . .

BIG DADDY: Why did Skipper crack up? Why have you?

(BRICK looks back at his father again. He has already decided, without knowing that he has made this decision, that he is going to tell his father that he is dying of cancer. Only this could even the score between them: one inadmissible thing in return for another.)

BRICK *(ominously)*: All right. You're asking for it, Big Daddy. We're finally going to have that real true talk you wanted. It's too late to stop it, now, we got to carry it through and cover every subject.

(He hobbles back to the liquor cabinet.)

Uh-huh.

(He opens the ice bucket and picks up the silver tongs with slow admiration of their frosty brightness.)

Maggie declares that Skipper and I went into pro-football after we left "Ole Miss" because we were scared to grow up . . .

(He moves downstage with the shuffle and clop of a cripple on a crutch. As MARGARET did when her speech became "recitative," he looks out into the house, commanding its attention by his direct, concentrated gaze — a broken, "tragically elegant" figure telling simply as much as he knows of "the Truth":)

— Wanted to — keep on tossing — those long, long! — high, high! — passes that — couldn't be intercepted except by time, the aerial attack that made us famous! And so we did, we did, we kept it up for one season, that aerial attack, we held it high! — Yeah, but —
  — that summer, Maggie, she laid the law down to me, said, Now or never, and so I married Maggie. . . .
BIG DADDY: How was Maggie in bed?
BRICK *(wryly)*: Great! the greatest!

(BIG DADDY nods as if he thought so.)

She went on the road that fall with the Dixie Stars. Oh, she made a great show of being the world's best sport. She wore a — wore a — tall bearskin cap! A shako, they call it, a dyed moleskin coat, a moleskin coat dyed red! — Cut up crazy! Rented hotel ballrooms for victory celebrations, wouldn't cancel them when it — turned out — defeat. . . .
  MAGGIE THE CAT! Ha ha!

(BIG DADDY nods.)

— But Skipper, he had some fever which came back on him which doctors couldn't explain and I got that injury — turned out to be just a shadow on the X-ray plate — and a touch of bursitis. . . .

I lay in a hospital bed, watched our games on TV, saw Maggie on the bench next to Skipper when he was hauled out of a game for stumbles, fumbles! — Burned me up the way she hung on his arm! — Y'know, I think that Maggie had always felt sort of left out because she and me never got any closer together than two people just get in bed, which is not much closer than two cats on a — fence humping. . . .

So! She took this time to work on poor dumb Skipper. He was a less than average student at Ole Miss, you know that, don't you?! — Poured in his mind the dirty, false idea that what we were, him and me, was a frustrated case of that ole pair of sisters that lived in this room, Jack Straw and Peter Ochello! — He, poor Skipper, went to bed with Maggie to prove it wasn't true, and when it didn't work out, he thought it *was* true! — Skipper broke in two like a rotten stick — nobody ever turned so fast to a lush — or died of it so quick. . . .

— Now are you satisfied?

(BIG DADDY *has listened to this story, dividing the grain from the chaff. Now he looks at his son.*)

BIG DADDY: Are *you* satisfied?
BRICK: With what?
BIG DADDY: That half-ass story!
BRICK: What's half-ass about it?
BIG DADDY: Something's left out of that story. What did you leave out?

(*The phone has started ringing in the hall.*)

GOOPER (*off stage*): Hello.

(*As if it reminded him of something,* BRICK *glances suddenly toward the sound and says:*)

BRICK: Yes! — I left out a long-distance call which I had from Skipper —
GOOPER: Speaking, go ahead.
BRICK: — In which he made a drunken confession to me and on which I hung up!
GOOPER: No.
BRICK: — Last time we spoke to each other in our lives . . .
GOOPER: No, sir.
BIG DADDY: You musta said something to him before you hung up.
BRICK: What could I say to him?
BIG DADDY: Anything. Something.
BRICK: Nothing.
BIG DADDY: Just hung up?
BRICK: Just hung up.
BIG DADDY: Uh-huh. Anyhow now! — we have tracked down the lie with which you're disgusted and which you are drinking to kill your disgust

with, Brick. You been passing the buck. This disgust with mendacity is disgust with yourself.

> *You!* — dug the grave of your friend and kicked him in it! — before you'd face truth with him!

BRICK: *His* truth, not *mine!*

BIG DADDY: His truth, okay! But you wouldn't face it with him!

BRICK: Who *can* face truth? Can *you?*

BIG DADDY: Now don't start passin' the rotten buck again, boy!

BRICK: *How about these birthday congratulations, these many, many happy returns of the day, when ev'rybody knows there won't be any except you!*

(GOOPER, *who has answered the hall phone, lets out a high, shrill laugh; the voice becomes audible saying: "No, no, you got it all wrong! Upside down! Are you crazy?")*

(BRICK *suddenly catches his breath as he realized that he has made a shocking disclosure. He hobbles a few paces, then freezes, and without looking at his father's shocked face, says:)*

Let's, let's — go out, now, and — watch the fireworks. Come on, Big Daddy.

(BIG DADDY *moves suddenly forward and grabs hold of the boy's crutch like it was a weapon for which they were fighting for possession.)*

BIG DADDY: Oh, no, no! No one's going out! What did you start to say?

BRICK: I don't remember.

BIG DADDY: "Many happy returns when they know there won't be any"?

BRICK: Aw, hell, Big Daddy, forget it. Come on out on the gallery and look at the fireworks they're shooting off for your birthday. . . .

BIG DADDY: First you finish that remark you were makin' before you cut off. "Many happy returns when they know there won't be any"? — Ain't that what you just said?

BRICK: Look, now. I can get around without that crutch if I have to but it would be a lot easier on the furniture an' glassware if I didn' have to go swinging along like Tarzan of th' —

BIG DADDY: FINISH! WHAT YOU WAS SAYIN'!

(An eerie green glow shows in sky behind him.)

BRICK (*sucking the ice in his glass, speech becoming thick*): Leave th' place to Gooper and Mae an' their five little same little monkeys. All I want is —

BIG DADDY: "LEAVE TH' PLACE," did you say?

BRICK (*vaguely*): All twenty-eight thousand acres of the richest land this side of the valley Nile.

BIG DADDY: Who said I was "leaving the place" to Gooper or anybody? This is my sixty-fifth birthday! I got fifteen years or twenty years left in me! I'll outlive *you!* I'll bury you an' have to pay for your coffin!

BRICK: Sure. Many happy returns. Now let's go watch the fireworks, come on, let's —

BIG DADDY: Lying, have they been lying? About the report from th' — clinic? Did they, did they — find something? — *Cancer.* Maybe?

BRICK: Mendacity is a system that we live in. Liquor is one way out an' death's the other. . . .

(He takes the crutch from BIG DADDY'S *loose grip and swings out on the gallery leaving the doors open.)*

(A song, "Pick a Bale of Cotton," is heard.)

MAE *(appearing in door)*: Oh, Big Daddy, the field hands are singin' fo' you!

BRICK: I'm sorry, Big Daddy. My head don't work any more and it's hard for me to understand how anybody could care if he lived or died or was dying or cared about anything but whether or not there was liquor left in the bottle and so I said what I said without thinking. In some ways I'm no better than the others, in some ways worse because I'm less alive. Maybe it's being alive that makes them lie, and being almost *not* alive makes me sort of accidentally truthful — I don't know but — anyway — we've been friends . . .

— And being friends is telling each other the truth . . . .

(There is a pause.)

You told *me!* I told *you!*

BIG DADDY *(slowly and passionately)*: CHRIST — DAMN —

GOOPER *(off stage)*: Let her go!

(Fireworks off stage right.)

BIG DADDY: — ALL — LYING SONS OF — LYING BITCHES!

(He straightens at last and crosses to the inside door. At the door he turns and looks back as if he had some desperate question he couldn't put into words. Then he nods reflectively and says in a hoarse voice:)

Yes, all liars, all liars, all lying dying liars!

(This is said slowly, slowly, with a fierce revulsion. He goes on out.)

— Lying! Dying! Liars!

(BRICK remains motionless as the lights dim out and the curtain falls.)

CURTAIN

ACT THREE

There is no lapse of time. BIG DADDY *is seen leaving as at the end of* ACT 2.

BIG DADDY: ALL LYIN' — DYIN'! — LIARS! LIARS! — LIARS!

(MARGARET enters.)

MARGARET: Brick, what in the name of God was goin' on in this room?

(DIXIE and TRIXIE enter through the doors and circle around MARGARET shouting. MAE enters from the lower gallery window.)

MAE: Dixie, Trixie, you quit that!

(GOOPER enters through the doors.)

Gooper, will y' please get these kiddies to bed right now!
GOOPER: Mae, you seen Big Mama?
MAE: Not yet.

(GOOPER and kids exit through the doors. REVEREND TOOKER *enters through the windows.)*

REVEREND TOOKER: Those kiddies are so full of vitality. I think I'll have to be starting back to town.
MAE: Not yet, Preacher. You know we regard you as a member of this family, one of our closest an' dearest, so you just got t' be with us when Doc Baugh gives Big Mama th' actual truth about th' report from the clinic.
MARGARET: Where do you think you're going?
BRICK: Out for some air.
MARGARET: Why'd Big Daddy shout "Liars"?
MAE: Has Big Daddy gone to bed, Brick?
GOOPER *(entering)*: Now where is that old lady?
REVEREND TOOKER: I'll look for her.

(He exits to the gallery.)

MAE: Cain'tcha find her, Gooper?
GOOPER: She's avoidin' this talk.
MAE: I think she senses somethin'.
MARGARET *(going out on the gallery to* BRICK*)*: Brick, they're goin' to tell Big Mama the truth about Big Daddy and she's goin' to need you.
DOCTOR BAUGH: This is going to be painful.

MAE: Painful things caint always be avoided.

REVEREND TOOKER: I see Big Mama.

GOOPER: Hey, Big Mama, come here.

MAE: Hush, Gooper, don't holler.

BIG MAMA (entering): Too much smell of burnt fireworks makes me feel a little bit sick at my stomach. — Where is Big Daddy?

MAE: That's what I want to know, where has Big Daddy gone?

BIG MAMA: He must have turned in, I reckon he went to baid . . .

GOOPER: Well, then, now we can talk.

BIG MAMA: What *is* this talk, *what* talk?

(MARGARET *appears on the gallery, talking to* DOCTOR BAUGH.)

MARGARET (musically): My family freed their slaves ten years before abolition. My great-great-grandfather gave his slaves their freedom five years before the War between the States started!

MAE: Oh, for God's sake! Maggie's climbed back up in her family tree!

MARGARET (sweetly): What, Mae?

(The pace must be very quick: great Southern animation.)

BIG MAMA (addressing them all): I think Big Daddy was just worn out. He loves his family, he loves to have them around him, but it's a strain on his nerves. He wasn't himself tonight, Big Daddy wasn't himself, I could tell he was all worked up.

REVEREND TOOKER: I think he's remarkable.

BIG MAMA: Yaiss! Just remarkable. Did you all notice the food he ate at that table? Did you all notice the supper he put away? Why he ate like a hawss!

GOOPER: I hope he doesn't regret it.

BIG MAMA: What? Why that man — ate a huge piece of cawn bread with molasses on it! Helped himself twice to hoppin' John.

MARGARET: Big Daddy loves hoppin' John. — We had a real country dinner.

BIG MAMA (overlapping MARGARET): Yaiss, he simply adores it! an' candied yams? Son? That man put away enough food at that table to stuff a *field* hand!

GOOPER (with grim relish): I hope he don't have to pay for it later on . . .

BIG MAMA (fiercely): What's *that*, Gooper?

MAE: Gooper says he hopes Big Daddy doesn't suffer tonight.

BIG MAMA: Oh, shoot, Gooper says, Gooper says! Why should Big Daddy suffer for satisfying a normal appetite? There's nothin' wrong with that man but nerves, he's sound as a dollar! And now he knows he is an' that's why he ate such a supper. He had a big load off his mind, knowin' he wasn't doomed t' — what he thought he was doomed to . . .

MARGARET (sadly and sweetly): Bless his old sweet soul . . .

BIG MAMA (vaguely): Yais, bless his heart, where's Brick?

MAE: Outside.

GOOPER: — Drinkin' . . .

BIG MAMA: I know he's drinkin'. Cain't I see he's drinkin' without you continually tellin' me that boy's drinkin'?

MARGARET: Good for you, Big Mama!

(She applauds.)

BIG MAMA: Other people *drink* and *have* drunk an' will *drink*, as long as they make that stuff an' put it in bottles.

MARGARET: That's the truth. I never trusted a man that didn't drink.

BIG MAMA: *Brick? Brick!*

MARGARET: He's still on the gall'ry. I'll go bring him in so we can talk.

BIG MAMA *(worriedly)*: I don't know what this mysterious family conference is about.

(Awkward silence. BIG MAMA looks from face to face, then belches slightly and mutters, "Excuse me . . . " She opens an ornamental fan suspended about her throat. A black lace fan to go with her black lace gown, and fans her wilting corsage, sniffing nervously and looking from face to face in the uncomfortable silence as MARGARET calls "Brick?" and BRICK sings to the moon on the gallery.)

MARGARET: Brick, they're gonna tell Big Mama the truth an' she's gonna need you.

BIG MAMA: I don't know what's wrong here, you all have such long faces! Open that door on the hall and let some air circulate through here, will you please, Gooper?

MAE: I think we'd better leave that door closed, Big Mama, till after the talk.

MARGARET: Brick!

BIG MAMA: Reveren' Tooker, will *you* please open that door?

REVEREND TOOKER: I sure will, Big Mama.

MAE: I just didn't think we ought t' take any chance of Big Daddy hearin' a word of this discussion.

BIG MAMA: I *swan!* Nothing's going to be said in Big Daddy's house that he caint hear if he want to!

GOOPER: Well, Big mama, it's —

(MAE gives him a quick, hard poke to shut him up. He glares at her fiercely as she circles before him like a burlesque ballerina, raising her skinny bare arms over her head, jangling her bracelets, exclaiming:)

MAE: *A breeze! A breeze!*

REVEREND TOOKER: I think this house is the coolest house in the Delta. — Did you all know that Halsey Banks's widow put air-conditioning units in the church and rectory at Friar's Point in memory of Halsey?

(General conversation has resumed; everybody is chatting so that the stage sounds like a bird cage.)

GOOPER: Too bad nobody cools your church off for you. I bet you sweat in that pulpit these hot Sundays, Reverend Tooker.

REVEREND TOOKER: Yes, my vestments are drenched. Last Sunday the gold in my chasuble faded into the purple.

GOOPER: Reveren', you musta been preachin' hell's fire last Sunday.

MAE *(at the same time to* DOCTOR BAUGH*)*: You reckon those vitamin B12 injections are what they're cracked up t' be, Doc Baugh?

DOCTOR BAUGH: Well, if you want to be stuck with something I guess they're as good to be stuck with as anything else.

BIG MAMA *(at the gallery door)*: *Maggie, Maggie, aren't you comin' with Brick?*

MAE *(suddenly and loudly, creating a silence)*: *I have a strange feeling, I have a peculiar feeling!*

BIG MAMA *(turning from the gallery)*: What feeling?

MAE: That Brick said somethin' he shouldn't of said t' Big Daddy.

BIG MAMA: Now what on earth could Brick of said t' Big Daddy that he shouldn't say?

GOOPER: Big Mama, there's somethin' —

MAE: NOW, WAIT!

(She rushes up to BIG MAMA *and gives her a quick hug and kiss.* BIG MAMA *pushes her impatiently off.)*

DOCTOR BAUGH: In my day they had what they call the Keeley cure for heavy drinkers.

BIG MAMA: Shoot!

DOCTOR BAUGH: But now I understand they just take some kind of tablets.

GOOPER: They call them "Annie Bust"[2] tablets.

BIG MAMA: *Brick* don't need to take *nothin'.*

*(*BRICK *and* MARGARET *appear in gallery doors,* BIG MAMA *unaware of his presence behind her.)*

That boy is just broken up over Skipper's death. You know how poor Skipper died. They gave him a big, big dose of that sodium amytal stuff at his home and then they called the ambulance and give him another big, big dose of it at the hospital and that and all of the alcohol in his system fo' months an' months just proved too much for his heart . . . I'm scared of needles! I'm more scared of a needle than the knife . . . I think more people have been needled out of this world than —

(She stops short and wheels about.)

Oh — here's Brick! My precious baby —

(She turns upon BRICK *with short, fat arms extended, at the same time uttering a loud, short sob, which is both comic and touching.* BRICK *smiles and bows slightly, making a*

2 *Antabuse: trade name for disulfiram, a pharmaceutical used for treating chronic alcoholism.*

burlesque gesture of gallantry for MARGARET *to pass before him into the room. Then he hobbles on his crutch directly to the liquor cabinet and there is absolute silence, with everybody looking at* BRICK *as everybody has always looked at* BRICK *when he spoke or moved or appeared. One by one he drops ice cubes in his glass, then suddenly, but not quickly, looks back over his shoulder with a wry, charming smile, and says:)*

BRICK: I'm sorry! Anyone else?

BIG MAMA *(sadly)*: No, son. I *wish* you wouldn't!

BRICK: I wish I didn't have to, Big Mama, but I'm still waiting for that click in my head which makes it all smooth out!

BIG MAMA: Ow, Brick, you — BREAK MY HEART!

MARGARET *(at same time)*: Brick, go sit with Big Mama!

BIG MAMA: I just cain't staiiiiii-nnnnnnnd-it . . .

(She sobs.)

MAE: Now that we're all assembled —

GOOPER: We kin talk . . .

BIG MAMA: Breaks my heart . . .

MARGARET: Sit with Big Mama, Brick, and hold her hand.

*(*BIG MAMA *sniffs very loudly three times, almost like three drumbeats in the pocket of silence.)*

BRICK: You do that, Maggie. I'm a restless cripple. I got to stay on my crutch.

*(*BRICK *hobbles to the gallery door; leans there as if waiting.)*

*(*MAE *sits beside* BIG MAMA, *while* GOOPER *moves in front and sits on the end of the couch, facing her.* REVEREND TOOKER *moves nervously into the space between them; on the other side,* DOCTOR BAUGH *stands looking at nothing in particular and lights a cigar.* MARGARET *turns away.)*

BIG MAMA: Why're you all *surroundin'* me — like this? Why're you all starin' at me like this an' makin' signs at each other?

*(*REVEREND TOOKER *steps back startled.)*

MAE: Calm yourself, Big Mama.

BIG MAMA: Calm you'self, *you'self*, Sister Woman. How could I calm myself with everyone starin' at me as if big drops of blood had broken out on m'face? What's this all about, annh! What?

*(*GOOPER *coughs and takes a center position.)*

GOOPER: Now, Doc Baugh.

MAE: Doc Baugh?

GOOPER: Big Mama wants to know the complete truth about the report we got from the Ochsner Clinic.

MAE *(eagerly)*: — on Big Daddy's condition!

GOOPER: Yais, on Big Daddy's condition, we got to face it.

DOCTOR BAUGH: Well . . .

BIG MAMA *(terrified, rising)*: Is there? Something? Something that I? Don't — know?

(In these few words, this startled, very soft, question, BIG MAMA reviews the history of her forty-five years with BIG DADDY, her great, almost embarrassingly true-hearted and simple-minded devotion to BIG DADDY, who must have had something BRICK has, who made himself loved so much by the "simple expedient" of not loving enough to disturb his charming detachment, also once coupled, like BRICK, with virile beauty.)

(BIG MAMA has a dignity at this moment; she almost stops being fat.)

DOCTOR BAUGH *(after a pause, uncomfortably)*: Yes? — Well —

BIG MAMA: I!!! — want to — *knowwwwww . . .*

(Immediately she thrusts her fist to her mouth as if to deny that statement. Then for some curious reason, she snatches the withered corsage from her breast and hurls it on the floor and steps on it with her short, fat feet.)

Somebody must be lyin'! — I want to know!

MAE: Sit down, Big Mama, sit down on this sofa.

MARGARET: Brick, go sit with Big Mama.

BIG MAMA: *What is it, what is it?*

DOCTOR BAUGH: I never have seen a more thorough examination than Big Daddy Pollitt was given in all my experience with the Ochsner Clinic.

GOOPER: It's one of the best in the country.

MAE: It's THE best in the country — bar *none!*

(For some reason she gives GOOPER a violent poke as she goes past him. He slaps at her hand without removing his eyes from his mother's face.)

DOCTOR BAUGH: Of course they were ninety-nine and nine-tenths per cent sure before they even started.

BIG MAMA: Sure of what, sure of what, sure of — *what?* — *what?*

(She catches her breath in a startled sob. MAE kisses her quickly. She thrusts MAE fiercely away from her, staring at the DOCTOR.)

MAE: Mommy, be a brave girl!

BRICK *(in the doorway, softly)*: "By the light, by the light, Of the sil-ve-ry mo-oo-n . . ."

GOOPER: Shut up! — Brick.

BRICK: Sorry . . .

(He wanders out on the gallery.)

DOCTOR BAUGH: But now, you see, Big Mama, they cut a piece off this
  growth, a specimen of the tissue and —
BIG MAMA: Growth? You told Big Daddy —
DOCTOR BAUGH: Now wait.
BIG MAMA *(fiercely)*: You told me and Big Daddy there wasn't a thing wrong
  with him but —
MAE: Big Mama, they always —
GOOPER: Let Doc Baugh talk, will yuh?
BIG MAMA: — little spastic condition of —

(Her breath gives out in a sob.)

DOCTOR BAUGH: Yes, that's what we told Big Daddy. But we had this bit of
  tissue run through the laboratory and I'm sorry to say the test was positive on it. It's — well — malignant . . .

(Pause.)

BIG MAMA: — Cancer?! Cancer?!

(DOCTOR BAUGH nods gravely. BIG MAMA gives a long gasping cry.)

MAE AND GOOPER: Now, now, now, Big Mama, you had to know . . .
BIG MAMA: WHY DIDN'T THEY CUT IT OUT OF HIM? HANH?
  HANH?
DOCTOR BAUGH: Involved too much, Big Mama, too many organs affected.
MAE: Big Mama, the liver's affected and so's the kidneys, both! It's gone way
  past what they call a —
GOOPER: A surgical risk.
MAE: — Uh-huh . . .

(BIG MAMA draws a breath like a dying gasp.)

REVEREND TOOKER: Tch, tch, tch, tch, tch!
DOCTOR BAUGH: Yes it's gone past the knife.
MAE: *That's why he's turned yellow, Mommy!*
BIG MAMA: *Git away from me, git away from me, Mae!*

(She rises abruptly.)

  I want Brick! Where's Brick? Where is my only son?
MAE: Mama! Did she say *"only* son"?

GOOPER: What does that make *me*?

MAE: A sober responsible man with five precious children! — *Six!*

BIG MAMA: I want Brick to tell me! Brick! Brick!

MARGARET (*rising from her reflections in a corner*): Brick was so upset he went back out.

BIG MAMA: *Brick!*

MARGARET: Mama, let *me* tell you!

BIG MAMA: No, no, leave me alone, you're not my blood!

GOOPER: *Mama, I'm your son!* Listen to *me!*

MAE: Gooper's your son, he's your first-born!

BIG MAMA: Gooper never liked Daddy.

MAE (*as if terribly shocked*): That's not TRUE!

(*There is a pause. The minister coughs and rises.*)

REVEREND TOOKER (*to* MAE): I think I'd better slip away at this point.

(*Discreetly*)

Good night, good night, everybody, and God bless you all . . . on this place . . .

(*He slips out.*)

(MAE *coughs and points at* BIG MAMA.)

DOCTOR BAUGH: Well, Big Mama . . .

(*He sighs.*)

BIG MAMA: It's all a mistake, I know it's just a bad dream.

DOCTOR BAUGH: We're gonna keep Big Daddy as comfortable as we can.

BIG MAMA: Yes, it's just a bad dream, that's all it is, it's just an awful dream.

GOOPER: In my opinion Big Daddy is having some pain but won't admit that he has it.

BIG MAMA: Just a dream, a bad dream.

DOCTOR BAUGH: That's what lots of them do, they think if they don't admit they're having the pain they can sort of escape the fact of it.

GOOPER (*with relish*): Yes, they get sly about it, they get real sly about it.

MAE: Gooper and I think —

GOOPER: Shut up, Mae! Big Mama, I think — Big Daddy ought to be started on morphine.

BIG MAMA: Nobody's going to give Big Daddy morphine.

DOCTOR BAUGH: Now, Big Mama, when that pain strikes it's going to strike mighty hard and Big Daddy's going to need the needle to bear it.

BIG MAMA: I tell you, nobody's going to give him morphine.

MAE: Big Mama, you don't want to see Big Daddy suffer, you know you —

(GOOPER, *standing beside her, gives her a savage poke.*)

DOCTOR BAUGH (*placing a package on the table*): I'm leaving this stuff here, so if there's a sudden attack you all won't have to send out for it.
MAE: I know how to give a hypo.
BIG MAMA: Nobody's gonna give Big Daddy morphine.
GOOPER: Mae took a course in nursing during the war.
MARGARET: Somehow I don't think Big Daddy would want Mae to give him a hypo.
MAE: You think he'd want *you* to do it?
DOCTOR BAUGH: Well . . .

(DOCTOR BAUGH *rises.*)

GOOPER: Doctor Baugh is goin'.
DOCTOR BAUGH: Yes, I got to be goin'. Well, keep your chin up, Big Mama.
GOOPER (*with jocularity*): She's gonna keep *both* chins up, aren't you, Big Mama?

(BIG MAMA *sobs.*)

Now stop that, Big Mama.
GOOPER (*at the door with* DOCTOR BAUGH): Well, Doc, we sure do appreciate all you done. I'm telling you, we're surely obligated to you for —

(DOCTOR BAUGH *has gone out without a glance at him.*)

— I guess that doctor has got a lot on his mind but it wouldn't hurt him to act a little more human . . .

(BIG MAMA *sobs.*)

Now be a brave girl, Mommy.
BIG MAMA: It's not true, I know that it's just not true!
GOOPER: Mama, those tests are infallible!
BIG MAMA: Why are you so determined to see your father daid?
MAE: Big Mama!
MARGARET (*gently*): I know what Big Mama means.
MAE (*fiercely*): Oh, do you?
MARGARET (*quietly and very sadly*): Yes, I think I do.
MAE: For a newcomer in the family you sure do show a lot of understanding.
MARGARET: Understanding is needed on this place.
MAE: I guess you must have needed a lot of it in your family, Maggie, with your father's liquor problem and now you've got Brick with his!

MARGARET: Brick does not have a liquor problem at all. Brick is devoted to Big Daddy. This thing is a terrible strain on him.

BIG MAMA: Brick is Big Daddy's boy, but he drinks too much and it worries me and Big Daddy, and, Margaret, you've got to co-operate with us, you've got to co-operate with Big Daddy and me in getting Brick straightened out. Because it will break Big Daddy's heart if Brick don't pull himself together and take hold of things.

MAE: Take hold of *what* things, Big Mama?

BIG MAMA: The place.

(There is a quick violent look between MAE and GOOPER.)

GOOPER: Big Mama, you've had a shock.

MAE: Yais, we've all had a shock, but . . .

GOOPER: Let's be realistic —

MAE: — Big Daddy would never, would *never*, be foolish enough to —

GOOPER: — put this place in irresponsible hands!

BIG MAMA: Big Daddy ain't going to leave the place in anybody's hand; Big Daddy is *not* going to die. I want you to get that in your heads, all of you!

MAE: Mommy, Mommy, Big Mama, we're just as hopeful an' optimistic as you are about Big Daddy's prospects, we have faith in *prayer* — but nevertheless there are certain matters that have to be discussed an' dealt with, because otherwise —

GOOPER: Eventualities have to be considered and now's the time . . . Mae, will you please get my brief case out of our room?

MAE: Yes, honey.

(She rises and goes out through the hall door.)

GOOPER *(standing over BIG MAMA.)*: Now, Big Mom. What you said just now was not at all true and you know it. I've always loved Big Daddy in my own quiet way. I never made a show of it, and I know that Big Daddy has always been fond of me in a quiet way, too, and he never made a show of it neither.

(MAE returns with GOOPER's brief case.)

MAE: Here's your brief case, Gooper, honey.

GOOPER *(handing the brief case back to her)*: Thank you . . . Of cou'se, my relationship with Big Daddy is different from Brick's.

MAE: You're eight years older'n Brick an' always had t' carry a bigger load of th' responsibilities than Brick ever had t' carry. He never carried a thing in his life but a football or a highball.

GOOPER: Mae, will y' let me talk, please?

MAE: Yes, honey.

GOOPER: Now, a twenty-eight-thousand-acre plantation's a mighty big thing t' run.

MAE: Almost singlehanded.

(MARGARET *has gone out onto the gallery and can be heard calling softly to* BRICK.)

BIG MAMA: You never had to run this place! What are you talking about? As if Big Daddy was dead and in his grave, you had to run it? Why, you just helped him out with a few business details and had your law practice at the same time in Memphis!

MAE: Oh, Mommy, Mommy, Big Mommy! Let's be fair!

MARGARET: Brick!

MAE: Why, Gooper has given himself body and soul to keeping this place up for the past five years since Big Daddy's health started failing.

MARGARET: Brick!

MAE: Gooper won't say it, Gooper never thought of it as a duty, he just did it. And what did Brick do? Brick kept living in his past glory at college! Still a football player at twenty-seven!

MARGARET (*returning alone*): Who are you talking about now? Brick? A football player? He isn't a football player and you know it. Brick is a sports announcer on T.V. and one of the best-known ones in the country!

MAE: I'm talking about what he was.

MARGARET: Well, I wish you would just stop talking about my husband.

GOOPER: I've got a right to discuss my brother with other members of MY OWN family, which don't include *you*. Why don't you go out there and drink with Brick?

MARGARET: I've never seen such malice toward a brother.

GOOPER: How about his for me? Why, he can't stand to be in the same room with me!

MARGARET: This is a deliberate campaign of vilification for the most disgusting and sordid reason on earth, and I know what it is! It's *avarice, avarice, greed, greed!*

BIG MAMA: *Oh, I'll scream! I will scream in a moment unless this stops!*

(GOOPER *has stalked up to* MARGARET *with clenched fists at his sides as if he would strike her.* MAE *distorts her face again into a hideous grimace behind* MARGARET's *back.*)

BIG MAMA (*sobs*): Margaret. Child. Come here. Sit next to Big Mama.

MARGARET: Precious Mommy. I'm sorry, I'm sorry, I — !

(*She bends her long graceful neck to press her forehead to* BIG MAMA's *bulging shoulder under its black chiffon.*)

MAE: How beautiful, how touching, this display of devotion! Do you know why she's childless? She's childless because that big beautiful athlete husband of hers won't go to bed with her!

GOOPER: You jest won't let me do this in a nice way, will yah? Aw right — I don't give a goddam if Big Daddy likes me or don't like me or did or never did or will or will never! I'm just appealing to a sense of common decency and fair play. I'll tell you the truth. I've resented Big Daddy's partiality to Brick ever since Brick was born, and the way I've been treated like I was just barely good enough to spit on and sometimes not even good enough for that. Big Daddy is dying of cancer, and it's spread all through him and it's attacked all his vital organs including the kidneys and right now he is sinking into uremia, and you all know what uremia is, it's poisoning of the whole system due to the failure of the body to eliminate its poisons.

MARGARET *(to herself, downstage, hissingly)*: *Poisons, poisons! Venomous thoughts and words! In hearts and minds! — That's poisons!*

GOOPER *(overlapping her)*: I am asking for a square deal, and, by God, I expect to get one. But if I don't get one, if there's any peculiar shenanigans going on around here behind my back, well, I'm not a corporation lawyer for nothing, I know how to protect my own interests.

(BRICK enters from the gallery with a tranquil, blurred smile, carrying an empty glass with him.)

BRICK: Storm coming up.

GOOPER: Oh! A late arrival!

MAE: Behold the conquering hero comes!

GOOPER: The fabulous Brick Pollitt! Remember him? — Who could forget him!

MAE: He looks like he's been injured in a game!

GOOPER: Yep, I'm afraid you'll have to warm the bench at the Sugar Bowl this year, Brick!

(MAE laughs shrilly.)

Or was it the Rose Bowl that he made that famous run in? —

(Thunder.)

MAE: The punch bowl, honey. It was in the punch bowl, the cut-glass punch bowl!

GOOPER: Oh, that's right, I'm getting the bowls mixed up!

MARGARET: Why don't you stop venting your malice and envy on a sick boy?

BIG MAMA: *Now you two hush, I mean it, hush, all of you, hush!*

DAISY, SOOKEY: Storm! Storm comin'! Storm! Storm!

LACEY: Brightie, close them shutters.

GOOPER: Lacey, put the top up on my Cadillac, will yuh?

LACEY: Yes, suh, Mistah Pollitt!

GOOPER *(at the same time)*: Big Mama, you know it's necessary for me t' go back to Memphis in th' mornin' t' represent the Parker estate in a lawsuit.

(MAE *sits on the bed and arranges papers she has taken from the brief case.*)

BIG MAMA: Is it, Gooper?

MAE: Yaiss.

GOOPER: That's why I'm forced to — to bring up a problem that —

MAE: Somethin' that's too important t' be put off!

GOOPER: If Brick was sober, he ought to be in on this.

MARGARET: Brick is present; we're present.

GOOPER: Well, good. I will now give you this outline my partner, Tom Bullitt, an' me have drawn up — a sort of dummy — trusteeship.

MARGARET: Oh, that's it! You'll be in charge an' dole out remittances, will you?

GOOPER: This we did as soon as we got the report on Big Daddy from th' Ochsner Laboratories. We did this thing, I mean we drew up this dummy outline with the advice and assistance of the Chairman of the Boa'd of Directors of th' Southern Plantahs Bank and Trust Company in Memphis, C. C. Bellowes, a man who handles estates for all th' prominent fam'lies in West Tennessee and th' Delta.

BIG MAMA: Gooper?

GOOPER (*crouching in front of* BIG MAMA): Now this is not — not final, or anything like it. This is just a preliminary outline. But it does provide a basis — a design — a — possible, feasible — *plan!*

MARGARET: Yes, I'll bet it's a plan.

(*Thunder*)

MAE: It's a plan to protect the biggest estate in the Delta from irresponsibility an' —

BIG MAMA: Now you listen to me, all of you, you listen here! They's not goin' to be any more catty talk in my house! And Gooper, you put that away before I grab it out of your hand and tear it right up! I don't know what the hell's in it, and I don't want to know what the hell's in it. I'm talkin' in Big Daddy's language now; I'm his *wife*, not his *widow*, I'm still his *wife!* And I'm talkin' to you in his language an' —

GOOPER: Big Mama, what I have here is —

MAE (*at the same time*): Gooper explained that it's just a plan . . .

BIG MAMA: I don't care what you got there. Just put it back where it came from, an' don't let me see it again, not even the outside of the envelope of it! Is that understood? Basis! Plan! Preliminary! Design! I say — what is it Big Daddy always says when he's disgusted?

BRICK (*from the bar*): Big Daddy says "crap" when he's disgusted.

BIG MAMA (*rising*): That's right — CRAP! I say CRAP too, like Big Daddy!

(*Thunder*)

MAE: Coarse language doesn't seem called for in this —

GOOPER: Somethin' in me is *deeply outraged* by hearin' you talk like this.

BIG MAMA: *Nobody's goin' to take nothin'!* — till Big Daddy lets go of it — maybe, just possibly, not — not even then! No, not even then!

(Thunder)

MAE: Sookey, hurry up an' git that po'ch furniture covahed; want th' paint to come off?

GOOPER: Lacey, put mah car away!

LACEY: Caint, Mistah Pollitt, you got the keys!

GOOPER: Naw, you got 'em, man. Where th' keys to th' car, honey?

MAE: You got 'em in your pocket!

BRICK: "You can always hear me singin' this song, Show me the way to go home."

(Thunder distantly)

BIG MAMA: Brick! Come here, Brick, I need you. Tonight Brick looks like he used to look when he was a little boy, just like he did when he played wild games and used to come home when I hollered myself hoarse for him, all sweaty and pink cheeked and sleepy, with his — red curls shining . . .

(BRICK *draws aside as he does from all physical contact and continues the song in a whisper, opening the ice bucket and dropping in the ice cubes one by one as if he were mixing some important chemical formula.*)

(Distant thunder.)

Time goes by so fast. Nothin' can outrun it. Death commences too early — almost before you're half acquainted with life — you meet the other . . . Oh, you know we just got to love each other an' stay together, all of us, just as close as we can, especially now that such a *black* thing has come and moved into this place without invitation.

(Awkwardly embracing BRICK, *she presses her head to his shoulder.)*

(A dog howls off stage.)

Oh, Brick, son of Big Daddy, Big Daddy does so love you. Y'know what would be his fondest dream come true? If before he passed on, if Big Daddy has to pass on . . .

(A dog howls.)

     . . . you give him a child of yours, a grandson as much like his son as his son is like Big Daddy . . .

MARGARET: I know that's Big Daddy's dream.

BIG MAMA: That's his dream.

MAE: Such a pity that Maggie and Brick can't oblige.

BIG DADDY (*off down stage right on the gallery*): Looks like the wind was takin' liberties with this place.

SERVANT (*off stage*): Yes, sir, Mr. Pollitt.

MARGARET (*crossing to the right door*): Big Daddy's on the gall'ry.

(BIG MAMA *has turned toward the hall door at the sound of* BIG DADDY's *voice on the gallery.*)

BIG MAMA: I can't stay here. He'll see somethin' in my eyes.

(BIG DADDY *enters the room from up stage right.*)

BIG DADDY: Can I come in?

(*He puts his cigar in an ash tray.*)

MARGARET: Did the storm wake you up, Big Daddy?

BIG DADDY: Which stawm are you talkin' about — th' one outside or th' hullaballoo in here?

(GOOPER *squeezes past* BIG DADDY.)

GOOPER: 'Scuse me.

(MAE *tries to squeeze past* BIG DADDY *to join* GOOPER, *but* BIG DADDY *puts his arm firmly around her.*)

BIG DADDY: I heard some mighty loud talk. Sounded like somethin' important was bein' discussed. What was the powwow about?

MAE (*flustered*): Why — nothin', Big Daddy . . .

BIG DADDY (*crossing to extreme left center, taking* MAE *with him*): What is that pregnant-lookin' envelope you're puttin' back in your brief case, Gooper?

GOOPER (*at the foot of the bed, caught, as he stuffs papers into envelope*): That? Nothin', suh — nothin' much of anythin' at all . . .

BIG DADDY: Nothin'? It looks like a whole lot of nothin'!

(*He turns up stage to the group.*)

You all know th' story about th' young married couple —

GOOPER: Yes, sir!

BIG DADDY: Hello, Brick —

BRICK: Hello, Big Daddy.

(The group is arranged in a semicircle above BIG DADDY, MARGARET *at the extreme right, then* MAE *and* GOOPER, *then* BIG MAMA, *with* BRICK *at the left.)*

BIG DADDY: Young married couple took Junior out to th' zoo one Sunday, inspected all of God's creatures in their cages, with satisfaction.

GOOPER: Satisfaction.

BIG DADDY *(crossing to up stage center, facing front)*: This afternoon was a warm afternoon in spring an' that ole elephant had somethin' else on his mind which was bigger'n peanuts. You know this story, Brick?

(Gooper nods.)

BRICK: No, sir, I don't know it.

BIG DADDY: Y'see, in th' cage adjoinin' they was a young female elephant in heat!

BIG MAMA *(at* BIG DADDY's *shoulder)*: Oh, Big Daddy!

BIG DADDY: What's the matter, preacher's gone, ain't he? All right. That female elephant in the next cage was permeatin' the atmosphere about her with a powerful and excitin' odor of female fertility! Huh! Ain't that a nice way to put it, Brick?

BRICK: Yes, sir, nothin' wrong with it.

BIG DADDY: Brick says th's nothin' wrong with it!

BIG MAMA: Oh, Big Daddy!

BIG DADDY *(crossing to down stage center)*: So this ole bull elephant still had a couple of fornications left in him. He reared back his trunk an' got a whiff of that elephant lady next door! — began to paw at the dirt in his cage an' butt his head against the separatin' partition and, first thing y'know, there was a conspicuous change in his *profile* — very *conspicuous!* Ain't I tellin' this story in decent language, Brick?

BRICK: Yes, sir, too fuckin' decent!

BIG DADDY: So, the little boy pointed at it and said, "What's that?" His mama said, "Oh, that's — nothin'!" — His papa said, "She's spoiled!"

*(*BIG DADDY *crosses to Brick at left.)*

You didn't laugh at that story, Brick.

*(*BIG MAMA *crosses to down stage right crying.* MARGARET *goes to her.* MAE *and* GOOPER *hold up stage right center.)*

BRICK: No, sir, I didn't laugh at that story.

BIG DADDY: What is the smell in this room? Don't you notice it, Brick? Don't you notice a powerful and obnoxious odor of mendacity in this room?

BRICK: Yes, sir, I think I do, sir.

GOOPER: Mae, Mae . . .

BIG DADDY: There is nothing more powerful. Is there, Brick?

BRICK: No, sir. No, sir, there isn't, an' nothin' more obnoxious.

BIG DADDY: Brick agrees with me. The odor of mendacity is a powerful and obnoxious odor an' the stawm hasn't blown it away from this room yet. You notice it, Gooper?

GOOPER: What, sir?

BIG DADDY: How about you, Sister Woman? You notice the unpleasant odor of mendacity in this room?

MAE: Why, Big Daddy, I don't even know what that is.

BIG DADDY: You can smell it. Hell it smells like death!

(BIG MAMA sobs. BIG DADDY looks toward her.)

What's wrong with that fat woman over there, loaded with diamonds? Hey, what's-you-name, what's the matter with you?

MARGARET *(crossing toward BIG DADDY)*: She had a slight dizzy spell, Big Daddy.

BIG DADDY: You better watch that, Big Mama. A stroke is a bad way to go.

MARGARET *(crossing to BIG DADDY at center.)*: Oh, Brick, Big Daddy has on your birthday present to him, Brick, he has on your cashmere robe, the softest material I have ever felt.

BIG DADDY: Yeah, this is my soft birthday, Maggie . . . Not my gold or my silver birthday, but my soft birthday, everything's got to be soft for Big Daddy on this soft birthday.

(MAGGIE kneels before BIG DADDY at center.)

MARGARET: Big Daddy's got on his Chinese slippers that I gave him, Brick. Big Daddy, I haven't given you my big present yet, but now I will, now's the time for me to present it to you! I have an announcement to make!

MAE: What? What kind of announcement?

GOOPER: A sports announcement, Maggie?

MARGARET: Announcement of life beginning! A child is coming, sired by Brick, and out of Maggie the Cat! I have Brick's child in my body, an' that's my birthday present to Big Daddy on this birthday!

(BIG DADDY looks at BRICK who crosses behind BIG DADDY to down stage portal, left.)

BIG DADDY: Get up, girl, get up off your knees, girl.

(BIG DADDY helps MARGARET to rise. He crosses above her, to her right, bites off the end of a fresh cigar, taken from his bathrobe pocket, as he studies MARGARET.)

Uh-huh, this girl has life in her body, that's no lie!

BIG MAMA: BIG DADDY'S DREAM COME TRUE!

BRICK: JESUS!

BIG DADDY *(crossing right below wicker stand)*: Gooper, I want my lawyer in the mornin'.

BRICK: Where are you goin', Big Daddy?

BIG DADDY: Son, I'm goin' up on the roof, to the belvedere on th' roof to look over my kingdom before I give up my kingdom — twenty-eight thousand acres of th' richest land this side of the valley Nile!

(He exits through right doors, and down right on the gallery.)

BIG MAMA *(following)*: Sweetheart, sweetheart, sweetheart — can I come with you?

(She exits down stage right.)

(MARGARET is down stage center in the mirror area. MAE has joined GOOPER and she gives him a fierce poke, making a low hissing sound and a grimace of fury.)

GOOPER *(pushing her aside)*: Brick, could you possibly spare me one small shot of that liquor?

BRICK: Why, help yourself, Gooper boy.

GOOPER: I will.

MAE *(shrilly)*: Of course we know that this is — a lie.

GOOPER: *Be still, Mae.*

MAE: I won't be still! I know she's made this up!

GOOPER: Goddam it, I said shut up!

MARGARET: Gracious! I didn't know that my little announcement was going to provoke such a storm!

MAE: *That* woman isn't *pregnant!*

GOOPER: Who said she was?

MAE: *She* did.

GOOPER: The doctor didn't. Doc Baugh didn't.

MARGARET: I haven't gone to Doc Baugh.

GOOPER: Then who'd you go to, Maggie?

MARGARET: One of the best gynecologists in the South.

GOOPER: Uh huh, uh huh! — I see . . .

(He takes out a pencil and notebook.)

— May we have his name, please?

MARGARET: No, you may not, Mister Prosecuting Attorney!

MAE: He doesn't have any name, he doesn't exist!

MARGARET: Oh, he exists all right, and so does my child, Brick's baby!

MAE: You can't conceive a child by a man that won't sleep with you unless you think you're —

(BRICK has turned on the phonograph. A scat song³ cuts MAE's speech.)

GOOPER: *Turn that off!*

---

3 *improvised jazz singing in wordless but expressive syllables.*

MAE: We know it's a lie because we hear you in here; he won't sleep with you, we hear you! So don't imagine you're going to put a trick over on us, to fool a dying man with a —

(A long drawn cry of agony and rage fills the house. MARGARET *turns the phonograph down to a whisper. The cry is repeated.)*

MAE: Did you hear that, Gooper, did you hear that?
GOOPER: Sounds like the pain has struck.
MAE: Go see, Gooper!
GOOPER: Come along and leave these lovebirds together in their nest!

(He goes out first. MAE *follows but turns at the door, contorting her face and hissing at* MARGARET *.)*

MAE: *Liar!*

(She slams the door.)

*(*MARGARET *exhales with relief and moves a little unsteadily to catch hold of* BRICK's *arm.)*

MARGARET: Thank you for — keeping still . . .
BRICK: O.K., Maggie.
MARGARET: It was gallant of you to save my face!

(He now pours down three shots in quick succession and stands waiting, silent. All at once he turns with a smile and says:)

BRICK: *There!*
MARGARET: What?
BRICK: The *click* . . .

(His gratitude seems almost infinite as he hobbles out on the gallery with a drink. We hear his crutch as he swings out of sight. Then, at some distance, he begins singing to himself a peaceful song. MARGARET *holds the big pillow forlornly as if it were her only companion, for a few moments, then throws it on the bed. She rushes to the liquor cabinet, gathers all the bottles in her arms, turns about undecidedly, then runs out of the room with them, leaving the door ajar on the dim yellow hall.* BRICK *is heard hobbling back along the gallery, singing his peaceful song. He comes back in, sees the pillow on the bed, laughs lightly, sadly, picks it up. He has it under his arm as* MARGARET *returns to the room.* MARGARET *softly shuts the door and leans against it, smiling softly at* BRICK.*)*

MARGARET: Brick, I used to think that you were stronger than me and I didn't want to be overpowered by you. But now, since you've taken to liquor — you know what? — I guess it's bad, but now I'm stronger than you and I can love you more truly! Don't move that pillow. I'll move it right back if you do! — Brick?

(She turns out all the lamps but a single rose-silk-shaded one by the bed.)

I really have been to a doctor and I know what to do and — Brick? — this is my time by the calendar to conceive?

BRICK: Yes, I understand, Maggie. But how are you going to conceive a child by a man in love with his liquor?

MARGARET: By locking his liquor up and making him satisfy my desire before I unlock it!

BRICK: Is that what you've done, Maggie?

MARGARET: Look and see. That cabinet's mighty empty compared to before!

BRICK: Well, I'll be a son of a —

(He reaches for his crutch but she beats him to it and rushes out on the gallery, hurls the crutch over the rail and comes back in, panting.)

MARGARET: And so tonight we're going to make the lie true, and when that's done, I'll bring the liquor back here and we'll get drunk together, here, tonight, in this place that death has come into . . . — What do you say?

BRICK: I don't say anything. I guess there's nothing to say.

MARGARET: Oh, you weak people, you weak, beautiful people! — who give up with such grace. What you want is someone to —

(She turns out the rose-silk lamp.)

— take hold of you. — Gently, gently with love hand your life back to you, like somethin' gold you let go of. I *do* love you, Brick, I *do*!

BRICK *(smiling with charming sadness)*: Wouldn't it be funny if that was true?

THE END

HAROLD PINTER

(1930–   )

*P*inter was born and raised in a working-class district in the East End of London. After leaving grammar school, he attended the Royal Academy of Dramatic Art and the Central School of Speech and Drama.

His first three plays were written and produced when he was 27. The Room *and* The Dumb Waiter *are short plays;* The Birthday Party, *a full-length play, was the only one to be produced in London, where it was a commercial failure. Three years later, in 1960, Pinter's second full-length play,* The Caretaker, *won critical and financial success on the London stage, and his career was launched. From 1959 to 1963 he also wrote scripts for radio and television; some of these, such as* A Slight Ache *(1961),* The Collection *(1962), and* The Lover *(1963), were later successfully adapted for the stage. Beginning in the mid-sixties he has written screenplays adapted from novels;* The Servant *(1963),* The Quiller Memorandum *(1966), and* The French Lieutenant's Woman *(1981) are the best known. He has also produced plays successfully, notably Robert Shaw's* The Man in the Glass Booth *(1967) and Simon Gray's* Butley *(1971).*

Pinter's work, from the beginning, did not follow conventional plot patterns and character development. Audiences were, and to some extent still are, baffled because his characters do not in any way provide biographies or explain their motives. Although Pinter is not unique in his mystification and non-verification, certainly he has had a significant influence on the contemporary theatre. He also uses the pause effectively; some actors claim that much happens in the pauses. Perhaps audiences experience similar responses. Because of these methods of presentation, dialogue is highlighted; and Pinter's dialogue is sharp, arresting, and effective.

In much of his work, Pinter creates a space and then depicts some outside force or forces that invade or threaten that space. Menace and violence emerge in a powerful way from these confrontations and the nature of power is displayed and examined.

Pinter is a dominant figure in the contemporary theatre because of the themes he has dealt with and his exploration of dramatic techniques. His themes are not only topical, they also touch upon the universal; his dramatic techniques aim at and frequently capture a modern idiom.

INTRODUCTION TO *THE HOMECOMING*

*T*he Homecoming, directed by Peter Hall, was produced by the Royal Shakespeare Company at the Aldwych Theatre on June 3, 1965. After a successful run, the production moved to the Music Box Theater in New York on January 5, 1967.

In his early plays, Pinter established the themes and moods that characterize his later works. In *The Room*, the room is surrounded by a hostile, vaguely defined world that threatens to overwhelm it. A similar menace exists in *The Dumb Waiter*, where the hired assassins await their orders in a basement room. In *The Caretaker* the outside world encroaches upon another basement room, where the characters struggle to establish territorial rights. In *The Homecoming*, we are still essentially in a single room. Now, however, we know more about the rest of the house and the outside world into which Sam and Lenny venture and in which they operate; and we hear more of the world from which Teddy and Ruth come. Nevertheless, we are still in a claustrophobic place and we know that Max, like Rose in *The Room*, will not leave this centre of his existence.

The violence that plays a significant part in Pinter's world also appears in the early works. *The Room* ends with a sudden, gratuitous act of violence, and *The Dumb Waiter* has a similar, although less unexpected, ending. In *The Caretaker*, the threat of violence is omnipresent in the coiled-spring character of Mick. Violence smoulders and erupts throughout *The Homecoming*. Max's references to his late wife alternate between sentimental reminiscences and vicious accusations. Lenny's accounts of his brutal, unmotivated actions are introduced abruptly, with powerful impact. While in many aspects the violence in the plays resembles that of the American gangster film, Pinter obviously intends us to recognize and face the violence that in fact surrounds us. As an element in this recognition, *The Homecoming* presents us with some effective contrasts to violence, first through Sam and then through Ruth, whose constant calm is the background for the tension of Lenny and the verbose violence of Max. (It is interesting to note that Pinter himself, when called up for national military service, was tried and fined as a conscientious objector.)

Pinter's plays have always puzzled some members of his audiences, for whom linear plots are the essence of drama. Despite their lack of conventional plot structures, his plays are rendered intensely dramatic by their violence and almost constant tension, and by powerful scenes such as the one between Ruth and Lenny concerning the glass of water. Moreover, while we watch his characters and, above all, listen to them, we accumulate information gradually through hints, suggestions — occasionally even statements of fact. But often in Pinter this "information" is not substantiated, and the audience may initially be frustrated by the accrued ambiguities. Eventually, however, this aspect of his work can have a compelling attraction.

Although Pinter's titles are simple to the point of taciturnity, they often capture a great deal of the play's significance. Thus we can ask: What is a homecoming? What is this particular homecoming? Who is really coming home? What is the home they are coming to? What has it been?

CAST OF CHARACTERS

MAX, *a man of seventy*
LENNY, *a man in his early thirties*
SAM, *a man of sixty-three*
JOEY, *a man in his middle twenties*
TEDDY, *a man in his middle thirties*
RUTH, *a woman in her early thirties*

SUMMER

An old house in North London.
A large room, extending the width of the stage.
The back wall, which contained the door, has been removed. A square arch shape remains. Beyond it, the hall. In the hall a staircase, ascending U.L., *well in view. The front door* U.R. *A coatstand, hooks, etc.*
In the room a window, R. *Odd tables, chairs. Two large armchairs. A large sofa,* L. *Against* R. *wall a large sideboard, the upper half of which contains a mirror.* U.L., *a radiogram.*

ACT ONE

(Evening.
LENNY is sitting on the sofa with a newspaper, a pencil in his hand. He wears a dark suit. He makes occasional marks on the back page.
MAX comes in, from the direction of the kitchen. He goes to sideboard, opens top drawer, rummages in it, closes it.
He wears an old cardigan and a cap, and carries a stick.
He walks downstage, stands, looks about the room.)

MAX: What have you done with the scissors?

(Pause.)

I said I'm looking for the scissors. What have you done with them?

(Pause.)

Did you hear me? I want to cut something out of the paper.
LENNY: I'm reading the paper.
MAX: Not that paper. I haven't even read that paper. I'm talking about last Sunday's paper. I was just having a look at it in the kitchen.

(Pause.)

Do you hear what I'm saying? I'm talking to you! Where's the scissors?
LENNY: *(looking up, quietly)* Why don't you shut up, you daft prat?[1]

---

1 *crazy fool; a British slang expression.*

(MAX lifts his stick and points it at him.)

MAX: Don't you talk to me like that. I'm warning you.

(He sits in large armchair.)

There's an advertisement in the paper about flannel vests.[2] Cut price. Navy surplus. I could do with a few of them.

(Pause.)

I think I'll have a fag. Give me a fag.

(Pause.)

I just asked you to give me a cigarette.

(Pause.)

Look what I'm lumbered with.

(He takes a crumpled cigarette from his pocket.)

I'm getting old, my word of honour.

(He lights it.)

You think I wasn't a tearaway? I could have taken care of you, twice over. I'm still strong. You ask your Uncle Sam what I was. But at the same time I always had a kind heart. Always.

(Pause.)

I used to knock about with a man called MacGregor. I called him Mac. You remember Mac? Eh?

(Pause.)

Huhh! We were two of the worst hated men in the West End of London. I tell you, I still got the scars. We'd walk into a place, the whole room'd stand up, they'd make way to let us pass. You never heard such silence. Mind you, he was a big man, he was over six foot tall. His family were all MacGregors, they came all the way from Aberdeen, but he was the only one they called Mac.

(Pause.)

He was very fond of your mother, Mac was. Very fond. He always had a good word for her.

2 *undershirts.*

(Pause.)

Mind you, she wasn't such a bad woman. Even though it made me sick just to look at her rotten stinking face, she wasn't such a bad bitch. I gave her the best bleeding years of my life, anyway.

LENNY: Plug it, will you, you stupid sod,[3] I'm trying to read the paper.

MAX: Listen! I'll chop your spine off, you talk to me like that! You understand? Talking to your lousy filthy father like that!

LENNY: You know what, you're getting demented.

(Pause.)

What do you think of Second Wind for the three-thirty?

MAX: Where?

LENNY: Sandown Park.

MAX: Don't stand a chance.

LENNY: Sure he does.

MAX: Not a chance.

LENNY: He's the winner.

(LENNY ticks the paper.)

MAX: He talks to me about horses.

(Pause.)

I used to live on the course. One of the loves of my life. Epsom?[4] I knew it like the back of my hand. I was one of the best-known faces down at the paddock. What a marvellous open-air life.

(Pause.)

He talks to me about horses. You only read their names in the papers. But I've stroked their manes, I've held them, I've calmed them down before a big race. I was the one they used to call for. Max, they'd say, there's a horse here, he's highly strung, you're the only man on the course who can calm him. It was true. I had a . . . I had an instinctive understanding of animals. I should have been a trainer. Many times I was offered the job — you know, a proper post, by the Duke of . . . I forget his name . . . one of the Dukes. But I had family obligations, my family needed me at home.

(Pause.)

---

3 *an abbreviation for sodomite, which is seldom meant to be insulting.*
4 *Epsom Downs is a famous English racecourse.*

The times I've watched those animals thundering past the post. What an experience. Mind you, I didn't lose, I made a few bob[5] out of it, and you know why? Because I always had the smell of a good horse. I could smell him. And not only the colts but the fillies. Because the fillies are more highly strung than the colts, they're more unreliable, did you know that? No, what do you know? Nothing. But I was always able to tell a good filly by one particular trick. I'd look her in the eye. You see? I'd stand in front of her and look her straight in the eye, it was a kind of hypnotism, and by the look deep down in her eye I could tell whether she was a stayer or not. It was a gift. I had a gift.

(Pause.)

And he talks to me about horses.
LENNY: Dad, do you mind if I change the subject?

(Pause.)

I want to ask you something. The dinner we had before, what was the name of it. What do you call it?

(Pause.)

Why don't you buy a dog? You're a dog cook. Honest. You think you're cooking for a lot of dogs.
MAX: If you don't like it get out.
LENNY: I am going out. I'm going out to buy myself a proper dinner.
MAX: Well, get out! What are you waiting for?

(LENNY looks at him.

LENNY: What did you say?
MAX: I said shove off out of it, that's what I said.
LENNY: You'll go before me, Dad, if you talk to me in that tone of voice.
MAX: Will I, you bitch?

(MAX grips his stick.)

LENNY: Oh, Daddy, you're not going to use your stick on me, are you? Eh? Don't use your stick on me, Daddy. No, please. It wasn't my fault, it was one of the others. I haven't done anything wrong, Dad, honest. Don't clout me with that stick, Dad.

(Silence.
MAX *sits hunched.* LENNY *reads the paper.*
SAM *comes in the front door. He wears a chauffeur's uniform. He hangs his hat on a hook in the hall and comes into the room. He goes to a chair, sits in it and sighs.)*

---

5 *slang for the name of the former English shilling — one-twentieth of a pound.*

Hullo, Uncle Sam.

SAM: Hullo.

LENNY: How are you, Uncle?

SAM: Not bad. A bit tired.

LENNY: Tired? I bet you're tired. Where you been?

SAM: I've been to London Airport.

LENNY: All the way up to London Airport? What, right up the M4?

SAM: Yes, all the way up there.

LENNY: Tch, tch, tch. Well, I think you're entitled to be tired, Uncle.

SAM: Well, it's the drivers.

LENNY: I know. That's what I'm talking about. I'm talking about the drivers.

SAM: Knocks you out.

(Pause.)

MAX: I'm here, too, you know.

(SAM looks at him.)

I said I'm here, too. I'm sitting here.

SAM: I know you're here.

(Pause.)

SAM: I took a Yankee out there today . . . to the Airport.

LENNY: Oh, a Yankee, was it?

SAM: Yes, I been with him all day. Picked him up at the Savoy at half past twelve, took him to the Caprice for his lunch. After lunch I picked him up again, took him down to a house in Eaton Square — he had to pay a visit to a friend there — and then round about tea-time I took him right the way out to the Airport.

LENNY: Had to catch a plane there, did he?

SAM: Yes. Look what he gave me. He gave me a box of cigars.

(SAM takes a box of cigars from his pocket.)

MAX: Come here. Let's have a look at them.

(SAM shows MAX the cigars. MAX takes one from the box, pinches it and sniffs it.)

It's a fair cigar.

SAM: Want to try one?

(MAX and SAM light cigars.)

You know what he said to me? He told me I was the best chauffeur he'd ever had. The best one.

MAX: From what point of view?

SAM: Eh?

MAX: From what point of view?

LENNY: From the point of view of his driving, Dad, and his general sense of courtesy, I should say.

MAX: Thought you were a good driver, did he, Sam? Well, he gave you a first-class cigar.

SAM: Yes, he thought I was the best he'd ever had. They all say that, you know. They won't have anyone else, they only ask for me. They say I'm the best chauffeur in the firm.

LENNY: I bet the other drivers tend to get jealous, don't they, Uncle?

SAM: They do get jealous. They get very jealous.

MAX: Why?

(Pause.)

SAM: I just told you.

MAX: No, I just can't get it clear, Sam. Why do the other drivers get jealous?

SAM: Because (a) I'm the best driver, and because . . . (b) I don't take liberties.

(Pause.)

I don't press myself on people, you see. These big businessmen, men of affairs, they don't want the driver jawing all the time, they like to sit in the back, have a bit of peace and quiet. After all, they're sitting in a Humber Super Snipe, they can afford to relax. At the same time, though, this is what really makes me special . . . I do know how to pass the time of day when required.

(Pause.)

For instance, I told this man today I was in the second world war. Not the first. I told him I was too young for the first. But I told him I fought in the second.

(Pause.)

So did he, it turned out.

(LENNY stands, goes to the mirror and straightens his tie.)

LENNY: He was probably a colonel, or something, in the American Air Force.

SAM: Yes.

LENNY: Probably a navigator, or something like that, in a Flying Fortress. Now he's most likely a high executive in a worldwide group of aeronautical engineers.

SAM: Yes.

LENNY: Yes, I know the kind of man you're talking about.

(LENNY *goes out, turning to his right.*)

SAM: After all, I'm experienced. I was driving a dust cart at the age of nineteen. Then I was in long-distance haulage. I had ten years as a taxi-
driver and I've had five as a private chauffeur.
MAX: It's funny you never got married, isn't it. A man with all your gifts.

(*Pause.*)

Isn't it? A man like you?
SAM: There's still time.
MAX: Is there?

(*Pause.*)

SAM: You'd be surprised.
MAX: What you been doing, banging away at your lady customers, have
you?
SAM: Not me.
MAX: In the back of the Snipe? Been having a few crafty reefs in a layby,
have you?
SAM: Not me.
MAX: On the back seat? What about the armrest, was it up or down?
SAM: I've never done that kind of thing in my car.
MAX: Above all that kind of thing, are you, Sam?
SAM: Too true.
MAX: Above having a good bang on the back seat, are you?
SAM: Yes, I leave that to others.
MAX: You leave it to others? What others? You paralysed prat!
SAM: I don't mess up my car! Or my . . . my boss's car! Like other people.
MAX: Other people? What other people?

(*Pause.*)

What other people?

(*Pause.*)

SAM: Other people.

(*Pause.*)

MAX: When you find the right girl, Sam, let your family know, don't forget,
we'll give you a number one send-off, I promise you. You can bring her
to live here, she can keep us all happy. We'd take it in turns to give her a
walk round the park.

SAM: I wouldn't bring her here.

MAX: Sam, it's your decision. You're welcome to bring your bride here, to the place where you live, or on the other hand you can take a suite at the Dorchester. It's entirely up to you.

SAM: I haven't got a bride.

(SAM stands, goes to the sideboard, takes an apple from the bowl, bites into it.)

Getting a bit peckish.

(He looks out of the window.)

Never get a bride like you had, anyway. Nothing like your bride . . . going about these days. Like Jessie.

(Pause.)

After all, I escorted her once or twice, didn't I? Drove her round once or twice in my cab. She was a charming woman.

(Pause.)

All the same, she was your wife. But still . . . they were some of the most delightful evenings I've ever had. Used to just drive her about. It was my pleasure.

MAX: *(softly, closing his eyes)* Christ.

SAM: I used to pull up at a stall and buy her a cup of coffee. She was a very nice companion to be with.

(Silence.
JOEY comes in the front door. He walks into the room, takes his jacket off, throws it on a chair and stands.
Silence.)

JOEY: Feel a bit hungry.

SAM: Me, too.

MAX: Who do you think I am, your mother? Eh? Honest. They walk in here every time of the day and night like bloody animals. Go and find yourself a mother.

(LENNY walks into the room, stands.)

JOEY: I've been training down at the gym.

SAM: Yes, the boy's been working all day and training all night.

MAX: What do you want, you bitch? You spend all the day sitting on your arse at London Airport, buy yourself a jamroll. You expect me to sit here waiting to rush into the kitchen the moment you step in the door? You've been living sixty-three years, why don't you learn to cook?

SAM: I can cook.
MAX: Well, go and cook!

(Pause.)

LENNY: What the boys want, Dad, is your own special brand of cooking, Dad. That's what the boys look forward to. The special understanding of food, you know, that you've got.
MAX: Stop calling me Dad. Just stop all that calling me Dad, do you understand?
LENNY: But I'm your son. You used to tuck me up in bed every night. He tucked you up too, didn't he, Joey?

(Pause.)

He used to like tucking up his sons.

(LENNY turns and goes toward the front door.)

MAX: Lenny.
LENNY: *(turning)* What?
MAX: I'll give you a proper tuck up one of these nights, son. You mark my word.

(They look at each other.
LENNY opens the front door and goes out.
Silence.)

JOEY: I've been training with Bobby Dodd.

(Pause.)

And I had a good go at the bag as well.

(Pause.)

I wasn't in bad trim.
MAX: Boxing's a gentleman's game.

(Pause.)

I'll tell you what you've got to do. What you've got to do is you've got to learn how to defend yourself, and you've got to learn how to attack. That's your only trouble as a boxer. You don't know how to defend yourself, and you don't know how to attack.

(Pause.)

Once you've mastered those arts you can go straight to the top.

(Pause.)

JOEY: I've got a pretty good idea . . . of how to do that.

(JOEY looks round for his jacket, picks it up, goes out of the room and up the stairs. Pause.)

MAX: Sam . . . why don't you go, too, eh? Why don't you just go upstairs? Leave me quiet. Leave me alone.

SAM: I want to make something clear about Jessie, Max. I want to. I do. When I took her out in the cab, round the town, I was taking care of her, for you. I was looking after her for you, when you were busy, wasn't I? I was showing her the West End.

(Pause.)

You wouldn't have trusted any of your other brothers. You wouldn't have trusted Mac, would you? But you trusted me. I want to remind you.

(Pause.)

Old Mac died a few years ago, didn't he? Isn't he dead?

(Pause.)

He was a lousy stinking rotten loudmouth. A bastard uncouth sodding runt. Mind you, he was a good friend of yours.

(Pause.)

MAX: Eh, Sam . . .
SAM: What?
MAX: Why do I keep you here? You're just an old grub.
SAM: Am I?
MAX: You're a maggot.
SAM: Oh yes?
MAX: As soon as you stop paying your way here, I mean when you're too old to pay your way, you know what I'm going to do? I'm going to give you the boot.
SAM: You are, eh?
MAX: Sure. I mean, bring in the money and I'll put up with you. But when the firm gets rid of you — you can flake off.
SAM: This is my house as well, you know. This was our mother's house.

MAX: One lot after the other. One mess after the other.

SAM: Our father's house.

MAX: Look what I'm lumbered with. One cast-iron bunch of crap after another. One flow of stinking pus after another.

(Pause.)

Our father? I remember him. Don't worry. You kid yourself. He used to come over to me and look down at me. My old man did. He'd bend right over me, then he'd pick me up. I was only that big. Then he'd dandle me. Give me the bottle. Wipe me clean. Give me a smile. Pat me on the bum. Pass me around, pass me from hand to hand. Toss me up in the air. Catch me coming down. I remember my father.

(BLACKOUT.

LIGHTS UP.

Night.

TEDDY *and* RUTH *stand at the threshold of the room.*

They are both well dressed in light summer suits and light raincoats.

Two suitcases are by their side.

They look at the room. TEDDY *tosses the key in his hand, smiles.)*

TEDDY: Well, the key worked.

(Pause.)

They haven't changed the lock.

(Pause.)

RUTH: No one's here.

TEDDY: *(looking up)* They're asleep.

(Pause.)

RUTH: Can I sit down?

TEDDY: Of course.

RUTH: I'm tired.

(Pause.)

TEDDY: Then sit down.

(She does not move.)

That's my father's chair.

RUTH: That one?

TEDDY: (smiling) Yes, that's it. Shall I go up and see if my room's still there?

RUTH: It can't have moved.

TEDDY: No, I mean if my bed's still there.

RUTH: Someone might be in it.

TEDDY: No. They've got their own beds.

(Pause.)

RUTH: Shouldn't you wake someone up? Tell them you're here?

TEDDY: Not at this time of night. It's too late.

(Pause.)

Shall I go up?

(He goes into the hall, looks up the stairs, comes back.)

Why don't you sit down?

(Pause.)

I'll just go up . . . have a look.

(He goes up the stairs, stealthily.
RUTH stands, then slowly walks across the room.
TEDDY returns.)

It's still there. My room. Empty. The bed's there. What are you doing?

(She looks at him.)

Blankets, no sheets. I'll find some sheets. I could hear snores. Really. They're all still here, I think. They're all snoring up there. Are you cold?

RUTH: No.

TEDDY: I'll make something to drink, if you like. Something hot.

RUTH: No, I don't want anything.

(TEDDY walks about.)

TEDDY: What do you think of the room? Big, isn't it? It's a big house. I mean, it's a fine room, don't you think? Actually there was a wall, across there . . . with a door. We knocked it down . . . years ago . . . to make an open living area. The structure wasn't affected, you see. My mother was dead.

(RUTH sits.)

Tired?

RUTH: Just a little.

TEDDY: We can go to bed if you like. No point in waking anyone up now. Just go to bed. See them all in the morning . . . see my father in the morning . . .

(Pause.)

RUTH: Do you want to stay?

TEDDY: Stay?

(Pause.)

We've come to stay. We're bound to stay . . . for a few days.

RUTH: I think . . . the children . . . might be missing us.

TEDDY: Don't be silly.

RUTH: They might.

TEDDY: Look, we'll be back in a few days, won't we?

(He walks about the room.)

Nothing's changed. Still the same.

(Pause.)

Still, he'll get a surprise in the morning, won't he? The old man. I think you'll like him very much. Honestly. He's a . . . well, he's old, of course. Getting on.

(Pause.)

I was born here, do you realize that?

RUTH: I know.

(Pause.)

TEDDY: Why don't you go up to bed? I'll find some sheets. I feel . . . wide awake, isn't it odd? I think I'll stay up for a bit. Are you tired?

RUTH: No.

TEDDY: Go to bed. I'll show you the room.

RUTH: No, I don't want to.

TEDDY: You'll be perfectly all right up there without me. Really you will. I mean, I won't be long. Look, it's just up there. It's the first door on the landing. The bathroom's right next door. You . . . need some rest, you know.

(Pause.)

I just want to . . . walk about for a few minutes. Do you mind?
RUTH: Of course I don't.
TEDDY: Well . . . Shall I show you the room?
RUTH: No, I'm happy at the moment.
TEDDY: You don't have to go to bed. I'm not saying you have to. I mean, you
    can stay up with me. Perhaps I'll make a cup of tea or something. The
    only thing is we don't want to make too much noise, we don't want to
    wake anyone up.
RUTH: I'm not making any noise.
TEDDY: I know you're not.

(He goes to her.)

(Gently.) Look, it's all right, really. I'm here. I mean . . . I'm with you.
    There's no need to be nervous. Are you nervous?
RUTH: No.
TEDDY: There's no need to be.

(Pause.)

They're very warm people, really. Very warm. They're my family.
They're not ogres.

(Pause.)

Well, perhaps we should go to bed. After all, we have to be up early, see
Dad. Wouldn't be quite right if he found us in bed, I think. *(He chuckles.)*
Have to be up before six, come down, say hullo.

(Pause.)

RUTH: I think I'll have a breath of air.
TEDDY: Air?

(Pause.)

What do you mean?
RUTH: *(standing)* Just a stroll.
TEDDY: At this time of night? But we've . . . only just got here. We've got to
    go to bed.
RUTH: I just feel like some air.
TEDDY: But I'm going to bed.
RUTH: That's all right.
TEDDY: But what am I going to do?

(Pause.)

The last thing I want is a breath of air. Why do you want a breath of
air?
RUTH: I just do.
TEDDY: But it's late.
RUTH: I won't go far. I'll come back.

(Pause.)

TEDDY: I'll wait up for you.
RUTH: Why?
TEDDY: I'm not going to bed without you.
RUTH: Can I have the key?

(He gives it to her.)

Why don't you go to bed?

*(He puts his arms on her shoulders and kisses her. They look at each other, briefly. She
smiles.)*

I won't be long.

*(She goes out of the front door.
TEDDY goes to the window, peers out after her, half turns from the window, stands,
suddenly chews his knuckles.
LENNY walks into the room from U.L. He stands. He wears pyjamas and dressing-
gown. He watches TEDDY.
TEDDY turns and sees him.
Silence.)*

TEDDY: Hullo, Lenny.
LENNY: Hullo, Teddy.

(Pause.)

TEDDY: I didn't hear you come down the stairs.
LENNY: I didn't.

(Pause.)

I sleep down here now. Next door. I've got a kind of study, workroom
cum bedroom next door now, you see.
TEDDY: Oh. Did I . . . wake you up?
LENNY: No. I just had an early night tonight. You know how it is. Can't
sleep. Keep waking up.

(Pause.)

TEDDY: How are you?
LENNY: Well, just sleeping a bit restlessly, that's all. Tonight, anyway.
TEDDY: Bad dreams?
LENNY: No, I wouldn't say I was dreaming. It's not exactly a dream. It's just that something keeps waking me up. Some kind of tick.
TEDDY: A tick?
LENNY: Yes.
TEDDY: Well, what is it?
LENNY: I don't know.

(Pause.)

TEDDY: Have you got a clock in your room?
LENNY: Yes.
TEDDY: Well, maybe it's the clock.
LENNY: Yes, could be, I suppose.

(Pause.)

Well, if it's the clock I'd better do something about it. Stifle it in some way, or something.

(Pause.)

TEDDY: I've . . . just come back for a few days.
LENNY: Oh yes? Have you?

(Pause.)

TEDDY: How's the old man?
LENNY: He's in the pink.

(Pause.)

TEDDY: I've been keeping well.
LENNY: Oh, have you?

(Pause.)

Staying the night then, are you?
TEDDY: Yes.
LENNY: Well, you can sleep in your old room.
TEDDY: Yes, I've been up.
LENNY: Yes, you can sleep there.

(LENNY yawns.)

Oh well.

TEDDY: I'm going to bed.

LENNY: Are you?

TEDDY: Yes, I'll get some sleep.

LENNY: Yes, I'm going to bed, too.

(TEDDY *picks up the cases.*)

I'll give you a hand.

TEDDY: No, they're not heavy.

(TEDDY *goes into the hall with the cases.*
LENNY *turns out the light in the room.*
The light in the hall remains on.
LENNY *follows into the hall.*)

LENNY: Nothing you want?

TEDDY: Mmmm?

LENNY: Nothing you might want, for the night? Glass of water, anything like that?

TEDDY: Any sheets anywhere?

LENNY: In the sideboard in your room.

TEDDY: Oh, good.

LENNY: Friends of mine occasionally stay there, you know, in your room, when they're passing through this part of the world.

(LENNY *turns out the hall light and turns on the first landing light.*
TEDDY *begins to walk up the stairs.*)

TEDDY: Well, I'll see you at breakfast, then.

LENNY: Yes, that's it. Ta-ta.

(TEDDY *goes upstairs.*
LENNY *goes off* L.
Silence.
The landing light goes out.
Slight night light in the hall and room.
LENNY *comes back into the room, goes to the window and looks out.*
He leaves the window and turns on a lamp.
He is holding a small clock.
He sits, places the clock in front of him, lights a cigarette and sits.
RUTH *comes in the front door.*
She stands still. LENNY *turns his head, smiles. She walks slowly into the room.*)

LENNY: Good evening.

RUTH: Morning, I think.

LENNY: You're right there.

(Pause.)

My name's Lenny. What's yours?
RUTH: Ruth.

(She sits, puts her coat collar around her.)

LENNY: Cold?
RUTH: No.
LENNY: It's been a wonderful summer, hasn't it? Remarkable.

(Pause.)

Would you like something? Refreshment of some kind? An aperitif,
anything like that?
RUTH: No, thanks.
LENNY: I'm glad you said that. We haven't got a drink in the house. Mind
you, I'd soon get some in, if we had a party or something like that.
Some kind of celebration . . . you know.

(Pause.)

You must be connected with my brother in some way. The one who's
been abroad.
RUTH: I'm his wife.
LENNY: Eh listen, I wonder if you can advise me. I've been having a bit of a
rough time with this clock. The tick's been keeping me up. The trouble
is I'm not all that convinced it was the clock. I mean there are lots of
things which tick in the night, don't you find that? All sorts of objects,
which, in the day, you wouldn't call anything else but commonplace.
They give you no trouble. But in the night any given one of a number
of them is liable to start letting out a bit of a tick. Whereas you look at
these objects in the day and they're just commonplace. They're as quiet
as mice during the daytime. So . . . all things being equal . . . this question of me saying it was the clock that woke me up, well, that could
very easily prove something of a false hypothesis.

(He goes to the sideboard, pours from a jug into a glass, takes the glass to RUTH.)

Here you are. I bet you could do with this.
RUTH: What is it?
LENNY: Water.

*(She takes it, sips, places the glass on a small table by her chair.
LENNY watches her.)*

Isn't it funny? I've got my pyjamas on and you're fully dressed.

(He goes to the sideboard and pours another glass of water.)

Mind if I have one? Yes, it's funny seeing my older brother again after all these years. It's just the sort of tonic my Dad needs, you know. He'll be chuffed⁶ to his bollocks in the morning, when he sees his eldest son. I was surprised myself when I saw Teddy, you know. Old Ted. I thought he was in America.

RUTH: We're on a visit to Europe.

LENNY: What, both of you?

RUTH: Yes.

LENNY: What, you sort of live with him over there, do you?

RUTH: We're married.

LENNY: On a visit to Europe, eh? Seen much of it?

RUTH: We've just come from Italy.

LENNY: Oh, you went to Italy first, did you? And then he brought you over here to meet the family, did he? Well, the old man'll be pleased to see you, I can tell you.

RUTH: Good.

LENNY: What did you say?

RUTH: Good.

(Pause.)

LENNY: Where'd you go to in Italy?

RUTH: Venice.

LENNY: Not dear old Venice? Eh? That's funny. You know, I've always had a feeling that if I'd been a soldier in the last war — say in the Italian campaign — I'd probably have found myself in Venice. I've always had that feeling. The trouble was I was too young to serve, you see. I was only a child, I was too small, otherwise I've got a pretty shrewd idea I'd probably have gone through Venice. Yes, I'd almost certainly have gone through it with my battalion. Do you mind if I hold your hand?

RUTH: Why?

LENNY: Just a touch.

(He stands and goes to her.)

Just a tickle.

RUTH: Why?

(He looks down at her.)

LENNY: I'll tell you why

(Slight pause.)

6 pleased.

One night, not too long ago, one night down by the docks, I was stand-ing alone under an arch, watching all the men jibbing the boom, out in the harbour, and playing about with the yardarm, when a certain lady came up to me and made me a certain proposal. This lady had been searching for me for days. She'd lost track of my whereabouts. How-ever, the fact was she eventually caught up with me, and when she caught up with me she made me this certain proposal. Well, this pro-posal wasn't entirely out of order and normally I would have subscribed to it. I mean I would have subscribed to it in the normal course of events. The only trouble was she was falling apart with the pox. So I turned it down. Well, this lady was very insistent and started taking lib-erties with me down under this arch, liberties which by any criterion I couldn't be expected to tolerate, the facts being what they were, so I clumped her one. It was on my mind at the time to do away with her, you know, to kill her, and the fact is, that as killings go, it would have been a simple matter, nothing to it. Her chauffeur, who had located me for her, he'd popped round the corner to have a drink, which just left this lady and myself, you see, alone, standing underneath this arch, watching all the steamers steaming up, no one about, all quiet on the Western Front, and there she was up against this wall — well, just slid-ing down the wall, following the blow I'd given her. Well, to sum up, everything was in my favour, for a killing. Don't worry about the chauffeur. The chauffeur would never have spoken. He was an old friend of the family. But . . . in the end I thought . . . Aaah, why go to all the bother . . . you know, getting rid of the corpse and all that, get-ting yourself into a state of tension. So I just gave her another belt in the nose and a couple of turns of the boot and sort of left it at that.

RUTH: How did you know she was diseased?

LENNY: How did I know?

(Pause.)

I decided she was.

(Silence.)

You and my brother are newly-weds, are you?

RUTH: We've been married six years.

LENNY: He's always been my favourite brother, old Teddy. Do you know that? And my goodness we are proud of him here, I can tell you. Doc-tor of Philosophy and all that . . . leaves quite an impression. Of course, he's a very sensitive man, isn't he? Ted. Very. I've often wished I was as sensitive as he is.

RUTH: Have you?

LENNY: Oh yes. Oh yes, very much so. I mean, I'm not saying I'm not sensi-tive. I am. I could just be a bit more so, that's all.

RUTH: Could you?

LENNY: Yes, just a bit more so, that's all.

(Pause.)

I mean, I am very sensitive to atmosphere, but I tend to get desensitized, if you know what I mean, when people make unreasonable demands on me. For instance, last Christmas I decided to do a bit of snow-clearing for the Borough Council, because we had a heavy snow over here that year in Europe. I didn't have to do this snow-clearing — I mean I wasn't financially embarrassed in any way — it just appealed to me, it appealed to something inside me. What I anticipated with a good deal of pleasure was the brisk cold bite in the air in the early morning. And I was right. I had to get my snowboots on and I had to stand on a corner, at about five-thirty in the morning, to wait for the lorry to pick me up, to take me to the allotted area. Bloody freezing. Well, the lorry came, I jumped on the tailboard, headlights on, dipped, and off we went. Got there, shovels up, fags on, and off we went, deep into the December snow, hours before cockcrow. Well, that morning, while I was having my mid-morning cup of tea in a neighbouring cafe, the shovel standing by my chair, an old lady approached me and asked me if I would give her a hand with her iron mangle.[7] Her brother-in-law, she said, had left it for her, but he'd left it in the wrong room, he'd left it in the front room. Well, naturally, she wanted it in the back room. It was a present he'd given her, you see, a mangle, to iron out the washing. But he'd left it in the wrong room, he'd left it in the front room, well that was a silly place to leave it, it couldn't stay there. So I took time off to give her a hand. She only lived up the road. Well, the only trouble was when I got there I couldn't move this mangle. It must have weighed about half a ton. How this brother-in-law got it up there in the first place I can't even begin to envisage. So there I was, doing a bit of shoulders on with the mangle, risking a rupture, and this old lady just standing there, waving me on, not even lifting a little finger to give me a helping hand. So after a few minutes I said to her, now look here, why don't you stuff this iron mangle up your arse? Anyway, I said, they're out of date, you want to get a spin drier. I had a good mind to give her a workover there and then, but as I was feeling jubilant with the snow-clearing I just gave her a short-arm jab to the belly and jumped on a bus outside. Excuse me, shall I take this ashtray out of your way?

RUTH: It's not in my way.

LENNY: It seems to be in the way of your glass. The glass was about to fall. Or the ashtray. I'm rather worried about the carpet. It's not me, it's my father. He's obsessed with order and clarity. He doesn't like mess. So, as I don't believe you're smoking at the moment, I'm sure you won't object if I move the ashtray.

(He does so.)

And now perhaps I'll relieve you of your glass.

RUTH: I haven't quite finished.

---

7 *"a machine for ironing laundry by passing it between heated rollers"* (Webster's).

LENNY: You've consumed quite enough, in my opinion.
RUTH: No, I haven't.
LENNY: Quite sufficient, in my own opinion.
RUTH: Not in mine, Leonard.

(Pause.)

LENNY: Don't call me that, please.
RUTH: Why not?
LENNY: That's the name my mother gave me.

(Pause.)

Just give me the glass.
RUTH: No.

(Pause.)

LENNY: I'll take it, then.
RUTH: If you take the glass . . . I'll take you.

(Pause.)

LENNY: How about me taking the glass without you taking me?
RUTH: Why don't I just take you?

(Pause.)

LENNY: You're joking.

(Pause.)

You're in love, anyway, with another man. You've had a secret liaison with another man. His family didn't even know. Then you come here without a word of warning and start to make trouble.

(She picks up the glass and lifts it towards him.)

RUTH: Have a sip. Go on. Have a sip from my glass.

(He is still.)

Sit on my lap. Take a long cool sip.

*(She pats her lap. Pause.
She stands, moves to him with the glass.)*

Put your head back and open your mouth.

LENNY: Take that glass away from me.

RUTH: Lie on the floor. Go on. I'll pour it down your throat.

LENNY: What are you doing, making me some kind of proposal?

(She laughs shortly, drains the glass.)

RUTH: Oh, I was thirsty.

(She smiles at him, puts the glass down, goes into the hall and up the stairs. He follows into the hall and shouts up the stairs.)

LENNY: What was that supposed to be? Some kind of proposal?

(Silence.
He comes back into the room, goes to his own glass, drains it.
A door slams upstairs.
The landing light goes on.
MAX comes down the stairs, in pyjamas and cap. He comes into the room.)

MAX: What's going on here? You drunk?

(He stares at LENNY.)

What are you shouting about? You gone mad?

(LENNY pours another glass of water.)

Prancing about in the middle of the night shouting your head off. What are you, a raving lunatic?

LENNY: I was thinking aloud.

MAX: Is Joey down here? You been shouting at Joey?

LENNY: Didn't you hear what I said, Dad? I said I was thinking aloud.

MAX: You were thinking so loud you got me out of bed.

LENNY: Look, why don't you just . . . pop off, eh?

MAX: Pop off? He wakes me up in the middle of the night, I think we got burglars here, I think he's got a knife stuck in him, I come down here, he tells me to pop off.

(LENNY sits down.)

He was talking to someone. Who could he have been talking to? They're all asleep. He was having a conversation with someone. He won't tell me who it was. He pretends he was thinking aloud. What are you doing, hiding someone here?

LENNY: I was sleepwalking. Get out of it, leave me alone, will you?

MAX: I want an explanation, you understand? I asked you who you got hiding here.

(Pause.)

LENNY: I'll tell you what, Dad, since you're in the mood for a bit of a . . . chat, I'll ask you a question. It's question I've been meaning to ask you for some time. That night . . . you know . . . the night you got me . . . that night with Mum, what was it like? Eh? When I was just a glint in your eye. What was it like? What was the background to it? I mean, I want to know the real facts about my background. I mean, for instance, is it a fact that you had me in mind all the time, or is it a fact that I was the last thing you had in mind?

(Pause.)

I'm only asking this in a spirit of inquiry, you understand that, don't you? I'm curious. And there's lots of people of my age share that curiosity, you know that, Dad? They often ruminate, sometimes singly, sometimes in groups, about the true facts of that particular night — the night they were made in the image of those two people *at it*. It's a question long overdue, from my point of view, but as we happen to be passing the time of day here tonight I thought I'd pop it to you.

(Pause.)

MAX: You'll drown in your own blood.
LENNY: If you prefer to answer the question in writing I've got no objection.

(MAX stands.)

I should have asked my dear mother. Why didn't I ask my dear mother? Now it's too late. She's passed over to the other side.

(MAX spits at him.
LENNY *looks down at the carpet.)*

Now look what you've done. I'll have to Hoover that in the morning, you know.

(MAX turns and walks up the stairs.
LENNY *sits still.*
BLACKOUT.
LIGHTS UP.)*

(Morning.
JOEY *in front of the mirror. He is doing some slow limbering-up exercises. He stops, combs his hair, carefully. He then shadowboxes, heavily, watching himself in the mirror.*
MAX *comes in from* U.L.
Both MAX *and* JOEY *are dressed.* MAX *watches* JOEY *in silence.* JOEY *stops shadowboxing, picks up a newspaper and sits.*
Silence.)

MAX: I hate this room.

(Pause.)

It's the kitchen I like. It's nice in there. It's cosy.

(Pause.)

But I can't stay in there. You know why? Because he's always washing up in there, scraping the plates, driving me out of the kitchen, that's why.
JOEY: Why don't you bring your tea in here?
MAX: I don't want to bring my tea in here. I hate it here. I want to drink my tea in there.

(He goes into the hall and looks towards the kitchen.)

What's he doing in there?

(He returns.)

What's the time?
JOEY: Half past six.
MAX: Half past six.

(Pause.)

I'm going to see a game of football this afternoon. You want to come?

(Pause.)

I'm talking to you.
JOEY: I'm training this afternoon. I'm doing six rounds with Blackie.
MAX: That's not till five o'clock. You've got time to see a game of football before five o'clock. It's the first game of the season.
JOEY: No, I'm not going.
MAX: Why not?

(Pause.
MAX *goes into the hall.)*

Sam! Come here!

*(*MAX *comes back into the room.*
SAM *enters with a cloth.)*

SAM: What?
MAX: What are you doing in there?
SAM: Washing up.
MAX: What else?
SAM: Getting rid of your leavings.
MAX: Putting them in the bin, eh?
SAM: Right in.
MAX: What point you trying to prove?
SAM: No point.
MAX: Oh yes, you are. You resent making my breakfast, that's what it is, isn't it? That's why you bang round the kitchen like that, scraping the frying-pan, scraping all the leavings into the bin, scraping all the plates, scraping all the tea out of the teapot . . . that's why you do that, every single stinking morning. I know. Listen, Sam. I want to say something to you. From my heart.

(He moves closer.)

I want you to get rid of these feelings of resentment you've got towards me. I wish I could understand them. Honestly, have I ever given you cause? Never. When Dad died he said to me, Max, look after your brothers. That's exactly what he said to me.
SAM: How could he say that when he was dead?
MAX: What?
SAM: How could he speak if he was dead?

(Pause.)

MAX: Before he died, Sam. Just before. They were his last words. His last sacred words, Sammy. A split second after he said those words . . . he was a dead man. You think I'm joking? You think when my father spoke — on his death-bed — I wouldn't obey his words to the last letter? You hear that, Joey? He'll stop at nothing. He's even prepared to spit on the memory of our Dad. What kind of a son were you, you wet wick? You spent half your time doing crossword puzzles! We took you into the butcher's shop, you couldn't ever sweep the dust off the floor. We took MacGregor into the shop, he could run the place by the end of a week. Well, I'll tell you one thing. I respected my father not only as a man but as a number one butcher! And to prove it I followed him into the shop.

I learned to carve a carcass at his knee. I commemorated his name in blood. I gave birth to three grown men! All on my own bat. What have you done?

(Pause.)

What have you done? You tit!

SAM: Do you want to finish the washing up? Look, here's the cloth.

MAX: So try to get rid of these feelings of resentment, Sam. After all, we are brothers.

SAM: Do you want the cloth? Here you are. Take it.

(TEDDY and RUTH come down the stairs. They walk across the hall and stop just inside the room.
The others turn and look at them. JOEY stands.
TEDDY and RUTH are wearing dressing-gowns.
Silence.
TEDDY smiles.)

TEDDY: Hullo . . . Dad . . . We overslept.

(Pause.)

What's for breakfast?

(Silence.
TEDDY chuckles.)

Huh. We overslept.

(MAX turns to SAM.)

MAX: Did you know he was here?

SAM: No.

(MAX turns to JOEY.)

MAX: Did you know he was here?

(Pause.)

I asked you if you knew he was here.

JOEY: No.

MAX: Then who knew?

(Pause.)

Who knew?

(Pause.)

I didn't know.

TEDDY: I was going to come down, Dad, I was going to . . . be here, when you came down.

(Pause.)

How are you?

(Pause.)

Uh . . . look, I'd . . . like you to meet . . .

MAX: How long you been in this house?

TEDDY: All night.

MAX: All night? I'm a laughing-stock. How did you get in?

TEDDY: I had my key.

(MAX whistles and laughs.)

MAX: Who's this?

TEDDY: I was just going to introduce you.

MAX: Who asked you to bring tarts[8] in here?

TEDDY: Tarts?

MAX: Who asked you to bring dirty tarts into this house?

TEDDY: Listen, don't be silly —

MAX: You been here all night?

TEDDY: Yes, we arrived from Venice —

MAX: We've had a smelly scrubber[9] in my house all night. We've had a stinking pox-ridden slut in my house all night.

TEDDY: Stop it! What are you talking about?

MAX: I haven't seen the bitch for six years, he comes home without a word, he brings a filthy scrubber off the street, he shacks up in my house!

TEDDY: She's my wife! We're married!

(Pause.)

MAX: I've never had a whore under this roof before. Ever since your mother died. My word of honour. *(To* JOEY.*)* Have you ever had a whore here? Has Lenny ever had a whore here? They come back from America, they bring the slopbucket with them. They bring the bedpan with them. *(To* TEDDY.*)* Take that disease away from me. Get her away from me.

---

8 *loose or immoral women.*

9 *an immoral woman.*

TEDDY: She's my wife.
MAX: *(to* JOEY*)* Chuck them out.

(Pause.)

A Doctor of Philosophy. Sam, you want to meet a Doctor of Philosophy? *(To* JOEY*)* I said chuck them out.

(Pause.)

What's the matter? You deaf?
JOEY: You're an old man. *(To* TEDDY.*)* He's an old man.

*(*LENNY *walks into the room, in a dressing-gown.*
He stops.
They all look round.
MAX *turns back, hits* JOEY *in the stomach with all his might.*
JOEY *contorts, staggers across the stage.* MAX, *with the exertion of the blow, begins to collapse. His knees buckle. He clutches his stick.*
SAM *moves forward to help him.*
MAX *hits him across the head with his stick.* SAM *sits, head in hands.*
JOEY, *hands pressed to his stomach, sinks down at the feet of* RUTH.
She looks down at him.
LENNY *and* TEDDY *are still.*
JOEY *slowly stands. He is close to* RUTH. *He turns from* RUTH, *looks round at* MAX.
SAM *clutches his head.*
MAX *breathes heavily, very slowly gets to his feet.*
JOEY *moves to him.*
They look at each other.
Silence.
MAX *moves past* JOEY, *walks towards* RUTH. *He gestures with his stick.)*

MAX: Miss.

*(*RUTH *walks towards him.)*

RUTH: Yes?

(He looks at her.)

MAX: You a mother?
RUTH: Yes.
MAX: How many you got?
RUTH: Three.

(He turns to TEDDY.*)*

MAX: All yours, Ted?

(Pause.)

Teddy, why don't we have a nice cuddle and kiss, eh? Like the old days? What about a nice cuddle and kiss, eh?

TEDDY: Come on, then.

(Pause.)

MAX: You want to kiss your old father? Want a cuddle with your old father?

TEDDY: Come on, then.

(TEDDY moves a step towards him.)

Come on.

(Pause.)

MAX: You still love your old Dad, eh?

(They face each other.)

TEDDY: Come on, Dad. I'm ready for the cuddle.

(MAX begins to chuckle, gurgling.
He turns to the family and addresses them.)

MAX: He still loves his father!

CURTAIN

ACT TWO

(Afternoon.
MAX, TEDDY, LENNY and SAM are about the stage, lighting cigars.
JOEY comes in from U.L. with a coffee tray, followed by RUTH. He puts the tray down.
RUTH hands coffee to all the men. She sits with her cup. MAX smiles at her.)

RUTH: That was a very good lunch.

MAX: I'm glad you liked it. *(To the others.)* Did you hear that? *(To RUTH.)* Well, I put my heart and soul into it, I can tell you. *(He sips.)* And this is a lovely cup of coffee.

RUTH: I'm glad.

(Pause.)

MAX: I've got the feeling you're a first-rate cook.
RUTH: I'm not bad.
MAX: No, I've got the feeling you're a number one cook. Am I right, Teddy?
TEDDY: Yes, she's a very good cook.

(Pause.)

MAX: Well, it's a long time since the whole family was together, eh? If only your mother was alive. Eh, what do you say, Sam? What would Jessie say if she was alive? Sitting here with her three sons. Three fine grown-up lads. And a lovely daughter-in-law. The only shame is her grandchildren aren't here. She'd have petted them and cooed over them, wouldn't she, Sam? She'd have fussed over them and played with them, told them stories, tickled them — I tell you she'd have been hysterical. (To RUTH.) Mind you, she taught those boys everything they know. She taught them all the morality they know. I'm telling you. Every single bit of the moral code they live by — was taught to them by their mother. And she had a heart to go with it. What a heart. Eh, Sam? Listen, what's the use of beating round the bush? That woman was the back-bone to this family. I mean, I was busy working twenty-four hours a day in the shop, I was going all over the country to find meat, I was making my way in the world, but I left a woman at home with a will of iron, a heart of gold and a mind. Right, Sam?

(Pause.)

What a mind.

(Pause.)

Mind you, I was a generous man to her. I never left her short of a few bob. I remember one year I entered into negotiations with a top-class group of butchers with continental connections. I was going into associ-ation with them. I remember the night I came home, I kept quiet. First of all I gave Lenny a bath, then Teddy a bath, then Joey a bath. What fun we used to have in the bath, eh, boys? Then I came downstairs and I made Jessie put her feet up on a pouffe — what happened to that pouffe, I haven't seen it for years — she put her feet up on the pouffe and I said to her, Jessie, I think our ship is going to come home, I'm going to treat you to a couple of items, I'm going to buy you a dress in pale corded blue silk, heavily encrusted with pearls, and for casual wear, a pair of pantaloons in lilac flowered taffeta. Then I gave her a drop of cherry brandy. I remember the boys came down, in their pyjamas, all their hair shining, their faces pink, it was before they started shaving, and they knelt down at our feet, Jessie's and mine. I tell you, it was like Christmas.

(Pause.)

RUTH: What happened to the group of butchers?
MAX: The group? They turned out to be a bunch of criminals like everyone else.

(Pause.)

This is a lousy cigar.

(He stubs it out.
He turns to SAM.*)*

What time you going to work?
SAM: Soon.
MAX: You've got a job on this afternoon, haven't you?
SAM: Yes, I know.
MAX: What do you mean, you know? You'll be late. You'll lose your job.
   What are you trying to do, humiliate me?
SAM: Don't worry about me.
MAX: It makes the bile come up in my mouth. The bile — you understand?
   (To RUTH.*)* I worked as a butcher all my life, using the chopper and the
   slab, the slab, you know what I mean, the chopper and the slab! To keep
   my family in luxury. Two families! My mother was bedridden, my
   brothers were all invalids. I had to earn the money for the leading psy-
   chiatrists. I had to read books! I had to study the disease, so that I could
   cope with an emergency at every stage. A crippled family, three bastard
   sons, a slutbitch of a wife — don't talk to me about the pain of child-
   birth — I suffered the pain, I've still got the pangs — when I give a little
   cough my back collapses — and here I've got a lazy idle bugger of a
   brother won't even get to work on time. The best chauffeur in the
   world. All his life he's sat in the front seat giving lovely hand signals.
   You call that work? This man doesn't know his gearbox from his arse!
SAM: You go and ask my customers! I'm the only one they ever ask for.
MAX: What do the other drivers do, sleep all day?
SAM: I can only drive one car. They can't all have me at the same time.
MAX: Anyone could have you at the same time. You'd bend over for half a
   dollar on Blackfriars Bridge.
SAM: Me!
MAX: For two bob and a toffee apple.
SAM: He's insulting me. He's insulting his brother. I'm driving a man to
   Hampton Court at four forty-five.
MAX: Do you want to know who could drive? MacGregor! MacGregor was
   a driver.

SAM: Don't you believe it.

(MAX *points his stick at* SAM.)

MAX: He didn't even fight in the war. This man didn't even fight in the
    bloody war!
SAM: I did!
MAX: Who did you kill?

(*Silence.*
SAM *gets up, goes to* RUTH, *shakes her hand and goes out of the front door.*
MAX *turns to* TEDDY.)

    Well, how you been keeping, son?
TEDDY: I've been keeping very well, Dad.
MAX: It's nice to have you with us, son.
TEDDY: It's nice to be back, Dad.

(*Pause.*)

MAX: You should have told me you were married, Teddy. I'd have sent you a
    present. Where was the wedding, in America?
TEDDY: No. Here. The day before we left.
MAX: Did you have a big function?
TEDDY: No, there was no one there.
MAX: You're mad. I'd have given you a white wedding. We'd have had the
    cream of the cream here. I'd have been only too glad to bear the
    expense, my word of honour.

(*Pause.*)

TEDDY: You were busy at the time. I didn't want to bother you.
MAX: But you're my own flesh and blood. You're my first born. I'd have
    dropped everything. Sam would have driven you to the reception in the
    Snipe, Lenny would have been your best man, and then we'd have all
    seen you off on the boat. I mean, you don't think I disapprove of mar-
    riage, do you? Don't be daft. (*To* RUTH.) I've been begging my two
    youngsters for years to find a nice feminine girl with proper credentials
    — it makes life worth living. (*To* TEDDY.) Anyway, what's the difference,
    you did it, you made a wonderful choice, you've got a wonderful family,
    a marvellous career . . . so why don't we let bygones be bygones?

(*Pause.*)

    You know what I'm saying? I want you both to know that you have my
    blessing.
TEDDY: Thank you.

MAX: Don't mention it. How many other houses in the district have got a
Doctor of Philosophy sitting down drinking a cup of coffee?

(Pause.)

RUTH: I'm sure Teddy's very happy . . . to know that you're pleased with
me.

(Pause.)

I think he wondered whether you would be pleased with me.
MAX: But you're a charming woman.

(Pause.)

RUTH: I was . . .
MAX: What?

(Pause.)

What she say?

(They all look at her.)

RUTH: I was . . . different . . . when I met Teddy . . . first.
TEDDY: No you weren't. You were the same.
RUTH: I wasn't.
MAX: Who cares? Listen, live in the present, what are you worrying about? I
mean, don't forget the earth's about five thousand million years old, at
least. Who can afford to live in the past?

(Pause.)

TEDDY: She's a great help to me over there. She's a wonderful wife and
mother. She's a very popular woman. She's got lots of friends. It's a
great life, at the University . . . you know . . . it's a very good life.
We've got a lovely house . . . we've got all . . . we've got everything we
want. It's a very stimulating environment.

(Pause.)

My department . . . is highly successful.

(Pause.)

We've got three boys, you know.

MAX: All boys? Isn't that funny, eh? You've got three, I've got three. You've got three nephews, Joey. Joey! You're an uncle, do you hear? You could teach them how to box.

(Pause.)

JOEY: *(to RUTH)* I'm a boxer. In the evenings, after work. I'm in demolition in the daytime.
RUTH: Oh?
JOEY: Yes. I hope to be full time, when I get more bouts.
MAX: *(to LENNY)* He speaks so easily to his sister-in-law, do you notice? That's because she's an intelligent and sympathetic woman.

(He leans to her.)

Eh, tell me, do you think the children are missing their mother?

(She looks at him.)

TEDDY: Of course they are. They love her. We'll be seeing them soon.

(Pause.)

LENNY: *(to TEDDY)* Your cigar's gone out.
TEDDY: Oh, yes.
LENNY: Want a light?
TEDDY: No. No.

(Pause.)

So has yours.
LENNY: Oh, yes.

(Pause.)

Eh, Teddy, you haven't told us much about your Doctorship of Philosophy. What do you teach?
TEDDY: Philosophy.
LENNY: Well, I want to ask you something. Do you detect a certain logical incoherence in the central affirmations of Christian theism?
TEDDY: That question doesn't fall within my province.
LENNY: Well, look at it this way . . . you don't mind my asking you some questions, do you?
TEDDY: If they're within my province.
LENNY: Well, look at it this way. How can the unknown merit reverence? In other words, how can you revere that of which you're ignorant? At the same time, it would be ridiculous to propose that what we *know* merits

reverence. What we know merits any one of a number of things, but it stands to reason reverence isn't one of them. In other words, apart from the known and the unknown, what else is there?

(Pause.)

TEDDY: I'm afraid I'm the wrong person to ask.

LENNY: But you're a philosopher. Come on, be frank. What do you make of all this business about being and not-being?

TEDDY: What do you make of it?

LENNY: Well, for instance, take a table. Philosophically speaking. What is it?

TEDDY: A table.

LENNY: Ah. You mean it's nothing else but a table. Well, some people would envy your certainty, wouldn't they, Joey? For instance, I've got a couple of friends of mine, we often sit round the Ritz Bar having a few liqueurs, and they're always saying things like that, you know, things like: Take a table, take it. All right, I say, *take* it, *take* a table, but once you've taken it, what you going to do with it? Once you've got hold of it, where you going to take it?

MAX: You'd probably sell it.

LENNY: You wouldn't get much for it.

JOEY: Chop it up for firewood.

(LENNY looks at him and laughs.)

RUTH: Don't be too sure though. You've forgotten something. Look at me. I . . . move my leg. That's all it is. But I wear . . . underwear . . . which moves with me . . . it . . . captures your attention. Perhaps you misinterpret. The action is simple. It's a leg . . . moving. My lips move. Why don't you restrict . . . your observations to that? Perhaps the fact that they move is more significant . . . than the words which come through them. You must bear that . . . possibility . . . in mind.

(Silence
TEDDY *stands.)*

I was born quite near here.

(Pause.)

Then . . . six years ago, I went to America.

(Pause.)

It's all rock. And sand. It stretches . . . so far . . . everywhere you look. And there's lots of insects there.

(Pause.)

And there's lots of insects there.

(Silence.
She is still.
MAX *stands.)*

MAX: Well, it's time to go to the gym. Time for your workout, Joey.
LENNY: *(standing)* I'll come with you.

*(*JOEY *sits looking at* RUTH.*)*

MAX: Joe.

*(*JOEY *stands. The three go out.*
TEDDY *sits by* RUTH, *holds her hand.*
She smiles at him.
Pause.)

TEDDY: I think we'll go back. Mmnn?

(Pause.)

Shall we go home?
RUTH: Why?
TEDDY: Well, we were only here for a few days, weren't we? We might as
    well . . . cut it short, I think.
RUTH: Why? Don't you like it here?
TEDDY: Of course I do. But I'd like to go back and see the boys now.

(Pause.)

RUTH: Don't you like your family?
TEDDY: Which family?
RUTH: Your family here.
TEDDY: Of course I like them. What are you talking about?

(Pause.)

RUTH: You don't like them as much as you thought you did?
TEDDY: Of course I do. Of course I . . . like them. I don't know what you're
    talking about.

(Pause.)

Listen. You know what time of the day it is there now, do you?
RUTH: What?
TEDDY: It's morning. It's about eleven o'clock.
RUTH: Is it?
TEDDY: Yes, they're about six hours behind us . . . I mean . . . behind the
    time here. The boys'll be at the pool . . . now . . . swimming. Think of
    it. Morning over there. Sun. We'll go anyway, mmnn? It's so clean
    there.
RUTH: Clean.
TEDDY: Yes.

RUTH: Is it dirty here?
TEDDY: No, of course not. But it's cleaner there.

(Pause.)

Look, I just brought you back to meet the family, didn't I? You've met them, we can go. The fall semester will be starting soon.
RUTH: You find it dirty here?
TEDDY: I didn't say I found it dirty here.

(Pause.)

I didn't say that.

(Pause.)

Look. I'll go and pack. You rest for a while. Will you? They won't be back for at least an hour. You can sleep. Rest. Please.

(She looks at him.)

You can help me with my lectures when we get back. I'd love that. I'd be so grateful for it, really. We can bathe till October. You know that. Here, there's nowhere to bathe, except the swimming bath down the road. You know what it's like? It's like a urinal. A filthy urinal!

(Pause.)

You liked Venice, didn't you? It was lovely, wasn't it? You had a good week. I mean . . . I took you there. I can speak Italian.
RUTH: But if I'd been a nurse in the Italian campaign I would have been there before.

(Pause.)

TEDDY: You just rest. I'll go and pack.

> *(TEDDY goes out and up the stairs.*
> *She closes her eyes.*
> *LENNY appears from U.L.*
> *He walks into the room and sits near her.*
> *She opens her eyes.*
> *Silence.)*

LENNY: Well, the evenings are drawing in.
RUTH: Yes, it's getting dark.

(Pause.)

LENNY: Winter'll soon be upon us. Time to renew one's wardrobe.

(Pause.)

RUTH: That's a good thing to do.
LENNY: What?

(Pause.)

RUTH: I always . . .

(Pause.)

Do you like clothes?
LENNY: Oh, yes. Very fond of clothes.

(Pause.)

RUTH: I'm fond . . .

(Pause.)

What do you think of my shoes?
LENNY: They're very nice.
RUTH: No, I can't get the ones I want over there.
LENNY: Can't get them over there, eh?
RUTH: No . . . you don't get them there.

(Pause.)

I was a model before I went away.
LENNY: Hats?

(Pause.)

I bought a girl a hat once. We saw it in a glass case, in a shop. I tell you what it had. It had a bunch of daffodils on it, tied with a black satin bow, and then it was covered with a cloche[1] of black veiling. A cloche. I'm telling you. She was made for it.
RUTH: No . . . I was a model for the body. A photographic model for the body.
LENNY: Indoor work?
RUTH: That was before I had . . . all my children.

---

1 *a woman's close-fitting, bell-shaped hat.*

(Pause.)

No, not always indoors.

(Pause.)

Once or twice we went to a place in the country, by train. Oh, six or seven times. We used to pass a . . . a large white water tower. This place . . . this house . . . was very big . . . the trees . . . there was a lake, you see . . . we used to change and walk down towards the lake . . . we went down a path . . . on stones . . . there were . . . on this path. Oh, just . . . wait . . . yes . . . when we changed in the house we had a drink. There was a cold buffet.

(Pause.)

Sometimes we stayed in the house but . . . most often . . . we walked down to the lake . . . and did our modelling there.

(Pause.)

Just before we went to America I went down there. I walked from the station to the gate and then I walked up the drive. There were lights on . . . I stood in the drive . . . the house was very light.

(TEDDY comes down the stairs with the cases. He puts them down, looks at LENNY.)

TEDDY: What have you been saying to her?

(He goes to RUTH.)

Here's your coat.

(LENNY goes to the radiogram and puts on a record of slow jazz.)

    Ruth. Come on. Put it on.
LENNY: *(to RUTH)* What about one dance before you go?
TEDDY: We're going.
LENNY: Just one.
TEDDY: No. We're going.
LENNY: Just one dance, with her brother-in-law, before she goes.

(LENNY bends to her.)

Madam?

(RUTH stands. They dance, slowly.
TEDDY stands, with RUTH's coat.
MAX and JOEY come in the front door and into the room.
They stand.
LENNY kisses RUTH. They stand, kissing.)

JOEY: Christ, she's wide open.

(Pause.)

She's a tart.

(Pause.)

Old Lenny's got a tart in here.

(JOEY goes to them. He takes RUTH's arm. He smiles at LENNY. He sits with RUTH on the sofa, embraces and kisses her.
He looks up at LENNY.)

Just up my street.

(He leans her back until she lies beneath him. He kisses her.
He looks up at TEDDY and MAX.)

It's better than a rubdown, this.

(LENNY sits on the arm of the sofa. He caresses RUTH's hair as JOEY embraces her.
MAX comes forward, looks at the cases.)

MAX: You going. Teddy? Already?

(Pause.)

Well, when you coming over again, eh? Look, next time you come over, don't forget to let us know beforehand whether you're married or not. I'll always be glad to meet the wife. Honest. I'm telling you.

(JOEY lies heavily on RUTH.
They are almost still.
LENNY caresses her hair.)

Listen, you think I don't know why you didn't tell me you were married? I know why. You were ashamed. You thought I'd be annoyed because you married a woman beneath you. You should have known me better. I'm broadminded. I'm a broadminded man.

(He peers to see RUTH's *face under* JOEY, *turns back to* TEDDY.)

Mind you, she's a lovely girl. A beautiful woman. And a mother too. A mother of three. You've made a happy woman out of her. It's something to be proud of. I mean, we're talking about a woman of quality. We're talking about a woman of feeling.

*(*JOEY *and* RUTH *roll off the sofa on to the floor.*
JOEY *clasps her.* LENNY *moves to stand above them. He looks down on them. He touches* RUTH *gently with his foot.*
RUTH *suddenly pushes* JOEY *away.*
She stands up.
JOEY *gets to his feet, stares at her.)*

RUTH: I'd like something to eat. *(To* LENNY.*)* I'd like a drink. Did you get any drink?
LENNY: We've got drink.
RUTH: I'd like one, please.
LENNY: What drink?
RUTH: Whisky.
LENNY: I've got it.

(Pause.)

RUTH: Well, get it.

*(*LENNY *goes to the sideboard, takes out bottle and glasses.*
JOEY *moves towards her.)*

Put the record off.

(He looks at her, turns, puts the record off.)

I want something to eat.

(Pause.)

JOEY: I can't cook. *(Pointing to* MAX.*)* He's the cook.

*(*LENNY *brings her a glass of whisky.)*

LENNY: Soda on the side?
RUTH: What's this glass? I can't drink out of this. Haven't you got a tumbler?
LENNY: Yes.
RUTH: Well, put it in a tumbler.

(He takes the glass back, pours whisky into a tumbler, brings it to her.)

LENNY: On the rocks? Or as it comes?
RUTH: Rocks? What do you know about rocks?
LENNY: We've got rocks. But they're frozen stiff in the fridge.

*(RUTH drinks.
LENNY looks round at the others.)*

Drinks all round?

*(He goes to the sideboard and pours drinks.
JOEY moves closer to RUTH.)*

JOEY: What food do you want?

(RUTH walks round the room.)

RUTH: *(to TEDDY)* Have your family read your critical works?
MAX: That's one thing I've never done. I've never read one of his critical
    works.
TEDDY: You wouldn't understand them.

(LENNY hands drinks all round.)

JOEY: What sort of food do you want? I'm not the cook, anyway.
LENNY: Soda, Ted? Or as it comes?
TEDDY: You wouldn't understand my works. You wouldn't have the faintest
    idea of what they were about. You wouldn't appreciate the points of ref-
    erence. You're way behind. All of you. There's no point in my sending
    you my works. You'd be lost. It's nothing to do with the question of
    intelligence. It's a way of being able to look at the world. It's a question
    of how far you can operate on things and not in things. I mean it's a
    question of your capacity to ally the two, to relate the two, to balance
    the two. To see, to be able to *see*! I'm the one who can see. That's why I
    can write my critical works. Might do you good . . . have a look at
    them . . . see how certain people can view . . . things . . . how certain
    people can maintain . . . intellectual equilibrium. Intellectual equilib-
    rium. You're just objects. You just . . . move about. I can observe it. I
    can see what you do. It's the same as I do. But you're lost in it. You
    won't get me being . . . I won't be lost in it.

*(BLACKOUT.
LIGHTS UP.
Evening.
TEDDY sitting, in his coat, the cases by him. SAM.
Pause.)*

SAM: Do you remember MacGregor, Teddy?
TEDDY: Mac?
SAM: Yes.
TEDDY: Of course I do.
SAM: What did you think of him? Did you take to him?
TEDDY: Yes. I liked him. Why?

(Pause.)

SAM: You know, you were always my favourite, of the lads. Always.

(Pause.)

When you wrote to me from America I was very touched, you know. I mean you'd written to your father a few times but you'd never written to me. But then, when I got that letter from you . . . well, I was very touched. I never told him. I never told him I'd heard from you.

(Pause.)

(Whispering.) Teddy, shall I tell you something? You were always your mother's favourite. She told me. It's true. You were always the . . . you were always the main object of her love.

(Pause.)

Why don't you stay for a couple more weeks, eh? We could have a few laughs.

(LENNY comes in the front door and into the room.)

LENNY: Still here, Ted? You'll be late for your first seminar.

(He goes to the sideboard, opens it, peers in it, to the right and the left, stands.)

Where's my cheese-roll?

(Pause.)

Someone's taken my cheese-roll. I left it there. *(To SAM.)* You been thieving?
TEDDY: I took your cheese-roll, Lenny.

(Silence.
SAM looks at them, picks up his hat and goes out of the front door.
Silence.)

LENNY: You took my cheese roll?

TEDDY: Yes.

LENNY: I made that roll myself. I cut it and put the butter on. I sliced a piece of cheese and put it in between. I put it on a plate and I put it in the sideboard. I did all that before I went out. Now I come back and you've eaten it.

TEDDY: Well, what are you going to do about it?

LENNY: I'm waiting for you to apologize.

TEDDY: But I took it deliberately, Lenny.

LENNY: You mean you didn't stumble on it by mistake?

TEDDY: No, I saw you put it there. I was hungry, so I ate it.

(Pause.)

LENNY: Barefaced audacity.

(Pause.)

What led you to be so . . . vindictive against your own brother? I'm bowled over.

(Pause.)

Well, Ted, I would say this is something approaching the naked truth, isn't it? It's a real cards on the table stunt. I mean, we're in the land of no holds barred now. Well, how else can you interpret it? To pinch your younger brother's specially made cheese roll when he's out doing a spot of work, that's not equivocal, it's unequivocal.

(Pause.)

Mind you, I will say you do seem to have grown a bit sulky during the last six years. A bit sulky. A bit inner. A bit less forthcoming. It's funny, because I'd have thought that in the United States of America, I mean with the sun and all that, the open spaces, on the old campus, in your position, lecturing, in the centre of all the intellectual life out there, on the old campus, all the social whirl, all the stimulation of it all, all your kids and all that, to have fun with, down by the pool, the Greyhound buses and all that, tons of iced water, all the comfort of those Bermuda shorts and all that, on the old campus, no time of the day or night you can't get a cup of coffee or a Dutch gin, I'd have thought you'd have grown more forthcoming, not less. Because I want you to know that you set a standard for us, Teddy. Your family looks up to you, boy, and you know what it does? It does its best to follow the example you set. Because you're a great source of pride to us. That's why we were so glad to see you come back, to welcome you back to your birthplace. That's why.

(Pause.)

No, listen, Ted, there's no question that we live a less rich life here than you do over there. We live a closer life. We're busy, of course. Joey's busy with his boxing, I'm busy with my occupation, Dad still plays a good game of poker, and he does the cooking as well, well up to his old standard, and Uncle Sam's the best chauffeur in the firm. But nevertheless we do make up a unit, Teddy, and you're an integral part of it. When we all sit round the backyard having a quiet gander at the night sky, there's always an empty chair standing in the circle, which is in fact yours. And so when you at length return to us, we do expect a bit of grace, a bit of je ne sais quoi,[2] a bit of generosity of mind, a bit of liberality of spirit, to reassure us. We do expect that. But do we get it? Have we got it? Is that what you've given us?

(Pause.)

TEDDY: Yes.

(JOEY comes down the stairs and into the room, with a newspaper.)

LENNY: *(to* JOEY*)* How'd you get on?
JOEY: Er . . . not bad.
LENNY: What do you mean?

(Pause.)

What do you mean?
JOEY: Not bad.
LENNY: I want to know what you *mean* — by not bad.
JOEY: What's it got to do with you?
LENNY: Joey, you tell your brother everything.

(Pause.)

JOEY: I didn't get all the way.
LENNY: You didn't get all the way?

(Pause.)

(With emphasis.) You didn't get all the way? But you've had her up there for two hours.
JOEY: Well?
LENNY: You didn't get all the way and you've had her up there for two hours!

---

2 *a French expression translated as "I do not know what." Hence, indescribable or an indefinable something. This is an example of Lenny's sometimes-surprising articulateness.*

JOEY: What about it?

(LENNY *moves closer to him.*)

LENNY: What are you telling me?
JOEY: What do you mean?
LENNY: Are you telling me she's a tease?

(*Pause.*)

She's a tease!

(*Pause.*)

What do you think of that, Ted? Your wife turns out to be a tease. He's had her up there for two hours and he didn't go the whole hog.
JOEY: I didn't say she was a tease.
LENNY: Are you joking? It sounds like a tease to me, don't it to you, Ted?
TEDDY: Perhaps he hasn't got the right touch.
LENNY: Joey? Not the right touch? Don't be ridiculous. He's had more dolly than you've had cream cakes. He's irresistible. He's one of the few and far between. Tell him about the last bird you had, Joey.

(*Pause.*)

JOEY: What bird?
LENNY: The last bird! When we stopped the car . . .
JOEY: Oh, that . . . yes . . . well, we were in Lenny's car one night last week . . .
LENNY: The Alfa.
JOEY: And er . . . bowling down the road . . .
LENNY: Up near the Scrubs.
JOEY: Yes, up over by the Scrubs . . .
LENNY: We were doing a little survey of North Paddington.
JOEY: And er . . . it was pretty late, wasn't it?
LENNY: Yes, it was late. Well?

(*Pause.*)

JOEY: And then we . . . well, by the kerb, we saw this parked car . . . with a couple of girls in it.
LENNY: And their escorts.
JOEY: Yes, there were two geezers in it. Anyway . . . we got out . . . and we told the . . . two escorts . . . to go away . . . which they did . . . and then we . . . got the girls out of the car . . .
LENNY: We didn't take them over the Scrubs.
JOEY: Oh, no. Not over the Scrubs. Well, the police would have noticed us there . . . you see. We took them over a bombed site.

LENNY: Rubble. In the rubble.
JOEY: Yes, plenty of rubble.

(Pause.)

Well . . . you know . . . then we had them.
LENNY: You've missed out the best bit. He's missed out the best bit!
JOEY: What bit?
LENNY: *(to* TEDDY*).* His bird says to him, I don't mind, she says, but I've got to
have some protection. I've got to have some contraceptive protection. I
haven't got any contraceptive protection, old Joey says to her. In that
case I won't do it, she says. Yes you will, says Joey, never mind about
the contraceptive protection.

*(*LENNY *laughs.)*

Even my bird laughed when she heard that. Yes, even she gave out a bit
of a laugh. So you can't say old Joey isn't a bit of a knockout when he
gets going, can you? And here he is upstairs with your wife for two
hours and he hasn't even been the whole hog. Well, your wife sounds
like a bit of a tease to me, Ted. What do you make of it, Joey? You satisfied? Don't tell me you're satisfied without going the whole hog?

(Pause.)

JOEY: I've been the whole hog plenty of times. Sometimes . . . you can be
happy . . . and not go the whole hog. Now and again . . . you can be
happy . . . without going any hog.

*(*LENNY *stares at him.*
MAX *and* SAM *come in the front door and into the room.)*

MAX: Where's the whore? Still in bed? She'll make us all animals.
LENNY: The girl's a tease.
MAX: What?
LENNY: She's had Joey on a string.
MAX: What do you mean?
TEDDY: He had her up there for two hours and he didn't go the whole hog.

(Pause.)

MAX: My Joey? She did that to my boy?

(Pause.)

To my youngest son? Tch, tch, tch, tch. How you feeling, son? Are you
all right?

JOEY: Sure I'm all right.

MAX: *(to* TEDDY*)* Does she do that to you, too?

TEDDY: No.

LENNY: He gets the gravy.

MAX: You think so?

JOEY: No he don't.

(Pause.)

SAM: He's her lawful husband. She's his lawful wife.

JOEY: No he don't! He don't get no gravy! I'm telling you. I'm telling all of you. I'll kill the next man who says he gets the gravy.

MAX: Joey . . . what are you getting so excited about? *(To* LENNY.*)* It's because he's frustrated. You see what happens?

JOEY: Who is?

MAX: Joey. No one's saying you're wrong. In fact everyone's saying you're right.

(Pause.

MAX *turns to the others.)*

You know something? Perhaps it's not a bad idea to have a woman in the house. Perhaps it's a good thing. Who knows? Maybe we should keep her.

(Pause.)

Maybe we'll ask her if she wants to stay.

(Pause.)

TEDDY: I'm afraid not, Dad. She's not well, and we've got to get home to the children.

MAX: Not well? I told you, I'm used to looking after people who are not so well. Don't worry about that. Perhaps we'll keep her here.

(Pause.)

SAM: Don't be silly.

MAX: What's silly?

SAM: You're talking rubbish.

MAX: Me?

SAM: She's got three children.

MAX: She can have more! Here. If she's so keen.

TEDDY: She doesn't want any more.

MAX: What do you know about what she wants, eh, Ted?

TEDDY: *(smiling)* The best thing for her is to come home with me, Dad. Really. We're married, you know.

(MAX walks about the room, clicks his fingers.)

MAX: We'd have to pay her, of course. You realize that? We can't leave her walking about without any pocket money. She'll have to have a little allowance.

JOEY: Of course we'll pay her. She's got to have some money in her pocket.

MAX: That's what I'm saying. You can't expect a woman to walk about without a few bob to spend on a pair of stockings.

(Pause.)

LENNY: Where's the money going to come from?

MAX: Well, how much is she worth? What we talking about, three figures?

LENNY: I asked you where the money's going to come from. It'll be an extra mouth to feed. It'll be an extra body to clothe. You realize that?

JOEY: I'll buy her clothes.

LENNY: What with?

JOEY: I'll put in a certain amount out of my wages.

MAX: That's it. We'll pass the hat round. We'll make a donation. We're all grown-up people, we've got a sense of responsibility. We'll all put a little in the hat. It's democratic.

LENNY: It'll come to a few quid, Dad.

(Pause.)

I mean, she's not a woman who likes walking around in second-hand goods. She's up to the latest fashion. You wouldn't want her walking about in clothes which don't show her off at her best, would you?

MAX: Lenny, do you mind if I make a little comment? It's not meant to be critical. But I think you're concentrating too much on the economic considerations. There are other considerations. There are the human considerations. You understand what I mean? There are the human considerations. Don't forget them.

LENNY: I won't.

MAX: Well don't.

(Pause.)

Listen, we're bound to treat her in something approximating, at least, to the manner in which she's accustomed. After all, she's not someone off the street, she's my daughter-in-law!

JOEY: That's right.

MAX: There you are, you see. Joey'll donate, Sam'll donate. . . .

(SAM looks at him.)

I'll put in a few bob out of my pension. Lenny'll cough up. We're laughing. What about you, Ted? How much you going to put in the kitty?

TEDDY: I'm not putting anything in the kitty.

MAX: What? You won't even help to support your own wife? I thought he was a son of mine. You lousy stinkpig. Your mother would drop dead if she heard you take that attitude.

LENNY: Eh, Dad.

(LENNY *walks forward.*)

I've got a better idea.

MAX: What?

LENNY: There's no need for us to go to all this expense. I know these women. Once they get started they ruin your budget. I've got a better idea. Why don't I take her up with me to Greek Street?

(*Pause.*)

MAX: You mean put her on the game?

(*Pause.*)

We'll put her on the game. That's a stroke of genius, that's a marvellous idea. You mean she can earn the money herself — on her back?

LENNY: Yes.

MAX: Wonderful. The only thing is, it'll have to be short hours. We don't want her out of the house all night.

LENNY: I can limit the hours.

MAX: How many?

LENNY: Four hours a night.

MAX: (*dubiously*). Is that enough?

LENNY: She'll bring in a good sum for four hours a night.

MAX: Well, you should know. After all, it's true, the last thing we want to do is wear the girl out. She's going to have her obligations this end as well. Where you going to put her in Greek Street?

LENNY: It doesn't have to be right in Greek Street, Dad. I've got a number of flats all around that area.

MAX: You have? Well, what about me? Why don't you give me one?

LENNY: You're sexless.

JOEY: Eh, wait a minute, what's all this?

MAX: I know what Lenny's saying. Lenny's saying she can pay her own way. What do you think, Teddy? That'll solve all our problems.

JOEY: Eh, wait a minute. I don't want to share her.

MAX: What did you say?

JOEY: I don't want to share her with a lot of yobs!

MAX: Yobs! You arrogant git! What arrogance. (*To* LENNY.) Will you be supplying her with yobs?

LENNY: I've got a very distinguished clientèle, Joey. They're more distinguished than you'll ever be.

MAX: So you can count yourself lucky we're including you in.

JOEY: I didn't think I was going to have to share her!

MAX: Well, you *are* going to have to share her! Otherwise she goes straight
back to America. You understand?

(Pause.)

It's tricky enough as it is, without you shoving your oar in. But there's
something worrying me. Perhaps she's not so up to the mark. Eh?
Teddy, you're the best judge. Do you think she'd be up to the mark?

(Pause.)

I mean what about all this teasing? Is she going to make a habit of it?
That'll get us nowhere.

(Pause.)

TEDDY: It was just love play . . . I suppose . . . that's all I suppose it was.

MAX: Love play? Two bleeding hours? That's a bloody long time for love
play!

LENNY: I don't think we've got anything to worry about on that score, Dad.

MAX: How do you know?

LENNY: I'm giving you a professional opinion.

(LENNY goes to TEDDY.)

LENNY: Listen, Teddy, you could help us, actually. If I were to send you some
cards, over to America . . . you know, very nice ones, with a name on,
and a telephone number, very discreet, well, you could distribute
them . . . to various parties, who might be making a trip over here. Of
course, you'd get a little percentage out of it.

MAX: I mean, you needn't tell them she's your wife.

LENNY: No, we'd call her something else. Dolores, or something.

MAX: Or Spanish Jacky.

LENNY: No, you've got to be reserved about it, Dad. We could call her something nice . . . like Cynthia . . . or Gillian.

(Pause.)

JOEY: Gillian.

(Pause.)

LENNY: No, what I mean, Teddy, you must know lots of professors, heads of departments, men like that. They pop over here for a week at the Savoy, they need somewhere they can go to have a nice quiet poke. And of course you'd be in a position to give them inside information.

MAX: Sure. You can give them proper data. I bet you before two months we'd have a waiting list.

LENNY: You could be our representative in the States.

MAX: Of course. We're talking in international terms! By the time we've finished Pan-American'll give us a discount.

(*Pause.*)

TEDDY: She'd get old . . . very quickly.

MAX: No . . . not in this day and age! With the health service? Old! How could she get old? She'll have the time of her life.

(RUTH *comes down the stairs, dressed.*
She comes into the room.
She smiles at the gathering, and sits.
Silence.)

TEDDY: Ruth . . . the family have invited you to stay, for a little while longer. As a . . . as a kind of guest. If you like the idea I don't mind. We can manage very easily at home . . . until you come back.

RUTH: How very nice of them.

(*Pause.*)

MAX: It's an offer from our heart.

RUTH: It's very sweet of you.

MAX: Listen . . . it would be our pleasure.

(*Pause.*)

RUTH: I think I'd be too much trouble.

MAX: Trouble? What are you talking about? What trouble? Listen, I'll tell you something. Since poor Jessie died, eh, Sam? we haven't had a woman in the house. Not one. Inside this house. And I'll tell you why. Because their mother's image was so dear any other woman would have . . . tarnished it. But you . . . Ruth . . . you're not only lovely and beautiful, but you're kin. You're kith. You belong here.

(*Pause.*)

RUTH: I'm very touched.

MAX: Of course you're touched. I'm touched.

(Pause.)

TEDDY: But Ruth, I should tell you . . . that you'll have to pull your weight a little, if you stay. Financially. My father isn't very well off.

RUTH: *(to* MAX*)* Oh, I'm sorry.

MAX: No, you'd just have to bring in a little, that's all. A few pennies. Nothing much. It's just that we're waiting for Joey to hit the top as a boxer. When Joey hits the top . . . well . . .

(Pause.)

TEDDY: Or you can come home with me.

LENNY: We'd get you a flat.

(Pause.)

RUTH: A flat?

LENNY: Yes.

RUTH: Where?

LENNY: In town.

(Pause.)

But you'd live here, with us.

MAX: Of course you would. This would be your home. In the bosom of the family.

LENNY: You'd just pop up to the flat a couple of hours a night, that's all.

MAX: Just a couple of hours, that's all. That's all.

LENNY: And you make enough money to keep you going here.

(Pause.)

RUTH: How many rooms would this flat have?

LENNY: Not many.

RUTH: I would want at least three rooms and a bathroom.

LENNY: You wouldn't need three rooms and a bathroom.

MAX: She'd need a bathroom.

LENNY: But not three rooms.

(Pause.)

RUTH: Oh, I would. Really.

LENNY: Two would do.

RUTH: No. Two wouldn't be enough.

(Pause.)

I'd want a dressing-room, a rest-room, and a bedroom.

(Pause.)

LENNY: All right, we'll get you a flat with three rooms and a bathroom.
RUTH: With what kind of conveniences?
LENNY: All conveniences.
RUTH: A personal maid?
LENNY: Of course.

(Pause.)

We'd finance you, to begin with, and then, when you were established, you could pay us back, in instalments.
RUTH: Oh, no, I wouldn't agree to that.
LENNY: Oh, why not?
RUTH: You would have to regard your original outlay simply as a capital investment.

(Pause.)

LENNY: I see. All right.
RUTH: You'd supply my wardrobe, of course?
LENNY: We'd supply everything. Everything you need.
RUTH: I'd need an awful lot. Otherwise I wouldn't be content.
LENNY: You'd have everything.
RUTH: I would naturally want to draw up an inventory of everything I would need, which would require your signatures in the presence of witnesses.
LENNY: Naturally.
RUTH: All aspects of the agreement and conditions of employment would have to be clarified to our mutual satisfaction before we finalized the contract.
LENNY: Of course.

(Pause.)

RUTH: Well, it might prove a workable arrangement.
LENNY: I think so.
MAX: And you'd have the whole of your daytime free, of course. You could do a bit of cooking here if you wanted to.
LENNY: Make the beds.
MAX: Scrub the place out a bit.
TEDDY: Keep everyone company.

(SAM comes forward.)

SAM: *(in one breath)* MacGregor had Jessie in the back of my cab as I drove them along.

(He croaks[3] *and collapses.*
He lies still.
They look at him.)

MAX: What's he done? Dropped dead?
LENNY: Yes.
MAX: A corpse? A corpse on my floor? Get him out of here! Clear him out of here!

(JOEY bends over SAM.)

JOEY: He's not dead.
LENNY: He probably was dead, for about thirty seconds.
MAX: He's not even dead!

(LENNY looks down at SAM.)

LENNY: Yes, there's still some breath there.
MAX: *(pointing at SAM)* You know what that man had?
LENNY: Has.
MAX: Has! A diseased imagination.

(Pause.)

RUTH: Yes, it sounds a very attractive idea.
MAX: Do you want to shake on it now, or do you want to leave it till later?
RUTH: Oh, we'll leave it till later.

(TEDDY stands.
He looks down at SAM.)

TEDDY: I was going to ask him to drive me to London Airport.

(He goes to the cases, picks one up.)

Well, I'll leave your case, Ruth. I'll just go up the road to the Underground.[4]
MAX: Listen, if you go the other way, first left, first right, you remember, you might find a cab passing there.
TEDDY: Yes, I might do that.
MAX: Or you can take the tube to Piccadilly Circus, won't take you ten minutes, and pick up a cab from there out to the Airport.

---

3 slang for "dies" and, in this case, indicates the sound he makes before collapsing.
4 subway or underground rail system.

TEDDY: Yes, I'll probably do that.
MAX: Mind you, they'll charge you double fare. They'll charge you for the return trip. It's over the six-mile limit.
TEDDY: Yes. Well, bye-bye, Dad. Look after yourself.

(*They shake hands.*)

MAX: Thanks, son. Listen. I want to tell you something. It's been wonderful to see you.

(*Pause.*)

TEDDY: It's been wonderful to see you.
MAX: Do your boys know about me? Eh? Would they like to see a photo, do you think, of their grandfather?
TEDDY: I know they would.

(MAX *brings out his wallet.*)

MAX: I've got one on me. I've got one here. Just a minute. Here you are. Will they like that one?
TEDDY: (*taking it*) They'll be thrilled.

(*He turns to* LENNY.)

Good-bye, Lenny.

(*They shake hands.*)

LENNY: Ta-ta, Ted. Good to see you. Have a good trip.
TEDDY: Bye-bye, Joey.

(JOEY *does not move.*)

JOEY: Ta-ta.

(TEDDY *goes to the front door.*)

RUTH: Eddie.

(TEDDY *turns.*
Pause.)

Don't become a stranger.

(TEDDY goes, shuts the front door.
Silence.
The three men stand.
RUTH sits relaxed in her chair.
SAM lies still.
JOEY walks slowly across the room.
He kneels at her chair.
She touches his head, lightly.
He puts his head in her lap.
MAX begins to move above them, backwards and forwards.
LENNY stands still.
MAX turns to LENNY.)

MAX: I'm too old, I suppose. She thinks I'm an old man.

(Pause.)

I'm not such an old man.

(Pause.)

(To RUTH.) You think I'm too old for you?

(Pause.)

Listen. You think you're just going to get that big slag all the time? You think you're just going to have him . . . you're going to just have him all the time? You're going to have to work! You'll have to take them on, you understand?

(Pause.)

Does she realize that?

(Pause.)

Lenny, do you think she understands . . .

(He begins to stammer.)

What . . . what . . . what . . . we're getting at? What . . . we've got in mind? Do you think she's got it clear?

(Pause.)

I don't think she's got it clear.

(Pause.)

You understand what I mean? Listen, I've got a funny idea she'll do the dirty on us, you want to bet? She'll use us, she'll make use of us, I can tell you! I can smell it! You want to bet?

(Pause.)

She won't . . . be adaptable!

(He begins to groan, clutches his stick, falls on to his knees by the side of her chair. His body sags. The groaning stops. His body straightens. He looks at her, still kneeling.)

I'm not an old man.

(Pause.)

Do you hear me?

(He raises his face to her.)

Kiss me.

(She continues to touch JOEY's *head, lightly.*
LENNY *stands, watching.)*

CURTAIN

ATHOL FUGARD

(1932–   )

orn in Middleburg, a small village in the Eastern Cape of South Africa, Harold Athol Lannigan Fugard comes from a white lower-middle-class background. His mother, Elizabeth Magdalena Potgieter, was Afrikaner and his father, Harold David Lannigan Fugard, came from a family of English immigrants. Fugard has remarked that the Afrikaner side of his background prevails in his sense of himself. Many of the details of Hally's life in "MASTER HAROLD" . . . and the boys mirror those of Fugard, who was also called Hally when he was growing up. The family moved to Port Elizabeth when Fugard was three, where his mother ran first the Jubilee Boarding House and then the St. George's Park Tea Room. His father played piano with jazz bands, the first of which was the Orchestral Jazzonians, the group that will play for the New Brighton ballroom dance championship in "MASTER HAROLD." When Fugard was seven or eight, his father hurt his hip and his leg was later amputated above the knee, in which respect he resembles Hally's father.

Fugard attended the University of Cape Town, a liberal, English-language university, where he read existentialist philosophers. He left before completing his degree. Educated in English, he chooses to write in English rather than Afrikaans. He came to national prominence in South Africa with the production of his play The Blood Knot *in 1961, which brought together onstage for the first time a white actor (Fugard himself) and a black actor. Over the years he has been involved in the development of experimental theatre in South Africa. His plays include* Boesman and Lena *(1969),* A Lesson from Aloes *(1981),* "MASTER HAROLD" . . . and the boys *(1983),* The Road to Mecca *(1988), and* My Children! My Africa! *(1989). An early novel,* Tsotsi, *was published in 1980.*

INTRODUCTION TO "*MASTER HAROLD*" . . . AND THE BOYS

*lthough Athol Fugard's works are embedded in the political context of South Africa, they begin with a very private moment or image and explore the dynamics of human relations as shaped and deformed by apartheid. "MASTER HAROLD" . . . and the boys builds on Fugard's memories of his relationship with a black servant, Sam Semela, who, he has written, was "the most significant — the only — friend of my childhood years" (*Notebooks*, 25). As in the play, this Sam made a kite for him, and read his books, yet in a moment of eternal shame he became a friend abused:

> *Can't remember now what precipitated it, but one day there was a rare quarrel between Sam and myself. In a truculent silence we closed*

the café, Sam set off home to New Brighton on foot and I followed
a few minutes later on my bike. I saw him walking ahead of me,
and coming out of a spasm of acute loneliness, as I rode up behind
him I called his name, he turned in mid-stride to look back and, as
I cycled past, I spat in his face. Don't suppose I will ever deal with
the shame that overwhelmed me the second after I had done that.
(Notebooks, 26)

In the St. George's Park Tea Room in Port Elizabeth on an afternoon in 1950, three male characters rework Fugard's autobiographical experience into an exploration of the terrible intimacy of racial politics in a white family.

The play focuses on men and manhood, the male body and the body politic. (Women, offstage, are represented as weak and ineffectual — Hally's mother — or stubborn but beaten — Willie's partner, Hilda.) Hally, the 17-year-old son of an alcoholic father with one leg, sees the world through the daily humiliation of his father's body. His father's drinking, his pain and querulousness, finally his need for help with his bodily functions all represent loss of control, and ultimately, for Hally, loss of manhood. Hally's view of the world is shaped by his relationship with his father and an obsession with bodily functions. He expresses an abstract commitment to social reform in revealing terms: "One day somebody is going to get up and give history a kick up the backside and get it going again." But, blind to his own participation in a system of domination, he actively exercises the power of being the white master — of metaphorically kicking the backsides of the 40-year-old "boys" — when the humiliation of being his father's son drives him to a violent, sometimes vicious despair.

Racism is obsessed with debasing the body. Sam, one of "the boys," knows only too well the punishment in jail of "strokes with a light cane," administered "with your trousers down." But Sam believes in looking up rather than focusing on the debased bottom; he constructs a kite for Hally after one particularly humiliating incident with his father, in order to teach him to look up like a man. Ironically, it is Sam, the butt of Hally's displaced rage, who articulates a liberal and humane vision of personal and social relations. And, too, Sam mediates the violence of the master and the resulting violence of the victim. Willie, his co-worker, plays "boy" to "Master Harold" in the tea room but beats his partner offstage, in a senseless parody of power. Sam works hard to educate both Hally and Willie to another way of being, based on individual dignity and mutual respect. Combining the roles of surrogate father, therapist, and artist, he offers a healing vision of personal and social harmony expressed through the metaphors of the kite and ballroom dancing.

If Fugard the child identifies with Hally, Fugard the writer identifies with Sam, crossing the racial divide. Hally learns by rote, and repeats the judgements of his class and race. In appropriating the ballroom dance competition as a topic for his essay, he quite unself-consciously rehearses typical racial stereotypes: "I'll point out . . . that in strict anthropological terms the culture of a primitive black society includes its dancing and singing. To put my thesis in a nutshell: The war-dance has been replaced by the waltz. But it still amounts to the same thing: the release of primitive emotions through movement." Sam refuses to engage with this analysis, proposing instead a utopian and political vision of ballroom dancing as "being in a dream about a world in which accidents don't happen." He subverts racist and rationalist attitudes toward a "primitive black society" and "primitive emotions" in a sophisticated appropriation of his own: the European waltz is turned back on itself and invoked as a model for global relations. Sam has learned Hally's lessons on civilization well.

Yet it is just this dance lesson that provokes uncomfortable questions. To what extent does the play challenge the institution and ideology of apartheid? The final, powerful image of the play is of two black men waltzing together, yet alone, in the St. George's Park Tea Room. It is a moment in which Willie takes the woman's position. Profoundly affected by the events of the afternoon, he promises to apologize to Hilda for beating her. But Hally has left the tea room in shame. The white man enters and exits at will, but the black men are enclosed in the space of the tea room, defined by the economic and social relations of apartheid.

Set in 1950, the play's context predates the social unrest of the 1970s and 1980s in South Africa and the development of what some have called a civil war between the townships and the security forces. In 1948, the Afrikaner National Party came to power with a platform that included apartheid. Apartheid (pronounced *apart-hate*) was coined as a term for racial separateness, but policies of racial segregation had been implemented throughout South Africa's colonial history. During the 1950s and 1960s, the state enacted increasingly stringent and repressive laws regulating every aspect of the lives of "non-whites": employment, housing, health, education, political, social, and sexual relationships, personal identity. Racial classifications devised by the government now determined the conditions of life an individual might expect and formed the basis for various attempts to divide and control the "non-white" population. People were classified in legal terms as African, Asian, Coloured, or White. "Black" referred to Africans specifically and more broadly to the three "non-white" groups: blacks constitute more than 80 percent of South Africa's population. The net effect of apartheid has been the total, ongoing impoverishment of all aspects of life for the vast majority of South Africans.

"MASTER HAROLD" . . . *and the boys* alludes to some of the consequences of racial segregation. Sam, for instance, has little formal education. He provides the social context that gives Hally's hypothetical short story about the kite its unexpected twist — the "whites only" park bench represents the racial

segregation of public amenities. (Ironically, the references to the music of Sarah Vaughan and Count Basie, black Americans, invoke similar institutions of racial segregation in the United States in the 1950s.) At the end of the play, with no cash to spare, Willie spends his bus fare on the jukebox and will walk the distance home to New Brighton, the black township outside the city of Port Elizabeth. Relative to other townships in the 1930s and 1940s, the population of New Brighton experienced a degree of freedom in that they were not subject to a curfew, to pass regulations, or to registration of employment. (The development of townships defined in terms of the South African racial classifications has been one aspect of a comprehensive state policy that also includes the creation of "homelands" to which many Africans have been moved.)

Apartheid, according to Nadine Gordimer, a noted white South African writer, has "slipped [a] special contact lens into the eyes of whites" that has induced a "distorted vision," distorted ways of seeing and not seeing blacks. Whites opposed to apartheid, she continues, are aware "that with the inner eye we have 'seen too much to be innocent' " (*Essential Gesture*, 265, 266). Fugard's play complements Gordimer's observation, showing with pain the crippling behaviour complicit with that distorted vision. Yet it also stays within the limitations of that vision. Set in 1950, first produced in 1982: are these limitations those of 1950 or the continuing distortions of the ideology of apartheid? One might argue that Sam's vision participates in the liberal belief in the possibility of a multiracial society prevalent in the 1950s. Yet Sam and Willie are circumscribed by the St. George's Park Tea Room, by the structure of apartheid. Offstage, the white man is crippled, reduced to his body; onstage, the force of his abusive power is challenged; but the structure of the room, invisible to its occupants, is taken for granted. From the point of view of the 1990s we need to ask difficult questions. Does the association of Sam and Willie with music, dance, and the emotions replicate racist stereotypes of blacks? Should Sam and Willie, who bear the brunt of apartheid's policies, have to bear the responsibility for educating Hally into humanity? Is Sam's role as surrogate father, as therapist who receives the child-client's blows and then blames himself for losing his sense of balance and manliness, not just a variant of the role of the subordinate as wise, intimate servant who knows his place? And finally, does the play represent a nostalgic desire to return to childhood's past, like Hally's desire to return to Sam's room in the Jubilee Boarding House where "life felt the right size"?

WORKS CITED

Fugard, Athol. *Notebooks 1960/1977*. Ed. Mary Benson. London: Faber, 1983.
Gordimer, Nadine. "Living in the Interregnum." *The Essential Gesture: Writing, Politics & Places*. Ed. Stephen Clingman. London: Penguin, 1989. 261–84.

"MASTER HAROLD" . . . and the boys

CAST OF CHARACTERS

HALLY

SAM

WILLIE

The St. George's Park Tea Room on a wet and windy Port Elizabeth afternoon.

Tables and chairs have been cleared and are stacked on one side except for one which stands apart with a single chair. On this table a knife, fork, spoon and side plate in anticipation of a simple meal, together with a pile of comic books.

Other elements: a serving counter with a few stale cakes under glass and a not very impressive display of sweets, cigarettes and cool drinks, etc.; a few cardboard advertising handouts — Cadbury's Chocolate, Coca-Cola — and a blackboard on which an untrained hand has chalked up the prices of Tea, Coffee, Scones, Milkshakes — all flavors — and Cool Drinks; a few sad ferns in pots; a telephone; an old-style jukebox.

There is an entrance on one side and an exit into a kitchen on the other.

Leaning on the solitary table, his head cupped in one hand as he pages through one of the comic books, is SAM. *A black man in his mid-forties. He wears the white coat of a waiter. Behind him on his knees, mopping down the floor with a bucket of water and a rag, is* WILLIE. *Also black and about the same age as Sam. He has his sleeves and trousers rolled up.*

The year: 1950

WILLIE: *(Singing as he works)*
    "She was scandalizin' my name,
    She took my money
    She called me honey
    But she was scandalizin' my name.
    Called it love but was playin' a game . . . "

(He gets up and moves the bucket. Stands thinking for a moment, then, raising his arms to hold an imaginary partner, he launches into an intricate ballroom dance step. Although a mildly comic figure, he reveals a reasonable degree of accomplishment)

Hey, Sam.

(SAM, *absorbed in the comic book, does not respond*)

Hey, Boet[1] Sam!

(SAM *looks up*)

I'm getting it. The quickstep. Look now and tell me. (*He repeats the step*) Well?

SAM: (*Encouragingly*) Show me again.

WILLIE: Okay, count for me.

SAM: Ready?

WILLIE: Ready.

SAM: Five, six, seven, eight . . . (WILLIE *starts to dance*) A-n-d one two three four . . . and one two three four . . . (*Ad libbing as* WILLIE *dances*) Your shoulders, Willie . . . your shoulders! Don't look down! Look happy, Willie! Relax, Willie!

WILLIE: (*Desperate but still dancing*) I am relax.

SAM: No, you're not.

WILLIE: (*He falters*) Ag no man, Sam! Mustn't talk. You make me make mistakes.

SAM: But you're too stiff.

WILLIE: Yesterday I'm not straight . . . today I'm too stiff!

SAM: Well, you are. You asked me and I'm telling you.

WILLIE: Where?

SAM: Everywhere. Try to glide through it.

WILLIE: Glide?

SAM: Ja, make it smooth. And give it more style. It must look like you're enjoying yourself.

WILLIE: (*Emphatically*) I wasn't.

SAM: Exactly.

WILLIE: How can I enjoy myself? Not straight, too stiff and now it's also glide, give it more style, make it smooth. . . . Haai! Is hard to remember all those things, Boet Sam.

SAM: That's your trouble. You're trying too hard.

WILLIE: I try hard because it *is* hard.

SAM: But don't let me see it. The secret is to make it look easy. Ballroom must look happy, Willie, not like hard work. It must . . . Ja! . . . it must look like romance.

WILLIE: Now another one! What's romance?

SAM: Love story with happy ending. A handsome man in tails, and in his arms, smiling at him, a beautiful lady in evening dress!

WILLIE: Fred Astaire, Ginger Rogers.[2]

SAM: You got it. Tapdance or ballroom, it's the same. Romance. In two weeks' time when the judges look at you and Hilda, they must see a man and a woman who are dancing their way to a happy ending. What

---

1 boet: *an Afrikaans word meaning brother or comrade.*

2 *Fred Astaire (1899–1987) and Ginger Rogers (1911–   ): famous American dance partners who starred in ten films (musicals), mainly in the 1930s, and who helped to popularize dance as an art form.*

I saw was you holding her like you were frightened she was going to run away.

WILLIE: Ja! Because that is what she wants to do! I got no romance left for Hilda anymore, Boet Sam.

SAM: Then pretend. When you put your arms around Hilda, imagine she is Ginger Rogers.

WILLIE: With no teeth? You try.

SAM: Well, just remember, there's only two weeks left.

WILLIE: I know, I know! (To the jukebox) I do it better with music. You got sixpence for Sarah Vaughan?[3]

SAM: That's a slow foxtrot. You're practicing the quick-step.

WILLIE: I'll practice slow foxtrot.

SAM: (Shaking his head) It's your turn to put money in the jukebox.

WILLIE: I only got bus fare to go home. (He returns disconsolately to his work) Love story and happy ending! She's doing it all right, Boet Sam, but is not me she's giving happy endings. Fuckin' whore! Three nights now she doesn't come practice. I wind up gramophone, I get record ready and I sit and wait. What happens? Nothing. Ten o'clock I start dancing with my pillow. You try and practice romance by yourself, Boet Sam. Struesgod, she doesn't come tonight I take back my dress and ballroom shoes and I find me new partner. Size twenty-six. Shoes size seven. And now she's also making trouble for me with the baby again. Reports me to Child Wellfed, that I'm not giving her money. She lies! Every week I am giving her money for milk. And how do I know is my baby? Only his hair looks like me. She's fucking around all the time I turn my back. Hilda Samuels is a bitch! (Pause) Hey, Sam!

SAM: Ja.

WILLIE: You listening?

SAM: Ja.

WILLIE: So what you say?

SAM: About Hilda?

WILLIE: Ja.

SAM: When did you last give her a hiding?

WILLIE: (Reluctantly) Sunday night.

SAM: And today is Thursday.

WILLIE: (He knows what's coming) Okay.

SAM: Hiding on Sunday night, then Monday, Tuesday and Wednesday she doesn't come to practice . . . and you are asking me why?

WILLIE: I said okay, Boet Sam!

SAM: You hit her too much. One day she's going to leave you for good.

WILLIE: So? She makes me the hell-in too much.

SAM: (Emphasizing his point) Too much and too hard. You had the same trouble with Eunice.

WILLIE: Because she also make the hell-in, Boet Sam. She never got the steps right. Even the waltz.

SAM: Beating her up every time she makes a mistake in the waltz? (Shaking his head) No, Willie! That takes the pleasure out of ballroom dancing.

---

3 Sarah Vaughan (1924–90): a black American singer noted for both jazz and commercial performances. She rose to stardom and international fame in the late 1940s and early 1950s.

WILLIE: Hilda is not too bad with the waltz, Boet Sam. Is the quickstep where the trouble starts.

SAM: *(Teasing him gently)* How's your pillow with the quickstep?

WILLIE: *(Ignoring the tease)* Good! And why? Because it got no legs. That's her trouble. She can't move them quick enough, Boet Sam. I start the record and before halfway Count Basie[4] is already winning. Only time we catch up with him is when gramophone runs down.

(SAM laughs)

Haaikona, Boet Sam, is not funny.

SAM: *(Snapping his fingers)* I got it! Give her a handicap.

WILLIE: What's that?

SAM: Give her a ten-second start and then let Count Basie go. Then I put my money on her. Hot favorite in the Ballroom Stakes: Hilda Samuels ridden by Willie Malopo.

WILLIE: *(Turning away)* I'm not talking to you no more.

SAM: *(Relenting)* Sorry, Willie . . .

WILLIE: It's finish between us.

SAM: Okay, okay . . . I'll stop.

WILLIE: You can also fuck off.

SAM: Willie, listen! I want to help you!

WILLIE: No more jokes?

SAM: I promise.

WILLIE: Okay. Help me.

SAM: *(His turn to hold an imaginary partner)* Look and learn. Feet together. Back straight. Body relaxed. Right hand placed gently in the small of her back and wait for the music. Don't start worrying about making mistakes or the judges or the other competitors. It's just you, Hilda and the music, and you're going to have a good time. What Count Basie do you play?

WILLIE: "You the cream in my coffee, you the salt in my stew."

SAM: Right. Give it to me in strict tempo.

WILLIE: Ready?

SAM: Ready.

WILLIE: A-n-d . . . *(Singing)*
"You the cream in my coffee.
You the salt in my stew.
You will always be my
    necessity.
I'd be lost without
    you. . . ." *(etc.)*

(SAM launches into the quickstep. He is obviously a much more accomplished dancer than WILLIE. HALLY enters. A seventeen-year-old white boy. Wet raincoat and school case. He stops and watches SAM. The demonstration comes to an end with a flourish. Applause from HALLY and WILLIE)

---

4 Count Basie (1904–84): a black American big-band leader and pianist, and a leading figure in the swing era in jazz.

HALLY: Bravo! No question about it. First place goes to Mr. Sam Semela.

WILLIE: *(In total agreement)* You was gliding with style, Boet Sam.

HALLY: *(Cheerfully)* How's it, chaps?

SAM: Okay, Hally.

WILLIE: *(Springing to attention like a soldier and saluting)* At your service, Master Harold!

HALLY: Not long to the big event, hey!

SAM: Two weeks.

HALLY: You nervous?

SAM: No.

HALLY: Think you stand a chance?

SAM: Let's just say I'm ready to go out there and dance.

HALLY: It looked like it. What about you, Willie?

(WILLIE groans)

What's the matter?

SAM: He's got leg trouble.

HALLY: *(Innocently)* Oh, sorry to hear that, Willie.

WILLIE: Boet Sam! You promised. *(WILLIE returns to his work)*

(HALLY deposits his school case and takes off his raincoat. His clothes are a little neglected and untidy: black blazer with school badge, gray flannel trousers in need of an ironing, khaki shirt and tie, black shoes. SAM has fetched a towel for HALLY to dry his hair)

HALLY: God, what a lousy bloody day. It's coming down cats and dogs out there. Bad for business, chaps . . . *(Conspiratorial whisper)* . . . but it also means we're in for a nice quiet afternoon.

SAM: You can speak loud. Your Mom's not here.

HALLY: Out shopping?

SAM: No. The hospital.

HALLY: But it's Thursday. There's no visiting on Thursday afternoons. Is my Dad okay?

SAM: Sounds like it. In fact, I think he's going home.

HALLY: *(Stopped short by SAM's remark)* What do you mean?

SAM: The hospital phoned.

HALLY: To say what?

SAM: I don't know. I just heard your Mom talking.

HALLY: So what makes you say he's going home?

SAM: It sounded as if they were telling her to come and fetch him.

(HALLY thinks about what SAM has said for a few seconds)

HALLY: When did she leave?

SAM: About an hour ago. She said she would phone you. Want to eat?

(HALLY doesn't respond)

Hally, want your lunch?

HALLY: I suppose so. *(His mood has changed)* What's on the menu? . . . as if I don't know.

SAM: Soup, followed by meat pie and gravy.

HALLY: Today's?

SAM: No.

HALLY: And the soup?

SAM: Nourishing pea soup.

HALLY: Just the soup. *(The pile of comic books on the table)* And these?

SAM: For your Dad. Mr. Kempston brought them.

HALLY: You haven't been reading them, have you?

SAM: Just looking.

HALLY: *(Examining the comics)* Jungle Jim . . . Batman and Robin . . . Tarzan . . . God, what rubbish! Mental pollution. Take them away.

(SAM exits waltzing into the kitchen. HALLY turns to WILLIE)

HALLY: Did you hear my Mom talking on the telephone, Willie?

WILLIE: No, Master Hally. I was at the back.

HALLY: And she didn't say anything to you before she left?

WILLIE: She said I must clean the floors.

HALLY: I mean about my Dad.

WILLIE: She didn't say nothing to me about him, Master Hally.

HALLY: *(With conviction)* No! It can't be. They said he needed at least another three weeks of treatment. Sam's definitely made a mistake. *(Rummages through his school case, finds a book and settles down at the table to read)* So, Willie!

WILLIE: Yes, Master Hally! Schooling okay today?

HALLY: Yes, okay. . . . *(He thinks about it)* . . . No, not really. Ag, what's the difference? I don't care. And Sam says you've got problems.

WILLIE: Big problems.

HALLY: Which leg is sore?

(WILLIE groans)

Both legs.

WILLIE: There is nothing wrong with my legs. Sam is just making jokes.

HALLY: So then you *will* be in the competition.

WILLIE: Only if I can find me a partner.

HALLY: But what about Hilda?

SAM: *(Returning with a bowl of soup)* She's the one who's got trouble with her legs.

HALLY: What sort of trouble, Willie?

SAM: From the way he describes it, I think the lady has gone a bit lame.

HALLY: Good God! Have you taken her to see a doctor?

SAM: I think a vet would be better.

HALLY: What do you mean?

SAM: What do you call it again when a racehorse goes very fast?

HALLY: Gallop?

SAM: That's it!

WILLIE: Boet Sam!

HALLY: "A gallop down the homestretch to the winning post." But what's that got to do with Hilda?

SAM: Count Basie always gets there first.

(WILLIE *lets fly with his slop rag. It misses* SAM *and hits* HALLY)

HALLY: *(Furious)* For Christ's sake, Willie! What the hell do you think you're doing!

WILLIE: Sorry, Master Hally, but it's him. . . .

HALLY: Act your bloody age! *(Hurls the rag back at* WILLIE*)* Cut out the non-sense now and get on with your work. And you too, Sam. Stop fooling around.

(SAM *moves away*)

No. Hang on. I haven't finished! Tell me exactly what my Mom said.

SAM: I have. "When Hally comes, tell him I've gone to the hospital and I'll phone him."

HALLY: She didn't say anything about taking my Dad home?

SAM: No. It's just that when she was talking on the phone . . .

HALLY: *(Interrupting him)* No, Sam. They can't be discharging him. She would have said so if they were. In any case, we saw him last night and he wasn't in good shape at all. Staff nurse even said there was talk about taking more X-rays. And now suddenly today he's better? If anything, it sounds more like a bad turn to me . . . which I sincerely hope it isn't. Hang on . . . how long ago did you say she left?

SAM: Just before two . . . *(His wrist watch)* . . . hour and a half.

HALLY: I know how to settle it. *(Behind the counter to the telephone. Talking as he dials)* Let's give her ten minutes to get to the hospital, ten minutes to load him up, another ten, at the most, to get home and another ten to get him inside. Forty minutes. They should have been home for at least half an hour already. *(Pause — he waits with the receiver to his ear)* No reply, chaps. And you know why? Because she's at his bedside in hospital helping him pull through a bad turn. You definitely heard wrong.

SAM: Okay.

(As far as HALLY *is concerned, the matter is settled. He returns to his table, sits down and divides his attention between the book and his soup.* SAM *is at his school case and picks up a textbook*)

Modern Graded Mathematics for Standards Nine and Ten. (Opens it at random and laughs at something he sees) Who is this supposed to be?

HALLY: Old fart-face Prentice.

SAM: Teacher?

HALLY: Thinks he is. And believe me, that is not a bad likeness.

SAM: Has he seen it?

HALLY: Yes.

SAM: What did he say?

HALLY: Tried to be clever, as usual. Said I was no Leonardo da Vinci and that bad art had to be punished. So, six of the best, and his are bloody good.

SAM: On your bum?

HALLY: Where else? The days when I got them on my hands are gone forever, Sam.

SAM: With your trousers down!

HALLY: No. He's not quite that barbaric.

SAM: That's they way they do it in jail.

HALLY: *(Flicker of morbid interest)* Really?

SAM: Ja. When the magistrate sentences you to "strokes with a light cane."

HALLY: Go on.

SAM: They make you lie down on a bench. One policeman pulls down your trousers and holds your ankles, another one pulls your shirt over your head and holds your arms . . .

HALLY: Thank you! That's enough.

SAM: . . . and the one that gives you the strokes talks to you gently and for a long time between each one. *(He laughs)*

HALLY: I've heard enough, Sam! Jesus! It's a bloody awful world when you come to think of it. People can be real bastards.

SAM: That's the way it is, Hally.

HALLY: It doesn't *have* to be that way. There is something called progress, you know. We don't exactly burn people at the stake anymore.

SAM: Like Joan of Arc.

HALLY: Correct. If she was captured today, she'd be given a fair trial.

SAM: And then the death sentence.

HALLY: *(A world-weary sigh)* I know, I know! I oscillate between hope and despair for this world as well, Sam. But things will change, you wait and see. One day somebody is going to get up and give history a kick up the backside and get it going again.

SAM: Like who?

HALLY: *(After thought)* They're called social reformers. Every age, Sam, has got its social reformer. My history book is full of them.

SAM: So where's ours?

HALLY: Good question. And I hate to say it, but the answer is: I don't know. Maybe he hasn't even been born yet. Or is still only a babe in arms at his mother's breast. God, what a thought.

SAM: So we just go on waiting.

HALLY: Ja, looks like it. *(Back to his soup and the book)*

SAM: *(Reading from the textbook)* "Introduction: In some mathematical problems only the magnitude . . . " *(He mispronounces the word "magnitude")*

HALLY: *(Correcting him without looking up)* Magnitude.

SAM: What's it mean?

HALLY: How big it is. The size of the thing.

SAM: *(Reading)* " . . . magnitude of the quantities is of importance. In other problems we need to know whether these quantities are negative or

positive. For example, whether there is a debit or credit bank balance . . . "

HALLY: Whether you're broke or not.

SAM: " . . . whether the temperature is above or below Zero . . . "

HALLY: Naught degrees. Cheerful state of affairs! No cash and you're freezing to death. Mathematics won't get you out of that one.

SAM: "All these quantities are called . . . " *(Spelling the word)* . . . s-c-a-l . . .

HALLY: Scalars.

SAM: Scalars! *(Shaking his head with a laugh)* You understand all that?

HALLY: *(Turning a page)* No. And I don't intend to try.

SAM: So what happens when the exams come?

HALLY: Failing a maths exam isn't the end of the world, Sam. How many
times have I told you that examination results don't measure
intelligence?

SAM: I would say about as many times as you've failed one of them.

HALLY: *(Mirthlessly)* Ha, ha, ha.

SAM: *(Simultaneously)* Ha, ha, ha.

HALLY: Just remember Winston Churchill didn't do particularly well at
school.

SAM: You've also told me that one many times.

HALLY: Well, it just so happens to be the truth.

SAM: *(Enjoying the word)* Magnitude! Magnitude! Show me how to use it.

HALLY: *(After thought)* An intrepid social reformer will not be daunted by the
magnitude of the task he has undertaken.

SAM: *(Impressed)* Couple of jaw-breakers in there!

HALLY: I gave you three for the price of one. Intrepid, daunted and magnitude. I did that once in an exam. Put five of the words I had to explain
in one sentence. It was half a page long.

SAM: Well, I'll put my money on you in the English exam.

HALLY: Piece of cake. Eighty percent without even trying.

SAM: *(Another textbook from* HALLY'S *case)* And history?

HALLY: So-so. I'll scrape through. In the fifties if I'm lucky.

SAM: You didn't do too badly last year.

HALLY: Because we had World War One. That at least had some action. You
try to find that in the South African Parliamentary system.

SAM: *(Reading from the history textbook)* "Napoleon and the principle of equality."
Hey! This sounds interesting. "After concluding peace with Britain in
1802, Napoleon used a brief period of calm to in-sti-tute . . . "

HALLY: Introduce.

SAM: " . . . many reforms. Napoleon regarded all people as equal before the
law and wanted them to have equal opportunities for advancement. All
ves-ti-ges of the feu-dal system with its oppression of the poor were
abolished." Vestiges, feudal system and abolished. I'm all right on
oppression.

HALLY: I'm thinking. He swept away . . . abolished . . . the last remains . . .
vestiges . . . of the bad old days . . . feudal system.

SAM: Ha! There's the social reformer we're waiting for. He sounds like a
man of some magnitude.

HALLY: I'm not so sure about that. It's a damn good title for a book, though. A man of magnitude!

SAM: He sounds pretty big to me, Hally.

HALLY: Don't confuse historical significance with greatness. But maybe I'm being a bit prejudiced. Have a look in there and you'll see he's two chapters long. And hell! . . . has he only got dates, Sam, all of which you've got to remember! This campaign and that campaign, and then, because of all the fighting, the next thing is we get Peace Treaties all over the place. And what's the end of the story? Battle of Waterloo, which he loses. Wasn't worth it. No, I don't know about him as a man of magnitude.

SAM: Then who would you say was?

HALLY: To answer that, we need a definition of greatness, and I suppose that would be somebody who . . . somebody who benefited all mankind.

SAM: Right. But like who?

HALLY: *(He speaks with total conviction)* Charles Darwin. Remember him? That big book from the library. *The Origin of the Species.*

SAM: Him?

HALLY: Yes. For his Theory of Evolution.

SAM: You didn't finish it.

HALLY: I ran out of time. I didn't finish it because my two weeks was up. But I'm going to take it out again after I've digested what I read. It's safe. I've hidden it away in the Theology section. Nobody ever goes in there. And anyway who are you to talk? You hardly even looked at it.

SAM: I tried. I looked at the chapters in the beginning and I saw one called "The Struggle for an Existence." Ah ha, I thought. At last! But what did I get? Something called the mistiltoe which needs the apple tree and there's too many seeds and all are going to die except one . . . ! No, Hally.

HALLY: *(Intellectually outraged)* What do you mean, No! The poor man had to start somewhere. For God's sake, Sam, he revolutionized science. Now we know.

SAM: What?

HALLY: Where we come from and what it all means.

SAM: And that's a benefit to mankind? Anyway, I still don't believe it.

HALLY: God, you're impossible. I showed it to you in black and white.

SAM: Doesn't mean I got to believe it.

HALLY: It's the likes of you that kept the Inquisition in business. It's called bigotry. Anyway, that's my man of magnitude. Charles Darwin! Who's yours?

SAM: *(Without hesitation)* Abraham Lincoln.

HALLY: I might have guessed as much. Don't get sentimental, Sam. You've never been a slave, you know. And anyway we freed your ancestors here in South Africa long before the Americans. But if you want to thank somebody on their behalf, do it to Mr. William Wilberforce.[5] Come on. Try again. I want a real genius. *(Now enjoying himself, and so is* SAM. HALLY *goes behind the counter and helps himself to a chocolate)*

---

5 *William Wilberforce (1759–1833): a prominent English member of Parliament who advocated the end of the slave trade. The British Parliament passed a law abolishing slavery in the British Empire, including the Cape Colony, in 1833. After a transitional period, slaves were legally freed in 1838.*

SAM: William Shakespeare.

HALLY: *(No enthusiasm)* Oh. So you're also one of them, are you? You're basing that opinion on only one play, you know. You've only read my *Julius Caesar* and even I don't understand half of what they're talking about. They should do what they did with the old Bible: bring the language up to date.

SAM: That's all you've got. It's also the only one *you've* read.

HALLY: I know. I admit it. That's why I suggest we reserve our judgment until we've checked up on a few others. I've got a feeling, though, that by the end of this year one is going to be enough for me, and I can give you the names of twenty-nine other chaps in the Standard Nine class of the Port Elizabeth Technical College who feel the same. But if you want him, you can have him. My turn now. *(Pacing)* This is a damned good exercise, you know! It started off looking like a simple question and here it's got us really probing into the intellectual heritage of our civilization.

SAM: So who is it going to be?

HALLY: My next man . . . and he gets the title on two scores: social reform and literary genius . . . is Leo Nikolaevich Tolstoy.

SAM: That Russian.

HALLY: Correct. Remember the picture of him I showed you?

SAM: With the long beard.

HALLY: *(Trying to look like Tolstoy)* And those burning, visionary eyes. My God, the face of a social prophet if ever I saw one! And remember my words when I showed it to you? Here's a *man*, Sam!

SAM: Those were words, Hally.

HALLY: Not many intellectuals are prepared to shovel manure with the peasants and then go home and write a "little book" called *War and Peace.* Incidentally, Sam, he was somebody else who, to quote, " . . . did not distinguish himself scholastically."

SAM: Meaning?

HALLY: He was also no good at school.

SAM: Like you and Winston Churchill.

HALLY: *(Mirthlessly)* Ha, ha, ha.

SAM: *(Simultaneously)* Ha, ha, ha.

HALLY: Don't get clever, Sam. That man freed his serfs of his own free will.

SAM: No argument. He was a somebody, all right. I accept him.

HALLY: I'm sure Count Tolstoy will be very pleased to hear that. Your turn. Shoot. *(Another chocolate from behind the counter)* I'm waiting, Sam.

SAM: I've got him.

HALLY: Good. Submit your candidate for examination.

SAM: Jesus.

HALLY: *(Stopped dead in his tracks)* Who?

SAM: Jesus Christ.

HALLY: Oh, come on, Sam!

SAM: The Messiah.

HALLY: Ja, but still . . . No, Sam. Don't let's get started on religion. We'll just spend the whole afternoon arguing again. Suppose I turn around and say Mohammed?

SAM: All right.

HALLY: You can't have them both on the same list!

SAM: Why not? You like Mohammed, I like Jesus.

HALLY: I *don't* like Mohammed. I never have. I was merely being hypothetical. As far as I'm concerned, the Koran is as bad as the Bible. No. Religion is out! I'm not going to waste my time again arguing with you about the existence of God. You know perfectly well I'm an atheist . . . and I've got homework to do.

SAM: Okay, I take him back.

HALLY: You've got time for one more name.

SAM: *(After thought)* I've got one I know we'll agree on. A simple straightforward great Man of Magnitude . . . and no arguments. And *he* really *did* benefit all mankind.

HALLY: I wonder. After your last contribution I'm beginning to doubt whether anything in the way of an intellectual agreement is possible between the two of us. Who is he?

SAM: Guess.

HALLY: Socrates? Alexandre Dumas? Karl Marx? Dostoevsky? Nietzsche?

(SAM shakes his head after each name)

Give me a clue.

SAM: The letter P is important . . .

HALLY: Plato!

SAM: . . . and his name begins with an F.

HALLY: I've got it. Freud and Psychology.

SAM: No. I didn't understand him.

HALLY: That makes two of us.

SAM: Think of mouldy apricot jam.

HALLY: *(After a delighted laugh)* Penicillin and Sir Alexander Fleming! And the title of the book: *The Microbe Hunters. (Delighted)* Splendid, Sam! Splendid. For once we are in total agreement. The major breakthrough in medical science in the Twentieth Century. If it wasn't for him, we might have lost the Second World War. It's deeply gratifying, Sam, to know that I haven't been wasting my time in talking to you. *(Strutting around proudly)* Tolstoy may have educated his peasants, but I've educated you.

SAM: Standard Four to Standard Nine.

HALLY: Have we been at it as long as that?

SAM: Yep. And my first lesson was geography.

HALLY: *(Intrigued)* Really? I don't remember.

SAM: My room there at the back of the old Jubilee Boarding House. I had just started working for your Mom. Little boy in short trousers walks in one afternoon and asks me seriously: "Sam, do you want to see South Africa?" Hey man! Sure I wanted to see South Africa!

HALLY: Was that me?

SAM: . . . So the next thing I'm looking at a map you had just done for homework. It was your first one and you were very proud of yourself.

HALLY: Go on.

SAM: Then came my first lesson. "Repeat after me, Sam: Gold in the Transvaal, mealies in the Free State, sugar in Natal and grapes in the Cape."[6] I still know it!

HALLY: Well, I'll be buggered. So that's how it all started.

SAM: And your next map was one with all the rivers and the mountains they came from. The Orange, the Vaal, the Limpopo, the Zambezi . . .

HALLY: You've got a phenomenal memory!

SAM: You should be grateful. That is why you started passing your exams. You tried to be better than me.

(They laugh together. WILLIE is attracted by the laughter and joins them)

HALLY: The old Jubilee Boarding House. Sixteen rooms with board and lodging, rent in advance and one week's notice. I haven't thought about it for donkey's years . . . and I don't think that's an accident. God, was I glad when we sold it and moved out. Those years are not remembered as the happiest ones of an unhappy childhood.

WILLIE: *(Knocking on the table and trying to imitate a woman's voice)* "Hally, are you there?"

HALLY: Who's that supposed to be?

WILLIE: "What you doing in there, Hally? Come out at once!"

HALLY: *(To SAM)* What's he talking about?

SAM: Don't you remember?

WILLIE: "Sam, Willie . . . is he in there with you boys?"

SAM: Hiding away in our room when your mother was looking for you.

HALLY: *(Another good laugh)* Of course! I used to crawl and hide under your bed! But finish the story, Willie. Then what used to happen? You chaps would give the game away by telling her I was in there with you. So much for friendship

SAM: We couldn't lie to her. She knew.

HALLY: Which meant I got another rowing for hanging around the "servants' quarters." I think I spent more time in there with you chaps than anywhere else in that dump. And do you blame me? Nothing but bloody misery wherever you went. Somebody was always complaining about the food, or my mother was having a fight with Micky Nash because she'd caught her with a petty officer in her room. Maud Meiring was another one. Remember those two? They were prostitutes, you know. Soldiers and sailors from the troopships. Bottom fell out of the business when the war ended. God, the flotsam and jetsam that life washed up on our shores! No joking, if it wasn't for your room, I would have been the first certified ten-year-old in medical history. Ja, the memories are coming back now. Walking home from school and thinking: "What can I do this afternoon?" Try out a few ideas, but sooner or later I'd end up in there with you fellows. I bet you I could still find my way to your room with my eyes closed. *(He does exactly that)* Down the corridor . . . telephone on the right, which my Mom keeps locked because somebody is using it on the sly and not paying . . . past the kitchen and unappet-

6 *Transvaal, Free State, Natal, Cape: the four states of South Africa.*

izing cooking smells . . . around the corner into the backyard, hold my breath again because there are more smells coming when I pass your lavatory, then into that little passageway, first door on the right and into your room. How's that?

SAM: Good. But, as usual, you forgot to knock.

HALLY: Like that time I barged in and caught you and Cynthia . . . at it. Remember? God, was I embarrassed! I didn't know what was going on at first.

SAM: Ja, that taught you a lesson.

HALLY: And about a lot more than knocking on doors, I'll have you know, and I don't mean geography either. Hell, Sam, couldn't you have waited until it was dark?

SAM: No.

HALLY: Was it that urgent?

SAM: Yes, and if you don't believe me, wait until your time comes.

HALLY: No, thank you. I am not interested in girls. *(Back to his memories . . . Using a few chairs he recreates the room as he lists the items)* A gray little room with a cold cement floor. Your bed against that wall . . . and I now know why the mattress sags so much! . . . Willie's bed . . . it's propped up on bricks because one leg is broken . . . that wobbly little table with the washbasin and jug of water . . . Yes! . . . stuck to the wall above it are some pin-up pictures from magazines. Joe Louis . . .

WILLIE: Brown Bomber. World Title. *(Boxing pose)* Three rounds and knockout.

HALLY: Against who?

SAM: Max Schmeling.

HALLY: Correct. I can also remember Fred Astaire and Ginger Rogers, and Rita Hayworth[7] in a bathing costume which always made me hot and bothered when I looked at it. Under Willie's bed is an old suitcase with all his clothes in a mess, which is why I never hide there. Your things are neat and tidy in a trunk next to your bed, and on it there is a picture of you and Cynthia in your ballroom clothes, your first silver cup for third place in a competition and an old radio which doesn't work anymore. Have I left out anything?

SAM: No.

HALLY: Right, so much for the stage directions. Now the characters. *(SAM and WILLIE move to their appropriate positions in the bedroom)* Willie is in bed, under his blankets with his clothes on, complaining nonstop about something, but we can't make out a word of what he's saying because he's got his head under the blankets as well. You're on your bed trimming your toenails with a knife — not a very edifying sight — and as for me . . . What am I doing?

SAM: You're sitting on the floor giving Willie a lecture about being a good loser while you get the checker board and pieces ready for a game. Then you go to Willie's bed, pull off the blankets and make him play with you first because you know you're going to win, and that gives you the second game with me.

---

7 *Rita Hayworth (1918–87): an American movie star who was moulded into a Hollywood goddess in the 1940s. She was Fred Astaire's dancing partner in two films in the 1940s.*

HALLY: And you certainly were a bad loser, Willie!

WILLIE: Haai!

HALLY: Wasn't he, Sam? And so slow! A game with you almost took the whole afternoon. Thank God I gave up trying to teach you how to play chess.

WILLIE: You and Sam cheated.

HALLY: I never saw Sam cheat, and mine were mostly the mistakes of youth.

WILLIE: Then how is it you two was always winning?

HALLY: Have you ever considered the possibility, Willie, that it was because we were better than you?

WILLIE: Every time better?

HALLY: Not every time. There were occasions when we deliberately let you win a game so that you would stop sulking and go on playing with us. Sam used to wink at me when you weren't looking to show me it was time to let you win.

WILLIE: So then you two didn't play fair.

HALLY: It was for your benefit, Mr. Malopo, which is more than being fair. It was an act of self-sacrifice. *(To SAM)* But you know what my best memory is, don't you?

SAM: No.

HALLY: Come on, guess. If your memory is so good, you must remember it as well.

SAM: We got up to a lot of tricks in there, Hally.

HALLY: This one was special, Sam.

SAM: I'm listening.

HALLY: It started off looking like another of those useless nothing-to-do afternoons. I'd already been down to Main Street looking for adventure, but nothing had happened. I didn't feel like climbing trees in the Donkin Park or pretending I was a private eye and following a stranger . . . so as usual: See what's cooking in Sam's room. This time it was you on the floor. You had two thin pieces of wood and you were smoothing them down with a knife. It didn't look particularly interesting, but when I asked you what you were doing, you just said, "Wait and see, Hally. Wait . . . and see" . . . in that secret sort of way of yours, so I knew there was a surprise coming. You teased me, you bugger, by being deliberately slow and not answering my questions!

(SAM laughs)

And whistling while you worked away! God, it was infuriating! I could have brained you! It was only when you tied them together in a cross and put that down on the brown paper that I realized what you were doing. "Sam is making a kite?" And when I asked you and you said "Yes" . . . ! *(Shaking his head with disbelief)* The sheer audacity of it took my breath away. I mean, seriously, what the hell does a black man know about flying a kite? I'll be honest with you, Sam, I had no hopes for it. If you think I was excited and happy, you got another guess coming. In fact, I was shit-scared that we were going to make fools of ourselves.

When we left the boarding house to go up onto the hill, I was praying
quietly that there wouldn't be any other kids around to laugh at us.

SAM: *(Enjoying the memory as much as* HALLY*)* Ja, I could see that.

HALLY: I made it obvious, did I?

SAM: Ja. You refused to carry it.

HALLY: Do you blame me? Can you remember what the poor thing looked
like? Tomato-box wood and brown paper! Flour and water for glue!
Two of my mother's old stockings for a tail, and then all those bits and
pieces of string you made me tie together so that we could fly it! Hell,
no, that was now only asking for a miracle to happen.

SAM: Then the big argument when I told you to hold the string and run
with it when I let go.

HALLY: I was prepared to run, all right, but straight back to the boarding
house.

SAM: *(Knowing what's coming)* So what happened?

HALLY: Come on, Sam, you remember as well as I do.

SAM: I want to hear it from you.

*(*HALLY *pauses. He wants to be as accurate as possible)*

HALLY: You went a little distance from me down the hill, you held it up
ready to let it go. . . . "This is it," I thought. "Like everything else in my
life, here comes another fiasco." Then you shouted, "Go, Hally!" and I
started to run. *(Another pause)* I don't know how to describe it, Sam. Ja!
The miracle happened! I was running, waiting for it to crash to the
ground, but instead suddenly there was something alive behind me at
the end of the string, tugging at it as if it wanted to be free. I looked
back . . . *(Shakes his head)* . . . I still can't believe my eyes. It was flying!
Looping around and trying to climb even higher into the sky. You
shouted to me to let it have more string. I did, until there was none left
and I was just holding that piece of wood we had tied to it. You came up
and joined me. You were laughing.

SAM: So were you. And shouting, "It works, Sam! We've done it!"

HALLY: And we had! I was so proud of us! It was the most splendid thing I
had ever seen. I wished there were hundreds of kids around to watch
us. The part that scared me, though, was when you showed me how to
make it dive down to the ground and then just when it was on the
point of crashing, swoop up again!

SAM: You didn't want to try yourself.

HALLY: Of course not! I would have been suicidal if anything had happened
to it. Watching you do it made me nervous enough. I was quite happy
just to see it up there with its tail fluttering behind it. You left me after
that, didn't you? You explained how to get it down, we tied it to the
bench so that I could sit and watch it, and you went away. I wanted you
to stay, you know. I was a little scared of having to look after it by
myself.

SAM: *(Quietly)* I had work to do, Hally.

HALLY: It was sort of sad bringing it down, Sam. And it looked sad again when it was lying there on the ground. Like something that had lost its soul. Just tomato-box wood, brown paper and two of my mother's old stockings! But, hell, I'll never forget that first moment when I saw it up there. I had a stiff neck the next day from looking up so much.

(SAM *laughs*. HALLY *turns to him with a question he never thought of asking before*)

Why did you make that kite, Sam?
SAM: *(Evenly)* I can't remember.
HALLY: Truly?
SAM: Too long ago, Hally.
HALLY: Ja, I suppose it was. It's time for another one, you know.
SAM: Why do you say that?
HALLY: Because it feels like that. Wouldn't be a good day to fly it, though.
SAM: No. You can't fly kites on rainy days.
HALLY: *(He studies SAM. Their memories have made him conscious of the man's presence in his life)* How old are you, Sam?
SAM: Two score and five.
HALLY: Strange, isn't it?
SAM: What?
HALLY: Me and you.
SAM: What's strange about it?
HALLY: Little white boy in short trousers and a black man old enough to be his father flying a kite. It's not every day you see that.
SAM: But why strange? Because the one is white and the other black?
HALLY: I don't know. Would have been just as strange, I suppose, if it had been me and my Dad . . . cripple man and a little boy! Nope! There's no chance of me flying a kite without it being strange. *(Simple statement of fact — no self-pity)* There's a nice little short story there. "The Kite-Flyers." But we'd have to find a twist in the ending.
SAM: Twist?
HALLY: Yes. Something unexpected. The way it ended with us was too straightforward . . . me on the bench and you going back to work. There's no drama in that.
WILLIE: And me?
HALLY: You?
WILLIE: Yes me.
HALLY: You want to get into the story as well, do you? I got it! Change the title: "Afternoons in Sam's Room" . . . expand it and tell all the stories. It's on its way to being a novel. Our days in the old Jubilee. Sad in a way that they're over. I almost wish we were still in that little room.
SAM: We're still together.
HALLY: That's true. It's just that life felt the right size in there . . . not too big and not too small. Wasn't so hard to work up a bit of courage. It's got so bloody complicated since then.

(The telephone rings. SAM *answers it)*

SAM: St. George's Park Tea Room . . . Hello, Madam . . . Yes, Madam, he's
here. . . . Hally, it's your mother.

HALLY: Where is she phoning from?

SAM: Sounds like the hospital. It's a public telephone.

HALLY: *(Relieved)* You see! I told you. *(The telephone)* Hello, Mom . . . Yes . . .
Yes no fine. Everything's under control here. How's things with poor
old Dad? . . . Has he had a bad turn? . . . What? . . . Oh, God! . . .
Yes, Sam told me, but I was sure he'd made a mistake. But what's all
this about, Mom? He didn't look at all good last night. How can he get
better so quickly? . . . Then very obviously you must say no. Be firm
with him. You're the boss. . . . You know what it's going to be like if he
comes home. . . . Well then, don't blame me when I fail my exams at
the end of the year. . . . Yes! How am I expected to be fresh for school
when I spend half the night massaging his gammy leg? . . . So am
I! . . . So tell him a white lie. Say Dr. Colley wants more X-rays of his
stump. Or bribe him. We'll sneak in double tots of brandy in
future. . . . What? . . . Order him to get back into bed at once! If he's
going to behave like a child, treat him like one. . . . All right, Mom! I
was just trying to . . . I'm sorry. . . . I said I'm sorry. . . . Quick, give
me your number. I'll phone you back. *(He hangs up and waits a few seconds)*
Here we go again! *(He dials)* I'm sorry, Mom. . . . Okay . . . But now
listen to me carefully. All it needs is for you to put your foot down.
Don't take no for an answer. . . . Did you hear me? And whatever you
do, don't discuss it with him. . . . Because I'm frightened you'll give in
to him. . . . Yes, Sam gave me lunch. . . . I ate all of it! . . . No, Mom
not a soul. It's still raining here. . . . Right, I'll tell them. I'll just do
some homework and then lock up. . . . But remember now, Mom.
Don't listen to anything he says. And phone me back and let me know
what happens. . . . Okay. Bye, Mom. *(He hangs up. The men are staring at
him)* My Mom says that when you've finished with the floors you must
do the windows. *(Pause)* Don't misunderstand me, chaps. All I want is
for him to get better. And if he was, I'd be the first person to say:
"Bring him home." But he's not, and we can't give him the medical care
and attention he needs at home. That's what hospitals are there for.
(Brusquely) So don't just stand there! Get on with it!

(SAM clears HALLY's table)

You heard right. My Dad wants to go home.

SAM: Is he better?

HALLY: *(Sharply)* No! How the hell can he be better when last night he was
groaning with pain? This is not an age of miracles!

SAM: Then he should stay in hospital.

HALLY: *(Seething with irritation and frustration)* Tell me something I don't know,
Sam. What the hell do you think I was saying to my Mom? All I can say
is fuck-it-all.

SAM: I'm sure he'll listen to your Mom.

HALLY: You don't know what she's up against. He's already packed his shaving kit and pajamas and is sitting on his bed with his crutches, dressed and ready to go. I know him when he gets in that mood. If she tries to reason with him, we've had it. She's no match for him when it comes to a battle of words. He'll tie her up in knots. (*Trying to hide his true feelings*)

SAM: I suppose it gets lonely for him in there.

HALLY: With all the patients and nurses around? Regular visits from the Salvation Army? Balls! It's ten times worse for him at home. I'm at school and my mother is here in the business all day.

SAM: He's at least got you at night.

HALLY: (*Before he can stop himself*) And we've got him! Please! I don't want to talk about it anymore. (*Unpacks his school case, slamming down books on the table*) Life is just a plain bloody mess, that's all. And people are fools.

SAM: Come on, Hally.

HALLY: Yes, they are! They bloody well deserve what they get.

SAM: Then don't complain.

HALLY: Don't try to be clever, Sam. It doesn't suit you. Anybody who thinks there's nothing wrong with this world needs to have his head examined. Just when things are going along all right, without fail someone or something will come along and spoil everything. Somebody should write that down as a fundamental law of the Universe. The principle of perpetual disappointment. If there is a God who created this world, he should scrap it and try again.

SAM: All right, Hally, all right. What you got for homework?

HALLY: Bullshit, as usual. (*Opens an exercise book and reads*) "Write five hundred words describing an annual event of cultural or historical significance."

SAM: That should be easy enough for you.

HALLY: And also plain bloody boring. You know what he wants, don't you? One of their useless old ceremonies. The commemoration of the landing of the 1820 Settlers,[8] or if it's going to be culture, Carols by Candlelight every Christmas.

SAM: It's an impressive sight. Make a good description, Hally. All those candles glowing in the dark and the people singing hymns.

HALLY: And it's called religious hysteria. (*Intense irritation*) Please, Sam! Just leave me alone and let me get on with it. I'm not in the mood for games this afternoon. And remember my Mom's orders . . . you're to help Willie with the windows. Come on now, I don't want any more nonsense in here.

SAM: Okay, Hally, okay.

(HALLY *settles down to his homework; determined preparations . . . pen, ruler, exercise book, dictionary, another cake . . . all of which will lead to nothing*)

(SAM *waltzes over to* WILLIE *and starts to replace tables and chairs. He practices a ballroom step while doing so.* WILLIE *watches. When* SAM *is finished,* WILLIE *tries*)

---

8 *In 1806, the British acquired control of the Cape Colony from the Dutch. In 1820, in response to social unrest and unemployment in Britain, the British Parliament provided funds to send about 4000 English, Scottish, Irish, and Welsh settlers to the Cape Colony. These settlers doubled the existing English-speaking population in the colony and helped to establish a significant English community and cultural presence in the Cape in an effort to buttress the Empire.*

Good! But just a little bit quicker on the turn and only move in to her after she's crossed over. What about this one?

(Another step. When SAM *is finished,* WILLIE *again has a go)*

Much better. See what happens when you just relax and enjoy yourself? Remember that in two weeks' time and you'll be all right.

WILLIE: But I haven't got partner, Boet Sam.

SAM: Maybe Hilda will turn up tonight.

WILLIE: No, Boet Sam. *(Reluctantly)* I gave her a good hiding.

SAM: You mean a bad one.

WILLIE: Good bad one.

SAM: Then you mustn't complain either. Now you pay the price for losing your temper.

WILLIE: I also pay two pounds ten shilling entrance fee.

SAM: They'll refund you if you withdraw now.

WILLIE: *(Appalled)* You mean, don't dance?

SAM: Yes.

WILLIE: No! I wait too long and I practice too hard. If I find me new partner, you think I can be ready in two weeks? I ask Madam for my leave now and we practice every day.

SAM: Quickstep non-stop for two weeks. World record, Willie, but you'll be mad at the end.

WILLIE: No jokes, Boet Sam.

SAM: I'm not joking.

WILLIE: So then what?

SAM: Find Hilda. Say you're sorry and promise you won't beat her again.

WILLIE: No.

SAM: Then withdraw. Try again next year.

WILLIE: No.

SAM: Then I give up.

WILLIE: Haaikona, Boet Sam, you can't.

SAM: What do you mean, I can't? I'm telling you: I give up.

WILLIE: *(Adamant)* No! *(Accusingly)* It was you who start me ballroom dancing.

SAM: So?

WILLIE: Before that I use to be happy. And is you and Miriam who bring me to Hilda and say here's partner for you.

SAM: What are you saying, Willie?

WILLIE: You!

SAM: But me what? To blame?

WILLIE: Yes.

SAM: Willie . . . ? *(Bursts into laughter)*

WILLIE: And now all you do is make jokes at me. You wait. When Miriam leaves you is my turn to laugh. Ha! Ha! Ha!

SAM: *(He can't take* WILLIE *seriously any longer)* She can leave me tonight! I know what to do. *(Bowing before an imaginary partner)* May I have the pleasure? *(He dances and sings)*

"Just a fellow with his pillow . . .
Dancin' like a willow . . .
In an autumn breeze . . . "
WILLIE: There you go again!

(SAM *goes on dancing and singing*)

Boet Sam!
SAM: There's the answer to your problem! Judges' announcement in two
weeks' time: "Ladies and gentlemen, the winner in the open section . . .
Mr. Willie Malopo and his pillow!"

(*This is too much for a now really angry* WILLIE. *He goes for* SAM, *but the latter is too
quick for him and puts* HALLY's *table between the two of them*)

HALLY: *(Exploding)* For Christ's sake, you two!
WILLIE: *(Still trying to get at* SAM*)* I donner you, Sam! Struesgod!
SAM: *(Still laughing)* Sorry, Willie . . . Sorry . . .
HALLY: Sam! Willie! *(Grabs his ruler and gives* WILLIE *a vicious whack on the bum*)
How the hell am I supposed to concentrate with the two of you behav-
ing like bloody children!
WILLIE: Hit him too!
HALLY: Shut up, Willie.
WILLIE: He started jokes again.
HALLY: Get back to your work. You too, Sam. *(His ruler)* Do you want
another one, Willie?

(SAM *and* WILLIE *return to their work.* HALLY *uses the opportunity to escape from his
unsuccessful attempt at homework. He struts around like a little despot, ruler in hand,
giving vent to his anger and frustration*)

Suppose a customer had walked in then? Or the Park Superintendent.
And seen the two of you behaving like a pair of hooligans. That would
have been the end of my mother's license, you know. And your jobs!
Well, this is the end of it. From now on there will be no more of your
ballroom nonsense in here. This is a business establishment, not a
bloody New Brighton dancing school. I've been far too lenient with the
two of you. *(Behind the counter for a green cool drink and a dollop of ice cream. He
keeps up his tirade as he prepares it)* But what really makes me bitter is that I
allow you chaps a little freedom in here when business is bad and what
do you do with it? The foxtrot! Specially you, Sam. There's more to life
than trotting around a dance floor and I thought at least you knew it.
SAM: It's a harmless pleasure, Hally. It doesn't hurt anybody.
HALLY: It's also a rather simple one, you know.
SAM: You reckon so? Have you ever tried?
HALLY: Of course not.
SAM: Why don't you? Now.
HALLY: What do you mean? Me dance?

SAM: Yes. I'll show you a simple step — the waltz — then you try it.

HALLY: What will that prove?

SAM: That it might not be as easy as you think.

HALLY: I didn't say it was easy. I said it was simple — like in simple-minded, meaning mentally retarded. You can't exactly say it challenges the intellect.

SAM: It does other things.

HALLY: Such as?

SAM: Make people happy.

HALLY: *(The glass in his hand)* So do American cream sodas with ice cream. For God's sake, Sam, you're not asking me to take ballroom dancing serious, are you?

SAM: Yes.

HALLY: *(Sigh of defeat)* Oh, well, so much for trying to give you a decent education. I've obviously achieved nothing.

SAM: You still haven't told me what's wrong with admiring something that's beautiful and then trying to do it yourself.

HALLY: Nothing. But we happen to be talking about a foxtrot, not a thing of beauty.

SAM: But that is just what I'm saying. If you were to see two champions doing, two masters of the art . . . !

HALLY: Oh, God, I give up. So now it's also art!

SAM: Ja.

HALLY: There's a limit, Sam. Don't confuse art and entertainment.

SAM: So then what is art?

HALLY: You want a definition?

SAM: Ja.

HALLY: *(He realizes he has got to be careful. He gives the matter a lot of thought before answering)* Philosophers have been trying to do that for centuries. What is Art? What is Life? But basically I suppose it's . . . the giving of meaning to matter.

SAM: Nothing to do with beautiful?

HALLY: It goes beyond that. It's the giving of form to the formless.

SAM: Ja, well, maybe it's not art, then. But I still say it's beautiful.

HALLY: I'm sure the word you mean to use is entertaining.

SAM: *(Adamant)* No. Beautiful. And if you want proof, come along to the Centenary Hall in New Brighton in two weeks' time.

(The mention of the Centenary Hall draws WILLIE *over to them)*

HALLY: What for? I've seen the two of you prancing around in here often enough.

SAM: *(He laughs)* This isn't the real thing, Hally. We're just playing around in here.

HALLY: So? I can use my imagination.

SAM: And what do you get?

HALLY: A lot of people dancing around and having a so-called good time.

SAM: That all?

HALLY: Well, basically it is that, surely.

SAM: No, it isn't. Your imagination hasn't helped you at all. There's a lot more to it than that. We're getting ready for the championships, Hally, not just another dance. There's going to be a lot of people, all right, and they're going to have a good time, but they'll only be spectators, sitting around and watching. It's just the competitors out there on the dance floor. Party decorations and fancy lights all around the walls! The ladies in beautiful evening dresses!

HALLY: My mother's got one of those, Sam, and, quite frankly, it's an embarrassment every time she wears it.

SAM: *(Undeterred)* Your imagination left out the excitement.

(HALLY *scoffs*)

Oh, yes. The finalists are not going to be out there just to have a good time. One of those couples will be the 1950 Eastern Province Champions. And your imagination left out the music.

WILLIE: Mr. Elijah Gladman Guzana and his Orchestral Jazzonions.

SAM: The sound of the big band, Hally. Trombone, trumpet, tenor and alto sax. And then, finally, your imagination also left out the climax of the evening when the dancing is finished, the judges have stopped whispering among themselves and the Master of Ceremonies collects their scorecards and goes up onto the stage to announce the winners.

HALLY: All right. So you make it sound like a bit of a do. It's an occasion. Satisfied?

SAM: *(Victory)* So you admit that!

HALLY: Emotionally yes, intellectually no.

SAM: Well, I don't know what you mean by that, all I'm telling you is that it is going to be *the* event of the year in New Brighton. It's been sold out for two weeks already. There's only standing room left. We've got competitors coming from Kingwilliamstown, East London, Port Alfred.

(HALLY *starts pacing thoughtfully*)

HALLY: Tell me a bit more.

SAM: I thought you weren't interested . . . intellectually.

HALLY: *(Mysteriously)* I've got my reasons.

SAM: What do you want to know?

HALLY: It takes place every year?

SAM: Yes. But only every third year in New Brighton. It's East London's turn to have the championships next year.

HALLY: Which, I suppose, makes it an even more significant event.

SAM: Ah ha! We're getting somewhere. Our "occasion" is now a "significant event."

HALLY: I wonder.

SAM: What?

HALLY: I wonder if I would get away with it.

SAM: But what?

HALLY: *(To the table and his exercise book)* "Write five hundred words describing an annual event of cultural or historical significance." Would I be stretching poetic license a little too far if I called your ballroom championships a cultural event?

SAM: You mean . . . ?

HALLY: You think we could get five hundred words out of it, Sam?

SAM: Victor Sylvester has written a whole book on ballroom dancing.

WILLIE: You going to write about it, Master Hally?

HALLY: Yes, gentlemen, that is precisely what I am considering doing. Old Doc Bromely — he's my English teacher — is going to argue with me, of course. He doesn't like natives. But I'll point out to him that in strict anthropological terms the culture of a primitive black society includes its dancing and singing. To put my thesis in a nutshell: The war-dance has been replaced by the waltz. But it still amounts to the same thing: the release of primitive emotions through movement. Shall we give it a go?

SAM: I'm ready.

WILLIE: Me also.

HALLY: Ha! This will teach the old bugger a lesson. *(Decision taken)* Right. Let's get ourselves organized. *(This means another cake on the table. He sits)* I think you've given me enough general atmosphere, Sam, but to build the tension and suspense I need facts. *(Pencil poised)*

WILLIE: Give him facts, Boet Sam.

HALLY: What you called the climax . . . how many finalists?

SAM: Six couples.

HALLY: *(Making notes)* Go on. Give me the picture.

SAM: Spectators seated right around the hall. *(WILLIE becomes a spectator)*

HALLY: . . . and it's a full house.

SAM: At one end, on the stage, Gladman and his Orchestral Jazzonions. At the other end is a long table with the three judges. The six finalists go onto the dance floor and take up their positions. When they are ready and the spectators have settled down, the Master of Ceremonies goes to the microphone. To start with, he makes some jokes to get the people laughing . . .

HALLY: Good touch! *(As he writes)* " . . . creating a relaxed atmosphere which will change to one of tension and drama as the climax is approached."

SAM: *(Onto a chair to act out the M.C.)* "Ladies and gentlemen, we come now to the great moment you have all been waiting for this evening. . . . The finals of the 1950 Eastern Province Open Ballroom Dancing Championships. But first let me introduce the finalists! Mr. and Mrs. Welcome Tchabalala from Kingwilliamstown . . . "

WILLIE: *(He applauds after every name)* Is when the people clap their hands and whistle and make a lot of noise, Master Hally.

SAM: "Mr. Mulligan Njikelane and Miss Nomhle Nkonyeni of Grahamstown; Mr. and Mrs. Norman Nchinga from Port Alfred; Mr. Fats Bokolane and Miss Dina Plaatjies from East London; Mr. Sipho Dugu and Mrs. Mable Magada from Peddie; and from New Brighton our very own Mr. Willie Malopo and Miss Hilda Samuels.

(WILLIE *can't believe his ears. He abandons his role as spectator and scrambles into position as a finalist*)

WILLIE: Relaxed and ready to romance!

SAM: The applause dies down. When everybody is silent, Gladman lifts up his sax, nods at the Orchestral Jazzonions . . .

WILLIE: Play the jukebox please, Boet Sam!

SAM: I also only got bus fare, Willie.

HALLY: Hold it, everybody. (*Heads for the cash register behind the counter*) How much is in the till, Sam?

SAM: Three shillings. Hally . . . your Mom counted it before she left.

(HALLY *hesitates*)

HALLY: Sorry, Willie. You know how she carried on the last time I did it. We'll just have to pool our combined imaginations and hope for the best. (*Returns to the table*) Back to work. How are the points scored, Sam?

SAM: Maximum of ten points each for individual style, deportment, rhythm and general appearance.

WILLIE: Must I start?

HALLY: Hold it for a second, Willie. And penalties?

SAM: For what?

HALLY: For doing something wrong. Say you stumble or bump into some-body . . . do they take off any points?

SAM: (*Aghast*) Hally . . . !

HALLY: When you're dancing. If you and your partner collide into another couple.

(HALLY *can get no further.* SAM *has collapsed with laughter. He explains to* WILLIE)

SAM: If me and Miriam bump into you and Hilda . . .

(WILLIE *joins him in another good laugh*)

Hally, Hally . . . !

HALLY: (*Perplexed*) Why? What did I say?

SAM: There's no collisions out there, Hally. Nobody trips or stumbles or bumps into anybody else. That's what that moment is all about. To be one of those finalists on that dance floor is like . . . like being in a dream about a world in which accidents don't happen.

HALLY: (*Genuinely moved by* SAM's *image*) Jesus, Sam! That's beautiful!

WILLIE: (*Can endure waiting no longer*) I'm starting! (WILLIE *dances while* SAM *talks*)

SAM: Of course it is. That's what I've been trying to say to you all after-noon. And it's beautiful because that is what we want life to be like. But instead, like you said, Hally, we're bumping into each other all the time. Look at the three of us this afternoon: I've bumped into Willie, the two of us have bumped into you, you've bumped into your mother, she bumping into your Dad. . . . None of us knows the steps and there's no music playing. And it doesn't stop with us. The whole world is doing it all the time. Open a newspaper and what do you read? America has bumped into Russia, England is bumping into India, rich man bumps into poor man. Those are big collisions, Hally. They make for a lot of bruises. People get hurt in all that bumping, and we're sick and tired of it now. It's been going on for too long. Are we never going to get it right? . . . Learn to dance life like champions instead of always being just a bunch of beginners at it?

HALLY: *(Deep and sincere admiration of the man)* You've got a vision, Sam!

SAM: Not just me. What I'm saying to you is that everybody's got it. That's why there's only standing room left for the Centenary Hall in two weeks' time. For as long as the music lasts, we are going to see six couples get it right, the way we want life to be.

HALLY: But is that the best we can do, Sam . . . watch six finalists dreaming about the way it should be?

SAM: I don't know. But it starts with that. Without the dream we won't know what we're going for. And anyway I reckon there are a few people who have got past just dreaming about it and are trying for something real. Remember that thing we read once in the paper about the Mahatma Gandhi? Going without food to stop those riots in India?

HALLY: You're right. He certainly was trying to teach people to get the steps right.

SAM: And the Pope.

HALLY: Yes, he's another one. Our old General Smuts[9] as well, you know. He's also out there dancing. You know, Sam, when you come to think of it, that's what the United Nations boils down to . . . a dancing school for politicians.

SAM: And let's hope they learn.

HALLY: *(A little surge of hope)* You're right. We mustn't despair. Maybe there's some hope for mankind after all. Keep it up, Willie. *(Back to his table with determination)* This is a lot bigger than I thought. So what have we got? Yes, our title: "A World Without Collisions."

SAM: That sounds good! "A World Without Collisions."

HALLY: Subtitle: "Global Politics on the Dance Floor." No. A bit too heavy, hey? What about "Ballroom Dancing as a Political Vision"?

(The telephone rings. SAM answers it)

SAM: St. George's Park Tea Room . . . Yes, Madam . . . Hally, it's your Mom.

HALLY: *(Back to reality)* Oh, God, yes! I'd forgotten all about that. Shit! Remember my words, Sam? Just when you're enjoying yourself, someone or something will come along and wreck everything.

---

9 *Jan Christian Smuts (1870–1950): a leading political figure in South Africa. He was a guerrilla leader in the South African (Anglo-Boer) War, 1899–1902 (from which he emerged a general), participated in the creation of the Union of South Africa (1910), was prime minister twice in 1919–24 and 1939–48, and gained an international reputation as a statesman, participating in the creation of both the League of Nations and the United Nations.*

SAM: You haven't heard what she's got to say yet.

HALLY: Public telephone?

SAM: No.

HALLY: Does she sound happy or unhappy?

SAM: I couldn't tell. *(Pause)* She's waiting, Hally.

HALLY: *(To the telephone)* Hello, Mom . . . No, everything is okay here. Just doing my homework. . . . What's your news? . . . You've what? . . . *(Pause. He takes the receiver away from his ear for a few seconds. In the course of* HALLY's *telephone conversation,* SAM *and* WILLIE *discretely position the stacked tables and chairs.* HALLY *places the receiver back to his ear)* Yes, I'm still here. Oh, well, I give up now. Why did you do it, Mom? . . . Well, I just hope you know what you've let us in for. . . . *(Loudly)* I said I hope you know what you've let us in for! It's the end of the peace and quiet we've been having. *(Softly)* Where is he? *(Normal voice)* He can't hear us from in there. But for God's sake, Mom, what happened? I told you to be firm with him. . . . Then you and the nurses should have held him down, taken his crutches away. . . . I know only too well he's my father! . . . I'm not being disrespectful, but I'm sick and tired of emptying stinking chamberpots full of phlegm and piss. . . . Yes, I do! When you're not there, he asks *me* to do it. . . . If you really want to know the truth, that's why I've got no appetite for my food. . . . Yes! There's a lot of things you don't know about. For your information, I still haven't got that science textbook I need. And you know why? He borrowed the money you gave me for it. . . . Because I didn't want to start another fight between you two. . . . He says that every time. . . . All right, Mom! *(Viciously)* Then just remember to start hiding your bag away again, because he'll be at your purse before long for money for booze. And when he's well enough to come down here, you better keep an eye on the till as well, because that is also going to develop a leak. . . . Then don't complain to me when he starts his old tricks. . . . Yes, you do. I get it from you on one side and from him on the other, and it makes life hell for me. I'm not going to be the peacemaker anymore. I'm warning you now: when the two of you start fighting again, I'm leaving home. . . . Mom, if you start crying, I'm going to put down the receiver. . . . Okay . . . *(Lowering his voice to a vicious whisper)* Okay, Mom. I heard you. *(Desperate)* No. . . . Because I don't want to. I'll see him when I get home! Mom! . . . *(Pause. When he speaks again, his tone changes completely. It is not simply pretense. We sense a genuine emotional conflict)* Welcome home, chum! . . . What's that? . . . Don't be silly, Dad. You being home is just about the best news in the world. . . . I bet you are. Bloody depressing there with everybody going on about their ailments, hey! . . . How you feeling? . . . Good . . . Here as well, pal. Coming down cats and dogs. . . . That's right. Just the day for a kip and a toss in your old Uncle Ned.[10] . . . Everything's just hunky-dory on my side, Dad. . . . Well, to start with, there's a nice pile of comics for you on the counter. . . . Yes, old Kemple brought them in. *Batman and Robin, Submariner* . . . just your cup of tea . . . I will. . . . Yes, we'll spin a few yarns tonight. . . . Okay, chum, see you in a little while. . . . No, I promise. I'll come straight home. . . . *(Pause — his mother*

---

10 *Uncle Ned: a colloquialism for "a nap in your bed (rhyming slang)."*

comes back on the phone) Mom? Okay. I'll lock up now. . . . What? . . . Oh, the brandy . . . Yes, I'll remember! . . . I'll put it in my suitcase now, for God's sake. I know well enough what will happen if he doesn't get it. . . . *(Places a bottle of brandy on the counter)* I *was* kind to him, Mom. I didn't say anything nasty! . . . All right. Bye. *(End of telephone conversation. A desolate* HALLY *doesn't move. A strained silence)*

SAM: *(Quietly)* That sounded like a bad bump, Hally.

HALLY: *(Having a hard time controlling his emotions. He speaks carefully)* Mind your own business, Sam.

SAM: Sorry. I wasn't trying to interfere. Shall we carry on? Hally? *(He indicates the exercise book. No response from* HALLY*)*

WILLIE: *(Also trying)* Tell him about when they give out the cups, Boet Sam.

SAM: Ja! That's another big moment. The presentation of the cups after the winners have been announced. You've got to put that in.

(Still no response from HALLY*)*

WILLIE: A big silver one, Master Hally, called floating trophy for the champions.

SAM: We always invite some big-shot personality to hand them over. Guest of honour this year is going to be His Holiness Bishop Jabulani of the All African Free Zionist Church.

*(*HALLY *gets up abruptly, goes to his table and tears up the page he was writing on)*

HALLY: So much for a bloody world without collisions.

SAM: Too bad. It was on its way to being a good composition.

HALLY: Let's stop bullshitting ourselves, Sam.

SAM: Have we been doing that?

HALLY: Yes! That's what all our talk about a decent world has been . . . just so much bullshit.

SAM: We did say it was still only a dream.

HALLY: And a bloody useless one at that. Life's a fuck-up and it's never going to change.

SAM: Ja, maybe that's true.

HALLY: There's no maybe about it. It's a blunt and brutal fact. All we've done this afternoon is waste our time.

SAM: Not if we'd got your homework done.

HALLY: I don't give a shit about my homework, so, for Christ's sake, just shut up about it. *(Slamming books viciously into his school case)* Hurry up now and finish your work. I want to lock up and get out of here. *(Pause)* And then go where? Home-sweet-fucking-home. Jesus, I hate that word.

*(*HALLY *goes to the counter to put the brandy bottle and comics in his school case. After a moment's hesitation, he smashes the bottle of brandy. He abandons all further attempts to hide his feelings.* SAM *and* WILLIE *work away as unobtrusively as possible)*

Do you want to know what is really wrong with your lovely little dream, Sam? It's not just that we are all bad dancers. That does happen to be perfectly true, but there's more to it than just that. You left out the cripples.

SAM: Hally!

HALLY: *(Now totally reckless)* Ja! Can't leave them out, Sam. That's why we always end up on our backsides on the dance floor. They're also out there dancing . . . like a bunch of broken spiders trying to do the quick-step! *(An ugly attempt at laughter)* When you come to think of it, it's a bloody comical sight. I mean, it's bad enough on two legs . . . but one and a pair of crutches! Hell, no, Sam. That's guaranteed to turn that dance floor into a shambles. Why you shaking your head? Picture it, man. For once this afternoon let's use our imaginations sensibly.

SAM: Be careful, Hally.

HALLY: Of what? The truth? I seem to be the only one around here who is prepared to face it. We've had the pretty dream, it's time now to wake up and have a good long look at the way things really are. Nobody knows the steps, there's no music, the cripples are also out there trip-ping up everybody and trying to get into the act, and it's all called the All-Comers-How-to-Make-a-Fuckup-of-Life Championships. *(Another ugly laugh)* Hang on, Sam! The best bit is still coming. Do you know what the winner's trophy is? A beautiful big chamber-pot with roses on the side, and it's full to the brim with piss. And guess who I think is going to be this year's winner.

SAM: *(Almost shouting)* Stop now!

HALLY: *(Suddenly appalled by how far he has gone)* Why?

SAM: Hally? It's your father you're talking about.

HALLY: So?

SAM: Do you know what you've been saying?

(HALLY can't answer. He is rigid with shame. SAM speaks to him sternly)

No, Hally, you mustn't do it. Take back those words and ask for for-giveness! It's a terrible sin for a son to mock his father with jokes like that. You'll be punished if you carry on. Your father is your father, even if he is a . . . cripple man.

WILLIE: Yes, Master Hally. Is true what Sam say.

SAM: I understand how you are feeling, Hally, but even so . . .

HALLY: No, you don't!

SAM: I think I do.

HALLY: And I'm telling you you don't. Nobody does. *(Speaking carefully as his shame turns to rage at SAM)* It's your turn to be careful, Sam. Very careful! You're treading on dangerous ground. Leave me and my father alone.

SAM: I'm not the one who's been saying things about him.

HALLY: What goes on between me and my Dad is none of your business!

SAM: Then don't tell me about it. If that's all you've got to say about him, I don't want to hear.

(For a moment HALLY *is at loss for a response)*

HALLY: Just get on with your bloody work and shut up.
SAM: Swearing at me won't help you.
HALLY: Yes, it does! Mind your own fucking business and shut up!
SAM: Okay. If that's the way you want it, I'll stop trying.

(He turns away. This infuriates HALLY *even more)*

HALLY: Good. Because what you've been trying to do is meddle in something you know nothing about. All that concerns you in here, Sam, is
   to try and do what you get paid for — keep the place clean and serve
   the customers. In plain words, just get on with your job. My mother is
   right. She's always warning me about allowing you to get too familiar.
   Well, this time you've gone too far. It's going to stop right now.

(No response from SAM*)*

You're only a servant in here, and don't forget it.

(Still no response. HALLY *is trying hard to get one)*

And as far as my father is concerned, all you need to remember is that
   he is your boss.
SAM: *(Needled at last)* No, he isn't. I get paid by your mother.
HALLY: Don't argue with me, Sam!
SAM: Then don't say he's my boss.
HALLY: He's a white man and that's good enough for you.
SAM: I'll try to forget you said that.
HALLY: Don't! Because you won't be doing me a favor if you do. I'm telling
   you to remember it.

(A pause. SAM *pulls himself together and makes one last effort)*

SAM: Hally, Hally . . . ! Come on now. Let's stop before it's too late. You're
   right! We *are* on dangerous ground. If we're not careful, somebody is
   going to get hurt.
HALLY: It won't be me.
SAM: Don't be so sure.
HALLY: I don't know what you're talking about, Sam.
SAM: Yes, you do.
HALLY: *(Furious)* Jesus, I wish you would stop trying to tell me what I do and
   what I don't know.

(SAM gives up. He turns to WILLIE)

SAM: Let's finish up.
HALLY: Don't turn your back on me! I haven't finished talking.

(He grabs SAM *by the arm and tries to make him turn around.* SAM *reacts with a flash of anger)*

SAM: Don't do that, Hally! *(Facing the boy)* All right, I'm listening. Well? What do you want to say to me?

HALLY: *(Pause as* HALLY *looks for something to say)* To begin with, why don't you also start calling me Master Harold, like Willie.

SAM: Do you mean that?

HALLY: Why the hell do you think I said it?

SAM: And if I don't?

HALLY: You might just lose your job.

SAM: *(Quietly and very carefully)* If you make me say it once, I'll never call you anything else again.

HALLY: So? *(The boy confronts the man)* Is that meant to be a threat?

SAM: Just telling you what will happen if you make me do that. You must decide what it means to you.

HALLY: Well, I have. It's good news. Because that is exactly what Master Harold wants from now on. Think of it as a little lesson in respect, Sam, that's long overdue, and I hope you remember it as well as you do your geography. I can tell you now that somebody who will be glad to hear I've finally given it to you will be my Dad. Yes! He agrees with my Mom. He's always going on about it as well. "You must teach the boys to show you more respect, my son."

SAM: So now you can stop complaining about going home. Everybody is going to be happy tonight.

HALLY: That's perfectly correct. You see, you mustn't get the wrong idea about me and my Dad, Sam. We also have our good times together. Some bloody good laughs. He's got a marvelous sense of humor. Want to know what our favorite joke is? He gives out a big groan, you see, and says: "It's not fair, is it, Hally?" Then I have to ask: "What, chum?" And then he says: "A nigger's arse" . . . and we both have a good laugh.

(The men stare at him with disbelief)

What's the matter, Willie? Don't you catch the joke? You always were a bit slow on the uptake. It's what is called a pun. You see, fair means both light in color and to be just and decent. *(He turns to* SAM) I thought *you* would catch it, Sam.

SAM: Oh ja, I catch it all right.

HALLY: But it doesn't appeal to your sense of humor.

SAM: Do you really laugh?

HALLY: Of course.

SAM: To please him? Make him feel good?

HALLY: No, for heaven's sake! I laugh because I think it's a bloody good joke.

SAM: You're really trying hard to be ugly, aren't you? And why drag poor old Willie into it? He's done nothing to you except show you the respect you want so badly. That's also not being fair, you know . . . and *I* mean just or decent.

WILLIE: It's all right, Sam. Leave it now.

SAM: It's me you're after. You should just have said "Sam's arse" . . . because that's the one you're trying to kick. Anyway, how do you know it's not fair? You've never seen it. Do you want to? (*He drops his trousers and underpants and presents his backside for* HALLY's *inspection*) Have a good look. A real Basuto arse . . . which is about as nigger as they can come. Satisfied? (*Trousers up*) Now you can make your Dad even happier when you go home tonight. Tell him I showed you my arse and he is quite right. It's not fair. And if it will give him an even better laugh next time, I'll also let *him* have a look. Come, Willie, let's finish up and go.

(SAM *and* WILLIE *start to tidy up the tea room.* HALLY *doesn't move. He waits for a moment when* SAM *passes him*)

HALLY: (Quietly) Sam . . .

(SAM *stops and looks expectantly at the boy.* HALLY *spits in his face. A long and heartfelt groan from* WILLIE. *For a few seconds* SAM *doesn't move*)

SAM: (*Taking out a handkerchief and wiping his face*) It's all right, Willie.

(*To* HALLY)

Ja, well, you've done it . . . Master Harold. Yes, I'll start calling you that from now on. It won't be difficult anymore. You've hurt yourself, Master Harold. I saw it coming. I warned you, but you wouldn't listen. You've just hurt yourself *bad*. And you're a coward, Master Harold. The face you should be spitting in is your father's . . . but you used mine, because you think you're safe inside your fair skin . . . and this time I don't mean just or decent. (*Pause, then moving violently towards* HALLY) Should I hit him, Willie?

WILLIE: (*Stopping* SAM) No, Boet Sam.

SAM: (*Violently*) Why not?

WILLIE: It won't help, Boet Sam.

SAM: I don't want to help! I want to hurt him.

WILLIE: You also hurt yourself.

SAM: And if he had done it to you, Willie?

WILLIE: Me? Spit at me like I was a dog? (*A thought that had not occurred to him before. He looks at* HALLY) Ja. Then I want to hit him. I want to hit him hard!

(*A dangerous few seconds as the men stand staring at the boy.* WILLIE *turns away, shaking his head*)

But maybe all I do is go cry at the back. He's little boy, Boet Sam. Little *white* boy. Long trousers now, but he's still little boy.

SAM: *(His violence ebbing away into defeat as quickly as it flooded)* You're right. So go on, then: groan again, Willie. You do it better than me. *(To* HALLY*)* You don't know all of what you've just done . . . Master Harold. It's not just that you've made me feel dirtier than I've ever been in my life . . . I mean, how do I wash off yours and your father's filth? . . . I've also failed. A long time ago I promised myself I was going to try and do something, but you've just shown me . . . Master Harold . . . that I've failed. *(Pause)* I've also got a memory of a little white boy when he was still wearing short trousers and a black man, but they're not flying a kite. It was the old Jubilee days, after dinner one night. I was in my room. You came in and just stood against the wall, looking down at the ground, and only after I'd asked you what you wanted, what was wrong, I don't know how many times, did you speak and even then so softly I almost didn't hear you. "Sam, please help me to go and fetch my Dad." Remember? He was dead drunk on the floor of the Central Hotel Bar. They'd phoned for your Mom, but you were the only one at home. And do you remember how we did it? You went in first by yourself to ask permission for me to go into the bar. Then I loaded him onto my back like a baby and carried him back to the boarding house with you following behind carrying his crutches. *(Shaking his head as he remembers)* A crowded Main Street with all the people watching a little white boy following his drunk father on a nigger's back! I felt for that little boy . . . Master Harold. I felt for him. After that we still had to clean him up, remember? He'd messed in his trousers, so we had to clean him up and get him into bed.

HALLY: *(Great pain)* I love him, Sam.

SAM: I know you do. That's why I tried to stop you from saying these things about him. It would have been so simple if you could have just despised him for being a weak man. But he's your father. You love him and you're ashamed of him. You're ashamed of so much! . . . And now that's going to include yourself. That was the promise I made to myself: to try and stop that happening. *(Pause)* After we got him to bed you came back with me to my room and sat in a corner and carried on just looking down at the ground. And for days after that! You hadn't done anything wrong, but you went around as if you owed the world an apology for being alive. I didn't like seeing that! That's not the way a boy grows up to be a man! . . . But the one person who should have been teaching you what that means was the cause of your shame. If you really want to know, that's why I made you that kite. I wanted you to look up, be proud of something, of yourself . . . *(Bitter smile at the memory)* . . . and you certainly were that when I left you with it up there on the hill. Oh, ja . . . something else! . . . If you ever do write it as a short story, there *was* a twist in our ending. I couldn't sit down there and stay with you. It was a "Whites Only" bench. You were too young, too excited to notice then. But not anymore. If you're not careful . . . Master Harold . . . you're going to be sitting up there by yourself for a long time to come, and there won't be a kite in the sky. (SAM *has got nothing more to say. He exits into the kitchen, taking off his waiter's jacket)*

WILLIE: Is bad. Is all all bad in here now.

HALLY: *(Books into his school case, raincoat on)* Willie . . . *(It is difficult to speak)* Will you lock up for me and look after the keys?

WILLIE: Okay.

(SAM returns. HALLY goes behind the counter and collects the few coins in the cash register. As he starts to leave . . .)

SAM: Don't forget the comic books.

(HALLY returns to the counter and puts them in his case. He starts to leave again)

SAM: *(To the retreating back of the boy)* Stop . . . Hally . . .

(HALLY stops, but doesn't turn to face him)

Hally . . . I've got no right to tell you what being a man means if I don't behave like one myself, and I'm not doing so well at that this afternoon. Should we try again, Hally?

HALLY: Try what?

SAM: Fly another kite, I suppose. It worked once, and this time I need it as much as you do.

HALLY: It's still raining, Sam. You can't fly kites on rainy days, remember.

SAM: So what do we do? Hope for better weather tomorrow?

HALLY: *(Helpless gesture)* I don't know. I don't know anything anymore.

SAM: You sure of that, Hally? Because it would be pretty hopeless if that was true. It would mean nothing has been learnt in here this afternoon, and there was a hell of a lot of teaching going on . . . one way or the other. But anyway, I don't believe you. I reckon there's one thing you know. You don't *have* to sit up there by yourself. You know what that bench means now, and you can leave it any time you choose. All you've got to do is stand up and walk away from it.

(HALLY leaves. WILLIE goes up quietly to SAM)

WILLIE: Is okay, Boet Sam. You see. Is . . . *(He can't find any better words)* . . . is going to be okay tomorrow. *(Changing his tone)* Hey, Boet Sam! *(He is trying hard)* You right. I think about it and you right. Tonight I find Hilda and say sorry. And make promise I won't beat her no more. You hear me, Boet Sam?

SAM: I hear you, Willie.

WILLIE: And when we practice I relax and romance with her from beginning to end. Non-stop! You watch! Two weeks' time: "First prize for promising newcomers: Mr. Willie Malopo and Miss Hilda Samuels." *(Sudden impulse)* To hell with it! I walk home. *(He goes to the jukebox, puts in a coin and selects a record. The machine comes to life in the gray twilight, blushing its way through a spectrum of soft, romantic colors)* How did you say it, Boet Sam? Let's dream. *(WILLIE sways with the music and gestures for SAM to dance)*

(Sarah Vaughan sings)

"Little man you're crying,
I know why you're blue,
Someone took your kiddy car away;
Better go to sleep now,
Little man you've had a busy day."
(etc. etc.)
   You lead. I follow.

(The men dance together)

"Johnny won your marbles,
Tell you what we'll do;
Dad will get you new ones
   right away;
Better go to sleep now,
Little man you've had a
   busy day."

WOODY ALLEN

(1935–   )

est known as a film director and actor, Woody Allen grew up in Brook-lyn and by the age of eighteen was writing gags for such famous perform-ers as Bob Hope, Guy Lombardo, and Sammy Kaye. At nineteen, he went to Hol-lywood where he was immersed in comedy writing for television as part of the NBC Writers' Program. In the early 1960s, Allen began to perform his own material in New York comedy clubs. Here he worked on comic material, timing, expression, and seeming spontaneity that was to stand him in good stead over a career of dramatic writing. Unlike the typically brash assertiveness of most 1960s comedi-ans, Allen cultivated a nervous, self-deprecating, even bookish manner of com-plaint, regret, and neurosis. His character has its roots in Jewish culture as the schlemiel: typically unprepossessing, ineffectual, spurned by family members, given to fantasy, but well-meaning.

This persona has also marked and guided his career in popular and critically acclaimed films such as Bananas *(1971),* Everything You Always Wanted to Know about Sex* (*but were afraid to ask) *(1972),* Play It Again, Sam *(1972),* Annie Hall *(1977),* Manhattan *(1979),* Hannah and Her Sisters *(1986),* Crimes and Misdemeanors *(1989),* Alice *(1990), and* Shadows and Fog *(1992).*

INTRODUCTION TO GOD

ollowing his two Broadway successes *Don't Drink the Water* (1966) and *Play It Again, Sam* (1969), Woody Allen penned his experimental one-act play *God* (1975). Subversive, surreal, chaotic in its plot and characterization, the play is a remarkable departure from Allen's more conventional comedy in the full-length Broadway plays. Here, the question of existence itself is at stake along with themes of creation, fiction, faith, meaning, and personal freedom.

The play takes place on quite different levels: self-consciously upon a New York stage as written by Woody Allen; in ancient Athens at the annual city Dionysia, a dramatic and religious festival; and within the rather inept play by Hepatitis of Rhodes entitled *The Slave,* an entry in the annual ancient theatre competition. Each level contains a frantic search for meaning in a sense of coherence and an acceptable conclusion. But, unfortunately, no script, direction, or meaningful resolution seems to exist. The actors are terribly on their own.

Confused, uncertain, ultimately impotent in the face of something they cannot control, the characters of the play blunder into real and fictional situations and characters with little sense of differentiation. They clearly do not know what to do or how to proceed, although they are aware that they must *act*. And the end of their actions is a total mystery to them. Consequently, the play *God* emerges as the main frame for the action, as arguments over meaning and direction become the script of the play. The audience is even appealed to for help, and a variety of actors "planted" in the audience take up the stage action. Thus, interruptions and false starts abound: Doris Levine, with a Brooklyn College minor in philosophy, emerges from the audience to try to resolve the question "is freedom chaos?"; playwright Woody Allen himself is consulted over the phone about the ending of the play, an ending of which he is uncertain; writer Lorenzo Miller claims to have invented the audience, members of whom protest their reality; Blanche DuBois, escaped from the conclusion of *A Streetcar Named Desire*, arrives in search of a play where God exists, only to be chased off stage by Groucho Marx; fresh from a metaphysical rebuttal by Socrates, Trichinosis claims to have invented the perfect ending for all plays in a *deus ex machina*, literally "God out of a machine."

Clearly indebted to the avant-garde procedures of absurdist theatre, *God* poses serious questions through the techniques of comedy. In this play, implausibility of situation couples with instability of character to effect a general ridiculousness. Self-conscious anachronism works against and for the characters of the play, who attempt to recover the religious certainties of ancient Greek theatre while also eating at Sardi's on Broadway or getting stabbed on public transit in New York. The ancient Greeks with their parodic names are also broad burlesque clowns with one eye ever on audience reaction; the Fates of ancient Greek tragedy are literalized as loud American tourists Bob and Wendy Fate; the Chorus provides conventional background as well as direct advice, all the while arguing with the direction of the play within entitled *The Slave*; King Oedipus himself enters delivering a roast beef sandwich; Diabetes, in the role of Phidipides, attempts to figure out how the king will react to his message of "Yes." Irony within absurd irony keeps the play from developing with any sense of coherence beyond unsustained and farcical dialogue.

Cause and effect break down. Ironic ripostes and deflations abound. Lively staging keeps the action going with surprise effects of audience interaction, unlikely characterization, the unwieldy God machine of Trichinosis, even the phone call put through to Woody Allen. But nobody — not the play's creator, not Hepatitis, the "created" creator, not Lorenzo Miller, the purported audience creator, not even a superhuman Creator — can save this play. Lack of direction is clearly this play's most significant feature. The inquiry into the existence of God becomes absurdist farce, playing on the insecurities, anxieties, and best wishes of human beings acting in an existence that is finally pointless to them. In the face of an intolerable, irresponsible freedom, the only recourse is laughter at the futile, improvisational quality of human reality. Thus the play ends as it begins, as the actor reiterates:

> The trick is to start at the ending when you write a play. Get a good strong ending and then write backwards.

The writer responds:

> *I've tried that. I got a play with no beginning.*
> ACTOR: *That's absurd.*
> WRITER: *Absurd? What's absurd?*

The play *God*, with its rollicking, manic, imaginative ironies, is itself the answer to the question at the blackout of the conclusion.

God
A Comedy in One Act

CAST
ACTOR

WRITER

GIRL

DORIS

MAID

TRICHINOSIS

PROMPTER

BURSITIS

MAN *(In Audience)*

LORENZO MILLER

WOMAN *(In Audience)*

BLANCHE DUBOIS

DIABETES

PHIDIPIDES *(A Slave, played by* DIABETES*)*

ANOTHER GREEK SLAVE

MASTER

BOB

WENDY

GUARD

WOMAN *(On Stage)*

KING

DOCTOR

WESTERN UNION DELIVERY BOY

STANLEY

ANOTHER MAN *(In Audience)*

ANOTHER WOMAN *(In Audience)*

GREEK CHORUS

GOD *(Non-speaking Role)*

GROUCHO MARX *(Non-speaking Role)*

SCENE: *Athens. Approximately 500 B.C. Two distraught Greeks in the center of enormous empty amphitheater. Sunset. One is the* ACTOR; *the other, the* WRITER. *They are both thinking and distracted. They should be played by two good, broad burlesque clowns.*

ACTOR: Nothing . . . just nothing . . .

WRITER: What?

ACTOR: Meaningless. It's empty.

WRITER: The ending.

ACTOR: Of course. What are we discussing? We're discussing the ending.

WRITER: We're always discussing the ending.

ACTOR: Because it's hopeless.

WRITER: I admit it's unsatisfying.

ACTOR: Unsatisfying!? It's not even believable. The trick is to start at the ending when you write a play. Get a good strong ending and then write backwards.

WRITER: I've tried that. I got a play with no beginning.

ACTOR: That's absurd.

WRITER: Absurd? What's absurd?

ACTOR: Every play must have a beginning, middle, and end.

WRITER: Why?

ACTOR: *(Confidently)* Because everything in nature has a beginning, middle, and end.

WRITER: What about a circle?

ACTOR: *(Thinks)* Okay . . . A circle has no beginning, middle, or end — but they're not much fun either.

WRITER: Diabetes, think of an ending. We open in three days.

ACTOR: Not me. I'm not opening in this turkey. I have a reputation as an actor, a following . . . My public expects to see me in a suitable vehicle.

WRITER: May I remind you, you're a starving, out-of-work actor whom I've generously consented to let appear in my play in an effort to assist your comeback.

ACTOR: Starving, yes . . . Out of work, perhaps . . . Hoping for a come-back, maybe — but a drunkard?

WRITER: I never said you were a drunkard.

ACTOR: Yes, but I'm also a drunkard.

WRITER: *(In a fit of sudden inspiration)* What if your character ripped a dagger from his robes and in a fit of frenzied frustration, tore away at his own eyes until he blinded himself?

ACTOR: Yeah, it's a great idea. Have you eaten anything today?

WRITER: What's wrong with it?

ACTOR: It's depressing. The audience will take one look at it and —

WRITER: I know — make that funny sound with their lips.

ACTOR: It's called hissing.

WRITER: Just once I want to win the competition! Once, before my life is over, I want my play to take first prize. And it's not the free case of ouzo I care about, it's the honor.

ACTOR: *(Suddenly inspired)* What if the king suddenly changed his mind? There's a positive idea.

WRITER: He'd never do it.

ACTOR: *(Selling him on it)* If the queen convinced him?

WRITER: She wouldn't. She's a bitch.

ACTOR: But if the Trojan Army surrendered —

WRITER: They'd fight to the death.

ACTOR: Not if Agamemnon[1] reneged on his promise?

WRITER: It's not in his nature.

ACTOR: But I could suddenly take up arms and make a stand.

WRITER: It's against your character. You're a coward — an insignificant wretched slave with the intelligence of a worm. Why do you think I cast you?

ACTOR: I've just given you six possible endings!

WRITER: Each more clumsy than the last.

ACTOR: It's the play that's clumsy.

WRITER: Human beings don't behave that way. It's not in their nature.

ACTOR: What does their nature mean? We're stuck with a hopeless ending.

WRITER: As long as man is a rational animal, as a playwright, I cannot have a character do anything on stage he wouldn't do in real life.

ACTOR: May I remind you that we don't exist in real life.

WRITER: What do you mean?

ACTOR: You are aware that we're characters in a play right now in some Broadway theater? Don't get mad at me, I didn't write it.

WRITER: We're characters in a play and soon we're going to see my play . . . which is a play within a play. And they're watching us.

ACTOR: Yes. It's highly metaphysical, isn't it?

WRITER: Not only is it metaphysical, it's stupid!

ACTOR: Would you rather be one of them?

WRITER: *(Looking at the audience)* Definitely not. Look at them.

ACTOR: Then let's get on with it!

WRITER: *(Mutters)* They paid to get in.

ACTOR: Hepatitis, I'm talking to you!

WRITER: I know, the problem is the ending.

ACTOR: It's always the ending.

WRITER: *(Suddenly to the audience)* Do you folks have any suggestions?

ACTOR: Stop talking to the audience! I'm sorry I mentioned them.

WRITER: It's bizarre, isn't it? We're two ancient Greeks in Athens and we're about to see a play I wrote and you're acting in, and they're from

---

1 *leader of the Greeks in the expedition against Troy. (See Homer's epics; also Aeschylus's* Oresteia.*)*

Queens or some terrible place like that and they're watching us in someone else's play. What if they're characters in another play? And someone's watching them? Or what if nothing exists and we're all in somebody's dream? Or, what's worse, what if only that fat guy in the third row exists?

ACTOR: That's my point. What if the universe is not rational and people are not set things? Then we could change the ending and it wouldn't have to conform to any fixed notions. You follow me?

WRITER: Of course not. *(To the audience)* You follow him? He's an actor. Eats at Sardi's.[2]

ACTOR: Play characters would have no determined traits and could choose their own characters. I wouldn't have to be the slave just because you wrote it that way. I could choose to become a hero.

WRITER: Then there's no play.

ACTOR: No play? Good, I'll be at Sardi's.

WRITER: Diabetes, what you're suggesting is chaos!

ACTOR: Is freedom chaos?

WRITER: Is freedom chaos? Hmm . . . That's a toughie. *(To the audience)* Is freedom chaos? Did anybody out there major in philosophy?

(A GIRL from the audience answers)

GIRL: I did.

WRITER: Who's that?

GIRL: Actually I majored in gym, with a philosophy minor.

WRITER: Can you come up here?

ACTOR: What the hell are you doing?

GIRL: Does it matter if it was Brooklyn College?

WRITER: Brooklyn College? No, we'll take anything.

(She's made her way up)

ACTOR: I am really pissed off!

WRITER: What's eating you?

ACTOR: We're in the middle of a play. Who is she?

WRITER: In five minutes the Athenian Drama Festival begins, and I have no ending for my play!

ACTOR: So?

WRITER: Serious philosophical questions have been raised. Do we exist? Do they exist? *(Meaning the audience)* What is the true nature of human character?

GIRL: Hi. I'm Doris Levine.

WRITER: I'm Hepatitis and this is Diabetes. We're ancient Greeks.

DORIS: I'm from Great Neck.

ACTOR: Get her off this stage!

WRITER: *(Really looking her up and down, as she's lovely)* She's very sexy.

---

2 *Broadway restaurant frequented by actors and show business people.*

ACTOR: What has that got to do with it?

DORIS: The basic philosophical question is: If a tree falls in the forest and no one is around to hear it — how do we know it makes a noise?

(Everyone looks around, puzzled over this)

ACTOR: Why do we care? We're on Forty-fifth Street.

WRITER: Will you go to bed with me?

ACTOR: Leave her alone!

DORIS: *(To ACTOR)* Mind your own business.

WRITER: *(Calling offstage)* Can we lower the curtain here? Just for five minutes . . . *(To the audience)* Sit there. It'll be a quickie.

ACTOR: This is outrageous! It's absurd! *(To DORIS)* Do you have a friend?

DORIS: Sure. *(Calling to the audience)* Diane, you want to come up here . . . I got something going with a couple of Greeks. *(No response)* She's shy.

ACTOR: Well, we have a play to do. I'm going to report this to the author.

WRITER: I *am* the author!

ACTOR: I mean the original author.

WRITER: *(Sotto voce to the ACTOR)* Diabetes, I think I can score with her.

ACTOR: What do you mean, score? You mean intercourse — with all these people watching?

WRITER: I'll lower the curtain. Some of them even do it. Not many, probably.

ACTOR: You idiot, you're fictional, she's Jewish — you know what the children will be like?

WRITER: Come on, maybe we can get her friend up here. *(The ACTOR goes to stage left to use the telephone)* Diane? This is a chance for a date with —————. *(Uses a real actor's name)* He's a big actor . . . lots of TV commercials . . .

ACTOR: *(Into the phone)* Get me an outside line.

DORIS: I don't want to cause any trouble.

WRITER: It's no trouble. It's just that we've seemed to have lost touch with reality here.

DORIS: Who knows what reality really is?

WRITER: You're so right, Doris.

DORIS: *(Philosophically)* So often people think they grasp reality when what they're really responding to is "fakeositude."

WRITER: I have an urge toward you that I'm sure is real.

DORIS: Is sex real?

WRITER: Even if it's not, it's still one of the best fake activities a person can do. *(He grabs her, she pulls back)*

DORIS: Don't. Not here.

WRITER: Why not?

DORIS: I don't know. That's my line.

WRITER: Have you ever made it with a fictional character before?

DORIS: The closest I came was an Italian.

ACTOR: *(He's on the phone. We hear the party on other end through a filter)* Hello?

PHONE: *(Maid's voice)* Hello, Mr. Allen's residence.

ACTOR: Hello, may I speak to Mr. Allen?

MAID'S VOICE: Who's calling, please?

ACTOR: One of the characters in his play.

MAID: One second. Mr. Allen, there's a fictional character on the phone.

ACTOR: *(To the others)* Now we'll see what happens with you lovebirds.

WOODY'S VOICE: Hello.

ACTOR: Mr. Allen?

WOODY: Yes?

ACTOR: This is Diabetes.

WOODY: Who?

ACTOR: Diabetes. I'm a character you created.

WOODY: Oh, yes . . . I remember, you're a badly drawn character . . . very one-dimensional.

ACTOR: Thanks.

WOODY: Hey — isn't the play on now?

ACTOR: That's what I'm calling about. We got a strange girl up on the stage and she won't get off and Hepatitis is suddenly hot for her.

WOODY: What does she look like?

ACTOR: She's pretty, but she doesn't belong.

WOODY: Blonde?

ACTOR: Brunette . . . long hair.

WOODY: Nice legs?

ACTOR: Yes.

WOODY: Good breasts?

ACTOR: Very nice.

WOODY: Keep her there, I'll be right over.

ACTOR: She's a philosophy student. But she's got no real answers . . . typical product of the Brooklyn College cafeteria.

WOODY: That's funny, I used that line in *Play It Again, Sam* to describe a girl.

ACTOR: I hope it got a better laugh there.

WOODY: Put her on.

ACTOR: On the phone?

WOODY: Sure.

ACTOR: *(To DORIS)* It's for you.

DORIS: *(Whispers)* I've seen him in the movies. Get rid of him.

ACTOR: He wrote the play.

DORIS: It's pretentious.

ACTOR: *(Into the phone)* She won't speak to you. She says your play is pretentious.

WOODY: Oh, Jesus. Okay, call me back and let me know how the play ends.

ACTOR: Right. *(He hangs up, then does a double take, realizing what the author said)*

DORIS: Can I have a part in your play?

ACTOR: I don't understand. Are you an actress or a girl playing an actress?

DORIS: I always wanted to be an actress. Mother hoped I'd become a nurse. Dad felt I should marry into society.

ACTOR: So what do you do for a living?

DORIS: I work for a company that makes deceptively shallow serving dishes for Chinese restaurants. *(A Greek enters from the wings)*

TRICHINOSIS: Diabetes, Hepatitis. It's me, Trichinosis. *(Ad-lib greetings)* I have just come from a discussion with Socrates at the Acropolis and he proved that I didn't exist, so I'm upset. Still, word has it you need an ending for your play. I think I have just the thing.

WRITER: Really?

TRICHINOSIS: Who's she?

DORIS: Doris Levine.

TRICHINOSIS: Not from Great Neck?

DORIS: Yes.

TRICHINOSIS: You know the Rappaports?

DORIS: Myron Rappaport?

TRICHINOSIS: *(Nodding)* We both worked for the Liberal party.

DORIS: What a coincidence.

TRICHINOSIS: You had an affair with Mayor Lindsay.

DORIS: I wanted to — he wouldn't.

WRITER: What's the ending?

TRICHINOSIS: You're much prettier than I imagined.

DORIS: Really?

TRICHINOSIS: I'd like to sleep with you right now.

DORIS: Tonight's my night. (TRICHINOSIS *takes her wrist passionately*) Please. I'm a virgin. Is that my line? *(The* PROMPTER *with book peeks out from the wings; is wearing a sweater)*

PROMPTER: "Please. I'm a virgin." Yes.

(Exits)

WRITER: What's the goddamn ending?

TRICHINOSIS: Huh? Oh — *(Calls off)* Fellas! *(Some Greeks wheel out an elaborate machine)*

WRITER: What the hell is that?

TRICHINOSIS: The ending for your play.

ACTOR: I don't understand.

TRICHINOSIS: This machine, which I've spent six months designing in my brother-in-law's shop, holds the answer.

WRITER: How?

TRICHINOSIS: In the final scene — when all looks black, and Diabetes the humble slave is in a position most hopeless —

ACTOR: Yes?

TRICHINOSIS: Zeus, Father of the Gods, descends dramatically from on high and brandishing his thunderbolts, brings salvation to a grateful but impotent group of mortals.

DORIS: *Deus ex machina.*[3]

TRICHINOSIS: Hey — That's a great name for this thing!

DORIS: My father works for Westinghouse.

WRITER: I still don't get it.

TRICHINOSIS: Wait'll you see this thing in action. It flies Zeus in. I'm going to make a fortune with this invention. Sophocles put a deposit on one. Euripides wants two.

WRITER: But that changes the meaning of the play.

---

3 *literally, "a god out of a machine." A stage device used especially by ancient Greek playwrights Euripides and Sophocles; or any contrived and implausible ending to a play.*

TRICHINOSIS: Don't speak till you see a demonstration. Bursitis, get into the flying harness.

BURSITIS: Me?

TRICHINOSIS: Do what I say. You won't believe this.

BURSITIS: I'm afraid of that thing.

TRICHINOSIS: He's kidding . . . Go ahead, you idiot, we're on the verge of a sale. He'll do it. Ha, ha . . .

BURSITIS: I don't like heights.

TRICHINOSIS: Get into it! Hurry up. Let's go! Get into your Zeus suit! A demonstration.

(Exiting as BURSITIS *protests)*

BURSITIS: I want to call my agent.

WRITER: But you're saying God comes in at the end and saves everything.

ACTOR: I love it! It gives the people their money's worth!

DORIS: He's right. It's like those Hollywood Bible movies.

WRITER: *(Taking center stage a little too dramatically)* But if God saves everything, man is not responsible for his actions.

ACTOR: You wonder why you're not invited to more parties . . .

DORIS: But without God, the universe is meaningless. Life is meaningless. We're meaningless. *(Deadly pause)* I have a sudden and overpowering urge to get laid.

WRITER: Now I'm not in the mood.

DORIS: Really? Would anyone in the audience care to make it with me?

ACTOR: Stop that! *(To the audience)* She's not serious, folks.

WRITER: I'm depressed.

ACTOR: What's bothering you?

WRITER: I don't know if I believe in God.

DORIS: *(To the audience)* I am serious.

ACTOR: If there's no God, who created the universe?

WRITER: I'm not sure yet.

ACTOR: Who do you mean, you're not sure yet!? When are you going to know?

DORIS: Anybody out there want to sleep with me?

MAN: *(Rising in the audience)* I'll sleep with that girl if nobody else will.

DORIS: Will you, sir?

MAN: What's wrong with everybody? A beautiful girl like that? Aren't there any red-blooded men in the audience? You're all a bunch of New York left-wing Jewish intellectual commie pinkos —

*(*LORENZO MILLER *comes out from wings. He is dressed in contemporary clothes)*

LORENZO: Sit down, will you sit down?

MAN: Okay, okay.

WRITER: Who are you?

LORENZO: Lorenzo Miller. I created this audience. I'm a writer.

WRITER: What do you mean?

LORENZO: I wrote: a large group of people from Brooklyn, Queens, Manhattan, and Long Island come to the Golden Theater and watch a play. There they are.

DORIS: *(Pointing to the audience)* You mean they're fictional too? *(LORENZO nods)* They're not free to do as they please?

LORENZO: They think they are, but they always do what's expected of them.

WOMAN: *(Suddenly a WOMAN rises in audience, quite angrily)* I'm not fictional!

LORENZO: I'm sorry, madam, but you are.

WOMAN: But I have a son at the Harvard Business School.

LORENZO: I created your son; he's fictional. Not only is he fictional, he's homosexual.

MAN: I'll show you how fictional I am. I'm leaving this theater and getting my money back. This is a stupid play. In fact, it's no play. I go to the theater, I want to see something with a story — with a beginning, middle, and end — instead of this bullshit. Good night.

(Exits up the aisle in a huff)

LORENZO: *(To the audience)* Isn't he a great character. I wrote him very angry. Later he feels guilty and commits suicide. *(Sound: gunshot)* Later!

MAN: *(Reenters with a smoking pistol)* I'm sorry, did I do it too soon?

LORENZO: Get out of here!

MAN: I'll be at Sardi's.

(Exits)

LORENZO: *(In the audience, dealing with various people of the actual audience)* What's your name, sir? Uh-huh. *(Ad-lib section, depending on what audience says)* Where are you from? Isn't he cute? Great character. Must remind them to dress him differently. Later this woman leaves her husband for this guy. Hard to believe, I know. Oh — look at this guy. Later he rapes that lady.

WRITER: It's terrible being fictional. We're all so limited.

LORENZO: Only by the limits of the playwright. Unfortunately you happen to have been written by Woody Allen. Think if you were written by Shakespeare.

WRITER: I don't accept it. I'm a free man and I don't need God flying in to save my play. I'm a good writer.

DORIS: You want to win the Athenian Drama Festival, don't you?

WRITER: *(Suddenly dramatic)* Yes. I want to be immortal. I don't want to just die and be forgotten. I want my works to live on long after my physical body has passed away. I want future generations to know I existed! Please don't let me be a meaningless dot, drifting through eternity. I thank you, ladies and gentlemen. I would like to accept this Tony Award and thank David Merrick[4] . . .

DORIS: I don't care what anybody says, I'm real.

LORENZO: Not really.

DORIS: I think, therefore I am. Or better yet, I *feel* — I have an orgasm.

LORENZO: You do?

DORIS: All the time.

LORENZO: Really?

DORIS: Very frequently.

LORENZO: Yes?

DORIS: Most of the time I do, yes.

LORENZO: Yes?

DORIS: At least half the time.

LORENZO: No.

DORIS: I do! With certain men . . .

LORENZO: Hard to believe.

DORIS: Not necessarily through intercourse. Usually it's oral —

LORENZO: Uh-huh.

DORIS: Of course I fake it too. I don't want to insult anybody.

LORENZO: Have you ever had an orgasm?

DORIS: Not really. No.

LORENZO: Because none of us are real.

WRITER: But if we're not real, we can't die.

LORENZO: No. Not unless the playwright decides to kill us.

WRITER: Why would he do something like that?

(From the wings, BLANCHE DUBOIS *enters)*

BLANCHE: Because, sugar, it satisfies something called their — aesthetic sensibility.

WRITER: *(All turn to look at her)* Who are you?

BLANCHE: Blanche. Blanche DuBois. It means "white woods." Don't get up, please — I was just passing through.

DORIS: What are you doing here?

BLANCHE: Seeking refuge. Yes — in this old theater . . . I couldn't help over-hearing your conversation. Could I get a coke with a little bourbon in it?

ACTOR: *(Appears. We didn't realize he'd slipped away)* Is a Seven-Up okay?

WRITER: Where the hell were you?

ACTOR: I went to the bathroom.

WRITER: In the middle of the play?

ACTOR: What play? *(To* BLANCHE*)* Will you explain to him we're all limited.

BLANCHE: I'm afraid it's all too true. Too true and too ghastly. That's why I ran out of my play. Escaped. Oh, not that Mr. Tennessee Williams is not a very great writer, but honey — he dropped me in the center of a nightmare. The last thing I remember, I was being taken out by two

---

4 *producer of Allen's two Broadway hits* Don't Drink the Water *(1966) and* Play It Again, Sam *(1969).*

strangers, one who held a strait jacket. Once outside the Kowalski residence, I broke free and ran. I've got to get into another play, a play where God exists . . . somewhere where I can rest at last. That's why you must put me in your play and allow Zeus, young and handsome Zeus to triumph with his thunderbolt.

WRITER: You went to the bathroom?

TRICHINOSIS: *(Enters)* Ready for the demonstration.

BLANCHE: A demonstration. How wonderful.

TRICHINOSIS: *(Calling offstage)* Ready out there? Okay. It's the end of the play. Everything looks hopeless for the slave. All other means desert him. He prays. Go ahead.

ACTOR: Oh, Zeus. Great god. We are confused and helpless mortals. Please be merciful and change our lives. *(Nothing happens)* Er . . . great Zeus . . .

TRICHINOSIS: Let's go, fellas! For Christ's sake.

ACTOR: Oh, great God.

(Suddenly there is thunder and fabulous lightning. The effect is wonderful: ZEUS *descends, hurling thunderbolts majestically)*

BURSITIS: *(As* ZEUS*)* I am Zeus, God of Gods! Worker of miracles! Creator of the universe! I bring salvation to all!

DORIS: Wait'll Westinghouse sees this!

TRICHINOSIS: Well, Hepatitis, what do you think?

WRITER: I love it! It's better than I expected. It's dramatic, it's flamboyant. I'm going to win the festival! I'm a winner. It's so religious. Look, I got chills! Doris!

(He grabs her)

DORIS: Not now.

(There is a general exit, a light change . . .)

WRITER: I must do some immediate rewrites.

TRICHINOSIS: I'll rent you my God machine for twenty-six fifty an hour.

WRITER: *(To* LORENZO*)* Can you introduce my play?

LORENZO: Sure, go ahead. *(They all exit.* LORENZO *stays behind and faces audience. As he speaks, a Greek* CHORUS[5] *enters and sits in the background of the amphitheater. White-robed, naturally)* Good evening and welcome to the Athenian Drama Festival. *(Sound: cheering)* We got a great show for you tonight. A new play by Hepatitis of Rhodes, entitled, "The Slave." *(Sound: cheers)* Starring Diabetes as the slave, with Bursitis as Zeus, Blanche DuBois, and Doris Levine from Great Neck. *(Cheers)* The show is brought to you by Gregory Londos' Lamb Restaurant, just opposite the Parthenon. Don't be a Medusa with snakes in *your* hair when you're looking for a place to dine out. Try Gregory Londos' Lamb Restaurant. Remember, Homer liked it — and he was blind.

---

5 in Greek drama, a group that mediates and comments upon the main action of the play.

(He exits. DIABETES *plays the slave named* PHIDIPIDES *and right now, he drifts on with another* GREEK SLAVE *as the* CHORUS *takes over)*

CHORUS: Gather round, ye Greeks, and heed the story of Phidipides — one so wise, so passionate, so steeped in the glories of Greece.

DIABETES: My point is, what are we going to do with such a big horse?

FRIEND: But they want to give it to us for nothing.

DIABETES: So what? Who needs it? It's a big wooden horse . . . What the hell are we going to do with it? It's not even a pretty horse. Mark my words, Cratinus — as a Greek statesman, I would never trust the Trojans. You notice they never take a day off?

FRIEND: Did you hear about Cyclops? He got a middle-eye infection.

VOICE OFF: Phidipides! Where is that slave?

DIABETES: Coming, Master!

MASTER: *(Enters)* Phidipides — there you are. There's work to be done. The grapes need picking, my chariot must be repaired, we need water from the well — and you're out schmoozing.

DIABETES: I wasn't schmoozing, Master, I was discussing politics.

MASTER: A slave discussing politics! Ha, ha!

CHORUS: Ha, ha . . . That's rich.

DIABETES: I'm sorry, Master.

MASTER: You and the new Hebrew slave clean the house. I'm expecting guests. Then get on with all the other tasks.

DIABETES: The new Hebrew?

MASTER: Doris Levine.

DORIS: You called?

MASTER: Clean up. Let's go. Hurry on.

CHORUS: Poor Phidipides. A slave. And like all slaves, he longed for one thing.

DIABETES: To be taller.

CHORUS: To be free.

DIABETES: I don't want to be free.

CHORUS: No?

DIABETES: I like it this way. I know what's expected of me. I'm taken care of. I don't have to make any choices. I was born a slave and I'll die a slave. I have no anxiety.

CHORUS: Boo . . . Boo . . .

DIABETES: Ah, what do you know, chorus boys.

(He kisses DORIS, *she pulls away)*

DORIS: Don't.

DIABETES: Why not? Doris, you know my heart is heavy with love — or as you Hebrews are fond of saying, I have a thing for you.

DORIS: It can't work.

DIABETES: Why not?

DORIS: Because you like being a slave and I hate it. I want my freedom. I want to travel and write books, live in Paris, maybe start a woman's magazine.

DIABETES: What's the big deal about freedom? It's dangerous. To know one's place is safe. Don't you see, Doris, governments change hands every week, political leaders murder one another, cities are sacked, people are tortured. If there's a war, who do you think gets killed? The free people. But we're safe because no matter who's in power, they all need someone to do the heavy cleaning.

(He grabs her)

DORIS: Don't. While I am still a slave I can never enjoy sex.

DIABETES: Would you be willing to fake it?

DORIS: Forget it.

CHORUS: And then one day the fates lent a hand. *(The* FATES *enter, a couple dressed like American tourists, wearing jazzy Hawaiian shirts;* BOB *has a camera around his neck)*

BOB: Hi, we're the Fates, Bob and Wendy Fate. We need someone to take an urgent message to the king.

DIABETES: The king?

BOB: You would be doing mankind a great service.

DIABETES: I would?

WENDY: Yes, but it's a dangerous mission, and even though you are a slave, you may say no.

DIABETES: No.

BOB: But it will give you a chance to see the palace in all its glory.

WENDY: And the reward is your freedom.

DIABETES: My freedom? Yes, well, I'd love to help you, but I have a roast in the stove.

DORIS: Let me do it.

BOB: It's too dangerous for a woman.

DIABETES: She's a very fast runner.

DORIS: Phidipides, how can you refuse?

DIABETES: When you're a coward, certain things come easy.

WENDY: We beg of you — please —

BOB: The fate of mankind hangs in the balance.

WENDY: We'll raise the reward. Freedom for you and any person of your choice.

BOB: Plus a sixteen-piece starter set of silverware.

DORIS: Phidipides, here's our chance.

CHORUS: Go ahead, you jerk.

DIABETES: A dangerous mission followed by personal freedom? I'm getting nauseous.

WENDY: *(Hands him an envelope)* Take this message to the king.

DIABETES: Why can't you take it?

BOB: We're leaving for New York in a few hours.

DORIS: Phidipides, you say you love me —

DIABETES: I do.

CHORUS: Let's go, Phidipides, the play is bogging down.

DIABETES: Decisions, decisions . . . *(The phone rings, and he answers it)* Hello?

WOODY'S VOICE: Will you take the goddamn message to the king. We'd all like to get the hell out of here.

DIABETES: *(Hangs up)* I'll do it. But only because Woody asked me to.

CHORUS: *(Sings)* Poor Professor Higgins —

DIABETES: That's the wrong show, you idiots!

DORIS: Good luck, Phidipides.

WENDY: You're really going to need it.

DIABETES: What do you mean?

WENDY: Bob here is really a practical joker.

DORIS: After we're free we can go to bed, and maybe for once I'll enjoy it.

HEPATITIS: *(Pops on stage)* Sometimes a little grass before you make it —

ACTOR: You're the writer!

HEPATITIS: I couldn't resist!

(Exit)

DORIS: Go!

DIABETES: I'm going!

CHORUS: And so Phidipides set out on his journey, bearing an important message for King Oedipus.[6]

DIABETES: King Oedipus?

CHORUS: Yes.

DIABETES: I hear he lives with his mother.

(Effects: Wind and lightning as SLAVE trudges on)

CHORUS: Over deep mountains, through high valleys.

DIABETES: High mountains and deep valleys. Where did we get this chorus?

CHORUS: At all times at the mercy of the Furies.[7]

DIABETES: The Furies are having dinner with the Fates. They went to Chinatown. The Hong Fat Noodle Company.

HEPATITIS: *(Enters)* Sam Wo's is better.

DIABETES: There's always a line at Sam Wo's.

CHORUS: Not if you ask for Lee. He'll seat you, but you have to tip him.

(HEPATITIS exits)

DIABETES: *(Proudly)* Yesterday I was a lousy slave, never having ventured beyond my master's property. Today I carry a message to the king, the king himself. I see the world. Soon I'll be a free man. Suddenly human possibilities are opening up to me. And because of it — I have an uncontrollable urge to throw up. Oh, well . . .

(Wind)

---

6 in Greek legend, a hero who unwittingly killed his father and married his mother (see Sophocles's play Oedipus the King).

7 in Greek myth, spirits of rightful punishment; the Fates presided dispassionately over the hard realities of human life.

CHORUS: Days turn into weeks, weeks into months. Still Phidipides struggles on.
DIABETES: Can you turn off the goddamn wind machine?
CHORUS: Poor Phidipides, mortal man.
DIABETES: I'm tired, I'm weary, I'm sick. I can't go on. My hand is shak-
ing . . . (The CHORUS begins humming a slow version of "Dixie") All around me
men dying, war and misery, brother against brother; the South, rich in
tradition; the North, mostly industrial. President Lincoln, sending the
Union Army to destroy the plantation. The Old Homestead. Cotton —
comin' down the river . . . (HEPATITIS enters and stares at him) Lawsy, lawsy,
Miss Eva — Ah can't cross the ice. It's General Beauregard and Robert
E. Lee . . . Ah — (Notices HEPATITIS staring at him) I — I . . . I got carried
away.

(HEPATITIS grabs him around the neck and pulls him to the side)

HEPATITIS: C'mere! What the hell are you doing!?
DIABETES: Where's the palace? I'm walking around for days! What kind of
play is this!? Where the hell is the goddamn palace? In Bensonhurst?
HEPATITIS: You're at the palace if you'd stop ruining my play! Guard! Come
on now, shape up.

(A powerful GUARD enters)

GUARD: Who are you?
DIABETES: Phidipides.
GUARD: What brings you to the palace?
DIABETES: The palace? I'm here?
GUARD: Yes. This is the royal palace. The most beautiful structure in all of
Greece, marble, majestic, and completely rent-controlled.
DIABETES: I bear a message for the king.
GUARD: Oh, yes. He is expecting you.
DIABETES: My throat is parched and I have not eaten in days.
GUARD: I will summon the king.
DIABETES: What about a roast-beef sandwich?
GUARD: I will get the king and a roast-beef sandwich. How do you want
that?
DIABETES: Medium.
GUARD: (Takes out a pad and writes) One medium. You get a vegetable with that.
DIABETES: What do you have?
GUARD: Let's see, today . . . carrots or baked potato.
DIABETES: I'll have the baked potato.
GUARD: Coffee?
DIABETES: Please. And a toasted bow tie — if you have one — and the king.
GUARD: Right. (As he exits) Let me have an RB to go with a regular coffee.

(The FATES cross, taking pictures)

BOB: How do you like the palace?
DIABETES: I love it.
BOB: *(Handing his wife the camera)* Take one of us together.

(As she does)

DIABETES: I thought you two were going back to New York.
WENDY: You know how fate is.
BOB: Unreliable. Take it easy.
DIABETES: *(Leans in to smell the flower in* BOB's *lapel)* That's a pretty flower. *(Gets an eyeful of water as* FATES *laugh)*
BOB: I'm sorry, I couldn't resist. *(Offers his hand.* DIABETES *shakes it. Gets a shock from a joy buzzer)*
DIABETES: Ahhhh!

(FATES exit laughing)

WENDY: He loves to play tricks on people.
DIABETES: *(To* CHORUS*)* You knew he was out to get me.
CHORUS: He's a scream.
DIABETES: Why didn't you warn me?
CHORUS: We don't like to get involved.
DIABETES: You don't like to get involved? You know, a woman was stabbed to death on the BMT while sixteen people looked on and didn't help.
CHORUS: We read it in the *Daily News*, and it was the IRT.
DIABETES: If one person had the guts to help her, maybe she'd be here today.
WOMAN: *(Enters with knife in her chest)* I am here.
DIABETES: I had to open my mouth.
WOMAN: A woman works her whole life on DeKalb Ave. I'm reading the *Post*, six hooligans — dope addicts — grab me and throw me down.
CHORUS: There weren't six, there were three.
WOMAN: Three, six — they had a knife, they wanted my money.
DIABETES: You should have given it to them.
WOMAN: I did. They still stabbed me.
CHORUS: That's New York. You give 'em the money and they still stab you.
DIABETES: New York? It's everywhere. I was walking with Socrates in downtown Athens, and two youths from Sparta jump out from behind the Acropolis and want all our money.
WOMAN: What happened?
DIABETES: Socrates proved to them using simple logic that evil was merely ignorance of the truth.
WOMAN: And?
DIABETES: And they broke his nose.
WOMAN: I just hope your message for the king is good news.
DIABETES: I hope so, for his sake.
WOMAN: For your sake.
DIABETES: Right and — what do you mean, for my sake?

CHORUS: *(Derisively)* Ha, ha, ha!

(The light becomes more ominous)

DIABETES: The light is changing . . . What is that? What happens if it's bad news?

WOMAN: In ancient times, when a messenger brought a message to the king, if the news was good, the messenger received a reward.

CHORUS: Free passes to the Loew's Eighty-sixth Street.

WOMAN: But if the news was bad . . .

DIABETES: Don't tell me.

WOMAN: The king would have the messenger put to death.

DIABETES: Are we in ancient times?

WOMAN: Can't you tell by what you're wearing?

DIABETES: I see what you mean. Hepatitis!

WOMAN: Sometimes the messenger would have his head cut off . . . if the king was in a forgiving mood.

DIABETES: A forgiving mood, he cuts your head off?

CHORUS: But if the news is really bad —

WOMAN: Then the messenger is roasted to death —

CHORUS: Over a slow fire.

DIABETES: It's been so long since I've been roasted over a slow fire, I can't remember if I like it or not.

CHORUS: Take our word for it — you won't like it.

DIABETES: Where's Doris Levine? If I get my hands on that Hebrew slave from Great Neck . . .

WOMAN: She can't help you, she's miles away.

DIABETES: Doris! Where the hell are you?

DORIS: *(In the audience)* What do you want?

DIABETES: What are you doing there?

DORIS: I got bored with the play.

DIABETES: What do you mean, you got bored? Get up here! I'm up to my ass in trouble because of you!

DORIS: *(Coming up)* I'm sorry, Phidipides, how did I know what happened in ancient history? I studied philosophy.

DIABETES: If the news is bad, I die.

DORIS: I heard her.

DIABETES: Is this your idea of freedom?

DORIS: Win a couple, lose a couple.

DIABETES: Win a couple, lose a couple? That's what they teach you at Brooklyn College?

DORIS: Hey, man, get off my back.

DIABETES: If the news is bad I'm finished. Wait a minute! The news! The message. I got it right here! *(Fumbles, takes a message from an envelope. Reads)* For Best Supporting Actor, the winner is ————. *(Use the name of the actor playing* HEPATITIS*)*

HEPATITIS: *(Pops on)* I want to accept this Tony Award and thank David Merrick —

ACTOR: Get off, I read the wrong message! *(Pulls out the real one)*
WOMAN: Hurry, the king's coming.
DIABETES: See if he has my sandwich.
DORIS: Hurry, Phidipides!
DIABETES: *(Reads)* The message is one word.
DORIS: Yes?
DIABETES: How'd you know?
DORIS: Know what?
DIABETES: What the message is, it's "yes."
CHORUS: Is that good or bad?
DIABETES: Yes? Yes is affirmative? No? Isn't it? *(Testing it) Yes!*
DORIS: What if the question is, Does the queen have the clap?[8]
DIABETES: I see your point.
CHORUS: His majesty, the king!

(Fanfare, big entrance of KING)

DIABETES: Sire, does the queen have the clap?
KING: Who ordered this roast beef?
DIABETES: I did, sire. Is that carrots? Because I asked for a baked potato.
KING: We're out of baked potatoes.
DIABETES: Then take it back. I'll go across the street.
CHORUS: The message. *(DIABETES keeps shhing them)* The message, he has the message.
KING: Humble slave, do you have a message for me?
DIABETES: Humble king, er . . . yes, as a matter of fact . . .
KING: Good.
DIABETES: Can you tell me the question?
KING: First the message.
DIABETES: No, you first.
KING: No, you.
DIABETES: No, you.
KING: No, you.
CHORUS: Make Phidipides go first.
KING: Him?
CHORUS: Yes.
KING: How can I?
CHORUS: Schmuck, you're the king.
KING: Of course, I'm the king. What is the message?

(The GUARD draws a sword)

DIABETES: The message is . . . ye-no — *(Trying to get an idea before spilling it)* no-yeah — maybe — maybe —
CHORUS: He's lying.
KING: The message, slave.

(The GUARD puts a sword to DIABETES' throat)

---

8 *venereal disease.*

DIABETES: It is one word, sire.

KING: One word?

DIABETES: Amazing, isn't it, because for the same money he's allowed fourteen words.

KING: A one-word answer to my question of questions. Is there a god?

DIABETES: That's the question?

KING: That — is the only question.

DIABETES: *(Looks at* DORIS, *relieved)* Then I'm proud to give you the message. The word is yes.

KING: Yes?

DIABETES: Yes.

CHORUS: Yes.

DORIS: Yes.

DIABETES: Your turn.

WOMAN: *(Lisp)* Yeth.

(DIABETES *gives her an annoyed look)*

DORIS: Isn't that fabulous!

DIABETES: I know what you're thinking, a little reward for your faithful messenger — but our freedom is more than enough — on the other hand, if you insist on showing your appreciation, I think diamonds are always in good taste.

KING: *(Gravely)* If there is a god, then man is not responsible[9] and I will surely be judged for my sins.

DIABETES: Pardon me?

KING: Judged for my sins, my crimes. Very horrible crimes, I am doomed. This message you bring me dooms me for eternity.

DIABETES: Did I say yes? I meant no.

GUARD: *(Seizes the envelope and reads the message)* The message is yes, sire.

KING: This is the worst possible news.

DIABETES: *(Dropping to his knees)* Sire, it's not my fault. I'm a lowly messenger, I don't create the message. I merely transmit it. It's like her majesty's clap.

KING: You will be torn apart by wild horses.

DIABETES: I knew you'd understand.

DORIS: But he's only the messenger. You can't have him torn apart by wild horses. You usually roast them over a slow fire.

KING: Too good for this scum!

DIABETES: When the weatherman predicts rain, do you kill the weatherman?

KING: Yes.

DIABETES: I see. Well. I'm dealing with a schizophrenic.

KING: Seize him.

(The GUARD *does)*

DIABETES: Wait, sire. A word in my defense.

KING: Yes?

---

9 *i.e. not in charge, not in control; not the final authority.*

DIABETES: This is only a play.

KING: That's what they all say. Give me your sword. I want the pleasure of this kill myself.

DORIS: No, no — oh, why did I get us into this?

CHORUS: Don't worry, you're young, you'll find somebody else.

DORIS: That's true.

KING: *(Raises the sword)* Die!

DIABETES: Oh, Zeus — God of Gods, come forward with your thunderbolt and save me — *(All look up; nothing happens, awkward moment)* Oh, Zeus . . . Oh, Zeus!!!

KING: And now — die!

DIABETES: Oh, Zeus — where the hell is Zeus!

HEPATITIS: *(He enters and looks up)* For Christ's sake, let's go with the machine! Lower him!

TRICHINOSIS: *(Enters from the other side)* It's stuck!

DIABETES: *(Giving the cue again)* Oh, great Zeus!

CHORUS: All men come to the same end.

WOMAN: I'm not gonna stand here and let him get stabbed like I was on the BMT!

KING: Grab her.

(The GUARD grabs her and stabs her)

WOMAN: That's twice this week! Son of a bitch.

DIABETES: Oh, great Zeus! God, help me!

(Effect. Lightning — ZEUS is lowered very clumsily and he jerks around until we see the lowering wire has strangled him. Everyone looks on, stunned)

TRICHINOSIS: Something's wrong with the machine! It's out of joint.

CHORUS: At last, the entrance of God!

(But he's definitely dead)

DIABETES: God . . . God? God? God, are you okay? Is there a doctor in the house?

DOCTOR: *(In the audience)* I'm a doctor.

TRICHINOSIS: The machine got screwed up.

HEPATITIS: Psst. Get off. You're ruining the play.

DIABETES: God is dead.

DOCTOR: Is he covered by anything?

HEPATITIS: Ad-lib.

DIABETES: What?

HEPATITIS: Ad-lib the ending.

TRICHINOSIS: Somebody pulled the wrong lever.

DORIS: His neck is broken.

KING: *(Trying to continue the play)* Er . . . well, messenger . . . see what you've done. *(Brandishes the sword. DIABETES grabs it)*

DIABETES: *(Grabbing sword)* I'll take that.
KING: What the hell are you doing?
DIABETES: Kill me, eh? Doris, get over here.
KING: Phidipides, what are you doing?
GUARD: Hepatitis, he's ruining the end.
CHORUS: What're you doing, Phidipides? The king should kill *you*.
DIABETES: Says who? Where is it written? No — I choose to kill the king.

(Stabs the KING, but the sword is fake)

KING: Leave me alone . . . He's crazy . . . Stop! . . . That tickles.
DOCTOR: *(Taking the pulse of the body of GOD)* He's definitely dead. We better
    move him.
CHORUS: We don't want to get involved.

(THEY start exiting, carrying GOD off)

DIABETES: The slave decides to be a hero!

(Stabs the GUARD; the sword is still a fake)

GUARD: What the hell are you doing?
DORIS: I love you, Phidipides. *(He kisses her)* Please, I'm not in the mood.
HEPATITIS: My play . . . my play! *(To CHORUS)* Where are you going?
KING: I'm going to call my agent at the William Morris Agency. Sol Mishkin.
    He'll know what to do.
HEPATITIS: This is a very serious play with a message! If it falls apart, they'll
    never get the message.
WOMAN: The theater is for entertainment. There's an old saying, if you
    want to send a message, call Western Union.
WESTERN UNION DELIVERY BOY: *(Enters on a bicycle)* I have a telegram for the
    audience. It's the author's message.
DIABETES: Who's he?
DELIVERY BOY: *(Dismounts, sings)* Happy birthday to you, happy birthday to
    you —
HEPATITIS: It's the wrong message!
DELIVERY BOY: *(Reads the wire)* I'm sorry, here it is. God is dead. Stop. You're
    on your own. And it's signed — The Moscowitz Billiard Ball Company?
DIABETES: Of course anything is possible. I'm the hero now.
DORIS: And I just know I'm going to have an orgasm. I know it.
DELIVERY BOY: *(Still reads)* Doris Levine can definitely have an orgasm. Stop. If
    she wants to. Stop.

(He grabs her)

DORIS: Stop.

(In the background a brutish man enters)

STANLEY: Stella! Stella!
HEPATITIS: There is no more reality! Absolutely none.

(GROUCHO MARX runs across stage chasing BLANCHE. A MAN in audience rises)

MAN: If anything's possible, I'm not going home to Forest Hills! I'm tired of working on Wall Street. I'm sick of the Long Island Expressway!

(Grabs a WOMAN in the audience. Rips her blouse off, chases her up the aisle. This could also be an usherette)

HEPATITIS: My play . . . *(The characters have left the stage, leaving the two original characters, the author and actor, HEPATITIS and DIABETES)* My play . . .
DIABETES: It was a good play. All it needed was an ending.
HEPATITIS: But what did it mean?
DIABETES: Nothing . . . just nothing . . .
HEPATITIS: What?
DIABETES: Meaningless. It's empty.
HEPATITIS: The ending.
DIABETES: Of course. What are we discussing? We're discussing the ending.
HEPATITIS: We're always discussing the ending.
DIABETES: Because it's hopeless.
HEPATITIS: I admit it's unsatisfying.
DIABETES: Unsatisfying!? It's not even believable. *(The lights start dimming)* The trick is to start at the ending when you write a play. Get a good, strong ending, and then write backwards.
HEPATITIS: I've tried that. I got a play with no beginning.
DIABETES: That's absurd.
HEPATITIS: Absurd? What's absurd?

BLACKOUT

SHARON POLLOCK

(1936–   )

A native of Fredericton, Pollock spent some of her youth at boarding school in Quebec's Eastern Townships and later attended the University of New Brunswick. Her father, a doctor, and community reformer, inspired one of Pollock's later plays, Doc *(1984)*. *Pollock eloped at age eighteen, two years after her mother, an alcoholic, committed suicide, but left the marriage ten years later. While living once again in her father's house, now with five children, she began acting in professional theatre. She had a sixth child, Amanda (who played Katie in the premiere of* Doc*). In 1966 she won a Dominion Drama Festival best acting award and moved to Calgary.*

In the 1970s, now living in Vancouver and acting in radio plays, Pollock began writing. Her first stage play, A Compulsory Option, *won the Alberta Culture Playwriting Competition in 1971. Pollock's first published play,* Walsh *(1973), is an historical account of Chief Sitting Bull's request for sanctuary in Canada after the Sioux victory at Little Big Horn. Her next three plays,* Out Goes You, *a political satire;* The Komagata Maru Incident *(1978), about a boatload of Sikh immigrants who were refused entry at Vancouver in 1914; and* My Name is Lisbeth, *a precursor of* Blood Relations, *were all produced in the Vancouver area. Pollock spent a year teaching playwriting at the University of Alberta before returning to Calgary in 1977. She was also director of the Playwrights' Colony at the Banff Centre.*

Three important plays that indicate a shift in Pollock's work from public to family politics, One Tiger to a Hill, Generations, *and* Blood Relations, *are published in* Blood Relations and Other Plays *(1981).* Whiskey Six Cadenza *was published in 1987. Although Pollock's plays are often based on historical incidents, they are not documentaries. Pollock explores characters by fictionalizing and inventing, and alters historical facts for dramatic purposes. Because she interprets historical incidents, however, she can be counted as one of Canada's dramatic mythmakers.*

Apart from writing (she also has numerous children's, radio, and television plays to her credit), Pollock gets involved with the process of staging plays in many ways: as director, playwright-in-residence, actor, and most recently as dramaturge for Alberta's Culture 1991 Mentorship Program. In the mid-1980s she was artistic director of Theatre Calgary and later Theatre New Brunswick, but quit both because she was unsatisfied with the administrative demands of the job. She has also been associate director of the Stratford Festival. Pollock, the winner of two Governor General's awards, one for Blood Relations *in 1982 and another for* Doc *in 1986, has said that "the most important thing for a playwright is to get inside the theatre, realize all the components. The spoken or written word is only one [component] and sometimes the least important."[1] Pollock is not afraid of new*

---

1 Suzanne Zwarun, "The Cats Came Back," Western Living *(September 1990): 37.*

challenges: In 1988 she performed in her one-woman show, Getting It
Straight, *about the mental wanderings of a schizophrenic; at the 1990 Edmonton
Fringe she played a bag lady in a one-act by her son, K.C. Campbell. She contin-
ues to reside in Calgary.*

INTRODUCTION TO *BLOOD RELATIONS*

*B*lood Relations is based on the true story of Lizzie Borden, who was
accused and acquitted of the 1892 axe murders of her father and
stepmother in a small town in Massachusetts. At that time, only two women
had ever been hanged for murder in the history of Massachusetts criminal
law. Pollock reopens the case in *Blood Relations* to find out what might have
motivated Lizzie Borden — 34 years old, trapped in her father's house with
no income or hope of a job, uninterested in marriage, antagonistic to a
stepmother who is eager to ensure that Lizzie is disinherited — to commit
the grisly double murder.

In structuring the play, Pollock takes liberties with the story, compressing
the killing of Lizzie's birds to the day before the murders, when Lizzie's
father had actually killed the birds some four months before. Pollock
introduces the character of the Actress, unnamed and anonymous, who visits
Lizzie ten years after the trial to re-create the scene of the murders. The
play becomes a metadrama, showing a play in progress, as the Actress takes
on Lizzie's part as the oppressed daughter being cheated out of her inheritance
by her stepmother's brother. The play-within-a-play unfolds seamlessly
despite occasional time shifts to the courtroom drama of Lizzie's trial. Lizzie
takes on the role of the only possible witness to the murders, Bridget, the
maid of the household. In doing so, the Lizzie who is accused of the murders
is an outsider, yet she also directs the action and the Actress who plays
her.

Pollock removes all the violence from the stage, preferring to concentrate
on the psychological motives and motifs presented by the Lizzie Borden
case. The bird-killing, which is also done with an axe, is created by an image
of the axe smashing into a table. Bird images are central to the play, signifying
female entrapment and beauty. Lizzie is so stifled by her society and her
predicament that she talks of running away with the town doctor, who
is married, or of death as possible escapes. Lizzie knows there is another
world beyond her own, having been away to school and to Europe. She
also knows how to play games, dance, and use her wit to get what she
wants. But the bottom line is that she cannot leave her father's house without
his money; he will not allow her to get a job, and she will not marry to
please him.

Pollock's presentation of Lizzie is sympathetic, but the question "Did
she or didn't she?" runs throughout the play. At the end, the clever structure
of the play allows an answer that is entirely satisfying to the metadrama.

Blood Relations

CHARACTERS

MISS LIZZIE, *who will play* BRIDGET, *the Irish maid.*

THE ACTRESS, *who will play* LIZZIE BORDEN.

HARRY, *Mrs. Borden's brother.*

EMMA, *Lizzie's older sister.*

ANDREW, *Lizzie's father.*

ABIGAIL, *Lizzie's step-mother.*

DR PATRICK, *the Irish doctor; sometimes* THE DEFENSE.

SETTING

The time proper is late Sunday afternoon and evening, late fall, in Fall River, 1902; the year of the "dream thesis", if one might call it that, is 1892.

The playing areas include (a) within the Borden house: the dining room from which there is an exit to the kitchen; the parlour; a flight of stairs leading to the second floor; and (b) in the Borden yard: the walk outside the house; the area in which the birds are kept.

PRODUCTION NOTE: *Action must be free-flowing. There can be no division of the script into scenes by blackout, movement of furniture, or sets. There may be freezes of some characters while other scenes are being played. There is no necessity to "get people off" and "on" again for, with the exception of The Actress and Miss Lizzie (and Emma in the final scene), all characters are imaginary, and all action in reality would be taking place between Miss Lizzie and The Actress in the dining room and parlour of her home.*

The Defense may actually be seen, may be a shadow, or a figure behind a scrim.

While Miss Lizzie exits and enters with her Bridget business, she is a presence, often observing unobtrusively when as Bridget she takes no part in the action.

ACT ONE

(Lights up on the figure of a woman standing centre stage. It is a somewhat formal pose. A pause. She speaks:)

"Since what I am about to say must be but that
Which contradicts my accusation, and
The testimony on my part no other
But what comes from myself, it shall scarce boot me
To say "Not Guilty".
But, if Powers Divine
Behold our human action as they do,
I doubt not than but innocence shall make
False accusation blush and tyranny
Tremble at . . . at . . . "

(She wriggles the fingers of an outstretched hand searching for the word.)

"Aaaat" . . . Bollocks!!

(She raises her script, takes a bite of chocolate.)

"Tremble at Patience", patience patience! . . . [1]

(MISS LIZZIE enters from the kitchen with tea service. THE ACTRESS' attention drifts to MISS LIZZIE. THE ACTRESS watches MISS LIZZIE sit in the parlour and proceed to pour two cups of tea. THE ACTRESS sucks her teeth a bit to clear the chocolate as she speaks:)

THE ACTRESS: Which . . . is proper, Lizzie?
MISS LIZZIE: Proper?
THE ACTRESS: To pour first the cream, and add the tea — or first tea and add cream. One is proper. Is the way you do the proper way, the way it's done in circles where it counts?
MISS LIZZIE: Sugar?
THE ACTRESS: Well, is it?
MISS LIZZIE: I don't know, sugar?
THE ACTRESS: Mmmn. *(MISS LIZZIE adds sugar.)* I suppose if we had Mrs. Beeton's *Book of Etiquette*, we could look it up.
MISS LIZZIE: I do have it, shall I get it?
THE ACTRESS: No. . . . You could ask your sister, she might know.
MISS LIZZIE: Do you want this tea or not?
THE ACTRESS: I hate tea.
MISS LIZZIE: You drink it every Sunday.
THE ACTRESS: I drink it because you like to serve it.
MISS LIZZIE: Pppu.
THE ACTRESS: It's true. You've no idea how I suffer from this toast and tea ritual. I really do. The tea upsets my stomach and the toast makes me fat because I eat so much of it.
MISS LIZZIE: Practice some restraint then.
THE ACTRESS: Mmmm . . . Why don't we ask your sister which is proper?
MISS LIZZIE: You ask her.

---

1 *the Actress is speaking as Hermione in Shakespeare's* A Winter's Tale *(3.2.21–31)*

THE ACTRESS: How can I? She doesn't speak to me. I don't think she even
    sees me. She gives no indication of it. *(She looks up the stairs.)* What do you
    suppose she does up there every Sunday afternoon?
MISS LIZZIE: She sulks.
THE ACTRESS: And reads the Bible I suppose, and Mrs. Beeton's *Book of Eti-*
    quette. Oh Lizzie. . . . What a long day. The absolutely longest day. . . .
    When does that come anyway, the longest day?
MISS LIZZIE: June.
THE ACTRESS: Ah yes, June. *(She looks at* MISS LIZZIE.*)* June?
MISS LIZZIE: June.
THE ACTRESS: Mmmmmm. . . .
MISS LIZZIE: I know what you're thinking.
THE ACTRESS: Of course you do. . . . I'm thinking . . . shall I pour the
    sherry — or will you.
MISS LIZZIE: No.
THE ACTRESS: I'm thinking . . . June . . . in Fall River.
MISS LIZZIE: No.
THE ACTRESS: August in Fall River? *(She smiles. Pause.)*
MISS LIZZIE: We could have met in Boston.
THE ACTRESS: I prefer it here.
MISS LIZZIE: You don't find it . . . a trifle boring?
THE ACTRESS: Au contraire.

(MISS LIZZIE *gives a small laugh at the affectation.*)

THE ACTRESS: What?
MISS LIZZIE: I find it a trifle boring . . . I know what you're doing. You're
    soaking up the ambience.
THE ACTRESS: Nonsense, Lizzie. I come to see you.
MISS LIZZIE: Why?
THE ACTRESS: Because . . . of us. *(Pause.)*
MISS LIZZIE: You were a late arrival last night. Later than usual.
THE ACTRESS: Don't be silly.
MISS LIZZIE: I wonder why.
THE ACTRESS: The show was late, late starting, late coming down.
MISS LIZZIE: And?
THE ACTRESS: And — then we all went out for drinks.
MISS LIZZIE: We?
THE ACTRESS: The other members of the cast.
MISS LIZZIE: Oh yes.
THE ACTRESS: And then I caught a cab . . . all the way from Boston. . . . Do
    you know what it cost?
MISS LIZZIE: I should. I paid the bill, remember?
THE ACTRESS: *(Laughs.)* Of course. What a jumble all my thoughts are.
    There're too many words running round inside my head today. It's
    terrible.
MISS LIZZIE: It sounds it.

(Pause.)

THE ACTRESS: . . . You know . . . you do this thing . . . you stare at me . . . You look directly at my eyes. I think . . . you think . . . that if I'm lying . . . it will come up, like lemons on a slot machine. *(She makes a gesture at her eyes.)* Tick. Tick . . . *(Pause.)* In the alley, behind the theatre the other day, there were some kids. You know what they were doing?

MISS LIZZIE: How could I?

THE ACTRESS: They were playing skip rope, and you know what they were singing? *(She sings, and claps her hands arythmically to:)*

"Lizzie Borden took an ax
Gave her mother forty whacks,
When the job was nicely done,
She gave her father forty-one."

MISS LIZZIE: Did you stop them?

THE ACTRESS: No.

MISS LIZZIE: Did you tell them I was acquitted?

THE ACTRESS: No.

MISS LIZZIE: What did you do?

THE ACTRESS: I shut the window.

MISS LIZZIE: A noble gesture on my behalf.

THE ACTRESS: We were doing lines — the noise they make is dreadful. Sometimes they play ball, ka-thunk, ka-thunk, ka-thunk against the wall. Once I saw them with a cat and —

MISS LIZZIE: And you didn't stop them?

THE ACTRESS: That time I stopped them.

(THE ACTRESS crosses to table where there is a gramophone. She prepares to play a record. She stops.)

THE ACTRESS: Should I?

MISS LIZZIE: Why not?

THE ACTRESS: Your sister, the noise upsets her.

MISS LIZZIE: And she upsets me. On numerous occasions.

THE ACTRESS: You're incorrigible, Lizzie.

(THE ACTRESS holds out her arms to MISS LIZZIE. They dance the latest "in" dance, a Scott Joplin composition. It requires some concentration, but they chat while dancing rather formally in contrast to the music.)

THE ACTRESS: . . . Do you think your jawline's heavy?

MISS LIZZIE: Why do you ask?

THE ACTRESS: They said you had jowls.

MISS LIZZIE: Did they.

THE ACTRESS: The reports of the day said you were definitely jowly.

MISS LIZZIE: That was ten years ago.

THE ACTRESS: Imagine. You were only thirty-four.

MISS LIZZIE: Yes.

THE ACTRESS: It happened here, this house.

MISS LIZZIE: You're leading.
THE ACTRESS: I know.
MISS LIZZIE: . . . I don't think I'm jowly. Then or now. Do you?
THE ACTRESS: Lizzie? Lizzie.
MISS LIZZIE: What?
THE ACTRESS: . . . did you?
MISS LIZZIE: Did I what?

(Pause.)

THE ACTRESS: You never tell *me* anything. *(She turns off the music.)*
MISS LIZZIE: I tell you everything.
THE ACTRESS: No you don't!
MISS LIZZIE: Oh yes, I tell you the most personal things about myself, my
    thoughts, my dreams, my —
THE ACTRESS: But never that one thing. . . . *(She lights a cigarette.)*
MISS LIZZIE: And don't smoke those — they stink.

*(THE ACTRESS ignores her, inhales, exhales a volume of smoke in MISS LIZZIE's
direction.)*

MISS LIZZIE: Do you suppose . . . people buy you drinks . . . or cast you
    even . . . because you have a "liaison" with Lizzie Borden? Do you sup-
    pose they do that?
THE ACTRESS: They cast me because I'm good at what I do.
MISS LIZZIE: They never pry? They never ask? What's she really like? Is she
    really jowly? Did she? Didn't she?
THE ACTRESS: What could I tell them? You never tell me anything.
MISS LIZZIE: I tell you everything.
THE ACTRESS: But that! *(Pause.)* You think everybody talks about you — they
    don't.
MISS LIZZIE: Here they do.
THE ACTRESS: You think they talk about you.
MISS LIZZIE: But never to me.
THE ACTRESS: Well . . . you give them lots to talk about.
MISS LIZZIE: You know you're right, your mind is a jumble.
THE ACTRESS: I told you so.

(Pause.)

MISS LIZZIE: You remind me of my sister.
THE ACTRESS: Oh God, in what way?
MISS LIZZIE: Day in, day out, ten years now, sometimes at breakfast as she
    rolls little crumbs of bread in little balls, sometimes at noon, or late at
    night . . . "Did you, Lizzie?" "Lizzie, did you?"
THE ACTRESS: Ten years, day in, day out?
MISS LIZZIE: Oh yes. She sits there where Papa used to sit and I sit there,
    where I have always sat. She looks at me and at her plate, then at me,
    and at her plate, then at me and then she says "Did you Lizzie?" "Lizzie,
    did you?"

THE ACTRESS: *(A nasal imitation of* EMMA's *voice.)* "Did-you-Lizzie — Lizzie-did-you." *(Laughs.)*

MISS LIZZIE: Did I what?

THE ACTRESS: *(Continues her imitation of* EMMA.*)* "You know."

MISS LIZZIE: Well, what do you think?

THE ACTRESS: "Oh, I believe you didn't, in fact I know you didn't, what a thought! After all, you were acquitted."

MISS LIZZIE: Yes, I was.

THE ACTRESS: "But sometimes when I'm on the street . . . or shopping . . . or at the church even, I catch somebody's eye, they look away . . . and I think to myself "Did-you-Lizzie — Lizzie-did-you."

MISS LIZZIE: *(Laughs.)* Ah, poor Emma.

THE ACTRESS: *(Dropping her* EMMA *imitation.)* Well, did you?

MISS LIZZIE: Is it important?

THE ACTRESS: Yes.

MISS LIZZIE: Why?

THE ACTRESS: I have . . . a compulsion to know the truth.

MISS LIZZIE: The truth?

THE ACTRESS: Yes.

MISS LIZZIE: . . . Sometimes I think you look like me, and you're not jowly.

THE ACTRESS: No.

MISS LIZZIE: You look like me, or how I think I look, or how I ought to look . . . sometimes you think like me . . . do you feel that?

THE ACTRESS: Sometimes.

MISS LIZZIE: *(Triumphant.)* You shouldn't have to ask then. You should know. "Did I, didn't I." You tell me.

THE ACTRESS: I'll tell you what I think. . . . I think . . . that you're aware there is a certain fascination in the ambiguity. . . . You always paint the background but leave the rest to my imagination. Did Lizzie Borden take an axe? . . . If you didn't I should be disappointed . . . and if you did I should be horrified.

MISS LIZZIE: And which is worse?

THE ACTRESS: To have murdered one's parents, or to be a pretentious small-town spinster? I don't know.

MISS LIZZIE: Why're you so cruel to me?

THE ACTRESS: I'm teasing, Lizzie, I'm only teasing. Come on, paint the background again.

MISS LIZZIE: Why?

THE ACTRESS: Perhaps you'll give something away.

MISS LIZZIE: Which you'll dine out on.

THE ACTRESS: Of course. *(Laughs.)* Come on, Lizzie. Come on.

MISS LIZZIE: A game.

THE ACTRESS: What?

MISS LIZZIE: A game? . . . And you'll play me.

THE ACTRESS: Oh —

MISS LIZZIE: It's your stock in trade, my love.

THE ACTRESS: Alright. . . . A game!

MISS LIZZIE: Let me think . . . Bridget . . . Brrridget. We had a maid then. And her name was Bridget. Oh, she was a great one for stories, stood

like this, very straight back, and her hair . . . and there she was in the courtroom in her new dress on the stand. "Do you swear to tell the truth, the whole truth, and nothing but the truth, so help you God?" *(Imitates Irish accent.)*
"I do sir," she said.
"Would you give the court your name."
"Bridget O'Sullivan, sir."

(Very faint echo of the voice of THE DEFENSE *under* MISS LIZZIE's *next line.)*

"And occupation."
"I'm like what you'd call a maid, sir. I do a bit of everything, cleanin' and cookin'."

(The actual voice of THE DEFENSE *is heard alone; he may also be seen.)*

THE DEFENSE: You've been in Fall River how long?
MISS LIZZIE: *(Who continues as* BRIDGET, *while* THE ACTRESS *(who will play* LIZZIE) *observes.)* Well now, about five years sir, ever since I came over. I worked up on the hill for a while but it didn't — well, you could say, suit me, too lah-de-dah — so I —
THE DEFENSE: Your employer in June of 1892 was?
BRIDGET: Yes sir. Mr Borden, sir. Well, more rightly, Mrs Borden for she was the one who —
THE DEFENSE: Your impression of the household?
BRIDGET: Well . . . the man of the house, Mr Borden, was a bit of a . . . tightwad, and Mrs B. could nag you into the grave, still she helped with the dishes and things which not everyone does when they hire a maid. *(*HARRY *appears on the stairs; approaches* BRIDGET *stealthily. She is unaware of him.)* Then there was the daughters, Miss Emma and Lizzie, and that day, Mr Wingate, Mrs B.'s brother who'd stayed for the night and was — *(He grabs her ass with both hands. She screams.)*
BRIDGET: Get off with you!
HARRY: Come on, Bridget, give me a kiss!
BRIDGET: I'll give you a good poke in the nose if you don't keep your hands to yourself.
HARRY: Ohhh-hh-hh Bridget!
BRIDGET: Get away you old sod!
HARRY: Haven't you missed me?
BRIDGET: I have not! I was pinched black and blue last time — and I'll be sufferin' the same before I see the end of you this time.
HARRY: *(Tilts his ass at her.)* You want to see my end?
BRIDGET: You're a dirty old man.
HARRY: If Mr Borden hears that, you'll be out on the street. *(Grabs her.)* Where's my kiss!
BRIDGET: *(Dumps glass of water on his head.)* There! *(*HARRY *splutters.)* Would you like another? You silly thing you — and leave me towels alone!

HARRY: You've soaked my shirt.

BRIDGET: Shut up and pour yourself a cup of coffee.

HARRY: You got no sense of fun, Bridget.

BRIDGET: Well now, if you tried actin' like the gentleman farmer you're supposed to be, Mr Wingate —

HARRY: I'm tellin' you you can't take a joke.

BRIDGET: If Mr Borden sees you jokin', it's not his maid he'll be throwin' out
on the street, but his brother-in-law, and that's the truth.

HARRY: What's between you and me's between you and me, eh?

BRIDGET: There ain't nothin' between you and me.

HARRY: . . . Finest cup of coffee in Fall River.

BRIDGET: There's no gettin' on the good side of me now, it's too late for
that.

HARRY: . . . Bridget? . . . You know what tickles my fancy?

BRIDGET: No and I don't want to hear.

HARRY: It's your Irish temper.

BRIDGET: It is, is it? . . . Can I ask you something?

HARRY: Ooohhh — anything.

BRIDGET: (Innocently.) Does Miss Lizzie know you're here? . . . I say does Miss
Lizzie —

HARRY: Why do you bring her up.

BRIDGET: She don't then, eh? (Teasing.) It's a surprise visit?

HARRY: No surprise to her father.

BRIDGET: Oh?

HARRY: We got business.

BRIDGET: I'd of thought the last bit of business was enough.

HARRY: It's not for —   [you to say]

BRIDGET: You don't learn a thing, from me or Lizzie, do you?

HARRY: Listen here —

BRIDGET: You mean you've forgotten how mad she was when you got her
father to sign the rent from the mill house over to your sister? Oh my.

HARRY: She's his wife, isn't she?

BRIDGET: (Lightly.) Second wife.

HARRY: She's still got her rights.

BRIDGET: Who am I to say who's got a right? But I can tell you this — Miss
Lizzie don't see it that way.

HARRY: It don't matter how Miss Lizzie sees it.

BRIDGET: Oh it matters enough — she had you thrown out last time, didn't
she? By jasus that was a laugh!

HARRY: You mind your tongue.

BRIDGET: And after you left, you know what happened?

HARRY: Get away.

BRIDGET: She and sister Emma got her father's rent money from the other
mill house to make it all even-steven — and now, here you are back
again? What kind of business you up to this time? (Whispers in his ear.)
Mind Lizzie doesn't catch you.

HARRY: Get away!

BRIDGET: *(Laughs.)* Ohhhh — would you like some more coffee, sir? It's the finest coffee in all Fall River! *(She pours it.)* Thank you sir. You're welcome, sir. *(She exits to the kitchen.)*

HARRY: There'll be no trouble this time!! Do you hear me!

BRIDGET: *(Off.)* Yes sir.

HARRY: There'll be no trouble. *(Sees a basket of crusts.)* What the hell's this? I said is this for breakfast!

BRIDGET: *(Entering.)* Is what for — oh no — Mr Borden's not economizin' to that degree yet, it's the crusts for Miss Lizzie's birds.

HARRY: What birds?

BRIDGET: Some kind of pet pigeons she's raisin' out in the shed. Miss Lizzie loves her pigeons.

HARRY: Miss Lizzie loves kittens and cats and horses and dogs. What Miss Lizzie doesn't love is people.

BRIDGET: *Some* people. *(She looks past HARRY to THE ACTRESS/LIZZIE. HARRY turns to follow BRIDGET's gaze. BRIDGET speaks, encouraging an invitation for THE ACTRESS to join her.)* Good mornin' Lizzie.

THE ACTRESS: *(She is a trifle tentative in the role of LIZZIE.)* Is the coffee on?

BRIDGET: Yes ma'am.

LIZZIE: I'll have some then.

BRIDGET: Yes ma'am. *(She makes no move to get it, but watches as LIZZIE stares at HARRY.)*

HARRY: Well . . . I think . . . maybe I'll . . . just split a bit of that kindling out back. *(He exits. LIZZIE turns to BRIDGET.)*

LIZZIE: Silly ass.

BRIDGET: Oh Lizzie. *(She laughs. She enjoys THE ACTRESS/LIZZIE's comments as she guides her into her role by "painting the background.")*

LIZZIE: Well, he is. He's a silly ass.

BRIDGET: Can you remember him last time with your Papa? Oh, I can still hear him: "Now Andrew, I've spent my life raisin' horses and I'm gonna tell you somethin' — a *woman* is just like a *horse*! You keep her on a tight rein, or she'll take the bit in her teeth and next thing you know, road, destination, and purpose is all behind you, and you'll be damn lucky if she don't pitch you right in a sewer ditch!"

LIZZIE: Stupid bugger.

BRIDGET: Oh Lizzie, what language! What would your father say if he heard you?

LIZZIE: Well . . . I've never used a word I didn't hear from him first.

BRIDGET: Do you think he'd be congratulatin' you?

LIZZIE: Possibly. *(BRIDGET gives a subtle shake of her head.)* Not.

BRIDGET: Possibly not is right. . . . And what if *Mrs B.* should hear you?

LIZZIE: I hope and pray that she does. . . . Do you know what I think, Bridget? I think there's nothing wrong with Mrs B. . . . that losing 80 pounds and tripling her intellect wouldn't cure.

BRIDGET: *(Loving it.)* You ought to be ashamed.

LIZZIE: It's the truth, isn't it?

BRIDGET: Still, what a way to talk of your mother.

LIZZIE: Step-mother.

BRIDGET: Still you don't mean it, do you?

LIZZIE: Don't I? *(Louder.)* She's a *silly ass* too!

BRIDGET: Shhhh.

LIZZIE: It's alright, she's deaf as a picket fence when she wants to be. . . . What's he here for?

BRIDGET: Never said.

LIZZIE: He's come to worm more money out of Papa I bet.

BRIDGET: Lizzie.

LIZZIE: What.

BRIDGET: Your sister, Lizzie. *(BRIDGET indicates EMMA, LIZZIE turns to see her on the stairs.)*

EMMA: You want to be quiet, Lizzie, a body can't sleep for the racket upstairs.

LIZZIE: Oh?

EMMA: You've been makin' too much noise.

LIZZIE: It must have been Bridget, she dropped a pot, didn't you, Bridget.

EMMA: A number of pots from the sound of it.

BRIDGET: I'm all thumbs this mornin', ma'am.

EMMA: You know it didn't sound like pots.

LIZZIE: Oh.

EMMA: Sounded more like voices.

LIZZIE: Oh?

EMMA: Sounded like your voice, Lizzie.

LIZZIE: Maybe you dreamt it.

EMMA: I wish I had, for someone was using words no lady would use.

LIZZIE: When Bridget dropped the pot, she did say "pshaw!" didn't you, Bridget.

BRIDGET: Pshaw! That's what I said.

EMMA: That's not what I heard.

(BRIDGET will withdraw.)

LIZZIE: Pshaw?

EMMA: If mother heard you, you know what she'd say.

LIZZIE: She's not my mother or yours.

EMMA: Well she married our father twenty-seven years ago, if that doesn't make her our mother —

LIZZIE: It doesn't.

EMMA: Don't talk like that.

LIZZIE: I'll talk as I like.

EMMA: We're not going to fight, Lizzie. We're going to be quiet and have our breakfast!

LIZZIE: Is that what we're going to do?

EMMA: Yes.

LIZZIE: Oh.

EMMA: At least — that's what I'm going to do.

LIZZIE: Bridget, Emma wants her breakfast!

EMMA: I could have yelled myself.

LIZZIE: You could, but you never do.

(BRIDGET serves EMMA, EMMA is reluctant to argue in front of BRIDGET.)

EMMA: Thank you, Bridget.

LIZZIE: Did you know Harry Wingate's back for a visit? . . . He must have snuck in late last night so I wouldn't hear him. Did you?

(EMMA shakes her head. LIZZIE studies her.)

LIZZIE: Did you know he was coming?

EMMA: No.

LIZZIE: No?

EMMA: But I do know he wouldn't be here unless Papa asked him.

LIZZIE: That's not the point. You know what happened last time he was here. Papa was signing property over to her.

EMMA: Oh Lizzie.

LIZZIE: Oh Lizzie nothing. It's bad enough Papa's worth thousands of dollars, and here we are, stuck in this tiny bit of a house on Second Street, when we should be up on the hill — and that's her doing. Or her's and Harry's.

EMMA: Shush.

LIZZIE: I won't shush. They cater to Papa's worst instincts.

EMMA: They'll hear you.

LIZZIE: I don't care if they do. It's true, isn't it? Papa tends to be miserly, he probably has the first penny he ever earned — or more likely *she* has it.

EMMA: You talk rubbish.

LIZZIE: Papa *can* be very warm-hearted and generous *but he needs encouragement.*

EMMA: If Papa didn't save his money, Papa wouldn't have any money.

LIZZIE: And neither will we if he keeps signing things over to her.

EMMA: I'm not going to listen.

LIZZIE: Well try thinking.

EMMA: Stop it.

LIZZIE: *(Not a threat, a simple statement of fact.)* Someday Papa will die —

EMMA: Don't say that.

LIZZIE: Some day Papa will die. And I don't intend to spend the rest of my life licking Harry Wingate's boots, or toadying to his sister.

MRS BORDEN: *(From the stairs.)* What's that?

LIZZIE: Nothing.

MRS BORDEN: *(Making her way downstairs.)* Eh?

LIZZIE: I said, nothing!

BRIDGET: *(Holds out basket of crusts. LIZZIE looks at it.)* For your birds, *Miss Lizzie.*

LIZZIE: *(She takes the basket.)* You want to know what I think? I think she's a fat cow and I hate her. *(She exits.)*

EMMA: . . . Morning, Mother.

MRS BORDEN: Morning Emma.

EMMA: . . . Did you have a good sleep?

(BRIDGET will serve breakfast.)

MRS BORDEN: So so. . . . It's the heat you know. It never cools off proper at night. It's too hot for a good sleep.

EMMA: . . . Is Papa up?

MRS BORDEN: He'll be down in a minute . . . sooo. . . . What's wrong with Lizzie this morning?

EMMA: Nothing.

MRS BORDEN: . . . Has Harry come down?

EMMA: I'm not sure.

MRS BORDEN: Bridget. Has Harry come down?

BRIDGET: Yes ma'am.

MRS BORDEN: And?

BRIDGET: And he's gone out back for a bit.

MRS BORDEN: Lizzie see him?

BRIDGET: Yes ma'am. *(Beats it back to the kitchen.)*

(EMMA concentrates on her plate.)

MRS BORDEN: . . . You should have said so. . . . She have words with him?

EMMA: Lizzie has more manners than that.

MRS BORDEN: She's incapable of disciplining herself like a lady and we all know it.

EMMA: Well she doesn't make a habit of picking fights with people.

MRS BORDEN: That's just it. She does.

EMMA: Well — she may —

MRS BORDEN: And you can't deny that.

EMMA: *(Louder.)* Well this morning she may have been a bit upset because no one told her he was coming and when she came down he was here. But that's all there was to it.

MRS BORDEN: If your father wants my brother in for a stay, he's to ask Lizzie's permission I suppose.

EMMA: No.

MRS BORDEN: You know, Emma —

EMMA: She didn't argue with him or anything like that.

MRS BORDEN: You spoiled her. You may have had the best of intentions, but you spoiled her.

(MISS LIZZIE/BRIDGET is speaking to ACTRESS/LIZZIE.)

MISS LIZZIE/BRIDGET: I was thirty-four years old, and I still daydreamed. . . . I did . . . I daydreamed . . . I dreamt that my name was Lisbeth . . . and I lived up on the hill in a corner house . . . and my hair wasn't red. I hate red hair. When I was little, everyone teased me. . . . When I was little, we never stayed in this house for the summer, we'd go to the farm. . . . I remember . . . my knees were always covered with scabs, god knows how I got them, but you know what I'd do? I'd sit in the field, and haul up my skirts, and my petticoat and my bloomers and roll down my stockings and I'd *pick* the scabs on my knees! And Emma would catch me! You know what she'd say? "Nice little girls don't have scabs on their knees!"

(They laugh)

LIZZIE: Poor Emma.

MISS LIZZIE/BRIDGET: I dreamt . . . someday I'm going to live . . . in a corner
house on the hill. . . . I'll have parties, grand parties. I'll be . . . witty,
not biting, but witty. Everyone will be witty. Everyone who is *anyone*
will want to come to my parties . . . and if . . . I can't . . . live in a
corner house on the hill . . . I'll live on the farm, all by myself on the
farm! There was a barn there, with barn cats and barn kittens and two
horses and barn swallows that lived in the eaves. . . . The birds I kept
here were pigeons, not swallows. . . . They were grey, a dull grey . . .
but . . . when the sun struck their feathers, I'd see blue, a steel blue
with a sheen, and when they'd move in the sun they were bright blue
and maroon and over it all, an odd sparkle as if you'd . . . grated a new
silver dollar and the gratings caught in their feathers. . . . Most of the
time they were dull . . . and stupid perhaps . . . but they weren't really.
They were . . . hiding I think. . . . They knew me. . . . They liked
me. . . . The truth . . . is . . .

ACTRESS/LIZZIE: The truth is . . . thirty-four is too old to daydream. . . .

MRS BORDEN: The truth is she's spoilt rotten. *(MR BORDEN will come down stairs
and take his place at the table.* MRS BORDEN *continues for his benefit.* MR BORDEN
*ignores her. He has learned the fine art of tuning her out. He is not intimidated or hen-
pecked.)* And we're paying the piper for that. In most of the places I've
been the people who pay the piper call the tune. Of course I haven't
had the advantage of a trip to Europe with a bunch of lady friends like
our Lizzie had three years ago, all expenses paid by her father.

EMMA: Morning Papa.

MR BORDEN: Mornin'.

MRS BORDEN: I haven't had the benefit of that experience. . . . Did you
know Lizzie's seen Harry?

MR BORDEN: Has she.

MRS BORDEN: You should have met him down town. You should never have
asked him to stay over.

MR BORDEN: Why not?

MRS BORDEN: You know as well as I do why not. I don't want a repeat of
last time. She didn't speak civil for months.

MR BORDEN: There's no reason for Harry to pay for a room when we've got
a spare one. . . . Where's Lizzie?

EMMA: Out back feeding the birds.

MR BORDEN: She's always out at those birds.

EMMA: Yes Papa.

MR BORDEN: And tell her to get a new lock for the shed. There's been
someone in it again.

EMMA: Alright.

MR BORDEN: It's those little hellions from next door. We had no trouble with
them playin' in that shed before, they always played in their own yard
before.

EMMA: . . . Papa?

MR BORDEN: It's those damn birds, that's what brings them into the yard.

EMMA: . . . About Harry . . .

MR BORDEN: What about Harry?

EMMA: Well . . . I was just wondering why . . . [*he's here*]

MR BORDEN: You never mind Harry — did you speak to Lizzie about Johnny MacLeod?

EMMA: I ah —

MR BORDEN: Eh?

EMMA: I said I tried to —

MR BORDEN: What do you mean, you tried to.

EMMA: Well, I was working my way round to it but —

MR BORDEN: What's so difficult about telling Lizzie Johnny MacLeod wants to call?

EMMA: Then why don't you tell her? I'm always the one that has to go running to Lizzie telling her this and telling her that, and taking the abuse for it!

MRS BORDEN: We all know why that is, she can wrap her father round her little finger, always has, always could. If everything else fails, she throws a tantrum and her father buys her off, trip to Europe, rent to the mill house, it's all the same.

EMMA: Papa, what's Harry here for?

MR BORDEN: None of your business.

MRS BORDEN: And don't you go runnin' to Lizzie stirring things up.

EMMA: You know I've never done that!

MR BORDEN: What she means —

EMMA: *(With anger but little fatigue.)* I'm tired, do you hear? Tired! *(She gets up from the table and leaves for upstairs.)*

MR BORDEN: Emma!

EMMA: You ask Harry here, you know there'll be trouble, and when I try to find out what's going on, so once again good old Emma can stand between you and Lizzie, all you've got to say is "none of your business!" Well then, it's *your* business, you look after it, because I'm not! *(She exits.)*

MRS BORDEN: . . . She's right.

MR BORDEN: That's enough. I've had enough. I don't want to hear from you too.

MRS BORDEN: I'm only saying she's right. You have to talk straight and plain to Lizzie and tell her things she don't want to hear.

MR BORDEN: About the farm?

MRS BORDEN: About Johnny MacLeod! Keep your mouth shut about the farm and she won't know the difference.

MR BORDEN: Alright.

MRS BORDEN: Speak to her about Johnny MacLeod.

MR BORDEN: Alright!

MRS BORDEN: You know what they're sayin' in town. About her and that doctor.

(MISS LIZZIE/BRIDGET *is speaking to* THE ACTRESS/LIZZIE.)

MISS LIZZIE/BRIDGET: They're saying if you live on Second Street and you need a housecall, and you don't mind the Irish, call Dr Patrick. Dr Patrick is very prompt with his Second Street house calls.

ACTRESS/LIZZIE: Do they really say that?

MISS LIZZIE/BRIDGET: No they don't. I'm telling a lie. But he is very prompt with a Second Street call, do you know why that is?

ACTRESS/LIZZIE: Why?

MISS LIZZIE/BRIDGET: Well — he's hoping to see someone who lives on Second Street — someone who's yanking up her skirt and showing her ankle — so she can take a decent-sized step — and forgetting everything she was ever taught in Miss Cornelia's School for Girls, and talking to the Irish as if she never heard of the Pope! Oh yes, he's very prompt getting to Second Street . . . getting away is something else. . . .

DR PATRICK: Good morning, Miss Borden!

LIZZIE: I haven't decided . . . if it is . . . or it isn't . . .

DR PATRICK: No, you've got it all wrong. The proper phrase is "good morning, Dr Patrick", and then you smile, discreetly of course, and lower the eyes just a titch, twirl the parasol —

LIZZIE: The parasol?

DR PATRICK: The parasol, but not too fast; and then you murmur in a voice that was ever sweet and low, "And how are you doin' this morning, Dr Patrick?" Your education's been sadly neglected, Miss Borden.

LIZZIE: You're forgetting something. You're married — and Irish besides — I'm supposed to ignore you.

DR PATRICK: No.

LIZZIE: Yes. Don't you realize Papa and Emma have fits every time we engage in "illicit conversation". They're having fits right now.

DR PATRICK: Well, does Mrs Borden approve?

LIZZIE: Ahhh. She's the real reason I keep stopping and talking. Mrs Borden is easily shocked. I'm hoping she dies from the shock.

DR PATRICK: *(Laughs.)* Why don't you . . . run away from home, Lizzie?

LIZZIE: Why don't you "run away" with me?

DR PATRICK: Where'll we go?

LIZZIE: Boston.

DR PATRICK: Boston?

LIZZIE: For a start.

DR PATRICK: And when will we go?

LIZZIE: Tonight.

DR PATRICK: But you don't really mean it, you're havin' me on.

LIZZIE: I do mean it.

DR PATRICK: How can you joke — and look so serious?

LIZZIE: It's a gift.

DR PATRICK: *(Laughs.)* Oh Lizzie —

LIZZIE: Look!

DR PATRICK: What is it?

LIZZIE: It's those little beggars next door. Hey! Hey get away! Get away there! . . . They break into the shed to get at my birds and Papa gets angry.

DR PATRICK: It's a natural thing.

LIZZIE: Well Papa doesn't like it.

DR PATRICK: They just want to look at them.

LIZZIE: Papa says what's his is his own — you need a formal invitation to get into our yard. . . . *(Pause.)* How's your wife?

DR PATRICK: My wife.

LIZZIE: Shouldn't I ask that? I thought nice polite ladies always inquired after the wives of their friends or acquaintances or . . . whatever.

(HARRY observes them.)

DR PATRICK: You've met my wife, my wife is always the same.

LIZZIE: How boring for you.

DR PATRICK: Uh-huh.

LIZZIE: And for her —

DR PATRICK: Yes indeed.

LIZZIE: And for me.

DR PATRICK: Do you know what they say, Lizzie? They say if you live on Second Street, and you need a house call, and you don't mind the Irish, call Dr Patrick. Dr Patrick is very prompt with his Second Street house calls.

LIZZIE: I'll tell you what I've heard them say — Second Street is a nice place to visit, but you wouldn't want to live there. I certainly don't.

HARRY: Lizzie.

LIZZIE: Well, look who's here. Have you had the pleasure of meeting my uncle, Mr Wingate.

DR PATRICK: No Miss Borden, that pleasure has never been mine.

LIZZIE: That's exactly how I feel.

DR PATRICK: Mr Wingate, sir.

HARRY: Dr . . . Patrick is it?

DR PATRICK: Yes it is, sir.

HARRY: Who's sick? *(In other words, "What the hell are you doing here?")*

LIZZIE: No one. He just dropped by for a visit; you see Dr Patrick and I are very old, very dear friends, isn't that so?

(HARRY stares at DR PATRICK.)

DR PATRICK: Well . . . *(LIZZIE jabs him in the ribs.)* Ouch! . . . It's her sense of humour, sir . . . a rare trait in a woman. . . .

HARRY: You best get in, Lizzie, it's gettin' on for lunch.

LIZZIE: Don't be silly, we just had breakfast.

HARRY: You best get in!

LIZZIE: . . . Would you give me your arm, Dr Patrick? *(She moves away with DR PATRICK, ignoring HARRY.)*

DR PATRICK: Now see what you've done?

LIZZIE: What?

DR PATRICK: You've broken two of my ribs and ruined my reputation all in one blow.

LIZZIE: It's impossible to ruin an Irishman's reputation.

DR PATRICK: *(Smiles.)* . . . I'll be seeing you, Lizzie . . .

MISS LIZZIE/BRIDGET: They're sayin' it's time you were married.

LIZZIE: What time is that?

MISS LIZZIE/BRIDGET: You need a place of your own.

LIZZIE: How would getting married get me that?

MISS LIZZIE/BRIDGET: Though I don't know what man would put up with your moods!

LIZZIE: What about me putting up with his!

MISS LIZZIE/BRIDGET: Oh Lizzie!

LIZZIE: What's the matter, don't men have moods?

HARRY: I'm tellin' you, as God is my witness, she's out in the walk talkin' to that Irish doctor, and he's fallin' all over her.

MRS BORDEN: What's the matter with you. For her own sake you should speak to her.

MR BORDEN: I will.

HARRY: The talk around town can't be doin' you any good.

MRS BORDEN: Harry's right.

HARRY: Yes sir.

MRS BORDEN: He's tellin' you what you should know.

HARRY: If a man can't manage his own daughter, how the hell can he manage a business — that's what people say, and it don't matter a damn whether there's any sense in it or not.

MR BORDEN: I know that.

MRS BORDEN: Knowin' is one thing, doin' something about it is another. What're you goin' to do about it?

MR BORDEN: God damn it! I said I was goin' to speak to her and I am!

MRS BORDEN: Well speak good and plain this time!

MR BORDEN: Jesus christ woman!

MRS BORDEN: Your "speakin' to Lizzie" is a ritual around here.

MR BORDEN: Abby —

MRS BORDEN: She talks, you listen, and nothin' changes!

MR BORDEN: That's enough!

MRS BORDEN: Emma isn't the only one that's fed to the teeth!

MR BORDEN: Shut up!

MRS BORDEN: You're gettin' old, Andrew! You're gettin' old! *(She exits.)*

(An air of embarrassment from MR BORDEN *at having words in front of* HARRY. MR BORDEN *fumbles with his pipe.)*

HARRY: *(Offers his pouch of tobacco.)* Here . . . have some of mine.

MR BORDEN: Don't mind if I do. . . . Nice mix.

HARRY: It is.

MR BORDEN: . . . I used to think . . . by my seventies . . . I'd be bouncin' a grandson on my knee. . . .

HARRY: Not too late for that.

MR BORDEN: Nope . . . never had any boys . . . and girls . . . don't seem to have the same sense of family. . . . You know it's all well and good to talk about speakin' plain to Lizzie, but the truth of the matter is, if Lizzie puts her mind to a thing, she does it, and if she don't, she don't.

HARRY: It's up to you to see she does.

MR BORDEN: It's like Abigail says, knowin' is one thing, doin' is another. . . . You're lucky you never brought any children into the world, Harry, you don't have to deal with them.

HARRY: Now that's no way to be talkin'.

MR BORDEN: There's Emma . . . Emma's a good girl . . . when Abbie and I get on, there'll always be Emma. . . . Well! You're not sittin' here to listen to me and my girls, are you, you didn't come here for that. Business, eh, Harry?

(HARRY *whips out a sheet of figures.*)

MISS LIZZIE/BRIDGET: I can remember distinctly . . . that moment I was undressing for bed, and I looked at my knees — and there were no scabs! At last! I thought I'm the nice little girl Emma wants me to be! . . . But it wasn't that at all. I was just growing up. I didn't fall down so often. . . . (*She smiles.*) Do you suppose . . . do you suppose there's a formula, a magic formula for being "a woman"? Do you suppose every girl baby receives it at birth, it's the last thing that happens just before birth, the magic formula is stamped indelibly on the brain — Ka Thud!! (*Her mood of amusement changes.*) . . . and . . . through some terrible oversight . . . perhaps the death of my mother . . . I didn't get that Ka Thud!! I was born . . . defective. . . . (*She looks at* THE ACTRESS.)

LIZZIE: (*Low.*) No.

LIZZIE/BRIDGET: Not defective?

LIZZIE: Just . . . born.

THE DEFENSE: Gentlemen of the Jury!! I ask you to look at the defendant, Miss Lizzie Borden. I ask you to recall the nature of the crime of which she is accused. I ask you — do you believe Miss Lizzie Borden, the youngest daughter of a scion of our community, a recipient of the fullest amenities our society can bestow upon its most fortunate members, do you believe Miss Lizzie Borden capable of wielding the murder weapon — thirty-two blows, gentlemen, thirty-two blows — fracturing Abigail Borden's skull, leaving her bloody and broken body in an upstairs bedroom, then, Miss Borden, with no hint of frenzy, hysteria, or trace of blood upon her person, engages in casual conversation with the maid, Bridget O'Sullivan, while awaiting her father's return home, upon which, after sending Bridget to her attic room, Miss Borden deals thirteen blows to the head of her father, and minutes later — in a state utterly compatible with that of a loving daughter upon discovery of murder most foul — Miss Borden calls for aid! Is this the aid we give her? Accusation of the most heinous and infamous of crimes? Do you believe Miss Lizzie Borden capable of these acts? I can tell you I do not!! I can tell you these acts of violence are acts of madness!! Gentlemen! If this gentlewoman is capable of such an act — I say to you — look to your daughters — if this gentlewoman is capable of such an act, which of us can lie abed at night, hear a step upon the stairs, a rustle in the hall, a creak outside the door. . . . Which of you can plump your pillow, nudge your wife, close your eyes, and sleep? Gentlemen, Lizzie Borden is not mad. Gentlemen, Lizzie Borden is not guilty.

MR BORDEN: Lizzie?

LIZZIE: Papa . . . have you and Harry got business?

HARRY: 'lo Lizzie. I'll ah . . . finish up later. *(He exits with the figures.* LIZZIE *watches him go.)*

MR BORDEN: Lizzie?

LIZZIE: What?

MR BORDEN: Could you sit down a minute?

LIZZIE: If it's about Dr Patrick again, I —

MR BORDEN: It isn't.

LIZZIE: Good.

MR BORDEN: But we could start there.

LIZZIE: Oh Papa.

MR BORDEN: Sit down Lizzie.

LIZZIE: But I've heard it all before, another chat for a wayward girl.

MR BORDEN: *(Gently.)* Bite your tongue, Lizzie.

(She smiles at him, there is affection between them. She has the qualities he would like in a son but deplores in a daughter.)

MR BORDEN: Now . . . first off . . . I want you to know that I . . . understand about you and the doctor.

LIZZIE: What do you understand?

MR BORDEN: I understand . . . that it's a natural thing.

LIZZIE: What is?

MR BORDEN: I'm saying there's nothing unnatural about an attraction between a man and a woman. That's a natural thing.

LIZZIE: I find Dr Patrick . . . amusing and entertaining . . . if that's what you mean . . . is that what you mean?

MR BORDEN: This attraction . . . points something up — you're a woman of thirty-four years —

LIZZIE: I know that.

MR BORDEN: Just listen to me, Lizzie. . . . I'm choosing my words, and I want you to listen. Now . . . in most circumstances . . . a woman of your age would be married, eh? have children, be running her own house, that's the natural thing, eh? *(Pause.)* Eh, Lizzie?

LIZZIE: I don't know.

MR BORDEN: Of course you know.

LIZZIE: You're saying I'm unnatural . . . am I supposed to agree, is that what you want?

MR BORDEN: No, I'm not saying that! I'm saying the opposite to that! . . . I'm saying the feelings you have towards Dr Patrick —

LIZZIE: What feelings?

MR BORDEN: What's . . . what's happening there, I can understand, but what you have to understand is that he's a married man, and there's nothing for you there.

LIZZIE: If he weren't married, Papa, I wouldn't be bothered talking to him! . . . It's just a game, Papa, it's a game.

MR BORDEN: A game.

LIZZIE: You have no idea how boring it is looking eligible, interested, and alluring, when I feel none of the three. So I play games. And it's a blessed relief to talk to a married man.

MR BORDEN: What're his feelings for you?

LIZZIE: I don't know, I don't care. Can I go now?

MR BORDEN: I'm not finished yet! . . . You know Mr MacLeod, Johnny MacLeod?

LIZZIE: I know his three little monsters.

MR BORDEN: He's trying to raise three boys with no mother!

LIZZIE: That's not my problem! I'm going.

MR BORDEN: Lizzie!

LIZZIE: What!

MR BORDEN: Mr MacLeod's asked to come over next Tuesday.

LIZZIE: I'll be out that night.

MR BORDEN: No you won't!

LIZZIE: Yes I will! . . . Whose idea was this?

MR BORDEN: No one's.

LIZZIE: That's a lie. She wants to get rid of me.

MR BORDEN: I want what's best for you!

LIZZIE: No you don't! 'Cause you don't care what I want!

MR BORDEN: You don't know what you want!

LIZZIE: But I know what you want! You want me living my life by the Farmers' Almanac; having everyone over for Christmas dinner; waiting up for my husband; and *serving at socials!*

MR BORDEN: It's good enough for your mother!

LIZZIE: She is *not* my *mother!*

MR BORDEN: . . . John MacLeod is looking for a wife.

LIZZIE: No, god damn it, he isn't!

MR BORDEN: Lizzie!

LIZZIE: He's looking for a housekeeper and it isn't going to be me!

MR BORDEN: You've a filthy mouth!

LIZZIE: Is that why you hate me?

MR BORDEN: You don't make sense.

LIZZIE: Why is it when I pretend things I don't feel, that's when you like me?

MR BORDEN: You talk foolish.

LIZZIE: I'm supposed to be a mirror. I'm supposed to reflect what you want to see, but everyone wants something different. If no one looks in the mirror, I'm not even there, I don't exist!

MR BORDEN: Lizzie, you talk foolish!

LIZZIE: No, I don't, that isn't true.

MR BORDEN: About Mr MacLeod —

LIZZIE: You can't make me get married!

MR BORDEN: Lizzie, do you want to spend the rest of your life in this house?

LIZZIE: No . . . No . . . I want out of it, but I won't get married to do it.

MRS BORDEN: (On her way through to the kitchen.) You've never been asked.

LIZZIE: Oh listen to her! I must be some sort of failure, then, eh? You had no son and a daughter that failed! What does that make you, Papa!

MR BORDEN: I want you to think about Johnny MacLeod!

LIZZIE: To hell with him!!!

(MR BORDEN *appears defeated. After a moment,* LIZZIE *goes to him, she holds his hand, strokes his hair.*)

LIZZIE: Papa? . . . Papa, I love you, I try to be what you want, really I do try, I try . . . but . . . I don't want to get married. I wouldn't be a good mother, I —

MR BORDEN: How do you know —

LIZZIE: I know it! . . . I want out of all this . . . I hate this house, I hate . . . I want out. Try to understand how I feel . . . Why can't I do something? . . . Eh? I mean . . . I could . . . I could go into your office . . . I could . . . learn how to keep books?

MR BORDEN: Lizzie.

LIZZIE: Why can't I do something like that?

MR BORDEN: For god's sake, talk sensible.

LIZZIE: Alright then! Why can't we move up on the hill to a house where we aren't in each other's laps!

MRS BORDEN: (Returning from kitchen.) Why don't you move out!

LIZZIE: Give me the money and I'll go!

MRS BORDEN: Money.

LIZZIE: And give me enough that I won't ever have to come back!

MRS BORDEN: She always gets round to money!

LIZZIE: You drive me to it!

MRS BORDEN: She's crazy!

LIZZIE: You drive me to it!

MRS BORDEN: She should be locked up!

LIZZIE: (Begins to smash the plates in the dining-room.) There!! There!!

MR BORDEN: Lizzie!

MRS BORDEN: Stop her!

LIZZIE: There!

(MR BORDEN *attempts to restrain her.*)

MRS BORDEN: For god's sake, Andrew!

LIZZIE: Lock me up! Lock me up!

MR BORDEN: Stop it! Lizzie!

(She collapses against him, crying.)

LIZZIE: Oh, Papa, I can't stand it.

MR BORDEN: There, there, come on now, it's alright, listen to me, Lizzie, it's alright.

MRS BORDEN: You may as well get down on your knees.

LIZZIE: Look at her. She's jealous of me. She can't stand it whenever you're nice to me.

MR BORDEN: There now.

MRS BORDEN: Ask her about Dr Patrick.

MR BORDEN: I'll handle this my way.

LIZZIE: He's an entertaining person, there're very few around!

MRS BORDEN: Fall River ain't Paris and ain't that a shame for our Lizzie!

LIZZIE: One trip three years ago and you're still harping on it; it's true, Papa, an elephant never forgets!

MR BORDEN: Show some respect!

LIZZIE: She's a fat cow and I hate her!

(MR BORDEN slaps LIZZIE. There is a pause as he regains control of himself.)

MR BORDEN: Now . . . now . . . you'll see Mr MacLeod Tuesday night.

LIZZIE: No.

MR BORDEN: God damn it!! I said you'll see Johnny MacLeod Tuesday night!!

LIZZIE: No.

MR BORDEN: Get the hell upstairs to your room!

LIZZIE: No.

MR BORDEN: I'm telling you to go upstairs to your room!!

LIZZIE: I'll go when I'm ready.

MR BORDEN: I said, Go!

(He grabs her arm to move her forcibly, she hits his arm away.)

LIZZIE: No! . . . There's something you don't understand, Papa. You can't make me do one thing that I don't want to do. I'm going to keep on doing just what I want just when I want — like always!

MR BORDEN: *(Shoves her to the floor to gain a clear exit from the room. He stops on the stairs, looks back to her on the floor.)* . . . I'm . . . *(He continues off.)*

MRS BORDEN: *(Without animosity.)* You know, Lizzie, your father keeps you. You know you got nothing but what he gives you. And that's a fact of life. You got to come to deal with facts. I did.

LIZZIE: And married Papa.

MRS BORDEN: And married your father. You never made it easy for me. I took on a man with two little ones, and Emma was your mother.

LIZZIE: You got stuck so I should too, is that it?

MRS BORDEN: What?

LIZZIE: The reason I should marry Johnny MacLeod.

MRS BORDEN: I just know, this time, in the end, you'll do what your Papa says, you'll see.

LIZZIE: No, I won't. I have a right. A right that frees me from all that.

MRS BORDEN: No, Lizzie, you got no rights.

LIZZIE: I've a legal right to one-third because I am his flesh and blood.

MRS BORDEN: What you don't understand is your father's not dead yet, your father's got many good years ahead of him, and when his time comes, well, we'll see what his will says then. . . . Your father's no fool, Lizzie. . . . Only a fool would leave money to you. *(She exits.)*

(After a moment, BRIDGET enters from the kitchen.)

BRIDGET: Ah Lizzie . . . you outdid yourself that time. *(She is comforting LIZZIE.)* . . . Yes you did . . . an elephant never forgets!
LIZZIE: Oh Bridget.
BRIDGET: Come on now.
LIZZIE: I can't help it.
BRIDGET: Sure you can . . . sure you can . . . stop your cryin' and come and sit down . . . you want me to tell you a story?
LIZZIE: No.
BRIDGET: Sure, a story. I'll tell you a story. Come on now . . . now . . . before I worked here I worked up on the hill and the lady of the house . . . are you listenin'? Well, she swore by her cook, finest cook in creation, yes, always bowin' and scrapin' and smilin' and givin' up her day off if company arrived. Oh the lady of the house she loved that cook — and I'll tell you her name! It was Mary! Now listen! Do you know what Mary was doin'? *(LIZZIE shakes her head.)* Before eatin' the master'd serve drinks in the parlour — and out in the kitchen, Mary'd be spittin' in the soup!
LIZZIE: What?
BRIDGET: She'd spit in the soup! And she'd smile when they served it!
LIZZIE: No.
BRIDGET: Yes. I've seen her cut up hair for an omelette.
LIZZIE: You're lying.
BRIDGET: Cross me heart. . . . They thought it was pepper!
LIZZIE: Oh, Bridget!
BRIDGET: These two eyes have seen her season up mutton stew when it's off and gone bad.
LIZZIE: Gone bad?
BRIDGET: Oh and they et it, every bit, and the next day they was hit with . . . *stomach flu!* so cook called it. By jasus Lizzie, I daren't tell you what she served up in their food, for fear you'd be sick!
LIZZIE: That's funny. . . . *(A fact — LIZZIE does not appear amused.)*
BRIDGET: *(Starts to clear up the dishes.)* Yes, well, I'm tellin' you I kept on the good side of cook.

(LIZZIE watches her for a moment.)

LIZZIE: . . . Do you . . . like me?
BRIDGET: Sure I do . . . You should try bein' more like cook, Lizzie. Smile and get round them. You can do it.
LIZZIE: It's not . . . *fair* that I have to.
BRIDGET: There ain't nothin' fair in this world.

LIZZIE: Well then . . . well then, I don't want to!

BRIDGET: You dream, Lizzie . . . you dream dreams . . . Work. Be sensible. What could you do?

LIZZIE: I could

MISS LIZZIE/BRIDGET: No.

LIZZIE: I could

MISS LIZZIE/BRIDGET: No.

LIZZIE: I could

MISS LIZZIE/BRIDGET: No!

LIZZIE: I . . . dream.

MISS LIZZIE/BRIDGET: You dream . . . of a carousel . . . you see a carousel . . . you see lights that go on and go off . . . you see yourself on a carousel horse, a red-painted horse with its head in the air, and green staring eyes, and a white flowing mane, it looks wild! . . . It goes up and comes down, and the carousel whirls round with the music and lights, on and off . . . and you watch . . . watch yourself on the horse. You're wearing a mask, a white mask like the mane of the horse, it looks like your face except that it's rigid and white . . . and it changes! With each flick of the lights, the expression, it changes, but always so rigid and hard, like the flesh of the horse that is red that you ride. You ride with no hands! No hands on this petrified horse, its head flung in the air, its wide staring eyes like those of a doe run down by the dogs! . . . And each time you go round, your hands rise a fraction nearer the mask . . . and the music and the carousel and the horse . . . they all three slow down, and they stop. . . . You can reach out and touch . . . you . . . you on the horse . . . with your hands so at the eyes. . . . You look into the eyes! *(A sound from LIZZIE, she is horrified and frightened. She covers her eyes.)* There are none! None! Just black holes in a white mask. . . . *(Pause.)* Only a dream. . . . The eyes of your birds . . . are round . . . and bright . . . a light shines from inside . . . they . . . can see into your heart . . . they're pretty . . . they love you. . . .

MR BORDEN: I want this settled, Harry, I want it settled while Lizzie's out back.

(MISS LIZZIE/BRIDGET draws LIZZIE's attention to the MR BORDEN/HARRY scene. LIZZIE listens, will move closer.)

HARRY: You know I'm for that.

MR BORDEN: I want it all done but the signin' of the papers tomorrow, that's if I decide to —

HARRY: You can't lose, Andrew. That farm's just lyin' fallow.

MR BORDEN: Well, let's see what you got.

HARRY: *(Gets out his papers.)* Look at this . . . I'll run horse auctions and a buggy rental — now I'll pay no rent for the house or pasturage but you get twenty percent, eh? That figure there —

MR BORDEN: Mmmn.

HARRY: From my horse auctions last year, it'll go up on the farm and you'll get twenty percent off the top. . . . My buggy rental won't do so well . . . that's that figure there, approximate . . . but it all adds up, eh? Adds up for you.

MR BORDEN: It's a good deal, Harry, but . . .

HARRY: Now I know why you're worried — but the farm will still be in the family, 'cause aren't I family? and whenever you or the girls want to come over for a visit, why I'll send a buggy from the rental, no need for you to have the expense of a horse, eh?

MR BORDEN: It looks good on paper.

HARRY: There's . . . ah . . . something else, it's a bit awkward but I got to mention it; I'll be severin' a lot of my present connections, and what I figure I've a right to, is some kind of guarantee. . . .

MR BORDEN: You mean a renewable lease for the farm?

HARRY: Well — what I'm wondering is . . . No offense, but you're an older man, Andrew . . . now if something should happen to you, where would the farm stand in regards to your will? That's what I'm wondering.

MR BORDEN: I've not made a will.

HARRY: You know best — but I wouldn't want to be in a position where Lizzie would be havin' anything to do with that farm. The less she knows now the better, but she's bound to find out — I don't feel I'm steppin' out of line by bringin' this up.

(LIZZIE *is within earshot. She is staring at* HARRY *and* MR BORDEN. *They do not see her.*)

MR BORDEN: No.

HARRY: If you mind you come right out and say so.

MR BORDEN: That's alright.

HARRY: Now . . . if you . . . put the farm — in Abbie's name, what do you think?

MR BORDEN: I don't know, Harry.

HARRY: I don't want to push.

MR BORDEN: . . . I should make a will . . . I want the girls looked after, it don't seem like they'll marry . . . and Abbie, she's younger than me, I know Emma will see to her, still . . . money-wise I got to consider these things . . . it makes a difference no men in the family.

HARRY: You know you can count on me for whatever.

MR BORDEN: If . . . *If* I changed title to the farm, Abbie'd have to come down to the bank, I wouldn't want Lizzie to know.

HARRY: You can send a note for her when you get to the bank; she can say it's a note from a friend, and come down and meet you. Simple as that.

MR BORDEN: I'll give it some thought.

HARRY: You see, Abbie owns the farm, it's no difference to you, but it gives me protection.

MR BORDEN: Who's there?

HARRY: It's Lizzie.

MR BORDEN: What do you want? . . . Did you lock the shed? . . . Is the shed locked? (LIZZIE *makes a slow motion which* MR BORDEN *takes for assent.*) Well you make sure it stays locked! I don't want any more of those god damned. . . . I . . . ah . . . I think we about covered everything, Harry, we'll . . . ah . . . we'll let it go till tomorrow.

HARRY: Good enough . . . well . . . I'll just finish choppin' that kindlin', give a shout when it's lunchtime. *(He exits.)*

(LIZZIE and MR BORDEN stare at each other for a moment.)

LIZZIE: *(Very low.)* What are you doing with the farm?

(MR BORDEN slowly picks up the papers, places them in his pocket.)

LIZZIE: Papa! . . . Papa. I want you to show me what you put in your pocket.

MR BORDEN: It's none of your business.

LIZZIE: The farm is my business.

MR BORDEN: It's nothing.

LIZZIE: Show me!

MR BORDEN: I said it's nothing!

(LIZZIE makes a quick move towards her father to seize the paper from his pocket. Even more quickly and smartly he slaps her face. It is all very quick and clean. A pause as they stand frozen.)

HARRY: *(Off.)* Andrew, there's a bunch of kids broken into the shed!

MR BORDEN: Jesus christ.

LIZZIE: *(Whispers.)* What about the farm.

MR BORDEN: You! You and those god damn birds! I've told you! I've told you time and again!

LIZZIE: What about the farm!

MR BORDEN: Jesus christ . . . You never listen! Never!

HARRY: *(Enters carrying the hand hatchet.)* Andrew!!

MR BORDEN: *(Grabs the hand hatchet from HARRY, turns to LIZZIE.)* There'll be no more of your god damn birds in this yard!!

LIZZIE: No!

(MR BORDEN raises the hatchet and smashes it into the table as LIZZIE screams.)

LIZZIE: No Papa!! Nooo!!

(The hatchet is embedded in the table. MR BORDEN and HARRY assume a soft freeze as ACTRESS/LIZZIE whirls to see MISS LIZZIE/BRIDGET observing the scene.)

LIZZIE: Nooo!

MISS LIZZIE: I loved them.

BLACKOUT

ACT TWO

(Lights come up on THE ACTRESS/LIZZIE *sitting at the dining room table. She is very still, her hands clasped in her lap.* MISS LIZZIE/BRIDGET *is near her. She too is very still. A pause.)*

ACTRESS/LIZZIE: *(Very low.)* Talk to me.

MISS LIZZIE/BRIDGET: I remember . . .

ACTRESS/LIZZIE: *(Very low.)* No.

MISS LIZZIE/BRIDGET: On the farm, Papa's farm, Harry's farm, when I was little and thought it was my farm and I loved it, we had some puppies, the farm dog had puppies, brown soft little puppies with brown ey . . . *(She does not complete the word "eyes".)* And one of the puppies got sick. I didn't know it was sick, it seemed like the others, but the mother, she knew. It would lie at the back of the box, she would lie in front of it while she nursed all the others. They ignored it, that puppy didn't exist for the others. . . . I think inside it was different, and the mother thought the difference she sensed was a sickness . . . and after a while . . . anyone could tell it was sick. It had nothing to eat! . . . And Papa took it and drowned it. That's what you do on a farm with things that are different.

ACTRESS/LIZZIE: Am I different?

MISS LIZZIE/BRIDGET: You kill them.

*(*ACTRESS/LIZZIE *looks at* MISS LIZZIE/BRIDGET. MISS LIZZIE/BRIDGET *looks towards the top of the stairs.* BRIDGET *gets up and exits to the kitchen.* EMMA *appears at the top of the stairs. She is dressed for travel and carries a small suitcase and her gloves. She stares down at* LIZZIE *still sitting at the table. After several moments* LIZZIE *becomes aware of that gaze and turns to look at* EMMA. EMMA *then descends the stairs. She puts down her suitcase. She is not overjoyed at seeing* LIZZIE, *having hoped to get away before* LIZZIE *arose, nevertheless she begins with an excess of enthusiasm to cover the implications of her departure.)*

EMMA: Well! You're up early . . . Bridget down? . . . did you put the coffee on? *(She puts her gloves on the table.)* My goodness, Lizzie, cat got your tongue? *(She exits to the kitchen.* LIZZIE *picks up the gloves.* EMMA *returns.)* Bridget's down, she's in the kitchen. . . . Well . . . looks like a real scorcher today, doesn't it? . . .

LIZZIE: What's the bag for?

EMMA: I . . . decided I might go for a little trip, a day or two, get away from the heat. . . . The girls've rented a place out beach way and I thought . . . with the weather and all . . .

LIZZIE: How can you do that?

EMMA: Do what? . . . Anyway, I thought I might stay with them a few days. . . . Why don't you come with me?

LIZZIE: No.

EMMA: Just for a few days, come with me.

LIZZIE: No.

EMMA: You know you like the water.

LIZZIE: I said no!

EMMA: Oh, Lizzie.

(Pause.)

LIZZIE: I don't see how you can leave me like this.

EMMA: I asked you to come with me.

LIZZIE: You know I can't do that.

EMMA: Why not?

LIZZIE: Someone has to *do* something, you just run away from things.

(Pause.)

EMMA: . . . Lizzie . . . I'm sorry about the — *[birds]*

LIZZIE: No!

EMMA: Papa was angry.

LIZZIE: I don't want to talk about it.

EMMA: He's sorry now.

LIZZIE: Nobody *listens* to me, can't you hear me? I said *don't* talk about it. I don't want to talk about it. Stop talking about it!!

(BRIDGET enters with the coffee.)

EMMA: Thank you, Bridget.

(BRIDGET withdraws.)

EMMA: Well! . . . I certainly can use this this morning. . . . Your coffee's there.

LIZZIE: I don't want it.

EMMA: You're going to ruin those gloves.

LIZZIE: I don't care.

EMMA: Since they're not yours.

(LIZZIE bangs the gloves down on the table. A pause. Then EMMA picks them up and smooths them out.)

LIZZIE: Why are you leaving me?

EMMA: I feel like a visit with the girls. Is there something wrong with that?

LIZZIE: How can you go now?

EMMA: I don't know what you're getting at.

LIZZIE: I heard them. I heard them talking yesterday. Do you know what they're saying?

EMMA: How could I?

LIZZIE: "How could I?" What do you mean "How could I?" Did you know?

EMMA: No, Lizzie, I did not.

LIZZIE: *Did-not-what.*

EMMA: Know.

LIZZIE: But you know now. How do you know now?

EMMA: I've put two and two together and I'm going over to the girls for a visit!

LIZZIE: Please Emma!

EMMA: It's too hot.

LIZZIE: I need you, don't go.

EMMA: I've been talking about this trip.

LIZZIE: That's a lie.

EMMA: They're expecting me.

LIZZIE: You're lying to me!

EMMA: I'm going to the girls' place. You can come if you want, you can stay if you want. I planned this trip and I'm taking it!

LIZZIE: Stop lying!

EMMA: If I want to tell a little white lie to avoid an altercation in this house, I'll do so. Other people have been doing it for years!

LIZZIE: You don't understand, you don't understand anything.

EMMA: Oh, I understand enough.

LIZZIE: You don't! Let me explain it to you. You listen carefully, you listen. . . . Harry's getting the farm, can you understand that? Harry is here and he's moving on the farm and he's going to be there, on the farm, living on the farm. *Our farm.* Do you understand that? . . . Do you understand that!

EMMA: Yes.

LIZZIE: Harry's going to be on the farm. That's the first thing. . . . No . . . no it isn't. . . . The first thing . . . was the mill house, that was the first thing! And *now* the farm. You see there's a pattern, Emma, you can see that, can't you?

EMMA: I don't —

LIZZIE: You can see it! The mill house, then the farm, and the next thing is the papers for the farm — do you know what he's doing, Papa's doing? He's signing the farm over to her. It will never be ours, we will never have it, not ever. It's ours by rights, don't you feel that?

EMMA: The farm — has always meant a great deal to me, yes.

LIZZIE: Then what are you doing about it! You can't leave me now . . . but that's not all. Papa's going to make a will, and you can see the pattern, can't you, and if the pattern keeps on, what do you suppose his will will say. What do you suppose, answer me!

EMMA: I don't know.

LIZZIE: Say it!

EMMA: He'll see we're looked after.

LIZZIE: I don't want to be looked after! What's the matter with you? Do you really want to spend the rest of your life with that cow, listening to her drone on and on for years! That's just what they think you'll do. Papa'll leave you a monthly allowance, just like he'll leave me, just enough to keep us all living together. We'll be worth millions on paper, and be stuck in this house and by and by Papa will die and Harry will move in and you will wait on that cow while she gets fatter and fatter and I — will — sit in my room.

EMMA: Lizzie.

LIZZIE: We have to do something, you can see that. We have to do something!

EMMA: There's nothing we can do.

LIZZIE: Don't say that!

EMMA: Alright, then, what can we do?

LIZZIE: I . . . I . . . don't know. But we have to do something, you have to help me, you can't go away and leave me alone, you can't do that.

EMMA: Then —

LIZZIE: You know what I thought? I thought you could talk to him, really talk to him, make him understand that we're people. *Individual people,* and we have to live separate lives, and his will should make it possible for us to do that. And the farm can't go to Harry.

EMMA: You know it's no use.

LIZZIE: I can't talk to him anymore. Everytime I talk to him I make everything worse. I hate him, no. No I don't. I hate her.

(EMMA *looks at her broach watch.*)

LIZZIE: Don't look at the time.

EMMA: I'll miss my connections.

LIZZIE: No!

EMMA: *(Puts on her gloves.)* Lizzie. There's certain things we have to face. One of them is, we can't change a thing.

LIZZIE: I won't let you go!

EMMA: I'll be back on the week-end.

LIZZIE: He killed my birds! He took the ax and he killed them! Emma, I ran out and held them in my hands, I felt their hearts throbbing and pumping and the blood gushed out of their necks, it was all over my hands, don't you care about that?

EMMA: I . . . I . . . have a train to catch.

LIZZIE: He didn't care how much he hurt me and you don't care either. Nobody cares.

EMMA: I . . . have to go now.

LIZZIE: That's right. Go away. I don't even like you, Emma. Go away! *(EMMA leaves, LIZZIE runs after her calling.)* I'm sorry for all the things I told you! Things I really felt! You pretended to me, and I don't like you!! Go away!! *(LIZZIE runs to the window and looks out after EMMA's departing figure. After a moment she slowly turns back into the room. MISS LIZZIE/BRIDGET is there.)*

LIZZIE: I want to die . . . I want to die, but something inside won't let me . . . inside something says *no.* (She shuts her eyes.) I can do anything.

DEFENSE: Miss Borden.

(Both LIZZIES turn.)

DEFENSE: Could you describe the sequence of events upon your father's arrival home?

LIZZIE: *(With no animation.)* Papa came in . . . we exchanged a few words . . . Bridget and I spoke of the yard goods sale down town, whether she would buy some. She went up to her room. . . .

DEFENSE: And then?

LIZZIE: I went out back . . . through the yard . . . I picked up several pears from the ground beneath the trees . . . I went into the shed . . . I stood looking out the window and ate the pears . . .

DEFENSE: How many?

LIZZIE: Four.

DEFENSE: It wasn't warm, stifling in the shed?

LIZZIE: No, it was cool.

DEFENSE: What were you doing, apart from eating the pears?

LIZZIE: I suppose I was thinking. I just stood there, looking out the window, thinking, and eating the pears I'd picked up.

DEFENSE: You're fond of pears?

LIZZIE: Otherwise, I wouldn't eat them.

DEFENSE: Go on.

LIZZIE: I returned to the house. I found — Papa. I called for Bridget.

(MRS BORDEN descends the stairs. LIZZIE and BRIDGET turn to look at her. MRS BORDEN is only aware of LIZZIE's stare. Pause.)

MRS BORDEN: . . . What're you staring at? . . . I said what're you staring at?

LIZZIE: *(Continuing to stare at MRS BORDEN.)* Bridget.

BRIDGET: Yes ma'am.

(Pause.)

MRS BORDEN: Just coffee and a biscuit this morning, Bridget, it's too hot for a decent breakfast.

BRIDGET: Yes ma'am.

(She exits for the biscuit and coffee. LIZZIE continues to stare at MRS BORDEN.)

MRS BORDEN: . . . Tell Bridget I'll have it in the parlour.

LIZZIE: *(Is making an effort to be pleasant, to be "good". MRS BORDEN is more aware of this as unusual behaviour from LIZZIE than were she to be rude, biting, or threatening. LIZZIE, at the same time, feels caught in a dimension other than the one in which the people around her are operating. For LIZZIE, a bell-jar effect. Simple acts seem filled with significance. LIZZIE is trying to fulfill other people's expectations of "normal".)*

LIZZIE: It's not me, is it?

MRS BORDEN: What?

LIZZIE: You're not moving into the parlour because of me, are you?

MRS BORDEN: What?

LIZZIE: I'd hate to think I'd driven you out of your own dining-room.

MRS BORDEN: No.

LIZZIE: Oh good, because I'd hate to think that was so.

MRS BORDEN: It's cooler in the parlour.

LIZZIE: You know, you're right.

MRS BORDEN: Eh?

LIZZIE: It is cooler. . . .

(BRIDGET enters with the coffee and biscuit.)

LIZZIE: I will, Bridget.

(She takes the coffee and biscuit, gives it to MRS BORDEN. LIZZIE watches her eat and drink. MRS BORDEN eats the biscuit delicately. LIZZIE's attention is caught by it.)

LIZZIE: Do you like that biscuit?

MRS BORDEN: It could be lighter.

LIZZIE: You're right.

(MR BORDEN enters, makes his way into the kitchen, LIZZIE watches him pass.)

LIZZIE: You know, Papa doesn't look well, Papa doesn't look well at all. Papa looks sick.

MRS BORDEN: He had a bad night.

LIZZIE: Oh?

MRS BORDEN: Too hot.

LIZZIE: But it's cooler in here, isn't it . . . *(Not trusting her own evaluation of the degree of heat.)* Isn't it?

MRS BORDEN: Yes, yes, it's cooler in here.

(MR BORDEN enters with his coffee. LIZZIE goes to him.)

LIZZIE: Papa? You should go in the parlour. It's much cooler in there, really it is.

(He goes into the parlour. LIZZIE remains in the dining-room. She sits at the table, folds her hands in her lap. MR BORDEN begins to read the paper.)

MRS BORDEN: . . . I think I'll have Bridget do the windows today . . . they need doing . . . get them out of the way first thing. . . . Anything in the paper, Andrew?

MR BORDEN: *(As he continues to read.)* Nope.

MRS BORDEN: There never is . . . I don't know why we buy it.

MR BORDEN: *(Reading.)* Yup.

MRS BORDEN: You going out this morning?

MR BORDEN: Business.

MRS BORDEN: . . . Harry must be having a bit of a sleep-in.

MR BORDEN: Yup.

MRS BORDEN: He's always up by — (HARRY *starts down the stairs.*) Well, speak of the devil — coffee and biscuits?
HARRY: Sounds good to me.

(MRS BORDEN *starts off to get it.* LIZZIE *looks at her, catching her eye.* MRS BORDEN *stops abruptly.*)

LIZZIE: (*Her voice seems too loud.*) Emma's gone over to visit at the girls' place. (MR BORDEN *lowers his paper to look at her.* HARRY *looks at her. Suddenly aware of the loudness of her voice, she continues softly, too softly.*) . . . Till the week-end.
MR BORDEN: She didn't say she was going, when'd she decide that?

(LIZZIE *looks down at her hands, doesn't answer. A pause. Then* MRS BORDEN *continues out to the kitchen.*)

HARRY: Will you be ah . . . going down town today?
MR BORDEN: This mornin'. I got . . . business at the bank.

(*A look between them. They are very aware of* LIZZIE's *presence in the dining-room.*)

HARRY: This mornin' eh? Well now . . . that works out just fine for me. I can . . . I got a bill to settle in town myself.

(LIZZIE *turns her head to look at them.*)

HARRY: I'll be on my way after that.
MR BORDEN: Abbie'll be disappointed you're not stayin' for lunch.
HARRY: 'Nother time.
MR BORDEN: (*Aware of* LIZZIE's *gaze.*) I . . . I don't know where she is with that coffee. I'll —
HARRY: Never you mind, you sit right there, I'll get it. (*He exits.*)

(LIZZIE *and* MR BORDEN *look at each other. The bell-jar effect is lessened.*)

LIZZIE: (*Softly.*) Good mornin' Papa.
MR BORDEN: Mornin' Lizzie.
LIZZIE: Did you have a good sleep?
MR BORDEN: Not bad.
LIZZIE: Papa?
MR BORDEN: Yes Lizzie.
LIZZIE: You're a very strong-minded person, Papa, do you think I'm like you?
MR BORDEN: In some ways . . . perhaps.
LIZZIE: I must be like someone.
MR BORDEN: You resemble your mother.
LIZZIE: I look like my mother?
MR BORDEN: A bit like your mother.
LIZZIE: But my mother's dead.

MR BORDEN: Lizzie —

LIZZIE: I remember you told me she died because she was sick . . . I was born and she died . . . Did you love her?

MR BORDEN: I married her.

LIZZIE: Can't you say if you loved her.

MR BORDEN: Of course I did, Lizzie.

LIZZIE: Did you hate me for killing her?

MR BORDEN: You don't think of it that way, it was just something that happened.

LIZZIE: Perhaps she just got tired and died. She didn't want to go on, and the chance came up and she took it. I could understand that. . . . Perhaps she was like a bird, she could see all the blue sky and she wanted to fly away but she couldn't. She was caught, Papa, she was caught in a horrible snare, and she saw a way out and she took it. . . . Perhaps it was a very brave thing to do, Papa, perhaps it was the only way, and she hated to leave us because she loved us so much, but she couldn't breathe all caught in the snare. . . . *(Long pause.)* Some people have very small wrists, have you noticed. Mine aren't . . .

(There is a murmur from the kitchen, then muted laughter. MR BORDEN looks towards it.)

LIZZIE: Papa! . . . I'm a very strong person.

MRS BORDEN: *(Off, laughing.)* You're tellin' tales out of school, Harry!

HARRY: *(Off.)* God's truth. You should have seen the buggy when they brought it back.

MRS BORDEN: *(Off.)* You've got to tell Andrew. *(Pokes her head in.)* Andrew, come on out here, Harry's got a story. *(Off.)* Now you'll have to start at the beginning again, oh my goodness.

(MR BORDEN starts for the kitchen. He stops, and looks back at LIZZIE.)

LIZZIE: Is there anything you want to tell me, Papa?

MRS BORDEN: *(Off.)* Andrew!

LIZZIE: *(Softly, an echo.)* Andrew.

MR BORDEN: What is it, Lizzie?

LIZZIE: If I promised to be a good girl forever and ever, would anything change?

MR BORDEN: I don't know what you're talking about.

LIZZIE: I would be lying . . . Papa! . . . Don't do any business today. Don't go out. Stay home.

MR BORDEN: What for?

LIZZIE: Everyone's leaving. Going away. Everyone's left.

MRS BORDEN: *(Off.)* Andrew!

LIZZIE: *(Softly, an echo.)* Andrew.

MR BORDEN: What is it?

LIZZIE: I'm calling you.

(MR BORDEN *looks at her for a moment, then leaves for the kitchen.* DR PATRICK *is heard whistling very softly.* LIZZIE *listens.*)

LIZZIE: Listen . . . can you hear it . . . can you?
MISS LIZZIE/BRIDGET: I can hear it. . . . It's stopped.

(DR PATRICK *can't be seen. Only his voice is heard.*)

DR PATRICK: *(Very low.)* Lizzie?
LIZZIE: *(Realization.)* I could hear it before [*you*]. *(Pause.)* It sounded so sad I wanted to cry.
MISS LIZZIE/BRIDGET: You mustn't cry.
LIZZIE: I mustn't cry.
DR PATRICK: I bet you know this one. *(He whistles an Irish jig.)*
LIZZIE: I know that! *(She begins to dance.* DR PATRICK *enters. He claps in time to the dance.* LIZZIE *finishes the jig.)*

(DR PATRICK *applauds.*)

DR PATRICK: Bravo! Bravo!!
LIZZIE: You didn't know I could do that, did you?
DR PATRICK: You're a woman of many talents, Miss Borden.
LIZZIE: You're not making fun of me?
DR PATRICK: I would never do that.
LIZZIE: I can do anything I want.
DR PATRICK: I'm sure you can.
LIZZIE: If I wanted to die — I could even do that, couldn't I.
DR PATRICK: Well now, I don't think so.
LIZZIE: Yes, I could!
DR PATRICK: Lizzie —
LIZZIE: You wouldn't know — you can't see into my heart.
DR PATRICK: I think I can.
LIZZIE: Well you can't.
DR PATRICK: . . . It's only a game.
LIZZIE: I never play games.
DR PATRICK: Sure you do.
LIZZIE: I hate games.
DR PATRICK: You're playin' one now.
LIZZIE: You don't even know me!
DR PATRICK: Come on Lizzie, we don't want to fight. I know what we'll do . . . we'll start all over. . . . Shut your eyes, Lizzie. *(She does so.)* Good mornin' Miss Borden. . . . Good mornin' Miss Borden. . . .
LIZZIE: . . . I haven't decided. . . . *(She slowly opens her eyes.)* . . . if it is or it isn't.
DR PATRICK: Much better . . . and now . . . would you take my arm, Miss Borden? How about a wee promenade?
LIZZIE: There's nowhere to go.

DR PATRICK: That isn't so. . . . What about Boston? . . . Do you think it's too far for a stroll? . . . I know what we'll do, we'll walk 'round to the side and you'll show me your birds. *(They walk.)* . . . I waited last night but you never showed up . . . there I was, travellin' bag and all, and you never appeared . . . I know what went wrong! We forgot to agree on an hour! Next time, Lizzie, you must set the hour. . . . Is this where they're kept?

(LIZZIE nods, she opens the cage and looks in it.)

DR PATRICK: It's empty. *(He laughs.)* And you say you never play games?
LIZZIE: They're gone.
DR PATRICK: You've been havin' me on again, yes you have.
LIZZIE: They've run away.
DR PATRICK: Did they really exist?
LIZZIE: I had blood on my hands.
DR PATRICK: What do you say?
LIZZIE: You can't see it now, I washed it off, see?
DR PATRICK: *(Takes her hands.)* Ah Lizzie. . . .
LIZZIE: Would you . . . help someone die?
DR PATRICK: Why do you ask that?
LIZZIE: Some people are better off dead. I might be better off dead.
DR PATRICK: You're a precious and unique person, Lizzie, and you shouldn't think things like that.
LIZZIE: Precious and unique?
DR PATRICK: All life is precious and unique.
LIZZIE: I am precious and unique? . . . I *am* precious and unique. You said that.
DR PATRICK: Oh, I believe it.
LIZZIE: And I am. I know it. People mix things up on you, you have to be careful. I am a person of worth.
DR PATRICK: Sure you are.
LIZZIE: Not like that fat cow in there.
DR PATRICK: Her life too is —
LIZZIE: No!
DR PATRICK: Liz —
LIZZIE: Do you know her!
DR PATRICK: That doesn't matter.
LIZZIE: Yes it does, it does matter.
DR PATRICK: You can't be —
LIZZIE: You're a doctor, isn't that right?
DR PATRICK: Right enough there.
LIZZIE: So, tell me, tell me, if a dreadful accident occurred . . . and two people were dying . . . but you could only save one. . . . Which would you save?
DR PATRICK: You can't ask questions like that.
LIZZIE: Yes I can, come on, it's a game. How does a doctor determine? If one were old and the other were young — would you save the younger one first?

DR PATRICK: Lizzie.

LIZZIE: You said you liked games! If one were a bad person and the other was good, was trying to be good, would you save the one who was good and let the bad person die?

DR PATRICK: I don't know.

LIZZIE: Listen! If you could go back in time . . . what would you do if you met a person who was evil and wicked?

DR PATRICK: Who?

LIZZIE: I don't know, Attila the Hun!

DR PATRICK: *(Laughs.)* Oh my.

LIZZIE: Listen, if you met Attila the Hun, and you were in a position to kill him, would you do it?

DR PATRICK: I don't know.

LIZZIE: Think of the suffering he caused, the unhappiness.

DR PATRICK: Yes, but I'm a doctor, not an assassin.

LIZZIE: I think you're a coward.

(Pause.)

DR PATRICK: What I do is try to save lives . . .

LIZZIE: But you put poison out for the slugs in your garden.

DR PATRICK: You got something mixed up.

LIZZIE: I've never been clearer. Everything's clear. I've lived all of my life for this one moment of absolute clarity! If war were declared, would you serve?

DR PATRICK: I would fight in a war.

LIZZIE: You wouldn't fight, you would kill — you'd take a gun and shoot people, people who'd done nothing to you, people who were trying to be good, you'd kill them! And you say you wouldn't kill Attila the Hun, or that that stupid cow's life is precious — *My life is precious!!*

DR PATRICK: To you.

LIZZIE: Yes to me, are you stupid!?

DR PATRICK: And hers is to her.

LIZZIE: I don't care about her! *(Pause.)* I'm glad you're not my doctor, you can't make decisions, can you? You are a coward.

*(*DR PATRICK *starts off.)*

LIZZIE: You're afraid of your wife . . . you can *only* play games. . . . If I really wanted to go to Boston, you wouldn't come with me because you're a coward! *I'm not a coward!!*

*(*LIZZIE *turns to watch* MRS BORDEN *sit with needlework. After a moment* MRS BORDEN *looks at* LIZZIE, *aware of her scrutiny.)*

LIZZIE: . . . Where's Papa?

MRS BORDEN: Out.

LIZZIE: And Mr Wingate?

MRS BORDEN: He's out too.

LIZZIE: So what are you going to do . . . Mrs Borden?

MRS BORDEN: I'm going to finish this up.

LIZZIE: You do that. . . . *(Pause.)* Where's Bridget?

MRS BORDEN: Out back washing windows. . . . You got clean clothes to go upstairs, they're in the kitchen.

(Pause.)

LIZZIE: Did you know Papa killed my birds with the ax? He chopped off their heads. *(MRS BORDEN is uneasy.)* . . . It's alright. At first I felt bad, but I feel better now. I feel much better now. . . . I am a woman of decision, Mrs Borden. When I decide to do things, I do them, yes, I do. *(Smiles.)* How many times has Papa said — when Lizzie puts her mind to a thing, she does it — and I do. . . . It's always me who puts the slug poison out because they eat all the flowers and you don't like that, do you? They're bad things, they must die. You see, not all life is precious, is it?

MRS BORDEN: *(After a moment makes an attempt casually to gather together her things, to go upstairs. She does not want to be in the room with LIZZIE.)*

LIZZIE: Where're you going?

MRS BORDEN: Upstairs. . . . *(An excuse.)* The spare room needs changing.

(A knock at the back door . . . A second knock.)

LIZZIE: Someone's at the door. . . . *(A third knock.)* I'll get it.

(She exits to the kitchen. MRS BORDEN waits. LIZZIE returns. She's a bit out of breath. She carries a pile of clean clothes which she puts on the table. She looks at MRS BORDEN.)

LIZZIE: Did you want something?

MRS BORDEN: Who was it? — the door?

LIZZIE: Oh yes. I forgot. I had to step out back for a moment and — it's a note. A message for you.

MRS BORDEN: Oh.

LIZZIE: Shall I open it?

MRS BORDEN: That's alright. *(She holds out her hand.)*

LIZZIE: Looks like Papa's handwriting. . . . *(She passes over the note.)* Aren't you going to open it?

MRS BORDEN: I'll read it upstairs.

LIZZIE: Mrs Borden! . . . Would you mind . . . putting my clothes in my room? *(She gets some clothes from the table, MRS BORDEN takes them, something she would never normally do. Before she can move away, LIZZIE grabs her arm.)* Just a minute . . . I would like you to look into my eyes. What's the matter? Nothing's wrong. It's an experiment. . . . Look right into them. Tell me . . . what do you see . . . can you see anything?

MRS BORDEN: . . . Myself.

LIZZIE: Yes. When a person dies, retained on her eye is the image of the last thing she saw. Isn't that interesting? *(Pause.)*

(MRS BORDEN slowly starts upstairs. LIZZIE picks up remaining clothes on tale. The hand hatchet is concealed beneath them. She follows MRS BORDEN up the stairs.)

LIZZIE: Do you know something? If I were to kill someone, I would come up behind them very slowly and quietly. They would never even hear me, they would never turn around. *(MRS BORDEN stops on the stairs. She turns around to look at LIZZIE who is behind her.)* They would be too frightened to turn around even if they heard me. They would be so afraid they'd see what they feared. *(MRS BORDEN makes a move which might be an effort to go past LIZZIE back down the stairs. LIZZIE stops her.)* Careful. Don't fall. *(MRS BORDEN turns and slowly continues up the stairs with LIZZIE behind her.)* And then, I would strike them down. With them not turning around, they would retain no image of me on their eye. It would be better that way.

(LIZZIE and MRS BORDEN disappear at the top of the stairs. The stage is empty for a moment. BRIDGET enters. She carries the pail for washing the windows. She sets the pail down, wipes her forehead. She stands for a moment looking towards the stairs as if she might have heard a sound. She picks up the pail and exits to the kitchen. LIZZIE appears on the stairs. She is carrying the pile of clothes she carried upstairs. The hand hatchet is concealed under the clothes. LIZZIE descends the stairs, she seems calm, self-possessed. She places the clothes on the table. She pauses, then she slowly turns to look at MRS BORDEN's chair at the table. After a moment she moves to it, pauses a moment, then sits down in it. She sits there at ease, relaxed, thinking. BRIDGET enters from the kitchen, she sees LIZZIE, she stops, she takes in LIZZIE sitting in MRS BORDEN's chair. BRIDGET glances towards the stairs, back to LIZZIE. LIZZIE looks, for the first time, at BRIDGET.)

LIZZIE: We must hurry before Papa gets home.

BRIDGET: Lizzie?

LIZZIE: I have it all figured out, but you have to help me, Bridget, you have to help me.

BRIDGET: What have you done?

LIZZIE: He would never leave me the farm, not with her on his back, but now *(She gets up from the chair)* I will have the farm, and I will have the money, yes, to do what I please! And you too Bridget, I'll give you some of my money but you've got to help me. *(She moves towards BRIDGET who backs away a step.)* Don't be afraid, it's me, it's Lizzie, you like me!

BRIDGET: What have you done! *(Pause. BRIDGET moves towards the stairs.)*

LIZZIE: Don't go up there!

BRIDGET: You killed her!

LIZZIE: Someone broke in and they killed her.

BRIDGET: They'll know!

LIZZIE: Not if you help me.

BRIDGET: I can't, Miss Lizzie, I can't!

LIZZIE: *(Grabs BRIDGET's arm.)* Do you want them to hang me! Is that what you want! Oh Bridget, look! Look! *(She falls to her knees.)* I'm begging for my life, I'm begging. Deny me, and they will kill me. Help me, Bridget, please help me.

BRIDGET: But . . . what . . . could we do?

LIZZIE: *(Up off her knees.)* Oh I have it all figured out. I'll go down town as quick as I can and you leave the doors open and go back outside and work on the windows.

BRIDGET: I've finished them, Lizzie.

LIZZIE: Then do them again! Remember last year when the burglar broke in? Today someone broke in and she caught them.

BRIDGET: They'll never believe us.

LIZZIE: Have coffee with Lucy next door, stay with her till Papa gets home and he'll find her, and then each of us swears she was fine when we left, she was alright when we left! — it's going to work, Bridget, I know it!

BRIDGET: Your papa will guess.

LIZZIE: *(Getting ready to leave for down town.)* If he found me here he might guess, but he won't.

BRIDGET: Your papa will know!

LIZZIE: Papa loves me, if he has another story to believe, he'll believe it. He'd want to believe it, he'd have to believe it.

BRIDGET: Your papa will know.

LIZZIE: Why aren't you happy? I'm happy. We both should be happy! *(LIZZIE embraces BRIDGET. LIZZIE steps back a pace.)* Now — how do I look?

(MR BORDEN enters. BRIDGET sees him. LIZZIE slowly turns to see what BRIDGET is looking at.)

LIZZIE: Papa?

MR BORDEN: What is it? Where's Mrs Borden?

BRIDGET: I . . . don't know . . . sir . . . I . . . just came in, sir.

MR BORDEN: Did she leave the house?

BRIDGET: Well, sir . . .

LIZZIE: She went out. Someone delivered a message and she left.

(LIZZIE takes off her hat and looks at her father.)

LIZZIE: . . . You're home early, Papa.

MR BORDEN: I wanted to see Abbie. She's gone out, has she? Which way did she go? *(LIZZIE shrugs, he continues, more thinking aloud.)* Well . . . I . . . I . . . best wait for her here. I don't want to miss her again.

LIZZIE: Help Papa off with his coat, Bridget. . . . I hear there's a sale of dress goods on down-town. Why don't you go buy yourself a yard?

BRIDGET: Oh . . . I don't know, ma'am.

LIZZIE: You don't want any?

BRIDGET: I don't know.

LIZZIE: Then . . . why don't you go upstairs and lie down. Have a rest before lunch.

BRIDGET: I don't think I should.

LIZZIE: Nonsense.

BRIDGET: Lizzie, I —

LIZZIE: You go up and lie down. I'll look after things here.

(LIZZIE smiles at BRIDGET. BRIDGET starts up the stairs, suddenly stops. She looks back at LIZZIE.)

LIZZIE: It's alright . . . go on . . . it's alright. *(BRIDGET continues up the stairs. For the last bit of interchange, MR BORDEN has lowered the paper he's reading. LIZZIE looks at him.)* Hello Papa. You look so tired. . . . I make you unhappy. . . . I don't like to make you unhappy. I love you.

MR BORDEN: *(Smiles and takes her hand.)* I'm just getting old, Lizzie.

LIZZIE: You've got on my ring. . . . Do you remember when I gave you that? . . . When I left Miss Cornelia's — it was in a little blue velvet box, you hid it behind your back, and you said, "guess which hand, Lizzie!" And I guessed. And you gave it to me and you said, "it's real gold, Lizzie, it's for you because you are very precious to me." Do you remember, Papa? *(MR BORDEN nods.)* And I took it out of the little blue velvet box, and I took your hand, and I put my ring on your finger and I said "thank you, Papa, I love you." . . . You've never taken it off . . . see how it bites into the flesh of your finger. *(She presses his hand to her face.)* I forgive you, Papa, I forgive you for killing my birds. . . . You look so tired, why don't you lie down and rest, put your feet up, I'll undo your shoes for you. *(She kneels and undoes his shoes.)*

MR BORDEN: You're a good girl.

LIZZIE: I could never stand to have you hate me, Papa. Never. I would do anything rather than have you hate me.

MR BORDEN: I don't hate you, Lizzie.

LIZZIE: I would not want you to find out anything that would make you hate me. Because I love you.

MR BORDEN: And I love you, Lizzie, you'll always be precious to me.

LIZZIE: *(Looks at him, and then smiles.)* Was I — when I had scabs on my knees?

MR BORDEN: *(Laughs.)* Oh yes. Even then.

LIZZIE: *(Laughs.)* Oh Papa! . . . Kiss me! *(He kisses her on the forehead.)* Thank you, Papa.

MR BORDEN: Why're you crying?

LIZZIE: Because I'm so happy. Now . . . put your feet up and get to sleep . . . that's right . . . shut your eyes . . . go to sleep . . . go to sleep . . .

(She starts to hum, continues humming as MR BORDEN falls asleep. MISS LIZZIE/ BRIDGET appears on the stairs unobtrusively. LIZZIE still humming, moves to the table, slips her hand under the clothes, withdraws the hatchet. She approaches her father with the hatchet behind her back. She stops humming. A pause, then she slowly raises the

hatchet very high to strike him. Just as the hatchet is about to start its descent, there is a
blackout. Children's voices are heard singing:)
"Lizzie Borden took an ax,
Gave her mother forty whacks,
When the job was nicely done,
She gave her father forty-one!
Forty-one!
Forty-one!"

(The singing increases in volume and in distortion as it nears the end of the verse till the
last words are very loud but discernible, just. Silence. Then the sound of slow measured
heavy breathing which is growing into a wordless sound of hysteria. Light returns to the
stage, dim light from late in the day. THE ACTRESS *stands with the hatchet raised in*
the same position in which we saw her before the blackout, but the couch is empty. Her
eyes are shut. The sound comes from her. MISS LIZZIE *is at the foot of the stairs. She*
moves to THE ACTRESS, *reaches up to take the hatchet from her. When* MISS LIZZIE's
hand touches THE ACTRESS's, THE ACTRESS *releases the hatchet and whirls around to*
face MISS LIZZIE *who is left holding the hatchet.* THE ACTRESS *backs away from* MISS
LIZZIE. *There is a flickering of light at the top of the stairs.)*

EMMA: *(From upstairs.)* Lizzie! Lizzie! You're making too much noise!

*(*EMMA *descends the stairs carrying an oil lamp.* THE ACTRESS *backs away from*
LIZZIE, *turns and runs into the kitchen.* MISS LIZZIE *turns to see* EMMA. *The hand*
hatchet is behind MISS LIZZIE's *back concealed from* EMMA. EMMA *pauses for a*
moment.)

EMMA: Where is she?
MISS LIZZIE: Who?
EMMA: *(A pause then* EMMA *moves to the window and glances out.)* It's raining.
MISS LIZZIE: I know.
EMMA: *(Puts the lamp down, sits, lowers her voice.)* Lizzie.
MISS LIZZIE: Yes?
EMMA: I want to speak to you, Lizzie.
MISS LIZZIE: Yes Emma.
EMMA: That . . . actress who's come up from Boston.
MISS LIZZIE: What about her?
EMMA: People talk.
MISS LIZZIE: You needn't listen.
EMMA: In your position you should do nothing to *inspire talk.*
MISS LIZZIE: People need so little in the way of inspiration. And Miss Corne-
    lia's classes didn't cover "Etiquette for Acquitted Persons".
EMMA: Common sense should tell you what you ought or ought not do.
MISS LIZZIE: Common sense is repugnant to me. I prefer uncommon sense.
EMMA: I forbid her in this house, Lizzie!

(Pause.)

MISS LIZZIE: Do you?
EMMA: *(Backing down, softly.)* It's . . . disgraceful.
MISS LIZZIE: I see.

(MISS LIZZIE turns away from EMMA a few steps.)

EMMA: I simply cannot —
MISS LIZZIE: You could always leave.
EMMA: Leave?
MISS LIZZIE: Move. Away. Why don't you?
EMMA: I —
MISS LIZZIE: You could never, could you?
EMMA: If I only —
MISS LIZZIE: Knew.
EMMA: Lizzie, did you?
MISS LIZZIE: Oh Emma, do you intend asking me that question from now till death us do part?
EMMA: It's just —
MISS LIZZIE: For if you do, I may well take something sharp to you.
EMMA: Why do you joke like that!
MISS LIZZIE: *(Turning back to EMMA who sees the hatchet for the first time. EMMA's reaction is not any verbal or untoward movement. She freezes as MISS LIZZIE advances on her.)* Did you never stop and think that if I did, then you were guilty too?
EMMA: What?

(THE ACTRESS will enter unobtrusively on the periphery. We are virtually unaware of her entrance until she speaks and moves forward.)

MISS LIZZIE: It was you who brought me up, like a mother to me. Almost like a mother. Did you ever stop and think that I was like a puppet, your puppet. My head your hand, yes, your hand working my mouth, me saying all the things you felt like saying, me doing all the things you felt like doing, me spewing forth, me hitting out, and you, you — !
THE ACTRESS: *(Quietly.)* Lizzie.

(MISS LIZZIE is immediately in control of herself.)

EMMA: *(Whispers.)* I wasn't even here that day.
MISS LIZZIE: I can swear to that.
EMMA: Do you want to drive me mad?
MISS LIZZIE: Oh yes.
EMMA: You didn't . . . did you?
MISS LIZZIE: Poor . . . Emma.
THE ACTRESS: Lizzie. *(She takes the hatchet from MISS LIZZIE.)* Lizzie you did.
MISS LIZZIE: I didn't. *(THE ACTRESS looks to the hatchet — then to the audience.)* You did.

BLACKOUT

DAVID FRENCH

(1939–   )

orn in Coley's Point, Newfoundland, David French moved with his family to Toronto when he was six years old. He began his life in the theatre as an actor, but eventually turned to writing for radio and television.

His first stage play, Leaving Home *(1972), is about a family not unlike his own, uprooted from Newfoundland and living in Toronto. The sequel,* Of the Fields, Lately *(1975), is dedicated to "all fathers and sons," and won a Chalmers Award. A third play,* Salt-Water Moon *(1984), actually comes first in the Mercer tetralogy, and is the story of how the patriarch of the Mercer family, Jacob, courted Mary, his wife, when she was a young girl. A fourth play,* 1949 *(1989), returns to the time of the title, four years after the Mercers have moved to Toronto from Newfoundland.*

French's family plays explore the destructive power of dominance and guilt, but their dark moments are balanced with comedy. French believes that "life is tragic and comic both at the same time, two interwoven threads. For example, you can be at a funeral and caught up in your own grief and look up and see the minister's fly at halfmast and his shirt-tail sticking out of it like a folded napkin. Now I may or may not laugh to myself at the time but I will see the humour of it later, in retrospect."[1] Writing Leaving Home *about his own people, in their own Newfoundland idiom, was in French's words "the most cathartic experience of my life."[2]*

Other stage plays include One Crack Out *(1976), about an aging pool hustler in Toronto;* Jitters *(1980), a backstage play; a translation of Chekhov's* The Seagull *(1978); and an adaptation of* The Forest *(1987) by another Russian writer, Alexander Ostrovsky.*

INTRODUCTION TO *LEAVING HOME*

*he first of the Mercer family plays, *Leaving Home* is written in the regional speech patterns of Newfoundland. The language is smooth and songlike in parts, and crashing and violent in others. The play is both tragic and comic; it chronicles the breakup of a family, the loss of two sons on one day, yet it contains comic details of everyday family life.

Jacob, the father, is the focus of the play. The first line refers to him, and before he sets foot on stage there is plenty of talk about Jacob, comparing him to others, anticipating his mood. This sets up the conflict later articulated by Jacob to his family of two sons, Ben and Billy, and wife, Mary: "The t'ree of you against the one of me." Competition for Mary's favour and attention is also apparent. Mary treats her husband and sons as if they were all children, and Jacob complains about his sons: "I've never counted.

---

1 Peter Neary, "Of many-coloured glass," Canadian Forum 53 (March 1974): 26.
2 Geraldine Anthony, ed., Stage Voices (Toronto: Doubleday, 1978): 246.

Not since the day they was born." Ben, the oldest son, is too aware of the tension in the household, and says to his mother: "It's always been him and us." At the end of the play, the pattern of lying, withholding, hiding, pretending has finally been broken. And although Jacob really believes that "all we got in this world is the family," he is incapable of holding the family together.

French plots his drama at converging life events for the sons in the family: Ben has just graduated from high school, and Bill is about to marry his sixteen-year-old pregnant girlfriend. Both events backfire, and both sons are driven away from the family home by their father. Even Mary, who is accustomed to protecting Jacob from the truth, is unable to block the sequence of events. In the end, however, she remains loyal to Jacob while supporting her sons in the choices they have made.

The past is as important as the present in *Leaving Home*. Jacob constantly refers back to his own experience, measuring the worth and value of what is before him by the standards of his own upbringing. Because Jacob's uncle was murdered by Catholics, Jacob holds it against Kathy, Billy's fiancée, who is Catholic in name only. Jacob often reminisces about his youth and how he courted Mary. His realm of experience is limited to love and marriage, work and family. He is bewildered by Ben's graduation, and feels left out, not only because Ben didn't think Jacob would want to attend his graduation ceremony, but because Jacob himself didn't get past Grade 3.

French continues the battle between father and sons in *Of the Fields, Lately*, returns to the past of Jacob and Mary's courtship in *Salt-Water Moon*, and then recounts the newly transplanted lives of the extended Mercer family living in Toronto as Newfoundland joins Confederation in *1949*.

Leaving Home

CAST OF CHARACTERS

MARY MERCER

BEN MERCER

BILLY MERCER

JACOB MERCER

KATHY JACKSON

MINNIE JACKSON

HAROLD

SCENE

The play is set in Toronto on an early November day in the late fifties.

ACT ONE

The lights come up on a working-class house in Toronto. The stage is divided into three playing areas: kitchen, dining room, and living room. In addition there is a hallway leading into the living room. Two bedroom doors lead off the hallway, as well as the front door which is offstage.

The kitchen contains a fridge, a stove, cupboards over the sink for everyday dishes, and a small drop-leaf table with two wooden chairs, one at either end. A plastic garbage receptacle stands beside the stove. A hockey calendar hangs on a wall, and a kitchen prayer.

The dining room is furnished simply with an oak table and chairs. There is an oak cabinet containing the good dishes and silverware. Perhaps a family portrait hangs on the wall — a photo taken when the sons were much younger.

The living room contains a chesterfield and an armchair, a T.V., a record player and a fireplace. On the mantle rests a photo album and a silver-framed photo of the two sons — then small boys — astride a pinto pony. On one wall hangs a mirror. On another, a seascape. There is also a small table with a telephone on it.

It is around five-thirty on a Friday afternoon, and MARY MERCER, *aged fifty, stands before the mirror in the living room, admiring her brand new dress and fixed hair. As she preens, the front door opens and in walk her two sons,* BEN, *eighteen, and* BILL, *seventeen. Each carries a box from a formal rental shop and schoolbooks.*

MARY: Did you bump into your father?

BEN: No, we just missed him, Mom. He's already picked up his tux. He's probably at the Oakwood. *(He opens the fridge and helps himself to a beer.)*

MARY: Get your big nose out of the fridge. And put down that beer. You'll spoil your appetite.

BEN: No, I won't. *(He searches for a bottle opener in a drawer.)*

MARY: And don't contradict me. What other bad habits you learned lately?

BEN: *(teasing)* Don't be such a grouch. You sound like Dad. *(He sits at the table and opens his beer.)*

MARY: Yes, well just because you're in university now, don't t'ink you can raid the fridge any time you likes.

(BILL crosses the kitchen and throws his black binder and books in the garbage receptacle.)

MARY: What's that for? *(BILL exits into his bedroom and she calls after him.)* It's not the end of the world, my son. *(pause)* Tell you the truth, Ben. We always figured you'd be the one to land in trouble, if anyone did. I don't mean that as an insult. You're more . . . I don't know . . . like your father.

BEN: I am?

(Music from BILL's room.)

MARY: *(calling, exasperated)* Billy, do you have to have that so loud? *(BILL turns down his record player. To BEN)* I'm glad your graduation went okay last night. How was Billy? Was he glad he went?

BEN: Well, he wasn't upset, if that's what you mean.

MARY: *(slight pause)* Ben, how come you not to ask your father?

BEN: What do you mean?

BILL: *(off)* Mom, will you pack my suitcase? I can't get everything in.

MARY: *(calling)* I can't now, Billy. Later.

BEN: I want to talk to you, Mom. It's important.

MARY: I want to talk to you, too.

BILL: *(Comes out of bedroom, crosses to kitchen.)* Mom, here's the deposit on my locker. I cleaned it out and threw away all my old gym clothes. *(He helps himself to an apple from the fridge.)*

MARY: Didn't you just hear me tell your brother to stay out of there? I might as well talk to the sink. Well, you can t'row away your old school clothes — that's your affair — but take those books out of the garbage. Go on. You never knows. They might come in handy sometime.

BILL: How? *(He takes the books out, then sits at the table with BEN.)*

MARY: Well, you can always go to night school and get your senior matric, once the baby arrives and Kathy's back to work. . . . Poor child. I talked to her on the phone this morning. She's still upset, and I don't blame her. I'd be hurt myself if my own mother was too drunk to show up to my shower.

BILL: *(a slight ray of hope)* Maybe she won't show up tonight.

MARY: *(Glances anxiously at the kitchen clock and turns to check the fish and potatoes)* Look at the time. I just wish to goodness he had more t'ought, your father. The supper'll dry up if he don't hurry. He might pick up a phone and mention when he'll be home. Not a grain of t'ought in his head. And I wouldn't put it past him to forget his tux in the beer parlour. *(Finally she turns and looks at her two sons, disappointed.)* And look at the two of you. Too busy with your mouths to give your mother a second glance. I could stand here till my legs dropped off before either of you would notice my dress.

BEN: It's beautiful, Mom.

MARY: That the truth?

BILL: Would we lie to you, Mom?

MARY: Just so long as I don't look foolish next to Minnie. She can afford to dress up — Willard left her well off when he died.

BEN: Don't worry about the money. Dad won't mind.

MARY: Well, it's not every day your own son gets married, is it? *(to BILL as she puts on large apron)* It's just that I don't want Minnie Jackson looking all decked out like the *Queen Mary* and me the tug that dragged her in. You understands, don't you, Ben?

BEN: Sure.

BILL: I understand too, Mom.

MARY: I know you do, Billy. I know you do. *(She opens a tin of peaches and fills five dessert dishes.)* Minnie used to go with your father. Did you know that, Billy? Years and years ago.

BILL: No kidding?

BEN: *(at the same time)* Really?

MARY: True as God is in Heaven. Minnie was awful sweet on Dad, too. She t'ought the world of him.

BILL: *(incredulously)* Dad?

MARY: Don't act so surprised. Your father was quite a one with the girls.

BEN: No kidding?

MARY: He could have had his pick of any number of girls. *(to BILL)* You ask Minnie sometime. Of course, in those days I was going with Jerome McKenzie, who later became a Queen's Counsel in St. John's. I must have mentioned him.

(The boys exchange smiles.)

BEN: I think you have, Mom.

BILL: A hundred times.

MARY: *(gently indignant–to BILL)* And that I haven't!

BILL: She has too. Hasn't she, Ben?

MARY: Never you mind, Ben. *(to BILL)* And instead of sitting around gabbing so much you'd better go change your clothes. Kathy'll soon be here. *(as BILL crosses to his bedroom)* Is the rehearsal still at eight?

BILL: We're supposed to meet Father Douglas at the church at five to. I just hope Dad's not too drunk. *(He exits.)*

MARY: *(Studies BEN a moment.)* Look at yourself. A cigarette in one hand, a bottle of beer in the other, at your age! You didn't learn any of your bad habits from me, I can tell you. *(pause)* Ben, don't be in such a hurry to grow up. *(She sits across from him.)* Whatever you do, don't be in such a hurry. Look at your poor young brother. His whole life ruined. Oh, I could weep a bellyful when I t'inks of it. Just seventeen, not old enough to sprout whiskers on his chin, and already the burdens of a man on his t'in little shoulders. Your poor father hasn't slept a full night since this happened. Did you know that? He had such high hopes for Billy. He wanted you both to go to college and not have to work as hard as he's had to all his life. And now look. You have more sense than that, Ben. Don't let life trap you.

(BILL enters. He has changed his pants and is buttoning a clean white shirt. MARY goes into the dining room and begins to remove the tablecloth from the dining room table.)

BILL: Mom, what about Dad? He won't start picking on the priest, will he? You know how he likes to argue.

MARY: He won't say a word, my son. You needn't worry. Worry more about Minnie showing up.

BILL: What if he's drunk?

MARY: He won't be. Your father knows better than to sound off in church. Oh, and another t'ing — he wants you to polish his shoes for tonight. They're in the bedroom. The polish is on your dresser. You needn't be too fussy.

BEN: I'll do his shoes, Mom. Billy's all dressed.

MARY: No, no, Ben, that's all right. He asked Billy to.

BILL: What did Ben do this time?

MARY: He didn't do anyt'ing.

BILL: He must have.

MARY: Is it too much trouble to polish your father's shoes, after all he does for you? If you won't do it, I'll do it myself.

BILL: *(indignantly)* How come when Dad's mad at Ben, I get all the dirty jobs? Jeez! Will I be glad to get out of here! *(Rolling up his shirt sleeves he exits into his bedroom.)*

(MARY takes a clean white linen tablecloth from a drawer in the cabinet and covers the table. During the following scene she sets five places with her good glasses, silverware and plates.)

BEN: *(slight pause)* Billy's right, isn't he? What'd I do, Mom?

MARY: Take it up with your father. I'm tired of being the middle man.

BEN: Is it because of last night? *(slight pause)* It is, isn't it?

MARY: He t'inks you didn't want him there, Ben. He t'inks you're ashamed of him.

BEN: He wouldn't have gone, Mom. That's the only reason I never invited him.

MARY: He would have went, last night.

BEN: *(angrily)* He's never even been to one lousy Parents' Night in thirteen years. Not one! And he calls *me* contrary!

MARY: You listen to me. Your father never got past Grade T'ree. He was yanked out of school and made to work. In those days, back home, he was lucky to get that much and don't kid yourself.

BEN: Yeah? So?

MARY: So? So he's afraid to. He's afraid of sticking out. Is that so hard to understand? Is it?

BEN: What're you getting angry about? All I said was —

MARY: You say he don't take an interest, but he was proud enough to show off your report cards all those years. I suppose with you that don't count for much.

BEN: All right. But he never goes anywhere without you, Mom, and last night you were here at the shower.

MARY: Last night was different, Ben, and you ought to know that. It was your high school graduation. He would have went with me or without me. If you'd only asked him.

(A truck horn blasts twice.)

There he is now in the driveway. Whatever happens, don't fall for his old tricks. He'll be looking for a fight, and doing his best to find any excuse. *(calling)* Billy, you hear that? Don't complain about the shoes, once your father comes!

BEN: *(urgently)* Mom, there's something I want to tell you before Dad comes in.

MARY: Sure, my son. Go ahead. I'm listening. What's on your mind?

BEN: Well . . .

MARY: *(smiling)* Come on. It can't be that bad.

BEN: *(slight pause)* I want to move out, Mom.

MARY: *(almost inaudibly)* . . . What?

BEN: I said I want to move out.

MARY: *(softly, as she sets the cutlery)* I heard you. *(pause)* What for?

BEN: I just think it's time. I'll be nineteen soon. *(pause)* I'm moving in with Billy and Kathy and help pay the rent. *(pause)* I won't be far away. I'll see you on weekends. *(MARY nods.)* Mom?

MARY: *(absently)* What?

BEN: Will you tell Dad? *(slight pause)* Mom? Did you hear me?

MARY: I heard you. He'll be upset, I can tell you. By rights you ought to tell him yourself.

BEN: If I do, we'll just get in a big fight and you know it. He'll take it better, coming from you.

(The front door opens and JACOB MERCER enters whistling 'I's the b'y'. He is fifty, though he looks older. He is dressed in a peaked cap, carpenter's overalls, thick-soled workboots, and a lumberjack shirt over a T-shirt. Under one arm he carries his black lunchpail.)

MARY: Your suit! I knowed it!

JACOB: Don't get in an uproar, now. I left it sitting on the front seat of the truck. *(He looks at BEN, then back to MARY.)* Is Billy home?

MARY: He's in the bedroom, polishing your shoes.

JACOB: *(Crosses to the bedroom door.)* Billy, my son, come out a moment.

(BILL enters, carrying a shoe brush.)

Put down the brush and go out in my truck and bring me back the tux on the seat.

BILL: What's wrong with Ben? He's not doing anything.

JACOB: Don't ask questions. That's a good boy. I'd ask your brother, but he always has a good excuse.

BEN: I'll go get it. *(He starts for the front door.)*

JACOB: *(calling after BEN)* Oh, it's too late to make up now. The damage is done.

MARY: Don't talk nonsense, Jacob.

JACOB: *(a last thrust)* And aside from that — I wouldn't want you dirtying your nice clean hands in your father's dirty old truck!

(The front door closes on his last words. BILL returns to his room. JACOB sets his lunchpail and his cap on the dining room table.)

JACOB: Did he get his diploma?

MARY: Yes. It's in the bedroom.

JACOB: *(Breaks into a smile and lifts his cap.)* And will you gaze on Mary over there. When I stepped in the door, I t'ought the Queen had dropped in for tea.

MARY: You didn't even notice.

JACOB: Come here, my dear, and give Jacob a kiss.

MARY: *(She darts behind the table, laughing.)* I'll give Jacob a swift boot in the rear end with my pointed toe.

(JACOB grabs her, rubs his rough cheek against hers.)

You'll take the skin off! Jake! You're far too rough! And watch my new dress! Don't rip it.

(JACOB releases her and breaks into a little jig as he sings.)

> I's the b'y that builds the boat
> And I's the b'y that sails her,
> I's the b'y that catches the fish
> And takes 'em home to Lizer.
>
> Sods and rinds to cover your flake
> Cake and tea for supper
> Codfish in the spring of the year
> Fried in maggoty butter.
>
> I don't want your maggoty fish
> Cake and tea for winter
> I could buy as good as that
> Down in Bona Vista.
>
> I took Lizer to a dance
> And faith but she could travel
> And every step that she did take
> Was up to her ass in gravel.

(JACOB ends the song with a little step or flourish.)

MARY: There's no mistakin' where you've been to, and it's not to church.

JACOB: All right, now, I had one little glass, and don't you start.

MARY: *(as she re-enters the kitchen)* How many?

JACOB: I can't lie, Mary. *(He puts his hand on his heart.)* As God is my witness — two. Two glasses to celebrate the wedding of my youngest son. *(He follows her into the kitchen.)*

MARY: Half a dozen's more like it, unless you expects God to perjure himself for the likes of you. Well, no odds: you're just in time. Kathy'll soon be here, so get cleaned up.

JACOB: I washed up on the job.

MARY: Well, change your old clothes. You're not sitting down with the likes of that on. *(She returns to the dining room with bread and butter for the dining room table.)*

JACOB: I suppose it's fish with Kathy coming and him now a bloody Mick. Next t'ing you knows he'll be expecting me to chant grace in Latin.

MARY: And I'll crown you if you opens your yap like that around Kathy. Don't you dare.

JACOB: *(Following MARY, he sits at the dining room table.)* 'Course we could have the priest drop by and bless the table himself. *(He makes the sign of the cross.)*

MARY: Jacob!

JACOB: Though I doubts he could get his Cadillac in the driveway.

MARY: *(back to kitchen)* If you comes out with the likes of that tonight, I'll never speak to you again. You hear?

JACOB: Ah, go on with you. What do you know? If you had nothing in your pockets but holes, a priest wouldn't give you t'read to sew it with.

BEN: *(Enters with the box.)* I put your toolbox down in the basement while I was at it, Dad. And rolled up the windows in your truck, in case it rains tonight.

JACOB: Did you, now? And I'm supposed to forget all about last night, is that it? Pretend it never occurred? Your brother's good enough for you but not your own father. *(as BEN crosses to kitchen)* Well, it would take more than that to stitch up the hurt, I can assure you. And a long time before it heals. Don't be looking to your mother for support.

BEN: I wasn't. *(He sits at kitchen table.)*

JACOB: Or for sympathy, either.

MARY: Jacob, it don't serve no purpose to look for a fight.

JACOB: *(to MARY)* You keep your two cents worth out of it. Nobody asked you. You got too much to say.

(Enter BILL, carrying the shined shoes, which he gives to his father.)

BILL: Hey, Dad, do me a favour? When Kathy gets here, no cracks about the Pope's nose and stuff like that. And just for once don't do that Squid-Jiggin' thing and take your teeth out. Okay? *(He sits at table across from his father and reads the evening paper.)*

JACOB: Well, listen to him, now. *(to MARY)* Who put him up to that? You? Imagine. Telling me what I can say and do in my own house.

MARY: *(returning to dining room)* Billy, my son, I got a feeling you just walked into it. *(She takes a polishing cloth from cabinet and rubs her good silverware, including a large fish-knife.)*

JACOB: *(to BILL)* If you only knowed what my poor father went t'rough with the Catholics. Oh, if you only knowed, you wouldn't be doing this. My own son a turncoat. And back home, when we was growing up, you wouldn't dare go where the Catholics lived after dark. You'd be murdered, and many's the poor boy was. Knocked over the head and drownded, and all they done was let night catch them on a Catholic road. My father's brother was one. Poor Isaac. He was just fifteen, that summer. Tied with his arms behind him and tossed in the pond like a stone. My poor father never forgot that to his dying day.

(The family wait out the harangue.)

And here you is j'ining their ranks! T'ree weeks of instructions. By the jumping Jesus Christ you don't come from my side of the family. I'm glad my poor father never lived to see this day, I can tell you. The loyalest Orangeman that ever marched in a church parade, my father. He'd turn over in his grave if he saw a grandson of his kissing the Pope's ass. Promising to bring up your poor innocent babies Roman Catholics and them as ignorant of Rome as earthworms.

Oh, it's a good t'ing for you, my son, that he ain't around to see it, because sure as you'm there he'd march into that church tomorrow with his belt in his hand, and take that smirk off your face! Billy, my son, I never expected this of you, of all people. No, I didn't. Not you. If it was your brother, now, I could understand it. He'd do it just for spite. . . .

MARY: Hold your tongue, boy. Don't you ever run down? I just hope to goodness Ben don't call on you at the wedding to toast the bride and groom. We'll all be old before it's over. *(slight pause)* Did you try on your tux?

JACOB: No, boy, it was too crowded.

MARY: Then try it on. You're worse than the kids. *(She hands him the box.)* Go on.

JACOB: *(to BILL, referring to the shoes)* T'anks. *(He exits into his bedroom.)*

MARY: Ben, do your mother a favour? Fill up the glasses. I left the jug in the kitchen. *(She sits at the dining room table, checks and folds five linen napkins.)* Look at him, Ben. The little fart. My baby. *(to herself)* How quick it all goes. . . . I can still see us to this day . . . the t'ree of us . . . coming up from Newfoundland . . . July of 1945 . . . the war not yet over. . . . Father gone ahead to look for work on construction . . . that old train packed with soldiers, and do you t'ink a single one would rise off his big fat backside to offer up his seat? Not on your life. There we was, huddled together out on the brakes, a couple, t'ree hours . . . with the wind and the soot from the engine blowing back . . . until a lady come out and saw us. 'Well, the likes of this I've never seen,' she says. 'I've got four sons in the war, and if one of mine was in that carriage, I'd disown 'im!'

We've never had anyt'ing to be ashamed of, my sons. We've been poor . . . but we've always stuck together. *(to BILL)* Is you frightened, my son?

BILL: No. Why should I be?

MARY: Don't be ashamed of it. Tomorrow you'll most likely wish you was back with your mother and father in your own soft bed.

BEN: He's scared shitless, Mom. *(to BILL)* Tell the truth.

MARY: Ben, is that nice talk?

BILL: *(to BEN)* I'll trade places.

MARY: Well, as long as you loves her, that's all that matters. Without that there's nothing, and with it what you don't have can wait. But a word of warning, Billy — don't come running to us with your squabbles, because we won't stick our noses into it. And before I forgets — you'd better not say a word to your father about Ben moving out. I'll tell him myself after the wedding.

JACOB: *(off)* Mary!

MARY: *(calling* What is it, boy?

JACOB: *(off)* Come here! I can't get this goddamn button fast!

MARY: *(shaking her head)* It's one of those mysteries how he made it t'rough life this far. If he didn't have me, he wouldn't know which leg of his pants was which. *(She exits.)*

BILL: *(slight pause)* You told her, huh? She doesn't seem to mind.

BEN: Keep your voice down. You want Dad to hear?

BILL: What did she say? Is she going to tell him?

BEN: Yeah, but do you think I ought to let her?

BILL: What do you mean?

BEN: Well, maybe I should tell him myself.

BILL: Are you crazy?

BEN: If I don't, you know what'll happen. Mom'll get all the shit.

BILL: *(pause)* Ben, you really want to do this? Are you sure?

BEN: Look — my books and tuition're paid for. All I got to worry about is the rent. I can handle that, waiting on tables. I'll make out. Listen, whose idea was it anyhow? Mine or yours? I wouldn't do it if I didn't want to.

BILL: Okay.

BEN: I need to, Billy. Christ, you know that. Either Dad goes, or I do.

BILL: I wish I felt that way. I don't want to move out. I don't want to get married. I don't know the first thing about girls. I mean, Kathy's the first girl I ever did it with. No kidding. The very first. We've only done it four or five times. The first time was in a cemetery, for Chrissake!

BEN: Well, at least you've been laid, Billy. I never.

BILL: Really? *(he laughs — pause)* I like Kathy. I like her a lot. But I don't know what else. What do you think Dad would do, if he was in my shoes? I think if Kathy was Mom he'd marry her, don't you?

MARY: *(Enters.)* Listen to me, you two. I don't want either one of you to say one word or snicker even when your father comes out. Is that understood?

BEN: What's wrong?

MARY: They give him the wrong coat. I suppose he was in such a rush to get to the Oakwood he didn't bother trying it on.

(Enter JACOB singing, now dressed in the rental tux and polished shoes. The sleeves are miles too short for him, the back hiked up. He looks like a caricature of discomfort.)

> Here comes the bride,
> All fat and wide,
> See how she wobbles
> From side to side.

(The boys glance at one another and try to keep from breaking up.)

JACOB: Well, boys, am I a fit match for your mother?

BEN: Dad, I wish I had a camera.

JACOB: Is you making fun?

MARY: No, he's not. The sleeves are a sight, but — *(giving* BEN *a censorious look)* — aside from that it's a perfect fit. Couldn't be better. Could it, Billy?

BILL: Made to measure, Dad.

JACOB: I t'ink I'll kick up my heels. I'm right in the mood. *(as he crosses to the record player)* What do you say, Mary? Feel up to it? *(He selects a record.)*

MARY: I'm willing, if you is, Jake.

JACOB: All right, boys, give us room. *(The record starts to play — a rousing tune with lots of fiddles.)* Your mother loves to twirl her skirt and show off her drawers! *(He seizes his wife, and they whirl around the room, twirling and stomping with enjoyment and abandon.)*

BEN: Go, Mom! *(He whistles.)*

(BILL *and* BEN *clap their hands to the music.)*

Give her hell, Dad!

MARY: Not so fast, Jacob, you'll make me dizzy!

*(*JACOB *stops after a few turns. He is slightly dizzy. He sits.)*

JACOB: *(to* BILL*)* Dance with your mother. I galled my heel at work. *(*BILL *does.)* You ought to have seen your mother in her day, Ben. She'd turn the head of a statue. There wasn't a man from Bareneed to Bay Roberts[1] didn't blink when she passed by.

MARY: Come on, Ben. Before it's over. *(She takes* BEN, *and they dance around the room.)*

JACOB: That's one t'ing about Ben, Mary. He won't ever leave you. The day he gets married himself he'll move in next door.

(Finally MARY *collapses laughing on the chesterfield. The music plays on.)*

JACOB: *(expansively)* I t'ink a drink's in order. What do you say, boys? To whet the appetite. *(He searches in the bottom of the cabinet. To* MARY*)* Where's all the whiskey to? You didn't t'row it out, did you?

MARY: You t'rowed it down your t'roat, that's where it was t'rowed.

JACOB: Well, boys, looks like there's no whiskey. *(He holds up a bottle.)* How does a little 'screech'[2] sound?

BEN: Not for me, Dad.

JACOB: Why not?

BEN: I just don't like it.

JACOB: *(sarcastically)* No, you wouldn't. I suppose it's too strong for you. Well, Billy'll have some, won't you, my son? *(He turns down the music.)*

---

1 *located on the south coast of Newfoundland.*
2 *a dark rum made in Newfoundland.*

BILL: *(surprised)* I will?

JACOB: Get two glasses out, then, and let's have a quick drink. *(BILL does and hands a glass to his father.)* Don't suppose you'd have a little drop, Mary, my love? *(He winks at BILL)*

MARY: Go on with you. You ought to have better sense, teaching the boys all your bad habits. And after you promised your poor mother on her death-bed you'd warn them off alcohol . . .

JACOB: Don't talk foolishness. A drop of this won't harm a soul. Might even do some good, all you know.

MARY: Yes, some good it's done you.

JACOB: At least I'd take a drink with my own father, if he was alive. I'd do that much, my lady.

MARY: *(quickly)* Pay no attention, Ben. *(to JACOB)* And listen, I don't want you getting tight and making a disgrace of yourself at the rehearsal tonight. You hear?

JACOB: Oh, I'll be just as sober as the priest, rest assured of that. And you just study his fingers, if they'm not as brown as a new potato from nicotine. I dare say if he didn't swallow Sen-Sen,[3] you'd know where all that communion wine goes to. *(to BILL)* How many drunks you suppose is wearing Roman collars? More than the Pope would dare admit. And all those t'ousands of babies they keep digging up in the basements of convents. It's shocking.

BEN: That's a lot of bull, Dad.

JACOB: It is, is it? Who told you that? Is that more of the stuff you learns at university? Your trouble is you've been brainwashed.

BEN: You just want to believe all that.

MARY: And you'd better not come out with that tonight, if you knows what's good for you.

JACOB: *(to BILL)* Mind — I'm giving you fair warning. I won't sprinkle my face with holy water or make the sign of the cross. And nothing in this world or the next can persuade me.

BILL: You don't have to, Dad. Relax.

JACOB: Just so you knows.

BEN: All you got to do, Dad, is sit there in the front row and look sweet.

JACOB: All right, there's no need to get saucy. I wasn't talking to you! *(He pours a little 'screech' in the two glasses. To BILL)* Here's to you, boy. You got the makings of a man. That's more than I can say for your older brother.

(JACOB downs his drink. BILL glances helplessly at BEN. He doesn't drink.)

Go on.

(BILL hesitates, then downs it, grimacing and coughing.)

You see that, Mary? *(his anger rising)* It's your fault the other one's the way he is. It's high time, my lady, you let go and weaned him away from the tit!

---

3 *a small breath-freshening candy with a strong flavour of licorice.*

MARY: *(angrily)* You shut your mouth. There's no call for that kind of talk!

JACOB: He needs more in his veins than mother's milk, goddamn it!

BEN: *(shouting at JACOB)* What're you screaming at her for? She didn't do anything!

JACOB: *(a semblance of sudden calm)* Well, listen to him, now. Look at the murder in his face. One harsh word to his mother and up comes his fists. I'll bet you wouldn't be half so quick to defend your father.

MARY: Be still, Jacob. You don't know what you're saying.

JACOB: He t'inks he's too good to drink with me!

BEN: All right, I will, if it's that important. Only let's not fight.

MARY: He's just taunting you into it, Ben. Don't let him.

JACOB: *(sarcastically)* No, my son, your mother's right. I wouldn't wish for your downfall on my account. To hear her tell it I'm the devil tempting Saul on the road to Damascus.

MARY: Well, the devil better learn his scripture, if he wants to quote it. The devil tempted our Lord in the wilderness, and Saul had a revelation on the road to Damascus.

JACOB: A revelation! *(He turns off the record.)* I'll give you a revelation! I'm just a piece of shit around here! Who is it wears himself out year after year to give him a roof over his head and food in his mouth? Who buys his clothes and keeps him in university?

MARY: He buys his own clothes, and he's got a scholarship.

JACOB: *(furious)* Oh, butt out! You'd stick up for him if it meant your life, and never once put in a good word for me.

MARY: I'm only giving credit where credit's due.

JACOB: Liar.

MARY: Ah, go on. You're a fine one to talk. You'd call the ace of spades white and not bat an eye.

JACOB: *(enraged)* It never fails. I can't get my own son to do the simplest goddamn t'ing without a row. No matter what.

BEN: It's never simple, Dad. You never let it be simple or I might. It's always a **test**.

JACOB: Test!

MARY: Ben, don't get drawn into it.

JACOB: *(to BEN)* The sooner you learns to get along with others, the sooner you'll grow up. Test!

BEN: Do you ever hear yourself? 'Ben, get up that ladder. You want people to think you're a sissy?' 'Have a drink, Ben. It'll make a man out of you!'

JACOB: I said no such t'ing, now. Liar.

BEN: It's what you **meant**. 'Cut your hair, Ben. You look like a girl.' The same shit over and over, and it never stops!

JACOB: Now it all comes out. You listening to this, Mary?

BEN: No, you listen, Dad. You don't really expect me to climb that ladder or take that drink. You want me to refuse, don't you?

JACOB: Well, listen to him. The faster you gets out into the real world the better for you. *(He turns away.)*

BEN: Dad, you don't want me to be a man, you just want to impress me with how much less of a man I am than you. *(He snatches the bottle from his father and takes a swig.)* All right, Look. *(He rips open his shirt.)* I still haven't got hair on my chest, and I'm still not a threat to you.

JACOB: No, and you'm not likely ever to be, either, until you grows up and gets out from under your mother's skirts.

BEN: No, Dad — until I get out from under **yours**.

(The doorbell rings.)

MARY: That's Kathy. All right, that's more than enough for one night. Let's have no more bickering. Jake, get dressed. And not another word out of anyone. The poor girl will t'ink she's fallen in with a pack of wild savages.

JACOB: *(getting in the last word)* And there's no bloody mistakin' who the wild savage is. *(With that he exits into his bedroom.)*

MARY: Billy, answer the door. *(to* BEN*)* And you — change your shirt. You look a fright.

*(*BEN *exits.* BILL *opens the front door, and* KATHY *enters. She is sixteen, very pretty, but at the moment her face is pale and emotionless.)*

KATHY: Hello, Mrs. Mercer.

MARY: You're just in time, Kathy. *(*MARY *gives her a kiss.)* Take her coat, Billy. I'll be right out, dear. *(She exits.)*

KATHY: Where is everyone?

BILL: *(taking her coat)* Getting dressed. *(As he tries to kiss her, she pulls away her cheek.)*

BILL: What's wrong? *(He hangs up her coat.)*

KATHY: Nothing. I don't feel well.

BILL: Why not? Did you drink too much at the party?

KATHY: What party?

BILL: Didn't the girls at work throw a party for you this afternoon?

KATHY: I didn't go to the office this afternoon.

BILL: You didn't go? What do you mean?

KATHY: Just what I said.

BILL: What **did** you say?

KATHY: Will you get off my back!

BILL: What did I say? *(slight pause)* Are you mad at me?

KATHY: *(Looks at him.)* Billy, do you love me? Do you? I need to know.

BILL: What happened, Kathy?

KATHY: I'm asking you a simple question.

BILL: And I want to know what's happened.

KATHY: If I hadn't been pregnant, you'd never have wanted to get married, would you?

BILL: So?

KATHY: I hate you.

BILL: For Chrissake, Kathy, what's happened?

KATHY: *(Sits on the chesterfield.)* I lost the baby. . . .

BILL: What?

KATHY: Isn't that good news?

BILL: What the hell happened?

KATHY: I started bleeding in the ladies' room this morning.

BILL: Bleeding? What do you mean?

KATHY: Haemorrhaging. I screamed, and one of the girls rushed me to the hospital. I think the people at work thought I'd done something to myself.

BILL: Had you?

KATHY: Of course not. You know I wouldn't.

BILL: What did the doctor say?

KATHY: I had a miscarriage. *(She looks up at him.)* You're not even sorry, are you?

BILL: I am, really. What else did the doctor say?

KATHY: I lost a lot of blood. I'm supposed to eat lots of liver and milk, to build it up. You should have seen me, Billy. I was white and shaky. I'm a little better now. I've been sleeping all afternoon.

BILL: *(slight pause)* What was it?

KATHY: What was what?

BILL: The baby.

KATHY: Do you really want to know?

(BILL *doesn't answer.*)

BILL: What'll we do?

KATHY: Tell our folks, I guess. My mother doesn't know yet. She's been at the track all day with her boyfriend. *(slight pause)* I haven't told anyone else, Billy. Just you.

(*Enter* JACOB *and* MARY. *He is dressed in a pair of slacks and a white shirt. He carries a necktie in his hand.* MARY *wears a blouse and skirt.*)

JACOB: Billy, my son, tie me a Windsor knot. That's a good boy. *(He hands* BILL *the necktie and* BILL *proceeds to make the knot. Shyly, to* KATHY*)* Hello, my dear. *(*KATHY *nods.)* Lovely old day.

MARY: Come on. We may as well sit right down before it colds off. I'll serve up the fish and potatoes. *(She transfers the fish and potatoes into serving dishes.)*

JACOB: *(calling)* Ben! *(to* KATHY, *referring to the tie)* I'm all t'umbs or I'd do it myself.

BEN: *(Enters, his shirt changed.)* Hi, Kathy.

KATHY: Hi, Ben. Congratulations.

BEN: For what?

KATHY: Didn't you graduate last night?

BEN: Oh. Yeah.

JACOB: I suppose if Ben ever becomes Prime Minister, I'll be the last to know unless I reads it in the newspapers.

MARY: Kathy, you sit right down there, dear. Billy, you sit next to her. And Ben's right here.

(BILL *hands his father the tie.* JACOB *slips it on as he approaches the table.*)

Father, why don't you say grace?

JACOB: Maybe Kathy would like to.

KATHY: We never say grace at our house.

JACOB: Is that a fact? Imagine.

BILL: *(jumping in)* 'Bless this food that now we take, and feed our souls for Jesus' sake. Amen.'

ALL: Amen. *(They dig in.)*

JACOB: Have an eye to the bones, Kathy. *(slight pause)* You was born in Toronto, wasn't you? Someday you'll have to take a trip home, you and Billy, and see how they dries the cod on the beaches. He don't remember any more than you. He was just little when he come up here.

MARY: That was a long time ago, Kathy. 1945.

KATHY: *(slight pause)* Have you been home since, Mr. Mercer?

JACOB: No, my dear, and I don't know if I wants to. A different generation growing up now. *(glancing at BEN)* A different brand of Newfie altogether. And once the oldtimers die off, that'll be the end of it. Newfoundland'll never be the same after that, I can tell you. *(slight pause)* Do you know what flakes is?

KATHY: No.

JACOB: Well, they'm spread over the shore — these wooden stages they dries the codfish on. Sometimes — and this is no word of a lie, is it, Mary? — the fishflies'll buzz around that codfish as t'ick as the hairs on your arm. *(slight pause)* T'icker. T'ick as tarpaper.

MARY: Jacob, we're eating. *(to KATHY)* He's just like his poor mother, Jacob is. She'd start on about the tapeworm as you was lifting the pork to your mouth. *(to JACOB)* Let the poor girl eat in peace, Father. *(to KATHY)* You've hardly touched your food, dear. Has he spoiled your appetite? It wouldn't be the first time.

KATHY: I'm just not too hungry, Mrs. Mercer.

MARY: I understands. Big day tomorrow. I was the same way, my wedding day. It's a wonder I didn't faint.

JACOB: *(slight pause — to KATHY)* You notice Ben don't look my way? He's sore.

(KATHY *glances at* BEN, *who goes on eating, oblivious.*)

JACOB: *(to KATHY)* Oh, he knows how to dish it out with the best, but he can't take it. You can joke with Billy, he likes a bit of fun, but with the other one you don't dare open your mouth.

BEN: Will you shut up, Dad?

JACOB: *(to KATHY)* I'll bet you didn't get sore with your poor father and talk back all the time when he was alive, did you, my dear? No, that's what you didn't. You had more respect. And I bet now you don't regret it.

MARY: Don't ask the child to choose sides, Jacob. You've got no right to do that. Anyhow, Kathy's got more sense than to get mixed up in it. Don't you, Kathy?

JACOB: The Bible says to honour thy father and thy mother. . . .

MARY: *(exasperated)* Oh, hold your tongue, for goodness sake. Don't your jaw ever get tired?

JACOB: *(to* KATHY*)* Well, you can see for yourself what happens, my dear. Anyone in this room is free to say what they likes about the old man, but just let him criticize back and you'd t'ink a fox had burst into the chicken coop, the way Mother Mercer here gathers her first-born under her wing. *(slight pause — to* KATHY, *but meant for his wife)* I suppose by now you've heard your mother and me once went together? I suppose Minnie's mentioned it often enough? Fine figure of a woman, Minnie. Still looks as good as ever.

BILL: I hear you used to be a real woman's man, Dad.

JACOB: Who told you that?

BILL: Mom.

MARY: *(quickly)* Liar. I told you no such t'ing.

BILL: You did so. Didn't she, Ben?

(BEN smiles at his mother.)

JACOB: Well, contrary to what your mother tells, that particular year I had only one sweetheart, and that was Minnie Jackson. Wasn't it, Mary?

MARY: *(nodding)* She was still a Fraser then. That was the same year I was going with Jerome McKenzie. Wasn't it, Jacob?

JACOB: Oh, don't forget the most important part, Mary, the Q.C., the Queen's Counsel. Jerome McKenzie, **Q.C.** *(to* KATHY*)* Jerome's a well-known barrister in St. John's, and Mrs. Mercer's all the time t'rowing him up in my face. Ain't you, Mary? Never lets me forget it, will you? *(to* KATHY*)* You see, my dear, she might have married Jerome McKenzie, **Q.C.**, and never had a single worry in the world, if it wasn't for me. Ain't that so, Mary?

MARY: If you insists, Jacob.

(BILL and KATHY stare silently at their plates, embarrassed. BEN looks from his father to his mother and then to BILL.)

BEN: Did you get the boutonnieres and cuff links for the ushers?

MARY: It's all taken care of, my son. *(pause)* What kind of flowers did your mother order, Kathy?

KATHY: Red roses.

MARY: How nice.

KATHY: I like yellow roses better, but — *(She stops abruptly.)*

BILL: But what?

KATHY: Nothing.

MARY: Yellow roses mean tears, my son.

KATHY: Did you carry roses, Mrs. Mercer?

MARY: I did. Red butterfly roses. And I wore a gown of white satin, with a lace veil. I even had a crown of orange blossoms.

KATHY: I'll bet you were beautiful.

JACOB: My dear, she lit up that little Anglican church like the Second Coming. I suppose I told you all about the wedding ring?

MARY: No, you didn't, and she don't want to hear tell of it, and neither do the rest of us. Don't listen to his big fibs, Kathy.

JACOB: I still remembers that day. I had on my gabardine suit, with a white carnation in the lapel. In those days Mary t'ought I was handsome.

MARY: Get to the point, Father.

JACOB: We was that poor I couldn't afford a ring, so when the Reverend Mr. Price got t'rough with the dearly beloveds and asked for the ring, I reached into my pocket and give him all I had — an old bent nail.

MARY: Last time it was a cigar band.

JACOB: *(still to KATHY)* And if you was to ask me today, twenty years later, if it's been worth it — my dear, my answer would still be the same, for all her many faults — that old rusty nail has brung me more joy and happiness than you can ever imagine. And I wouldn't trade the old woman here, nor a blessed hair of her head, not for all the gold bullion in the Vatican.

BILL: Dad.

JACOB: And my name's not Jerome McKenzie, Q.C., either. And the likes of Ben here may t'ink me just an old fool, not worth a second t'ought —

(BEN shoves back his plate, holding back his temper.)

— and run me down to my face the first chance he gets —

BEN: Ah, shut up.

JACOB: — and treat me with no more respect and consideration than you would your own worst enemy! —

BEN: Will you grow up! *(He knocks over his chair and exits into his bedroom.)*

JACOB: *(shouting after him)* — but I've always done what I seen fit, and no man can do more! *(The door slams — slight pause)* I won't say another word.

MARY: You've said enough, brother. *(slight pause)* What Kathy must t'ink of us! *(slight pause)* And then you wonders why he's the way he is, when you sits there brazen-faced and makes him feel like two cents in front of company. You haven't a grain of sense, you haven't!

JACOB: Did I say a word of a lie? Did I?

MARY: No, you always speaks the gospel truth, you do.

JACOB: I never could say two words in a row to that one, without he takes offence. Not two bloody words!

(MARY collects the supper plates. BILL and KATHY remain seated.)

Look. He didn't finish half his plate. *(calling)* Come out and eat the rest of your supper, Ben. There's no food wasted in this house. *(slight pause)* Take it in to him, Mary.

MARY: *(picking up BEN's chair)* You — you're the cause of it. You're enough to spoil anyone's appetite.

JACOB: Ah, for Christ's sake, he's too damn soft, and you don't help any. I was out fishing on the Labrador when I was ten years old, six months of the year for ten dollars, and out of that ten dollars had to come my rubber boots. *(to KATHY)* Ten years old, and I had to stand up and take it like a man. *(to MARY)* That's a lot tougher than a few harsh words from his father!

MARY: *(as she serves the dessert)* And you'll make him hard, is that it, Jacob? Hard and tough like yourself? Blame him for all you've suffered. Make him pay for all you never had.

JACOB: Oh, shut up, Mary, you don't understand these matters. He won't have you or me to fall back on once he gets out into the world. He'll need to be strong or — *(He winks at BILL.)* — he'll end up like your cousin Israel.

MARY: And don't tell **that** story, Jacob. You're at the table.

JACOB: *(to KATHY)* Israel Parsons was Mrs. Mercer's first cousin.

MARY: Might as well talk to a log.

JACOB: He was a law student at the time, and he worked summers at the pulp and paper mill at Corner Brook, cleaning the machines. Well, one noon hour he crawled inside a machine to clean the big sharp blades, and someone flicked on the switch. Poor young Israel was ground up into pulp. They didn't find a trace of him, did they, Mary? Not even a hair. Mary's poor mother always joked that he was the only one of her relatives ever to make the headlines — if you knows what I mean.

MARY: She knows. And just what has Israel Parsons got to do with Ben, pray tell?

JACOB: Because that's what the world will do to Ben, Mary, if he's not strong. Chew him up alive and swallow him down without a trace. Mark my words. *(He lifts the bowl to his mouth and drinks the peach juice.)*

(The front door bursts open.)

MINNIE: *(off)* Anybody home?

JACOB: Minnie! *(He glances at MARY, then rises.)*

(MINNIE enters. She is in her late forties, boisterous and voluptuous, a little flashily dressed.)

MINNIE: Is you still eating?

JACOB: No, come in, come in.

MINNIE: If you is — guess what? — I brung along me new boyfriend to spoil your appetites. . . . Where's he to? Can't keep track of the bugger! *(She returns to the hallway, and shouts offstage.)* For Christ's sake, you dirty t'ing, you! You might have waited till you got inside!

KATHY: *(to BILL)* What's **she** doing here?

MINNIE: *(off)* Come on. There's no need to be shy.

(HAROLD enters with MINNIE. He is conservatively dressed but sports a white carnation.)

MINNIE: *(to HAROLD)* That's Jacob and Mary. This here's Harold. *(They shake hands.)*

JACOB: Here, give me your coats. *(He takes the coats.)*

MINNIE: T'anks, boy. *(to KATHY)* Hello, sister! Still mad at me?

(KATHY *doesn't answer.*)

MINNIE: *(to* MARY*)* Harold works in a funeral parlour. He's an embalmer.
    Imagine. We met when poor Willard died. He worked on his corpse.
MARY: *(incredulously)* You made that up, Minnie. Confess.
MINNIE: As God is me witness, maid!
JACOB: Just so long as you'm not drumming up business, Harold.

(HAROLD *doesn't crack a smile.*)

MINNIE: He ain't got an ounce of humour in his body, Harold. *(looking at*
    JACOB*)* But he's got two or t'ree pounds of what counts. Don't you,
    Lazarus?[4]
KATHY: *(sharply)* Mother!
MINNIE: 'Mother' yourself. *(sitting on arm of chesterfield next to* HAROLD*)* I calls him
    Lazarus because he comes to life at night. And what a resurrection. Ah,
    I'm so wicked, Mary. To tell you the truth, I haven't been exactly
    mourning since Willard died, as sister over there can testify. And I'll tell
    you why. I took a good solid look at Willard — God rest his soul! —
    stretched out in his casket the t'ree days of his wake, all powdered and
    rouged and made up like a total stranger, and I says to myself, Minnie,
    live it up, maid. This is all there is, this life. You're dead a good long
    time. *(to* JACOB*)* And I for one wouldn't bet a t'in dime on the hereafter,
    and God knows I've t'rowed hundreds of dollars away on long shots in
    my day.
JACOB: Now, Minnie, enough of the religion. Would you both care for a
    whiskey? *(*MARY *reacts.)*
MINNIE: *(meaning* HAROLD*)* Look at his ears pick up. Sure, Jake. That's one of
    the reasons we come early.

(JACOB *crosses to the cabinet during* MINNIE's *speech and brings out a bottle of whiskey.*
He pours three drinks.)

And Mary, I got to apologize for last night. I suppose I'll never live it
down. I don't know what happened, maid. I laid down with a drink in
me hand after supper and the next t'ing I know it's this morning and
I'm in the doghouse.
MARY: That's okay, Minnie. *(She sits.)*
JACOB: Billy, my son, bring me the ginger ale. That's a good boy.

(During the dialogue BILL *fetches the ginger ale from the fridge and returns to the dining*
room table.)

How do you like your drink, Minnie?
MINNIE: A little mix in mine, and not'ing in Harold's. The ginger ale tickles
    his nose and gets him all excited.

---

4 *in the New Testament, Lazarus, the brother of Mary Magdalene, was raised from the dead by Jesus (John 11:*
1–44).

JACOB: What is he, Minnie? Newfie?

MINNIE: No, boy — Canadian.

JACOB: Harold, there's only two kinds of people in this world — Newfies and them that wishes they was.

MINNIE: That's what I tells him, boy.

JACOB: Why else would Canada have j'ined us in '49? Right, Minnie? *(JACOB crosses to chesterfield with the drinks.)*

MARY: I t'ought you didn't have no whiskey? I t'ought all you had in the house was 'screech'? Do you mean to tell me that was deliberate, what you put Ben t'rough?

JACOB: *(quickly changing the subject)* Minnie, don't you want to see the shower gifts?

MINNIE: Sure, boy. Where's they to?

JACOB: They're in the bedroom. Show her, Mary. Now's a good time.

(MARY rises and crosses to the bedroom door. MINNIE follows.)

MINNIE: *(indicating HAROLD)* Don't give him any more to drink, Jacob, till I gets back. The bugger likes to get a head start.

(They exit.)

MINNIE: *(off)* Maid, will you look! A gift shop! Jesus!

JACOB: *(slight pause–to HAROLD, embarrassed)* Well.

(HAROLD nods. They drink.)

MINNIE: *(off)* Even a rolling pin! *(She pokes out her head.)* My Jesus, Harold, I finally found somet'ing that compares!

(JACOB glances at HAROLD. HAROLD glances at JACOB. They drink.)

JACOB: *(after a moment)* Grand old day.

(HAROLD nods. Silence.)

JACOB: *(after a moment)* Couldn't ask for better.

(HAROLD nods. Silence.)

JACOB: *(after a moment)* Another grand day tomorrow.

(HAROLD clears his throat.)

JACOB: Pardon?

(HAROLD shakes his head. Silence.)

JACOB: *(embarrassed)* Well, why don't we see what mischief the women are up to?

(HAROLD nods. With visible relief both men exit together.)

BILL: Tomorrow's off! We've got to tell them, Kathy! And right now!

KATHY: We don't have to call it off.

BILL: What do you mean?

KATHY: You know what I mean.

BILL: You mean you'd get married without having to?

KATHY: I work, you know. I'll be getting a raise in two months, and another six months after that. I'll be making good money by the time you get into university. I could help put you through. *(slight pause)* I wouldn't be in the way. *(slight pause)* Billy? Don't you even care for me?

BILL: Sure.

KATHY: How much?

(Enter HAROLD. During the dialogue he helps himself to another drink from the dining room and crosses to the chesterfield.)

BILL: A lot. But I still don't want to get married. I'm not ready. We're too young. Christ, you can't even cook!

KATHY: And you're just a mama's boy!

(HAROLD is now seated. KATHY stares at him a moment. Then she smiles.)

KATHY: Well, Harold wants me, even if you don't. Don't you, Harold? *(She rises and crosses to the chesterfield, flaunting herself.)*

BILL: Kathy!

KATHY: *(to HAROLD)* I've seen the way you look at me. *(She drops on the chesterfield beside HAROLD.)* You'd like to hop in the sack with me, wouldn't you? Tell the truth.

BILL: Why are you doing this?

KATHY: You think he's any different than you?

BILL: What do you mean?

KATHY: This make you jealous, Billy? *(She caresses the inside of HAROLD's thigh.)*

BILL: *(grabbing her by the wrist)* I don't understand you, Kathy.

KATHY: I understand you, Billy. Only too well. Poor trapped Billy.

BILL: I'm not trapped.

KATHY: Aren't you?

BILL: No! I'll call it off!

KATHY: Yes! Why don't you?

BILL: I will!

KATHY: I wouldn't want you to waste your life. I'll bet now you wished you'd never met me, don't you? You wish you'd never touched me. All this trouble because you didn't have the nerve to go to the drugstore!

BILL: Well, why did you let me do it if it wasn't a safe time? Answer me that!

(Enter MINNIE, JACOB, and MARY.)

MINNIE: Well, kids, you're well off now. More than we got when we started out, heh, Mary? Willard and me didn't have a pot to piss in or a window to t'row it out. *(to* JACOB, *as she sits)* Where's your eldest? I ain't met him yet.

JACOB: Ben? Oh, he's in his bedroom — *(He glances at* MARY *who is now sitting in the armchair.)* — studying. He's in university, Minnie. *(He calls to* BEN'S *door.)* Ben, come out. *(slight pause)* And bring your diploma. *(He glances sheepishly at* MARY *and looks away.* MARY *shakes her head, amused.)*

(Enter BEN, *dressed in a sport jacket. He carries his rolled-up diploma tied with a ribbon.)*

Graduated from Grade T'irteen last night, Minnie. That's Ben. Ben, this is Mrs. Jackson, and that's Harold.

(They all nod hello.)

MINNIE: *(appraising* BEN *with obvious delight)* So this is the best man, heh? Well. Well, well, well. What a fine-looking boy, Jacob. He'll be tall.

JACOB: A little too t'in, Minnie. And not much colour to his face.

MINNIE: What odds? You was a skeleton yourself at his age. Tell you what, Ben. Be over some Saturday night and give you a scrubbing down in the tub. We'll send your father and mother to the pictures. *(to* MARY) Oh, how wicked, maid. Don't mind me, I've got the dirtiest tongue. The t'ings I comes out with. That's what comes of hanging around race-tracks and taverns with the likes of the Formaldehyde Kid here. *(slight pause)* You looks like your mother's side of the family, Ben.

JACOB: I kind of t'ought he looked like my side. *(to* BEN) Show Minnie your diploma.

(BEN hands the diploma to MINNIE.)

MINNIE: *(to* BEN) Proud father.

BEN: *(to* JACOB) I thought you didn't have any whiskey?

JACOB: *(ignoring* BEN *and glancing over* MINNIE'S *shoulder as she reads the diploma)* He got honours all the way t'rough high school, Minnie. He got a scholarship.

MINNIE: Where'd he get his brains to? *(embarrassed silence — to* BEN) Told you you look like your mother's side. *(She hands back the diploma, rises, and hands her glass to* JACOB) Next round less ginger ale, Jacob. Gives me gas. *(crossing to the record player)* And I'd hate to start cracking off around Father Douglas. *(She puts on a record — 'Moonglow' theme from 'Picnic'.)* What a face he's got on him, already, the priest. Pinched little mouth. You'd t'ink he just opened the Song of Solomon and found a fart pressed between the pages like a rose. *(She starts to move slowly to the music.)*

KATHY: Mother, do you have to?

MINNIE: Do I have to what, sister?

KATHY: Make a fool of yourself.

MINNIE: Listen to who's talking! *(slight pause)* I'd dance with Harold except the only tune he knows is the Death March. And the only step he knows is the foxtrot. Imagine foxtrotting to the Death March. *(to* JACOB*)* Jacob, you was a one for dancing years ago. Wasn't he, Mary?

MARY: He still is, Minnie.

MINNIE: Did he ever tell you how I first got to go out with him?

MARY: I don't believe he did.

MINNIE: He didn't? Well, remember Georgie Bishop? He took me out one night — to the Salvation Army dance at Bay Roberts. It was in the wintertime, and cold as a nun's tit. I saw Jacob there, hanging about, and now and then he'd look my way and I'd wink. Oh, I was some brazen.

JACOB: I t'ought you had somet'ing in your eye, Minnie.

MINNIE: Yes, boy, the same as was in yours — the devil! . . . To make a long story short, Mary, when it come time to go home, Georgie and me went outside where his horse and sled was hitched to the post. He'd tied it fast with a knot, and do you know what this bugger had gone and done?

JACOB: Now don't tell that, Minnie.

MINNIE: Pissed on the knot! He had, maid. A ball of ice as big as me fist. And who do you suppose walks up large as life and offers to drive me home in his sled? *(pause)* Poor Georgie. The last I remembers of him he was cursing the dirty son-of-a-bitch that had done it and was stabbing away at the knot with his jack-knife! *(She notices* BEN's *amused reaction to her story.)* Come dance with me, Ben. Don't be shy. Come on. If I'm not mistaken, you've got the devil in your eye, too. Just like your father. *(She puts* BEN's *arm around her waist and they dance.)* Look, Harold. You might learn a t'ing or two. *(She presses close against* BEN.*)* Mmm. You know, Jacob, this is no longer a little boy. He's coming of age.

KATHY: Mother, you're **dirty**.

MINNIE: How fast you've grown, Ben. How tall and straight. Do you want to hear a funny one? I could have been your mother. Imagine. But your grandfather — Jacob's father — put his foot down. I was a Catholic, and that was that in no uncertain terms. Wasn't it, Jacob? *(slight pause)* So I married Willard. . . . .

(They break apart.)

MINNIE: *(to* JACOB, *as she sits)* Ah well, boy, I suppose it all worked out for the best. Just t'ink, Jacob — if you had married me it might have been you Harold pumped full of fluids.

JACOB: That it might, Minnie. That it might.

MINNIE: But you can't help marvel at the way t'ings work out. Makes you wonder sometimes.

JACOB: *(Turns off music.)* What's that, Minnie?

MINNIE: *(slyly)* Your son marrying my daughter and turning Catholic in the bargain. Serves you right, you old bugger. The last laugh's on you. **And** your poor old father.

JACOB: You'm not still carrying that grudge around inside you, is you? I'm getting a fine girl in the family. That's the way I looks at it.

MINNIE: *(rising to help herself to another drink)* I don't mind telling you, Jacob, I've had my hands full with **that** one. Not a moment's peace since the day poor Willard died. She was kind of stuck on her father, you know. Jesus, boy, she won't even speak to Harold. Won't let him give her away tomorrow, will you, sister? Her uncle's doing that. Oh, she snaps me head off if I as much as makes a suggestion. T'inks she knows it all. And now look. All I can say is I'm glad her father ain't alive, this night.

JACOB: Now, Minnie, you knows you don't mean all that. Own up to it.

MINNIE: Oh, I means it, boy, and more. T'ank God it's only the second month. At least she don't show yet. If she's anyt'ing like me, she'll have a bad time. Well, a little pain'll teach her a good lesson.

KATHY: I wish you wouldn't talk about me like that, Mother.

MINNIE: Like what?

KATHY: Like I was invisible. I don't like it; I've told you before.

JACOB: Now, now, Kathy.

MINNIE: Listen to her, will you? Invisible. Sister, you may soon wish you **was** invisible, when the girls from work start counting back on the office calendar.

KATHY: Let them count!

MINNIE: See, Jacob? See what I'm up against? No shame!

JACOB: Minnie, let's not have any hard feelings. It's most time for church. I'll get the coats.

MARY: Yes, do.

(JACOB gets MINNIE's and MARY's coats.)

MINNIE: *(crossing to BEN)* You don't know, Mary, how fortunate you is having sons. That's the biggest letdown of me life, not having a boy. . . . We couldn't have any but the one . . . *(bitterly)* and that had to be the bitch of the litter. How I curse the day. A boy like this must be a constant joy, Mary.

MARY: And a tribulation, maid.

MINNIE: Yes, but look at all the worry a daughter brings. *(as JACOB helps her into her coat)* This is the kind of fix she can get herself into.

KATHY: Mother, I just asked you not to.

BILL: Tell her, Kathy.

MINNIE: And then to top it off who gets the bill for the wedding? Oh, it's just dandy having a daughter, just dandy. I could wring her neck.

BILL: Kathy.

KATHY: *(to BILL)* You tell her.

MINNIE: If I had my own way I know what I'd do with all the bitches at birth. I'd do with them exactly what we did back home with the kittens —

KATHY: I'm not pregnant!

MINNIE: What?

KATHY: *(bitterly)* You heard me. I'm not pregnant.

MINNIE: What do you mean you're not? You are so, unless you've done somet'ing to yourself. . . .

KATHY: I didn't.

MARY: Kathy.

MINNIE: I took you to the doctor myself. I was in his office. Why in hell do you suppose you're getting married tomorrow, if it's not because you're having a baby?

KATHY: *(turning to* MARY*)* Mrs. Mercer, I had a miscarriage. . . .

MINNIE: A miscarriage . . .

MARY: When, Kathy? *(She puts her arms around* KATHY*.)*

KATHY: This morning. I went to the doctor. There's no mistake. And I didn't do anything to myself, Mother.

MINNIE: *(quietly)* Did I say you did, sister?

MARY: Sit down, dear. *(She helps* KATHY *sit — long pause.)* This may not be the right moment to mention it, Minnie, but . . . well, it seems to me t'ings have altered somewhat. *(She looks at* BEN*)* T'ings are back to the way they used to be. The youngsters don't need to get married. There's no reason to, now.

(Pause. No one moves except HAROLD *who raises his glass to drink.)*

BLACKOUT

ACT TWO

(A moment later. As the lights come up, the actors are in the exact positions and attitudes they were in at end of Act One. The tableau dissolves into action.)

JACOB: Sit down, Minnie. We've got to talk this out. *(to* KATHY*)* Can I get you anyt'ing, my dear?

*(*KATHY *shakes her head.* MINNIE *sits.)*

MINNIE: *(slight pause)* What time is it getting to be?

BEN: Seven-fifteen.

MINNIE: The priest expects us there sharp at eight. He's got a mass to say at half-past.

MARY: Now wait just a minute. I t'ink you're being hasty, Minnie. The children can please themselves, now, what they wants to do. Maybe they don't want to get married.

JACOB: Mary's right, Minnie. Ask them.

MINNIE: For someone who don't like to butt in, maid, you got a lot to say sometimes. Stay out of it or I might say somet'ing I'm sorry for.

MARY: I can't stay out of it. I wouldn't advise my worst enemy to jump into marriage that young, and neither would you, Minnie. They'd be far better off waiting till Billy finishes university. . . .

MINNIE: Well, maybe **they** can afford to put it off, but **I** sure as hell can't. The invitations are out . . . the cake's bought, and the dress . . . the flowers arranged for . . . the photographer . . . the priest and organist hired . . . the church and banquet hall rented . . . the food —

KATHY: *(jumping up)* I don't want to get married!

MARY: What?

MINNIE: What? Don't believe her, Mary. She do so. She's got a stack of love comics a mile high. *(to KATHY)* Now you shut your mouth, sister, or I'll shut it for you.

KATHY: I won't.

MINNIE: You knows what'll happen if you backs out now? I'll be made a laughing stock. Is that what you wants, you little bitch?

KATHY: Don't call me a bitch, you old slut!

MARY: Kathy.

MINNIE: *(to JACOB)* Did you hear that? Why, I'll slap the face right off her! *(She goes after KATHY.)*

JACOB: *(keeping MINNIE away from her daughter)* All right, now. This is no way to behave. Tonight of all nights!

KATHY: That's what you are, an old cow! He only wants you for your money. *(indicating HAROLD)*

MINNIE: That's a lie.

KATHY: Is it?

MINNIE: That's a lie. Let me at her, Jacob. I'll knock her to kingdom come.

JACOB: Enough, goddamn it! Both of you!

(Silence.)

That's better. Let's all ca'm down. We could all learn a lesson from Harold here. He's civilized. *(slight pause)* What we need's a drink.

MINNIE: *(as JACOB refills the glasses)* Imagine. My own flesh and blood, and she's got it in for me. She's never had much use for me, and even less since I took up with Harold here. She'll say anyt'ing to get back at me. Anyt'ing!

JACOB: Kathy's had a bad time of it, Minnie. No doubt she's upset. *(to MARY)* Remember how you was, when we lost our first? Didn't care if she lived or died. Didn't care if she ever laid eyes on me again, she was that down in the dumps. And I'm surprised, Billy. Not once have you come to her defence or spoken a word of comfort. You've got to be more of a man than that.

BEN: Why can't they get married and Billy still go to school?

MARY: *(to BEN)* Mind you business.

MINNIE: You hear that, Jacob? That's the one with all the brains.

BEN: *(to MARY)* I'm just trying to help.

MARY: Who? Yourself?

KATHY: I want him to, Mrs. Mercer. He doesn't have to quit school. I like to work. Honest.

MARY: Well, Billy, you're the only one we haven't heard from. What do you say?

JACOB: Ah, what's it matter if he gets married now or after university? He won't do much better than Kathy.

MINNIE: She's a good girl, in spite of what I said about her. A hard worker. She always pays her board sharp. And clean as a whistle.

JACOB: That's settled, then.

MARY: Is it, Billy?

JACOB: For God's sake, Mary.

MARY: He's got a tongue of his own. Let him answer. The poor child can't get a word in edgewise.

JACOB: Stop mothering him. He's a man now. Let him act like one. *(amused)* Besides, he's just getting cold feet. Ain't you, my son?

BEN: Did you get cold feet, Dad?

JACOB: All men do. *(MARY glances at JACOB who nudges her.)* Even the best of us. Billy'll be fine after tomorrow.

MINNIE: T'anks, Jacob. I could kiss you. Now, Harold, wait your turn, and don't be jealous. *(as she crosses to the record player and selects a record)* The mother of the bride and the father of the groom will now have the next dance. With your permission, Mary?

MARY: With my blessing, maid.

JACOB: *(glancing at MARY)* I don't know whether I'm up to it, Minnie.

MINNIE: Go on, Jacob. You'll be dancing a jig at your own wake.

(Music: 'Isle of Newfoundland'. JACOB takes MINNIE in his arms and they dance. BILL goes to KATHY, takes her hand and leads her into the darkened kitchen. They make up.)

MINNIE: Ah, Jacob, remember when we'd hug and smooch in the darkest places on the dance floor? The way he stuck to the shadows, Mary, you'd swear he was a bat. Dance with her, Harold. *(indicating MARY)* She won't bite. *(to JACOB)* He's some wonderful dancer, boy. Went to Arthur Murray's. He's awful shy, though.

(MARY and HAROLD exchange glances. HAROLD clears his throat.)

Ah, boy, Jacob, I'd better give Harold a turn. He'd sit there all night looking anxious. He likes a good foxtrot. Fancies himself Valentino. Come on, Lazarus.

(MINNIE and HAROLD dance. JACOB crosses to MARY who is sitting behind dining room table.)

JACOB: Dance, Mary?

MARY: You make a good match, the two of you.

JACOB: Mary, I t'ink you'm jealous.

MARY: Don't be foolish. And don't start showing off. That's the next step.

JACOB: 'How beautiful are thy feet with shoes, O prince's daughter! The j'ints of thy t'ighs are like jewels, the work of the hands of a cunning workman.
'Thy navel is like a round goblet, which wanteth not liquor; thy belly is like — [1]

---

1 *from the biblical Song of Solomon 7:1–2.*

MARY: *(sharply)* Jacob!

JACOB: ' — an heap of wheat set about with lilies.
'Thy two breasts — '

MARY: All right, boy — enough!

JACOB: *(sitting)* Do you remember, Mary, when you was just a piss-tail maid picking blueberries on the cliffs behind your father's house, your poor knees tattooed from kneeling? Did you ever t'ink for a single minute that one day you'd be the mother of grown-up sons and one of 'em about to start a life of his own?

MARY: No, and that I didn't. In those days I couldn't see no further ahead than you charging down Country Road on your old white horse to whisk me away to the mainland.

JACOB: Any regrets?

MARY: What does you t'ink?

JACOB: Ah, go on with you. *(pause)* The old house seems smaller already, don't it?

MARY: Empty.

MINNIE: *(still dancing)* Tomorrow's a landmark for us all, Jacob. I lose me only daughter and you lose your two sons. *(JACOB reacts.)* Somehow I don't envy you, boy. I t'ink it'll be harder on you. If I had sons . . .

(JACOB crosses quickly to the record player and switches it off.)

JACOB: What was that you just said, Minnie? Did I hear you correct? Whose sons?

MINNIE: Yours.

JACOB: Mine? Only one's going.

MINNIE: Didn't anybody tell you?

JACOB: Tell me what? I'm lucky to get the time of day. *(to MARY)* Tell me what?

MARY: Ben's moving in with Bill and Kathy. Taking their spare room.

JACOB: He is like hell!

BEN: I am!

JACOB: You'm not!

BEN: I am!

JACOB: Don't be foolish!

MINNIE: I t'ought he knowed, Mary. I t'ought the kids had told him.

JACOB: No, Minnie, they neglected to mention it. I'm not surprised!

MINNIE: I wouldn't have put me big foot in me mouth otherwise.

JACOB: Why should I know any more what goes on in my own house than the stranger on the street? I'm only his father. I'm not the one they all confides in around this house, I can tell you. I'm just the goddamn old fool. That's all! The goddamn fool.

BEN: I wanted to tell you after the wedding.

JACOB: Yes, you did so.

BEN: I would have sooner, but this is what happens.

JACOB: Oh, so now it's all my fault?

BEN: I didn't say that. Stop twisting what I say.

JACOB: How quick you is to shift the blame, my son. *(to* MARY*)* How come you to know? He was quick enough to run to you with the news, wasn't he?

MARY: I can't help that.

JACOB: Yes, you can. I'm always the last to find out, and you'm the reason, Mary. You'm the ringleader. The t'ree of you against the one of me.

MARY: And you talks about shifting the blame.

JACOB: Wasn't I the last to find out Billy was getting married? He told you first, but did you come and confide in me? That you didn't. If I hadn't found that bill from Ostranders for Kathy's engagement ring . . . !

BILL: We would have told you . . .

JACOB: A lot of respect you show for your father. A lot of respect. You'm no better than your brother.

MARY: Ca'm down, boy. You're just getting yourself all worked up.

JACOB: I won't ca'm down. Ca'm down. All I ever does is break my back for their good and comfort, and how is it they repays me? A slap in the face! *(to* BEN*)* What did you have in mind to do, my son? Sneak off with all your belongings, like a t'ief, while your father was at work?

BEN: Go to hell.

JACOB: What did you say?

BEN: You heard me. I don't have to take shit like that from anyone. And I don't care who's here!

*(*JACOB *takes a threatening step toward his son.* MARY *steps between.)*

JACOB: I'll knock your goddamn block off!

MARY: Now just stop it, the both of you! Stop it!

MINNIE: I'd never have gotten away with that from my father. He'd have tanned me good.

MARY: And Minnie — mind your own business. This is none of your concern.

JACOB: Talking like that to his own father . . .

BEN: And if you ever hit me again . . . !

JACOB: I'll hit you in two seconds flat, if you carries on. Just keep it up. Don't t'ink for one minute you'm too old yet!

BEN: Come on. Hit me. I'm not scared. Hit me. You'd never see me again!

MARY: *(slapping* BEN*)* Shut right up. You're just as bad as he is!

MINNIE: Two of a kind, maid. Two peas in a pod. That's why they don't get on.

JACOB: Why the hell do you suppose we slaved to buy this house, if it wasn't for you two? And now you won't stick around long enough to help pay back a red cent. You'd rather pay rent to a stranger!

BILL: Dad, I'm leaving to get married, in case you forgot.

JACOB: You don't need to. Put if off. Listen to your mother!

BILL: A minute ago you said —

JACOB: Forget a minute ago! This is now!

BEN: He'll have converted for nothing, if he does!

JACOB: You shut your bloody mouth! *(to* BILL*)* Put it off, my son. There's no hurry. Don't be swayed by Minnie. She's just t'inking of herself. Getting revenge for old hurts.

MINNIE: And you're full of shit, Jacob.

JACOB: You goddamn Catholics, you don't even believe in birth control. Holy Jumping Jesus Christ. The poor young boy'll be saddled with a gang of little ones before he knows it! And all because my poor father hated the Micks!

MINNIE: Come on, sister, we don't need that. Get your coat. You, too, Harold. Let's go, Billy. The priest can't wait on the likes of us.

*(*BILL *and* KATHY *move to go.)*

JACOB: Don't go, Billy. There's no need!

BILL: First you say one thing, Dad, and then you say something else. Will you please make up your mind! *(to* BEN*)* Ben, what should I do? Tell me.

BEN: I can't help you, Billy.

*(*KATHY *looks at* BILL, *then runs out, slamming the door.)*

MARY: *(to* BILL*)* Go after her, my son. Now's the time she needs you. We'll see you in church. Go on, now.

BILL: Ben?

BEN: In a minute. I'll see you there.

BILL: Dad?

*(*JACOB *turns away.* BILL *runs out.)*

MINNIE: I'll take the two kids with me, Mary. See you in a few minutes.

JACOB: You won't see me there tonight, Minnie, and you can count on that. And not tomorrow, either.

MINNIE: That's up to you, Jacob, though I hope you changes your mind for Billy's sake. *(slight pause)* We oughtn't to let our differences interfere with the children. *(slight pause)* Come along, Lazarus. It's time we dragged our backsides to the church.

(They exit. Silence. MARY *removes her coat, then slowly begins to clear the table.* BEN *looks over at his father. Finally he speaks.)*

BEN: Dad . . .

JACOB: What?

BEN: I want to explain. Will you let me?

JACOB: I should t'ink you'd be ashamed to even look at me, let alone open your mouth. *(slight pause)* Well? What is it? I suppose we'm not good enough for you?

BEN: Oh, come on.

JACOB: *(to* MARY*)* If you's going to the church, you'd better be off.

BEN: We still have a few minutes.

JACOB: *(to MARY)* And no odds what, I won't go to church. They can do without me.

MARY: Suit yourself. But I'm going. Just don't come back on me afterwards for not coaxing you to.

JACOB: You can walk in that church tonight, feeling the way you does? Oh, you'm some two-faced, Mary.

MARY: Don't you talk. You was quite willing to see Billy go, till it slipped out that Ben was going, too.

JACOB: That's a lie!

MARY: Is it?

JACOB: That's a damn lie!

MARY: I'll call a cab. *(She crosses to the phone, picks up the receiver. To JACOB)* We can't always have it our way. *(She dials and ad libs softly while dialogue continues between father and son.)*

JACOB: A lifetime spent in this house, and he gives us less notice than you would a landlord! And me about to wallpaper his room like a goddamn fool! *(slight pause)* And don't come back broke and starving in a week or two and expect a handout, 'cause the only way you'll get t'rough that door is to break it in! *(slight pause)* You'll never last on your own. You never had to provide for yourself.

BEN: I'll learn.

JACOB: You'll starve.

BEN: All right, I'll starve. And then you can have the satisfaction of being right. *(slight pause)* You're always telling me it's time I got out on my own and grew up.

JACOB: Sure, t'row up in my face what I said in the past!

BEN: Dad, will you listen to me for once? It's not because home's bad, or because I hate you. It's not that. I just want to be independent, that's all. Can't you understand that? *(slight pause)* I had to move out sometime.

JACOB: Was it somet'ing I said? What was it? Tell me. I must have said somet'ing!

BEN: No, it was nothing you said. Will you come off it?

JACOB: Can you imagine what our relatives will say, once they hears? They'll say you left home on account of me.

BEN: Well, who the hell cares?

JACOB: And you any idea what this'll do to your mother? You'm her favourite. *(The last syllable rhymes with 'night'.)*

MARY: Jacob! That's not fair!

JACOB: What odds? It's true, and don't deny it. *(to BEN)* Your mother's always been most fond of you. She even delivered you herself. Did you know that?

MARY: There's no time for family history, Father.

(JACOB moves quickly to the mantel and takes the photo album. He is slightly desperate now. He flicks open the album.)

JACOB: *(intimately, to BEN)* Look. Look at that one. You could scarcely walk. Clinging for dear life to your mother's knee. *(turing the page)* And look at this. The four of us. Harry Saunders took that of us with my old box camera the day the Germans marched into Paris. *(Turns the photo over.)* There. You'm good with dates. June 14, 1940. Look how lovely your mother looks, my son. No more than ninety pounds when she had you.

MARY: Ninety-one.

JACOB: She was that t'in, you'd swear the wind would carry her off. We never believed we'd have another, after the first died. He was premature. Seven months, and he only lived a few hours.

MARY: Enough of the past, boy.

JACOB: That was some night, the night you was born. Blizzarding to beat hell. The doctor lived in Bay Roberts, and I had to hitch up the sled —

MARY: He's heard all that.

JACOB: Some woman, your mother. Cut and tied the cord herself. Had you scrubbed to a shine and was washed herself and back in bed, sound asleep, before we showed up.

MARY: Took all the good out of me, too.

JACOB: And wasn't she a picture? She could have passed for her namesake in the stained glass of a Catholic window, she was that radiant.

MARY: Get on with you.

JACOB: Your mother'd never let on, but you can imagine the state she'll be in if you goes. You'm all that's left now, Ben. The last son. *(a whisper)* I t'ink she wishes you'd stay.

MARY: I heard that. Look, you speak for yourself. I've interfered enough for one night.

JACOB: Your mother has always lived just for the two of you.

MARY: *(pained)* Oh, Jacob.

JACOB: Always.

BEN: Come on, Dad, that's not true.

JACOB: It is so, now. It is so.

MARY: Well, it's not, and don't you say it is. The likes of that!

JACOB: Confess, Mary. I don't count, I've never counted. Not since the day they was born.

BEN: If that's true, Dad, you should be glad to get rid of both of us. Have Mom all to yourself again.

JACOB: Don't be smart.

MARY: Who's the one making all the fuss? Me or you? Answer me that.

JACOB: No, you'd sit by silent and let me do it for you and take all the shit that comes with it. I'm wise to your little games.

MARY: I can't stop him, if he wants to go. I don't like it any more than you do. I can't imagine this house without our two sons. But if what Ben wants is to go, he's got my blessing. I won't stand in his way because I'm scared. And if you can't speak for yourself, don't speak for me. I'm out of it.

JACOB: If he's so dead set on going, he can march out the door this very minute.

MARY: He will not! Don't be foolish!

JACOB: He will so, if I say so!

(JACOB charges into BEN's bedroom and returns with a suitcase which he sets on the floor.)

There! Pack your belongings right this second, if we'm not good enough for you

MARY: Ben, don't pay him no mind.

JACOB: I don't want you in this house another minute, if you'm that anxious to be elsewhere. Ingrate!

MARY: If you don't shut your big yap, he just might, and then you'd be in some state.

JACOB: Oh, I would, would I? Well, we'll just see about that. I'll help him pack, if he likes! *(He charges into BEN's bedroom.)*

MARY: Ben, don't talk back to him when he's mad. It only makes it worse, you knows that.

(JACOB comes out with a stack of record albums which he hurls violently to the floor.)

JACOB: There. Enough of that goddamn squealing and squawking. Now I can get some peace and quiet after a hard day's work.

BEN: Dad, I think I ought to . . .

JACOB: Don't open your mouth. I don't want to hear another word!

BEN: All right, make a fool of yourself!

JACOB: *(to MARY)* And that goes for you, too! *(He charges back into the bedroom.)*

BEN: What'll we do, Mom? We got to get out of here. Can't you stop him?

MARY: All you can do, when he gets like this, is let him run down and tire himself out. His poor father was the same. He'd hurl you t'rough the window one minute and brush the glass off you the next.

(JACOB comes out with a stack of new shirts still in the cellophane.)

JACOB: And look at this, will you? Talk about a sin. I walks around with my ass out, and here's six new shirts never even opened. *(He hurls the shirts on the pile of records.)*

BEN: I don't want to spoil your fun, Dad, but so far all that stuff belongs to Billy.

(JACOB stares at the scattered records and shirts, alarmed.)

MARY: Now you've done it, boy. Will you sit down now? You're just making a bigger fool of yourself the longer you stands.

JACOB: *(Her reproach is all he needs to get back in stride.)* Sure, mock me when I'm down. Well, I'll show you who the fool is. We'll just see who has the last laugh! *(He charges into his own bedroom.)*

(MARY picks up the records and shirts.)

BEN: *(pause)* I wanted to tell him, Mom, a week ago. I kept putting it off.

MARY: I wish you had, Ben. This mightn't have happened.

BEN: It's all our fault, anyhow.

MARY: What do you mean?

BEN: We've made him feel like an outsider all these years. The three of us. You, me, Billy. It's always been him and us. Always. As long as I can remember.

MARY: Blame your father's temper. He's always had a bad temper. All we done was try our best to avoid it.

BEN: Yeah, but we make it worse. We feed it. We shouldn't shut him out the way we do.

MARY: And what is it you're not saying, that it's my fault somehow? Is that what you t'inks? Say it.

BEN: I didn't say that.

MARY: Your father believes it. He calls me the ringleader.

BEN: Well, you set the example, Mom, a long time ago. When we were little.

MARY: Don't you talk, Ben. You're some one to point fingers. *(slight pause)* Perhaps I did. Perhaps your father's right all along. But you're no little child any longer, and you haven't been for years. You're a man now, and you never followed anyone's example for too long unless you had a mind to. So don't use that excuse.

BEN: I'm not. I'm just as much to blame as anybody. I know that.

MARY: I always tried to keep the peace. And that wasn't always easy in this family, with you and your father at each other's t'roats night and day. And to keep the peace I had to sometimes keep a good many unpleasant facts from your father. Small, simple t'ings, mostly.

BEN: You were just sparing yourself.

MARY: I was doing what I considered the most good! And don't tell me I wasn't. Oh, Ben, you knows yourself what he's like. If you lost five dollars down the sewer, you didn't dare let on. If you did, he'd dance around the room like one leg was on fire and the other had a bee up it. It was just easier that way, not to tell him. Easier on the whole family. Yes, and easier on myself.

BEN: But it wasn't easier when he found out. On him **or** us.

MARY: He didn't always, Ben.

BEN: No, but when he does, like tonight — it's worse!

(JACOB enters from the bedroom, slowly, carrying a small cardboard box. He removes the contents of the box — a neatly folded silk dressing-gown — and throws the box to one side.)

JACOB: I won't be needing the likes of this. Take it with you. I've got enough old junk cluttering up my closet.

BEN: I don't want it, either.

MARY: He gave you that for your birthday. You've never even worn it.

JACOB: Take it!

(He hurls it violently in BEN's face. Then he notices the diploma lying on the table. He grabs it.)

MARY: Not the diploma, Jacob! No!

(BEN *says nothing. He just stares at his father, who stares back the whole time he removes the ribbon, unfolds the diploma, and tears it into two pieces, then four, then eight. He drops the pieces to the floor.*)

MARY: God help you. This time you've gone too far.

(*Pause. Then* BEN *crosses to the suitcase. He picks it up.*)

BEN: I'll pack. (*He exits into his bedroom.*)
MARY: All right. You satisfied? You've made me feel deeply ashamed tonight, Jacob, the way you treats Ben. I only hopes he forgives you. I don't know if I would, if it was me.
JACOB: I always knowed it would come to this one day. He's always hated me, and don't say he hasn't. Did you see him tonight? I can't so much as lay a hand on his shoulder. He pulls away. His own father, and I can't touch him. All his life long he's done nothing but mock and defy me, and now he's made me turn him out in anger, my own son. (*to* MARY, *angrily*) And you can bugger off, too, if you don't like it. Don't let me keep you. Just pack your bag and take him with you. Dare say you'd be happier off. I don't give a good goddamn if the whole lot of you deserts me.
MARY: You don't know when to stop, do you? You just don't know when to call a halt. What must I do? Knock you senseless? You'd go on and on until you brought your whole house tumbling down. I suppose it's late in the day to be expecting miracles, but for God's sake, Jacob, control yourself. For once in your life would you just t'ink before you speaks? **Please!** (*slight pause*) I have no sympathy for you. You brought this all on yourself. You wouldn't listen. Well, listen now. Have you ever in your whole life took two minutes out to try and understand him? Have you? Instead of galloping off in all directions? Dredging up old hurts? Why, not five minutes ago he stood on that exact spot and stuck up for you!

(JACOB *looks at her, surprised, slightly incredulous.*)

JACOB: Ben did . . . ?
MARY: Yes, Ben did, and don't look so surprised. Now it may be too late, but there are some t'ings that just have to be said, right now, in the open. Sit down and listen. Sit down. (JACOB *sits.*) For twenty years now I've handled the purse strings in this family, and only because you shoved it off on me. I don't like to do it any more than you do. I'm just as bad at it, except you're better with the excuses. (JACOB *rises.*) I'm not finished. Sit down. (*He does — slight pause.*) Last fall you tumbled off our garage roof and sprained your back. You was laid up for six months all told — November to May — without a red cent of Workmen's Compensation, because the accident didn't happen on the job. And I made all the payments as usual — the mortgages, your truck, the groceries, life insur-

ance, the hydro and oilman, your union dues. All that, and more. I took care of it all. And where, Jacob, do you suppose the money came from? You never once asked. Did you ever wonder?

JACOB: Where? From the bank.

MARY: The bank! We didn't have a nickel in the bank. Not after the second month.

JACOB: What is you getting at, Mary?

MARY: Just this. *(She lowers her voice.)* If Ben hadn't got a scholarship, he wouldn't have went to college this fall. He couldn't have afforded to. It was his money that took us over the winter. All those years of working part-time and summers. All of it gone.

JACOB: Ben did that?

MARY: And you says he hates you!

JACOB: I don't want no handouts from him. I'll pay him back every cent of it.

MARY: Shut up. He'll hear you! He never wanted you to know, so don't you dare let on I told you, you hear? He knowed how proud you is, and he knowed you wouldn't want to t'ink you wasn't supporting your family. *(slight pause)* Now, boy, who's got the last laugh? *(MARY takes her coat and puts it on as she crosses to BEN's door.)* Hurry up, Ben. The taxi ought to be here any second.

(She turns and looks at JACOB. There is anguish in her face. When she speaks her voice is drained.)

I'm tired, Jacob. And you ought to be, too, by all rights. It's time to quit it. A lifetime of this is enough, you and Ben. Declare it an even match for your own sake, boy, if for nothing else. I don't want to see you keep getting the worst of it. You always did and you still do.

(Enter BEN, carrying his suitcase.)

BEN: *(to MARY)* Isn't the cab here yet? It's almost eight.

MARY: He'll beep his horn. *(slight pause)* You don't need to take that now, my son. Pick it up later.

BEN: That's okay, Mom. I've got all I want. The rest you can throw out. *(He sits on his suitcase.)*

JACOB: Your mother told me what you done last winter. I —

MARY: *(sharply)* Jacob!

JACOB: I wants to t'ank you. I'll pay you back.

MARY: You promised you — *(She stops, shakes her head in exasperation.)*

JACOB: *(slight pause)* I'm sorry what happened here tonight. I wants you to know that. I'll make it up to you. I will.

BEN: *(meaning it)* It's nothing. Forget it.

MARY: Let him say he's sorry, Ben. He needs to.

JACOB: Maybe I've been wrong. I suppose I ain't been the best of fathers. I couldn't give you all I'd like to. But I've been the best I could under the circumstances.

BEN: Dad.

JACOB: Hear me out, now. We never seen eye to eye in most cases, but we'm
still a family. We've got to stick together. All we got in this world is the
family — *(He rises.)* — and it's breaking up, Ben. *(slight pause)* Stay for a
while longer. For a few more years.

BEN: I can't.

JACOB: You can. Why not?

BEN: I just can't.

JACOB: Spite! You'm just doing this out of of spite!

(BEN shakes his head.)

Then reconsider . . . like a good boy. Let your brother rent his room to
a stranger, if he's that hard up. Don't let him break us up.

(The taxi sounds its horn.)

MARY: There's the taxi now.

JACOB: *(desperately)* You don't have to go, my son. You knows I never meant
what I said before. You'm welcome to stay as long as you likes, and you
won't have to pay a cent of rent. *(even more desperately)* Come back
afterwards!

BEN: No, Dad.

JACOB: Yes, come back. Like a good boy. I never had a choice in my day, Ben.
You do.

BEN: I don't!

JACOB: You do so! Don't contradict me!

BEN: What do you know? You don't know the first thing about me, and you
don't want to. You don't know how I feel, and you don't give a shit!

JACOB: In my day we had a duty to —

BEN: In your day! I'm sick of hearing about your fucking day! **This** is **my**
day, and we're strangers. You know the men you work with better than
you do me! Isn't that right? Isn't it?

JACOB: And you treats your friends better than you do me! I know **that**
much, I can tell you. A whole lot better! And with more respect. Using
language like that in front of your mother!

(The taxi honks impatiently. BEN moves to go. JACOB grabs the suitcase.)

MARY: Jacob! The taxi's waiting!

JACOB: *(to BEN)* You'm not taking that suitcase out of this house! Not this
blessed day! *(He puts the suitcase down at a distance.)*

MARY: That's okay, Ben. Leave it. You can come back some other time.
(MARY exits.)

JACOB: He will like hell. Once he goes, that's it. He came with nothing, he'll
go with nothing!

BEN: *(slight pause)* Do you know why I want to be on my own? The real
reason?

JACOB: To whore around!

BEN: Because you're not going to stop until there's nothing left of me. It's not the world that wants to devour me, Dad — it's you!

(JACOB whips off his belt.)

JACOB: *(as he brings it down hard on BEN's back)* Then go!

(BEN instinctively covers his head, crouching a little, unprotesting.)

JACOB: *(sobbing, as he brings the belt down again and again.)* Go! Go! Go! Go! Go!

(Finally, as JACOB swings again for the sixth time, BEN whirls and grabs the belt from his father's hand. Then with a violent motion he flings it aside.)

BEN: You shouldn't have done that, Dad. You shouldn't. *(He exits.)*

(Silence. JACOB retrieves his belt. A slight pause.)

JACOB: *(fiercely striking the chesterfield with his belt)* Holy Jumping Jesus Christ!

(Silence. MARY enters from the hallway. JACOB begins to put on his belt. He notices MARY.)

What's you doing here? Isn't you going? *(He crosses into the dining room and sits at the table.)*

(Slowly MARY puts down her purse and enters the dining room, crossing behind JACOB and sitting at the table beside him. She says nothing.)

JACOB: *(anguished)* In the name of Jesus, Mary, whatever possessed you to marry the likes of me over Jerome McKenzie?

(MARY says nothing. Pause.)

I've never asked you before, but I've always wondered.

(Pause.)

MARY: It was that day you, me, and Jerome McKenzie was all sitting around my mother's kitchen and in walked my brother Clifford. He was teaching Grade Six in St. John's that year, and he told of a story that occurred that very morning at school. You've most likely forgotten. A little girl had come into his class with a note from her teacher. She was told to carry the note around to every class in the school and wait till every teacher read it. Clifford did, with the child standing next to him. The note had t'ree words on it: **Don't she smell**? Well, Jacob, boy, when you heard that, you brought your fist down so hard on the tabletop it cracked one of Mother's good saucers, and that's when I knowed Jerome McKenzie hadn't a hope in hell. *(slight pause)* Q.C. or no Q.C.!

(Slowly MARY *lifts one foot then the other onto the chair in front of her. The lights slowly dim into darkness.)*

END

WRITING ESSAYS ABOUT LITERATURE

PUTTING THE JOB IN PERSPECTIVE

*W*riting well on any academic subject is demanding work, and writing about literature is among the most demanding kinds of academic writing. It helps to remember, however, that confronting the task seriously will improve not only the way you express what you think but your ability to think, as well. Mastering the critical and interpretive essays required in English courses will prepare you to handle other writing jobs with comparative ease. Whether you are committed to specializing in English or interested mainly in doing as well as you can in a required English course before going on to other areas of study, the advice that follows will help you make your choices sensibly and get the most from the work you do.

Writing about literature often starts with a feeling — you either like something or not — or an intuition about how a piece of writing works. In expressing these inklings in writing, you clarify them for yourself, identify the assumptions behind them, and learn how well they are grounded in the work you are considering. In the process, you not only come to understand better how literature works, but you also discover a good deal about how you think. Writing about literature is challenging for the same reasons it is rewarding — because it requires you to confront yourself as well as what you read.

When you explore literature in essays, you will rarely be looking for answers that are absolutely right or wrong. Depending on the approach taken and the questions asked, a wide variety of conclusions can be drawn about an individual work of literature, and because of the personal element in responses, even writers approaching questions in similar ways will often come up with quite different answers. Think of your essays about literature as part of an ongoing search for understanding, a process that begins when an author, poet, or playwright confronts his or her perceptions about the world in writing and continues as long as somebody is reading and writing about the original creation. Remembering that you are taking part in a continuing dialogue rather than solving a problem with a single, predetermined answer will help you resist obvious conclusions and make your confrontation with a demanding subject less intimidating.

But again, "less intimidating" does not mean easy. The lack of pat answers, though reassuring in some ways, is no excuse for either slack thinking or sloppy writing. On the contrary, because your essays will be judged more by the quality of thought and expression they demonstrate than by how close they come to some established position, care is especially important.

Originality is a start, but your original perceptions have to be supported scrupulously with evidence from the work in question; you must impress you audience by convincing it.

PREPARING TO WRITE

An essay about a literary work should say something illuminating about it, and an illumination depends on focus as well as initial brilliance. Thoughtful insights take time to develop, and an essential step in writing about literature involves clarifying for yourself what it is you want to say. Only when you are sure of your message can you decide how best to present it clearly and convincingly to your readers. The work cannot be rushed at this stage, so it is essential to leave yourself adequate time, not only to draft and revise, but to think, to plan, and to criticize your own ideas, as well.

PROCESS IN SUMMARY
PREPARING TO WRITE

Step 1:   Prepare for writing assignments in advance by reading all assigned texts in a course as early as possible and by including speculation about potential lines of argument in your notes.

Step 2:   Once you receive a writing assignment, evaluate it carefully to determine special requirements and anticipate problems.

Step 3:   Choose a subject that interests you.

Step 4:   Choose a topic you can handle well in the time available.

Step 5:   If you are confused about any aspect of an assignment or if you anticipate deviating in any way from the directions, check with your instructor.

Step 6:   Review the primary works you are writing about carefully, taking notes and identifying key passages as you read.

Step 7:   Read whatever background material you consider necessary.

DRAFTING

Step 1:   Begin generating ideas in writing while you still have more time than you need to complete your essay.

Step 2:   Focus your ideas into a manageable thesis and state this thesis clearly in a single sentence.

Step 3:   Prepare a simple, tentative outline. Do not spend a lot of time on this outline because it will probably have to be modified later. Repeat Step 2 if necessary.

Step 4:   Working from your outline and keeping your thesis statement clearly in mind, complete a rough draft of the entire essay without stopping to revise.

REVISING AND EDITING

Step 1:   Review your essay to identify any parts that do not relate clearly to your thesis; cut or adapt these as necessary.

Step 2:   Add support at any point where your conclusions seem to need it.

Step 3:   Revise your opening to ensure that the main points of your essay are clear and supply any additional information your reader may need to follow your approach.

Step 4:   When you are satisfied with the content of your essay, continue revising it for clarity and style until you are satisfied that it is the best you can make it or until the deadline requires you to commit yourself to a final version.

Step 5:   When you are rested and free from distractions, proofread your essay carefully, making neat changes on the manuscript where necessary.

READING WITH AWARENESS

The most fundamental preparation for writing about literature is reading. Read the piece you intend to write about, and then reread it. Read not just superficially to get a basic idea of what the piece says, but carefully, with an awareness of implications beneath the surface and of how the way it is written determines the way it affects you. Taking English courses and studying what others write about literature will teach you the kinds of things to look for, but you will need more. Serious reading, like serious writing, takes practice and cannot be rushed: putting off thinking about literature in general until you are required to write about a particular piece is like putting off training for a race until just before you have to run it. Developing the habit of reading seriously will put you far ahead of students who read only when forced to by an assignment, and it will also yield a great deal of satisfaction in itself.

TAKING NOTES

While reading thoughtfully is essential, it is not enough. You will find that your reading translates more readily into essays if you record your responses. Take notes as you read, perhaps on the text itself if it is your own copy and an inexpensive one. Marking particularly interesting passages will be a great help when you come back later to sort out evidence for an idea you are developing in an essay. When taking notes in class, record not only what your instructor says but the ideas that occur to you as well. If what is said about one work suggests comparison with another, take note of the possibility. Remark contradictions and unanswered questions. Your dissenting opinions, which you might well forget if you neglected to write them down at the time, will often provide the foundation for your most original essays and may in the long run prove to be the most valuable material you record in class.

An excellent practice for bridging the gap between the sketchy notes you write in class and fully developed essays is to extend your notes in a journal. Rather than reviewing class notes only when you are preparing for an exam, take time between classes to review and expand on the ideas your notes record. Consider which of your ideas may yield topics for essays, and test the manageability of these topics by sketching outlines. Elaborate in a paragraph or two on ideas you have had time to record in only a sentence. If you have recorded questions in your notes, attempt to answer them yourself in writing. The best time to develop your notes into something more useful occurs when the ideas they record are still fresh in your mind. While keeping a literary journal is not so different from taking notes, it allows you time to develop your ideas more thoughtfully and provides practice that will help you become more comfortable with critical writing.

EVALUATING ASSIGNMENTS

Before attempting a writing assignment, you must first determine exactly what it requires and whether you can carry out any approach you are considering in the time available. The time you invest in evaluating assignments is rarely wasted. However eager you may be to get started, be cautious; enthusiasm is great, but you will win few races by sprinting off in the wrong direction.

Be especially careful when choosing topics from a list, a point at which the work of a few minutes can make the difference between success and failure. While you can assume that your instructor considers all suggested topics suitable for some students in your class, you cannot assume that all the topics will be suitable for all the students. Resist the temptation to commit yourself to the first topic that catches your interest. Evaluate all your options, eliminating the obvious impossibilities first. It will usually be clear that some works and some approaches are too difficult for you to manage. Personal taste is also an important consideration: until you gain more experience as a critic, you will rarely write successful essays about literary works you dislike. Once you have narrowed the choice to a few possibilities, sketch brief outlines to give yourself a better idea of where you might go with each topic. Determine whether you can meet all the requirements in each case. For example, even though you admire a certain poem, you may not be capable of handling a topic that requires you to produce a successful essay about how that poem's metrical patterns reinforce its meaning. While there can be long-term benefits in taking the extra time required to prepare for specialized topics, be sure you can manage the workload. Be wary of ambitious failures.

Once you find an assignment you think you can handle well, consider its wording carefully. Are you sure what all the terms mean? If not, ask your instructor to explain. Is there anything about the approach you are considering that seems at odds with the assignment as stated? Perhaps, for example, an assignment asks you to compare characterization in two stories, only one of which particularly impresses you. It may be permissible to concentrate on the one you like while using the other to illuminate by contrast what you admire in your favourite, but, then again, your instructor may want a more balanced comparison. Find out before you devote a lot of time to a questionable approach. Similarly, even though you plan no deviations from the stated requirements, you may find an assignment ambiguous in some respect. If you are told to compare two poems, for example, does this mean you are obligated to consider all aspects of the two poems? Or will you be permitted to devote most of your comparison to some aspect that seems especially revealing? While the more focused approach may seem more interesting to you, your instructor may have left the comparison general to test your understanding of a variety of elements in the poems. Any number of misunderstandings can occur, and you will be wise to anticipate them while you still have plenty of time to adapt.

Think early. Check early. Doing so can save you time, effort, and disappointment.

RESEARCH

In a very limited sense, any essay you write on a literary subject will involve research: you will have to read the works you intend to write about very carefully, probably a number of times, and even with an assignment that does not formally require research, you will often read other works by the same writer and explore his or her personal and historical background.

In a formal research paper, however, you will also be expected to find and evaluate what others have written about your subject. In this case, finding and properly acknowledging your debt to secondary material — writings about literature rather than the literature itself — will be a major part of your job. A detailed explanation of research methods and the format for acknowledging sources is beyond the scope of this chapter, but most college-level writing textbooks cover such material thoroughly. If you plan to take more than a few English courses, *The MLA Handbook for Writers of Research Papers*, which provides an exhaustive guide to the standard format used in English essays, is a good investment. Here it will suffice to provide a few general hints that can save you a lot of time and trouble.

Many students get into difficulty by confusing random sampling with research. They find the call number of a book on their topic, go to the specified shelf in the library, pull out several books on the same general subject, and consider their search complete. The one advantage of this approach — speed — cannot compensate for the problems it will almost certainly create. Books chosen at random rarely provide more than brief, general comment on an essay topic; what relevant comment they do include is often slanted according to their focal concerns. In addition, books stay on library shelves long after what they say has been qualified by later observations, and the material you find in a random selection will certainly not be the most recent available. This is not to say that books are of no value; the point is that books must be chosen carefully and supplemented by reference to up-to-date articles from scholarly journals.

The annotated bibliographies and the periodical indexes available in reference libraries will allow you to find material relevant to your topic quickly, and they will also give you an overview of the kinds of approaches to the work in question that others have found useful. But, as valuable as they are in saving you the trouble of reviewing irrelevant or barely relevant material, these resources will not solve all your problems. Often, they will list far more apparently relevant resources than you have time to consult. How are you to choose? In some cases your instructor will make suggestions, but such advice may still leave you guessing about which comments are most important and influential. One of the easiest ways into ongoing critical debates is to look first at the most recent writings you can find on your topic, taking careful note of the earlier works these cite. When two or three recent sources refer to an older one, it will usually be worth your while to check what it says directly. No method of sampling is a substitute for an exhaustive review of criticism, but methods that allow you to make an informed selection should be sufficient for most of your essays. They will certainly serve you better than random choice.

Seeking out the most pertinent material is not the only challenge in research, however. When you set out to research critical comment, remember that you are in at least as much danger from what you find as from what you miss. Discovering a source that carries on your line of argument so well that it leaves you little to add will take the satisfaction out of your work as well as the challenge, and you will learn little from basing your essay on such a source. Moreover, depending heavily on a source increases the chances of unintentional plagiarism — not making it entirely clear which ideas are really yours and which are borrowed. Thus, finding a published essay that covers much of what you intend to say about a topic is a good reason to consider changing topics or at least modifying your approach.

Much more serious than occasional reliance on secondary sources for ideas is developing a habit of dependency. It is all too easy to drift into a pattern of reviewing criticism before you begin to form your own ideas, thereby allowing others to shape your views. Always keep in mind when dealing with critical opinions that they are just that — opinions. Be impressed if you like, but never be intimidated. Even the best critics are human and therefore fallible. They are influenced by the prevailing critical assumptions of their times and often by specific theoretical affiliations. You have every right to disagree with published critics or, for that matter, with your instructors, provided you state your case clearly and support it conscientiously with references to the text in question. Consider other views carefully and with the respect any honest effort to advance understanding deserves, but then, when writing your essays, think for yourself.

STARTING TO WRITE

In contrast with the many difficulties involved in completing a good critical essay on time, putting off getting started is one of the easiest things you will ever do — easy and risky. It is human nature to put off the more difficult of competing tasks until the straightforward ones are out of the way, but with writing, the difficult jobs are precisely the ones to start first. Start early. Leave yourself time to explore blind alleys and, when you feel you are getting nowhere, to allow your subconscious mind to work on the problem while you are consciously engaged with other concerns. You will almost always find that ten hours invested in a writing project over a week will yield better results than a single ten-hour stretch of writing immediately before the deadline for submission.

WRITER'S BLOCK

Unfortunately, even when you are well aware of the advantages of an early start, you may be held up by a psychological quirk commonly referred to as "writer's block."

Writer's block usually sets in at the earliest stages of a project, making it impossible to begin writing at all or, at best, to carry on past the first page or two. Because fear of failure is part of the cause, writer's block often strikes when you can least afford it — when you are involved in an especially important project or working under pressure. If you have never experienced writer's block, you may find the idea amusing, but sooner or later it affects most writers, and when it does, it can be both unpleasant and costly. Moreover, the anxiety created by one experience can lead to others, creating a steadily worsening problem. It makes sense, therefore, to prepare for writer's block before it strikes by experimenting with methods of resistance in order to determine which work best for you.

The methods described below are primarily intended to help you generate and shape ideas, but because they also encourage you to start writing early, not just when you have time to complete a project but when you have time to waste, they help eliminate writer's block as well. So, even if you find it fairly easy to think of things to say without writing, writing will usually help, and it will certainly make your work no harder.

QUESTIONS

Perhaps the most straightforward way to clarify what you think about a subject is to ask yourself questions about it. In order to avoid writer's block, not to mention loss and confusion, keep a record of your questions and answers in writing.

Beginning with very general questions, such as why you like or dislike something, progress gradually to questions that are more specific, quickly abandoning lines of inquiry that lead away from manageable topics. If you need help devising questions, you will find the lists included in writing textbooks many and varied, and most of them will work adequately up to a point. Watch for that point. At first, any question that forces you to examine your ideas will be better than none, but the further you carry on with a ready-made list, the more likely the questions are to limit your answers. As soon as a suggested line of inquiry begins to get in the way of your developing ideas, abandon it and strike off on your own. Such lists are generally more useful for getting started than for leading you to conclusions.

Be wary also of lists of questions not designed for students of literature. For example, lists are often based on the journalistic standard: Who? What? Where? When? Why? How? While such lists encourage thoroughness in getting at the facts of a situation, an essay about literature is, of course, far more subtle than a news story. Normally, your readers will be familiar with the facts of the works you are discussing and will not require a review. Thus you will be wise to pass quickly over the Who? What? Where? and When? and concentrate on questions concerned with Why? and How? More often than not, you will begin forming a useful argument only when you begin addressing these last two.

INTERACTION

If asking and answering questions by yourself seems lonely work, you may prefer to involve others. Approaches vary according to circumstances and temperament.

One common method of generating ideas, sometimes called brainstorming, involves gathering a group together, with tape recorder running or one member taking notes, and throwing out ideas. The exchange is kept as informal as possible to avoid inhibiting creativity. This sort of exercise works better in developing advertising slogans than critical essays, and a lot of what results will be useless, but finding and rejecting inappropriate approaches to a subject will often help you progress towards forming better ones. At least such an exchange of ideas will get you started.

If you lack the informed group required for brainstorming, you can sometimes develop ideas and free yourself from writer's block by talking to a single listener. Even if this person knows little about your subject, his or her responses can help you decide where your views lack clarity or need support. Remember, however, that in the end it should be you who judges and refines the ideas: using another person as a sounding board for your own ideas is not the same thing as allowing another person to tell you what to think. For the sake of honesty and your development as a critical thinker, avoid working with someone whose superior knowledge of your subject may make it hard to rely on your own judgement.

FREE WRITING

One of the most reliable ways of breaking writer's block is called "free writing." Free writing is a way of freeing yourself from worry about imperfections in expression that can inhibit the flow of ideas early in a project. It involves committing yourself to writing for a predetermined period of time. You simply sit down in a place where you will not be interrupted and, keeping your subject in mind, write until the time is up. Resist pausing for reflection or stopping to revise. At best, you will be well into a rough draft by the time you finish. At worst, what you produce will be only vaguely relevant to your subject, but, even if the written result is of little value, you will still have broken your writer's block and moved closer to understanding what you want to say. You can always begin a second session of free writing by reacting to the shortcomings of your first.

FOCUSING

Once you put your early inhibitions behind you and begin accumulating ideas, you will soon find yourself with more than you can hope to bring together in a paper. This is the time to turn your attention from generating ideas to pruning and focusing. Handling the focusing stage of a writing project well can save you a great deal of time later on, but it takes discipline. Piling up ideas becomes so easy once you get started that it is tempting to carry on too long, deluding yourself that you are accomplishing something when in fact you are rambling out of control. While writing anything is better than writing nothing at the start of the writing process, this does not remain true throughout. Avoid the common mistake of trying to substitute quantity for quality.

You can approach the job of focusing from two general directions — working from a thesis or toward one. If you are lucky, you will discover one particularly interesting line of argument early along. Stating your main ideas as a proposition to be proved — a proposition often referred to as a "thesis" and commonly announced near the beginning of an essay in a sentence termed a "thesis statement" — will provide you with a guide as you write, a premise to refer to as you choose which of your secondary ideas to expand, which to subordinate, and which to cut. If no clear thesis has emerged by the time you are ready to start focusing, you can develop one by grouping the most promising ideas and then pruning obvious loose ends. The more loose ends you cut, the more clearly you will see the best potential lines of argument. By the time you have narrowed the possibilities to two or three, you will not only be in a good position to choose the best, but you will also have developed a general idea of how best to support the one you choose.

Be certain, however, that you do not stop before the job is done. Just as it is important to begin focusing before you are overwhelmed with an unmanageable accumulation of ideas, it is also vital to carry on to the desired end — a single, supportable thesis:

> **Not** *"Although Andrew Marvell's 'To His Coy Mistress' is manipulative to some extent in taking advantage of flattery, sophistry, and shocking images of mutability, it sometimes reveals a genuine regard for the object of passion and leaves the reader wondering how fully the object of Marvell's affection — or lust — would be capable of appreciating what is going on in the poem."*

> **But** *"In 'To His Coy Mistress,' Andrew Marvell is addressing a well-educated woman whose intelligence he respects."*

> **Or** *"Andrew Marvell's most compelling means of seduction in 'To His Coy Mistress' is neither flattery nor shock, but logic."*

The first statement above has more than its share of interesting ideas, but it would likely yield either two or three papers tacked loosely together or, worse still, a muddled blend. Parting with ideas can be hard, but attempting to fit more notions into an essay than you can explain and support adequately will be much harder. Saving a few minutes by rushing the focusing stage can cost you many hours later on.

OUTLINES

Quite a few writing textbooks advise preparing a detailed outline before attempting the first draft, a practice that is usually less effective for critical arguments than expository essays. In essays devoted mainly to reviewing large amounts of factual information, information that is readily gathered and organized in advance of writing, a detailed outline will prove an invaluable tool, one that can greatly speed the process of writing and revision. In more speculative essays, however, the kind of essays commonly written about literature, the difficulty of deciding what you are going to say in what order without a certain amount of groping on paper will often make a detailed outline harder to produce than a draft.

Therefore, using outlines for essays on literature requires flexibility. If planning is one of your strengths, beginning your writing with an outline will definitely speed the work that follows. But if you find preparing outlines more difficult than diving in and writing a draft without one, you will be wise not to spend too much time struggling to follow advice that is more appropriate for some types of writers and for some types of writing than others. Do what works for you.

TREE-DIAGRAMMING

If you like working from an outline yet find outlines difficult to organize while you are still generating ideas, try "tree-diagramming," a method that can help you form an outline in something the same way free writing helps you progress towards a first draft. Place a word or phrase representing your central idea in the middle of a large sheet of paper and work outward, connecting related ideas through a series of branches. Though the result of this exercise will rarely resemble a tree, it will provide you with an overview of relationships, revealing both dead ends and useful lines of inquiry quickly. (See figures 1 and 2.)

WRITING AND REVISING

If you start early and use your time efficiently, you should have developed and focused your ideas several days before your essay is due. At this point, you will have at least a general idea of how your essay will be organized to support your thesis, and you will have probably done some drafting. The next step, completing your first draft, should be fairly straightforward if you resist the temptation to stop and polish style.

Once you have a completed draft that makes sense and includes all your main points, distance yourself from what you have written by leaving it alone for a day or two. Then, coming back to the project relatively fresh, you will be able to decide more quickly and reliably whether what you have written needs cutting, expansion, or restructuring. After you are satisfied with the form and the essential content, it will be time for polishing style and fine-tuning your argument.

Remember: an essay you write over a week or ten days will almost always be better than one you produce in a single marathon effort, even though you invest the same number of hours in total.

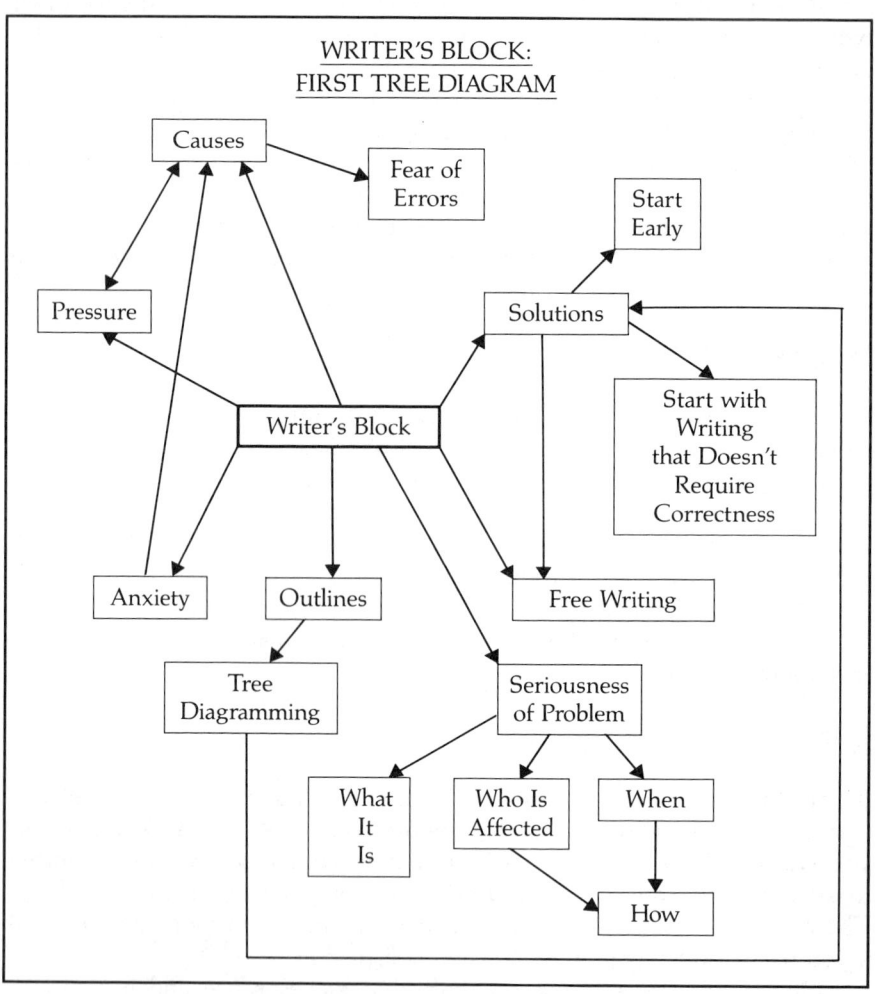

WRITER'S BLOCK:
FIRST TREE DIAGRAM

AUDIENCE

As you revise your essay, you will have two main concerns — making your argument clear and forceful, and maintaining one consistent appropriate style throughout. Style can be the trickier of the two, especially when you try to affect it. Do not assume an overly sophisticated, erudite style which may not be appropriate even for literary critics. You will find that an unnatural

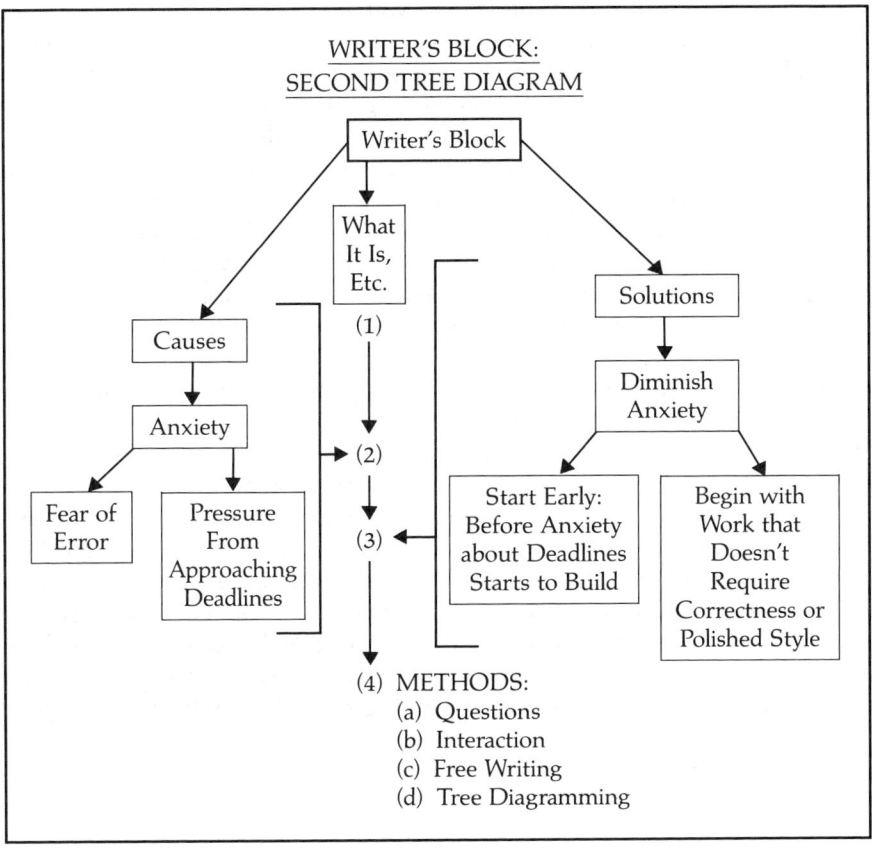

WRITER'S BLOCK:
SECOND TREE DIAGRAM

Writer's Block

What It Is, Etc.

(1)

Causes

Anxiety

Solutions

Diminish Anxiety

Fear of Error

Pressure From Approaching Deadlines

(2)

(3)

Start Early: Before Anxiety about Deadlines Starts to Build

Begin with Work that Doesn't Require Correctness or Polished Style

(4) METHODS:
(a) Questions
(b) Interaction
(c) Free Writing
(d) Tree Diagramming

style will be very difficult to maintain for an entire essay. A much easier and more reliable approach is to let your audience and your relationship with it control your style automatically, as they would your voice if you were speaking.

What audience do you write for? The answer is less obvious than you might think. While you probably want most to impress the instructor who will eventually give your work a grade, you may well find that writing with another audience in mind makes this easier. Consider the unnaturalness of explicating literature for someone who knows a great deal more about it than you and who has probably encountered views similar to yours many times before. Will this situation inspire you with confidence? Or is it more likely to make you adopt an apologetic tone and be slightly dismissive about your ideas? How do you feel about writing for someone who can be expected to note technical errors and lower your grade in consequence? Will this audience encourage a confident, forceful style? Hardly.

It makes more sense to write for an audience you can persuade and enlighten, one at about your own level of ability. An audience made up of the better students in your class is a sensible choice. You know this audience well, you can assume it will be familiar with the works you are considering, and you can be confident that it will find your insights fresh and interesting. Writing for an audience of equals will also make it easier for you to adopt a natural, unpretentious style — your own.

In addition to helping you find an appropriate style, writing for an audience of equals will also help you decide what needs to be explained and what does not. For example, since your audience has read and understood the surface meaning of the works you are writing about, you will not need to summarize plot or review other obvious facts. When you need to make specific references to plot or character in support of your developing argument, you will keep these references brief — reminders, rather than revelations. On the other hand, you cannot assume that your audience has seen reasoning similar to yours before, and you should therefore make your line of thinking and the connections between evidence and the conclusions you draw from it more explicit than you might if you were writing exclusively for your instructor.

OPENINGS

Inexperienced writers often get into trouble by working on the assumption that the parts of an essay should be finished one at a time from first to last. This assumption is wrong on two counts. First, if you have the time, it is almost always easier to improve all the parts of an essay at about the same rate as you work through a series of drafts. Second, when lack of time makes a series of drafts impossible and you have to finish sections in sequence, it is usually easier to write the rest of the essay before you put the finishing touches on the opening.

If you are like most student writers, you have more difficulty with openings than with any other part of your essays. Your opening paragraphs may be wordy, vague, and repetitive, even though they receive more attention line for line than other sections. The problem is poor timing. While good essays generally require several drafts, inexperienced writers working under pressure hope to arrive at a final version in as few drafts as possible. In this hope, they attempt to produce a final, polished version when they have only an incomplete or very rough draft to revise, and they naturally start with the opening, struggling to introduce what they will say before they are sure of precisely what this will be. The time-consuming tinkering with wording and groping for ideas that ensue can take more time than revising the whole essay less meticulously. Even worse, having put so much effort into the opening, they are reluctant to make necessary changes once they finish the rest of the essay. The result: a vague, inflated introduction followed by a hastily composed argument that had to be dashed off because of all the time wasted in introducing it. There is nothing wrong with including an opening paragraph containing a clear thesis statement in your first draft; in fact it helps to keep your argument on topic. But, having done that, you will usually find it easiest to leave the opening rough until the rest of your essay is polished to its conclusion. At this point, you will have a much more certain idea of what you want to introduce in the opening, and you will find writing it much easier in consequence.

Keep in mind as you complete your opening that it should actually accomplish something — excite your reader's interest, persuade your reader of the value of your approach, prepare your reader to grasp what follows. You can achieve these aims only when you yourself fully understand where your essay is going.

REVISING FOR CORRECTNESS

While your first concerns throughout most of the writing process should be to make sense and express yourself in an appropriate, consistent style, you cannot afford to ignore correctness — following the accepted conventions of grammar, punctuation, and spelling. While correctness cannot in itself guarantee success, carelessness or incompetence in handling basic writing will certainly ensure failure.

Fortunately, whether they believe it or not, most students who are penalized for errors know enough about grammar and punctuation to write correctly. Attitude more than ignorance is the cause. If you tend to make a lot of mistakes, do not let discouragement or frustration exaggerate your weakness. Convincing yourself that you lack the ability to write correctly is simply an excuse for not investing the time and the work required to master correctness. Seriously confronted, the job of revising for correctness will become easier and less time-consuming with practice.

TEN COMMON MISTAKES TO AVOID IN WRITING ABOUT LITERATURE

Occasionally, even when you start early and work conscientiously, you will still get into difficulty in writing an essay about literature. More often than not this stems from one of the common errors below. While being on guard against these mistakes cannot guarantee success, it will greatly increase your chances.

1. TAKING ON UNREALISTICALLY AMBITIOUS PROJECTS

Be realistic in choosing topics. Avoid topics that will take more space, time, specialized knowledge, or research than you can put into them. If you are not sure whether your plans are manageable, check with your instructor.

2. PLAGIARIZING BY MISTAKE

Be careful not to drift into plagiarism by keeping sloppy records of your research. Record complete information for references immediately upon encountering a source you may want to refer to later. When taking notes, make a clear distinction between recorded information, paraphrases, and quotations.

3. RETAINING IRRELEVANT MATERIAL FROM EARLY DRAFTS

If sections of an essay seem loosely connected with each other or with the controlling thesis, try to put the essay in order by supplying clear transitions showing the reader how each part relates to the whole. If you find it difficult to justify a section, cut or shorten it. The ideas that could produce two or three good essays will usually make one bad one.

4. ATTEMPTING TO POLISH STYLE TOO EARLY

Do not attempt to perfect style while you are still unsure of what you want to say. Be especially wary of polishing openings before you have a clear idea of what will follow.

5. WRITING ABOUT YOURSELF RATHER THAN YOUR TOPIC

Concentrate on your topic rather than your feelings, doubts, or difficulties as you write. Avoid such redundant insertions as "it seems to me that" and "I think that"; your reader will know you are doing the thinking that goes into your essay without constantly being reminded.

Time is the key factor. To write correctly you must know your limitations and allow yourself time to compensate for them. If you find yourself penalized

6. SUMMARIZING PLOT AND EXPLAINING THE OBVIOUS

Avoid boring your reader by summarizing what happens in literary works and reviewing obvious facts at length. Assume an audience of intelligent readers familiar with the works you are analyzing and supply only the information this audience will need to evaluate your argument.

Do not be influenced by the summaries provided in various publications termed "notes." These summaries do not constitute serious criticism and should not be imitated.

7. CONFUSING VERB TENSES

Keep the sequences of verb tenses within long sentences as simple as possible, and avoid shifting tenses unnecessarily. Using the conventional present tense to describe characters, circumstances, and events in literary works will help greatly.

8. INFLATING STYLE

Inflated style is no substitute for good ideas. Impress your readers with the clarity and sense of your thinking rather than the sophistication of your presentation. Strive to write in your own voice; keep your sentence structure as straightforward as you can without being choppy and repetitive; use only those literary terms that you understand. If you work with a thesaurus, use it to find the most accurate and readily understood terms available rather than as a shortcut to pretentiousness and obscurity.

9. FAILING TO FOLLOW CONVENTIONS OF MANUSCRIPT FORM

Follow the accepted conventions for presenting your work on the page and acknowledging sources. It helps to remember that these conventions are not merely decorative; rather, they are an essential code for communicating information efficiently and accurately.

10. PROOFREADING INATTENTIVELY

Proofread when you are rested, preferably after a good night's sleep, rather than immediately after you finish an essay. Proofread in a place free from distractions, and give the job the full attention it requires. The half hour or so you take to proofread an essay properly will often have more effect on the grade than any other half hour of work you invest in the project.

for errors regularly, understand why. Is it carelessness in the final stages of writing? Or do you lack the background in the basics of writing? If you know what you are doing but make careless mistakes, you need merely improve your proofreading skills and find an appropriate proofreading time, which is to say a time when you will not be too tired to concentrate or likely to be distracted. If your problem is more serious and you are uncertain of what is correct in some cases, budget the extra time you will need to check. Checking your own work is a good way to learn, and you will probably find once you confront the problem of errors that you know more than you think you do. Like most students who are penalized for errors, you probably make the same types of errors again and again, although you handle most elements correctly. Take note of the types of things that go wrong and concentrate on these. Make a checklist of things to watch for. Review the relevant rules as you approach the final stages of writing. Ignorance, in this case, is no excuse: all the information you need about grammar and punctuation can be found easily in writing handbooks, and spelling can, of course, be checked in a dictionary — provided you allow yourself time to do the work.

Once you are satisfied that your own writing is correct, turn your attention to another aspect of your essay that requires care. Most instructors consider the format and accuracy of quotations and references to be just as important as the correctness of your own writing, so check these carefully before submitting your essay. Have you provided all the requirements, such as a title and title page, that are mentioned in the assignment? Are all your quotations recorded exactly? Have you consistently followed the correct format in supplying notes and bibliographical references? Taking care with such details shows that you are serious about your work; allowing even a few mistakes can call the accuracy of all your work into question.

One further word of warning, however: remember that timing is just as important as taking time in correcting your essays. It is as serious a mistake to let your concern with correctness preoccupy you during the earlier stages of writing as it is to neglect correctness later on. Worrying about errors early along will distract you from the important work of forming ideas, and it may also encourage you to adopt an overly cautious style aimed more at avoiding errors than communicating. So leave the job of checking for correctness till the end of your project, and then take it seriously.

*   *   *

While you cannot avoid the basic fact that writing well about literature involves hard work, you can, by following the advice supplied here, avoid wasting the work you do and ensure that your hard work yields the good results it deserves. But be skeptical: this advice is a basis, not a formula, for success. Keep in mind that writing is a personal endeavour and that no one method will work best for every person and every occasion. Treat this and all advice on writing critically, measuring its usefulness against your experience of what works best for you as you continue to grow as a writer.

GLOSSARY OF LITERARY TERMS

ACCENT: The stress that makes a syllable more emphatic or prominent in pronunciation than neighbouring syllables.

ACT: A main division of a drama.

ACTION: What happens in a drama; the physical activity represented on the stage, but also the mental activity stimulated in a reader or audience.

ALLITERATION: The repetition of consonant sounds, particularly at the beginning of words close to one another.

ALLUSION: A reference to characters, places, events, or objects from history, religion, mythology, or literature, which the reader is supposed to recognize and connect to the subject of the work in which the allusion appears.

AMBIGUITY: The presence of multiple meanings in a word or phrase, whether intentional or accidental.

AMPHIBRACH (AMPHIBRACHIC): A poetic foot of three syllables, only the middle one being accented. See FOOT and Figure 1, "The Metrical Feet," in the Introduction to Poetry.

AMPHIMACER (AMPHIMACRIC): A poetic foot of three syllables, the first and last being accented; also called a cretic. See FOOT and Figure 1, "The Metrical Feet," in the Introduction to Poetry.

ANAPEST (ANAPESTIC): A poetic foot of three syllables, only the last being accented. See FOOT and Figure 1, "The Metrical Feet," in the Introduction to Poetry.

ANTAGONIST: Any character who opposes another; most often applied to one opposing the main character (the protagonist).

APOSTROPHE: An address to an absent or dead person, to an object, or to an abstraction.

ARCHETYPE: A character type, symbol, plot, or theme that appears frequently in works of literature and therefore seems to have universal meaning.

ASIDE: Words delivered by one character to another or to the audience, and understood not to be heard by other characters on the stage.

ASSONANCE: Repetition of similar vowel sounds.

BALLAD: A form of narrative poetry used continuously since medieval times, consisting of four-line stanzas usually alternating iambic tetrameter and iambic trimeter and rhyming *abcb*, often characterized by repetition and repeated refrains. Ballads are usually classed as either popular or literary ballads. Popular ballads were transmitted orally and were frequently intended to be sung; they originated with anonymous authors among the folk, or common people of rural society. Literary ballads are conscious imitations of these popular ballads and are intended to be read or recited, not sung. Because they are often composed by individuals familiar with literary traditions, however, they may employ complex symbolism lacking in the popular ballads.

BLANK VERSE: Lines of unrhymed iambic pentameter.

BLOCKING: The planning of movement on the stage for a production of a drama.

CAESURA: A pause within a poetic line, created by punctuation, by the phrasing of ideas, or by the manipulation of metre.

CARPE DIEM: A Latin phrase, meaning "seize the day," often used to describe poems that urge the enjoyment of the moment because time is fleeting.

CHARACTER: A person in a work of literature or one of the *dramatis personae* of a play; also the moral, psychological, and intellectual traits of such a person. A *round* character possesses the complexities, contradictions, and subtle depths of personality associated with actual human beings. A *flat* character, in contrast, seems relatively two dimensional: the character is presented briefly and has little depth of personality. Both kinds may be *dynamic* — a character who changes, for better or worse, during the course of a literary work — or *static*, a character who undergoes no development.

CHARACTERIZATION: The techniques used to depict the traits of a character in a literary work. See CHARACTER.

CHORUS: In ancient Greek drama, a group of characters who comment in unison upon and sometimes take part in the action of a drama.

CLASSIC: A work considered to be the best of its class.

CLASSICAL LITERATURE: The literature of ancient Greece and Rome.

CLASSICISM: The application of artistic principles supposedly derived from the classical literatures of Greece and Rome, including formal control, proportion, simplicity, unity, and rationality. Classicism emerged in the Continent and England among the humanists of the fifteenth and sixteenth centuries. See NEOCLASSICISM.

CLIMAX: The crucial or high point of tension, understanding, or recognition in a plot and the turning point of the action.

CLOSED COUPLET: See COUPLET.

COMEDY: A literary mode, especially in drama, that ends happily, with the resolution of difficulties, the restoration of fortunes, and the unity of the community, often symbolized by one or more marriages. Comedy can celebrate or satirize the values of a society or individual, but it affirms life through its presentation of good fortune, positive pleasures, meaningful societal values, and individuals as significant parts of society.

COMPLICATION: The problem near the beginning of a story or drama that causes the conflict.

CONCEIT: An elaborate or extended comparison, whether simile or metaphor; known as Petrarchan conceits (after Petrarch, the poet who popularized them in his sonnets) when they are conventional, as with the comparison of a lover to a ship, and as metaphysical conceits (after the metaphysical poets of the seventeenth century) when they are elaborate or ingenious comparisons of things not traditionally linked, as with the comparison of separated lovers to a compass.

CONFLICT: The opposition of forces within a character, or the struggles either between characters (protagonists) and other characters (antagonists) or between characters and natural or supernatural forces.

CONNOTATION: The implications of a word; that is, the feelings, ideas, or associations suggested by a word in addition to its denotation, or dictionary meaning.

CONSONANCE: Repetition of consonants within or at the end of words.

CONTEXTUAL SYMBOL: See SYMBOL.

CONVENTION: A technique or feature included frequently in specific types of literature or in literature from a particular historical period. The Petrarchan conceit is a conventional feature in some Renaissance poetry; the use of heroic couplets is a conventional technique in eighteenth-century poetry.

CONVENTIONAL SYMBOL: See SYMBOL.

COUPLET: Two adjacent lines of poetry that rhyme; called a closed couplet when the pair is end-stopped by significant punctuation and contains a complete thought; called heroic couplet when the rhymed lines are in iambic pentameter.

CRETIC: See AMPHIMACER.

DACTYL (DACTYLIC): A poetic foot of three syllables, only the first being accented. See FOOT and Figure 1, "The Metrical Feet," in the Introduction to Poetry.

DACTYLIC RHYME: See RHYME.

DENOTATION: The dictionary meaning of a word, which depends significantly on context, without reference to its implications and associations.

DÉNOUEMENT: See RESOLUTION.

DEUS EX MACHINA: Literally, "the god out of the machine"; the descent of a god, represented by an actor lowered to the main level of the stage in a mechanical device, to intercede and conclude an ancient Greek drama; by extension, any contrived and improbable ending.

DIALOGUE: The direct presentation of the spoken words of characters in a story or play.

DICTION: The choice of types of words, specific words, and levels of language. Levels may be formal (lofty language such as that used in epics and in the speeches of nobles in Shakespearean drama), informal (the speech and idiom of daily life), or colloquial (the speech and idioms of particular social classes or groups, such as the Cockneys in England).

DIMETER: A term of poetic measurement indicating a line containing two feet. See FOOT, METRE, and Figure 2, "Line Lengths," in the Introduction to Poetry.

DOUBLE RHYME: See RHYME.

DRAMATIC MONOLOGUE: A form of poetry in which a character speaks to a definite but silent listener and thereby reveals his or her own character.

DRAMATIS PERSONAE: Literally, "the characters of the drama"; a descriptive list of characters prefixed to a drama; see CHARACTER.

DYNAMIC CHARACTER: See CHARACTER.

ELEGY: In classical Greece, a poem on any serious theme that was written in a couplet form known as elegiac metre; since the Renaissance, used to refer to a lyric that laments a death.

END RHYME: See RHYME.

END-STOPPED LINE: A line terminated with a relatively strong pause, usually indicated by the presence of a comma, semicolon, dash, or period; the opposite of enjambment.

ENJAMBMENT: The running over of meaning from one line to another unhindered by punctuation or syntactical pauses; opposite of an end-stopped line.

EPIC: A long narrative poem recounting in elevated language the deeds of heroes; settings are vast, sometimes extending beyond earth, and episodes may involve the gods or other supernatural beings.

EPILOGUE: The concluding, summarizing section of a drama in which all the strands of the plot are drawn together; sometimes the epilogue is an actual addition.

EPIPHANY: A religious term meaning a "manifestation" or "showing forth"; western Christianity celebrates the

Feast of the Epiphany on January 6 to mark Christ's manifestation of divinity to the Magi; James Joyce applied the term to short fiction to describe the moment when events show forth their meaning, bringing illumination or revelation to a character.

EXEUNT: The plural form of the Latin *"exit"*; literally, "they go out"; a stage direction signalling the exit of all characters in a scene; sometimes expressed as *"exeunt omnes"* ("all go out"); when names or categories follow the term, as in *"exeunt Lords,"* only the named group leaves the stage.

EXPOSITION: The presentation, usually at or near the beginning of a narrative or drama, of necessary background information about characters and situations.

EXPRESSIONISM: An early twentieth-century artistic movement that emphasized the inner world of emotions and thought and projected this inner world through distortions of real-world objects; unlike impressionism, expressionist literature and drama distorts and abstracts the external world, creating works that are symbolic, anti-realistic, and often nightmarish in vision; in prose, stream of consciousness narration is one of its major techniques.

EYE RHYME: See RHYME.

FEMININE RHYME: See RHYME.

FIGURATIVE LANGUAGE: Language that uses figures of speech (such as metaphors or similes) so that it means more than the simple denotation of the words and, therefore, must be understood in more than a literal way.

FLASHBACK: An interruption of the chronological sequence of events to present an event that occurred at an earlier time.

FLAT CHARACTER: See CHARACTER.

FOOT: The basic metrical unit in poetry, consisting of one or more syllables, usually with one stressed or accented; a basic pattern of stressed and unstressed syllables commonly identified by names derived from Greek poetics, the most common being the iamb, the trochee, the dactyl, the anapest, and the spondee. See METRE and Glossary entries for each kind, or see Figure 1, "The Metrical Feet," in the Introduction to Poetry for a list.

FORESHADOWING: The presentation of incidents, characters, or objects that hint at important events that will occur later.

FREE VERSE: Poetry that is free of regular rhythm, rhyme pattern, and verse form; often called *vers libre*.

FREYTAG'S PYRAMID: A structural diagram, resembling a pyramid in shape, devised by the nineteenth-century German playwright and critic Gustav Freytag to illustrate the rising and falling action of a five-act drama:

          3. Climax
  2. Rising Action 4. Falling Action
1. Exposition   5. Resolution

GENRE: A classification of literature into separate kinds, such as drama, poetry, and prose fiction; a major literary form that sometimes contains other related forms, which are known as subgenres.

HEPTAMETER: A term of poetic measurement indicating a line containing seven feet. See FOOT, METRE, and Figure 2, "Line Lengths," in the Introduction to Poetry.

HEROIC COUPLET: See COUPLET.

HEROIC QUATRAIN: See QUATRAIN.

HEXAMETER: A term of poetic measurement indicating a line containing six feet. See FOOT, METRE, and Figure 2, "Line Lengths," in the Introduction to Poetry.

HYPERBOLE: A figure of speech depending on exaggeration, the overstatement of the literal situation, to achieve dramatic or comic effects.

IAMB (IAMBIC): A poetic foot of two syllables, the second being accented. See FOOT and Figure 1, "The Metrical Feet," in the Introduction to Poetry.

IMAGE: See IMAGERY.

IMAGERY: At its most basic, the verbal creation of images, or pictures, in the imagination; also applied to verbal appeals to any of the senses.

IMPERFECT RHYME: See RHYME.

INTERNAL RHYME: See RHYME.

IRONY: A figure of speech that creates a discrepancy between appearance and reality, expectation and result, or surface meaning and implied meaning; traditionally categorized as verbal irony (a reversal of denotative meaning in which the thing stated is not the thing meant), dramatic irony (in which the discrepancy is between what a character believes or says and the truth possessed by the reader or audience), and situational irony (in which the result of a situation is the reverse of what a character expects).

ITALIAN SONNET: See SONNET and SONNET, PETRARCHAN.

LEITMOTIF: A recurring word, phrase, situation, or theme running through a literary work. Also see MOTIF.

LINE LENGTH: See Figure 2, "Line Lengths," in the Introduction to Poetry for a list; consult this Glossary for descriptions of individual kinds.

LYRIC: A form of poetry that is relatively short and that emphasizes emotions, moods, and thoughts, rather than story.

MASCULINE RHYME: See RHYME.

METAPHOR: A figure of speech that makes a comparison by equating things, as in "His heart is a stone."

METAPHYSICAL CONCEIT: See CONCEIT.

METAPHYSICAL POETS: Seventeenth-century poets who linked physical with metaphysical or spiritual elements in their poetry.

METONYMY: A figure of speech that substitutes one idea or object for a related one, such as saying "the Crown" when referring to the monarchy or the government.

METRE: A measure of the feet in a line of poetry, and thus a term expressing the number of feet in a line and the pattern of the predominant feet in that line; the rhythmic pattern of a line. See Figure 1, "The Metrical Feet," in the Introduction to Poetry.

MODERNISM: An artistic movement of the early twentieth century that deliberately broke from the reliance on established forms and insisted that individual consciousness, not something objective or external, was the source of truth; modernist literature may be structurally fragmented; its themes tend to emphasize the philosophy of existentialism, the alienation of the individual, and the despair inherent in modern life.

MONOMETER: A term of poetic measurement indicating a line containing one foot. See FOOT, METRE, and Figure 2, "Line Lengths," in the Introduction to Poetry.

MOOD: A general emotional atmosphere created by the characters and setting and by the language chosen to present these.

MOTIF: An image, character, object, setting, situation, or theme recurring in many works. Also see LEITMOTIF.

MOTIVATION: The psychological reason behind a character's words or actions.

MYTH: A traditional story embodying ideas or beliefs of a people; also a story setting forth the ideas or beliefs of an individual writer.

NARRATION: The recounting, in summarized form, of events and conversations.

NARRATIVE POEM: A poem that tells a story.

NARRATOR: The person telling a story, either a fictional character or the implied author of the work; see POINT OF VIEW.

NATURALISM: A literary movement based on philosophical determinism, the belief that the lives of ordinary people are determined by biological, economic, and social factors; naturalists tend to use the techniques of realism in order to present a tragic vision of the fate of individuals crushed by forces they cannot control.

NEAR RHYME: See RHYME.

NEOCLASSICISM: The principles of those writers who emerged with the restoration of Charles II to the throne of England in 1660 and who sought to restore classical restraint in all areas of life. The literature of the Neoclassical Period, which extends until about the 1798 publication of Wordsworth and Coleridge's *Lyrical Ballads*, was highly formal (frequently being based on the heroic couplet), praised reason over emotion, and often used satire and irony to criticize deviations from decorum and propriety. See CLASSICISM.

OBLIQUE RHYME: See RHYME.

OCTAMETER: A term of poetic measurement indicating a line containing eight feet. See FOOT, METRE, and Figure 2, "Line Lengths," in the Introduction to Poetry.

OCTAVE: An eight-line stanza in any metre or any rhyme scheme; any eight-line unit of poetry, rhymed or unrhymed; the initial eight lines of a sonnet united by the rhyme scheme.

ODE: A long, often elaborate, lyric poem that uses a dignified tone and style in treating a lofty or serious theme; regular forms not frequently used in English include the Greek Pindaric ode, which was divided into three repeated types of stanzas (strophe, antistrophe, and epode), each with its own metrical pattern, and the Horatian ode, which retained a single pattern throughout every stanza.

OFF RHYME: See RHYME.

ONOMATOPOEIA: Words that imitate the sounds that they describe.

OXYMORON: An ironic figure of speech containing an overt contradiction, as in the word *oxymoron* itself, which means "sharp stupidity" in Greek, or in such phrases as "fearful joy" or "paper coin"; see IRONY and PARADOX.

PARADOX: An apparent contradiction that, upon deeper analysis, contains a degree of truth.

PARODY: A humorous imitation that mocks a given literary work by exaggerating or distorting some of its salient features.

PENTAMETER: A term of poetic measurement indicating a line containing five feet. See FOOT, METRE, and Figure 2, "Line Lengths," in the Introduction to Poetry.

PERSONA: Literally, the mask; the speaking personality through which the author delivers the words in a poem or other literary work; the fictional "I" who acts as the actual author's mouthpiece in a literary work.

PERSONIFICATION: The attribution of human traits to inanimate objects or abstract concepts.

PETRARCHAN CONCEIT: See CONCEIT.

PETRARCHAN SONNET: See SONNET and SONNET, PETRARCHAN.

PLOT: The arrangement of actions in a drama or story, often in a sequence according to cause and effect.

POINT OF VIEW: The angle of vision or perspective from which a story is told. The point of view may be first person (in which the narrator is a character within the story), third person (a character or an implied author outside the story), or very rarely, second person (in which the narrator, as in "choose-your-adventure" books, addresses the reader as "you"). Narrative point of view also involves questions of knowledge and reliability. Narrators may be omniscient, knowing both external events and internal thoughts and motivations, or they may be limited to some degree, knowing only some external details. Reliable narrators (a category that includes omniscient narrators) tell the truth completely. Unreliable narrators have personal limitations, such as youth or lack of education, that make them misunderstand what they narrate.

PROLOGUE: The preface or introduction to a play, often containing a plot summary.

PROTAGONIST: The main character of a drama or story.

PYRRHIC: A poetic foot of two syllables, neither of which is accented. See FOOT and Figure 1, "The Metrical Feet," in the Introduction to Poetry.

QUATRAIN: A four-line stanza in any metre or any rhyme scheme, except the heroic quatrain, which is in iambic pentameter and rhymes *abab*; any four-line unit of poetry, rhymed or unrhymed; four lines of a sonnet united by the rhyme scheme.

QUINTET: A five-line stanza in any metre or any rhyme scheme; any five-line unit of poetry, rhymed or unrhymed.

REALISM: The attempt to represent accurately the actual world; a literary movement that developed in reaction to the artificialities of romantic literature and melodramatic drama and that tended to focus on the lives of ordinary people, to use the language of daily speech, and to develop themes that offered social criticism and explored the problems of mundane life.

RESOLUTION: A portion of a story or drama occurring after the climax that reveals the consequences of the plot and resolves conflicts.

RHYME (RIME): The repetition of identical or similar final sounds in words, particularly at the end of lines of poetry. Single, or masculine, rhymes repeat only the last syllable of the words; double, or feminine, rhymes (also sometimes called trochaic rhymes) repeat identical sounds in both an accented syllable and the following unaccented syllable; triple, or dactylic, rhymes repeat identical sounds in an accented syllable and the two following unaccented syllables. End rhyme occurs when the rhyming words are at the end of their respective lines; internal rhyme occurs when one or both of the rhyming words are within a line. Most rhyme involves the exact repetition of sounds; near rhyme (also known as slant, off, imperfect, or oblique rhyme) depends upon the approximation, rather than duplication, of sounds: it repeats either the final consonant (but not the preceding vowels) or the vowels (but not the following consonants) of the words. Eye, or sight, rhyme depends on the similar spelling of words, not their pronunciation, as in *gone* and *lone*.

RHYTHM: The flow of stressed and unstressed syllables; the patterned repetition of beats.

RISING ACTION: The progression of events and development of the conflict of a story or play up to the point of the climax.

ROMANTICISM: A literary movement that began in England sometime around the 1798 publication of Wordsworth and Coleridge's *Lyrical Ballads* and was a reaction to the restraint and order of neoclassicism. The Romantics praised emotion over reason and celebrated the imagination; their literature used a diction that was less formal and elevated than that of the classicists (see CLASSICISM), employed themes based on the supernatural, nature and nature's influence on human beings, and the power of the liberated imagination. "Romantic" and "romanticism" are applied to works that exhibit emotional and imaginative exuberance or that use such themes, whether or not written during the Romantic period.

ROUND CHARACTER: See CHARACTER.

SATIRE: A literary form that uses wit and humour to ridicule persons, things, and ideas, frequently with the declared purpose of effecting a reformation of vices or follies.

SCANSION: The analysis and marking of the metres and feet in a poem; see METRE and FOOT; see also Figure 1, "The Metrical Feet," and Figure 2, "Line Lengths," in the Introduction to Poetry.

SEPTET: A seven-line stanza in any metre or any rhyme scheme; any seven-line unit of poetry, rhymed or unrhymed.

SESTET: A six-line stanza in any metre or any rhyme scheme; any six-line unit of poetry, rhymed or unrhymed; the final six lines of a Petrarchan sonnet, which are united by the rhyme scheme.

SETTING: Emotional, physical, temporal, and cultural context in which the action of the story or play takes place.

SHAKESPEAREAN SONNET: See SONNET and SONNET, ENGLISH.

SIGHT RHYME: See RHYME.

SIMILE: A figure of speech making a direct comparison between things by using *like* or *as* or similar words, as in "His heart is like a stone."

SINGLE RHYME: See RHYME.

SLANT RHYME: See RHYME.

SOLILOQUY: The thoughts and impulses of a character, voiced aloud on stage and shared with the audience.

SONNET: A lyric form of fourteen lines, traditionally of iambic pentameter and following one of several established rhyme schemes; see SONNET, ENGLISH; SONNET, MILTONIC; SONNET, PETRARCHAN.

SONNET, ENGLISH: Also called the Shakespearean sonnet; a sonnet consisting of three quatrains and a couplet, rhyming *abab cdcd efef gg;* when the quatrains employ linked rhyme (*abab bcbc cdcd ee*), known as the Spenserian Sonnet.

SONNET, MILTONIC: A variation of the Petrarchan sonnet that eliminates the pause at the end of the octave; thus, the *volta*, when it occurs, usually appears in the middle of the ninth line.

SONNET, PETRARCHAN: Also called the Italian sonnet: the first eight lines (the octave) state a problem, and the final six lines (the sestet) frequently begin with a *volta*, or turn, such as *but, yet,* or *however,* and resolve or comment on the problem; originally limited to five rhymes, with the rhyme scheme of the octave usually being *abba abba* (thus dividing into two quatrains), and the rhyme scheme of the sestet varying, but generally being either *cde cde* (thus dividing into two tercets, or three-line units) or *cdcdcd*.

SPONDEE (SPONDAIC): A poetic foot of two syllables, both of which are accented. See FOOT and Figure 1, "The Metrical Feet," in the Introduction to Poetry.

STANZA: A division of a poem into a group of lines; traditionally, a grouping of lines according to rhyme scheme, number of lines, or metrical pattern that frequently is repeated in each stanza; a unit of two or more lines that are grouped together visually in any poem by being separated from preceding and following lines. See Figure 3, "Names of Stanzas and Line Groupings," and Figure 4, "Notable Fixed and Complex Forms," in the Introduction to Poetry.

STATIC CHARACTER: See CHARACTER.

STREAM OF CONSCIOUSNESS: A narrative presenting the flow of thoughts and emotions of a character.

STRUCTURE: The arrangement of elements within a work; the organization of and relationship between parts of a work; the plan, design, or form of a work.

STYLE: A writer's selection and arrangement of words.

SUSPENSE: The anxiety created by a situation in which the outcome is uncertain.

SYMBOL: A figure of speech that links a person, place, object, or action to a meaning that is not necessarily inherent in it; a word so charged with implication that it means itself and also suggests additional meanings, which are the product of convention (the culture traditionally associates a particular image with a particular meaning) or of context (the placement of the image in a work and the details and emphases within that work add suggestiveness to the image, making it symbolic).

SYNECDOCHE: A figure of speech in which a part stands for the whole or the whole stands for the part, as when the term "hands" signifies "sailors."

TERCET: A three-line stanza in any metre or any rhyme scheme, but usually called a triplet when all three lines rhyme; any three-line unit of poetry, rhymed or unrhymed; three lines united by the rhyme scheme in the sestet or a Petrarchan sonnet.

TETRAMETER: A term of poetic measurement indicating a line containing four feet. See FOOT, METRE, and Figure 2, "Line Lengths," in the Introduction to Poetry.

THEME: The central idea or meaning of a work; a generalization, or statement of underlying ideas, suggested by the concrete details of language, character, setting, and action in a work.

TONE: The speaker's attitude towards the subject matter or audience, as revealed by the choice of language and the rhythms of speech.

TRAGEDY: A literary work, especially a drama, presenting the failure and downfall of a character. Tragedy is a serious form demonstrating moral choice, error of judgement, and, in many cases, heroic death, as well as the enlightened understanding resulting from such considerations. Tragedy tends to deal with right and wrong, life and death, and the remorselessness of the universe in relationship to the puniness of human beings.

TRIMETER: A term of poetic measurement indicating a line containing three feet. See FOOT, METRE, and Figure 2, "Line Lengths," in the Introduction to Poetry.

TRIPLE RHYME: See RHYME.

TRIPLET: A tercet; usually applied to one in which all three lines rhyme.

TROCHAIC RHYME: See RHYME.

TROCHEE (TROCHAIC): A poetic foot of two syllables, the first being accented. See FOOT and Figure 1, "The Metrical Feet," in the Introduction to Poetry.

UNDERSTATEMENT: A figure of speech, the opposite of exaggeration, that intensifies meaning ironically by deliberately minimizing, or underemphasizing, the importance of ideas, emotions, and situations.

UNITY: The cohesiveness of a literary work in which all the parts and elements harmonize.

VERS LIBRE: See FREE VERSE.

VOLTA: The turn of thought in a poem, especially after the octave of a Petrarchan sonnet.

Index of Authors, Titles, and First Lines of Poetry

To the Owner of this Book:

We are interested in your reaction to *The Harbrace Anthology of Literature* by Rick Bowers, Raymond E. Jones, and Jon C. Stott. With your comments, we can improve this book in future editions. Please help us by completing this questionnaire.

1. Please indicate which version of this anthology you used: Literature
   Poetry
   Drama
   Short Fiction

2. What was your reason for using this book?
   _____ university course
   _____ college course
   _____ continuing education course
   _____ personal interest
   _____ other (specify)

3. If you used this text for a program, what was the name of that program?

4. Which school do you attend?

5. Approximately how much of the book did you use?
   _____ ¼   _____ ½   _____ ¾   _____ all

6. Which chapters or sections were omitted from your course?

7. What is the best aspect of this book?

8. Is there anything that should be added?

9. Please add any comments or suggestions.

(fold here)

(fold here and tape shut)

0116870399-M8Z4X6-BR01

Heather McWhinney
Publisher, College Division
HARCOURT BRACE & COMPANY, CANADA
55 HORNER AVENUE
TORONTO, ONTARIO
M8Z 9Z9